REAL ESTATE DEVELOPMENT LAW

■ ■ ■

By

Rick Daley

Senior Lecturer in Law
The Moritz College of Law
at The Ohio State University

Also available on Law School Exchange at:
http://exchange.westlaw.com/

AMERICAN CASEBOOK SERIES®

WEST®

A Thomson Reuters business

Mat #41060152

610 Opperman Drive
St. Paul, MN 55123
1–800–313–9378

Printed in the United States of America

ISBN: 978–0–314–26742–9

DEDICATION

This book is dedicated to the memory of James P. Mulroy. Jim taught me what practicing business law is all about. His unexpected death in February 2006 gave me both pause for reflection and the impetus to get on with a new stage of my life by agreeing to join the Moritz College of Law faculty and write this book. Jim, I salute you for being a good Marine and a great lawyer and friend.

PREFACE

The fact that I am writing a book on real estate development law comes as a huge surprise to me. When I graduated from law school in June of 1978, I said a hearty goodbye and good riddance to academia and the Socratic method and jumped headlong into the practice of law. For the next 12 years, I immersed myself in the private practice of business law, working 80 hour weeks and, for the most part, successfully convincing myself that I was having a good time. I spent most of those 80 hour weeks representing real estate developers and watching them make a great deal of money doing something they all seemed to love.

In 1990, I finally had an epiphany and realized that life might be more lucrative and, certainly more fun, if I were to exit the private practice of law and go to work for a developer. I had the good fortune of being offered the opportunity to become Executive Vice President and General Counsel for The Pizzuti Companies, a real estate development company headquartered in Columbus, Ohio.

From 1990 through 2003, I had the time of my professional life, wearing the hats of both lawyer and businessman for a rapidly growing and wildly successful real estate development company. During my stint with Pizzuti, the company grew its revenue base more than tenfold and opened regional offices in Orlando, Chicago and Indianapolis. The people I worked with were smart, passionate and a helluva lot of fun to be around. Best of all, I made a goodly sum of money without having to fill out a time sheet accounting for my life down to the 1/10th of an hour.

In 2003, I decided to take a respite from the workaday world to become, in the words of my then 12 year old son, a "housewife." The previous 25 years had been a wild and very rewarding ride, but I felt like a needed a break from the demands of real estate development business. For the next two and one half years, I devoted most of my time to being a chauffeur for my son and daughter, while still dangling my feet in the real estate development pool by serving as a consultant on a number of new real estate ventures. As the time passed, I became more and more convinced that my time as a full-time practicing lawyer was in the rear view mirror and that I needed to move on to something new and different to keep my mind from turning to mush (which some have said actually happened years ago).

While I was trying to figure out what I wanted to do when and if I ever grew up, I received a totally unexpected telephone call from Dean Nancy Rogers at The Moritz College of Law at The Ohio State University. Although I am a graduate of Ohio State's law school, the last time I had stepped into the law school building was when I graduated in 1978. I had made the occasional donation to the law school during my years of practice and assumed that Dean Rogers was calling to ask me to up the ante on the amount of my donations.

I was shocked to hear Nancy ask if I would be interested in teaching a course in real estate development law at the Moritz College of Law. According to Nancy, a distinguished College of Law alum named Ken Zeisler had made a sizable contribution to the school to fund the teaching of a class in real estate development law. Ken graduated from the OSU law school in 1961 and had gone on to achieve great success as a shopping center developer in Cleveland, Ohio. Ken's contribution proposal to Nancy noted that the 35 years he had spent working as a real estate lawyer and developer had left him "very disappointed with the competence of the attorneys on the other side of the transaction (as it pertained to their knowledge of a real estate transaction and what it takes to make a successful deal)." Ken told Nancy that he wanted to do his part to rectify this sad state of affairs by providing the funding necessary for the Moritz to hire someone to teach a "practical, hands-on" course in real estate development law during the 2006 and 2007 school years. Nancy had been unable to find anyone to teach the course among the usual suspects in the academic world, so she decided to take a flyer and ask an old, washed-up vet like me if I would be willing to sign on to help Ken Zeisler achieve his vision.

During our first telephone conversation, Nancy also noted in passing that one of Ken's hopes was that whoever was hired to teach the course might also end up writing a book on the topic of real estate development law. It was this comment by Nancy that really piqued my interest in the job. I have long dreamed of being the next Robert Parker and waking up each morning to sit down at the computer to crank out one great mystery novel after another. [For those of you who are unfamiliar with Parker's Spenser character, you should stop reading this drivel right now and head to your favorite bookstore to pick up one of Parker's more than 30 books featuring the tough Boston private eye with a soft, intellectual side]. Unfortunately, I have absolutely no creative talent whatsoever—which is probably why I ended up becoming a lawyer in the first place.

When Nancy first mentioned the possibility of writing a book on real estate development law, the proverbial light bulb went off in my head. Here was the perfect opportunity for me to live my dream of being a writer, without having to summon up even one lick of creativity. After all, what could be less creative than regurgitating in written form all the things about the practice of law that it had taken me 25 years to learn?

Long story short, I told Nancy Rogers that I would take the job and promptly started writing a book on real estate development law. The first thing I needed to do was to figure out what is "real estate development law." The first chapter of this book is devoted to my somewhat feeble attempt to explain (or maybe justify) what it is I did for the first 25 years of my professional life.

As I started to think about what I wanted to convey in this book, I became increasingly more appreciative of how prescient Ken Zeisler was in his perception that law schools don't teach students how to be business lawyers. Students who think they might be interested in pursuing a business law practice after graduation have little, if any, opportunity during their law school years to gain an appreciation of what it is truly like to be a business lawyer. Aspiring litigators have moot court and litigation practicum to expose them in some limited fashion to what the litigation practice is all about (to say nothing of the seemingly endless array of *Law & Order* shows on TV). The aspiring business lawyer has virtually nothing of a comparable nature to give him a taste of what it means to be a business lawyer.

It is my hope that this book can help in some small measure to fill this void in the curriculum of this country's law schools. As an area of the practice where the "deal is king" and a practicing lawyer must bring to bear a solid working knowledge of several legal disciplines, real estate development law is an ideal platform to provide students with a practical understanding of how the legal concepts that they mastered in law school can be used by them to help their clients achieve their business objectives–and that, after all, is what being a business lawyer is all about.

Lest there be any doubt in your minds, let me now make it clear that this book is being written from a practical and not a scholarly perspective. Over the years, I have been called by a lot of different names–most of them couched in mildly profane terms to take due note of my natural wit and mental acuity. However, rest assured that the word "scholar" has never before been uttered in the same sentence as "Rick Daley." Although I now have the privilege of being a member of the faculty of a wonderful law school like Moritz, the fact of the matter is that my knowledge of the topic of this book has been wholly formed by my 25 years representing real estate developers, first as a lawyer in private practice and then as in-house counsel. The voice in which this book is written is, therefore, undeniably and without choice that of a practicing lawyer.

While this book will not be filled with scholarly analysis or insightful legal queries, neither is it intended to be a primer on the technical aspects of real estate development law. Rather, the focus will be on examining why the real estate development lawyer takes certain positions and how a real estate development lawyer's actions and judgments can serve to enhance (or detract from) the ultimate success of a real estate deal.

Let me make several, final comments about the style, approach, and organization of this book.

- For the most part, the topics addressed in this book will be examined from the viewpoint of the lawyer representing a real estate developer. The competing perspectives of the other players in the real estate development process will, however, be highlighted when and where appropriate.

- Real estate development law is not a discrete, substantive area of the law, but rather it is an amalgamation of a multitude of legal disciplines that a real estate development lawyer must master if he is to successfully represent his client. This book will, therefore, explore not just traditional real estate topics, such as the leasing, acquisition and conveyance of real property, but also issues related to tax, partnership, bankruptcy, environmental, finance, zoning, construction and public law.

- A mantra that will be repeated often in this book is that "if you want to succeed as a real estate development lawyer, you first need to understand the real estate development business." As such, the first three chapters of this book are devoted to an exploration of the real estate development business, including a full chapter on what the real estate development lawyer needs to know about the economics of a real estate development project.

- The role played by the real estate development lawyer will be examined during each of the ten stages of a real estate project, beginning with the acquisition of the land on which the project will be developed and ending with the ultimate sale of the project.

- The best way to appreciate the lawyer's role in the real estate development process is to look at that process against the backdrop of a "real world" case study. I have chosen as the primary case study a 350 acre mixed use project located in Orlando, Florida, having over two million square feet of developed office space, two apartment complexes, two hotels, and a neighborhood retail and dining center. I worked on this deal (the "Heathrow International Business Center") from its inception in 1992 when Pizzuti first acquired an ownership position in Heathrow through 2002 when the project was sold in its entirety.

- The heart and soul of real estate development law is represented by the documents prepared, reviewed and negotiated by the real estate development lawyer. A significant part of this book will be dedicated to (a) looking at the key provisions of those legal documents that evidence the real estate development deal and (b) discussing how those provisions can be structured and manipulated to serve the legitimate business needs of the real estate development lawyer's client. The Document Appendix to this book includes a number of standard transactional documents that the real estate development lawyer will encounter during the course of his representation of a developer.

- I have made a conscious attempt to sprinkle throughout the book some *"Practice Tips"* that I have learned during my career. The tips are not intended to be intellectually inspiring or particularly insightful–just useful.

- The 12 chapters of this book are liberally footnoted with citations not to appellate cases, but rather to practitioner-authored articles on topics that are of interest to practicing lawyers (and not just law school professors).

- Terms of art commonly used by developers and their lawyers are highlighted in ***boldface print and italics*** when they first appear in the text.

- The practice of transactional business law does not lend itself to absolutes or legal imperatives. As a result, the text is liberally sprinkled with terms like "typically," "normally," and "customarily."

- Finally, when I started writing this book in the spring of 2006, life was really good for real estate developers and their lawyers. Cap rates were low, rents were high and debt and equity capital was flowing like champagne at a well-attended wedding reception. The good times came to a sudden halt when the subprime meltdown began taking its toll on the commercial real estate markets in the later part of 2007. Life today is very difficult for my friends and former colleagues in the real estate development business and will likely remain challenging for at least the next couple of years. However, as I finish writing this text, I do so with a profound confidence that the practice of real estate development law will soon become as rewarding and profitable for today's practitioners as it was for me during my 25 years in the practice. I say that both because I believe it to be true and because I need to somehow justify having spent the last five years of my life writing about a practice area that is currently in the toilet.

You will note that I refer throughout this book to the real estate development lawyer as a "he." This is done solely for the sake of convenience and is not in any way intended to derogate or minimize the participation of women in the real estate development business. I had a choice of either using the annoying "he or she" reference or just settling on one gender reference. The fact that I have been a "he" throughout my professional life seemed to make the gender choice both easy and natural

I would like to thank a number of people for their roles in the writing of this book. First there is Ken Zeisler, a prince of a fellow and someone I have grown extremely fond of during the course of my writing of this book. But for Ken's initial idea to sponsor a course at Moritz on real estate development law, I would never have had the opportunity to live my dream of waking up every morning to work on a book (albeit one with few plot twists and zero creativity). Then there is Nancy Rogers, who, for some inexplicable reason, had the crazy idea of asking a semi-retired, real estate development lawyer to join the Moritz faculty. Thank you, Nancy, for giving me my second career.

I would be remiss if I didn't take the time to list some of the people who have directed and inspired me during my professional career. Thanks to all of my early mentors (particularly Dave Sidor, Jim King, Jim Mulroy and Kim Swanson), my friends and colleagues at Pizzuti (including Cliff Aiken, Jim Cramer, Dean Kissos, Jim Miller and Scott West) and to all those lawyers who showed me the right way to practice law (Jim Seay, Dick Murphey and Fred Smith among a long list of exemplary professionals). A special thank you goes to Ron Pizzuti, who, by rescuing me from private practice, provided me with the platform to expand my talents and make some money along the way.

Finally, I must thank my wife Sandy and my wonderful kids, Jill and Michael, for the patience, understanding and love they have shown me as I sat staring at my laptop these last few years. I couldn't have done it without you (nor would I have wanted to).

Oh by the way, I wrote this Preface on a flight to Kauai, Hawaii. Life in academia really is pretty cool.

RICK DALEY
Daley.54@osu.edu

October 1, 2010 (my son's 19th birthday)

Summary of Contents

Page

TABLE OF CONTENTS

Page

REAL ESTATE DEVELOPMENT LAW

CHAPTER 1

WHAT IS REAL ESTATE DEVELOPMENT LAW?

■ ■ ■

I. INTRODUCTION

The logical place for me to start this book is with a nice, tidy definition of exactly what is meant by the term "real estate development law." Try as I might, I have yet to come up with such a definition.

Most areas of the practice can be defined by reference to the substantive body of law that serves as the foundation for the practitioner's day-to-day activities. For example, we all think we have a pretty good idea of what securities law is all about—that is, a legal specialty that is centered on the application of the Securities Act of 1933 and the Securities Exchange Act of 1934. The same goes for most other defined areas of the practice—environmental law, estate planning, tax law, criminal law, real estate law, etc. The well-defined bodies of law that serve as the context for those practice areas are summarized and explicated in legal treatises that line the walls of libraries in every law firm and law school in this country.

One can scan the shelves of those law libraries without ever finding a single book wholly dedicated to the topic of real estate development law. The reason for this is quite simple—real estate development law is a practice area that is defined not by matters of substantive law, but rather by the business activities of the lawyer's client. In essence, real estate development law is nothing more than a massing of all those legal disciplines that a lawyer must call upon when seeking to help a real estate developer achieve its business objectives.

Real estate developers are impatient folks, who have no tolerance for the rigor or niceties of legal specialties. As a young lawyer, I once made the mistake of pointing out to a developer client that his proposed project triggered a host of complex legal issues crossing several, distinct practice areas. He looked me in the eye and said, "Son, I don't really care which way the wind is blowing, just bring the damn ship in."

Real estate development law is, therefore, all the "stuff" that a lawyer must know in order to help his developer client "bring the ship in." On

1

any given project, a real estate development lawyer may be called upon to advise his client not only on traditional real estate law topics, such as the acquisition, leasing and conveyance of real property, but also on matters involving all of the following legal disciplines:

- Tax law (federal, state and local);

- Finance law;

- Contract law;

- Corporate, partnership and limited liability company law;

- Securities law;

- Environmental law;

- Bankruptcy law;

- Government relations and public law;

- Land use and zoning law;

- Insurance law;

- Construction law; and

- Litigation (hopefully, precious little of this one).

Let me quickly disabuse any aspiring real estate development lawyer of the notion that he will have the luxury of spending all of his time managing so-called "experts" in each of the above disciplines. The economics of the real estate development business simply do not lend themselves to the use of a phalanx of lawyers, each of whom is a specialist in a discrete area of the law. The lead real estate development lawyer must have a strong working knowledge of each of the legal disciplines that comprise the area of real estate development law. Without such a broad working knowledge, the real estate development lawyer will simply not be able to help his client "bring the ship in."

It is not, however, enough for a real estate development lawyer to master all of the areas of the law listed above. One of my senior partners once told me that one cannot be a good business lawyer, unless he first understands the client's business. His point was that it is the business lawyer's job to not only keep the client out of trouble, but also to create a legal platform to permit the client to achieve its business objectives—in other words, make money and grow and stabilize its business. There is no area of business law where my former partner's wise words ring more true than that of real estate development law. A lawyer who fancies himself an expert in all of the legal disciplines noted above will be an abysmal failure as a real estate development lawyer, unless he becomes equally adept at understanding the business goals of his developer client. He may end up being a highly sought out speaker at bar association functions, but he won't help his client make any money and, hence, won't make any himself. If you take only one thing from this book, it should be this:

If you want to succeed as a real estate development lawyer, you first need to understand the real estate development business.

II. THE REAL ESTATE DEVELOPMENT BUSINESS

At its essence, real estate development is the process of crafting solutions to satisfy the real estate needs of a defined customer class (be it Corporate America[1] or the ordinary Joe who lives down the street). The process starts with the developer identifying an unsatisfied customer demand. Once that demand is identified, the developer's job then becomes taking an unproductive, vacant tract of land and manipulating it in some fashion (by subdividing it, building a building on it, etc.) to satisfy the customer's needs. This process of marrying a customer's real estate needs with a newly-created real estate product is what the real estate development business is truly all about.

The value-add for which the developer is ultimately compensated is twofold:

- Its correct identification of the customer's unsatisfied, real estate need; and

- Its design and execution of a business plan to meet the customer's need in a cost-effective and otherwise appropriate manner.

In his book about the demise of the Olympia and York real estate company, Peter Foster neatly sums up the developer's role in the following manner:

> They are not necessarily architects or contractors, engineers or financiers, but their skill lies in bringing these specialties together to satisfy the demands of those who need space to carry out their businesses. They do not draw up blueprints or erect steel or pour concrete, but they cause these things to happen.[2]

A. WHO ARE THE REAL ESTATE DEVELOPER'S CUSTOMERS?

Like any other business, the real estate development business is driven by the needs, attitudes, likes and dislikes of its customers. The old saw about "build it and they will come" never was true and certainly holds no sway in today's dynamic, global economy. The bankruptcy court records are replete with stories of real estate developers, who ignored the basic needs of their customers and, instead, became obsessed with building their dream projects in pioneering locations. No matter how beautiful or creative a particular real estate project may be, it will not work, unless a customer somewhere deems it worthy of plunking down its real cash for the right to use or own that project.

---

1. For the purposes of this discussion, "Corporate America" is used as a short-hand reference for all of those operating entities that have a business need to house their employees and product in buildings constructed by developers. The breadth of that term is not limited to domestic U.S. corporations, but is intended to include all those business organizations, both foreign and domestic, whose financial standing and operating history make them a natural target for a real estate developer's avarice.

2. Peter Foster, Towers of Debt: The Rise and Fall of the Reichmanns 19 (1993).

Who then are the real estate developer's customers? The developer's customers can be broken down into two broad categories.

- ***Tenants***—These are the folks who are willing to pay rent to *USE* for a specified period of time all or some portion of a project created by the developer. Tenants from Corporate America are the lifeblood of commercial real estate projects, such as office buildings, warehouses and shopping centers.

- ***Buyers***—These are the people who want to *OWN* the developer's project, because they believe that owning real estate is a good investment. These buyers (commonly referred to as ***institutional investors***) generally come from the ranks of life insurance companies, pension plans, equity funds and other financial institutions, both domestic and foreign, who have huge sums of money to invest in real estate each year.

The focus of this book will be on the development of commercial real estate projects that meet the needs of two distinct classes of customers— (1) tenants from Corporate America and (2) buyers from the ranks of the institutional investor community. The success of a real estate development project is largely predicated upon the developer's ability to create a product that simultaneously satisfies the needs of each of these customers.

B. WHAT ARE THE CUSTOMER'S NEEDS?

The needs of a real estate developer's customers are subject to many of the same societal shifts and attitudinal changes that characterize the needs of the customers of any other business. Due to the lag time in the development and construction of a real estate project, the life cycle of a trend in the real estate business is usually a little longer than in other businesses. But make no mistake about it, trends do exist in the real estate business and any developer who ignores those trends will see its projects end up in the same trash heap as the pet rock and beehive hairdo. Again, it is not the size, beauty or location of the product created by the developer that is important, but rather whether the created product appropriately meets the needs of the targeted customer class.

What then are the needs of the developer's two customers—that is, Corporate America and the institutional investor? The next section of this Chapter will look at the general, real estate needs of each of those customers.

1. Corporate America as Tenants

Corporate America usually opts to satisfy its real estate needs by leasing product created by developers.[3] There are two basic reasons that

---

3. There are, of course, many exceptions to this general rule. By way of example, a company might choose to own a real estate project if the project is highly customized to suit its operational needs—e.g., a manufacturing plant or a research and development facility. In the years following the financial crisis of 2008, many companies found that it was more cost-efficient for them to build and own their new real estate facilities, because real estate developers could not access

support a company's decision to lease (rather than own) the real estate it needs to operate its business.[4]

- It costs less for a company to lease real estate than it does for it to own the same real estate (at least in the short-term). Members of Corporate America generally want to preserve their financial resources to fund the operation and growth of their core businesses and not the acquisition and ownership of real estate.

- For similar reasons, companies generally do not want to deploy their human resources to deal with the myriad of operational and financial issues and risks involved with the ownership of real estate—for example, the replacement of a leaky roof, the retrofitting of an obsolete air conditioning system or the disposition of unwanted real estate assets. It is easier for a company to lease real estate and leave all of those risks to developers or financial institutions who are accustomed to dealing with real estate issues. A common refrain voiced by members of Corporate America is that "We are in the business of selling widgets and not in the real estate business."

At the risk of stating the obvious, it is the rent paid by the tenants of a real estate project that creates the value inherent in that project. The rent must be sufficient to cover the project's expenses, plus provide an operating return or profit to the developer to compensate it for the entrepreneurial risk it took in developing the project in the first instance.[5] While no real estate project can be considered risk-free, the real estate developer can significantly ameliorate the risk of a real estate project by leasing it as soon as possible to creditworthy tenants. With this tenet in mind, it is easy to see why developers thirst for the opportunity to have Corporate America as tenants in their projects.

---

capital to develop those facilities at competitive rates. The norm, however, is for companies to meet their real estate needs by leasing and not owning that real estate. As such, the focus of this text will be on Corporate America being a tenant customer of the real estate developer.

4. *See* WILLIAM B. BRUEGGEMAN AND JEFFREY D. FISHER, REAL ESTATE FINANCE AND INVESTMENTS 445–450 (13th ed. 2008) for a discussion of additional factors that a company weighs when making its lease vs. own decision. One factor cited by the authors as favoring the "lease" decision is that, under generally accepted accounting principles, most commercial real estate leases do not have any affect on the tenant's balance sheet. *See id.* at 448–449. However, the accounting treatment historically afforded commercial real estate leases may be changing. On August 17, 2010, the Financial Accounting Standards Board and the Internal Accounting Standards Board issued a joint proposal that would require most tenants to reflect on their balance sheets the right to use the space over the lease term as an asset and the obligation to pay rent as a liability. *See* FASB AND IASB, FASB EXPOSURE DRAFT, *Proposed Accounting Standards Update, Leases* (August 17, 2010), available online at http://www.fasb.org. If adopted, the proposed lease rules could lead some members of Corporate America to at least temporarily favor owning real estate (due in large measure to the complexity associated with the implementation of the proposed accounting rules). In the long run, most practitioners and accountants believe that the proposed accounting rules will not usher in any fundamental change in the lease vs. own decision faced by Corporate America.

5. *See infra* Chapter 3, Pages 39–50, for a further discussion of the economics associated with the development and leasing of commercial real estate projects.

2. Institutional Investors as Buyers

Life insurance companies, pension plans and other foreign and domestic financial institutions have vast cash resources that they need to invest to achieve the financial return targets set by their governing boards. The managers of such institutional portfolios seek to diversify their investments among different asset classes (for example, stocks, bonds and real estate), so that they can avoid compounding the risk associated with the poor financial performance of any one class of assets.[6]

Institutional investors look for two things when they invest in real estate:

- Current operating profits represented by the excess of rents over property expenses (***net operating income***); and

- The potential increase in the value of the real estate over the investor's cost of acquiring and carrying that asset (***residual value***).[7]

The price the institutional investor is willing to pay for a real estate asset is directly tied not only to the amount of the net operating income and residual value flowing from that asset, but also to the relative predictability that the projected income and value will be realized. Stated differently, the more confident the investor is that the expected income and value will be achieved, the higher the price the investor will pay for the underlying asset. To the extent the investor believes that the asset's achievement of the projected financial performance is somewhat risky, the acquisition price will be reduced accordingly. At some point, the investor's lack of confidence in the predictability of the asset's financial performance may lead the investor to decide to wholly back away from making any investment in the subject real estate asset.

Institutional investors seek to lessen the risk associated with their real estate investments by insisting that any project acquired by them be ***institutional-grade***. An institutional grade, real estate project is one where:

- The creditworthiness of the project's tenant roster is sufficiently solid as to give the investor comfort that the expected income stream from the project will be realized; and

- The project location, design and quality of construction are such that it is reasonable to assume that replacement tenants will be found if and when the existing tenants vacate the project.

---

6. In the years leading up to the financial crash of 2008, institutional investors had an almost insatiable appetite for investment in real estate. While the immediate after effects of the 2008 crisis led institutional investors to temporarily exit the real estate capital markets, those investors are now once again pursuing strategic investments in quality commercial real estate assets. *See generally* ANTHONY DOWNS, REAL ESTATE AND THE FINANCIAL CRISIS: HOW TURMOIL IN THE CAPITAL MARKETS IS RESTRUCTURING REAL ESTATE FINANCE (Urban Land Institute 2009); and URBAN LAND INSTITUTE AND PRICEWATERHOUSECOOPERS, EMERGING TRENDS IN REAL ESTATE 2010 (October 2009).

7. The concepts of net operating income and residual value are discussed in more detail *infra* Chapter 3, Page 39.

The price that an investor is willing to pay for a particular real estate asset is directly tied to where that asset falls on the institutional-grade continuum.

An institutional investor's purchase of a project is almost always the developer's ultimate *exit strategy* for that project. The concept of an exit strategy will be developed at much greater length in *Chapter 12—Stages 8–10: Selecting an Exit Strategy*. At this point, what is important to keep in mind is that the institutional investor's purchase of the developer's created project provides the developer with an opportunity (1) to wring out the last dollar of profit from its created project and (2) to end all of the developer's risk on that project.

The real estate developer must, at all times during the course of its development of a particular project, keep in mind not only the needs and wants of the tenants it is wooing for that project, but also the needs and wants of the investors who will provide the developer with its exit strategy for that project. If the developer disregards the needs of the institutional investor community by failing to develop an institutional-grade property, the developer's exit strategy might disappear. An otherwise well-executed project can very quickly fall into the "loser" category if the absence of an exit strategy leaves the developer in limbo and, hence, exposes the profitability of its project to erosion from unanticipated, future market risks.

C. THE CUSTOMERS' NEEDS DEFINED BY PRODUCT TYPE

The foregoing section of this Chapter talked in general terms about the identity and needs of the real estate developer's customers. That discussion intentionally avoided any reference to the specific nature of the real estate product and instead focused on the process whereby a real estate developer identifies an unsatisfied need of a customer and then creates a product to meet that customer's needs. It is that process which defines the real estate development business. The building constructed by the developer is simply a by-product of the development process.

Having made that philosophical point (perhaps once too often), it is certainly important to take note of the various product types created by real estate developers. Set forth below is a chart which identifies (a) the general types of products created by real estate developers (referred to in the remainder of this book as *projects*) and (b) the class of customers typically served by those projects. The listed product types are limited to those commercial real estate projects that are traditionally viewed as being institutional-grade and, hence, subject to acquisition by the previously-discussed institutional investor.

Type of Project	Customers Served by Project[8]

Office:
   Downtown Office Buildings
   Suburban Office Buildings
	Corporate America[9]

Industrial:
   Warehouses
   Manufacturing/R & D Facilities
	Corporate America

Retail:
   Regional Malls
   Neighborhood Strip Centers
   Lifestyle Centers
   Big Box Centers
	Corporate America and private consumers

Multi-family Residential (Apartments)	Private consumers

Hospitality/Entertainment:
   Hotels
   Restaurants
	Corporate America and private consumers

Mixed Use (i.e., a combination of some or all of the foregoing project types)	Corporate America and private consumers

The above table is not intended to be an exhaustive listing of all of the various project types currently being developed by real estate developers. Rather, it is merely an attempt to highlight the principal project categories that have historically attracted the attention of the institutional real estate investor.

One development activity that is not specifically highlighted in the above list is land development.[10] While land development is an essential component of the real estate development business, it is not one that typically attracts independent, investor capital.[11] Land development is the process of taking a vacant parcel of land and readying it for the construction of ***vertical improvements*** (developer-speak for buildings). The developer adds value to the vacant parcel by: subdividing the parcel into smaller, usable tracts; extending roads, utilities and other infrastructure throughout the parcel; and securing all governmental approvals required for the development of the parcel.[12] Land development can occur as a free-

---

8. The listing of the "customers served" addresses only the direct user of the listed property type. The other customer served by each of the listed product types is the institutional investor, who is a potential buyer of these institutional-grade projects.

9. The reference in the table to "Corporate America" is intended to include the entire panoply of business entities, ranging from large global enterprises like Microsoft or Deutsche Bank to the small local accounting firm or tanning salon.

10. Land development is to be sharply contrasted with land speculation, where an individual or company buys land hoping that it will significantly increase in value in the future, at which time the owner will quickly sell it for a profit. Land speculators don't attempt to add value to the land through their development efforts, but simply make a market bet that something will occur in the future that will make the purchased land more valuable.

11. Institutional investors do, however, frequently invest on the front side of large, mixed use land developments in an effort to position themselves for a later investment in the vertical improvements constructed on the developed land.

12. For an excellent exposition of how a developer can add value to land by its development activities, *see* John D. Hastie, *Real Estate Acquisition, Development and Disposition form the Developer's Perspective*, in ALI–ABA COURSE OF STUDY MATERIALS, MODERN REAL ESTATE TRANSACTIONS:

standing development activity (with the developer selling off the developable tracts to other developers or users) or as a necessary adjunct for the development of a vertical improvement project of some type on the land. For the purposes of this book, the assumption will be made that the developer's land development efforts will be a precursor to its development of a vertical improvement project on the land.

III. PLAYERS IN THE REAL ESTATE DEVELOPMENT PROCESS

The development of a real estate project requires the coordinated efforts of a number of real estate professionals. The role the developer plays in the process is analogous to the role of the conductor of a symphony orchestra. It is the developer's job to select the various members of the orchestra (the "players" described below); to provide them with the sheet music for the performance (the overall development plan); and to coordinate the nature, timing and scope of the performance of each of the players. Upon the completion of a successful performance, the conductor takes a bow amidst a standing ovation—and the real estate developer makes a hefty deposit of cash at its local bank.

Every real estate development project has as its genesis a developer-generated vision as to how to best satisfy a real estate need of a targeted class of customers. Sinclair Lewis characterized this "vision" in the following caustic terms in his book *Babbitt*:

> Babbitt spoke well—and often—at these orgies of commercial righteousness about the "realtor's function as a seer of the future development of the community, and as a prophetic engineer clearing the pathway for inevitable changes"—which meant that a real estate broker could make money by guessing which way the town would grow. This guessing he called Vision.[13]

The stereotypical real estate developer is Charlie Croker, the lead character in Tom Wolfe's book *A Man in Full*.[14] Charlie was an ex-All American football player, who was able to parlay his status as an athletic hero and an all-round "good old boy" into the creation of a real estate empire and the acquisition of all the toys symbolic of his position at the top of the real estate heap. Unfortunately for Charlie, he forgot about the "customer" thing, fell in love with a real estate product (a pioneering high-rise office building far outside the Atlanta business district) and ended up having all of his toys auctioned off to the highest bidder by his lender.

Today's real estate developers (at least the successful ones) are a far cry from the Charlie Croker and Babbit stereotypes. The business is now

---

PRACTICAL STRATEGIES FOR REAL ESTATE ACQUISITION, DISPOSITION, AND OWNERSHIP, Course No. SS–012, 16–19 (July 2010).

13. *See* SINCLAIR LEWIS, BABBIT 40 (1922).

14. *See* TOM WOLFE, A MAN IN FULL (1998).

dominated by Harvard and Duke MBA grads (and I dare say a fair number of law school grads) and not by glad-handers and back-slappers like Charlie Croker. The "vision" possessed by today's developer is not simply a matter of Babbit's gut instinct (although I would be remiss if I did not recognize the importance of an "educated gut" in the development business), but more a function of a detailed analysis of demographics, logistics, financial returns and market research.[15] The aspiring real estate development lawyer is, therefore, forewarned that his future client is likely to be someone who can not only talk about "dirt", but is also equally conversant on the topics of discounted cash flow, commercial mortgage backed securities, preferred returns and tax increment financing.

The developer is charged not only with defining the vision of the development plan, but also with executing that development plan. The following is a brief description of the various players whose activities and contributions must be orchestrated by the developer during the real estate development process.

A. DESIGN PROFESSIONALS[16]

Once the developer crystallizes its vision for satisfying the needs of its customer, it must turn to architects, engineers and land planners to give life and definition to that vision. These design professionals, working in close concert with the developer, create preliminary schematic plans for the design and structure of the project. Once the preliminary plans are approved by the developer, the designers (usually headed by the architect) then prepare a more detailed set of plans and specifications that serve as the blueprint for the execution of the project. The plans and specifications are a fluid set of documents that are modified over time to reflect changes to make the project more cost-effective and to better hone in on satisfying both the perceived and actual needs of the customer. During the construction of the project, the architect's role shifts from that of a designer to that of an inspector, as it fulfills the responsibility of seeing to it that the project, as actually constructed, conforms to the design plan approved by the developer.

B. CONSTRUCTION PROFESSIONALS[17]

The construction of the project envisioned in the architect's plans and specifications is the job of construction professionals, who generally fall into one of the following three sub-categories.

---

15. In the aftermath of the 2008 financial crisis, at least one commentator indicated a longing for the "good old days" by noting that "Real estate . . . is a good business for B students who work hard, not for PhDs with computer models." *See* URBAN LAND INSTITUTE, *supra* note 6, at 10.

16. *See infra* Chapter 10, Pages 402–403, 405, for a more detailed discussion of the roles played by the architect and other design professionals.

17. See infra Chapter 10, Pages 403–406, for a more detailed discussion of the roles played by the contractor, subcontractors and suppliers.

- *Contractor*—The contractor is the person who has the overall responsibility for constructing the project in accordance with the plans and specifications. While the contractor's specific title may vary depending on the specific structure of its contractual arrangement with the developer (general contractor, construction manager and design-builder are the most common position titles),[18] its job remains the same—to construct the project on time, on budget and in strict accordance with the approved plans and specifications. Once the plans and specifications are completed (ideally with significant input from the contractor), the contractor's task is to prepare a construction cost budget and a construction schedule. If approved by the developer, the submitted budget and schedule then become the bible for the project, with the contractor being contractually committed to build the project on budget and on time.

- *Subcontractors*—Subcontractors are the trade groups that are charged with performing the actual work of constructing the project. Examples of some customary trades found on a commercial real estate project are plumbers, electricians, steel erectors, cement contractors, landscapers, drywallers and roofers. Each subcontractor enters into a contractual arrangement directly with the general contractor, with such arrangement obligating the subcontractor to perform its piece of the work at the cost and within the time frame specified in the bid it submitted at the inception of the construction project.

- *Suppliers*—Suppliers provide the materials and supplies needed by the contractor and subcontractors to perform their respective construction tasks. Examples of construction firms falling into this sub-category are steel fabricators, concrete suppliers and window and door companies.

C. RISK MANAGERS

Real estate projects are rife with risk, ranging from the most basic (being that the project misses the mark in its attempt to meet an unsatisfied customer need) to those involving a specific aspect of the execution of the project development plan (for example, the risk that the project will not be completed on time and on budget). As will be discussed at great length later on in this book, the management of these risks is the special province of the real estate development lawyer, who must not only identify all of the potential risks of a particular project, but then also try to hedge the developer's risk through a combination of creative deal structuring and accomplished document drafting. There are, however, a

---

18. *See infra* Chapter 10, Pages 409–417, for a discussion of the different ways in which the contractor's role on a commercial real estate project can be structured.

number of specific project risks that can be addressed through the receipt of insurance or certifications from the following third party, risk managers.[19]

- ***Property Insurers***[20]—Insurance companies will provide insurance protecting the developer from risks associated with damage to the project from fire and other casualties both during and after the construction of the project. Liability insurance protecting the developer from exposure to lawsuits for the traditional "slip and fall" and other on-site injuries can also be obtained from insurance companies.

- ***Title Insurers***[21]—Thirty years ago, a developer's comfort that it had good title to its land was generally provided in the form of a title abstract put together by a sole practitioner. The abstract purported to show all the title documents found with respect to the parcel of land in the county courthouse. The protection afforded by such an abstract was only as good as the malpractice coverage maintained by the preparer of the title abstract (which was usually minimal at best). Today, the quality of title to real estate is insured by mammoth title insurance companies, who are obligated to compensate the real estate owner for any loss incurred if title to the real estate ends up falling short of the title quality insured by the title insurance company. The receipt of title insurance is an essential component of every commercial real estate transaction.

- ***Surveyors***[22]—Surveyors provide the developer with a visual depiction of the boundaries of the land that it is buying and the location of any roadways, utility lines and other improvements located on both the developer's land and adjacent land parcels. The survey, when read in conjunction with the title policy provided by the title insurance company, serves to confirm that the size, location and character of the land are consistent with the developer's overall development plan for the land.

- ***Environmental Firms***[23]—A standard part of every real estate acquisition is the receipt of an environmental assessment from a qualified environmental firm certifying that the property is free of any environmental contaminants or other hazardous substances (or

---

19. This list of risk managers is intended to be representative (but not all-inclusive) of the categories of firms that a developer might retain to help mitigate its risk during the development process. Depending on the nature of the underlying development project, the developer might also retain the services of a traffic engineer, a market research company, a public relations firm or a zoning consultant.

20. *See generally* Richard R. Goldberg, *Insurance*, in ALI–ABA COURSE OF STUDY MATERIALS, MODERN REAL ESTATE TRANSACTIONS: PRACTICAL STRATEGIES FOR REAL ESTATE ACQUISITION, DISPOSITION, AND OWNERSHIP, Course No. SS–012, 861 (July 2010).

21. *See infra* Chapter 5, Pages 125–132, and Chapter 8, Pages 293–295, 305 for a more detailed discussion of the use of a title insurance policy in connection with the developer's acquisition of the project land.

22. *See infra* Chapter 5, Pages 127–128, and Chapter 8, Pages 295–297, for a more detailed discussion of the use of a survey in connection with the developer's acquisition of the project land.

23. *See infra* Chapter 5, Page 115, and Chapter 8, Pages 297–298, for a more detailed discussion of the use of an environmental assessment in the context of the developer's acquisition of the project land.

if, any such contaminant or substance is present, a statement as to the identity, location and concentration of such contaminant or substance). The receipt of a well-crafted, environmental certification from a qualified and financially-sound environmental firm goes a long way toward ameliorating the project risk associated with adverse environmental conditions.

- *Wetland Consultants*—Wetlands are now recognized as being an integral part of our ecosystem. Laws have been adopted which protect the destruction or alteration of areas falling with the definition of "protected wetlands."[24] There are few occurrences which can have a more deleterious impact on the budget and schedule of a development project than a determination that the developer's construction activities have improperly disturbed a wetlands area. As a result, it is now part of every developer's standard, pre-acquisition checklist to receive a certification from a qualified wetlands consultant that the parcel to be acquired does not infringe on any protected wetlands.

- *Appraisers*—Every development project has at its core a projection of the ultimate fair market value of the project. Central to the validity of that value projection are the financial and demographic assumptions made by the developer concerning matters such as the amount of the rent that it will be able to collect from its tenants and the length of time it will take to fully lease the project. Developers are a fairly confident lot, who do not believe that they need any third party confirmation concerning the accuracy of their financial projections. Banks and other financial institutions that provide the developer with the funds necessary to develop its projects tend not to be quite as sanguine about the rectitude of the developer's financial conclusions. As a result, lenders routinely require, as a condition to the making of a real estate loan, that a qualified appraiser issue an appraisal report confirming the accuracy of the developer's financial projections.[25] While an appraisal is not a guaranty of project value, it does provide some comfort to the lender (and also indirectly to the developer) that the project's economics have a solid basis in financial and market reality.

D. LENDERS

Simply stated, developers love to use "other people's money" when they develop real estate projects. In the typical real estate deal, 70–90% of the project's development costs are funded through a construction loan obtained by the developer.[26] The construction loan is almost always

---

24. *See* Clean Water Act, § 404, 33 U.S.C. § 1344. Many states have also passed legislation designed to supplement the federal statute on wetlands. *See generally* Jeanne M. Christie, *State Wetland Programs*, in ALI–ABA COURSE OF STUDY MATERIALS, WETLANDS LAW AND REGULATION, Course No. SK–081, 329 (June 2005).

25. *See infra* Chapter 9, Page 388.

26. During the early and mid–1980's, it was common for 100% (and sometimes more) of a project's development costs to be funded by debt. This extreme over-leveraging of real estate

secured by a first mortgage on the subject real estate and is typically for a term of 24–36 months (being the time period generally considered sufficient to complete construction and fully lease the project to rent-paying tenants). Construction loans are generally fully recourse to the developer or some other creditworthy entity affiliated with the developer (meaning that all of such entity's assets can be attacked to pay off the loan). Commercial banks are the usual providers of construction loans.[27]

Once the project is fully leased, the developer customarily turns to a permanent lender to provide the funds necessary to pay off the short-term construction loan. In contrast to construction debt, permanent debt is generally nonrecourse to the developer (meaning that the developer is not personally liable for the repayment of the loan) and has a term of five to ten years. Historically, the primary providers of permanent debt have been insurance companies, pension plans and other financial institutions.[28]

Construction and permanent loans are the traditional forms of debt used to finance the development, ownership and operation of commercial real estate projects. There are, however, countless other loan arrangements used to finance real estate projects. Among the techniques that are most in vogue in the current lending environment are mezzanine debt and securitized loans. Those arrangements are all designed to give the developer greater options and more flexibility when structuring the financing of its project development costs.[29]

E. INVESTORS

This Chapter has already discussed at some length the role that institutional investors (life insurance companies, pension plans and other financial institutions) play as a customer of the real estate developer. As stated in that earlier discussion, the institutional investor's purchase of a completed real estate project represents the ultimate exit strategy for the developer. The investor's purchase of the project can take many forms, ranging from the outright purchase of fee simple title to the project to the investor's formation of a joint venture with the developer.[30] In a real estate joint venture, the developer usually cashes out a portion of its

---

projects led to an unprecedented number of both project and lender bankruptcies. *See* MIKE E. MILES, GAYLE L. BERENS AND MARC A. WEISS, REAL ESTATE DEVELOPMENT, PRINCIPLES AND PROCESS 170 (4th ed. 2007). The onset of the financial crisis of 2008 caused those lenders who remained willing to loan money to real estate developers to sharply reduce the percentage of development costs funded with debt dollars from 70–90% to 50–70%. *See* URBAN LAND INSTITUTE, *supra* note 6, at 19. Because I do not consider lender policies adopted in the wake of the 2008 crash to necessarily be the "new normal," I will continue throughout this book to describe the typical loan-to-cost ratio as being somewhere between 70–90%.

27. *See infra* Chapter 9 for a thorough discussion of construction loans.

28. *See infra* Chapter 12, Pages 553–563, for a further discussion of permanent loans.

29. *See infra* Chapter 12, Pages 561–563, for a discussion of securitized loans and mezzanine debt.

30. *See infra* Chapter 12, Pages 563–565, for a discussion of the interim exit strategies available to the developer.

interest in the project, but still retains a limited interest in the project's future, financial performance.

As noted earlier, developers generally finance the majority of their development costs with construction debt. The remaining project costs are funded with equity provided either by the developer or by third party investors.[31] Historically, the only investors who were willing to provide the developer with upfront equity were the developer's "family and friends"— for example, doctors, dentists, in-laws, and golfing buddies. Institutional investors were reluctant to invest in a project before the income stream from committed project tenants was fully stabilized. However, as institutional investors continue to chase ways to increase the yield on their real estate investments, it has become much more commonplace for the institutional investor to invest in development projects from their inception, thereby giving the developer yet another avenue to satisfy its desire to use "other people's money" to finance its development activities.

F. OPERATORS

Once construction of a real estate project is completed (and, in reality, even before then), the developer has to insure that the following two distinct functions are properly performed.

- *Leasing.* The responsibility for performing this function is generally assigned to a licensed real estate broker, whose job it is to find tenants to lease space in the developer's project. This is the real estate developer's version of the marketing department found in other businesses.

- *Property Management.* Every completed project needs someone to make sure that the toilets flush, building security is maintained and the rent is collected. These tasks are generally assigned to a property manager.

The developer can either hire independent brokerage and property management firms or put people on its own payroll to perform these two tasks. The decision as to which of these alternatives to select is largely a matter of the developer's personal preference and business style.[32]

G. ECONOMIC DEVELOPMENT OFFICERS

Until recently, governmental officials were seldom, if ever, viewed as positive contributors to a real estate development project. Rather, they were perceived as obstacles that the developer had to overcome in order to

---

31. *See infra* Chapter 7 for a discussion of the equity capitalization of the entity owning the development project.

32. Small development companies often choose to outsource these two jobs to third parties. This permits them to offload to others the ongoing cost of paying the overhead and other general administrative expenses of the personnel required to perform the leasing and management functions. As the developer's business grows, operating and cost efficiencies can often be achieved by pulling those functions in-house.

bring its development project to fruition. However, over the last several years, it has suddenly dawned on appointed and elected officials that one way to augment a state or local government's revenue base (without having to raise taxes on the citizenry) is to entice developers to build job-producing projects within its boundaries. This recognition has caused virtually every political subdivision in the country to create a new staff position for an economic development officer. It is the economic development officer's job to put together a menu of tax abatements, grants and other financial and governmental incentives to entice a developer to build its project in a particular locale.[33] The existence of some level of governmental assistance quite often proves to be the difference between a project that never gets off the ground and one that becomes a tremendous success.

H. PUBLIC SECTOR

The involvement of the public sector in the real estate development process is highlighted in the following quote from *Real Estate Development: Principles and Process*:

> Private sector real estate developers have a public sector partner in every deal—no exceptions—whether or not they choose to recognize that partner. The government—federal, state, and local—controls the U.S. system of capitalism under which private developers operate. Real estate development is a highly regulated process. Property law, public infrastructure, financial market rules, zoning, building permits, and impact fees are all part of the public sector's realm.... [I]f developers do not work hand in hand with local governments, giving them the same amount of respect and attention they would give a private sector partner delays and problems are likely to occur.... Time is money in real estate development, and overlooking or antagonizing ... public partners often costs a developer time, which translates into more interest payments and more significant costs. More important, the public sector can permanently delay a developer and can even change the rules in the middle of the game.... For these reasons, it pays for private developers to treat the public sector as a partner from the outset. The partnership is like a marriage: it can take many forms, but if it fails, it is painful.[34]

I. LAWYERS

Oh yeah, I almost forgot to mention one last player in the real estate development process—the real estate development lawyer.

---

33. *See infra* Chapter 6, Pages 158–173, for an examination of the various incentives that a governmental unit can use to assist a private development project.

34. *See* MILES, *supra* note 26, at 12–13.

IV. THE REAL ESTATE DEVELOPMENT LAWYER

A real estate development lawyer's job is, quite simply, to represent the interests of his developer client in all aspects of the real estate development process. In this respect, the role of the real estate development lawyer is similar to the role played by every transactional business lawyer, be he a merger and acquisition specialist, securities lawyer or some other type of transactional lawyer. He assumes primary responsibility for papering the terms and conditions of his client's business transaction and advising the client on how best to deal with the various business and legal risks inherent in that transaction.

A real estate development lawyer's practice is, however, markedly different in a number of respects from the practices of other transactional business lawyers.

- The real estate development lawyer is involved in virtually every aspect of his client's business. A securities lawyer handling a debt offering for a retail clothing store has little, if any, reason to become involved with or knowledgeable about the client's core business. Because the real estate development business is essentially nothing more than an endless stream of legal transactions, the real estate development lawyer necessarily finds himself continually immersed in his client's business activities. As such, the mantra introduced at the inception of this Chapter about the necessity of understanding the client's business takes on heightened significance for the real estate development lawyer.

- A real estate development lawyer must be proficient in a number of legal fields in order to effectively represent his client. The practices of most transactional lawyers involve specializing in one fairly-limited area of the law—for example, securities law for the lawyer mentioned above who is handling a debt offering for his retail client. That degree of specialization is not feasible for a real estate development lawyer. The nature of the real estate development business is such that a lawyer representing a developer must have a thorough comprehension of a broad array of legal disciplines, including real estate, tax, securities, finance, environmental, bankruptcy, zoning, construction and partnership law.

- A real estate development lawyer generally must "go it alone" in representing his developer client. Unlike a merger or a securities offering, most real estate development deals cannot support an army of highly-specialized lawyers. Both the economics and intertwining nature of the various components of the real estate development process dictate that the real estate development lawyer not only assume direct, hands-on responsibility for the structuring of the development deal, but also for its execution.

- A real estate development lawyer's actions can have a dramatic impact on the profitability (or lack thereof) of his client's development project. The lawyer handling the clothing merchant's debt offering does not have any real impact on how many sweaters his client sells. It is the color, style and composition of the sweater that dictates the profit the client derives from its sweater sales. In the real estate development business, it is as much the developer's skill in managing the risks inherent in the development process as it is the nature of the product produced by that process that ultimately dictates how much money the developer makes on the project. The real estate lawyer's efforts have a direct impact on the quality of his client's risk management efforts and, hence, on the overall success of his client's project.

The differences noted above between the practice of the real estate development lawyer and that of other types of transactional business lawyers are intended to be just that—differences between practice types, without any value judgments being made as to which practice type is more interesting, challenging or lucrative. The fact of the matter is that "beauty truly is in the eye of the beholder" when it comes to a young lawyer's selection of the practice area in which he wants to concentrate. As a lawyer who has spent 30 years representing developers, I do, however, admit to a bias in favor of real estate development law.

A. ROLES PLAYED BY THE REAL ESTATE DEVELOPMENT LAWYER

The real estate development lawyer plays a wide variety of roles in the representation of his developer client. Each of those roles requires the lawyer to learn and continually fine-tune an equally diverse set of skills.

1. Advisor

I love to read trashy lawyer novels for the pure escape value of reading about lawyers who not only devise ingenious legal strategies, but also end up physically taking down the bad guy. I recently came upon the following passage in the Steve Martini novel *Double Tap* that I found to be wonderfully descriptive of the essence of being a transactional business lawyer.

> What do you think I should do? You can hurdle the bar exam and sally forth to spend decades in front of the bench. You can deflect thunderbolts tossed by the gods in black robes and do battle daily with other lawyers. But in the end it is this question posed by [a client] that is the riddle most feared by every attorney I have ever met.[35]

Rest assured that your developer client will frequently ask you that fear-inducing question—what do you think I should do? Moreover, the question will not be limited to so-called "legal" issues on which you can wax eloquently for hours, without ever coming to any real conclusion. No,

---

35. STEVE MARTINI, DOUBLE TAP 182 (2005).

the developer is much more likely to ask you the dreaded "what do you think I should do" question about fundamental business issues, such as whether it should waive the contingencies in a purchase contract and proceed to close on the purchase of a multi-million dollar parcel of land. While the real estate development lawyer cannot make the decision for his client, the lawyer must be willing to step up and give his honest, unvarnished advice when his client asks for it. Trust me when I tell you that developers do not tolerate lawyers who are incapable of providing direct answers to the client's equally direct questions. When the inevitable question is asked by your client, just keep in mind the admonition leveled at me by the client I mentioned at the outset of this Chapter—"Frankly son, I don't care which way the wind is blowing, just bring the damn ship in."

2. Deal Designer

The real estate development lawyer is responsible for concocting the deal design and structure for a real estate project. The structure ultimately put in place by the lawyer must be tax-efficient and consistent with the developer's tolerance for risk. The structure must also effectively integrate all of the developer's relationships with the other project participants— that is, lenders, investors, construction professionals, etc. Finally, the selected structure must provide the developer with an acceptable exit strategy at each stage of the deal. The development of the right deal design requires the lawyer to marshal not only his knowledge of real estate, tax and partnership law concepts, but also his knowledge of the client's business and its overall financial condition.

3. Risk vs. Reward Analyst

As mentioned earlier in this Chapter, the success of any real estate project is dependent on how well the developer manages project risk. The real estate development lawyer should take the lead in identifying and then dealing with all project risks in a fashion that is appropriate within the context of the particular deal. This does not mean that it is the lawyer's role to eliminate all risks attendant to a particular real estate project. In truth, the only way to eliminate all project risks is to kill the deal—something that bad lawyers do way too often. The real estate development lawyer's job is to lead his client through a risk-reward analysis, so that the risks ultimately taken by the developer are reasonably justifiable in light of the rewards to be derived by the developer from its participation in the project.

4. Negotiator

The real estate development lawyer usually serves as the developer's chief negotiator on all deal issues (legal and business). In performing this role, the lawyer must put aside his competitive drive to "win" every issue and instead focus on those issues which are essential to the client being in a position to move forward with the project. Nowhere is the concept of a "win-win" outcome of more consequence than in the context of a real estate development deal. In his efforts to produce such a "win-win" result, it is incumbent upon the real estate development lawyer to not only understand the business objectives of his client, but also those of the business person and lawyer sitting across the table from him.

5. Drafter

If a lawyer is going to be successful in the practice of real estate development law, he must master the art of communicating his thoughts in writing in a clear and concise manner. One only needs to look at the mounds of documents cluttering the table at a real estate closing to realize that a real estate development lawyer without exceptional drafting skills is like a singer with laryngitis.

6. Enforcer

Every client occasionally needs its lawyer to act as the "bad cop" when trying to enforce the provisions of a contract. It is crucial for the real estate development lawyer to keep this fact in mind when designing the structure of his client's development deal. As stated by one noted development lawyer:

> If the transaction was structured and the documents prepared with enforcement in mind, [litigating the documents] will present no major trauma for the attorney or the client; if not, both of them might be in for major surprises.[36]

B. TEN CHARACTERISTICS OF A SUCCESSFUL REAL ESTATE DEVELOPMENT LAWYER

The following are ten characteristics that any successful real estate development lawyer must possess.

- He must have a sound understanding of the entirety of the business deal and, in particular, the project economics.

- He must have a solid working knowledge of the multiple legal disciplines that impact a real estate development deal—that is, real estate, tax, finance, contract, securities, environmental, bankruptcy, public, zoning, insurance and construction and public law.

- He must be able to communicate his thoughts and positions in writing in a clear, concise and strategic manner.

- He must be a *deal maker* and not a *deal killer.*

- He must be able establish and maintain solid, mutually respectful, working relationships with all of the players in the real estate development process.

- He must never hide behind the law when his client asks for his advice.

---

36. *See* HASTIE, *supra* note 12, at 13.

- He must avoid the temptation to show off his legal acumen by overlawyering a deal.

- He must have both the ability and the inclination to make quick decisions.

- He must feel comfortable working alone, without the safety net provided by the presence of an army of supporting lawyers.

- He must understand that success is measured not by the brilliance and creativity of his deal structure or by the comprehensiveness of his documents, but rather by how well his deal structure and documents serve his client's business objectives.

V. SUMMARY

There is no precise definition of the area of practice known as real estate development law. At its most basic level, real estate development law is the compendium of knowledge and skills that a lawyer must possess in order to help his real estate developer client achieve its business goals. A real estate development lawyer must have not only a thorough understanding of a number of substantive areas of the law, but also a solid working knowledge of his client's development business. Always remember the mantra—***if you want to succeed as a real estate development lawyer, you must first understand the real estate development business.***

CHAPTER 2

THE TEN STAGES OF A REAL ESTATE DEVELOPMENT PROJECT

■ ■ ■

I. INTRODUCTION

Chapter 1 touched upon some of the general roles a real estate development lawyer plays in representing his developer client. That discussion necessarily started with an examination of the business of real estate development. The real estate development business is, in essence, made up of a series of real estate projects, each of which is a micro-business in and of itself.

This Chapter will take a look in a more specific and focused manner at what a real estate development lawyer actually does in the course of his practice. That inquiry will be prefaced with an examination of the nature and scope of the business activity that is supported by the real estate development lawyer's efforts—that is, the ***real estate project***.[1]

II. WHAT IS A REAL ESTATE PROJECT?

Each real estate project developed by a real estate developer is, in effect, a separate business. Some projects involve the development of a single building for one customer. Such projects can have duration of two years or less and often have a fully-dedicated development staff of only one or two people. Then there are projects that involve the development of a massive, mixed use site for a multitude of customers, involving the developer's expenditure of hundreds of millions of dollars. Those projects can take upwards of ten years to complete and frequently involve a fully-dedicated development staff of ten or more people.

Regardless of its size, each real estate project starts in the same fashion—by the developer identifying an unsatisfied need of a targeted customer or customer class and then coming up with an idea of how best

---

1. For the purposes of this book, a real estate "project" will be deemed to be an institutional-grade, commercial real estate project that is leased to tenants from Corporate America—*see supra* Chapter 1, Page 4. The discussion in this Chapter is, however, equally applicable to other types of real estate development projects—e.g., the construction of a four-unit apartment building.

22

to satisfy that need. Once the developer devises its initial vision for a particular project, the project then advances through a series of stages, which, by and large, are consistent for every project, regardless of product type or location. Those stages will be the focus of the remainder of this Chapter.

III. THE TEN STAGES OF A REAL ESTATE DEVELOPMENT PROJECT

Many books and articles have been written about the various elements and stages of a real estate development project.[2] Most of those works are written from the perspective of the real estate developer and, hence, are heavily weighted toward the stages of a project's life cycle having to do with the developer's formulation of its initial vision and its subsequent testing of that vision to determine the feasibility of moving forward with the development project.[3] The vision and feasibility stages of the real estate development process are uniquely the province of the developer as entrepreneur and visionary. The lawyer (almost by definition, neither a visionary, nor an entrepreneur) rarely plays anything but a minor, peripheral role in these initial two stages of the real estate development process.

The lawyer's role starts once his developer client has come up with its initial idea for the project and reached at least a preliminary conclusion as to the project's feasibility. From the perspective of the real estate development lawyer, the ten stages of a real estate development project are as follows:

1. Gaining control of the site;
2. Securing essential governmental approvals and incentives;
3. Forming and capitalizing the project entity;
4. Closing the land acquisition;
5. Securing construction financing;
6. Designing and constructing the project;
7. Negotiating the project lease;
8. Executing an interim exit strategy;
9. Operating the project; and
10. Selling the project.

---

2. *See, e.g.,* MIKE E. MILES, GAYLE L. BERENS AND MARC A. WEISS, REAL ESTATE DEVELOPMENT: PRINCIPLES AND PROCESS (4th ed. 2007). The Miles book talks about an eight-stage model of real estate development, with those eight stages being (1) inception of an idea, (2) refinement of the idea, (3) feasibility, (4) contract negotiation, (5) formal commitment, (6) construction, (7) completion and formal opening and (8) property, asset and portfolio management. *See id.* at 5–8.

3. For real estate purists, the classic definition of feasibility was proffered by James A. Grasskamp in 1972, when he wrote that a "real estate project is 'feasible' when the real estate analyst determines that there is a reasonable likelihood of satisfying explicit objectives when a selected course of action is tested for fit to a context of specific constraints and limited resources." *See* James A. Grasskamp, *A Rational Approach to Feasibility Analysis,* APPRAISAL JOURNAL 515 (1972). Developers tend to reduce this definition to a more simple statement of feasibility—"the deal works."

These ten stages are present, in some fashion, in every real estate project. They do not, however, occur in any neat, sequential order.[4] It is a rare deal indeed where at least three of the stages do not converge and play themselves out over exactly the same period of time. By way of example, it is far from unusual for the real estate development lawyer to be negotiating a contract with a landowner seeking control of the site at the exact same time he is negotiating a construction loan commitment with a bank and the specifics of a tax abatement package with representatives of the local municipality. The overlapping and relative fluidity of these development stages is yet another reason why the real estate developer lawyer must gain an early and thorough understanding of all the components of the underlying business deal.

The Pages that follow will examine in summary fashion each of the ten stages of a real estate development project. That examination will first focus on the developer's business objectives and then will move on to a discussion of the lawyer's activities in support of those business objectives.[5]

A. STAGE 1: GAINING CONTROL OF THE SITE

Developer's Business Objectives. It is assumed for the purposes of this discussion that the developer has already selected a site that it believes is an ideal (or at least acceptable) location for the creation of a project to satisfy the needs of its targeted customer. Once that site is selected, the developer's business objective is to gain control of that site as quickly and cheaply as possible.

It is quite likely at this stage of the project's life that the developer has made only a preliminary decision on the feasibility of the project. While the developer probably feels pretty good about the location of the site and the existence of the customer's unsatisfied real estate need, the developer has likely not yet worked out the final project economics, secured debt or equity financing or actually locked down a customer for the project. All it knows is that the project has potential if it is located on the selected site. The developer's goal at this stage of the game is simply to tie up the site long enough to permit the developer to do all those things which are necessary to permit it to reach a final conclusion on whether the project is a "go" or a "no go." All the developer has in mind when he tells his lawyer to "tie up" the site is the taking of whatever minimal actions are required to prevent its competitors from swooping in to gain control of the land and, therefore, the project's potential.

---

4. *See* MILES, *supra* note 2, at 6, for an excellent discussion of the free-flowing, non-linear nature of the development process.

5. A separate chapter of this book is devoted to each of the ten stages of a real estate development project. Reference should be made to the applicable chapter for a more detailed analysis of the business and legal considerations inherent in each such stage.

Lawyer's Job. This stage is where the real estate development lawyer has the first opportunity to add value to his client's project. The lawyer's activities during this stage are as follows:

- *Learn the Business Deal*—Before putting pen to paper (or, in today's world, "fingers to keyboard"), the real estate development lawyer must first acquire a solid working knowledge of all aspects of his client's project, including the project's targeted customer, product type, financial projections and development schedule.

- *Prepare the What If List*—This is where the lawyer's value-add shines at its brightest. It falls to the real estate development lawyer to go through the mental gymnastics of identifying all those foreseeable events and conditions, the occurrence or existence of which could lead the developer to decide to scrap the project. These are what my first mentor called *what ifs*—what if the land is not zoned for commercial development, what if hazardous substances are found on the site, what if title to the land is unmarketable, etc. Once those what ifs are identified, the lawyer must then figure out how best to protect his client from their occurrence by either (1) identifying a method to confirm their non-existence in the subject project (for example, by requiring the receipt of a clean environmental report certifying that no adverse environmental condition exists on the land) or (2) providing an acceptable exit strategy for his client if the what ifs are found to exist in the project (for example, the grant to the developer of a right to terminate its obligation to purchase the land if an adverse environmental condition is found to exist on the land).

- *Select the Right Form of Contract*—Purchase agreements are a lot like clothing, in that there is no one agreement that is right for every occasion. Just as one would not wear flannel pajamas to a wedding, the real estate development lawyer should not use his 100 Page, *killer form*, purchase agreement[6] to paper his client's purchase of a two acre tract from an unsophisticated farmer.

- *Prepare and Negotiate a Contract That Serves His Client's Objective*—In preparing the purchase contract, the real estate development lawyer must always keep in mind what his client's business objective is at this stage of the project—that is, to gain legal control of the land long enough to permit the developer to figure out if the project is feasible. Preparing a contract that serves this business objective, while at the same time protecting the client from the existence of the dreaded what ifs, is an art form that must be mastered by any lawyer who aspires to success in the real estate development field.

---

6. *See infra* Chapter 5, Page 8, for a discussion of the so-called "killer" form of purchase contract.

B. STAGE 2: SECURING GOVERNMENTAL APPROVALS AND INCENTIVES

Developer's Business Objectives. Before the developer purchases the land, it wants to have in hand all those governmental approvals that are essential to the developer's decision to move forward with the development of the project. The identity of the "essential" governmental approvals will vary from deal to deal, depending on the uniqueness of the deal and the political climate in the jurisdiction in which the project is situated. At the bare minimum, the developer will want to know that the property is zoned to permit its development in the contemplated manner and that any governmental incentives needed to make the project's economics work are in place (for example, the grant of a tax abatement or the government's agreement to fund the construction of needed off-site infrastructure). In an ideal world, the developer will have received all requisite governmental approvals prior to its purchase of the land (culminating in the issuance of a building permit for the full construction of the project). However, the real estate developer does not live in an ideal world and is almost always willing to proceed with the land purchase before its receipt of those governmental approvals that are either perfunctory in nature or that the developer's experience tells it will eventually be issued without any controversy or unreasonable delay.

Lawyer's Job. This is the one stage where the extent of the real estate development lawyer's participation can vary a great deal from project to project. The real estate development lawyer must first sit down with his developer client to determine which governmental approvals fall into the "essential" category mentioned above. It is quite common for the developer to take the lead in securing those governmental approvals, which, while essential to the project, are not perceived to be the subject of much political controversy. Unfortunately, in today's politically divisive culture, very few governmental actions fall into the uncontroversial category. It is the real estate development lawyer's job to be sufficiently well-versed in the legal parameters surrounding the sought after governmental approval, so that he can come to his client's rescue if and when things get sticky. To the extent things get really sticky (for example, if the developer wants to build a Walmart superstore adjacent to a high-end residential subdivision), the developer should strongly consider bringing in political muscle in the form of separate zoning counsel, who can leverage his relationship with the local politicos to secure the desired approval.[7]

C. STAGE 3: FORMING AND CAPITALIZING THE PROJECT ENTITY

Developer's Business Objectives. Few developers profess to be experts when it comes to structuring either the entity that will own the project or the manner in which any outside equity investors will partici-

---

7. In my experience, a good zoning lawyer possesses a unique combination of the networking skills of a lobbyist and the analytical and presentation skills of a litigator. While it is important for the real estate development lawyer to have a thorough understanding of zoning law and procedure, it is equally important for him to know when to turn matters over to a full-time zoning lawyer.

pate in that entity. Developers do, however, have some very specific expectations (some might say "demands" is a better word choice) as to the outcome of that structuring:

- The structure must be ***tax efficient*** (lawyer-speak for the developer's desire to maximize its profits, while minimizing the tax it pays on those profits);

- The structure must limit the developer's personal liability for project risks;

- The structure must vest as much decision-making control as possible with the developer (developers give whole new meaning to the term "control freak"); and

- The structure must result in any investment by outside equity providers being ***cheap capital*** (meaning that the financial return paid to the outside equity providers is as low as possible and, in all events, less than the return paid to the developer).

Lawyer's Job. This is the project stage where the development lawyer gets the chance to truly showcase the breadth of his legal knowledge. He is much more a tax, securities, corporate and partnership lawyer during this stage than he is a real estate lawyer. It is this project stage, more than any other, which demands that the development lawyer have a full and effective understanding of the economics of the subject real estate project. The development lawyer must first select the proper form of the legal entity that will own the project. He must then draft legal documents to govern (a) the manner in which the entity is capitalized and managed and (b) the way in which the project's profits and losses are allocated among the developer and its outside equity investors. In doing so, the development lawyer must be mindful at all times of meeting the aforementioned expectations of his developer client, no matter how unrealistic certain of those expectations may be. The real estate development lawyer must also seek to imbue the entity's governing documents with sufficient flexibility to cover the future twists and turns in the project's development and the maturation of the relationship among the developer and the equity investors. Designing appropriate exit strategies to deal with those twists and turns is one of the development lawyer's biggest challenges during this project stage.

D.   STAGE 4: CLOSING THE LAND ACQUISITION

Developer's Business Objectives. The closing of the land acquisition is the watershed moment when the developer effectively makes the decision to proceed with the project. Before it commits the funding necessary to acquire the land, the developer must have first reached a comfort level that the project is indeed feasible—that is, that the rewards of moving forward with the project sufficiently outweigh the risks associated with the project. Once the decision has been made that the project is feasible, it then becomes time for the developer to begin executing its development plan for the project. In most situations, that means closing on the purchase of the land and promptly beginning on-site construction of the project.

Lawyer's Job. As the keeper of the what if list, it is the real estate development lawyer's job to make sure that all of the conditions specified in the purchase contract have been met to the developer's reasonable satisfaction.[8] These conditions include (1) the successful conclusion of all project due diligence, (2) the determination that title to the land is marketable, (3) the securing of all requisite governmental approvals for the project, (4) the validation of all representations and warranties made in the contract by the land seller and (4) the occurrence of all other events specifically identified as conditions precedent to the developer's obligation in the purchase contract. Once it has determined that all such contractual conditions have been satisfied, the real estate development lawyer must next turn his attention to orchestrating all of the moving parts and players that make up a real estate closing. Much of what a lawyer does in preparing for and then effecting the land acquisition closing is more logistical than legal in nature. The closing checklist, which itemizes all those things that have to be done and all those documents that have to be executed and delivered at or before closing, is the lawyer's best friend during the closing process. As one author so aptly put it when describing why clients turn over the closing process to their lawyers—"Lawyers are diligent, obsessive and careful."[9] While these characteristics sometimes get in the way in one's personal life, they are the perfect skills for the real estate development lawyer to possess when serving in his role as the coordinator of the closing process.

E. STAGE 5: OBTAINING CONSTRUCTION FINANCING

Developer's Business Objectives. Most developers try to fund somewhere between 70–90% of their development costs with construction debt obtained from a commercial bank or some other financial institution. The developer wants to achieve four basic goals when securing construction financing for the project:

- It wants the cost of the debt to be as cheap as possible;
- It wants to be able to draw down on the construction loan when and as it needs to pay its bills;

---

8. Even if all of the contractual conditions have been satisfied, the developer may determine that the project is not feasible for other reasons—for example, a sudden worsening of the general economy or an unexpected financial loss being incurred on the developer's other projects. If the developer decides that it does not want to go forward with the land acquisition even though all of the conditions specified in the purchase contract have been satisfied, it then will fall to the real estate development lawyer to get creative and try to find an out for the developer under the purchase contract. *See infra* Chapter 5, Pages 108–110, for a discussion of some potential ways in which a real estate development lawyer can craft the land purchase contract to try to address such unexpected occurrences.

9. *See* JOSHUA STEIN, A PRACTICAL GUIDE TO REAL ESTATE 173 (2001).

- It wants to make sure that it can pay all of its bills (including soft costs and fees payable to the developer) with debt and defer the use of its equity until as late in the process as possible;[10] and

- It wants to try to limit in some fashion its personal liability on the construction debt.

Lawyer's Job. The focus of the lawyer's attention during the course of negotiating the construction loan documents should be threefold—(1) addressing all those specific situations where the funding needs of the developer's project are at odds with the standard loan disbursement provisions of the documents (for example, the funding of the developer's fees upfront and not pro rata over the construction term)[11], (2) trying to insert as much flexibility as reasonably practicable in the loan documents, so as to give the developer the ability to respond in an effective manner to unexpected developments during the construction period (for example, reserving the right to use cost savings in one category of construction expense to fund budget busts in another category) and (3) including provisions in the loan documents that seek to limit the circumstances under which the developer will be personally liable for the repayment of the loan (for example, providing that the loan will become partially non-recourse[12] upon the leasing of some portion of the project to creditworthy tenants). In performing his job at this project stage, it is imperative that the real estate development lawyer understand not only the business objectives of his developer client, but also those of the lender. If he understands the perspectives of both parties, the development lawyer will be better able to successfully negotiate changes to the loan documents that serve his client's interests, without eviscerating the legitimate business needs of the lender.

F.   STAGE 6: DESIGNING AND CONSTRUCTING THE PROJECT

Developer's Business Objectives. The developer wants to accomplish two basic goals during Stage 6—

- The creation of a project design that is both aesthetically and functionally attractive to the developer's targeted customers;[13] and

---

10. The cost of obtaining equity capital from outside investors is almost always higher than the cost of the construction debt. The relative cost of debt and equity is discussed *infra* at Chapter 3, Pages 49–50.

11. It is, therefore, absolutely essential that the real estate development lawyer review and understand the developer's proposed draw schedule—that is, the developer's proposal as to when it will receive disbursements under the construction loan and what categories of development costs will be funded with those disbursements. *See infra* Chapter 9, Pages 359–362, 364–367, 392–393.

12. A non-recourse loan is one where the sole remedy of the lender upon a default under the loan is to foreclose on the project. The personal assets of the developer are not, therefore, subject to being attached to pay off a non-recourse loan. In almost all instances, construction loans are recourse to the developer—at least until such time as the construction of the project is completed and some significant portion of the project is leased to rent-paying tenants. *See infra* Chapter 9, Pages 321–322.

13. As noted in Chapter 1 of this book, the project design must pass muster with both of the developer's customers—that is, tenants who are interested in leasing space in the project and institutional investors who are interested in purchasing the project. *See supra* Chapter 1, Page 4.

- The completion of project construction on budget and on time.

Achieving these two objectives requires the developer to be extremely hands on during this stage of the project, meeting at least weekly with both the project architect and contractor to review the progress of construction and to prepare an action plan to address any unexpected developments.

Lawyer's Job. The task falls to the real estate development lawyer to prepare contracts with all of the design and construction professionals (principally the architect and general contractor). The contracts must spell out in a consistent and complete manner the respective roles and responsibilities of every person who participates in some manner in the design and construction of the project. The documents should also make it clear that it is the developer and neither the architect, nor the contractor, who ultimately controls this project stage. Finally, it is the real estate development lawyer's job to add sufficient teeth to the documents, so as to incentivize the design and construction professionals to complete construction of the project on time, on budget and in full accordance with the project design selected by the developer.

G. STAGE 7: NEGOTIATING THE PROJECT LEASE

Developer's Business Objectives. The prior six project stages are all centered on the cost side of the developer's business. Stage 7 is where the developer makes its money. The profitability of a project is directly tied to the developer's success in meeting the following three leasing objectives:

- The project should be leased at rents that are consistent with or better than the project's initial financial projections;

- The lease-up of the project should occur within the time frames set forth in the project's business plan; and

- The project should be leased on business and legal terms that are consistent with the expectations of the developer's "other customer"—that is, the institutional investor, who will ultimately invest either debt or equity in the project.[14]

The developer's profit on the project will suffer if it fails to meet any of these objectives.

Lawyer's Job. The first thing that the real estate development lawyer needs to understand at this project stage is that he is part of the

---

14. The inclusion in the lease of certain "out of the mainstream" provisions could limit (or in extreme situations, eliminate) the appetite of the institutional investor to buy or invest in the project. For example, the inclusion of a provision giving the tenant a right to terminate its lease in advance of the stated expiration of the tenant's lease term could have a dramatic impact on the price that an institutional investor would be willing to pay for the project (because such provisions diminish the institutional-grade status of the project).

developer's marketing team. In Stages 1 through 6, the developer is the consumer (buying land, seeking governmental approvals, securing construction financing, etc.). At the leasing stage, the developer is selling its product to its customer. The last thing a developer needs at this crucial, money-making stage of the project is a lawyer who revels in playing the role of the hard-ass lawyer by preparing the most egregious, one-sided lease imaginable and then being intractable in his resolve to win the negotiation of every point in the lease document. Tenants always have choices and one choice they often make is not to deal with a developer that is represented by a lawyer who chooses to kill rather than make deals.

Conversely, a lawyer can add real value to his client's project if he:

- Prepares a relatively short lease document[15] that covers the essential deal points and protects the developer's legitimate business interests, but is still readable and relatively user-friendly;

- Focus the lease negotiations on those provisions that make or save the developer real money (for example, the rent, operating expense and tenant improvement provisions) and limit the amount of time spent on the negotiation of relatively insignificant legal issues (for example, the attempt to craft a pluperfect subordination or eminent domain clause);[16]

- Make sure that the terms of the lease conform to the expectations and requirements of the institutional investor community; and

- Include provisions that make the lease easier (and therefore, more cost effective) for the developer's property manager to administer.

Real estate development lawyers who follow these four simple rules will make their clients money in both the short and long-term.

H.   STAGE 8: EXECUTING AN INTERIM EXIT STRATEGY

Developer's Business Objectives. Once the project is fully leased and cash flowing, the developer faces the question of what to do next— should it sell the project outright or should it retain full or partial ownership of the project for some extended period of time.

---

15.   Anyone can go to a form book and prepare a 50 Page lease document. It takes much more time, patience and skill to distill into ten Pages the essential points of the 50–Page document. *See infra* Chapter 11, Pages 456–457 for *a* narrative on the author's efforts to prepare a crisp, yet effective office lease for the Heathrow International Business Center (the case study that is used throughout this book).

16.   If the lawyer is going to accomplish this objective, he must understand both the overall economics of the project and the practices followed by institutional investors in underwriting a project's value. For example, an institutional investor will commonly discount a project's rental income by as much as $.10 per square foot if a lease places the obligation on the landlord to maintain and repair the structural components of a building (e.g., the roof and floors). A lawyer who concedes this point to a tenant on the perfectly reasonable theory that it is unlikely that the structural components of a new building will need any significant maintenance and repair just cost his client a significant amount of money (represented by the lower purchase price that an institutional investor will pay for the project as a result of the $.10 per square foot rental discount).

- ***Sale of Project***—The advantages of a quick project sale are that (a) it puts cash into the pockets of the developer in an amount equal to the sum of its capital contributions to the venture, plus the incremental value of the project over its development costs and (b) it eliminates any risk that a future occurrence (for example, a tenant bankruptcy or a downturn in the economy) will erode the profit inherent in the project. An outright sale of the project will, however, be a taxable event and will subject the developer to income tax on the excess of the project's sales price over the project's adjusted tax basis (which, at this early stage in the project's history, is generally equal to the project's development costs).[17]

- ***Retention of Ownership***—Many developers prefer to hold on to their developed projects for an extended period of time, so as to take advantage of both (a) the continuing positive cash flow produced from the project and (b) the anticipated increase in the value of the project over time. By doing so, the developer postpones the imposition of any tax on the project's profit, until the date of its ultimate sale. The retention of an ownership interest in the project does, however, subject the developer to the ongoing risk that some event will occur in the future which will decrease (or wholly eliminate) both the project's positive cash flow and its incremental value. Some developers try to limit this risk by retaining only partial ownership of the project.

If the developer opts to retain an ownership position in the project, it will nonetheless want to pay off its construction loan as soon as possible after the project is fully leased. The typical construction loan has three features that do not comport with the developer's continuing ownership of a fully-leased project:

- The developer (or one of its affiliates) is personally liable for the repayment of the construction loan;

- The interest rate of a construction loan is a variable rate that is subject to increase if the financial index to which it is tied increases (e.g., the prime rate or the London Interbank Offered Rate); and

- The construction loan provides for the full repayment of the loan within a relatively short period after the completion of the project (usually no more than one or two years).

A developer who wants to retain ownership of a project (in full or in part) can do so and still pay off the construction loan by (a) replacing the construction loan with a permanent, non-recourse loan (b) contributing

---

17. *See* INTERNAL REVENUE CODE § 1001. An important factor to take into consideration is whether the project sale will produce a capital gain or ordinary income for the developer and its outside equity investors. Capital gains are currently taxed at a maximum rate of 15%, while the maximum rate applicable to ordinary income is currently 35%. *See id.* § 1. A gain on the sale of a real estate project will normally qualify for capital gain treatment, unless (a) the project has been held for less than 12 months after the date on which it was placed in service or (b) the project was held primarily for sale to customers. *See id.* §§ 1221–1223.

the project to a newly-formed joint venture with an institutional investor, with the investor making a cash contribution to the venture sufficient to retire any construction debt[18] or (c) a combination of (a) and (b). Under each of these alternatives, the developer will have positioned itself to continue to enjoy the economic benefits from the project (positive cash flow in the short-term and continuing appreciation in the value of the project in the long-term). A developer who wishes to cash out a significant part of its equity in the project (represented by both its initial cash contribution to the project and its interest in the incremental value of the project over its development costs) will likely choose either alternative (b) or (c). If the developer has no particular desire or need to realize on its equity in the project, then it is more apt to simply refinance the project with a nonrecourse, permanent loan and retain ownership of 100% of the project.

Lawyer's Job. At this stage, the real estate development lawyer's first mission is to advise his developer client as to which of the available interim exit strategies will best achieve the developer's business objectives. In order to render effective advice on this topic, the development lawyer must be well-versed not only on the economics of the subject project, but also on the economics of the developer's business as a whole. The development lawyer must also determine if there are any outside equity investors, whose approval is required as a condition precedent to the implementation of an interim exit strategy (and, if there are, what options are available to the developer if they fail to approve the developer's selected strategy). Finally, the development lawyer must once again put on his tax lawyer hat to make sure that the selected exit strategy does not result in any unexpected tax consequences to the developer or any of its equity investors. Once the decision is made as to which interim exit strategy will be implemented, the real fun starts for the real estate development lawyer. Regardless which interim exit strategy is selected, the legal documents required to evidence the transaction will be complex and voluminous—two words that are music to the lawyer's ears.

I.   STAGE 9: OPERATING THE PROJECT

Developer's Business Objectives. The developer's economic desires for the project during this operational stage are relatively simple and straightforward—(1) to maximize and stabilize the project's annual cash flow and (2) to enhance the long-term residual value of the project. In order to actualize these goals, the developer wants its project operations to proceed in accordance with the following guiding principles:

- Keep the project full with tenants paying rent at or above the pro forma rents;

- Hold project expenses at or below the pro forma expenses;

---

18. The investor's cash contribution may also be used to fund a full or partial return of the developer's equity in the project equity. *See infra* Chapter 12, Pages 563–564.

- Maintain the project in a good condition and order of repair; and
- Keep both its tenants and its equity investors happy

The job of keeping the project full usually falls to a licensed real estate broker, while the remaining three tasks are assigned to a property manager. Whether the developer staffs these roles internally or externally is largely a matter of the developer's personal preference and business style.

Lawyer's Job. If the developer opts to staff project operations externally (that is, by outsourcing these functions to independent third parties), the development lawyer will need to put together the agreements retaining the broker and property manager. Those agreements should clearly delineate what is expected from the broker and the property manager and should be for relatively short terms, so that the developer can go a different direction if the third party's performance is not acceptable. During the operations stage, the development lawyer also assumes the role of a legal handyman, taking on whatever legal matters might arise with respect to the day-to-day management of the project. By way of example, the development lawyer might have to deal with a tenant bankruptcy one day and with an on-site environmental spill the next.

J. STAGE 10: SELLING THE PROJECT

Developer's Business Objective. Forget about the maxim that real estate is all about "location, location, location." The reality is that timing is an equally important contributor to the ultimate success of a real estate project. The developer's business objective at this final project stage is quite simple—to try to maximize its profit by picking the optimal time to sell the project. Selecting that optimal date is, however, much more of an art than it is a science.[19] Real estate is an inherently cyclical business, with the up and down cycles each lasting for not just months, but years. The developer who waits too long to pull the trigger on its project sale may end up seeing all of the value of its project permanently eroded during a lengthy downturn in the real estate markets.[20] The moral of this story is that the successful developer should err on the side of selling its project too early rather than too late.

---

19.   There are many considerations that factor into the determination of when a project should be sold. The most important consideration is market timing—that is, selling the project at a time when the demand for commercial real estate like the project is at its peak, thereby maximizing the purchase price that an institutional investor will pay for the project. Project-specific conditions also influence the selection of the time when a project should be marketed for sale. By way of example, it would not be advisable to try to sell a project at a time when the project's anchor tenant has only one year left on its lease term (because of the uncertainty about the future income stream generated from the project). Conversely, a project that has no leases expiring for the next five years would be an ideal candidate for sale. The art of selecting the optimal time to put a project up for sale involves balancing the general state of the economy with the project-specific conditions that also impact a project's marketability.

20.   This was the unfortunate fate meted out to those developers who continued to own stabilized real estate projects after the 2008 financial crisis. The consensus of most real estate economists is that real estate values decreased by somewhere between 40–50% in the wake of the 2008 downturn. *See* URBAN LAND INSTITUTE AND PRICEWATERHOUSECOOPERS, EMERGING TRENDS IN REAL ESTATE 9 (October 2009.

Lawyer's Job. In the first instance, it is the real estate development lawyer's job to create the legal flexibility to permit his developer client to sell its project when the developer decides that the time is right to do so. Developers do not take kindly to hearing from their lawyers that the provision of some lease, financing agreement or other legal document makes the sale of a project at the time selected by the developer economically infeasible.[21] The real estate development lawyer mission is to anticipate the developer's ultimate sale of the project by creating contractual exits for the developer at each of the prior nine project stages.

The project sale also presents the real estate development lawyer with a unique and interesting opportunity to have a significant body of his legal work scrutinized and critiqued by an army of lawyers, accountants and other real estate professionals retained by the buyer to perform due diligence on the project.[22] To the extent he did his job properly in the prior nine project stages, this process will be relatively painless for the development lawyer (and maybe even a bit rewarding). To the extent he failed to do his job in those earlier stages, the development lawyer will get to witness first-hand the economic impact that poor lawyering can have on a real estate project.

IV.   SUMMARY

This Chapter laid the groundwork for the remainder of this book by identifying the ten stages of the lawyer's participation in a real estate development project. The role played by the real estate development lawyer during each of those ten stages of a development project will be examined in later chapters of this book.

---

21.   By way of example, a project mortgage might include a prepayment penalty that requires the developer to pay a hefty additional sum to its lender if the project is sold early in the loan term. *See infra* Chapter 12, Pages 556–558.

22.   A significant part of a buyer's due diligence is its review of legal documents such as project leases, reciprocal easement agreements and title conditions and restrictions. Legal documents that create uncertainty about the predictability of the project's future income stream will have a direct, negative impact on the purchase price an investor will pay for the project. Examples of such circumstances are a lease that does not clearly set forth the rent applicable to a tenant's extension term or a lease that leaves up in the air the issue of whether the landlord or the tenant has the economic obligation to pay for any required upgrading of the project's heating and air conditioning system.

CHAPTER 3

WHAT THE REAL ESTATE DEVELOPMENT LAWYER NEEDS TO KNOW ABOUT PROJECT ECONOMICS

■ ■ ■

I. INTRODUCTION

The mantra for this book is *if you want to succeed as a real estate development lawyer, you first need to understand the real estate development business.* With that admonition in mind, Chapter 1 examined the nature of the real estate development business and the various players who are involved in that business. Chapter 2 looked at the ten stages of a real estate development project. This Chapter will conclude the initial study of the business aspects of real estate development by examining the fundamentals of real estate project economics.

The following topics will be covered in this Chapter:

- The reasons the real estate development lawyer should care about project economics;

- The basic concepts of net operating income and residual value;

- The funding of development costs with construction debt and equity contributions;

- The concept of financial leverage;

- The theory of the time value of money; and

- The methodologies used to value real estate projects.

As was the case in Chapters 1 and 2, the discussion of project economics will be undertaken primarily from the perspective of the real estate development lawyer.

II. WHY SHOULD A REAL ESTATE DEVELOPMENT LAWYER CARE ABOUT PROJECT ECONOMICS?

By now you are probably asking yourself a couple of questions.

- Why is this crazy person making me learn about economics?

- Isn't that what accountants and financial analysts are for?

While I will refrain from commenting on my mental state or hazarding a guess as to the relative usefulness of accountants or financial analysts, I will be happy to try to answer the fundamental question— "Why should a real estate development lawyer care about project economics?"

The discussion of project economics properly starts with the concepts embodied in the following quotes from two well-regarded books on real estate finance.

> Valuation is a function of the future income stream and the risk associated with that stream.[1]

> An investor who buys a particular property is in effect buying a set of assumptions about the ability of the property to generate cash flows over the period and the likely market value of the property at the end of the holding period. That the physical structure is tangential to the investment decision is sometimes difficult for students to grasp. But soundness of construction, distinguished architecture and harmonious surroundings are relevant to the investment decision only to the extent those factors affect the flow of benefits from ownership and control.[2]

The common thread running through both of these quotes is that the value of commercial real estate is a function not of the project's location, design or construction, but rather of the income stream generated from that project.

It should, therefore, come as little surprise that the first thing that an institutional investor wants to see when deciding whether it will buy a project and, if so, what it will pay for that project, is not a photograph of the building, the project plans and specifications or even the demographics for the market in which the project is located. No, what the institutional investor is most interested in are the project leases. The institutional investor knows that the leases define both the amount of the income stream generated from a project and the various risks associated with the investor's receipt of that income stream.

---

1. *See* MICHAEL E. MILES, GAYLE L. BERENS AND MARC A. WEISS, REAL ESTATE DEVELOPMENT: PRINCIPLES AND PROCESS 93 (3rd ed. 2000).

2. *See* GAYLON E. GREER AND MICHAEL D. FARRELL, INVESTMENT ANALYSIS FOR REAL ESTATE DECISIONS 16–17 (2nd ed. 1988).

Given the fact that the single most important determinant of the value of a real estate project is the work product of the real estate development lawyer, it seems rather obvious why the lawyer should feel compelled to learn something about project economics. The following are four additional reasons why an aspiring real estate development lawyer should read the remainder of this Chapter.

- An essential element of the structuring of any real estate development deal is the allocation of a project's economic benefits and financial risks among the various providers of capital to the project—that is, the developer, the lender and the outside equity investors. Without a sound understanding of project economics, the lawyer will be at a loss in seeking to properly allocate those benefits and risks among the parties.[3]

- As stated at the outset of this Chapter, the value of a project is not determined by the quality of its construction or design (the "bricks and mortar" equation), but rather is a function of two things—(1) the project's current income stream (represented by the lease) and (2) the sales proceeds realized upon the ultimate disposition of the project (represented by the sales contract). The real estate development lawyer is a key participant in both the leasing of the project and its ultimate sale. As a result, there is perhaps no other industry where the profitability of the client's business is more closely tied to the lawyer's job performance.

- Real estate documents in today's marketplace are filled with financial formulas and definitions. A real estate development lawyer who understands project economics can add real value to his client's deal by manipulating those definitions and formulas in a manner which redounds to his client's benefit.

- Developers love lawyers who speak their lingo.

III. REAL ESTATE ECONOMICS 101—THE BASIC CONCEPTS

The lawyer's course in real estate economics begins with a reiteration of the prior statement that the value of a commercial real estate project is a function of two basic economic concepts:

- The ***net operating income*** generated from the project; and

- The ***residual value*** of the project.

The next section of this Chapter will take a brief look at each of these concepts.

---

3. *See* John D. Hastie, *Real Estate Acquisition, Development and Disposition from the Developer's Perspective,* in ALI–ABA COURSE OF STUDY MATERIALS, MODERN REAL ESTATE TRANSACTIONS: PRACTICAL STRATEGIES FOR REAL ESTATE ACQUISITION, DISPOSITION, AND OWNERSHIP, Course No. SS–012, 15 (July 2010).

A. NET OPERATING INCOME

Net operating income (NOI) is the term used to measure the current income stream generated by a project. Net operating income is defined as follows:

Net operating income = Gross revenues − Operating expenses.

Gross revenues are the sum of all rents and other income received by the owner of the project. *Operating expenses* are all those expenses that are paid by the owner to operate and maintain the project, including real estate taxes, janitorial fees, maintenance and repair costs, insurance premiums, utility costs and property management fees. Expressly excluded from the definition of "operating expenses" are the principal and interest paid on the project debt and capital expenditures (for example, leasing commissions and the cost of adding to or replacing the structural components of the project).[4]

B. RESIDUAL VALUE

Residual value is the cash produced on the sale of the project. For this purpose, residual value is defined as follows:

Residual value = Gross sales proceeds − Selling expenses.

Gross sales proceeds are generally equal to the purchase price payable on the sale of the project. *Selling expenses* are those transactional costs that reduce the amount of cash available for distribution to the project participants (i.e., the developer and its lender and equity investors) and include real estate brokerage commissions, legal fees and title insurance premiums.

C. USE OF NET OPERATING INCOME AND RESIDUAL VALUE

A project's net operating income and residual value are the cash sources used by the project owner (1) to repay the funds advanced by the lender, developer and equity investors to pay the costs of developing the project and (2) to pay an additional return to those parties to compensate them for the risks they took in funding the development costs. The amount and timing of the payments to be received by these three categories of fund providers are directly linked to the risk taken by the provider

---

4. When calculating a project's net operating income, an institutional investor will commonly add two fictional line item expenses to its calculation, both of which have the effect of decreasing a project's net operating income—(1) a so-called "vacancy allowance" to reflect its expectation of the normal vacancy and uncollectable rents associated with a project (typically an amount equal to 5% of the total projected gross revenues) and (2) a so-called "structural reserve" to reflect the average cost of repairing and replacing the project's structural components over the life of the project (typically an amount equal to $.05–.10 per square foot contained within the project, depending upon the age and physical condition of the project). The existence and amounts of these two reserves will vary depending upon the provisions of the project's lease and the investor's perception of the project's risk.

when the funds were committed to the project. The adage "the greater the risk, the greater the return" certainly holds true in the real estate development business.

IV. THE FUNDING OF DEVELOPMENT COSTS

The funds used to pay the costs of developing a real estate project come from three principal sources—(1) the project lender, (2) the developer and (3) the outside equity investors. This section will examine the risk and return expectations and requirements of each of these funding sources. As a stepping off point for that discussion, one first needs to gain an appreciation for the cost categories that are included in the development cost budget.

A. DEVELOPMENT COST BUDGET

The development cost budget should include all those costs that are directly related to the development of a real estate project. There are three basic categories of development costs.[5]

- ***Land costs*** are the costs incurred by the developer in connection with its acquisition and ownership of the land on which the developer's project will be located.

- ***Hard costs*** are those expenses that are directly incurred in connection with the construction of the building, the build-out of the tenant space and the making of other site improvements and include the contractor's fee and the cost of all labor and materials provided to the project.

- ***Soft costs*** are all those costs, other than hard costs, which would not have been incurred, but for the development of the subject project. Soft costs include the following:
  - Interest, fees and other carrying charges paid on any loan secured to acquire the land or construct the building;
  - Fees paid to architects, engineers and other design professionals;
  - Appraisal fees, title insurance premiums and surveying costs;
  - Due diligence costs paid to environmental consultants, soils engineers, land planners, etc.;
  - Development fees paid to the developer;[6]

---

5. *See generally* DAVID M. GELTNER, NORMAN G. MILLER, JIM CLAYTON AND PIET EICHHOLTZ, COMMERCIAL REAL ESTATE ANALYSIS AND INVESTMENTS 767 (2nd ed. 2007).

6. The developer's fees are not only a component of the project's overall development costs, but also a source of the economic return garnered by the developer from its participation in the project. The fact that the construction lender and outside equity investors are customarily responsible for funding the vast majority of the developer's fees leads to a natural tension between the developer and its lender and outside investors concerning both the amount of the

- Real estate brokerage and leasing commissions;

- Impact fees and other governmental charges;

- Advertising and other marketing costs;

- Legal fees;

- Construction period operating expenses such as real estate taxes, insurance premiums and utility charges;

- An operating reserve to pay the projected deficit in the project's net operating income during the period after completion of construction, but before the project is sufficiently leased to cover the project's operating expenses; and

- A contingency reserve to cover any unexpected costs incurred during the development process.

B.　CONSTRUCTION FINANCING

The developer typically funds 70–90% of its project development costs through a construction loan.[7] Commercial banks are the biggest suppliers of construction loans in the United States. The risk/return parameters of the typical construction loan are described below.

1.　Risks Faced by Construction Lender

Construction lenders face two basic risks:

- The risk that construction of the project will not be completed on budget and on time; and

- The risk that, even if completed on budget and on-time, the project will not produce sufficient cash flow or possess sufficient value to pay off the construction loan.

Construction lenders are, by their very nature, the least risk tolerant of the three main funding sources for the typical real estate development project (the other two being the developer and its outside equity investors). Construction lenders seek to mitigate their lending risk in a number of ways, including those discussed below.[8]

- ***Requiring a First Mortgage on Project***—The primary way that the construction lender limits its risk exposure is by securing the repayment of its loan with a first mortgage on the project. If any default occurs under the construction loan, the construction lender

---

development fee and the time at which it is paid to the developer. *See infra* Chapter 9, Pages 364–367, for a further discussion of this point.

7. In the aftermath of the 2008 financial crisis, construction lenders limited began to limit their loan amounts to 50–70% of the project's development costs. *See supra* Chapter 1, note 26; and *infra* Chapter 9, Page 398. This Chapter will use the historical 70–90% loan-to-cost ratio to describe the portion of a project's development costs that is funded under a construction loan.

8. The risks faced by a construction lender and the various ways that it seeks to mitigate those risks are discussed in greater detail *infra* Chapter 9, Pages 331–397.

can then foreclose on the project and, if necessary, contract with a third party for the completion of the project.[9]

- ***Receiving Personal Guaranties from Developer***—The construction lender further addresses the risk inherent in a construction loan by requiring the developer (or a creditworthy affiliate of the developer) to provide the lender with personal guaranties that the project will be completed on budget and on time and that the loan will be repaid.

- ***Limiting the Length of the Loan Term***—The construction lender does not want to take any long-term risk on the project. For this reason, most construction loans are for a term of no more than 36 months. The relatively short term of the construction loan forces the borrower to either sell the project prior to the maturity of the construction loan or obtain a permanent loan to refinance its construction loan position.[10]

- ***Limiting the Loan Amount***—Obviously, a construction lender can limit its risk by reducing the amount of its loan. As noted earlier, lenders typically seek to mitigate their loan risk by loaning less than all of a project's development costs (historically in the 70–90% range). The next section of this Chapter explores two other tests commonly used by a construction lender to limit the amount of its construction loan and, hence, its risk that the loan will not be fully repaid by the developer.

2. Loan Ratios

A construction lender relies on two ratios to place a ceiling on the amount of its construction loan—(1) the ***loan-to-value ratio*** (***LTV***) and (2) the ***debt service coverage ratio*** (***DSC***). The first such ratio (LTV) limits the loan amount by reference to the projected residual value of the developer's project, while the second ratio (DSC) limits the loan amount by reference to the projected net operating income of that project.

The loan-to-value ratio is a test that a construction lender uses to determine whether its collateral for the repayment of the loan (the first mortgage on the project) will produce sufficient value to pay off the loan, if and when it should ever have to foreclose on the project.[11] Most lenders use an LTV ratio in the vicinity of 60–80%. A construction loan made at a 70% LTV means that the maximum amount of the construction loan will be 70% of the project's projected value. The value differential (that is, the 30% by which the projected value exceeds the loan amount) is the

---

9. A sale of an uncompleted project at foreclosure will rarely produce sufficient cash to cover the full amount of the outstanding construction debt. The lender is, therefore, often left with little choice but to protect its loan position by completing construction of the project.

10. *See infra* Chapter 12, Page 553.

11. *See infra* Pages 55–62, for a discussion of some of the methods used by construction lenders to value real estate projects.

"cushion" that the construction lender relies on to lessen its risk exposure on the construction loan.[12]

The use of a debt service coverage ratio is designed to give the lender comfort that the income stream from the project will be sufficient to permit the developer to pay all debt service payments, when and as they become due during the term of the construction loan. Most lenders use a debt service coverage ratio of somewhere between 1.20 and 1.40. A construction loan made at a DSC of 1.30 means that the projected net operating income must be at least 130% of the debt service the developer is required to pay on its construction loan. This 30% differential gives the lender comfort that the project will produce sufficient cash flow to service its debt.

Once the maximum debt service the project can support is determined by applying the DSC ratio, the maximum loan amount can then be determined by using what lenders commonly refer to as a ***mortgage constant***. The mortgage constant is the percentage of an original loan that must be paid every year to repay all principal and interest over a stated period of time (commonly referred to as the ***amortization period***). To calculate the mortgage constant, the lender must first make certain assumptions about the interest rate payable on the loan and the time period over which the loan is to be amortized.[13] Once those assumptions are made, the determination of the mortgage constant is simply a matter of doing the math.[14] The maximum loan amount supported by a particular project under the DSC test is equal to the project's maximum debt service (determined by dividing the project's projected NOI, by the stipulated DSC ratio), divided by the mortgage constant.[15]

The operation of the LTV and DSC tests is illustrated in the following example.

> **Example 3–1**: Assume that a project being underwritten by a construction lender has the following financial characteristics:
>
> - Total development costs of $4,200,000;
> - Projected value of $5,000,000; and
> - Projected annual net operating income of $450,000.

Further assume that the lender proposes to set its maximum loan amount for the project by employing a LTV ratio of 80% and a DSC ratio of 1.20 (using a mortgage constant of 10%).[16]

---

12. *See* MILES, *supra* note 1, at 84.

13. The construction lender will select an interest rate and amortization period based on the rate and period then being used on permanent loans for similar project types. *See infra* note 17.

14. For those compulsive mathematicians in the reading audience, a monthly mortgage constant can be calculated using a hand-held calculator by solving for payment (PMT), where PV = $1; FV = 0; n = the number of months in the selected amortization period; and i = the stated interest rate payable under the loan (divided by 12—accomplished by using the "g" key on an HP 12–C calculator). *See* WILLIAM B. BRUEGGEMAN AND JEFFREY D. FISHER, REAL ESTATE FINANCE AND INVESTMENTS 79 (13th ed. 2008).

15. When fully-armed with this knowledge, the real estate development lawyer should try to manipulate the "mortgage constant" definition in a loan agreement in his client's favor by increasing the assumed amortization period and decreasing the assumed interest rate, thereby decreasing the mortgage constant and increasing his client's available loan amount.

With all these assumptions in mind, the maximum loan amount under the LTV test is $4 million [project value of $5 million, multiplied by the 80% LTV ratio]. The maximum loan amount produced under the DSC test is $3.75 million [([NOI of $450,000, divided by the 1.2 DSC ratio), divided by the mortgage constant of 10%]. A construction lender, being the risk averse animal that it is, will almost always set the loan amount at the lower of the two maximum loan amounts produced by the LTV and DSC tests ($3.75 million in this example).[17]

3. Return Expectations of the Construction Lender

The construction lender's return for taking the risk of making a construction loan is represented by the interest payments it receives under the loan.[18] The construction lender makes its money off of the spread between its *cost of funds*[19] and the interest rate it receives on its project loan. Reduced to its simplest and most basic statement, a bank makes money when it receives a deposit from a customer for a CD paying 5% and then takes that deposit and uses it to make a construction loan to a developer at an interest rate of 8%. The bank's positive return in this scenario is, however, wholly dependent on the developer being able to pay off the construction loan at maturity. The uncertainty that this desired outcome will occur is the risk that was addressed in the preceding section of this Chapter.[20] While a construction lender will always require a

---

16. A 10% mortgage constant is produced by the use of an assumed annual interest rate of 8% and an assumed amortization period of 20 years. For those untrusting souls, the assumed interest rate and amortization period can be run through the formula set forth in note 14, *supra*, to produce a monthly mortgage constant of .0084. That monthly figure is then multiplied by 12 to produce an annual mortgage constant of 10.04% (which, for the purposes of the textual illustration, has been rounded down to 10%).

17. The LTV and DSC tests are also commonly used by permanent lenders to determine the amount of the loan it will make on a project. Indeed, construction lenders regularly canvass the permanent lender community to determine what LTV and DSC ratios are being used to set the principal amount of permanent loans. By keeping abreast of what is going on in the permanent loan market, the construction lender tries to insure that it does not make a construction loan on a project in an amount in excess of that which a permanent lender will make on that same project (once it is completed and leased in accordance with the developer's initial projections). Unlike the construction lender, the permanent lender has the relative luxury of applying the LTV and DSC tests based on actual net operating income numbers and not on those projected by the developer in advance of the development of the project. As such, the making of a permanent loan is an inherently less risky activity than is the making of a construction loan.

18. The construction lender passes through to the borrower all of the costs incurred by the lender in connection with the making of its construction loan, thereby preserving the interest paid on its loan as the lender's true economic return. The costs customarily passed on to the borrower include the lender's legal fees, appraisal costs, title insurance premiums and construction inspection costs. Construction lenders also frequently charge upfront "loan origination" fees, which, as little more than prepaid interest, serve to augment the lender's return on its construction loan.

19. A lender's "cost of funds" is a factor of (a) the interest rate it needs to pay on money deposited with it by its depositor customers and (b) the interest rate it needs to pay on any money borrowed by it from the Federal Reserve Bank or any other source. There are a number of indexes which try to track the average "cost of funds" of lending institutions—*see e.g.*, the 11th District Monthly Weighted Average Cost of Funds Index, available online at http://www.fhlbsf. com.

20. The construction lender's risk is further compounded by the fact that it ordinarily does not receive the return represented by the project's interest payments until the construction loan

positive spread between the rate of interest charged on a construction loan and its cost of funds (it is, after all, in the business of making money), the size of that spread will vary depending on the lender's perception of its risk in making the loan. This is just another way of saying that the lender expects a return commensurate with its assumed risk. Put in real world terms, the interest rate charged on a project that is pre-leased to Microsoft will be significantly lower than the interest rate charged on a project where no such pre-leasing exists.

Another risk faced by a construction lender is that a change in the economy will occur during the term of the construction loan that will increase the lender's cost of funds above that which existed when the loan was closed. The construction lender addresses this risk by providing that the interest rate payable under its construction loan will be adjusted from time to time to reflect an increase in a financial index selected by the lender that is representative of the lender's cost of funds. The prime rate, the federal funds rate and the London Inter-bank Offered Rate (**LIBOR**) are examples of benchmarks commonly used for this purpose by construction lenders.[21]

C. EQUITY CONTRIBUTIONS

Construction debt usually covers somewhere between 70–90% of a project's development costs. That leaves 10–30% of the development costs to be funded through equity contributions[22] made to the project by the developer and its outside equity investors. The discussion that follows will first examine the risk profile and return expectations of equity providers. It will then look at how the principle of financial leverage can be used to enhance the economic return on the invested equity.

The developer almost always makes some level of equity contribution to the project. Large, national developers often contribute 100% of the equity needed to fund the gap between the amount of the construction loan and the project's total development costs. Even in those projects where the vast majority of the needed equity is provided by outside investors, the outside investors normally insist that the developer make some significant equity contribution to the venture, so as to insure that

---

is fully paid off. Developers habitually request (and lenders often agree) that the construction loan budget include all interest payable during the term of the construction loan. In this scenario, the developer simply borrows from the construction lender an amount sufficient to permit it to make the interest payments on the construction loan, thereby subjecting the lender's interest rate return to the risk that the loan will not be paid off at maturity.

21. Astute developers are also concerned about the impact that a "floating" interest rate can have on the economics of its project. Developers can limit their exposure to interest rate increases by buying a "cap" or a "swap" from a financial institution that either puts a ceiling on the amount of any interest rate increase or effectively substitutes a fixed interest rate for a variable one. This protection comes at a significant cost and, therefore, is used somewhat sparingly by developers. *See infra* Chapter 9, Pages 369–372.

22. The terms "equity" and "capital" are used interchangeably throughout this Chapter to refer to cash or other property contributed by an investor to the entity that owns the real estate development project.

the developer has an economic stake in seeing to it that the project is successful.[23]

Who are the outside equity investors that serve as an additional source for the funding of a project's development costs? On smaller projects, they tend to fall into the category of "family and friends" of the developer. On larger projects, the bulk of the outside capital is provided by the type of institutional investors discussed in Chapter 1 of this book—e.g., life insurance companies, pension funds, equity funds and other financial institutions.[24] Regardless whether the investor is the developer's family dentist or a life insurance company, all capital providers share a common investment goal—they want to "achieve the maximum ownership interest and share of returns from the development while making the minimum possible financial exposure."[25]

By making its investment in a project, the equity investor is effectively buying a share of the project's net operating income and residual value. As Professor Greer notes in *Investment Analysis for Real Estate Decisions*:

> The price an investor is prepared to pay for a defined property interest depends in part upon the amount and timing of these anticipated receipts and upon the degree of confidence with which expectations are held. It also depends upon the investor's tolerance for bearing risk and upon the relative attractiveness of alternative opportunities.[26]

The next two sections of this Chapter will look at the risks associated with the making of an equity investment in a real estate development project and the commensurate economic return demanded by the equity investor.

1. Risks Faced by the Equity Investor

The equity investor faces the same basic project risks that are faced by the construction lender—(a) the risk that the project will not be completed on budget and on time and (b) the risk that, even if the project is completed on budget and on time, the project will not produce sufficient cash flow or possess sufficient value to pay the projected economic return to the investor. The level of risk associated with the making of an equity investment in a real estate project is, however, significantly greater than that associated with the making of a construction loan. The reasons the equity investor has a heightened level of risk are discussed below.

- *No Fixed Obligation to Repay*—Unlike the loan dollars advanced by the construction lender, the funds committed by the outside capital provider are truly at risk with the success of the project. There is no fixed obligation on the part of the project owner or any

---

23. In the vernacular of the real estate industry, this is known as requiring that the developer have "some skin in the game."

24. *See supra* Chapter 1, Pages 6–7.

25. *See* MILES, *supra* note 1, at 48.

26. *See* GREER, *supra* note 2, at 6.

other person to repay either the contributed capital or any return on that capital.[27]

- *No Security for Repayment*—In return for its capital contribution, the capital provider receives an ownership interest in the entity that owns the real estate project. It does not, however, receive any collateral interest in the underlying project to secure its hope of receiving a return of its equity contribution or its share of the project's cash flow.

- *No Cushion for Repayment*—The previous discussion of the construction lender's risk profile spoke about the lender's attempt to mitigate its risk by using certain lending tests to create "cushions" between the value of the project and the amount of the construction loan (the loan-to-value test) and the project's cash flow and the lender's debt service payments (the debt service coverage test). No such cushion exists for the capital provider, who, in effect, is the construction lender's cushion. The capital provider gets paid only after all requisite payments are made to the construction lender. Moreover, the only way that the capital provider will receive any profit from its investment is if the project ultimately has a value in excess of its accrued development costs (which includes any unexpected cash deficits from the project).

- *Lack of Marketability for Equity Interests*— There is no market for the sale of equity interests in private real estate projects. The owner of stock in a publicly-traded company can cut its losses by selling its stock when it sees the company beginning to lose value. The investor in a private real estate project has almost no ability whatsoever to limit its loss in that fashion.[28]

2. Return Expectations of the Equity Investor

The risk assumed by the equity investor is much greater than that assumed by the construction lender. As such, the return expectations of the equity investor are much higher than those of the construction lender.

In order to fully appreciate how the risk/return continuum plays out in the context of a real estate project, one must take a look at three standard, economic return measurements.

---

27. An investor may seek to lessen this risk by establishing some type of "super priority" status for its contributed capital. Under that scenario, the first dollars of available project cash flow will be used to pay an agreed-upon sum to the investor (commonly referred to as a "preferred return"), before the developer receives any cash distributions from the project. *See infra*, Chapter 7, Pages 243–245.

28. The creation of publicly-traded, real estate investment trusts has permitted the small investor to purchase a highly marketable equity ownership interest in real estate. Real estate investment trusts or "REITS" such as Simon Property Group Inc., ProLogis and Duke Realty Corp. own vast portfolios of commercial real estate. By definition, however, a REIT must have at least 100 shareholders and, therefore, is not an entity suited for the garden variety, closely-held real estate development venture that is the subject of this book. *See* INTERNAL REVENUE CODE 856(a)(5). For a general discussion of the REIT ownership vehicle, *see* GEORGE LEFCOE, REAL ESTATE TRANSACTIONS, FINANCE, AND DEVELOPMENT 683–688 (6th ed. 2009).

- ***Return on Total Costs—*** This return standard measures the overall productivity of the project. A project's return on total costs is equal to the project's net operating income, divided by the project's total development costs. In Example 3–1, it was assumed that a project produced annual net operating income of $450,000 and that its aggregate development costs were $4.2 million. Using these same assumptions, the project's overall rate of return would be 10.71% (the NOI of $450,000, divided by the development costs of $4,200,000). This 10.71% project return must then be divided between the two principal funding sources for the project—that is, the construction lender and the equity investors (which, for this purpose, will be deemed to include the developer).[29]

- ***Return on Debt—*** The construction lender's return on its advancement of the construction loan proceeds is roughly equal to the rate of interest being charged on the construction loan. In Example 3–1, the return on debt would be the 8% interest rated charged to the project by the construction lender.[30]

- ***Return on Equity***[31]***—*** This financial standard measures the return to the equity investor and is often referred to as the ***cash on cash return***.[32] The return on equity is equal to the cash that is available for distribution to the equity investors (commonly referred to as ***before tax cash flow***), divided by the total capital contributed to the project by the investors. For this purpose, before tax cash flow is equal to the project's net operating income, less (a) the debt service payments required to be paid to the project lender and (b) those other project costs that are not part of the operating expense component of the project's net operating income—e.g., the cost of replacing a roof or acquiring additional land. This calculation is consistent with the requirement that the project's cash flow must be applied to the payment of the project's debt service costs, before any cash distributions are made to the equity investors.

The following example shows how an investor's return on equity is calculated.

Example 3–2: Assume the following facts produced under Example 3–1:

------

29. The purpose of this Chapter is to point out the difference in the return expectations of the construction lender and the equity investor. A significant portion of Chapter 7, *Stage 3: Forming and Capitalizing the Project Entity* is devoted to an analysis of the various ways in which the overall equity return can be allocated among the developer and its outside equity investors. *See infra* Chapter 7, Pages 239–249.

30. As pointed out in note 18 *supra*, the construction lender may enhance its percentage return on debt by charging loan origination and other fees on the front-end of the loan transaction.

31. The return "on" the investor's equity needs to be contrasted with the return "of" the investor's equity. The return "on" equity can be likened to interest earned on a bank deposit. The return "of" equity is akin to the withdrawal of the bank deposit principal.

32. *See* Thomas F. Kaufman, *Understanding Real Estate Economics*, in ALI–ABA COURSE OF STUDY MATERIALS, MODERN REAL ESTATE TRANSACTIONS: PRACTICAL STRATEGIES FOR REAL ESTATE ACQUISITION, DISPOSITION, AND OWNERSHIP, Course No. SS–012, 1301, 1307 (July 2010).

- Total development costs— $4,200,000
- Construction loan amount— $3,750,000[33]
- Amount of invested equity— $450,000[34]
- Annual net operating income— $450,000
- Annual debt service payments— $375,000[35]

Under these facts, the project's before tax cash flow is $75,000 (the annual NOI of $450,000, less the annual debt service payments of $375,000). The project's return on equity is 16.67%, calculated as follows:

$$\text{Return on Equity (16.67\%)} \quad = \quad \frac{\text{Before tax cash flow (\$75,000)}}{\text{Amount of invested equity (\$450,000)}}$$

D. COMPARATIVE RATES OF RETURN— DEBT vs. EQUITY

The relative return expectations of the construction lender and the equity investor are nicely highlighted in Example 3–2. Under the facts of that example, the project's return on total costs is 10.71% (the annual NOI of $450,000, divided by the total development costs of $4.2 million). The construction lender's return on its debt is 8% (the assumed interest rate on the lender's construction loan) and the investor's return on equity is 16.67%.

The disparity in the returns of the construction lender and the equity investors mirrors the disparity in the risks taken by those parties in funding their respective shares of the project's development costs. The greater risk assumed by the equity investor justifies the greater return paid to the equity investor.[36]

The higher level of risk assumed by the equity investor is further underscored by making one minor change to the facts of Example 3–2. If it is assumed that the actual, annual net operating income from the project

---

33. The $3,750,000 loan amount was produced by the application of the LTV and DSC tests under the facts assumed in Example 3–1. *See supra* Pages 43–44.

34. The amount of the invested equity equals the total development costs ($4,200,000) minus the portion of such development costs funded under the construction loan ($3,750,000).

35. The annual debt service payments are determined by multiplying the loan amount ($3,750,000) by the lender's mortgage constant of 10% (calculated based on an assumed annual interest rate of 8% and an assumed amortization period of 20 years).

36. The investor's actual return on equity during the term of the construction loan is probably even higher than the 16.67% figure produced under the assumed facts of Example 3–2. Most construction loans are "interest only," meaning that the borrower is not required to make any principal payments during the construction loan term. The return on equity formula assumes that periodic principal payments are being made in an amount sufficient to repay the loan over an assumed amortization period of 20 years, thereby producing a mortgage constant of 10% versus an interest only payment of 8%. If the construction loan's interest only payment of 8% were to be substituted for the assumed mortgage constant of 10%, the investor's annual return on equity under the above example would skyrocket to 33.33% [(the annual NOI of $450,000 minus the reduced debt service payments of $300,000), divided by the investor's equity investment of $450,000]. The investor's return on equity would revert back to the 16.67% level upon the refinancing of the construction debt with a permanent loan carrying an interest rate of 8% and an amortization period of 20 years.

is only \$375,000 (and not \$450,000 as initially projected by the developer), the respective returns to the debt and equity components would be as follows:

Lender's return on debt—	8%
Investor's return on equity—	0%

Under that scenario, the entirety of the project's net operating income (\$375,000) would be used to pay debt service on the loan (the loan amount of \$3,750,000, multiplied by the mortgage constant of 10%), leaving no cash whatsoever for distribution to the investor. The lender's return would remain fixed at its 8% interest rate and the investor would bear the full brunt of the risk of a decrease in the project's net operating income.

V. FINANCIAL LEVERAGE

The majority of a real estate project's development costs are usually funded with debt. The use of borrowed funds to finance a project is called ***leverage***.

From the equity investor's perspective, there are two fundamental advantages of the use of leverage to fund a project's development costs.

- Leverage permits the equity investor to diversify its real estate investments by funding 10–30% of the development costs in several deals, rather than 100% of those costs in just one project. This diversification lowers the investor's real estate risk by permitting it to spread that risk over several different projects.

- Leverage can be used to increase the investor's percentage return on equity.

A. IMPACT OF LEVERAGE ON
RETURN ON EQUITY

Leverage, if properly used, can significantly increase the financial return to the equity investor. This point can be illustrated by revisiting three economic concepts discussed earlier in this Chapter:

- ***Return on Total Costs***—The project's net operating income divided by its total development costs;

- ***Mortgage Constant***—The percentage of the loan amount that is required to be paid annually to fully repay all principal and interest over an assumed amortization period; and

- ***Return on Equity***—The investor's before tax cash flow, divided by its equity contributions.

With these concepts in mind, three basic propositions can be stated concerning the impact of leverage on a real estate development deal:

- ***Proposition #1***—If the project has no leverage whatsoever (that is, all development costs are funded by capital contributions from equity investors), the investor's return on equity will be identical to the project's return on total costs;

- *Proposition #2*—So long as the project's return on total costs is greater than the mortgage constant on the project debt, the use of leverage will serve to increase the investor's return on equity (so-called *positive leverage*); and

- *Proposition #3*—Conversely, once the mortgage constant exceeds the project's return on total costs, the use of further leverage will cause the investor's return on equity to decrease (*negative leverage*).[37]

The impact financial leverage has on an investor's equity return can best be understood by going back to the example that has been used throughout this Chapter. Remember that the return on total costs for the hypothetical project addressed in Examples 3–1 and 3–2 was 10.71%. Proposition #1 provides that a wholly unleveraged project (that is, one funded 100% with equity contributions) would produce a return on equity to the investor at the same 10.71% level. The return on equity for the hypothetical investor in Example 3–2 was 16.67%. The placement of debt on the project of $3,750,000 caused the investor's return on equity to increase by almost 6%. This is true because, under proposition #2, the hypothetical project produced a return on cost (10.71%) that was higher than the mortgage constant (10%) applicable to the project debt.

What happens if the leverage on the hypothetical project is increased by an additional $250,000 to $4 million? The answer is that the increased leverage will continue to enhance the investor's returns as long as the cost of the debt (represented by the mortgage constant) remains less than the project's return on total costs. The result will, however, be markedly different if the lender decides that the higher loan amount merits an increase in its interest rate from 8 to 9% (to compensate the lender for the additional risk of making the higher loan). The impact of this interest rate increase is that the project's mortgage constant goes from 10% to 10.8%. At this leverage level, the project has fallen over the precipice of negative leverage, because the project's return on total costs (10.71%) is less than the mortgage constant on the project debt (10.8%). Under proposition #3, an increase in the assumed leverage to $4 million, coupled with an increase in the interest rate to 9%, should result in a reduction in the investor's return on equity—which it does, decreasing the investor's return on equity form 16.67% to 9%.[38]

---

37. *See generally* GELTNER, *supra* note 5, at 310; and BRUEGGEMAN, *supra* note 13, at 349–354.

38. The investor's return on equity of 9% is calculated as follows:

$$\frac{\text{Investor's before tax cash flow (NOI of \$450,000} - \text{debt service of \$432,000)}}{\text{Investor's capital contributions (\$200,000)}},$$

with the project's debt service being equal to the project debt of $4 million, multiplied by the mortgage constant of 10.8%, and the investor's capital contributions being equal to the difference between the project's total development costs of $4.2 million and the $4 million principal amount of the project's construction debt.

Reducing the leverage on the hypothetical project from \$3.75 million to \$3.5 million should, consistent with the principle enunciated in proposition #2, cause a reduction in the investor's return on equity (because the project still has positive leverage at the \$3.75 million debt level). The computation set forth in the footnote validates this proposition by showing that a \$250,000 reduction in the project's leverage will cause the investor's return on equity to fall from 16.67% to 14.29%.[39]

B. CAUTIONARY WORDS OF WISDOM

The preceding discussion seems to indicate that determining the proper amount of leverage for a project is simply a matter of math. All one has to do is to run the numbers to reach the leverage level that maximizes the return on equity to the investor.[40] In the vernacular of the real estate investor, this mathematical process is called "chasing yield."

Pushing up leverage levels to chase yield has non-mathematical consequences due to the always lurking presence of the "r" word—that is, risk. The greater the leverage, the greater the risk that (1) the project's net operating income will not be sufficient to cover the project's debt service and (2) the project's residual value will be less than the amount of the project debt. The characterization of leverage as being positive or negative relates strictly to the math of the return on equity calculation and has nothing to do with qualitative levels of project risk.[41]

The developer must also remember that the viability of the financial calculations discussed in this section is totally dependent on the accuracy of the projections and assumptions on which such calculations are based. If the developer's zest to increase its return on equity causes it to overstate its projected net operating income, the fact that its calculations show that leverage is still mathematically positive will be of little import

---

39. The investor's return on equity of 14.29% is calculated as follows:

$$\frac{\text{Investor's "before tax cash flow" (NOI of \$450,000} - \text{debt service of \$350,000)}}{\text{Investor's capital contributions (\$700,000),}}$$

with the project's debt service being equal to the project debt of \$3.5 million, multiplied by the mortgage constant of 10%, and the investor's capital contributions being equal to the difference between the project's total development costs of \$4.2 million and the \$3.5 million principal amount of the project's construction debt.

40. One should not assume that investors will automatically reduce project debt to a level that produces positive leverage. While doing so will increase the percentage of the investor's rate of return, it will also mean that the investors will have to find additional cash to fund their increased equity contributions. For investors who are strapped for cash or who just want to spread their cash over a wider range of investments, investment in deals with negative leverage is neither unheard of, nor necessarily inadvisable.

41. There are real world consequences to increasing leverage on a deal. The interest rate charged on a construction loan having a loan-to-value ratio of 90% will likely be higher than the interest rate charged on a loan on the same project that has a loan-to-value ratio of 60%. The construction lender will also be much more inclined to place stringent conditions on its loan disbursements under the 90% LTV loan than it would under a lower-leveraged project. When chasing yield, the developer must be cognizant of both the economic and non-economic deal changes that may be triggered by an increase in the project's leverage ratio. *See infra* Chapter 9, Pages 376–387.

in the ensuing work-out negotiations with the construction lender and the outside equity investor.

VI. AFTER–TAX ECONOMIC RETURNS

All of the return measurements discussed in this Chapter have been pre-tax computations—that is, the financial impact of federal, state and local income tax laws has not been taken into consideration in any way. There are three reasons why real estate economic models generally adopt a pre-tax bias.

- Most real estate projects are owned by so-called ***pass-through entities***—that is entities that do not directly pay any taxes, but rather pass on all tax attributes and consequences to its equity owners.[42]

- The tax consequences of a real estate investment vary widely from investor to investor. It is, therefore, virtually impossible to create an economic model of general applicability that accurately measures the after-tax return produced from a real estate investment.

- The tax laws governing the development and ownership of real estate change so rapidly as to make the formulation of any enduring after-tax economic model extremely difficult.[43]

Although the tax consequences of investing in real estate may not be susceptible to inclusion in any tight economic model, those consequences can nonetheless significantly impact the overall economic benefits of a particular taxpayer's investment in real estate. The provisions of the Internal Revenue Code governing depreciation deductions, passive losses, like-kind exchanges and capital gains are of particular import to the real estate investor.[44] While these and other tax law provisions can impact a real estate investor's financial returns, they seldom are the driving force behind an investor's decision whether it will or will not invest in a particular project.[45]

---

42. *See infra* Chapter 7, Pages 201–204 for a further discussion of the tax treatment of "pass-through entities.".

43. Examples of major tax legislation passed during the period of the author's practice of law are the Tax Reform Act of 1976, The Economic Recovery Tax Act of 1981, The Deficit Reduction Act of 1984, The Tax Reform Act of 1986, and the Growth and Tax Relief and Reconciliation Act of 2001. Each of these acts significantly altered the way that real estate investments are treated for federal income tax purposes.

44. *See* INTERNAL REVENUE CODE. §§ 168 (depreciation), 469 (passive losses), 1031 (like-kind exchanges), 1221–1223 and 1231 (capital gains). For a solid, general discussions of the federal tax rules applicable to real estate investments, *see* GEORGE LEFCOE, REAL ESTATE TRANSACTIONS, FINANCE, AND DEVELOPMENT, Chapter 28 (6th ed. 2009); and BRUEGGEMAN, *supra* note 13, at 336–344.

45. During the early 1980's, many high-income taxpayers invested in real estate solely because the provisions of the federal income tax laws permitted them to garner tax deductions (primarily depreciation deductions) that they could then use to reduce their tax obligations on other income. These were the so-called "tax shelters" that were so prevalent in the years following the Reagan administration's passage of the Economic Recovery Tax Act of 1981. The era of the real estate tax shelter came to a close with the enactment of the Tax Reform Act of 1986, which limited both (a) the level of a taxpayer's depreciation deductions and (b) the taxpayer's

VII. TIME VALUE OF MONEY

Dr. Mike Miles, a noted real estate finance expert, once described the fundamentals of real estate investment in the following simple, but sage way:

> When comparing alternatives for investment, investors are motivated by two preferences:
>
> *More is better than less*; and
> *Sooner is better than later.*[46]

Dr. Miles provided the following gloss on the two simple axioms set forth above.

> When comparing alternative investments that carry comparable risk and require an equal capital investment, investors prefer the alternative that will produce the most total income from operations and resale; hence more is better than less. And among alternatives for investment with comparable risk and equal total income, investors prefer the option that will produce income more quickly; hence, sooner is better than later.[47]

This Chapter has thus far focused on the magnitude of economic returns, measured both from the perspective of the project as a whole (the concepts of net operating income, residual value and return on total costs) and from the separate perspectives of the construction lender (return on debt) and the investor (return on equity). The magnitude of the cash flows is what Dr. Miles was referring to when he made his "more is better than less" statement.

This Chapter has also discussed how the element of project risk affects the investment decisions and return expectations of the parties. Implicit in Dr. Miles' quoted statement is the proposition that, if the magnitude and timing of the receipt of cash flows from two investment alternatives are comparable, the investor will select the alternative that has the least risk. In this context, risk is defined in terms of the relative predictability of the investor's actual receipt of the projected cash flows from the project. Once an investor begins to question the likelihood that a project will produce cash flow in the projected magnitude and at the projected times, its choice is either to decline the investment opportunity as being too risky or to demand that its percentage return from the investment be increased to reward it for its acceptance of increased project risk.

One consideration that has not yet been factored into this Chapter's discussion of project economics is the impact that the timing of the

---

ability to use those deductions to reduce the taxes paid on non-real estate income. *See* BRUEGGE-MAN, *supra* note 14, at 343.

46. *See* MILES, *supra* note 1, at 83 (emphasis added).

47. *See id.*

projected cash flows has on (a) the value of a real estate project and (b) the investor's economic return from its investment in that project. The remainder of this Chapter will be devoted to a review of the implications to the investor of the ***time value of money***.[48]

Dr. Miles' statement that "sooner is better than later" is the essence of the time value of money concept. As explained by Dr. Miles, "three major concepts drive the notion that a dollar received today is more valuable than a dollar received in the future: 1) opportunity cost, 2) inflation and 3) risk."[49]

- ***Opportunity cost*** is the "foregone opportunity to earn interest on funds committed to other investments."[50] In other words, if a particular investment calls for a deferral of the investor's receipt of a payment, that investor is deprived for the period of the deferral of the ability to invest the amount of that payment in an interest-bearing account or some other investment vehicle.

- ***Inflation*** is one economic concept with which everyone is fairly familiar. Inflation is generally defined as an increase in prices that results in a decline in purchasing power. In the context of the valuation of real estate, inflation simply means that if a payment is to be received in the future, its value in today's dollars is reduced by the percentage of inflation that occurs through the period ending with the future payment date.

- ***Risk*** is the concept that acknowledges the chance that a future payment may not be received at the projected time or in the projected amount.

All three of these factors must be taken into account when determining how much less valuable a future payment is when compared to a current payment in a like amount (its so-called ***present value***).[51] The ***discounted cash flow model***, which is the subject of the next section of this Chapter, is a real estate valuation methodology that is designed to take all of these time value of money concepts into consideration.

VIII.   REAL ESTATE VALUATION METHODOLOGIES[52]

A.   DISCOUNTED CASH FLOW MODEL

The discounted cash flow model (***DCF***) is "[a]n investment evaluation technique that incorporates adjustments for both volume and timing of

---

48. The time value of money is defined by Professor Greer as the "[p]reference for more immediate rather than delayed receipt of funds, so that investment benefits are more valued the sooner they are received." *See* Greer, *supra* note 2, at 520.

49. *See* Miles, *supra* note 1, at 83.

50. *See* Greer, *supra* note 2, at 512

51. "Present value" is the term used to denote the discounted current value of a future cash flow. *See generally* Brueggeman, *supra* note 14, at 49–53; and Greer, *supra* note 2, at 247–249.

52. For a good discussion of the various valuation methodologies used to analyze real estate investments, *see generally* Kaufman, *supra* note 32, at 1306–1319.

anticipated future cash flows and is generally accepted as the most desirable approach to evaluating opportunities."[53] The DCF model requires the financial analyst to undertake each of the following tasks.

- First, all future revenues and expenses of the real estate project must be forecasted with as much accuracy and foresight as possible. It is common for the forecasting period to be at least ten years in duration, with the end point of that forecasting period being the projected sale of the project.

- Once the financial forecast is completed, all of the forecasted revenue and expense items are then discounted (or reduced) to determine their present value under the time value of money concepts discussed above.

The forecasting of future cash flows is a very time-consuming and painstaking process. In effect, the DCF method requires the analyst to try to predict in great detail both the amount and the timing of each item of revenue and expense generated from a project over an extended period of time. In preparing this forecast, the analyst must make a number of assumptions concerning future occurrences—e.g., the level of inflation that will occur in both rents and operating expenses; the timing and degree to which the building will be leased; the likelihood that a tenant will default in the payment of its rent; the financial terms of a permanent loan on the project; the projected cost of maintaining and repairing the building in future periods; and the purchase price at which the project will ultimately be sold. This is an extremely arduous task that requires the participation of an analyst, who is both experienced in the real estate industry generally and intimately acquainted with the financial and legal details associated with the specific project in question.[54] Aspiring real estate development lawyers should be forewarned that the developer often calls upon its lawyer to review and bless the analyst's assumptions as they relate to the various economic rights, obligations and liabilities spelled out in the leases and other legal documents governing the project's operations.

Once the financial forecast is completed, the financial analyst must then select an appropriate rate at which to discount all of the future cash flows (both income and expenses). Determining the appropriate discount rate is a function of the three time value of money concepts discussed above—that is, opportunity cost, inflation and risk. Each of these elements (and, hence, the discount rate used to evaluate a particular project) will vary from investor to investor and from project to project. The value assigned to a particular real estate project has an inverse relationship with

---

53. *See* GREER, *supra* note 2, at 503.

54. The reliability of the results produced by a DCF analysis is wholly dependent upon the accuracy of the various financial assumptions made concerning future project revenues and expenses. The old adage of "garbage in, garbage out" is very descriptive of the DCF process. For an excellent discussion of some of the pitfalls of the DCF approach, *see* J. Douglas Timmons and Wayne R. Archer, *Discounted Cash Flow Analysis and Unpredictable Cash Flows,* 18 REAL ESTATE REVIEW 26 (Fall 1988) and Vernon Martin III, *Nine Abuses Common in Pro Forma Cash Flow Projections,* 18 REAL ESTATE REVIEW 20 (Fall 1988).

the discount rate used in the DCF modeling—that is, the higher the discount rate, the lower the value.

The operation of a discounted cash flow model is best illustrated by reference to a few rudimentary examples.

Example 3–3: Assume that a real estate project has the following financial characteristics:

- Equity contributions— $2,000,000
- Annual cash flows—
    - Year 1— $200,000
    - Year 2— $225,000
    - Year 3— $250,000
    - Net proceeds of sale in Year 4— $3,000,000
- Total cash flows— $3,675,000

The project generates a net return for its investors (before the application of any time value of money concepts) of $1,675,000 (total cash flows of $3,675,000, less the investors' equity contributions of $2 million).

The next two examples show how the time value of money concepts impact an investor's real financial returns.

Example 3–4: Assume that a discount rate of 10% is determined to be a fair reflection of the opportunity cost, inflation and risk associated with a deferral of the cash flows generated from the project that was the subject of Example 3–3. The following table shows the present values of the project's annual cash flows in Years 1–3 and the net proceeds of the sale of the project in Year 4.[55]

Future Cash Flows	Actual Amount of Cash Flow	Present Value of Cash Flow
Year 1	$200,000	$181,818
Year 2	$225,000	$185,950
Year 3	$250,000	$187,828
Year 4 Sale	$3,000,000	$2,049,040
Total Cash Flows	$3,675,000	$2,604,636

The operation of the DCF model shows that the investors' net return on their equity contributions (adjusted to take into consideration the time value of money) is $604,636 (the present value of all of the project's cash flows, less the investors' initial equity contributions of $2 million).

Example 3–5: Assume that the investors' equity contributions ($2 million) and the selected discount rate (10%) are the same as in Example 3–4, but that the cash flows produced from the project are as follows:

---

55. For the purposes of Examples 3–4 through 3–6, it is assumed that the annual cash flows are received once a year on the last day of the year and that the net proceeds of sale are received on the last day of Year 4 (with the project not producing any other cash flow in Year 4).

- Year 1 cash flow— $100,000
- Year 2 cash flow— $150,000
- Year 3 cash flow— $275,000
- Net proceeds of sale in Year 4— $3,150,000
- Total cash flows— $3,675,000

The total cash flows payable to the investors in Example 3–5 are the same as in Example 3–4—that is, $3,675,000. The difference between the cash flows in the two examples is that the cash flows in Example 3–5 are more back-loaded than those assumed in Example 3–4—that is, the net proceeds of sale in Example 3–5 are $150,000 higher than those in Example 3–4, but its annual cash flows in Years 1–3 are $150,000 lower than those produced from the project in Example 3–4.

The implications under a DCF analysis of the back-loading of the cash flows in Example 3–5 are evidenced in the following table.

Future Cash Flows	Actual Amount of Cash Flow	Present Value of Cash Flow
Year 1	$100,000	$90,909
Year 2	$150,000	$123,966
Year 3	$275,000	$206,611
Year 4 Sale	$3,150,000	$2,151,492
Total Cash Flows	$3,675,000	$2,571,978

The net present value return on the investors' equity contributions in Example 3–5 is $571,978 (the present value of all of the project's cash flows, less the investors' equity contributions of $2 million). This result is $32,385 less than the total discounted return produced for the investors under Example 3–4—a differential that exists even though the aggregate cash flows payable to the investors under both examples is $3,675,000. The difference in the net present value numbers produced in the two examples is attributable to the fact that the Example 3–4 project produced cash flows to its investors quicker than did the project illustrated in Example 3–5. Under the time value of money concept represented by Dr. Miles' "sooner is better than later" maxim, a rational investor should select the Example 3–4 project for investment over the Example 3–5 project.

The present values of the cash flows in both Examples 3–4 and 3–5 were calculated using the same 10% discount rate—meaning that an investment in the two hypothetical projects was determined to be of equal risk. What would happen if the project in Example 3–4 were determined to be more risky than the Example 3–5 project? Example 3–6 shows how the element of risk affects a project's value under a DCF analysis.

Example 3–6: Assume all of the same facts applicable to Example 3–4, with one exception—the investor determines that the location of the project makes its receipt of the projected cash flows much less predictable than was the case with respect to the Example 3–4 project. As a result, the investor determines that the proper discount rate to evaluate its future cash flows is 12% (and not 10% as used in Example 3–4). The impact of this adjustment to the project's discount rate is illustrated in the following table.

Future Cash Flows	Actual Amount of Cash Flow	Present Value of Cash Flow
Year 1	$200,000	$178,571
Year 2	$225,000	$179,368
Year 3	$250,000	$177,945
Year 4 Sale	$3,000,000	$1,906,554
Total Cash Flows	$3,675,000	$2,442,438

The adjustment of the discount rate to reflect greater project risk causes the net present value of the Example 3–6 project to be $162,198 less than that of the Example 3–4 project—despite the fact that both the amount and timing of the cash flows in those two examples are identical.

The DCF model is an invaluable tool to help an investor rank the relative attractiveness of a variety of real estate investment alternatives. The Example 3–4 project is the most attractive investment alternative with a net present value of $604,636, followed by the Example 3–5 project with a net present value of $571,998, and the Example 3–6 project with a net present value of $442, 438.

It should be noted, however, that the above DCF calculations indicate that all three of the investment alternatives should be acceptable to an investor with unlimited financial resources (assuming that such a theoretical investor actually exists). The discount rate selected by an investor to evaluate a particular investment opportunity generally represents the investor's minimum acceptable rate of return for that project (commonly referred to as a **_hurdle rate_**).[56] If a DCF calculation shows that an investment opportunity produces a net present value in excess of the investor's required equity contributions, then that opportunity should theoretically be acceptable to the investor. An investment that has a net present value less than the investor's required equity contributions means that the return generated from the investment alternative is less than the investor's hurdle rate and, therefore, should be rejected by the investor.[57]

B.   INTERNAL RATE OF RETURN

The end result of a DCF analysis is a net present value number that can then be compared to the investor's original cash outlay to determine

---

56. *See* Kaufman, *supra* note 32, at 1314.

57. The establishment of the appropriate "hurdle rate" for a particular investment is largely a matter of the investor's perception of the risk that the projected return from an investment will, in fact, be realized. By way of example, an investor's hurdle rate for its investment in a AAA-rated corporate bond will be significantly less than its hurdle rate for an investment in an unleased, regional shopping mall.

whether the subject investment generates a return which is greater or less than the investor's minimum hurdle rate for such investment. The DCF analysis does not, however, show the exact percentage rate of return that is generated from an investment alternative. An investor who wants to know the percentage return on equity of a particular investment opportunity must, instead, use an ***internal rate of return*** calculation.

An investment's internal rate of return (**IRR**) is the percentage rate at which the net present value of a series of future cash flows is exactly equal to the required initial cash investment.[58] An investment that has a net present value in excess of the amount of the investor's initial equity contribution should have an internal rate of return in excess of the investor's hurdle rate for that investment, while an investment that has a net present value less than the initial equity contribution should have an IRR below the investor's hurdle rate. Consistent with the above DCF discussion, a project that has an IRR less than the investor's hurdle rate should be rejected, while a project having an IRR in excess of the investor's hurdle rate should theoretically be acceptable to the investor who has unlimited financial resources.

The DCF and IRR calculations, when properly used, should provide the prospective investor with the same signals as to those projects that are suitable for its equity investment. The primary difference between these two evaluation techniques is that the DCF of a prospective investment is expressed in terms of dollars, while the IRR is expressed in percentage terms. In most situations, a prospective equity investor (particularly an institutional investor) will use both DCF and IRR calculations to determine the acceptability of a particular investment opportunity.[59]

C.   CAPITALIZATION RATE

The use of a ***capitalization rate*** to determine a project's value is another commonly used valuation method. This method determines the value of a project by "capitalizing" (i.e., dividing) a stabilized project's NOI[60] by a percentage rate that is used to determine the price payable for the sale of comparable properties. The capitalization rate valuation formula is as follows:

$$\text{Project Value} = \frac{\text{Project NOI}}{\text{Capitalization Rate}}$$

The capitalization rate (or ***cap rate***) is intended to represent the percentage return a buyer will demand as a condition to its purchase of a particular project. The selected cap rate is determined by looking at sales

---

58. *See* GREER, *supra* note 2, at 507–508.

59. For a comparison of the DCF and IRR methodologies, see Kaufman, *supra* note 32, at 1310–1313; and GREER, *supra* note 2, at 275–289.

60. A project is generally deemed "stabilized" when it is fully leased and all of its tenants have begun paying rent.

of comparable properties and calculating the ratio between the purchase price paid for each such property and its net operating income in the year of sale.

Example 3–7: Assume that the sale of two office projects have the following economic characteristics:

Office Building A:

- Sales Price = $5,000,000; and
- NOI = $550,000.

Office Building B:

- Sales Price = $6,500,000; and
- NOI = $700,000.

The sale of Office Building A for $5 million produces a cap rate of 11% (NOI of $550,000 divided by the sales price of $5 million), while the sale of Office Building B produces a cap rate of 10.77% (NOI of $700,000, divided by the sales price of $6.5 million). Under the capitalization rate valuation method, the value of a development project considered comparable to Office Buildings A and B could be determined by dividing the project's stabilized NOI by a capitalization rate of 10.88% (the average of the two capitalization rates produced from the sales of Office Buildings A and B).

The attraction of the cap rate model is its simplicity. While it is not quite to the point of being a "back of the napkin" valuation, it certainly is nowhere near as complex or involved as is above. For this reason, the capitalization rate method is more likely to be used by brokers trying to put a general price tag on a listed property than it is by an equity investor or lender evaluating a project for potential investment. Lenders and investors tend to rely on DCF valuations for the following three reasons.[61]

- DCF models require the preparer to make very explicit assumptions about every aspect of a project's future operations. The reasonableness of the assumptions can be evaluated by a lender or investor and then subjected to a sensitivity analysis to determine the impact of changed assumptions on the project's value.

- The cap rate method is premised on the relative stability and equality of a project's NOI from year to year—an assumption that is frequently ill-founded. The DCF analysis not only expressly allows for variations in a project's annual cash flows, but also discounts those cash flows to properly account for the time value of money.

- The cap rate methodology is based on the assumption that it is possible to identity comparable sales of comparable properties. Given the complexity of today's real estate markets, the process of identifying such comparability is extremely difficult and uncertain.

---

61. *See* MILES, *supra* note 1, at 84; and Kaufman, *supra* note 32, at 1308.

D. DANGERS ASSOCIATED WITH ECONOMIC MODELS

Before leaving the topic of project economics, one quick note should be made about the dangers inherent in preparing and relying on financial models for a proposed development project. All financial models are based on **projections** of a project's financial performance. Projections are nothing more than a developer's guess (hopefully, an educated one) about how a particular project will fare in the future—for example, how much will the project cost to build, when will it lease and at what rents, and what will the economy look like when the finished project is brought online. There are no definitive answers to these questions when the projections are being prepared. Developers and investors should, therefore, be careful not to place too much stock in a project's initial financial projections.

A practitioner, who is well-acquainted with the world of real estate finance, offered up the following critique of the role that financial models play in the real estate investment arena.

> Models are important for evaluating real estate and great care should be exercised in creating, reviewing and relying on them. Nevertheless the best real estate investors do not necessarily have the best models. If the key to real estate was the best models, then the best spreadsheet or model would create the most successful investor and that is clearly not the case. Common sense, single-minded conviction, hard work, intuition and luck are all key elements of a successful real estate investment portfolio.[62]

In the aftermath of the financial crisis of 2008, one particularly jaundiced, real estate observer made much the same point by noting that "[r]eal estate is a good business for B students who work hard, not PhDs with computer models."[63]

IX. SUMMARY

After slogging your way through this Chapter, you are undoubtedly once again asking "do I really need to know all of these economic concepts and formulas?" Like it or not, the answer to that question is an unequivocal "yes." Today's loan and equity documents are strewn with definitions of net operating income, present value, internal rates of return, loan-to-value ratio, debt service coverage and the like. The real estate development lawyer must understand these concepts, so that he can manipulate the variables and assumptions implicit in such definitions in a manner that favors his client. A real estate development lawyer who enters into negotiations with counsel for a lender or equity investor without a solid

---

62. *See* Kaufman, *supra* note 32, at 1304.

63. *See* URBAN LAND INSTITUTE AND PRICEWATERHOUSECOOPERS, EMERGING TRENDS IN REAL ESTATE 10 (October 2009). For what it is worth, I believe that a good real estate development lawyer must possess both the moxie and drive of the exalted developer and the grades and intellect of the disparaged PhD.

understanding of all of these economic concepts is akin to the fellow who goes to a gunfight with a knife—he will lose the fight in a quick and very spectacular fashion.

Chapter 4

The Heathrow International Business Center: a Case Study

■ ■ ■

I. DESCRIPTION OF PROJECT

The Heathrow International Business Center ("HIBC") is an approximately 400 acre, mixed use, commercial real estate project located off of Interstate Route 4, just north of Orlando, Florida. At the time of its sale in 2002 (at which time the author's direct involvement in the project largely ceased), the HIBC project included the following components:

Office—15 office buildings containing over 2 million square feet of space;

Hotel—A full service Marriott hotel and a Marriott Courtyard hotel;

Multi-family—Two apartment complexes;

Retail—A neighborhood strip center and a boutique shopping plaza; and

Land—Over 100 acres of undeveloped commercial land.

II. PROJECT'S EARLY HISTORY

HIBC was the brainchild of Jeno Paulucci (of Jeno's Pizza Rolls and Chun–King Foods fame). Paulucci had the dream of developing a high-end, master planned residential and golf community north of Orlando. Paulucci believed (correctly as it turned out, although not in the time frames he originally contemplated) that the golf and residential community should be complemented by a commercial component—hence the creation of HIBC located directly adjacent to the Heathrow golf course and just off of the main north-south highway in Orlando—Interstate Route 4. Paulucci managed to work his way through the State of Florida's complicated zoning and governmental entitlement process and by 1985 had received all of the requisite governmental approvals to kick off development of HIBC.

Paulucci immediately built an elaborate entranceway to the park and oversaw the construction of a Marriott Courtyard Hotel, a neighborhood

64

retail center (grocery store, pharmacy and local space) and three office buildings.[1] Development of the neighboring golf course and gated residential community was proceeding along smoothly under Jeno's guidance when the real estate markets hit the wall in the late 1980's. Given the depressed state of the real estate economy, a pioneering project such as HIBC was doomed for failure. Jeno became frustrated with the whole HIBC project and decided to exit the Orlando real estate business and take with him whatever still existed of the fortune he had made in the frozen food industry. Once his dalliance with the real estate development world ended, Paulucci went on to found yet another fast food company—Luigino's, Inc., which now sells frozen food under the Michelina and Budget Gourmet brand names.[2]

Over a period of about seven years, Paulucci was able to extract himself from all entanglements with both the Heathrow residential community and the neighboring HIBC commercial development. His departure was executed through a mixture of sales, foreclosures and other arrangements with his real estate creditors and partners. Two of those transactions are particularly germane to this case study.

- *HIBC 300 Office Building*—The 300 building was the second office building constructed in HIBC. The development of the 300 building was undertaken by a joint venture between Paulucci and Cabot, Cabot and Forbes, a prominent Boston-based real estate developer. The Bank of New England provided the construction loan on the 300 building and ended up taking over ownership of that building by way of a deed in lieu of foreclosure in 1990. The Bank of New England then failed in January of 1991 and was taken over by the FDIC. The FDIC quickly began actively marketing for sale all of the Bank of New England's real estate assets, including the HIBC 300 building.[3]

---

1. Two of those buildings were speculative office buildings, each of which contained approximately 85,000 square feet of rentable space. The third office building was built by AAA to serve as its new national headquarters. In his self-published biography, *The Power of the Peddler,* Paulucci recounts a story about having to scale a 12–foot high, barbed wire fence at AAA's then corporate headquarters outside of Washington D.C. in order to arrive on time for a meeting with AAA's CEO to make a pitch that AAA should relocate its headquarters to the HIBC site. *See* JENO PAULUCCI, THE POWER OF THE PEDDLER 429–433 (Paulucci International 2006).

2. In an interesting side note, Jeno's daughter filed a lawsuit against her father in 2006, alleging, among other things, that Jeno looted her trust fund to pay for the "tens of millions of dollars" he lost on the Heathrow project (including HIBC). His daughter's characterization of the Heathrow development as "an abject business and aesthetic failure" stands in stark contrast to Jeno's statement that Heathrow is a "successful new city which covers ten square miles and serves as the hub for Central Florida's growth." *See* Neal St. Anthony, *Family Feud Opens New Front in Local Court,* STAR TRIBUNE, January 30, 2006, available online at http://www.StarTribune.com.

3. The author had occasion in early 1992 to talk to a loan officer who had handled Bank of New England's construction loan on the HIBC 300 building. The loan officer admitted that neither he, nor anyone else at the bank, had ever visited HIBC. When I asked him why a site inspection had not been scheduled, he replied that he considered such a trip to be unnecessary in light of the fact that the project was "located in downtown Orlando," a location which he and others at the bank felt was a fail-safe market for office development. The fact that the HIBC project was located in a pioneering location about 20 miles north of downtown Orlando was apparently a fact that never reared its ugly head during Bank of New England's underwriting of

- **_Undeveloped HIBC Land_**—Paulucci's ownership of the undeveloped HIBC land (then consisting of approximately 350 acres) was subject to a mortgage loan in favor of Chemical Bank. After lengthy and often strident work-out negotiations, Paulucci agreed in the late spring of 1994 to convey the undeveloped HIBC land to Chemical Bank by way of a deed in lieu of foreclosure. Chemical Bank immediately put the land on the market for sale.

III. AUTHOR'S HISTORY WITH HIBC

In 1992, I was Executive Vice President and General Counsel of The Pizzuti Companies ("Pizzuti"), a real estate development company that was headquartered in Columbus, Ohio and had a satellite office in Orlando, Florida. In early 1992, Pizzuti became aware that the FDIC was planning to put the HIBC 300 building up for sale as part of its attempt to liquidate its ownership of the Bank of New England's real estate portfolio. Through a whole host of fortunate circumstances, Pizzuti was able to circumvent the normal FDIC bidding process and acquire the exclusive right to bid on the purchase of the HIBC 300 building. Thirty days later,[4] Pizzuti closed on its acquisition of the HIBC 300 building and approximately 14 acres of vacant land located immediately adjacent to the 300 building.

As part of its due diligence on the 300 building acquisition, Pizzuti assigned the general manager of its Florida office to conduct interviews with the tenants of the 300 building (which didn't take that long given the building's 45% vacancy rate). During the course of those interviews, one of the tenants (an executive compensation consulting firm known as Newport Partners) passed on to Pizzuti's representative the desire of its principals to become partners in the purchase of the 300 building.

At the time, I was in the process of negotiating the terms of an acquisition loan for the 300 building from Barnett Bank. Because of the high vacancy rate in the building (and hence the lack of an income stream to support its loan), Barnett was insisting that Pizzuti assume personal liability for the repayment of the full loan. When I got the call from our Florida general manager telling me that Newport was interested in becoming a 50% partner in the 300 building acquisition, I somewhat cavalierly told him to pass on to the Newport principals that we would only consider having them as partners if their financial wherewithal was such that Barnett Bank would be willing to have them take over 50% of Pizzuti's personal liability on the acquisition loan (on a several basis). I viewed this as a quick way to get the Newport folks out of our hair, because I thought it was highly unlikely that two executive compensation

the construction loan on the HIBC 300 building. Given this type of laissez-faire loan due diligence, there is little wonder why the low quality of its real estate loan portfolio led to the FDIC's seizure of the bank in 1991.

4. The short closing period was the trade-off that Pizzuti was forced to agree to in order to secure the exclusive right to bid on the purchase of the 300 building.

consultants would have the kind of money to allow Barnett to accept them as guarantors of a 50% several liability position under the acquisition loan. Lo and behold, I received a call later that day from our contact at Barnett Bank asking if I knew the two principals of Newport. They had apparently just deposited $10 million in cash at a Barnett Bank branch office and had given instructions that I be made immediately aware of the deposit. Long story short,[5] Newport became Pizzuti's 50% partner on the 300 building acquisition and would serve as Pizzuti's 50% partner in the development of 11 HIBC office buildings over the next ten years.[6]

The next step in Pizzuti's involvement in HIBC came when Pizzuti received a Request for Proposal ("RFP") from Cincinnati Bell inquiring whether Pizzuti had an interest in submitting a proposal for the development of a 125,000 square foot office building and a 60,000 square foot data center in Orlando for Cincinnati Bell's information services division ("CBIS").[7] The RFP was sent to Pizzuti because it owned 14 acres of developable acreage located adjacent to the 300 building.[8] Pizzuti's management team viewed the CBIS RFP as an ideal opportunity for Pizzuti (1) to get out from under its ownership of the 14 acres and (2) to make its mark in the Orlando office market.[9] Unfortunately, after looking at the proposed plans and specifications for the CBIS project, Pizzuti quickly concluded that there was no way that the two CBIS buildings could be configured to fit on Pizzuti's 14 acre site. As the Pizzuti management team desperately tried to figure out some alternative land play that would permit it to respond to the CBIS RFP, yet another fortuitous event occurred that would prove to be pivotal to Pizzuti's development of the HIBC project.

Shortly after its receipt of the CBIS RFP, Pizzuti received a phone call from Chemical Bank asking if Pizzuti had any interest in buying the approximately 350 acre HIBC tract that Chemical had just acquired from Jeno Paulucci. The convenient juxtaposition of Pizzuti's receipt of the call from Chemical Bank only days after its receipt of the RFP from CBIS was typical of the good fortune that Pizzuti experienced throughout its involvement with the HIBC project. Pizzuti's development department hounded the management team unmercifully, until they finally agreed to contact Chemical Bank to see if it would agree to sell Pizzuti the 20 or so acres that it needed to construct the CBIS office and data center project.

---

5. This was one of Ron Pizzuti's favorite phrases and, therefore, may show up frequently in this book.

6. The two principals of Newport partners would assume a 50% several liability position on the construction loan for each of the 11 office development projects. Several liability (wherein each guarantor is liable for only its designated portion of a loan) stands in sharp contrast to the normal lender practice of requiring each of the loan guarantors to be jointly and severally liable for the repayment of 100% of the loan.

7. CBIS would end up being the named tenant on the lease, although of its lease obligations were personally guaranteed by its parent company, Cincinnati Bell.

8. Cincinnati Bell sent RFP to about 20 other developers, who owned developable, office ground in the greater Orlando area.

9. Pizzuti had developed two office buildings south of Orlando in the mid–1980's and was determined to significantly expand its presence in the Orlando office market.

Unfortunately (or, as it later turned out, fortunately), Chemical indicated that it was not willing to sell the HIBC land in bits and pieces and that it would only consider offers for the acquisition of the entire 350 acres. My initial reaction to Chemical's position was "Who the hell is going to be crazy enough to buy 350 acres of undeveloped land located 20 miles north of Orlando at a time when office vacancy rates nationwide and in Orlando are topping out at over 20%?"

Again, long story short, Pizzuti was just that crazy. It put the entirety of the HIBC land under contract at a purchase price of $7.5 million, won the bidding for the CBIS project and somehow convinced its good friends at Newport to become a 50% partner in the land acquisition and in all future office building projects at HIBC (including the CBIS project). As the one principal from Newport said to me when we closed on the acquisition of the HIBC land, "It feels like we just decided to go over Niagra Falls in a barrel." Six years later, the Pizzuti/Newport partnership had developed well over 1 million square feet of office space at HIBC. My buddy at Newport still has the wine barrel I sent him following the HIBC land closing and I have one helluva case study for my book on Real Estate Development Law.

IV. HIBC TRANSACTIONAL TIMELINE

The following timeline highlights some of the more important milestones that occurred during Pizzuti's participation in the HIBC project.

1992   Purchase from FDIC of 300 building and adjacent 14 acre tract.
Formation of partnership with Newport Partners to own the 300 building and adjacent tract.

1994   Receipt of RFP from Cincinnati Bell for CBIS build-to-suit project.[10]
Acquisition from Chemical Bank of 350 acres of undeveloped HIBC land.

1995   Kick-off of CBIS buildings.
Closing of land acquisition and development loan with First Union National Bank.
Kick-off of 400 building (100,000 square feet of speculative office space)[11] that was fortuitously 100% leased by Veritas Software Corp. prior to the completion of the building's construction.[12]

1996   Sale of CBIS facilities to New York Life Insurance and Annuity Corp.
Kick-off of 500 building (75,000 square feet of speculative space).
Kick-off of HTE building (87,000 square foot build-to-suit for HTE).[13]

1997   Kick-off of 600 building (125,000 square foot build-to-suit for First USA Inc.).[14]

---

10. A "build-to-suit" project is one that is 100% leased to one tenant before construction is commenced.

11. A "speculative" project is one that is not pre-leased before construction is commenced.

12. Veritas Software Corp. was merged into Symantec Corporation in 2005.

13. HTE Inc. was acquired by SunGard Data Systems, Inc. in 2003.

             Kick-off of 701 building (125,000 square feet of speculative space). Placement of permanent loan on 300, 400, 500, 600 and HTE buildings with Connecticut General Life Insurance Corp.

1998   Kick-off of 901 building (159,000 square feet of speculative space). Kick-off of 550 building (125,000 square foot build-to-suit for First USA, Inc.).

1999   Kick off of HIBC 801 building (150,000 square feet of speculative space).

2000   "Divorce" from Newport Partners.[15] Formation of equity fund with Nationwide Realty Investors, Ltd.[16] Sale of C 550 and 600 buildings to Lexington Partners.

2001   Kick-off of 1001 building (192,000 square feet of speculative space). Sale of hotel and retail land to third party developers.

2002   Sale of entirety of HIBC project (eight office buildings and 100 acres of undeveloped land) to Colonial Properties Trust.

2003   The author's retirement from Pizzuti.

V. THE HIBC CASE STUDY

Two important lessons can be gleaned from reading the above history of the HIBC project—(1) the developer who has the initial grand vision for a project seldom is the one who makes the big bucks from that project (say hello to Jeno Paulucci) and (2) as in any other business, success in the real estate development business requires a blend of luck and skill. The foregoing discussion touched upon some of the luck that Pizzuti was blessed to receive during its involvement with the HIBC project. The HIBC project will be used as a case study throughout the remainder of this text to examine the skill that the real estate development lawyer must bring to the representation of a developer client.

I selected HIBC as the primary case study for this book for the following reasons.

- First and foremost, HIBC is a "real deal" and not a hypothetical created solely for academic purposes. I am an ardent believer that the best way to learn about a particular practice area is to look at how real lawyers conducted themselves in the face of the challenges presented by real business transactions.

---

14. First USA Inc. was acquired by Bank One Corp. in 1997. Bank One was merged into J.P. Morgan Chase & Co. in 2004.

15. As will be discussed in greater detail later in this book (*see infra* Chapter 7, Pags 219–220, 282–284), Newport Partners was Pizzuti's partner in both the HIBC land and the HIBC 300, 400, 500, 550, 600, 701, 801, 901 and HTE buildings, as well as in 12 office and industrial projects located in the Columbus, Ohio metropolitan area. In February, 2000, Pizzuti and Newport entered into a series of complex documents to evidence a "divorce" in their partnership relationship, thereby affording Pizzuti the ability to form a new equity fund with Nationwide Realty Investors, Ltd.

16. The equity fund with Nationwide Realty Investors, Ltd. is discussed in more detail *infra* Chapter 12, Pages 565–567. As part of the Nationwide equity deal, Pizzuti gave Nationwide a partial ownership interest in its office and industrial portfolio (expressly including its HIBC office buildings) in exchange for Nationwide's agreement to provide the capital required (a) to partially return Pizzuti's equity in its existing portfolio and (b) to fund Pizzuti's new development efforts.

- I was intimately involved in every stage of the HIBC project. I am, therefore, in the unique position of being able to provide answers to the all-important questions of "why" the documents were structured in a particular way and "why" the parties took certain legal and business positions.

- HIBC was a big, complex project, in which the economic stakes of all of the participants were quite high. As a result, intense lawyering was the norm, producing a set of legal documents that, although far from perfect, are the product of ardent negotiations by sophisticated practitioners.

- HIBC is a great case study to examine the ten stages of a real estate development project. The HIBC project involved a little bit of everything from a transactional perspective, which makes it an excellent tool for examining the various trials and tribulations of the real estate development lawyer. Each of the ensuing chapters of this book will include an anecdotal discussion of (1) the legal and business issues faced by Pizzuti at each stage of the development of the HIBC project and (2) the solutions crafted by Pizzuti's lawyers to respond to those issues.

My hope is that the HIBC case study will be as instructive to the reader of this text as it was to me during my ten year involvement with the project.

VI. PLAYERS IN THE DEVELOPMENT OF HIBC

In the chapters that follow, frequent reference will be made to the "players" in the HIBC development process. Those players are summarized below.

- ***Developer:*** The Pizzuti Companies, Columbus, Ohio.
- ***Architect:*** Hunton Brady Architects, Orlando, Florida.
- ***Contractor:*** Brasfield & Gorrie General Contractors, Birmingham, Alabama
- ***Construction Lenders***: Barnett Bank, First Union National Bank, Wells Fargo National Bank, Bank One and Huntington National Bank.
- ***Initial Equity Partner:*** The two principals of Newport Group, Orlando, Florida.
- ***Institutional Investor Partner:*** Nationwide Realty Investors, Ltd., Columbus, Ohio.
- ***Permanent Lender:*** Connecticut General Life Insurance Company.
- ***Title Insurance Company:*** First American Title Insurance Company, Orlando, Florida.

- ***Surveyor:*** Tinkelpaugh Surveying, Orlando, Florida.
- ***Project Buyer:*** Colonial Properties Trust, Birmingham, Alabama.
- ***Outside Legal Counsel:*** Holland & Knight, Orlando, Florida.
- ***Leasing Broker:*** Pizzuti Realty, Orlando, Florida.
- ***Property Manager:*** Pizzuti Management, Orlando, Florida.

As the above list illustrates, the same basic team developed the entirety of the HIBC project. Indeed, the only player that changed from project to project was the construction lender (with such change being driven by the developer's need to occasionally test the market to insure that it was receiving the most favorable loan terms).[17] The maintenance of a consistent development team allowed Pizzuti to more easily control the quality of the HIBC project and to quickly adapt to changes in the real estate marketplace.

From a personal perspective, I want to applaud and thank all of the team members for the incredible knowledge, skill, dedication and integrity that they brought to the dance every day throughout the ten year history of the HIBC project. The project would not have been a success (and this book certainly would not have been written) but for the hard work and wise counsel provided by the entire HIBC team.

---

17. Even then, First Union National Bank provided the financing for the acquisition and development of the HIBC land, plus construction financing for the majority of the HIBC office buildings.

CHAPTER 5

STAGE 1: GAINING CONTROL OF THE SITE

■ ■ ■

I. INTRODUCTION

Stage 1 is ground zero in the real estate development lawyer's participation in the real estate development process. In most cases, the first time that the development lawyer hears about a project is when he receives a call from his developer client asking for help in "tying up a site." The story the developer tells his lawyer in this first phone call is almost always the same.

- I have a hot lead on a project and need to eliminate my competition for the project by tying up a site ASAP.

- No, I don't yet know whether the project is feasible. I can't take the time or spend the money to make that decision until I have control of the site.

- I know some of the challenges that lie ahead for the deal, but not all of them.

- I don't want to scare the landowner away, so keep whatever document you put together short and sweet—but make sure I am protected.

- In case I didn't mention it, I told the landowner that we would have something for him to take a look at first thing tomorrow morning.

Once he gets this call, the real estate development lawyer is fully immersed in the deal. The documents he puts together in Stage 1 will not only serve as the road map for the project, but will also set the tone for the entirety of the deal. In the parlance of the developer, this is the real estate development lawyer's first test to see whether he is a ***deal maker*** or a ***deal killer***.

II. BUSINESS OBJECTIVES OF THE PARTIES

The developer's business objective in Stage 1 is clear—it simply wants to tie up the site as quickly and as cheaply as possible. Gaining control of the site provides the developer with an advantage over its competitors as

72

it goes about the process of seeing whether its project is feasible. The developer will want to delay its actual acquisition of the land for as long as possible, so that it has sufficient time to complete its feasibility study and otherwise be in a position to start construction of the project immediately following the land acquisition closing. Delaying the purchase of the development site in such a fashion accomplishes two basic goals of the developer—(1) it lessens the developer's risk that something might happen prior to commencement of construction that will make the project infeasible[1] and (2) it lowers the developer's overall development costs by eliminating the costs of owning the land (for example, real estate taxes and interest on any land acquisition financing) prior to the land being put into production.[2]

The landowner's business goals are even more simply stated. The free agent, wide receiver in the 1996 movie *Jerry Maguire* could have been speaking for every landowner in the world when he issued his now famous incantation to "show me the money."[3] Land sellers come in every form, ranging from the unsophisticated farmer, whose farm just happens to be in the path of development, to the institutional investor, who invests millions of dollars to try to find land that will eventually be in that proverbial path of development. Regardless of their level of business sophistication, every land seller wants the same two things—(1) the highest price for the land and (2) its receipt of the purchase price as quickly as possible and without conditions.

It does not take the most ingenious of lawyers to figure out that the business objectives of the developer and the landowner are diametrically opposed to each other. The real estate developer's job is to craft a solution which, given the needs and relative bargaining power of the landowner, still serves his developer client's legitimate business interests.

HIBC Case Study—Stage 1

Our study of the ten stages of the HIBC project begins in 1994 when Pizzuti first started thinking about buying the 350 acre tract known as the "Heathrow International Business Center" (so named by Jeno Paulucci,

---

1. *See supra* Chapter 2, note 3 for a definition of feasibility—which, from the developer's perspective, essentially means that "the deal works."

2. John Hastie, a prominent real estate development lawyer from Oklahoma, comments that "[l]and is and should be viewed by developers as a commodity which is consumed in the development process." *See* John D. Hastie, *Real Estate Acquisition, Development and Disposition from the Developer's Perspective*, in ALI–ABA COURSE OF STUDY MATERIALS, MODERN REAL ESTATE TRANSACTIONS: PRACTICAL STRATEGIES FOR REAL ESTATE ACQUISITION, DISPOSITION, AND OWNERSHIP, Course No. SS–012, 19 (July 2010). For this reason, Hastie goes on to note that "[m]ost developers are either unable or unwilling to inventory land for long-term capital appreciation." *Id.* While Hastie's comment is generally accurate, the trend in recent years has been for large, national and regional developers to inventory sufficient land to feed their development efforts for a period of five to ten years.

3. JERRY MAGUIRE, directed and written by Cameron Crowe (TriStar Pictures 1996)

the Pizza Roll king). As noted in Chapter 4 of this book, an interesting confluence of events occurred in the summer of 1994 that served to jump start Pizzuti's development of the HIBC project. First, Pizzuti received a letter from Cincinnati Bell Information Services ("CBIS") requesting a proposal from Pizzuti concerning the development of an approximately 125,00 square foot office building and a 60,000 square foot data center for CBIS' use in Orlando, Florida. Pizzuti received the CBIS request for proposal because of its ownership of a 14 acre tract located adjacent to the HIBC office building that it had acquired in 1992. Unfortunately, Pizzuti's development team quickly realized that the CBIS buildings were simply too big to be built on that 14 acre tract. Shortly thereafter, Pizzuti was contacted by Chemical Bank to see whether Pizzuti had any interest in buying the 350 acre HIBC tract that Chemical had just acquired from Jeno Paulucci by way of a deed in lieu of foreclosure.[4]

Pizzuti's receipt of the request for proposal from CBIS and the land sale call from Chemical Bank represents the classic beginning of the first stage of a real estate development project—that is, the developer's identification of an unsatisfied customer need (CBIS' desire to occupy new two buildings in Orlando, Florida) and its formulation of a preliminary plan to satisfy that need (the acquisition of a portion of the HIBC tract to serve as the site for the CBIS buildings). The CBIS project presented a wonderful development opportunity for Pizzuti because the project had the potential to be extremely profitable and because it would also serve as a high profile kick-off for Pizzuti's plans to become a major player in the office development market in Central Florida.

There were, however, many hurdles to be cleared before Pizzuti could make a determination that its development of the CBIS project was feasible—not the least of which was the fact that approximately 20 other developers had also received the CBIS request for proposal. Promptly after being contacted by Chemical Bank, Pizzuti dispatched its development team to figure out whether some part of the HIBC acreage could support the CBIS development. Its development team quickly targeted an approximately 20 acre parcel in the southeast quadrant of HIBC as being the perfect location for the CBIS project. Pizzuti was confident that tying up the 20 acre HIBC parcel would give it a competitive edge in its efforts to be awarded the CBIS project,

There was, however, one glitch in Pizzuti's grand development plan— Chemical Bank was adamant that it would not entertain any offer to purchase less than the entirety of the 350 acre tract. Chemical's goal was to get the HIBC land off of its books as quickly as possible. It believed that the best alternative for it to accomplish this goal was to sell the entire tract at one time to one buyer. As a result, Chemical was intent on finding a qualified buyer who had the financial wherewithal to pay a fair price for the 350 acres and to do so quickly without the need for a financing

---

4. Chemical Bank made similar inquiries to several other developers doing business in the Central Florida market.

contingency (in other words, someone who could just write a check to cover the price of the land).

It was against this factual backdrop that Pizzuti made its first phone call to its real estate development lawyer—me. The assignment that I was given by Pizzuti's development team was to "tie up the HIBC property ASAP." The dynamics of the ensuing negotiation with Chemical Bank will be alluded to throughout this Chapter.

III. THE LETTER OF INTENT

After receiving the call from his client, the real estate development lawyer must first decide whether he will use a ***letter of intent*** or go straight to a more formal real estate purchase contract or option. The letter of intent vs. purchase contract conundrum has long been and still is a favorite topic for debate among real estate lawyers.[5]

Let me try to put an end to that debate. As will be discussed later in this Chapter,[6] there are indeed some very good legal reasons why a letter of intent should not be used in certain cases. However, any lawyer who routinely advises his client to never use a letter of intent has either not practiced real estate development law for very long or not practiced it very successfully. The fact of the matter is that the letter of intent is now a widely accepted, preliminary step in the acquisition and disposition of commercial real estate. Whether lawyers like it or not, their clients (both sellers and buyers) are going to continue to insist on using letters of intent. The job of the real estate development lawyer is to make sure that the letter of intent achieves its intended goal (and nothing more).

A. WHAT ARE LETTERS OF INTENT AND WHY DO CLIENTS LIKE THEM?

The letter of intent goes by a number of names—"term sheet," "deal letter," "written handshake," and, my personal favorite, the "hug."[7] The letter of intent (referred to in the remainder of this Chapter by the

---

5. *See e.g.*, Gregory G. Gosfield, *The Structure and Use of Letters of Intent as Prenegotiation Contracts for Prospective Real Estate Transactions,* 38 REAL PROPERTY, PROBATE AND TRUST JOURNAL 130 (2003); Thomas C. Homburger and James R. Schueller, *Letters of Intent—A Trap for the Unwary,* 37 REAL PROPERTY, PROBATE AND TRUST JOURNAL 509 (2002); Georgette C. Poindexter, *Letters of Intent in Commercial Real Estate,* in ALI–ABA COURSE OF STUDY MATERIALS, MODERN REAL ESTATE TRANSACTIONS: PRACTICAL STRATEGIES FOR REAL ESTATE ACQUISITION, DISPOSITION, AND OWNERSHIP, Course No. SS–012, 61 (July 2010); and David A. Fenley, *Letters of Intent: A Survey of Their Enforceability and Desirability in Real Estate Transactions,* in ACREL PAPERS (ALI–ABA, April 2002), available online at http://www.acrel.org/Documents/Seminars/Spring2002Tab10.pdf.

6. *See infra* Pages 76–81.

7. *See* Nina B. Matis and Elliot M. Surkin, *The Hug: "There is Commercial Utility to Allowing Persons to Hug before They Marry." A Discussion of Letters of Intent in Purchase and Sale Transactions,* in ALI–ABA COURSE OF STUDY MATERIALS, MODERN REAL ESTATE TRANSACTIONS: PRACTICAL STRATEGIES FOR REAL ESTATE ACQUISITION, DISPOSITION, AND OWNERSHIP, Course No. SS–012, 89 (July 2010).

acronym ***LOI***) is generally a two to three page document that is viewed by both the seller and the buyer as nothing more than a preliminary expression of certain key deal points on which they have reached a consensus. While an LOI is customarily signed by both the seller and the buyer, there is seldom an expectation on the part of either the seller or the buyer that the LOI will in any way legally bind them to consummate the purchase and sale of the property that is the subject of the LOI.[8]

The foregoing description makes the LOI seem like a rather innocuous, if not wholly useless document. Why then have LOIs become so commonplace in today's commercial real estate industry? The following are the benefits, both actual and perceived, of using an LOI.

- The LOI is a relatively quick and inexpensive way for the buyer and seller to see if they have some common ground on the essential deal points (e.g., the purchase price, deal contingencies and the anticipated closing date). The alternative of paying lawyers to prepare and negotiate a complex purchase agreement is distasteful to both the seller and the buyer (if not to their respective counsel).

- For the land seller, the LOI is a useful tool for it to evaluate the levels of interest of potential buyers.

- For the buyer, the LOI presents it with an opportunity to tie up the property while it tries to make a determination as the feasibility of its development project.

- The LOI is a quick way to create ***deal momentum***. Deal momentum is the circumstance where the parties feel committed mentally and emotionally to doing a deal, even though they are not legally committed to do so. This is the "hug" effect mentioned earlier in this Chapter.

- Finally, the LOI serves as the parties' CliffsNotes for the deal. Once an LOI is signed, the lawyers for the buyer and seller are then charged with responsibility for writing a novel (i.e., a purchase contract) that is consistent with those notes.

B. DANGERS ASSOCIATED WITH THE USE OF A LETTER OF INTENT

As noted above, both the seller and the buyer generally view an LOI as a non-binding document. As a result, the parties are sometimes rather careless in their wording of the LOI. The lack of attention to the content of the LOI can cause some unintended, adverse consequences for the parties. The case of *Goren v. Royal Investments Incorporated* illustrates what can happen if the parties fail to bring the same attention to detail to the LOI that they customarily do to purchase contracts and other documents that they perceive to be binding.

----

8.   A few exceptions to this general rule are discussed *infra* at Pages 82–83.

GOREN v. ROYAL INVESTMENTS INCORPORATED[9]

Appeals Court of Massachusetts, Suffolk
516 N.E.2d 173
Decided December 9, 1987

Once again we consider in what circumstances a writing, which by context or by terms, contemplates a more formal agreement, may nonetheless serve as a binding contract.

We summarize the facts which present the problem. After a course of negotiations during May, 1984, Piatt Associates and Richard A. Goren (collectively called "Opera") as buyer, and Royal Investments Incorporated ("Royal"), as seller, signed a document as of June 6, 1984, contemplating the sale by Royal to Opera of the premises at 565–567 Washington Street, Boston (the "locus"). That document bore the caption "Offer to Purchase." Over the signature of Opera were the words "SUBMITTED BY" and over the signature of Royal there appeared the words "ACCEPTED BY." Prior to the signed document of June 6, 1984, there had been four drafts which successively offered improved terms to the seller but which were not acceptable to it.

The fifth, and accepted, draft, i.e., that of June 6, 1984, offered a price of $762,000, entirely in cash. There were provisions which provided for: sequential deposits (aggregating $50,000); the handling of then current leases and the making of new ones; a closing date; and payment of a broker's commission by the seller. Under a caption which read, "PURCHASE AND SALE," there appeared the following sentence: "A mutually acceptable Purchase and Sale Agreement shall be executed within four weeks of acceptance of this offer."

Before a purchase and sale agreement was signed, Royal received an offer to buy its property that was $78,000 higher than that which Opera had made. Royal became inattentive to calls from Opera or the broker. Although it had expected Royal, as seller, to proffer a purchase and sale agreement, Opera had an agreement prepared (on the 1978 edition of the Greater Boston Real Estate Board form), which incorporated the terms of the June 6th document. Opera then tendered signed copies of that agreement to Royal. On July 11, 1984, twenty-four hours after it had signed an agreement to sell to the party that had offered the better price, Royal informed Opera that their deal was off. "[W]e cannot sign this agreement," Royal explained, "in that we cannot guarantee the removal of the Moto–Photo tenant from the building." Two days earlier on July 9th, Royal had, for a price, in fact secured the agreement of Moto–Photo to vacate its space in the locus.

Among his detailed findings the trial judge found as follows: The document dated June 6, 1984, and countersigned by the seller on July 7, 1987, had been the end product of active negotiations. It constituted more

---

9. All footnotes and citations have been omitted from this opinion.

than a preliminary expression of intent or draft for discussion purposes. Rather, the parties intended to be bound as of June 7, 1984, by the provisions of the June 6th document, and execution of a purchase and sale agreement was no more than a formality intended to tidy up ministerial and nonessential terms of the bargain. The transaction was not particularly complex and did not require intricate final documents. Assertions by ... Royal's principal officer that he would not have agreed to boilerplate provisions in the agreement tendered by Opera (relating, e.g., to state of the title, insurance, liquidated damages in the event of buyer's default) were not credible because the same provisions appeared in the agreement Royal signed to get the higher price.

The provision in the June 6th document looking to execution of a purchase and sale agreement, the judge concluded, contemplated that the parties would exercise good faith in attempting to draft and negotiate such an agreement. Royal, the judge found, did not act in good faith. In its refusal to execute the agreement tendered by Opera, it "was motivated entirely by the increased financial benefits which Royal would realize if it were able to convey the property to Paramount Associates at a purchase price of $840,000...." ...

On appeal Royal prudently does not dissipate its energy in rebutting the implicit finding of the judge that it suffered a spell of moral abandon. Rather ... Royal urges that the judge was clearly in error in finding that the parties had agreed on all significant points. The clause contemplating execution of a purchase and sale agreement, Royal contends, was a talisman of the inchoate quality of the June 6th document.

To be sure ..., language looking to execution of a final written agreement justifies a strong inference that significant items on the agenda of the transaction are still open and, hence, that the parties do not intend to be bound. If, however, the parties have agreed upon all material terms, it may be inferred that the purpose of a final document which the parties agree to execute is to serve as a polished memorandum of an already binding contract....

Here ... all significant economic issues were resolved in the preliminary agreement. The additional matters with which the form purchase and sale agreement treated were subjects such as state of the title, conformance with local law, condition of the premises, extension provision to allow seller time to remove title defects, buyer's right of election to accept a deficient title, performance to be merged in delivery of the deed, use of purchase money to clear title, maintenance of insurance at not less than eighty percent of sound insurable value, assignment of insurance, closing adjustments, holding of deposit by broker, and disclaimer of implied warranties. These points are not without importance and may, on occasion, be the subjects of bargaining. They are, however, subsidiary matter and norms exist for their customary resolution. The form of agreement tendered by Opera conformed to those norms, and the seller does not suggest that at the time of the preliminary agreement there were differences of position on any of the subsidiary points.

Royal argues that the highly material matter of delivering the premises free of the tenancy of In and Out Photo of New England, Inc. (known as Moto–Photo), was not resolved. It may not have been resolved between Royal and Moto–Photo (the latter, after the preliminary agreement, appears to have jacked up the price of being bought out), but it was surely resolved in the preliminary agreement, which provided: "Current leases must be terminated by the seller and premises now occupied by Moto–Photo will be delivered vacant at or prior to the closing date."

On the basis of the judge's findings, for which there is support in the record, that the preliminary agreement covered all material points and that the parties so regarded it, the case falls into that category where execution of a more formal instrument "was hardly more than a formality."

This is not to say that parties to a preliminary agreement may not provide that they do not intend to be bound until the transaction is buttoned up by a more detailed and formal agreement. There is commercial utility to allowing persons to hug before they marry. If "[p]arties to what would otherwise be a bargain and a contract ... agree that their legal relations are not to be affected [,] [i]n the absence of any invalidating cause, such a term is respected by the law like any other term...." Restatement (Second) of Contracts § 21 comment b (1979). A proviso of that sort should speak plainly, e.g., "The purpose of this document is to memorialize certain business points. The parties mutually acknowledge that their agreement is qualified and that they, therefore, contemplate the drafting and execution of a more detailed agreement. They intend to be bound only by the execution of such an agreement and not by this preliminary document."

[T]he judgment ... is affirmed. Royal Investments Incorporated ... shall ... deliver to the plaintiffs or their nominee, good and marketable title by quitclaim deed to the premises at 565–567 Washington Street, Boston, in exchange for payment of $762,000.

Nᴏᴛᴇꜱ ᴀɴᴅ Qᴜᴇꜱᴛɪᴏɴꜱ Aʙᴏᴜᴛ ᴛʜᴇ Gᴏʀᴇɴ Cᴀꜱᴇ

The facts of the *Goren* case present the classic situation where the enforceability of an LOI is called into question—that is, a seller ends negotiations with the buyer named in an LOI and then moves immediately to a contract to sell its property to another buyer at a higher price. Particularly interesting is the finding by the court in *Goren* that the Royal's contentions that it "would not have agreed to boilerplate provisions in the agreement tendered by Opera (relating, e.g., to state of the title, insurance, liquidated damages in the event of the buyer's default) were not credible because the same provisions appeared in the agreement Royal signed to get the higher price."[10] The provisions characterized by the *Goren* court as "boilerplate" are frequently the subject of intense and very meaningful negotiations by the parties.[11] Would the *Goren* case have been decided differently if the purchase agreement signed by Royal with its new buyer had contained "boilerplate" provisions that were markedly different from those contained in the purchase agreement tendered to Royal by Opera just before Royal cut off negotiations under the LOI? What would the court have decided if Opera had never gotten around to submitting a draft purchase agreement to Royal?

The lesson to be learned from the *Goren* case is not, as one lawyer stated, that "a letter of intent is an invention of the devil and should be avoided at all costs."[12] The real lesson to be learned from the *Goren* case is that the real estate development lawyer should heed the words of wisdom espoused by the adorably insightful Humpty Dumpty, when he gave this great advice to Alice—"When I use a word ... it means just what I choose it to mean— neither more nor less."[13]

The parties in *Goren* made the mistake of not clearly articulating their intentions as to whether they were or were not legally bound by the provisions of the LOI.[14] There are other cases like *Goren* where the courts have refused to fully accept one party's claim that an LOI was nothing more than a preliminary, non-binding recital of certain key business terms.[15] In all those cases, however, the parties failed to include in the LOI a clear, unambiguous statement that it was their shared intentions that the provisions of the LOI would not be legally binding on either party. The inclusion of a clause similar to the one below will go a long way toward assuring the parties that the LOI will not be enforceable against either of them.[16]

---

10. *See* Goren v. Royal Investments Incorporated, 516 N.E.2d 173, 174 (App. Ct. Mass. 1987).

11. The "boilerplate" provisions referred to in the *Goren* decision included those relating to the condition of the property, closing adjustments and a disclaimer of implied warranties. *See id.* at 178. As will be discussed in some length in subsequent sections of this Chapter, those provisions are customarily viewed from widely divergent perspectives by the buyer and the seller. *See infra* Pages 145–148.

12. *See* Steven Volk, *The Letter of Intent*, 16 INSTITUTE ON SECURITIES REGULATION 145 (1985). *See also* Gregory G. Gosfield, *A Primer on Real Estate Options*, 35 REAL PROPERTY, PROBATE AND TRUST JOURNAL 129, 133–134 (2000) where the author states that "[l]etters of intent are indubitably the devil's work ... [and] the letters are wolves in sheep's clothing, plastique that can fit any shape and explode with fatal consequences, vipers poised to bite the fool who tries to collar them."

13. *See* LEWIS CARROLL, THROUGH THE LOOKING GLASS: AND WHAT ALICE FOUND THERE 205 (1872).

14. Indeed, the opinion handed down by the court in *Goren* specifically acknowledges that its ruling would have been different if Royal and Opera had included the following provision in their LOI.

> The purpose of this document is to memorialize certain business points. The parties mutually acknowledge that their agreement is qualified and that they, therefore, contemplate the drafting and execution of a more detailed agreement. They intend to be bound only by the execution of such an agreement and not by this preliminary document.

See Goren, 516 N.E.2d at 177.

15. *See* Fenley, *supra* note 5, at 5–6; and Michael Hamilton, *Purchase and Sale Transactions*, in COMMERCIAL REAL ESTATE TRANSACTIONS HANDBOOK 5–3 through 5–6 (Mark A. Senn ed., 4th ed. 2009).

16. There is a strain of case law that raises the possibility that the doctrine of promissory estoppel can be used to enforce the provisions of an LOI, even if the LOI specifically recites that it is non-binding. *See* Poindexter, *supra* note 5, at 69; and Budget Marketing v. Centronics, 927 F.2d 421 (8th Cir. 1991). In the *Budget Marketing* case, the defendant repeatedly made oral assurances

This letter of intent is merely an expression of certain preliminary basic business points discussed by the parties in connection with a potential purchase and sale of the subject property and is not intended in any way to create any obligations of any kind on either of the parties to this letter of intent. The parties will not be bound to each other in any way, unless and until a formal agreement for the purchase and sale of the property is executed by both parties. This provision as to the non-binding nature of this letter of intent supersedes any provisions herein or any past or future actions of the parties to the contrary.[17]

Practice Tip #5–1: When and How to Use an LOI

The real estate development lawyer should generally trust the instincts of his developer client as to when the submission of an LOI is an appropriate, preliminary step in the land purchase negotiations. Developers have a more refined sensitivity for the dynamics of deal negotiations than do lawyers (even those who have read this book) and, as such, are better equipped than their lawyers to make the decision as to whether a particular deal is sufficiently simple and straightforward as to merit skipping the LOI stage and moving directly to the preparation of a purchase contract.

Once a decision is made to use a letter of intent, the real estate development lawyer must resist his natural inclination to overlawyer a deal and, instead, prepare a very short and simple LOI. A sample of a skeletal LOI is included as Document #1 in the Document Appendix. An LOI should address only the most essential terms of the proposed land acquisition—(a) a description of the land, (b) the amount of the purchase price and how it will be paid, (c) the allocation of responsibility for the payment of various closing costs, (d) the scope of the buyer's contingencies, (e) the scheduled closing date and, of course, (f) a clear statement of the non-binding nature of the LOI. Keeping the LOI "short and sweet" serves two important purposes—(1) it enhances the possibility that the landowner might create the desired "deal momentum" by signing the LOI without first running that document by its lawyer and (2) it significantly reduces

---

to the plaintiff of its intention to close the subject sales transaction. The court in *Budget Marketing* ruled that such oral assurances were sufficient to render the issue of whether the plaintiff reasonably relied on those assurances as a question of fact to be determined by the trial court. It should be noted that not only were the oral statements made by the defendant quite specific and frequent, but also that such statements were apparently made for the express purpose of inducing the plaintiff to expend a significant amount of money to prepare for a closing of the transaction contemplated under the LOI. In light of the relatively egregious conduct of the defendant in *Budget Marketing,* that case should not discourage a real estate development lawyer from using an LOI (although it should caution the lawyer to make sure that his client does not act in a manner which is wholly inconsistent with the non-binding nature of the LOI crafted by such lawyer).

17. *See* Matis, *supra* note 7, at 95.

the chance that some court might decide that the document is so detailed that all or some portion of it should be deemed to be binding on the parties to the LOI.[18]

C. PARTIALLY BINDING LETTERS OF INTENT

As stated at the very outset of this Chapter, the developer's goal in Stage 1 is to tie up the site, so that its competitors cannot steal the developer's business opportunity by buying the targeted land from the landowner. The execution of a non-binding letter of intent, while creating some positive deal momentum, does not actually tie up the site (at least not to the extent desired by the developer). Under a true, non-binding LOI, the landowner is free to continue to market its land and accept purchase offers from third parties, until such time as the developer and the landowner execute a definitive land purchase agreement.

The developer's desire to try to tie up the land under an LOI has led to the creation of a legal document that is often referred to as a "partially binding, non-binding letter of intent." This oxymoronic document name simply means that some elements of the LOI are non-binding, while others are binding. The following are two provisions that a real estate development lawyer often tries to insert into an otherwise non-binding LOI.

- *"No Shopping" Clause—* By placing a ***no-shopping clause*** in an LOI, the real estate development lawyer seeks to create a binding obligation on the landowner to refrain for a specified period of time from entering into or continuing any negotiations or discussions with any party other than the developer concerning the sale of the landowner's land. The no-shopping clause is, therefore, intended to prevent the landowner from shopping the developer's deal to other potential buyers to see if a better deal can be had. The term of the typical no shopping clause begins on the date the LOI is signed by the landowner and expires on the earlier of (1) the date on which the parties execute a fully-binding purchase agreement or (2) an outside date specified in the LOI (e.g., 30 days after the effective date of the LOI).[19]

---

18. *See* Teachers Insurance and Annuity Association of America v. Tribune Company, 670 F.Supp. 491 (S.D.N.Y. 1987), where the court held that a very detailed LOI (which expressly included a statement that the LOI was a "binding agreement" subject to certain conditions) obligated the parties to negotiate in good faith to reach a definitive, formal agreement and to refrain from "renouncing the deal, abandoning the negotiations, or insisting on conditions that do not conform to the preliminary agreement." *Id.* at 499. An important contributing factor to the court's decision in *Teachers Insurance* was the fact that the LOI in that case tried to cover those contractual terms not specifically addressed in the LOI by saying that such terms would be those which were "usual and customary in this type of transaction." *Id.* The use of such a clause does little to aid a party's future negotiating position and, as seen in the *Teachers Insurance* case, can create some unintended legal consequences for the parties to the LOI.

19. In order for a no-shopping clause to be enforceable against the landowner, the landowner's promise to refrain from shopping the deal to third parties must be supported by adequate consideration. *See e.g.,* OfficeMax v. Sapp, 132 F. Supp.2d 1079 (M.D. Georgia 2001), where a Georgia court refused to enforce a no shopping obligation due to the lack of consideration given

- ***Obligation to Negotiate in Good Faith***—As one might expect, landowners often reject the developer's attempt to include a binding, no shopping clause in the LOI. On occasion, the developer will try to circumvent the landowner's rejection of its no shopping clause by including a provision in the LOI that seeks to impose a binding obligation on the parties "to negotiate the terms of a definitive purchase agreement in good faith and to use reasonable efforts to cause a definitive purchase agreement to be prepared and executed within ___ days after the parties' execution of the letter of intent." By inserting such a provision in the LOI, the developer seeks to gain some quantum of leverage against the landowner if the landowner ends up agreeing to sell the land to someone other than the developer. The real estate development lawyer should, however, be mindful that a mutual obligation to negotiate in good faith can come back to haunt his developer client if, for instance, the developer finds a cheaper or better land alternative for its project and, accordingly, seeks to abandon negotiations with the LOI landowner. The insertion of a good faith negotiation clause in an LOI creates a slippery slope for both the seller and the buyer and, as such, should be included in an LOI only with great caution and a full awareness of its potential consequences.

If an attempt is made to insert a binding clause into an otherwise non-binding LOI, it is absolutely imperative that the real estate development lawyer make it clear within the four corners of the LOI document what provisions are binding and what provisions are non-binding. If that distinction is not made clear in the LOI, the developer may be exposed to the type of unexpected consequences faced by the defendant in the *Goren* case.

IV. PAPERING THE DEAL

The preliminaries are now over and the seller and the buyer are ready to move on to the preparation and execution of a binding land acquisition document. Before beginning an examination of the key provisions of the land acquisition document, this Chapter will first discuss three topics which are central to the real estate development lawyer's ability to prepare a solid first draft of the acquisition document:

- The questions the lawyer must ask his developer client in order to gain a proper understanding of the business deal and the risks associated with that deal;

- The lawyer's selection of the right form of contract for the deal; and

- An overview of some valuable rules to follow and techniques to use when drafting legal documents.

---

for such obligation. Developer's counsel should, therefore, be careful to include a recital of adequate consideration in any no-shopping clause that he inserts into an LOI (e.g., the payment of a nominal sum of cash or a promise on the developer's part to take or refrain from taking some specific action).

A. LEARNING THE BUSINESS DEAL

A real estate development lawyer is not in a position to start drafting the purchase contract, until he thoroughly understands his client's business deal. In this context, the business deal encompasses both (1) the essential business terms of the land acquisition and (2) the nature, status and timing of the project that will be developed on the acquired land.

The signed LOI (assuming there is one) will provide the real estate development lawyer with the basic business points that define the land acquisition—for example, the property description, purchase price, deal contingencies and projected closing date. To learn the rest of the business deal, the real estate development lawyer needs to sit down with his client and ask a series of questions designed by the lawyer to augment his understanding of the overall deal. Among the principal questions which the lawyer should ask his client are the following.

- What is the projected end use of the land (e.g., an office building or shopping center)?

- Is the property zoned to permit the developer's projected end use?

- Are all needed utilities, roads and other infrastructure already extended to the boundaries of the land? If not, who has the responsibility to arrange for such infrastructure extension?

- What are the biggest risks associated with the deal?

- What has to happen for the deal to become a reality?

- Is the developer willing to close on the acquisition of the land before all aspects of its broader deal have come together?

- What events could cause the project deal to blow up?

- Does the developer need to secure financing for the acquisition of the land and the development of the project? If so, has the developer received a commitment for the required financing?

- Will the developer have any equity partners in the development project?

- Are there any governmental incentives or approvals which are essential components of the business deal?

- What is the status of the site due diligence (soils tests, environmental assessments, etc.)?

- What is the developer's projected time line for the acquisition of the land and the commencement of construction of the project?

The real estate development lawyer will find that this question and answer session will serve two valuable purposes—(1) it will provide the lawyer with the level of understanding of the overall business deal and its associated risks and challenges that the lawyer needs in order to protect his client's business interests and (2) it will bring into focus certain issues that the developer has not previously thought of or resolved.

B. SELECTING THE RIGHT FORM OF CONTRACT

The next question faced by the real estate development lawyer is what form of document should he use to evidence the business deal he just learned about from meeting with his client? That question has three parts to it.

- Should the document take the form of a purchase contract or an option?

- Should the lawyer use a pre-printed form (modified to reflect the specifics of his client's deal) or his own customized form?

- Should the lawyer use a "killer" form[20] that is designed to protect his client from every conceivable risk, or should he use a more user-friendly contract form that seeks to accommodate the legitimate interests of the landowner?

The answer to this three-part question depends upon the complexity of the deal and the sophistication and experience of the landowner.

1. Purchase Contract vs. Option

A purchase contract establishes an obligation of the buyer to buy, subject to the satisfaction of those conditions set forth in the purchase contract.[21] An option, on the other hand, creates a right, but not an obligation, to buy that the prospective buyer can exercise unilaterally at any time within the fixed period set forth in the option agreement. Under an option, the buyer must provide consideration for the option that is separate and distinct from the purchase price payable following the exercise of the option. Most commentators believe that the payment of a relatively nominal amount of cash can provide the requisite consideration needed to establish the enforceability of an option.[22]

Based on the definitional difference between an option and a purchase contract, it would at first blush seem obvious that a lawyer representing a buyer/developer should always select an option as the form to use when preparing the first draft of the land acquisition document. After all, what person in his right mind would select "obligations" over "rights"? The reality, however, is that the land acquisition document typically used in

---

20. The term "killer" document was originally coined by the New York Bar Association to describe the pro-landlord form of lease that was widely used in the 1980's. *See* JOHN B. WOOD AND ALAN M. DI SCIULLO, NEGOTIATING AND DRAFTING OFFICE LEASES 1–2 and 1–3 (2002).

21. Conditions in a purchase contract are frequently referred to as "contingencies." While the term "contingency" has a less refined legal meaning than does the term "condition," this Chapter will nonetheless follow the vernacular of the real estate developer and use those two terms interchangeably to refer to the situation where a party's obligation to perform under a contract is dependent upon the occurrence or existence of some specified event or circumstance.

22. *See* Gosfield, *Primer on Real Estate Options, supra* note 12, at 141; and Harvey L. Temkin, *Too Much Good Faith in Real Estate Purchase Agreements? Give Me an Option,* 34 UNIVERSITY OF KANSAS LAW REVIEW 43 (1985).

the commercial real estate development world is a purchase contract and not an option.

The reasons why the purchase contract is the favored document form for a commercial real estate deal are discussed below.

- Many sophisticated landowners/sellers simply will not agree to use an option agreement. In consideration of its agreement to take its land off the market, the seller wants the buyer to have an obligation to buy and not just the right to buy. If the seller can somehow be convinced to go with the option form, it will usually seek to extract such an exorbitant cash consideration for the grant of the option as to render the option untenable from the buyer's perspective.[23]

- The legal distinction between an option and a purchase agreement is one with limited practical difference for either the seller or the buyer. As will be discussed in more detail later in this Chapter, the courts have consistently recognized the validity of a purchase contract which sets forth the buyer's determination of the "suitability" or "feasibility" of the land as a condition to the buyer's purchase obligation.[24] From the buyer's perspective (as opposed to that of his anal-retentive lawyer), there is little significant difference between this sort of broad contingency in a purchase contract and the unilateral right to buy set forth in the option agreement.

- Except for the "option" versus "contingency" language noted in the above paragraph, the provisions of the option agreement and the purchase contract are virtually identical. If an option is used by the development lawyer, it is incumbent upon him to include in the option agreement all of the terms and conditions that will govern the purchase and sale of the land, if and when the buyer exercises its purchase option. Those terms and conditions generally are the same under both the purchase contract and the option agreement.

The bottom line is that, in the ideal world, the buyer/developer is probably marginally better off going with an option than with a purchase contract. Unfortunately, the real estate development lawyer seldom is afforded the luxury of functioning in the ideal world. For this reason, the remainder of this Chapter will assume that the selected form for the land acquisition is the purchase contract and not the option (although as noted

---

23. Option consideration, once paid, is by its terms non-refundable to the prospective buyer, even if the buyer never exercises its option to purchase the optioned land. This should be contrasted to the typical situation where the deposit paid under a purchase contract is fully refundable to the buyer if the buyer's contingency is not satisfied or waived within the specified time period.

24. The trade-off for the courts' blessing of broad "suitability" contingencies is often the imposition of an implied obligation that the holder of such contingency must exercise good faith in its determination that the property is suitable. *See infra* Pages 102–109, for a discussion of two cases dealing with this issue—Mattei v. Hopper, 330 P. 2d 625 (Sup. Ct. Cal. 1958); and Sheridan v. Crown Capital Corp., 554 S.E.2d 296 (Ga. App. 2001). For a discussion of the legal theory underlying contingent purchase arrangements, *see* Temkin, *supra* note 22 at 43–51.

above, there really is not much practical difference between those two forms).

2.　Pre-printed Form vs. Lawyer's Own Form

Each jurisdiction usually has at least one pre-printed purchase contract form that is disseminated either by the local bar association or the board of realtors. Most of these pre-printed contracts are for the sale of residential dwellings and, as such, have limited utility for commercial real estate transactions. There are, however, some jurisdictions where a state or local trade association has prepared and blessed a fairly simple form of purchase contract for commercial transactions. The Orlando, Florida area is one jurisdiction that has pre-printed forms that can be used for commercial real estate acquisitions.[25]

My experience has been that the use of a pre-printed purchase contract form works quite well for the simple acquisition of a relatively small tract from a landowner who is not accustomed to selling real estate. A two or three page pre-printed form with the logo of the local bar association in the upper right hand corner is much less intimidating to the inexperienced landowner than is the slick, multi-page document that most real estate development lawyers use as their standard purchase contract form. In this limited circumstance, the use of a pre-printed form can expedite negotiations with the landowner and produce the developer's desired result of tying up the site as quickly and as cheaply as possible.

The real estate development lawyer is, however, cautioned not to make the mistake of assuming that the pre-printed form can work for the deal just because it has the imprimatur of the local board of realtors or bar association. The lawyer must carefully review the form and make sure it works to protect his client's interests. To the extent the form needs to be revised in any way (for example, the inclusion of additional contingencies or representations and warranties), those revisions should be reflected in riders to the pre-printed form. Keep in mind, however, that employing too many riders defeats the whole purpose of using the pre-printed form in the first place—that is, making the proposed acquisition seem less threatening to the landowner. The use of excessive riders can also produce a document that is internally inconsistent and, hence, fraught with the potential for being interpreted in an unexpected and unwanted manner.

In situations other than the limited circumstance described above (that is, a small, straightforward deal with an unsophisticated seller), the pre-printed form has little value to the real estate development lawyer. Most land acquisitions are simply too unique and complex to be governed by a two or three page, pre-printed, purchase contract form. For this reason, it will be assumed for the remainder of this Chapter that the real

---

25. Two pre-printed forms commonly used in Florida are (1) the "FAR/BAR" form that has the blessing of both the state realtors association and the state bar association, but has a decided residential bias and (2) the FAR form promulgated by the Florida Board of Realtors that is specifically tailored for commercial transactions.

estate development lawyer is using his original purchase contract form and not a pre-printed form.

3.   Using the "Killer" Form of Purchase Contract

Experienced practitioners are all too familiar with the lawyer who insists on using his so-called ***killer purchase contract*** form for every transaction. The killer form is the 50 page document that the lawyer (or more likely one of his senior partners) has labored over for years. It has ten pages of definitions (mostly arcane legal terms) and an intentionally intricate (albeit, virtually indecipherable) set of cross-references to other internal sections of the document. The killer form seeks to place every marginally conceivable deal risk and responsibility squarely on the shoulders of the seller and to give the buyer the right to do whatever it pleases throughout the acquisition process—usually "in its sole and absolute discretion."

In my view, the killer form is aptly named because the lawyer who insists on its use is more likely to kill the deal than make the deal. The submission of the killer form to the unsophisticated seller will so intimidate the seller that making a deal will become at best difficult and on occasion impossible. Sending a killer form to the sophisticated seller will unnecessarily increase the tension and combativeness of the acquisition negotiations, thereby potentially wasting two things that the developer holds most precious—time and money.

As has been said many times in prior chapters, the real estate development lawyer's job is to help his client achieve its business objectives. At Stage 1, that objective is to tie up the targeted site quickly and in a cost-effective manner. The successful real estate development lawyer should not waste the time of either his client or the seller by preparing a purchase contract draft that is commercially unreasonable, overreaching or unnecessarily complex. To be sure, the development lawyer must adopt a form that protects his client from legitimate deal risks. The insecure lawyer too frequently seeks to protect his client by using a killer form that he has been told will insulate his client from every risk, both real and imagined. This lawyer has likely never taken the time to understand his client's business deal, because he feels sufficiently comforted by his perception that the killer document will serve as a substitute for knowledge of the deal. Unfortunately, the insecure lawyer finds that, once the negotiations start, he is ill-equipped to rebuff the requested document modifications by seller's counsel for the simple reason that he does not understand how the acquisition fits into his client's bigger business deal or what is commercially reasonable under the circumstances. The insecure lawyer's choice at that point is either (1) to risk killing the deal by digging his heels in and refusing to change any substantive provision of the contract or (2) to chance looking stupid in the eyes of the developer by letting the seller's counsel run roughshod over him during the negotiations.

The challenge presented to the real estate development lawyer in Stage 1 is to prepare a purchase contract that appropriately manages the delicate balance between his client's desire to tie up the property as quickly and as cheaply as possible and his responsibility to protect his developer client from legitimate project risks. There is no purchase contract form that is appropriate for every occasion or every deal. The real estate development lawyer's job is to match the occasion with the proper form, so that both of the above objectives can be achieved.

C. DRAFTING RULES AND TECHNIQUES

The purchase contract is the first document that is going to be analyzed in depth in this book. Before embarking on a review of the substantive provisions of a purchase contract, let me digress and take the opportunity to discuss some drafting rules and techniques that have held me in good stead over the years. This is not a book on legal writing and, therefore, I will not be talking about clarity, concision, syntax or punctuation. What I will be presenting are my thoughts on what the real estate development lawyer can do to improve his document drafting. The importance of the real estate development lawyer being a skilled draftsman cannot be overstated.[26] Simply put, a lawyer who is not an accomplished draftsman should look for a field of practice other than real estate development law.

Here are ten rules that a real estate development lawyer should follow when preparing a legal document.

- *Think Before You Write*—Before the lawyer begins drafting, he must think through the following points—(1) what are the deal risks faced by his client and how can those risks best be handled (the so-called "what if" list referred to in Chapter 2)[27] and (2) what conditions must be satisfied before his client will be willing to buy the land.

- *Know What Each Provision Means and Why It Is in the Document*—Every provision in a legal document has a consequence. The real estate development lawyer's job is to make sure that the consequence of each contractual provision is consistent with his client's business interests. This is especially true with respect to the inclusion in a document of so-called "boilerplate" language, such as provisions on "governing law," "assignability" and "notice." Nothing is more embarrassing than having to respond to a question as to why a particular provision is in the contract by saying "I don't know—we just always put it in."

---

26. For an exceptional, practical discussion of the important role that document drafting plays in the real estate lawyer's practice, *see* JOSHUA STEIN, A PRACTICAL GUIDE TO REAL ESTATE PRACTICE Chapters 5 and 6 (2001).

27. *See supra* Chapter 2, Page 25.

- ***Don't Try To Sound Like a Lawyer***—The excessive use of legalese makes a lawyer look pompous, not smart.

- ***Use Standard Forms Judiciously***—A standard form can be a very valuable starting point to help the development lawyer identify legal issues and create a structure and format for his document. A standard form should not, however, be used as a crutch or held sacrosanct in any way. The document prepared by the lawyer must be tailored to fit his client's business deal. Too many young lawyers make the mistake of trying to make the client's business deal fit within the standard form rather than taking the proper approach of customizing the document to fit the deal.

- ***Keep the Document As Short and Simple As Possible***—This point was previously made in the course of the discussion of the killer form of contract. Quite simply, it takes a lot more skill and talent to cover all of the appropriate issues in a ten page document than it does in a 50 page document. While clarity should never be sacrificed strictly for the sake of brevity,[28] the thoughtful draftsman should always seek to convey his message in as few words as possible.

- ***Use Defined Terms To Make the Document Easier To Read and Understand***—Most legal documents repeat certain important concepts and terms multiple times. For example, a purchase contract will need to refer to the property being sold and the person to whom it is being sold on literally dozens of occasions. The use of defined terms to refer to these two concepts ("Property" and "Buyer") can greatly aid both the internal consistency and readability of the purchase contract. The real estate development lawyer must, however, avoid falling prey to the temptation to define every other word in a document. As one practitioner has noted, "overuse of defined terms imparts significance to terms which are not of significance, injects confusion instead of clarity and results in a document which is at best silly and at worst offensive to the reader."[29]

- ***Avoid Excessive Cross-references***—Each section of an agreement should be understood simply by reading the words contained in that section. Excessive cross-references to other sections of the document can make the document utterly unreadable.

- ***Always Use Good Grammar***—A lawyer who is respected by his peers is given much greater latitude throughout the deal negotiations. Nothing can cause a lawyer to lose the respect of his peers quicker than his violation of basic rules of grammar in his drafted documents (for example, a lack of parallelism or the use of dangling modifiers).

---

28. *See* JOSHUA STEIN, *supra note 26*, at 63.

29. *See* Hastie, *supra* note 2, at 14.

- ***Adopt an "Inverted Pyramid" Structure for the Document—*** Every legal document needs to be organized in some logical order. I have found that the "inverted pyramid" format works best—that is, including the most important concepts at the beginning of the document and the least important at the end.[30] The relative importance of the various provisions of a document should be evaluated from the perspective of the lawyer's client. Years of experience have taught me that no client actually reads the entire document and, therefore, it is wise to include the provisions of most interest to the client as early in the document as possible.

- ***Don't Ignore the Look of the Document—***As is the case in every business, style sells in the legal profession. Just as a lawyer wearing a $2,000 Armani suit is initially given more credence than is his peer wearing a J.C. Penny design replete with gravy stains, a document that looks crisp and professional is afforded much greater deference than is a document that has never been introduced to the wonders of font manipulation under Microsoft Word.

V. IDENTIFYING AND MITIGATING DEAL RISKS

Drafting rule #1 is that before the real estate development lawyer starts drafting the purchase contract, he should first take the time to identify the risks of the subject deal and figure out how best to protect his client from the existence of those risks. With the sagacity of that admonition in mind, this Chapter will turn to an exploration of deal risks and what methods are available to the lawyer in his quest to eliminate or at least minimize his client's exposure to those risks.

There are six categories of risk associated with the real estate development process.

- ***Business Risk—***This is the risk that the developer's business plan is flawed in some way—for example, the perceived customer need doesn't exist or the developer's proposal to satisfy that need doesn't work. In other words, this is the risk that the developer had a bad idea.

- ***Market Risk—***This is the risk that an otherwise good idea by the developer is negatively impacted by a future change in the real estate or capital markets—for example, an economic recession brought on by some unforeseeable occurrence like a war or natural disaster or a dislocation in the targeted real estate market caused by the construction of a new highway interchange just down the road from the developer's project.

- ***Land Risk—***This is the risk that the acquired land is for some reason not suitable for its intended purpose—that is, for the cre-

---

30. See Joshua Stein, *supra* note 26, at 61.

ation on the land of an income-producing real estate project. Examples of site-specific, land risks are noted in the next section of this Chapter.

- *Financial Risk*—This is the risk discussed in Chapter 3 concerning the impact of opting to fund development costs with debt.[31] Simply put, financial risk is the possibility that the development project will not have sufficient value to pay off the project loan at maturity or will not produce sufficient cash flow to pay the interim debt service on that loan.

- *Execution Risk*—This is the risk that the developer does not properly execute one or more elements of its project business plan— for example, it fails to lease the project within the time frames or at the rent levels projected in its initial economic model or it falls short of its goal of constructing the project on time and on budget.

- *Operational Risk*—This is the risk that, once the project is constructed and leased, events occur that impact the project's profitability—for example, a tenant files for bankruptcy or the building is partially destroyed by a fire.[32]

At this first stage of the real estate development process, the real estate development lawyer's focus should be on preparing a land purchase contract that protects the developer against the onset of any of the above risks prior to its closing on the land acquisition. The lawyer's role in helping mitigate the developer's exposure to these risks once the land is acquired will be explored in subsequent chapters of this book.

A. LAND RISK

Before drafting the purchase contract, the real estate development lawyer should pause and ask himself "What could go wrong that would cause the developer to conclude that it no longer wants to acquire the land?" The circumstances that could lead the developer to reach such a conclusion fall under the broad category of *land risk*. For this purpose, land risks include both circumstances that are specific to the to-be acquired land and circumstances that relate in a broader sense to the viability of the developer's proposed real estate project.

The following are examples of some typical *site-specific land risks*:

- The site is not zoned to permit construction and use of the project;

- Utilities have not been extended to the site;

- The site soils will not support construction of the project;

- There is no access to the site from a public roadway;

---

31. *See supra* Chapter 3, Page 52. *See also* GAYLON E. GREER AND MICHAEL D. FARRELL, INVESTMENT ANALYSIS FOR REAL ESTATE DECISIONS 324–328 (2nd ed. 1988).

32. Operational risks can sometimes be partially mitigated by purchasing insurance against such risks—for example, casualty and rent loss insurance. For this reason, operational risks are sometimes referred to as "insurable risks." *See* GREER, *supra* note 31, at 328.

- The site is contaminated with hazardous substances or other environmental contaminants;

- Protected wetlands are present on part of the site;

- The site is part of a larger tract that cannot be subdivided without receipt of a governmental approval; and

- Title to the site is unmarketable or otherwise not suited for the development of the intended project.

Most developers do not want to acquire land, unless the land can be promptly commoditized as part of a development project.[33] Therefore, when contemplating the risks associated with a proposed land acquisition, the real estate development lawyer also needs to consider those non-site specific factors that could cause his developer client to jettison its plans to develop a project on the land.[34] The following are some common examples of *non-site-specific land risks* that might lead the developer to conclude that it does not want to buy a particular parcel of land:

- The developer cannot secure debt or equity funding for the project development costs;

- The developer fails to secure a governmental incentive or approval that is considered central to making the project economics work;

- The developer cannot lease the project within the projected time frames or at the projected rental;

- The developer discovers that it cannot build the project on time and on budget;

- The economy tanks, with the end result that there is no appreciable demand for the developer's project;

- A project that is directly competitive with the developer's project is started by another firm, leaving the developer with a significantly diminished class of targeted customers for its project; and

- The developer suffers a major financial loss on another deal and, as a result, no longer has the financial wherewithal to develop the proposed project.

All of these land risks (both site-specific and non-site-specific) are frequently lumped together in the contingency provision of a purchase contract and referred to as events which would cause a buyer to determine that the land is not "suitable" or "feasible" for its intended use—*see infra* Pages 100–114 for a detailed examination of the buyer's contingency clause.

---

33. *See supra* note 2.

34. This is one more reason why it is important that the real estate development lawyer understand the business side of the proposed development project. A land purchase contract that protects the developer only from site-specific land risks could result in the developer being forced to buy land for which it has no present development use—a circumstance that is sure to infuriate even the most mild-mannered of developers (of which there are precious few).

B. STRATEGIES TO MITIGATE LAND RISK

The real estate development lawyer can employ three, separate strategies to try to mitigate the categories of land risk discussed above:

- The establishment of the non-existence of certain risks as a ***contingency*** to the buyer's obligation to purchase the land;
- The receipt of a ***representation and warranty*** from the seller that certain risks do not exist; and
- The receipt of a ***certification*** from a third party that certain risks do not exist.

The ways in which the real estate development lawyer utilizes these risk mitigation methods when drafting the land purchase contract will be examined in much more detail in the next section of this Chapter.

VI. THE PURCHASE CONTRACT

The purchase contract is the road map for the land acquisition. It should show anyone picking up the purchase contract not only where the developer wants to go, but also how and when it proposes to get there and what interim stops it needs to make on the way.

The pages that follow will undertake a detailed analysis of each of the key provisions of the land purchase contract. The divergent approaches of the seller and the buyer on the main deal points will be highlighted in the course of that analysis. The order in which such provisions will be examined is roughly based on the order in which they appear in the Standard Form of Real Estate Purchase Agreement included as Document #2 in the Document Appendix (referred to in the remainder of this Chapter as the "Form Purchase Agreement"). Parenthetical reference is made in the caption of each of the following provisions to the section of the Form Purchase Agreement where such provision is addressed.

A. IDENTIFICATION OF PARTIES. *(Preamble)*

The identities of the seller and the buyer are customarily referred to in the first paragraph of the purchase contract. To insure enforceability of the various obligations and liabilities set forth in the contract, it is important to accurately identify each party to the contract by using such party's full legal name. If one of the parties is a legal entity of some type (which is usually the case), care should be taken to not only use the right legal name for that entity, but also to identify the party by entity type and the jurisdiction in which it was formed—for example, "a Delaware corporation" or "an Ohio limited liability company." Counsel representing each of the buyer and the seller should also try to get some information as to the financial creditworthiness of the identified party. To the extent the named party is a single purpose entity,[35] with little, if any, net worth, consideration should be given to requiring that either (a) the named party

---

35. *See infra* Chapter 7, Page 217, for a further discussion of single purpose entities.

to the purchase contract must be changed to a financially viable entity or (b) the obligations of the named party must be guaranteed by a financially viable entity. Crafting an elaborate set of obligations and liabilities to be placed on a particular party to a purchase contract will be to no avail if that party is an entity without significant assets.

B.   EFFECTIVE DATE OF EXECUTION. *(Preamble)*

Most of the time frames set forth in a purchase contract (for example, the date for delivery of a title insurance commitment and the outside date for the satisfaction of contingencies) are described by using the **effective date** of the parties' execution of the contract as the starting point. The effective date is usually the date on which both the buyer and the seller have executed the purchase contract.

C.   DESCRIPTION OF PROPERTY. *(§1)*

The description of the property to be sold must accomplish two things.

- It must describe the land in sufficient detail, so that no question exists as to its size, location or boundaries. This is most often accomplished by referencing the number of acres contained with the land parcel and attaching a legal description of the land as an exhibit to the purchase contract.[36]

- It must reference all other property rights that, although tangential to the land parcel, are nonetheless required for the full, legal and beneficial use of the land. These additional property rights include easements, access rights, development rights, mineral rights and all other "appurtenances and privileges" related to the land.[37]

D.   DEPOSIT. *(§2)*

There is no legal requirement that the buyer pay a deposit coincident with the parties' execution of the purchase contract. In practice, most land acquisitions of any significance will provide for the buyer's payment of a so-called **earnest money** or **good faith deposit** to evidence to the seller that the buyer is serious about buying the land. In the commercial setting, there is no rule of thumb as to the size of the deposit (unlike residential transactions, where a deposit equal to 10% of the purchase price is fairly

---

36. A legal description is generally prepared by a licensed surveyor and describes the property either by means of (a) a metes and bounds description (a description of the property by reference to the length and compass bearings of each of the perimeter boundaries of the property) or (2) a by reference to a subdivision map already filed of record in the local real estate records.

37. "Appurtenances and privileges" is an often-used catchall intended to capture all other property rights and interests associated with a particular land parcel. The term "appurtenance" is defined in THE ICSC DICTIONARY OF SHOPPING CENTER TERMS 5 (3rd ed. 2008) as an "extension, such as an easement or right-of-way, that is outside of the property itself, but is considered to be part of the property and adds to its greater use or enjoyment."

standard). The seller and buyer weigh in on the issue of the size of the deposit in obvious, predictable ways—the seller wants to see as big a deposit as possible, while the buyer would like to keep the deposit at a relatively nominal amount.[38]

The provisions of the contract dealing with the payment of the deposit should address all of the following topics.

- ***Who Should Hold the Deposit?*** The holder of the deposit (commonly referred to in this capacity as the ***escrow agent***) should be a title company or some other independent third party, who is unrelated to either the buyer or the seller.[39] The terms under which the third party holds the deposit are usually spelled out in a separate escrow agreement among the escrow agent, the seller and the buyer.

- ***What Form Should the Deposit Take?*** The deposit is usually paid in cash. However, in large transactions, it is often more cost-effective for the buyer to post the deposit in the form of an irrevocable, standby letter of credit.[40]

- ***Should the Deposit Be Held In an Interest-bearing Account?*** The answer to this question is almost always "yes," with any interest earned on the deposit accruing to the benefit of the buyer.

- ***When Should the Deposit Be Refunded To the Buyer?*** The deposit (and any interest earned on the deposit) should be returned to the buyer upon the termination of buyer's obligation under the purchase contract as a result of either (1) the buyer's failure to satisfy or waive certain conditions specified in the purchase contract or (2) the seller's default under the purchase contract. The drafter of the purchase contract should take great care to specify the exact circumstances under which the deposit must be returned to the buyer. The buyer will typically want the escrow agent to be required to refund the deposit immediately upon the buyer instruct-

---

38. A common compromise position is to provide that the deposit will be paid by the buyer in installments over a stated period of time—for example, one third of the total deposit being payable every 30 days during the buyer's 90 day due diligence period. This type of arrangement is particularly appealing to a buyer, who can opt not to make the additional deposits if its due diligence during the prior 30–day period was unsatisfactory.

39. The lawyer for the buyer or the seller should normally not act as the escrow agent. In the event a dispute arises under the purchase contract, a lawyer acting as escrow agent runs the very real risk of being disqualified from the continuing representation of his client, because it holds a deposit that is the object of desire of both the seller and the buyer. *See* GREGORY M. STEIN, MORTON P. FISHER, JR. AND GAIL M. STERN, A PRACTICAL GUIDE TO COMMERCIAL REAL ESTATE TRANSACTIONS—FROM CONTRACT TO CLOSING 23–24 (2001); and Andrew L. Herz, Bruce B. May and Gail Livingston Mills, *When Good Deals Go Bad—Purchase Contracts, Defaults, Waivers and Remedies*, in ACREL PAPERS (ALI–ABA, October 2004), available online at http://www.acrel.org/Documents/Seminars/Spring2004.

40. An irrevocable, standby letter of credit is a guaranty by a financial institution (usually a bank) that it will pay the holder of the letter of credit a fixed sum of money upon the holder's presentation to the financial institution of a demand for payment. The issuance of a letter of credit does not constitute a current borrowing by the person requesting such letter and, therefore, does not subject that person to ongoing interest charges on the amount of the letter. However, a fee (typically 1% of the maximum amount disbursable under the letter of credit) will be payable to the financial institution upon the issuance of the letter of credit.

ing the escrow agent to do so (usually in writing), while the seller will not want the escrow agent to be empowered or obligated to refund the deposit, without first receiving the seller's blessing to do so. A frequently used compromise requires the buyer to send any refund notice to both the escrow agent and the seller, with the escrow agent then being prohibited from paying the deposit to buyer for some period of time after its receipt of the refund demand. This procedure gives the seller the time and opportunity to take whatever action it believes is appropriate to prevent an improper refund of the deposit.

- **_When Should the Deposit Be Paid To the Seller?_** The deposit should be paid to the seller upon the closing of the buyer's purchase of the land, with the buyer receiving a credit on the purchase price in an amount equal to the deposit. The question of whether the deposit is to be paid to the seller upon the buyer's default under the purchase contract is a question which will be explored in more detail as part of the discussion later in this Chapter of liquidated damages and other contractual remedies.[41]

E. PURCHASE PRICE. _(§3)_

This is the one provision of the purchase contract that it is sure to be read by both the seller and the buyer. The purchase price provision should specifically address the following considerations.

- **_Amount_**—The purchase price can be stated either as a fixed sum or as a product of a formula. It is very common for a commercial land acquisition to have the purchase price determined by multiplying the number of acres contained within the site by a per acre price. If the price is calculated in this manner, the parties need to stipulate in the contract who will make the determination of the number of acres contained within the site (usually the surveyor) and, somewhat more controversially, whether that determination will be made on the basis of the land parcel's "gross" or "net" acreage. The seller will always want the purchase price to be determined based on gross acreage. The buyer, on the other hand, will generally want the per acre price to be applied against only those net acres that it can develop, subtracting out any portion of the land that is burdened by an easement or right-of-way or is otherwise not developable (for example, because it is located in a protected wetlands).

- **_Method of Payment_**—A stock phrase contained in virtually all purchase contracts is that the purchase price will be "paid in cash at closing." This does not mean that the buyer needs to bring a suitcase full of $20 bills with it to the closing. In this context, "cash" means any method of payment where there is no risk of

---

41. _See infra_ Pages 139–141.

collection on the payment (as there is with a personal check or credit card). In today's environment, the "cash" payment is almost always made by means of a wire transfer of funds through an electronic system maintained by the Federal Reserve System. The careful lawyer should specify in the purchase contract that the buyer will pay the purchase price by means of a wire transfer to a specific account which is either identified in the purchase contract or to be designated at some later date by the escrow agent.[42] Although not as common as a cash payment, the contract may recite that all or some portion of the purchase price will be "paid" by means of either the seller's provision to the buyer of purchase money financing[43] or the buyer's assumption of an existing mortgage debt on the land.[44]

Practice Tip #5–2: Contractual Techniques to Deal With Land Risk

As was mentioned earlier in this Chapter, the real estate development lawyer uses three basic techniques to try to mitigate his client's exposure to deal risks prior to the land acquisition closing. Those three techniques are (1) the establishment of the non-existence of certain risks as a **contingency** *to the buyer's obligation to purchase the property, (2) the receipt of a* **representation and warranty** *from the seller confirming that certain risks do not exist and (3) the receipt of a* **certification** *from a third party that certain risks do not exist. The charts set forth below illustrate which of these three techniques is available to help the real estate developer deal the principal categories of both site-specific and non-site specific, land risks*

---

42. In most situations, responsibility for disbursing the closing funds will fall on the escrow agent. If that is to be the case, the purchase contract should require the buyer to make its payment to the escrow agent's trust account.

43. Purchase money financing is nothing more than a loan made by the seller to the buyer to pay all or some portion of the purchase price for the land. A purchase money loan is almost always secured by a mortgage on the land. If purchase money financing is involved in a land acquisition, the real estate development lawyer should make sure that the essential terms of such financing are specified in the purchase contract—that is, the principal amount of the loan, the interest rate, the amount and timing of all required debt service payments and all other important business terms related to the extension of the purchase money financing.

44. If the buyer is going to assume an existing mortgage debt on the land, the purchase contract should recite that the cash portion of the purchase price payable by the buyer will be credited with an amount equal to the outstanding principal balance of the mortgage debt as of the date of closing. The purchase contract should also require the seller to fully comply with the terms of the existing mortgage debt at all times prior to closing and to cooperate with the buyer in its efforts to effect an assumption of the mortgage debt. Finally, the purchase contract should require that the existing mortgage lender certify in writing to the buyer that: (a) the seller is not in default under the mortgage debt; (b) the loan is fully assumable by the buyer, without the payment by buyer of any additional fees or, if any such fees are payable, the amount of such fees and who will be required to pay them; and (c) the mortgage debt will, from and after the date of buyer's assumption of such debt, be on the economic and business terms and conditions set forth in the lender's certification to the buyer (e.g., the interest rate, debt service payments and maturity date of the assumed loan).

Site-specific Risks	*Contingency*	*Representation/ Warranty*	*Certification*
The site is not zoned to permit development of project.	*Yes*	*Yes*	*Yes*
Utilities are not available to the site.	*Yes*	*Yes*	*Yes*
The site soils will not support construction of the project.	*Yes*	*Yes*	*Yes*
There is no access to the site from a public roadway.	*Yes*	*Yes*	*Yes*
The site has environmental problems.	*Yes*	*Yes*	*Yes*
The site has protected wetlands.	*Yes*	*Yes*	*Yes*
The site cannot legally be subdivided from a larger tract.	*Yes*	*Yes*	*Yes*
Title to the site is unmarketable.	*Yes*	*Yes*	*Yes*

Non-site-specific Risks	*Contingency*	*Representation/ Warranty*	*Certification*
The developer cannot secure financing for the project.	*Yes*	*No*	*No*
The developer cannot lease the project.	*Yes*	*No*	*No*
The developer is unable to obtain governmental incentives/approvals.	*Yes*	*No*	*No*
The developer cannot construct the project on time and on budget.	*Yes*	*No*	*No*
The economy tanks.	*Yes*	*No*	*No*
A competitive project is started in the vicinity of the developer's project.	*Yes*	*No*	*No*
The developer loses big on another project.	*Yes*	*No*	*No*

As the above charts clearly illustrate, the real estate development lawyer can, if he so elects, use a "belt and suspenders" approach by simultaneously using all three risk mitigation techniques to try to ameliorate his client's risk exposure to site-specific risks. However, the only way the real estate development lawyer can deal with non-site-specific risks is to use a contingency mechanism to provide his client with an out under the contract should one of those risks occur.

This Practice Tip is placed here because the next several pages of this Chapter will be devoted to an analysis of the four principal provisions of the purchase contract that deal with risk mitigation issues—that is, the provisions on contingencies, due diligence, representations and warranties, and title and survey. The "cheat sheet" provided by the above table is intended to be a handy reference tool to aid the reader's understanding of how a real estate development lawyer can craft the provisions of the purchase contract to try to protect his client from the land risks noted above.

F. BUYER CONTINGENCIES. *(§4)*

A contingency is defined in *The Real Estate Dictionary* as "the dependence upon a stated event which must occur before a contract is binding."[45] As noted earlier in this Chapter, the terms "contingency" and "condition" are used interchangeably by real estate developers to describe the situation where a party's obligation to perform under a purchase contract is dependent upon the occurrence of some specified event or circumstance.

In most situations, it is the buyer who seeks to create contingencies to its contractual obligation to purchase the land. The typical contingency provision will state that the buyer has a specified period of time in which to "satisfy or waive" the stated contingency. If the contingency is not satisfied or waived by the buyer within the contingency period, then the buyer will have the right to terminate its obligations under the purchase contract and receive a refund of its earnest money deposit.

The buyer's contingency clause is the second most hotly negotiated provision found in the purchase contract—right after the provision on the purchase price. When it comes to the issue of a buyer contingency, the interests of the buyer and seller are wildly divergent. The buyer wants as broad a contingency for as long a period as possible. The seller, on the other hand, does not want the buyer's purchase obligation to be contingent upon anything that the seller does not believe it can control (for example, the seller's delivery of good title to the land). If the seller is willing to grant the buyer any contingency to its purchase obligation, the seller will want the scope of the contingency to be as narrow as possible and the duration of the contingency period to be as short as possible.

Notwithstanding the seller's natural distaste for buyer contingencies, clauses setting forth some type of contingency to the buyer's purchase obligation have become quite commonplace in contracts for the purchase and sale of commercial real estate. The primary reason why buyer contingency clauses are customarily found in purchase contracts is that even the seller recognizes that there are certain things about the land which the buyer cannot learn until the buyer is given access to the land to conduct its due diligence—for example, whether the site soils can support construction of the contemplated development project. The knowledgeable seller also knows that the buyer will not spend the money necessary to

---

45. *See* JOHN TALAMO, REAL ESTATE DICTIONARY 50 (7th ed. 2001).

perform its costly due diligence, unless the buyer has a legally enforceable, contractual right to purchase the property. As a result, the real dynamic of the negotiations over the buyer's contingency clause is not whether such a clause is going to be included in the purchase contract, but rather what that clause is going to look like. In order to gain an appreciation of that dynamic, one must first look at how both the developer/buyer and the landowner/seller view contingency clauses.

1. Developer's Perspective on Contingency Clauses

Ideally, the developer would like a contingency clause that effectively converts the purchase contract into a long-term, unilateral option agreement—an "I'll buy if I want to" arrangement. An option agreement effectively eliminates the developer's land risk, because the developer does not have an obligation to purchase the land—it merely has the right to purchase the land if it elects to exercise the option.

As discussed earlier in this Chapter, the typical landowner is unwilling to grant an open-ended option on its land, unless it is paid a handsome, nonrefundable option fee for doing so. The landowner is, however, usually willing to agree to the inclusion in the purchase contract of some type of buyer contingency clause, because the landowner realizes that it would be commercially unreasonable to expect a developer to bind itself to purchase a parcel of land before it has had the opportunity to gain access to the land to conduct its due diligence. The question, therefore, becomes how far the developer can go in structuring a contingency clause which, for all intents and purposes, converts the purchase contract into an "I'll buy if I want to" option.

2. The Suitability Contingency

It is quite common for the first draft of a purchase contract prepared by a real estate development lawyer to contain a clause such as the following (often referred to as a *free look*):

> *Buyer's obligation to purchase the Land is contingent upon Buyer determining within ___ days after the Effective Date that the Land is suitable for Buyer's intended use.*

This type of broadly-worded buyer contingency would, on its face, seem to allow a buyer to come very close to achieving its goal of converting a purchase obligation into an option right. The question, however, is whether such a clause will be viewed by the courts as being an "illusory promise," which would then have the effect of rendering the purchase contract wholly unenforceable.

The *Mattei v. Hopper* case examines the illusory promise issue in the context of a purchase contract that purported to condition the purchaser's obligation to buy a parcel of land upon "obtaining leases satisfactory to the purchaser."[46]

---

46. *See* Mattei v. Hopper, 330 P.2d 625, 626 (California 1958).

MATTEI v. HOPPER[47]

Supreme Court of California
330 P.2d 625
Decided on October 24, 1958

Plaintiff brought this action for damages after defendant allegedly breached a contract by failing to convey her real property in accordance with the terms of a deposit receipt which the parties had executed. After a trial without a jury, the court concluded that the agreement was 'illusory' and lacking in 'mutuality.' . . .

Plaintiff was a real estate developer. He was planning to construct a shopping center on a tract adjacent to defendant's land. For several months, a real estate agent attempted to negotiate a sale of defendant's property under terms agreeable to both parties. After several of plaintiff's proposals had been rejected by defendant because of the inadequacy of the price offered, defendant submitted an offer. Plaintiff accepted on the same day.

The parties' written agreement was evidenced on a form supplied by the real estate agent, commonly known as a deposit receipt. Under its terms, plaintiff was required to deposit $1,000 of the total purchase price of $57,500 with the real estate agent, and was given 120 days to 'examine the title and consummate the purchase.' At the expiration of that period, the balance of the price was 'due and payable upon tender of a good and sufficient deed of the property sold.' The concluding paragraph of the deposit receipt provided: 'Subject to Coldwell Banker & Company obtaining leases satisfactory to the purchaser.' This clause and the 120–day period were desired by plaintiff as a means for arranging satisfactory leases of the shopping center buildings prior to the time he was finally committed to pay the balance of the purchase price and to take title to defendant's property.

Plaintiff took the first step in complying with the agreement by turning over the $1,000 deposit to the real estate agent. While he was in the process of securing the leases and before the 120 days had elapsed, defendant's attorney notified plaintiff that defendant would not sell her land under the terms contained in the deposit receipt. Thereafter, defendant was informed that satisfactory leases had been obtained and that plaintiff had offered to pay the balance of the purchase price. Defendant failed to tender the deed as provided in the deposit receipt.

Initially, defendant's thesis that the deposit receipt constituted no more than an offer by her, which could only be accepted by plaintiff notifying her that all of the desired leases had been obtained and were satisfactory to him, must be rejected. Nowhere does the agreement mention the necessity of any such notice. Nor does the provision making the agreement 'subject to' plaintiff's securing 'satisfactory' leases necessarily

---

47. All footnotes and citations have been omitted from this opinion.

constitute a condition to the existence of a contract. Rather, the whole purchase receipt and this particular clause must be read as merely making plaintiff's performance dependent on the obtaining of 'satisfactory' leases. Thus a contract arose, and plaintiff was given the power and privilege to terminate it in the event he did not obtain such leases....

However, the inclusion of this clause, specifying that leases 'satisfactory' to plaintiff must be secured before he would be bound to perform, raises the basic question whether the consideration supporting the contract was thereby vitiated. When the parties attempt, as here, to make a contract where promises are exchanged as the consideration, the promises must be mutual in obligation. In other words, for the contract to bind either party, both must have assumed some legal obligations. Without this mutuality of obligation, the agreement lacks consideration and no enforceable contract has been created. Or, if one of the promises leaves a party free to perform or to withdraw from the agreement at his own unrestricted pleasure, the promise is deemed illusory and it provides no consideration. Whether these problems are couched in terms of mutuality of obligation or the illusory nature of a promise, the underlying issue is the same consideration.

While contracts making the duty of performance of one of the parties conditional upon his satisfaction would seem to give him wide latitude in avoiding any obligation and thus present serious consideration problems, such 'satisfaction' clauses have been given effect. They have been divided into two primary categories and have been accorded different treatment on that basis. First, in those contracts where the condition calls for satisfaction as to commercial value or quality, operative fitness, or mechanical utility, dissatisfaction cannot be claimed arbitrarily, unreasonably, or capriciously and the standard of a reasonable person is used in determining whether satisfaction has been received.... However, it would seem that the factors involved in determining whether a lease is satisfactory to the lessor are too numerous and varied to permit the application of a reasonable man standard.... Illustrative of some of the factors which would have to be considered in this case are the duration of the leases, their provisions for renewal options, if any, their covenants and restrictions, the amounts of the rentals, the financial responsibility of the lessees, and the character of the lessees' businesses.

This multiplicity of factors which must be considered in evaluating a lease shows that this case more appropriately falls within the second line of authorities dealing with 'satisfaction' clauses, being those involving fancy, taste, or judgment. Where the question is one of judgment, the promisor's determination that he is not satisfied, when made in good faith, has been held to be a defense to an action on the contract. Although these decisions do not expressly discuss the issues of mutuality of obligation or illusory promises, they necessarily imply that the promisor's duty to exercise his judgment in good faith is an adequate consideration to support the contract. None of these cases voided the contracts on the ground that they were illusory or lacking in mutuality of obligation.

Defendant's attempts to distinguish these cases are unavailing, since they are predicated upon the assumption that the deposit receipt was not a contract making plaintiff's performance conditional on his satisfaction. As seen above, this was the precise nature of the agreement. Even though the 'satisfaction' clauses discussed in the above-cited cases dealt with performances to be received as parts of the agreed exchanges, the fact that the leases here which determined plaintiff's satisfaction were not part of the performance to be rendered is not material. The standard of evaluating plaintiff's satisfaction—good faith—applies with equal vigor to this type of condition and prevents it from nullifying the consideration otherwise present in the promises exchanged. . . .

We conclude that the contract here was neither illusory nor lacking in mutuality of obligation because the parties inserted a provision in their contract making plaintiff's performance dependent on his satisfaction with the leases to be obtained by him.

***

NOTES AND QUESTIONS ABOUT THE MATTEI CASE

The *Mattei* case supports the proposition that a broad **suitability contingency** will not render a purchase contract unenforceable. The buyer will, however, have the implied duty to use good faith when making its determination of the suitability of the land. Theoretically, the existence of the implied duty of good faith makes a purchase contract with a broad suitability contingency less desirable to a buyer than a pure option agreement, where the buyer could seemingly use bad faith in deciding not to exercise its purchase option. However, does this theoretical distinction between an option and a broad suitability contingency have any practical significance to a buyer? The following discussion questions are intended to serve as a guide in evaluating the practical difference between a broad contingency clause and an option.

- Would it make any difference if the contingency clause stated that the determination of the suitability of the land was to be made by the buyer "in its sole discretion?"[48]

- Would a buyer violate its implied duty of good faith if it decided to back out of the purchase contract for any of the following reasons:

    - The buyer can't find a lead tenant for the project;

---

48. *See* Allen D. Shandron, Inc. v. Cole, 416 P.2d 555 (Ariz. 1966), where the court held that the "use of the word 'discretion' specifically means that the Landlord will not act arbitrarily, unreasonably or capriciously." *See also* Bryant v. City of Atlantic City, 707 A.2d 1072 (N.J. 1998) where the court held that, despite the presence of the modifier "in its sole discretion," a developer still had to act reasonably in making its decision as to whether the costs of an environmental remediation were unreasonable. *But see* Reedy v. Reedy, 264 P.2d 913 (Kan. 1953), where the Kansas court held that the use of the word "discretion" to describe a party's review of a contractual matter effectively made the party's promise illusory and that, in such instance, the court would not imply an obligation of good faith to create an enforceable agreement among the parties. *See also* Michael G. O'Flaherty, *Real Estate Contracts from Execution to Closing*, in ACREL PAPERS (ALI–ABA, October 1999), available online at http://www.acrel.org/Documents/Seminars/a002107.pdf.

- There is a sudden downturn in the real estate market where the land is located;

- The buyer decides that the purchase price agreed to in the purchase contract is too high;

- The buyer is able to get an option to buy another parcel that is better suited for the project than is the parcel which is the subject of the purchase contract; or

- The buyer decides to move to Tahiti and start a sailboat charter business.

The following case illustrates what can go wrong when a buyer presumes that a broad suitability contingency places it in a position that is wholly tantamount to the "I'll buy if I want to" position of an option holder.

SHERIDAN v. CROWN CAPITAL CORPORATION[49]

Court of Appeals of Georgia
554 S.E.2d 296
Decided on August 22, 2001

This is an appeal from cross-motions for summary judgment in an interpleader action brought by Christopher B. Manos, Jr., P.C., escrow agent, holding $25,000 in earnest money for the purchase of property, between Paul Sheridan, seller, and Crown Capital Corporation, purchaser, because Crown refused to go through with the purchase of 2.26 acres of commercial real estate and buildings in Carrollton, Carroll County, for $1,075,000. Crown, the author of the contract, contended that it had the right to a free look at the property under the agreement; had the right "to determine if the Property is satisfactory for the Purchaser's intended use" by inspection of the property; and had the right to terminate for failure to secure an anchor tenant, making the property development unsatisfactory. Sheridan contended that the inspection provision limited the satisfactory intended use to conditions set forth in the clause for inspection and for the commercial use of the property and did not include economical feasibility for any reason. The trial court erroneously granted summary judgment to Crown and against Sheridan. We reverse.

The property was zoned commercial, containing commercial buildings on the 2.26 acres. On August 24, 1998, the agreement prepared by Crown's representatives was executed by Crown's president and presented to Sheridan as an offer to purchase the property as zoned. On September 4, 1998, Sheridan accepted the offer and executed the agreement. Crown deposited $25,000 as earnest money with Christopher B. Manos, Jr. as escrow agent. Crown had 120 days from the acceptance to inspect the property and to determine if it was satisfactory to its intended use under the agreement. After the one hundred twenty-first day, Crown had to

---

49.   All footnotes and citations have been omitted from this opinion.

deposit an additional $75,000 in earnest money, unless it had earlier given notice of termination after inspection if the property was not satisfactory to the purchaser's intended use.

On December 8, 1998, Crown gave [Sheridan] notice that ... Purchaser hereby terminates the Contract, effective immediately.

Cub Foods, a potential anchor tenant of Crown's, withdrew its interest; this caused the development, and not the property, to be economically unsuitable for Crown's development, because now the development was "not economically feasible for any reason." Thus, Crown exercised what it believed was its opportunity (free look) to tie up the property for 120 days under what it believed was its absolute discretion to terminate the agreement for any reason without any liability, but there was no inspection performed for it....

The cardinal rule of construction is to ascertain the intent of the parties, which is to formulate an enforceable agreement. A key element of contract construction is that the trial court must give a fair and reasonable construction to the contract that upholds the contract rather than causing it to have no binding effect, because the intent of the parties is to enter into a valid contract and not an unenforceable illusionary agreement.... [T]he law will not construe a contract so as to give [one party] the right to destroy it by a simple refusal to comply with it, unless the terms of the contract are so clear and unambiguous as to make irresistible the conclusion that no other result could possibly be reached, and that such was the intention of the parties."

Contracts are construed most strongly against the drafter, which, here, was Crown. Thus, Section 8(a) should be construed in pari materia with Section 10(c) so that satisfactory use intended by the purchaser is defined and limited to "[u]se of premises as a commercial shopping center development" and not an unrestricted discretionary use that would permit the destruction of the contract without contractually defined justification. Further, the inspection under Section 8(a) specifies determination of those physical conditions of the property necessary to the development for a commercial shopping center. The agreement was not an illusion, terminable on the exercise of unfettered discretion by Crown, as Crown would have us believe, but a binding contract.

Thus, the contract must be construed as a whole rather than in separate and distinct parts, giving effect to all terms; the contract should not be determined by examining isolated clauses and provisions as the trial court has done. Therefore, Section 10(c) must be construed with Section 8(a) to disclose the intent of the parties as to the purchaser's intended use, i.e., use as a commercial shopping center development. When the four corners of the instrument are searched, the meaning of the purchaser's intended use becomes clearly manifest as the intent of the parties from construing Section 8(a) with Section 10(c). Thus, economic unsuitability for use intended by failure to obtain an anchor tenant was never within the manifest intent of the parties as a meaning of "use intended" when the limited scope of the purpose of the inspection under Section 8(a) and of the development under Section 10(c) are construed together. The purchaser did not have any discretion as to the use intended outside the commercial shopping center development, because Section 8(a) limited satisfactory use intended to the physical conditions of the property revealed on inspection as set forth in such paragraph for the development of the property. . . .

This agreement clearly provided for a condition subsequent for the termination of the contract in the event that the inspection of the property revealed that the property could not be satisfactorily physically developed for commercial shopping center use. If the physical condition of the land would not permit development as a commercial shopping center, revealed upon timely inspection and notice, then the agreement terminated automatically upon such notice by the purchaser to the seller. In the event that no inspection was made, the condition subsequent could not be invoked to terminate the contract. In this case, no inspection was ever made by the purchaser nor were any physical conditions identified that could prevent the development of a commercial shopping center by Crown had an inspection been timely conducted. Thus, the condition subsequent never occurred.

Therefore, under the express terms of the agreement, Crown's notice of unauthorized termination and refusal to close the purchase of the property constituted an un-excused failure to perform the agreement, i.e., a default. Thus, Crown was in default under Section 19. Sheridan was entitled to recover the earnest money as reasonable liquidated damages under the agreement.

Nᴏᴛᴇs ᴀɴᴅ Qᴜᴇsᴛɪᴏɴs Aʙᴏᴜᴛ ᴛʜᴇ Sʜᴇʀɪᴅᴀɴ Cᴀsᴇ

It is interesting to note that the buyer in the *Sheridan* case was apparently so sanguine in its view that the purchase contract gave it a "free look" that it never even bothered to inspect the property once it found out that its anchor tenant had backed out of the deal. Moreover, the buyer never provided the seller with any notice (written or verbal) as to any physical conditions on the property that it had determined were unsuitable for its proposed shopping center development.

Two interesting questions emerge from the *Sheridan* case:

• Would the court in *Sheridan* have decided the case differently if the purchase contract had stated that the buyer's obligation to purchase the property was contingent upon the buyer determining that the property was both "physically and economically" suitable for development as a shopping center?

• What would have been the result if the buyer had gone through the motions of inspecting the property and then issued a letter to the seller listing certain physical conditions which were unacceptable to the buyer?[50]

---

3. Lessons to Be Learned From *Mattei* and *Sheridan* Cases

The case law represented by the *Mattei* and *Sheridan* line of decisions[51] establish four important considerations that the real estate development lawyer must keep in mind when drafting a buyer contingency clause.

- Broad suitability contingency clauses are enforceable.

- The party benefiting from such a contingency will, however, be obligated to act in good faith in making its decision as to the suitability of the property.

- The contingency clause must be carefully and artfully drafted, so as to avoid the unintended consequences that befell the defendant in the *Sheridan* case. The lawyer drafting the buyer's contingency clause would be well-advised to use language that will, at least arguably, encompass both site-specific and non-site-specific land risks. The following is an example of such a contingency clause:

  > *The Buyer's obligation to purchase the land is expressly made contingent upon the Buyer determining within ___ days after the Effective Date that the condition of the Land is suitable for Buyer's intended use and that Buyer's intended development of the Land is economically feasible.*[52]

- A buyer who wants to back out of a deal in reliance upon a broad contingency clause must be extremely vigilant and thorough in both the conduct of its property due diligence and its communication of the unsatisfactory results of that due diligence to the seller. There can be no guaranty, however, that such vigilance and thoroughness will serve to validate the legality of the buyer's contract termination, if the real reason behind the buyer's decision to back out of the contract is wholly unrelated to any matter within the scope of the buyer's contractual contingency.

---

50. *See* Zygar v. Johnson, 169 Or.App. 638 (2000) in which the buyer reasonably believed that the results of the termite inspection were unsatisfactory and, therefore, was able to get out of a contract to buy a house even though it was submitted that the "real" reason for his terminating the contract was that his fiancé had decided she did not want to live there. *See also* GRANT S. NELSON, DALE A. WHITMAN, ANN M. BURKHART AND R. WILSON FREYERMUTH, REAL ESTATE TRANSFER, FINANCE, AND DEVELOPMENT, CASES AND MATERIALS 116–126 (8th ed. 2009). For additional cases examining the issue of whether a buyer's lackluster pursuit of its due diligence constituted a violation of its implied obligation to proceed in good faith, *see* Liuzza v. Panzer, 333 So.2d 689 (La. App. 1976); Barber v. Jacobs, 753 A.2d 430 (Conn. Ct. App. 2000); and Loma Linda University v. District–Realty Title Insurance Corp., 443 F.2d 773 (C.A.D.C. 1971).

51. For a general discussion of the case law on the enforceability and interpretation of contingency clauses, *see generally* Herz, *supra* note 39; and O'Flaherty, *supra* note 48.

52. I prefer to use the term "feasible" when referring to economic issues because "feasibility" is a well-recognized concept of real estate economics. *See supra* Chapter 3, note 3, for a definition of feasibility.

If the real estate development lawyer remains mindful of the above propositions, he will find that a broad suitability contingency is an invaluable tool to be used in his attempt to minimize his client's exposure to land risks. When structured in an appropriate manner, such a clause can provide the buyer with almost as much contractual flexibility as a pure option, without the financial downside of the buyer having to pay a nonrefundable option fee.[53]

4. Drafting the Contingency Clause—Other Considerations

The following are additional points that the real estate development lawyer should take into consideration when drafting the buyer contingency clause.

- It is neither necessary, nor wise to include a specific contingency in the purchase contract for every conceivable land risk. As noted in *Practice Tip #5–2*, the developer's exposure to most site-specific land risks can be addressed through seller representations and warranties, required third party certifications and a broad suitability contingency. Throwing a laundry list of site-specific contingencies into the purchase contract creates unnecessary clutter and complexity and frequently scares off the landowner, who generally regards any contingency as a signal that the developer is just trying to tie up the landowner's site and that there is no realistic prospect that the developer will actually close on the land acquisition.[54]

- Notwithstanding the general advice noted in the preceding paragraph, the real estate development lawyer should consider supplementing the suitability contingency clause with an additional, topic-specific contingency if he believes that a particular land risk (for example, a rezoning of the land or the obtaining of project financing[55]) will not be resolved during the stated duration of the suitability contingency. In such a circumstance, developer's counsel should try to either (1) extend the length of the suitability contingency period to cover the time needed by the developer to resolve the

---

53. A recent California case illustrates that there are limits that will be placed on a lawyer's attempt to use a broad suitability contingency to achieve all of the "I'll buy if I want to" benefits of an option. In Steiner v. Thexton, 226 P.3d 359 (California 2010), the Supreme Court of California held that a contingency clause that gave the buyer the right to terminate the contract at any time and for any reason "in its absolute and sole discretion" was a unilateral option that was not enforceable absent the buyer's provision of independent, bargained-for consideration for the grant of that option.

54. In making this statement, I am assuming that the landowner has agreed to the inclusion in the purchase contract of a broad suitability contingency of some stated duration. If the landowner is unwilling to agree to a broad suitability contingency, then the buyer has no choice but to try to include topic-specific contingencies in the purchase contract. *See infra* Page ___, for a discussion of tactics often employed by the landowner's lawyer to defeat the buyer's attempt to include a broad suitability contingency in the purchase contract.

55. Sellers of commercial land tend to view the inclusion in a purchase contract of a specific financing contingency as a sign that the proposed buyer is not a financially viable entity and, hence, that there is not much chance that the buyer will actually close on its purchase of the seller's land. As such, most developers will opt not to include a financing contingency in the purchase contract if they are otherwise able to get the seller to agree to a broad suitability and economic feasibility contingency of the type mentioned earlier in this Chapter.

particular land risk or (2) include a free-standing contingency of a longer duration to address that particular risk.

- Finally, the real estate development lawyer should be careful to not get too specific in its description of the buyer's contingencies. Change happens quickly during the real estate development process. Contingency language that seems perfectly on point on the date the purchase contract is initially prepared and executed may be hopelessly outdated and overly limiting months later when the time is at hand for the developer to decide whether it will purchase the land.[56] The real estate development lawyer's job is to prepare a contingency clause that affords his client the maximum flexibility to react to whatever land risks might surface during the contingency period, while at the same time not being so broad as to run afoul of the illusory promise rule discussed earlier in this Chapter.[57]

5. Landowner's Perspective on Contingency Clauses

For the purpose of the following discussion, assume that the real estate development lawyer has prepared a draft purchase contract that contains the following contingency clause:

> *Buyer's obligation to purchase the Land is contingent upon it determining within 270 days after the Effective Date that the Land is suitable for its intended use.*

How will the typical landowner react to this type of contingency clause? If the landowner is represented by competent counsel, the usual reaction will be that the contingency is "too broad" and that the contingency period is "too long."

It is important to remember what the inclusion of a contingency clause means to a landowner. By agreeing to a purchase contract with a buyer contingency, the landowner is agreeing to take its property off the market for the duration of the contingency period, without any assurance that the buyer will actually close on its purchase of the land. It is this lost opportunity that counsel representing the landowner will attempt to avoid when negotiating the terms of a buyer contingency clause.

As stated earlier in this Chapter, most landowners are willing to grant the buyer a limited contingency to permit the buyer to perform its site due diligence—soils tests, an environmental assessment, etc. The customary duration of a due diligence contingency of this type is 20–45 days after the contract's effective date. Hence, a typical, landowner counter-measure to

---

56. The *Sheridan* decision is a case in point. When the purchase contract was initially executed, the developer had a tenant in place for its project (Cub Foods) and, therefore, legitimately believed that the only land risk that it needed to cover in the contingency clause was the risk that the land was not physically capable of handling the proposed development. Unfortunately, Cub Foods backed out of the deal, leaving the developer with a situation where its contractual contingency was not sufficiently broad to cover the legitimate business reason it wanted to terminate its obligation to purchase the land.

57. John Hastie nicely addresses this point in his general advice that the "attorney should simultaneously plan for the maximum realization of profits by the client and the fire sale liquidation of the project." *See* Hastie, *supra* note 2, at 122.

the type of broad suitability contingency clause referenced at the outset of this section would be a clause similar to the following:

> *Buyer's obligation to purchase the Land is contingent upon it determining within 30 days after the Effective Date that the Land is physically capable of supporting Buyer's construction of a four story, 100,000 square foot office building on the Land.*

The above clause is the landowners' way of telling the real estate development lawyer that its contingency clause is "too broad" and "too long."

How do the parties bridge the obvious gap that exists between the developer's 270 day suitability contingency and the landowner's 30 day due diligence contingency? As is the case in any contractual negotiation, that answer ultimately is tied to the parties' relative negotiating leverage. Is the land an in-fill site that is fully zoned and permitted? If so, the leverage swings in favor of the landowner. If the land is neither zoned, nor permitted and is a pioneering development location, then the negotiating leverage lies with the developer.

The landowner wants to make sure that the buyer is seriously committed to buying the landowner's site and is not just trying to tie up that site for as long as possible in the hope that some spectacular development or resale opportunity fortuitously falls into the buyer's lap. The landowner's lawyer is, therefore, given the assignment of negotiating a contingency clause that is as far-removed as possible from the "I'll buy if I want to" form of a pure option.

The following are some negotiating techniques regularly used by seller's counsel to limit buyer contingency clauses.

- A negotiating tactic commonly used by the landowner's lawyer is to try to get the developer (or its lawyer) to specifically identify those land risks that are the most troubling to the developer. The landowner's counsel will then try to turn the table on the developer by pointing out which of the identified risks can be handled by third party certifications or some limited representations from the seller. The landowner's lawyer will grudgingly deal with any remaining risk that it believes to be legitimate in the context of the proposed land acquisition by drafting contingency language that is limited as to both the scope of the contingency and the period in which the contingency must be satisfied or waived by the buyer.

- Seller's counsel will seek to limit the scope of the buyer's contingency to those risks that any person seeking to develop the land would encounter—for example, a rezoning of the land from an agricultural to a commercial classification. Contingencies covering risks specifically associated with the buyer's proposed project (for example, the receipt of acceptable tenant leases, construction financing or governmental incentives) are routinely rejected by seller's counsel as being "your problem, not mine."

- If a contingency involves an approval that the developer must secure for the project (for example, a rezoning of the land), seller's counsel will try to place an affirmative obligation on the developer to take whatever interim action is required as a prerequisite for the ultimate granting of such approval. By way of example, seller's counsel might insert a clause saying that the buyer will be obligated to submit its request for a rezoning of the property within 30 days after the effective date and that developer's failure to do so will result in an automatic termination of the purchase contract.

- Finally, seller's counsel may require a "stair-stepping" of the deposit paid by the developer. Stair-stepping a deposit usually entails either (a) the developer paying additional deposits periodically throughout the contingency period (for example, every 60 days), (b) some portion of the developer's deposit becoming nonrefundable at designated points of the contingency period (this is often referred to as the deposit "going hard") or (c) some combination of (a) and (b).

The negotiations over the buyer's contingency clause are all about breadth and length, as buyer's counsel tries to structure the contingency clause so as to protect his client from all land risks (both site-specific and non-site-specific), while seller's counsel seeks to limit the buyer's contingency clause to only those items that any buyer of the subject land would have to accomplish in order to justify the amount of the purchase price set forth in the purchase contract.

HIBC Case Study—The Buyer's Contingency

Pizzuti wanted a contingency clause that was sufficiently broad and long to address both the normal land risks associated with the purchase of a large commercial tract (remember the HIBC parcel was 350 acres) and the non-site-specific risk related to Pizzuti's attempt to land the CBIS build-to-suit project. Chemical Bank, on the other hand, wanted to make sure that (1) it was dealing with a serious and financially capable buyer and (2) the deal would close as quickly as possible. Chemical Bank, as an experienced seller of real estate, fully appreciated that Pizzuti needed a contingency period to permit it to do its due diligence and otherwise figure out if its development of the HIBC land was feasible. Chemical Bank was also adamant that it would not make any contractual representations and warranties about the condition of the land and that Pizzuti would be buying the land in its "as is" condition.[58]

---

58. Chemical's negotiating stance was to be expected, because it had acquired the land by way of a deed in lieu of foreclosure from Jeno Paulucci. As such, Chemical's knowledge about the property was limited to whatever its loan officer had learned when the land loan was first made and whatever Paulucci had been willing to share with it during the foreclosure negotiations (presumably worse than nothing). The "take it as is" approach adopted by Chemical is typical of

Given all of the above factors, counsel for Pizzuti and Chemical had little difficulty agreeing to a broad contingency clause that gave Pizzuti the right to terminate its contractual obligations if it determined that the land was not "suitable for Buyer's intended purpose." The Pizzuti–Chemical land purchase contract defined "suitability" in the following manner:

Determination of the Property's suitability shall include, but not be limited to, Buyer's consideration of the following matters:

a.   Suitability of soils, access, visibility and other physical characteristics of the Property;

b.   Satisfactory results of environmental test and site investigations regarding the Property;

c.   Availability of permits, licenses, variances and other governmental approvals, including land use and zoning approvals, necessary for Buyer's intended use of the Property; and

d.   Economic and market analysis to determine feasibility of the Property for Buyer's development purposes.

Chemical Bank even went so far as to agree that Pizzuti could make the determination of the suitability of the land "in its sole discretion."

The real negotiation on the HIBC contingency clause was over the length of the contingency period. Pizzuti asked for a 270 day contingency period, which, in its mind, would give it sufficient time to secure CBIS' commitment to locate its office building and data center on the HIBC parcel. Chemical Bank initially took the position that the contingency period (for both the due diligence and feasibility contingencies) would be only 30 days. The compromise ultimately agreed to by Pizzuti and Chemical Bank was that the contingency period would be 90 days—a time period that Pizzuti believed would be sufficient to complete its due diligence, but not long enough to lock up the CBIS project.

The final part of the negotiation over the HIBC contingency clause related to Chemical Bank's insistence that Pizzuti evidence the seriousness of its interest in acquiring the HIBC land by posting a sizable earnest money deposit—$750,000. Chemical initially took the position that the entirety of the $750,000 deposit would have to be paid upfront upon contract execution and that 1/3 of that deposit (or $250,000) would become nonrefundable 30 days after contract execution, with another 1/3 becoming nonrefundable 60 days after contract execution. Pizzuti ultimately agreed to pay the $750,000 deposit, but retained the right to pay it in three installments over the first 60 days of the contingency period. More importantly, Pizzuti was also able to get Chemical Bank to agree to keep the contingency clause as a "free look" by making the entirety of the deposit refundable throughout the 90–day contingency period.

The HIBC contingency clause is a nice illustration of how a buyer and a seller can resolve their competing business objectives to make a deal. The

---

the negotiating position taken by any lender whose ownership of a land parcel is gained through a confrontational, negotiated work-out with its borrower.

points in the contingency clause negotiations which were "won" and "lost" by Pizzuti are noted below.

"Won"	*"Lost"*
A broad suitability contingency	*Only a 90 day contingency period*
Deposit fully refundable for 90 days	*Purchase on an "as is" basis*
Deposit paid in three installments	*Deposit of $750,000*

6. Terminating the Contract at End of Contingency Period

The whole point of a buyer contingency clause is to give the buyer the ability to terminate its obligations under the purchase contract if the stated contingency is not satisfied or waived by the buyer. It is imperative that the purchase contract specifically identify the method to be used by buyer if it elects to terminate its purchase obligation. The land seller generally prefers a provision which states that the buyer will be deemed to have waived its contingency, unless it gives seller written notice within the contingency period that it is affirmatively electing to terminate the purchase contract. Conversely, a land buyer favors a provision which presumes that the contingency has not been satisfied or waived (and, hence, that the purchase contract is terminated), unless the buyer provides written notice to the contrary to the seller within the contingency period. The selected presumption should be clearly articulated in the contingency provision of the purchase contract.

G. DUE DILIGENCE. *(§5)*

Due diligence is the investigatory process that a land buyer goes through to determine whether a particular parcel of land is suitable for the buyer's intended use of such parcel. As discussed under the immediately prior section of this Chapter, a buyer's successful completion of its site due diligence is frequently a contingency to the buyer's obligation to purchase the land.

The buyer must have access to the land in order to perform its site due diligence. The buyer does not automatically gain such access simply by its execution of a purchase contract. The purchase contract should explicitly state that the buyer and its consultants will have access to the land at all reasonable times after contract execution so that the buyer and its consultants can conduct appropriate site tests and inspections. The following is a list of those site tests and inspections typically conducted by a land buyer:

- A ***survey*** prepared by a licensed land surveyor that identifies the dimensions and boundaries of the land and the location of any improvements, easements, roads and encroachments affecting the land;

- An *environmental assessment* prepared by a qualified environmental engineering firm that identifies any environmental problems detected from an inspection of the site and a review of the appropriate federal and state environmental protection agency files;

- A *soils report* and topographical study prepared by a qualified soils engineer that confirms that the site soils will support the construction of the buyer's proposed project on the land;

- A *wetlands report* prepared by a qualified wetlands consultant that identifies the location, size and nature of any protected wetlands located on the land;

- An *access and utility study* prepared by the buyer or a consultant hired by the buyer (sometimes the buyer's general contractor) that confirms that the land has direct access to public roads and that utilities of sufficient size and capacity to service buyer's proposed project are available to the boundaries of the land; and

- A *zoning report* prepared by the buyer or a land use consultant hired by the buyer that recites the current zoning classification of the land and confirms that the buyer's development plans conform to all requirements imposed by such zoning classification.

A word of caution should be noted about the written reports produced by the buyer's consultants during the due diligence process. As noted earlier in this Chapter, the developer seeks to limit its exposure to various land risks by retaining experts to provide it with written certifications that the subject land risks do not exist with respect to the land. The issuers of those certifications (be it, the surveyor, environmental engineer or some other outside consultant) regularly try to subject their certifications to a litany of assumptions, limitations and qualifications, all of which are intended to essentially render the certifications meaningless.[59] It often falls to the real estate development lawyer to negotiate a form of certification that can, in fact, provide some true comfort to the developer. In addition to tightening down the terms of the consultant's certification, the lawyer must also determine whether the consultant has sufficient assets (either personally or through some form of malpractice insurance coverage) to reimburse the developer for any loss it incurs as a result of the consultant's report being wrong.

A buyer's due diligence efforts will also be aided by its receipt of permission from the landowner to review any prior third party reports and certification in the landowner's possession concerning the condition of the land. The landowner is often hesitant to grant the buyer access to such documents based on the landowner's fear that its sharing of such reports and certifications will somehow constitute a guaranty by the landowner of the completeness and accuracy of the furnished reports and certifications.

---

59. For example, it is common for an environmental engineer's first draft of its certification letter to state that the consultant's liability for any errors or omissions contained in the report is limited to the amount of the fee paid to the consultant by the land buyer—maybe $10,000 on a project like HIBC, which carried a land purchase price of $7,500,000.

In some instances (e.g., the HIBC land acquisition), the landowner may agree to provide the buyer with copies of such reports and certifications in exchange for the buyer's acceptance of a relatively short contingency period.[60]

In exchange for its agreement to grant the buyer access to its land and records, the landowner customarily requires the following buyer covenants to be spelled out in the purchase contract:

- The buyer's agreement that it will provide the landowner with reasonable prior notice of its entry onto the property for the conduct of its due diligence tests;

- The buyer's agreement to repair any damage to the land caused by its entry onto the land;

- The buyer's indemnification of the landowner against any loss or expense associated with the conduct of any on-site tests;

- The buyer's acknowledgement that any and all tests conducted by buyer and its consultants will be paid for by the buyer; and

- Finally, the buyer's agreement that, if its acquisition of the land is not closed due to the exercise of its option to terminate the purchase contract, the buyer will provide the landowner with copies of all third party reports and certifications received by the buyer during the course of its due diligence efforts.[61]

The due diligence process will be examined in more detail in Chapter 8 of this book—*Stage 4: Closing the Land Acquisition.*[62]

H. REPRESENTATIONS AND WARRANTIES. *(§6)*

The seller representation and warranty is the third and final weapon available to the real estate development lawyer to try to mitigate his client's exposure to the various risks associated with a proposed land acquisition.[63] A ***representation*** is a statement of a current fact, while a ***warranty*** is a promise of a future fact.[64] An example of a seller representation is "there are no hazardous materials or toxic substances located on the Land." A seller warranty on the same topic would read as follows—

---

60. The receipt of such historical reports is not a substitute for the buyer securing new reports from its consultants. The buyer will not have any right to hold the issuer of the old reports liable for any error or omission, because of a lack of privity between such issuer and the buyer. If the seller's lawyer does his job, he will also make it clear in the four corners of the purchase contract that the seller's delivery of such reports to the buyer will not in any way render the seller liable to the buyer for any mistakes or omissions contained in such reports.

61. In light of the case law on illusory promises examined earlier in this Chapter (*see supra* Pages 101–105), the careful buyer's lawyer should refuse this landowner request out of concern that the buyer's delivery of such reports and certifications to the landowner might provide the landowner with evidence of buyer's violation of its implied duty to exercise good faith in determining whether the land is suitable for buyer's intended purposes.

62. *See infra* Chapter 8, Pages 292–300.

63. The buyer contingency and third party certifications are the other two, risk mitigation weapons at the lawyer's disposal. *See supra* Pages 100–114 and 114–118, respectively.

64. *See* GREGORY STEIN, *supra* note 39, at 26.

"there will be no hazardous materials or toxic substances located on the Land on the closing date." Most purchase contracts require the seller to make a statement concerning a particular fact both as of the date on which the contract was executed (a representation) and as of the closing date (a warranty). For this reason, the terms "representation" and "warranty" are usually lumped together and treated interchangeably in the purchase contract. For the sake of simplicity, the term "representations" will be used throughout the remainder of this Chapter as a shorthand reference to include both representations and warranties.[65]

Any substantive discussion of seller representations must first start with the principle of *caveat emptor*—"let the buyer beware." The doctrine of caveat emptor remains generally applicable to the sale of commercial real property (although significant inroads on that principle have been made in the context of the purchase and sale of residential real property).[66] In its simplest terms, the doctrine of caveat emptor stands for the dual proposition that (1) a seller has no obligation to disclose to the buyer any defects or other problems related to the condition of the real property being sold to the buyer and (2) the buyer has no inherent legal right to sue the seller if the condition of the real property purchased by the buyer ultimately proves to be at odds with the buyer's expectations.

While the doctrine of caveat emptor does not require a commercial land seller to make any disclosures about the condition of the land, that doctrine does not permit the seller to lie or make any affirmative misrepresentations about the land.[67] A buyer of commercial real estate can, therefore, partially negate the application of the doctrine of caveat emptor by including in the purchase contract specific seller representations concerning the seller's status and authority and the condition and character of its land.[68]

1.   Seller's Perspective on Representations and Warranties

Landowners are quick to embrace the doctrine of caveat emptor. As stated at the outset of this Chapter, the business objective of the landown-

---

65. For a discussion of the different remedies which may be available to a buyer for the seller's breach of a representation versus its breach of a warranty, *see infra* Pages 123–125.

66. *See* GREGORY STEIN, *supra* note 39, at 10; Hamilton, *supra* note 15, at 5–14 through 5–17; GERALD KORNGOLD AND PAUL GOLDSTEIN, REAL ESTATE TRANSACTIONS, CASES AND MATERIALS ON LAND TRANSFER, DEVELOPMENT AND FINANCE 206–211 (4th ed. 2002); and Kathleen McNamara Tomcho, *Commercial Real Estate Buyer Beware: Sellers May Have the Right to Remain Silent*, 70 SOUTHERN CALIFORNIA LAW REVIEW 1571 (1997). For an argument in favor of the implication of a seller duty to disclose certain latent defects in commercial real property, *see* Frona M. Powell, *The Seller's Duty to Disclose in Sales of Commercial Real Estate*, 28 AMERICAN BUSINESS LAW JOURNAL 245 (1990).

67. *See* GREGORY STEIN, *supra* note 39, at 10. As one practicing lawyer points out, the major purpose of representations and warranties is to cause the seller to reveal facts that, together with a program of due diligence, is designed to disclose risks that can be assessed by the purchaser in order to make an informed decision as to whether the purchase will be consummated. *See* Edward A. Peterson, *The Effective Use of Representations and Warranties in Commercial Real Estate Contracts,* in ACREL PAPERS (ALI–ABA, October 1999), available online at http://www.acrel.org/Documents/Seminars/a002089.pdf.

68. *See generally* Billie J. Ellis and Douglas A. Yeager, *Practical Implications of a Seller's Representations and Warranties in a Highly Competitive Commercial Real Estate Transaction,* in ACREL PAPERS 68 (ALI–ABA, October 2006).

er is to sell its land for the highest price, as quickly as possible and without conditions. In addition, the land seller wants to make sure that, once the land sale is closed, it will have no further liability or obligation relative to the sold land.

The landowner's love affair with the doctrine of caveat emptor is evidenced by the inclusion in the standard, seller form of purchase contract of a provision similar to the following:

> *EXCEPT AS OTHERWISE EXPRESSLY PROVIDED IN THIS CONTRACT, BUYER ACKNOWLEDGES THAT IT HAS EXAMINED THE PROPERTY AND IS BUYING THE PROPERTY "AS IS", WITHOUT WARRANTY OR REPRESENTATION OF ANY KIND WHATSOEVER, EXPRESS OR IMPLIED, INCLUDING, WITHOUT LIMITATION, ANY IMPLIED WARRANTY OF FITNESS OF THE PROPERTY FOR A PARTICULAR PURPOSE, WHETHER BY SELLER OR BY AN AGENT, BROKER, EMPLOYEE OR OTHER REPRESENTATIVE OF SELLER. ALL UNDERSTANDINGS AND AGREEMENTS HERETOFORE BETWEEN THE PARTIES ARE HEREBY MERGED IN THIS CONTRACT, WHICH ALONE SHALL FULLY AND COMPLETELY EXPRESS THE PARTIES' AGREEMENT.*

> *BUYER ACKNOWLEDGES THAT IT HAS RECEIVED AN ADEQUATE OPPORTUNITY TO INSPECT THE PROPERTY AND TO MAKE SUCH LEGAL, FACTUAL AND OTHER INQUIRIES AND INVESTIGATIONS AS BUYER DEEMS APPROPRIATE WITH RESPECT TO THE PROPERTY. BUYER HEREBY WAIVES, RELEASES AND DISCHARGES ANY CLAIMS THAT IT HAS OR MAY HAVE AGAINST SELLER WITH RESPECT TO ANY CONDITION ON OR ABOUT THE PROPERTY OR ANY OTHER STATE OF FACTS WHICH EXISTS WITH RESPECT TO THE PROPERTY. BUYER FURTHER ACKNOWLEDGES AND AGREES THAT THERE SHALL BE NO ADJUSTMENTS IN THE PURCHASE PRICE FOR ANY PHYSICAL, FUNCTIONAL, ECONOMIC OR ENVIRONMENTAL CONDITION RELATING TO THE PROPERTY.*

The above language (taken directly from the purchase contract entered into by Pizzuti and Chemical Bank for the HIBC land acquisition, replete with all of its wonderful references to "heretofore," "hereby," and "herein") is commonly referred to as an *"as is"* clause.[69] An "as is" clause is basically the landowner's homage to the doctrine of caveat emptor.

The sophisticated land seller often starts its negotiations with a buyer by taking the position that the buyer must purchase the land (a) without any contingencies and (b) subject to an "as is" clause of the type noted above. The land seller is seldom able to successfully defend both of these positions against the entreaties of the land buyer. A seller who is steadfast in its refusal to make any substantive representations will usually have to

---

69. As one practitioner correctly notes, the importance of an "as is" clause to the seller is often "demonstrated by the use of all capital fonts and the requirement for the buyer to expressly acknowledge the same by initialing the relevant page." *See* Hamilton, *supra* note 15, at 5–14.

give the land buyer a fairly broad suitability contingency, so that the buyer can conduct on-site due diligence to gain a full understanding of the condition and character of the land.[70] Conversely, if the land seller's primary negotiating objective is to severely limit the scope and duration of the buyer's contingencies, it will likely find that the best way for it to accomplish that objective is to provide the buyer with a fairly complete set of seller representations.

To the extent the landowner is willing to include certain representations in the purchase contract, its lawyer will try to limit both the number and scope of the included representations. The landowner's lawyer will also likely object to the inclusion in the purchase contract of any representation that speaks in absolute terms about the condition or character of the land. The seller does not want to be in a position of insuring or guarantying that any aspect of the land is consistent with the buyer's expectations. The seller's lawyer will, therefore, often insist that any representation be couched in terms of the "seller's knowledge" of the subject matter of the representation.

The following are the operative issues that should be considered when attaching a knowledge limitation to a seller representation.[71]

- Does the seller's knowledge extend not only to information that it actually knows, but also to information which it reasonably should know?

- Is the seller under a good faith obligation to make some level of inquiry or investigation concerning the subject matter of the representation?

- In the context of a representation being made by an entity, whose knowledge is imputed to the named seller—that of all its current and former employees, officers, directors and consultants or just a limited subset of that group.

Because state courts differ in their interpretation of knowledge qualifiers, most practitioners now seek to include in the purchase contract an express definition of what is meant by the term "seller's knowledge."[72]

2. Buyer's Perspective on Representations and Warranties

As discussed earlier in this Chapter, the seller representation is a device that the real estate development lawyer uses to try to limit the developer's land risk. The development lawyer's counterpoint to the landowner's "as is" clause is the *full warranty sale*,[73] where the seller

---

70. This is what occurred during the course of the Pizzuti–Chemical Bank negotiation for the purchase of the HIBC land. Chemical Bank agreed to provide Pizzuti with a very broad suitability contingency in exchange for Pizzuti's agreement that the transaction would be an "as is" sale.

71. *See* Kevin L. Shepherd, *Top 10 "Gotchas" in Comprehensive Contracts of Sale*, 17 No. 5 PRACTICAL REAL ESTATE LAWYER 17, 19 (2001); and Peterson, *supra* note 67, at 14.

72. *See e.g.*, Peterson, *supra* note 67, at 30–31; and Ellis *supra* note 68, at 63–64. *See also* Hamilton, *supra* note 15, at 5–65 and 5–66, for an example of a definition of "seller's knowledge."

73. *See* Hastie, *supra* note 2, at 44.

is not only asked to make representations on the complete litany of the developer's potential land risks, but is also asked to provide the buyer with the following "full disclosure" representation:

The Seller has fully and accurately disclosed to the Buyer in writing any and all material facts and circumstances relating to the transaction that is the subject of this Agreement or the ownership, operation, condition or character of the Land.

The real estate development lawyer's dream world consists of a purchase contract that includes both a set of full warranty sale representations and a broadly stated suitability contingency. In reality, the real estate development lawyer successfully achieves that level of contractual Nirvana just about as often as seller's counsel gets a buyer to agree to an "as is" sale without any contingencies.

The land risks that are intended to be covered by a full warranty sale fall into two distinct categories:[74]

- *Category 1*—Site-specific risks that *CAN* be resolved by the developer's receipt of clean certifications from third party consultants during its site due diligence;[75] and

- *Category 2*—Site-specific risks that *CANNOT* be resolved as part of the developer's due diligence efforts.

Representations covering the first category of land risks are intended to provide the land buyer with back-up support for the conclusions reached by its consultants during the due diligence process. In legal parlance, this is a classic "belt and suspenders" tactic, where the buyer seeks protection against a particular land risk from two separate sources—the third party certifications of its consultants and the representations made in the purchase contract by the seller.[76]

The receipt of seller representations on category 1 land risks is generally viewed by the buyer as a luxury and not a necessity. If the purchase contract gives the buyer a right to terminate its obligations if the results of its due diligence are unsatisfactory, then the buyer can safely entertain the notion of dropping from the purchase contract those seller representations that are solely intended to address category 1 land risks.

Assume for the moment that the purchase contract includes a broad suitability contingency that provides the buyer with a contractual out if it determines that the land is not suitable for its intended use. In that

---

74. Land risks that are not site-specific (for example, risks related to the general state of the economy or the status of the developer's lease-up of its proposed project) can only be addressed through use of a buyer contingency clause. Neither the land seller, nor a third party expert is equipped to provide the buyer with any comfort on such non-site-specific risks. *See supra Practice Tip #5–2.*

75. For a partial listing of such third party certifications, *see supra* Pages 114–115.

76. A developer should not consider a seller representation to be a wholesale substitute for conducting its independent due diligence on a particular land risk. The developer should rely primarily on the investigations and expertise of its third party consultants (and not on statements made by the landowner) when making a determination as to whether the land is suitable for the developer's proposed project.

circumstance, the real estate development lawyer's attention should be primarily focused on how he can structure the seller's representations to deal with category 2 land risks—that is, those site-specific risks that cannot be resolved as part of the developer's due diligence. The following are some examples of facts or circumstances that fall into that second risk category:

- Notices received by the seller from a governmental agency concerning some condition or circumstance that could have an adverse effect on the utility of the land for the buyer's project (e.g., a notice of a proposed condemnation or a notice of a violation of a local zoning ordinance);

- Circumstances or conditions known solely by the seller (and not the general public) that could impact the usability of the land for buyer's project (e.g., the seller's knowledge of a threatened lawsuit affecting the land); and

- The seller's unrecorded grant to a third party of a legal or equitable interest in the land.

The one common thread running through all of the above examples is that the seller has knowledge of a land risk that is not readily discoverable by the buyer through an inspection of the land or a review of the public real estate records. Under the doctrine of caveat emptor, the landowner has no common law obligation to disclose its knowledge of those land risks to the prospective buyer. The only strategy available to the buyer to protect itself against the category 2 land risk is to include representations in the purchase contract that are intended to flush out the seller's knowledge of those risks.[77]

There is one additional deal risk that the buyer can cover only by the inclusion in the purchase contract of appropriate seller representations— that is, the risk that the seller does not have the requisite status or authority to sell the land to the buyer.[78] The real estate development lawyer should, therefore, be sure to include in the purchase contract specific seller representations confirming that:

- The seller is not required to obtain any third party approval as a condition precedent to its sale of the land to the buyer;

- There are no pending or threatened lawsuits, bankruptcy proceedings or governmental orders that could adversely affect the seller's authority to sell the land to the buyer; and

- If the seller is an entity, the entity is in good standing in the state of its formation and the state in which the land is located and the

---

77. For a thorough discussion of how a real property buyer can protect itself against certain land risks by the use of representations and warranties, *see generally* Peterson, *supra* note 67 at 6–11; and Ellis *supra* note 68, at 14–27.

78. *See* Peterson, *supra* note 67, at 3–6.

persons executing the purchase contract are duly authorized to act on the seller's behalf.[79]

3. "As Is" vs. Full Warranty Sale—A Common Compromise

Counsel for the seller and buyer are usually able to carve out a mutually acceptable middle ground between the two extremes of an absolute "as is" sale (the seller's preference) and a full warranty sale (the buyer's preference). Seller's counsel is typically willing to provide a limited set of seller representations and warranties addressing (1) those category 1 land risks that are peculiarly within the realm of the seller's knowledge and, hence, cannot be eliminated by the buyer's receipt of third party certifications and (2) risks associated with the seller's status and authority to sell the land, which, again, involve matters that are known only to the seller and are not accessible in any way by the buyer.[80] Similarly, buyer's counsel is usually amenable to limiting the scope of at least some of the representations to the "seller's knowledge."[81]

Resolving these largely uncontroversial matters still leaves much to be negotiated between the parties concerning the scope of the seller's representations. The real estate development lawyer will push for the inclusion in the purchase contract of a laundry list of representations that are designed (1)to force the seller to disclose everything it knows about the land and (2) to provide the buyer with added "belt and suspenders" comfort on a variety of matters related to the condition and character of the land. The landowner's counsel will counter by trying to limit the seller's representations to those matters mentioned in the preceding paragraph that are solely within the province of the landowner's knowledge.[82]

The outcome of the parties' negotiations on the seller's representations will be greatly influenced by what they agreed to on the subject of the buyer's contingency—with the number and scope of the seller's representations having an inverse relationship with the breadth and duration of the buyer's contingency. The parties' haggling over the seller representations will effectively come down to an exercise in the allocation

---

79. Even with this representation in hand, the real estate development lawyer should conduct an independent review of the public records to confirm the status in good standing of the selling entity. As discussed *supra* Chapter 8, Pages 304–305, the contract should also require the selling entity to provide the buyer with entity resolutions authorizing the sale of the land and confirming the authority of all persons executing documents on the seller's behalf.

80. Some large institutional sellers are not willing to make even these limited representations. By way of example, Chemical Bank absolutely refused to make any representations whatsoever concerning the HIBC land (premised, at least in part, on its relatively modest involvement in the development of the HIBC project). *See supra HIBC Case Study—The Buyer's Contingency.*

81. The exact definition of a "seller's knowledge" is often a topic of heated negotiations between counsel for the seller and the buyer—particularly when the seller is a large entity that employs hundreds of potential sources of "knowledge." *See supra* text accompanying notes 71 and 72.

82. *See* Hamilton, *supra* note 15, at 5–17, 5–18 and 5–58 through 5–65, for an interesting ranking (from the least to the most controversial) of the representations and warranties customarily requested by the buyer.

of risk—that is, how much risk is each party willing to assume under the land purchase contract in order to get the deal done.[83]

4. Effective Date of Representations and Warranties

Most purchase contracts provide that the seller's representations are deemed to be made both as of the date of the parties' execution of the contract and as of the date of the land acquisition closing. A provision of this type effectively burdens the seller with the risk that something happens between the date of the execution of the contract and the date of closing to cause a once true representation to become false. The implications of this type of provision on the remedies that are available to the buyer to deal with the seller's breach of a representation are discussed later in this Chapter.

5. Survival of Representations and Warranties

Under the common law doctrine of merger, a seller's representations will be deemed to have merged into the deed delivered to the buyer at closing and, as such, will not support any post-closing legal action that the buyer might otherwise want to bring against the seller for a breach of a representation.[84] The effective disappearance of the seller's representations after closing rarely, if ever, is consistent with the buyer's intentions.

As such, it is the real estate development lawyer's job to make sure that the purchase contract contains a *survival clause* that recites that the seller's representations (as well as any other seller covenants that are not fully performed prior to closing) will survive the closing. The length of the survival period is a subject of negotiation, with the outside survival date being the statute of limitations applicable to any action on the breached representation. Land buyers customarily ask for a survival period of at least two years, while sellers seek to limit the survival period to 12 months or less.

The purchase contract should also recite what actions must be taken by the buyer during the agreed-upon survival period in order to keep alive its legal action for a breach of a representation. The options range from simply sending the seller a written notice alleging a breach to actually filing a lawsuit on or before the outside date of the survival period.

6. Remedies for a Breach of a Representation and Warranty

Before closing, the buyer's primary remedies for the seller's breach of a representation are to terminate its purchase obligation, receive a refund of its earnest money deposit and sue the seller for damages. In practice, the buyer customarily places a price tag on the breached representation

---

83. *See* Ellis, *supra* note 68, at 62.

84. *See* GEORGE LEFCOE, REAL ESTATE TRANSACTIONS, FINANCE AND DEVELOPMENT (6th ed. 2009) at 147–150; Lawrence Berger, *Merger By Deed—What Provisions of a Contract for Sale of Land Survive the Closing*, 21 REAL ESTATE LAW JOURNAL 22 (Summer 1992); and Peterson, *supra* note 67, at 14–15.

and then tries to negotiate a reduction in the purchase price for the land.[85]

As noted earlier in this Chapter, it is commonplace for representations to be deemed remade as of the date of closing. What remedy should be available to the buyer if a seller representation, which was true when made on the date of the execution of the purchase contract, turns out to be false as of the date of closing? By way of example, assume that the purchase contract contained the following seller representation—"There are no hazardous materials or toxic substances located on the Land." What should be the buyer's remedy if an unrelated third party dumps toxic waste on the land after the effective date of the contract, but before the closing? What if the seller told the third party that it was OK to dump the toxic waste on the land?

Common sense dictates that the seller should be subject to a damages action for a post-effective date breach of the above representation, only if it intentionally did something during the contract period that caused the representation to become false—for example, giving its approval to the dumping of the waste on the land. The remedy section for the breach of a representation usually addresses this scenario by specifically stating that:

> *Seller will not be deemed to be in default under this Agreement if any fact or circumstance occurs after the Effective Date that renders any of Seller's representations and warranties false, so long as any such fact or circumstance is not within the reasonable control of Seller; provided, however, that the occurrence of any such fact or circumstance will nonetheless permit Buyer to terminate its obligations to perform under this Agreement as a result of the failure to satisfy the condition precedent that all of Seller's representations and warranties must be true as of the date of closing.*

The proviso in the above clause is needed because the buyer does not want to be obligated to purchase contaminated land, regardless whether the dumping of the toxic waste on the site was the fault of the seller or a third party.

The buyer's primary remedy for a breach of a representation that is discovered after the date of closing is a damages action. Sellers who are concerned about being nickeled and dimed to death with post-closing allegations of breached representations should consider protecting themselves by inserting in the purchase contract some threshold of materiality that a breached representation must satisfy before an action may be instituted against the seller.[86] By way of example, a seller might negotiate a provision that says that no action may be brought against the seller for the breach of any representation, unless the aggregate money damages which would be owed to the buyer as a result of such breach exceeds $50,000.

---

85. *See* Hastie, *supra* note 2, at 44.

86. *See* Ellis, *supra* note 68, at 65.

The effectiveness of a buyer's remedy for the seller's breach of a representation is, of course, worthless if the seller has no assets at the time that the buyer files its damages action—a circumstance which is quite common in today's marketplace where most sellers are single purpose entities that disburse all of the sales proceeds immediately following the closing. A buyer can protect the viability of its damages remedy by either (1) insisting that a creditworthy entity guaranty the accuracy of the seller's representations and warranties or (2) holding back payment of a portion of the purchase price for a period of time after the closing to make sure that funds are available to cover any losses incurred by the buyer as a result of a breach that is discovered post-closing.[87]

I. TITLE AND SURVEY ISSUES. *(§7)*

This section will tackle the topic of what a purchase contract should say about the state of the land title to be conveyed to the buyer at closing. The details of the real estate development lawyer's review of the land title are discussed in Chapter 8—*Stage 4: The Land Acquisition Closing.*[88]

1. Quality of Title to Be Conveyed to the Buyer

The purchase contract should clearly recite the quality of the title to the land that the seller is obligated to convey to the buyer at the land acquisition closing. The following is a commonly-used statement of the requisite quality of title:[89]

Seller will convey to Buyer marketable title to the Land, free and clear of all liens and encumbrances other than the Permitted Exceptions.

The quoted provision establishes a two-pronged standard for the quality of the land title to be conveyed to the buyer.

- First, title to the land must be ***marketable.*** Marketability of title is a base-line concept that is intended to describe a generic state of title that is legally presumed to be acceptable to all owners of real estate. Title to real estate is generally said to be marketable if it permits the owner to possess, use and dispose of the subject property, without any unreasonable legal impediment.[90] Most jurisdictions have promulgated standards for determining whether title to a parcel is marketable.[91] It is important to keep in mind that title can be marketable, even though it is subject to certain liens, easements, restrictions and other exceptions to title.

---

87. The purchase price holdback can either be retained by the buyer or held in escrow by an independent third party. *See id.*

88. *See infra* Chapter 8, Pages 293–295.

89. The quoted excerpt is from the Form Purchase Agreement included in the Document Appendix as Document #2.

90. *See* LEFCOE, *supra* note 84, at 127–128.

91. *See e.g.,* OHIO TITLE STANDARDS, www.ohiobar.org/Pages/staticPageviewer.aspx?articleid= 101.

- Second, title to the land must be free of all liens and encumbrances other than ***permitted exceptions***. This requirement is intended to describe the state of title that is required by a particular buyer and is a step up from the base-line concept of marketable title. As will be discussed later in this section, the defined term "permitted exceptions" is generally intended to encompass only those liens, easements, restrictions and other exceptions to a perfectly clean title that the buyer determines will not unreasonably interfere with its ownership and use of the land.

2. Delivery of Title Commitment

Purchase contracts governing the purchase and sale of commercial real estate almost universally provide that the quality of the title being conveyed to the buyer will be evidenced by an ***owner's title insurance policy***. An owner's title insurance policy is a contract in which a title insurance company[92] indemnifies an owner of real estate against any loss that an owner may suffer due to the quality of the owner's title being other than that specified in the title insurance policy.[93] A one-time insurance premium is paid to the title insurance company coincident with the closing of the buyer's acquisition of the land and the insurance company's issuance of its title insurance policy.[94]

The first step in the process of insuring a buyer's title to land is the issuance by the title insurer of its preliminary ***title commitment***. The title commitment is the insurer's promise to issue a title insurance policy to the buyer at the land acquisition closing. The title commitment sets forth a legal description of the land and then lists as exceptions to the insurer's promised insurance coverage every lien, encumbrance, restriction, condition, easement and other adverse interest disclosed during the course of the insurer's review of the public real estate records applicable to the land.

The purchase contract should address the following issues relative to the title commitment.

- ***Who Has the Responsibility for Causing the Title Commitment To Be Issued?*** This responsibility generally falls on the seller.

- ***When Must the Title Commitment Be Delivered to the Buyer?*** Purchase contracts typically require that a title commitment be delivered to the buyer somewhere between 10–30 days after the date of the parties' execution of the contract.

---

92. The insurance companies who write title insurance policies are huge national and international companies with billions of dollars of reserves. Examples of some of the leading title insurance companies are Chicago Title Insurance Company, First American Corporation and Stewart Title Guaranty Company.

93. *See* Shannon J. Skinner, *A Practical Guide to Title Review*, in ALI–ABA COURSE OF STUDY MATERIALS, MODERN REAL ESTATE TRANSACTIONS, Course No. SL–004, 361, 363 (July 2005).

94. In a number of states, title insurance premiums are regulated by the state's insurance department. *See* AMERICAN LAND TITLE ASSOCIATION, TITLE INSURANCE REGULATORY SURVEY (2010).

- ***Who Gets To Select the Title Insurance Company?*** For obvious reasons, the identity of the title insurance company is usually selected by the party who is contractually responsible to pay the title insurance premiums at closing. While the issue of who pays the title premiums is always subject to negotiation, local custom often dictates whether the seller or the buyer will be required to pay those costs.

- ***What Is the Insured Amount of the Title Insurance Policy?*** The insured amount represents the maximum amount that the title insurer will ever have to pay to its insured.[95] The purchase contract should recite that the insured amount will be equal to the purchase price.

- ***What Type of Title Insurance Policy Will Be Issued?*** Most sophisticated buyers will want to make sure that the policy that will be issued to it at closing is on a form sanctioned by the American Land Title Association ("ALTA"). The 2006 version of the ALTA owner's policy is now the title policy of choice for owners of commercial real estate.[96]

3. Furnishing of Survey

A survey is a visual depiction of the boundaries of the land. It shows the acreage contained within the land parcel and the specific legal description of the parcel (usually called out either by means of a subdivision map or a metes and bounds description).[97]

The provision of a survey to the buyer should be a requirement of every commercial land purchase contract. While a title commitment can identify all exceptions to a parcel's title, a survey is needed to identify the location of such exceptions in relation to the land's boundary lines. A survey is also the vehicle used by the real estate development lawyer to determine where each physical improvement related to the parcel is located—for example, the location of utility lines and public roads. The title commitment excludes from its coverage any "matters which would be revealed by an accurate survey of the property."[98] It is, therefore, essential that the survey be provided to the title insurance company, so that this exception to its insurance coverage can be deleted from the final title insurance policy to be issued to the buyer at the closing of its land acquisition.

The purchase contract should address the following matters related to the preparation of the survey of the land.[99]

---

95. *See* Skinner, *Title Review, supra* note 93, at 365.

96. *See* Jeffrey G. Gurren, *2006 ALTA Title Insurance Policies: The Significant Changes*, 24 No. 5 PRACTICAL REAL ESTATE LAWYER 17, 24 (September 2008).

97. *See supra* note 36.

98. *See* Schedule B to the ALTA OWNER'S TITLE INSURANCE POLICY (2006).

99. For a general discussion of the role that a survey plays in the land acquisition process, *see generally* Shannon J. Skinner, *A Practical Guide to Survey Review*, in ALI–ABA COURSE OF STUDY MATERIALS, MODERN REAL ESTATE TRANSACTIONS, Course No. SL–004, 385 (July 2005).

- ***Who Has the Responsibility for Causing the Survey To Be Prepared and Issued to the Buyer?*** There is no widely-accepted custom concerning who has the responsibility for ordering the survey for the land. The purchase contract should simply identify whether the buyer or seller is assigned that responsibility.

- ***When Must the Survey Be Delivered to the Buyer?*** The time period for the delivery of the survey to the buyer is usually similar to the time period for the delivery of the title commitment—that is, typically around 10–30 days after contract execution. As will be discussed later in this section, it is, however, key that the period for the buyer's review of title matters not start until it has in its hands both the title commitment and the survey.[100]

- ***Who Gets to Select the Surveyor?*** As is the case with the title commitment, the party responsible for paying for the survey usually gets to determine the identity of the surveyor. The assignment of responsibility for paying the surveyor's fees is open to negotiation between the parties.

- ***What Type of Survey Should Be Required?*** As will be discussed in some detail in Chapter 8—*Stage 4: Closing the Land Acquisition*,[101] there are many different types of land surveys. In order to make sure that the title insurer is able to remove the preprinted survey exception from Schedule B of the final title policy, the purchase contract should recite that the survey to be furnished to the buyer (and the title company) should be an ALTA survey, which complies with the *Minimum Standard Detail Requirements for ALTA/ACSM Land Title Surveys*.[102]

- ***What Should Be Included in the Surveyor's Certification?*** Unlike a title commitment, a survey is not, in and of itself, a contract of insurance or indemnification, but rather simply a depiction of certain matters related to the boundaries and configuration of the land. In an attempt to establish a right of action in the buyer (and its lender) for any mistakes in the survey, it is advisable to recite in the purchase contract that the surveyor will be required to certify, at a minimum, that the survey was prepared in accordance with the *Minimum Standard Detail Requirements for ALTA/ ACSM Land Title Survey*. The real estate development lawyer should also consult with his client's prospective construction lender to see if the lender has any additional certifications that it wants to see included in the survey.

---

100. *See infra* Page 129.

101. *See infra* Chapter 8, Pages 295–296.

102. See AMERICAN LAND TITLE ASSOCIATION AND THE AMERICAN CONGRESS ON SURVEYING & MAPPING, MINIMUM STANDARD DETAIL REQUIREMENTS FOR ALTA/ACSM LAND TITLE SURVEYS (2005), also found in Skinner, *Survey Review, supra* note 99, at Appendix C.

4. Review of Title Commitment and Survey[103]

The purchase contract should specifically address (a) the time period within which the buyer must notify the seller of any objections it has to anything contained within the title commitment or the survey and (b) the standard for determining the title and survey objections which the buyer is permitted to lodge under the purchase contract.

a. *Title Review Period*

It is crucial that the real estate development lawyer review the title commitment and survey together. The development lawyer should, therefore, make sure that the purchase contract specifically states that the period for the buyer's review of the title commitment and survey will not begin until such time as *BOTH* the title commitment and the survey have been received by the buyer. The length of the title review period is a matter of negotiation between the parties, but usually runs anywhere from ten to 30 days after the buyer's receipt of the last of the survey and the title commitment. The purchase contract should recite that, in order for a title objection to be effective, a written notice specifying the objection must be delivered to the seller within the title review period. Any title exception that is not addressed in a written objection notice delivered within the stated review period will be conclusively presumed to be acceptable to the buyer (and, as such, considered a "permitted exception"). The well-represented seller will usually want to make sure that the title review period must, in all events, terminate no later than the outside date for the satisfaction of the buyer's non-title contingencies under the purchase contract.

b. *Standard for Title Review*

The articulation of the standard that will govern the buyer's review of the title commitment and survey is one aspect of the title provisions on which the buyer and seller frequently disagree. The seller's primary fear is that an overly broad title review standard can effectively give the buyer an unintended out under the contract by allowing the buyer to object to a title exception that cannot readily be cured by the seller (for example, the location of a utility easement). As one might expect, the "unintended out" is precisely what the real estate development lawyer has in mind when it comes to defining the title review standard in the purchase contract. The relative intransigence of counsel for the seller and buyer on the scope of the title review standard is, of course, significantly lessened to the extent the purchase contract already has in place a broad suitability contingency in buyer's favor (so long as the title review period does not extend beyond the outside date for the satisfaction or waiver of the suitability contingency).

---

103. The practical aspects of a lawyer's review of title and survey matters are discussed supra Chapter 8, Pages 293–297. *See also* Skinner, *Title Review, supra* note 93; and Skinner, *Survey Review,* supra note 99.

The argument between the seller and buyer over the title review standard is usually centered on the definition of those title exceptions that will be considered ***permitted exceptions*** under the purchase contract. In this context, permitted exceptions are those title matters that may be included as exceptions in both the deed conveying title to the land to buyer at closing and in the final title insurance policy issued by the title insurance company. The following are four definitions of permitted exceptions that are sometimes found in purchase contracts. They are listed in order of preference from the seller's perspective:

- Exceptions that do not render the title unmarketable;[104]

- Exceptions other than those existing as of the date of the parties' execution of the purchase contract (with the existing exceptions usually being identified in an exhibit attached to the purchase contract);

- Exceptions that, in the buyer's judgment, will not adversely affect its intended use of the land; and

- Exceptions to which the buyer does not specifically object in a notice delivered to seller prior to the expiration of buyer's title review period.

If the seller and the buyer are each represented by experienced counsel, the negotiations are usually focused on coming up with a mutually satisfactory compromise between the second and third alternatives noted above (unless the purchase contract contains a broad suitability contingency, in which case it is common for the parties to opt for the fourth alternative). One category of title exception that should never be treated as a permitted exception is a mortgage or other monetary lien against the land that can be satisfied by the payment of an ascertainable sum of money.

5. Curing of Title Defects

Once a prospective buyer has delivered its title objections to the seller, the question that next arises is whether the seller will be obligated to cure those objections, regardless of the cost or effort which must be expended to effect such a cure. Curing a title objection simply means taking whatever action is required to terminate a lien, encumbrance, restriction or other exception to title.

The only category of title objections that the purchase contract should, in all instances, require the seller to cure are those mortgages or other monetary liens that can be cured by the payment of an ascertainable sum of money (so-called ***monetary liens***). Purchase contracts typically give a buyer the right to remedy any failure by the seller to cure a monetary lien by paying off such lien at closing and then offsetting the full amount of that payment against the cash portion of the purchase price otherwise payable by the buyer at closing.

---

104. *See supra* Page 125 for a discussion of the concept of "marketable title."

Most purchase contracts do not obligate a seller to cure title defects other than monetary liens. Depending on the title defect in question, a seller may not be able to cure the defect or may only be able to do so by paying an exorbitant sum. Given these uncertainties, it is quite common for purchase contracts to give the seller an option (rather than an obligation) to cure the buyer's title objections. If the seller fails to cure the buyer's legitimate title objections within the curative period specified in the purchase contract, then the buyer will customarily be given the option to either (1) waive the title objection and proceed to closing or (2) terminate the purchase contract and receive a refund of its earnest money deposit. A middle ground frequently seen in purchase contracts is the creation of an obligation on the seller to use "commercially reasonable efforts" to cure the buyer's title objections. Some purchase contracts even go so far as to try to define "commercially reasonable efforts" by requiring the seller to expend up to some specified amount of money in the attempt to cure the buyer's title objections.

Before leaving the topic of the curing of title defects, brief mention should be made of the seller's practice of getting the title insurance company to "affirmatively insure over" certain title defects. Financially strong sellers are frequently able to secure the title company's commitment to delete a title exception from the title insurance policy, even though the title exception in question has not actually been cured. A seller can sometimes achieve this result by supplying the title company with its guaranty that it will reimburse the title company for the amount of any insurance payment that the title company might ultimately have to pay to the buyer with respect to the title defect in question. On first blush, this arrangement would seem as if it should be perfectly acceptable to the buyer, because the buyer is receiving a clean title policy, which contains the title insurance company's agreement to indemnify it against any losses it might suffer because of the existence of the subject title defect. However, the reality is that the next buyer of the insured property may not be able to get its title company to similarly insure over the uncured title defect. Additionally, the loss of the buyer's opportunity to sell the property may not be a loss that is covered by the title company's affirmative insurance commitment. In view of this uncertainty, buyer's counsel should be extremely reluctant to accept a title policy that affirmatively insures over any title defect.

6. Issuance of the Final Title Insurance Policy

Most purchase contracts contain language contemplating that the final title insurance policy will be issued to buyer at the closing. The reality is, however, that the actual issuance of the final owner's policy usually lags the closing and the insurer's receipt of its full title insurance premium by a period of one or two weeks (as is the case with virtually all other insurance policies). The careful real estate development lawyer should address this reality by including in the list of the documents to be delivered to buyer at closing an instrument that both (a) confirms the fact that all conditions to the title insurance company's obligation to issue a title insurance policy have been satisfied and (b) clearly delineates all of the title exceptions that will be included in the final title insurance policy. These requirements can be evidenced in the form of either a pro forma title insurance policy or a marked-up copy of the title commitment.[105]

J. CLOSING ISSUES. *(§§8, 9 and 10)*

In the vernacular of the real estate lawyer, the ***closing*** refers to the consummation of all of the transactions contemplated in the purchase contract, including, most significantly, the buyer's payment of the purchase price to the seller and the seller's execution and delivery of the deed and other documents vesting title to the land in buyer. A well-drafted purchase contract should address six elements of the closing process:

- The conditions to the parties' respective obligations to close the transaction;

- The scheduled date of closing;

- The documents and other items required to be delivered by the parties at closing;

- The allocation of responsibility for the payment of the costs of closing the transaction;

- The income and expense prorations and related purchase price adjustments required to be made at closing; and

- The style of the closing.

1. Conditions to Closing. *(§8)*

The purchase contract should contain a separate section that lists the parties' respective conditions to closing. The inclusion of such a provision helps manage the expectations of each of the buyer and the seller by providing them with a central repository to which they can refer to identify those legal and business matters that must be addressed before the transaction can close.

2. Date of Closing. *(§9)*

The purchase contract should recite the outside date by which the closing of the land acquisition must occur. The outside closing date may be described by reference to a certain number of days after the occurrence of some contractual milestone (for example, the effective date of the contract execution or the date of the satisfaction of all closing conditions) or a fixed date in time (for example, December 31, 2011). The setting of an outside closing date is important for a couple reasons:

- First, it establishes the parties' expectations concerning the time frame within which the land acquisition will be consummated; and

---

105. *See infra* Chapter 8, Page 305.

- Second, it establishes the date on which a non-performing party will be deemed to be in default for its failure to fully perform all of its obligations under the purchase contract

In addition, the normative rule is that possession and all other benefits and burdens of ownership will pass to the buyer on the date of the closing of the land acquisition.

3. Closing Deliverables. *(§§10(a)–(g))*

The purchase contract should specifically list in one section all of the documents and other materials that each of the buyer and the seller is responsible for executing and delivering at the closing (the so-called ***closing deliverables***). The real estate development lawyer should be able to identify the vast majority of those documents at the time of the initial drafting of the purchase contract based on his prior experience in closing real estate transactions.[106] It is nonetheless advisable for the drafter of the purchase contract to create some wiggle room for the parties by inserting contractual language that confirms that "each party will execute and deliver at closing such other documents as are reasonably requested by the other party to further evidence or effect the purchase and sale of the Land in the manner contemplated in this Agreement."

4. Payment of Closing Costs. *(§10(h))*

In addition to the buyer's payment of the purchase price, there are a number of other costs that are typically paid at closing. The purchase contract becomes a much more readable and user friendly document if it contains a separate subsection that calls out all such costs and stipulates who has the responsibility for paying them at closing. The following are examples of costs that are customarily paid at closing:

- Fees that are payable to state and local governments with respect to the conveyance of real property (i.e., transfer taxes or conveyance fees) and the recording of legal documents in the public real estate records (i.e., recording costs);

- Commissions payable to any brokers involved in the land acquisition;

- The premium and other costs that are payable to the title insurance company in connection with its issuance of a title insurance policy; and

- The fees payable to the surveyor for its furnishing of the survey.[107]

Local custom usually influences which of the above costs will be paid by the seller and which will be paid by the buyer. However, assignment of responsibility for the payment of these costs is always subject to the

---

106. *See infra*, Chapter 8, Pages 302–305, for a discussion of the legal documents that are customarily executed at closing to evidence the sale and conveyance of the land to the buyer—e.g., a general warranty deed and a closing statement.

107. *See infra* Chapter 8, Pages 306–307 for a discussion of the customary treatment of these and other closing costs.

negotiation of the parties. As such, the responsibility for the payment of known closing costs (such as those noted above) should always be specifically assigned in the purchase contract.

It is also quite common for the parties to agree to include a catch-all clause in the purchase contract that provides that any costs associated with the purchase and sale of the land that are not specifically addressed in the purchase contract, will be paid by the party "who, in accordance with custom and practice in the jurisdiction in which the Land is located, is normally required to pay such closing costs." Including a default clause of this type is sometimes useful in helping the parties resolve a conflict related to the payment of a closing cost that was not within the parties' contemplation at the time of the drafting of the purchase contract.

5. Closing Prorations and Adjustments. *(§10(i))*

In determining the amount of the cash to be paid to the seller at closing, an adjustment to the purchase price needs to be made to deduct the principal amount of any purchase money financing being provided by the seller or the principal amount of any existing mortgage loan that is being assumed by the buyer. No such deduction need be made for any new loan obtained by buyer to fund its acquisition of the land, because, from the seller's perspective, cash is cash regardless whether it is being paid by the buyer or by the buyer's lender.

The cash portion of the purchase price payable by the buyer at closing also needs to be adjusted to deal with those periodic payment obligations that cover a period of time both before and after the date of closing. Examples of such periodic obligations are:

- Real estate taxes;
- Ground lease rentals;
- Interest on any existing mortgage loan being assumed by the buyer;
- Owner's association dues and assessments; and
- Certain utility charges (for example, water and sewer costs), when the utility provider will not agree to create separate bills for the periods before and after closing.

The norm in handling these periodic costs is to apportion such costs between the seller and the buyer based on the respective portions of such costs that are attributable to the periods pre- and post-closing, with the seller being liable for the portion of such costs that are attributable to the period on or before the closing date and the buyer being liable for the portion of such costs that are attributable to the period after the closing date.[108] By way of example, if real estate taxes are paid annually and if the

---

108. The purchase contract should address in a similar manner the apportionment of items of income that span the period both before and the date of closing (e.g., rentals payable under a farm lease). Such income items are relatively rare in a land acquisition, but are an extremely important component of the sale of improved real property such as an office building. *See infra* Chapter 12, Page 578, for a discussion of the apportionment of rents in connection with the developer's sale of a stabilized project.

land acquisition closing occurs on the 100th day of the year, then an appropriate apportionment of the real estate tax bill for the year of closing would result in the seller being responsible for 100/365 of the tax bill and the buyer being responsible for 265/365 of such bill. If the seller has already paid a periodic cost (meaning that the cost was "paid in advance"), then the buyer's prorated share of such cost should increase the amount of cash that the buyer will be required to pay to the seller at closing. Conversely, if the periodic cost will have to be paid by the buyer after the closing date (meaning the cost is "paid in arrears"), then the amount of buyer's cash payment at closing should be decreased by an amount equal to the seller's prorated share of such cost.

The vagaries associated with the levying of real estate taxes by local taxing authorities create a number of issues that should be addressed in the purchase contract. In many jurisdictions, real estate taxes are imposed and become a lien on real estate at the beginning of the calendar year, even though such taxes are not due and payable until later in such calendar year (or, in some extreme cases, in the succeeding calendar year). In some locales, the actual amount of the real estate taxes payable by a landowner is not established until well after the date of their initial imposition against the land. Indeed, in some jurisdictions, the amount of the real estate taxes payable with respect to a particular parcel can be revised upwards or downwards months after the date of such parcel's sale.[109]

The confluence of all of these circumstances often creates a scenario where, at the time of their execution of the purchase contract, the buyer and seller are unable to determine the exact amount of the real estate taxes to be apportioned between them at closing. The purchase contract should address this possibility by specifically stating that the closing apportionment of real estate taxes will be done either on the basis of (a) the most currently available real estate tax information (frequently the taxes for the prior taxable year) or (b) the parties' best estimate of what the taxes will ultimately prove to be for the taxable year in question. The lawyer for the landowner will customarily seek to have the real estate tax apportionment calculated on the basis of the most current tax information and to have the resulting apportionment be final and conclusive on the parties, regardless whether the actual real estate taxes are subsequently adjusted. Counsel for the buyer, on the other hand, will want either to have the taxes prorated on the basis of some multiple of the prior year's taxes (e.g., 110% of such prior year figures) or to subject the apportionment of such taxes to some type of post-closing adjustment in the event

---

109. *See e.g.,* OHIO REVISED CODE ANNOTATED §§ 5715.19 (West 2010). Under Ohio law, a complaint can be filed to revise a parcel's real estate taxes a full 15 months after the initial assessment of such taxes, even if an intervening sale of such parcel has occurred. Indeed, it has become common practice in Ohio for lawyers representing local school boards (whose funding is dependent upon real estate tax collections) to file complaints seeking to have the real estate taxes increased for any large commercial property that is sold during such 15 month period for a purchase price that exceeds the amount of the existing valuation of such property for real estate tax purposes.

the actual real estate taxes prove to be higher than those used for the apportionment calculation at closing.[110]

6. Style of Closing. *(§9)*

When I first started practicing law 30 + years ago, the word "closing" brought forth a vision of a large conference room (usually smoke-filled back then) in which representatives of the seller and the buyer and their respective lawyers gathered to hammer out the final details of the land acquisition and sign all those documents called for in the purchase contract. This type of all-hands gathering of lawyers and clients is often referred to as a ***New York style closing***.[111] Alas, in today's impersonal, electronic age, New York style closings are few and far between—even in New York.

Virtually all commercial real estate transactions are now closed via an ***escrow closing***.[112] In an escrow closing, the parties do not get together at one time in one place for the purpose of signing documents. Instead, each party executes whatever documents it needs to sign at a time and place of its choosing prior to the scheduled closing date and then forwards the executed documents to the title insurance company or some independent third party (with such party commonly being referred to as the ***escrow agent***). The buyer deposits into the escrow agent's trust account (usually via an electronic wire transfer of funds) whatever cash is required to close the deal. Counsel for each of the buyer and the seller then send detailed written instructions (***escrow instructions***) to the escrow agent, specifying the circumstances under which the escrow agent is authorized and directed (a) to release the documents from escrow, (b) to forward the appropriate purchase price payment to the seller and (c) to take whatever other actions are required to consummate the land acquisition in the manner contemplated in the purchase contract.

Some purchase contracts go into excruciating detail describing the precise manner in which the escrow closing will be structured and implemented. My experience has been that playing out the closing mechanism in all its glory (or lack thereof) in the purchase contract detracts from the real issues at hand and is generally just a waste of time and words. If the parties intend to close the land acquisition in escrow (and they almost always do), the purchase contract should simply identify who will serve as the escrow agent and leave the details of the escrow closing for the lawyers to address in detailed escrow instructions prepared by them just prior to closing when all of the salient factors to be incorporated into such instructions are better known by the parties. Some lawyers shortcut the whole matter by opting to establish a New York style closing as the default rule in the purchase contract, with the full knowledge that they

---

110. *See* § 10(i) of the Form Purchase Agreement for an example of such a post-closing adjustment clause.

111. *See* GREGORY STEIN, *supra* note 39, at 279–280.

112. In keeping with the geographical theme, escrow closings are sometimes referred to as "California style closings." *See* LEFCOE, *supra* note 84, at 314.

will later work out a mutually satisfactory escrow arrangement, so that they can spare their clients (and themselves) the agony of ever having to sit across the table from each other and exchange closing day pleasantries.

K. DEFAULTS AND REMEDIES. *(§11)*

The purchase contract should contain specific provisions that (1) define when a party will be deemed to be in default in the performance of its obligations under the purchase contract and (2) specify the remedies available to the other party upon the occurrence of such a default.

1. Event of Default

Most land purchase contracts condition the occurrence of an event of default on:

- The receipt by the defaulting party of a written notice from the non-defaulting party describing the exact nature of the alleged default; and

- The defaulting party's failure to cure such default within some stated period of time following its receipt of the aforementioned written notice.

The requirement for prior written notice and an opportunity to cure is usually something that is desirable from both the seller's and the buyer's perspectives. Depending on the nature of the alleged default, the applicable cure period commonly ranges from ten to 30 days after receipt of the written notice alleging the existence of the default.

2. Remedies

Absent some provision in the purchase contract to the contrary, each of the buyer and the seller will have the following remedies available to it upon the occurrence of an event of default by the other party to the purchase contract:

- Rescission;

- Damages; and

- Specific performance.[113]

An in-depth analysis of the case law discussing the nature and scope of these three remedies is clearly beyond the scope of this Chapter. However, the point needs to be made that it is incumbent upon the real estate development lawyer to understand how the courts in his jurisdiction have interpreted each of these remedies, so that he can properly advise his client about both (1) the risks faced by the developer if it defaults in the performance of its contractual obligations and (2) the ways in which the developer can protect itself against the risk of a default by the seller.

---

113. *See* Herz, *supra* note 39, at 12–14; and LEFCOE, *supra* note 84, at 157–166.

3. Contractual Limitation of Remedies

The courts have made it clear that the parties to a real estate purchase contract have the ability to limit their legal remedies by including in the purchase contract clear, unequivocal statements of their intentions to do so.[114] The following are some examples of contractual limitations on remedies often seen in land purchase contracts.

- ***Limitations on the Seller's Remedies:***
  - Remedies limited to retention of earnest money deposit as liquidated damages (*see* discussion of liquidated damages in the next section of this Chapter); and
  - Specific performance eliminated as an available remedy.

- ***Limitations on the Buyer's Remedies:***
  - Remedies limited to liquidated damages, with the amount of the liquidated damages being equal to a fixed percentage of purchase price;
  - Remedy for the seller's breach of a representation and warranty limited to buyer's termination of the contract and receipt of a refund of its earnest money deposit, so long as such breach is attributable to the occurrence after the date of the contract execution of some event which is not within the seller's control;[115] and
  - Action for damages eliminated as an available remedy, except in the instance of a willful failure to perform by seller, in which event the buyer can pursue recovery of the direct, out-of-pocket costs incurred by the buyer in connection with its due diligence efforts.

The topic of contractual remedies is one area of the purchase contract where lawyers commonly make the mistake of "failing to see the forest for the trees." Lawyers often fall in love with the intricacy of their prose in describing the parties' available remedies, without stepping back to consider whether a party's financial standing effectively negates the utility of the stated contractual remedies. A lawyer representing the buyer of property from a financially-troubled seller should, if possible, require a guaranty of the seller's obligations by a well-healed affiliate of the seller and, in all events, ardently resist any attempt by the seller's counsel to eliminate specific performance as a remedy available to the buyer. The lawyer representing the seller of property to a newly-formed entity should take one or both of the following approaches to protect his client's interests—(1) secure a guaranty of the buyer's obligations from some entity having a substantial net worth or (2) insist upon the posting of a sizable earnest money deposit and the inclusion in the contract of a

---

114. *See* 77 AMERICAN JURISPRUDENCE 2D *Vendor and Purchaser* § 453 (2010); and Herz, *supra*, footnote 35, at 12–14.

115. *See supra* Page 124.

provision that makes it clear that the deposit may be retained by the seller in the event of a default by the buyer.

4. Liquidated Damages

Liquidated damage clauses are extremely common in land purchase contracts. A liquidated damage clause is simply "a contract provision by which the parties agree in advance to the amount of damages payable on a breach."[116] While occasionally used to redress seller's breaches, liquidated damage clauses are far more often utilized as the seller's remedy for the buyer's failure to perform under the land purchase contract. The typical seller liquidated damage clause calls for the posting by the buyer of a significant earnest money deposit (5–10% of the purchase price) and for the receipt by the seller of the entirety of that deposit as liquidated damages in the event of a contractual default by the buyer.

The following are reasons why a liquidated damage clause is an attractive method to redress a buyer's default.

- The typical liquidated damage clause is designed to protect the seller from the credit risk of contracting to sell its land to a newly-formed, single purpose entity. By requiring the buyer to pay a significant deposit into escrow, the seller has the comfort of knowing that money will be available to cover its losses if the buyer fails to perform.

- A liquidated damage clause allows both the buyer and the seller to avoid the pain and cost associated with protracted litigation.

- Finally, under a liquidated damage clause, both parties know the exact consequences of the buyer failing to perform its obligation to purchase the land. This level of predictability stands in sharp contrast to the uncertainty associated with the pursuit of other legal remedies.

It is relatively settled law that an enforceable liquidated damage clause must satisfy both of the following requirements:[117]

- The liquidated sum must be a reasonable forecast of the financial loss caused by the breach;[118] and

---

116. *See* Lefcoe, *supra* note 84, 62, at 159.

117. *See* Frank C. Dunbar, Jr., Drafting *the Liquidated Damage Clause—When and How*, 20 Ohio State Law JOURNAL 221 (1959). An emerging trend in the case law on liquidated damages is to ignore the traditional, two-pronged legal test noted above and, instead, to focus on the relative bargaining power of the seller and the buyer. That trend is illustrated by Uzan v. 845 UN Limited Partnership, 778 N.Y.S.2d 171 (2004), in which the illustrious Donald Trump triumphed one more time by getting the New York Supreme Court to agree to enforce a liquidated damage clause that resulted in two Turkish billionaires forfeiting an $8 million earnest money deposit (25% of the $32 million purchase price for two penthouse apartments in Manhattan). In that case, it was held that a liquidated damage clause (at least in the factual context of the purchase of luxury condominium units) is enforceable absent a showing of "disparity of bargaining power, or of duress, fraud, illegality or mutual mistake." *See id.* at 178.

118. The courts are divided on the issue of whether the liquidated sum must be a reasonable approximation of damages both at the time the contract was executed and at the time of the default. *See* Nelson, *supra* note 50, at 62–64

- The harm caused by the breach must be difficult to estimate accurately.[119]

The typical liquidated damage clause attempts to react to these two requirements in the following manner:

The Seller will be entitled to receive the entire amount of the Deposit as full and complete liquidated damages to redress a default by the Buyer in the performance of its obligations under this Agreement; it being expressly acknowledged by the parties hereto that the Seller's damages in the event of a default by the Buyer will be difficult to ascertain and that the receipt of the Deposit constitutes a reasonable liquidation of such damages and is not intended as a penalty.

5. Exclusivity of Liquidated Damages Remedy

One interesting question concerning the liquidated damage clause is, does such a clause need to be the sole and exclusive remedy of the seller? Is a liquidated damage clause enforceable if the purchase contract purports to preserve the seller's right to pursue (a) an action for specific performance against the buyer, (b) an action for damages or (c) both (a) and (b)? The majority rule is that the inclusion of a liquidated damages clause in a purchase contract precludes the seller from pursuing an action for damages, even if the purchase contract purports to give the seller that option.[120] However, somewhat surprisingly (at least to this author), the rule is just the opposite as it relates to the remedy of specific performance. There the majority rule is that, unless otherwise clearly stated to the contrary in the purchase contract, the presence in a purchase contract of a liquidated damages clause does not serve as a legal bar to the seller's pursuit of an action for the specific performance of its contract.[121]

The parties to a real estate purchase contract should not leave to chance the issue of whether liquidated damages will be the exclusive

---

119. The courts have almost uniformly determined that the harm caused by the breach of a real estate sales contract is difficult to estimate. *See* Jeffrey B. Coopersmith, *Refocusing Liquidated Damage Law for Real Estate Contracts: Return to the Historical Roots of the Penalty Doctrine*, 39 EMORY L. J. 267 (1990), where the author persuasively notes that "the market for real property often fluctuates across relatively short time frames, making any pre-estimate rather meaningless." *See id.* at 286.

120. *See* Catholic Charities of Archdiocese of Chicago v. Thorpe, 741 N.E.2d 651 (Ill. App. 2000) in which the court noted that a clause purporting to give the seller a choice between retaining a deposit as liquidated damages or instituting a damages action against the buyer is unenforceable because it is nothing more than an attempt by the seller "to have his cake and eat it too." *See also* Linda A. Francis, Annotation, *Provision in Land Contract for Liquidated Damages upon Default of Purchaser as Affecting Right of Vendor to Maintain Action for Damages for Breach of Contract*, 39 A.L.R. 5th 33 (1996).

121. *See* LEFCOE, *supra* note 84, at 160–161. *But see* Hatcher v. Panama City Nursing Center, Inc., 461 So.2d 288 (Fla. Dist. Ct. App. 1985), where the court held that the presence of a liquidated damages clause in a purchase contract precluded a seller from pursuing a specific performance action, even though the contract did not specifically state that specific performance was unavailable to redress a buyer default. *See also* Coopersmith, *supra* note 119, at 302, where the author comments that "[i]f the seller has the choice of either . . . liquidated damages or suing for specific performance, the concept of liquidated damages as a form of risk allocation is destroyed. Upon a breach by the buyer, the seller would simply elect the more lucrative alternative."

remedy of the seller. A clear, unequivocal statement in the purchase contract that liquidated damages will be the seller's "sole and exclusive remedy to redress a default by the buyer" and that the seller "waives all other remedies, including the remedy of specific performance" will put an end to any uncertainty concerning the seller's remedial options. Absent such a clause, the seller might be able to "have its cake and eat it too"—a situation that a buyer will always find to be intolerable.

HIBC Case Study—Remedies

Chemical Bank was initially adamant that Pizzuti's sole remedy for Chemical's default under the HIBC purchase contract should be specific performance. Chemical Bank wanted no part of a damages action that might expose it to some extraordinarily high level of damages based on an argument that the fair market value of the HIBC land far exceeded the purchase price being paid by Pizzuti. The only inroad that Pizzuti was able to make on this point was to get counsel for Chemical to agree that, in the event of a "willful refusal to close" by Chemical, Pizzuti could supplement its specific performance action with a damages action, so long as the amount of the collectible damages was capped at the sum of Pizzuti's "direct out-of-pocket expenses to unaffiliated third parties incurred by Buyer in reliance on this Contract." The remedies clause ultimately agreed to by Chemical and Pizzuti is representative of the type of clause a seller should insist on when it has the fear that appraisers might differ wildly on how to value a large parcel of land that is being sold in bulk to one buyer (versus piecemeal to a number of different purchasers).

Conversely, Chemical sought to "have its cake and eat it too" when it came to its remedies for a default by Pizzuti. The Contract for Sale and Purchase of Real Estate provides that Chemical had the choice to either (a) retain the deposit as liquidated damages or (b) "pursue all of its legal and equitable remedies against Buyer, including an action for specific performance." Based on the Hatcher case cited and described supra note 121, this clause was probably unenforceable when entered into by Chemical and Pizzuti in 1992—although I profess to not have heard of the Hatcher case at the time.

Pizzuti's position on the seller remedies clause was fairly typical for a buyer of commercial land. Pizzuti took the position that it was not worth getting into a long negotiation with Chemical on the seller remedies, so long as Pizzuti was given a broad contingency that permitted it to terminate its purchase obligation if it decided the project was not feasible for some reason.[122] The Contract for Sale of Purchase and Real Estate speci-

---

122. Refraining from arguing about the seller's remedies also permits the real estate development lawyer to claim the high ground in the negotiations by asserting that he doesn't care about the seller's remedies, because his client will never default on a deal. Such moral high ground is

fied that the closing would take place a mere 27 days after the expiration of Pizzuti's contingency period. Pizzuti believed that if it felt comfortable enough to waive its feasibility contingency at the end of the 90 day review period, the likelihood was that nothing would occur in the subsequent 27 days to change its mind about closing on the acquisition of the HIBC land.

L. RISK OF LOSS. *(§12)*

What happens if a serious flood damages the land or a governmental authority commences an eminent domain proceeding against the land after the date of the parties' execution of the purchase contract, but before the actual land acquisition closing? Does the risk of such a loss fall on the buyer or the seller?

Under the age-old principle of equitable conversion,[123] the risk of loss due to the occurrence during the contract period of a flood, eminent domain proceeding or some other casualty falls on the buyer.[124] Simply stated, this means that the buyer remains obligated to purchase the land at the price set forth in the purchase contract, even though, due to the interim occurrence of the casualty,[125] the land no longer has the same value to the buyer as it did when the purchase contract was executed. There is a strong minority position that the doctrine of equitable conversion has no application to the purchase and sale of land if the prospective buyer of the land has neither taken possession, nor actually acquired legal title to the land.[126] The Uniform Vendors and Purchasers Risk Act codifies the minority rule.[127]

The careful real estate development lawyer should take pains to negate the potential impact of the doctrine of equitable conversion by making it clear within the context of the purchase contract that the risk of loss remains with the seller until closing.[128] The Form Purchase Agreement contains the following clause:

The risk of loss to the Property from the occurrence of a casualty or a taking by any public authority under the power or right of eminent

---

more easily attained when a broad suitability contingency gives the developer a relatively easy out under the purchase contract.

123. "The rule underlying the doctrine of equitable conversion is that a contract to sell real property vests the equitable ownership of the property in the purchaser; and thus, where there is any loss by a destruction of the property through casualty during the pendency of the contract (neither party being guilty of causing the destruction) such loss must be borne by the purchaser." *See* Sanford v. Breidenbach, 173 N.E.2d 702, 707 (Ohio App. 1960).

124. *See* Randy R. Koenders, Annotation, *Risk of Loss by Casualty Pending Contract for Conveyance of Real Property Modern Cases*, 85 A.L.R.4th 233 (2001).

125. The doctrine of equitable conversion has also been applied to allocate to the buyer the risk of changes in a parcel's "legal status"—e.g., a change in a zoning or building code. *See* NELSON, *supra* note 50, at 95.

126. *See id.* at 94–95.

127. *See* LEFCOE, *supra* note 84, at 122–123.

128. *See id.* at 123.

domain (or by the threat thereof) will be borne by Seller until the closing of Buyer's purchase of the Property.

The purchase contract should button up this point by specifically stating that the buyer will have the right to terminate the purchase contract if a property loss occurs during the contract period. Quite often the seller will try to limit the buyer's termination option by introducing a materiality concept that effectively provides that the buyer will remain obligated to purchase the land if the occurrence of the subject casualty or taking has no significant impact on the value of the land.[129] If the contract remains in place following the occurrence of a casualty or taking (either due to the immaterial nature of the resulting loss or the buyer's election not to exercise its termination option), then the seller should be obligated by the purchase contract to assign to the buyer all insurance claims, condemnation awards and other potential recoveries related to the casualty or taking.

M. MUTUAL REPRESENTATION ON BROKERAGE COMMISSIONS. *(§13)*

There is generally no requirement that a brokerage agreement be recorded in the chain of title to a land parcel in order for the broker to be entitled to a commission on the sale of such parcel. Indeed, in some jurisdictions, the doctrine of promissory estoppel supplies the broker with the ability to enforce its alleged right to a sale commission even if no written agreement of any kind was ever entered into by the broker and a party to the sales transaction.[130] Given these two facts, it is not at all uncommon for a broker to unexpectedly show up at closing (or even worse after the closing) with his hand outstretched asking for a commission.

In order to safeguard against the unexpected commission claim, counsel for the buyer and the seller should include in the purchase contract a mutual representation and warranty confirming that neither party has taken any action or entered into any agreement that could result in a brokerage commission, finder's fee or similar charge being owed with respect to the sale of the land to the buyer. To the extent either the seller or the buyer has an agreement to pay a commission to some third party, the commitment of such party to pay such commission in full on or before the date of closing should be clearly spelled out in the purchase contract.

Finally each party should indemnify the other party against any liability for any commission claimed in breach of its "no commission" representation and warranty. This is yet another area where lawyers are well-advised to inquire into the creditworthiness of the party making the representation and warranty.

---

129. The materiality of the loss can be described in a variety of ways—e.g., a loss of at least $____ or a taking of at least ____ acres.

130. *See* Orlando Lucero, *The Brokerage Agreements—What You Don't Know Can Hurt You,* 20 No. 2 PRACTICAL REAL ESTATE LAWYER 39, 40 (March 2004).

N. OPERATION OF THE PROPERTY DURING THE CONTRACT PERIOD. *(§14)*

The real estate development lawyer should try to insert in the purchase contract a clear statement limiting the seller's ability to take any action with respect to the land after contract execution that could adversely affect the value or utility of the land to the buyer. A clause such as that set forth in § 13 of the Form Purchase Agreement seeks to protect the buyer from the seller taking any of the following actions during the pendency of the purchase contract:

- Granting any easements, licenses or other contract rights or property interests with respect to the land that could survive the buyer's purchase of the land;

- Performing any excavation or construction activities on the land or taking any other action that could affect the natural condition of the land as it existed on the date of the execution of the purchase contract; or

- Seeking a rezoning or other change in any governmental rule or approval applicable to the land.

Some sellers take the position that they should have the right to take any of the above actions, without the buyer's consent, at any time prior to the date on which the buyer has waived all of the contingencies to its obligation to purchase the property. If such a provision is agreed to (in most cases it should not be), the real estate development lawyer should insert into the purchase contract a specific requirement that its client be given prompt written notice of the seller's taking of any such action, so that the buyer will have ample time to terminate the contract prior to the expiration of the contingency period if the buyer determines that the seller's action has made its project infeasible in some manner.

During the contract period, the developer is often busy trying to get governmental agencies, utility companies and other third parties to agree to take some affirmative action with respect to the land. By way of example, the developer may be trying to rezone the land to permit its proposed development project or to get the local water company to agree to pay for the extension of water lines to the boundaries of the land. It is often difficult for the developer to make any headway in its negotiations over these types of land changes, unless the seller is willing to cooperate in at least a minimal fashion in the developer's efforts to secure the desired project approvals. It is, therefore, recommended that the real estate development lawyer include in the purchase agreement a requirement that the seller and its representatives cooperate in good faith with the buyer's efforts to effect a change in the condition or character of the land. A thoughtful lawyer for the seller will, however, want to make sure that his client's obligations are limited in the following two respects:

- The seller will not be required to incur any out-of-pocket expense in connection with its cooperation with the buyer's efforts; and

- The seller will not be obligated to consent to buyer's taking of any action that would legally bind the seller or its land prior to the buyer's closing on the acquisition of the land.

O. BOILERPLATE PROVISIONS. *(§§15–24)*

We now come to one of my least favorite topics of all time—the so-called ***boilerplate*** provisions included in the purchase contract. Merriam–Webster's Collegiate Dictionary defines "boilerplate" as "standardized, formulaic, or hackneyed language."[131] Too many lawyers (particularly young lawyers), boilerplate clauses are those standard provisions that are stuck in the back of every agreement "just because they always are." The consensus is that, although nobody ever takes the time to understand or even read the boilerplate provisions, some wise old lawyer years ago determined that the provisions were essential to an agreement and that excising those provisions from a document could have unknown, but extremely disastrous consequences. Boilerplate provisions are, therefore, viewed as the quintessential "cover your ass" clauses.

I am here to tell you that there is no such thing as a boilerplate clause—at least if that term is used to describe a provision that the lawyer does not have to understand, but which should be included in every agreement a lawyer drafts. One of the most embarrassing experiences I ever had as a young lawyer was when one of my senior partners began his review of a draft document that I had worked on all night by turning to the last page of the document and asking me what the "Complete Agreement" provision meant and why I had included it in my draft. I assure you that the senior partner was less than impressed with my response that "I just thought I was supposed to include that boilerplate in every document."

The lesson to be learned from the above story is that the real estate development lawyer should never include a clause in purchase contract without having a legitimate reason for doing so. Before discussing those clauses which, although often referred to as boilerplate, nonetheless should be included in most purchase contracts, let me throw out an example of the danger of using the same old boilerplate language in every document. One of the standard provisions contained at the back of many contracts is the following clause.

> *The rights and remedies of the parties to this Agreement are cumulative and are not in lieu of, but are in addition to, any other rights or remedies that the parties may have at law or otherwise.*

This certainly sounds like the kind of nice, safe clause that should be included in every contract. What would happen, however, if this nice, safe clause were to be included in a purchase contract that contained a

---

131. *See* Mᴇʀʀɪᴀᴍ-Wᴇʙsᴛᴇʀ's Cᴏʟʟᴇɢɪᴀᴛᴇ Dɪᴄᴛɪᴏɴᴀʀʏ 165 (10th ed. 2001).

provision purporting to establish liquidated damages as the seller's sole and exclusive remedy for the buyer's default under the purchase contract?

OK, it is now time for me to get off my high horse and mention several clauses that I believe should be included at the end of most purchase contracts. Please, however, indulge my sensitivities and let me call them "miscellaneous" and not "boilerplate" provisions. The clauses discussed briefly below are set forth in their entirety at the end of the Form Purchase Agreement.

- *Assignment of Agreement (§15)*—This clause negates the common law rule that all contracts are freely assignable, unless otherwise stated in the contract.[132] In most (but not all) situations, the buyer and the seller will share the view that the other party to the purchase contract should not be able to assign its rights, duties or obligations under the contract to any other person without first obtaining the consent of the other contracting party.[133] It is, however, important to think this point through to determine whether any exceptions to this general rule should be set forth in the purchase contract—e.g., the exception contained in the Form Purchase Agreement for the buyer's assignment of its interest in the purchase contract to its affiliates.

- *Governing Law (§16)*—The general rule is that the law of the jurisdiction in which the land is located will govern the interpretation of the purchase contract.[134] This provision should be included in the miscellaneous provisions to remind the lawyer that he needs to give thought to whether any portion of the purchase contract should be construed in accordance with some other state's laws. By way of example, if the property is located in the State of Florida, but both the seller and the buyer are headquartered in Ohio, it might be appropriate to provide that any disputes over the purchase contract will be determined in accordance with Ohio law.

- *Counterparts (§17)*—This provision is intended to permit a document to become effective as soon as each party has signed a purchase contract and sent it to the other party. It does not, however, require that both the seller and the buyer sign the same document. The use of counterparts regularly saves the parties a full day in making the document effective—the day that it would take

---

132. *See* 6 AMERICAN JURISPRUDENCE 2D, *Assignments*, §46 (2010).

133. The seller, in particular, generally wants to prohibit the buyer from having any right to assign its rights under the purchase contract. Otherwise, the buyer who obtains a contractual right to purchase land at a favorable price would able to "flip" its contract rights to a third party and make a substantial profit, without ever having to acquire the land. *See* discussion of this point at GREGORY STEIN, *supra*, note 39, at 103.

134. *See* AMERICAN JURISPRUDENCE 2D *Conflict of Laws*, § 35 (2010). The law of the state where the land is located will usually cover the interpretation of the conveyance documents that are required to be placed of public record. However, the parties to a real estate purchase contract are free to select another state's law to govern the construction of the purchase contract, so long as that other state has some reasonable relationship to the subject matter of the purchase contract.

for one party to send its signed document to the other party so that both signatures can be affixed to the same document.

- ***Attorney's Fees (§18)***—This clause should be included in those jurisdictions that permit the prevailing party in a lawsuit to recover its legal fees—particularly if attorney's fees can only be recovered in the jurisdiction if the contract expressly sanctions such a recovery. The Form Purchase Contract is the form I used for transactions in Florida, where prevailing party legal fees are recoverable.[135]

- ***Entire Agreement (§19)***—This clause is intended to negate the effect of any prior letters of intent or other written documents entered into by the buyer and the seller and to make it clear that the purchase contract can only be amended by a document signed by both such parties.

- ***Reasonableness of Consent (§20)***—I consistently include this clause in my documents. I find that requiring both parties to act reasonably gives me access to the higher ground in negotiations, without putting my client at any particular disadvantage—in part because my clients are always reasonable and in part because the law often implies a duty for a party to a purchase contract to act reasonably.[136] While this clause fits my style and that of my clients, I assure you that the majority of today's practicing lawyers would never countenance the inclusion of this clause in their package of "boilerplate" provisions.

- ***Notices (§21)***—Especially in today's electronic age where communication by e-mail is the norm, it is important to specify in the purchase contract how each notice called for in the contract may be sent and when it is deemed to be effective. The notices called out in the purchase contract normally have a significant legal impact on the purchase and sale transaction (for example, the buyer's notice terminating the contract or identifying its title objections). For this reason, many practitioners have been hesitant to treat an e-mail transmission as a permitted method of sending contractual notices. Fax transmissions are, however, regularly included in purchase contracts as an acceptable mode for sending notices to the other party.[137]

- ***Date for Performance (§22)***—It is common for purchase contracts to call out the time for a party's performance of a particular

---

135. *See e.g.*, Moritz v. Hoyt Enterprises, Inc., 604 So.2d 807 (Fla. 1992).

136. Some states permit the parties to act arbitrarily and capriciously if the purchase contract expressly permits them to do so. *See supra* note 48. Even when working in one of those jurisdictions, I tend to include a "reasonableness" clause in my documents, because I prefer to focus on the meat of the negotiations and not get bogged down in an argument about whether and when a party can act unreasonably.

137. *See* GREGORY STEIN, *supra* note 39, at 107; and Herz, *supra* note 39, at 14–16. For an example of a purchase contract that includes e-mail as an approved method of sending contractual notices, *see* Peter Aitelli, *Purchase and Sale Agreement for Real Property*, in ALI–ABA COURSE OF STUDY MATERIALS, MODERN REAL ESTATE TRANSACTIONS: PRACTICAL STRATEGIES FOR REAL ESTATE ACQUISITION, DISPOSITION, AND OWNERSHIP, Course No. SS–012 167, § 22 (July 2010).

obligation by reference to a stated number of days after some fixed date—for example, the obligation to deliver the title commitment within 20 days after the date of the parties' execution of the purchase contract. Lawyers often find it to be a useful and pleasant shortcut to include a provision in the purchase contract saying that if any such time period ends on a weekend or holiday, the time period will automatically be pushed back to the next business day.

- ***Confidentiality*** *(§23)*—I have found that most of my developer clients prefer to keep their potential land acquisitions a secret until they are ready to go to the press with a full-blown story about their planned projects. Including a confidentiality clause in the purchase contract is intended (and sometimes even works) to prevent the seller from stealing the developer's thunder by prematurely going public about the proposed land sale.

- ***Defined Terms*** *(§24)*—Except in the most complex agreements, I prefer to define terms when they are first used in the text of the document. I find that this approach enhances the flow and readability of the purchase contract. Having said that, I do like to list all of the defined terms in one place with appropriate section cross-references, so that if the reader ever gets lost when trying to figure out the meaning of a defined term, there is one central place he can go for guidance.

The above is not intended to be an exhaustive list of every miscellaneous clause to be included in a purchase contract. Nor is it intended as a directive that every purchase contract should include the listed clauses. The only absolute associated with these types of miscellaneous clauses is that the real estate development lawyer absolutely must include only those clauses that are appropriate to serve his client's business objective.

Practice Tip #5–3: Contract Negotiations

Lawyers often seek to elevate the nature of what they do on a daily basis by characterizing contract negotiations as an "art form." While I certainly accept the fact that there is not a lot of "science" to negotiating a contract, referring to a lawyer as an "artist" seems to me to be a bit of misdirected hyperbole. Likening contract negotiations to a game of chess is a much more apt analogy. Strategy and consistency are the hallmarks of a good negotiator, not creativity and spontaneity.

The following are some guidelines that can help make a real estate development lawyer a more successful negotiator.

- ***Control the Drafting of the Document.*** *Preparing the initial draft of the purchase contract presents the real estate development lawyer with an opportunity to set the agenda for the negotiations and to incorporate contractual language that is responsive to his* *client's business interests. Assuming responsibility for subsequent redrafts of the purchase contract also allows the real estate development lawyer to both dictate the pace of the negotiations and craft the negotiated changes in a manner which is most favorable to his client.*

- ***Understand and Take advantage of Your Negotiating Leverage.*** *In the context of a real estate deal, "leverage" simply means that a party has the upper hand on some subject of the negotiations. Negotiations are all about understanding the relative leverage of the parties on each negotiating topic. It is important for the real estate development lawyer to understand when he has the leverage on a particular point and when he does not. In order to make that determination, the real estate development lawyer must understand (1) the competing business positions and objectives of the buyer and the seller and (2) the strengths and weaknesses of opposing counsel. By way of example, if a landowner is desperate to sell its land so that it can pay off the creditors of its separate operating business, the real estate development lawyer will be in a unique position to structure a deal which is highly beneficial to the developer.*

- ***Be a Consequential Thinker.*** *Before taking a position in any negotiation, the lawyer must anticipate how the other side will react to that position. Much like a good chess player, the real estate development lawyer must think several steps ahead to make sure that he does not find himself so hemmed into one negotiating strategy that he ends up with a document that effectively "checkmates" the business interests of his client. For instance, a real estate development lawyer needs to be careful that his insistence on a full slate of seller representations and warranties does not result in the seller refusing to provide the buyer with a broad suitability contingency clause.*

- ***Adopt Your Own Negotiating Style and Stick With It.*** *Just as the real estate development lawyer needs to understand the strengths and weaknesses of his opposing counsel, so must he understand and accept his own negotiating strengths and weaknesses. Over the years, I have learned that I tend to grow tired and lose focus during lengthy, meandering negotiations conducted over the phone or in person. As a result, I always try to articulate my position (and minimize the wisdom of the other side's position) in some written communication with the other side, so that our in-person or telephonic negotiations can be more focused and shorter in duration. The lesson to be learned is that there is more than one way to successfully conduct a negotiation and the lawyer who most often succeeds is the one who frames the negotiations to highlight his strengths and expose the weaknesses of opposing counsel.*

- ***Don't Take Unreasonable Positions.*** *There is nothing that damages a lawyer's reputation more quickly than his insistence on* *consistently taking unreasonable positions. A lawyer who adopts extreme positions on behalf of his client, without any real rationale for doing so, runs the very real risk of earning the worst of all possible reputations in the real estate bar—that of being a deal killer.*

VII. SUMMARY

This Chapter began with the statement that Stage 1 of the real estate development process presents the real estate development lawyer with his first opportunity to exhibit the skills and inclination of a "deal maker." The efforts of the real estate development lawyer at this first stage are focused on helping his developer client achieve two basic objectives:

- Tying up the identified site as quickly and as cheaply as possible; and

- Doing so in a fashion that minimizes the developer's exposure to project risks.

The developer's goal of tying up the site can be achieved in a variety of ways—by using a preliminary letter of intent or by going straight to a binding purchase document (be it a purchase contract or an option). While there are legitimate legal risks associated with the use of a letter of intent, the commercial reality is that the use of a letter has become a commonly accepted first step in the developer's attempt to gain legal control of land. The real estate development lawyer must, therefore, learn how to utilize the letter of intent format in a way that serves his client's interests, without creating any unexpected and unwanted legal obligations for the developer.

A significant part of this Chapter was devoted to a discussion of how a real estate development lawyer can use the land purchase contract as a vehicle to protect his client against land risk—that is, the risk that something occurs that causes the developer to decide not to buy the land. Land risk comes in two basic forms—(1) risk involving a circumstance that is specific to the subject site—e.g., the presence on the site of environmental contaminants, and (2) risk involving a circumstance that has nothing to do with the site itself, but which relates in a broader fashion to the feasibility of the developer's overall development project— e.g., a fall-off in tenant demand for the project because of the kick-off of a nearby, competitive project, or a sudden, unexpected downturn in the real estate economy. The real estate development lawyer's efforts to minimize his client's exposure to both of these categories of land risk revolve around his artful use of buyer contingencies, third party certifications and seller representations and warranties.

As stated at the outset of this Chapter, the land purchase contract serves as the road map for the real estate development project. The real estate development lawyer must bring to bear all of his skill and knowledge if he is to succeed in his effort to produce a purchase contract that, like any good road map, gets the developer where he wants to go.

CHAPTER 6

STAGE 2: SECURING GOVERNMENTAL APPROVALS AND INCENTIVES

■ ■ ■

I. INTRODUCTION

The real estate development business is a heavily regulated industry in which the involvement of the public sector often is the determining factor in a project's success or failure. When I first started practicing law more than 30 years ago, the government's participation in the development process was typically limited to its issuance of zoning letters, building permits and other administrative clearances. In today's real estate industry, federal, state and local governments are proactive players at every stage of the development process, ranging from the initial visioning of the project to its ultimate funding, construction and operation.

The focus of this Chapter will be on how the government[1] can provide incentives to aid the development of a private real estate project.[2] Those incentives will be examined from the perspectives of both the developer who asks for help and the government that then needs to decide whether the developer's project merits such help.[3] The Chapter will conclude by straying into an area that is quite unique for this text—that is, those issues of public policy that affect (or at least should affect) the government's decision to provide aid to a private development project.

---

1. The term "government" is used in this Chapter as an all-inclusive, shorthand reference to all levels of government, including federal, state, county, city, village and township governments, and to all of the constituent agencies and offices at each such governmental level.

2. This Chapter has as its focus government assistance provided to a private development project. As such, there will be no attempt to discuss development projects undertaken directly by the government or by a quasi-governmental agency, where the ultimate driver for the project is different from the seeking of bottom line profits that is the focus of this book (e.g., an urban redevelopment agency established by a municipality to spearhead the redevelopment of a distressed area of the city).

3. This Chapter will not make reference to the Heathrow International Business Center project that serves as a focal point for our examination of the other nine stages of a real estate development project. The HIBC case study is not a good platform for the discussion of Stage 2 because the key governmental approvals secured for the HIBC project (and there were plenty of them) were all linked to the peculiarities of the State of Florida's growth management rules— none of which have any particular application to the practice of real estate development law in jurisdictions other than Florida.

152

II. DEVELOPER'S BUSINESS OBJECTIVE

Prior to closing on its acquisition of the land, the developer will want to make sure that it has received all those governmental approvals that it considers to be essential conditions precedent to a kick-off of its development project. Those approvals generally fall into one of two categories:

- Approvals that are required to permit the project to be constructed in accordance with the developer's development plan (commonly referred to in the real estate industry as **entitlements**); and

- Approvals that are required to make the project economics work or otherwise make the project feasible[4] (better known as *incentives*).

The threshold question for the developer during Stage 2 is what governmental approvals are "essential" to its decision to move forward with the project. In an ideal, risk-free world, the developer will have received final and irrevocable governmental approvals for all components of the project before the developer is required to commit to purchase the land on which the project will be constructed (including a full-blown building permit authorizing the developer to prosecute and complete construction of the entirety of the project). However, commercial real estate developers are seldom afforded the luxury of operating in a risk-free environment. Developers routinely make judgments that certain approvals are so insignificant, ministerial in nature or otherwise free of political controversy that their receipt can be deferred until after the project land is purchased. All other approvals (be they related to entitlements or incentives) fall into the "essential" category and should be the focus of the developer's efforts during Stage 2 of the development process.

III. DIFFERENCE BETWEEN
AN ENTITLEMENT AND
AN INCENTIVE

While entitlements and incentives both fit within the definition of those essential approvals that a developer should secure prior to the onset of its commitment to purchase the project land, the two categories of approvals are markedly different. An entitlement approval is issued when the government determines that a proposed real estate project satisfies a set of governmental rules that are applicable to all similarly situated projects.[5] The developer is legally required to secure the entitlement approval before it can proceed with the construction of the project. The

---

4. For a discussion of the concept of "feasibility" in the context of a real estate development project, *see* Chapter 2, note 3.

5. The following are examples of entitlement approvals that are frequently viewed by the developer as being essential to its decision to commit to purchase the project land—(a) a rezoning required for the developer's use of the project in a particular manner, (b) development plan approval (to the extent the government has any discretion to disapprove the design or layout of the proposed project), (c) environmental or wetlands clearances required as a condition precedent

government's primary power in the area of entitlements is its limited right to say "no." The developer's receipt of an entitlement approval simply means that it can proceed to build its project—it does not mean that it should do so. The grant of an entitlement makes the project possible, but not necessarily feasible.

An incentive approval is in many ways the flip side of the entitlement coin. There is no legal imperative for the developer to request the grant of an incentive, nor is there typically any set of fixed governmental rules to determine whether the incentive should be granted to a particular project. The government's primary power in the area of incentives is its right to favor a particular project by saying "yes" to the grant of a benefit to that project that is not shared in common with similarly situated projects. The developer's receipt of an incentive approval does not mean that it can build its project, but it often goes a long way toward answering the question of whether it should do so. The grant of an incentive makes the project feasible, but not necessarily possible.

There is not much instructive guidance that can be given in this Chapter about the developer's efforts to receive an entitlement approval, other than—(1) the developer needs to get the approval before it proceeds with the project and (2) it must employ all appropriate measures to insure that its proposed development plan complies with the governmental rules that govern the grant of the subject entitlement. I have now exhausted my advice on the topic of entitlements, so the remainder of this Chapter will be devoted to the topic of primary interest during Stage 2 of a development project—the developer's enhancement of its project's feasibility through its receipt of governmental incentives.[6]

IV. WHY DOES THE DEVELOPER WANT (OR NEED) INCENTIVES?

The wildly popular book *Freakonomics* contains the following passage that nicely encapsulates the developer's quest for governmental incentives:

> Economics is, at root, the study of incentives: how people get what they want, or need, especially when other people want or need the same thing.[7]

---

to the start of construction on the project site, and (d) the grant of development rights consistent with state-wide, growth management rules.

6. This Chapter is not intended to be a primer on zoning and land use law. Those interested in the intricacies of Euclidean zoning, new urbanism and growth management regimes are urged to consult the following resources—DANIEL P. SELMI, JAMES A. KUSHNER AND EDWARD H. ZEIGLER, LAND USE REGULATION (3rd ed. 2008); GEORGE LEFCOE, REAL ESTATE TRANSACTIONS, FINANCE, AND DEVELOPMENT, 795–852 (6th ed. 2009); Stephen T. Janik, *The Regulatory Structure of New Urbanism: the Evolution Away from Euclidean Zoning*, in ACREL PAPERS (ALI–ABA, Spring 2002), available online at http://www.acrel.org/Documents/Seminars/Spring2002Tab6.pdf; and Gurdon Buck, *The Latest Buzz in the Land Development Cocktail Parties "Smart Growth," "Urban Sprawl," "New Urbanism" and "The Village Districts,"* in ACREL PAPERS (ALI–ABA, Spring 1999), available online at http://www.acrel.org/Documents/Seminars/a000014(1).pdf.

7. *See* STEVEN D. LEVITT AND STEPHEN J. DUBNER, FREAKONOMICS 16 (2005).

For the commercial real estate developer, the receipt of governmental incentives can satisfy one (and sometimes both) of the following wants and needs:[8]

- Give its project a competitive advantage over similar projects that do not receive the incentive;[9] or

- Make feasible a project which would not be so, but for the receipt of the incentive.[10]

So how can the developer's receipt of governmental incentives serve the two goals mentioned above? The following is a list of the four principal ways in which a developer's project can be benefited by the receipt of governmental incentives:

- ***Lower the developer's cost of capital*** through the provision of low-interest loans, grants or other financial subsidies;

- ***Reduce the project's development costs*** through direct government funding of land acquisition or infrastructure costs or the use of tax increment financing or other creative financing tools to fund a portion of the project's development costs;

- ***Increase the project's net operating income*** by providing tax and financial incentives to attract new tenants, reduce the project's operating costs or increase the project's revenues; and

- ***Eliminate barriers to entry for the project*** by streamlining the approval and permitting process, using the government's eminent domain powers to assist the developer in its land assemblage, constructing infrastructure to enhance the marketability and functionality of the project site or assisting the developer in its clean-up of environmentally contaminated sites.

The specific incentive techniques that are available to help the developer achieve these four objectives will be discussed in more detail later in this Chapter.

---

8. The distinction between the real estate developer's "wants" and "needs" is neatly summed up in the following refrain from a Rolling Stones song—"You can't always get what you want, but, if you try, sometimes you just might find that you get what you need." MICK JAGGER AND KEITH RICHARDS, *You Can't Always Get What You Want*, on LET IT BLEED (ABKCO 1969).

9. This point is illustrated by looking at two identical, suburban office buildings located within close proximity of each other. The only difference between the two buildings is that the municipality in which Building A is located has agreed to abate all real estate taxes on the building for a period of ten years (producing a $200,000 annual savings), while the municipality in which Building B is located is unwilling to grant any tax abatement for Building B. Solely due to the existence of the tax abatement, the owner of Building A can lower its rents by $200,000 per year and still achieve the same annual return on costs that flows to the owner of Building B—a clear competitive advantage that will result in tenants flocking to Building A (and away from Building B).

10. This objective is particularly important with respect to urban development projects, because the cost of developing a project in an urban setting is typically much higher than the cost of doing so in the suburbs (for a whole host of reasons, including higher land costs, outdated infrastructure, environmental problems and constrained work sites). The receipt of incentives is, therefore, frequently needed to level the playing field between a downtown project and a competing project constructed in the suburbs. *See generally* CHRISTOPHER B. LEINBERGER, TURNING AROUND DOWNTOWN: TWELVE STEPS TO REVITALIZATION (The Brookings Institute, 2005).

V. WHY IS THE GOVERNMENT WILLING TO PROVIDE INCENTIVES?

It is easy to understand why a developer is happy to receive governmental incentives for its project. But why does the government want to provide incentives to a developer? What possible public interests can be served by the government's provision of aid to a private development project? Is the provision of incentives favoring a single developer over its competitors really a valid exercise of the government's powers?

The reason why governments put together incentive packages to aid the development of a private project can be understood by again referring to a quote from *Freakonomics*.

> An incentive is simply a means of urging people to do more of a good thing and less of a bad thing.[11]

By providing incentives to a private developer, the government hopes that it will cause the developer to "do a good thing" by developing a project of a type and in a location desired by the government (and not "do a bad thing" by developing a project of a type or in a location that is not favored by the government). It is this simple concept that has provoked virtually every political subdivision in the United States, from large states like California to the smallest of townships in Maine, to staff an office of economic development to try to craft incentives to encourage private development within its boundaries.

But why does the government care whether a particular type of a project is developed within its geographic borders? There are both economic and social policy justifications for a government's decision to try to direct the course of real estate development in its jurisdiction.

A. ECONOMIC REASONS

The primary purpose of government is to provide for the health, education, welfare and safety of its citizens. Government serves that purpose by operating schools, staffing police and fire departments and offering a variety of services intended to foster the well-being of those living within its boundaries. Performing those tasks costs money, which must be funded out of the government's revenues (largely generated from taxes and fees imposed on the general populace). Over the last few decades, it has become the job of the government's economic development officer to figure out inventive ways to increase the government's revenue base, without having to impose additional taxes on its citizens. It is this goal of increasing government revenues that has given rise to the offering of governmental incentives to spur the development of private real estate projects.

The development of the right real estate project can augment the government's revenues in a variety of ways. The most obvious source of

---

11. *See* LEVITT, *supra* note 7, at 17.

additional revenue is the property taxes that will be imposed on the new project's value. Even more important are the additional property taxes that will be generated from surrounding properties if (and it's a big "if") the developer's project has the desired dual effect of (1) increasing the value of existing, surrounding properties and (2) serving as the catalyst for the development of new projects inside the government's borders.[12]

Property taxes are not the only source of additional revenue that a government hopes to generate by offering incentives to a private real estate project. It is the government's objective when structuring its incentive package to encourage (and sometimes actually require) the creation of new jobs—jobs for the construction workers employed by the developer's contractor, jobs for the occupants of the developer's project (be it an office building, retail center or warehouse) and jobs for the occupants of all of the new development projects that are hopefully spawned by the construction of the incentivized project. The creation of new jobs produces two results that are equally important to the government—(1) it increases the government's income and sales tax revenues (because the more money people make, the more they will spend on both commodities and taxes) and (2) it produces a content citizenry that, hopefully, will be inclined to cast its votes to keep the existing officeholders in power.

The one point made obvious by the above discussion is that the government's goal of enhancing its revenue base will only be achieved if the incentivized project actually has the intended effect of spurring additional development and increasing property values in the surrounding neighborhood. The dynamics and magnitude of the bet that government makes when it identifies a project as a candidate to trigger additional development is discussed in more detail later in this Chapter.[13]

B. SOCIAL POLICY REASONS

Governments also use incentives to promote certain social policy agendas. As noted in the previously-quoted excerpt from *Freakonomics*, governments create incentives to urge developers to "do more of a good thing and less of a bad thing."[14]

The following are some of the "good things" that governments have encouraged developers to do by offering incentives:

- Rebuild blighted areas;
- Clean up and redevelop environmentally contaminated sites;
- Use "green" and other sustainable building practices;
- Construct affordable housing;

---

12. *See* Theodore J. Novak, *Magnet Public/Private Projects: Does the Pull Really Work,* in ACREL PAPERS (ALI–ABA, Fall 2002), available online at http://www.acrel.org/Documents/Semi nars/2002%20Novak%20-%20Magnet%20projects.pdf.

13. *See infra* Pages 185–187.

14. *See* LEVITT *supra* note 7, at 17.

- Dedicate parkland and other public space;
- Preserve and renovate historic structures;
- Design projects consistent with the new urbanism zoning model;[15]
- Build downtown (and not in suburbs or exurbs); and
- Invest in low-income communities.

In all of the above cases, the government offers up something that the developer wants (for example, financial subsidies, tax abatements or increased project density) in exchange for the developer behaving in a certain, governmentally-prescribed way.[16]

VI. TYPES OF GOVERNMENTAL INCENTIVES

The incentives that a government can use to assist a private development project fall into four general categories.

- Financial incentives;
- Tax incentives;
- Regulatory assistance; and
- Development assistance.

The purpose, nature and scope of each of these incentive categories are discussed below.[17]

VII. FINANCIAL INCENTIVES

There are a wide variety of financial incentives that a government can offer to a developer of a private real estate project. The purpose of all such financial incentives is to improve the developer's project economics by lowering either its cost of capital or its project development costs.

The precise nature and scope of the financial incentives that are available for use by a particular governmental entity are typically defined in enabling legislation adopted by such entity. Because the specifics of such financial incentives vary substantially by jurisdiction, it is impracti-

---

15. For a discussion of the theories embraced within the concept of new urbanism, *see* the authorities cited *supra* note 6.

16. The government could, of course, better advance its policy agenda if it were to mandate that developers act in the prescribed fashion (rather than simply encouraging them to do so through the use of incentives). The policy debate over the use of mandates versus incentives is an interesting one that is discussed at length in the following articles—Denise J. Lewis, Thomas J. Coyne and Dwight H. Merriam, *Tax and Other Inducements for the Development of Real Estate—"Carrots and Sticks: How Governments Cajole and Bludgeon Developers into Submission,"* in ACREL PAPERS 1 (ALI–ABA, Fall 2006); and Carl J. Circo, *Using Mandates and Incentives to Promote Sustainable Construction and Green Building Projects in the Private Sector: A Call for More State Land Use Policy Initiatives,* 112 PENN STATE LAW REVIEW 731 (2008).

17. The particulars of the various governmental incentives discussed in this Chapter vary widely by jurisdiction. This Chapter will not analyze any specific state statute or local ordinance, but rather will discuss governmental approvals and incentives in general terms in an attempt to highlight the principal issues that a practitioner must address in the jurisdiction in which he is practicing.

cal to list in this text all of the financial incentives available at each level of federal, state and local government. It can, however, be stated that those financial incentives generally fall in one of the following three buckets:

- ***Direct grants and subsidies,*** where the government makes a direct payment or property contribution either to the developer or to one of the developer's vendors;

- ***Low-cost financing,*** where the government provides debt to the developer at below-market pricing and terms;[18] and

- ***Tax increment financing,*** where the government uses the enhanced revenues generated from the new project to fund some portion of the project's development costs.

Depending on the size and complexity of the project, a developer of a single project might receive several financial incentives from different governmental entities. By way of example, the developer of an industrial park might receive the benefit of a state grant to pay for the cost of needed road improvements, a low-interest bond financing sponsored by the county to cover the cost of extending sewer and water lines to the project and a tax increment financing agreement from the city to fund its land acquisition and other site-wide infrastructure costs. The end result of the developer's receipt of such financial incentives is that its lower cost structure will give it a competitive advantage over other nearby industrial parks.[19]

A. TAX INCREMENT FINANCING

Tax increment financing is an incentive tool that has become immensely popular in recent years.[20] Given the prevalence of its use and

---

18. Two common ways that a governmental entity can provide low-cost financing for the benefit of a private project are through (1) its issuance of tax-exempt bonds (either backed by the full faith and credit of the governmental entity issuing the bonds or by the revenue created from the new project) and (2) its creation of a special assessment district where the cost of public infrastructure required by the incentivized project is funded by the assessment of taxes and fees against all property owners that benefit from construction of such infrastructure. The specifics of both of these financing techniques are beyond both the scope of this Chapter. Those interested in learning more about these governmental financing alternatives are referred to the following resources—Novak, *supra* note 12, at 5–6; J. Murphy McMillan III, William S. Mendenhall and James A. Richardson, *Use of Public Incentive Finance in Commercial Real Estate Developments: A Developer's Perspective,* REAL ESTATE FINANCE JOURNAL 10 (Summer 2007); and URBAN LAND INSTITUTE, INFO PACKET No. 308, INFRASTRUCTURE FINANCING (February 2006).

19. The receipt of financial incentives is particularly important during times when private sources of debt and equity funding for the development of a real estate project are limited because of a dislocation in a particular market or a general economic malaise. In times of restricted capital flows (such as the years following the financial crisis of 2008), the receipt of a governmental grant or other financial subsidy is often much more than merely a way to enhance the developer's financial returns—it may, in fact, be the only way that the developer can get enough money to start its project. *See* Charles A. Long, *Using Public–Private Partnerships to Create Value–Added Conversions,* an Urban Land Institute Webinar (April 30, 2010) (background statement and supporting PowerPoint slides are available online at http://www.uli.peachnewmedia.com/store/provider/provider.09/php).

20. A recent study commissioned by the Chicago Metropolitan Agency for Planning noted that, as of January 2006, there were 530 TIF districts in the greater Chicagoland area and 140

the significance of the benefit it can bestow on the private developer, the topic of tax increment financing (a *TIF*) deserves special mention in this Chapter.

A TIF is a financing device that uses the ***incremental taxes***[21] derived from a new real estate project to pay for a portion of the project's development costs. The incremental taxes consist of the additional future taxes imposed on the project over and above the taxes attributable to the pre-development value of the project (usually the "land only" value of the project site).[22] In other words, the incremental taxes are those taxes which would not be payable BUT FOR the development of the new project.

In a TIF arrangement, the project owner pays its annual real estate taxes on the full value of the completed project (and not just the pre-existing, land only value of the project site). The incremental piece of those taxes (commonly referred to as the ***increment***)[23] is then diverted from the government's normal pool of tax revenues and specifically used to repay the TIF-financed project costs.

The following example illustrates how a TIF works.

Example 6–1: Assume that Developer plans to construct an office building in Downtown. In order for its cost structure to be competitive with other Downtown office buildings, Developer believes that it needs to reduce its development costs by $5 million (which, conveniently for this illustration, is the exact amount of the infrastructure costs that Developer needs to incur for the project's road and utility improvements). The existing value of the land on which Developer's office building will be constructed is $1 million. This land only value currently produces an annual real estate tax bill of $25,000. Developer estimates that the value of its new project at completion will be $28 million. At that number, the completed project would generate an annual real estate tax liability of $700,000.

Based on the above facts, Downtown could agree to use a TIF to fund $5 million of Developer's infrastructure costs. The annual tax increment of $675,000 (the projected annual tax bill on the completed project of $700,000, minus the existing land only tax bill of $25,000) would be

---

such districts in the City of Chicago. *See* CHICAGO METROPOLITAN AGENCY FOR PLANNING, ECONOMIC DEVELOPMENT INCENTIVES (June 2009) (available online at http://www.goto2040.org/incentives).

21. The subject of a TIF is typically real estate taxes. However, some jurisdictions have experimented with creating a TIF to capture incremental sales or other business taxes. *See* Novak, *supra* note 12, at 2.

22. The calculation of the taxes attributable to the pre-development value of the project is not as clear-cut as it might seem. The principal issue that the negotiators of a TIF must address is what happens if the applicable tax rate increases during the term of the TIF, either as a result of a specific vote of the electorate or some automatic adjustment for inflation. Should the additional taxes produced from the tax rate increase (including those related to the pre-development value of the project) be included in the tax increment? The answer to that question is the product of the specific language of the applicable TIF statute and the negotiating skills of the lawyers for the developer and the government.

23. In some jurisdictions such as Ohio, the incremental taxes are referred to as "payments in lieu of taxes" or "PILOTs." *See* Price D. Finley, *Don't Let Your "TIF" Cause a "Tiff,"* 15 FINLEY'S OHIO MUNICIPAL SERVICE, Issue 4, at 2 (July/August 2003).

captured and used by Downtown to pay off the $5 million of infrastructure costs financed under the TIF (plus interest calculated at whatever level is sanctioned under the TIF statute applicable to Downtown). Assuming that the interest rate on the TIF is 5.5% and that the actual, annual tax increment matches Developer's pre-development estimate of $675,000, the $5 million TIF amount would be fully repaid in approximately ten years.

The tax dollars produced from Developer's project during each year of the ten year term of the TIF would be used in the following fashion—(1) $675,000 to repay the TIF costs; and (2) $25,000 to fund the government's general operating costs (schools, police and fire, etc.). Upon the repayment of all of the TIF costs, the entirety of the tax payment (including the increment of $675,000) would then revert back into the government's coffers to pay its general operating costs.

Example 6–1 begs one very important question—who bears the risk that the actual tax increment is not sufficient to pay off the TIF-financed costs?[24] Does the developer bear that risk or is the governmental entity that provided the TIF at risk for the unreimbursed TIF costs? The answer to that question depends, at least in part, on whether the TIF is structured as a ***pay as you go TIF*** or as a ***bonded TIF***.

- ***Pay as You Go TIF***—With this type of TIF, the developer is responsible for the upfront payment of the full amount of the TIF costs ($5 million in the previous example) and then is reimbursed for such payment by its receipt of the actual tax increment over the term of the TIF.[25] Under the pay as you go arrangement, the developer bears the full risk that the tax increment actually produced from the project is less than initially projected (and, hence, not big enough to fully reimburse the developer for its earlier payment of the TIF costs).

- ***Bonded TIF***—Developers frequently ask the government to structure its TIF as a bonded arrangement. Under a bonded TIF, the government uses its borrowing power to issue bonds[26] in an amount equal to the TIF costs. The TIF provider pays the proceeds of the bond sale to the developer to cover the full amount of the developer's TIF-covered costs. The government provider then uses the tax

---

24.   This risk can be produced under either of the following scenarios—(1) the developer fails to complete construction of the project or (2) the completed project doesn't produce the value initially projected by the developer.

25.   A well-drafted, pay as you go TIF agreement will make it clear that the developer cannot benefit economically if the actual amount of the increment is greater than projected. As a result, the excess of the actual increment over the projected increment will usually be available to the government's non-TIF taxing districts to pay their general operating costs.

26.   The government can fund the TIF costs by its issuance of either general obligation bonds or revenue bonds. General obligation bonds are backed by the full faith and credit of the issuing governmental entity and, hence, can be issued at a very low interest rate. Revenue bonds are backed by the revenues created from the incentivized project and are not supported by the full faith and credit of the government. Therefore, the interest rate on revenue bonds is normally slightly higher than that payable on general obligation bonds (but is still below that typically charged by banks and other construction lenders). *See* Lewis, *supra note* 16, at 32–33; Novak, *supra* note 12, at 3; and MIKE E. MILES, GAYLE L. BERENS AND MARC A. WEISS, REAL ESTATE DEVELOPMENT: PRINCIPLES AND PROCESS 259 (3rd ed. 2000).

increment actually paid by the project owner during the TIF term to retire the principal and interest due on the bonds. A typical, unvarnished, bonded TIF serves two primary developer objectives— (1) it places the risk that the actual tax increment is insufficient to pay the TIF costs on the government and (2) it relieves the developer of the cash flow burden of having to make an upfront payment equal to the TIF-covered costs. In an attempt to shift the risk of a lower than projected increment back to the developer, many governmental entities insist that the developer personally guaranty all or some portion of the shortfall between the TIF costs and the actual increment.[27]

B. TIF LEGAL ISSUES

A TIF is a statutory creation. While all 50 states have statutes in place authorizing a local government's use of a TIF,[28] the provisions of those statutes vary widely. It is, therefore, essential for a real estate practitioner to master the intricacies of his state's TIF statute before he enters into negotiations with a governmental entity concerning that entity's provision of a TIF for the benefit of the practitioner's client.

The following are the principal issues that are presented under state TIF statutes.

- ***What governmental entities can use a TIF?*** Is a TIF a tool that can be used by all state or local governmental entities (state, county, municipal, village and township governments, as well as instrumentalities and agencies of such governmental units) or only by a limited subset of such entities?

- ***What types of projects are eligible for a TIF?*** Here the question is whether the use of a TIF is limited to certain types of projects— for example, only non-residential properties or only those properties to which the public has access (e.g., a performing arts center or stadium).

- ***What conditions warrant the use of a TIF?*** All states require the presence of a public purpose for the diversion of tax revenues to pay for the development costs of a private project. The issue is whether that public purpose is satisfied simply by the developer and the governmental entity agreeing and stipulating that the construction of the project will promote ***economic development*** (i.e., potentially create new jobs and spur further development in the vicinity of the incentivized project) or whether a more restrictive definition of public purpose is imposed—for example, the remediation of blight.[29] The resolution of this issue will largely determine

---

27. Depending on the developer's credit standing, the government may also ask that the developer collateralize its guaranty with a letter of credit, a mortgage on the project property or the pledge of some additional property interest.

28. *See* LEFCOE, *supra* note 6, at 864.

29. The question whether economic development is a sufficient public purpose to support a government's provision of incentives to a private development project came to the forefront of

whether a TIF can be used for a suburban, greenfield project or whether it is only available for development in higher density urban areas. In addition, several state statutes require a specific government finding that the development of the incentivized project would not occur "but for" the government's creation of the TIF.[30]

- ***What costs are eligible for funding under a TIF?*** TIFs have traditionally been used to fund the costs of constructing public infrastructure, such as sewer and water lines and public roadways.[31] However, the statutes of many states have in recent years been interpreted to permit a much more expansive view of the development costs that can be funded under a TIF.[32] Costs that are frequently permitted to be funded under a TIF now include not only roadway, utility and other infrastructure costs, but also the costs of acquiring the project land, cleaning up environmental contamination, demolishing existing site improvements and, in some circumstances, even the cost of financing the construction of new buildings. Ultimately the precise wording of a particular state's statute (and the creative interpretation of that statutory language by real estate lawyers) will provide the answer to the question of what costs are eligible for TIF funding.

- ***What are the geographical boundaries of the TIF district?*** Some states provide the government with broad authority to establish the boundaries of the TIF district beyond the site on which the construction of the funded improvements are being erected (on the theory that those improvements will provide a direct or indirect benefit to surrounding properties). Setting the boundaries of the TIF district beyond those of the specific, incentivized project creates a larger increment that can then be used to fund more development costs over a quicker period of time (good for the developer). The downside from the government's perspective of creating a larger

public policy debate following the United States Supreme Court's decision in the case of Kelo v. City of New London, 545 U.S. 469 (2005). In *Kelo*, the Supreme Court confirmed the constitutionality of a municipality's exercise of its eminent domain powers to aid a private project on the grounds that the municipality's objective of spurring economic development was a valid public purpose. The *Kelo* case is set out and discussed later in this Chapter at Page 173. For a discussion of the impact of the *Kelo* decision on a government's use of a TIF, *see* George Lefcoe, *After Kelo, Curbing Opportunistic TIF–Driven Economic Development: Foregoing Ineffectual Blight Tests; Empowering Property Owners and School Districts*, 83 TULANE LAW REVIEW 1 (2008).

30. *See* Richard Ward, *To TIF or Not To TIF: Debating the Issues*, DEVELOPMENT STRATEGIES REVIEW 1, 2 (Summer 2000), reprinted in URBAN LAND INSTITUTE, INFO PACKET NO. 357, TAX INCREMENT FINANCING (February 2006). Two interesting questions related to the statutory "but for" test are (1) what quantum of information must the developer provide to satisfy that test and (2) is that information then available for public review under a local public information statute.

31. Indeed one of the original theories supporting the adoption of TIF statutes was that a TIF could potentially level the playing field between potential sites located in different communities where one site had adequate infrastructure in place and the other did not. *See* Finley, *supra* note 23, at 2.

32. *See* Novak, *supra* note 12, at 3; and Ward, *supra* note 30, at 3. *Also see e.g.*, JG St. Louis West Limited Liability Company v. City of Des Peres, 41 S.W.3d 513 (Mo. App. Ct.), where a Missouri court upheld the use of a TIF to finance the costs of constructing a parking garage to serve a retail center.

than required TIF district is that the increment created from new development in areas surrounding the incentivized project will be diverted to the repayment of the TIF costs and will not be available to fund the government's general operating costs.

- ***What is the maximum term of a TIF?*** Some jurisdictions place a cap on the length of the term for the repayment of the TIF-covered costs—for example, Ohio's TIF statute provides for a maximum TIF term of 30 years.[33] Most developers prefer to push the term out as far as possible in an effort to maximize the amount of the development costs that can be covered under the TIF (an approach which runs counter to the government's desire for a quick payback of the TIF-funded costs).

- ***What percentage of the tax increment can be used to repay the TIF costs?*** Some governments seek during their negotiations with developers to limit the percentage of the tax increment that can be used to repay the TIF costs—for example, to 50% of the increment. Doing so means that the remaining 50% of the increment will immediately be available to pay the government's general operating costs.

- ***Is the consent of the school district or any other taxing district required prior to the adoption of a TIF?*** As noted at the outset of this section, the effect of a TIF is to divert the tax increment generated by the incentivized project away from school districts, police and fire departments and other taxing districts that get their funding from the government's general operating revenues. In order to protect the interests of such taxing districts, some state statutes specifically require that a TIF cannot become operative, unless all or some portion of those taxing districts consent to the creation of the TIF. By way of example, Washington's statute provides that the consent of the fire department and at least 75% of the other affected taxing districts is required for the creation of a TIF.[34] Ohio takes a middle ground position by providing that the school district's consent is required if the term of the TIF is greater than ten years or the percentage of the diverted tax increment is more than 75%.[35]

The TIF enabling statute in a particular state will provide the answers to all of the above questions. Once those answers are provided, the negotiating teams representing the developer and the government will then need to structure the terms of a TIF in a manner that both complies with the statutory constraints and serves the respective interests of the developer and the government.

---

33. *See* OHIO REVISED CODE ANNOTATED § 5709.40(C), (4) (West 2010).

34. *See* Novak, *supra* note 12, at 3.

35. *See* OHIO REVISED CODE ANNOTATED § 5709.40(B) (West 2010).

C. TIF POLICY ISSUES

The use of TIFs to encourage private development has been the source of an ongoing public policy debate. TIF proponents argue that a TIF is an ideal governmental incentive, because it encourages economic development without negatively impacting the government's operating revenues. They point out that the tax increment that is used to finance the TIF costs would not have existed BUT FOR the developer's construction of its new project—which, in turn, would not have been kicked off BUT FOR the incentives provided to the project by the sponsoring governmental entity. In other words, the use of a TIF doesn't cost the government anything at all during the TIF term and provides it with (1) the use of the tax increment on the TIF project once the term of the TIF expires and (2) the unfettered use both during and after the TIF term of the additional tax revenues created from the increased property values and additional development spawned by the incentivized project. To TIF supporters, the use of a TIF is a perfect example of a government "making a development pay for itself."[36]

TIF opponents argue that a TIF is nothing more than a convenient way for government officials to allocate tax revenues away from schools and other taxing districts to the benefit of politically well-connected developers—and to do so without having to obtain the consent of the electorate. These opponents discount the "but for" argument of the TIF proponents by asserting that, in almost all instances, the developer would have moved forward with the project with or without the TIF.[37] In their view, a TIF permits private developers to improve the bottom line profitability of their projects by getting the government to fund project development costs that are strictly private in nature and serve no valid public purpose.[38] While TIF opponents may not object to the use of a TIF to finance the construction of roads and sewer lines that serve the public at large, they object strenuously to the use of a TIF for the benefit of a private development project.[39]

---

36. *See* MILES, *supra* note 26, at 314.

37. TIF opponents assert that statutory provisions conditioning the use of a TIF on findings that (1) the TIF district constitutes a "blighted area" and (2) the incentivized project would not have occurred "but for" the passage of the TIF provide little protection against the misuse of the TIF incentive. As two leading TIF experts have noted "[i]t is only a bit of an overstatement to characterize the 'blight' and 'but for' findings as merely *pro forma* exercises, since specialized consultants can produce the needed evidence in almost all cases." *See* Richard F. Dye and David F. Merriman, *Tax Increment Financing: A Tool for Local Economic Development,* 18 LAND LINES 2 (Lincoln Institute of Land Policy 2006).

38. TIF opponents also point out that the existence of a TIF has the potential of creating a deficit in the government's operating revenues if the government has to provide additional services and facilities for the occupants of the TIF project (something which is usually a very real prospect). Because the increment from the TIF project is not available to pay for the additional services and facilities provided to the TIF project, the government could find itself in the politically unenviable position of having to increase taxes to deal with the additional demands placed upon it by the occupants of the incentivized real estate project.

39. For a more detailed discussion of the policy arguments of TIF opponents, *see generally* Lefcoe, *After Kelo, supra* note 29; Alyson Tomme, *Tax Increment Financing: Public Use or Private Abuse,* 90 MINNESOTA LAW REVIEW 213 (2005); and Dye, *supra* note 37.

In recent years, the public policy debate over the pros and cons of TIFs has spilled over into the courts. Taxpayers have filed numerous lawsuits seeking to restrain the government's use of TIFs to support private development projects.[40] Local taxing districts are also beginning to get into the act by resorting to the courts to try to prevent municipalities from creating TIFs that have the effect of diverting revenues away from such taxing districts.[41] While no judicial decision has come down to date, which would in any way significantly impede the government's latitude to assist private development projects through the use of tax increment financing, practitioners would be well-advised to diligently monitor judicial developments on this topic in the years to come.

VIII. TAX INCENTIVES

The grant of tax incentives is probably the technique most commonly used by the government to encourage the construction of a private development project. While tax incentives take many forms, they all share the attribute of reducing the tax burden of either the owner of the incentivized project or the tenants of that project. Taxes which are typically the subject of governmental incentive packages include real estate taxes, income taxes (at the federal, state and local levels) and sales taxes.

Tax incentives afford the developer of a private development project the opportunity to enhance its net operating income and, hence, the ultimate value of its project.[42] A reduction in the real estate taxes that a developer will have to pay on its newly-developed project will boost the developer's NOI by reducing its operating expenses. A government-sponsored reduction in the income and sales taxes payable by tenants of a particular project will make the developer's project more attractive to potential tenants and may permit the developer to charge premium rents to those tenants who decide to relocate to the new project.

There are three basic categories of tax incentives that can be used to benefit the development of a private real estate project.[43]

---

40. *See* Novak, *supra* note 12, at 3. One very high profile project that was the subject of taxpayer litigation contesting the use of a TIF was the Florida Marlins stadium project in Miami. The Florida Supreme Court in Braman v. Miami–Dade County, 18 So.3d 1259 (2009), affirmed a lower court's decision upholding the use of a TIF to fund a portion of the costs of developing the Florida Marlins new stadium complex in Miami.

41. In 2009, Jackson County, Missouri sued the Kansas City Tax Increment Financing Commission, alleging improprieties in the manner in which TIF decisions were being made by Kansas City officials. *See* David Stokes, *Counties, Not Municipalities Should Decide TIFs*, 6 SHOW-ME INSTITUTE No. 8 (March 24, 2010), available online at http://showmeinstitute.org/publication/id. 250/pub_detail.asp. *See also A Tiff over TIF in Northern California*, GIDEON'S TRUMPET, A BLOG ON TAKINGS OF PROPERTY BY EMINENT DOMAIN AND INVERSE CONDEMNATION (April 15, 2010), http://www. mercurynews.com/milpitas/ci_14883612, discussing a threatened lawsuit by Santa Clara County against the city of Milpitas concerning the city's creation of TIF districts within its boundaries.

42. *See supra* Chapter 3, Pages 37–39.

43. The tax incentive categories are listed in the order of developer preference—from the most to the least desirable. The developer's preference is based largely on time value of money considerations, with the abatement creating the best time-valued benefit to the developer

- **Abatement**—An abatement reduces (or wholly eliminates) a taxpayer's tax liability for some fixed period of time. An example of a typical tax abatement that a government might use to incentivize a private development project is the abatement for ten years of 100% of the real estate taxes that would otherwise be assessed on improvements constructed on the project site.[44] An abatement can be issued either on a single project site or offered on a blanket basis for all projects constructed within some designated geographical area (for example, a community reinvestment area or an enterprise zone).[45]

- **Credit**—This incentive provides the taxpayer with a credit that it can apply as an offset against its existing tax liability.[46] Examples of tax credits used to incentivize private real estate projects are the federal income tax credits included in the Internal Revenue Code for costs incurred by a taxpayer in connection with the rehabilitation of a certified historic structure[47] or the construction of a low-income housing project.[48]

- **Rebate**—A rebate is a governmental refund of taxes previously paid by a taxpayer. The rebate can be used with respect to any kind of tax, including sales and income taxes. In recent years, it has become commonplace for municipalities to try to entice a user to relocate to a particular project by offering the user a full or partial rebate of all income taxes paid to the municipality by the user's employees during some designated period of time.[49]

(because it never has to pay the tax) and the rebate providing the least time-valued benefit (because it has to pay the taxes before it is entitled to an eventual refund and, therefore, loses the use of the funds for a period of time).

44. Care must be taken to make sure that the grant of abatement does not defeat the purpose of other governmental incentives provided for a particular development project. For example, a real estate tax abatement should not be given to any project that is the subject of a TIF because the abatement would reduce the amount of the tax increment available to be captured to finance the TIF-funded costs.

45. *See* Novak, *supra* note 12, at 3–4.

46. A taxpayer is ordinarily not entitled to receive any direct payment if the amount of its tax credit exceeds its tax liability for the current tax period. Unused credits are, however, frequently permitted to be carried forward by the taxpayer and used to offset its tax liability in future tax periods.

47. Section 47 of the Internal Revenue Code provides for a federal income tax credit equal to 20% of the "qualified expenditures" incurred in connection with a "certified rehabilitation of certified historic structures." *See* discussion of rehabilitation tax credit in Lewis, *supra* note 16, at 2–6.

48. Section 42 of the Internal Revenue Code provides for a federal income tax credit for certain costs incurred in connection with the construction of low-income housing projects. The amount of the credit will vary based on the value and category of the project. *See* discussion of low-income housing tax credit in Lewis, *supra* note 16, at 24–27.

49. By way of example, the City of Columbus, Ohio has adopted a policy that rebates payroll taxes to companies that agree to relocate to office space in downtown Columbus from somewhere outside of the city limits. The amount of the rebate is tied to the length of a company's commitment to its new space and the number of new jobs created by its move. A general description of the City's downtown office incentive can be found online at http://econdev. columbus.gov/business_services/financial_assistance.aspx.

The end result of the government's use of any of these incentives is the same—the developer's net operating income is increased and the government's tax revenues are decreased.

IX. REGULATORY ASSISTANCE

As noted at the outset of this Chapter, there are a variety of governmentally-imposed rules that a developer must comply with when constructing a real estate project. Local zoning laws restrict the manner in which a project can be used and the dimensions and components of the improvements that can be constructed on the project site. State and federal laws govern the timing and scope of the remediation of environmental contamination found on a particular site. State building codes impose constraints on materials and practices used during the construction of project improvements. State and local authorities impose fees and establish timelines for the developer's application for and receipt of building permits and other development approvals.

Complying with these and other governmental rules has the effect of costing the developer both time and money. One way that a governmental entity can provide meaningful assistance to a private real estate project is by loosening the strictures that a developer must follow during the course of its development efforts. The following are three examples of techniques frequently utilized by governmental entities to help private development projects make their way through the maze of governmental regulation.

- *Zoning and Building Code Variances*—Oftentimes, the most beneficial contribution that a government can make to a private development project is the grant of a variance permitting the developer to avoid some particularly troublesome rule. By way of example, a municipality's decision to reduce the number of parking spaces required in a project or to permit construction of improvements within ten feet (instead of 20 feet) of the site's side boundary line could make the difference between a project being feasible or infeasible.

- *Streamlined Approval Process*—To the developer, time really is money. In recognition of that fact, many governmental entities have begun to promise developers relaxed submission requirements and expedited development approvals.[50]

- *Waiver/Reduction of Development and Building Permit Fees*—One way in which the government has sought to reduce its financial deficits is by significantly increasing the level of develop-

---

50. One example of a government streamlining its approval process to benefit a private developer can be found in the actions taken by the City of Chicago during its efforts in 2000 to convince Boeing to relocate its corporate headquarters from Seattle to Chicago. Chicago agreed to provide Boeing with a single governmental point of contact, which was then given the authority to orchestrate and expedite the grant of all required permits from all of the governmental agencies having jurisdiction over the Boeing project. The end result of this "single point of contact" arrangement was that Boeing was able to significantly lessen the prospect of government-caused delays in getting its project completed. *See* Novak, *supra* note 12, at 6.

ment and building permit fees it charges for the construction of a new project in its jurisdiction. In some states such as California, governmentally-imposed fees represent a significant line item cost for a developer. A full or partial waiver of those fees can, therefore, be a very meaningful benefit to a developer.[51]

The next two sections examine regulatory assistance techniques that can have a dramatic impact on the developer's bottom line economics.

A. INCENTIVE ZONING

An interesting phenomenon of recent vintage has been the rise of *incentive zoning* as a vehicle to cause developers to design and construct their projects in a certain way. Incentive zoning consists of a local government providing a bonus to a developer in exchange for the developer agreeing to do something that the government believes is desirable. The primary bonus handed out by local governments is the right of the developer to increase the density of its project—i.e., the number of square feet in "for lease" projects or the number of units in "for sale" projects.[52] Governments also sometimes agree to provide developer bonuses in the form of a reduction in development fees or a waiver of some construction requirement otherwise mandated in the government's zoning and building codes (for example, lowering the number of parking spaces the developer is required to provide for the project). The adoption of green building practices,[53] the dedication of land for parks and the contribution of public art are types of private developer conduct that are often encouraged under incentive zoning programs.[54]

B. BROWNFIELD REDEVELOPMENT

One of the more difficult challenges facing governments in the 21st century is the task of revitalizing areas of their communities that flourished in the past as industrial sites, but are now vacant as a result of a decline in the U.S. manufacturing sector. A high percentage of these vacant properties (commonly referred to as *brownfield* sites) have at least some moderate level of potential, environmental contamination. The

---

51. *See* Miles, *supra* note 26, at 316–318.

52. In the idiom of the developer, increased density equates to increased project profits. If a developer is allowed to increase the quantity of its revenue-producing product (and that is what density is all about), without any concomitant increase in its land, infrastructure or soft costs, then the developer's projected net operating income from the project will be augmented by an amount equal to the increased revenues produced by the bonus density, less the actual cost of the developer's compliance with the government's incentive zoning program.

53. The use of incentives to encourage developers to "go green" has been the topic of numerous practitioner-authored articles in the last few years. *See e.g.*, Circo, *supra* note 16; Roger Schwenke, *Green Building Regulations: The Mandatory, The Voluntary and Some Incentives*, in ACREL Papers 325 (ALI–ABA, Fall 2009); and Yuanshu Deng and Jared Eigerman, *Non–Federal Green Building Incentives*, Real Estate Finance Journal 54 (Spring 2010).

54. *See* Lewis, *supra* note 16, at 33–34; and Miles, *supra* note 25, at 304. *Also see supra* Pages 157–158, for a listing of other "good things" that a government might decide to reward through the grant of zoning bonuses.

"brownfield" tag is given to "real property, the expansion, redevelopment, or reuse of which may be complicated by the presence or potential presence of a hazardous substance, pollutant or contaminant."[55] Brownfield sites occupy a position somewhere between those properties with no environmental problems whatsoever (so-called **greenfield** sites) and those properties that are so severely contaminated that they "present an imminent and substantial endangerment to health or the environment."[56]

Developers were historically hesitant to buy and develop brownfield sites, because of the uncertain application to such sites of federal and state environmental laws. In the late 1970's and early 1980's, the federal government (and most state governments) adopted expansive legislation intended to give government the authority to impose liability on a broad array of persons to clean up severely contaminated properties. Unfortunately, laws such as the Resource Conservation and Recovery Act ("RCRA"),[57] the Comprehensive Environmental Response, Compensation, and Liability Act ("CERCLA")[58] and state laws patterned after those two pieces of federal legislation snared within the scope of their liability and clean-up provisions all properties having any level of environmental contamination (and not just those properties that were so severely contaminated as to present a real risk to human health). Developers legitimately feared that, despite the relatively moderate level of contamination present on most brownfield sites, they might be required under applicable environmental laws to immediately convert brownfields into greenfields by removing all vestiges of hazardous substances from those sites. The potential cost associated with such wholesale remediation efforts made it too risky for developers to commit to redevelop brownfield sites, no matter how well located or configured those sites were.[59]

In an effort to encourage the redevelopment of brownfield sites (and, hence, the expansion of the government's revenue base), virtually every state has now enacted legislation and designed programs intended to eliminate (or at least reduce) the barriers to the redevelopment of brownfield sites.[60] The state brownfield initiatives are generally referred to as **voluntary action programs** or **VAPs**. The following are some common elements of state voluntary action programs.[61]

- **Limited Clean-up Standards**—An essential component of each state program is the development of limited clean-up standards that do not require brownfield developers to remove all hazardous

---

55. *See* 42 U.S.C. § 9601(39)(B).

56. *See* 42 U.S.C. § 6991.

57. *See* 42 U.S.C. § 6901 *et seq.*

58. *See* 42 U.S.C. § 9601 *et seq.*

59. *See* Wendy E. Wagner, *Chapter 2: Overview of Federal and State Law Governing Brownfield Cleanups*, in BROWNFIELDS—A COMPREHENSIVE GUIDE TO REDEVELOPING CONTAMINATED PROPERTY (Todd S. Davis ed., 2002).

60. *See* ENVIRONMENTAL PROTECTION AGENCY, STATE BROWNFIELDS AND VOLUNTARY RESPONSE PROGRAMS: AN UPDATE FROM THE STATES, PUBLICATION NUMBER: EPA–560–R–09–522 (November 2009).

61. *See* Amy Edwards, *Brownfields Redevelopment Initiatives*, 19 No. 2 PRACTICAL REAL ESTATE LAWYER 47 (March 2003).

substances from the affected site. The state programs adopt risk-based approaches intended to limit the population's exposure to dangerous environmental conditions, without imposing on the developer the unrealistic obligation to return the site to a fully pristine condition. By way of example, a developer might be relieved of an obligation to remove mildly contaminated soils from a site if it stipulates that all areas containing such contaminated soils will be capped with a concrete pad (either as part of the main building pad or a parking lot), thereby effectively eliminating any real risk that anyone will ever be exposed to the contaminated soils. Development practices such as this are commonly referred to as ***institutional controls*** and go a large way to reducing the cost of redeveloping brownfield sites.

- ***Covenants Not to Sue***—Most states have regulations in place authorizing the state's environmental officer to issue a covenant not to sue to a developer that completes a voluntary clean-up of a brownfield site in accordance with the limited clean-up standards mentioned under the prior heading. The developer's receipt of a covenant not to sue has the effect of insulating it from any further liability to the state with respect to the environmental condition of the site.

- ***Expedited Governmental Review***—The VAPs of most states have implemented shortened regulatory timelines for the state environmental agency's review and approval of a developer-sponsored remediation plan, thereby mitigating the risk to the developer that an interminable governmental review process will effectively kill its development project (under the old, but still true, adage that "time kills all deals").

- ***Financial and Tax Incentives***—Many states go the extra step of providing financial and tax incentives designed to encourage the redevelopment of brownfield sites. By way of example, the State of Ohio provides (1) project-specific grants of up to $3 million to fund the developer's costs of cleaning up certain select brownfield sites and (2) tax abatements to those brownfield projects that qualify for the government's issuance of a covenant not to sue.[62]

The United States Congress has also sought to encourage the development of brownfield sites by the passage of legislation such as the Small Business Liability Relief and Brownfields Revitalization Act of 2001 (the "Revitalization Act").[63] The Revitalization Act provides funding to assist state and local governments in the administration of their voluntary action programs and grants relief from liability under CERCLA for per-

---

62. *See* Todd S. Davis and Jennifer Kwasniewski, *Chapter 57: Ohio*, in BROWNFIELDS—A COMPREHENSIVE GUIDE TO REDEVELOPING CONTAMINATED PROPERTY, (Todd S. Davis, ed., 2002).

63. *See* PUBLIC LAW NO. 107–118, 115 STAT. 2356 (codified as amended in scattered sections of 42 U.S.C. §§ 9601 et seq.).

sons buying and then cleaning up brownfield sites in compliance with a state's VAP.[64]

All of the state and federal efforts mentioned above are intended to permit a brownfield site to be developed in a much cheaper[65] and liability-free manner. The conversion of vacant, environmentally-troubled sites into vital redevelopment projects can also have a dramatic impact on the revenue bases of the affected governmental subdivisions.

X. DEVELOPMENT ASSISTANCE

The final category of incentives that a government can provide to support a private real estate project is development assistance. There are two principal sources of development assistance that a private developer might want to consider seeking from a governmental entity.

- ● *Construction of Public Infrastructure.* The feasibility of certain development projects is inextricably tied to the addition or enhancement of public infrastructure improvements that serve the project. By way of example, the development of a retail center in the suburbs may not work unless the state and federal governments agree to fund and construct a new freeway interchange which feeds into the retail site. Similarly, a downtown residential complex may not be feasible unless oversized sewer lines are extended to the boundary of the project site or a stoplight with right and left turn lanes is installed at the intersection of the two roads bordering the site. The government can assist such a development project by agreeing to design and construct the requisite infrastructure improvements at its cost.

- ● *Eminent Domain.* A developer's grand plans are often stymied by its inability to assemble all of the land required for the subject development project. Land assemblage problems are particularly prevalent in the context of an urban redevelopment project, where the land targeted as the site for the project is frequently owned by numerous property owners (and not just one farmer, as is the case in many greenfield projects). One or two recalcitrant or unreachable property owners can thwart an otherwise promising real estate project. The government's exercise of its eminent domain powers can be a solution of last resort for the developer's land assemblage problems.

Federal, state and local governments generally have the right to acquire private property without the property owner's consent, so long as the government acquires the property for a valid "public use" and pays the property owner "just compensation" for such acquisition.[66] While the

---

64. *See generally* Edwards, *supra* note 61.

65. The costs of cleaning up a brownfield site may also be eligible for funding under a state's TIF statute. *See supra* Page ___.

66. The takings clause of the Fifth Amendment to the United States Constitution creates these two conditions to the government's exercise of its eminent domain powers. *See* U.S.

issue of what constitutes "just compensation" is itself an interesting and complex topic,[67] it is the "public use" issue that is most germane to the question whether a government can exercise its eminent domain powers to aid a private development project. The U.S. Supreme Court's decision in Kelo v. City of New London[68] tackled that issue head on and, in doing so, framed a public policy debate which will rage on for years to come concerning the legitimacy of the government's use of its powers to encourage the development of a private real estate project. For that reason, I have opted to include edited copies of both Justice Stevens' majority opinion and Justice O'Connor's dissenting opinion in the text of this Chapter.

<hr>

KELO v. CITY OF NEW LONDON[69]

Supreme Court of the United States
545 U.S. 469
Decided June 23, 2005

JUSTICE STEVENS delivered the opinion of the Court.

In 2000, the city of New London approved a development plan that, in the words of the Supreme Court of Connecticut, was "projected to create in excess of 1,000 jobs, to increase tax and other revenues, and to revitalize an economically distressed city, including its downtown and waterfront areas." In assembling the land needed for this project, the city's development agent has purchased property from willing sellers and proposes to use the power of eminent domain to acquire the remainder of the property from unwilling owners in exchange for just compensation. The question presented is whether the city's proposed disposition of this property qualifies as a "public use" within the meaning of the Takings Clause of the Fifth Amendment to the Constitution.

The city of New London (hereinafter City) sits at the junction of the Thames River and the Long Island Sound in southeastern Connecticut. Decades of economic decline led a state agency in 1990 to designate the City a "distressed municipality." ... These conditions prompted state and local officials to target New London, and particularly its Fort Trumbull area, for economic revitalization. To this end, respondent New London Development Corporation (NLDC), a private nonprofit entity established some years earlier to assist the City in planning economic development, was reactivated.... [Shortly thereafter] the pharmaceutical company

<hr>

CONSTITUTION amendment V. The constitutions of most states have provisions similar to the takings clause found in the U.S. Constitution.

67. *See e.g.* Jack R. Sperber, *Just Compensation and the Valuation Concepts You Need to Know to Measure It*, in ALI–ABA COURSE OF STUDY MATERIALS, CONDEMNATION 101: HOW TO PREPARE AND PRESENT AN EMINENT DOMAIN CASE, Course #SP–007, 1 (January 2009).

68. *See* Kelo v. City of New London, 545 U.S. 469 (2005).

69. All footnotes and citations have been omitted from Justice Stevens' and Justice O'Connor's opinions.

Pfizer Inc. announced that it would build a $300 million research facility on a site immediately adjacent to Fort Trumbull; local planners hoped that Pfizer would draw new business to the area, thereby serving as a catalyst to the area's rejuvenation.... NLDC finalized an integrated development plan focused on 90 acres of the Fort Trumbull area....

The development plan ... [contemplated the construction of] a waterfront conference hotel, ... marinas, ... [a] pedestrian "riverwalk," ... 80 new residences organized into an urban neighborhood, ... at least 90,000 square feet of research and development office space ... [and] land for office and retail space, parking, and water-dependent commercial uses. The NLDC intended the development plan to capitalize on the arrival of the Pfizer facility and the new commerce it was expected to attract. In addition to creating jobs, generating tax revenue, and helping to "build momentum for the revitalization of downtown New London," the plan was also designed to make the City more attractive and to create leisure and recreational opportunities on the waterfront and in the park....

Petitioner Susette Kelo has lived in the Fort Trumbull area since 1997. She has made extensive improvements to her house, which she prizes for its water view.... In all, the nine petitioners own 15 properties in Fort Trumbull.... There is no allegation that any of these properties is blighted or otherwise in poor condition; rather, they were condemned only because they happen to be located in the development area.

We granted certiorari to determine whether a city's decision to take property for the purpose of economic development satisfies the "public use" requirement of the Fifth Amendment.

Two polar propositions are perfectly clear. On the one hand, it has long been accepted that the sovereign may not take the property of A for the sole purpose of transferring it to another private party B, even though A is paid just compensation. On the other hand, it is equally clear that a State may transfer property from one private party to another if future "use by the public" is the purpose of the taking; the condemnation of land for a railroad with common-carrier duties is a familiar example. Neither of these propositions, however, determines the disposition of this case.

As for the first proposition, the City would no doubt be forbidden from taking petitioners' land for the purpose of conferring a private benefit on a particular private party. Nor would the City be allowed to take property under the mere pretext of a public purpose, when its actual purpose was to bestow a private benefit. The takings before us, however, would be executed pursuant to a "carefully considered" development plan. The trial judge and all the members of the Supreme Court of Connecticut agreed that there was no evidence of an illegitimate purpose in this case.

On the other hand, this is not a case in which the City is planning to open the condemned land—at least not in its entirety—to use by the general public.... [T]his "Court long ago rejected any literal requirement that condemned property be put into use for the general public." ... Not only was the "use by the public" test difficult to administer (e.g., what proportion of the public need have access to the property? at what price?), but it proved to be impractical given the diverse and always evolving needs of society. Accordingly, when this Court began applying the Fifth Amendment to the States at the close of the 19th century, it embraced the broader and more natural interpretation of public use as "public purpose." . . .

The disposition of this case therefore turns on the question whether the City's development plan serves a "public purpose." Without exception, our cases have defined that concept broadly, reflecting our longstanding policy of deference to legislative judgments in this field.

In Berman v. Parker, this Court upheld a redevelopment plan targeting a blighted area of Washington, D. C., in which most of the housing for the area's 5,000 inhabitants was beyond repair. Under the plan, the area would be condemned and part of it utilized for the construction of streets, schools, and other public facilities. The remainder of the land would be leased or sold to private parties for the purpose of redevelopment, including the construction of low-cost housing. The owner of a department store located in the area challenged the condemnation, pointing out that his store was not itself blighted and arguing that the creation of a "better balanced, more attractive community" was not a valid public use. Writing for a unanimous Court, Justice Douglas refused to evaluate this claim in isolation, deferring instead to the legislative and agency judgment that the area "must be planned as a whole" for the plan to be successful. The Court explained that "community redevelopment programs need not, by force of the Constitution, be on a piecemeal basis-lot by lot, building by building." The public use underlying the taking was unequivocally affirmed:

> "We do not sit to determine whether a particular housing project is or is not desirable. The concept of the public welfare is broad and inclusive. . . . The values it represents are spiritual as well as physical, aesthetic as well as monetary. It is within the power of the legislature to determine that the community should be beautiful as well as healthy, spacious as well as clean, well-balanced as well as carefully patrolled. In the present case, the Congress and its authorized agencies have made determinations that take into account a wide variety of values. It is not for us to reappraise them. If those who govern the District of Columbia decide that the Nation's Capital should be beautiful as well as sanitary, there is nothing in the Fifth Amendment that stands in the way."

In Hawaii Housing Authority v. Midkiff, the Court considered a Hawaii statute whereby fee title was taken from lessors and transferred to lessees (for just compensation) in order to reduce the concentration of land ownership. We unanimously upheld the statute and rejected the Ninth Circuit's view that it was "a naked attempt on the part of the state of Hawaii to take the property of A and transfer it to B solely for B's private use and benefit." Reaffirming Berman's deferential approach to legislative judgments in this field, we concluded that the State's purpose of eliminating the "social and economic evils of a land oligopoly" qualified as a valid public use. Our opinion also rejected the contention that the mere fact that the State immediately transferred the properties to private individuals upon condemnation somehow diminished the public character of the taking. "[I]t is only the taking's purpose, and not its mechanics," we explained, that matters in determining public use. . . .

Viewed as a whole, our jurisprudence has recognized that the needs of society have varied between different parts of the Nation, just as they have evolved over time in response to changed circumstances. Our earliest cases in particular embodied a strong theme of federalism, emphasizing the "great respect" that we owe to state legislatures and state courts in discerning local public needs. . . . For more than a century, our public use jurisprudence has wisely eschewed rigid formulas and intrusive scrutiny in favor of affording legislatures broad latitude in determining what public needs justify the use of the takings power.

Those who govern the City were not confronted with the need to remove blight in the Fort Trumbull area, but their determination that the area was sufficiently distressed to justify a program of economic rejuvenation is entitled to our deference. The City has carefully formulated an economic development plan that it believes will provide appreciable benefits to the community, including-but by no means limited to-new jobs and increased tax revenue. As with other exercises in urban planning and development, the City is endeavoring to coordinate a variety of commercial, residential, and recreational uses of land, with the hope that they will form a whole greater than the sum of its parts. To effectuate this plan, the City has invoked a state statute that specifically authorizes the use of eminent domain to promote economic development. Given the comprehensive character of the plan, the thorough deliberation that preceded its adoption, and the limited scope of our review, it is appropriate for us, as it was in Berman, to resolve the challenges of the individual owners, not on a piecemeal basis, but rather in light of the entire plan. Because that plan unquestionably serves a public purpose, the takings challenged here satisfy the public use requirement of the Fifth Amendment.

To avoid this result, petitioners urge us to adopt a new bright-line rule that economic development does not qualify as a public use. Putting aside the unpersuasive suggestion that the City's plan will provide only purely economic benefits, neither precedent nor logic supports petitioners' proposal. Promoting economic development is a traditional and long-accepted function of government. There is, moreover, no principled way of distinguishing economic development from the other public purposes that we have recognized. . . . It would be incongruous to hold that the City's interest in the economic benefits to be derived from the development of the Fort Trumbull area has less of a public character than any of those other interests. Clearly, there is no basis for exempting economic development from our traditionally broad understanding of public purpose.

Petitioners contend that using eminent domain for economic development impermissibly blurs the boundary between public and private takings. Again, our cases foreclose this objection. Quite simply, the government's pursuit of a public purpose will often benefit individual private parties. For example, in Midkiff, the forced transfer of property conferred a direct and significant benefit on those lessees who were previously unable to purchase their homes.... The owner of the department store in Berman objected to "taking from one businessman for the benefit of another businessman. Our rejection of that contention has particular relevance to the instant case: "The public end may be as well or better served through an agency of private enterprise than through a department of government—or so the Congress might conclude. We cannot say that public ownership is the sole method of promoting the public purposes of community redevelopment projects."

It is further argued that without a bright-line rule nothing would stop a city from transferring citizen A's property to citizen B for the sole reason that citizen B will put the property to a more productive use and thus pay more taxes. Such a one-to-one transfer of property, executed outside the confines of an integrated development plan, is not presented in this case. While such an unusual exercise of government power would certainly raise a suspicion that a private purpose was afoot, the hypothetical cases posited by petitioners can be confronted if and when they arise. They do not warrant the crafting of an artificial restriction on the concept of public use.

Alternatively, petitioners maintain that for takings of this kind we should require a "reasonable certainty" that the expected public benefits will actually accrue. Such a rule, however, would represent an even greater departure from our precedent. "When the legislature's purpose is legitimate and its means are not irrational, our cases make clear that empirical debates over the wisdom of takings-no less than debates over the wisdom of other kinds of socioeconomic legislation-are not to be carried out in the federal courts." ... The disadvantages of a heightened form of review are especially pronounced in this type of case. Orderly implementation of a comprehensive redevelopment plan obviously requires that the legal rights of all interested parties be established before new construction can be commenced. A constitutional rule that required postponement of the judicial approval of every condemnation until the likelihood of success of the plan had been assured would unquestionably impose a significant impediment to the successful consummation of many such plans.

Just as we decline to second-guess the City's considered judgments about the efficacy of its development plan, we also decline to second-guess the City's determinations as to what lands it needs to acquire in order to effectuate the project. "It is not for the courts to oversee the choice of the boundary line nor to sit in review on the size of a particular project area. Once the question of the public purpose has been decided, the amount and character of land to be taken for the project and the need for a particular tract to complete the integrated plan rests in the discretion of the legislative branch."

In affirming the City's authority to take petitioners' properties, we do not minimize the hardship that condemnations may entail, notwithstanding the payment of just compensation. We emphasize that nothing in our opinion precludes any State from placing further restrictions on its exercise of the takings power. Indeed, many States already impose "public use" requirements that are stricter than the federal baseline. Some of these requirements have been established as a matter of state constitutional law, while others are expressed in state eminent domain statutes that carefully limit the grounds upon which takings may be exercised. As the submissions of the parties and their amici make clear, the necessity and wisdom of using eminent domain to promote economic development are certainly matters of legitimate public debate. This Court's authority, however, extends only to determining whether the City's proposed condemnations are for a "public use" within the meaning of the Fifth Amendment to the Federal Constitution. Because over a century of our case law interpreting that provision dictates an affirmative answer to that question, we may not grant petitioners the relief that they seek.

The judgment of the Supreme Court of Connecticut is affirmed.

JUSTICE O'CONNOR ... dissenting.

Over two centuries ago, just after the Bill of Rights was ratified, Justice Chase wrote:

"An ACT of the Legislature (for I cannot call it a law) contrary to the great first principles of the social compact, cannot be considered a rightful exercise of legislative authority.... A few instances will suffice to explain what I mean.... [A] law that takes property from A. and gives it to B: It is against all reason and justice, for a people to entrust a Legislature with SUCH powers; and, therefore, it cannot be presumed that they have done it."

Today the Court abandons this long-held, basic limitation on government power. Under the banner of economic development, all private property is now vulnerable to being taken and transferred to another private owner, so long as it might be upgraded—i.e., given to an owner who will use it in a way that the legislature deems more beneficial to the public—in the process. To reason, as the Court does, that the incidental public benefits resulting from the subsequent ordinary use of private property render economic development takings "for public use" is to wash out any distinction between private and public use of property—and thereby effectively to delete the words "for public use" from the Takings Clause of the Fifth Amendment. Accordingly I respectfully dissent....

The Fifth Amendment to the Constitution, made applicable to the States by the Fourteenth Amendment, provides that "private property [shall not] be taken for public use, without just compensation." ... [W]e have read the Fifth Amendment's language to impose two distinct conditions on the exercise of eminent domain: "[T]he taking must be for a 'public use' and 'just compensation' must be paid to the owner." ...

While the Takings Clause presupposes that government can take private property without the owner's consent, the just compensation requirement spreads the cost of condemnations and thus "prevents the public from loading upon one individual more than his just share of the burdens of government." The public use requirement, in turn, imposes a more basic limitation, circumscribing the very scope of the eminent domain power: Government may compel an individual to forfeit her property for the public's use, but not for the benefit of another private person. This requirement promotes fairness as well as security.

Where is the line between "public" and "private" property use? We give considerable deference to legislatures' determinations about what governmental activities will advantage the public. But were the political branches the sole arbiters of the public-private distinction, the Public Use Clause would amount to little more than hortatory fluff. An external, judicial check on how the public use requirement is interpreted, however limited, is necessary if this constraint on government power is to retain any meaning.

Our cases have generally identified three categories of takings that comply with the public use requirement, though it is in the nature of things that the boundaries between these categories are not always firm. Two are relatively straightforward and uncontroversial. First, the sovereign may transfer private property to public ownership-such as for a road, a hospital, or a military base. Second, the sovereign may transfer private property to private parties, often common carriers, who make the property available for the public's use-such as with a railroad, a public utility, or a stadium. But "public ownership" and "use-by-the-public" are sometimes too constricting and impractical ways to define the scope of the Public Use Clause. Thus we have allowed that, in certain circumstances and to meet certain exigencies, takings that serve a public purpose also satisfy the Constitution even if the property is destined for subsequent private use.

This case returns us for the first time in over 20 years to the hard question of when a purportedly "public purpose" taking meets the public use requirement. It presents an issue of first impression: Are economic development takings constitutional? I would hold that they are not. We are guided by two precedents about the taking of real property by eminent domain. In Berman, we upheld takings within a blighted neighborhood of Washington, D.C. The neighborhood had so deteriorated that, for example, 64.3% of its dwellings were beyond repair. It had become burdened with "overcrowding of dwellings," "lack of adequate streets and alleys," and "lack of light and air." Congress had determined that the neighborhood had become "injurious to the public health, safety, morals, and welfare" and that it was necessary to "eliminat[e] all such injurious conditions by employing all means necessary and appropriate for the purpose," including eminent domain. Mr. Berman's department store was not itself blighted. Having approved of Congress' decision to eliminate the harm to the public emanating from the blighted neighborhood, however, we did not second-guess its decision to treat the neighborhood as a whole rather than lot-by-lot.

In Midkiff, we upheld a land condemnation scheme in Hawaii whereby title in real property was taken from lessors and transferred to lessees. At that time, the State and Federal Governments owned nearly 49% of the State's land, and another 47% was in the hands of only 72 private landowners. Concentration of land ownership was so dramatic that on the State's most urbanized island, Oahu, 22 landowners owned 72.5% of the fee simple titles. The Hawaii Legislature had concluded that the oligopoly in land ownership was "skewing the State's residential fee simple market, inflating land prices, and injuring the public tranquility and welfare," and therefore enacted a condemnation scheme for redistributing title.

In those decisions, we emphasized the importance of deferring to legislative judgments about public purpose. Because courts are ill equipped to evaluate the efficacy of proposed legislative initiatives, we rejected as unworkable the idea of courts' " 'deciding on what is and is not a governmental function and . . . invalidating legislation on the basis of their view on that question at the moment of decision, a practice which has proved impracticable in other fields.' Likewise, we recognized our inability to evaluate whether, in a given case, eminent domain is a necessary means by which to pursue the legislature's ends.

Yet for all the emphasis on deference, Berman and Midkiff hewed to a bedrock principle without which our public use jurisprudence would collapse: "A purely private taking could not withstand the scrutiny of the public use requirement; it would serve no legitimate purpose of government and would thus be void." To protect that principle, those decisions reserved "a role for courts to play in reviewing a legislature's judgment of what constitutes a public use. . . .

The Court's holdings in Berman and Midkiff were true to the principle underlying the Public Use Clause. In both those cases, the extraordinary, precondemnation use of the targeted property inflicted affirmative harm on society—in Berman through blight resulting from extreme poverty and in Midkiff through oligopoly resulting from extreme wealth. And in both cases, the relevant legislative body had found that eliminating the existing property use was necessary to remedy the harm. Thus a public purpose was realized when the harmful use was eliminated. Because each taking directly achieved a public benefit, it did not matter that the property was turned over to private use. Here, in contrast, New London does not claim that Susette Kelo's . . . well-maintained home [is] the source of any social harm. Indeed, it could not so claim without adopting the absurd argument that any single-family home that might be razed to make way for an apartment building, or any church that might be replaced with a retail store, or any small business that might be more lucrative if it were instead part of a national franchise, is inherently harmful to society and thus within the government's power to condemn.

In moving away from our decisions sanctioning the condemnation of harmful property use, the Court today significantly expands the meaning of public use. It holds that the sovereign may take private property currently put to ordinary private use, and give it over for new, ordinary private use, so long as the new use is predicted to generate some secondary benefit for the public-such as increased tax revenue, more jobs, maybe even esthetic pleasure. But nearly any lawful use of real private property can be said to generate some incidental benefit to the public. Thus, if predicted (or even guaranteed) positive side effects are enough to render transfer from one private party to another constitutional, then the words "for public use" do not realistically exclude any takings, and thus do not exert any constraint on the eminent domain power. . . .

The Court protests that it does not sanction the bare transfer from A to B for B's benefit. It suggests two limitations on what can be taken after today's decision. First, it maintains a role for courts in ferreting out takings whose sole purpose is to bestow a benefit on the private transfer-ee-without detailing how courts are to conduct that complicated inquiry . . . The trouble with economic development takings is that private benefit and incidental public benefit are, by definition, merged and mutually reinforcing. In this case, for example, any boon for Pfizer or the plan's developer is difficult to disaggregate from the promised public gains in taxes and jobs.

Even if there were a practical way to isolate the motives behind a given taking, the gesture toward a purpose test is theoretically flawed. If it is true that incidental public benefits from new private use are enough to ensure the "public purpose" in a taking, why should it matter, as far as the Fifth Amendment is concerned, what inspired the taking in the first place? How much the government does or does not desire to benefit a favored private party has no bearing on whether an economic development taking will or will not generate secondary benefit for the public. And whatever the reason for a given condemnation, the effect is the same from the constitutional perspective-private property is forcibly relinquished to new private ownership.

A second proposed limitation is implicit in the Court's opinion. The logic of today's decision is that eminent domain may only be used to upgrade-not downgrade-property. At best this makes the Public Use Clause redundant with the Due Process Clause, which already prohibits irrational government action. The Court rightfully admits, however, that the judiciary cannot get bogged down in predictive judgments about whether the public will actually be better off after a property transfer. In any event, this constraint has no realistic import. For who among us can say she already makes the most productive or attractive possible use of her property? The specter of condemnation hangs over all property.

Nothing is to prevent the State from replacing any Motel 6 with a Ritz–Carlton, any home with a shopping mall, or any farm with a factory.

The Court also puts special emphasis on facts peculiar to this case: The NLDC's plan is the product of a relatively careful deliberative process; it proposes to use eminent domain for a multipart, integrated plan rather than for isolated property transfer; it promises an array of incidental benefits (even esthetic ones), not just increased tax revenue; it comes on the heels of a legislative determination that New London is a depressed municipality.... But none has legal significance to blunt the force of today's holding. If legislative prognostications about the secondary public benefits of a new use can legitimate a taking, there is nothing in the Court's rule ... to prohibit property transfers generated with less care, that are less comprehensive, that happen to result from less elaborate process, whose only projected advantage is the incidence of higher taxes, or that hope to transform an already prosperous city into an even more prosperous one.

Finally, in a coda, the Court suggests that property owners should turn to the States, who may or may not choose to impose appropriate limits on economic development takings. This is an abdication of our responsibility. States play many important functions in our system of dual sovereignty, but compensating for our refusal to enforce properly the Federal Constitution (and a provision meant to curtail state action, no less) is not among them.

It was possible after Berman and Midkiff to imagine unconstitutional transfers from A to B. Those decisions endorsed government intervention when private property use had veered to such an extreme that the public was suffering as a consequence. Today nearly all real property is susceptible to condemnation on the Court's theory. In the prescient words of a dissenter from the infamous decision in Poletown, "[n]ow that we have authorized local legislative bodies to decide that a different commercial or industrial use of property will produce greater public benefits than its present use, no homeowner's, merchant's or manufacturer's property, however productive or valuable to its owner, is immune from condemnation for the benefit of other private interests that will put it to a 'higher' use. This is why economic development takings "seriously jeopardiz[e] the security of all private property ownership."

Any property may now be taken for the benefit of another private party, but the fallout from this decision will not be random. The beneficiaries are likely to be those citizens with disproportionate influence and power in the political process, including large corporations and development firms. As for the victims, the government now has license to transfer property from those with fewer resources to those with more. The Founders cannot have intended this perverse result. "[T]hat alone is a just government," wrote James Madison, "which impartially secures to every man, whatever is his own."

I would hold that the takings ... are unconstitutional, reverse the judgment of the Supreme Court of Connecticut, and remand for further proceedings.

NOTES AND QUESTIONS ABOUT THE KELO CASE

The primary reason for including the Kelo decision in this Chapter was to set the stage for the ensuing discussion of the public policy issues that weigh on the government's decision to provide incentives to aid a private development project. The four key questions raised and answered by the Supreme Court in Kelo are summarized below.

- ***Can the government exercise its eminent domain powers to assist a project which will be owned by a private party?*** Justice Stevens' majority opinion makes it clear that the fact that the land taken by the government will ultimately find its way into the hands of private ownership does not, in and of itself, invalidate the government's exercise of its eminent domain powers.[70] Justice Stevens did, however, issue an important caveat in his aside that a city would not be "allowed to take property under the mere pretext of a public purpose, when its actual purpose was to bestow a private benefit."[71] Since the date of the Kelo decision, a number of challenges have been mounted seeking to override a government's exercise of its eminent domain powers on the theory that its finding of a public use to support the taking was a mere pretext for the grant of a purely private benefit to a real estate developer.[72]

- ***Does economic development qualify as a public use?*** The affirmative answer provided to that question in Justice Stevens' majority opinion[73] has served as the trigger for a populist outrage in many parts of the country. The counterpoint in the debate concerning the sufficiency of economic development as a public use is presented by Justice O'Connor's now famous assertion that, under the majority opinion in Kelo, "Nothing is to prevent the State from replacing any Motel 6 with a Ritz–Carlton, any home with a shopping mall, or any farm with a factory."[74] As will be discussed in the next section of this Chapter, a resolution of the Motel 6/Ritz–Carlton quandary has particular significance to the political determination when and whether it makes sense

---

70. *See* Kelo, 545 U.S. at 485–486.

71. *See id.* at 478.

72. *See e.g.*, Goldstein v. Pataki, 516 F.3d 50 (2d Cir. 2008); Franco v. National Capital Revitalization Corp., 930 A.2d 160 (DC 2007); and Kaur v. N.Y.S. Urban Development Corp., 72 A.D.3d 1 (1 Dept. N.Y. 2009). For a more detailed discussion of post-*Kelo* cases adopting the "pretext" challenge, *see* Daniel B. Kelly, *Supreme Court Economics Review Symposium on Post–Kelo Reform: Pretextual Takings: Of Private Developers, Local Governments and Impermissible Favoritism*, 17 SUPREME COURT ECONOMIC REVIEW 173 (2009).

73. *See Kelo* 545 U.S. at 484–486.

74. *See id.* at 503.

for a government to provide incentives to assist a private development project.

- **What level of deference is to be afforded a governmental finding of the existence of a public use?** The majority opinion in Kelo placed a great deal of emphasis on the fact that the City of New London "carefully formulated an economic development plan that it believes will provide appreciable benefits to the community, including—but by no means limited to—new jobs and increased tax revenue."[75] Justice Steven then noted that "we decline to second-guess the City's considered judgment about the efficacy of its development plan."[76] The emphasis on the deference to be afforded a "carefully formulated plan" has been seized upon by other courts to justify governmental takings in a number of post-Kelo decisions.[77]

- **Can states adopt a more restrictive interpretation of the nature of the public use required to justify a governmental taking of private property?** Justice Stevens comment that "nothing in our opinion precludes any State from placing further restrictions on its exercise of the takings power"[78] has served as an opening for a number of states to impose significant judicial and legislative limitations on the eminent domain powers of state and local governments.[79] The Ohio Supreme Court in Norwood v. Horney embraced the sentiments expressed by Justice O'Connor in her Kelo dissent in its holding that "any taking based solely on financial gain is void as a matter of law and the courts owe no deference to a legislative finding that the proposed taking will provide financial benefit to the community."[80] Other courts have invalidated government takings in the post-Kelo environment based on the "pretextual" argument mentioned earlier in this section.[81]

The real incursions on the substance of the Kelo holding have taken place not in the courts, but in state legislatures. An overwhelming majority of the states have adopted some type of statutory or constitutional limitations on the government's eminent domain powers.[82] The legislative approaches adopted

---

75. *See id.* at 483.

76. *See id.* at 489.

77. *See generally* Amy Brigham Boulris and Annette Lopez, *2007–2008 Update on Judicial Reactions to Kelo,* in ALI–ABA COURSE OF STUDY MATERIALS, EMINENT DOMAIN AND LAND VALUATION LITIGATION, Course #SP–006, 63 (January 2009); and Ross F. Moskowitz and Joan H. Kim, *Eminent Domain: The Taking of Private Property for Public Use—An Examination of Recent New York State Decisions in Light of Kelo v. City of New London,* REAL ESTATE FINANCE JOURNAL 82 (Spring 2010).

78. *Kelo,* 545 U.S. at 489.

79. *See generally* Boulris, *supra* note 77; and Steven J. Eagle and Lauren A. Perotti, *Coping with Kelo: A Potpourri of Legislative and Judicial Responses,* 42 REAL PROPERTY, PROBATE AND TRUST JOURNAL 799 (Winter 2008).

80. *See* Norwood v. Horney, 110 Ohio St.3d 353, 378.

81. *See* sources cited *supra* note 77.

82. According to one professor, since the *Kelo* decision was handed down in June, 2005, 42 states have enacted legislation or constitutional amendments attempting to limit the ability of state and local governments to exercise their eminent domain powers. *See* Andrew P. Morriss, *Supreme Court Economic Review Symposium on Post–Kelo Reform: Symbol or Substance? An Empirical Assessment of State Responses to Kelo,* 17 SUPREME COURT ECONOMIC REVIEW 237 (2009).

by the states generally fall into one of two categories—(1) a flat-out prohibition on the government's exercise of its eminent domain powers to aid any project that will be owned by a private developer or (2) a restriction that a government may only use eminent domain to help a private development project if the purpose of that project is the remediation of "blight" (with the definition of "blight" being very specifically and narrowly defined to exclude economic development).[83] Based on the actions taken in the last few years by state legislatures, it is safe to say that the government's use of its eminent domain powers to aid a private development project has a more limited application today than it did in the immediate aftermath of Kelo.[84]

XI. PUBLIC POLICY ISSUES

This Chapter has now addressed two of the three questions that always characterize any discussion of Stage 2 of a real estate development project—(1) why does a private development project need governmental incentives (and why does the government want to make those incentives available to the developer) and (2) what can the government do to aid the private development project? A much tougher to answer question is should the government provide incentives to a private development project? Answering that question requires a closer examination of the various public policy issues that a government must weigh each time a developer asks it for help

A. THE GOVERNMENT'S BET

Before venturing into the thorny entanglement of public policy issues, it is important to first focus on the nature of the "bet" that the government makes each time it decides to provide incentives to a private development project. As noted earlier in this Chapter,[85] a government lends its support to a private development project to grow its revenue base and advance its social policy agenda. The use of incentives to serve these goals creates the following two-pronged dilemma for the government:

However, Professor Morriss notes in his article that about half of the adopted restrictions were more symbolic than substantive. *See id.* at 240.

83. *See* Eagle, *supra* note 79, at 802–803.

84. In an interesting aside to the *Kelo* case, the New York Times reported in November 2009 that the Pfizer Company is planning to close its offices in New London and move approximately 1,400 jobs out of the city. Pfizer was, of course, the anchor of the economic development project that the City of New London was attempting to support when it opted to use its eminent domain powers to take Susette Kelo's house. Pfizer's departure will leave the City of New London with an empty office complex and acres of vacant land that were cleared to make room for hotels, shops, offices and condominiums that were never built. In a final irony, Pfizer now plans to consolidate its Connecticut operations in Groton, the town where Susette Kelo now lives—some people just can't catch a break. *See* Patrick McGeehan, *Pfizer to Leave City that Won Land Use Case*, New York Times, November 13, 2009, at A1.

85. *See supra* Pages 156–158.

- In the short-term, the government's decision to provide incentives to a private project either (1) depletes the government's existing revenue base (if it uses existing revenues to provide grants or other financial subsidies to the incentivized project) or (2) defers the government's access to the new revenues generated from the private project (if it uses tax abatements or a TIF to incentivize the private project); and

- The byproduct of the government's use of incentives to serve its social policy objectives is frequently an increase in the project's development costs—a circumstance that almost always causes the developer to return to the well and ask for more financial and tax giveaways, which, in turn, further depletes the government's existing revenue base.

In other words, by using incentives to serve its long-term objectives, the government inevitably worsens its short-term, revenue position.

When it provides public incentives to a private development project, the government is effectively betting that the incentivized project will be a long-term success and that the existence of that project will create jobs, increase property values and spur additional development in the surrounding neighborhood. If those things do not occur, then the government will lose its bet, with the end result that its coffers will be less full than when it first decided to sponsor the incentivized project. The importance of the government making the right bet is highlighted by the fact that it is estimated that state and local governments expend somewhere in the neighborhood of $50 BILLION ANNUALLY in an effort to stimulate economic development.[86]

One economist has characterized the government's bet in the following manner.

> The issue isn't whether economic development incentives can work; empirical evidence suggests they can. The issues are whether benefits of incentives outweigh costs, and how benefits and costs are affected by local conditions and incentive design.[87]

Although Mr. Bartik's statement is both thoughtful and succinct, I prefer to think about the government's bet in much less academic terms. As one who greatly enjoys sitting down at a blackjack table in Vegas, I view the decision of a government to give incentives to a private development project as being a bit like doubling down on an eleven—it produces a

---

86. *See* CHICAGO METROPOLITAN AGENCY FOR PLANNING, *supra* note 19, at 3. The $50 billion figure does not take into account any incentives made available by the federal government. An additional measure of the significance of the government's bet is provided by a recent study commissioned by the Ohio Department of Development, which estimated that the property taxes foregone by school districts in Ohio as a result of the grant of property tax abatements and the use of TIFs is approximately $2.6 billion. *See* OHIO DEPARTMENT OF DEVELOPMENT, OHIO ECONOMIC DEVELOPMENT INCENTIVE STUDY 39 (May 2009).

87. *See* Timothy J. Bartik, *Eight Issues for Policy toward Economic Development Incentives,* W.E. UPJOHN INSTITUTE FOR EMPLOYMENT RESEARCH (1996). Mr. Bartik's paper was published by the Minneapolis Federal Reserve for a conference held in Washington D.C. on May 21–22, 1996, on the topic of *The Economic War among the States.*

wonderful result if your next card has a picture on it, but it will likely cost you twice as much money if the next card is a deuce. The economic development officer's challenge is to figure out what the next card turned over by the dealer will be—a deuce or a jack. The public policy discussion that follows is intended to describe the context in which the economic development officer makes that judgment.[88]

B. PUBLIC PURPOSE

The first policy question that the economic development officer must answer when weighing the use of governmental incentives to aid a private development project is, does the provision of incentives serve a valid public purpose? In answering that question, the economic development officer (with a little help from the ever friendly real estate development lawyer) needs to consult three different sources—(1) the statute that creates the incentive, (2) case law interpreting the public purpose doctrine and (3) the one most often ignored by lawyers, the body politic. If any one of those sources provides a "no" answer to the proffered question, the economic development officer should reject the notion of providing incentives to the private development project.

1. Statutory Definition

Most statutory and constitutional provisions authorizing the use of a governmental incentive establish the existence of a public purpose as a precondition to the government's provision of such incentive. The lawyers representing both the developer and the government must begin their respective analyses of the public purpose issue with a close examination of the definition of and context in which such term is used in the enabling statutory or constitutional provision. By way of example, if the operative state statute provides that the only public purpose supporting the creation of a TIF is the remediation of blight, it then becomes the lawyers' jobs to divine whether the private development project being proposed by the developer satisfies the blight remediation test.

2. Judicial Interpretation

There is a rich body of case law interpreting the doctrine of public purpose in the context of a variety of different governmental incentives.[89]

---

88. In keeping with the blackjack analogy, I would be remiss if I didn't point out that there is nothing that forces the economic development officer to sit down at the betting table in the first place. Government can avoid making its bet if it "just says no" when it is asked to provide incentives to a private development project. The downside of that approach is, of course, that the government may lose the opportunity to enhance its long-term revenue base by helping a private developer kick off a project that ultimately proves to be wildly successful for both the developer and the government. The upside of "just saying no" is that another developer may come along at some point down the road with an idea for an even better project (and, even better yet, one that doesn't require the government's provision of any incentives).

89. *See e.g.*, Maready v. City of Winston–Salem, 467 S.E.2d 615 (N.C. 1996) (finding a valid public purpose for the provision of approximately $13.2 million in governmental incentives for businesses agreeing to locate in Winston–Salem, North Carolina); Blinson v. State, 651 S.E.2d 268 (N.C. App. 2007) (upholding the existence of a valid public purpose for the government's provision

Some of that case law was alluded to earlier in this Chapter as part of the discussion of tax increment financing and the Kelo case.[90] The remainder of the case law on the public purpose topic is sufficiently nuanced and varied by jurisdiction that a lawyer spending time structuring and negotiating incentive packages has no choice but to become and stay fully versed on the decisions rendered by the courts of his state.

It should be noted, however, that there is a common theme running throughout most of the case law on the public purpose doctrine—specifically, that the courts are extremely hesitant to overturn a legislative finding that the provision of a public incentive to a private project is supported by a valid public purpose.[91] Whether the judiciary's extreme deference to legislative findings of public purpose will continue in the post-Kelo legal and political environments is a question that will likely play out in the courts over the next decade.[92]

3. Political Decision

The most important definition of public purpose is found not in the language of an enabling statute or the text of an appellate court decision, but rather in the constantly evolving opinions of the true gatekeepers of governmental incentive packages—the mayors, city council members, county commissioners, township trustees, economic development officers and other government officials, who are asked on a daily basis to make an evaluation as to whether a particular private development project merits the receipt of a governmental incentive. There is, unfortunately no guidebook that the real estate lawyer can consult to provide him with the specifics of this political definition of public purpose. The political definition of public purpose changes daily (and sometimes hourly) based on the sentiments of the electorate and the perceptions of such sentiments by the government's elected and appointed officials. An incentive package that is meticulously crafted by the developer's lawyer to comply with the public purpose parameters specified by applicable statutory and case law will

---

of approximately $242 million in incentives to induce Dell, Inc. to build a facility in North Carolina); Poe v. Hillsborough County, 695 So.2d 672 (Fla. 1997) (confirming the existence of a public purpose to support the government's issuance of approximately $180 million in bonds to finance the construction of a stadium for the Tampa Bay Buccaneers). For a general discussion of the evolution of the public purpose doctrine, *see* Anne C. Choe, *Recent Development: Blinson v. State and the Continued Erosion of the Public Purpose Doctrine in North Carolina*, 87 NORTH CAROLINA LAW REVIEW 644 (2009); Thaddeus Pitney, *Loans, and Takings, and Buildings—Oh My: A Necessary Difference between Public Purpose and Public Use in Economic Development*, 56 SYRACUSE LAW REVIEW 321 (2006);and Gregory W. Fox, *Note, Public Finance and the West Side Stadium: The Future of Stadium Subsidies in New York*, 71 BROOKLYN LAW REVIEW 477 (2005).

90. *See supra* Pages 162–166 and 183–185.

91. *See* Pitney, *supra* note 89, at 330–332; and Audrey G. McFarlane, *Local Economic Development Incentives in an Era of Globalization: The Exploitation of Decentralization and Mobility*, 35 URBAN LAWYER 305, 312–313 (2003).

92. There is little doubt that courts post-*Kelo* have shown less deference to legislative findings related to the topic of governmental takings than they did before *Kelo* decision was handed down. *See* Boulris, *supra* note 77, at 1–2. However, some commentators have noted that the public purpose doctrine should be construed more strictly in the context of a governmental taking than it should in the context of the provision of other governmental incentives (principally because of the more direct involvement of private property rights in the eminent domain arena). *See generally* Pitney, *supra* note 89.

nonetheless be doomed for rejection if the developer is unable to convince four of seven township trustees to vote for it. No truer words were ever spoken than when a city council member commented to me in the middle of a heated discussion that "public purpose is what I say it is."

Practice Tip #6–1: Hiring Political Clout

The grant of governmental incentives is, at its essence, a political process. In almost every instance, a developer's receipt of an incentive is dependent upon a discretionary, legislative or regulatory determination being made that the developer's project is worthy of assistance from the public sector. That determination is part legal (i.e., are the tests set forth in the enabling statute satisfied), but even more political. When casting their vote for or against the grant of an incentive, the government officials tasked with that responsibility must answer two basic questions—(1) is the grant of the incentive good public policy and (2) will the grant of the incentive poll favorably with the officials' voting constituency? The real estate development lawyer's job is to persuade the government officials that the answer to both those questions is "yes."

It has been my experience that a real estate development lawyer is usually well-advised to retain outside counsel to help its developer client secure the sought after incentives. This is especially true when the development project is located outside of the lawyer's primary, practice jurisdiction. In hiring outside counsel, the development lawyer should look for someone who knows local politics and has personal access to those government officials, who will be making the ultimate determination on the grant of the incentives to assist the developer's project. While hiring such political clout is important, the real estate development lawyer must make sure to retain someone that he is comfortable with becoming the public face for the developer during the course of the incentive negotiations. Hiring the mayor's best drinking buddy won't work, unless that person also has the talent and style to do the job in a manner commensurate with the developer's overall approach to the real estate development business. Stated differently, it is crucial that outside incentive counsel be retained not just for who he knows, but also for what he knows.

C.   THE BUT FOR TEST

It is quite common for a developer to approach its state and local economic development officers with a simple proposition—that is, the government needs to provide a whole laundry list of incentives to support the developer's private project or the project will never be built. When braced with such a comment, the economic development officers (and, ultimately, the members of the legislative and regulatory bodies that must cast their votes for or against the incentive grant) must decide whether the project satisfies or fails the political but for test.[93] Is the developer correct in saying that the development will not occur but for the provision of governmental incentives or is developer just bluffing in an attempt to further feather its already plush nest? Ultimately, the success of the government's bet on the project will be dependent on how accurately it answers the but for test.[94]

If the economic development officers decide to call the developer's bluff based on their belief that the project will proceed with or without incentives and the developer then pulls the plug on the project, the development officers probably should start looking for another job. However, their tenure as civil servants will also be called into question if they give into the developer's demands and further deplete the government's coffers, only to subsequently learn that the project was destined to go full speed ahead with or without the assistance of the state and local governments.

It is a commonly accepted notion that government should not provide incentives to a project if the project would have been developed without the incentives.[95] A recent study issued by the Ohio Department of Development sums up this point by in the following fashion.

> [N]ot all development requires direct public assistance, and public assistance is not an entitlement. Incentives should be concentrated on encouraging those projects that would not go forward in our state without incentives.[96]

However, as noted in a report presented to the Federal Reserve Bank of Atlanta, "it is impossible to know what might have happened without incentives."[97] In order to realistically assess whether a project would have occurred without public support, government officials need to get inside the developer's head by receiving, reviewing and analyzing all of the financial, demographic, marketing and other development information that the developer took into account when making its decision concerning the feasibility of the proposed project. Obvious questions abound as to both the completeness and accuracy of the information provided to the government by the developer, and the government's capability of reviewing that information to make a well-reasoned decision of the project's feasibility. Therefore, while government must always confront the but for

---

93. *See* Pages 163, 165, *supra*, for a discussion of the "but for" test in the specific context of a TIF.

94. The application of the "but for" test assumes, in the first instance, that the government wants the developer's project to go forward. If the government doesn't care whether a particular project ever happens, then it never has to solve the "but for" test.

95. *See* CHICAGO METROPOLITAN AGENCY FOR PLANNING, *supra* note 19, at 3.

96. *See* OHIO DEPARTMENT OF DEVELOPMENT, *supra* note 86, at 41.

97. *See* Jessica LeVeen Farr, *Attracting Economic Development—At What Cost?* 15 No. 3 PARTNERS IN COMMUNITY AND ECONOMIC DEVELOPMENT 1 (December 22, 2005). *See also* Timothy J. Bartik and Richard D. Bingham, *Can Economic Development Programs Be Evaluated,* DILEMMAS OF URBAN ECONOMIC DEVELOPMENT, 246, 250 (Richard D. Bingham and Robert Miers eds., 1997).

test when deciding whether it will provide assistance to a private development project, the application of that test is inherently much more ad hoc and political in nature than it is empirical.

D. THE ZERO SUM GAME

On the public policy front, the *zero sum game* is a close relative to the but for test. As noted under the previous heading, the but for test requires governmental officials to determine whether a developer's project would happen with or without the provision olf governmental incentives. The zero sum game comes into play when the question is not whether the developer's project will happen (the but for test), but rather whether it will happen in jurisdiction A or jurisdiction B? The zero sum game is played when the developer successfully pits one jurisdiction against another in a crusade to maximize the amount of incentives the developer receives for the project.[98] The "zero sum" nomenclature refers to the fact that the larger economy (be it global, federal or state) will not be affected one way or the other by the developer's decision where to locate its project. If the developer selects jurisdiction A over jurisdiction B, the gains flowing to jurisdiction A will be directly and equally offset by the losses flowing to jurisdiction B.[99] In the zero sum game, the developer wins, the larger economy loses (or at best breaks even) and jurisdictions A and B are the recipient of offsetting gains and losses.

The public policy issue presented by the zero sum game is whether a legitimate public purpose is served by a governmental entity's provision of incentives to cause a developer to choose one jurisdiction over another as the location for its project. Should a particular political subdivision be required to think about the greater good which would best be served if no incentives were provided to the developer, thereby maximizing the tax revenues generated from the project and forcing the developer to make a location decision on the merits and not on the artifice of a particular jurisdiction's incentive package? Or is it legitimate for a local governmental official to fashion whatever incentives are required to cause a developer to select its community over a neighboring community?

Some very scholarly articles have been written about the policy merits of permitting political subdivisions to compete for private development

---

98. The bidding war that breaks out when jurisdictions compete for a particular project has been pejoratively referred to by some commentators as the "economic race to the bottom." These commentators assert that jurisdictions are unnecessarily giving away their tax bases by engaging in incentive competitions with other jurisdictions. *See e.g.*, Farr, *supra* note 97, at 2. *But see* Bartik, *supra* note 87, at 3–4, for a presentation of the opposing view that "competition should bid business taxes down to equal the marginal cost of providing businesses with public services, . . . minus the marginal social benefit the businesses provide by creating jobs. Such a business tax system is economically efficient."

99. One writer has noted that what results from interstate competition for a particular business or project is "at best, not job creation but job relocation from one area in the Unites States to another." *See* Peter D. Enrich, *Business Tax Incentives: A Status Report,* 34 URBAN LAWYER 415, 416 (2002)

projects through the offering of incentives.[100] Most of those articles take the position that the zero sum game is detrimental to the economy as a whole and that legislation should be adopted that prevents states[101] and local jurisdictions[102] from offering incentives designed to cause a business to relocate to a particular state or locale. However, as long as tax revenues are generated and spent at the local level, it seems likely that governmental entities will continue to play the zero sum game.[103]

E. EFFICACY OF INCENTIVES

The final public policy question that must be addressed by government officials is whether governmental incentives really work.[104] A fair amount of analysis and self-examination has occurred in recent years concerning the efficacy of the use of governmental incentives. A 2009 study commissioned by the Chicago Metropolitan Agency for Planning concluded that "on balance, the available research on the effectiveness and impacts of economic development incentives yields mixed results."[105] Recent reports examining the governmental incentive programs offered in Michigan and Ohio have reached similar, inconclusive conclusions.[106]

---

100. *See* literature summary discussed in CHICAGO METROPOLITAN AGENCY FOR PLANNING, *supra* note 19, at 32–36. *See also* Bartik, supra note 87; and McFarlane, *supra* note 91.

101. *See* Melvin L. Burnstein and Arthur J. Rolnick, *Congress Should End the Economic War Among the States,* 96 STATE TAX NOTES 125–44 (June 27, 1996) for a discussion of the perceived need for Congress to pass federal legislation prohibiting states from competing with one another to retain and attract businesses through the provision of tax and other financial incentives. Also, a number of taxpayer lawsuits have been filed in the last several years seeking to use the Commerce Clause of the United States Constitution to invalidate a state's use of tax incentives to convince a business to locate within its borders. *See e.g.*, DaimlerChrysler Corp. v. Cuno, 547 U.S. 332 (2006), *vacating and remanding in part* 386 F.3d 738 (6th Cir. 2004); Olson v. State, 742 N.W.2d 681 (Minn. Ct. App. 2007); and Blinson v. State, 651 S.E.2d 268 (N.C. App. 2007). Those cases have all been decided in the government's favor. *See generally*, Morgan L. Holcomb and Nicholas Allen Smith, *Community Efforts to Attract and Retain Corporations: Legal and Policy Implications of State and Local Tax Incentives and Eminent Domain: The Post–Cuno Litigation Landscape,* 58 CASE WESTERN RESERVE LAW REVIEW 1157 (Summer 2008).

102. *See* CHICAGO METROPOLITAN AGENCY FOR PLANNING, *supra* note 19, at 19.

103. The impetus to play the game is particularly pronounced in states such as Pennsylvania, Ohio and Michigan that are experiencing high unemployment and large revenue deficits. Given those circumstances, it is wholly unrealistic to expect that elected and appointed government officials will not use every available public incentive to lure private development projects to their particular jurisdictions in an effort to spur job creation and raise additional tax revenues. If they don't do so, they will, in all likelihood, be looking for private sector jobs in the very near term.

104. As noted earlier in this Chapter, governmental incentives work only if (1) the revenues generated from the incentivized project are greater than the government's cost of providing the incentives and (2) the project would not have been developed but for the grant of the incentives. A more lofty public policy issue is whether "instead of paying cash to corporations or foregoing tax revenues, the better approach is to focus on educating and training a state's citizens as well as making the environment a safe and attractive place to live with amenities that would be attractive to the type of personnel employed by business corporations." *See* McFarlane, *supra* note 91, at 315. A resolution of that issue is well beyond the scope of this Chapter and, most certainly, the competency of the author.

105. *See* CHICAGO METROPOLITAN AGENCY FOR PLANNING, *supra* note 19, at 18.

106. *See* OHIO DEPARTMENT OF DEVELOPMENT, *supra* note 86; and ANDERSON ECONOMIC GROUP LLC, MICHIGAN'S BUSINESS TAX INCENTIVES (2009).

The real question is whether the incentives provided by the government truly impact developer and user conduct. Does a developer decide to proceed with a particular type of project in a particular location as a direct result of its receipt of governmental incentives or are the provided governmental incentives just a way for the developer to increase its NOI and otherwise enhance the value of its project? Does a prospective tenant or buyer decide to lease or buy space in a project because of its receipt of incentives or are those incentives truly incidental to its space decision and, as such, just a pot sweetener?

The answers to these questions depend, in large part, on the identity of the responder. Most government officials take the position that "incentives remain one of the only tools available to localities attempting to create jobs and enhance their revenue streams."[107] Legal scholars and representatives of taxpayer groups tend to conclude that "they don't work—no business executive worth his salt will make a location decision based on state ... incentives."[108] Economists tend to equivocate (imagine that) by pointing out that the "upshot ... is that on this most basic question of all—whether incentives induce significant new investment or jobs—we simply do not know the answer."[109] Finally the intended recipient of the governmental incentive (a developer or user) characteristically responds by saying "they work for me."

My own 30+ years of experience in the private sector tells me that incentives do, in fact, work—sometimes. There are good projects that create jobs, add to the government's revenue base and advance socially important goals, which would simply not be feasible without the receipt of governmental incentives. There are also plenty of projects that do not serve any of the government's economic, social or political objectives, but which nonetheless receive governmental incentives because that is simply the way business is now done in the 21st century. It is the government's job to examine all of the existing facts and circumstances surrounding a particular development project to try to ferret out which incentives work and when those incentives are needed to encourage a private development project.

A related issue is what happens if the benefits produced from the use of governmental incentives don't materialize in the intended manner—for example, the project doesn't produce the 500 new jobs heralded by the developer or the developer delays its construction of the affordable hous-

---

107. *See* CHICAGO METROPOLITAN AGENCY FOR PLANNING, *supra* note 19, at 3.

108. *See* David Brunori, *The Politics of State Taxation: Helping States to Hurt Themselves,* STATE TAX NOTES 752 (June 6, 2005).

109. *See* Alan Peters and Peter Fisher, *The Failures of Economic Development Incentives,* 70 JOURNAL OF AMERICAN PLANNING ASSOCIATION 1, 27 (2004). In defense of economists generally (and Messrs. Peters and Fisher specifically), it should be noted that there is a growing consensus among economists that "there are very good reasons—theoretical, empirical and practical—to believe that economic development incentives have little or no impact on firm location and investment decisions." *See id.* There is also a developing consensus that, while incentives "rarely tip the location choice ... across different regions ... [they] do contribute somewhat to interregional business location decisions." *See* CHICAGO METROPOLITAN AGENCY FOR PLANNING, *supra* note 19, at 32.

ing units that were central to its receipt of a density bonus? The trend in recent years is to clearly articulate in a development agreement signed by the developer and the government the specific actions that must be taken by the developer to establish its entitlement to and continued retention of the benefit of the governmental incentives.[110] By way of example, the development agreement could recite that the project's payroll tax rebate is contingent upon the project producing 500 new jobs and the developer completing its affordable housing units within three years from the date of the parties' execution of the development agreement.

The key from the government's perspective is that the development agreement must contain effective governmental remedies for the developer's failure to meet the conditions recited in the agreement. The following are some examples of remedies that can be used to protect the interests of the government if the developer fails to comply with all of the conditions and obligations placed upon it under the terms of the applicable development agreement:[111]

- A denial of a governmental certificate of occupancy for the project;

- An automatic suspension of the continued operation of the incentive; or

- A required repayment by the developer of the economic benefit of the incentive.[112]

All of the above protections are intended to allocate to the developer the risk that the project fails to generate the intended governmental benefit due to the developer's failure to perform. The same protections are not, however, typically afforded the government if the project fails to produce the anticipated benefit because of a dislocation in the market or some other cause beyond the developer's control (including an initial misreading of the market dynamics by the government).

XII. THE PERILS OF A PUBLIC–PRIVATE PARTNERSHIP

The focus of this Chapter has thus far been on the benefits produced for both the private and public sectors by the government's provision of incentives to encourage the development of a private real estate project. When all the stars align properly, the collaborative efforts of a private developer and the government (a so-called ***public-private partnership*** or a ***PPP***)[113] can produce wonderful results for both the public and private

---

110. *See* Theodore C. Taub, *The ABC's of PPP's: How to Structure Public–Private Partnerships for Real Estate Development Projects,* in ALI–ABA COURSE OF STUDY MATERIALS, LAND USE INSTITUTE: PLANNING, REGULATION, LITIGATION, EMINENT DOMAIN AND COMPENSATION, Course #SR–004, 903 (August 2009).

111. *See* McMillan, *supra* note 18, at 14.

112. This is a so-called "clawback" provision, where the developer has to refund to the government the full economic benefit of the granted incentive—e.g., the taxes exempted under a real estate tax abatement or the infrastructure costs funded through a TIF.

113. The growing trend of government adopting a more active role in the development of private real estate projects has given rise to the coining of the term "public-private partnership."

sectors—witness such high profile PPP projects as Faneuil Hall Marketplace in Boston, the Inner Harbor redevelopment in Baltimore and the Arena District project in Columbus, Ohio.[114] There is, however, a definite downside to the creation of a PPP from the perspectives of both the developer and the government.

From the government's perspective, the negatives associated with the creation of a PPP are mostly political in nature. A governmental entity that is interested in supporting development within its borders has little choice but to collaborate in some fashion with the private sector—for the simple reason that government does not possess the expertise, experience or staffing needed to pull off a complicated real estate development project.[115] The necessity underlying its participation in a PPP does not, however, insulate the government from the cries of the general public that the government has sold out to rich developers and is not looking out for the best interests of its citizenry. If a PPP with a private developer fails, the end result is often the one thing that both appointed and elected government officials fear most—the loss of the incumbent party at the next election.

Participation in a PPP also has a decided downside for the private developer. Developers who are used to controlling their own destinies and being able to respond quickly to market changes and development challenges will find their collaboration with the public sector to be frustrating and sometimes excruciatingly painful. The following are some of the negatives associated with a developer's participation in a PPP.

- **_Loss of Development Control_**—An inevitable consequence of a developer's request for governmental incentives is the developer's loss of some level of control over the design, construction and operation of its development project. A governmental entity providing economic and development support for a private project typically demands some role in the development process (in much the same way that a private equity investor demands a presence at the table when it provides funding for a private development project). From the developer's perspective, the participation of the public sector in the development process is particularly rankling for two reasons—(a) development is a dynamic and often chaotic process that is a bit like the making of sausage—in other words, a process which, by definition, does not stand up well to public scrutiny and (b) most developers believe that government officials are clueless when it comes to the reality of project economics and private real estate markets.

As the term is used in today's real estate culture, a public-private partnership or PPP refers to any project in which the government provides some project-specific support (as opposed to its general oversight of all similarly situated real estate projects).

114.   For a discussion of these and other PPP projects, see Miles, *supra* note 26, *Chapter 14: Meshing Public and Private Roles in the Development Process.*

115.   *See* Leinberger, *supra* note 10, at 8.

- ***Protracted Development Schedules***—Negotiating and approving a PPP is an exacting and complex process that often takes an inordinate amount of the developer's time. The end result is that a PPP project takes much longer to plan and complete than does the typical private development project—a circumstance that can call into question the ultimate profitability of the project.

- ***Increased Project Costs***—PPP projects customarily cost more than wholly private development projects for two reasons—(1) the extraordinary legal and other transactional costs associated with the negotiation and approval of the governmental incentive package and (2) the direct costs of complying with those governmentally-mandated construction practices that are frequently part and parcel of a PPP-supported project—for example, the adoption of "green" building practices or the compliance with local prevailing wage rules.

The confluence of these three circumstances means that it is much tougher for a developer of a PPP project to properly respond to market conditions and complete the project on budget and on time—all hallmarks of a successful real estate project. For these reasons, most private developers are hesitant to enter into a PPP, unless doing so is necessary to make the project feasible.

Practice Tip #6–2: Preparing the Developer for a PPP

If a developer decides to embark on the path of developing its project as a PPP (despite the above warnings about the downside of doing so), the real estate development lawyer should counsel his client to abide by the following rules.

- ***Make sure your public partner is capable of doing the deal***— *As is the case when selecting a private sector partner, it is essential that the developer make a realistic assessment as to whether its putative public partner has the requisite expertise, financial standing and political command to deliver on its promise to provide incentives and other governmental support for the developer's project.*

- ***Protect the pro forma at all costs***—*The developer should not be bashful about the level of financial return it needs to receive from the project. While it certainly does not want to openly flaunt the projected profitability of a PPP project, the developer must also resist the public sector's attempt to get the developer to agree to concessions that will negatively impact the project's NOI.*

- ***Sell the "big picture" and the "moment"***—*When seeking to secure public incentives for its project, the developer needs to refine its sales pitch to cater to the tastes of the intended public audience.*

That audience is unlikely to be swayed by details concerning the quality of the project's construction or the efficiency of the project's cost structure. The public wants to know three things—(1) how many jobs the project might create (note the use of the word "might"), (2) how many dollars the project might (there's that word again) add to the government's revenue base and (3) how the project will positively impact the city's landscape (lots of pretty pictures required for this one). In selling its public audience on the benefits of its project, the developer should stick with big picture, talking points and avoid putting too much detail into the public domain concerning the developer's development plan.[116] Finally, the developer must sell the "moment"—that is, what the proposed project can do for the government right now (wholly ignoring how the site might be developed by someone else in the future).

- ***Always count your votes**—Obtaining the requisite governmental approvals and incentives for a private development project is, at its essence, a political process. It is all about getting a majority of the ordinary people serving on city council, the county commission or township board of trustees to vote for your project. Every action taken by the developer and its legal team throughout the incentive negotiation process must be directed to getting and keeping the votes needed to secure passage of the developer's incentive package.*

XIII. SUMMARY

The government is an active player in the development of every commercial real estate project. Indeed, one author has accurately stated that the "government is always a partner in any real estate development."[117] Regardless whether the government's participation is limited to it serving as a gatekeeper in the issuance of those approvals required for the commencement and prosecution of project construction or as a more full-bodied provider of governmental incentives, it is incumbent upon the real estate development lawyer to appreciate the business, legal and political considerations that surround the government's participation in the development process. As such, this important second stage of a real estate development project requires the lawyer to be part legal technician and part political advisor.

I want to end this Chapter with one concluding thought about the role that governmental incentives play in the development of private real estate projects. While legal scholars and economists continue to debate the issue of whether the government should provide incentives to aid private

---

116. One of my former co-workers used to describe this "big picture" approach as refusing to let the public "peek under your kimono."

117. *See* MILES, *supra* note 26, at 297.

development projects, the fact of the matter is that such incentives are more prevalent in today's marketplace than they have ever been. Indeed, the receipt of governmental incentives is fast becoming the "new normal" for the real estate development industry. The successful real estate lawyer of the future will be the practitioner who is as comfortable counseling his client about TIFs, abatements and incentive zoning as he is representations, warranties and title defects.

CHAPTER 7

STAGE 3: FORMING AND CAPITALIZING THE PROJECT ENTITY

■ ■ ■

I. INTRODUCTION

I recently ran across the following quote from a seasoned real estate lawyer:

> [C]ontrary to what some attorneys might believe, very few attorneys make money for a client; the reverse is ordinarily true. It is more probable that an attorney will lose money for a client by being untimely or so complicating a factor as to render the transaction uneconomical.[1]

Stage 3 of the real estate development process presents the real estate development lawyer with an opportunity to disprove the accuracy of this quote (which I nonetheless believe to be generally true). When it comes to structuring the entity that will ultimately own the project, a real estate development lawyer who is well-versed in tax, corporate, finance and partnership law can add real value to the developer's project.

This Chapter will first look at those tax and non-tax factors that serve as the guideposts for the lawyer in his effort to design the ownership and capital structure that best serves his client's business objectives. It will then move on to an examination of the "bewildering array of ownership entity choices"[2] and how the selection of the appropriate entity is influenced by the investment goals and business objectives of the providers of the capital that is needed to kick off the developer's project. The Chapter will conclude with a detailed discussion of the myriad of economic, operational and tax issues that must be taken into consideration by the real estate development lawyer when drafting the documents that will

---

1. *See* John D. Hastie, *Real Estate Acquisition, Development and Disposition from the Developer's Perspective*, in ALI–ABA COURSE OF STUDY MATERIALS, MODERN REAL ESTATE TRANSACTIONS: PRACTICAL STRATEGIES FOR REAL ESTATE ACQUISITION, DISPOSITION AND OWNERSHIP, Course No. SS–012, 1, 54 (July 2010).

2. *See* PHILLIP T. KOLBE AND GAYLON E. GREER, INVESTMENT ANALYSIS FOR REAL ESTATE DECISIONS 196 (7th ed. 2009).

199

govern the formation and conduct of the owning entity and the relationship between the developer and its outside equity investors.[3]

II. BUSINESS OBJECTIVES SERVED BY THE CHOICE OF ENTITY

There are three business objectives that must be taken into consideration when selecting the optimal structure for the entity that will own the developer's real estate project. Those three objectives are discussed below.

A. AVOIDANCE OF DOUBLE TAXATION

In most situations, the positive cash flow produced from a real estate project is distributed to the beneficial owners of that project no less frequently than annually. It should always be the goal of the person designing the ownership entity structure to try to avoid subjecting the project's income to taxation both when earned by the project entity and then again when the cash flow associated with that income is distributed to the project's beneficial owners. Subjecting the same income stream to this type of ***double taxation*** reduces the amount of cash that can be pocketed by the developer and its investors by increasing the tax dollars paid to the federal, state and local tax authorities.

The negative impact that double taxation has on the investors' economic returns is illustrated in the following simple example.

Example 7–1: Assume that Project X generates the following annual returns from its rental operations:

- Net cash flow from operations—$500,000; and

- Taxable income—$400,000.

Assume further that the investors in Project X are two individuals, who have agreed that all available cash flow from the project will be distributed to them at the end of each calendar year. Finally, assume that the investors in Project X are both in the 35% tax bracket for federal income tax purposes.[4]

If Project X is subject to only one level of taxation (imposed at the individual investor level), then the annual after-tax return to the investors from their investment in Project X is $360,000, computed as follows:

---

3. It should be noted that it is not unusual for the developer to provide all of the capital initially required to develop a commercial real estate project. However, for instructional purposes, this Chapter will proceed on the assumption that the majority of the capital needed to fund the development project will be provided by one or more outside equity investors, with the remainder of the required capital being provided by the developer. References to the "owners" or "investors" will, where the context permits, include both the developer and its outside equity investors. As was the case in earlier chapters of this book, the terms "equity" and "capital" will be used interchangeably to refer to the cash or other property contributed to the project by the investors.

4. As of the date of the writing of this Chapter, the 35% rate is the maximum marginal tax rate imposed on ordinary income earned by an individual taxpayer. *See* INTERNAL REVENUE CODE § 1(i), (2).

Net cash flow from project operations	$500,000
Less: Federal income tax paid by investors	
(Taxable income of $400,000 * 35% tax rate)	($140,000)
After-tax return to investors	**$360,000**

If, however, the project is subjected to two levels of tax on its earnings (once at the entity level at an assumed tax rate of 35% and then again at the investor level at the current maximum dividend tax rate of 15%)[5], the annual after-tax return to the investors is reduced to $306,000, computed as follows:

Net cash flow from project operations	$500,000
Less: Federal income tax paid by investors	
(Taxable income of $400,000 * 35% tax rate)	($140,000)
Cash flow available for distribution to investors	$360,000
Less: Federal income tax paid by investors	
(Dividend income of $360,000 * 15% tax rate)	($54,000)
After-tax return to investors	**$306,000**

Under the above example, the imposition of a second level of tax at the entity level results in $54,000 of project cash flow being taken away from the investors and placed in the coffers of the IRS—a result that is anathema to all taxpayers, but particularly so to real estate investors. The impact of double taxation was even more extreme before the adoption by Congress in 2003 of a maximum tax rate on dividends of 15%.[6] Before the passage of the 2003 tax bill, the imposition of a second layer of tax at the entity level at a 35% rate would have produced a total deflection of project cash flow to the IRS of $126,000, thereby reducing the investors' after-tax return to $234,000.

Practice Tip #7–1: Pass-through Tax Entities

Example 7–1 illustrates how subjecting the income stream of a real estate project to double taxation has the effect of "robbing Peter to pay Paul," with Peter being the poor real estate owner and Paul being the monolithic force known as the Internal Revenue Service. The real estate development lawyer's job is to design an entity structure that eliminates a second tax imposed at the entity level.

The need to avoid subjecting the project's income to two levels of tax leads the real estate development lawyer into the confounding world of

------

5. *See id.* § 1(h)(11). The 15% limit on dividend income is scheduled to expire in 2011 (along with other tax cuts ushered in during the Bush administration). As of the date of this writing, no action had yet been taken on the extension of the Bush tax cuts.

6. *See* Jobs and Growth Tax Relief Reconciliation Act, Public Law No. 108–27. 117 Stat. 752 (2003).

partnership taxation under Subchapter K of the Internal Revenue Code.[7] *If the goal of subjecting the real estate project's income to a single level of tax is to be achieved, the entity selected to hold title to the project must be taxed as a "partnership."*[8]

Before focusing on what it means for an entity to be taxed as a partnership, it is advisable to first take note of how Judge Raum of the United States Tax Court characterized the workings of Subchapter K:

> *The distressingly complex and confusing nature of the provisions of subchapter K present a formidable obstacle to the comprehension of these provisions without the expenditure of a disproportionate amount of time and effort even by one who is sophisticated in tax matters with many years of experience in the tax field. . . . Surely, a statute has not achieved "simplicity" when its complex provisions may confidently be dealt with by at most only a comparatively small number of specialists who have been initiated into its mysteries.*[9]

Given Judge Raum's cautionary note about Subchapter K, it would seem senseless to try to summarily describe the fundamental principles of partnership taxation. Unfortunately, I have no choice but to try to do so. This is, after all, a treatise on real estate development law and not on partnership taxation. Therefore, I do not have the luxury (or undoubtedly the competence) to explore the complexities of Subchapter K in a multi-volume text as did Messrs. McKee, Nelson and Whitmire in their landmark book FEDERAL TAXATION OF PARTNERSHIPS AND PARTNERS.[10] *Having said that, the principles of partnership taxation are so fundamental to the practice of the real estate development lawyer that I am left with the unenviable option of trying in 1,000 words or less to give the reader an overall sense of what it means to be taxed as a partnership.*

The following is a quick, bullet point summary of the basics of partnership taxation under Subchapter K of the Code. All references in the following summary to "partnerships" and "partners" include all entities subject to Subchapter K and all of the equity participants in such entities.

- *A partnership is not a taxable entity. As such, a partnership does not pay any federal income tax.*

- *All of the partnership's items of taxable income and loss are "passed through" to its partners (hence, the characterization of an entity*

---

7. *See* INTERNAL REVENUE CODE §§ 701–777.

8. A "partnership" includes all those business entities that are taxed under Subchapter K of the Code and includes general partnerships, limited partnerships and limited liability companies. Corporations (both C and S corporations) are the principal, non-partnership, tax entities. *See* INTERNAL REVENUE CODE § 761(a).

9. *See* David A. Foxman, 41 TC 535, 551, note 9 (1964).

10. *See* WILLIAM S. MCKEE, WILLIAM F. NELSON AND ROBERT L. WHITMIRE, FEDERAL TAXATION OF PARTNERSHIPS AND PARTNERS (4th ed. 2007). I heartily recommend the McKee book to all those wanting to understand both the intricacies of Subchapter K and the logic on which it was constructed. During my 30 + years of practice, I relied on the McKee treatise more than any other resource material.

*taxed as a partnership under Subchapter K as **a pass-through entity**).*

- *Each partner reports its share of the partnership's income and loss on the partner's separate income tax return. The federal income tax payable on the income and loss generated by the partnership's activities is, therefore, calculated based on the personal tax situation of each partner (including the marginal tax rate applicable to such partner).*

- *The amount, character and timing of the income and loss passed through to the partners is, however, determined at the partnership level.[11] The partnership (and not any individual partner) is responsible for adopting the accounting method, taxable year and other tax elections that are necessary to determine the amount and character of the income or loss to be passed through to the partners.*

- *Each partner's share of the partnership's income and loss is determined based upon the allocation provisions contained in the partnership agreement.[12]*

- *A partner may not deduct its share of partnership losses to the extent such losses exceed the partner's basis in its partnership interest.[13] For this purpose, a partner's initial basis in its partnership interest is generally equal to the amount of cash and the fair market value of property contributed by it to the partnership, plus its share of partnership liabilities.[14] The basis of the partner's partnership interest is thereafter adjusted to reflect the partner's share of the partnership's income and loss, any contributions made to or distributions received from the partnership and any changes in the amount of the partnership's liabilities.*

- *Contributions made to the partnership by a partner (whether in cash or in-kind) are generally made tax-free.[15]*

---

11. The reason why such items are determined at the entity level has been described as being "necessary to avoid the administrative nightmare that would result if each partner had to calculate her own share of partnership income using her own accounting method, taxable year, method of depreciation, etc." *See* L. Cunningham and N. Cunningham, The Logic of Subchapter K: A Conceptual Guide to the Taxation of Partnerships 8 (3rd ed. 2006).

12. Under the Treasury Regulations promulgated under Section 704(b) of the Internal Revenue Code, the tax allocation provisions of the partnership agreement will be respected for federal income tax purposes, so long as such provisions either have "substantial economic effect" or are otherwise in accordance with the "partners' interests in the partnership." *See* Treasury Regulation § 1–704–1(b), (1) and (3). The rules governing the allocation of items of taxable income and loss among the equity participants in a pass-through tax entity are extremely complex and clearly beyond the scope of this Chapter. For an excellent discussion of those tax rules, *see* McKee, *supra* note 10, at ¶ 11.02; and Gary E. Fluhrer and Robert G. Gottlieb, *Until the Tax Lawyer Arrives: Understanding Tax Provisions in LLC Agreements,* in ACREL Papers 595 (ALI–ABA, March 2004).

13. *See* Internal Revenue Code § 704(d).

14. A partner's share of the partnership's liabilities are determined in accordance with a complex set of rules set forth in Treasury Regulation §§ 1.752–1, 2 and 3.

15. *See* Internal Revenue Code § 721(a).

- *Distributions made to the partner (whether in cash or in-kind) are tax-free, except to the extent the amount of such distributions exceed the partner's basis in its partnership interest.[16]*

- *Although the partnership is not a taxable entity, it is required to file an informational tax return (IRS Form 1065) with the IRS reporting all items of income, gain, loss, deduction and credit generated from the partnership's activities. The partnership is also required to provide each partner with a statement (Schedule K–1) of its share of such partnership tax items.*

The above is a quick summary of some of the more salient tax considerations that a real estate development lawyer must take into consideration during Stage 3 of the real estate development process (designed to stay within the self-imposed "1,000 words or less" regimen). Discussions of other partnership tax issues are embedded in later sections of this book that address matters affected by Subchapter K of the Code.

B. LIMITED LIABILITY

One way a real estate development lawyer can mitigate the risk associated with an investor's investment in real estate (thereby enhancing the attractiveness of the investment) is to devise an ownership structure that limits the investor's liability to the amount of the capital it contributes to the project. The worst case scenario for a real estate investor is that it not only loses the capital it contributed to the project, but also exposes its other assets to the claims of a failed project's creditors. The entity structure ultimately put into place by the real estate development lawyer must, in all events, seek to insulate the investors from personal liability for the debts of the project.[17]

C. OPERATIONAL AND INVESTMENT FLEXIBILITY

If there is one word that a lawyer should always keep in mind when representing a real estate developer it is "flexibility." The development business is extremely dynamic in nature and is conducted by a particularly mercurial class of individuals. For this reason, the real estate development

---

16. *See id.* § 731(a)(1).

17. No entity choice can provide an investor with an absolute shield against personal liability to project creditors. If an entity is thinly capitalized, the possibility exists under applicable case law that a creditor of the entity might be able to "pierce the corporate veil" and seek recovery of its claim against the entity's equity owners. *See generally* Franklin E. Gevurtz, *Piercing Piercing: An Attempt to Lift the Veil of Confusion Surrounding the Doctrine of Piercing the Corporate Veil,* 76 OREGON LAW REVIEW 853 (1997); and JACK S. LEVIN, STRUCTURING VENTURE CAPITAL, PRIVATE EQUITY AND ENTREPRENEURIAL TRANSACTIONS § 3.01.1.2 (2004). Because significant equity contributions are customarily required to start a real estate development project, it is unlikely that the "piercing the corporate veil" line of cases would have any applicability to an entity's ownership of a real estate project.

lawyer must imbue the project documents with as much flexibility as possible to permit his developer client to quickly chance course to deal with unexpected occurrences. Nowhere during the development process is this axiom more applicable than when the real estate development lawyer is tasked with the assignment of crafting an ownership structure that is both (a) attractive to potential equity investors, who yearn for predictability and certainty and (b) acceptable to his developer client, who almost always has a total aversion to being pinned down in any way

When seeking to attract outside equity investors to its development project, the developer wants its lawyer to design an ownership structure that affords the developer two distinct types of contractual flexibility.

- ***Investment Flexibility***—The developer needs to have the flexibility to allocate the various tax and economic attributes associated with the project in whatever manner is required to meet the unique business objectives and economic return parameters of the outside equity investors.

- ***Operational Flexibility***—The developer also wants the flexibility to devise an entity governance scheme that grants the investors some level of dominion over major project decisions (for example, a sale or refinancing of the project), without unduly restricting the developer's freedom to manage the project's day-to-day operations in a manner that it deems appropriate to maximize the chances for the project's overall success.

The investment and operational wants and needs of equity investors vary widely from project to project. The real estate development lawyer must be extremely vigilant so as not to choose an entity form that unduly handcuffs his client in its pursuit of outside equity investors.

III. ENTITY CHOICES

As mentioned at the outset of this section, the real estate development lawyer has a "bewildering array of ownership entity choices"[18] available to him when he sets about selecting the appropriate form of entity to own the real estate project. Recent legal developments have, however, significantly simplified the lawyer's choice of entity analysis.[19] In most instances, the entity of choice to hold title to a privately-held real estate project is a limited liability company.[20] Later sections of this

---

18. *See* KOLBE, *supra* note 2.

19. The most significant of these developments was the IRS' promulgation in 1996 of the so-called "check the box regulations." Prior to the advent of the check the box regulations, practitioners were required to engage in a complicated analysis based on a number of state law considerations to determine whether an unincorporated entity was entitled to be treated as a partnership for federal income tax purposes. Under the check the box regulations, most newly-formed, unincorporated businesses (expressly including limited liability companies) will automatically be classified as partnerships for federal income tax purposes, unless they expressly elect to be taxed as a C corporation by "checking the box" to be excluded from the operation of the Subchapter K of the Internal Revenue Code. *See* Treasury Regulation §§ 301.7701–1–3.

20. *See* L. Andrew Immerman and Ethan D. Millar, *Why Not Form a Business as an LLC?*, 19 No. 3 PRACTICAL TAX LAWYER 21 (Spring 2005); Elliot M. Surkin, John E. Blyth, Gary E. Fluhrer,

chapter will discuss the reasons why a limited liability company is today's favored entity and will also highlight those limited instances where an entity other than a limited liability company should be used.

Before tackling the subject of limited liability companies, this Chapter will first review the entity choices that are available to the real estate development lawyer.[21] The advantages and disadvantages of each entity type will be highlighted by describing how such entity fares in achieving the three business objectives noted at the inception of this Chapter—that is, (1) the avoidance of double taxation, (2) the existence of limited liability and (3) the creation of operational and investment flexibility.[22]

A. TENANTS IN COMMON

Tenancy in common is defined in THE REAL ESTATE DICTIONARY as "an undivided ownership interest in real estate by two or more persons."[23] When two or more parties hold title to a real estate project as tenants in common, the deed conveying title to them must specify the percentage ownership interest of each of the parties (with the presumption that, unless otherwise stated, each of the named tenants in common will own an equal percentage interest in the property).[24] Each tenant in common has a direct ownership interest in the real property (as contrasted to a situation where an entity holds title to the real estate and the individual owns an interest only in the entity and not directly in the real estate).

- ***Avoidance of Double Taxation***: There is no double taxation of the taxable income of a project held as tenants in common. Each

---

Kenneth M. Jacobson, Robert A. Nix II and James A. Winkler, *The LLC Vehicle—Is There Ever a Reason Not to Use It?*, in ACREL PAPERS (ALI–ABA, April 2000), available online at http://www. acrel.org/Documents/Seminars/a002132.pdf; and James A. Winkler and Gary E. Fluhrer, *Limited Liability Companies—Management Structures and Selected Issues in Using LLCs*, in ACREL PAPERS (ALI–ABA, October 2000), available online at http://www.acrel.org/Documents/Seminars/a 002162.pdf.

21. The discussion which follows is premised on the assumption that the real estate project will be beneficially owned by the developer and one or more outside equity investors. If the project is to be 100% owned by the developer, the decision as to how to hold title to that project will involve an analysis of how successfully each ownership format achieves two of the three business objectives discussed at the outset of this chapter—that is, the avoidance of double taxation and the existence of limited liability. Investment and operational flexibility is, by definition, not an issue in a one-owner setting. In most situations, a single owner of a real estate project will be best-served by forming a single member limited liability company to hold title to its project. *See infra Practice Tip #7–2: The Single Member LLC*, for a discussion of single member limited liability companies. *See also* Norton L. Steuben, *Choice of Entity for Real Estate after Check-the-Box and the Entity Explosion*, 37 REAL PROPERTY, PROBATE AND TRUST JOURNAL 54, 86 (Spring 2002).

22. For a further discussion of choice of entity issues, *see generally* ROBERT KEATINGE AND ANN E. CONWAY, KEATINGE AND CONWAY ON CHOICE OF BUSINESS ENTITY: SELECTING FORM AND STRUCTURES FOR A CLOSELY HELD BUSINESS (2006); and Stefan F. Tucker and Tammara F. Langlieb, *The Best of Times and the Worst of Times: Tax Planning for Real Estate Transactions in the Current Economy*, in ALI–ABA COURSE OF STUDY MATERIALS, MODERN REAL ESTATE TRANSACTIONS: PRACTICAL STRATEGIES FOR REAL ESTATE ACQUISITION, DISPOSITION, AND OWNERSHIP, Course No. SS–012, 1077, 1092 (July 2010)

23. *See* JOHN TALAMO, THE REAL ESTATE DICTIONARY 187 (7th ed. 2001).

24. *See* 20 AMERICAN JURISPRUDENCE 2D, *Cotenancy and Joint Ownership* § 117 (2010).

individual tenant in common reports its proportionate share of the project's income and expense items directly on its individual tax return.

- **Limited Liability**: A tenancy in common does not provide the co-owners of a project with limited liability. Each tenant in common is vicariously liable for the liabilities of the project, unless otherwise agreed to by the creditor.[25] A tenant in common will also be personally liable for its proportionate share of any debt or expense incurred by another co-tenant for the benefit of the co-tenancy property (for example, a mortgage loan or real estate taxes).[26] For these reasons, commercial real estate development projects are rarely, if ever, titled in the names of tenants in common.

- **Operational and Investment Flexibility**: The lack of operational and investment flexibility is another reason why tenancy in common arrangements are seldom selected as an ownership entity for real estate development projects.[27] The general rule is that all decisions that must be made with respect to a tenancy in common project must be made with the consent of all of the tenants in common. While this rule may be modified in some jurisdictions by the agreement of the parties, it is questionable whether that rule can be changed to any significant degree without causing the

---

25. *See* KEATINGE AND. CONWAY, *supra* note 22, at § 18.8.

26. *See* GEORGE LEFCOE, REAL ESTATE TRANSACTIONS, FINANCE, AND DEVELOPMENT 675 (6th ed. 2009); and NORTON L. STEUBEN, REAL ESTATE PLANNING, CASES, MATERIALS, QUESTIONS AND COMMENTARY 8 (4th ed. 2006).

27. While tenancy in common is not generally thought of as a suitable ownership vehicle for a real estate development project (because it exposes its owners to personal liability and has little of the desired investment or operational flexibility), syndicated tenancy in common arrangements (referred to in the industry as a "TIC") became quite the rage in the mid–2000's as an ownership structure for certain stabilized, single tenant, real estate projects. The surge in popularity of TICs was directly tied to the ever-increasing desire of taxpayers to defer recognition of taxable gain on the disposition of their real estate holdings by reinvesting the proceeds of such disposition in other "like kind" real estate. Section 1031 of the Internal Revenue Code provides that no current tax is imposed on a taxpayer's sale of real estate if the proceeds of such sale are effectively placed in escrow and then used to purchase other "like kind" property within 180 days after the date of the sale. An equity interest in an entity that holds title to a real estate project (be it a partnership, corporation or limited liability company) is not considered to be "like kind" property for the purposes of § 1031 of the Internal Revenue Code. However, as noted above, a tenancy in common involves a direct ownership interest in real estate and not an equity interest in any entity. As such, a tenant in common interest can be a proper subject of a tax-free, like kind exchange of real estate under § 1031. However, per Revenue Procedure 2002–22, 2002–2 C.B. 438, a TIC interest will only qualify as like-kind real estate if certain conditions are met, which, for the most part, makes the use of the TIC arrangement wholly impractical for the typical real estate development project. By way of example, Revenue Procedure 2002–22 states that (a) each tenant in common must share all economic and tax attributes generated from a project in direct proportion to its percentage TIC interest (thereby destroying the desired investment flexibility) and (b) the unanimous consent of all tenants in common is required for the sale, lease or mortgaging of the underlying real estate project (the total opposite of the type of operational flexibility considered so necessary for a real estate development project). For a further discussion of TIC syndications, *see* Bradford Updike, *Exploring the Frontier of Non-traditional Real Estate Investments: A Closer Look at Section 1031 Tenancy-in-common Arrangements*, 22 TAX MANAGEMENT REAL ESTATE JOURNAL No. 9 (September 6, 2006); and Terrence Floyd Cuff, *Avoiding Ticky Tacky TICs: Some Comments on Investing in TICs and Avoiding the Pig in a Poke*, in ALI–ABA COURSE OF STUDY MATERIALS, CREATIVE TAX PLANNING FOR REAL ESTATE TRANSACTIONS, Course No. SM–034, 795 (September 2006).

tenancy in common arrangement to be treated as a partnership for both state law and federal income tax purposes.[28] Moreover, a tenancy in common arrangement does not afford the developer the ability to allocate economic or tax attributes of the project in any way other than in strict accordance with the specific percentage ownership interests of the individual tenants in common. This lack of investment flexibility makes the tenancy in common format a difficult vehicle to use when trying to raise outside equity to fund a project's development costs. Finally, one of the hallmarks of a tenancy in common structure is the reserved right of each tenant in common to petition the courts to partition or sell the co-tenancy property. A right of partition is the antithesis of the type of contractual flexibility that the real estate development lawyer strives to achieve in selecting an entity to hold title to his client's real estate project.

B. C CORPORATION

Title to a real estate project can be held by a corporation in which the developer and the outside equity investors are the shareholders. Most corporations are taxable under Subchapter C of the Internal Revenue Code[29] and, therefore, are commonly referred to as *C corporations*.

- *Avoidance of Double Taxation*: A C corporation is a separate taxable entity. As such, the income stream of a real estate project held by a C corporation is subject to double taxation—first when the income is earned by the corporate titleholder and second when a distribution of the related cash flow is made to the shareholders. In addition, tax deductions and losses generated from the real estate project (including depreciation deductions) cannot be passed through to the shareholders of a C corporation, but rather may be used only to offset the positive taxable income of the C corporation (which may not exist if the sole asset of the C corporation is the real estate project). For these reasons, commercial real estate projects are seldom owned by C corporations (unless the project is built solely for the use and occupancy of the corporation).

- *Limited Liability:* The one advantage of a C corporation is that its shareholders are not personally liable for the corporation's debts and claims. As such, an investor's liability on a real estate project titled in the name of a C corporation is limited to the amount of the investor's capital contribution to the corporation.[30]

- *Operational and Investment Flexibility:* Corporate governance issues are covered by the corporate statute of the state where the corporation is incorporated. The specificity of such statutory provi-

---

28. *See* Steuben, *Choice of Entity, supra* note 21, at 6; and Tucker, *supra* note 22, at 1092.

29. *See* INTERNAL REVENUE CODE §§ 301–395.

30. *See supra* note 17 for a discussion of "piercing of the corporate veil" doctrine.

sions places an inherent limitation on the operational flexibility available under the C corporation ownership option. The C corporation format also significantly restricts the creativity of the parties with respect to the allocation of economic and tax attributes associated with the ownership and operation of a real estate project. Some level of investment flexibility can, however, be achieved through the use of multiple classes of stock and the issuance of corporate debt instruments.

C. S CORPORATION

An *S corporation* is a corporation that elects to be taxed for federal income tax purposes under Subchapter S of the Internal Revenue Code[31] (and not Subchapter C). Subchapter S of the Internal Revenue Code was adopted by Congress in an attempt to achieve tax neutrality between the taxation of partners and Subchapter S shareholders.[32] However, as will be noted later in this discussion, there remain significant differences in the tax treatment afforded to partnerships and S corporations, all of which weigh heavily against the use of an S corporation to hold title to a real estate development project.

- *Avoidance of Double Taxation*: As a general rule, an S corporation is not treated as a separate taxpayer for federal income tax purposes. In most situations, a single layer of tax is imposed at the shareholder level on the income generated from a real estate project owned by the S corporation. There are, however, a couple of exceptions to this general rule, which negate the wisdom of using an S corporation as the ownership entity for a real estate project.[33]

  - First, unlike the tax treatment afforded to an equity participant in a partnership or limited liability company, a shareholder of an S corporation cannot increase the tax basis of his stock by his percentage interest in the S corporation's debt. The S shareholder's right to receive tax-free cash distributions and deduct entity-generated losses is limited to the amount of his tax basis in his stock. The fact that the tax basis of a partner's or LLC member's equity interest (but not that of an S shareholder's stock) includes its allocable share of the entity's debt means that the ability of a partner or LLC member to receive tax-free cash distributions[34] and deduct entity tax losses is much greater than the ability of the S shareholder to do so.

---

31. *See* INTERNAL REVENUE CODE §§ 1361–1379.

32. *See* McKEE, *supra* note 10, at ¶ 2.02[3].

33. *See generally* Tucker, *supra* note 22, at 1093–1109.

34. This distinction is particularly important as it relates to the distribution to the equity holders of the proceeds of a refinancing, where the amount of the new debt exceeds the amount of the refinanced debt (a situation which is quite common in the real estate development business). In a partnership or limited liability company context, the distribution of the excess refinancing

- Second, Subchapter S imposes an entity level tax on the distribution of any appreciated property to its shareholders.[35] Entities taxed as partnerships under Subchapter K (which includes general and limited partnerships and limited liability companies) are not subject to any separate entity tax upon the distribution to its equity owners of appreciated property.

- *Limited Liability*: An S corporation shareholder has the same limited liability as a C corporation shareholder.

- *Operational and Investment Flexibility*: The operational and investment flexibility afforded by the S corporation format is even less than that which exists for a C corporation. Unlike a C corporation, an S corporation can only have 10 shareholders, all of whom must either be individuals, estates or qualifying trusts.[36] As such, the use of an S corporation denies the developer access to its most important source of seed capital for its project—that is, life insurance companies, pension funds, venture capital firms, foreign nationals and other large, non-individual taxpayers. Subchapter S also expressly provides that an S corporation can only have one class of stock.[37] The "once class of stock" restriction effectively means that all allocations and distributions made by the S corporation to its shareholders must be made in direct proportion to the shareholders' respective ownership interests in the S corporation's stock. These statutory restrictions on the capital structure of an S corporation effectively prevent the S corporation from attaining anywhere near the level of operational and investment flexibility afforded regular C corporations, let alone that available in the partnership and LLC formats.[38]

D. GENERAL PARTNERSHIP

A *general partnership* is an unincorporated organization in which two or more persons agree to share profits and losses associated with the conduct of a business or investment activity.[39] The conduct and

---

proceeds is almost always tax-free to the partners or limited liability members (because the tax bases of their respective equity interests generally include their allocable share of the entity's debt). Because the S corporation shareholder is not able to include any portion of the corporation's debt in the basis of his stock, the distribution of refinancing proceeds by a S corporation is much more likely to trigger taxable gain at the equity holder level than is a distribution of refinancing proceeds by a partnership or limited liability company.

35. *See* INTERNAL REVENUE CODE § 311(b). *See also* Tucker, *supra* note 22, at 1093.

36. *See* INTERNAL REVENUE CODE § 1361(b)(1)(A) and (B).

37. *See id.* § 1361(b) (1) (D).

38. The lack of operational and investment flexibility, when coupled with the negative tax attributes of the S corporation noted earlier in this section, have caused the authors of the pre-eminent treatise on partnership taxation to comment that "there is rarely a reason to create a corporation with the intention of electing to be taxed under Subchapter S." *See* McKEE, *supra* note 10, at § 2.02[3].

39. *See* UNIFORM PARTNERSHIP ACT (1997) § 101(6).

activities of a general partnership are governed by state statutes, almost all of which are patterned after the Uniform Partnership Act. A general partnership is taxed under Subchapter K, unless an affirmative election to be taxed as a C corporation is filed with the IRS.[40]

- *Avoidance of Double Taxation*: A general partnership is treated as a pass-through entity for federal income tax purposes. As such, there is no federal income tax imposed at the partnership level. All items of income and expense generated by the general partnership are passed through to and reported on the personal tax returns of its partners. The income stream generated from a real estate project held by a general partnership is, therefore, subject to a single layer of tax.

- *Limited Liability*: In a general partnership, each general partner is personally liable for all partnership debts and claims.[41] The fact that each partner's separate, individual assets are potentially at risk if the real estate project proves to be unsuccessful generally makes a general partnership a poor choice for an entity to hold title to a real estate development project.[42]

- *Operational and Investment Flexibility*: The Uniform Partnership Act provides for a series of default rules which, unless otherwise provided in the partnership agreement, will determine how the partnership's profits and losses will be split and how the partnership will otherwise conduct its affairs and activities.[43] By way of example, absent a provision to the contrary in the partnership agreement, the Uniform Partnership Act provides that (1) all partnership profits and losses will be shared equally by its partners[44] and (2) each partner will have "equal rights in the management and conduct of the partnership business."[45] These default rules can, however, be modified by a written partnership agreement, thereby giving the partnership ample operational flexibility with respect to the manner in which the partnership's economic profits and losses

---

40. *See* Treasury Regulation § 301.7701–3(c).

41. *See* Uniform Partnership Act (1997) § 306.

42. Most states have now enacted statutes which permit a general partnership to register as a "limited liability partnership." Those statutes (which vary from jurisdiction to jurisdiction) seek to limit the partners' personal liability for certain partnership debts and claims, most notably the partners' joint and several liability for tort claims. In many states, the limited liability partnership election is only available to persons engaged in a professional service business—e.g., lawyers and accountants. Moreover, in most states, the protection against a partner's personal liability is limited to tort claims occasioned by the negligent of willful acts of other partners and do not insulate the partner from liability for other partnership debts and claims. As such, limited liability partnerships are usually not a suitable vehicle to own a real estate development project. *See generally* Carter G. Bishop and Daniel S. Kleinberger, Limited Liability Companies: Tax and Business Law, Chapter 15 (2003). *See also* Steuben, *supra* note 21, at 68.

43. *See* Uniform Partnership Act (1997) § 103(a).

44. *See id.* § 401(b).

45. *See id.* § 401(f).

will be split and the way in which the partnership's business will be managed and operated. In addition, Subchapter K of the Internal Revenue Code permits the partners to allocate items of taxable income and expense among themselves in any fashion they see fit (including in a manner different from the way they share the partnership's underlying economic profits and losses), as long as any such allocation has "substantial economic effect"—that is, it substantially affects the value of the partners' partnership interests independent of tax consequences.[46] A general partnership, therefore, is engrained with as much operational and investment flexibility as any tax pass-through entity (including a limited partnership or a limited liability company) and much more than the tenancy in common or corporate ownership arrangements discussed previously in this Chapter.

E. LIMITED PARTNERSHIP

A ***limited partnership*** differs from the general partnership primarily because it affords potential limited liability status to a group of investors referred to as ***limited partners***. Limited partnerships are also treated as pass-through entities for federal income tax purposes under Subchapter K. Until the advent of the limited liability company in the early 1990's, the combined features of limited liability and treatment as a pass-through entity for tax purposes made the limited partnership the favored ownership entity for commercial real estate projects.

- ***Avoidance of Double Taxation***: A limited partnership is taxed for federal income tax purposes in the same manner as a general partnership. Vesting title to a real estate project in a limited partnership will, therefore, avoid the imposition of any double tax on the project's income stream.

- ***Limited Liability***: Under the most recent version of the Uniform Limited Partnership Act, a limited partner has a "full, status-based liability shield . . ., even if the limited partner participates in the management and control of the limited partnership."[47] A limited partnership must, however, by statute, have at least one general partner, who is generally liable for all of the entity's debts and claims.[48] A common gamut employed during the limited partner-

---

46. *See* INTERNAL REVENUE CODE § 704(b) and Treasury Regulation § 1.704–1(b). For an extended discussion of the tax allocation rules of Subchapter K, *see* MCKEE, *supra* note 10, at Chapter 11, *Determining the Partners' Distributive Shares*; and Mark Stone, *Partnership Allocations—Getting It Drafted Simple, But Right*, 21 TAX MANAGEMENT REAL ESTATE JOURNAL 206 (July 6, 2005).

47. *See* COMMENT TO UNIFORM LIMITED PARTNERSHIP ACT (2001) § 303. Prior versions of the Uniform Limited Partnership Act subjected a limited partner to a potential loss of its limited liability if it participated in the control of the business. Limited partnerships formed in states that have not adopted the Uniform Limited Partnership Act (2001) may, therefore, not be able to provide a complete liability shield for its limited partners.

48. *See* UNIFORM LIMITED PARTNERSHIP ACT (2001) § 404.

ship's heyday in the 1970's and 1980's was to make the sole general partner of the partnership a shell corporation without any significant assets, thereby effectively giving limited partnerships the same limited liability status as corporations. This approach was the subject of a great deal of litigation as the IRS sought to have such limited partnerships taxed as corporations (and not as pass-through entities)[49] and creditors sought to pierce the corporate veil and collect damages against the limited partners of the partnership and the shareholders of the corporate general partner.[50] As noted earlier in this chapter, the IRS' adoption of the check-the-box regulations has now rendered moot the issue of whether a thinly-capitalized corporate general partner might cause a limited partnership to be taxed as a corporation. However, the use of a minimally capitalized shell entity as the sole general partner of a limited partnership still creates the theoretical risk under state law that the limited partners or the equity owners of the shell entity might be held personally liable for the debts and claims of the limited partnership.[51] This theoretical risk marginally detracts from the attractiveness of the limited partnership as an entity to hold title to a real estate development project.[52]

- ***Operational and Investment Flexibility***: The investment flexibility of a limited partnership is as complete as it is in a general partnership. In those states that have enacted the 2001 version of the Uniform Limited Partnership Act (with its absolute liability shield for all limited partners),[53] the operational flexibility of a limited partnership is effectively the same as that of a general partnership. However, in all other jurisdictions, the prohibition on a limited partner's participation in the control of the business is a factor that limits the operational flexibility of a limited partnership and, hence, weighs against the selection of a limited partnership as an owner of a real estate development project.

---

49. *See* McKee, *supra* note 10, at ¶ 3.02

50. *See* Steuben, *Choice of Entity*, *supra* note 21, at 80.

51. *See id.*, where the author notes that the theories underlying the IRS' attack on thinly capitalized corporate general partners "might be resurrected and applied to impose sham or thin treatment on limited partnerships having corporate general partners possibly resulting in the limited partners having general liability or the partnership failing to comply with RULPA and, therefore, not being treated as a limited partnership."

52. A few states have authorized the formation of limited liability limited partnerships ("LLLPs"). LLLPs are identical to limited partnerships, except that there is no requirement that the general partner be personally liable for the partnership's debts and claims. Of the few states that have adopted LLLP statutes, most have limited the use of LLLPs to activities other than the ownership of real estate. *See id.* at 84.

53. The 2001 version of the Uniform Limited Partnership Act has been enacted in 16 states and introduced into legislation in three other states. *See* Uniform Law Commissioners, A Few Facts about the Uniform Limited Partnership Act (2001), http://www.nccusl.org/Update/uniformact_factsheets.

F. LIMITED LIABILITY COMPANY

A *limited liability company* (*LLC*) is a relatively recent statutory creation. The first LLC statute was adopted by the Wyoming legislature in 1977. Today all 50 states, plus the District of Columbia, have statutes in place that permit the creation of a limited liability company.[54] The LLC is an entity that seeks to take the best of both the corporate and partnership worlds, by combining the limited liability status of corporations, with the pass-through tax status and operational and investment flexibility of partnerships. It has, therefore, quickly become the entity of choice for real estate developers.

- *Avoidance of Double Taxation*: An LLC is automatically taxed as a partnership for federal income tax purposes, unless its members make an affirmative election to be taxed as a C corporation under the check-the-box regulations. As such, no federal income tax is imposed at the LLC level.

- *Limited Liability Status*: The liability of a member in a LLC is akin to that of a shareholder in a corporation. The LLC member's personal assets are immune from attack by the creditors of the LLC, even if the member directly participates in the management and control of the LLC's business.[55]

- *Operational and Investment Flexibility*: An LLC has all of the same operational and investment flexibility as does a general partnership. There are effectively no limits on how the LLC's business operations will be managed. Indeed the members of an LLC may elect to delegate to a non-member manager all or any part of the authority to manage the LLC's activities.[56] The members of an LLC also have the same flexibility as do the partners in general and limited partnerships to allocate the entity's economic and tax attributes in whatever fashion they deem appropriate.

IV. LLC AS ENTITY OF CHOICE FOR REAL ESTATE DEVELOPERS

It is clearer today than at any time in recent history that there is one entity that should almost always be chosen to own a real estate development project—an LLC. As the chart set forth below reveals, the LLC does not possess any of the negative characteristics that are associated with the other potential entity choices. For example, unlike a tenancy in common arrangement, the LLC does not expose its members to any personal liability for the project's debts or claims, nor does it require the unanimous consent of its members to the sale, leasing or mortgaging of the project. An LLC does not have the general liability concerns of a general partnership, nor does it have the double taxation problems associated with

---

54. *See* LARRY E. RIBSTEIN AND ROBERT R. KEATINGE, RIBSTEIN AND KEATINGE ON LIMITED LIABILITY COMPANIES Appendix A (2nd ed. 2010).

55. *See e.g.,* REVISED UNIFORM LIMITED LIABILITY COMPANY ACT (2006), § 304.

56. *See id.* § 407(c)(6).

a C corporation. An LLC is superior to an S corporation both because of the S corporation's lack of operational and investment flexibility and because of the previously-discussed ways in which the S corporation's tax treatment falls short of a full pass-through of its tax attributes to the shareholders. Finally, even the once favored limited partnership format fails to measure up against the LLC due to (1) the requirement that there be at least one entity (the general partner) that has general liability for the entity's debts and claims and (2) to a lesser extent, the rule followed in the majority of jurisdictions that a limited partner may not participate in the control of the business, without risking the loss of its limited liability.

Entity Type	No Double Taxation	Limited Liability	Operational/Investment Flexibility
Tenancy in Common	Yes	No	No
C Corporation	No	Yes	Limited
S Corporation	Limited	Yes	Limited
General Partnership	Yes	No	Yes
Limited Partnership	Yes	Limited	Limited
Limited Liability Company	Yes	Yes	Yes

The above chart clearly shows that the LLC is the only entity that fully satisfies all three of the business objectives noted at the outset of this Chapter—that is, (1) the avoidance of double taxation of the income stream generated from the operation of the real estate project, (2) the limitation of the equity participant's personal liability for project debts and claims and (3) the creation of sufficient operational and investment flexibility to permit the developer and its outside equity investors to structure their business deal in whatever fashion best suits their needs.

V. WHEN SHOULD AN ENTITY OTHER THAN AN LLC BE USED?

As stated above, the LLC is almost always the ownership entity of choice for closely-held real estate development projects. Indeed, when six seasoned lawyers were asked in 2000 to prepare a paper for the American College of Real Estate Lawyers on the traditional "choice of entity" topic, they ended up entitling their article *The LLC Vehicle—Is There Ever a Reason Not to Use It?*[57] The answer they provided to that question was— "[w]e came to believe that many of the instances where the ownership vehicle in a closely-held real estate deal was an entity other than an LLC resulted from habit or conservatism (resistance to change) of either the lawyer or the client and not from careful analysis."[58]

There are three relatively isolated instances where a real estate development lawyer might want to consider having an entity other than an LLC hold title to a development project.

---

57. *See* Surkin, *The LLC Vehicle, supra* note 20.

58. *See id.* at 2.

- ***Publicly-held Property***—To the extent the developer desires to raise capital by accessing the public markets, an LLC format will not be the most desirable entity choice. Most publicly-held real estate in the United States is owned by ***real estate investment trusts (REITs)***.[59] REITs are creatures of the federal income tax laws and may be organized as either a corporation or unincorporated trust or association for state law purposes. A REIT is not subject to any entity-level tax, as long as it satisfies a series of complex tests, including the requirement that the REIT distribute at least 90% of its qualifying income each year to its shareholders.[60] As of October, 2010, shares of stock in 133 REITs were treaded on the New York Stock Exchange at a total market capitalization value of approximately $328 billion.[61]

- ***State Tax Law Barriers***—There are a handful of states that subject LLCs to an entity-level state income or franchise tax.[62] The instances of double taxation for state tax purposes are often anomalies resulting from the existing state tax laws not yet being revised to take cognizance of the relatively new LLC entity form. Nonetheless, in those states where the LLC is afforded unfavorable state tax treatment, the real estate development lawyer should consider using a limited partnership or some other entity type to hold title to the developer's real estate project.

- ***Deal-specific Investor Concern***: Some real estate deals are structured to appeal to a particular investor or investor class, who may for some reason not want to become a member in an LLC.[63] Some conservative investors may also be leery of the LLC format, because the body of case law addressing the application of federal and state law to LLCs is not nearly as well-developed as those related to other entity types, such as a corporation or a general or limited partnership.[64] This concern will presumably wane as the passage of time results in more judicial decisions being handed down on legal topics involving LLCs.

The limited exceptions noted above make up the universe of the 1% of occasions on which the rational developer will decide not to use an LLC to

---

59. *See* the following website sponsored by the National Association of Real Estate Investment Trusts for a general discussion of the impact of REITs in the real estate marketplace—www.investinreits.com.

60. *See generally* LEFCOE, *supra* note 26, at 683–688.

61. *See* NAREIT REITWATCH, A MONTHLY STATISTICAL REPORT ON THE REAL ESTATE INVESTMENT TRUST INDUSTRY 1 (October 2010), available online at http://returns.reit.com/reitwatch/rw1010.pdf. The topic of REITs and other publicly-held real estate is beyond the scope of this book. However, it is important to recognize the enormity of the role of REITs in the development and ownership of commercial real estate in this country.

62. *See* Surkin, *The LLC Vehicle, supra* note 20, at 4–7; and RIBSTEIN, *supra* note 49, at § 16.29 and Appendix 16–1.

63. The TIC syndication described *supra* note 27, is an example of a situation where an investor's objective (securing a tax deferral under the like-kind exchange rules of Section 1031 of the Internal Revenue Code) makes the LLC the wrong entity choice.

64. *See* Steuben, *supra* note 21, at 88.

hold title to a privately-held commercial real estate project. Our focus for the remainder of this Chapter will be on the 99% of occasions when the entity of choice is the LLC.

Practice Tip #7–2: The Single Member LLC

One additional advantage of the LLC format is the ability to have an LLC owned by a single member.[65] This contrasts markedly with either a general or a limited partnership in which, by definition, there must be two partners in order for there to be a validly formed entity.

*The **single member LLC (SMLLC)** is commonly used by a real estate developer to hold title to each of its real estate project in a separate, discrete ownership vehicle.[66] This ownership structure is similar to a corporation's formation of a wholly-owned subsidiary. The advantages of forming an SMLLC as a subsidiary of another LLC are as follows.*

- *The assets of the parent LLC (including its ownership of other SMLLCs) are not at risk to satisfy the claims and debts of an SMLLC.*

- *Under the partnership tax rules of Subchapter K of the Internal Revenue Code, the SMLLC is wholly ignored for federal income tax purposes, with the end result that a separate informational tax return does not have to be filed by the SMLLC.[67] An SMLLC that is disregarded for federal income tax purposes is commonly referred to as a **tax nothing entity**.*

- *The existence of the SMLLC will conform to the typical requirement of a lender that any project on which it is making a secured loan must be owned by a separate entity (commonly referred to by lenders as a **single purpose** or **bankruptcy remote entity**), so as to preclude the possibility that the entity owning the real estate project might be forced into bankruptcy for reasons having to do with financial problems not directly associated with the project that secures the lender's loan.[68]*

---

65. *See e.g.,* REVISED UNIFORM LIMITED LIABILITY COMPANY ACT (2006) § 201(d)(1). *See also* RIBSTEIN, *supra* note 54 at § 4.2

66. By way of example, Pizzuti Properties LLC was a limited liability company formed in 2000 by The Pizzuti Companies and Nationwide Realty Investors, Ltd. to acquire ownership of Pizzuti's existing portfolio of office and industrial properties and to develop new projects in the future. It was agreed that each existing and new real estate project would be held in a separate SMLLC, in which the sole member would be Pizzuti Properties LLC. *See* discussion of the Pizzuti Properties venture *infra* Page 220, and *infra* Chapter 12, Pages 565–567.

67. *See* Treasury Regulation § 301–7701–3(a).

68. *See infra* Chapter 12, Page 562, for a further discussion of bankruptcy remote entities.

VI. SOURCES OF PROJECT EQUITY

Approximately 70–90% of the development costs of a typical real estate project are funded through a construction loan secured by the developer from a bank or other commercial lending source. This leaves 10–30% of a project's development costs to be funded through capital contributions made by the equity owners of the real estate project.[69]

A project's capital can be provided by (a) the developer, (b) outside equity investors or (c) most typically, a combination of (a) and (b). For the purpose of the following discussion, it will be assumed that the needed capital is being provided by a combination of the developer and its outside equity investors.[70]

Historically, the developer's cadre of outside equity investors fell into the category of the developer's "family and friends"—that is, the developer's extended family, his country club buddies, his doctor and dentist and a host of other people who are personally acquainted with the developer. This category of investor is usually willing to take a fair amount of entrepreneurial risk on a real estate investment, in large part due to the investor's personal familiarity with and confidence in the developer.

Institutional investors, such as life insurance companies and pension funds, have historically been hesitant to assume the level of risk attendant to an investment of seed capital on the front-end of a development project. These investors were fully content to invest only in mature, stabilized real estate projects that were fully leased and producing predictable income streams. The reticence of the institutional investment community to invest in development projects has eroded due to the saturation of the investment market for stabilized real estate projects and the never-ending quest of the institutional investor to increase the yield from its real estate investments. As alluded to in Chapter 3, one way for an investor to increase its investment yield is to increase its tolerance for project risk.[71]

As a result, the commercial real estate developer now has two available sources of outside equity investment—(1) family and friends and (2)

---

69. The ratio of development costs funded by debt vs. equity varies from period to period based on the then prevailing condition of the real estate finance markets. The 70–90% and 10–30% ratios mentioned in the text are historical averages and are clearly more heavily weighted in favor of debt funding than is the reality in the current (vintage 2010) capital markets, where debt funding is hovering in the 50–70% range. *See supra* Chapter 1, note 26; and *infra* Chapter 9, Page 398.

70. An outside equity investor will generally insist that the developer make a significant equity contribution to the real estate venture. The equity investor wants to make sure that the developer has a financial stake in making the project a success for all its investors. This financial stake is colloquially referred to as the developer's "skin in the game." The amount of the developer's co-investment is typically in the 10–15% range, but will vary depending on the nature of the deal and the relative liquidity of the developer. *See* Dean C. Pappas, Steven A. Waters, Vicki R. Harding, Gary E. Fluhrer and Robert G. Gottleib, *The Changing World of Real Estate Equity Investment*, in ACREL PAPERS 45, 50, note 12 (ALI–ABA, Spring 2008).

71. *See supra* Chapter 3, Page 52.

institutional investors.[72] The risk tolerance and economic return expectations of these two groups are, however, markedly different. The differing perspectives of these two investor groups will be highlighted where appropriate in the discussion that follows concerning the key provisions of an LLC operating agreement.

HIBC Case Study—Two Very Different Equity Sources

Pizzuti relied on two very different equity sources during its development of the HIBC project. At the inception of the HIBC project, the principals of Newport Partners, an executive compensation consultant headquartered in Orlando, Florida, served as Pizzuti's outside equity investor.[73] The Newport principals fit squarely within the "family and friends" category of investors discussed in the previous section of this Chapter. They were rich entrepreneurs, who were looking for a way to diversify their investments and increase the yield on their overall portfolios. They wanted to invest in the HIBC project due to their perception that Pizzuti was an accomplished developer with a proven track record of producing above-market returns on its development projects. As one of the Newport principals mentioned to me over and over again during the course of the Pizzuti–Newport relationship, "We are comfortable investing with you as long as we know that you are putting your own money into the deals and are assuming the same investment risk that we are." It was this fundamental premise that served as the genesis for the following unusual equity deal struck by Pizzuti and Newport.

- *Pizzuti and Newport formed a general partnership to own and operate each office project in which they were co-investors. The general partnership vehicle was selected for two reasons—(1) an LLC was not yet a viable entity choice in the State of Florida[74] and (2) Pizzuti wanted Newport to be generally liable for all project debts and liabilities (a proposition that would have been anathema to an institutional investor).*

- *Pizzuti and Newport each provided 50% of the equity capital required for the office projects.*

- *The principals of Newport agreed to personally guaranty (on a several basis) 50% of each construction loan obtained by a Pizzuti–*

---

72. The public sector is yet another source for the funding of those development costs that are not covered by construction debt—for example, by way of a government's direct payment of certain project infrastructure costs or by its provision of financing to pay such infrastructure costs. The public sector's involvement as the developer's "partner" in a commercial real estate project is addressed *supra* in Chapter 6.

73. For the story of how Pizzuti was introduced to Newport Partners, *see supra* Chapter 4.

74. Florida imposed an entity-level state income tax on LLCs until 1998. In addition, the Florida limited liability statute that was in effect in the early and mid 1990s was perceived as being both overly complex and not sufficiently flexible. *See* Gregory J. Marks, *New Florida Limited Liability Company Act*, Greenberg Traurig Alert (June 1999).

Newport general partnership (something that would have been absolutely beyond the pale for any institutional investor).

This unique capital structure was used for ten office projects developed in the HIBC office park during the period from 1992 through 1999.

For a host of reasons discussed later in this text,[75] *Pizzuti decided in 1999 to pursue a more traditional equity arrangement for the funding of its existing portfolio and its future development efforts. In February 2000, Pizzuti formed a new equity venture with Nationwide Realty Investors, Ltd. ("NRI"). NRI was the real estate arm of Nationwide Insurance Company, a large institutional investor headquartered in Columbus, Ohio. The new venture entity (known as "Pizzuti Properties LLC") acquired all of the HIBC office projects (plus the entirety of Pizzuti's portfolio of industrial properties scattered throughout the Midwest). Pizzuti and NRI agreed that all of Pizzuti's future development projects would be owned by Pizzuti Properties LLC and that NRI would provide 90% and Pizzuti would provide10% of all equity capital required to fund the new projects. Pizzuti was required to provide all personal guaranties required by any construction lender for a new project.*

The deal struck between Pizzuti and NRI typifies the distinction customarily drawn in institutional equity deals between the developer as the "service partner" and the investor as the "money partner." It was Pizzuti's job to identify new development opportunities and then use its personal resources to bring the project to fruition. NRI's job was to provide most of the money needed to fund the projects.

The specifics of Pizzuti's relationship with these two very different equity sources will be examined in more detail in the remaining pages of this Chapter.

VII.   THE FORMATION OF THE LLC

For the remainder of this Chapter, it will be assumed that (1) the capital needed for the kick-off the real estate development project is being provided 25% by the developer and 75% by one or more outside equity investors and (2) the parties have made the rational choice to use an LLC to own the real estate project. The decision to use an LLC as the owning entity gives rise to following two basic questions.

- In which jurisdiction should the LLC be formed?

- Do the parties need to prepare a written agreement to govern the activities of the LLC?

---

75. *See infra* Page 287 and *infra* Chapter 12, Pages 565–567.

A. IN WHICH JURISDICTION SHOULD THE LLC BE FORMED?

The answer to the first question usually comes down to three choices:

1. The state where the developer is headquartered;

2. The state where the project is located (if different than #1); or

3. Delaware.

Real estate development lawyers often choose the first or second alternative, because they are familiar with that state's LLC laws or because they perceive it to be easier from an administrative perspective to form an LLC in a state that has some logical nexus with the developer and its project. Each state's LLC statute is a little different. Therefore, before forming the LLC in either of the states noted under choice #1 or choice #2, the real estate development lawyer must review that state's LLC statute to make sure that the provisions of the statute are suitable for the developer's project.

Delaware has long been known for adopting legislation considered favorable to the formation and operation of business entities.[76] This is certainly true when it comes to the Delaware Limited Liability Company Act (referred to in this Chapter as the "Delaware Act.").[77] Perhaps the most attractive feature of the Delaware Act is its whole-hearted embracing of the principle of contractual flexibility. Section 18–1101(b) of the Delaware LLC act provides that:

> It is the policy of this chapter to give the maximum effect to the principle of freedom of contract and to the enforceability of limited liability company agreements.[78]

In effect, the Delaware Act creates a blank slate for the parties to craft the terms of a business deal that are acceptable to them. The Delaware Act also lays out a set of statutory default rules that will govern those matters that are either intentionally or unintentionally not addressed within the confines of the written operating agreement entered into by the LLC members. For this reason, Delaware has become the jurisdiction of choice for many practitioners when forming an LLC.[79] For the remainder of this Chapter, it will be assumed that the developer and its outside equity investors have elected to use a Delaware LLC to own their real estate project

---

76. *See* Steven A. Waters and Robert R. Nix II, *Letting the Statute Be the Deal: The Delaware Statutory LLC Default Rules*, in ACREL Papers 473, 474 (ALI–ABA, March 2004).

77. *See* Delaware Code Annotated, Title 6, Chapter 18 (West 2010).

78. *See id.* § 18–1101(b).

79. *See* Waters, *supra* note 76, at 474; Surkin, *The LLC Vehicle, supra* note 20, at 3; and Scott A. Lindquist, *A Real Estate Lawyer's Guide to Equity Investment (with Forms)*, 25 No. 2 Practical Real Estate Lawyer 41, 45 (March 2009).

B. IS A WRITTEN OPERATING AGREEMENT NECESSARY?

The simple answer to the above question is—no, there is no legal requirement that the members enter into a formal, written operating agreement. All that is required to form an LLC under the Delaware Act is the filing of a certificate of formation with the Delaware Secretary of State.[80] The Delaware Act establishes a series of default rules that will govern an LLC's operations if a written operating agreement is not executed by the LLC's members.[81] Those default rules are quite extensive and include, among others, provisions stipulating that (a) profits and losses will be allocated to the members in proportion to the amounts of their respective capital contributions,[82] (b) the LLC will be managed by its members, with the decision of those members who have contributed more than 50% of the capital being controlling[83] and (c) the members will not have personal liability for the debts and claims of the LLC.[84] The Delaware Act makes it clear that each of these default rules may be modified by the terms of a written operating agreement executed by the members.[85]

While the default rules might work for the simplest of deals, I would never recommend dispensing with a written operating agreement in any real estate development deal in which there is a member other than the developer (in other words, any LLC other than a developer-owned SMLLC). The default rules of the Delaware Act are generally ill-suited to reflect the scope and depth of the business deal typically struck by the developer and the outside equity investors. Moreover, even in the simplest of deals, there is real intrinsic value to including the entirety of the parties' business understanding in one document that the parties are required to review and sign. The likelihood that the parties to a business deal will read the operating agreement (at least the key provisions of that agreement) is much greater than the prospect that they will ever look at the default rules of the governing LLC statute.

VIII. KEY PROVISIONS OF AN LLC OPERATING AGREEMENT

The document that governs the relationship of the members of an LLC and the operation of the LLC's business is called an ***operating agreement***. A sample Operating Agreement for a Delaware LLC is included in the Document Appendix as Document #3 (the "Form Operating Agreement").

The remainder of this Chapter will focus on an analysis of the following key provisions of an LLC operating agreement:

---

80. *See* DELAWARE CODE § 18–103.

81. *See generally* Waters, *supra* note 76.

82. *See* DELAWARE CODE §§ 18–503 and 18–504.

83. *See id.* § 18–402.

84. *See id.* § 18–303.

85. *See id.* § 18–1101.

- The provisions that describe the nature and scope of the members' obligations to make capital contributions to the LLC—Article 2 of the Form Operating Agreement;

- The provisions that govern the manner and order of priority in which the LLC's cash flow will be distributed to its members—Article 3 of the Form Operating Agreement; and

- The provisions that delineate who will be responsible for the day-to-day management of the LLC's business and what limitations, if any, will be placed on such person's management authority—Article 5 of the Form Operating Agreement.

The typical LLC operating agreement contains numerous provisions other than the three articles highlighted above. By way of example, the Form Operating Agreement has separate articles addressing the requirements for the initial organization of the LLC (Article 1), the allocation of items of taxable income and loss among the members (Article 4), the handling of the LLC's accounting and fiscal affairs (Article 6), the placement of restrictions on the transferability of the LLC membership interests (Article 7) and the procedures attendant to the dissolution and liquidation of the LLC's business (Article 9). While certainly important, these provisions tend to be more technical in nature[86] and, hence, are seldom the subject of much controversy between the developer and its outside equity investor.

Because the stated mission of this book is to examine the principal issues that a real estate development lawyer will encounter during the course of his representation of a developer, the choice has been made to focus on just those provisions of the operating agreement that are most often the subject of extended negotiations between the real estate development lawyer and counsel for the outside equity investor. The reader is, however, urged to carefully read through the other sections of the Form Operating Agreement in order to gain a sense of the legal and business issues underlying such sections.[87]

---

86. Such provisions are, for the most part, covered by a fairly specific set of statutory or regulatory rules. For example, most of the provisions contained in Articles 1, 6, 7 and 9 of the Form Operating Agreement are in the nature of either a confirmation of the default rules set forth in the Delaware Act or a specific divergence from those default rules. Additionally, the essence of the provisions of Article 4 of the Form Operating Agreement (those relating to the allocation of items of taxable income and loss among the members for federal income tax purposes) is governed by the highly complex rules set forth in the Treasury Regulations promulgated under Section 704(b) of the Internal Revenue Code. While it is absolutely essential that the real estate development lawyer master these statutory and regulatory doctrines in order to effectively represent his developer client, a detailed discussion of those highly technical rules is simply beyond the scope of this Chapter.

87. For an excellent discussion of such "other" provisions, *see* Kenneth M. Jacobson, *Sweating the Details: Issue and Negotiation Point Checklist for Limited Liability Company Operating Agreement Matters Pertaining to Capital Contributions, Management Structures and Decision-Making, Distributions, Exit Strategies and Indemnification*, in ACREL PAPERS 102 (ALI–ABA, March 2004); and Gary E. Fluhrer, Jan K. Gruben, Kenneth M. Jacobson, Lewis R. Kaster, Keith E. Osber, Joel M. Reck and Jonathon Rivin, *Multi-party Limited Liability Company Operating Agreement*, in ACREL PAPERS 133 (ALI–ABA, March 2004).

The three key provisions of the LLC operating agreement (that is, the provisions relating to the LLC's capital structure, its cash distribution scheme and its management plan) will be examined from the perspective of both the developer and the outside equity investor. The Form Operating Agreement will serve as the template for the discussion of those three provisions. The section of the Form Operating Agreement where the provision under discussion can be found will be identified in a parenthetical reference in the caption heading.

IX. CAPITALIZATION OF THE LLC. *(Article 2)*

Article 2 of the Form Operating Agreement covers the topic that is the central reason why the developer and its investors come together in the first instance—money. This article addresses two fundamental questions—(1) how will the LLC initially be capitalized, and (2) under what circumstances will additional capital be contributed to the LLC by its members?

A. INITIAL CAPITAL CONTRIBUTIONS. *(§2.1)*

An LLC is initially capitalized through cash, property and services contributed to the LLC by the developer and its outside equity investors (referred to collectively in the remainder of this Chapter as the ***members***). The legal and business issues related to each of these capital contributions are addressed separately in the next several sections of this Chapter.

1. Cash Contributions

In the typical real estate development deal, the members contribute cash to the LLC in an amount equal to the project's total development costs, minus the principal amount of the project's construction loan. The section of the operating agreement that covers the members' cash capital contributions needs to address the following three considerations:

- The amount of the cash contribution to be made by each member;

- The timing for the making of such cash contributions; and

- Any conditions precedent to a member's obligation to fund its cash contribution.

The developer generally wants to receive the equity investor's cash contribution without condition and as soon as possible—preferably coincident with the members' execution of the operating agreement.[88] The outside equity investor, on the other hand, often seeks to have its obligation to fund its cash contribution made expressly contingent upon

---

88. An exception to this general rule exists when the outside equity investors are entitled to a "preferred return" on their cash contributions, effective as of the date on which the cash is contributed to the LLC. The topic of an investor's preferred return is discussed in more detail *infra* Pages 243–245.

the occurrence of an event that confirms that the project is a "real deal"—e.g., the closing of the construction loan or the obtaining of an essential governmental approval. In all events, the lawyer representing the outside investor should require the developer to fund its cash contribution at the same time that the outside investor funds its contribution.

The provisions of the construction loan documents will also have an impact on the issue of the timing of the members' cash contributions. Some construction loans require ***front-end equity***, while others expressly permit ***back-end equity***. A requirement for front-end equity simply means that the members' cash contributions must be funded by the members and expended by the LLC to pay project development costs, before any loan proceeds will be disbursed to the LLC by the construction lender. Conversely, back-end equity refers to the situation where the members are required to fund their respective cash contributions only after the entire principal amount of the construction loan has been disbursed to the LLC. A construction lender will normally require front-end equity, because doing so lessens the lender's risk that the members will default in their obligation to fund the required cash contributions. A construction lender will agree to a back-end funding of the project equity only if (a) the funding member is extremely creditworthy and (b) the lender receives a personal guaranty from such member that it will fund its cash contribution to the LLC when and as needed to pay unpaid project costs.[89]

The developer's take on the issue of the timing of the member's funding of their cash contributions is driven by the developer's overriding objective of paying its development costs in the cheapest manner possible. This means that the developer will first want to pay the project's development costs with whatever source of funds has the lowest ***pay rate***. The pay rate on the construction loan is represented by the interest rate payable under the loan. The pay rate on the equity investor's capital contribution is the rate of return, if any, that has to be paid to the equity investor before any cash distributions are made to the developer. The required, priority return payable to an equity investor is known as a ***preferred return***.[90]

The developer's thought process on this timing issue is highlighted in the following example.

Example 7–2: Assume that Project X is owned by ABC LLC. The total development costs for Project X are $10 million, $8 million of which will be funded by a construction loan from Lender and $2 million of which will be funded by Investor's cash contributions. The interest rate payable on the construction loan is fixed at 8%. The operating agreement for ABC LLC provides that a preferred return of 10% will accrue on Investor's cash contributions, beginning on the date on which such contributions are first funded. If Lender were to

---

89. *See infra* Chapter 9, Page 349.

90. *See infra* Pages 243–245, for a more detailed discussion of the equity investor's preferred return.

approve back-end equity for the project, Investor's cash contribution would not have to be funded until 12 months after the construction loan closing.

Under the facts of the above example, the developer would achieve a cost savings of $40,000 if Lender were to permit Investor's cash contribution to be back-ended (that is, funded only after the full amount of the construction loan is disbursed to pay Project X's development costs). This cost savings is calculated by multiplying the amount of Investor's capital contribution ($2 million), by the difference between the preferred return payable on Investor's equity and the interest rate payable under the construction loan (10% − 8% = 2%). If ABC's operating agreement were not to require the payment of any preferred return on Investor's cash contribution (or more likely, were to defer the accrual of a preferred return until completion of the project's construction), then the developer would want Investor's equity to be front-ended, because it could use Investor's $2 million cash contribution interest-free for a period of 12 months—thereby saving the developer $160,000 in project development costs (the investor's $2 million equity contribution, multiplied by the 8% interest rate payable on the construction loan).

2. Property Contributions

While the capital contribution of the outside equity investor almost always take the form of cash (that is, after all, the one thing the equity investor has that the developer most wants), the developer frequently contributes property to the LLC (either as its sole capital contribution or in addition to its cash contribution). The following are the two most common property interests contributed to the capital of an LLC by a developer:

- The land on which the project will be constructed (if the land is already owned by the developer); and

- Intangible personal property related to the project—e.g., the developers contractual rights under the land purchase contract; architectural plans and specifications; and building permits and other governmental approvals.

If the developer is going to make a property contribution to an LLC, the operating agreement should address the following considerations.

- ***Agreed-upon Fair Market Value of Property Contribution***— Under financial accounting principles, the contributor of property is deemed to have made a capital contribution to the LLC in an amount equal to the fair market value of the property as of the date of its contribution. Because the determination of the fair market value of contributed property will have a direct impact on the computation of the members' respective distributive shares of the LLC's profits and losses, the topic of the agreed-upon fair market value of the contributed property is often the subject of intense negotiations. The agreed-upon value of the developer's property contribution should be clearly spelled out in the operating agreement, in order to preempt any future attempt by either the developer or the other member to renegotiate the fair market value of the contributed property. If the members decide that the property contribution has no discernible fair market value (as is often the case when the developer's property contributions consists of contractual and development rights related to the project), the parties should be equally assiduous in reflecting in the operating agreement their mutual agreement that the contributed rights have a $0 value.

- ***LLC's Assumption of Liabilities***. The developer will want to make sure that the LLC assumes all of the liabilities and obligations of the developer with respect to the contributed property— e.g., any mortgage loan that encumbers the contributed land or any contractual obligation placed on the developer under the land purchase contract. An indemnification from the LLC with respect to such liabilities and obligations should be included in the applicable provisions of the operating agreement.

- ***Representations and Warranties***. The other members of the LLC will want to receive contractual assurances from the developer concerning the status and condition of the contributed property. To the extent land is being contributed to the LLC, the developer should expect the outside equity investors to insist that the developer make representations and warranties to the LLC similar to those customarily contained in a land purchase contract.[91] If the property contribution consists of contractual and development rights associated with the LLC's proposed project, the representations and warranties are usually limited to an affirmation that the developer has the ability to transfer such rights to the LLC and that no default exists under the transferred rights. The outside equity investor should also ask for the inclusion in the operating agreement of a right to reduce any cash distributions owed to the developer by the amount of any damages incurred by the LLC due to the developer's breach of its representations and warranties.

3. Tax Consequences of Property Contributions

A contribution of property to an LLC in exchange for the contributor's receipt of an LLC membership interest is generally a tax-free event at both the LLC and property contributor level.[92] Exceptions to this general rule may apply if (a) the contributor receives cash in return for its contribution of property to the LLC or (b) the contributor is relieved of liabilities in excess of its tax basis in the contributed property. The tax rules governing these two scenarios are extremely complex.[93] A lawyer

---

91. *See supra* Chapter 5, Pages 116–125, for a discussion of the land seller's representations and warranties.

92. *See* INTERNAL REVENUE CODE § 721(a).

93. *See generally* MCKEE, supra note 10, at § 4.01.

representing a developer who either receives cash or is relived of a liability as the result of its contribution of property to an LLC should consult those tax rules to determine their applicability to the developer's property contribution.

The tax basis of the property contributor's membership interest will be equal to the sum of (a) any cash contributed by it to the LLC, plus (b) the tax basis of the contributed property in its hands immediately prior to such contribution.[94] The tax basis of the contributed property in the hands of the LLC is similarly deemed to be equal to the adjusted tax basis of that property in the hands of the property contributor immediately prior to its contribution to the LLC.[95] These tax rules stand in sharp contrast to the financial accounting principles mentioned earlier, which require that the property contributor's capital account be credited with an amount equal to the agreed-upon fair market value of the contributed property. There is, as a result, a disparity between the value of the contributed property on the LLC's books and the LLC's tax basis in such property. The difference between the value and the tax basis of the property on the date of its contribution to the LLC is referred to as a ***book/tax disparity***.[96] Any taxable gain realized by the LLC on its ultimate sale of the contributed property must first be allocated to the property contributor in an amount equal to such book/tax disparity.[97]

The operation of this tax rule is illustrated by the following example.

Example 7–3: Developer contributes land to ABC LLC. The contributed land has an agreed fair market value of $1 million. Developer's tax basis in the land on the date of its contribution to ABC LLC is $800,000.[98] Investor makes a cash contribution to ABC LLC of $3 million. Developer and Investor agree that they will split all profits and losses generated by the activities of ABC in the same 75–25% ratio that characterizes the respective values of their capital contributions to ABC. The land is later sold by ABC for $1 million, triggering a taxable gain of $200,000 (the $1 million purchase price, less ABC's adjusted tax basis in the land of $800,000).

Under Section 704(c) of the Internal Revenue Code, the entire $200,000 gain realized by ABC LLC must be allocated to Developer and reported on its federal income tax return. If the land had been sold for $1.2 million (thereby triggering a taxable gain of $400,000), the first $200,000 of such gain would have been allocated to Developer, with the

---

94. *See* INTERNAL REVENUE CODE § 722.

95. *See id.* § 723.

96. *See* Robert R. Casey, Kelly M. Bender and John T. Albers, *Partnership Allocations—Introduction*, in ALI–ABA COURSE OF STUDY MATERIALS, PARTNERSHIPS, LLCS AND LLPS: UNIFORM ACTS, TAXATION, DRAFTING, SECURITIES, AND BANKRUPTCY, Course No. SR–012, 249, 260–265 (July 2009).

97. *See* INTERNAL REVENUE CODE § 704(c).

98. The tax basis of a real estate asset is generally equal to its initial cost, plus the cost of any additions or improvements made to the asset, and less any depreciation deductions taken by the asset owner. Because land is by definition a non-depreciable asset, Developer's adjusted basis of the contributed land is equal to the developer's cost of acquiring the land. *See generally* LEFCOE, *supra* note 24, at 624.

remaining $200,000 of gain being allocated 75% to Investor and 25% to Developer.

4. Service Contributions

The developer is often granted an LLC membership interest in consideration of its past efforts in putting the deal together (for example, putting the land under contract, getting the property rezoned and attracting tenants to the project) and its agreement to continue to work in the future to bring the project to a successful conclusion. The equity interest given to the developer in consideration of its provision of services to the LLC is usually in addition to the equity interest received by the developer in exchange for its contribution of cash or property to the LLC. By way of example, the developer might receive (1) a 25% membership interest in exchange for its contribution of 25% of the LLC's total required capital, plus (2) an additional 15% membership interest in consideration of its provision of past and future services to the LLC.

There are two types of membership interests that can be granted to a developer in exchange for its contribution of services to the LLC—a *capital interest* and a *profits interest*. A capital interest entitles the developer to an immediate share of the value of all existing LLC assets. In contrast, a profits interest only entitles the developer to a share of the profits that are attributable either to the LLC's future operations or a future appreciation in the value of the LLC's assets.

The following simple example highlights the difference between these two interests.

> **Example 7–4:** Assume that ABC LLC's sole asset is a parcel of land purchased by ABC on the date of its formation for $1 million. Assume further that Investor contributes cash of $1 million to fund ABC's land acquisition and that Developer makes no cash or property contribution whatsoever. Investor is given a 70% interest in the LLC and that Developer receives a 30% LLC interest. Finally, assume that ABC sells its land one year later for $1.5 million.

If Developer's membership interest were to be characterized as a capital interest, the proceeds of the land sale would be distributed to the members as follows:

- Developer—$450,000
- Investor—$1,050,000

If, on the other hand, the developer's membership interest were to be treated as a profits interest, the proceeds of the land sale would be distributed to the members as follows:

- Developer—$150,000
- Investor—$1,350,000

The difference between the two types of interests is that a capital interest gives Developer a 30% interest in all of the land sale proceeds (including both the portion of such proceeds attributable to the initial land value of $1 million and the portion attributable to the land appreciation of $500,000), while a profits interest restricts Developer's share of the land sales proceeds to 30% of the land appreciation of $500,000.

5. Tax Consequences of Service Contributions

For the last 40 years, legal scholars and practitioners have engaged in a vigorous debate as to whether the grant of an equity interest in exchange for a contribution of services should result in the recognition of current income to the service provider.[99] While the courts and legal commentators long ago agreed that the grant of a capital interest to a service provider should be a taxable event, no such consensus existed until recently on the issue of whether a service provider's receipt of a profits interest should be taxable.[100]

In 1993, the IRS finally provided some certainty on the issue of the tax consequences of a taxpayer's receipt of a profits interest in exchange for services. In Revenue Procedure 93–27, the IRS stated that it will generally not treat a partner's receipt of a profits interest as a taxable event.[101] The IRS defined a profits interest as being any interest other than a capital interest. It then described a capital interest as "an interest that would give the holder a share of the proceeds if the partnership's assets were sold at fair market value and then the proceeds were distributed in complete liquidation of the partnership. This determination is generally made at the time of the receipt of the partnership interest."[102]

In May of 2005, the IRS issued Proposed Regulations that also sought to deal with the tax consequences of a service provider's receipt of an equity interest from a pass-through tax entity.[103] The Proposed Regulations start out by rejecting the notion embraced by Revenue Procedure 93–27 that a person's receipt of a profits interest in exchange for the performance of services is not a taxable event. Rather the Proposed Regulations expressly state that capital and profits interests (collectively referred to in the Proposed Regulations as "compensatory partnership

---

99. The debate started in 1971 when the Tax Court held that the receipt of a profits interest was taxable to a service partner. *See* Sol Diamond v. Commissioner, 56 T.C. 530 (1971), *aff'd* 492 F.2d 286 (7th Cir. 1974). For a discussion of subsequent court decisions addressing the tax consequences of the grant of a profits interest to a service partner, *see* McKEE, *supra* note 10, at § 5.02.

100. The putative treatment of the receipt of a profits interest as a taxable event is a developer's worst nightmare—i.e., its required payment of taxes at a time when it has not yet received any cash benefit from its ownership of the profits interest.

101. *See* Revenue Procedure 93–27, 1993–2 C.B. 343, § 4.01. Revenue Procedure 93–27 states that its pronouncements do not apply to the receipt of a profits interest if—(1) the profits interests relates to a "substantially certain and predictable stream of income from high quality debt securities or a high-quality net lease", (2), within two years of receipt, the partner disposes of the profits interest, or (3) the profits interest is a limited partnership interest in a "publicly traded limited partnership." *See id.* at § 4.02.

102. *See id.* at § 2.01. The reference in Revenue Procedure 93–27 and other IRS pronouncements to a "partnership interest" includes a membership interest in a limited liability company that is taxed as a partnership under Subchapter K of the Internal Revenue Code.

103. *See* Proposed Treasury Regulation §§ 1.721–1(b)(1) and 1.83–3(e) (2005).

interests") will be treated in a like manner for federal income tax purposes, with the recipient of either such interest being deemed to have received taxable income in an amount equal to the excess of the fair market value of such interest over the amount paid for such interest by the service provider.[104]

At first blush, the Proposed Regulations seem to be a drastic departure from the tax treatment afforded to a member's receipt of a profits interest under Revenue Procedure 93–27. Fortunately, however, the IRS simultaneously released an IRS Notice,[105] which, when read together with the Proposed Regulations, creates a safe harbor that effectively provides the same tax result for the recipient of a profits interest as that currently mandated under Revenue Procedure 93–27.[106]

The Proposed Regulations state that the fair market value of a compensatory partnership interest will be deemed to be equal to its "liquidation value."[107] In IRS Notice 2005–43, the IRS defines "liquidation value" in a manner that is virtually identical to the definition given to a "capital interest" in Revenue Procedure 93–27. Specifically, IRS Notice 2005–43 states that:

> Liquidation value . . . means the amount of cash that the recipient of the Compensatory Partnership Interest would receive if, immediately after the transfer, the partnership sold all of its assets (including goodwill, going concern value, and any other intangibles associated with the partnership's operations) for cash equal to the fair market value of those assets and then liquidated.[108]

As discussed in the previous section of this Chapter, a profits interest does not give a member the right to receive any cash upon a liquidation of the LLC immediately following the member's receipt of its membership interest.[109] Under the Proposed Regulations and IRS Notice 2005–43, a profits interest will, by definition, have a $0 liquidation value.[110] Therefore, while the member's receipt of the profits interest may be a taxable event within the meaning of the Proposed Regulations, no tax will be payable as a result of the member's receipt of that profits interest.

---

104. *See* MCKEE, *supra* note 10, at § 5.02[8].

105. *See* IRS Notice 2005–43, 2005–1 C.B. 1221 (May 24, 2005).

106. The safe harbor established for profits interest under IRS Notice 2005–43 will only be available to those entities that affirmatively elect to be covered by its provisions. The procedures to be followed in making such election are specified in the IRS notice and specifically include the insertion in an LLC's operating agreement of a provision authorizing and validating the LLC's safe harbor election. *See id.* at § 3.03(2). Section 6.3 of the Form Operating Agreement contains such a safe harbor election (based on the premise the Proposed Regulations will become final in their current form).

107. The "fair market value = liquidation value" safe harbor is not, however, applicable to the three types of profits interests described *supra,* at note 101, that were excluded from the application of Revenue Procedure 93–27. *See* IRS Notice 2005–43, *supra* note 105, at § 3.02(1).

108. *See* IRS Notice 2005–43, *supra* note 105, at § 4.02.

109. *See supra* Page 229, Example 7–4.

110. *See* CUNNINGHAM, *supra,* note 11, at 135.

A member's receipt of a capital interest will, however, clearly produce taxable income for that member under the Proposed Regulations and IRS Notice 2005–43. A recipient of a capital interest gains an immediate share in the value of the entity's existing assets. If the entity were to sell its assets and liquidate immediately following the issuance of a capital interest to one of its members, that member would be entitled to a share of the liquidation proceeds—with that share being deemed to be the "liquidation value" of the member's capital interest under IRS Notice 2005–43. Under the rules set forth in the Proposed Regulations, the recipient of the capital interest would be deemed to have taxable income in the year of its receipt of such interest in an amount equal to the interest's liquidation value.

If final regulations are adopted that are wholly consistent with the Proposed Regulations (as supplemented by IRS Notice 2005–43), Revenue Procedure 93–27 will automatically become obsolete.[111] The Proposed Regulations are currently in the comment stage and, as of the date of the writing of this Chapter, no date has been publicly projected for the issuance of final Regulations.[112]

There are two general propositions that are clear under whichever tax regime is ultimately in force (that is, either Revenue Procedure 93–27 or the Proposed Regulations):

- The receipt of a profits interest in exchange for the performance of services will not result in the recognition of any taxable income by the recipient of that profits interest;[113] and

- The receipt of a capital interest in exchange for the performance of services will result in the recipient's recognition of taxable income in an amount equal to recipient's share of the liquidation value of the entity's assets, less the amount of any cash or other property contributed by it to the entity.

The practitioner should, however, be mindful that, if and when the Proposed Regulations become effective, the rules that will govern the qualification of a profits interest for tax-free treatment will be considerably more complex and administratively exacting than is the case under current tax practice.

6. The Importance of Profits Interests

So why the big fuss about a profits interest? The answer lies in the fact that the developer's receipt of a profits interest in exchange for its

---

111. *See* IRS Notice 2005–43, *supra* note 105, at § 7.

112. According to Professor McKee, "a representative of the U.S. Treasury Department has stated publicly that they are waiting to see what happens with the carried interest legislation proposed in early 2009 before acting to finalize the 2005 Proposed Regulations." *See* McKee, *supra* note 10, at § 5.02[8]. *See infra* Pages 252–256, for a discussion of the proposed carried interest legislation.

113. This statement is subject to the caveat that a profits interest of a type described in note 101, *supra,* might be subject to current tax based on the theory that such an interest has a readily determinable value on the date of its grant.

provision of services to the LLC is the most commonly used method to economically reward the developer for its efforts in putting the real estate deal together. Key employees of the developer are also frequently given profits interests to reward them for their past performance and to incentivize them to perform in the future in a manner intended to maximize the profitability of the LLC's real estate project.

The existence of a generous profits interest is often the linchpin of the economics supporting a developer's decision to move forward with a particular project. A profits interest affords the developer and its senior staff with the opportunity to reap significant financial rewards, without having to take any commensurate capital risk. The fact that a profits interest can be doled out in an extremely tax efficient manner is an added reason why the grant of a profits interest is an indispensable component of most equity deals struck between the developer and its outside equity investor.[114]

HIBC Case Study—Profits Interests

The equity deal struck in February 2000 by The Pizzuti Companies (the developer) and Nationwide Realty Investors, Ltd. (its outside equity investor) stands as an excellent example of how the grant of profits interests can be structured to benefit the developer and its key employees. The operating agreement for the Pizzuti–Nationwide LLC provided that profits generated from new development projects would be split as follows:

Nationwide	*55%*
Pizzuti	*30 %*
Key Pizzuti Employees	*15 %*

*While Pizzuti and its key employees received an aggregate profit split of 45%, they were only obligated to contribute 10% of the required capital (10% by Pizzuti and 0% by the key employees). The 35% incremental profit share (referred to by real estate investment bankers as a **promoted interest** or **promote**)[115] was granted to Pizzuti and its employees in exchange for their performance of services for the benefit of the LLC. Nationwide was more than willing to grant the 35% promoted interest to the developer and its employees for two reasons:*

- *The promote would only kick in after Nationwide had first received a 10% preferred return on its capital contributions;[116] and*

---

114. A profits interest is considered tax efficient for two reasons—(1) it can be granted without triggering any current tax consequences to either the grantor or recipient of the interest (*see supra* Pages 230–232) and (2) a significant portion of the cash distributions payable under a profits interest (specifically the proceeds payable on a sale of the project) will ordinarily be taxed as a capital gain (currently taxed at a maximum rate of 15%) and not as compensation income (currently taxed at a maximum rate of 35%). *See infra* Pages 252–256.

115. The size of a developer's promote is determined by subtracting from its percentage interest in the LLC's profits (its "profit split") its percentage share of the capital contributions required to be made to the LLC (its "capital split").

> • *The promote would incentivize Pizzuti and it senior executives to do everything within their power to make the new projects a success— thereby producing a true win-win for all the equity participants.*

Because the promoted interests were properly structured as profits interests in accordance with the guidelines laid out in Revenue Procedure 93–27, the grant of the 35% promote was effected in a wholly tax-free manner.

The Pizzuti–Nationwide equity structure was markedly different from the arrangement that Pizzuti had struck with its prior equity investor— Newport Partners. The equity deal that Pizzuti negotiated with Newport did not provide for the grant of ANY profits interests to either Pizzuti or its employees. The profits generated from their jointly-owned projects were split in the same 50–50 ratio that governed their respective obligations to contribute capital to the entities that owned such projects. The absence of any promote was directly attributable to Newport's willingness to serve as a general partner of each project entity and to personally guaranty 50% of all construction debt. The trade-off for Newport's agreement to reduce Pizzuti's overall project risk was the concomitant reduction in Pizzuti's overall economic return from the project (manifested in the elimination of any disproportionate profits interest in Pizzuti's favor). While Pizzuti deemed this to be an acceptable trade-off during the early years of its work on the HIBC project (when the risk associated with that project was at its peak), it was the absence of a profits interest for itself and its key employees that drove Pizzuti in 2000 to replace Newport with Nationwide as its principal outside equity provider for the HIBC project.[117]

B. ADDITIONAL CAPITAL CONTRIBUTIONS. *(§2.2)*

The discussion thus far in this section has focused on the capital contributed by the members at the inception of the LLC's formation. The next topic to be addressed is the post-formation capitalization of an LLC in the form of additional capital contributions made by the members. Many of the principles and concepts addressed in the initial capitalization section have equal applicability to the topic of additional capital contributions. For example, additional capital contributions can take the form of cash, property or service contributions and the tax consequences of any such additional contributions are the same as those discussed earlier with respect to the initial capitalization of the LLC.

Additional capital contributions involve the funding of those project costs that were not sufficiently foreseeable on the date of the LLC's

---

116. *See infra* Pages 243–245, for a discussion of preferred returns.

117. *See infra* Pages 282–284, and *infra* Chapter 12, Pages 565–567, for a further discussion of Pizzuti's termination of its relationship with Newport.

formation, so as to be included in the company's initial capital budget. Unforeseeable project costs generally fall into one of two categories:

- Costs attributable to project cost overruns or operating deficits; or

- Costs attributable to an unexpected expansion or change in the LLC's business.

The category in which a particular project cost falls will go a long way toward determining whether such cost will be funded through additional capital contributions made to the LLC by its members.

1. Optional vs. Mandatory Contributions

The first question that must be answered is whether a member is obligated to make an additional capital contribution to the LLC and, if so, under what circumstances does that obligation exist? The answer to that question is pretty clear as it relates to the second category of costs referenced above—that is, those costs which are related to an unexpected expansion or change in the LLC's business. A member will rarely, if ever, be obligated to make an additional contribution to fund the payment of a cost in that category. Indeed, in most negotiated deals, whoever is managing the LLC will be prohibited from incurring any cost in that second category, without first obtaining the consent of the outside equity investor.[118]

The funding of costs attributable to project cost overruns or operating deficits raises an entirely different and more difficult set of questions. The following are two classic examples of this category of project costs:

- Debt service payments that were not included in the project budget either due to (a) an unexpected increase in the floating rate of interest on the project's construction debt or (b) a slower than anticipated lease-up of the project, thereby postponing the budgeted onset of rental income to cover the debt service payments; and

- Construction costs incurred to address adverse soils conditions or some other project condition that was unknown at the time of the formation of the LLC.

The developer typically tries to hedge the LLC's financial risk by including in the project's initial capitalization budget a contingency reserve or other miscellaneous account to deal with the funding of such cost overruns.[119] However, despite such preventive measures, cost overruns occur on a fairly regular basis on real estate development projects. If left unfunded, such cost overruns can delay the timely completion of the project and, in the most extreme of situations, lead to the construction lender's foreclosure of the project. The question, therefore, becomes not whether, but how to fund such cost overruns.

---

118. *See infra* Pages 263–266.

119. *See supra* Chapter 3, Page 41. All references in this section to "cost overruns" are also intended to include operating deficits produced by the project's operating expenses being greater than its rental receipts.

The members' customary first option for the funding of cost overruns is debt—either an increase in the amount of the project's construction loan or a new loan. However, debt may not be available in sufficient amounts to fund the payment of the cost overruns or may be available only on prohibitive economic and business terms. In recognition of this fact, the members of an LLC usually include in the LLC operating agreement a provision which deals in some fashion with the members' making of additional capital contributions to fund the payment of cost overruns. As might be expected, the views of the developer and the outside equity investor on how those provisions should be crafted are usually quite divergent.

2. Investor's Perspective on Additional Capital Contributions

The outside equity investor's posture on additional capital contributions is influenced by its belief that any cost overrun is invariably the fault of the developer. After all, didn't the developer market the project to the investor by selling itself as a real estate development expert, who was eminently qualified to complete and operate the project on time and on budget?

Given this mind set (which is, at least to some extent, logically justifiable), it should not be surprising that the equity investor's typical starting point in negotiations about additional capital contributions is that:[120]

- The investor will have no obligation whatsoever to make any additional capital contributions to the LLC;

- The developer will be required to make additional capital contributions to cover 100% of any cost overruns; and

- Any additional capital contributions made by the developer will be subordinate to the investor's capital position (meaning that such additional capital will only be repaid to the developer after the investor has received a full return "of" all of its initial capital and maybe even some minimum percentage of a return "on" its invested capital.[121]

By adopting this stance, the outside equity investor is effectively asking the developer to guaranty the accuracy of the project budget on which the LLC's initial capitalization was based.

3. Developer's Perspective on Additional Capital Contributions

The developer's view of cost overruns is colored by its pragmatic world view that "stuff happens." In the developer's mind, a project budget

---

120. *See* Caryl B. Welborn, *Limited Liability Company Operating Agreement*, in ALI–ABA COURSE OF STUDY MATERIALS, MODERN REAL ESTATE TRANSACTIONS, Course No. SR–001, 1033, ARTICLE 3 (August 2009) for an example of an additional capital contribution clause that incorporates these concepts.

121. A return "of" an investor's capital refers to the distribution to the investor of its original invested capital. A return "on" the investor's capital refers to the periodic earnings received by the investor on its invested capital.

is not a financial guaranty, but rather simply a reasonable estimate of the costs that will be incurred during the course of the development of a real estate project. While the developer is willing to take certain actions designed to limit the prospects of a cost overrun (e.g., the execution of a guaranteed maximum price construction contract that places an upper ceiling on the construction price payable to the project's general contractor),[122] it also knows that real estate development is not an exact science and that it cannot control all of the variables that can impact the financial performance of a commercial real estate project.

With these thoughts in mind, the real estate development lawyer's first draft of the additional capital contribution section of the operating agreement will customarily have the following flavor:

- The developer will have unilateral, unconditional right to call for the members to make additional capital contributions to fund any project cost overrun; and

- The members' funding of such additional capital contributions will be made in the same ratio and with the same relative priority as the funding of their initial capital contributions to the LLC.

A particularly cheeky developer might take this position one step further by asserting that the outside equity investors should be responsible for funding 100% of the cost overruns, without any financial participation whatsoever by the developer.

4. Possible Compromises

While the developer and its equity investor may differ on who should be responsible for funding cost overruns, they share the objective of wanting to make sure that those overruns are ultimately funded in some manner (because they know that if the overruns aren't funded, the project's commercial viability may be threatened). The following is a list of some compromise provisions that are often used to bridge the parties' differences on the additional capital contribution subject.[123]

- The members can agree to a limited number of cost categories that will be subject to mandatory, additional capital contributions—e.g., debt service costs; costs set forth in an approved operating budget; real estate taxes and other costs that, if not timely paid, will produce significant, adverse legal consequences to the LLC; and any other costs that are not within the reasonable control of the developer.

- The members can stipulate that certain types of cost overruns must be funded by the developer—e.g., those overruns that are caused by the developer's negligence or misconduct.[124]

---

122. *See infra* Chapter 10, Pages 430–431, for a discussion of guaranteed maximum price contracts.

123. *See generally,* Jacobson, *supra* note 87, at 108–113.

124. *See e.g.,* Welborn, *supra* note 120, at § 3.4. *See also* H. Edward Hales, Jr., *Drafting Partnership Agreements and Operating Agreements: Selected Issues—Form Operating Agreement:*

- The members can agree to place a cap on the amount of the additional capital contributions that a member is obligated to make to the LLC; or

- The members can agree to afford a priority return status to certain additional capital contributions—e.g., a requirement that any additional capital contributions made by the outside equity investor must be repaid in full, with interest, before any cash distributions are made to the developer.

Each of the suggested compromise provisions can be used separately or in conjunction with one or more of the other provisions. By way of example, § 2.2 of the Form Operating Agreement adopts a hybrid approach by limiting each member's mandatory capital contribution obligation to the funding of those costs that are incurred for an "approved purpose"—generally meaning any cost that is consistent with a budget previously approved by the members.

5. Remedies for Failure to Contribute Additional Capital. *(§2.3)*

The Operating Agreement should identify the remedies that will be available to the LLC and the non-defaulting members to redress a member's failure to make a mandatory additional capital contribution. The following is a menu of contractual rights and prohibitions that are commonly included in an operating agreement to remedy a member's failure to make a required additional capital contribution to an LLC:[125]

- The right of a non-defaulting member to make up the shortfall in the defaulting member's additional capital funding, either in the form of an additional capital contribution to the LLC or a loan to the defaulting member;[126]

- The loss by the defaulting member of certain rights granted to it in the Operating Agreement—e.g., the right to vote on proposed LLC actions or the right to trigger a buy-sell provision;

- The grant to the LLC of the right to offset the amount of a defaulted additional capital contribution obligation against any cash or property distributions otherwise due to the defaulting member under the terms of the Operating Agreement;

- The grant of an option to the non-defaulting members to buy the membership interest of the defaulting member in accordance with

---

Pro–Developer, in ALI–ABA COURSE OF STUDY MATERIALS, PARTNERSHIPS, LLCS AND LLPS: UNIFORM ACTS, TAXATION, DRAFTING, SECURITIES AND BANKRUPTCY, Course No. SL–013, 245, § 4.2 (April 2006).

125. The listed alternatives may be used separately or in conjunction with each other and are in addition to the normal remedies triggered by any contractual default—e.g., damages, specific performance and rescission.

126. This remedy is contained in an operating agreement in recognition of the LLC's continuing need to pay its bills, regardless whether all the members comply with their additional funding obligations. A non-defaulting member who makes up the funding shortfall will customarily receive an exalted priority return status on the amount of its shortfall funding, with interest accruing on such funding at a relatively high rate.

the provisions of a buy-sell provision contained in the operating agreement;[127]

- A so-called **squeeze-down** right, pursuant to which the non-defaulting member may elect to cause the LLC to recalculate the ratios in which the members will share in the LLC's future profits and losses. A squeeze-down provision usually seeks to punish the defaulting member for its failure to fund its share of the required additional capital by reducing the defaulting member's future economic sharing ratio below its share of the total capital contributed to the LLC. By way of example, a squeeze-down provision might state that the defaulting member's future participating percentage will be equal to 50% of the ratio that the defaulting member's total funded capital contributions bears to the total funded capital contributions of all the members.[128]

One consideration that a lawyer representing the developer must keep in mind when negotiating remedy provisions is that, in most instances, the outside equity investor has greater financial strength and liquidity than does the developer. As such, the careful real estate development lawyer should never allow his developer client to be placed in a situation where the outside equity investor can make a unilateral call for additional capital to the disadvantage of the developer. This advice is particularly crucial if the operating agreement contains a squeeze-down provision that would permit the outside equity investors to significantly reduce or wholly eliminate the developer's interest in the project if the developer is unwilling or unable to satisfy the investor's capital call.

X. CASH DISTRIBUTIONS. *(Article 3)*

The cash distribution sections of the operating agreement are the one set of provisions that are sure to be read (over and over again) by the developer and the outside equity investor. These provisions address the two topics that hold the most interest for the members—how the cash flow created by the development project will be split among the members and when that cash flow will be paid to them? As noted in an earlier chapter of this book, a real estate development project's value is ultimately determined based upon the amount and timing of the cash flows

---

127. Provisions permitting the non-defaulting member to buy the membership interest of the defaulting member frequently provide that the price payable to the defaulting member on any such buy-out will be discounted in some fashion from the price otherwise payable under the operating agreement's buy-sell provision. A discount of this type is often referred to as a "haircut." *See infra* Pages 278–282, for a general discussion of buy-sell clauses.

128. *See* Fluhrer, *Multi-party Limited Liability Company Operating Agreement, supra* note 87, at § 4.3, for an example of a "squeeze-down" provision. Depending on the level of the squeeze-down, an argument could be made by the defaulting member that the squeeze-down is an unenforceable penalty. *See* ROBERT L. WHITMIRE, WILLIAM F. NELSON, WILLIAM S. MCKEE, MARK A. KULLER, SANDRA W. HALLMARK AND JOE GARCIA, JR., STRUCTURING AND DRAFTING PARTNERSHIP AGREEMENTS (INCLUDING LLC AGREEMENTS) § 3.06970 (3rd ed. 2003); and Lindquist, *supra* note 79, at 49. If the defaulting member is the manager or managing member of the LLC, the application of a squeeze-down provision will customarily also result in the defaulting member's loss of all of its management authority.

generated from that project.[129] Article 3 of the Form Operating Agreement spells out the manner in which each member will participate in the project's cash flow and, hence, in the overall value of the development project.[130]

A. CATEGORIES OF CASH FLOW

There are two basic categories of cash flow that an LLC derives from its ownership and operation of a real estate development project:

- Cash flow attributable to the LLC's day-to-day conduct of its rental and development operations (***Operating Cash Flow***); and

- Cash flow attributable to the occurrence of certain capital transactions, such as the sale of all or a part of the project, the refinancing of project debt, a condemnation or casualty related to the project, or the occurrence of some other event outside the realm of the LLC's regular business activities (***Capital Proceeds***).

Cash flow is separated into these two separate categories, because the members will often want to distribute Operating Cash Flow and Capital Proceeds in significantly different ways. If the members opt to distribute Operating Cash Flow and Capital Proceeds in the same way (for example, in proportion to their respective capital contributions to the LLC), there is no need to create two categories of cash flow in the Operating Agreement and both such categories can be included under a single, umbrella definition of ***Cash Flow***.

The Form Operating Agreement contains the following definitions of Operating Cash Flow and Capital Proceeds.[131]

"Capital Proceeds" means the gross cash receipts of the Company produced from the occurrence of a Capital Event,[132] reduced by the sum of the following: (a) all cash expenditures paid in connection with

---

129. *See supra* Chapter 3, Page 37.

130. It is important to take note of the difference between "cash flow" and "profit and loss." Profit and loss is an accounting and tax concept that measures the overall economic profitability (or lack thereof) of the LLC's business activities. Cash flow is the amount of cash that is actually available to be distributed to the LLC's members after deducting from the LLC's gross cash revenues any and all cash expenditures made by the LLC. Over the entirety of the LLC's existence, the profits and losses incurred by the LCC will, by definition, equal the LLC's cash flow during such entire period (less the amount of such cash flow consisting of a return of the members' capital contributions to the LLC). There can, however, be significant timing differences between the amount of the LLC's profits and its cash flow during a particular interim period of the LLC's existence. By way of example, the members of an LLC could opt to use a portion of the cash generated in a particular period to purchase an adjacent tract of land for future development—a decision which would decrease the LLC's cash flow, without decreasing the LLC's profits for such period. The attention of the members will generally be focused on the timing and amount of the cash distributions they receive from the LLC and not on the more ethereal, tax and accounting concepts of profit and loss.

131. *See* Form Operating Agreement, Exhibit A—Definitions.

132. A "Capital Event" generally refers to a sale or refinancing of a project or the occurrence of some other event outside of the course of the LLC's normal business activities (for example, a condemnation or casualty), which produces cash proceeds to the LLC. *See id.*

the Capital Event, including, without limitation, any brokerage commissions or fees paid to any party; (b) the repayment of the principal and any accrued and unpaid interest on any debt being refinanced or retired as part of the Capital Event; and (c) such cash reserves as Developer may decide to establish, with the consent of the Investor, to cover future occurrences and contingencies.

"Operating Cash Flow" means, with respect to each Fiscal Quarter of the Company, the sum of the gross cash receipts of the Company from any source other than Capital Proceeds, plus the amount of any previously-established, but unused cash reserves, reduced by the sum of the following items paid by the Company: (a) all principal and interest payments and all other sums paid on or with respect to any indebtedness; (b) all operating expenses incurred incident to the operation of the Project; (c) all capital expenditures incurred incident to the construction, repair or replacement of the Project; (d) such cash reserves as Developer may from time to time decide to establish, with the consent of the Investor, to cover future occurrences and contingencies; and (e) all other cash expenditures made by the Company related to the ownership, operation or management of the Project and the Company's business (other than any expenditure made in connection with the occurrence of a Capital Event).

Note that there is a reduction in both definitions for "cash reserves" established by the developer (in this case, with the investor's consent). A ***cash reserve*** is a deposit made by the LLC into a "rainy day" bank account. Cash reserves are usually created for one of two reasons—either as (1) a general reserve to hedge the LLC's exposure to unknown and unforeseeable contingencies or (2) a specific reserve to deal with a reasonably foreseeable future occurrence that could result in the LLC not having sufficient cash on hand to pay all of its expenses (such as a tenant moving out of the project). A natural tension exists on the topic of cash reserves between the developer (who is generally loath to set up any reserves) and its outside equity investors (who regularly push for the establishment of fairly significant cash reserves). The developer is, by nature, more optimistic than the typical conservative equity investor, who sees financial catastrophe lurking around every corner. This inherent difference in approach is amplified by the fact that the outside equity investor usually is entitled to receive its cash distributions from the LLC before the developer has the right to receive its cash distributions. As such, the establishment of a cash reserve will hit the developer in the pocketbook well before it affects the outside investor. A carefully crafted operating agreement should specifically address which of the members has the authority to establish a cash reserve and what, if any, limitations are placed on that authority.

B. SCHEMES FOR THE DISTRIBUTION OF CASH FLOW

The previous section focused on the calculation of the amount of cash flow that is available for distribution to the LLC's members. The next question that the real estate development lawyer must address is how that cash flow will be divided among the members of the LLC. In answering that question, the first place to look is the default rules contained in the applicable state LLC statute. By way of example, the Delaware Act provides that:

> Distribution of cash or other assets of a limited liability company shall be allocated among the members ... in the manner provided in the limited liability company agreement. If the limited liability company agreement does not so provide, distributions shall be made on the basis of the agreed value (as stated in the records of the limited liability company) of the contributions made by each member to the extent they have been received by the limited liability company and have not been returned.[133]

The default rule, therefore, is that all cash flow will be distributed to the members in proportion to the respective amounts of their capital contributions (the so-called **capital split**). Outside equity investors are typically more than happy to follow the default rule, because doing so means that it will receive a percentage of the LLC's cash flow that is commensurate with its capital split (which, in the typical situation is much higher than the developer's capital split). The default rule is not viewed with the same level of acceptance by the developer, who has contributed his "blood, sweat and tears"[134] to making the project successful and is likely personally guarantying repayment of the project's construction loan. The developer ardently believes that its relative contribution to the project is far greater than its stated capital split and, therefore, that its share of the project's cash flow should be set at a percentage well in excess of that capital split.

As discussed earlier in this Chapter, the conflicting viewpoints of the developer and its outside equity investor are usually resolved by granting the developer an additional profits interest in the venture. The remainder of this discussion will assume that the handshake agreement between the developer and its outside equity investor is that cash contributions will be made 75% by the outside equity investor and 25% by the developer, while the LLC's profits will be split 50–50. The 25% difference between the developer's capital split and its profits split is the promote discussed earlier in this Chapter.[135] Because the grant to the developer of a profits

---

133. *See* DELAWARE CODE ANNOTATED, Title 6, § 18–504 (West 2010).

134. The developer's contribution of such blood, sweat and terms has given rise to the term "sweat equity" to describe the services contributed to a real estate venture by the developer. *See* Lindquist, *supra* note 79, at 46.

135. *See supra* Pages 242–243.

interest greater than its capital split takes the deal outside of the scope of the default rule of the Delaware Act, the members will need to specifically address in the operating agreement the manner in which the LLC's cash flow will be distributed to its members.

Translating the parties handshake agreement on the grant to the developer of a 25% promote into a comprehensive scheme for the distribution of the LLC's cash flow requires a resolution of the following issues.

- Will the members be entitled to a preferred return on the amount of their capital contributions?

- When will the members' capital contributions be returned?

- Will the same distribution scheme apply to both Operating Cash Flow and Capital Proceeds?

1. Preferred Return

It is fairly common for the outside equity investor to insist that it must receive a minimum cash return on its capital contributions before the developer gets to receive any distributions attributable to its 25% promoted interest. This minimum cash return is commonly referred to as a ***preferred return***. There are several subsets of questions related to the setting of the preferred return.[136]

- ***Is the payment of the preferred return guaranteed by the LLC or the developer?*** In Chapter 3, it was noted that the primary difference between debt and equity is that there is no fixed obligation to repay the capital contributed to the LLC by a member or to pay any return on that contributed capital.[137] As a general rule, the only source for the repayment of a member's capital contribution (including the payment of any return on such contribution) is the cash flow generated by the LLC's business activities. If there is no cash flow, then no payments are due to the equity investor. While it is not unheard of for a developer to agree to guaranty the payment of some minimal preferred return to the equity investor for a limited period of time (for example, the first two years of the LLC's existence), the real estate development lawyer should agree to the inclusion of such a guaranty only in those very rare instances where such a guaranty is absolutely essential to the developer's ability to secure the funding commitment of its equity investor.

- ***What is the amount of the preferred return?*** Historically, the rate of the annual preferred return rate on real estate development deals has run somewhere between 8 and 12% of the contributed capital.[138] The setting of the preferred return rate is, in large

---

136. For a wide-ranging discussion of the various issues associated with preferred returns, *see* Hales, *supra* note 124, at 247; Jacobson, *supra* note 87, at 122; WHITMIRE, *supra* note 128, at § 5.03; and Lindquist, supra note 79, at 46–47.

137. *See supra* Chapter 3, Page 147.

138. The investment in real estate by Wall Street opportunity funds has also introduced the concept of a minimum internal rate of return being achieved by an investor on its contributed

measure, dependent upon the parties' perception of the risk of the subject real estate investment, with the preferred return rate being higher for riskier projects.

- ***Is the preferred return cumulative?*** The LLC's obligation to make a preferred return payment to its investors is conditioned upon the LLC having sufficient cash on hand to make such payments. The question, therefore, becomes what if the LLC does not have enough cash available in a particular year to pay the investors the full amount of the stipulated preferred return? Does the shortfall carry over to the next LLC year, thereby increasing the amount of the preferred return to be paid to the investors in the subsequent year? In most situations, the outside equity investor will carry the day in its insistence that the preferred return be calculated on a cumulative basis, with the end result that any shortfalls in the payment of the required preferred return will carry over to the next calculation period.

- ***Is the preferred return calculated on a compounded basis? If so, how frequently will it be compounded?*** The compounding of the preferred return simply means that any preferred return that is not paid when due (presumably because the LLC does not have cash currently available to make such payment) will thereafter be added to the base amount against which the preferred return is calculated. The frequency of the compounding of any unpaid preferred return commonly falls somewhere between monthly and annually, although, on rare occasions, a particularly aggressive capital provider may be able to get the concept of daily compounding incorporated into the documents. The good news for the real estate developer is that it usually stands a better chance of successfully eliminating the compounding feature from the investor's preferred return than it does the cumulative feature of that return.

- ***When does the accrual of the preferred return begin?*** The preferred return will customarily begin accruing on the date that the capital is first contributed to the LLC. However, it is not unheard of for an operating agreement to recite that the investors' preferred return will not begin to accrue until after the real estate project is completed and ready to be occupied by tenants. The theory posited by the real estate development lawyer in his attempt to so defer the beginning date for the accrual of the preferred return is that, by definition, a real estate project cannot produce any cash to pay the investor a return on its capital, until it is capable of being occupied by rent paying tenants. The countervailing point made by counsel for the equity investor is that the

---

capital, before the developer gets to participate in any cash flow attributable to its promoted interest. *See* LEVIN, *supra* note 16, at ¶ 1001.1; Lindquist, supra note 79, at 46; and Dale Ann Reis, Deborah Levinson and Sanford Presant, *Opportunistic Investing and Private Equity Funds*, 6 WHARTON REAL ESTATE REVIEW 39 (Spring 2002). *See supra* Chapter 3, Pages 59–60, for a discussion of the calculation and use of the internal rate of return standard.

investor is simply not in a business of providing its capital to anyone on an interest-free basis—and that includes capital invested during the construction period of a commercial real estate project.

- ***Will the developer's preferred return have the same priority as that of the outside equity investor?*** The hypothetical developer introduced at the beginning of this section, as the contributor of 25% of the LLC's capital, should also be entitled to a preferred return on its cash contribution. The real question is will the developer be entitled to receive its preferred return only after the preferred return of the outside equity investor has been fully paid? My experience has been that the real estate development lawyer has a decent shot (although far from a guaranty) of getting the investor to agree that the developer's preferred return will be entitled to the same priority as that of the outside investor (albeit in the same 75–25 ratio that characterizes the respective amounts of their capital contributions).[139] Aficionados of arcane legalese often use the Latin term *pari passu* (meaning "of equal step") to describe the grant of equal priority to the developer's preferred return.[140]

2.   Return of Capital Contributions[141]

The question here is twofold—

- Will the return of the outside equity investor's capital contributions be required before any return of capital is made to the developer?

- Will the return of the outside equity investor's capital contributions be required before any distributions are made with respect to the developer's profits interest?

The answers to these questions vary depending on the relative negotiating leverage of the parties. That negotiating leverage tilts in favor of the outside equity investor if the project has a high risk quotient and if the outside equity investor agrees to provide virtually all of the required capital. For example, a venture capitalist investing in a high-risk, high-growth, start-up business customarily structures its venture capital investment so that it receives a full return of its capital contributions, plus some type of minimum return on that capital (frequently measured by an

---

139. If the investor's preferred return is granted a priority over that of the developer, a situation could arise where the entirety of the LLC's cash flow for a particular fiscal period is used to pay the investor's preferred return. This could present the developer with a circumstance where it has taxable income from its participation in the LLC, but no cash flow from the LLC to pay the resulting tax. To combat such a possibility, the lawyer for the developer often seeks to include in the operating agreement a requirement that a mandatory distribution be made to the developer to cover its tax liability, even if that distribution results in the investor not receiving its full preferred return payment. *See* Fluhrer, *Multi-party Limited Liability Company Operating Agreement, supra* note 87, at 174–175 (5.6); and Stone, *supra* note 46, at 206.

140. See Investor Words Investing Glossary, *http://www.investorwords.com/*.

141. The word "return" is customarily used to refer to the cash paid to an investor by reason of its status as a contributor of capital to the LLC. Words like "payment" and "repayment" are more typically used to describe the cash paid by an LLC to those creditors who hold a fixed debt obligation from the LLC.

internal rate of return calculation) before the service partner is entitled to participate in any cash distributions.[142] In the venture capital context, the economic interest of the service partner is commonly referred to as a ***carried interest***, because it is "carried" by the service partner without any economic benefit, until the venture capitalist has received all of its money back, plus a negotiated level of return on that money.[143] It is important to note that, in the context of a venture capital deal, the service provider seldom makes any significant cash contribution to the venture.

Because the real estate development business is far less risky than the typical start-up business targeted by venture capitalists and because the real estate developer usually makes a significant capital contribution to the deal, the developer is frequently able to negotiate return of capital provisions that fall well short of the pure carried interest arrangement discussed above. The real estate development lawyer's success in crafting distribution provisions which provide "no" answers to both of the questions posed at the beginning of this section is dependent upon how much capital the developer has committed to the deal and the level of risk associated with its proposed project (with the lawyer's chance for success being better the greater the developer's capital and the lower the project risk).

3. Distribution of Operating Cash Flow vs. Capital Proceeds

It is quite common for an LLC Operating Agreement to establish different distribution schemes for Operating Cash Flow and Capital Proceeds. The reason for this differing treatment is, at least in part, driven by the tax consequences associated with the grant to the developer of a percentage interest in the LLC's profits that is disproportionate to the developer's percentage interest in the total capital committed to the LLC (i.e., the developer's promote). As discussed earlier in this Chapter, a developer will not be subject to any current tax upon its receipt of a profits interest, so long as that profits interest does not give the developer any right to share in the existing value of the LLC's assets as of the date of its grant.[144] In the context of a profits interest granted on the date of the formation of the LLC, the value of the LLC's assets generally will equal the aggregate value of the members' capital contributions (i.e., the sum of all cash and the agreed-upon value of all property contributed to the LLC).

In deference to the tax treatment afforded profits interests, the typical LLC Operating Agreement requires that the proceeds of the sale or refinancing of the LLC's assets (i.e., Capital Proceeds) first be used to return the members' capital contributions. By including this provision in the operating agreement, the members are virtually assured that the

---

142. *See e.g.,* Reis, *supra* note 138, at 41.

143. *See infra* Pages 252–256, for a discussion of the tax controversy currently surrounding carried interests.

144. *See supra* Pages 230–232.

developer will not be currently taxed on its receipt of a promoted interest in the LLC's profits.

There is no similar tax driver in play when it comes to how the members decide to share in the LLC's Operating Cash Flow. So long as the members' split of the Capital Proceeds is structured in the above-noted fashion, the inclusion in the operating agreement of a provision stating that the developer will be entitled to share in Operating Cash Flow at its profits interest split (and not its lower capital split) will not result in any unwanted tax consequences being imposed upon the developer. Indeed, it is quite common for operating agreements for real estate development LLCs to provide that, while Capital Proceeds must first be distributed to the members in proportion to their respective capital splits (until such time as the investors have recouped a full return of their contributed capital), all Operating Cash Flow of the LLC will be distributed to the members in accordance with the members' agreed-upon profit splits.

The distribution of Operating Cash Flow to the developer in accordance with its higher, promoted, profits interest can, under certain circumstances, trigger unintended business consequences for the parties. The following example illustrates a problem that can arise if the operating agreement provides that the developer is entitled to receive its share of Operating Cash Flow based upon its promoted profits interest.

Example 7–5: Assume that ABC LLC is formed to buy an office building and that the purchase price of the building is $5 million, all of which is paid through capital contributions from ABC's members. The members agree that Investor will supply 75% of the required capital ($3.75 million) and that Developer will provide the remaining 25% ($1.25 million). The members' handshake agreement is that they will split all profits 50–50. Because the members have read this Chapter, they know that Developer cannot be given more than a 25% interest in the existing value of the office building ($5 million), unless Developer is willing to recognize taxable income coincident with its receipt of a membership interest in ABC (which it clearly doesn't want to do). As such, they agree that, while Operating Cash Flow will be split 50–50, Capital Proceeds will first be used to return the members' capital contributions, with the remainder then being split in accordance with the agreed-upon 50–50 profit sharing ratio.

All goes well for ABC's business during the first two operating years. The financial results for those two years are as follows;

Year 1:	Operating Cash Flow	$450,000
	Developer's 50% share	$225,000
	Investor's 50% share	$225,000
Year 2:	Operating Cash Flow	$550,000
	Developer's 50% share	$275,000
	Investor's 50% share	$275,000

At the beginning of Year 3, the office building's anchor tenant goes bankrupt and ABC is forced to sell the office building for $4 million—$1 million less than it paid for the same building two years previously. Per their agreement, the sales proceeds are split between the members in accordance with their capital interests (that is, 75% to Investor and 25% to Developer).

Year 3:	Capital Proceeds	$4,000,000
	Developer's 25% share	$1,000,000
	Investor's 75% share	$3,000,000

The following recap shows how Developer and Investor fared on their respective investments in ABC.

Developer's Cash Flow:

Year 1 Operating Cash Flow	$225,000
Year 2 Operating Cash Flow	$275,000
Year 3 Capital Proceeds	$1,000,000
Total Cash Distributions	$1,500,000
Less: Initial Capital Contribution	$1,000,000
Net Investment Profit	**$500,000**

Investor's Cash Flow:

Year 1 Operating Cash Flow	$225,000
Year 2 Operating Cash Flow	$275,000
Year 3 Capital Proceeds	$3,000,000
Total Cash Distributions	$3,500,000
Less: Initial Capital Contribution	$4,000,000
Net Investment Loss	**($500,000)**

The above example shows what can happen under a fairly typical cash distribution scheme when early project profits are followed by subsequent project losses. The LLC basically broke even on its investment in the office building (putting aside for a second everything the reader learned in Chapter 3 about the time value of money). The LLC generated Operating Cash Flow of $1 million in Years 1 and 2 and then was forced to sell its only asset in Year 3 at a loss of $1 million. One would think that the parties' handshake agreement that they would share any profits 50–50 should result in neither of them making any money on its investment—because the LLC failed to earn an overall profit. However, as the above example illustrates, the operation of ABC's cash distribution scheme actually resulted in Developer making $500,000 on its investment, while Investor lost $500,000.

While Developer probably thinks that its lawyer did a helluva job in drafting the cash distribution provisions of ABC's operating agreement, the end result is clearly inconsistent with the original tenor of the business deal struck by Developer and Investor. There are a couple ways that the members could have fixed this problem.

- The members could have established a cash reserve from Operating Cash Flow to partially hedge the risk of a future downturn in the project's overall financial condition. In Example 7–5, the establishment of a cash reserve of $500,000 out of the $1 million of aggregate Operating Cash Flow distributions made in Years 1 and 2 would have cut the inappropriate shifting of cash to Developer from $500,000 to $375,000.

- The members could have agreed to a *clawback* provision, which would have allowed the LLC to deduct from Developer's share of the Capital Proceeds the $250,000 of Operating Cash Flow distributed to the developer in Years 1 and 2 with respect to its 25% promoted profits interest.[145]

4. Distribution Provisions of Form Operating Agreement. *(§§3.1–3.3)*

The distribution provisions of the Form Operating Agreement are fairly typical for a real estate development LLC. Those provisions prescribe the following simple schemes for the distribution of the LLC's Operating Cash Flow and Capital Proceeds.

- *Distribution of Operating Cash Flow*:
  - First, 25% to the developer and 75% to the investor, until each member has received the full amount of its unpaid preferred return (calculated at a cumulative, compounded rate of 10%); and
  - The remainder 50% to the developer and 50% to the investor.

- *Distribution of Capital Proceeds*:
  - First, 25% to the developer and 75% to the investor, until each member has received a full return of its capital contributions;
  - Second, 25% to the developer and 75% to the investor, until each member has received a full return of its unpaid preferred return; and
  - The remainder 50% to the developer and 50% to the investor.

The cash distribution provisions of the Form Operating Agreement are, to some extent, pro-developer. The Form Operating Agreement does not authorize the establishment of any investor-mandated cash reserves, nor does it contain a clawback provision. Moreover, the Form Operating Agreement provides that the developer and the investor will be given the same priority on a *pari passu* basis in the LLC's distribution of all preferred return and return of capital distributions.

---

145. If the distribution of Operating Cash Flow attributable to the developer's promoted interest exceeds the developer's share of the Capital Proceeds, a "clawback" provision customarily permits the investor to institute a legal action against the developer to recover the excess distributions. *See* Reis, *supra* note 138, at 49.

5. Timing of Cash Distributions

The default rule set forth in the Delaware Act calls for the making of distributions on the withdrawal of a member or on the dissolution of the LLC.[146] This default rule clearly will not work for either the developer or its outside equity investors and, thus, must be changed in the operating agreement.

Distributions of Operating Cash Flow should be made no less frequently than annually. Many investors push to have Operating Cash Flow distributed on a quarterly or monthly basis. Capital Proceeds should generally be distributed roughly coincident with the occurrence of the capital event giving rise to such Capital Proceeds (e.g., the sale of the project or the refinancing of the project debt). With respect to the distribution of both Operating Cash Flow and Capital Proceeds, the drafter of the operating agreement should specify that the distributions will be made within a specified number of days after the end of the selected fiscal period or the occurrence of the capital event, as the case may be. The period so selected should be sufficiently long to permit the LLC's financial officers ample time to make an accurate calculation of the amount of the cash flow which is available for distribution to the members.

HIBC Case Study—Cash Distributions

The cash distribution provisions of the Pizzuti–Newport general partnership agreement stated that all cash flow would be distributed 50% to Pizzuti and 50% to Newport. Pizzuti did not receive any promoted profits interest as part of its relationship with Newport. As a result, there was simply no need to address any of the complexities discussed in the prior section.

The distribution provisions of the Pizzuti–Nationwide operating agreement, on the other hand, were quite complex. Promoted profits interests were granted to both Pizzuti and a separate LLC formed by its key employees. The specifics of these promoted interests are discussed in the prior section of this Chapter captioned "HIBC Case Study—Profits Interests." The existence of such promoted interests necessitated the inclusion in the Pizzuti–Nationwide operating agreement of provisions on (a) the accrual and payment of a preferred return to the equity investors and (b) the separate calculation of Operating Cash Flow and Capital Proceeds. The basics of those provisions were, in most respects, comparable to the pro-developer provisions of the Form Operating Agreement summarized in the previous section of this Chapter.

Most of the complexity found in the distribution provisions of the Pizzuti–Nationwide operating agreement was attributable to the fact that

---

146. *See* DELAWARE CODE ANNOTATED, Title 6, § 18–601 (West 2010).

the new entity was formed to own: (a) more than 20 existing real estate projects; (b) an unlimited number of real estate projects to be newly developed under the ownership umbrella of the newly formed entity; and (c) a real estate operating company assigned with the responsibility for developing, leasing and managing all of Pizzuti's and Nationwide's jointly-owned real estate projects. Pizzuti and Nationwide negotiated different economic sharing ratios and conditions for each of the three classes of properties owned by the new Pizzuti–Nationwide entity. For example, the preferred return on the existing properties was set at 9.5%, while the preferred return for newly developed properties was pegged at 10% (illustrating the point made earlier in this Chapter that the setting of the preferred return rate is linked to the perceived risk of the subject real estate investment). The promoted interests granted to Pizzuti and its employees also differed by property class—e.g., an aggregate 35% promote for the operating company and the newly-developed projects versus a 5% promote on the existing properties.

The disparate treatment afforded each of these three property classes required that the cash flow attributable to the activities of each of those classes be separately calculated. The issue which consumed an inordinate amount of time during the drafting and negotiation of the Pizzuti–Nationwide operating agreement was how the calculation of one category of cash flow should impact the calculation of cash flow for another property category. There were two specific questions that counsel for Pizzuti and Nationwide spent hours discussing (sometimes in civil tones).

- *Should a loss realized on the sale of one property impact the distribution of Capital Proceeds on the later sale of another property?*

- *Should the positive Operating Cash Flow produced from one property category (e.g., the existing properties) be used to subsidize the payment of the preferred return payable on another property category (e.g., the newly-developed properties)?*

Pizzuti argued passionately that each cash flow category should be calculated and distributed on a totally free-standing basis and that the level of Capital Proceeds produced on the sale or refinancing of one property should never be taken into consideration when determining the proper distribution of Capital Proceeds attributable to another property. Why was Pizzuti so adamant in its position? If you were representing Nationwide, what grounds would you have postulated to support your position that both of the above questions should be answered in the affirmative?[147]

---

147. FYI—Pizzuti lost the argument on both of these points.

C. THE CARRIED INTEREST TAX CONTROVERSY

As noted in an earlier section of this Chapter, the developer's receipt of a profits interest that is disproportionate to its share of the LLC's contributed capital is not subject to tax at the time such interest is granted, because that interest does not entitle the developer to any share of the "liquidation value" of the LLC's existing assets.[148] The rules of Subchapter K of the Internal Revenue Code further provide that an LLC's taxable income and loss are passed through to its members, with the character of such items in the hands of the members being determined at the partnership level.[149] As such, a sale of a commercial real estate project that produces a long-term capital gain at the LLC level will be treated as a long-term capital gain on the tax returns of the LLC's constituent members. Under current federal tax law, long-term capital gains are taxed at a maximum rate of 15%, while ordinary compensation income is subjected to a maximum tax rate of 35%.[150]

The convergence of the above-described tax rules results in an extremely favorable treatment for the developer's promote. The following example illustrates the effect that these rules have upon the after-tax return earned by a developer from its receipt of a promoted profits interest.

> **Example 7–6:** Assume Developer makes a capital contribution to ABC LLC of $500,000 (representing 25% of the total capital contributed to ABC by all its members). ABC uses the contributed capital to purchase land at an initial cost of $2 million. Developer receives a 50% profits interest in ABC, which consists of its 25% capital interest and a promoted profits interest of 25% (which was properly structured to avoid Developer's current recognition of income). Two years later, ABC sells the land for $4 million, producing a long-term capital gain of $2 million. Immediately following the sale, ABC distributes the $4 million in land sales proceeds to its members, with Developer receiving a total distribution of $1.5 million (its invested capital of $500,000, plus its 50% share of the $2 million profit generated on ABC's sale of the land).

The after-tax profit generated from Developer's investment in ABC is quite impressive—a net return to Developer's bottom line of $850,000.

Developer's Cash Distribution on Sale of Land	$1,500,000
Less: Developer's Capital Contribution to ABC	$500,000
Less: Developer's Income Tax Payment	
(Developer's 50% Share of $2 million	
capital gain * the 15% capital gains tax rate)	$150,000
Developer's Net After-tax Return	**$850,000**

The results produced in Example 7–6 stand as a testament to (1) the financial importance of a developer's receipt of a promote[151] and (2) the

---

148. *See supra* Page 231.

149. *See* INTERNAL REVENUE CODE § 702(b). *See also supra* Page 203.

150. *See* INTERNAL REVENUE CODE §§ 1(h) and (i).

beneficial tax treatment afforded to a developer's receipt of a distribution attributable to the occurrence of a project sale at the entity level.[152] If Developer's share of the gain produced on the sale of ABC's land had been taxed at the 35% rate applicable to ordinary compensation income (instead of the advantaged capital gains rate of 15%), Developer's net after-tax return from its investment in ABC would have been decreased by $200,000 (its 50% share of the $2 million gain produced on the sale of the land * the 20% differential between the tax rates payable on capital gains vs. ordinary income).

The favorable tax treatment imparted to a developer's receipt of a promoted profits interest is being threatened by proposed legislation introduced in Congress in 2007 (and re-introduced in a variety of forms since that date).[153] Earlier that year, Blackstone Group, a leading private equity firm that was in the process of going public, filed reports with the SEC indicating, among other things, that Steven Schwarzman, Blackstone's CEO, had earned approximately $400 million in 2006—most of which was apparently produced from profits interests held by Mr. Schwarzman in a variety of ventures and, therefore, was taxed at the maximum capital gains rate of 15%. The disclosure of the tax benefits achieved by Schwarzman's use of what in private equity and hedge fund circles is called a carried interest (a promote in the vernacular of the real estate investor) triggered a public outcry that led Representative Sander Levin to introduce H.R. 2834 in an attempt to better serve "tax fairness" by subjecting all income produced under a carried interest to taxation as ordinary compensation income (and not, under any circumstances, as capital gain).[154]

H.R. 2834 and its progeny[155] cover profits interests (referred to in the proposed legislation as "investment services partnership interests") that are "held by any person if it was reasonably expected at the time such person acquired such interest that such person (or any person related to such person) would provide (directly or indirectly) a substantial quantity of services" related to the investment, purchase, sale, management, fi-

---

151. In Example 7–6, the 25% promote produced an additional pre-tax distribution to Developer of $500,000—i.e., the 25% promote the $2 million land profit.

152. The developer would also be entitled to capital gain treatment on the sale of its membership interest in the LLC. *See* INTERNAL REVENUE CODE § 741. *See generally* McKEE, *supra* note 10, at § 16.01.

153. *See generally,* Carol Kulish Harvey, *Proposals on Carried Interests: The Currents State of Play,* in ALI–ABA COURSE OF STUDY MATERIALS, CREATIVE TAX PLANNING FOR REAL ESTATE TRANSACTIONS, Course No. SR–032, 569 (October 2009); and Pappas, *supra* note 70, at 102–103.

154. *See* H.R. 2834, 110th Congress (2007). *See also* Pappas, *supra* note 70, at 102.

155. Representative Levin reintroduced the bill in substantially the same form in 2009—*see* H.R. 1935, 111th Congress (2009). The language of the 2009 bill was then incorporated into the American Jobs and Closing Tax Loopholes Act of 2010, H.R. 4213, 112th Congress (2010), which was passed by the House of Representatives in May 2010. The Senate has considered several versions of anti-carried interest proposals, including one circulated in the summer of 2010 by Senator Max Baucus. As of the date of this writing, no final action has been taken by either house of Congress on definitive legislation addressing the taxation of carried interests.

nancing or disposition of "specified assets."[156] For this purpose, the "specified assets" covered by the proposed legislation expressly include not just securities, commodities and other interests generally dealt with by the targeted hedge fund managers and private equity firms, but also "real estate held for rental or investment."[157]

The proposed legislation holds both good news and bad news for real estate developers and investors:

- ***The Good News***—The pending bills would confirm the tax treatment of capital and profits interests suggested in the Proposed Regulations referred to earlier in this Chapter (i.e., the current recognition of income on the receipt of a capital interest, but not a profits interest);[158] and

- ***The Bad News***—The proposed legislation would require all income produced under an "investment services partnership interest" (the term coined by Representative Levin to describe the promote/carried interests referred to earlier in this Chapter) to be taxed as ordinary compensation income—and specifically not as capital gains.[159] This mandated, ordinary income treatment expressly includes any gain produced on the sale of an entity's assets or an investor's sale of its equity interest in such entity.

If legislation is passed that is consistent with the Representative Levin's bill, Developer's tax charge under the facts of Example 7–6 would increase by $100,000—an approximate 12% reduction in its net, after-tax return from its investment in ABC.[160]

The argument proffered in support of the proposed legislation is that the economic benefit received by a taxpayer under a carried interest or promote is, in essence, nothing more than compensation received by the holder of that interest in exchange for its provision of services to the entity. The proponents of the approach adopted in Representative Levin's bill assert that rich developers and hedge fund managers should not be "paying lower tax rates than their secretaries or the janitor that cleans up the building."[161] Supporters of the Levin bill also point out that added tax revenues are desperately needed to help reduce the federal deficit.

---

156. *See* H.R. 1935, *supra* note 155, at § 2.

157. *See id.*

158. *See id.* § 1. *See also supra* Pages 230–232.

159. The legislation introduced by Representative Levin makes an exception for a "qualified capital interest," which is generally defined as the portion of a person's equity interest that is granted in consideration of the person's contribution of cash or property to a pass-through entity. As such the passage of the Levin bill would impact only the promoted portion of the equity interest granted to Developer in Example 7–6 and not the portion of such interest that was directly proportionate to its capital split.

160. Developer's additional tax obligation is calculated as follows—the percentage of Developer's promoted profits interest (25%) ABC's land sale gain ($2 million) the increase in the tax rate applicable to the sale under the proposed legislation (20%). The imposition of this additional tax liability would decrease Developer's net, after-tax return from $850,000 to $750,000.

161. *See* Jann S. Wenner, *Obama Fights Back: The Rolling Stone Interview*, ROLLING STONE, October 15, 2010 (quote from President Obama).

The proposed legislation on carried interests is being met with fierce opposition from both private equity firms[162] and real estate industry groups.[163] The essence of the opponents' argument is twofold—(1) a carried interest subjects the holder of that interest to the same type of entrepreneurial risk that characterizes a taxpayer's investment in stocks, bonds and other investment assets that are afforded capital gain treatment, and (2) subjecting carried interests to taxation as ordinary income will severely retard economic growth in the already depressed, financial and commercial real estate sectors of the U.S. economy.

As of the date of this writing, it is uncertain whether legislation will ultimately be passed subjecting carried interests to ordinary income taxation or whether that legislation will extend to commercial real estate investments.[164] The resolution of that issue will likely depend less on principles of "tax fairness" than on the comparative strength of the lobbyists hired by the proponents and opponents of the proposed legislation.[165]

Equally uncertain is what impact the passage of the Levin bill would have on the commercial real estate industry. Stated differently, will changing the manner in which promotes are taxed actually cause developers to refrain from kicking off a development project or will it just add a different flavor to the economic negotiations between the developer and its outside equity investors? My experience tells me that the latter conclusion is closer to the truth than the former. The developer is likely to ask for a

---

162. Steven Schwarzman, the CEO of Blackstone Group, whose 2006 receipt of millions of dollars of carried interest benefits prompted the introduction of the carried interest legislation, has stated that President Obama's support for that legislation "is like when Hitler invaded Poland." *See* Jonathon Alter, *A "Fat Cat" Strikes Back*, NEWSWEEK, August 15, 2010.

163. A website maintained by the Building Owners and Managers Association ("BOMA") urges its members to call their senators and representatives to protest Congress' consideration of the carried interest legislation and sets out the following suggested banter.

I'm calling to ask the senator/representative to oppose the proposal to double the tax on carried interest, which is commonly used in commercial real estate development. You may have heard that it's a Wall Street issue, but it's really a Main Street issue that's bad for our state's real estate market because it will further hurt job creation by hindering economic development. The state and local governments will not collect as much tax revenue either because it will reduce the number of real estate transactions.

See http://www.boma.org/Advocacy/carriedinterest/default.aspx (last visited on October 20, 2010).

164. The proposal adopted by the House of Representatives in May 2010 called for the application of a blended tax rate to the tax profits produced under a carried interest. Specifically, H.R. 4213 (*see supra* note 155) contemplated that 50% of income or gain attributable to a carried interest would be subjected to ordinary income tax rates, while the remaining 50% of such income or gain would be subjected to capital gains rates. The applicable percentage for ordinary income tax treatment would be increased to 75% beginning in 2013. At least one real estate trade group has expressed general support for this approach. See Ryan J. Donmoyer, *Real Estate Group Pushes to Soften "Carried Interest" Tax Rise*, BLOOMBERG BUSINESS WEEK (May 8, 2010), available online at http://www.businessweek.com/news/2010–05–08/real-estate-group-pushes-to-soften-carried-interest-tax-rise.html.

165. In the interests of full disclosure, I should note that my 2003 retirement from the active practice of real estate development law was greatly aided and supported by my prior receipt of promotes on projects such as HIBC. For a detailed analysis of the carried interest issue (albeit one that is strongly supportive of the proposed legislation), *see* Aviva Aron–Dine, *An Analysis of the "Carried Interest" Controversy*, CENTER ON BUDGET AND POLICY PRIORITIES (July 31, 2007), available online at http;//www.cbpp.org/7-31-07tax.pdf.

higher percentage promote or some other increase in its overall share of the entity's cash flow (e.g., an increased property management fee) to offset the higher tax that it will have to pay on the financial fruits of that promote. The equity investor is likely to say "no" to that request. The negotiation that follows will focus on whose "ox will be gored" by the diversion of a portion of the project profits to the IRS' coffers—the developer, its equity investor, or, more likely, both of them.

XI.   MANAGEMENT OF THE LLC. *(Article 5)*

The LLC ownership format provides its members with a high degree of flexibility to select a management structure that best suit their needs.[166] The Delaware Act provides that an LLC can be managed by either: (1) its members (a ***member-managed LLC***); or (2) a manager chosen in the manner provided in the operating agreement (a ***manager-managed LLC***).[167] The default rule established in Section 18–402 of the Delaware Act states that:

> Unless otherwise provided in a limited liability company agreement, the management of a limited liability company shall be vested in its members in proportion to the then current percentage or other interest of members in the profits of the limited liability company owned by all of the members, the decision of members owning more than 50 percent of the said percentage or other interest in the profits controlling.[168]

As is the case with most of the Delaware Act's default rules, the members are free to dispense with this member-managed, default rule and adopt another management structure for the LLC. The operating agreement should expressly recite whether the LLC will be member-managed or manager-managed.

A.   MEMBER-MANAGED LLC

A member-managed LLC is an LLC in which all control over the management of the LLC's business is vested in its members. In its purest form, a member-managed LLC would function much like a general partnership, with each member having the right to approve all LLC decisions and each member having the unfettered right to bind the LLC by its actions. At the other end of the management spectrum would be a member-managed LLC in which the members appoint a ***managing member*** and delegate to such managing member plenary authority to make all decisions and to take all actions in the name and on behalf of the LLC. This type of an arrangement would be akin to a limited partnership in which the general partner is given full authority to manage the business of the limited partnership.

---

166.   *See* Winkler, *supra* note 20, at 1.

167.   *See* DELAWARE CODE ANNOTATED, Title 6, § 18–402 (West 2010).

168.   *See id.*

In most cases, the management structure of a member-managed LLC falls somewhere between these two extremes. In the context of a member-managed LLC formed by a developer and one outside equity investor to own and operate a single real estate development project, the developer is usually appointed as the managing member of the LLC.[169] In its capacity as the managing member, the developer is given fairly broad authority to take most actions in the name and on behalf of the LLC. The developer's authority will however, typically be limited by the requirement that it must obtain the equity investor's consent before taking certain so-called *major decisions*.[170]

A hybrid of the member-managed structure that has become quite popular in recent years is a corporate-like structure, whereby the members delegate most of their rights and powers to manage and control the business and affairs of the LLC to a board of directors or executive committee comprised of individuals selected by the members to represent their respective interests. Those equity investors who are accustomed to interacting with corporate boards of directors might find such a corporate-like structure to be to their liking. The use of a quasi-corporate structure might also prove useful in an LLC in which there are multiple outside investors, who have varying voting interests and approval rights.[171] However, in the context of a single asset deal between a developer and one outside investor, following the formalities associated with a corporate-like management structure usually proves to be unproductive and overly cumbersome.

B.   MANAGER-MANAGED LLC

A manager-managed LLC is an LLC in which the management and control of the business and affairs of the LLC is centralized in one or more managers. A manager of an LLC may, but need not be, a member of the LLC.[172] A manager (regardless whether it is also a member) is not liable for any debt, obligation or liability of the LLC, solely by reason of acting as the manager of the LLC.[173]

Once the members decide to appoint a manager to manage and control the business and affairs of the LLC, they must next determine the scope of the manager's authority.[174] This is the same issue that the

---

169. The reason that the developer (and not the investor) is typically designated as the managing member is driven not by legal reasons (there is no legal impediment to the outside equity investor being appointed as the managing member), but rather by the mere fact that most investors do not have the time or the expertise to manage the day-to-day affairs of a local real estate venture. *See generally* Pappas, *supra* note 70, at 60–61.

170. For a sample laundry list of those LLC actions that could fall under the "major decision" umbrella, *see infra* Pages 264–265.

171. The Delaware Act provides that an operating agreement may provide for classes, groups and series of members, all of whom have different voting rights. *See* Delaware Code §§ 18–215 and 18–302. *See also* Winkler, *supra* note 20, at 12–14.

172. *See* Delaware Code § 18–403.

173. *See id.* at § 18–303.

174. The Delaware Act provides that the scope of the manager's responsibilities and authority will be determined by the provisions of the operating agreement. *See id.* at § 18–402

members of a member-managed LLC must face following the designation of one of its members to serve as a managing member of the LLC. The customary approach is to give the manager the full power to take all actions on behalf of the LLC, except for those specifically-designated major decisions for which it must first obtain the consent of the members.

Finally, the Delaware Act expressly permits a manager to delegate its management rights and powers to other persons, including its agents, officers or employees.[175] Given this broad delegation power, a manager-managed LLC can also implement a corporate-like management structure of the type discussed earlier under the *Member-managed LLC* caption.

C. THE SELECTION OF A MANAGEMENT STRUCTURE

Developers often prefer a manager-managed LLC structure for two reasons.

- Under the LLC statutes of some states, a non-managing member of a member-managed LLC is given apparent authority to execute documents and take other actions that bind the LLC. A member's apparent authority to bind the LLC can largely be eliminated by implementing a manager-managed LLC structure.[176]

- The developer frequently conducts its development business in an entity separate from the entity in which it opts to hold title to its real estate portfolio. In that circumstance, all of the personnel, technology and other management tools required to manage the LLC's business and affairs would be housed in a non-member entity. For this reason, the developer may want to select a manager-managed format[177] and have its operating company named as the non-member manager of the LLC, while its investment company serves as a member of that LLC.

---

175. *See id.* at § 18–407.

176. *See* RIBSTEIN AND KEATINGE, *supra* note 54, at § 2.4, where the authors conclude that "where there is a concern with who has the ability to bind the organization, it is preferable to use a ... manager-managed LLC." It should be noted that the Delaware Act does not make a distinction between the apparent authority of a member in a member-managed versus that of a member in a manager-managed LLC. *See* DELAWARE CODE § 18–402, which states that "[u]nless otherwise provided in the limited liability company agreement, each member and manager has the authority to bind the limited liability company." Because a legal question exists as to whether a private operating agreement can lawfully restrict the broad apparent authority granted to a member by statute, a leading California real estate development lawyer has commented that "[b]ecause it is not clear that Delaware has a surefire way of restricting authority and management to a select group, Delaware may not offer the statute of choice despite its otherwise contract-based approach." See Caryl B. Welborn, *Managing Investor's Liabilities in the Real Property Venture*, in ALI–ABA COURSE OF STUDY MATERIALS, MODERN REAL ESTATE TRANSACTIONS, Course No. SL–004, 681/ 685 (July 2005). In the context of a closely-held real estate project between a developer and one or two outside equity investors, this nuance of the Delaware Act would not seem to be sufficient reason to avoid Delaware as the state of choice for the formation of an LLC.

177. As noted earlier in this section, a manager does not have to be a member of the LLC. *See* DELAWARE CODE § 18–403.

Conversely, there are a couple reasons why the outside equity investor might want the LLC to adopt a member-managed structure.

- A member-managed format is generally considered more conducive to the establishment of a quasi-corporate structure, where management oversight is provided by a board of directors or an executive committee appointed by the members. Large equity investors, such as insurance companies and pension funds, who are accustomed to dealing with corporate bodies, often prefer a member-managed format in which the members delegate their management authority to a board of directors or an executive committee.

- A member-managed structure is also the structure of choice if the outside equity investor reserves the authority to take certain affirmative actions to bind the LLC. By way of example, an equity investor might want to both control the LLC's executive committee and reserve the right to take the lead in negotiations for the sale of the LLC's property (*see e.g.,* the discussion of *The Prudential Case Study–Investor Dominance* that follows this section).

The choice between a member-managed LLC and a manager-managed LLC frequently comes down to the relative negotiating strength of the developer and the outside equity investor, with the developer customarily preferring a manager-managed arrangement and the equity investor frequently favoring a member-managed structure. Each of those structures is, however, sufficiently flexible that the developer and the equity investor can achieve their business objectives under whichever management structure is ultimately selected.

The discussion in the remainder of this section will focus on the management issues faced by the parties in the context of the development of a single real estate project by an LLC that is owned by the developer and one outside equity investor. For the purposes of that discussion, it will be assumed that the developer will serve as either the manager or managing member of the LLC and that the parties have opted not to form an executive committee or board of directors to oversee the developer's activities.

Before embarking on a discussion of the management provisions that should be addressed in the operating agreement for a traditional real estate development venture, this Chapter will take a slight detour by introducing a new case study involving a much less traditional development style.

The Prudential Case Study—Investor Dominance

This Chapter has thus far focused on the usual circumstance where a developer and an equity investor of relatively equal bargaining strength elect to blend their particular talents (the developer's development expertise and the investor's cash resources) to jointly develop a real estate project. In such a circumstance, the developer is typically given broad control over the management of the LLC, with the investor's role being limited to its exercise of a veto right over certain major decisions. As the following case study illustrates, the equity investor is not always content to assume such a passive role in the management of the LLC's business.

In 1999, Pizzuti decided to expand its warehouse development business into the greater Chicagoland market. Because of its lack of familiarity with the dynamics and players in the Chicagoland market (one of the top three warehouse markets in the United States), Pizzuti was hesitant to take on anywhere near the level of risk that it assumed when it acquired the HIBC land four years earlier.

In the same time frame, The Prudential Insurance Company of America was trying to devise ways to enhance the economic yield of its vast real estate portfolio. Prudential had historically centered its real estate investment efforts on the purchase of fully leased real estate projects. By doing so, Prudential effectively insulated itself from two of the most pervasive real estate risks—namely that (a) the development of the project is not completed on budget and on time and (b) the project is not leased within the time frame and at the rental rates identified in the project's financial projections. The trade-off for limiting its risk in that regard was its acceptance of a lower rate of return on its investment dollars. Prudential decided that the only way for it to increase its investment return was for it to change its investment style and accept more risk.

It was against the backdrop of these changes in their normal risk profiles that Pizzuti and Prudential struck an interesting deal to jointly participate in the development of a warehouse project in Joliet, Illinois. The essential terms of that deal are outlined below.

- *Pizzuti would develop a warehouse project in accordance with plans and specifications and a development budget pre-approved by Prudential. The development cost budget would include a development fee to Pizzuti of 4% of the project's total costs.*

- *Upon completion of the project's construction, Pizzuti and Prudential would form a Delaware LLC for the purpose of acquiring the completed project from Pizzuti. The purchase price for the LLC's acquisition of the warehouse project would be equal to the lesser of the pre-approved cost budget or the actual project development costs.*

- *The purchase price would be funded by cash capital contributions made to the LLC by its members in the following percentages—95% by Prudential and 5% by Pizzuti.*

- *Upon the LLC's acquisition of the warehouse project, the LLC's operating cash flow would be split in accordance with the members' capital contribution percentages (that is, the 95–5 ratio mentioned above), until such time as the members had received a preferred return on their capital contributions of 9.75%, at which time further operating cash flow distributions would be split 70% to Prudential and 30% to Pizzuti. Capital proceeds would be paid 95% to Prudential and 5% to Pizzuti, until each of them had received cash distributions sufficient to fully return its capital contributions and provide it with an internal rate of return on its investment of 12.5%.*[178] *Thereafter, the economic split would shift to 70% for Prudential and 30% for Pizzuti. The effect of this arrangement was to provide Pizzuti with a 25% promote (after Prudential's receipt of the specified priority distributions).*

- Any funds needed by the LLC over and above the cash contributions funded coincident with the formation of the LLC would be provided through additional capital contributions made 70% by Prudential and 30% by Pizzuti.

From Pizzuti's perspective, the above-described deal structure (commonly referred to as a "pre-sale")[179] *afforded it with a relatively risk-free opportunity to get is feet wet in the Chicago warehouse market. Pizzuti's only required financial commitment to the project was the 5% capital contribution that it was required to fund on the date of the LLC's acquisition of the Joliet warehouse project. The amount of Pizzuti's capital contribution was only slightly more than the 4% development fee it was entitled to receive under the pre-approved development cost budget. Therefore if the deal went poorly, Pizzuti's principal risk was the loss of its development fee. If the deal proved to be successful, Pizzuti would profit nicely from its 25% promoted interest in the LLC.*

The primary benefit to Prudential of the pre-sale structure was that it provided Prudential with the potential to garner a higher than normal return on its investment dollars.[180] *In order to position itself to achieve the higher return, Prudential had to do something that it was not accustomed to doing—that is, subject its investment to the risk that the project would not produce the desired rental stream.*[181] *Prudential attempted to deal with this unaccustomed risk by negotiating a string of very advantageous provisions in its operating agreement with Pizzuti.*

---

178. The Prudential–Pizzuti operating agreement granted Prudential a priority status over Pizzuti as to each component of the LLC's capital proceeds—e.g., Prudential was entitled to receive a return of all of its capital contributions before Pizzuti had the right to receive a return of any portion of its capital contributions. Cash distribution provisions that create a series of distribution priorities (14 in all in the Prudential–Pizzuti operating agreement) are commonly referred to in real estate investment circles as a "waterfall."

179. The "pre-sale" tag is given to deals of this type because of the upfront, binding commitment made by the equity investor to buy the project on its completion.

180. The potential for earning a higher return on its investment existed because Prudential was buying into the Joliet project at cost (and not at fair market value, as would be the case if it were buying a fully leased project).

181. The pre-sale structure insulated Prudential from any risk associated with the construction of the project not being completed on time and on budget. Prudential was not required to commit any dollars to the project until it was completed. Moreover, its funding commitment was capped based on the development cost budget established at the outset of the project, thereby placing the entire risk associated with construction cost overruns on Pizzuti (something that Pizzuti, as an experienced developer, was accustomed to handling).

Prudential held the upper hand in its negotiations with Pizzuti because it was willing to fund 95% of the project's development costs and limit Pizzuti's downside risk on the project. Prudential opted to use its dominant negotiating leveraged to fashion management provisions that placed it in a position to actively control the management of the business and affairs of the LLC. The Prudential–Pizzuti operating agreement contained the following provisions:

- *The LLC adopted a member-managed structure;*

- *A five member executive committee was appointed to exercise control over all aspects of the LLC's business and affairs, with Prudential having the right to appoint three of the executive committee members;*

- *Prudential reserved the unilateral right to call for additional capital contributions to be made to the LLC;*

- *Prudential reserved the unilateral right to sell the project; and*

- *Prudential reserved the unilateral right to secure financing for the project.*

The Prudential–Pizzuti operating agreement was a stark example of an investor using its negotiating leverage to secure two characteristics that are uniquely available under the LLC ownership format—(a) control over the management of the LLC's business and (b) limited liability.

So whatever came of this investor-dominated real estate development project? Unfortunately, the Joliet warehouse project never generated the level of rents initially projected for the project. The following was the end result of the project's dismal lease-up.

- *Prudential used its control of the executive committee to replace Pizzuti as the property manager and leasing representative for the project.*

- *Prudential made a call for additional capital and, following Pizzuti's refusal to fund the call, exercised its squeeze-down right to effectively eliminate Pizzuti's ongoing percentage interest in the project's cash flow (which was non-existent anyway).*

- *Prudential exercised its right to put the project on the market for sale. There were, however, no takers for the building.*

- *Prudential and Pizzuti terminated their relationship when Pizzuti withdrew from the LLC and transferred all of its remaining interest in the Joliet project to Prudential.*

As of the date of the writing of this Chapter, Prudential still owns the Joliet project. It is still less than 50% leased. While the legal provisions inserted into the Prudential–Pizzuti operating agreement gave Prudential its desired management control, that control was not enough to overcome the fact that the Joliet building was simply a bad real estate project—yet another reminder of the subordinate role that the lawyer plays in the real estate development process.

D. THE MANAGEMENT PROVISIONS OF THE OPERATING AGREEMENT

The following is a discussion of the key provisions of the management section of the operating agreement. Where appropriate, a parenthetical reference is made to the section of the Form Operating Agreement where such provision is addressed.[182] Unless otherwise specifically stated, all references in the following discussion to the *manager* have equal applicability to both the manager of a manager-managed LLC and the managing member of a member-managed LLC.

1. Grant of Management Authority to Manager. *(§5.1)*

The operating agreement should contain an express grant to the manager of the authority to manage and control the business and affairs of the LLC. There are two basic methods to accomplish that objective:

- The inclusion in the operating agreement of a simple statement that the manger will have the full and exclusive right, power and authority to manage and control the business and affairs of the LLC and to take all actions that an LLC is authorized to take under the applicable state LLC statute; or

- The recital in the operating agreement of a laundry list of the general powers granted to the manager.

Regardless which drafting method is adopted, the grant of management authority should make specific cross-reference to any limitations on the manager's management authority.[183]

2. Limitations on Manager's Authority—Major Decisions. *(§5.2)*

This provision is one of the most hotly negotiated provisions of the entire operating agreement. The real estate development lawyer wants the list of limitations on his client's management authority to be short and specific. Counsel for the investor typically prefers to use the terms "long" and "general" to characterize his proffered list of limitations on the manager's authority.

The general theory behind this section of the operating agreement is that there are certain decisions that are so significant to the LLC's

---

182. The Form Operating Agreement incorporates a manager-managed management structure. There is, however, little practical difference between a manager-managed arrangement and a member-managed arrangement where the members designate a managing member.

183. The Form Operating Agreement adopts the first of these drafting methods. For an example of a management provision employing the second drafting method, *see* Pappas, *supra* note 70, at 65–67.

business that they should not be made without the consent of all the members. While the developer and the investor can (and almost always will) disagree on the identity and scope of the major decisions, they generally are in agreement that there are, in fact, certain decisions that should be made jointly by both members. By way of example, one area of common consensus between the members is that the manager should not be able to admit a new member to the LLC, without first obtaining the consent of the other member.

The major decisions clause of the operating agreement is intended to give the outside equity investor a veto right over certain actions that the developer proposes to take on behalf of the LLC. The outside investor is not empowered under this section to either (1) to take any independent, affirmative action on behalf of the LLC or (2) compel the manager to act in any prescribed manner.[184] All the investor can do under this section is say "no" to a proposal presented to it by the manager.

What then are LLC decisions that an investor might try to include within the definition of those major decisions that require its prior consent? The following are examples of certain decisions that arguably fall into that category:[185]

- The sale of the LLC's real estate project;

- The obtaining of a mortgage loan secured by the LLC's assets;

- The entering into of any contract for the construction or design of the LLC's project;

- The acquisition of a significant new asset;

- The admission of a new member to the LLC;

- The selection or replacement of the project's leasing agent or property manager;

- The filing of a bankruptcy for the LLC;

- The execution of an amendment to the operating agreement;

- The implementation of a material change in the nature of the LLC's business;

- The merger or consolidation of the LLC with another entity;

- The institution or settlement of a lawsuit in which the LLC is a named party;

---

184. *See supra The Prudential Case Study—Investor Dominance,* for an example of a situation where the investor reserved both the right to take affirmative actions on behalf of the LLC and to compel the developer to undertake certain actions under the direction of the investor. As noted in the discussion of that case study, an investor's reservation of the right to control the management of an LLC's business and affairs has no impact on the investor's limited liability status. The type of arrangement described in the *Prudential Case Study* is, however, not the norm for a traditional developer-investor relationship on a commercial real estate project (certainly not one in which the developer agrees to make a significant equity contribution to the LLC).

185. For other sample listings of "major decisions," *see* Pappas, *supra* note 70, at 68–73; Jacobson, *supra* note 87, at 116–117; and Lindquist, *supra* note 79, at 59–62.

- The taking of any action that would cause the LLC's dissolution and termination;
- The hiring of an affiliate of the manager to perform services for the LLC;
- The filing of any tax election that would result in the LLC being taxed as a corporation;
- The determination of the types and levels of insurance coverage to be maintained by the LLC;
- The execution of a significant lease of space in the LLC's project;
- The incurring of any significant, unbudgeted expenditure;
- The approval of annual operating and capital budgets;
- The demolition or significant alteration of the LLC's real estate project;
- The distribution of any cash or assets to any member or affiliate of any member in a manner that is not formally prescribed by the terms of the operating agreement;
- The grant of the LLC's guaranty of any third party debt;
- The execution of an agreement with any governmental authority that would significantly alter the project's zoning or other governmental entitlements;
- The establishment of a cash reserve;
- The compromise of a significant claim held by or asserted against the LLC;
- The retention of legal counsel or an accountant;
- The taking of any action that would violate the terms of the operating agreement or make it impossible for the LLC to conduct its business; and
- The taking of any other action that is outside of the ordinary course of the LLC's business.

The above sampling is neither an exhaustive list of those decisions that the investor should try to include within the category of major decisions, nor a representative list of those decisions that the developer might be willing to accept in that category. The identity and scope of such major decisions will vary depending on both the nature of the LLC's business and the relative negotiating leverage of the developer and the equity investor.

The continuing use in the above list of the adjective "significant" is meant to serve as a reminder that, even if the members can agree that a particular matter should be treated as a major decision, the precise scope of such item is sure to be the subject of intense negotiations between the lawyers representing the developer and the equity investor. To better illustrate this point, take a look at typical developer and investor versions of the definition of a major decision involving the LLC's execution of a "significant" lease.

- ***Investor Version***—"The execution of any lease of more than 5,000 square feet of rentable space."

- ***Developer Version***—"The execution of any lease of more than 100,000 square feet of rentable space if the average, annual, net rental generated during the first five years of the lease term is less than $15 per rentable square foot."

This example highlights the nature of the negotiations that regularly occur between the real estate development lawyer and the attorney representing the outside investor. The real estate development lawyer wants to subject his client's actions to oversight by the outside investor only if it is a "really big deal" and then only if that "really big deal" adversely affects the LLC's projected economics. Counsel for the investor obviously wants his client's approval to be required for a much broader spectrum of transactions and circumstances.

Practice Tip #7–3: Drafting Limitations on the Manager's Authority

When representing a real estate developer, I always tried to incorporate the following three points into the provisions of the operating agreement that purported to limit my client's management authority:

- *An exclusion for any action that is either required by law (e.g., the payment of real estate taxes) or otherwise required by the terms of any agreement previously approved by the investor (e.g., the construction of tenant improvements in accordance with an approved lease);*

- *An exclusion for any action taken by the manager that is consistent with leasing guidelines and cost budgets approved by the investor at the outset of the project; and*

- *The use of dollar amounts or some other objective measurement standard to determine whether a particular decision is sufficiently significant to justify its inclusion within the definition of those major decisions that require the consent of the outside investor—e.g., the right of the manager to settle a lawsuit for less than $100,000 or to buy land containing less than five acres.*

Including these types of provisions in the operating agreement greatly enhances the flexibility of the developer to manage the ordinary, day-to-day activities of the LLC, without interference from the outside investor. Examples of the use of this technique can be found in §5.2 of the Form Operating Agreement.

---

3. Manager's Duties. *(§5.3)*

It is advisable from the perspectives of both members to itemize in the operating agreement any specific duties that are assigned to the manager. A specific itemization of those duties will go a long way toward clarifying the understanding of both the developer and the investor as to exactly what is expected of the developer when acting in its capacity as the manager of the LLC. By way of example, if the manager is expected to put together annual operating budgets for the LLC, the operating agreement should say so and should specify both the required content and the timing for the delivery of such budgets. Examples of other specific duties to be performed by the manager are set forth in § 5.3 of the Form Operating Agreement.

4. Manager's Compensation. *(§5.4)*

The fees that are to be paid to the manager should be specifically recited in the operating agreement. In the context of a real estate development deal, the following is a representative list of fees that are potentially payable to a manager:

- A development fee to compensate the manager for services provided in connection with the overall development of the LLC's real estate project—customarily stated as a percentage of total development costs (typically, anywhere from 3 to 10% of such costs);

- A property management fee to compensate the manager for services provided in connection with the oversight of the project's operations following completion of construction, including collection of rent, maintenance of the project and preparation of operating budgets— customarily stated either as a fixed sum or as a percentage of project's total rentals (typically anywhere from 2 to 6% of such rentals);

- A leasing fee to compensate the manager for services provided in connection with the leasing of the project—customarily stated as a percentage of the total rents payable under the leases (typically, anywhere from 3 to 10% of such rents); and

- A construction management fee to compensate the manager for services provided in connection with either the initial construction of the project or the later construction of tenant improvements— customarily stated as a percentage of construction costs (typically anywhere from 3 to 10% of such costs).

If any of the above services are to be provided by an affiliate of the manager (which is often the case), the LLC and such affiliate should enter into a separate services agreement that describes the scope of the services to be provided to the LLC and the amount of the fees to be paid to the affiliate.

The outside investor will want to limit the fees paid to the manager. One of the most common gripes heard from an investor is that the developer is trying to "fee up" the deal. "Feeing up the deal" is investor jargon for the developer charging fees to the LLC in an amount in excess of those fees that would be charged by an independent third party for the provision of comparable services. If the investor's lawyer is in a particularly aggressive mood, he may also argue that any fees payable to the developer or its affiliates should be set at below market rates, because the developer is already receiving a profits interest in the venture to compensate it for its contribution of services to the LLC. Whether any credence should be given to this argument is dependent upon the size and scope of the developer's profits interest. For example, the investor's point may be well taken if the developer is contributing only one percent of the LLC's capital in return for a 50% profits interest in a fully pre-leased project that has little risk of failure. However, in the typical development deal, the investor is usually willing to acknowledge that the developer is entitled to both a profits interest to reward it for its entrepreneurial risk and market rate fees to compensate it for the services it provides to the LLC.

5. Removal of the Manager

The equity investor will frequently seek to reserve a right to revoke the developer's authority to manage the LLC's business if the developer is failing to achieve the promised financial results for the project, either due to its malfeasance, misfeasance, nonfeasance or simply the vagaries of the marketplace.[186] The investor can achieve its objective of terminating the developer's management control by either (1) reserving the right to appoint itself as the new manager of the LLC or (2) removing the developer as the manager of the LLC and substituting a third party as the new manager of the entity.

The developer will, of course, strongly resist any attempt by the investor to wrest away the developer's control of the management of the LLC's business. As noted in earlier sections of this Chapter, the developer's primary economic interest in a real estate venture is typically represented by its receipt of a promoted profits interest in the LLC. The developer views its retention of control over the management of the LLC's business as the best way for it to preserve and maximize the value of its promote.[187]

The real estate development lawyer will find it difficult to resist the investor's request for the right to remove the developer as the manager of the LLC "for cause"—at least as long as a "for cause" removal is limited to the developer's fraud or other willful misconduct. To the extent the

---

186. *See generally* Pappas, *supra* note 70, at 61–62.

187. Counsel for the investor will frequently try to impose an economic penalty against the developer if the investor exercises a contractual right to remove the developer as the manager of the LLC. That economic penalty is usually couched in terms of a reduction or elimination of the developer's promote, because the investor realizes that it may have to offer a similar promote to entice a third party to take over the developer's role as the manager of the LLC. *See id.* at 62. The developer's loss of the right to receive ongoing property management, leasing and construction management fees from the LLC is another potential penalty that can be imposed by the investor.

investor wants to reserve the right to terminate the developer's management authority for less egregious reasons (e.g., the project's failure to produce positive cash flow at a targeted level), the investor should be prepared to engage in a long and arduous negotiating session with counsel for the developer, who will give on this point only if the negotiating leverage is strongly tilted in the investor's favor.[188]

6. Dealing With Affiliates. *(§5.5)*

The Delaware Act establishes the following default rule for a manager's or member's self-dealing with the LLC:

> Except as provided in a limited liability company agreement, a member or manager may lend money to, borrow money from, act as a surety, guarantor or endorser for, guarantee 1 or more obligations of, provide collateral for, and transact other business with, a limited liability company and, subject to other applicable law, has the same rights and obligations with respect to any such matter as a person who is not a member or manager.[189]

Under the Delaware Act, a manager or a member is, therefore, free to negotiate any type of self-dealing arrangement with the LLC and, in doing so, put its self-interest above that of the LLC and the other members.[190]

Despite (or, more accurately, because of) the broad blessing of self-dealing set forth in the Delaware Act, most operating agreements include a general prohibition against the manager entering into any agreement with any of its affiliates, unless such agreement is first approved by the investor.[191] This prohibition is intended to preclude the manager from hiring an unqualified affiliate to perform services or provide materials to the LLC or agreeing to pay any such affiliate an above market fee for its services or materials. The real estate development lawyer should make sure that any affiliate agreements that he knows the developer intends to sign are excluded from the general prohibition set forth in this section. Investor's counsel will frequently seek to have a clause inserted into the operating agreement which says that the investor (and not the manager) will have the right to administer and enforce any affiliate contract on the LLC's behalf.[192]

---

188. The reader will note that the Form Operating Agreement is totally silent on the issue of the removal of the manager. I simply could not bring myself to include a removal provision in the Form Operating Agreement, which, except for this point, is a fairly balanced, unbiased document.

189. *See* Delaware Code Annotated, Title 6, § 18–107 (West 2010).

190. *See* Waters, *supra* note 76, at 1–2.

191. The Form Operating Agreement adopts a less restrictive approach to the developer's engagement of affiliates to provide services to the LLC. Instead of prohibiting any affiliate contract that is not pre-approved by the outside investor, § 5.5 of the Form Operating Agreement authorizes the developer to enter into any agreement with an affiliate, as long as the terms and conditions of such agreements are "comparable to those which would govern the provision by an independent third party in an arm's length transaction of comparable services and materials in the locale in which the Project is located."

192. *See e.g.,* §5.5 of the Form Operating Agreement.

7. Other Business Ventures. *(§5.6)*

Both the developer and its equity investor may have interests in other ventures that are competitive with the LLC's business. For example, it would not be unusual for an office developer to own more than one office building in the same office park and for the developer to have different equity investors for each such building. Similarly, the equity investor may have investments in any number of competing projects in the same submarket in which the LLC's project is located.

A member's ownership of an interest in a business venture that is competitive with the LLC's project creates an obvious conflict of interest for that member. The legal questions are (a) does the existence of such a conflict of interest constitute a breach of the fiduciary duty owed by a member to the other members of the LLC and (b) if so, can the members expressly waive such fiduciary duty in the LLC's operating agreement?

The following case involving the Columbus Blue Jackets hockey team addresses these precise issues.

McCONNELL v. HUNT SPORTS ENTERPRISES[193]

Court of Appeals of Ohio, Tenth District
725 N.E.2d 1193
Decided on August 31, 1999

... In 1996, the National Hockey League ("NHL") determined it would be accepting applications for new hockey franchises. In April 1996, Gregory S. Lashutka, the mayor of Columbus, received a phone call from an NHL representative inquiring as to Columbus's interest in a hockey team. As a result, Mayor Lashutka asked certain community leaders who had been involved in exploring professional sports in Columbus to pursue the possibility of applying for an NHL hockey franchise. Two of these persons were Ronald A. Pizzuti and [John H.] McConnell.

Pizzuti began efforts to recruit investors in a possible franchise. Pizzuti approached Lamar Hunt, principal of Hunt Sports Group, as to Hunt's interest in investing in such a franchise for Columbus. Hunt was already the operating member of the Columbus Crew, a professional soccer team whose investors included Hunt Sports Group, Pizzuti, McConnell, and Wolfe Enterprises, Inc. Hunt expressed an interest in participating in a possible franchise. The deadline for applying for an NHL expansion franchise was November 1, 1996.

On October 31, 1996, CHL was formed when its articles of organization were filed with the secretary of state.... The members of CHL were McConnell, Wolfe Enterprises, Inc., Hunt Sports Group, Pizzuti Sports

---

193. All footnotes and citations have been omitted from this opinion. In addition, all references to "appellant" have been replaced with "Hunt" and all references to "appellees" have been replaced with "McConnell and Wolfe."

Limited, and Buckeye Hockey, L.L.C. Each member made an initial capital contribution of $25,000. CHL was subject to an operating agreement that set forth the terms between the members. Pursuant to section 2.1 of CHL's operating agreement, the general character of the business of CHL was to invest in and operate a franchise in the NHL.

On or about November 1, 1996, an application was filed with the NHL on behalf of the city of Columbus. In the application, the ownership group was identified as CHL, and the individuals in such group were listed as Pizzuti Sports Limited, McConnell, Wolfe Enterprises, Inc., and Hunt Sports Group. A $100,000 check from CHL was included as the application fee. Also included within the application package was Columbus's plan for an arena to house the hockey games. There was no facility at the time, and the proposal was to build a facility that would be financed, in large part, by a three-year countywide one-half percent sales tax. The sales tax issue would be on the May 1997 ballot.

On May 6, 1997, the sales tax issue failed. The day after, Mayor Lashutka met with Hunt, and other opportunities were discussed. The mayor also spoke with Gary Bettman, commissioner of the NHL, and they discussed whether an alternate plan for an arena was possible. Also on May 7, 1997, Dimon McPherson, chairman and chief executive officer of Nationwide Insurance Enterprise ("Nationwide"), met with Hunt, and they discussed the possibility of building the arena despite the failure of the sales tax issue . . . . . Hunt was interested, and Nationwide began working on an arena plan. On or about May 9, 1997, the mayor spoke with Bettman and let him know that alternate plans would be pursued, and Mr. Bettman gave Columbus until June 4, 1997 to come up with a plan.

By May 28, 1997, Nationwide had come up with a plan to finance an arena privately and on such date, Nationwide representatives met with representatives of Hunt Sports Group. Hunt Sports Group did not accept Nationwide's lease proposal. . . . On May 29, 1997, Nationwide representatives again met with representatives of Hunt Sports Group. Again, Hunt Sports Group indicated that the lease proposal was unacceptable and that the NHL team would lose millions with this proposal. The June 4, 1997 NHL deadline was discussed. Hunt Sports Group stated that it would continue to evaluate the proposal, and it wanted the weekend to do so. Nationwide informed appellant that it needed an answer by close of business Friday, May 30.

On May 30, 1997, McPherson called McConnell and requested that they meet and discuss "where [they] were on the arena." McPherson "could see that the situation now was slipping away, and [he] just didn't want that to happen," so he went to see McConnell for advice and counsel. . . . McConnell stated that if Hunt would not step up and lease the arena and, therefore, get the franchise, McConnell would. Hunt Sports Group did not contact Nationwide on May 30, 1997. . . .

[O]n June 2, 1997, McPherson met with Bettman and told him that Nationwide would be building an arena in downtown Columbus. McPherson also told Bettman that if need be, McConnell would purchase the franchise on his own ... On June 3 ... Hunt Sports Group told Nationwide that it still found the terms of the lease to be unacceptable. On June 3 or June 4, McConnell, in a conversation with the NHL, orally agreed to apply for a hockey franchise for Columbus. On June 4, McPherson returned a call from Hunt, and Hunt informed McPherson that he was still interested in pursuing an agreement with Nationwide.

On June 4, 1997, the NHL franchise expansion committee met. Bettman informed the committee that Nationwide would build an arena, and McConnell was prepared to go forward with the franchise even if he had to do it himself. The committee was told that Hunt Sports Group's involvement was an open issue, but McConnell as an owner was more than adequate. The expansion committee recommended Columbus to the NHL board of governors as one of four cities to be granted a franchise.

On June 5, 1997, the NHL sent Hunt a letter requesting that he let the NHL know by Monday, June 9, 1997 whether he was going forward with his franchise application. In a June 6, 1997 letter to the NHL, Hunt responded that CHL intended to pursue the franchise application. Hunt informed the NHL that he had arranged a meeting with the members of CHL to be held on June 9, 1997. Hunt indicated that the application was contingent upon entering into an appropriate lease for a hockey facility.

On June 9, 1997, a meeting took place at Pizzuti's office. Those present at the meeting included McConnell, Hunt, Pizzuti, John F. Wolfe, chairman of Wolfe Enterprises, Inc., and representatives of Buckeye Hockey, L.L.C. and Ameritech. The NHL required that the ownership group be identified and that such ownership group sign a lease term sheet by June 9, 1997. Brian Ellis, president and chief operating officer of Nationwide, presented the lease term sheet to those present at the meeting, left the meeting, and went to a different room.

Hunt indicated the lease was unacceptable. Ameritech and Buckeye Hockey, L.L.C. indicated that if Hunt found it unacceptable, then they too found it unacceptable. Pizzuti and Wolfe agreed to participate along with McConnell. John Christie, president of JMAC, Inc., the personal investment company of the McConnell family, left the meeting and joined Ellis. Christie informed Ellis that McConnell had accepted the term sheet and was signing it in his individual capacity. The term sheet contained a signature line for "Columbus Hockey Limited" as the franchise owner. Ellis phoned his secretary and had her omit the name "Columbus Hockey Limited" on her computer from under the signature line and fax the change to Ellis at Pizzuti's office. McConnell then signed the term sheet as the owner of the franchise. Christie faxed the signed lease term sheet to Bettman that day along with a cover letter and a description of the ownership group. Such ownership group was identified as John H. McConnell, majority owner, Pizzuti Sports, L.L.C., John F. Wolfe, and "[u]p to seven (7) other members." The cover letter indicated that the attached material signified an amendment to the November 1, 1996 application from the city.

On June 17, 1997, the NHL expansion committee recommended to the NHL board of governors that Columbus be awarded a franchise with McConnell's group as owner of the franchise. On the same date, the complaint in the case at bar was filed. On or about June 25, 1997, the NHL board of governors awarded Columbus a franchise with McConnell's group as owner. Hunt Sports Group, Buckeye Hockey, L.L.C. and Ameritech have no ownership interest in the hockey franchise. . . .

In their complaint, McConnell and Wolfe Enterprises, Inc. requested a declaration that section 3.3 of the CHL operating agreement allowed members of CHL to compete with CHL. Specifically, McConnell and Wolfe Enterprises, Inc. sought a declaration that under the operating agreement, they were permitted to participate in COLHOC [, the new limited liability company formed by McConnell, Pizzuti and Wolfe to own the Columbus Hockey franchise,] and obtain the franchise. . . .

[T]he trial court found that section 3.3 of the operating agreement was clear and unambiguous and allowed McConnell and Wolfe Enterprises, Inc. to compete against CHL and obtain the NHL franchise. In addition, the trial court found McConnell did not breach the operating agreement by competing against CHL. . . . Hunt Sports Group filed a notice of appeal. . . .

McConnell and Wolfe contend section 3.3 is plain and unambiguous and allows what occurred here-COLHOC competing for and obtaining the NHL franchise. Hunt asserts, in part, that the trial court's interpretation of section 3.3 was incorrect and that section 3.3 is ambiguous and subject to different interpretations. Therefore, Hunt contends extrinsic evidence should have been considered, and such evidence would have shown the parties did not intend section 3.3 to mean members could compete against CHL and take away CHL's only purpose. . . .

For the reasons that follow, we conclude that section 3.3 is plain and unambiguous and allowed members of CHL to compete against CHL for an NHL franchise.

Section 3.3 of the operating agreement states:

"Members May Compete. Members shall not in any way be prohibited from or restricted in engaging or owning an interest in any other business venture of any nature, including any venture which might be competitive with the business of the Company."

Hunt emphasizes the word "other" in the above language and states, in essence, that it means any business venture that is different from the business of the company. Appellant points out that under section 2.1 of the operating agreement, the general character of the business is "to invest in and operate a franchise in the National Hockey League." Hence, Hunt contends that members may only engage in or own an interest in a venture that is not in the business of investing in and operating a franchise with the NHL.

Hunt's interpretation of section 3.3 goes beyond the plain language of the agreement and adds words or meanings not stated in the provision. Section 3.3, for example, does not state "[m]embers shall not be prohibited from or restricted in engaging or owning an interest in any other business venture that is different from the business of the company." Rather, section 3.3 states: "any other business venture *of any nature.*" (Emphasis added.) It then adds to this statement: "including any venture which might be competitive with the business of the Company." The words "any nature" could not be broader, and the inclusion of the words "any venture which might be competitive with the business of the Company" makes it clear that members were not prohibited from engaging in a venture that was competitive with CHL's investing in and operating an NHL franchise. Contrary to Hunt's contention, the word "other" simply means a business venture other than CHL. The word "other" does not limit the type of business venture in which members may engage.

Hence, section 3.3 did not prohibit McConnell and Wolfe from engaging in activities that may have been competitive with CHL, including their participation in COLHOC. Accordingly, summary judgment in favor of McConnell and Wolfe was appropriate, and they were entitled to a declaration that section 3.3 of the operating agreement permitted them to request and obtain an NHL hockey franchise to the exclusion of CHL.....

We now address the substance of the trial court's [finding] ... that the evidence did not show McConnell and Wolfe interfered with Hunt's prospective business relationships with Nationwide or the NHL. As to the fiduciary duty issue, the trial court found ... that McConnell and Wolfe had not engaged in any kind of willful misconduct, misrepresentation, or concealment. Therefore, the trial court concluded that McConnell and Wolfe had not breached any fiduciary duty in seeking and obtaining the NHL franchise and in negotiating with Nationwide concerning the arena lease. For the reasons that follow, we conclude that ... [the trial court's decision] was appropriate.

Before we can review the propriety of the ... [trial court's decision], the law on fiduciary duty and interference with a prospective business relationship must be addressed. The term "fiduciary relationship" has been defined as a relationship in which special confidence and trust is reposed in the integrity and fidelity of another, and there is a resulting position of superiority or influence acquired by virtue of this special trust. In the case at bar, a limited liability company is involved which, like a partnership, involves a fiduciary relationship. Normally, the presence of such a relationship would preclude direct competition between members of the company. However, here we have an operating agreement that by its very terms allows members to compete with the business of the company.

Hence, the question we are presented with is whether an operating agreement of a limited liability company may, in essence, limit or define the scope of the fiduciary duties imposed upon its members. We answer this question in the affirmative.

A fiduciary has been defined as a person having a duty, *created by his or her undertaking,* to act primarily for the benefit of another in matters *connected with such undertaking.* A claim of breach of fiduciary duty is basically a claim for negligence that involves a higher standard of care. In order to recover, one must show the existence of a duty on the part of the alleged wrongdoer not to subject such person to the injury complained of, a failure to observe such duty, and an injury proximately resulting therefrom. These principles support our conclusion that a contract may define the scope of fiduciary duties between parties to the contract.

Here, the injury complained of by Hunt was, essentially, McConnell's and Wolfe's competing with CHL and obtaining the NHL franchise. The operating agreement constitutes the undertaking of the parties herein. In becoming members of CHL, Hunt, McConnell and Wolfe agreed to abide by the terms of the operating agreement, and such agreement specifically allowed competition with the company by its members. As such, the duties created pursuant to such undertaking did not include a duty not to compete. Therefore, there was no duty on the part of McConnell and Wolfe to refrain from subjecting Hunt to the injury complained of herein.

We find further support for our conclusion in case law concerning close corporations and partnerships.... [Ohio courts have supported] the proposition that close corporation employment agreements may limit the scope of fiduciary duties that otherwise would apply absent certain provisions in such agreements. The same principle has been applied in situations involving partnerships that are subject to partnership agreements.

"Operating agreement" is defined in R.C. 1705.01(J) as all of the valid written or oral agreements of the members as to the affairs of a limited liability company and the conduct of its business. R.C. 1705.03(C) sets forth various activities limited liability companies may engage in and indicates such are subject to the company's articles of organization or operating agreement. Indeed, many of the statutory provisions in R.C. Chapter 1705 governing limited liability companies indicate they are, in various ways, subject to and/or dependent upon related provisions in an operating agreement Here, the operating agreement states in its opening paragraph that it evidences the mutual agreement of the members in consideration of their contributions and promises to each other. Such agreement specifically allowed its members to compete with the company.

Given the above, we conclude as a matter of law that it was not a breach of fiduciary duty for McConnell and Wolfe to form, COLHOC and obtain an NHL franchise to the exclusion of CHL. In so concluding, we are not stating that *no* act related to such obtainment could be considered a breach of fiduciary duty. In general terms, members of limited liability companies owe one another the duty of utmost trust and loyalty. However, such general duty in this case must be considered in the context of members' ability, pursuant to operating agreement, to compete with the company. . . .

This evidence shows that McConnell and Wolfe obtained the NHL franchise to the exclusion of CHL. This constituted direct competition with CHL. However, McConnell and Wolfe were permitted under the operating agreement to compete with CHL and, as discussed above, this in and of itself cannot constitute a breach of fiduciary duty. Further, in so competing, McConnell and Wolfe did not engage in any acts that would otherwise constitute wrongful behavior. Nationwide contacted McConnell only after appellant indicated the lease terms were unacceptable. Even then, McConnell stated he would accept the lease terms and obtain the franchise on his own only if Hunt did not. There is no evidence that McConnell acted in any secretive manner in his actions leading up to the franchise award or that he used CHL assets for personal gain. In short, the evidence shows that McConnell and Wolfe obtained the NHL franchise to the exclusion of CHL.

Notes and Questions About the McConnell Case

The *McConnell* court made three interesting findings.

- The Court stated that "in general terms, members of a limited liability companies owe one another the duty of utmost trust and loyalty."[194]

- The Court also found that "normally, the presence of such a [fiduciary] relationship would preclude direct competition between members of the company."[195]

- Finally, the Court ruled that the members could waive such fiduciary duties by including a provision in the operating agreement that such direct competition was permitted.[196]

The key lesson to be learned from the *McConnell* case is that, if the members want to have the right to engage in outside ventures that are competitive with the LLC's business, a specific clause sanctioning such competitive conduct must be included in the operating agreement. Absent the inclusion of such a clause, a member's engagement in an activity that is competitive with the LLC's business could subject that member to a lawsuit for the breach of the fiduciary duty owed by it to other members of the LLC.

It should be noted that the Ohio LLC statute that was in force when the *McConnell* decision was handed down makes no express mention of any fiduciary duties owed by one member to another in the context of a member-managed LLC (which the LLC in *McConnell* was).[197] The Revised Uniform

---

194. *See* McConnell v. Hunt Sports Enterprises, 725 N.E.2d 1193, 1216 (Ohio App. 1999).

195. *See id.* at 1214.

196. *See id.* at 1212.

197. *See* Ohio Revised Code Annotated Chapter 1705 (West 1996).

Limited Liability Company Act, however, expressly provides that a member of a member-managed LLC has "the duty of loyalty ... to refrain from competing with the company in the conduct of the company's activities."[198] The Revised Uniform Limited Liability Company Act further states that "if not manifestly unreasonable, the operating agreement may restrict or eliminate ... the duty to refrain from competing with the company in the conduct of the company's activities."[199] The unanswered question under the quoted provisions of the Revised Uniform Limited Liability Company Act is whether it is "manifestly unreasonable" to permit a member to engage in conduct that is directly competitive with the LLC's business.[200]

The Delaware Act makes no mention whatsoever of either the existence or absence of any fiduciary duties owed to the members of an LLC by a member or a manager. The Delaware Act would, however, seem to clearly validate the enforceability of an operating agreement clause that permits a member or a manager to engage in conduct that is competitive with the business of the LLC. The Delaware Act expressly provides that:

> To the extent that, at law or in equity, a member or a manager ... has duties (including fiduciary duties) to a limited liability company or to another member or manager ..., the member's or manager's ... duties may be expanded or restricted or eliminated by provisions in the limited liability company agreement.[201]

The *McConnell* case and the statutory provisions discussed above validate the ability of the members of an LLC to contractually permit each other to own interests in other projects that are directly competitive with the project being developed by the LLC. To the extent both members want to permit the other member to engage in conduct that is competitive with the LLC's business, it is essential that a clause blessing such competitive activities be inserted into the operating agreement. An example of such a clause is set forth in § 5.6 of the Form Operating Agreement.

There are circumstances that warrant a carve-out from the "freedom to compete" provision of the operating agreement. For example, an investor in a grocery-anchored, neighborhood shopping center might want to prohibit the developer from developing another grocery-anchored center (presumably with another grocer) in the immediate vicinity of the LLC's project. Conversely, the developer of a suburban office building might want to try to preclude its equity investor from being the primary funding source for the development of a competitive office project in the same sub-

---

198. *See* Revised Uniform Limited Liability Company Act (2006) § 409(b) (3).

199. *See id.* § 110(d) (1) (c).

200. The Revised Uniform Limited Liability Company Act also provides that "[a]ll of the members ... may authorize or ratify, after full disclosure of all material facts, a specific act or transaction that would otherwise violate the duty of loyalty." *See id.* § 409(f).

201. *See* Delaware Code Annotated, Title 6, § 18–1101(c) (West 2010). It should be noted, however, that § 18–1101(c) of the Delaware act expressly provides that the limited liability company agreement "may not eliminate the implied covenant of good faith and fair dealing." *See id.*

market where the developer's project is located. To the extent a member wants to limit another member's competitive activities, it would be well-advised to buttress whatever legal arguments it might have under *McConnell* and its statutory and judicial progeny by including a specific non-competition covenant in the operating agreement.

---

8.   Deadlocks and Buy-sell Provisions. *(§5.11)*

As noted earlier in this Chapter, most operating agreements put in place a management structure that requires the consent of all or a super-majority of the members to the making of certain major decisions. In drafting the operating agreement, a key question that the real estate developer must ask is what happens if the parties simply cannot reach agreement on a major decision? The point at which the parties "agree to disagree" is commonly referred to in operating agreements as a ***deadlock.***

At the beginning of a business deal, the members are usually totally in sync on all matters related to the LLC's real estate development project. Talking about the potential for future disagreements is a real downer that both parties would prefer to skip. It is, however, a topic which the real estate development lawyer absolutely must force his client to confront.[202] The occurrence of a deadlock can be a death knell for even the most successful of real estate projects, unless the parties have taken the time to construct a pre-determined plan to deal with the consequences of the deadlock.[203]

Once agreement is reached on the list of those major decisions that require the parties' mutual consent, the real estate development lawyer must take the time to sit down and ask himself the "what if they can't agree" question as it relates to each of the major decisions. The lawyer must devise and incorporate into the operating agreement two separate strategies to deal with each potential deadlock situation:

- One strategy that is designed to permit the conduct of the LLC's business to continue in some orderly fashion while the members try to work out their differences (the ***interim strategy***); and

- A second strategy that addresses how the parties can terminate their relationship (hopefully in an amicable and profitable fashion) if they are ultimately unable to resolve their disagreements (the ***exit strategy***).

---

202.   *See* Hales, *supra* note 124, at 1.10.

203.   *See generally* Elliot M. Surkin, *How Do I Get Out of Here? A Discussion of Exit Strategies in Closely-held Real Estate LLCs*, in ALI–ABA COURSE OF STUDY MATERIALS, MODERN REAL ESTATE TRANSACTIONS, Course No. SP–002, 1241 (August 2008); Stevens A. Carey, *Buy/Sell Provisions in Real Estate Joint Venture Agreements*, 39 REAL PROPERTY, PROBATE AND TRUST JOURNAL 651 (2004); and Pappas, *supra* note 70, at 61.

The following example shows why it is important for the members to incorporate mutually acceptable interim and exit strategies into the operating agreement.

> **Example 7–7:** Developer and Investor form ABC LLC to develop an office building in Columbus, Ohio. Eighty percent of ABC's development costs are financed under a construction loan obtained from Buckeye Bank. The construction loan has a term of three years and is personally guaranteed by Developer.
>
> The office building is 100% leased at above pro forma rents to a AAA-credit tenant. At the beginning of ABC's third year of operations, Developer requests Investor's approval to refinance the construction loan with a permanent, non-recourse loan from Heartland Insurance Company. The refinancing with Heartland will (a) lock in a high level of operating cash flow for the members of ABC (b) let Developer get off the hook on its guaranty to Buckeye Bank and (c) produce refinancing proceeds sufficient to pay off the Buckeye Bank loan and provide a partial return of capital to ABC's members.
>
> Investor refuses to consent to the Heartland financing, because it wants to realize all of its investment profit "right now" by selling the building. In an effort to try to force the Developer to agree to sell the building, Investor also refuses to approve Developer's operating budget for the office building. The construction loan, which is still fully guaranteed by Developer, is scheduled to mature in nine months. Developer calls his lawyer in a panic and asks—"What do I do now?"

The easy way out would be for Developer to accede to Investor's demands and sell the building. A building sale would pay off the loan, retire Developer's guaranty and probably produce a nice payday for both Developer and Investor. But Developer doesn't pay its lawyer to show it the easy way out of a dilemma. It still wants to hold onto the building by doing the refinancing with Heartland and it tells its lawyer to figure out a way to "get it done."

Hopefully, the operating agreement prepared by Developer's lawyer incorporated interim and exit strategies of the type found in the Form Operating Agreement. The three strategies contained in the Form Operating Agreement that could help Developer achieve its business objective are described below.

- *Cooling-off Period*—The Form Operating Agreement provides that promptly following Investor's refusal to consent to Developer's refinancing proposal, Developer and Investor are required to meet and negotiate in good faith for a period of up to 30 days to try to resolve their differences. This 30–day cooling off period is intended to provide Developer with an opportunity to try to convince Investor of the wisdom of its ways.[204]

---

204. Some operating agreements go so far as to include a provision requiring the parties to submit their disagreement to mandatory mediation. I am not the biggest fan of mediation and, therefore, did not include such a requirement in the Form Operating Agreement. My apologies on

- ***Budget Approval Carryover***—ABC cannot stop paying its bills just because Investor refuses to approve Developer's operating budget for the upcoming year. The Form Operating Agreement addresses this point by providing that Developer is authorized to act in accordance with the budget approved for the prior year, adjusted to reflect (a) any actual increases in the amount of ***uncontrollable expenses***, such as debt service, real estate taxes, utilities, insurance premiums and the like and (b) increases in all other line item expenses to reflect any upward movement during the prior year in the Consumer Price Index.[205] While not perfect, this type of budget carryover provision will let Developer attempt to conduct business as usual while it attempts to resolve its business dispute with Investor.

- ***Push-pull Buy-sell***— The above two provisions are examples of interim strategies intended to permit ABC to continue to conduct its business while the parties see if they can somehow work out their differences. Section 5.11 of the Form Operating Agreement is an example of an exit strategy that can be triggered if the parties simply cannot resolve their disagreements. The exit strategy set forth in the Form Operating Agreement is commonly referred to as a ***push-pull, buy-sell*** provision. Its purpose is to provide deadlocked members with a mechanism they can use to go their separate ways, with one member acquiring the LLC's assets and the other member liquidating its membership interest.

A push-pull buy-sell is triggered when one member notifies the other member of the price at which it is willing to either buy the other member's interest or sell its interest. The member receiving the buy-sell notice has the option of either selling its interest or buying out the other member at the price stated in the initial buy-sell notice. The "push-pull" nature of this buy-sell is intended to enhance the fairness of the buy-out by letting one member set the buy-out price, while the other member gets to decide whether it will be a buyer or a seller. The theory underlying the push-pull buy-sell is that the member who sends the buy-sell notice will be reluctant to lowball its buy-out price, because it fears that the other member will turn around and opt to purchase its membership interest at the lowball number.

The following points should be noted about the buy-sell provision contained in § 5.11 of the Form Operating Agreement.

- The buy-sell can only be triggered after the occurrence of a deadlock. A deadlock is deemed to occur only if the parties are unable to resolve their differences over a proposed major decision during the 30–day cooling-off period mentioned earlier in this section.

---

this point to Nancy Rogers, the former dean of the Moritz College of Law, who created one of the leading alternative dispute resolution programs in the country during the term of her leadership at Moritz.

205. *See* Form Operating Agreement §5.8.

- The buy-sell cannot be exercised at any time during the first three years of the LLC's existence (regardless whether a deadlock occurs during that three year period). This so-called **lock-out period** is designed to provide time to permit the developer to complete construction and fully lease the project, without any disruption caused by a disgruntled investor.

- The operation of the buy-sell provision contained in the Form Operating Agreement can only be opened up by the developer. The buy-sell provisions are applicable following the occurrence of a deadlock and the developer controls whether a deadlock exists. If the investor disapproves a major decision proposal presented to it by the developer, the developer then has the choice either to withdraw the proposal (in which event no deadlock will be deemed to exist) or to formally notify the investor that a deadlock has occurred and, accordingly, the buy-sell may be exercised by either member. The developer's ability to control the availability of the buy-sell is intended to provide the developer with a tool to help it overcome the timing problem described in the next paragraph.

- In most real estate development LLCs, the investor is financially stronger than the developer and almost always much more liquid. The investor is, therefore, usually in a much better position than the developer to make a "buy" election under the push-pull buy-sell. The developer is seldom capable of simply writing a check out of its available cash resources to buy out the interest of the malcontent investor. The developer needs time to arrange debt or equity financing for a purchase of the investor's membership interest. The Form Operating Agreement gives the developer a minimum of 210 days after its receipt of a buy-sell notice from the investor in which to put together the requisite funding to purchase the investor's LLC interest (180 days in which to respond to the buy-sell notice and another 30 days in which to close on the purchase following its notice to the investor that it will be a "buyer" on the transaction). The investor's lawyer will try to shorten this time period, so as to limit the developer's ability to be something other than a "seller" under the push-pull, buy-sell. As noted in the prior bulleted paragraph, the developer's ability to control when the buy-sell first becomes available for exercise gives it another tactical weapon to try to buy time to find the requisite funding to purchase the investor's membership interest.

- Finally, in many situations the warring members are so concerned about the inherent uncertainties associated with the exercise of the push-pull provision (will I be a buyer or a seller and should I lowball the purchase price) that they end up hammering out a negotiated settlement of their disagreements. This *in terrorem* effect of the push-pull buy-sell is why it is often labeled a **Russian roulette** provision. The question whether there really is a bullet in the chamber serves as a very real incentive for the parties to sit down at the negotiating table to structure a mutually acceptable resolution of their differences. As such, the threat of the use of the buy-sell is frequently more effective than the actual exercise of that provision.

There are an unlimited number of other mechanisms that can be employed to provide the members with an exit strategy.[206] Two of the most commonly used alternative exit strategy methods are:

- A ***forced sale***, where a member has the right to force the LLC to market its project for sale to third parties; and

- The ***drag along*** approach, where a member has the right to sell its membership interest to a third party and to compel the other member to sell its membership interest to the third party purchaser on the same terms.

Both of these methods can work to achieve the members' objectives of terminating their venture relationship.[207] For my money, however, neither method is as reliable or effective as the push-pull, buy-sell provision.

HIBC Case Study—The Value of a Push-pull Buy-sell

The Pizzuti–Newport general partnership agreement contained a classic example of a push-pull, buy-sell provision. The buy-sell was only exercisable upon the declaration of an impasse between the partners (simply another word for a deadlock). By 1999, Pizzuti and Newport jointly owned nine office projects in the HIBC office park and another 12 office and warehouse projects in various locations in Ohio. All of those properties were owned by general partnerships, whose activities were governed by partnership agreements containing push-pull, buy-sell provisions.

By 1999, Pizzuti had decided that it needed to tap into a more substantial equity source than Newport in order to permit it to expand its development business throughout the eastern half of the United States. Pizzuti had also become disenchanted with the cost of Newport's capital. As noted earlier in this Chapter,[208] Newport's capital was given the exact same return and priority as was Pizzuti's—that is, Pizzuti was not receiving any promoted profits interest under its arrangement with Newport.

For these reasons, Pizzuti approached Newport in early 1999 to discuss Pizzuti's desire to find a new capital partner. The proposal that Pizzuti

---

206. For a discussion of other exit strategies, *see generally* Lindquist, *supra* note 79, at 51–56; Surkin, *How Do I Get out of Here*, supra note 203; Carey, *supra* note 203; and Pappas, *supra* note 70, at 61.

207. A variation commonly used under both the forced sale and drag along methods is to provide the other member a limited preemptive right to purchase the LLC's assets (in the case of a forced sale) or the member's equity interest (in the case of a drag along) at either a predetermined strike price or at the price offered by the third party purchaser. *See* Pappas, *supra* note 70, at 79–80.

208. *See supra HIBC Case Study—Profits Interests.*

presented to Newport was that Newport would have the right to continue to invest in Pizzuti's development deals, but that it would have to do so under the same economic return parameters agreed to by the new capital partner. Newport indicated that, while it was not thrilled with the concept, it would be willing to look at any equity proposal that Pizzuti was ultimately able to negotiate with an institutional equity investor.

In July, 1999, Pizzuti struck an equity deal with Nationwide Realty Investors, Ltd. that called for Nationwide to invest in all of the existing Pizzuti–Newport deals and provide the lion's share of all capital needed for Pizzuti's new development projects. The deal initially struck by Pizzuti and Nationwide contemplated that Newport would (1) contribute its interests in the existing portfolio to the new venture and (2) have the right to invest in new deals on the same basic terms as Nationwide (albeit at a much smaller level). After several extremely contentious meetings with Pizzuti representatives, Newport ultimately balked and told Pizzuti that it was not willing to participate in the Nationwide equity deal. Newport's refusal to participate put the entirety of the Nationwide deal in jeopardy, because Newport's contribution of its interests in the existing portfolio to the new Pizzuti–Nationwide entity was a condition precedent to Nationwide doing the deal.[209]

Pizzuti's relationship with Newport quickly soured following Newport's refusal to participate in the new venture with Nationwide. Pizzuti felt that it was absolutely essential to the long-term health of its development business that the deal with Nationwide be consummated. As a result, Pizzuti met with Nationwide and received its agreement to buy out all of Newport's interests in the combined Pizzuti–Newport portfolio. Newport, however, refused to sell its interests to Nationwide.

Pizzuti was, therefore, left between the proverbial rock and a hard place. Its relationship with Newport had disintegrated to the point that there was no realistic prospect of going back to a business as usual posture and doing co-investment development deals with Newport. Moreover, Nationwide was adamant that it would not fund Pizzuti's new development deals, unless it also received the sweetener of an interest in the stabilized and highly profitable real estate portfolio that Pizzuti co-owned with Newport. A classic deadlock situation existed that cried out for the implementation of an exit strategy for the Pizzuti–Newport relationship. Pizzuti found that exit strategy in the push-pull, buy-sell provisions contained in all of the Newport general partnership agreements.

In the late summer of 1999, Pizzuti delivered 19 separate buy-sell notices to Newport.[210] *Each such buy-sell notice set forth a purchase price*

---

209. The trade-off for Nationwide's agreement to provide 90% of the capital needed for Pizzuti's new development projects was its receipt of an approximately 65% equity interest in the stabilized portfolio of Pizzuti's existing office and industrial projects. The economics of the deal simply did not work unless Newport agreed to contribute its 50% equity interests in the HIBC office projects and its 25% interest in the Ohio industrial projects.

210. Buy-sell notices were not delivered for the two office projects co-owned by Pizzuti and Newport in Columbus, Ohio, because Nationwide was not interested in investing in those two projects.

for the Pizzuti–Newport project that was equal to the price that Nationwide had indicated it was willing to pay for such project. In delivering the buy-sell notices, Pizzuti was gambling that (1) Newport did not have the required liquidity to effect a buy-out of all of Pizzuti's interests in all of the19 projects and (2) Newport's previously-stated disinterest in taking on the management of a real estate project would deter it from becoming a buyer of some (but not all) of Pizzuti's partnership interests. This was a significant gamble by Pizzuti, but one that it felt that it had no choice but to take.

Long story, short, the delivery of the buy-sell notices to Newport had the desired effect. Newport returned to the negotiating table and an agreement was ultimately reached for Nationwide's buy-out of Newport's entire interest in the Pizzuti–Newport portfolio. Newport received a nice bit of cash and Pizzuti gained the freedom to close its equity deal with Nationwide.[211]

The Newport story highlights the importance of incorporating an exit strategy into the entity documents. If the Newport general partnership agreements had not contained push-pull, buy-sells, Pizzuti would have had zero leverage in its efforts to force Newport to go along with the Nationwide deal—something that Pizzuti correctly believed was a necessary next step in the progression of its business model. Pizzuti would have been forced to try to strike a deal with Nationwide or some other equity provider for the funding of its new pipeline deals, without being able to throw in the deal sweetener of the grant to the equity provider of an interest in an existing real estate portfolio. The end result would have been an equity deal which was far less favorable to Pizzuti than was the combined deal which it ultimately struck with Nationwide.

XII. SUMMARY

A limited liability company is almost always the entity of choice for real estate development deals. Because of its wholesale embracing of freedom of contract principles, the Delaware Limited Liability Company Act provides the practitioner with a virtually unlimited ability to craft an operating agreement that serves the economic, business, tax and legal interests of his client. The lawyer who brings to bear a thorough under-standing of tax and legal principles and superior negotiating and drafting skills can help his client attract cheap, efficient and undemanding capital to its development project.

---

211. Newport did, however, use its negotiating leverage to also require Pizzuti to buy out its 25% interest in the two Ohio office projects and its 50% interest in the undeveloped HIBC land (neither of which held any investment interest for Nationwide). *See supra* Chapter 12, Pages 565–567 for a further narrative on the Pizzuti–Newport divorce.

CHAPTER 8

STAGE 4: CLOSING THE LAND ACQUISITION

■ ■ ■

I. INTRODUCTION

Stage 4 is the point in the real estate development process where the proverbial "rubber meets the road" for the developer. The developer has made the determination that its development project is feasible and that the time is at hand to buy the land and kick off its construction efforts. It is the real estate development lawyer's job to make sure that all of the various land risks identified in the purchase contract are either eliminated or otherwise dealt with in a manner that is acceptable to his client. Once that portion of his job is done, the lawyer next turns to the task of doing that which is necessary to close the land acquisition as quickly and professionally as possible.

The following are the general topics that will be addressed as part of our discussion of Stage 4 of the development process:

- The identification of all of the players involved in the process of closing the land acquisition;
- The preparation of the checklist that will serve as the lawyer's guidebook throughout the closing process;
- The successful completion of the due diligence process, including the review of title, survey, environmental and land use matters;
- The preparation of those closing documents that are required to evidence and consummate the developer's acquisition of the land, including the deed, entity authority documents, seller's affidavits and the closing statement;
- The allocation and apportionment of the economics of the closing process, including the making of all appropriate closing prorations and the provision for the payment of all applicable closing costs; and
- The orchestration of all of the moving parts that make up the actual real estate closing.

For the purposes of simplifying the analysis of the real estate development lawyer's activities in Stage 4, it will be assumed that the buyer is

285

using its own cash to purchase the land and is not obtaining outside debt or equity funding. It should, however, be noted that the buyer frequently uses "other people's money" to fund at least a portion of the land acquisition price. The deal requirements imposed by debt and equity providers can significantly expand both the scope and complexity of those items which need to be included on the land closing checklist.

The practical context for our examination of the land closing process will, once again, be provided by the HIBC case study introduced in Chapter 4 and, specifically, the Pizzuti Companies' acquisition of the 350 acres of undeveloped land[1] known as the Heathrow International Business Center. In that regard, it will be assumed that the developer has made a positive determination that the development project planned for the land is economically feasible and that the developer is ready to waive its purchase contract contingencies,[2] buy the land and begin construction of its project as soon as its lawyer advises that it is time to do so.

II. WHAT IS A CLOSING?

The term ***closing*** is used by lawyers and businesspersons to refer to the event that represents the final consummation of an agreed-upon legal transaction. In the context of a land acquisition, the closing occurs when title to the land is formally conveyed from the seller to the buyer and the buyer pays the purchase price to the seller.

The land purchase contract executed by the buyer and the seller typically goes into great detail specifying the conditions that must be satisfied prior to closing and when and how the closing will be effected. In that sense, the purchase contract represents the road map to be followed by the buyer and the seller in their quests to reach their final destination points—for the seller, the receipt of the negotiated purchase price and, for the buyer, the acquisition of legal title to the land so that it can start construction of its real estate project.

While a "closing" technically refers to the specific moment in time when title to the land is conveyed to the buyer in exchange for its payment of the purchase price to the seller, that term is commonly used by practitioners to also include all those preliminary actions that must be taken by the buyer and the seller to arrive at their final destination

---

1. The closing of a purchase of improved property (that is, land on which an office building, retail center, warehouse or other structure is situated) introduces a host of additional issues that will not be discussed in this Chapter (for example, the soundness of the design and construction of the improvements and the predictability and integrity of the income stream evidenced by the leases of space in the project improvements). *See generally* Andrew N. Jacobson, *A Narrative Real Estate Acquisition Due Diligence Checklist*, 17 No. 6 PRACTICAL REAL ESTATE LAWYER 7 (November 2001); and Alan Wayte, *Real Property Acquisition Due Diligence Checklist*, in ALI–ABA COURSE OF STUDY MATERIALS, MODERN REAL ESTATE TRANSACTIONS, Course No. SB–08, Volume 1 (August 1996). *See also infra* Chapter 12, Pages 576–579.

2. For the purposes of this Chapter, it will be assumed that the land seller and land buyer have executed a purchase contract that is consistent with the Standard Form of Purchase Agreement included as Document #2 in the Document Appendix, including the broad suitability contingency clause set forth in § 4 and the due diligence clause set forth in § 5 of that agreement.

points. The closing is, therefore, both an event and a process. In order to gain the reputation of being a good "closer" (a highly sought after moniker in the legal business), a lawyer must learn how to master both the closing process and the ultimate closing event. One noted real estate practitioner, who has written extensively on the closing process, notes that "commercial real estate closings require management skills and techniques much like those you would need to produce a Broadway show, build a building or invade a small country."[3]

III.   THE PLAYERS

The closing process involves the participation of many players beyond the buyer and the seller. The identity and role served by each of those players is briefly discussed below.

- *Buyer's Counsel*—The lawyer for the buyer plays a leading role in closing his client's acquisition of the land. As will be discussed in the next section of this Chapter, it is buyer's counsel who customarily assumes primary responsibility for preparing and monitoring the closing checklist, which often includes not only those tasks that must be performed prior to and at the actual land acquisition closing, but also those additional tasks related to the raising of debt and equity to fund the broader set of project development costs.[4] In this capacity, the buyer's counsel serves as the director of the Broadway play that is the land acquisition closing.

- *Local Counsel for Buyer*—The buyer should consider hiring local counsel in one of two situations—(1) buyer's customary counsel does not regularly practice in the jurisdiction where the land is located or (2) the nature of the subject land acquisition requires the hiring of a legal expert in a field which is outside of the core competency of the buyer's counsel (for example, zoning or environmental law).[5]

- *Seller's Counsel*—The land seller has a very singular goal at Stage 4 of a development project—give me the money. The seller's limited goal usually (but not always)[6] produces a relatively limited role for

---

3. *See* Joshua Stein, *Preparing for the Commercial Real Estate Closing (Part 1)*, 15 No. 4 PRACTICAL REAL ESTATE LAWYER 1 (July 1999).

4. Lenders and equity investors frequently provide their own separate checklists for their provision of funds for a commercial real estate project. However, it remains the job of buyer's counsel to coordinate the activities of all of the players in the closing process to see to it that all of the items contained on those separate checklists are timely performed to the satisfaction of the debt and equity providers.

5. *See infra* Pages 300–301, for a discussion of the crucial rule served by Florida local counsel when Pizzuti acquired the HIBC land.

6. The role of seller's counsel in the closing process is heightened when the subject of the sale is improved property. For example, I prepared and rigorously enforced the closing checklist (and, hence, tried to control the closing process) when The Pizzuti Companies sold the entirety of the Heathrow International Business Center (eight office buildings and approximately 100 acres of undeveloped ground) to Colonial Properties in 2002. Beyond my normal penchant to act as a

its counsel in the land acquisition closing. In the typical land sale, the role of the seller's lawyer is confined to preparing the conveyance documents and arranging for their execution and delivery by the seller at closing.

- **Title Insurance Company**—The title insurance company is the deep pocketed expert that is responsible for insuring the quality of the title to the land that is being conveyed to buyer. The selection of the title company is a matter that should be addressed in the land purchase contract.[7]

- **Surveyor**—The surveyor is the local party who is responsible for making a land visit and producing a precise drawing showing the location of the land's boundaries and any improvements, easements or other conditions affecting the title or use of the land.

- **Escrow Agent**—This is a neutral third party assigned with the task of holding the earnest money deposit posted by the buyer and helping the buyer and seller close the land acquisition.[8] The escrow agent (frequently the title company) is routinely also assigned the task of holding and disbursing the various legal documents signed by the seller and buyer in advance of the actual land closing. The conditions governing the escrow agent's handling of the earnest money deposit and closing documents are typically spelled out in written escrow instructions prepared by buyer's or seller's counsel (or both of them).[9]

- **Real Estate Broker(s)**—In today's marketplace, most commercial land is sold with the involvement of a licensed real estate broker hired by the seller (the **listing broker**) and often with the cooperation of a licensed broker retained to represent the interests of the buyer (the **cooperating broker**). In almost every commercial sales transaction, the broker(s) are commissioned salespersons who only get paid if the transaction actually closes.[10]

---

control freak, I felt the need to take the lead on the HIBC sale because of the overarching business need of my client to close the transaction and get paid ASAP.

7. *See supra* Chapter 5, Page 127.

8. Best practices would discourage either seller's counsel or buyer's counsel from agreeing to serve as the escrow agent. Absent a specific agreement to the contrary, a lawyer who both represents a party to the land purchase contract and acts as the escrow agent will likely be disqualified from representing its client (be it the seller or the buyer) if a dispute arises between the buyer and the seller under the purchase contract. *See* GREGORY M. STEIN, MORTON P. FISHER, JR. AND GAIL M. STERN, A PRACTICAL GUIDE TO COMMERCIAL REAL ESTATE TRANSACTIONS: FROM CONTRACT TO CLOSING, §§ 2.28 and 8.03 (2001). When Pizzuti bought the HIBC land in 1994, the attorney representing the land seller also acted as the escrow agent for the transaction. However, the HIBC purchase contract also specifically provided that "Buyer acknowledges that Escrow Agent is the attorney for Seller and agrees that in the event of a dispute between the parties regarding this Contract, Escrow Agent shall be entitled to represent Seller without claim of conflict of interest by Buyer due to the service by Seller's counsel as Escrow Agent hereunder"—a provision that should work, unless the specific subject of the seller-buyer dispute is objectionable conduct by the escrow agent.

9. *See infra* Page 310.

10. While many real estate brokers are extremely knowledgeable real estate professionals, the nature of their "if come" compensation arrangements tends to color their judgment as to the

- ***Environmental Engineer***—Virtually every purchase of commercial land is now dependent upon the buyer's receipt of a report from an environmental engineer stating that no hazardous substances are present on the land. The environmental engineer is usually hired and compensated by the buyer.

- ***Other Site Consultants***—Depending on the location and configuration of the land and the nature of the buyer's planned development project, the buyer may also want to retain other independent consultants to provide it with advice as to whether the land is suitable for the buyer's intended use. The following are some of the areas on which the buyer might want to receive the advice of an independent site consultant—(1) the absence of any protected wetlands or endangered wildlife on the parcel, (2) the availability of adequate access and utilities to the site, (3) the ability of the site's soils to support the buyer's planned improvement, and (4) the compliance of the land (and the buyer's intended use of the land) with all applicable zoning and land use laws.[11]

It falls to the real estate development lawyer (the "buyer's counsel" at this Stage 4) to coordinate and oversee the activities of all of the above players to make sure that the developer/buyer has all the information it needs to make the right decision as to whether to purchase the seller's land. One interesting aspect of the land closing process is that, once the buyer decides to move forward with the acquisition, all of the above players share the same objective of making the closing happen as quickly and efficiently as possible. As the director of the closing "play," the real estate development lawyer has the ultimate responsibility for reigning in the enthusiasm of all the players to see to it that the closing occurs only when and as appropriate to protect the legitimate interests of the developer.

IV. THE CLOSING CHECKLIST

The second thing that the real estate development lawyer should do after the execution of the purchase contract is to prepare a closing checklist.[12] The checklist should recite all those tasks that must be performed and all those conditions that must be satisfied prior to the actual closing of the land acquisition. The tasks to be addressed on any useful closing checklist include not just those purely legal matters that

wisdom of closing a particular transaction. It has been my experience that a broker rarely says "no" and almost always says "yes" when asked whether a particular purchase and sale transaction makes sense for his client. Both the buyer and the seller are, therefore, usually well-advised to rely on brokers to find a buyer or a seller for a particular tract of land, but not to advise them as to the propriety of the subject transaction.

11. *See* Jacobson, *supra* note 1, at 10–13; and Dorothea W. Dickerman, *Navigating Commercial Real Estate Closings (Part 1)*, 26 No. 2 PRACTICAL REAL ESTATE LAWYER 45, 54–55 (March 2010).

12. The first thing that the real estate development should do is to engage in some type of self-congratulatory conduct, be it a good meal, a stout drink or some other indulgent act. The closing process begins immediately thereafter.

must be performed by lawyers (e.g., the preparation of a deed or a bill of sale), but also logistical matters that are the province of non-lawyers (e.g., the issuance of an environmental report or the funding of an earnest money deposit).

Once completed, the closing checklist will endure as the script to be followed by all the players participating in the closing process. It is the real estate development lawyer's responsibility not only to prepare the first draft of the closing checklist, but also to constantly monitor the players' progress in accomplishing the listed tasks (and, when appropriate, to supplement and modify the description of such tasks). The march toward the land acquisition closing is a constantly evolving process and the closing checklist maintained by the real estate development lawyer must keep pace with every twist and turn that occurs during the course of the purchase and sale transaction.

As noted earlier, the closing checklist should reference all those tasks that must be performed in order for the buyer and seller to close on the land acquisition. Those tasks can be broken down into the following three components:

- Due diligence;
- Third party approvals; and
- Legal documents.

Each of those components will be discussed in further detail in the next section of this Chapter.

The closing checklist must list not only what has to be done (i.e., the closing tasks generally described above), but also who has to do it and when it must be done. If it is going to be useful closing tool, it is essential that the closing checklist allocate performance responsibility to the person best suited to perform each listed task[13] and set forth a target date for the completion of that task that is consistent with the requirements of the purchase contract and the dictates of the parties' business objectives.

Practice Tip #8–1: How to Prepare a Closing Checklist

The drivers for the preparation of the closing checklist are (1) the applicable provisions of the land purchase contract and (2) those business considerations that are germane to the development business, generally, and to the developer's proposed project, specifically. The starting place for the lawyer's preparation of a closing checklist is the purchase contract executed by his client and the land seller. A well-crafted purchase contract should provide even the novice lawyer with a clear road map to help him

---

13. It is important that the closing checklist differentiate between tasks to be performed by the "buyer" and those tasks to be performed by "buyer's counsel" (as opposed to lumping all those tasks under one, general "buyer" category). Failing to do so can lead to confusion as to the specific person who, in fact, is responsible for achieving each closing task.

complete the majority of the "what," "who" and "when" columns of the closing checklist. By way of example, the closing checklist should specifically recite the dates on which the buyer is required to post its earnest money deposit, deliver its title objections and waive its contractual contingencies.

The remaining items in the closing checklist must be fleshed out through a combination of the lawyer's past deal experience and his client's project-specific, business objectives. The inexperienced lawyer should consult closing checklists prepared by other lawyers in his firm or company (or standard checklists reproduced in practitioner-authored literature)[14] to highlight those tasks that need to be achieved in all similar transactions. The only way to unearth the client's project-specific checklist items is for the lawyer to sit down with representatives of the developer to review the project and ask the developer pointed questions about what must happen to make the project a reality.

The following are a few tips about how to prepare a closing checklist that is both user-friendly and user-productive:

- *Organize the listed tasks in chronological order according to their respective targeted completion dates;*

- *Include specific contact information for each person assigned responsibility for the performance of any closing task (e.g., name, email address, telephone and fax numbers);*

- *Include cross-references to sections of the purchase contract that discuss each checklist item;*

- *Keep the checklist as short as possible by not replicating the entirety of the purchase contract or restating the painfully obvious;[15]*

- *Circulate the checklist to all the players in the closing process (including opposing counsel) to keep them advised as to the parties' progress toward closing;[16] and*

- *Find the most anal person in your office (if it's not you) and assign him the job of monitoring and updating the closing checklist on a regular basis.[17]*

---

14. *See e.g.,* Jacobson, *supra* note 1; GREGORY STEIN, *supra* note 8, at Appendix J; and Dorothea W. Dickerman, *Navigating Commercial Real Estate Closings (Part 2) (With Forms),* 26 No. 13 PRACTICAL REAL ESTATE LAWYER 15 (May 2010).

15. By way of example, it is unnecessary to repeat the provisions of the land purchase contract that identify the specific form of title insurance commitment to be furnished by the title company or the specific content of the buyer's title objection notice—because both of those items should already be adequately addressed in the purchase contract.

16. Buyer's counsel may want to maintain two checklists—one edited version that can be circulated to the seller and all the other players and one more detailed version that is for the buyer's "eyes only" (due to the deal-sensitive, buyer considerations included in the more detailed version of the closing checklist).

17. In his excellent article on the closing process, Joshua Stein embraces this bit of advice by asking and answering the following question—"[W]hy do clients use lawyers for closings? Answer: Lawyers are diligent, obsessive and careful." *See* Joshua Stein, *Closings: Step by Step,* 45 No. 7 PRACTICAL REAL ESTATE LAWYER 77, at 79.

The closing checklist can (and should be) the bible of the real estate development lawyer throughout Stage 4 of a development project. That goal will, however, only be realized if the closing checklist is both thorough and succinct when first prepared and regularly reviewed and updated throughout the period leading up to the actual closing of the land acquisition.

V. DUE DILIGENCE

Due diligence involves the gathering and analysis of information that permits the buyer to decide whether it wants to purchase a particular tract of land. For the purposes of the following discussion of the due diligence process, two baseline assumptions will be made concerning the purchase contract entered into by the seller and the buyer—(1) the contract expressly gives the buyer and its representatives a right to enter onto the seller's land for the purpose of inspecting and performing tests on the land (*see e.g.,* § 5 of the Standard Form of Purchase Agreement) and (2) the contract contains a broad suitability contingency that affords the buyer the right to terminate the contract if it makes a determination that the land is not suitable for its intended use (*see e.g.,* § 4 of the Standard Form of Purchase Agreement).[18] Finally, as noted at the outset of this Chapter, an assumption is also being made that the buyer has concluded that the development project it has planned for the land is economically feasible—so the only issue that remains is whether the land itself is physically and legally suitable for the buyer's planned project.

The due diligence process is focused on resolving the issue of the suitability of the land for buyer's intended use. In their efforts to resolve that issue, the buyer and its counsel will customarily undertake the following due diligence tasks:

- A review of the status of the title to the land;

- The performance of a survey of the boundaries, improvements and attributes affecting the land;

- An assessment of the environmental condition of the land;

- An inspection of the physical condition of the land; and

- An analysis of the land's compliance with zoning and land use regulations.

The real estate development lawyer's job is to coordinate the performance of these five due diligence tasks (as well as any others that may be necessitated by the peculiar nature of the land or the proposed project), so that the buyer is in a position to make a well-reasoned decision concerning the suitability of the land prior to the expiration of the contingency period

---

18. *See supra* Chapter 5, Pages 100–101, 109–110, 114–116, for a more detailed discussion of the factors that need to be taken into consideration when drafting and negotiating the due diligence and contingency provisions of the land purchase contract.

specified in the purchase contract.[19] To the extent possible, the real estate development lawyer should visit the site as soon as possible during the closing process (or better yet prior to the execution of the purchase contract) to better acquaint himself with the possible due diligence issues associated with the subject land parcel.

A. TITLE INSURANCE[20]

The first step in the title review process is usually the issuance of a title insurance commitment by a title insurance company selected in accordance with the applicable provisions of the purchase contract.[21] A title insurance commitment represents an agreement by the title insurance company to issue a title insurance policy at the closing of the land acquisition, subject to those terms, conditions, exceptions and limitations specifically set forth in the title commitment. The purchase contract customarily provides the buyer and its counsel a limited period of time to review the title commitment and convey their title objections to the seller. It then falls to the seller to either cure the buyer's title objections or take the risk that the buyer may elect to terminate its obligation to buy the land.

Buyer's counsel should first confirm that the commitment correctly recites the facts surrounding the proposed transaction—specifically the name of the proposed insured (the legal entity that will take title to the property at closing), the insured amount of the title insurance policy (almost always the purchase price being paid for the land), the nature of the estate being conveyed to the buyer (typically fee simple) and the legal description of the land (which must match the legal description of the land provided on the survey described in the next section of this Chapter). All of these factual items are covered in Schedule A of the title insurance policy.

Once the accuracy of the facts set forth in Schedule A are verified, buyer's counsel must next turn to the real heart of the title review—

---

19. As noted *supra* Chapter 5, Pages 116–117, the buyer's due diligence efforts can be supplemented by its receipt in the purchase contract of specific representations and warranties from the seller concerning a variety of conditions related to the land. Such representations and warranties should not, however, serve as a substitute for the buyer's conduct of thorough due diligence of the condition of the land. As noted by one author, "[p]ractitioners should use warranties and representations as "come clean" provisions rather than as an alternate for detailed inquiry." *See* James W. Theobald, *Land Use Due Diligence Considerations for Transactional* Cross *Attorneys*, in ACREL Papers 85, 87 (ALI–ABA, Spring 2004).

20. The review of a title insurance policy is a very complex undertaking. The details of the practitioner's review of the title insurance policy (and the underlying commitment) are beyond the scope of this Chapter, which has as its limited purpose the introduction of the reader to some of the issues that a practicing lawyer needs to take into consideration during the course of his review of the status of the title to the land. For a more thorough discussion of the title review process, *see* Shannon J. Skinner, *A Practical Guide to Title Review (With Checklist)*, in ALI–ABA Course of Study Materials, Modern Real Estate Transactions, Course No. SN–001, 377 (July 2007); and John C. Murray, *Title Insurance in Commercial Real Estate Transactions*, in Commercial Real Estate Transactions Handbook, Chapter 7 (Mark A. Senn ed., 4th ed. 2009).

21. *See supra* Chapter 5, Pages 125–132, for a discussion of the title review provisions of a land purchase contract.

Schedule B of the commitment, which recites all those exceptions to the title insurance company's insurance of absolutely clean title to the land. The title exceptions recited in Schedule B fall into two categories—(1) general exceptions that are applicable to all properties (the ***Schedule B–1 exceptions***) and (2) the specific exceptions applicable to the parcel of land that is the subject of the title commitment (the ***Schedule B–2 exceptions***).

The four general exceptions most typically set forth in Schedule B–1 of a standard ALTA owner's policy are exceptions for the following matters that do not appear of record in the public real estate files maintained by the jurisdiction in which the land is situated:

- Rights of parties in possession of the land;

- Encroachments, boundary disputes and other matters that an accurate survey of the land would disclose;

- Easements not shown by public record; and

- Mechanics and other construction-related liens.

Buyer's counsel can usually arrange for the title company to agree to delete these general exceptions from the title insurance policy by providing the title company with an acceptable current survey of the land and an affidavit executed by the land seller certifying that there are no liens, conditions, easements or other exceptions to title other than those specifically recorded in the public real estate records.[22]

The special exceptions listed in Schedule B–2 of the commitment are those mortgages, liens, encumbrances, conditions, easements, restrictions, taxes, lawsuits and other matters affecting the title to the land that appear of public record. Buyer's counsel should insist on receiving legible copies of the complete legal documents that evidence the Schedule B–2 exceptions. He should then closely review those documents to determine whether any of the listed special exceptions could adversely affect the buyer's use of the land for its proposed development project. Mortgages, delinquent real estate taxes and other recorded liens that can be discharged by the payment of money should always be objected to by buyer's counsel (with the end result that the title commitment will require that they be paid off at or prior to closing).[23] The following are examples of reasons why buyer's counsel might object to other special exceptions listed in Schedule B–2:

- A utility easement runs through the middle of the proposed building pad for the buyer's planned structure;

- Recorded covenants, conditions and restrictions (*CCRs*) restrict the use of the land in a fashion which is inconsistent with the buyer's proposed use;

---

22. *See infra* Page 304, for a discussion of the land seller's affidavit.

23. *See infra* Page 305.

- A reciprocal easement agreement (*REA*)[24] requires the owner of the land to make an unacceptably high, financial contribution to the construction and maintenance of some infrastructure improvement that benefit both the land and an adjoining property;

- A recorded covenant requires the approval of a third party as a condition to the seller's sale of the land; or

- A lease gives a third party the right to extract subsurface minerals located beneath the land.

Once buyer's counsel determines which, if any, of the special exceptions referenced in the title commitment are objectionable to the buyer, he should then send written notice of such title objections to both the seller and the title insurance company, making sure that the notice is delivered within the time period specified in the purchase contract. Negotiations will then ensue among counsel for the seller, buyer and title company in an effort to produce a modified set of title exceptions that are achievable by the seller and the title company and acceptable to the buyer.

Depending on the jurisdiction where the property is located, buyer's counsel may also be able to obtain endorsements to the title commitment and policy, which will provide his client with expanded protection against potential title defects. By way of example, in most states, a title company can issue endorsements confirming that the buyer's proposed use of the land will comply with all applicable zoning laws and that the land has access to a public roadway. The availability, scope and cost of such endorsements vary widely by jurisdiction. When considering obtaining any such title endorsement, buyer's counsel must engage in a detailed cost-benefit analysis to determine whether the added benefit of getting a particular title endorsement (which is often minimal) outweighs the cost of paying for it (which can be astronomical).[25]

B. SURVEY

A survey is a visual depiction of the location, boundaries and size of a particular tract of land that is produced by a surveyor physically visiting the site and taking field measurements related to the land. As such, the survey often represents the only opportunity that buyer's counsel will have to "see" the land prior to closing.[26]

There are two basic types of surveys—(1) a boundary or land survey that simply identifies the boundary lines of a particular tract, and (2) an as-built survey that goes one step further than the boundary survey by

---

24. CCRs and REAs can be particularly troublesome to a buyer because of their length, complexity and overreaching nature. *See* Everett S. Ward, *Legal Due Diligence Issues in Real Estate Purchase Transactions*, REAL ESTATE FINANCE JOURNAL 9, 10–11 (Spring 2007).

25. *See* Skinner, *Title Review*, *supra* note 20, at 380–382; and GREGORY STEIN, *supra* note 8, at §§ 3.23–3.24.

26. *See* Shannon J. Skinner, *A Practical Guide to Survey Review*, in ALI–ABA COURSE OF STUDY MATERIALS, MODERN REAL ESTATE TRANSACTIONS, Course #SN–01, 401, 408 (July 2007).

identifying all improvements and other legal attributes affecting the tract. An as-built survey is considerably more costly and usually takes more time to complete than a boundary survey.

The most common form of as-built survey is an ***ALTA survey***, which is prepared in accordance with surveying standards jointly promulgated by American Land Title Association and the American Congress on Surveying and Mapping. In addition to showing the location of all boundary lines and improvements located on the land, an ALTA survey also locates all adjacent infrastructure improvements, driveways and means of access and shows all easements and other locatable title matters of record affecting the land.[27] If requested by the party ordering the survey, an ALTA survey can also show: any portion of the land is located within a flood zone; the acreage contained within the land's boundaries; the location of all building setback lines mandated by applicable zoning codes; the location and number of spaces contained within any parking area; the location of all utility lines existing on or serving the land; and any observable evidence of the use of the land as a solid waste dump or landfill.[28] The provision of an ALTA survey is now a standard requirement of most sophisticated, commercial real estate transactions.[29]

Upon his receipt of the survey (which for the purposes of this Chapter will be assumed to be an ALTA survey), buyer's counsel should first compare it to the title insurance commitment to make sure that the legal description included in the commitment matches that shown on the survey. Buyer's counsel should next physically locate on the survey all those easements and other title exceptions listed in Schedule B–2 of the title commitment, that are capable of being plotted on a survey. Once those two tasks are completed, buyer's counsel should conduct a qualitative review of the survey in an effort to answer the following questions.[30]

- Does the acreage and configuration of the land conform to the buyer's expectations when it entered into the purchase contract?

- Do any of the improvements located on the land encroach upon the boundaries of adjoining properties (or vice versa)?

- Is the location of any existing easement, building setback line, improvement, etc. in any way inconsistent or otherwise at odds with the buyer's development plans for the land?

---

27. *See generally* Shannon J. Skinner and Gary R. Kent, *Surveys*, in COMMERCIAL REAL ESTATE TRANSACTIONS HANDBOOK, Chapter 6, 6–6 through 6–10 (Mark A. Senn ed., 4th ed. 2009).

28. All of these items (and more) are listed as "optional survey responsibilities and specifications" in Table A of the MINIMUM STANDARD DETAIL REQUIREMENTS FOR ALTA/ACSM LAND TITLE SURVEYS, as adopted by AMERICAN LAND TITLE ASSOCIATION AND NATIONAL SOCIETY OF PROFESSIONAL ENGINEERS (2006). Lenders typically require that the borrower provide it with an ALTA survey which incorporates all (or most all) of the optional Table A items. *See* Skinner, *Survey Review*, *supra* note 26, at 410.

29. *See supra* Chapter 5, Pages 127–128, for a discussion of survey issues to be addressed in the purchase contract. It should also be noted that the provision of an ALTA survey is normally required by the title company as a condition to its acquiescence in the buyer's request to delete the survey exception in Schedule B–1 of the standard ALTA title commitment. *See* Skinner and Kent, *supra* note 27, at 6–6 and 6–7.

30. *See* Ward, *supra* note 24, at Appendix 2, for a sample checklist for the review of a survey.

- Are easements or publicly-dedicated rights-of-way in place to provide utility and vehicular access to the boundaries of the tract?[31]

- Are the requisite utility lines and roadways located within the aforementioned easement or right-of-way areas?

- Does the survey show that any portion of the land is located within a flood plain?

Any title objections produced by buyer's counsel's review of the ALTA survey should be incorporated into the title objection notice sent to the title company and the seller's counsel.

Buyer's counsel should also make sure that the survey is signed by a surveyor licensed to do business in the jurisdiction in which the land is located and that it is dated sometime after the date of the parties' execution of the purchase contract.[32] An ALTA survey should also include above the surveyor's signature a certification, at the minimum, that the survey was performed in accordance with the ALTA/ACSM standards. Additional surveyor certifications concerning the items shown in the survey and the manner in which the survey was performed are often subject of heated negotiations between the surveyor and the buyer and its lender.[33]

C. ENVIRONMENTAL ASSESSMENT

The buyer should not waive its purchase contract contingency, unless it has received written confirmation from a qualified environmental engineer that there is no evidence of hazardous substances having been discharged on the land in violation of any environmental law.[34] The receipt of such an environmental assessment is the best way for the buyer to insulate itself from risk under environmental laws such as the Comprehensive Response, Compensation and Liability Act,[35] which seek to impose strict liability on landowners for environmental problems, unless the landowner has made "all appropriate inquiry into the previous ownership and use of the property consistent with good commercial or customary practice."[36]

The report typically furnished to the buyer by an environmental engineer in the context of a land acquisition is a so-called *Phase One*

---

31. If that is not the case, the buyer should require that the purchase contract be amended to provide that its obligation to purchase the land is expressly conditioned upon the provision of such easements or the obtaining of such dedications.

32. *See* Ward, *supra* note 24, at 11.

33. *See* Skinner and Kent, *supra* note 27, at 6–8.

34. A review of all applicable federal and state, environmental laws and regulations is well beyond the scope of this Chapter. For a discussion of the impact of environmental laws on commercial real estate transactions, *see* Jack Fersco and Robert A. Stout, Jr., *Environmental Issues in Commercial Real Estate Sales and Leases*, in COMMERCIAL REAL ESTATE TRANSACTIONS HANDBOOK, Chapter 12 (Mark A. Senn ed., 4th ed. 2009)

35. *See* 42 U.S.C. §§ 9601–9675 (2010).

36. *See id.* at § 9601 (35) (A).

Environmental Assessment. In preparing a Phase One assessment, the environmental engineer reviews public records and engages in a routine walk-through of the land in an effort to determine if there is any indication of any existing or historical environmental problem on the land. If the environmental engineer identifies any potential environmental problems, it will then recommend that a more rigorous environmental investigation be conducted, which may include the taking of core samples and the testing of ground water. The results produced by such an additional round of testing are then summarized in what is commonly referred to as a ***Phase Two Environmental Assessment***.

Because the performance of a Phase One assessment (and certainly any follow-up Phase Two assessment) can take a long time to complete, it is imperative that the buyer order its environmental assessment as early as possible following the full execution of the purchase contract. In any event, unless the environmental engineer is able to provide the buyer with written assurance in the form of either a Phase One or Phase Two report that there are no environmental problems associated with the land,[37] the buyer would be well-advised to promptly send written notice to the seller terminating the buyer's obligation to purchase the land.

D. OTHER TESTS OF PHYSICAL CONDITION OF LAND

As part of its due diligence efforts, the buyer may also want to receive written confirmation from qualified experts that the physical condition of the land is conducive to the development project that the buyer has planned for the land. By way of example, the buyer might commission a geotechnical engineer to test the quality, composition and compactness of the site soils to verify that the soils will support the type and intensity of the improvements that the buyer intends to construct on the land. The buyer might also want to receive an engineer's written analysis confirming that the site is served by utilities and roadways that are adequate to service the buyer's proposed development project. Land buyers also now routinely seek written assurances from independent third parties that no portion of the land is located within a protected wetland, flood zone or other specially-protected district and that there are no endangered or potentially endangered animals or plants present on any part of the land.[38] The receipt of such written assurances gives the buyer additional comfort that it will not incur the additional cost and time delay that would be triggered by the presence of any of these negative conditions on the land.

---

37. *See supra* Chapter 5, Page 115, for a discussion of the challenges faced by the real estate development lawyer when trying to negotiate the form and content of an environmental assessment. *See also* Dickerman, *(Part 1), supra* note 11, at 53–54.

38. For a discussion of these and other site-specific reports that the buyer may want to consider obtaining during its site due diligence, *see* Jacobson, *supra* note 1, at 8–11; and Dickerman, *(Part 1), supra* note 11, at 54–55.

E. LAND USE MATTERS

Land use considerations are the last piece to the buyer's due diligence puzzle.[39] The buyer must verify at some point during its due diligence process that the property is zoned to permit the improvement and use of the land in a manner consistent with the buyer's development plan. This inquiry goes well beyond just confirming that the property is zoned for commercial use (as opposed to strictly residential or agricultural use). The buyer must also receive comfort that the specific uses it has planned for the site (for example, a three-story office building and two free-standing casual restaurants) and the location, design, composition and density of its proposed project improvements are all sanctioned under the applicable zoning code. Provisions of the zoning code mandating standards for parking, signage and building setback lines and imposing impact and other development fees should be of particular concern for the buyer/developer. Additional land use issues are created by statute in those states that have adopted state-wide, growth management systems[40] and in CCRs put in place by prior landowners in an attempt to regulate the nature, scope and intensity of the use of the land in question.

The requisite solace sought by the buyer on these and similar land use due diligence matters can be provided in a number of different ways. First, on certain matters, the buyer may be able to get an affirmative statement from a governmental entity confirming the validity of the buyer's plans for the site.[41] Additional comfort might be provided by the title company's issuance of a zoning endorsement or some other form of affirmative insurance on a particular land use matter. Finally, the buyer can request a certification from a land use consultant or a legal opinion from special counsel on a particularly difficult or vexing land use issue. Ultimately, however, responsibility for performing the land use due diligence will fall upon the real estate development lawyer, who must exercise prudence in identifying the land use issues of most concern to the buyer and then figure out the most effective and cost efficient way to resolve those issues to the buyer's satisfaction.

F. CONCLUSION OF DUE DILIGENCE

It is essential that the buyer and its counsel secure all requisite due diligence reports as soon as possible and, in all events, prior to the expiration of the buyer's contingency period. Each such report must be final and signed by an authorized representative of the provider of the subject report. The buyer and its counsel should jointly evaluate whether

---

39. *See generally*, Theobald, *supra* note 19.

40. *See e.g.* Florida's Local Government Comprehensive Plan and Land Development Regulation Act, FLORIDA STATUTES §§ 163.3164–163.3247 (2010).

41. One practitioner urged lawyers who make the mistake of relying solely on short-form government clearance letters to "remember (i) there is no estoppel against governmental entities in the exercise of their normal duties, and (ii) the phone number of your malpractice carrier." *See* Theobald, *supra* note 19, at 6.

their combined due diligence efforts justify the buyer waiving its contingency and proceeding to close on its purchase of the land. Assuming that the answer to that question is "yes,"[42] buyer's counsel should promptly prepare and send to the land seller and its counsel a formal written notice waiving the buyer's contingency and scheduling a closing date in accordance with the terms of the purchase contract.

HIBC Case Study—Assembling the Due Diligence Team

The land purchase contract governing The Pizzuti Companies' purchase of the 350 acre HIBC tract gave it only 90 days in which to perform its due diligence and make a determination whether to waive its suitability contingency and proceed to close on its purchase of the tract.[43] Its chore of completing its due diligence on such a sprawling tract in only three short months was made even more daunting by the facts that (1) title to the HIBC tract was extremely complicated, with more than 50 special exceptions appearing in Schedule B–2 of the title commitment, including more than 30 roadway and utility easements and a 40+ page set of convoluted CCRs, (2) part of the land was located in and subject to the jurisdiction of the municipality of Lake Mary, while the remainder of the land was subject to the jurisdiction of Seminole County[44] and (3) Pizzuti had very little experience developing property in the State of Florida and zero experience doing so in Seminole County and the City of Lake Mary. Pizzuti's challenge, therefore, was to try to figure out how to complete its due diligence on the HIBC land in only 90 days (an incredibly exacting proposition in and of itself), without having a tried and true development team in place to lead its due diligence efforts.

The first call I made following the execution of the HIBC land purchase contract was to Jim Seay, an Orlando lawyer with whom I had worked on a couple of prior occasions.[45] I quickly explained to him the

---

42. If it's a "no", buyer's counsel should either send the seller a written notice terminating the purchase contract or seek to negotiate an amendment to the purchase contract that extends the buyer's contingency period or otherwise solves its due diligence objections.

43. The HIBC land purchase contract included a very broad suitability contingency that gave Pizzuti an out should it determine "in its sole discretion that the Property is not suitable for Buyer's intended purpose," with the determination of the Property's "suitability" including, but not limited to "suitability of soils, access, visibility and other physical characteristics of the Property ... [and] economic and market analysis to determine feasibility of the Property for Buyer's development purposes." The purchase contract did not, however, contain any seller representations and warranties and, instead, required the buyer to purchase the property in its "as is" condition. *See supra* Chapter 5, Page 118.

44. The dual jurisdiction status of the property resulted in two separate (and often conflicting) development orders being issued with respect to the future use and development of the HIBC land—one by the City of Lake Mary and one by Seminole County. The development orders were issued pursuant to the directives contained in the State of Florida's state-wide growth management rules. *See supra* note 41 and accompanying text.

45. In 1994, Jim Seay was practicing with the Orlando-based firm of Maguire, Voorhis & Wells (later merged into Holland & Knight). To this day, Jim remains one of the best lawyers that I have ever known and, I am proud to say, is also a great friend.

challenge that Pizzuti was facing and asked whether he would be willing to head up our due diligence efforts. Fortunately for me and the Pizzuti organization, Jim Seay was not only incredibly competent, but also extremely well-connected in the Orlando real estate market. Within a matter of hours, Jim was able to put together a due diligence team that included all of the best third party experts in the Orlando market, all of whom had prior experience in working on the HIBC tract.[46] As a result, the Pizzuti organization was able to successfully complete its due diligence within the 90 day period (with hours to spare) and proceed to close on the purchase of a 350 acre tract of land that would dramatically improve its business prospects for years to come.

There are two important points that should be taken from the above discussion. First, sometimes the single best thing that a practicing lawyer can do on a transaction is to hire special counsel who has the expertise and local contacts needed to get the job done. While doing so may be a bit of a blow to the lawyer's ego ("there is actually somebody out there who is better suited to do the job than I am") and will likely result in a significant reduction in the lawyer's fees, it is absolutely essential that the real estate development lawyer realize when he is out of his element and needs help. Second, when putting together the team to conduct the buyer's due diligence, the lawyer's objective should always be to hire the best available consultants (even if they are not the cheapest). The long-term benefit of being advised by the best people in their respective fields far outweighs the short-term savings that might be achieved by hiring a less qualified person (who just happens to be related to the boss).

VI. THIRD PARTY APPROVALS

The second task involved in the closing process is the identification and receipt from third parties of all those approvals that are required for the buyer to consummate its acquisition of the land. The required third party approvals fall into two basic categories—(1) those governmental approvals that the buyer considers to be essential conditions precedent to a kick-off of its development project[47] and (2) those public and private approvals that are required to permit the seller and the buyer to close the land acquisition in the manner contemplated in the purchase contract. Examples of each of those categories of approvals are set forth below.

---

46. Jim's task in selecting the members of Pizzuti's due diligence team was made somewhat easier by the fact that we had been able to negotiate into the HIBC land purchase contract a provision requiring the seller to furnish us with "all reports, studies, plans, licenses, permits, correspondence and other documents or information in the possession of Seller regarding the Property" and to "authorize its consultants to cooperate with Buyer . . . with regard to questions or clarifications respecting the Property." As a result, Jim Seay was able to quickly look through the many boxes of information provided to Pizzuti by the land seller and identify and contact those third party consultants who had prior, substantive experience evaluating the condition of the HIBC land.

47. *See supra* Chapter 6 for a discussion of those governmental approvals that are essential to a developer's decision to move forward with a development project.

Essential Governmental Approvals Required for the Kick-off of the Project	Public and Private Approvals Required for the Closing of the Land Acquisition
Rezoning of land to change permitted use.	Governmental approval permitting a subdivision of the land from a larger tax parcel owned by the seller.
Approval of tax and financial incentives for the development project.	Consent of a partner, shareholder or other equity owner to the sale of the land by seller or the purchase of the land by buyer.
Development plan approval.	Consent of a lender to the buyer's assumption of an existing land loan.
Clearance letter from state EPA or Army Corps of Engineers[48]	Approval of sale by adjoining property owners under a Reciprocal Easement Agreement or Covenants, Conditions and Restrictions.

The identity of the third party approvals that must be obtained as part of the closing process will vary depending on the jurisdiction in which the land is located and the nature of the development project that the buyer intends to construct on the land.[49]

The real estate development lawyer's goal should be to meet with his client as early in the process as possible to identify all those third party approvals that are important to the overall transaction and that vest real discretion in the third party to grant or withhold its approval.[50] Ideally, all the required approvals will be identified prior to the execution of the purchase contract, so that buyer's counsel can structure the contract to provide ample time for the buyer to obtain the approvals prior to the required waiver of its purchase contract contingencies. To the extent the need for a certain approval is unearthed after the execution of the contract, buyer's counsel may have no choice but to go back to the seller on bended knee asking to amend the purchase contract to make the buyer's receipt of the missed third party approval an additional condition to the buyer's obligation to purchase the land.

VII. LEGAL DOCUMENTS

The final part of the closing process that needs to be addressed in the closing checklist relates to the identification of those legal documents that must be prepared, negotiated, executed and delivered to convey the land to the buyer and otherwise close the land acquisition in accordance with the

---

48. The Army Corps of Engineers is the governmental agency that is principally tasked with administering the federal government's oversight of wetlands under the Clean Water Act. *See* 33 U.S.C. §§ 1311(a)–1362(7).

49. *See generally* Joshua Stein, *Preparing for the Commercial Real Estate Closing, supra* note 3, at 9–10.

50. The lawyer's closing checklist should not be cluttered with the inclusion of ministerial or otherwise non-essential governmental approvals. *See supra* Chapter 6, Page 153.

terms of the purchase agreement.[51] The closing checklist should not only list each required legal document, but also make it clear who has the responsibility for drafting such document and when the document needs to be drafted, executed and delivered.[52] The legal documents that are customarily part of a land acquisition closing are briefly discussed in the next several sections of this Chapter.

A. DEED

The deed is the document that conveys legal title to the land from the seller to the buyer. There are three basic types of deeds—a ***general warranty deed***, a ***limited warranty deed*** and a *quitclaim deed*. All three deeds accomplish the same basic objective of conveying title to the land to the buyer. The difference in the three deed forms relates to the warranty made by the seller concerning the state of title to the land that it is conveying to the buyer.[53]

In a general warranty deed, the seller warrants that it is conveying good title to the land to the named buyer and that the buyer may bring a cause of action against the seller if the title is defective, regardless whether the title defect arose during or prior to the seller's ownership of the land. In a limited warranty deed, the seller's title warranty only extends to defects caused by an act or omission of the seller during the period of its ownership of the land (and specifically not to any defects caused by the seller's predecessors-in-title). Finally, a quitclaim deed contains no warranty of title whatsoever, but just purports to convey to the buyer whatever interests the seller owned at the time of its execution and delivery of the quitclaim deed.

From the above description, it is apparent that a seller would prefer to use a quitclaim deed, while a buyer would opt in favor of using a general warranty deed. In actual practice, the deed choice in a land sale usually comes down to either a general warranty deed or a limited warranty deed and depends on the custom of the locale in which the land is located and the relative bargaining strength of the seller and the buyer. It is important to keep in mind, however, that a title warranty (be it a general or limited warranty) is only as good as the credit standing of the

---

51. These legal documents are referred to in Chapter 5 as the "closing deliverables." *See supra* Chapter 5, Page 133.

52. It is important for the parties to try to reach agreement on the form and content of all the legal documents prior to the outside date for the buyer's waiver of its contractual contingencies. The parties to the land contract can accomplish this objective by either attaching forms of all required legal documents as exhibits to the executed purchase contract or requiring that drafts of the legal documents be delivered and approved prior to the expiration of the buyer's contingency period. The one legal document that tends to be in play right up until the actual funding of the purchase price is the closing statement. It is, therefore, advisable for the lawyers to include as much detail as possible in the purchase contract concerning the manner in which the various financial calculations, prorations and adjustments will be made in the final closing statement executed at closing. *See supra* Chapter 5, Pages 134–136, *supra*.

53. The title warranty made by the seller is typically made subject to the existence of certain "permitted exceptions" to title. *See* supra Chapter 5, Page 130, for a discussion of the concept of permitted exceptions.

seller making the warranty. In today's marketplace where most commercial real estate is owned by single purpose entities having little or no net worth, the buyer's true recourse for title defects is against the title insurance company that issued the title insurance policy on the land. As a result, the negotiations between the buyer and the seller over the form of the deed to be used in a particular transaction are usually quite short-lived and relatively insignificant.[54]

B. BILL OF SALE/ASSIGNMENT OF INTANGIBLE PROPERTY

The deed is intended to convey a real property interest to the buyer. If the buyer is also being transferred personal property (for example, a shed, tractor or landscaping supplies located on the land), then the seller will need to execute and deliver at closing a *bill of sale* transferring all of its rights to such personal property to the buyer. Similarly, if the deal specified in the purchase contract contemplates the transfer to the buyer of various contractual rights or intangible property (for example, a farm lease, development rights or a trade name), then the legal documents to be executed and delivered at closing should also include an ***assignment of intangible property***.

C. CLOSING AFFIDAVITS

In the typical land acquisition closing, the seller is required to execute three different affidavits—(1) a ***title affidavit*** certifying the absence of any off-record title matters to both the buyer and the title company,[55] (2) a so-called ***FIRPTA affidavit***, confirming that the seller is not a "foreign person" subject to the withholding of taxes under the Foreign Investment in Real Property Tax Act[56] and (3) a ***bring-down certificate*** that confirms that all of the representations and warranties made by the seller in the purchase contract remain true as of the date of the closing.[57]

D. ENTITY AUTHORITY DOCUMENTS

To the extent either the seller or the buyer is an entity, the list of closing documents should also include (1) a ***certificate of good standing*** from the state in which such entity was formed affirming that the entity exists and is in good standing under the laws of such state[58] and (2) a

---

54. Many states have statutes prescribing the required form and content of the various types of deeds. *See e.g.*, OHIO REV. CODE ANN. §§ 5302.01–5302.11 (West 2010). In those states, the practitioner should use the statutory deed form whenever possible.

55. An off-record title matters affidavit is usually required by the title company as a condition to its deletion of the preprinted, general exceptions to title set forth in Schedule B–1 of an ALTA owner's title policy. *See* GREGORY STEIN, *supra* note 8, at § 2.94.

56. *See* INTERNAL REVENUE CODE § 1445.

57. *See supra* Chapter 5, Page 123, for a discussion of the effective date for the making of representations and warranties.

58. To the extent the land is located in a state other than the state in which the entity was formed, the entity authority documents typically also include a governmental certificate affirming

resolution certified by an authorized officer of the entity confirming that all requisite action has been taken by the entity to authorize its participation in the purchase and sale transaction and that the person who will be signing the closing documents on behalf of the entity is duly authorized to do so. A legal opinion provided by the entity's lawyer is frequently required to further confirm that the entity exists and is authorized to close the deal.

E. APPROVED TITLE INSURANCE DOCUMENTS

An essential component of the closing process is the production of a written document that embodies the parties' agreement concerning the precise form and content of the title insurance policy that the title company is obligated to issue to the buyer at closing (including the deletion of any Schedule B title exceptions and the issuance of any required endorsements). The title company typically satisfies this requirement by either putting drafting a pro forma title insurance policy or marking up the title commitment to indicate exactly what the title policy will look like when issued. The title company will then indicate on either the pro forma policy or the marked-up commitment that the title company will be obligated to issue the title insurance policy upon the closing of the subject transaction and the payment of the title company's insurance premiums.[59]

F. CLOSING STATEMENT

The ***closing statement*** is the document which shows how much money the buyer needs to pay to close the land acquisition and to whom that money is to be disbursed. Too many lawyers make the egregious mistake of focusing on the purely "legal" documents (like the deed and entity resolutions) and leaving the preparation and review of the closing statement to the principals of the buyer and the seller and their respective financial analysts and accountants. The lawyer who fails to give due regard to the admonition to "follow the money" does so at his own peril— and to the potential financial detriment of his client, who may have to pay more or receive less than it otherwise should.

A well-drafted purchase contract will provide counsel for the buyer and the seller with an instruction manual to determine the exact amount of the buyer's cash payment at closing and the manner in which that cash payment will then be distributed to the seller and other participants in the closing process.[60] If the purchase contract fails to clearly describe how the money should be handled at closing, the parties will be faced with the

---

that the entity is lawfully registered to do business in the state in which the land is located. *See* GREGORY STEIN, *supra* note 8, at § 3.63.

59. *See generally*, GREGORY STEIN, *supra* note 8, at § 8.06.

60. *See supra* Chapter 5, Pages 133–136, for a review of the provisions of the purchase contract that impact the financial calculations called for in the closing statement.

prospect of having to enter into fresh negotiations at the closing table, which could, in turn, threaten the viability of the entire purchase and sale transaction.[61]

The first line of any closing statement is the purchase price being paid for the land by the buyer. The stated purchase price establishes the threshold for the calculation of both the net amount of cash required to be funded at closing by the buyer and the net sales proceeds payable to the seller. The buyer's net funding obligation is reduced by the amount of its previously-paid earnest money deposits, while the seller's share of the net sales proceeds is reduced by the pay-off balance of any mortgage loan that encumbers the land.[62]

The next step in the lawyer's preparation of the closing statement is the allocation of responsibility between the seller and the buyer for the payment of those third party costs that are payable at closing. Third party costs regularly paid at the land acquisition closing include the following:

- Title insurance premiums (payable to the title company);[63]

- Surveying fees (payable to the surveyor);

- Real estate commissions (payable to the licensed real estate brokers involved in the transaction);[64]

- Transfer taxes and recording fees (payable to the local governmental agency charged with administering and maintaining the public real estate records);[65] and

---

61. *See* Stein, *Closings: Step by Step, supra* note 17, at 83. Careless lawyers will, on occasion, take a short-cut by seeking to leave the financial closing calculations to "community custom"—a singularly bad idea because there is no such thing as "community custom" in commercial real estate transactions.

62. The amount of the loan pay-off will be indicated in a letter provided by the lender to the seller and the escrow agent, which letter will indicate (1) the balance of the outstanding principal and interest due under the loan as of a specific, projected closing date and (2) the amount of the per diem interest carry that will have to be added to the amount of the loan pay-off if the loan is not fully repaid on the projected closing date. The pay-off letter will also usually contain the lender's agreement that it will take all requisite actions to discharge its recorded mortgage on the land promptly after its receipt of the loan pay-off balance.

63. The calculation of the title insurance premiums will vary depending on whether the state in which the land is situated is a "rate locked" or "rate competitive" state. *See* Dickerman, *(Part 1), supra* note 11, at 53. In a rate locked state, the premiums that a title company can charge for its issuance of an owner's title insurance policy are fixed by state regulations and, therefore, are not subject to negotiation by the affected parties. In rate competitive states, the title company has a fair amount of latitude to set its title insurance premiums based on its negotiations with whichever party has the obligation to pay the title insurance premiums.

64. In most situations, the broker's commission is computed as a fixed percentage of the stated purchase price for the land. By way of example, the total broker's commission payable on the HIBC land acquisition was 7% of the $7.5 million purchase price, or $525,000.

65. The charges payable to the government in connection with a land acquisition closing generally fall into two classes—(1) recording fees charged to record the deed and other legal documents in the public real estate records of the jurisdiction where the land is located (usually a fairly small number that is calculated based on the number of pages contained in the recorded document) and (2) taxes/fees imposed upon the parties for the privilege of conveying real property in a particular subdivision (referred to in different jurisdictions as "conveyance fees," "documentary stamps" or "transfer taxes"). This second class of governmental charges can be quite significant in amount. By way of example, in Seminole County, Florida (where the HIBC land is situated), documentary stamps at the rate of $.70 per $100 of the purchase price must be obtained

- Legal fees (payable to counsel for the buyer and the seller, respectively).[66]

The allocation of responsibility for paying all of these closing costs is a matter of negotiation between the seller and the buyer and should be clearly specified in the executed purchase contract. Closing costs assigned to the buyer increase the net cash payable by it at closing, while closing costs assigned to the seller decrease its share of the net sales proceeds.

The final closing statement entries are those relating to closing adjustments that must be made to the purchase price to reflect the proration of those periodic payment obligations, such as real estate taxes, which cover a period of time both before and after the date of closing. To the extent the seller has pre-paid any such obligation, the amount of the cash payable by the buyer and the net proceeds payable to the seller at closing will typically be increased by an amount equal to the portion of such prepayment that is attributable to the period after the date of closing. Conversely, to the extent the any such obligation remains unpaid at closing, the amount of the cash payable by the buyer and the net proceeds payable to the seller at closing will typically be decreased by an amount equal to the portion of the outstanding obligation that is attributable to the period prior to the date of closing.[67]

Once completed, the closing statement should set forth a figure for the "net cash payable by buyer at closing." That figure should equal the sum of (1) the various closing costs payable by seller and buyer at closing and (2) the "net sales proceeds payable to seller at closing."[68]

Practice Tip #8–2: Getting Paid at Closing

I have always been amazed at how infrequently legal fees appear as a line item on a closing statement. For some reason, lawyers representing both the buyer and the seller are often hesitant to include their fees as costs that must be paid out of the proceeds of the closing. I have never figured out if those lawyers are bashful or just plain embarrassed about the amount of their bills. I do know, however, that real estate brokers, title

------

for the conveyance of any real property located in that county (producing a total documentary stamp charge of $52,500 on a land purchase price of $7.5 million).

66. *See infra Practice Tip #8–2: Getting Paid at Closing.*

67. *See supra* Chapter 5, Pages 134–136, for a more detailed discussion of closing prorations and adjustments.

68. The format of the closing statement is a matter of individual preference. Some lawyers use the HUD–1 settlement statement created by the Department of Housing and Urban Development for use on residential transactions. *See* Gregory Stein, *supra* note 8, at § 7.25. I always found the HUD–1 form to be inadequate for most commercial real estate transactions and instead preferred to use a more extensive form of closing statement that incorporated a detailed schedule of all cash disbursements made at closing and a series of notes explaining the support for and method of calculation of the various closing costs, prorations and adjustments set forth in the closing statement. A sample Closing Statement applicable to the sale of the HIBC land by The Pizzuti Companies is included as Document #4 in the Document Appendix.

insurance companies, surveyors and other players in the closing process rarely share the lawyers' reluctance to get paid at closing. Indeed, my experience has been that those other players actually seem quite proud to submit their bills and get paid at closing.

My own personal view is that the fees of both buyer's and seller's counsel should regularly appear on the closing statement and be paid at closing. A client wants to be able to quantify its all-in costs of the transaction and deserves to know what its legal bill is going to be at the same time as it learns of its other transactional costs. From the lawyer's perspective, it is fitting that the person who has labored the most to close the transaction gets to walk away from the closing with a check in hand. I have also found over the years that there is no better time to get paid than when your client is in the midst of celebrating the closing of a transaction.

HIBC Case Study—Negotiating the Closing Numbers

The $7.5 million purchase price for the HIBC land was established very early in the negotiations between Pizzuti and the land seller—indeed, I seem to clearly remember the words "take it or leave it" being muttered by the Chemical Bank loan officer assigned responsibility for negotiating the land sale. In an attempt to save some negotiating face, I decided to take a crack at easing Pizzuti's financial burden by getting Chemical Bank to agree to a few concessions concerning the manner in which responsibility for various closing costs would be allocated between the seller and the buyer.

The first draft of the land purchase contract (prepared, of course, by Chemical Bank's counsel) sought to place the obligation on Pizzuti to pay all closing costs, other than the seller's legal fees and the 7% real estate commission that Chemical had agreed to pay to its listing broker. Based less on my negotiating prowess than on the fact that I had already acceded to Chemical's insistence on a purchase price of $7.5 million, I was able to win a few small victories in the negotiation over the allocation of responsibility for the payment of closing costs. Specifically, Chemical Bank agreed that it would pay one-half of the title insurance premiums payable to the title company and one-half of the documentary stamps payable to Seminole County (an aggregate savings for Pizzuti of approximately $50,000).

The biggest financial concession I was able to secure cost Chemical nothing, but benefitted Pizzuti to the tune of $150,000. As noted earlier, Chemical had previously agreed with its listing broker that it would pay a real estate commission of 7% of the purchase price upon a closing of the sale of the HIBC land. Based on a $7.5 million purchase price, this meant that Chemical was on the hook for the payment of a real estate commission of $525,000. Because The Pizzuti Companies owned a licensed real estate brokerage firm in Orlando (creatively named "Pizzuti Realty"), I asked Chemical to recognize Pizzuti Realty as a cooperating broker on the HIBC *land sale and pay it a commission of 2% of the purchase price, or $150,000. Because the terms of its commission agreement with the listing broker expressly permitted Chemical to deduct the amount of any cooperating broker commission from the commission otherwise payable to the listing broker, Chemical was relatively quick to agree to my request to divert a portion of the committed real estate commission to Pizzuti Realty. The end result was that The Pizzuti Companies' out-of-pocket funding at closing was reduced by $150,000, while Chemical's share of the net sales proceeds remained unaffected.*

The bottom line impact of the closing cost negotiations was that Pizzuti saved approximately $200,000 (at least when compared to the positions put forth in Chemical's first draft of the purchase contract). I actually felt pretty good about that—at least until my boss reminded me that the agreed-upon purchase price of $7.5 million was $300,000 higher than the maximum price that he wanted to pay for the HIBC land.

VIII. THE ACTUAL CLOSING

The actual closing is the point in time where all of the closing preliminaries have been concluded[69] and the buyer is prepared to pay its money and receive title to the land. In the "olden days" when I first started practicing law, the next step would be for the lawyers to negotiate where the closing would be held ("your place or mine") and, once that was decided, to notify their respective client representatives to book their flights and hotel rooms and be prepared to spend a couple of days cloistered away in a conference room drinking coffee, eating deli sandwiches and watching the lawyers compile closing documents, haggle over the remaining open issues and generally act lawyerly.

While a full sit-down closing of the type described above is certainly "interesting" (describing it as "fun" would be a bit of an overstatement), clients and lawyers have come to realize that, in most instances, it is an extremely inefficient way to close a real estate deal. The norm in today's fast-paced, commercial world is for the transaction to be closed *in escrow* (a *California closing* instead of a *New York closing* where everybody gathers around the table and eats those deli sandwiches). In an escrow closing, the buyer and seller stay put at their respective places of business and the lawyers use overnight couriers to deliver the signed closing documents to the local escrow agent who is handling the closing—a much more efficient style of closing which benefits all concerned (except for the owner of the local deli who would otherwise be supplying all of the sandwiches for the closing).

---

69. The statement that the "closing preliminaries" have been concluded means that the buyer has successfully completed its due diligence, identified all needed third party approvals, agreed to the form of all the closing documents (with the probable exception of the closing statement—*see* note 55, *supra*), checked and re-checked its closing checklist and waived its contractual contingencies.

The logistics of conducting an escrow closing (viewed principally from the perspective of counsel for the buyer) are described below.

- **Document Execution**—The lawyer's first step is to sit down with his client and get the client to sign all those closing documents that require its execution. The lawyer should make sure that all blanks in the documents are completed, all exhibits are attached and all execution formalities are followed.[70] The executed originals of the closing documents should then be sent to the escrow agent via overnight courier, along with the written escrow instructions described in the next paragraph.

- **Escrow Instructions**—Counsel for the buyer and the seller (acting separately or jointly) will prepare and deliver to the escrow agent detailed written instructions setting forth the conditions under which the escrow agent is to hold, disburse and, ultimately, record the signed closing documents (as well as the funds wired to the escrow agent by the buyer under the next paragraph). Escrow instructions prepared by buyer's counsel will typically address the following topics—(1) a listing of those documents and funds being delivered to the escrow agent by the buyer, (2) a recital of the specific conditions that must be satisfied before the escrow agent is authorized to disburse the escrowed documents and funds (e.g., the receipt of all requisite signed documents from the seller, the escrow agent's delivery to buyer's counsel of a letter indicating that it is prepared to issue a title insurance policy to buyer in the exact form of the marked-up title commitment or pro forma title policy and the escrow agent's receipt via fax of a signed letter from buyer's counsel specifically authorizing the escrow agent to "break escrow"), (3) a statement of what the escrow agent is to do once it is authorized to break escrow—i.e., disburse the buyer's wired funds in accordance with the closing statement signed by representatives of the buyer and seller,[71] record the deed and any other specifically-designated documents in the public real estate records of the jurisdiction in which the property is located and distribute copies of the recorded documents and executed originals of all other documents to buyer and seller in accordance with a document disbursement schedule appended to the escrow instructions and (4) a statement of what the escrow agent should do if all of the escrow conditions have not been satisfied by a specified outside date (usually send all the signed documents back to buyer's counsel and wire the buyer's funds back to the buyer's bank account).

---

70. Special care needs to be taken to insure that all documents that are to be recorded in the public real estate records have been formatted, executed and acknowledged in strict accordance with the recording requirements of the jurisdiction in which the land is located.

71. As noted previously (*see supra* note 52), the closing statement is frequently not finalized and available for execution until the actual day of closing. As a result, the norm in commercial real estate transactions is for the closing statement to be signed by a client representative (or occasionally the client's lawyer) on the date of closing and faxed to the other party and the escrow agent.

- ***Wiring of Funds***—Upon his receipt of a copy of the escrow instructions signed by the escrow agent, counsel for the buyer should then arrange for his client to send the money required to close the land acquisition to the escrow agent's designated bank account. The buyer's payment is typically sent directly to the escrow agent's account by means of a wire transfer of funds through an electronic system maintained by the Federal Reserve. The escrow instructions sent to the escrow agent by buyer's counsel (or a supplemental set of written instructions) should specify the manner in which the buyer's funds should be invested during the pendency of the escrow (e.g., in a liquid, interest-bearing account of some type).[72]

- ***Giving the "Green Light"***—Once all the conditions specified in the escrow instructions have been satisfied, the lawyers representing the buyer and the seller will give the "green light" to the escrow agent to release the documents and funds from escrow and disburse them in the manner specified in the escrow instructions.

- ***Closing the Escrow***—Once it gets the green light from buyer's and seller's counsel, the escrow agent will then close the escrow by recording the deed, disbursing the escrowed funds and distributing the remaining documents as instructed in the escrow instructions.

Once the deed is recorded and the funds are disbursed, it is time for: the seller to celebrate (it has, after all, gotten paid for its contributions); the buyer to get to work developing its real estate project on the acquired land; and the lawyers to do it all over again on behalf of other clients.

HIBC Case Study—A Hybrid Closing

The closing of the HIBC land purchase was a hybrid between a New York-style, sit-down closing and a California-style, escrow closing. The closing was structured as an escrow closing, with all the business principals staying at home and all the closing documents and funds being placed in escrow with the escrow agent pursuant to carefully drawn escrow instructions prepared by counsel for the seller and the buyer. However, unlike a pure escrow closing, all the lawyers representing the seller and the

---

72. The parties need to be acutely aware of the deadlines imposed by the banks involved in the wiring of closing funds. It is quite common for a bank to take the position that it cannot guaranty the same-day receipt of a closing disbursement, unless the bank triggers the wire transfer to the intended recipient of the disbursement by a specific time in the afternoon (typically 3–4 p.m.). A wire transfer triggered after the specified deadline may result in a disbursement "hanging in space overnight rather than invested at interest"—a particularly troublesome predicament if the intended recipient of the disbursement is an existing mortgage lender whose loan will continue to accrue interest until paid in full. *See* Dickerman, *(Part 1)*, *supra* note 11, at 60. For this reason, practitioners try to stay away from scheduling closings on Friday afternoons when the financial impact of a late wire of funds is compounded by a factor of three (for every day over the weekend that the wired funds cannot be invested in the intended manner).

buyer (including yours truly) gathered around the table in the escrow agent's offices in Orlando to compile the documents, haggle over the remaining open issues and, yes, consume plenty of coffee and deli sandwiches.

Over the years, I have developed a strong preference for conducting commercial real estate closings in a style similar to the hybrid arrangement employed for the HIBC land purchase. While an escrow closing is infinitely more efficient than an all-hands, sit-down closing, there is still something very comforting about being physically present to make sure that it really is the right time for the actual closing to occur.

IX. POST-CLOSING MATTERS

A lawyer's natural temptation once a transaction closes is to put the land acquisition file aside and immediately move on to the next deal. It is important, however, that the lawyer take a few minutes (after finishing his celebratory libations) to organize his thoughts and address a variety of post-closing matters.

It is not unusual for a closing to occur despite the existence of some minor loose ends that must be addressed by the parties—for example, notifying an owner's association of the identity of the new landowner or splitting a pending water bill for the property which was discovered at the last moment. Before putting the file away for good, the lawyers should document all the loose ends in a brief letter agreement and establish responsibility and a timeline for taking care of those matters (and maybe escrow some of the closing proceeds until all the loose ends are successfully tied up).[73]

Buyer's counsel also needs to attend to the following three post-closing items—(1) the preparation and distribution to his client of **closing bibles** that include copies of all of the pertinent legal documents related to the land acquisition, (2) the calendaring of any pertinent post-closing dates (e.g., the outside date for the reproration of real estate taxes or the filing of a claim for the breach of a representation or warranty) and (3) the receipt from the title company of a final title insurance policy for the land. Once those items are handled, buyer's counsel can comfortably move on the next transaction.

X. SUMMARY

Stage 4 requires the real estate development lawyer to be prepared, organized, diligent and, quite frankly, anal. While preparing a closing checklist and working out the logistics of a land acquisition closing may not be the most intellectually stimulating of tasks, there is a wonderful

---

73. *See* Stein, *Closings: Step by Step, supra* note 17, at 84–85.

dual reward waiting for the real estate development lawyer who successfully manages the process that is the closing of the land acquisition—the self-satisfaction of knowing that he is a deal closer (and not a deal killer) and, of course, the closing dinner with his client at the local steakhouse.

CHAPTER 9

STAGE 5: OBTAINING CONSTRUCTION FINANCING

■ ■ ■

I. INTRODUCTION

A developer typically funds approximately 70–90% of its development costs by obtaining a construction loan from a commercial bank or other financing source.[1] The remaining development costs are paid with equity contributions made to the development entity by either the developer or its investors.[2]

It is important to start with a quick review of why the developer wants (or, more accurately, needs) to fund the majority of its development costs with dollars borrowed from a construction lender—the use of so-called "other peoples' money" or "OPM."[3] There are three basic reasons supporting a developer's use of OPM (referred to in more elite, academic circles as *leverage*).

- Leverage permits the developer to diversify its real estate investments by funding 10–30% of the development costs in several deals, rather than 100% of those costs in just one project. This diversification lowers the developer's real estate risk by permitting it to spread that risk over several different projects. This approach is similar to a stock investor purchasing a mutual fund versus putting the entirety of his investment in a single stock.

- Leverage can be used to increase or "juice" the developer's return on equity.[4] This is true because construction lenders ordinarily

---

1. As this Chapter is being written, the United States is experiencing a credit crunch of unparalleled consequence. In today's market (third quarter 2010), the percentage of development costs typically financed with a construction loan has dropped rather precipitously to more like 50–70% (if construction financing can be obtained at all). It is unclear how long the financial markets will remain clogged and, hence, how long the leverage used on development projects will remain suppressed. However, the fundamentals of construction lending discussed in this Chapter are the same regardless whether the developer is able to borrow 90% of its development costs or just 50% of those costs.

2. *See supra* Chapter 7, for a detailed discussion of equity contributions.

3. *See supra* Chapter 3, Pages 50–52, for a further discussion of the impact that leverage has on the economics of a real estate development project.

4. *Id.* at Page 51.

require a lower percentage return on their loan dollars than equity investors require on their equity contributions (largely because of the greater risk borne by the equity investor).

- Finally, most developers just flat out *NEED* to obtain a construction loan to get their projects done. Real estate is an incredibly capital-intensive business requiring the long-term investment of significant dollars. A typical suburban office building may easily cost $10 million or more, with the building owner being required to keep its investment intact for a period of upward of five to ten years if it is going to maximize its financial return from that project. Moreover, few developers develop only one project at a time. Indeed, the diversification principle mentioned at the outset of this section frequently results in a developer having a number of projects in its development pipeline at the same time. The need for leverage can be illustrated by looking at an office developer who has five projects being developed in the same 12–month period at an aggregate cost of more than $50 million—a situation that is far from atypical in the development world. How many people do you know who can personally write a check for $50 million without using other peoples' money?

Given the above considerations, it is easy to see why the securing of a construction loan is a key element of virtually every real estate development project.[5]

This Chapter will begin with an examination of the many ways in which a construction loan is different from the conventional mortgage loan with which most people are familiar. It will then move on to a quick discussion of the business objectives of both the construction lender and the borrower and the typical way in which most construction loans are structured and papered. The remainder of the Chapter will be devoted to an in-depth analysis of the unique risks faced by a construction lender and the various techniques that the lender can use to help mitigate those risks—and, of course, the developer's "pushback" on each of those risk mitigation techniques. All of these topics will be discussed against the backdrop of two similar (but, in many ways, starkly different) suburban office projects developed in Orlando, Florida by my former employer—one being an 87,000 square foot building designed for occupancy by a single tenant and the other being a 75,000 square foot, speculative, multi-tenant building.

---

5. Large national developers often finance their real estate projects through the use of lines of credit provided by a consortium of financial institutions. These lines of credit are intended to provide the developers with flexible financing for the concurrent acquisition and development of multiple projects. Although they present some unique legal issues (for example, cross-default and financial covenant issues), the negotiation of acquisition and development lines of credit centers on most of the same issues that characterize the negotiation of the single asset, construction loan that is the focus of this Chapter.

II. THE UNIQUE NATURE OF A CONSTRUCTION LOAN

The typical home buyer finances 70–90% of the price of buying his or her personal residence by getting a residential mortgage loan from a local bank or savings and loan association. In return for the lender providing loan dollars to cover the majority of the purchase price of the home, the borrower commits to repay the loan over a term of 30 years, with the amount of the borrower's monthly principal and interest payments being fixed in a manner set forth in the loan documents. If the borrower for some reason fails to keep current on its monthly loan payment, the lender's principal recourse is to foreclose on the mortgage and take over ownership of the residence (at least until it finds someone who will buy the residence back from the lender).

In the commercial real estate context, the second cousin of the residential mortgage loan is a financing structure commonly referred to as a ***conventional permanent loan***. The permanent lender (typically an insurance company, pension fund or other financial institution) makes a loan to permit a borrower either to pay a significant portion of the price of acquiring a completed, commercial real estate project or to refinance an existing loan on the project. The borrower agrees to use the net operating income produced from its operation of the commercial property to make monthly payments of principal and interest to repay the loan over a fixed period of years (typically significantly less than the 30 year term commonly seen in residential mortgage loans). The permanent lender's principal remedy for the borrower's failure to make its monthly mortgage payments is to foreclose on the mortgage and take over ownership and operation of the commercial project that was pledged as collateral to secure the borrower's repayment obligation.

A construction loan is vastly different from a conventional permanent loan. The only characteristic that is common to both a construction loan and a conventional permanent loan is that the lender takes a mortgage on the underlying real estate in order to provide it with a level of security in case the borrower fails to repay its loan. This is not a book on mortgage financing, so this Chapter will not address either the fundamentals associated with a borrower's pledging of real estate collateral to secure its loan or the manner in which the priority of those having competing claims to the underlying real estate is determined.[6] Suffice it to say that many of the same legal principles related to the grant of the mortgage and the determination of the mortgage's priority are common to both construction loans and conventional permanent loans.

That is, however, where the similarity between a construction loan and a conventional permanent loan ends. The following is a list of the fundamental differences between a construction loan and a conventional permanent loan. Those differences, which are highlighted in a somewhat

---

6. There are a number of excellent law school texts devoted to the topic of mortgage financing. *See, e.g.*, STEVEN W. BENDER, CELESTE M. HAMMOND, MICHAEL T. MADISON AND ROBERT M. ZINMAN, MODERN REAL ESTATE FINANCE AND LAND TRANSFER: A TRANSACTIONAL APPROACH (4th ed. 2008); AND GRANT S. NELSON, DALE A. WHITMAN, ANN M. BURKHART AND R. WILSON FREYERMUTH, REAL ESTATE TRANSFER, FINANCE, AND DEVELOPMENT: CASES AND MATERIALS (8th ed. 2009).

cursory and conclusory fashion below, will be examined in greater detail later on in this Chapter as part of the discussion of the unique risks faced by the construction lender and the techniques that are available to help mitigate its exposure to those risks.

A. NATURE OF UNDERLYING COLLATERAL

The most fundamental and consequential difference between a construction loan and a conventional permanent loan revolves around the nature of the real estate collateral which secures the borrower's obligation to repay its loan. In the case of a conventional permanent loan, the permanent lender holds a mortgage on real property having a defined income stream and, hence, a readily realizable value. In the context of a construction loan, the value of the lender's collateral is tied to the completion and leasing of the project for which the construction loan proceeds are being disbursed. In a very real sense, therefore, the construction loan proceeds are being used to *CREATE* the value of the lender's underlying collateral.

Another way to think about the difference between a construction loan and a conventional real estate loan is to imagine that one bank (akin to the construction lender) is asked to make a loan of $5 million to Jasper Johns[7] to fund the costs associated with his painting of a new mural on the side of a building in downtown Chicago, while another financial institution (similar to the permanent lender) is asked to make a loan of $5 million to permit an art enthusiast to buy an existing Jasper Johns painting. In the first instance, there is no existing value in the "to be created" work of art, while in the second situation, the collateral is an actual painting which has a readily determinable, financial value in the art world. The bank that makes the "creative" loan to Jasper Johns will have its loan adequately collateralized only if Johns actually paints the proposed mural *AND* that mural is enthusiastically embraced by the modern art community. It is, therefore, absolutely essential from the perspective of the "creative" lender that Johns use the loan proceeds to fund the costs of completing his new masterpiece. The same state of affairs exists for the real estate construction lender who wants to make sure that its loan proceeds are used by the developer to construct and lease a commercial real estate project in accordance with the developer's project schematics and financial pro forma.[8] As will be discussed in later sections of this Chapter, it is this evolving, creative nature of the construction lender's collateral that is the primary driver for most of the provisions of the lender's construction loan agreement.

---

7. Jasper Johns is one of the most successful, living American artists. Two of his best known works are "The Flag" and "Savarin Cans," both of which are prime examples of the American Pop Art movement.

8. Please accept my apology for the blasphemous comparison of the work of Jasper Johns to a suburban office building. Comparing the two "creative" scenarios is simply my clumsy attempt to clarify the difference between a construction loan and a permanent loan and is not intended in any way to minimalize the artistry of Mr. Johns.

B.   BASIS OF LOAN UNDERWRITING

When a lender is asked to make a permanent loan on a commercial real estate project, the primary focus of its analysis as to the wisdom of making the loan (commonly referred to as the ***underwriting*** of the loan) is the project's existing income stream. Is the project leased and on what terms? What is the amount of the project's annual net operating income? Are there any foreseeable circumstances which could cause the project's revenues to decrease or its expenses to increase in the future?

A construction lender, on the other hand, is not afforded the luxury of underwriting a construction loan based on actual, historical data. While the permanent lender gets to inspect a completed facility and look at historical, financial information, the construction lender is forced to make an up or down decision on a proposed construction loan based solely on the developer's projections as to both the physical appearance and the financial performance of the imagined project. As a result, the focus of the construction lender's attention when underwriting a loan is not only on the relative merits of the proposed development project (e.g., are the projected construction costs reasonable and can space in the project be leased at the projected rents), but also on the capability and financial wherewithal of the borrower and its development team (e.g., can this development team complete and lease the project in the proposed manner). The end result is that a construction loan is inherently part real estate loan and part personal loan.

C.   DISBURSEMENT OF LOAN PROCEEDS

The principal amount of a conventional permanent loan is fully disbursed at closing to allow the borrower to either purchase an existing project or refinance the debt that then encumbers the project. Conversely, the principal amount of a construction loan is disbursed incrementally over time when and as the project's development costs are incurred.[9] A construction loan for a typical office building might involve ten to 15 separate monthly disbursements of loan proceeds, while a regional mall project could easily require the construction lender to make twice that number of monthly disbursements.

D.   LENGTH OF LOAN TERM

A typical loan term for a permanent mortgage loan is anywhere from five to 15 years. While five to 15 years may not seem like a particularly

---

9.   There are two reasons why the construction loan is not disbursed in a lump sum at closing. First, the periodic disbursement of the construction loan proceeds helps the borrower reduce the interest it pays on the construction loan (because it doesn't have to pay interest on the undisbursed portion of the construction loan). Second, if the construction lender were to disburse the entire principal amount of the construction loan at closing, it would be exposed to an even greater risk that the borrower might use those proceeds for some reason other than the completion of the proposed real estate project (and, hence, the creation of the value of the lender's loan collateral).

long time to the reader, in the eyes of a real estate investor, it is an eternity. The permanent lender has the ability to make a loan having a term of that magnitude because it is dealing with a completed asset that has a proven, financial track record and a relatively predictable financial future.[10]

The customary term of a construction loan is much shorter than that of a permanent loan—12 to 36 months as opposed to five to 15 years. The shorter duration of the construction loan term is primarily attributable to the uncertain future value of the "to be constructed" project and the lender's concomitant desire to get its loan repaid as soon as construction of the project is completed.

E. IDENTITY OF LENDER

Construction loans are, for the most part, the province of commercial banks. As noted earlier in this section, a construction loan is part real estate loan and part personal loan. A commercial bank is much more apt than a life insurance company or pension fund to have the local knowledge, experience and personal relationships required to properly underwrite and administer such a combination loan. In addition, commercial banks naturally gravitate to the shorter terms of construction loans due to their need to maintain liquidity to meet the more immediate cash needs of their retail customers.[11]

Permanent loans, on the other hand, are made based upon an evaluation of the physical and financial components of an existing real estate asset and, as such, do not require the same level of local knowledge or hands-on administration that a construction loan does. As a result, permanent loans are typically made not by commercial banks, but rather by financial institutions, such as life insurance companies and pension funds, that tend to have a longer-term investment perspective.

F. CALCULATION OF INTEREST RATE

The norm in the permanent loan market is for interest to be set at a fixed annual percentage (for example 8%) for the entire duration of the loan term. Fixed pricing works in the permanent loan arena because the permanent lender disburses the entire principal amount of its loan in a lump sum on a date which is in close proximity to the date on which it accesses the funds it uses to make that loan disbursement. As a result, the permanent lender is in a position to quantify and fix upfront both its cost of funds[12] and the interest rate it charges to its borrower. The permanent

---

10. The predictability of a project's future financial prospects is truly "relative." For a discussion of the many challenges created for the permanent lender by a lengthy loan term, *see generally* Frank Crance and Patricia J. Frobes, *Anticipating the Future and Retaining the Ability to Change Your Mind*, in ALI–ABA COURSE OF STUDY MATERIALS, REAL ESTATE FINANCING DOCUMENTA-TION—STRATEGIES FOR CHANGING TIMES, Course No. SL–007, 165 (January 2006).

11. *See* BENDER, *supra* note 6, at 295.

12. A permanent lender's cost of funds is determined by reference to the comparative levels of its cash inflows (for example, from insurance premiums or pension contributions) and its cash

lender's profit on the permanent loan transaction (assuming that the loan is kept current and is paid in full at maturity) is equal to the excess of the permanent loan's fixed interest rate over the lender's cost of funds as of the date of the permanent loan closing.

As mentioned earlier in this section, the principal amount of the construction loan is disbursed not in a lump sum at closing, but rather incrementally over the 12 to 36 month term of the construction loan. Because its loan disbursements are spread over a lengthy period of time, the construction lender (unlike the permanent lender) is not in a position to determine its cost of funds[13] and fix its interest rate at the time of the initial construction loan closing. By way of example, assume that the construction lender's cost of funds as of the date of the initial construction loan closing is 4% and that the construction lender would be happy to receive a profit on the construction loan of 3% of the loan balance. If the lender's cost of funds remains constant throughout the full term of the construction loan, the lender could achieve its desired loan profit by fixing the borrower's interest rate at 7% (the lender's cost of funds of 4%, plus its desired profit spread of 3%). But what happens if the construction lender's cost of funds increases to 6% after it has disbursed only 25% of the total proceeds available under the construction loan? If the lender fixes its interest rate at 7% at the time of the construction loan closing, the subsequent increase in its cost of funds would result in the lender's profit margin on the loan being reduced by an amount equal to 2% of the 75% portion of the loan proceeds remaining to be disbursed after the cost of funds increase—a result which would certainly not be acceptable to the construction lender.

For the above reason, construction loans typically provide for a variable or ***floating interest rate*** that is adjusted during the loan term to reflect changes in a specified financial index. The ***prime rate***[14] and the London Interbank Offered Rate (***LIBOR***)[15] are the two financial indices

---

outflows (for example, for the payment of death or pension benefits). A permanent lender's cost of funds is generally more stable than that of a commercial bank because of the long-term nature of the permanent lender's business model. *See generally* DAVID M. GELTNER, NORMAN G. MILLER, JIM CLAYTON AND PIET EICHOLTZ, COMMERCIAL REAL ESTATE ANALYSIS AND INVESTMENTS 389–390 (2nd ed. 2007).

13. A construction lender's cost of funds is generally a blended rate tied to the interest that it has to pay on its customer's deposits and the interest rate at which it borrows funds from other financial institutions.

14. The "prime rate" is generally viewed as the interest rate charged on loans made by a financial institution to its most creditworthy customers. The specific prime rate used as the benchmark for the setting of the interest rate on a construction loan is routinely expressed in terms of either (i) the prime rate announced by the subject construction lender, (ii) the prime rate published by a national bank other than the construction lender (for example, Bank of America) or (iii) the prime rate referenced in a national publication (for example, the *Wall Street Journal*).

15. LIBOR is a daily reference rate based on the interest rates at which banks borrow unsecured funds from other banks in the London wholesale money market (or interbank market). Because LIBOR is based on the borrowing rates afforded to other banks (and not a bank's commercial customers, as is the case with the prime rate), LIBOR is almost always lower than the prime rate. As such, the spreads quoted on LIBOR are historically higher than those quoted on the prime rate—for example, LIBOR plus 3% versus the prime rate plus 1%.

most commonly used by construction lenders to set their floating interest rates.[16]

By tying its floating interest rate to the variable performance of a financial index,[17] the construction lender is able to protect the amount of its potential construction loan profit from any unanticipated increase in the lender's cost of funds that occurs during the term of the construction loan.

It should also be noted that the numerical interest rate charged on construction loans is customarily higher than the numerical interest charged by permanent lenders. Why do you suppose that is the case? Does the phrase "the greater, the risk, the greater the reward" mean anything to you?

G. IMPOSITION OF LOAN FEES

Construction and permanent lenders both charge upfront loan fees to all but their best customers (who frequently have enough negotiating leverage to get those fees waived). Loan fees are typically expressed in terms of a percentage of the principal amount of the loan—e.g., a fee of 1%[18] on a $10 million permanent loan means that the borrower will have to pay a $100,000 upfront fee to the lender. These upfront fees are in addition to the borrower's required interest payments and are typically referred to as ***origination, commitment*** or ***loan processing fees***. The fees are imposed to achieve one or both of the following lender objectives— (i) the reimbursement of the lender's cost of making the loan and (ii) the augmentation of the lender's profit on the loan transaction.

Construction lenders typically charge higher upfront fees on their loans than do permanent lenders. The construction lender's imposition of such higher fees is justified (at least in the construction lender's mind) by the facts that (1) a construction loan is inherently more risky than a permanent loan and (2) the post-closing administration of a construction loan is much more labor-intensive than that of a permanent loan.

H. BORROWER'S RECOURSE ON LOAN

Most permanent loans are ***nonrecourse*** to the borrower. What this means is that the borrower has no personal liability for the repayment of the permanent loan. The permanent lender's sole remedy for a loan

---

16. The following is a common example of how the construction loan documents might describe the variable rate of interest charged under the construction loan—"the Lender's Prime Rate in effect from time to time, plus 1%, with any change in the rate of interest due to a change in the Prime Rate being effective on the date such change is announced by the Lender."

17. The financial index selected by the construction lender (be it LIBOR, prime or some other index) is not intended to tie exactly to the lender's cost of funds. Rather, the lender's goal is simply to choose an index that will fluctuate in a manner which is roughly predictive of future fluctuations in the lender's cost of funds.

18. One percent is frequently referred to in the lending industry as a "point" or "100 basis points."

default is to foreclose on its mortgage and take over ownership and operation of the underlying real estate project. The permanent lender is in a position to grant this concession to its borrower because the project which serves as collateral for the loan presumably has a predictable stream of income that the lender can look to as a reliable source for the loan's repayment.[19]

The construction loan borrower is seldom in a position to demand (or even reasonably request) the inclusion in the construction loan of a nonrecourse provision. Indeed, the norm is for the construction loan to be fully recourse to both the named borrower[20] and to some other creditworthy entity under a personal guaranty. The reason behind the construction lender's insistence that its loan be fully recourse is quite simple—the construction lender's collateral is an amorphous, "to be created" asset that is producing no current revenue and, hence, has no existing value. The requirement that somebody with a relatively deep pocket be personally liable for the repayment of the construction loan is one way for the construction lender to hedge its bet on the ultimate successful completion and lease-up of the development project.

I. VALUE OF FORECLOSURE REMEDY

Both construction and permanent lenders reserve the right to foreclose on the borrower's mortgage if the borrower defaults under the loan. The value of that foreclosure remedy is, however, markedly different for the construction lender versus the permanent lender.

When the permanent lender successfully forecloses on its permanent loan mortgage, it inherits full control and ownership of a completed project, which, presumably, has an existing income stream (although maybe not at the level which was present when the loan was initially made). What does the construction lender get when it forecloses on its construction loan mortgage? The answer to that question is "not much." A partially constructed development project has little, if any, existing value and is frequently worth less than the principal amount of the construction loan. The only thing that the construction lender gains from foreclosing on its mortgage is the right to complete construction of the project and then try to lease it to rent-paying tenants—a right which is more in the nature of a daunting challenge than it is any positive, current benefit to the construction lender. It is for this reason that the typical construction loan is not only secured by a mortgage on the underlying real estate, but also further secured by a personal guaranty posted by a creditworthy affiliate of the borrower.

---

19. *See infra* Chapter 12, Pages 554–556, for a more focused discussion of the nonrecourse provisions of a permanent loan.

20. The entity which owns the real estate project (and, hence, the entity which must serve as the borrower on the construction loan) is frequently a newly-formed entity whose only asset is the real estate project that is being developed with the use of the proceeds of the construction loan. *See infra* Page 377, for a discussion of the use of single purpose entities in construction loan transactions.

J. FUNDING OF DEBT SERVICE PAYMENTS

As is the case with residential mortgage loans, permanent loans require the borrower to make monthly principal and interest payments in an amount designed to pay off the loan at maturity.[21] The permanent loan borrower uses the net operating income generated by its commercial real estate project to fund these debt service payments.

A construction loan project does not have any net operating income that the borrower can use to fund the debt service payments owed on the construction loan. In recognition of this fact, debt service payable under a construction loan is traditionally "interest only"—meaning that the borrower is not required to make any payments of principal during the term of the construction loan. But if the development project is not producing any income stream whatsoever (which is usually the case during at least the first 12 months or so of the construction loan term), where does the borrower get the funds to make its interest payments? The answer is quite simple—it borrows them from the construction lender. As a result, most construction loan budgets contain a line item expense for the payment of the borrower's construction period interest. The fact that the borrower typically pays its interest carry with borrowed funds is further underscored by a provision routinely included in construction loan documents that expressly grants the construction lender the right to make payments to its own account to pay the borrower's construction interest.[22]

III. BUSINESS OBJECTIVES OF LENDER AND BORROWER

The following is a summary of the business objectives of the lender and the borrower during the construction financing stage of the development process.

A. BORROWER/DEVELOPER

The following are the four main business objectives of the developer/borrower[23] during Stage 5.

- ● *Cheap Debt*—The developer wants the cost of its construction debt to be as cheap as possible. In the simplest of terms, the developer

---

21. Most permanent loans provide for a final "balloon" or "bullet" payment to be made at the maturity of the loan, with that final payment being significantly greater than the installment of principal and interest payable during each month of the permanent loan term. An oversized final payment is required because the periodic principal and interest payments due under a construction loan are typically computed based on a 15–30 year amortization schedule, while the term of the permanent loan is usually only five to ten years.

22. *See, e.g.,* §6.1(f) of the Form Construction Loan Agreement contained in the Document Appendix as Document #5.

23. The terms "borrower" and "developer" are frequently used interchangeably in this Chapter. The one exception to that rule is where specific reference is made to the "borrower" being a newly-formed affiliate of the developer that is created solely for the purpose of serving as the nominal borrower under the construction loan.

wants the interest rate and any loan fees or other costs payable by the developer under the construction loan to be as low as possible. All other things being equal, a construction loan which bears interest at 1 point over LIBOR is obviously more advantageous to the borrower than a construction loan which bears interest at 2 points over LIBOR. On a $10 million construction loan having a term of two years and a construction period of one year, such a one percentage point interest rate differential should save the borrower somewhere in the vicinity of $150,000.[24]

- ***Ready Access to Loan Disbursements***—The developer wants to be able to draw down on the construction loan when and as needed to pay its bills. It does not want the construction loan documents to present any obstacles or impediments to its ability to promptly receive disbursements of loan proceeds in the exact amount required to pay its contractors, consultants and itself.[25]

- ***Preferential Use of Debt***—The developer will strive to fund as many of its development costs as possible (including soft costs and fees payable to the developer) with debt and defer the use of its equity contributions until as late in the process as possible. Because the relative return required by equity investors (including a self-funding developer) is typically higher than the cost of the construction debt, the use of debt dollars on a "first in" basis effectively reduces the developer's overall project costs and leaves more profit to be divided among the developer and its equity investors.[26]

- ***Limitation of Personal Liability***—The developer wants to try to limit its personal liability on the construction loan. In this respect, it is the developer's goal to make the construction loan more a real estate loan than a personal loan.

The developer is not always in a position to perfectly achieve all of these objectives. Counsel to the developer must nonetheless be fully cognizant of the developer's business objectives as he seeks to massage the construction loan documents to achieve those objectives to the maximum extent possible.

---

24. The precise amount of the cost savings achieved by the lower interest rate will depend upon both the timing and magnitude of the loan disbursements made during the term of the construction loan. A loan which is 80% funded during the first six months of the loan term will have a significantly higher interest carry expense than will a loan which is only 40% funded during that same six month period. For this purpose, a loan which is "80% funded" means that the construction lender has made loan disbursements to the borrower in an amount equal to 80% of the maximum principal amount of the construction loan.

25. The reference to payments "to itself" specifically includes disbursements of loan proceeds to pay the developer its development fee and the unrealized profit on the land it contributes to the venture. The competing perspectives of the borrower and the lender on the wisdom of using loan proceeds to pay the development fee and land profit is examined in some detail later on in this Chapter. *See infra* Pages 364–367.

26. *See supra* Chapter 7, Pages 225–226.

B. CONSTRUCTION LENDER

The construction lender has one fundamental business objective—to maximize the positive *spread* between its cost of funds and the payments it receives from the borrower. It is this spread that represents the construction lender's profit on the transaction. The construction lender makes money when it receives a deposit from a customer to purchase a CD earning 3% and then turns around and makes a construction loan to one of its developer customers at an interest rate of 8%.

A bank's profit on a construction loan transaction is dependent not only on the rate at which it prices the construction loan (which is obviously always higher than its cost of funds), but just as importantly on the construction loan being paid off in its entirety at maturity. It doesn't take a mathematical genius to figure out that a construction loan with a wonderful, theoretical spread of 5% will not produce a profit to the lender if the borrower cannot repay the loan on maturity and the lender ends up having to sell the loan at 60 cents on the dollar.[27]

C. SHARED BUSINESS OBJECTIVES

There is a natural tension between the business objectives of the construction lender and the borrower. The remainder of this Chapter will be devoted to an analysis of those strategies and techniques which are available to the parties to try to bridge the gap between their competing business objectives. One important consideration to keep in mind is that the construction lender and the borrower share one very important business objective—achieving the completion of the development project in accordance with the developer's initial projections and leasing plan. One prominent Texas practitioner underscores this point in a very interesting and telling fashion by noting that "the construction lender's lawyer should always remember the admonition of the typical developer/borrower that once the lender has advanced the first million dollars the construction lender and the borrower are partners."[28]

HIBC Case Study—The Tale of Two Construction Loans[29]

The HIBC project will provide the factual context for the discussion of construction financing throughout the remainder of this Chapter. In 1996, The Pizzuti organization was committed to increasing the velocity of office

---

27. While this result seems both rudimentary and obvious, it is a point that the best and the brightest on Wall Street apparently failed to recognize in the ten year stretch from 1998–2008 when the subprime/CMBS crisis almost gutted the global economy. *See infra Practice Tip 9–3: The Credit Crisis of 2008 (and Beyond).*

28. *See* Phillip D. Weller, *Fundamentals of Construction Lending*, in ALI–ABA Course of Study Materials, Modern Real Estate Transactions: Practical Strategies for Real Estate Acquisition, Disposition, and Ownership, Course No. SS–012, 1470, 1478 (July 2010).

29. Some of the specific facts associated with the development and financing of the HTE and 500 projects have been "massaged" to better serve the educational directives of this Chapter. However, the overall substance of the negotiations between Pizzuti and its construction lender is

development in its HIBC office park located in Orlando, Florida. As mentioned in Chapter 4, Pizzuti acquired the 350 acre HIBC tract in 1994 and successfully built and leased two office buildings in 1995 to solid credit tenants—Cincinnati Bell Information Services and Veritas Software. Pizzuti y believed that there was a tremendous pent-up demand for office space in the north Orlando submarket and that its HIBC project was ideally positioned to soak up that demand.

In early 1996, Pizzuti commissioned its architects to begin the design of two new HIBC office buildings, each of which would contain approximately 75,000 square feet of rentable space. At the same time, Pizzuti began an intense marketing blitz to identify and secure office tenants for the two proposed buildings. Pizzuti's marketing efforts turned up a number of tenant prospects, the hottest of which was HTE, Inc., a software development firm that was interested in leasing somewhere around 70–90,000 square feet of space in the north Orlando submarket.[30] HTE's targeted occupancy date was March 1, 1997. While HTE's business seemed to be booming, its balance sheet wasn't—its net worth was just barely into eight figures.

In addition to HTE, Pizzuti's leasing agents turned up a long list of other tenants who had expressed an interest in relocating their businesses to HIBC. A consistent refrain heard from those prospective tenants was that, while they were definitely intrigued by the possibility of moving to HIBC, they wouldn't view the alternative as being "real," unless and until they saw a new HIBC building under construction. None of the prospective tenants (other than HTE) was willing to enter into lease negotiations based on artist renderings and Pizzuti's other projections of what its new office buildings would look like.

Based on that feedback from its leasing agents, Pizzuti took the following steps—

- *It immediately instructed its architects and leasing agents to work directly with HTE to come up with a design and ten-year lease structure for a building to be 100% occupied by HTE. The building ultimately designed for HTE contained approximately 87,000 square feet of rentable space.*

- *It also announced that it would immediately begin construction of a 75,000 square foot "spec"[31] office building to be known as the "500 Building." The "spec building" parlance meant that Pizzuti was committed to beginning construction of the 500 Building even though it had not secured leasing commitments from any tenants.*

Pizzuti's next task was to try to identify banks who might be interested in providing construction financing for both the 500 Building and the HTE

---

reported as accurately as possible given the almost 13 year passage of time and my feeble memory.

30. HTE, Inc. was acquired by SunGard Data Systems, Inc. in 2003.

31. "Spec" is short for "speculative" and connotes the fact that the developer is willing to "speculate" that it will be able to secure rent-paying tenants for its project.

project. Pizzuti knew that this would be a bit of a challenge because the country (and the Orlando office market in particular) was just beginning to emerge from the real estate recession of the early 1990's,[32] and most commercial banks were extremely hesitant to re-enter the construction lending fray. Nonetheless, Pizzuti persevered and identified two lenders who expressed a preliminary interest in providing construction loans for both buildings—Barnett Bank[33] and First Union National Bank.[34] Pizzuti immediately submitted the following construction loan proposals to both Barnett and First Union.

PROPOSED LOAN TERMS	*HTE BUILDING*	*500 BUILDING*
Loan Amount	*$9,000,000 (90% of cost)*[35]	*$8,000,000 (80% of cost)*
Loan Term	*24 months with one 12 month extension option*	*36 months with one 24 month extension option*
Interest Rate	*Interest only payments at LIBOR[36] plus 1%*	*Interest only payments at LIBOR plus 1.5%*
Commitment Fee	*Waived*	*1%*
Equity	*$1 million of back-end equity*	*$2 million of front-end equity*
Credit Enhancement	*Completion and payment guaranties from affiliates of borrower*	*Completion and payment guaranties from affiliates of borrower*
Projected Date of Completion of Construction	*12 months after loan closing*	*12 months after loan closing*

The substance of Pizzuti's construction loan negotiations with Barnett and First Union will be addressed later in this Chapter as part of the examination of the various risk mitigation techniques commonly used by construction lenders to advance and protect their business objectives. Until then, I will just give the reader the main story lines (HTE's less than stellar credit and the whole "spec building thing") and the ultimate punch line (First Union made construction loans on both the HTE and 500

---

32. Unlike the 2008 financial crisis, the early 1990's real estate downturn was directly attributable to a huge overbuilding in all sectors of the real estate industry—especially the office sector. The result of the overbuilding in the late 1980's was that office vacancy rates rose to a national average of more than 18% in 1991 and construction of new office space came to a total halt during the period from 1992 through 1994. The construction of new office space fell 93.8% from a high of almost 120 million square feet in 1989 to a low of 7.4 million square feet in 1994. *See* ANTHONY DOWNS, REAL ESTATE AND THE FINANCIAL CRISIS: HOW TURMOIL IN THE CAPITAL MARKETS IS RESTRUCTURING REAL ESTATE 76–77 (Urban Land Institute 2009).

33. In 1996, Barnett Bank was considered the dominant real estate lender in Orlando. Barnett was acquired by NationsBank in 1997, with Nations Bank being merged into Bank of America one year later.

34. First Union National Bank was headquartered in Charlotte and was anxious to expand its market share in Orlando. First Union was merged into Wachovia Corp. in 2001. Wachovia was sold to Wells Fargo in a garage sale in the worst days of the 2008 financial crisis.

35. The projected cost of each building was $10 million. Due to its higher-end finishes, the per square foot cost of the 500 Building was, however, $18 more than that of the HTE building ($133 psf vs. $115 psf).

36. he requested use of LIBOR as a financial index was something quite new in 1996 for a secondary market such as Orlando. While later loans between Pizzuti and First Union used LIBOR, the loans made by First Union on the HTE and 500 Building projects used the more traditional "prime rate" benchmark for the setting of the borrower's floating interest rate.

Buildings, as well as six other office buildings ultimately developed by Pizzuti at HIBC).

IV. DOCUMENTING THE CONSTRUCTION LOAN

Before launching into a discussion of the unique risks attendant to the making of a construction loan, it first makes sense to set the platform for that discussion by talking about the documents used to paper a construction loan. The general categories of loan documents and the constituent components of those document categories are set forth below.

A. COMMITMENT LETTER

The ***commitment letter*** serves a purpose comparable to that served by the letter of intent in the land acquisition stage of the development process. It sets forth the principal terms on which the construction loan will be made and creates the platform for counsel's later drafting and negotiation of the loan documents that will be executed by the borrower and the lender at the closing of the construction loan. In most situations, the commitment letter is executed somewhere between 20 to 180 days in advance of the construction loan closing.

The commitment letter prepared by lender's counsel customarily addresses the following topics:[37]

- ***Loan amount*** (including any overriding limitations on the loan amount based on lender-imposed requirements such as loan-to-value and loan-to-cost ratios, debt service coverage tests, etc.);

- ***Loan term*** (including the length of the initial term and the conditions to the exercise of any extension options);

- ***Interest rate*** (including a description of the financial index on which the rate will be calculated and a provision addressing the manner in which adjustments will be made to the floating rate);

- ***Payment obligations*** (including the due dates for all of the borrower's payment obligations and whether the loan will be interest only (the norm) or require some principal amortization (usually only applicable during an extension of the construction loan term));

- ***Equity requirements*** (including both the amount of the borrower's required equity contributions and when those contributions must be made—i.e., before or after the lender's disbursement of the proceeds of the construction loan);

---

37. For an overview of the content of construction loan commitment letters, *see* Patricia J. Frobes, *Construction Loan Commitment Letters*, in ALI–ABA COURSE OF STUDY MATERIALS, REAL ESTATE FINANCING DOCUMENTATION: STRATEGIES FOR CHANGING TIMES, Course No. SM–008, 155 (January 2007).

- *Fees and reimbursable costs* (including the amount of any origination, commitment or loan processing fees and the identification of all costs to be paid/reimbursed by borrower—e.g., the lender's legal fees, title insurance premiums, survey costs, environmental charges, etc.);

- *Guaranties* (including the general terms of any completion or payment guaranties and the identity of the guarantor);

- *Conditions to closing and loan funding* (including any pre-leasing standard and a listing of all required closing deliverables, such as soils tests, title policy, survey, environmental assessment, construction and design contracts, insurance policies, etc.);

- *Loan disbursement procedures* (including the timing of the disbursements, the documentation that must be submitted in support of any requested disbursement and the approval process applicable to each submitted draw request);

- *Identification of collateral* (including a first mortgage, conditional assignment of leases, collateral assignment of construction and design contracts, payment and performance bonds, letters of credit, etc.); and

- *Closing date and procedures* (including the outside date for the loan closing and a listing of all those documents that must be executed and delivered at closing).

The commitment letter is usually signed by both the lender and the borrower.[38] However, as is the case with the land purchase letter of intent, the commitment may or may not be binding on the parties. Even if the lender and the borrower evidence their agreement to be bound by the specific provisions of the commitment letter, both sides to the transaction (particularly the lender) regularly seek to reserve a high level of discretion to back out of the deal based on a change in market conditions or other events outside of the skin of the commitment letter—e.g., the disapproval of the deal by the lender's loan committee or the borrower's receipt of a more competitive loan offer from another construction lender. The construction lender will invariably seek to impose an obligation on the borrower to pay the lender's fees and costs, even if the loan does not close for a reason expressly sanctioned in the body of the commitment letter.[39]

B. EVIDENCE OF INDEBTEDNESS

The borrower's obligation to repay the principal and interest due under the construction loan is evidenced by the borrower's execution of a

---

38. On occasion, the commitment letter will not be signed by the parties, but rather will serve in the nature of an unsigned term sheet. In those situations, the borrower and the lender will adopt a "let's just go to the loan documents" attitude and dispense with the formality of executing a detailed commitment letter.

39. *See* Susan G. Talley, *Selected Issues in Construction Lending*, in ALI–ABA COURSE OF STUDY MATERIALS, COMMERCIAL REAL ESTATE FINANCING: STRATEGIES FOR CHANGING MARKETS AND UNCERTAIN TIMES, Course No. SP–008, 125, 128 (January 2009).

promissory note. The ***promissory note*** is the document that sets forth the maximum loan amount, the maturity date of the loan, the borrower's interest rate and the amount and timing of the periodic debt service payments due under the construction loan.

C. COLLATERAL DOCUMENTS

The primary collateral document used in both conventional permanent loans and construction loans is a mortgage,[40] pursuant to which the borrower grants the lender a first priority lien on the borrower's real estate project. Other collateral documents frequently used to secure the borrower's obligations under a construction loan are:

- ***An assignment of leases***, whereby the borrower assigns to the construction lender the right to receive rents and otherwise enforce the performance of the tenants under all project leases;

- ***A collateral assignment of all construction and design contracts***, which authorizes the lender to take over the borrower's position under these contracts and complete the project in the event of a default by the borrower;

- ***UCC financing statements***, which, when filed in the required state and local offices, will perfect the lender's security interest in any fixtures and personal property associated with the project;[41]

- ***A completion guaranty***, pursuant to which a creditworthy entity affiliated with the borrower agrees to do whatever is necessary to complete the project in accordance with the agreed-upon plans and specifications and construction schedule; and

- ***A payment guaranty***, pursuant to which a creditworthy entity affiliated with the borrower agrees to guaranty the borrower's payment obligations under the construction loan documents.

D. CONSTRUCTION LOAN AGREEMENT

The ***construction loan agreement*** is the document that sets the construction loan apart from conventional permanent loan. As will be discussed in great detail in the ensuing sections of this Chapter, the construction lender faces a series of unique risks when it makes a construction loan—many of which revolve around the earlier-discussed phenomenon that the loan proceeds disbursed under the construction loan are used to CREATE the value of the lender's loan collateral.

---

40. In some jurisdictions, the mortgage may be called a "deed of trust." A discussion of the operation and provisions of a mortgage/deed of trust are beyond the scope of this Chapter on construction financing. For those interested in doing further reading on the mortgage financing topic, *see* Robert A. Thompson and Brian D. Smith, *Negotiating Loan Transactions*, in Commercial Real Estate Transactions Handbook § 9.03[C] (Mark A. Senn ed., 4th ed. 2009) and BENDER, *supra* note 7, at 93–130.

41. The actual grant of the security interest that is perfected by the filing of the UCC financing statements is typically contained in the mortgage/deed of trust.

One practicing lawyer described the challenges faced by counsel for the borrower and the lender in drafting and negotiating the construction loan documents in the following way:

> Construction loans are one of the most difficult kinds of loan for a lender and a borrower to negotiate, document and carry out to conclusion. There are many reasons for this phenomenon. Construction projects are subject to change, delays, cost overruns and unanticipated events. The construction loan documentation must be structured so as to anticipate the unforeseen.[42]

A sample construction loan agreement is contained in the Documents Appendix as Document #5. The various provisions of the construction loan agreement will be the dominant focus of the rest of this Chapter.

V.   UNIQUE RISKS FACED BY THE CONSTRUCTION LENDER

The construction lender must confront and navigate its way through a series of risks that are not presented in the context of a conventional permanent loan. These unique risks are all driven by two fundamental considerations—(1) the construction lender is forced to conduct its loan underwriting on the basis of the developer's projections of what the project is going to look like and how it will perform financially (and not based on an inspection of an existing real estate asset or an analysis of in-place leases and other historical, financial data) and (2) the proceeds of the construction loan will be used to create the value of the collateral for that loan.

The following are five unique risks faced by the construction lender:

- The project is not completed on time;
- The actual completed cost of the project is greater than its budgeted cost;
- The actual value of the completed project is less than its projected value;
- The borrower uses the construction loan proceeds for a purpose other than the completion of the project; and
- A lien filed by a third party after the date of the loan closing gains priority over the construction lender's mortgage.

The possible causes and consequences of each of these risk scenarios are discussed below.

A.   COMPLETION RISK

The nature and consequences of the completion risk faced by the construction lender are best illustrated by reference to the two HIBC

---

42. *See* Talley, *supra* note 39, at 127.

development projects that are serving as the case study for this Chapter—the 500 and HTE projects. Both of those projects were projected to cost $10 million and to be completed within 12 months. The following are examples of how completion risk might play out in the context of these two projects.

- *Non-completion Risk*—Construction of the 500 Building is permanently halted six months into the construction period after the borrower has taken down $4 million in loan proceeds (40% of the overall projected costs of the 500 project).

- *Late Completion Risk*—Construction of the HTE project is completed nine months later than anticipated (and six months after the date of HTE's scheduled occupancy of the building).

The onset of these completion risks can be triggered by any number of events and circumstances, including those described below.

- *Execution Risk*–This is the risk that the developer fails to execute on its construction schedule for some reason, including—

  - An overly optimistic, construction schedule (frequently triggered by the developer's motivation to meet a completion deadline established by a third party—e.g., HTE's targeted occupancy date);

  - The general contractor's incompetency;

  - The developer's failure to timely secure all essential governmental permits and approvals (e.g., a rezoning of the site or the issuance of a building permit to begin work on the project); or

  - The developer's failure to conduct all appropriate site due diligence, with the end result that adverse environmental, soils or other site-related conditions present insurmountable obstacles to the developer's completion of the project in accordance with its construction schedule.

- *Financial Risk*—This is the risk that the developer runs out of money and cannot fund its required equity contributions. The financial position of a well-heeled developer can quickly deteriorate after the construction loan closing for any number of reasons, including: a sudden drop in the stock market; a severe loss suffered by the developer on another real estate project; a falling out between the developer and one of its principal equity investors; or a drunken (and unlucky) weekend in Las Vegas. Regardless of the reason for the developer's financial straits, the bottom line is that construction of the project cannot go forward if the developer doesn't have the funds to pay its share of the project's development costs.

- *Unforeseen Risk*—This is the risk that lawyers are referring to when they use the fancy legal term force majeure—i.e., the risk of the occurrence of an event which is beyond the developer's anticipation or control, but which nonetheless delays or prevents the construction of the developer's project. Examples of typical force majeure events are a fire, hurricane, strike, arson or embargo.

So what are the consequences of the occurrence of the above risks? That question can be answer by reflecting once again on the two HIBC case studies introduced at the beginning of this section.

- *Non-completion of 500 Building*—In this scenario, the value of the collateral for the construction lender's loan is never created because construction of the building is never finished. The value of a half-finished building is almost always less than its cost. As a result, what the construction lender hoped would be a real estate loan supported by valuable collateral turns into a personal loan where the construction lender's only viable alternative is a legal action against the borrower/guarantor under the loan.

- *Late Completion of HTE Building*—At first blush, it would seem that the construction lender is in a much better position on its HTE loan than on the 500 Building loan. After all, the lender has a first mortgage on a finished office building in a first-class business park. But is there any true value to that finished office building? What if the developer's lease with HTE includes a clause permitting HTE to terminate its lease if the building is not completed by its targeted occupancy date? From a construction lender's perspective, there are few things worse than being left with a mortgage on a single tenant building that doesn't have a tenant. This is especially true where the building's design has been tailored to meet the particular needs and eccentricities of the putative tenant and, hence, is not usable by other prospective tenants, unless the lender is willing to incur the additional costs needed to retrofit the building.[43]

B. RISK OF COST OVERRUNS

What if the cost of completing construction of the 500 Building ends up being $12 million (instead of the projected $10 million)? The specter of project cost overruns is not only the most common risk faced by a construction lender, but also one of the most significant.

A cost overrun on a development project can be attributable to the occurrence of both foreseeable and unforeseeable events. The following are common examples of events that can trigger a project cost overrun:

- An incomplete listing in the developer's project budget of those development costs that must be incurred to complete construction of the project;

---

43. The HTE building serves as an excellent example of a single-tenant building that is not readily usable by other users. The design of the HTE building included a three-story atrium, an employee cafeteria and some very strangely-configured conference rooms (laid out in a fashion intended to accommodate the unique operational needs of a computer software company). The cost of renovating the building to suit the needs of a larger class of potential space users would have been substantial (well into seven figures).

- An inaccurate construction cost estimate provided by the developer's general contractor;

- A change in the nature or scope of the construction project (commonly referred to as a ***change order***);[44]

- The occurrence of a force majeure event (see the earlier discussion of force majeure events under the Completion Risk subheading); or

- Higher than anticipated interest carry costs.[45]

From the construction lender's perspective, the existence of a cost overrun is not overly consequential if the developer steps up and funds the excess costs out of its own pocket. But what happens if the developer is either unable or unwilling to pay the amount of the project cost overruns? Under that scenario, the construction lender is faced with two relatively bad choices:

- It can refuse to provide the additional loan dollars needed to fund the cost overruns, in which event construction of the project will likely never be completed (thereby converting a cost overrun risk into the non-completion risk mentioned under the prior heading of this section); or

- It can agree to provide the additional loan dollars to fund the cost overruns, in which event the lender's "cushion" between the amount of the construction loan and the ultimate value of the completed project will be significantly reduced.[46]

Regardless which course of action the lender opts to pursue to deal with a cost overrun, the impact on the net value of its collateral under the construction loan will be the same—the net value of its collateral position will go down.

C. RISK OF INSUFFICIENT PROJECT VALUE

For the purposes of looking at the next risk faced by a construction lender, assume that construction of the 500 Building is completed on-time and on-budget (meaning that the construction lender has successfully managed to avoid both the completion and cost overrun risks). But what happens if the fair market value of the completed 500 Building project (originally projected by the developer to be $12 million) turns out to be $9 million—or $1 million less than the cost of constructing the 500 Building?

---

44. A change order is usually initiated either due to (a) the developer's perception that a change is necessary to respond to an evolving market condition (e.g., a perceived need for an office building to have an on-site fitness center) or (b) a prospective tenant's operational needs (e.g., a tenant's decision that it needs a separate, computer server room).

45. An unbudgeted increase in the developer's construction loan interest costs can result from either (a) an increase in the financial index specified in the construction loan documents (e.g., LIBOR, prime rate, etc.), (b) a longer than anticipated lease-up period (which would have the effect of decreasing the revenue stream that would otherwise be used to pay the construction loan interest) or (c) the developer's front-loading of its development costs (which would increase the daily average of the outstanding principal balance during the construction loan term and, hence, the amount of the borrower's overall interest expense).

46. For a discussion of the lender's "cushion," *see infra* Pages 387–388.

The following are some of the more common causes that can trigger such a marked decline in a building's value upon completion.

- A failure of the project to lease up in accordance with the developer's initial projections (e.g., a lease-up that is slower than projected or at lower rental rates than projected);

- A change in general market conditions (e.g., the advent of an across-the-board reduction in the pricing of commercial real estate due to a credit crunch of the type experienced in the U.S. during 2008); or

- The occurrence of an event that adversely affects the position of the building in the marketplace (e.g., the construction of a newer, bigger and better office building two blocks down the road from the project being financed under the construction loan).

A decline in the actual versus projected value of a commercial real estate project may effectively eliminate the construction lender's exit strategy for its construction loan.[47]

The 500 Building case study can be used to illustrate how a decline in the actual value of a completed project can eviscerate the construction lender's hope for an exit under its construction loan. First, assume that the loan-to-value ratio[48] prevailing in the permanent loan market as of the date the construction lender committed to make a construction loan on the 500 Building is 66%—meaning that a permanent lender would be willing to make an $8 million permanent loan on the 500 Building (an amount which would be sufficient to fully retire the construction loan), if the value of the 500 Building at completion is at least $12 million. If, as assumed in the prior hypothetical, the value of the completed 500 Building is only $9 million, the permanent loan market would only support a loan on that building of $6 million—the $9 million value multiplied by the loan-to-value ratio of 66%. That state of affairs leaves a noticeable gap of $2 million between the outstanding principal balance of the construction loan ($8 million) and the maximum principal amount that could be obtained under a permanent loan ($6 million)—a gap which largely takes away the refinancing exit strategy customarily afforded the construction lender by the permanent loan market.

The decision tree created by the above fact situation is as follows:

- If the developer has a deep pocket, it can refinance the construction loan with a $6 million permanent loan and pay off the remaining $2

---

47. As will be discussed later in this Chapter (*see infra* Page 376), the typical sources for the repayment of a construction loan (the lender's "exit strategies") are either (a) the outright sale of the project to a third party buyer or (b) the refinancing of the construction loan with a conventional permanent loan. A marked decline in the completed value of a project will call into question the efficacy of both of these exit strategies.

48. A loan-to-value ratio is a mechanism used by lenders to set the maximum amount of a commercial real estate loan at a specified percentage of the value of the project that serves as collateral for the repayment of the loan. *See infra* Pages 387–388, for a discussion of the way in which a construction lender uses a loan-to-value ratio to mitigate its risk that the value of the project at completion will be less than that initially projected by the developer.

million balance with its separate, personal funds (something that would make the construction lender happy, but would certainly not please the developer); or

- If the developer doesn't have a deep pocket, it could either—
  - Try to sell the project for a price sufficient to pay off the $8 million construction loan;[49] or
  - If it can't sell the project for at least $8 million, ask the construction lender to either—
    - Extend the maturity of the construction loan to give the developer time to increase the project's value, or
    - Take up to a $2 million loss on the construction loan.

It is this last branch of the decision tree that the construction lender wants to avoid at all costs.

D. RISK OF MISAPPLICATION OF FUNDS

The next construction loan risk can be illustrated by assuming that the construction lender fully disburses the $9 million loan amount under the HTE construction loan only to subsequently find out that the developer applied a mere $6 million of the loan proceeds to the payment of development costs on the HTE project. The first question that comes to mind is how could that possibly happen?

The answer to that question lies in the manner in which the principal amount of a construction loan is disbursed to the borrower. Under a conventional permanent loan, the lender customarily disburses 100% of the loan amount at closing. The permanent lender pays the portion of the permanent loan that is required to pay off any existing mortgage loans directly to the holders of those loans, with the remaining proceeds then being deposited to the borrower's account. By making a lump sum payment directly to the account of the existing lien holders, the permanent lender can controls its risk that the borrower absconds with the funds and fails to pay off the existing project loans (which is the permanent lender's only real concern about the borrower's use of the proceeds of the permanent loan).

Unlike a conventional permanent loan, the principal amount of a construction loan is disbursed incrementally over a period of many months. As a result, the construction lender is not in a position to protect itself against the risk of a misapplication of funds by simply dictating on a one-time only basis that the loan proceeds will be disbursed in a lump sum to a party or parties designated by the lender.

What would cause a developer to misuse the loan proceeds in the manner described above? The simplest answer to that question is the three-headed monster of avarice, greed and evil. In other words, the

---

49. *See supra* Chapter 2, Page 32, and *infra* Chapter 12, Pages 550–553, for an examination of the reasons why a developer might not want to sell the project at completion.

developer sees the construction loan process as a convenient way to feed its gambling, drug or sex addictions.

A more common cause of a developer's misappropriation of construction loan proceeds is not evil, but desperation. Real estate development is a very capital-intensive business and one where cash flow is quite unpredictable. Absent any restrictions on its conduct, a developer might be tempted to take construction loan proceeds from one project to try to stem a cash flow problem it is experiencing on another project. The well-intentioned developer would, of course, fully expect to repatriate the proceeds to the lender's construction project as soon as the developer resolves its temporary cash flow problems on its other project.

So what happens to the construction lender if the developer's temporary cash flow problems become permanent? In that situation, the proceeds of the loan which were intended to be used to create the value of the lender's loan collateral will forever be diverted for another purpose. Ultimately, the developer's misapplication of the construction loan proceeds will leave the construction lender with the exact dilemma it faces when the project experiences a cost overrun—it either provides the additional loan dollars needed to complete the project or it accepts the very real prospect that it will be forced to take a sizable loss on the construction loan transaction.

E.   RISK OF INTERVENING LIENS

The primary source of a construction lender's security for the borrower's repayment of the construction loan is the mortgage that is recorded against the borrower's real estate project. The goal of the construction lender in requiring the execution, delivery and recordation of that mortgage is to establish in its favor a first priority lien on the project that secures the developer's obligation to repay the full amount of the construction loan.

This seemingly simple, clear-cut goal is potentially undercut by the manner in which the loan proceeds are disbursed under a construction loan. As previously discussed, disbursements under a construction loan may be made months and, in some cases, years after the date of the recordation of the construction lender's mortgage. The extended time frame for the making of disbursements under a construction loan gives rise to the possibility that a third party might file a lien against the underlying real estate project AFTER the date of the recordation of the construction lender's mortgage, but BEFORE the date on which the loan proceeds are fully disbursed by the construction lender. The issue that confronts the construction lender is whether the lender's first mortgage position extends to all disbursements made under the construction loan (because the construction loan mortgage was recorded prior to the recording of the third party's lien) or just to those disbursements made prior to the recording of the third party lien.

The import of this issue is best understood by looking at a timeline involving the loan disbursements made pursuant to one of our case study construction loans. Assume that the timeline for the 500 Building construction loan plays out as follows.

- *June 1*—A mortgage securing a construction loan of $8 million is recorded in the real estate records of Seminole County, Florida.

- *June 2 through December 31*—The construction lender makes periodic disbursements of loan proceeds totaling $4 million.

- *January 1*—A third party files a lien against the project for $2 million.

- *January 2 through May 31*—The construction lender disburses the remaining $4 million of loan proceeds to the borrower.

- *August 1*—The third party lien holder forecloses on its lien and the real estate project is sold at a sheriff's sale for $8 million.

Under this hypothetical timeline, who gets the proceeds of the sheriff's sale? Is the construction lender entitled to all $8 million or just $6 million, with the remaining $2 million going to the intervening lien holder? If the third party's lien is given priority over construction loan disbursements made after the January 1 lien filing date, then the construction lender's collateral position under its construction loan will be adversely affected to the tune of $2 million.

Fortunately (at least for the construction lender), many states have statutes on the books that confirm the priority of all advances made under a construction loan over liens that are perfected after the date of the recording of the construction loan mortgage.[50] Those statutes expressly provide that a construction loan mortgage (variously referred to in statutes as **construction, future advance, or open-end mortgages)**[51] will have priority over all subsequently recorded liens to the full extent of all amounts secured by the mortgage, regardless whether the disbursements are made before or after the date of the perfection of the intervening lien.[52] Liens which take on a subordinate position under these state statutes include subsequent mortgages, judgment liens and vendor liens.

There is, however, one type of intervening lien that is afforded special protection under the statutes and case law of many states—the **mechanics' lien.** A mechanics' lien is a right created by statute whereby a person who works on or provides labor or materials to a real estate project can file a lien against that project if such person is not paid in full for his or her efforts.[53] The genesis for the adoption of mechanics' lien statutes was the principle that "those whose work or materials go into an improvement

---

50. *See* NELSON, *supra* note 6, at 1017.

51. *See* Harold E. Leidner, *An Overview of Mechanics' Liens and Future Advance Mortgages*, 3 PRACTICAL REAL ESTATE LAWYER 39, 42 (1987).

52. *See* BENDER, *supra* note 6, at 317; and NELSON, *supra* note 6, at 1017.

53. *See generally* Leidner, *supra* note 51.

to real estate should be permitted, in fairness, to satisfy their unpaid bills out of that real estate."[54]

Mechanics' lien law varies widely from state to state, as to both the content of the statute creating the mechanics' lien and the judicial gloss placed on the statute by local courts. That variance is particularly noteworthy on the primary topic that attracts the construction lender's attention—that is, can a mechanics' lien ever gain priority over a construction mortgage filed of public record before the filing of the mechanics' lien?[55]

Before attempting to answer the construction lender's priority question, a practitioner must first become thoroughly acquainted with the particulars of the mechanics' lien statute of the state where the underlying real estate project is located. The practitioner's first point of inquiry is to determine the date on which the applicable state statute says a mechanics' lien is deemed to have attached to the owner's real estate project. The "attachment date" (referred to in some jurisdictions as the "effective date" or "priority date" of the mechanics' lien) is the date which is used to determine the relative priorities of the mechanics' lien and the construction mortgage. If the mechanics' lien's attachment date pre-dates the date of the recordation of the construction mortgage, the mechanics' lien will be treated as having full priority over the construction mortgage.

Most liens (including construction mortgages) are deemed to have attached as of the date on which the lien is first filed in the real estate records of the county in which the real estate is located.[56] If this rule were to be applied to mechanics' liens, the comparative priority of a mechanics' lien and a construction mortgage would almost always be determined in favor of the construction mortgage (because a mechanics' lien is typically filed months after the recording of the construction mortgage and the start of construction on the mortgaged site). Unfortunately for the construction lender, only a handful of state statutes provide that a mechanics' lien attaches as of the date on which the mechanics' lien is filed of public record.

In a majority of states, the attachment date of a mechanics' lien relates back to the date of the "commencement of work" on the project.[57]

---

54. *See* Nelson, *supra* note 6, at 1007.

55. There are a host of other legal issues related to the validity of a mechanics' lien—for example, who can file a mechanics' lien, when and where the lien must be filed, what form the filing must take, etc. Those issues are beyond the scope of this Chapter, which is very intentionally limited to a discussion of the comparative priorities of a mechanics' lien and construction loan mortgage. For a more detailed discussion of the law of mechanics' liens, *see* George Lefcoe, Real Estate Transactions, Finance, and Development Chapter 26 (6th ed. 2009); and Nelson, *supra* note 6, at 1006–1025.

56. *See* Lefcoe, *supra* note 55, at 258–263.

57. *See id.* at 572. The jurisdictions which do not follow the "visible commencement of work" rule define the effective date for a mechanics lien in a wide variety of ways. Some states take the position that the effective date of a mechanics lien is the date on which the specific mechanic lien claimant first performed work at the site. Other states establish the effective date as the date on which the owner/developer first files a notice of commencement in the public real estate records.

There are two important components to the "commencement of work" test.

- First, the commencement date is the first date that ANYBODY performs any work on the site. It does not refer just to work performed by a particular lien claimant. Therefore, if excavation of the site first began on January 1, 2009, the effective date of a roofer's mechanics lien will be January 1, 2009—even if the roofer didn't perform any work on the project until October 1, 2009.

- Second, state law is far from consistent as what constitutes "commencement of work." A standard commonly used by state courts to determine when work has commenced is that the work must be sufficiently "conspicuous and substantial" to be apparent to all observers that improvements are being constructed on the site. The courts have not, however, been able to articulate with any clarity what specific improvements satisfy that "conspicuous and substantial" standard.[58]

The above rule can wreak havoc on the priority of the construction lender's mortgage. In today's fast-paced development world, many developers routinely start site work on a project before the construction loan is closed and the construction lender's mortgage is recorded. If that work is later found to constitute a "commencement of work" under the applicable state statute, the construction lender may well find itself in a position where the lien of its mortgage is subordinate to all subsequently-filed mechanics liens.

The measures that a construction lender can take to protect itself against a loss of priority for its mortgage in those jurisdictions that follow the "commencement of work" rule will be reviewed at some length later in this Chapter.[59] Suffice it to say at this point that a lender working in those jurisdictions should be extremely hesitant to permit any work to be done on the site before its construction mortgage is recorded.

The construction lender cannot, however, solve all of its mechanics' lien problems simply by recording its construction mortgage prior to the start of any work on the mortgaged property. In many jurisdictions, the courts have extended the construction mortgage loan's priority over subsequently-filed mechanics liens only to an ***obligatory advance*** which the construction lender is contractually required to make under the applicable provisions of the loan documents.[60] If the construction lender is not

---

There are also a handful of jurisdictions which say that the priority date of a mechanics lien is the date on which the lien is first filed in the public real estate records. Finally, in Missouri, construction loans are apparently always deemed to be subordinate to a filed mechanics lien, regardless of when the work was first started or the lien first filed of record. See NELSON, *supra* note 6, at 1010.

58. *See* BENDER, *supra* note 6, at 308; LEFCOE, *supra* note 55, at 572; and David A. Schmudde, *What You Should Know about Construction Financing*, 20 No. 2 PRACTICAL REAL ESTATE LAWYER 51, 55 (September 2004).

59. *See infra* Pages 394–397.

60. *See generally* Leidner, *supra* note 51, at 42; NELSON, *supra* note 6, at 1016–1025; and BENDER, *supra* note 6, at 308–323. Several states have enacted statutes which abolish the

contractually obligated to make a future advance, then any loan advance made by the construction lender after its receipt of notice of the existence of an intervening mechanics lien will be categorized as an *optional advance* and held to be subordinate to the mechanics' lien.[61]

The implication to the construction lender of the optional versus obligatory advance dichotomy is illustrated by referring back to the prior example where the 500 Building construction lender has disbursed $4 million of its construction loan when it receives notice that a subcontractor on the project has filed a $2 million mechanics lien against the underlying real estate. The construction lender is motivated to continue to make loan disbursements under its construction loan because if it fails to do so the project will not be completed—and, as discussed previously, the lender will then face the prospect of suffering a loss on its construction loan due to the meager value attributed to a partially completed development project. However, if the construction lender is not contractually obligated to make the future loan advances, its security for the disbursement of the last $4 million of loan proceeds might be subordinate to the subcontractor's $2 million mechanics lien. If that is the case, the relative priorities of the construction lender and the mechanics lien claimant in the borrower's real estate project will take on the look of what one author has called an "Oreo cookie."[62] The construction lender will have a first priority position in the real property collateral for $4 million (the amount of the loan disbursed before its receipt of notice of the intervening mechanics lien) and a third priority position in that collateral for another $4 million (the amount of the loan disbursed after its receipt of notice of the intervening mechanics lien). Sandwiched between the construction lender's first and third priority positions will be the contractor's second priority position of $2 million—the cream filling between the construction lender's two cookies.

In those jurisdictions that recognize a distinction between obligatory and optional advances, the operative issue for the construction lender becomes when a future is advance obligatory and when is it optional? A resolution of that issue becomes particularly problematic given the fact that most construction loan agreements contain numerous conditions to the construction lender's obligation to disburse proceeds under the loan—for example, the continuing accuracy of certain borrower representations and warranties, the borrower's submission of documentation evidencing its compliance with the approved project budget and the absence of any borrower default under the construction loan documents.[63] Several states

---

obligatory vs. optional advance distinction and make it clear that all disbursements made under a construction loan will have priority over a mechanics' lien, as long as the construction loan mortgage is recorded prior to the attachment date of the mechanics' lien. *See* LEFCOE, *supra* note 55, at 584. THE RESTATEMENT (THIRD) OF PROPERTY (*Mortgages*) § 2.3 (1997) also adopts this approach.

61. States differ on whether the construction lender's notice of the intervening lien must be actual or constructive. *See* NELSON, *supra* note 6, at 1021.

62. *See* NELSON, *supra* note 6, at 1017.

63. *See, e.g.,* §§ 3.2 and 4.1 of the Form Construction Loan Agreement.

have sought to add clarity to that issue by amending their mechanics' lien statutes to specifically sanction certain conditions that will not cause a loan advance to be considered optional.[64] A lawyer representing a construction lender in the remaining states has no choice but to carefully read the applicable case law and then attempt to tailor the provisions of the construction loan agreement to avoid a determination that the lender's construction loan advances are optional.[65]

VI. THE CONSTRUCTION LENDER'S RISK MITIGATION TECHNIQUES

The point has now been repeatedly and emphatically made that a construction lender faces a myriad of unique risks when it makes a construction loan on a commercial real estate project. The remainder of this Chapter will be devoted to an examination of the multitude of ways in which the construction lender can seek to mitigate its exposure to those risks.

In developing its risk mitigation strategy, the construction lender's primary objective is to do that which is necessary to hasten and enhance its profitable exit from the loan. The construction lender's exit strategy is inextricably tied to the willingness of institutional investors to provide the capital necessary to pay off the construction loan either through a purchase of the completed real estate project or a refinancing under a permanent loan or some other secured debt arrangement.[66] The construction lender must, therefore, structure and price its construction loan with

---

64. *See* LEFCOE, *supra* note 55, at 585. By way of example, Ohio's open end mortgage statute contains the following language—"a holder of a mortgage is 'obligated' to make an advance if such holder . . . has a contractual commitment to do so, even though the making of such advance may be conditioned upon the . . . occurrence or existence, or the failure to occur or exist, of any event of fact." *See* OHIO REVISED CODE ANNOTATED § 5301.232(E) (4) (West 2010).

65. *See* Patricia J. Frobes, *Selected Issues in Secured Construction Lending*, in ALI–ABA COURSE OF STUDY MATERIALS, REAL ESTATE FINANCING DOCUMENTATION: STRATEGIES FOR CHANGING TIMES, Course No. SL–007, 123, 126–127 (January 2006); and LEFCOE, supra note 55, at 583–584.

66. In the years leading up to the 2008 credit crunch, Wall Street began providing a new source of capital to fund the construction lender's exit strategy—the securitization of mortgage loans. Securitization essentially involves the purchase by an investment banker of a mortgage loan, which it then includes in a pool of similar loans that are "securitized" into separate debt certificates and sold to the public. Wall Street initially avoided securitizing construction loans, preferring instead to focus on the securitization of residential mortgage loans and conventional permanent loans, which were viewed by investment bankers and credit rating agencies as being less risky and having more homogeneous terms. However, beginning in 2005, certain Wall Street firms started putting together securitized construction loan pools in an effort to further increase the profitability of their securitization business units. The credit crisis of 2008 put an end (at least temporarily) to the securitization business. In one short year, new issues of commercial mortgage-backed securities ("CMBS") dropped 95% (from $230 billion in 2007 to only $12 billion in 2008). As of the date this Chapter is being written (the third quarter of 2010), the CMBS market remains largely moribund. While it is reasonable to assume (and even hope) that the mortgage securitization business will be resuscitated at some point in the future, it is likely that CMBS issues will stay away (at least in the near term) from the risky construction loan market. As a result, the discussion of the securitization of construction loans (which a few years ago would have received several pages of coverage in this Chapter) has now been reduced to this single footnote. *But see infra* Chapter 12, Page ___, for a discussion of the securitization of permanent loans.

an eye toward the needs and desires of the institutional investor community. Moreover, if the project is going to attract the interest of institutional investors, the construction lender must do everything within its limited powers to insure that (1) the project is completed within the time and cost parameters set forth in the developer's initial development projections, (2) the project is completed lien-free and in accordance with the approved plans and specifications and (3) the completed project has a value consistent with the value assigned to the project as part of the construction lender's original underwriting of its construction loan.

The discussion that follows will separately examine the lender's attempt to protect itself from each of the five categories of loan risk mentioned in the previous section of this Chapter. The template for that discussion will include—(a) a description of the techniques available to the lender to deal with the cited risk, (b) a cross-reference to the section of the Form Construction Loan Agreement that seeks to implement the discussed technique,[67] (c) typical borrower "pushbacks"[68] to the lender's proposed use of each such technique and (d) a brief overview of the way in which each of the noted risks was handled in the context of the two HIBC construction loans that are the subject of the case study being utilized throughout this Chapter.

A. DEALING WITH COMPLETION RISK

The construction lender has a host of ways in which it can seek to insulate itself from the risk that the real estate project is not completed—either at all or not on time. The range of the lender's risk mitigation methods is described below.

1. Project Due Diligence. *(§§2.2 and 3.2)*

The first thing that a construction lender must do to protect itself against completion risk is to undertake a thorough due diligence of the developer's proposed project. The purpose of the lender's due diligence is to validate both the general feasibility of the proposed project (i.e., can it be built) and the specific construction schedule proffered by the developer in its loan request (i.e., can it be completed on time).

The construction lender's due diligence efforts can be separated into two distinct undertakings. First the construction lender typically retains its own consultant (an architect or engineer) to conduct an independent

---

67. The Form Construction Loan Agreement is a plain vanilla agreement that, very intentionally, is neither tremendously pro-lender nor pro-developer. As such, the Form Construction Loan Agreement does not contain provisions on every risk mitigation technique discussed in this Chapter.

68. A "pushback" is industry jargon to describe one party's response to a proposal made by the other party to a negotiation. I have opted to use the slang term in this Chapter because it is wonderfully descriptive of what actually occurs during the course of a negotiation—where one party pushes and the other party "pushes back." MSN Encarta's definition of "pushback" is "opposition or resistance to something such as an initiative, plan or strategy." *See* MSN ENCARTA DICTIONARY (2010), http://encarta.msn.com/.dictionary.

review of the borrower's plans and specifications and construction schedule. The consultant's job is to answer the following questions.

- Has the developer missed anything that would prevent the project from being completed within the projected time period—e.g., an unscheduled requirement that a water line be extended to the project's boundaries from an off-site location?

- Is the developer's proposed construction schedule reasonable—e.g., does it permit sufficient time to complete all of the required construction tasks before the onset of winter weather conditions?

The construction lender will seek to further protect itself from completion risk by inserting in its commitment letter a requirement that, as a condition to lender's obligation to close the construction loan, the borrower must furnish the lender with a variety of third party certifications and approvals concerning the suitability and readiness of the project site for development.[69] The following are some examples of certifications and approvals customarily required by a construction lender:[70]

- A title insurance commitment confirming the quality of the borrower's title to the land on which the project will be constructed and insuring the first priority position of the lender's construction mortgage;[71]

- A survey showing the boundaries of the borrower's land and further indicating that there are no encroachments or other physical impediments to the borrower's proposed development;

- An environmental site assessment certifying that there are no adverse environmental conditions existing on the site that could prevent or delay the borrower's development efforts or subject the borrower or lender to any liability for the cost of remediating such conditions;

- A wetlands report stating that there are no protected wetlands on the site;

- A soils report saying that the soils on the site are of a sufficient type and level of compaction to support the proposed improvements;

---

69. The construction loan agreement will also customarily condition the lender's obligation to make any loan disbursements on its receipt of all the required certifications and approvals—just in case the parties opt to close (but not fund) the construction loan before such certifications and approvals are received by the lender. *See e.g.,* § 3.1 of the Form Construction Loan Agreement.

70. Lender's counsel should customize the list of required certifications and approvals to deal with the specifics of each loan transaction. For example, if the proposed development project is located in the State of Florida, the construction lender will likely require the receipt of certifications from state and local officials that the project site is both "concurrent" and "consistent" with Florida's state-wide growth management regulations. *See* Florida's Local Government Comprehensive Plan and Land Development Regulation Act, FLORIDA STATUTES §§ 163–3164–163.3247 (2010).

71. *See supra* Chapter 5, Pages 126–127, and Chapter 8, Pages 293–295, for a more detailed discussion of title insurance. *See also* Jeffrey G. Gurren, *Maintaining and Enhancing Title Insurance Coverage,* in ALI–ABA COURSE OF STUDY MATERIALS, COMMERCIAL REAL ESTATE FINANCING: STRATEGIES FOR CHANGING MARKETS AND UNCERTAIN TIMES, Course No. SP–008, 471 (January 2009).

- Letters from local utility companies stating that all requisite utilities will be available to service the borrower's real estate project;

- A zoning letter provided by the local zoning authority affirming that the property is zoned to permit the construction and intended use of the proposed project;[72] and

- All building permits and other governmental approvals required for the construction and use of the proposed improvements.[73]

The lender will also want to reserve the right to approve both (a) the identity of all the firms providing the third party certifications and (b) the form and content of the furnished certifications and approvals. Quite predictably, the lender will also require that the borrower pick up the cost of providing all of the required certifications and approvals.[74]

Borrower's Pushback: The borrower is seldom in a position to resist the construction lender's insistence on the above due diligence requirements. Instead, the borrower focuses its negotiating efforts on trying to get the lender's blessing that the required certifications can be provided by consultants previously hired by the borrower.[75] By prevailing on this point, the borrower controls the process (presumably its consultants will not give the lender any unnecessary bad news) and limits its costs (by not having to reimburse the lender for duplicate due diligence reports from a second set of independent consultants). My experience has been that most lenders will accede to such a request by the borrower so long as (1) the borrower's consultants are firms with proven track records and (2) the consultants provide separate written certifications addressed directly to the lender in a format approved by the lender.

2. Conditions to Loan Advances. *(§§3.1, 4.1, 5.1 and 5.2)*

The construction lender will condition its obligation to make the initial loan advance[76] upon its receipt of all the certifications and approv-

---

72. Some construction lenders seek to augment their due diligence on zoning matters by requiring the borrower to obtain a zoning endorsement to the lender's title insurance policy, which endorsement will specifically insure the lender that the proposed project complies with all applicable zoning laws. Depending on the jurisdiction where the project is located, the cost of such a zoning endorsement can be quite exorbitant. Counsel for the borrower is, therefore, usually well-advised to resist the required provision of a zoning endorsement to the title policy.

73. For an overview of the lender's due diligence process, *see* David A. Weissmann, *The Construction Lending Process (With Forms)*, 24 No. 2 PRACTICAL REAL ESTATE LAWYER 39 (March 2008).

74. For a construction loan of the size provided to the borrower on the HIBC 500 Building ($8 million), the cost of providing the lender's required certifications and approvals will typically run well into five figures. It is essential that the borrower include all such costs in its development budget for the project.

75. *See supra* Chapter 5, Pages 114–116, where it is noted that the well-represented developer should already have received most (if not all) of the listed certifications as part of the developer's due diligence for its acquisition of the land on which the project will be developed.

76. A ''loan advance'' is lender-speak for a disbursement to the borrower of a portion of the principal amount of the construction loan. It is quite common for the borrower and the lender to close the construction loan by executing and delivering all of the requisite loan documents, before the lender is prepared to make its initial advance of construction loan proceeds. As such, the construction loan agreement almost always includes a provision conditioning its obligation to

als referred to in the preceding section. The lender will also require the borrower to make a series of representations and warranties that are intended to further protect the lender against the risk that the project is not completed on time. The lender will then complete the loop by conditioning its obligation to make any loan advance (either the initial advance or any subsequent advance) upon the continuing accuracy of all of the borrower's representations and warranties at the time of each advance. The borrower representations and warranties repeat the substance of the affirmations addressed in the above-described third party certifications (e.g., the soils are suitable for construction, there are no hazardous substances on the site, etc.) and further attempt to elicit from the borrower generalized, broadly phrased statements concerning the project construction schedule (e.g., the borrower has obtained all approvals required for the timely completion of the project in accordance with the plans and specifications).

The construction loan agreement typically includes one additional provision that is designed to mitigate the lender's completion risk. Section 5.2(d) of the Form Construction Loan Agreement contains the following prototypical borrower covenant concerning the borrower's adherence to its projected construction schedule:

> *Borrower covenants and agrees with Lender that Borrower will ... commence construction of the Improvements no later than 30 days from the date hereof ...; cause the construction ... to be prosecuted with diligence and continuity in a good and workmanlike manner in accordance with the Plans; ... and complete construction of the Improvements ... on or before the Completion Date.*

Borrower's ongoing compliance with this covenant is then expressly stated to be a condition to the construction lender's obligation to continue disbursing proceeds under the loan.[77]

Borrower's Pushback: In the ideal world, the borrower will have in hand prior to the loan closing all of the certifications and approvals required for it to move forward with the construction of the improvements. A borrower living in that ideal world will not be troubled by provisions of a construction loan agreement that condition the lender's obligation to make loan advances on (1) the lender's receipt and approval of all requisite certifications and approvals and (2) the borrower's compliance with all of the representations, warranties and covenants contained in the construction loan agreement.

Unfortunately, commercial real estate developers seldom reside in such an ideal world. This is especially true on so-called "fast-track" construction projects, where the developer has little choice but to start construction of its project well before it has finalized the construction plans and specifications or received all of the requisite project approvals

---

make its initial loan advance on its receipt and approval of the certifications and approvals discussed in the prior section of this Chapter.

77. *See* §4.1(f) of the Form Construction Loan Agreement.

and certifications. The HTE case study is an example of such a fast track project. In order to get HTE to sign its lease, Pizzuti had to agree that it would have the building completed and ready for HTE's occupancy by no later than March 1, 1997. Pizzuti knew that the only way that it could meet that targeted occupancy date was to begin construction before all the construction schedule niceties had been put to bed.

A borrower like Pizzuti on the HTE project has no choice but to ask the lender to agree to disburse a portion of the construction loan proceeds before all of the required certifications and approvals are obtained.[78] While a construction lender is usually hesitant to grant the borrower such a concession, a lender such as First Union on the HTE project needs to balance the resulting increase in its completion risk against the risk that the project value will dissipate (or perhaps totally disappear) if construction of the project cannot proceed on a fast-track schedule.

3. Underwriting of Development Team. *(§§3.2(f)–(h) and (k))*

An aspect of a construction loan that distinguishes it from a conventional permanent loan is the construction lender's urgent need to analyze and underwrite not only the real estate project that will serve as collateral for its loan, but also the competency and creditworthiness of the borrower and its development team.[79] The construction lender's due diligence on the development team is especially pertinent to the lender attempt to limit its exposure to completion risk.

The focus of the construction lender's underwriting of the development team is initially on the developer. The developer is responsible for overseeing and coordinating the efforts of all of the various players in the development process, including architects, engineers, contractors, leasing brokers and, yes, even lawyers. Before committing to a construction loan, the lender must get affirmative answers to all of the following questions about the developer's capabilities:

- Does the developer have the requisite experience and expertise to pull off the proposed development project;[80]

- Does the developer have a reputation for honesty and professionalism; and

- Does the developer have enough money to get the job done?

---

78. An alternative solution would be for the borrower to self-fund the initial construction costs with equity and then receive a reimbursement of those costs out of the loan proceeds when the lender-imposed funding conditions are finally satisfied. This too is part of that ideal world where most cash-strapped developers cannot afford to live.

79. I do not mean to minimize the importance to the permanent lender of the quality of its borrower (referred to in institutional investor circles as the loan's "sponsorship"). The permanent lender is intensely focused during its underwriting on the track record and financial standing of its borrower. However, the "creative" dynamic and unique risks associated with a construction loan make the developer's competency and creditworthiness more important to the construction lender than they are to the permanent lender.

80. The developer's experience and expertise must be validated both as to product type and locale. A shopping center developer may not have the necessary competency to develop an industrial park. Similarly, an Ohio-based office developer may not have the requisite skills and contacts to develop an office project in the State of Florida.

The development process seldom proceeds without some bumps in the road. The construction lender should be extremely focused on whether the developer has the talent, background, inclination and financial staying power to overcome those bumps and still complete the project on schedule.

Once the lender gets comfortable with the developer, the next step in its loan underwriting is a review of the construction, design and marketing team put together by the developer to work on the project. The lender will demand that it have the right to approve both the identity of the project architect and general contractor and the form and content of their respective contracts with the borrower. Depending on the nature and complexity of the project, the lender may also require approval rights for certain major subcontracts. The focal point of the lender's review of the resumes of the development team is on whether the team members have a proven track record for timely completing projects comparable to the project for which the lender will be providing the bulk of the development funding. The relative financial strength of the general contractor is also a major subject of the lender's underwriting analysis—particularly if the developer's balance sheet is somewhat suspect.

The final bit of personal underwriting done by the construction lender relates to the named borrower under the construction loan. The construction lender may insist that the borrower be a single purpose entity that is formed solely for the purpose of holding title to the project that is the subject of the lender's construction loan. The lender's reason for wanting a single purpose entity as the borrower is its belief that such an entity will be more "bankruptcy remote" than an entity which has ownership interests in a variety of assets and businesses. A ***bankruptcy remote entity*** is an entity that has little risk of becoming embroiled in a bankruptcy proceeding for any reason that is not directly related to the financial success of the real estate project on which the construction lender holds a first mortgage.[81]

Borrower's Pushback: This is the one aspect of the lender-borrower relationship where there really is no pushback from the developer. The borrower is in a full-throttle sales mode as it tries to convince the construction lender that the developer and its entire development team are eminently well-qualified to shepherd the project to completion. Golf with the lender's loan officer and members of its credit committee is the norm at this stage of the construction loan process. The only part of the sales process that is the least bit partisan is the developer's enticing promise that, if the lender cooperates on the pricing and structuring of the

---

81. For a discussion of the "bankruptcy remote" borrower, *see generally* Thompson, *supra* note 40, at 9–134. It should be noted that the "bankruptcy remote" nature of a single purpose entity has been called into question by a decision handed down in May, 2009, by the Bankruptcy Court for the Southern District of New York in the General Growth Properties, Inc. bankruptcy proceeding. In that proceeding, the Bankruptcy Court approved the upstreaming to the parent corporation's cash management account of rents produced from properties held by separate, single purpose entities. By effectively overriding the separateness of the single purpose entities from their corporate parent, the Bankruptcy Court's order has raised concerns within the practicing bar about the efficacy of bankruptcy remote entities. *See* Kris Hudson and Lingling Wei, *Move by General Growth Rattles Malls' Investors*, WALL STREET JOURNAL, May 8, 2009, at B1.

subject construction loan, the developer will provide the lender with plenty of additional loan business in the future.

4. Front-end Equity

One of the construction lender's biggest fears when underwriting a construction loan is that the developer loses interest in completing its development project. The developer may realize after the fact that its vision for the project was inaccurate or that the project has simply missed its mark in some fashion. The lender wants to make sure that, in such instances, the developer has the proper incentives to direct all of its attention and skills to righting the ship and making the project a success.

One of the best ways for the construction lender to keep the developer interested in the project is to require the developer to make its entire equity contribution (the 10–30% of the development costs not funded through the construction loan), before the lender is required to make any disbursement of construction loan proceeds. This *front-end equity* is often referred to by construction lenders as the developer's "skin in the game."

The alternative funding mechanism favored by all developers is *back-end equity,* where the developer is required to use its equity to fund development costs only after the construction lender has fully disbursed the entirety of the construction loan amount. It is easy to fathom how a developer with a back-end equity requirement might be sorely tempted to divert its attention away from a project that the developer thinks is a loser to a project where the developer has a larger, more direct financial interest at stake—even though it is at that precise juncture that the lender most wants the developer to focus all of its energy on turning the loser project into a winner. For this reason, most construction lenders are extremely loath to grant their borrowers the luxury of back-end equity funding.

Construction lenders often attempt to further focus the developer's attention on the project at hand by taking the position that the developer's front-end equity can only be used to fund the project's hard costs— i.e., those construction costs that are directly tied to the construction of actual, physical improvements on the developer's land.[82] This "hard cost only" funding limitation is imposed by the lender to prevent the borrower from applying its equity contributions to defray two categories of costs that the lender views as "phantom equity"—(1) development, leasing and other fees payable to the developer and its affiliates, and (2) the appreciation in the value of the contributed land over its initial cost. The construction lender wants the developer's skin in the game to consist of real cash and not non-cash, income items which redound to the developer's favor.[83]

---

82. *See supra* Chapter 3, Page 40.

83. *See* Frobes, *Selected Issues in Secured Construction Lending, supra* note 65, at 124; and Weissmann, *supra* note 72, at 52.

Borrower's Pushback: The borrower will strongly resist the construction lender's call for front-end equity. The point has been made both earlier in this Chapter and in the discussion of project economics in Chapter 3 that equity typically demands a higher return than debt.[84] What this means is that the use of equity dollars is a more expensive way for the borrower to fund its development costs. Requiring the borrower to fund its equity upfront causes an increase in the borrower's development costs and a concomitant decrease in the borrower's project profit.

It is, therefore, clear why the borrower prefers to fund its equity at the back-end of the construction process. Getting the lender to agree to forego its requirement for front-end equity is, however, a very dicey challenge for the borrower. In today's lending environment, only the most financially sound of borrowers have any hope of prevailing on the topic of back-end equity.[85] In all other situations, the lender will usually prevail on its assertion that the borrower's equity contribution must be fully expended before the lender becomes obligated to make any disbursement of construction loan proceeds.

The negotiating table is similarly slanted in favor of the lender's position that borrower's upfront equity can only be used to pay hard costs. The best result that most borrowers can hope to achieve on this issue is the receipt of lender's acknowledgement that the developer's fees and its land profit are legitimate project costs that can be paid with the proceeds of the construction loan—but only after all of the borrower's required equity contributions have first been used to pay project hard costs.[86]

5. Completion Guaranty

As noted earlier, the construction loan agreement customarily contains a provision requiring the borrower to complete construction of the project by a fixed outside date.[87] However, as also noted earlier, the borrower is frequently a shell entity that has no assets other than the project under development. For this reason, the construction lender routinely insists that the borrower also furnish the lender with a ***completion guaranty*** from a creditworthy affiliate of the borrower.

A completion guaranty is a promise by the guarantor that it will do whatever is necessary to complete construction of the project in accordance with the approved plans and specifications and by the outside

---

84. *See supra* Chapter 3, Pages 49–50, and *supra* Page 315.

85. If the borrower somehow succeeds in getting the lender to agree that its equity can come in at the back-end of the loan, the borrower will have to provide the lender with a personal guaranty of its funding of the back-end equity contributions.

86. The borrower has a better chance of including its land profit as part of its equity contributions if the borrower has owned the land for an extended period of time or has made substantial improvements to the land (e.g., the extension of roads, utilities and other infrastructure to the boundaries of the land).

87. The completion deadline should be a date by which the developer is reasonably comfortable it will be able to complete construction of the project (unless an existing lease specifies an earlier completion deadline, in which event that earlier date will customarily be used in the construction loan agreement).

completion date specified in the construction loan agreement. A well-drafted completion guaranty will make it clear that, although the completion guarantor may not be obligated to repay the construction loan,[88] it will be obligated to pay whatever costs are needed to finish construction of the project. This obligation specifically includes the obligation to fund additional equity contributions if the construction loan has been fully disbursed prior to project completion.

A completion guaranty should not be viewed by the construction lender as a panacea for its completion risk. In the first instance, a completion guaranty (like any other guaranty) is often difficult to enforce.[89] Moreover if the borrower has defaulted on its completion obligation, it is likely that its affiliated completion guarantor will do the same thing.[90] The real purpose of the completion guaranty is not to insure the construction lender that the project will be completed as required under the construction loan agreement, but rather to keep the attention of a person or entity related to the borrower, who, hopefully, has a deep pocket. The other negative associated with a completion guaranty is that, if the guarantor's supposed deep pocket has a hole in it, the completion guaranty will not be worth the paper it is written on.

Borrower's Pushback: If the borrower is a single purpose entity, borrower's counsel will have little choice but to accept the construction lender's requirement for the furnishing of a completion guaranty by an affiliate of the borrower. The issue typically becomes not whether a completion guaranty will be furnished, but who will provide it, with the borrower preferring to offer up a lesser credit in the developer's constellation and the lender insisting that the completion guaranty be provided by the deepest of deep pockets in developer's organizational structure.

6. Payment and Performance Bonds

One of the lender's best protections against completion risk is the borrower's selection (and the lender's approval) of an experienced general contractor who has both the financial strength and industry knowledge to timely complete construction of the borrower's proposed project. But what if the general contractor selected by the borrower fails for whatever reason to finish the job? Is there anything the construction lender could

---

88. A completion guaranty does not, in and of itself, place any repayment obligation on the completion guarantor. The completion guarantor is, however, often asked to also provide the lender with a payment guaranty, pursuant to which it guaranties repayment of the construction loan. *See infra* Pages 377–378.

89. *See* Patricia J. Frobes, *Completion Guarantees and Carry Guarantees*, in ALI–ABA Course of Study Materials, Real Estate Financing Documentation: Strategies for Changing Times, Course No. SL–007, 139, 140–142 (January 2006).

90. This is especially true in those jurisdictions in which the measure of damages for the breach of a completion guaranty is deemed to be limited to the incremental value that would have been added to the lender's security if the project had been completed (and not the full cost of completing the project). If the cost of completing the project exceeds the incremental value that would inure to the lender's benefit from completion of the improvements (which is typically the case on a troubled project), the completion guarantor has a clear motivation not to abide by the express terms of its completion guaranty. *See id.* at 141.

have required as part of the construction loan closing to mitigate the risk of a default by the general contractor?

The answer that counsel for the construction lender frequently trots out to the above question is the ***payment and performance bond***.[91] Under payment and performance bonds, a surety company agrees to guaranty that construction of the project will be completed in accordance with the terms of the general contractor's contract and that all persons owed money under such contract for the performance of work or the provision of materials to the project will be paid. In exchange for the surety's issuance of such guaranties, the purchaser pays the surety an upfront fee, which is ordinarily equal to a percentage of the total price of the bonded construction contract. The amount of the surety's fee is directly tied to its perception of the degree to which it is at risk that the general contractor will not complete its performance under the construction contract. If the surety perceives that the risk is too great (generally because of the general contractor's lack of financial standing), it will simply refuse to issue payment and performance bonds—regardless of the amount of its promised fee.

Borrower's Pushback: Borrower's counsel's immediate reaction when it sees a requirement for the posting of payment and performance bonds in a construction loan agreement is to hit the delete button for the entire section. From the borrower's perspective, payment and performance bonds are guilty of two cardinal sins in the development business—(1) they increase the borrower's project costs and, even worse, (2) they don't add any real value to the project from anyone's perspective (other than the surety company that collects its fee for issuing the bonds).

The gist of the borrower's problem with payment and performance bonds is that a surety company will usually only issue its bonds if the general contractor is so financially strong as to make the existence of the bonds wholly meaningless. It is analogous to Bill Gates guarantying that Warren Buffet won't go bankrupt. Moreover, the fine print of the payment and performance bonds creates a plethora of defenses to any attempt by the bondholder to enforce the terms of the bonds against the surety.[92]

A borrower can frequently negotiate a waiver of the requirement that it obtain payment and performance bonds—unless the borrower's general contractor has a low net worth, in which case the lender will legitimately stand firm on its requirement that the project be bonded. Unfortunately, if the relative financial strength of the general contractor scares the construction lender, it is a safe bet that the surety company will refuse to issue payment and performance bonds for the project. The end result of

---

91. The payment and performance bond is technically two separate bonds—(a) a payment bond where the surety guaranties payment of all construction costs owed to subcontractors, laborers, suppliers and material providers under the general contractor's construction contract and (b) a performance bond where the surety guaranties that the construction of the project will be completed at the time and otherwise in accordance with the terms of the general contractor's construction contract with the owner. The two bonds are usually issued jointly by the surety for a single combined fee. *See* BENDER, *supra* note 6, at 333–336; and Weissmann, *supra* note 72, at 47.

92. *See* Weissmann, *supra* note 72, at 47; and LEFCOE, *supra* note 55, at 512.

this charade is that, if the borrower wants to secure a construction loan for its proposed project, it should select a financially-strong general contractor.[93]

7. Collateral Assignment of Construction and Design Contracts *(§3.2(l))*

The "worst day ever" for a construction lender is when it is left with no other option than to foreclose on its mortgage on an uncompleted development project. The value of a partially completed, commercial real estate project is usually less than the outstanding principal balance of the construction loan. If the foreclosing construction lender has any hope of getting its loan fully repaid, it needs to accomplish the singular goal of completing construction of the project.

The best path for the construction lender to follow to complete construction of the project is to retain the borrower's development team to finish the job they started.[94] The construction lender's fear is that the project architect or the general contractor will refuse to continue work on the project or will agree to do so only if it is able to extract an exorbitant, additional fee from the construction lender. The construction lender counters this fear by inserting in the construction loan agreement a requirement that the borrower collaterally assign to the construction lender all of the borrower's right, title and interests in its contracts with the architect, general contractor and other essential design and construction professionals. The foreclosing construction lender will then stand in the shoes of the borrower in its efforts to compel the borrower's development team to complete construction of the project.[95]

Construction and design contracts regularly contain provisions prohibiting a party from assigning its interest in the contract without first obtaining the consent of the other party. A fairly standard provision of an architect's contract is that the ownership of the plans and specifications remains in the architect, although the owner is given a license to use those plans and specifications in connection with the construction of the designed project. In order to avoid being stymied by either of these contractual provisions following the foreclosure of its construction mortgage, the prudent lender will condition its obligation to close and fund the construction loan upon its receipt of (1) the written consent of the architect and general contractor to the borrower's collateral assignment of its construction and design contracts (including the architect's affirmation

---

93. Payment and performance bonds are, however, typically required as a matter of public policy on jobs involving the construction of publicly-owned improvements—e.g. courthouses and schools.

94. This obviously assumes that the contractor and architect were not the causes of the project's failure.

95. Most construction lenders will also require the borrower to collaterally assign to them all governmental approvals, building permits, construction bonds and other intangibles and contract rights that the lender may require to complete the project. The assignment of those rights can be effected either in the mortgage or in a free-standing assignment document. *See* Weissmann, *supra* note 72, at 52.

that the lender will have the right to use the project plans and specifications) and (2) the acknowledgements of the architect and general contractor that they will remain obligated to perform under their respective contracts following the construction lender's foreclosure of its construction mortgage.

Borrower's Pushback: To use an old Texas political saying,[96] borrowers "really don't have much of a dog in that fight." While there are a number of issues that trigger intense negotiations between the construction lender and the architect/general contractor concerning the form and content of the aforementioned acknowledgement and consent,[97] the borrower's sole concern is that the architect and contractor provide the lender with something that makes the lender happy enough to close and fund the loan.

8. Retainage. *(§§2.1 and 4.2)*

It is in the best interests of both the borrower and the lender to create a strong incentive for the general contractor and its subcontractors to fully complete their work and remedy all defective construction conditions. A common way to accomplish that objective is for the construction lender to withhold from its loan advance a portion of the payment that would otherwise be payable to the general contractor. The withheld amounts (commonly referred to as ***retainage***) will be released by the lender only after the project is completed. Retainage characteristically falls somewhere between five to ten percent of each of the contractor's requested construction draws.[98] The exact amount of the retainage will vary depending on the nature of the work, the creditworthiness of the contractor and the percentage of completion of the project.[99] The general contractor should withhold a like amount of retainage from each payment it owes to its subcontractors, thereby giving each of those parties an incentive to remain on call to do whatever follow-up work may be necessary to complete the project.

Borrower's Pushback: It is the responsibility of borrower's counsel to make sure that the retainage provisions of the construction loan agreement are fully consistent with those set forth in the borrower's construction contract with the general contractor. The borrower will not be pleased if the construction loan agreement recites that the construction

---

96. This saying is most commonly attributed to either George H.W. Bush or James Baker.

97. *See* Alfred G. Kyle, *Commercial Real Estate Construction Lending (With Forms) (Part 3)*, 22 No. 4 PRACTICAL REAL ESTATE LAWYER 7, 9–10 (July 2006).

98. A "draw" is the amount of a construction loan advance that is payable to the general contractor to fund its previously-incurred costs. A "draw request" is the document submitted by the general contractor that identifies the amount of the requested loan advance and provides documentation supporting the construction costs incurred by the general contractor.

99. Some states such as Texas have statutes which condition the priority of the construction mortgage over subsequently filed mechanics liens on the construction lender's holding of a certain level of retainage until the project is completed. For the reasons stated in our earlier discussion of mechanics liens (*see supra* Pages 337–342), it is imperative that counsel for the construction lender incorporate those retainage requirements into the construction loan agreement. *See* Weller, *supra* note 28, at 1750.

lender will withhold 10% of each construction draw, while the general contractor's contract sets the applicable retainage percentage at 5%—because the borrower will have to temporarily fund the differential out of its own separate funds until the lender disburses the retainage on final completion.

The borrower frequently requests that (1) the retainage percentage only apply to the first 50% of the work[100] and (2) the retainage applicable to certain discrete portions of the work be fully released upon the completion of that portion of the work (e.g., the completion of all site work by an excavation contractor).[101] The construction lender is usually inclined to work with the borrower to make these changes, so long as it does not believe that the requested changes will unduly impair its overall objective of getting the project completed on schedule.

9. Builder's Risk Insurance. *(§3.2(e))*

One aspect of the lender's completion risk that has not yet been addressed is the risk that some natural occurrence beyond the control of the borrower's development team causes construction of the project to be halted or delayed. What happens if a tornado rips off the roof of a warehouse in the middle of construction or a fire destroys all of a building's interior improvements? Dealing with such natural risks is particularly important on a single tenant, build-to-suit project such as the HTE building, where a delay in completing construction may call into question the tenant's obligation to take occupancy and begin paying rent on the facility.

Construction lenders deal with this category of risk by requiring either the borrower or the general contractor (or sometimes both of them) to obtain insurance coverage commonly referred to as ***builders risk insurance,*** which insures the owner against damage caused to a development project by fire, wind, explosion, lightning, hail, and other causes beyond the parties' control.[102] The premium for obtaining builder's risk insurance is yet another development cost to be included in borrower's overall project budget, either as a direct cost or as a cost subsumed in the general contractor's price for the project. The insured amount of a

---

100. This effectively reduces the overall retainage to be funded as part of the final disbursement from 10% to 5% of the cost of the work.

101. If this modification is not made to the lender's standard retainage clause, a subcontractor whose work is completed early in the construction period will have to wait to receive the retainage on its contract until the final disbursement is made under the construction loan—a date which could easily be six to 24 months after the subcontractor's final exit from the project site.

102. The lender may also force the borrower to obtain an endorsement to the builder's risk policy that specifically confirms that the insurer will pay all insurance proceeds directly to the construction lender. *See e.g.,* § 3.2(e) of the Form Construction Loan Agreement. The receipt of this endorsement will allow the construction lender to assert control over the funding of the costs of reconstructing the damaged project. For a list of other potential endorsements to the builder's risk policy, *see* Aaron Johnston, Jr. and Charles E. Comiskey, *Property and Liability Insurance and Indemnities in Real Estate Transactions,* in Commercial Real Estate Transactions Handbook 11–41 through 11–43 (Mark A. Senn, ed., 4th ed. 2009)

builder's risk policy is customarily capped at the value of the completed project.[103]

Borrower's Pushback: The borrower acknowledges the need for a builder's risk policy. Its only issue is keeping the cost of obtaining that coverage as low as possible. That goal will sometimes dictate that the general contractor obtain the builder's risk policy, while at other times will weigh in favor of the borrower doing so.[104]

HIBC Case Study—Dealing With Completion Risk

First Union National Bank was the construction lender on both the HTE and 500 projects. The selection of First Union over Barnett Bank was the direct result of two factors—(1) First Union's determination to gain a foothold in the Orlando market and (2) Pizzuti's desire to establish a "go to" construction lender for all of its HIBC projects.

First Union was an aggressive bank headquartered in Charlotte, North Carolina. The bank had targeted Orlando as a growth market in which it wanted to significantly expand its construction lending business. It dispatched one of its young, aggressive loan officers (for the purposes of this case study, he will be known as "Abe") to try to originate construction loan business from the Orlando real estate development community. Abe's style was a bit too flashy (and pushy) for the staid, good old boy developers who still dominated the Orlando market in the mid–1990's. As a result, First Union wasn't making much of a mark in Orlando, until Abe ran into the troops from Pizzuti, who were also viewed in the Orlando community as outsiders and a bit too aggressive and trendy for their own good. The burgeoning relationship between Pizzuti and First Union was also helped along by the fact that Abe and his counterparts at Pizzuti shared a passion for three things—creative real estate deals, golf and beer.

At the same time that First Union was trying to expand its Orlando business base, Pizzuti was trying to figure out how to best deal with the massive development project that was HIBC. It concluded that, if it was going to be able to develop office projects at HIBC with its desired velocity, it needed to put together a development team that would work on the entirety of the project. In Pizzuti's view, a major player on its development team needed to be a construction lender that was both capable of doing multiple deals in the same location[105] and willing to issue loan commit-

---

103. *See* LEFCOE, *supra* note 55, at 513.

104. The premiums payable for builder's risk insurance will be based on a number of variables, including the nature and cost of the insured project and the volume of business done with the insurer by the insured (be it the general contractor or the owner).

105. The selection of a lender willing to do multiple deals in the same business park was particularly important because Pizzuti envisioned the HIBC development playing out with a mix of single tenant projects (attractive to even the most conservative of lenders) and speculative projects (anathema at the time to virtually all lenders). By blending these two different classes of projects under the umbrella of a single lender, Pizzuti hoped to be able to finance speculative

ments with a fair amount of alacrity and consistency. It didn't take long for Pizzuti to realize that Barnett Bank (the then dominant construction lender in Orlando) was not a viable candidate to become the construction lender on the Pizzuti team. Barnett was leery of taking on too much construction loan exposure in one business park[106] and was also well-known for its ponderous, lengthy and overly cumbersome underwriting process—something which was a clear turn-off for an aggressive and very impatient developer like Pizzuti.

Abe and First Union were much more smitten than was Barnett with Pizzuti's pitch that it was looking for one lender to do the HTE and 500 Building loans and its dangling carrot that "there will be plenty more where these came from." The coupling of Pizzuti and First Union in 1996 was a marriage made in heaven[107] between two aggressive real estate outsiders, each of whom wanted to make a big splash in the Orlando market. It certainly didn't hurt that First Union (unlike Barnett) was willing to make a land loan[108] to help Pizzuti fund the cost of extending roads, utility lines and other infrastructure throughout the undeveloped portions of the HIBC tract.

Having established how and why First Union agreed to make construction loans on the HTE and 500 Building projects, the discussion next turns to how First Union and Pizzuti dealt with the lender's completion risk on the two projects. Pizzuti made two strategic decisions on the frontside of its negotiations with First Union that paved the way for a relatively quick and easy negotiation on the various completion risk pushbacks described earlier in this Chapter.

First, Pizzuti selected Brasfield & Gorrie, a construction company headquartered in Birmingham, Alabama, to serve as its general contractor on both projects. Although a bit of an outsider to the Orlando market (a status it shared with both Pizzuti and First Union), Brasfield had two attributes which greatly appealed to First Union—(1) it had a lot of money and (2) it had a wonderful reputation for both competency and timeliness in its construction of projects throughout the Southeast.

---

office buildings, which, on a free-standing basis, might otherwise have not been financeable in the lending climate that permeated the Central Florida market in the mid–1990's.

106. Lenders like Barnett try to balance their loan portfolios by assiduously avoiding taking too much financing risk on one location or one developer.

107. The First Union–Pizzuti "marriage" ended in divorce a few years after the closing of the HTE and 500 Building loans. The cause of that divorce was twofold—(1) Abe moved on to bigger and better things and was replaced by a loan officer whose approach to the construction lending business was too conservative and slow-moving for Pizzuti's tastes and (2) the economy picked up in a very noticeable fashion creating a whole new set of construction loan "dance partners" for the HIBC development.

108. Land loans are tough to obtain even in the best of economic times, because vacant land does not produce a predictable income stream that can be used to service the debt. The only revenue source that is available to retire a land loan are sales of parcels to developers or land speculators—a market that was, at best, dismal at the time that Pizzuti was trying to secure financing for its development of the HIBC tract. As a result, Barnett was certainly not alone in its reluctance to make a land loan on the HIBC tract—in fact, it was joined in that sentiment by every Orlando lender other than First Union.

The second decision Pizzuti made that helped get First Union comfortable with its completion risk on the two buildings was its decision to offer up a completion guaranty on both projects from Pizzuti Equities Inc., a company that had a sizable net worth. The combined financial strengths of Brasfield and Pizzuti Equities gave First Union a great deal of comfort that the projects would be completed in a timely fashion.

So what did Pizzuti ask for in exchange for its agreement to select a financially strong general contractor and provide a completion guaranty from an equally strong entity? First and foremost, it asked for (and received) First Union's commitment to provide construction loans on both projects—one being a build-to-suit with the single tenant having OK but not great credit and the other being a 100% speculative project—something that was far from the norm in the Orlando lending market. It also received First Union's continuing commitment (more of a "handshake" than an actual contractual commitment) that it would work with Pizzuti on a restructuring and expansion of its existing HIBC land loan.

On the specific topic of the lender's completion risk, Pizzuti asked for the following lender concessions:

- *The back-ending of the $1 million of equity required for the HTE project (even Pizzuti wasn't so bold as to request a back-ending of equity on the speculative 500 Building);*

- *A waiver of the payment and performance bond requirement;*

- *The elimination of the 10% retainage requirement once the project was 50% complete;*

- *A loosening of the loan advance conditions on the HTE project to permit $2 million to be disbursed prior to the receipt of all the project certifications and approvals required in the construction loan agreement (including the final development plan approval from Seminole County and the issuance of a building permit for the 87,000 square foot office building); and*

- *The setting of completion deadlines for both projects as the date that was 12 months after the construction loan closing (which, as to the HTE project, was approximately three months after HTE's targeted occupancy date).*

So how did Pizzuti fare on its requests? Actually, it did pretty well. First Union agreed to back-end 50% of the equity required on the HTE project. It granted all of Pizzuti's other requests, with the obvious exception that First Union insisted that the completion deadline on the HTE loan coincide with the targeted commencement date specified in the HTE lease. First Union did, however, agree to extend that completion deadline for the same force majeure delays specifically sanctioned in the HTE lease. All in all, not a bad day's work for Pizzuti's overworked and underpaid general counsel.

B. DEALING WITH THE RISK
OF COST OVERRUNS

The next risk that the construction lender must protect itself against is the risk that the project will cost more than originally projected. The end result of that risk becoming reality is that either the project cannot be completed or the net value of the lender's collateral is compromised by the amount of the cost overrun. Some of the same techniques discussed with respect to the lender's completion risk are equally applicable to help insulate the lender from the risk of cost overruns—for example, the required provision of a completion guaranty and payment and performance bonds and the underwriting of the competency and financial strength of the borrower's development team. There are, however, a number of new tools that the construction lender can use to deal with the risk of project cost overruns.

1. Approval of Project Budget. *(§§2.1, 2.2 and 3.2(o))*

The construction lender begins its efforts to combat the risk of a cost overrun by instructing its financial analysts and consultants to closely review the borrower's proposed development budget (including the general contractor's detailed construction budget) to validate the accuracy and completeness of the various line item expenses noted in the budget. Do the developer's proposed costs square with the normative unit pricing that the lender has seen on similar projects? Does the budget include all those costs that must be incurred if the project is going to be completed in accordance with the approved plans and specifications and project schedule? Are the budgeted construction and design costs consistent with the fees and costs listed in the borrower's design and construction contracts?

Once the lender has approved a development budget for the project, it is essential that the approved budget thereafter serve as the benchmark for determining the amount of all future disbursements made under the construction loan. The lender accomplishes this goal by attaching a copy of the approved budget as an exhibit to its construction loan agreement and then including provisions in the construction loan agreement specifying that (1) the budget cannot be changed without the lender's consent, (2) all disbursements requested by borrower under the construction loan must be specifically linked to a particular line item in the approved budget and (3) unless otherwise expressly approved by the lender, the aggregate of all disbursements for a particular line item cost may not exceed the amount specified for that line item in the approved budget.

Borrower's Pushback: There is nothing that drives a borrower crazier than to have its construction lender try to change the borrower's development budget. Borrowers are not generally known for their deference to or respect for the financial and development expertise of their lenders. Moreover, the borrower clearly understands the lender's end game when the lender attempts to increase the borrower's development costs (by the way, it never goes the other way). I have never known a lender to couple its insistence on an increase in the borrower's development costs with a related offer to increase the loan amount on a dollar-for-dollar basis. The end result is that every lender-sponsored increase in the amount of the approved development costs triggers a like increase in the amount of the borrower's required equity contribution.

The borrower often voices one additional, specific objection to the lender's demand that the construction budget serve as the bible for the making of all construction loan disbursements. As will be discussed in more detail later on in this Chapter,[109] it is the borrower's reasoned judgment that the lender's proper point of inquiry should be the borrower's aggregate development costs and not each line item cost. Stated differently, the borrower takes the position that it should be able to fund a cost overrun in one line item with the cost savings achieved in another line item. The borrower, of course, seeks to employ a rather expansive definition of "cost savings" to effectively include any excess in a budgeted line item cost over the amount of that line item cost that has already been disbursed under the construction loan.[110]

2. Contingency Reserve

The construction lender's concern when making a construction loan is that something bad happens which causes the project to cost more than originally anticipated—regardless whether that bad thing is triggered by an act or omission of the borrower or the occurrence of an event or circumstance that is outside of the borrower's control. The knee jerk reaction of many lenders to the specter that "something bad might happen" is to require the borrower to include in its construction budget a new line item for the funding of a ***contingency reserve.***

Depending on the nature of the project and the persistence of the lender, a contingency reserve can run anywhere from one to ten percent of the project's total development costs. The lender views the insertion of a contingency reserve in the development budget as its cushion or hedge against "something bad happening" that could adversely affect the value of its collateral for the construction loan. The lender's bottom line, of course, is that the economics of its position under the construction loan still need to work after the insertion in the borrower's development budget of the added cost for a contingency reserve.

---

109. *See infra* Pages 372–374, for a discussion of the loan balancing provision.

110. Taken to its logical conclusion, the import of the borrower's expansive definition of "cost savings" is that a cost overrun can never exist until late in the construction process (because the borrower will always have a theoretical cost savings until all of the construction loan proceeds have been disbursed). Experienced lender's counsel will counter the borrower's position by asserting that a cost savings is achieved on a particular line item only when all work associated with that line item has been completed—e.g., only if 100% of the site work has been completed at a cost that is less than the projected site work cost set forth in the approved budget. A provision similar to §2.7 of the Form Construction Loan Agreement would be more to the liking of lender's counsel than would the borrower-sponsored definition of cost savings referred to in the text. *See* Frobes, Selected Issues in Secured Construction Lending *supra* note 65, at 125.

Borrower's Pushback: To quote Ronald Reagan in his 1980 presidential debate with Jimmy Carter, "there you go again." The borrower once again knows that the end result of the lender's insistence on the establishment of a contingency reserve will be an increase in the borrower's equity requirement in an amount equal to the dollar amount of the contingency reserve.[111] As a result, the borrower will mightily resist the creation of a contingency reserve by saying things like—"the prospect for cost overruns are already covered by the completion guaranty," "the general contractor has a contingency reserve in its construction contract" (assuming that is true) and "my numbers are solid so there's no need to include any additional cushion." Most of the developer's objections will, of course, fall by the wayside if the construction lender permits the borrower to fund the contingency reserve with back-end equity dollars.

3.   Limitation on Change Orders. *(§5.2(k))*

Cost overruns can also occur due to a change or addition made to the plans and specifications for a particular project. Such change and additions are commonly referred to in the real estate industry as ***change orders.*** Change orders can be as simple as replacing carpet tiles in the building lobby with marble or as complex as adding a structured parking garage in lieu of a surface parking lot. Similarly a change order can be sponsored by either the contractor (to correct an error or deficiency in the existing plans and specifications), the developer (to respond to an evolving market condition by adding a health club or upgrading building finishes) or a tenant of the project (to better serve its use of the leased space by adding a computer server room).

The construction lender has a natural and quite legitimate aversion to change orders. When it signs the construction loan agreement, the construction lender is agreeing to finance construction of a project whose nature, scope, dimension and cost are specifically defined by plans and specifications approved by the lender. A change order can negatively impact the lender's collateral position under the construction loan by either (1) reducing the value of the completed project (e.g., by means of a change order that downgrades the quality of the building's interior and exterior finishes) or (2) increasing the project's total development costs (e.g., by means of a change order that upgrades the quality of such building finishes).

The construction lender's preferred way to deal with the change order risk is to say that the plans and specifications are inviolate and may not be changed in any way without the lender's prior written consent. By taking this extreme approach, the lender puts itself firmly in control of the project that will ultimately be built with its loan proceeds.

---

111.   The savvy borrower will often include a small contingency reserve in its initial development budget to try to assuage the lender's concern over the prospect of cost overruns. The amount of the borrower's proposed contingency reserve is merely intended as "eye candy" to lend its budgeting processes an air of fairness and legitimacy and is seldom of a magnitude sufficient to give the lender any real comfort on the cost overrun issue.

Borrower's Pushback: A recurring theme in the borrower's negotiations with the construction lender is the borrower's need to reserve flexibility throughout the development period to do that which the borrower believes is necessary or desirable to optimize the project's value by responding in an appropriate fashion to market conditions or the desires of prospective tenants. The borrower also wants to maintain the right to make minor changes to the plans and specifications to keep the project on schedule and on budget (e.g., changing the light fixtures in the building lobby because the originally selected light fixtures are on back order).

The borrower's desire for construction and design flexibility runs directly counter to the lender's desire to retain control over the development process by prohibiting all change orders that are not expressly sanctioned by the lender. A compromise often requested by the borrower (and commonly granted by the lender) involves the establishment of a materiality standard to identify those change orders that will require the lender's prior consent. The materiality standard can be stated either numerically (any change order which causes a change of more than $X in the project's development costs) or descriptively (any change order that significantly alters the structural components or exterior aesthetics of the improvements or could result in the borrower not being able to complete construction of the improvements by the completion deadline). The borrower's goal in crafting the materiality standard is to maximize its development flexibility, while the lender's goal is to preserve its control over the development process. There is, obviously, a fair amount of negotiating room between these two extremes.

4. Receipt of a Fixed Construction Price from General Contractor

The largest single line item in any development budget is the general contractor's price for constructing the improvements. As a result, one of the construction lender's greatest concerns is that the general contractor's actual construction price will exceed the construction price identified in the approved development budget.

The price component of a construction contract can be described in a variety of ways.[112] Two of the most common pricing alternatives are—

- ***Stipulated Sum Pricing***—that is, a fixed price, regardless of the amount of the contractor's actual construction costs; or

- ***Cost Plus a Fee Pricing***—that is, the contractor's actual construction costs, plus a contractor fee equal to a stated percentage of the actual costs.

Given a choice, the construction lender will always prefer a stipulated sum contract. A stipulated sum contract largely eliminates any prospect of a cost overrun in the general contractor's pricing.[113] The cost plus a fee

---

112. *See infra* Chapter 10, Pages 427–431, for a detailed discussion of the different ways in which the construction price can be structured.

113. The construction lender's risk under a stipulated sum pricing model is that project experiences cost overruns and the general contractor does not have the requisite financial

arrangement is especially troublesome for a construction lender, because it invites a significant negative variance between the budgeted construction price and the actual price paid to the general contractor.[114] It is, therefore, quite common for the construction loan agreement to include a requirement that the agreement between the borrower and the general contractor include a stipulated sum construction price in an amount that is no greater than the amount of the hard costs of construction set forth in the approved project budget.

Borrower's Pushback: Why would the borrower have a problem with the lender's insistence on a stipulated sum construction price? Isn't the interest of the borrower also served by putting into place a pricing mechanism which effectively eliminates the prospect of a construction cost overrun? The answer to those questions is "yes, but. . . ."

The "but" part of this answer is tied to the borrower's accurate perception of the following two realities of the construction industry—

- A general contractor will seldom agree to a stipulated sum price, unless it first has the opportunity to bid out the final plans and specifications to a pool of subcontractors to fix its costs on the project; and

- The universal reaction of a contractor that is asked to provide fixed pricing is to hedge its position by increasing its construction price over the price that it realistically believes would be produced under a cost plus a fee pricing arrangement.

Given these commercial realities, the developer will argue that the lender's insistence on a stipulated sum construction contract will cost the developer money and will effectively eliminate its ability to land a deal such as the HTE project, where the need to fast track construction does not lend itself to a time-consuming bid process.

A middle ground between the two pricing extremes that can appeal to both the construction lender and the borrower is a ***guaranteed maximum price.*** In a guaranteed maximum price contract, the contractor is paid for its cost of work plus a fee, up to but not exceeding a fixed, aggregate number.[115] It is, therefore, a hybrid of the cost plus and stipulated sum pricing models.

---

strength to cover those overruns. A construction lender can try to protect itself against this contractor credit risk by requiring a completion guaranty or payment and performance bonds. *See supra* Pages 350–352.

114. *See* Lynn Axelroth, *The Owner's Perspective*, in FUNDAMENTALS OF CONSTRUCTION LAW Chapter 1 (Carina Y. Enhada, Cheri Turnage Gatlin and Fred D. Wilshusen, eds. 2001).

115. The setting of a guaranteed maximum price is often more art than science and involves intense negotiations between the developer and its selected general contractor. The developer's goal is to secure a guaranteed maximum price that fits within the financial parameters set forth in its development budget. The general contractor's objective is to provide a guaranteed maximum price that is low enough for it to get the job, but high enough to give it a cushion if construction costs unexpectedly spike after the construction contract is signed. The guaranteed maximum price established for a project where the construction plans and specifications are in their formative stage (such as the HTE project) will, therefore, almost always be higher than the

The construction lender will accept a guaranteed maximum price contract as long as the guaranteed maximum price is the number inserted into the approved budget as the developer's hard costs of construction. The benefit to the borrower of a guaranteed maximum price arrangement is that its actual construction costs may prove to be less than the stated maximum price. The cynical borrower (are there any other kind) knows, however, that it is highly likely that the final construction price will equal the guaranteed maximum price, unless the general contractor is economically incentivized to minimize its construction costs. The cynical, but smart, borrower tackles this issue head on by offering to increase the amount of the contractor's fee if the general contractor completes construction of the project for less than the guaranteed maximum price.[116]

5. Limitations on Funding of Soft Costs

The prior section addressed one of the ways that a construction lender can protect itself against cost overruns related to the hard costs of construction. But how does the lender deal with its obligation to provide loan disbursements to cover soft costs, such as legal fees, development fees, architectural fees, interest carry, the developer's land profit and leasing commissions?

As stated on countless occasions in this Chapter, the construction lender's overriding business objective is to make sure that the borrower's project is completed so that it can be leased to rent-paying tenants. Soft costs, by definition, do not directly involve the construction of an asset having an enduring value. As such, the construction lender's preferred position on the funding of the borrower's soft costs is typically represented by one or some combination of the following three verbs—"eliminate," "decrease" and "defer."

At the outset, it needs to be acknowledged that there are "soft costs" and then there are "really soft costs." The former category of soft costs includes those costs that the lender generally does not object to funding. These soft costs are customarily owed to third parties unrelated to the borrower and are attributable to the third party's performance of a service which is essential to the creation of the borrower's real estate project— e.g., architectural and engineering fees, title insurance premiums, survey costs, brokerage commissions and even the legal fees of borrower's counsel. While the construction lender intellectually would prefer to defer the funding of those soft costs until after construction of the project is fully completed, the lender usually recognizes that such a deferral is neither practical, nor realistic.

There is another group of soft costs that the lender not only does not object to funding, but actually insists be funded on a special priority basis.

---

maximum price set for a comparable project with a well-developed set of plans and specifications (like the 500 Building).

116. *See* Axelroth, *supra* note 114, at 23. By way of example, a borrower might agree to share 50% of any cost savings with the general contractor, with the cost savings being the excess of the guaranteed maximum price over the actual costs of construction.

These soft costs are the interest carry and loan fees payable to the lender and the fees payable to the lender's consultants—e.g. its lawyer, appraiser and inspecting architect.[117]

That leaves the "really soft costs." These are costs which inure in some fashion to the benefit of the borrower and its affiliates. The two most glaring examples of these "really soft costs" are (1) the development fees paid to the borrower/developer and (2) the borrower's unrealized profit on the land on which the project is being built.

Development fees are payable to developer in recognition of its past services in putting the deal together and its future services in overseeing the ongoing development of the project. Development fees are usually expressed as a percentage of the project's total development costs— anywhere from two to ten percent, depending on the nature of the project. Due to the illiquid nature of commercial real estate assets,[118] many developers rely on the receipt of development fees funded with construction loan proceeds to cover their overhead and other operating expenses.

The construction lender views development fees as being part of the profit which the developer will make from its real estate project. The lender does not want to fund any portion of the developer's profit before a realistic determination can be made that the project's actual cost structure is consistent with the development cost budget. Therefore, the construction lender will typically seek to either wholly ELIMINATE its obligation to fund development fees, DECREASE the amount of the development fees to be included in the approved development budget or DEFER the date of the funding of the development fees until the project is fully completed.

The lender's view of the borrower's unrealized land profit is frequently even less favorable than its view of development fees. What exactly is the borrower's unrealized land profit? The following example based on the HIBC case study is an illustration of the perspectives of the borrower and the lender on the subject of unrealized land profit.

Example 9–1: Assume that Pizzuti's cost basis[119] in the ten acre tract underlying the HTE building is $1 million. Assume further that Pizzuti believes that the fair market value of the ten acre tract is $2.5 million. Pizzuti's proposed development cost budget includes a line item for land of $2.5 million. Pizzuti's intention is to draw down the full $2.5 million land value as part of its initial loan advance under the First Union construction loan.

So how would a construction lender react to the scenario described in the above example? That's right—

---

117. *See e.g.*, §6.1(f) of the Standard Form of Construction Loan Agreement.

118. The point being made here is that the developer cannot sell a real estate project every time it needs to make payroll or purchase office supplies.

119. The developer's cost basis in its land is generally equal to the cost of its initial acquisition of the subject tract, plus any capital expenditures it makes to improve the land (e.g., the extension of roads, utility lines and other infrastructure to service the tract).

- *Choice #1*—ELIMINATE its obligation to fund the unrealized land profit,

- *Choice #2*—DECREASE the value of the land included in the development budget (say to $1.5 million), and

- *Choice #3*—DEFER its funding of loan dollars to pay the land profit until final completion of the development project.[120]

Borrower's Pushback: From the developer's perspective, the issue of the lender's funding of the borrower's "really soft costs" is all about cash flow. The borrower desperately wants to front-load the lender's funding of those costs that will ultimately find a home in the developer's pocket. Ideally, the borrower wants the lender to fund 100% of the borrower's development fee and the full fair market value of the borrower's land as part of the initial loan advance made at the construction loan closing. Under the HTE example noted above, this would mean that Pizzuti would receive a cash payment at the construction loan closing of $3 million—a land payment of $2.5 million and a development fee of $500,000 (assuming that Pizzuti's proposed development fee is 5% of its $10 million development cost budget).

So how can a developer possibly justify its receipt of such a sizable cash payment out of the initial loan advance? The developer has three possible (and maybe even plausible) arguments that it can make to support its receipt of the development fee and land profit at the initial loan closing. First, it can, with a totally straight face, contend that it has fully earned its development fee by putting the deal together and getting the tenant to sign its lease. Second, it can point out that it would be well within its rights to sell the land to the borrower at its full fair market value (instead of conveying the land to the newly-formed entity as a capital contribution).[121] Finally, the developer can argue that the issue of the timing of the disbursement of the "really soft costs" is a matter of little overall consequence to the lender, because the construction loan is fully recourse to the borrower and probably also supported by completion and payment guaranties provided by creditworthy affiliates of the developer.

When confronted with these compelling arguments, the construction lender either repeats its mantra of "eliminate, decrease and defer" or tries to find a mutually acceptable middle ground. A solution that often works for both the borrower and the lender is for (1) a portion of the development fee to be funded in the initial loan advance (e.g., 50%), with the disbursement of the remainder of the fee to be spread over the construc-

---

120. The construction lender frequently responds to the developer's request that its unrealized land profit be funded with loan dollars by combining choices #'s 2 and 3—that is, by decreasing the amount of the land profit included in the development budget and then insisting that funding for the reduced land profit be deferred until the date of the final loan disbursement.

121. The reason that a developer generally contributes the land to the borrowing entity is tax-driven. By making a capital contribution of the land to the venture, the developer is able to defer its recognition of a taxable gain on its land profit. *See* INTERNAL REVENUE CODE § 721(a). *See also supra* Chapter 7, Pages 227–229.

tion period in proportion to the project's percentage of completion and (2) the unrealized land profit to be included in the approved development budget, but its funding deferred until later in the construction period.[122]

6. Establishment of Generous Interest Reserve

A unique feature of a construction loan is its floating interest rate— i.e., an interest rate that changes over the term of the construction loan based upon changes in a financial index that is designed to measure the lender's cost of funds. The floating interest rate is intended (1) to protect the lender's profit margin against a post-loan closing increase in its cost of funds and (2) to permit the borrower to benefit from a post-loan closing decrease in the lender's cost of funds.

Another unique feature of a construction loan is that the interest that accrues under the loan is treated as a development cost and is typically funded through construction loan advances. The reason that construction period interest is funded out of the proceeds of the construction loan is quite simple—the commercial real estate project that is being developed with the aid of the construction loan does not produce any income during the construction period.

The combination of these two unique features creates a cost overrun risk for the borrower and the construction lender. What happens if inflation significantly drives up the borrower's floating interest rate during the construction loan term, with the result that the borrower's interest carry costs are dramatically higher than originally contemplated in the borrower's development cost budget? By way of illustration, assume that the interest rate identified in the commitment letter is LIBOR plus 2% and that, at the time of the parties' execution of the commitment letter, LIBOR stands at 4%. Based on these facts, the borrower's development budget includes an interest carry cost calculated on the assumption that the interest rate under the construction loan will be 6% throughout the loan term.[123] That assumption produces a projected, aggregate interest carry over the 24 month term of a $10 million construction loan of $900,000.[124] If LIBOR suddenly surges from 4% to 6%, the impact on the borrower's interest carry costs can be dramatic—a cost overrun of $300,000 based on the assumptions used in the above illustration.

---

122. A common trigger for the funding of the land profit is the execution of binding leases on a designated percentage of the rentable square footage contained within the project's improvements. The achievement of a leasing threshold provides comfort to the lender that the project will ultimately be profitable and that its loan can be refinanced at maturity.

123. Such an assumption by the borrower is quite logical given the fact that, although the interest rate may change during the course of the loan term, it is theoretically as likely that the rate will go down as it is that the rate will go up.

124. Interest accrues on only the disbursed portion of the construction loan. The borrower's aggregate interest carry costs will, therefore, vary not only based on increases and decreases in the applicable financial index, but also based on the pace at which the borrower draws down its loan advances. The calculation in the text is based on a commonly-used rule of thumb that the average daily balance of a 24 month construction loan (assuming an actual construction period of 12 months) will be 75% of the loan's maximum principal amount.

A cost overrun triggered by an increase in the borrower's floating interest rate creates the same problem for the construction lender as does any other cost overrun—that is, if the borrower isn't able to fund the increased interest carry, the lender is left with the dilemma of either advancing additional loan dollars to cover the additional interest (in which event the net value of its collateral position will suffer) or putting the progress of the development project on hold until the borrower can identify an alternative funding source to cover its increased carry costs.

Is there anything the construction lender can do to try to protect itself against the prospect of a cost overrun attributable to a jump in the financial index used to price its loan? The prophylactic measure customarily used by construction lenders is to make sure that the interest carry number included in the approved development budget assumes a reasonable increase in the borrower's interest rate during the construction loan term. In the example used earlier in this section, a construction lender trying to protect itself against an interest carry cost overrun might require that the borrower calculate its interest carry costs based on an assumption that the interest rate payable during the loan term will be 7% (rather than the 6% figure produced by utilizing the applicable LIBOR rate as of the date of the construction loan closing).

Borrower's Pushback: As is the case with respect to any lender-sponsored attempt to alter the borrower's proposed development budget, the borrower's primary pushback on the calculation of its interest reserve is grounded in the comparative development expertise and experience of the borrower and the lender—in other words, "I know what I am doing and you don't." This response is particularly predictable given the fact that the borrower is acutely aware that any increase in its interest reserve will more than likely lead to a similar increase in its upfront equity requirement.

It should be noted that the borrower and the construction lender share a desire to avoid a cost overrun triggered by a dramatic increase in the financial index. From the borrower's perspective, the best way to avoid a precipitous increase in its interest carry costs is to get the lender to agree to fix the interest rate for the entirety of the construction loan term—i.e., setting the interest rate at a fixed rate of 6% and not LIBOR plus 2%. However, fixing the interest rate exposes the construction lender to the risk that its loan profit will be eroded by an increase in its costs of fund, without a concomitant increase in the interest rate being paid by the borrower. This dilemma leads to the discussion in Practice Tip #9–2 of interest rate hedges that are sometimes put in place at the volition of the borrower and sometimes implemented as a lender-imposed condition to the making of a construction loan.[125]

---

125. The reason that a borrower would voluntarily purchase an interest rate hedge is obvious—it wants to protect itself against the risk that its return on its development project will

Practice Tip #9–1: Interest Rate Hedges

There are a variety of financial products (more pejoratively referred to as "derivatives") that are designed to provide a hedge against the risk associated with a fluctuation in floating interest rates. The three basic categories of interest rate hedges are (1) an interest rate cap, (2) an interest rate collar and (3) an interest rate swap.[126] All three of these hedge techniques are intended to protect the borrower against the ravages of an unbudgeted increase in its floating interest rate, while at the same time preserving the integrity of the construction lender's spread between its cost of funds and the interest payable to it by the borrower under the construction loan. Hedge products can be purchased from a variety of financial institutions, including the derivatives department of the bank that makes the construction loan.

*<u>Interest Rate Cap:</u>[127] An interest rate cap is essentially what it sounds like—the placing of a cap or a ceiling on the maximum interest rate that the borrower will ever have to pay on its construction loan,[128] regardless of the level of increases in the base financial index used in the construction loan. By way of example, if the floating interest rate specified in the construction loan documents is LIBOR plus 200 basis points and the borrower buys a 7% interest rate cap (commonly-referred to as the **strike price**), then the maximum level of interest that the borrower will ever have to pay is 7%, even if LIBOR increases to 6% at some time during the construction loan term. It is important to note, however, that a borrower who buys an interest rate cap still retains the benefit of a decline in the floating interest rate. Therefore, if LIBOR falls from 4% to 3%, the hypothetical borrower's interest rate will be decreased to 5%, irrespective of its purchase of an interest rate cap.*

The protection afforded to the borrower by an interest rate cap obviously does not come free. In most situations, the borrower has to pay a sizable

---

be adversely affected by a future increase in its floating interest rate. It is, however, also fairly common for a construction lender to require a borrower to purchase an interest rate hedge to guard against the borrower defaulting on its loan if interest rates rise dramatically during the term of the construction loan.

126. *See generally* Steven R. Davidson and Eric M. Schiller, *Interest Rate Hedging Products*, in ALI–ABA COURSE OF STUDY MATERIALS, COMMERCIAL REAL ESTATE FINANCING: STRATEGIES FOR CHANGING MARKETS AND UNCERTAIN TIMES, Course No. SP–008, 555 (January 2009).

127. The interest rate cap discussed in this *Practice Tip* is different from a negotiated cap where the construction lender simply agrees in the construction loan documents that the interest rate payable by the borrower will never exceed a fixed maximum rate, regardless of the level of future increases in the applicable financial index. Negotiated caps were fairly common before the prime rate increased by more than 12 points during a two year period from April 1978 to April 1980. That period of rapidly escalating interest rates resulted in the virtual demise of negotiated caps in construction loan transactions.

128. The discussion in this *Practice Tip* assumes that the borrower purchases an interest rate hedge to cover the full amount of its construction loan (and just the construction loan). There is no requirement that the borrower limit the principal amount of its interest rate hedge (known as the "notional amount") in that fashion. A borrower may (and frequently does) purchase an interest rate hedge to cover a broader portfolio of its construction loans. Similarly a borrower could acquire a hedge for just a portion of its construction loan (although borrowers seldom do so due to the high legal and other transactional costs associated with the purchase of an interest rate hedge).

upfront fee to the party that is providing the cap—be it an affiliate of the construction lender or some unrelated bank, insurance company or other financial institution. The size of that fee is directly related to the level of the purchased cap, with the amount of the fee increasing as the strike price decreases. In return for its receipt of the upfront fee, the provider of the interest rate cap will agree to make payments to the borrower if the floating interest rate under the construction loan ever rises above the strike price of the purchased cap.[129]

Interest Rate Collar: *The interest rate collar is a variation of the interest rate cap. An interest rate collar places both a ceiling and a floor on the level of the borrower's floating interest rate exposure. By way of example, an interest rate collar might place a ceiling of 8% and a floor of 4% on the floating interest rate that the borrower will be obligated to pay during the term of the collar. If the interest rate computed in accordance with the floating rate methodology used in the construction loan exceeds 8%, then the provider of the cap will be obligated to make a payment to the borrower in the amount of that excess.*[130] *Conversely, if the floating interest rate falls below the 4% floor, then the borrower will be obligated to make a payment to the collar provider in an amount equal to that difference.*[131] *If the interest rate floats between the 4% floor and the 8% ceiling, no payments will be made under the collar.*[132]

As is the case with an interest rate cap, the provider of an interest rate collar typically charges the borrower an upfront fee for the collar. The amount of that fee is generally less than the fee payable for an interest rate cap, because the provider of the collar has bargained for its receipt of a portion of the benefit associated with declining interest rates—unlike the situation with an interest rate cap where 100% of the benefit of falling interest rates remains with the borrower.

Interest Rate Swap: *A swap is the most frequently purchased hedge against fluctuations in floating interest rate indices. In a typical interest rate swap, the borrower agrees to make a fixed interest rate payment to the*

---

129. It is important to keep in mind that the interest carry payable by the borrower to the construction lender is not directly affected by the borrower's purchase of an interest rate cap. In the example used in the text, if LIBOR goes to 6%, then the borrower will be obligated to pay interest to its construction lender at an 8% rate (LIBOR plus 2%). However, the borrower will also be entitled to receive a payment from the provider of the interest cap in an amount equal to the product of (a) the principal amount of the purchased cap, multiplied by (b) the excess of the construction loan interest rate over the strike price of the cap. The end result is that the borrower's net interest carry on its development project is effectively capped at the 7% level, but the construction lender still gets to receive the full economic benefit provided by the floating interest rate feature of the construction loan.

130. The amount of the payments made to or by the borrower will be dependent both on the level of the floating interest rate and the notional amount of the collar. *See supra* note 128.

131. Because an interest rate collar contemplates the possibility that the borrower may have to make future payments to the collar provider, an issue presented by the collar that is not present with a cap is the credit standing of the borrower. If the borrower's credit is not sufficiently solid, the provider of the collar will insist that the borrower post collateral to secure its future payment obligations. The borrower's financial standing will also have a direct bearing on the level of the upfront fee that the borrower will have to pay for the collar.

132. Under a collar, the borrower retains the benefit of a decline in its floating interest rate until such time as the floating rate falls below the collar's floor.

provider of the swap and the swap provider agrees to make an interest payment to the borrower based on a floating rate of interest.[133] *To illustrate how a swap works, assume that the borrower decides to swap out its floating rate exposure on the entirety of a fully-funded $10 million construction loan where the interest rate on the loan is stated to be a variable rate equal to a spread over LIBOR. Finally, assume that the swap provider is willing to swap out the floating rate interest rate for a fixed rate of 6%.*[134]

Under an interest rate swap, the borrower remains obligated to make its floating interest rate payment to the construction lender throughout the construction loan term. Therefore, under the above example, the borrower would make a monthly interest payment to the construction lender based on the then level of LIBOR regardless of the existence of the swap. The borrower and the swap provider would then make payments to each other depending on whether the borrower is **in the money** *or* **out of the money** *on the swap. If the floating interest rate in a particular month is more than the fixed rate of the swap, then the swap provider would be obligated to make a payment to the borrower who would be considered to be "in the money" on the swap. If, however, the floating rate for the month is less than the swap's fixed rate, then the borrower would be obligated to make a payment to the swap provider and the borrower would be considered to be "out of the money" on the swap.*

The following chart illustrates the impact that a move in the floating interest rate will have on the operation of the hypothetical interest rate swap mentioned at the outset of this discussion (that is, a swap of a floating interest rate on a fully-funded $10 million construction loan for a fixed rate of 6%).

Floating Interest Rate%	*Borrower's Monthly Interest Payment to Construction Lender*	*Swap Provider's Monthly Payment to Borrower*	*Borrower's Monthly Payment to Swap Provider*	*Borrower's Net Monthly Interest Payment*
5%	*$41,667*	*None*	*$8,333*	*$50,000*
6%	*$50,000*	*None*	*None*	*$50,000*
7%	*$58,333*	*($8,333)*	*None*	*$50,000*

By entering into the swap, the borrower has fixed its net monthly interest payment at $50,000, thereby effectively converting its floating rate construction loan to a 6% fixed rate loan. Under a swap, the borrower

---

133. The description of the swap implies that there are two payments being made during each month of the swap term—one by the borrower and one by the swap provider. In fact, most swaps are structured so that only one net payment is made during the applicable month of the swap term. *See* Davidson, *supra* note 126, at 559.

134. When a borrower asks a financial institution to provide it with a fixed rate that it is willing to swap for the borrower's floating interest rate, the swap provider will calculate what it believes to be a proper fixed rate match based on (a) the financial index used to calculate the floating interest rate, (b) the creditworthiness of the borrower and any security pledged to support the borrower's payment obligation, (c) its perception of future economic conditions, (d) the notional amount of the swap and (e) the length of the swap term (with the fixed rate of the swap usually increasing as the swap term gets longer). The swap provider will, obviously, also factor its desired profit into its fixed rate quote.

protects itself against a dramatic increase in its floating interest rate, but totally surrenders any benefit that it might otherwise receive from a decrease in the applicable financial index.

An interest rate swap can often be obtained without the need for the borrower to make any upfront fee to the swap provider.[135] *The absence of an upfront fee causes many borrowers to favor a swap over an interest rate cap or collar (both of which require the payment of a sizable fee to the swap provider).*

__Summary__: Interest rate hedges are valuable tools for use by both the borrower and the construction lender to hedge the risk of a cost overrun occasioned by a rapid rise in the level of the financial index specified in the construction loan documents. There are, however, a host of complex legal and business issues associated with swaps, caps, collars and other hedge techniques, all of which are beyond the scope of this discussion. Anyone considering the use of an interest rate hedge should consult the sources cited in the footnote for a more detailed examination of those issues.[136]

---

7. Loan Balancing Provision. *(§6.1(c))*

The ***loan balancing provision*** is the capstone of a lender's protection against the risk of a project cost overrun. The following is a typical loan balancing provision:

> *If at any time Lender notifies Borrower that, in Lender's sole judgment, the undisbursed balance of the Loan proceeds allocated to any line item in the Project Budget is insufficient to complete and fully pay the remaining Hard or Soft Costs represented by such line item, then Borrower shall promptly deposit with Lender cash in an amount equal to such deficiency. Lender shall have no obligation to make any further Loan advances, until it has received the required cash deposit from Borrower.*

Under the above clause, a construction loan will be considered ***out of balance*** if the lender's projection of the actual cost of fully funding a particular line item expense is more than the amount allotted for such expense in the approved development budget.

From the perspective of a construction lender, the purpose of a loan balancing provision is to permit the lender to suspend its obligation to make disbursements under the loan if it believes that a cost overrun has called into question whether the project can be completed for the budgeted cost. The lender does not want to compound its problems by having to

---

135. A borrower can try to buy down the percentage of the fixed rate swap by offering to pay an upfront fee to the swap provider. By way of example, if the swap provider offers to exchange a floating prime rate interest payment for a fixed rate payment of 6%, the borrower may be able to lower the fixed rate payment to 5.5% by agreeing to pay the swap provider an additional, upfront fee.

136. *See* Davidson, *supra* note 126; and BENDER, *supra* note 6, at 305–306.

"throw good money after bad" on a project whose completion is questionable because of the existence of a cost overrun. The lender's suspended funding obligation will only be reinstated if and when the borrower provides assurances acceptable to the lender that there are sufficient proceeds (whether debt or equity or a combination of both) to pay all costs needed to complete the project in accordance with the approved plans and specifications.

When structuring its loan balancing provision, the construction lender ideally looks to serve a number of objectives.[137]

- It wants to have the ability to make a determination that the loan is out of balance as early in the construction process as possible based on its projection of future costs. It does not want to have to wait to suspend its funding obligation until there is an actual (as opposed to a projected) cost overrun.

- It wants to preserve the right to make an unrestricted, independent determination that the loan is out of balance, without having to receive any validation of its decision from any other party (for example, the project architect or the general contractor).

- It wants to have the right to enforce the balancing remedy as to each separate line item of the approved project budget, without regard to any arguable cost savings in another line item of the budget.

- It wants to retain control over the use of any contingency reserve and the reallocation of any actual, verified cost savings in other line items.[138]

- It wants to make it clear that the only acceptable cure for a loan that is out of balance is the borrower's immediate deposit of cash with the construction lender in an amount sufficient to fund the projected cost overrun.

A loan balancing provision structured along the above lines[139] will provide the lender with significant protection against the risk of a project cost overrun—at least if the borrower/guarantors have the requisite financial standing and liquidity to put the loan back into balance by committing additional equity to the project. Even if the borrower/guarantors are incapable of putting additional cash into the project, a well-crafted loan balancing provision should give the lender the right to suspend its funding obligation while it seeks out other solutions to the cost overrun.

Borrower's Pushback: Developers view a cost overrun as just one more challenge that must be overcome as part of the dynamics of the

---

137. *See* Frobes, *Selected Issues in Secured Construction Lending, supra* note 65, at 123–125.

138. The loan balancing provision brings out an interesting dichotomy in the construction lender's thought process. It wants to be able to make a determination that a loan is out of balance based on "projected" costs, while at the same time insisting that any offsetting cost savings must be determined on the basis of "actual" costs.

139. For an example of a loan balancing provision which serves all of the lender's listed objectives, *see* Talley, *supra* note 39, at 143–144.

development process. Most developers ardently believe that they will eventually figure out a way to deal with an apparent cost overrun, either by shaving costs in other areas of the project or by identifying an unbudgeted revenue source to cover the cost overrun. All the developer asks is that the construction lender continue to provide funding to advance the project toward completion while the developer works on devising an acceptable way to resolve the cost overrun problem.

Given its perspective on the development process, it is not surprising that the borrower finds much to object to in the construction lender's typical loan balancing provision. The following are objections frequently raised by borrower's counsel to the lender's loan balancing provision.[140]

- The loan should be deemed out of balance based only on actual (and not projected) cost overruns.

- The existence of a cost overrun must be validated by a written statement from the project architect or the general contractor (or, at the bare minimum, made by the lender in the exercise of its reasonable judgment).

- The loan balancing remedy should apply only if there is an overrun in the developer's aggregate development costs (and not just in any one line item).

- The borrower should have the unfettered right to use the contingency reserve and projected cost savings[141] in other line items to offset any cost overrun.

- If the loan is legitimately determined to be out of balance, the borrower should have the right to cover the cost overruns in a variety of ways, expressly including (i) posting a letter of credit or other collateral to secure its obligation to fund a cost overrun with a back-end equity contribution and (ii) securing of secondary financing to fund the cost overrun.[142]

While the differences between the lender and the borrower on the loan balancing provision might seem irreconcilable, the lawyers representing the borrower and the lender are usually able to structure a mutually acceptable compromise.[143] By way of example, most lenders are willing to agree to act reasonably when making a determination that the loan is out of balance; to give the borrower a degree of flexibility to use cost savings and the contingency reserve to offset a project cost overrun; and to provide the borrower with a reasonable range of alternatives to put the

---

140. *See* Frobes, *Selected Issued in Secured Construction Lending, supra* note 765, at 125; and Thompson, *supra* note 40, at 9–112 and 9–113.

141. The borrower's thought process on the issue of whether and when projected or actual costs should be used in the implementation of the loan balancing provision is just as inconsistent as is the lender's thought process on that topic. *See supra* note 138.

142. *See* Thompson, *supra* note 40, at 9–113.

143. Section 6.1(c) of the Form Construction Loan Agreement is an example of a clause that is bit more balanced and fair to the developer than is the clause set forth at the beginning of this section or the clause included at the end of the article by Susan Talley referred to *supra* note 139.

loan back in balance.[144] The construction lender's willingness to make these concessions is, in large measure, driven by its recognition that, even when faced with a potential cost overrun, its best course of action is to do that which is necessary to insure the completion of the project.

HIBC Case Study—Dealing With the Risk of a Cost Overrun

*Reaching agreement on the cost overrun mitigation techniques discussed in this section did not prove to be a particularly challenging endeavor for Pizzuti and First Union. Much of the pressure normally felt by a construction lender to tighten the screws on possible cost overruns was relieved because Pizzuti was able to produce a guaranteed maximum price (**GMP***) contract from, its general contractor, Brasfield & Gorrie, on both the HTE and the 500 projects. Brasfield's GMP on both projects included a fairly significant contingency reserve—1.5% of the total construction costs for the HTE project and 1% of such costs for the 500 Building project. Finally, Brasfield's GMP was then further backed by a completion guaranty from Pizzuti Equities.*

With this anti-cost overrun support in place, Pizzuti was able to get First Union to agree to the following concessions to its standard cost overrun provisions:

- *The grant to Pizzuti of the right to make change orders up to a stipulated dollar amount without having to obtain First Union's consent;*

- *First Union's acknowledgement that Pizzuti could use the contingency reserve and verifiable cost savings in any line item to defray a cost overrun in another line item of the development budget;*

---

144. A topic which can, on occasion, become the subject of intense negotiations between the construction lender and the borrower is the standard prohibition contained in the construction loan documents against the existence of any secondary project financing (i.e., any borrowing in addition to the construction loan). If the borrower is unable (or unwilling) to provide equity to fully fund the gap between its overall development costs and the amount of the construction loan (which gap can exist either at the outset of the loan or as a result of the construction lender's exercise of its loan balancing right), the borrower will need to negotiate revisions to the secondary financing prohibition so that the borrower can source additional debt financing to help fund the cost gap. A common source for the funding of that gap is mezzanine financing where a financial institution provides debt to help a borrower defray its equity requirements in exchange for the borrower's agreement (a) to pay an above-market interest rate to the mezzanine lender (sometimes in the form of a profit participation) and (b) to pledge ownership interests in the borrower as collateral for the mezzanine loan. The placement of mezzanine financing on a real estate project raises a host of very complex issues regarding the construction and mezzanine lenders' respective interests and priorities in the underlying real estate project. Those issues are typically addressed in an intercreditor agreement entered into by the mezzanine and construction lenders. An exploration of the many issues associated with mezzanine financing is beyond the scope of this Chapter. For a discussion of those issues, *see generally* Kyle, *supra* note 97, at 130–131; Michael Weinberger, *Mezzanine Finance*, in ALI–ABA COURSE OF STUDY MATERIALS, COMMERCIAL REAL ESTATE FINANCING: STRATEGIES FOR CHANGING MARKETS AND UNCERTAIN TIMES, Course No. SP–008, 357 (January 2009); and K.C. McDaniel, *Intercreditor Remedies—When and How*, in ALI–ABA COURSE OF STUDY MATERIALS, COMMERCIAL REAL ESTATE FINANCING: STRATEGIES FOR CHANGING MARKETS AND UNCERTAIN TIMES, Course No. SP–008, 1445 (January 2009).

- *First Union's agreement that it would fund 50% of Pizzuti's development fee in the initial loan advance, with the remainder to be allocated proportionately over the remaining draws based on the percentage of completion of each project; and*

- *First Union's acceptance of Pizzuti's estimate of the fair market value of the land as the "land cost" included in the approved development budget. Pizzuti was also able to get First Union to agree to treat the full fair market value of the land as a credit against its required equity contribution on both projects.*

Thus, by addressing First Union's primary cost overrun concerns by providing the lender with an acceptable GMP contract and a completion guaranty, Pizzuti was able to get significant relief from the more draconian provisions of First Union's standard construction loan provisions on cost overruns. This is an instructive lesson for the new practitioner—if you understand and try to satisfy the legitimate business needs of the other side to a negotiation, you will be well-positioned to negotiate contractual concessions that are essential to your client's achievement of its primary business objectives.

C. DEALING WITH THE RISK OF INSUFFICIENT VALUE ON COMPLETION

The prior two sections addressed the issue of what the construction lender can do to try to protect itself against the risks that the project may not be completed on time or on budget. Once it has dealt with those two issues, the construction lender is faced with yet another significant risk— what happens if the project is completed on time and on budget, but its value is less than the value projected by the borrower at the inception of the loan underwriting process?

The diminished value of the underlying real estate collateral is an issue which, in some measure, is faced by all real estate lenders—both construction and permanent lenders. However, the risk is elevated in the context of a construction loan, because there is no income stream in place when the construction lender has to make its decision to commit to make a particular construction loan. Therefore, unlike the permanent lender, who only has to worry about a future deterioration in a project's existing income stream, the construction lender must also be concerned with the creation of the value of the project in the first instance. If that value is not created to the extent projected in the lender's initial loan underwriting, the construction lender may be left without a viable exit strategy for the repayment of its construction loan.

The next several sections of this Chapter will examine the risk mitigation techniques that a construction lender can use to lessen its exposure to this value risk

1. Credit Enhancement. *(§§3.2(b) and (b), 5.1(d) and 5.3)*

The best way for a construction lender to limit its value risk is to shift its primary security for the loan's repayment away from the value of the underlying real estate collateral and toward the balance sheet of the borrower/guarantor. In other words, the construction lender should try to make its construction loan less a real estate loan and more a personal loan. The value risk faced by a construction lender on a $10 million construction loan to build a warehouse in Columbus, Ohio is very different if the borrower is Warren Buffet versus yours truly. If I am the borrower, the lender will be forced to pull out all the stops in using the other techniques discussed in this section to mitigate its value risk. If Mr. Buffet is the borrower, the construction lender will have the luxury of being somewhat lax on its structuring of the risk mitigation provisions of the construction loan agreement.

The following discussion highlights the two credit enhancement techniques that are most commonly used by a construction lender to lessen its value risk—(1) the payment guaranty and (2) a letter of credit.

Payment Guaranty: The norm in today's lending environment is for the borrower to be a single purpose entity with no net worth beyond the value of the project that is the subject of the construction loan. The credit standing behind a construction loan is, therefore, typically provided by an affiliate of the borrower, who executes a payment guaranty that unconditionally obligates the guarantor to repay the construction loan.[145]

The construction lender will try to secure a payment guaranty from the most creditworthy person associated with the developer—which typically is the developer's principal equity owner. Once the identity of an acceptable guarantor is determined, the lender will next turn its attention to including provisions in the payment guaranty that are designed to buttress the utility and enforceability of that document—for example:

- A clause making it clear that the lender need not exhaust its remedies against the borrower or the collateral before pursuing a collection action against the guarantor;

- A statement acknowledging that the construction loan and the underlying collateral documents may be modified or dealt with in any fashion without notice to the guarantor and without affecting the ongoing liability of the guarantor;

- A provision affirming that the guaranty will survive the bankruptcy of the borrower;

---

145. The many issues associated with the structuring and enforcement of payment guaranties are beyond the scope of this Chapter. For a more detailed discussion of payment guaranties in the context of real estate financing transactions, *see generally* Andrea M. Mattei, *Credit Enhancements in Turbulent Times*, in ALI–ABA COURSE OF STUDY MATERIALS, COMMERCIAL REAL ESTATE FINANCING: STRATEGIES FOR CHANGING MARKETS AND UNCERTAIN TIMES, Course No. SP–008, 663 (January 2009) and Diana C, Liu, *An Annotated Guaranty*, 17 No. 5 PRACTICAL REAL ESTATE LAWYER 45 (September 2001).

- A representation confirming the guarantor's current net worth and a warranty obligating the guarantor to maintain that level of net worth throughout the term of the construction loan; and

- A covenant requiring the guarantor to provide the lender with its current financial statements at least annually throughout the term of the construction loan.

Borrower's Pushback: Most borrowers acknowledge that they will not be able to secure construction financing, unless they furnish the lender with a payment guaranty from a creditworthy entity. From the borrower's perspective, the principal issue comes down to who will have to provide the guaranty—the individual owners of the borrower/developer or, preferably, some lesser credit entity owned and controlled by the individual owners.

A borrower will occasionally seek to place an upper limit on the dollar amount of the guarantor's exposure under its payment guaranty. The following are examples of some common guaranty limitations:[146]

- A guaranty of the "top 50% of the loan";[147]

- A guaranty of the "bottom 50% of the loan";[148]

- A several guaranty limited to the guarantor's percentage equity interest in the deal;

- A reduction of the guaranty to 25% of the loan upon the completion of the project; or

- An elimination of the guaranty upon the project achieving a lease-up of more than 90% of its rentable space.

The guarantor's ability to negotiate a limited guaranty is a function of the creditworthiness of the borrowing entity, the lender's perception of the risk associated with the underlying real estate project, and the competitiveness of the construction loan market. In the current lending climate, a guarantor of a construction loan will seldom be able to negotiate any limitation on its payment guaranty, until the project is completed and substantially leased.

Letter of Credit: If the borrower is either unable or unwilling to fully satisfy the lender's demand for the provision of a payment guaranty from a creditworthy person, the construction lender might ask the borrow-

---

146. *See* RICHARD B. PEISER WITH ANNE B. FREJ, PROFESSIONAL REAL ESTATE DEVELOPMENT: THE ULI GUIDE TO THE BUSINESS 187–188 (2nd ed. 2003). The specific percentages used in the text are purely for illustrative purposes and should not be interpreted as being industry norms.

147. A guaranty of the "top" 50% of a $10 million loan means that the guarantor protects the lender against the first $5 million of loss. As such, if the borrower forecloses on a project and sells it at a sheriff's sale for $4 million (producing a lender loss of $6 million), the guarantor will be obligated to pay $5 million to the lender (thereby reducing the lender's net loss to $1 million). *See id.,* at 187.

148. A guaranty of the "bottom" 50% of a $10 million loan means that the guarantor protects the lender against the last $5 million of loss. As such, the guarantor will not have any liability to the lender under its payment guaranty, unless the sale of the project at a sheriff's sale produces sales proceeds of less than $5 million. *See id.* at 188. For obvious reasons, construction lenders seldom, if ever, agree to a guaranty of the bottom portion of a loan.

er to further secure the loan by posting a letter of credit from a commercial bank or other financial institution. The letter of credit will typically be for an amount less than the full amount of the construction loan.[149]

The topics of the structuring and enforcement of letters of credit are again beyond the scope of this Chapter.[150] Having said that, it should be observed that the construction lender will customarily insist that the letter of credit be an ***irrevocable, standby letter of credit,*** whereby the issuer is unconditionally obligated to pay the amount of the letter of credit upon its receipt of a lender demand for payment that says nothing more than "the borrower is in default under the construction loan."[151]

Borrower's Push-back: The borrower's principal concern with a letter of credit is its cost. The bank issuing the letter of credit will usually charge the borrower an annual fee of 1–3% of the letter of credit amount ($40–120,000 per year for a $4 million letter of credit).[152] Moreover, if the construction lender cannot get comfortable with the credit of the person whose payment guaranty is being offered up by the borrower, it is likely that the borrower will have similar difficulty in obtaining a letter of credit.

The one instance where a borrower might want to agree to provide the lender with a letter of credit is where the individual owners of the developer have ample net worth, but do not want to subject themselves to personal liability for the full repayment of the construction loan. In such a circumstance, a borrower may be able to satisfy the lender's credit concerns by buttressing a payment guaranty from a marginally creditworthy entity with the issuance of a letter of credit for a limited portion of the construction loan amount (e.g., 10–20% of the loan).[153]

2. Underwriting to the Permanent Loan Market

The construction lender's business model contemplates that a life insurance company, pension fund or other financial institution will step up to provide the necessary debt or equity dollars to pay off the construction loan once the developer's project is completed and leased.[154] In order to properly position the construction loan for refinancing with a perma-

---

149. *See generally* Lefcoe, *supra* note 55, at 510.

150. For a more in-depth discussion of letters of credit, *see id.* at 585–588; and Mattei, *supra* note 145, at 671–674.

151. A sample irrevocable standby letter of credit is attached to the Mattei article, *supra* note 181, at 679–682.

152. The letter of credit fee will vary based on (a) the amount and duration of the letter of credit and (b) the financial strength of the person requesting the issuance of the letter of credit (who will also be the person ultimately responsible for the repayment of the letter of credit amount to the issuing financial institution if the construction lender ever draws down on the letter of credit).

153. This approach, if accepted by the construction lender, would permit the individual owners to reduce their contingent liability on a $10 million construction loan from a full $10 million to $1–2 million (the amount of the guaranty that the owners would be required to provide to the bank issuing the letter of credit)—a result that might justify the borrower's payment of an additional fee of $10–20,000 per year to obtain a letter of credit.

154. As used in the remainder of this section, the term "permanent loan" will include both a conventional permanent loan and the sale to an institutional investor of all or a portion of the real estate project.

nent loan, it is essential that the construction lender underwrite its loan based on those lending principles and guidelines that are then prevailing in the permanent loan market. A construction lender that fails to adhere to this simple rule runs the risk of having a bad loan on its books that is not susceptible to being refinanced by a permanent loan. By way of example, if a construction lender makes a loan in a principal amount equal to 90% of a project's total development costs at a time when the permanent loan market is pricing its loans at no more than 70% of project costs, the construction lender will have rely on the credit of the borrower/guarantor to provide the funds necessary to pay off the portion of the construction loan that cannot be retired with the proceeds of a permanent loan—a scenario that may not be realistic when the construction loan matures.

There are two strategies that a construction lender can adopt to increase the odds that its underwriting of the construction loan will square with the prevailing underwriting practices of the permanent loan market. One such strategy—a ***permanent take-out commitment***—operates prospectively, while the other strategy—a ***loan remargining***—works retroactively.

Permanent Take-out Commitment: Until the mid–1980's, the required presence of a permanent loan take-out commitment was a staple of most construction loans.[155] A permanent take-out commitment is an agreement by a permanent lender that it will close a permanent loan to the borrower and pay off the construction loan upon the occurrence of certain conditions.

Ideally, the take-out commitment is issued by the permanent lender before the construction loan is closed (or at least before the initial advance of construction loan proceeds). The permanent lender's obligation to "take out" the construction loan can be documented either by a tri-party agreement entered into by the construction and permanent lenders and the borrower or a buy-sell agreement to which just the construction and permanent lenders are parties.[156] The substance of both of these agreements is the same—a recitation of when and under what circumstances the permanent lender is required to close and fund its permanent loan.

The key issue to be addressed in the agreement between the construction and permanent lenders is the scope of the conditions to the permanent lender's take-out commitment.[157] The construction lender wants the conditions to the permanent lender's funding obligation to be as limited as possible and relate solely to the physical condition of the project—i.e., the lien-free completion of the project in accordance with the approved plans and specifications. If the conditions to the permanent lender's funding obligation are limited to objectively achievable events, then the existence of a permanent take-out commitment provides the construction lender

---

155. *See* PEISER, *supra* note 146, at 182.

156. *See* Weller, *supra* note 28, at 1753.

157. *See* Talley, *supra* note 39, at 140–141.

with its best protection against the risk that the actual value of the completed project is less than that initially projected by the borrower.

The permanent lender, on the other hand, wants the conditions to its funding obligation to be as expansive as possible to provide the permanent lender with a host of outs if something occurs after its issuance of the take-out commitment that causes the permanent lender to change its mind concerning the funding of the permanent loan.[158] The permanent lender wants the funding conditions to extend not just to the completed status of the project, but also to issues that impact the project's income stream—specifically including (1) the lease-up of the project at net rental rates consistent or better than the developer's financial projections and (2) the absence of any change in prevailing market conditions that would make its funding of the permanent loan inadvisable (e.g., a marked increase in capitalization rates used to value commercial real estate projects similar to the developer's project).

The permanent lender's reticence to furnish the construction lender with a condition-free take-out stems from the fact that the permanent lender is being asked to make its loan commitment well in advance of the anticipated permanent loan closing—typically at least 12 months and many times 24–36 months in advance of the closing date. As witnessed by the sudden downturn in the economy in 2008, a lot can happen in 12–36 months to cause a permanent lender to re-think its initial underwriting decision. Following the 2008 disruption of the capital markets, real estate values plummeted and the permanent loan market totally dried up. Given that type of circumstance, it is clear why construction lenders want to rigorously restrict the permanent lender's funding discretion, while the permanent lender wants to instill its take-out commitment with an unending series of contractual escape hatches.

The first sentence in this discussion referenced the fact that take-out commitments were the norm 25–30 years ago. Implicit in that comment is the fact that take-out commitments have lost their luster in recent years.[159] What happened to cause take-out commitments to go out of favor? In addition to the broadening of its take-out conditions, what else can a permanent lender to do to hedge its risk that something untoward occurs between the date of its issuance of the take-out commitment and the anticipated date of the permanent loan closing? The answers to those questions are provided below in the discussion of the *Borrower's Pushback*.

Borrower's Pushback: The borrower shares the construction lender's desire to refinance the construction loan with a permanent loan. Implementing a permanent loan exit strategy permits the borrower to replace a short-term, fully recourse debt obligation with a longer-term,

---

158. *See* PEISER, *supra* note 146, at 183

159. The inexperienced, underfunded developer is still frequently faced with a requirement that it obtain a permanent take-out commitment (debt or equity) as a condition to the funding of its construction loan. *See* PEISER, *supra* note 146, at 182.

nonrecourse mortgage loan.[160] Having a take-out commitment in hand before starting construction on the project effectively eliminates most of the borrower's risk that something will occur to decrease the borrower's prospects of implementing its permanent loan exit strategy.

So, given the theoretical attractiveness of the permanent loan take-out to both the construction lender and the borrower, why isn't the existence of a binding take-out commitment a required condition of every construction loan? The answer to that question lies in the way in which permanent lenders react to a request that they provide a take-out commitment on a development project. When asked to commit to making a permanent loan 12–36 months in advance of the anticipated permanent loan closing date (and, more importantly, before construction of the project has even begun), a cautious permanent lender will routinely do three things:

- Set the permanent loan interest rate at a generous spread over the permanent lender's cost of funds;

- Require the borrower to pay a sizable, non-refundable commitment fee at the time of the issuance of the permanent take-out commitment; and

- Subject its funding obligation to a plethora of conditions, many of which are designed to convert the loan "commitment" into a loan "option" for the permanent lender.[161]

From the borrower's perspective, a take-out commitment issued along the lines outlined above is simply not worth the cost of obtaining that commitment. Why, asks the borrower, should I pay an exorbitant, upfront commitment fee to obtain an over-priced loan that the permanent lender is only nominally obligated to fund? Moreover, because a take-out commitment is almost always enforceable by the permanent lender (even though it may not be particularly enforceable against the permanent lender), the existence of the take-out effectively precludes the borrower from benefiting from any change in interest rates or market conditions that might otherwise motivate it to look elsewhere for permanent financing.[162]

For all of the above reasons, the existence of a take-out commitment is no longer commonly required as a condition to the funding of a construction loan.[163] One type of project where a take-out commitment is

---

160. *See infra* Chapter 12, Page 553, for a further discussion of the developer's desire to refinance its construction loan with a permanent loan.

161. The following is an example of the breadth of the funding conditions found in the standard take-out commitments of most permanent lenders—"[a]s a condition to the initial disbursement of loan proceeds under this Agreement, there shall be no material adverse change in Borrower's financial condition, prospects, profits or operations or the physical condition of the Property." *See* Michael Hamilton, *Representing Borrowers in Changing Time*, in ALI–ABA COURSE OF STUDY MATERIALS, COMMERCIAL REAL ESTATE FINANCING: STRATEGIES FOR CHANGING MARKETS AND UNCERTAIN TIMES, Course No. SP–008, 159, 167–168 (January 2009).

162. *See* Thompson, *supra* note 40, at 9–14.

163. This may change in the immediate future as construction lenders adopt more conservative underwriting practices to respond to the 2008 credit crunch. *See infra Practice Tip #9–2— The Credit Crisis of 2008 (and Beyond).*

still frequently used is a project that is 100% pre-leased to a credit tenant.[164] In that situation, the borrower may try to increase the amount of its construction loan[165] and decrease its exit strategy risk by securing a take-out commitment from a life company or other institutional investor. A take-out commitment issued on a project that is fully leased to a creditworthy tenant will typically cost less and be subject to a much less expansive set of funding conditions than will a commitment issued on a project that is not blessed with either of those characteristics.[166]

Remargining the Construction Loan: A second strategy employed by construction lenders to try to be more responsive to the underwriting guidelines being practiced in the permanent loan market is something called a ***loan remargining*** provision. A remargining provision obligates the borrower/guarantor to make additional equity contributions to pay down the principal amount of the construction loan to the extent the lender determines that the created value of a development project is less than that projected at the inception of the lender's underwriting for the loan. The following is an example of a fairly standard remargining provision.[167]

> *If at any time during the term of the Loan, Lender obtains an appraisal of the Project, which shows that the Loan-to-Value Ratio of the Loan is greater than 70%, then Borrower will immediately be required to make a principal payment to reduce such Loan-to-Value Ratio to 70% or less.*

Under the excerpted remargining provision, a construction lender would have the right to require the borrower to make a $700,000 principal payment on its $7 million construction loan if an appraisal obtained by the lender at the completion of the project shows that the fair market value of the project is $9 million (and not $10 million as initially projected by the borrower).

A remargining provision is commonly attached to a provision giving the borrower an option to extend the loan's maturity date for an additional term of two to three years (sometimes referred to as a ***mini-perm loan***). The construction lender will frequently condition the borrower's right to exercise that extension option upon an objective determination being made that the completed project satisfies certain value and income standards—e.g., loan-to-value and debt service coverage tests. If the con-

---

164. In the context of a single tenant project, the take-out will frequently take the form of an institutional investor's commitment to buy the project upon completion.

165. If the terms of the take-out commitment are sufficiently tight, a construction lender might be willing to increase the principal amount of the construction loan to 90–100% of the project's development costs.

166. The construction lender's goal would be to limit the take-out conditions to (a) the lien-free completion of the project in accordance with the approved plans and specifications and (b) the receipt of an estoppel certificate from the project's sole tenant affirming that the lease is in full force and effect and that the tenant has begun paying rent.

167. The quoted provision uses a loan-to-value test to determine whether the loan needs to be remargained. Construction lenders often use a debt service coverage ratio and other income stream measurements as benchmarks for triggering a remargining of the construction loan.

struction loan agreement gives the borrower a right to remargain the loan, the borrower can preserve its right to exercise its extension option by paying down the principal amount of the construction loan to a level that causes its project to come into compliance with the stated financial conditions.[168]

One point to keep in mind with respect to the remargining technique is that it is only as good as the credit of the borrower/guarantor. Therefore, while the remargining provision is designed to enhance the lender's exit strategy under the construction loan by retroactively bringing the loan into compliance with the underwriting practices of the permanent loan community, that provision is rendered wholly ineffective if the borrower/guarantor doesn't have the money required to make the mandated principal payment.

Borrower Pushback: A borrower has two principal objectives in negotiating a remargining provision (assuming it is unable to get the lender to agree to delete the entire provision). First, the borrower will resist an attempt by the construction lender to require the borrower to pay down the principal during the construction loan term. While most borrowers are willing to accept a remargining provision as an adjunct to its mini-perm conversion right, they will insist that the lender not have the right to change the rules of the game and reduce the construction loan amount prior to the loan's original maturity date. Otherwise, the borrower will never know whether it has the funding needed to complete the construction and leasing of its real estate project.

As noted, most borrowers will accede to the lender's requirement that a remargining provision be included as a condition to the borrower's exercise of its right to convert the construction loan into a mini-perm loan. The devil is, however, in the details when it comes to the substance of the remargining provision. What are the specific financial ratios included in the remargining provision—e.g., is the extension of the loan term conditioned on the project satisfying a loan-to-value ratio of 80% or 70%? Is the project's compliance with the mandated financial ratios determined strictly under executed leases or can the borrower factor in projected rentals on vacant space? What other parameters will be used to test the project's compliance with the financial ratios—e.g., the identification of a specific capitalization rate for determining the project's value, the recital of the debt amortization period used to determine the project's debt service coverage ratio, etc.?[169]

3. Control of Project Lease-up

The value of a commercial real estate project is wholly dependent on the level of the income stream produced from the project's leases. There-

---

168. *See* Talley, *supra* note 39, at 141–142; and Alfred G. Kyle, *Commercial Real Estate Construction Lending (With Forms) Part I*, 22 No. 2 PRACTICAL REAL ESTATE LAWYER 7, 9 (March 2006).

169. For a discussion of the various financial tests used by a lender to determine the maximum amount of a construction loan, *see supra* Chapter 3, Pages 42–44, and *infra* Pages 387–389.

fore, one way for the construction lender to protect itself against value risk is to exercise its powers under the loan documents to cause the borrower to lease its project within the time periods and at the rental rates specified in the borrower's initial financial projections.

The construction lender can exert its control over the lease-up of the project in two distinct ways. First, the lender can establish a pre-leasing requirement as a condition to its obligation to fund advances under the construction loan. The following is a sample of a clause establishing such a pre-leasing requirement:

> *Lender shall not be obligated to make any loan advance until at least ___% of the rentable space contained in the Project has been leased pursuant to written leases approved by Lender.*

The creation of a pre-leasing requirement provides the construction lender with a significant buffer against the risk that the value of the completed project will be less than its underwritten value. In the perfect world, the construction lender would condition its obligation to make any loan advances upon the borrower's prior execution of leases at or above pro forma rents for 100% of the rentable space in the project. Under that scenario, the construction lender's value risk would be limited to the risks that (1) the project is not completed at the time required under the executed leases (thereby permitting the tenants to terminate their leasing commitments) and (2) a change or dislocation in the real estate market leads to a decline in the relative value assigned to the income stream produced under the signed leases (e.g., an increase in capitalization rates or the advent of runaway inflation). While most construction lenders do not expect to achieve the perfect world of a 100% pre-leasing condition, the insertion into the construction loan agreement of a lesser pre-leasing requirement (e.g., the required pre-leasing of 60% of the rentable space in the project) will n provide the construction lender with a substantial hedge against the lease-up risk that is at the heart of the lender's value quandary.

The second technique utilized by the construction lender to advance its interest in seeing the project leased in a manner consistent with the developer's initial projections is the lender's reservation of a right to approve all leases of space in the project.[170] The following is an example of such a provision:

> *Borrower shall not enter into any lease of space in the Project, without first obtaining the written consent of Lender as to both the form and content of such lease. Borrower's breach of the foregoing covenant shall constitute an Event of Default, with Lender thereafter having all rights and remedies available to it at law or in equity to redress such breach, including, without limitation, the right to suspend its obligation to make any further advances under the Loan.*

---

170. The construction lender will usually further condition its consent to any lease of space in the project to the tenant executing a subordination, non-disturbance and attornment agreement

Such a borrower covenant provides the construction lender with added protection against the risk that the borrower will lease space in the project for a rent which is less than that projected in the developer's approved leasing plan.

Borrower's Pushback: The negotiations will take a contentious turn when the construction lender seeks to place limitations on the flexibility that the developer feels it needs to lease its project. A pre-leasing requirement particularly rankles a developer who believes (rightly or wrongly) in the old adage of "build it and they will come." It is exceedingly difficult for a developer to get a prospective tenant to sign a lease for space in a building before construction of the building has begun. Tenants tend to be fairly cautious and cynical people, who are unwilling to make long-term leasing decisions based on an artist's rendering of a proposed building or a developer's promise that the building will be completed "real soon." A pre-leasing requirement places the developer in a classic Catch 22—it can't get the prospective tenant to sign a lease until construction has started and it can't get the construction lender to give it the money it needs to start construction until the lease is signed. A borrower who is forced to accept a pre-leasing requirement will expend considerable negotiating energy in an attempt to place a reasonable limit on the pre-leasing requirement (e.g., the leasing of 20% of the project's rentable space rather than 70% of such space).

A borrower is generally more accepting of the construction lender's insistence that it retain the right to pre-approve any lease signed by the borrower. The borrower, does not, however, want the lender's approval right to deprive the borrower of the discretion that it needs to effectively market its building. The prudent borrower seeks to limit the lender's lease approval rights in a variety of ways, including the following:[171]

- A limitation that the lender has the right to approve only "major leases"—e.g., leases of at least 20,000 rentable square feet;

- A provision authorizing the borrower to sign a lease, so long as the lease terms are consistent with leasing guidelines[172] previously approved by the lender;

- The lender's pre-approval of the borrower's standard lease form and the lender's further agreement that the borrower can make reasonable, negotiated modifications to such form, as long as such modifications do not materially, adversely impair the rental stream created under the lease; and

- A requirement that the lender act reasonably and with dispatch in reviewing any lease requiring its approval under the construction loan documents.

("SNDA"). For a discussion of the purposes served by an SNDA, *see infra* Chapter 11, Pages 545–546.

171. *See* Kyle, *Part 3, supra* note 97, at 10; and Crance, *supra* note 10, at 175–177.

172. The approved guidelines usually stipulate a minimum lease term, a maximum tenant improvement allowance, a minimum net rental and those other legal and business terms that hold particular significance for the construction lender.

One issue related to the lender's lease approval rights that engenders extensive discussion is the issue of who gets to decide whether a prospective tenant's credit is acceptable, with each of parties predictably taking the position that it should have the final say on that issue. A common compromise is for the construction loan agreement to recite that the lender's approval of the identity of a particular tenant (as opposed to the terms of that tenant's lease) is not required if the prospective tenant meets a minimum net worth standard (e.g., a net worth computed in accordance with generally accepted accounting principles of not less than $25 million).

4. Limitations on Amount of Construction Loan

The most obvious way for a construction lender to limit its value risk is by reducing the amount of the construction loan. A construction loan of $10 million on Project A is by definition more risky than a loan of $8 million on the same project. By the same token, a construction lender makes its money by maximizing the amount of money it loans to borrowers—so long as that money is repaid in full on the maturity of the loan. A construction lender whose risk aversion causes it to unduly limit the amount of its construction loans will discover that it is outbid on project after project by more aggressive construction lenders.

The key for the construction lender is to set its loan amount at a level that gives it reasonable assurance that the loan will be repaid. The construction lender accomplishes that objective by creating a "cushion" between the principal amount of the loan and the anticipated value of the underlying development project.[173]

Construction lenders have devised a series of financial tests to help them create the optimal level of loan cushion. The four most common underwriting techniques used by construction lenders to establish the maximum amount of a construction loan (and, hence, the amount of the lender's loan cushion) are set forth below.

- *Loan-to-Cost*—Under this test, the loan amount is stated as a percentage of the borrower's total development costs. Loan-to-cost ratios have traditionally hovered in the 70–90% range, although the economic downturn of the late 2000's has many experts predicting that loan-to-cost ratios will drop precipitously.[174] A loan-to-cost ratio of 80% will produce a maximum loan amount of $8 million on a project having a total development cost of $10 million.

- *Loan-to-Value*—This test ties the maximum loan amount to a percentage of the projected value of the underlying development project. Loan-to-value percentages are normally slightly lower than loan-to-cost ratios based on the theory that a development project should always have a projected value that is well in excess of its

---

173. *See* MICHAEL E. MILES, GAYLE L. BERENS AND MARC A. WEISS, REAL ESTATE DEVELOPMENT: PRINCIPLES AND PROCESS 93 (3rd ed. 2000).

174. *See infra Practice Tip #9–2—The Credit Crisis of 2008 (and Beyond),* at Page 397.

cost. A loan-to value ratio of 70% on a project having an anticipated value of $12 million will produce a maximum construction loan amount of $8.4 million. The construction lender implements its loan-to-value criterion by conditioning its funding obligation on its receipt of an appraisal from a qualified appraiser showing that the appraised fair market value of the project at completion will be equal to or greater than the projected value used by the lender during its underwriting of the construction loan.[175]

- **Debt Service Coverage**—This test establishes the upper boundary of the construction loan amount by requiring that the project's annual, anticipated, net operating income comfortably exceed the annual debt service payable under the loan.[176] A debt service coverage ratio of somewhere between 1.1 and 1.3 is fairly typical in the underwriting of construction loans.[177]

- **Debt Yield**—In recent years, the debt yield test has become a popular tool used by lenders in the underwriting of construction loans. Under the debt yield test, the maximum amount of a construction loan is determined by dividing the project's projected annual, net operating income by some fixed percentage yield. By way of example, a debt yield percentage of 10% on a project having an anticipated NOI of $1 million would produce a maximum loan amount of $10 million.

The specific percentages selected by a construction lender for each of these four tests will depend upon its own risk profile, its perception of the risk quotient of the subject project and the conditions then prevailing in the construction financing and permanent loan markets. It is the norm for construction lenders to adopt a lowest common denominator approach by establishing the maximum amount of the construction loan as the lowest figure produced under the four tests (or at least those tests used by the construction lender in its underwriting of the construction loan).

Borrower Pushback: The typical borrower cares deeply about maximizing the principal amount of its construction loan[178] and cares hardly at all about the lender's need for a loan cushion. A borrower who wants to push the envelope on the outer boundary of the construction loan amount will be well-served by (1) establishing a reputation among construction lenders for preparing accurate financial projections, (2) offering up loan guaranties backed by a financially solid guarantor, (3) convincing the construction lender to use an appraiser with whom the developer has an established relationship and (4) hiring legal counsel who understands the financial tests used by construction lenders and, therefore, is well-

---

175. *See, e.g.,* §3.2(m) of the Form Construction Loan Agreement.

176. *See supra* Chapter 3, Page 43, for a description of how the maximum principal amount of a loan is calculated under the debt service coverage test.

177. A debt service coverage of 1.1 means that the project's net operating income must be at least 110% of the debt service payable by the borrower under the construction loan.

178. For a discussion of the borrower's reasons for wanting to maximize the amount of its construction loan, *see supra* Pages 51–52.

equipped to rebuff any overbearing attempts made in the commitment letter and construction loan agreement to unreasonably limit the amount of the borrower's construction financing.

HIBC Case Study—Dealing With Value Risk

A significant part of the Pizzuti–First Union loan negotiations revolved around First Union's ardent attempts to protect itself against the risk that the HTE and 500 Building projects would not have sufficient value upon completion to facilitate a refinancing of First Union's construction loans. Given the disparate nature of the two projects, the discussion which follows will separately examine First Union's attempt to use value risk mitigation techniques for each of the HTE and 500 projects.

__Limitation of Loan Amount__: The loan proposals submitted by Pizzuti to First Union asked for a 90% loan-to-cost loan for the HTE project and an 80% loan-to-cost loan for the 500 Building. First Union gave its approval to the requested loan amount for the 500 Building, but refused to go along with Pizzuti's request for a 90% loan amount on the HTE project. First Union's position on the HTE loan was largely driven by its concern about HTE's credit (or lack thereof). Long story short, First Union agreed to provide an 85% loan-to-cost loan for the HTE project, subject, however, to a 75% loan-to-value override based on an appraisal to be obtained by First Union. Unfortunately for Pizzuti, the appraisal came in unreasonably low (at least from Pizzuti's perspective) because of the concern over HTE's net worth. The lower than anticipated appraised fair market value for the HTE project resulted in a further reduction of the loan amount to $8.2 million.

__Control of Project Lease-up__: First Union's approach to the lease-up issue on the HTE project was relatively simple and straightforward. Due to the single tenant nature of that project, First Union required Pizzuti to collaterally assign its interest in the HTE lease to First Union, so that, if necessary, First Union could complete construction of the project and enforce HTE's lease obligations. The construction loan agreement also established the receipt of HTE's signed estoppel certificate and subordination, non-disturbance and attornment agreements as conditions to the initial loan advance.[179]

First Union's initial approach to the lease-up of the 500 Building was much more rigorous. The first draft of its commitment letter recited that no loan disbursements would be made under the construction loan until at least 60% of the rentable space in the 500 Building was leased pursuant to written leases approved by First Union. The commitment letter purported to give First Union the right to disapprove any lease in its sole discretion.

---

179. *See infra* Chapter 11, Pages 545–547, for a discussion of the contents of a typical tenant estoppel certificate and subordination, non-disturbance and attornment agreement.

After lengthy negotiations on the point, Pizzuti was able to get First Union to agree to drop the pre-leasing agreement in its entirety. The bargaining chips Pizzuti played to achieve this result were (1) the financial strength of the parties guarantying repayment of the construction loan (see discussion infra) and (2) a marketing report prepared by Pizzuti's leasing broker stating that there was ample, pent-up demand for leased space in the north Orlando office market, but that the prospective tenants they had contacted were leery of committing to lease space in a project until they saw a building coming out of the ground. Pizzuti was also able to get First Union to agree to loosen its lease approval rights to exempt (a) any lease with average base rents of at least $19 psf and a term of at least five years and (b) up to 20,000 square feet of space which could be leased on any terms determined by Pizzuti in its sole discretion.

___Permanent Take-out Commitment___: First Union's initial reaction to Pizzuti's loan proposal for the HTE project was to require Pizzuti to obtain a take-out commitment as a condition precedent to First Union's funding obligation under its construction loan.[180] First Union was concerned about the mediocre credit standing of HTE and felt that the receipt of a take-out commitment from a permanent lender would serve as a needed confirmation of the acceptability of the HTE lease to the permanent loan market. While First Union's position on the HTE take-out condition was eminently logical, Pizzuti was able to eliminate that condition from the loan commitment based on two considerations—(1) the HTE loan was backed by a full payment guaranty from extremely creditworthy persons and (2) Pizzuti could not get a bankable, take-out commitment[181] from a permanent lender on the HTE project (in part because of the permanent loan market's concern with HTE's credit). In the end, First Union had no choice but to back off on its requirement for a take-out commitment on the HTE project.

___Loan Remargining/Conversion to Mini-perm___: In its initial loan submissions, Pizzuti had asked for a 12 month extension option on the HTE loan and a 24 month extension option on the 500 Building loan. First Union compromised on these two requests by agreeing to provide an 18 month extension option under each of the construction loans, subject, however, to (1) Pizzuti making fixed, monthly, principal payments on each loan throughout the extension term and (2) Pizzuti providing First Union with evidence that the subject building had been completed in accordance with the approved plans and specifications. Neither loan conditioned the exercise of Pizzuti's extension option on the project's satisfaction of any financial tests or lease-up standards, nor did either loan contain a remar-

---

180. First Union acknowledged that a take-out commitment was infeasible on the 500 building project because it was a purely speculative building with no existing income stream.

181. A "bankable commitment" is a take-out commitment from a permanent lender that the construction lender believes obligates the permanent lender to fund its permanent loan upon the satisfaction of a limited number of objective conditions. A "non-bankable commitment", on the other hand, is a commitment from a permanent lender that is so riddled with subjective conditions as to make the funding of the permanent loan a matter of the permanent lender's inclination and discretion as of the date of the maturity of the construction loan. *See* BENDER, *supra* note 6, at 300.

gining provision. Pizzuti's primary goal in negotiating for the extension options was to buy itself time to refinance the underlying construction loans if the permanent loan market was soft when the construction loans matured. Because First Union was comfortable with the credit it had on the two construction loans, it was not as concerned as it normally would have been about pricing its loans to the permanent loan market.

__Payment Guaranties__: Pizzuti was able to gain the upper hand in its negotiations on the value risk issue by agreeing to furnish First Union with payment guaranties from three very creditworthy persons—Pizzuti Equities (Pizzuti's real estate holding company)[182] and the two principals of Newport Partners, Pizzuti's 50% equity partner in both the 500 Building and HTE projects. Having payment guaranties from guarantors having a combined net worth of just shy of nine figures provided First Union with a great deal of comfort that the loans would be repaid at maturity, even if the underlying projects were not as successful as originally projected.

Pizzuti injected a potential point of contention into its negotiations with First Union when it informed First Union that the guaranties of Pizzuti Equities and the two Newport principals had to be 50% several guaranties (and not joint and several guaranties of the full loan amounts as originally anticipated by First Union). What this meant is that Pizzuti Equities guaranty would be limited to 50% of each construction loan and that the Newport guaranties would also be limited to 50% of the outstanding construction loan balances.[183]

The several nature of the guaranties was an essential component of the overall equity deal struck by Pizzuti and Newport Partners[184] and, as such, was a non-negotiable point from the borrower's perspective. The implication to First Union of accepting several guaranties was that its credit support on the construction loans would be severely impacted if either Pizzuti Equities or the Newport principals (but not all of them) experienced a significant loss of net worth. Although First Union was far from thrilled with the several guaranties, it was nonetheless still comfortable that the net worth of each of the guarantors was sufficient on a stand-alone basis to support the repayment of the construction loans.

---

182. It is the goal of most developers to create an entity that has sufficient net worth to provide completion and payment guaranties for the developer's construction loans (in lieu of the provision of such guaranties by the individual owners of the developer). *See supra* Page 378. The accomplishment of this goal was a principal focus of Ron Pizzuti and the organization that he founded in 1976 and was ultimately met when Pizzuti Equities was capitalized with a number of profitable real estate projects in the early 1990's.

183. The two Newport principals were jointly and severally liable for the repayment of their 50% several share of the construction loans.

184. *See supra* Chapter 4, Page 66, and Chapter 7, Page 219.

D. DEALING WITH THE RISK OF A MISAPPLICATION OF FUNDS

The next risk that needs to be addressed by the construction lender is the risk that the borrower does not use the proceeds disbursed under the construction loan to complete the project. The borrower's misapplication of loan proceeds can be triggered by any number of reasons, including greed, temporary cash flow problems, desperation or carelessness. Regardless of the reason underlying the misapplication, the impact on the lender's position on its construction loan is the same—the value of the project that serves as collateral for the repayment of its loan will either never be fully created or will be created with a lower net value than originally anticipated by the lender.

The construction lender deals with the misapplication of funds risk by implementing a detailed and tightly supervised process for the review, approval and funding of the borrower's periodic draw requests. The borrower's ***draw requests*** are the written requests periodically delivered to the construction lender by the borrower asking the lender to disburse loan proceeds to pay development costs incurred by the borrower during the preceding period. The various elements of the construction lender's administration of the borrower's draw requests are described below.

1. Development Budget and Draw Schedule. *(§§3.2(n) and (o))*

The construction loan agreement requires the borrower to provide the lender with a detailed development budget and its projected draw schedule. The development budget identifies by line item all of the hard and soft costs that will be incurred in connection with the development of the borrower's commercial real estate project. The draw schedule is the borrower's projection as to the amount of each monthly draw request that the borrower anticipates submitting to the construction lender during the term of the construction loan. Once finalized and approved by the lender, the budget and projected draw schedule become the templates for the submission and funding of all future draw requests.[185]

2. Applications for Payment. *(§§1.1 and 2.1)*

Whenever the borrower wants to receive a disbursement of loan proceeds to pay development costs, the borrower must submit an ***application for payment*** to the lender on a form prescribed in the construction loan agreement.[186] Each application for payment must identify the development costs to be funded by reference to a specific line item contained in the approved development budget. Moreover, the application for payment can only cover costs which have already been incurred by the borrower and incorporated into the project (and not costs which may be incurred in the future).[187] The applications for payment are typically submitted by the borrower on a monthly basis.[188]

---

185. *See* Weller, *supra* note 28, at 1752; and Weissmann, *supra* note 72, at 48.

186. The application for payment is most commonly made on AMERICAN INSTITUTE OF ARCHITECTS DOCUMENT G–702 (1992). *See* Weller, *supra* note 28, at 1753.

187. Most lenders resist the funding of loan disbursements to cover materials that have been purchased, but not yet incorporated into the construction project (e.g., steel, drywall, roofing, etc.). *See, e.g.,* § 2.5 of the Form Construction Loan Agreement. An exception to this general rule

3. Required Certifications. *(§2.2)*

Prior to its approval of any application for payment, the construction lender will require the borrower, its general contractor and its architect to certify that the development costs identified in the application have actually been incurred in the indicated amounts and that the work related to such costs has been incorporated into the borrower's development project. The construction lender will then furnish its inspecting architect with the borrower's application for payment and require the inspecting architect to visit the project site to verify that the costs referenced in the application have, in fact, been incurred and incorporated into the work. Only after it as received all of the above certifications will the construction lender approve and agree to fund the costs covered in the application for payment.[189]

4. Funding of Draw Requests. *(§§2.1, 2.3 and 6.1)*

Once it has approved the borrower's draw request and received all of the aforementioned certifications, the construction lender will then disburse loan proceeds equal to the costs covered by the draw request, less any retainage required to be withheld from the disbursements per the construction loan agreement.[190] The construction lender[191] can fund the draw requests in any one of three ways:

- A direct deposit into a checking account designated by the borrower;

- Dual payee checks made out jointly to the borrower and the end recipient of each component of the funded draw request; or

- Checks made payable directly to each intended recipient of a portion of the loan proceeds—e.g., directly to the contractor, subcontractor, etc.

The three methods noted above are listed from the least to the most conservative approach for the lender's disbursement of its loan proceeds. While a construction lender will customarily reserve the right in the construction loan agreement to make payments of loan proceeds directly to contractors, subcontractors and material providers, few lenders actually do so, because of a concern that they might be subjecting themselves to

---

may be made if (a) the materials are stored on-site and covered by the borrower's builder's risk insurance policy and (b) all requisite steps are have been taken to create a first priority security interest in the stored materials in favor of the lender. *See* Weissmann, *supra* note 72 at 51.

188. For a general discussion of the application for payment process, *see* Weller, *supra* note 28, at 1753; and Weissman, *supra* note 72, at 50–51.

189. *See* Schmudde, *supra* note 58, at 56.

190. *See supra* Page 354.

191. A construction lender will frequently engage the services of a title company to oversee the funding of the draw requests. *See, e.g.,* § 2.3 of the Form Construction Loan Agreement. *See also* Weissmann, supra note 72, at 51.

some form of lender liability if the project goes awry and the various firms providing work on the project do not get paid.[192]

Borrower's Pushback: The borrower's primary concern about the lender's mandated draw process is that it not be so rigorous and complex as to delay or otherwise negatively impact the borrower's ability to fund the payment of its development costs on a timely basis. Borrower's counsel should consult with the borrower's in-house finance staff to determine whether the logistics of the draw process being suggested by lender work for the borrower.

HIBC Case Study—Dealing With the Risk of a Misapplication of Funds

Only one issue of any significance surfaced during Pizzuti's review and negotiation of First Union's standard loan disbursement procedures. The initial draft of First Union's construction loan agreement gave First Union the right at any time during the loan term to make loan disbursements directly to the general contractor, subcontractors or any other third party performing work or providing services or materials related to the HTE and 500 projects. Pizzuti objected to First Union's reservation of such an unconditional right based on the assertion that Pizzuti, as the developer, needed to at all times possess the ultimate form of leverage over its general contractor and all other persons involved in the development process—that is, the right to withhold payment to such persons until their performance met Pizzuti's satisfaction. First Union recognized Pizzuti's concern as being legitimate and agreed to condition its right to make such direct disbursements upon the prior occurrence of an event of default under the construction loan.

E. DEALING WITH THE RISK OF INTERVENING LIENS

The construction lender's security can be significantly impaired if a mechanics' lien gains priority over the lien of the lender's construction mortgage. The various ways in which the construction mortgage might become subordinate to a subsequently-filed mechanics' lien are described in some detail in an earlier division of this Chapter.[193] As noted in that discussion, the rules governing the perfection and priority of mechanics' liens vary widely from state to state. The differing treatments afforded mechanics' liens in various states make it dangerous to try to be too

---

192. *See Schmudde, supra note 58, at 57–58; Frobes, Selected* Issues in Secured Construction Lending, *supra note 65, at 126–127; and Talley, supra note 39, at 136–137.*

193. *See supra* Pages 337–347.

specific in laying out the techniques that a construction lender can rely on to try to mitigate its risk of an intervening lien. However, some general comments may be made concerning what a construction lender can do to try to insulate itself from the risk that its mortgage loses priority to an intervening mechanics' lien.

1. Compliance With State Law. *(§5.1(r))*

First and foremost, counsel for the construction lender must master the mechanics' lien statute of the state where the subject real estate project is located and take whatever protective measures are sanctioned in that statute to preserve the priority of the construction mortgage over a subsequently filed mechanics' lien. Depending on the particular jurisdiction, this may entail labeling the mortgage as an "open-end" or "construction" mortgage and filing a notice of commencement after the date on which the mortgage is first recorded. It may also involve successfully working one's way through the often confusing and frequently inconsistent judicial gloss on the distinction between optional and obligatory loan advances.[194] Finally, it may require the lender to hold back a certain level of retainage from its loan disbursements or to provide certain statutorily prescribed notices to the project's general contractor. Whatever the specific circumstances, the key is that the construction lender must rigorously comply with the specific mandates of the state's mechanics' lien law.[195]

2. Early Work Prohibition. *(§§5.1(n))*

The most common way that a mechanics' lien can gain priority over the construction lender's mortgage is if some work on the project is started before the date on which the lender's mortgage is recorded.[196] As a result, the surest way for a lender to protect itself against the risk of an intervening mechanics' lien is to prohibit the borrower from starting work on the project prior to the recordation of the construction mortgage. The construction lender should require the borrower to sign a ***no work affidavit*** at the construction loan closing attesting to the fact that neither it, nor any contractor, subcontractor, supplier or material provider has performed any work or provided any materials to the site prior to the closing of the construction loan. The careful lender will also dispatch one of its underlings to the site on the day of the construction loan closing to visually confirm that no work has been started on the project.[197]

3. Lien Waivers. *(§§1.1 and 5.1(i))*

Most construction lenders require receipt of written ***lien waivers*** as a condition to the funding of any construction loan draw.[198] A lien waiver

---

194. *See supra* Pages 340–341, for a discussion of the difference between obligatory and optional loan advances and the potential significance of that difference.

195. *See generally* Weller, *supra* note 28, at 1750; Schmudde, *supra* note 58, at 55; Kyle, *Part 3, supra* note 97, at 12–13, and Leidner, *supra* note 51, at 44–45.

196. *See* Leidner, *supra* note 51, at 41.

197. *See* Schmudde, *supra* note 58, at 55.

198. *See e.g.,* §1.1 of the Form Construction Loan Agreement (the definition of "Draw Request").

should be signed by each contractor, subcontractor, supplier and material provider that receives any payment under the funded draw and should specifically state that such person has been fully paid for all work performed on the project and that it waives the right to file a mechanics' lien against the project to the extent of such prior or contemporaneous payments.[199]

4. Title Endorsements. *(§§3.2(c) and 4.1(c))*

The construction lender should look to its title insurer to provide it with affirmative insurance that the lien of its construction mortgage has full priority over any intervening mechanics lien. The title insurer can provide the lender with the desired protection by (1) deleting from the loan policy the standard exception for mechanics' liens[200] and (2) providing a so-called ***date-down endorsement*** at the time of each loan disbursement confirming that no mechanics' lien has been filed against the project since the date of the recordation of the construction mortgage.[201]

5. Bonding of Liens

Most state statutes contain provisions permitting an owner to remove a mechanics' lien against its property if it posts a surety bond in the full amount of the perfected mechanics' lien. If the project is located in a state that permits the bonding of mechanics' liens, the construction lender would be well-advised to include a requirement in the construction loan agreement that the borrower post such a bond within a fixed number of days following the filing of a mechanics' lien against the project.[202]

Borrower's Pushback: With one notable exception, the borrower ordinarily has no particular objection to the legal measures employed by the construction lender to protect itself against the risk of an intervening mechanics' lien. The exception relates to the construction lender's attempt to prohibit the borrower from beginning any work on its project prior to the recordation of the construction loan mortgage. Developers often have to begin work on the site before all the details of the construction loan closing have been finalized. As a result, borrower's counsel is regularly challenged with devising a scenario that will permit the borrower to begin its construction activities before the recordation of the construction mortgage, without exposing the construction lender to any undue risk that its mortgage will lose its priority to an intervening mechanics lien. The techniques used to achieve those objectives are dependent upon the provisions of the mechanics' lien statute of the state in which the project is located. If counsel for the borrower and the lender assiduously follow

---

199. See Weissmann, *supra* note 72, at 46–47.

200. For a discussion of the standard exceptions to a title insurance policy, *see supra* Chapter 8, Page 294. *See also* Shannon J. Skinner, *A Practical Guide to Title Review (With Checklist),* in ALI–ABA COURSE OF STUDY MATERIALS, MODERN REAL ESTATE TRANSACTIONS, Course No. SN–001 377,379 (July 2007).

201. *See* Leidner, *supra note* 51, at 45–46.

202. *See* Weller, *supra* note 28, at 1751.

those statutory rules, the risk that work done on a site before the construction loan closing can cause a subsequently filed lien to gain priority over the lien of the construction lender's mortgage can often be eliminated or, at the very least, limited to a lien securing the actual cost of the early work.[203]

Practice Tip #9–2: The Credit Crisis of 2008 (and Beyond)

A chapter on construction financing written in 2010 would be incomplete without at least some small mention being made of the financial crisis experienced by the real estate industry beginning in earnest in 2008. By the same token, an analysis of the causes and underpinnings of the credit crisis is well beyond both the scope of this text and my level of expertise. Therefore, I have no intention of wasting my time or yours trying to dissect what got us into this mess or what it will take to get us out of it. If you are interested in finding out how sub-prime loans, credit default swaps, mortgage securitizations, housing market speculation and the general divorcing of the principles of risk and reward brought the global economy to the brink of failure, I strongly commend reading Anthony Downs, Real Estate and the Financial Crisis: How Turmoil in the Capital Markets is Restructuring Real Estate Finance (2009).

My frame of reference when thinking about the financial crisis is much more anecdotal than theoretical. A developer buddy recently told me a story about his efforts to secure construction financing for the development of an office building in Columbus that is 80% pre-leased to a solid credit tenant. He commented that three years ago he would have received ten or more extremely competitive offers from local lenders to provide financing for a project of that ilk. Today, the only proposal he has managed to secure is on pricing and other business terms that would have been considered laughable prior to the onset of the current credit crisis.

My friends in the practicing real estate bar have shared countless similar stories about the sorry state of the construction financing market. All of the stories have the same basic punch line—there simply are no deals being done in today's market. Part of the lack of deal flow is certainly attributable to a decline in the demand for new commercial space brought on by the overall recession in the U.S. economy. However, the real cause for

---

203. This limited risk is often dealt with by the borrower (1) covering the early work under a separate contract entered into by the borrower and the person performing that work (2) obtaining a lien waiver from the person performing the early work, (3) convincing the title company to delete the standard mechanics' lien exception from the lender's loan policy (usually in exchange for its delivery to the title company of a guaranty from a creditworthy entity that it will pay the cost of the early work), and (4) paying the full cost of the early work out of the initial loan advance made under the construction loan. Pizzuti used all of these techniques (and more) to permit it to begin work on the HTE project before the closing of its construction loan from First Union. Those techniques were, however, specifically tailored to satisfy the unique provisions contained in the Florida mechanics' lien statute—*see* FLORIDA STATUTES §§ 713.01–713.37 (2010). I have, therefore, opted to not address the specifics of how Pizzuti dealt with the early work risk in this text of general application.

the present malaise in the commercial real estate market is not a lack of demand as much as it is a lack of available financing for both new and existing projects. The folks that have capital to invest in commercial real estate (and there are plenty of them out there)[204] have, at least temporarily, decided to remain on the sidelines until they get a better sense of where the bottom is for the economy, in general, and the commercial real estate sector, in particular. I will leave it to people like Tony Downs to try to figure out what it will take to resolve the current stand-off between the real estate development and institutional investment communities and when the end of that stand-off might occur.

I am, however, confident that the commercial real estate industry in the U.S. will thrive once again in the not too distant future (I just don't know when that will be). The reasons for my optimism are:

- *The U.S. commercial property markets are not over-built like they were in the real estate recession of 1991;*

- *There is an abundant amount of capital being set aside by institutional investors to invest (eventually) in U.S. real estate;*

- *The commercial real estate business is local in nature and, as such, is not in danger of being outsourced to India or other countries having low labor costs; and*

- *The core fundamentals of the U.S. commercial real estate industry (unlike the auto and investment banking industries) remain tied to an enduring consumer demand—that is, the need of its citizens for shelter to live and work.*

While I am guardedly optimistic about the eventual recovery of the commercial real estate markets, I do not expect the recovery to bring about a reinstatement of "business as usual" for the construction financing business (nor should it). The prior pages of this Chapter have been peppered with references to what is "typical," "customary" and "usual" in the construction loan arena. The following are some of my thoughts on how the "typical" construction loan might change in the near term.[205]

- *Loan amounts will be dramatically reduced as the U.S. commercial real estate industry undergoes "massive deleveraging."[206] The new "typical" construction loan may require a loan-to-cost ratio of 60%, a loan-to-value ratio of 65%, a debt service coverage ratio of 1.3 and a debt yield of 14%.*

---

204. One real estate advisor recently reported that "more than $300 billion of capital is ready to buy distressed real estate assets and mis-priced loans in the U.S. alone." *See* Simon Ziff, President, Ackerman–Ziff Real Estate Group, *presentation at the Urban Land Institute's webinar on Refinancing Your Project in Today's Credit Crisis (May 7, 2009). See also* DOWNS, *supra* note 32, at 97and 195.

205. For a discussion of others' views on how the real estate finance industry may change in reaction to the credit crisis, *see* Richard R. Goldberg, *The Future of Real Estate Financing: What to Expect After the Crash,* IN ALI–ABA COURSE OF STUDY MATERIALS, MODERN REAL ESTATE TRANSACTIONS: PRACTICAL STRATEGIES FOR REAL ESTATE ACQUISITION, DISPOSITION, AND OWNERSHIP, Course No. SS–012, 1505 (July 2010); URBAN LAND INSTITUTE AND PRICEWATERHOUSECOOPERS, EMERGING TRENDS IN REAL ESTATE, Chapter 2 (2010); and DOWNS, *supra* note 32, at Chapter 9.

206. *See* URBAN LAND INSTITUTE, *supra* note 205, at 5.

- *Construction lenders will be much more selective in their identification of developers to whom they will extend construction financing. Loan committees will insist that developers have very deep pockets and established track records of success in the industry.*

- *Pre-leasing requirements will become the norm for most development projects. So-called "spec" projects will simply not be financeable.*

- *Construction lenders will seek to reinstate the pre–1980's requirement of a permanent take-out commitment for individual construction loans.*[207]

- *Back-end equity will be eliminated from the lender's vocabulary.*

- *Lenders will refuse to fund the borrower's "really soft costs" (that is, the developer's fees and unrealized land profit).*

- *Lenders will ratchet up both their underwriting practices and loan due diligence, with the end result that closing a construction loan will take longer and cost more.*

- *The pricing of interest rate spreads will increase significantly as both construction and permanent lenders seek to extract higher returns on their real-estate based loans.*

How long will construction lenders continue to employ these conservative underwriting practices? The cynical realist in me says it probably won't be all that long before a new generation of construction lenders comes along, forgets the lessons of the past, leaps headfirst onto the bandwagon of "irrational exuberance"[208] *and begins once again to make construction loans at 100% of project costs.*

VII. SUMMARY

Because the construction loan is such an enduring staple of the real estate development business, it behooves all lawyers participating in any fashion in the real estate development process to gain a full understanding of both the unique risks faced by the construction lender and the various strategies at the construction lender's disposal to help shield it from those risks. Once such an understanding of the underlying business and legal principles is achieved, counsel for the borrower and the lender can then have at it in their shared quest to negotiate a financing deal that serves the legitimate business needs of both their respective clients.

---

207. This trend will be hastened by the almost total demise of the mortgage securitization business. Pre–2007, many construction lenders were able to lessen their real estate risk by selling off a pool of construction loans to investment bankers, who would then securitize the loans and sell them off in bits and pieces to individual investors. *See supra* note 66. *See also* Goldberg, *supra* note 205, at 1508–1509.

208. Any discussion of the credit crisis certainly merits at least one quote from Alan Greenspan. *See* Alan Greenspan, Remarks at the Annual Dinner and Francis Boyer Lecture of The American Enterprise Institute for Public Policy Research, in Washington, D.C. (December 5, 1996).

CHAPTER 10

STAGE 6: DESIGNING AND CONSTRUCTING THE PROJECT

■ ■ ■

I. INTRODUCTION

Stage 6 is when the developer's vision for its project is refined and translated first into a specific architectural design and then into a constructed building. One noted real estate author has described this stage by noting that "the developer moves from the role of creator/promoter to that of manager, ensuring time and budget are as tightly controlled as possible, accounting for the performance and payment of all the players in the process."[1]

This Chapter is not intended to be a primer on the drafting of design and construction documents. The specific language to be incorporated into the developer's contracts with its selected design and construction professionals is dependent on the particulars of the developer's project and, as such, is not an appropriate topic for a text of this type. Rather, this Chapter will attempt to create a base line of knowledge for the practitioner tasked with the responsibility for drafting and negotiating those contracts by first exploring the nature of the construction and design process and then examining the primary contractual issues that the practitioner must address as part of his efforts to help the developer convert its theoretical business plan into a bricks and mortar reality.

II. DEVELOPER'S BUSINESS OBJECTIVES

The developer's business objectives during Stage 6 are threefold:

- The articulation of a project design that is both aesthetically and functionally attractive to the developer's customers (including the institutional investor community, which will ultimately be called upon to make a debt or equity investment in the project);[2]

---

1. *See* MIKE E. MILES, GAYLE L. BERENS AND MARC A. WEISS, REAL ESTATE DEVELOPMENT: PRINCIPLES AND PROCESS 447 (3rd ed. 2000).

2. *See supra* Chapter 1, Pages 6–7, for a discussion of the developer's "second customer" (i.e., the institutional investor).

400

- The receipt of satisfactory assurances that the project, as designed, can be built on time and on budget; and

- The construction of the project in accordance with the articulated project design and sound construction practices.

If the developer is to achieve these three objectives, it must put together a strong team of design and construction professionals; adopt a delivery system that is well-suited for the developer's project; and put in place contracts that are designed to properly incentivize and regulate the conduct of the selected design and construction professionals. The remainder of this Chapter will be devoted to a discussion of these developer responsibilities.

III. THE DESIGN AND CONSTRUCTION PROCESS

A real estate development lawyer cannot properly serve his developer client during the sixth stage of a development project, unless he first understands the process involved in designing and constructing that project. The design and construction process[3] involves the developer's expenditure of great sums of money to create a final, tangible product that is acceptable to its customers. From start to finish, the process can take anywhere from six months for a simple, commercial project, to upwards of ten years for a large, mixed use project.

The word that most aptly describes the construction process is "dynamic"—that is, a process which is "characterized by continuous change, activity or progress," and which is also "marked by intensity and vigor."[4] The dynamic nature of the construction process is nicely illustrated in the following quote from a 1981 judicial opinion:

> [E]xcept in the middle of a battlefield, nowhere must men coordinate the movement of such chaos and with such limited certainty of present facts and future occurrences as in a huge construction project.... Even the most painstaking planning frequently turns out to be mere conjecture and accommodation to changes must necessarily be of the rough, quick and *ad hoc* sort, analogous to ever-changing commands of the battlefield.[5]

The dynamic nature of the construction process produces an environment that is more conducive than any other stage of a development project to the generation of disputes among the various participants in that process.[6] It is the job of the real estate development lawyer to try to

---

3. The term "construction process" will be used throughout this Chapter as a short-hand reference to the design and construction process—merely my attempt to save words and certainly not an intended slight of my architect friends.

4. *See* THE FREE DICTIONARY (2010), at http://www.thefreedictionary.com.

5. *See* Blake Construction Co. v. C.J. Coakley Co., 431 A.2d 569, 575 (D.C. App. 1981), quoted in Stanley P. Sklar, *Drafting and Negotiating Construction Contracts*, in DRAFTING AND NEGOTIATING TOMORROW'S CONSTRUCTION CONTRACTS TODAY 31, 35 (Stanley P. Sklar Chair, 2009).

6. *See* Phillip E. Beck and John M. Mastin, Jr., *Construction Contracts*, in COMMERCIAL REAL ESTATE TRANSACTIONS HANDBOOK, Chapter 4, 4–7 (Mark A. Senn ed., 4th ed. 2009); and Patrick J.

fashion contract documents that have as their core objective the avoidance of unnecessary construction disputes—a job which the lawyer can only perform if he fully understands both his client's business objectives and the inherently risky nature of the construction process.

The construction process consists of three phases—(1) the planning phase, (2) the design phase and (3) the construction phase.[7] During the planning phase, the developer determines the location and general nature, size and scope of its proposed project (e.g., a four story, Class A, office building in Orlando, Florida). This is the work that the developer must complete early on in the development process (and certainly before it waives its purchase contract contingencies).[8] For the purposes of the discussion in this Chapter, it will be assumed that the developer has successfully concluded the planning phase and is ready to embark on the design and construction phases of the process.

A. DESIGN PHASE

At the inception of the design phase, the developer provides the architect with the developer's requirements for the contemplated development project. Those requirements (commonly referred to in the real estate industry as the developer's **_program_**)[9] include the specific location of the project land; the type and size of the project (e.g., a four-story, speculative, office building); the developer's construction budget and schedule for the project; any aesthetic factors that the developer wants to see incorporated into the project (e.g., a glass curtain wall exterior or a two-story, interior atrium); any performance requirements that the developer has for the project (e.g., an HVAC system that complies with a specific industry standard); the developer's marketing strategy for the building (e.g., the targeting of mostly full-floor tenants); and any other considerations that the developer wants to see incorporated into the architect's final design package.[10]

With the details of the developer's program in hand, the architect then assumes responsibility for preparing plans and specifications that specifically delineate all aesthetic and functional components of the design of the project.[11] Following its initial meeting with the developer, the architect will prepare general design drawings and guidelines (known as

---

O'Connor, _Integrated Project Delivery: Collaboration Through New Contract Forms_, DRAFTING AND NEGOTIATING TOMORROW'S CONSTRUCTION CONTRACTS TODAY 31, 35 (Stanley P. Sklar Chair, 2009).

7. In a nod to the litigious nature of the construction process, one practitioner notes that the construction process actually consists of four stages, with the fourth stage being "litigation." _See_ Beck, _supra_ note 6, at 4–7.

8. _See supra_ Chapter 5, Pages 100–101.

9. _See_ Thomas M. Keranen, _The Design Professional_, in FUNDAMENTALS OF CONSTRUCTION LAW 49, 62–63 (Carina Y. Enhada, Cheri Turnage Gatlin and Fred D. Wilshusen, eds., 2001).

10. _See_ JOHN C. CAMERON, JR., A PRACTITIONER'S GUIDE TO CONSTRUCTION LAW 5–1 and 5–2 (2000 with 2009 Cumulative Supplement).

11. For an excellent exposition of the architect's responsibilities, _see generally id._ at 5–1 through 5–4.

schematic drawings) for the developer's review, including a site plan, building elevations, outline specifications, floor plans and exterior renderings. Once the schematic drawings are approved by the developer, the architect will then move on to the preparation of more detailed drawings (*design development drawings*), which will incorporate all of the approved aspects of the schematic drawings, plus add new detail concerning the building's architectural design and the specifics of the building's structural, mechanical and electrical systems.

The final stage of the design phase involves the architect's preparation of final plans, which will then serve as the blueprint for the actual construction of the project by the contractor selected by the developer. The final plans prepared by the architect will include all of the following components:

- A site plan showing the precise footprint of the building and all driveways, parking lots and other exterior, common areas serving the building;

- Civil engineering drawings detailing all site work required for the project (including utility work);

- Architectural drawings indicating the precise look of all exterior and interior improvements, including floor plans for each floor of the building and exterior building elevations;

- Engineering drawings depicting the specific location and nature of all structural, mechanical, electrical, plumbing and fire protection systems associated with the project;

- Landscaping plans displaying all plantings and other landscaping of the site; and

- Detailed, narrative specifications identifying the methods to be followed in constructing the project and the type, quality and quantity of all materials to be incorporated into the project.[12]

All aspects of the final plans (as well as all previous plans prepared by the architect) will be subject to the developer's approval.

B. CONSTRUCTION PHASE

During the construction phase, the contractor selected by the developer takes over and builds the project in accordance with the approved final plans. The construction phase (which, for the typical commercial real estate project will last between six to 12 months) begins when a shovel is

---

12. The project specifications can be further broken down into the following three categories: (1) design specifications, which state "precise measurements, tolerances, materials, construction methods, sequences, quality control, inspection requirements, and other information" (*see* JUSTIN SWEET, LEGAL ASPECTS OF ARCHITECTURE, ENGINEERING AND THE CONSTRUCTION PROCESS § 19.01(d) (1994)); (2) performance specifications setting forth the performance standards that must be satisfied in the completed building (e.g., those relating to the building's HVAC system); and (3) purchase specifications that specifically identify by product name materials required to be used in constructing the building. *See* CAMERON, A PRACTITIONER'S GUIDE, *supra* note 10, at 9–6.

first placed in the dirt and ends when the building is fully completed and all required certificates of occupancy[13] and other governmental approvals are received to permit the developer to use the project for its intended purpose. The contractor's job is to orchestrate the activities of a variety of trades (excavators, steelworkers, plumbers, roofers, electricians, drywallers, carpet installers, etc.) to make sure that the project is completed on time, on budget and in strict accordance with the quality parameters established by the developer. The challenges faced by the contractor and the developer during the construction phase will be fleshed out in ample detail in later sections of this Chapter.[14]

C. FAST-TRACK CONSTRUCTION

It is important to keep in mind that the three phases of the construction process (that is, planning, design and construction) occur in neat, sequential order in only the rarest of commercial real estate projects. The norm in today's fast-paced real estate industry is for there to be at least some overlap in each of the three phases. The compression of the construction process in this manner is frequently referred to as ***fast-track construction***, which, in essence, means that construction of a portion of the project is commenced before the planning and design of the entirety of the project is completed.[15] By way of example, the contractor might be given the go-ahead to begin excavation of the site before the developer and the architect have reached final agreement on the exterior appearance of the developer's proposed building or on the capacity and design of the building's HVAC system. Fast tracking construction in this manner makes the construction process even more dynamic and, hence, significantly more risky for every participant in that process.[16]

IV. PLAYERS IN THE DESIGN AND CONSTRUCTION PROCESS

The single most vital ingredient of a successful construction process is the developer's selection of the right people to serve on its design and construction team. The developer needs to not only choose highly qualified professionals to serve on its team, but to also make sure that all of the

---

13. In most jurisdictions, a tenant/user cannot occupy any portion of a commercial building for the conduct of its business until a certificate of occupancy for the tenant/user's space has been issued by the building department of the political subdivision where the building is located. A certificate of occupancy can be either temporary (meaning that the tenant/user can use the space for the conduct of its business as long as certain punchlist work is completed to the satisfaction of the building department within a designated period of time) or permanent (meaning that all work required to satisfy the building department's regulations has been completed). *See infra* Chapter 11, Page 474, for a discussion of certificates of occupancy in the context of the developer's construction of tenant improvements under a lease.

14. *See infra* Pags 427–438.

15. *See* CAMERON, A PRACTITIONER'S GUIDE, *supra* note 10, at 8–119 of the 2009 Supplement; and Joyce K. Hackenbrach and Clark Whitney, *How to Control the Owner's Risk in a Commercial or Industrial Construction Contract*, 23 No. 6 PRACTICAL REAL ESTATE LAWYER 3 (November 2007).

16. *See* MILES, *supra* note 1, at 427.

chosen professionals work together in a cooperative and collaborative fashion for the benefit of the project as a whole. As will be discussed in later sections of this Chapter,[17] the real estate development lawyer's mission is to craft contract documents that encourage the various players in the construction process to function as a team and not as isolated adversaries.

The complexity of the construction process is driven, in large measure, by the sheer number of the players who make indispensable contributions to the design and construction of a commercial real estate project. The identity of those players is briefly summarized below.

- *Architect*—The architect is the licensed professional who is principally responsible for the design of the project. The architect's duties extend not just to the aesthetics of the project (how pretty does it look), but also to its functionality (does it work for the developer's customers).

- *Engineers*—While the architect serves as the lead professional on all aspects of the project's design, a significant portion of the design work is typically farmed out by the architect to engineers, whose primary foci are on the design and performance of the project's systems and infrastructure.[18] By way of example, the architect may retain a civil engineer to design the utilities and other site improvements serving the project; a mechanical and electrical engineer to design the building's HVAC and electrical systems; and a structural engineer to design the structural components of the building. The required engineering services are typically provided either by members of the architect's in-house staff or by independent engineering firms hired by the architect as subcontractors.[19]

- *Contractor*—The contractor is the person who is responsible for constructing the project in accordance with the plans and specifications prepared by the architect and engineers. It falls to the contractor to schedule and coordinate the activities of all firms providing construction services or materials for the project. The contractor is sometimes referred to as the "general" or "prime contractor."

- *Subcontractors*—The contractor typically subcontracts components of the work to specialized trade contractors (e.g., site excavators, steel erectors, plumbers, electricians, drywallers, carpenters, painters and HVAC installers).

- *Suppliers*—The contractor will also enter into contractual arrangements with a variety of suppliers to acquire materials for incorporation into the building being constructed on the project site. By way of example, the contractor may assume direct responsi-

---

17. *See infra* Pages 419–421.

18. Architects also frequently subcontract the performance of landscape design services to architects who specialize in the field of landscape design.

19. *See* Keranen, *supra* note 9, at 57–58.

bility for buying all cabinetry and floor covering, which will then be furnished to those subcontractors who are assigned the jobs of installing those materials in the building.

- *Government*—Federal, state and local governments play a very important role in regulating the manner in which a commercial project is designed and constructed. The two pieces of federal legislation that most directly affect the construction process are The Americans with Disabilities Act (governing required means of access for persons with disabilities)[20] and The Occupational Safety and Health Act (setting forth standards for workers' safety and health on jobsites).[21] State building codes provide standards governing the practices and materials used in connection with the construction of commercial projects, and local zoning and building codes regulate matters of design (e.g., building height, setback lines and required parking areas) and set forth the requirements that must be met for the issuance of a building permit and a certificate of occupancy for a project.

- *Construction Lender*—The construction lender is the person who provides the funds required to pay a significant portion of the costs of designing and constructing the developer's project.[22] The construction lender imposes on the developer its own, separate set of requirements concerning the design and construction of the project. Principal among such requirements is the lender's insistence that no construction loan proceeds will be disbursed until such time as an independent architect or engineer hired by the lender has visited the jobsite to confirm that the construction work that is the subject of the developer's draw request has, in fact, been completed.[23]

- *Developer*—As the person with the most at stake on any construction project, the developer must exercise extreme vigilance in the oversight of all aspects of the project design and construction and the orchestration of the activities of all the players involved in that endeavor. It is essential that all substantive aspects of the design and construction process be subject to the developer's final approval.[24]

---

20. *See* 42 U.S.C. §§ 12101–12213 (2010).

21. *See* 29 U.S.C. §§ 651–678 (2010).

22. *See generally supra* Chapter 9.

23. *See id.* at Page 393.

24. The standard form contract documents prepared for commercial construction projects by the American Institute of Architects (the "AIA") contemplate that the developer will delegate a significant degree of its authority over the construction process to the architect and contractor. However, as will be discussed in more detail later in this Chapter (*see infra* Page 439), "it is supercilious to suggest that the developer who is responsible for paying the design and construction costs and satisfying the ultimate requirements of end users should have little or no voice in the implementation of the construction contract." *See* John D. Hastie, *Architectural and Construction Contracts—The Developer's Perspective*, in ALI–ABA COURSE OF STUDY MATERIALS, MODERN REAL ESTATE TRANSACTIONS, Course #SB–08, 4 (August 1996).

- ***Real Estate Development Lawyer***—The real estate development lawyer's primary job during Stage 6 is the preparation and negotiation of design and construction documents that empower the developer to oversee the construction process and require and incentivize the various players in that process to perform their services in a collaborative fashion that is consistent with the developer's business needs. Unfortunately, the developer all too often fails to involve its lawyer in those contract negotiations and, instead, opts to execute construction and design documents prepared by its counterpart based on the theory that the documents are "standard forms that everyone uses." In those instances, the role of the real estate development lawyer is reduced to fighting battles with the contractor and architect over disputes which could have been avoided if the lawyer had been given the opportunity to craft the contract documents in the first instance.

Practice Tip #10–1: Learning the Construction Process

My biggest regret about my years in practice is that I never understood the construction process as well as I should have. While I forced myself to learn all that I could about the development business (including a decent "walking around" knowledge of project economics), I for some reason did not apply the same effort to acquaint myself with the intricacies involved in the design and construction of a commercial building. As a result, I found myself acting during Stage 6 as more of a legal technician than a true, well-rounded, advisor and counselor. I knew my way around the standard design and construction documents and felt comfortable dealing with the key "legal issues" that typically surfaced during negotiations with counsel for the contractor and architect. However, my limited knowledge of the design and construction disciplines often put me at a disadvantage in those negotiations and forced me to interrupt the flow of the discussions by making the hapless statement that "I will have to get back to you on that point after I check with my construction folks." I had, in other words, forgotten the mantra set forth in the first chapter of this book—if you want to succeed as a real estate development lawyer, you first need to understand the real estate development business.[25]

My advice to aspiring real estate lawyers is to do everything within their power to learn about the construction and design process (advice which I took to heart only in the last couple years of my practice career). Here are some tips on how the young (or not so young) lawyer can go about doing just that.

---

25. The following practitioner-authored quote further illustrates the point made in the text—"The best fisherman in the world will not fare well in unfamiliar waters. Likewise, the best attorney in the world cannot provide sufficient counsel with respect to the construction process if he is unfamiliar with it." *See* Beck, *supra* note 6, at 4–9.

- *Visit the jobsite (and experience the pleasure of putting on a hard hat);*
- *Buy an architect or contractor lunch to talk about his business;*
- *Read whatever you can get your hands on describing the design and construction process;*[26]
- *Attend job meetings where the contractor, architect and other professionals talk about the progress of the construction project; and*
- *Ask questions of the developer and anyone else involved in the construction process.*

One bit of final advice—make it clear to your client that you are doing all of these things "off the clock." Your reward will be that you will become a better lawyer—and, by the way, get more business as a result.

V. SELECTING THE DESIGN AND CONSTRUCTION TEAM

There are two basic ways to select members of the developer's design and construction team—bidding and negotiation.[27] In a bidding arrangement, the developer sends its program requirements to a select group of qualified professionals and asks each of them to submit its best bid for the project within a fixed period of time. The "bid" will generally consist of the bidder's proposed price and schedule for the performance of the programmed work and, if the subject of the bid is design work, minimally required design drawings and specifications. Once the developer receives all of the submitted bids, it will select the bidder's proposal that it believes is best suited for the project in question.[28] The selected bidder will then be formally hired to perform the job on terms and conditions that are consistent with the developer's program requirements and the bidder's submitted bid.[29]

A bid arrangement is normally used by a developer to select its general contractor only when the project design is fully complete and the developer is, therefore, in a position to deliver final construction plans to the contractors on its bid list. In such a situation, the developer hopes that

---

26. Publications issued by trade associations representing architects and contractors (e.g., the American Institute of Architects and the Associated General Contractors of America) are particularly good sources of reading material. *See e.g.* the bookstore listings at www.AIA.org and www.AGC.org.

27. *See generally*, MILES, *supra* note 1 at 425–426; and CAMERON, A PRACTITIONER'S GUIDE, *supra* note 10, at 8–2 through 8–7.

28. In the context of contractors' bids, the developer usually accepts the lowest bid or, if the bidders have not been sufficiently pre-qualified, the "lowest responsible bid." *See* CAMERON, A PRACTITIONER'S GUIDE, *supra* note 10, at 8–7.

29. The developer will usually include its preferred form of contract in its bid package. The bidder will then be required to accept that form of contract or to point out any modifications which the bidder will require to be made as a condition to its bid. *See id.* at 8–5 and 8–6.

the competition spawned by the bid process will produce the lowest possible price for the construction work. The bidding process is also frequently used by the general contractor to select subcontractors and suppliers for certain components of the construction job.

As alluded to above, the bid process only works if the design of the work being bid out is fully complete (or very nearly so). If the design is incomplete, a bid recipient will be unable to determine with the desired precision how long it will take to complete the work and what it will cost it to do so. As a result, the bidder will not be in a position to "sharpen its pencil" on its bid and will either refuse to bid on the project or will submit a high-ball bid, which is replete with assumptions, qualifications, limitations and contingencies.

Selecting a design or construction professional through negotiation means exactly what it sounds like—the developer selects a firm that it believes has the financial wherewithal and technical expertise and experience to do the job and then sits down with the selected firm to see if the parties can reach a mutually acceptable arrangement for the performance of the work. The architect and other design professionals are customarily selected by negotiation, as are contractors, subcontractors and suppliers when the design of the work has not yet been completed.

There are many reasons why a developer might opt to select its contractor by negotiation, even if the project design is complete. Foremost among those reasons is that the developer may have an established working relationship with a contractor that it believes is ideally suited to perform the work, because of the contractor's financial strength and its expertise and experience in developing similar projects. The developer may also want to involve the selected contractor in discussions with the architect concerning the design of the project and in sales presentations to potential users of space in the developed project. Finally, the developer may need to fast-track the construction process and cannot afford to take the extra time required to wade its way through the cumbersome and time-consuming bid process.

The trend in recent years is for a private developer to select its design and construction team by means of negotiation and not a bidding process.[30] For that reason, the discussion in the remainder of this Chapter will assume that the developer has opted to select its team through a process of individualized negotiations.

VI. PROJECT DELIVERY SYSTEMS

Once the members of the design and construction team are selected by the developer, the next question that arises is what contract structure will be utilized to establish the responsibilities and authorities of the three

---

30. The bidding process remains the norm on public projects, such as schools, courthouses and hospitals, where the timing of completion of the project is not as crucial and the use of a transparent bid process satisfies the public's objective of keeping its costs as low as possible. *See* Miles, *supra* note 1, at 425.

prime players in the construction process—that is the developer, architect and contractor. The method for assigning construction and design responsibility and authority to those three players is referred to in the construction industry as a ***project delivery system***.[31]

There are three basic categories of project delivery systems—(1) ***design-bid-build***, (2) ***construction management*** and (3) ***design-build***.[32] The definition and respective advantages and disadvantages to the developer of each of these project delivery systems are discussed below.[33]

A.   DESIGN–BID–BUILD

The design-bid-build delivery system is also referred to as the ***traditional delivery method***. The "traditional" designation is assigned to the design-bid-build system because it reflects the historical norm of the developer assigning responsibility for the design function to the architect under one contract and the responsibility for the construction function to the contractor under a separate contract. In the design-bid-build arrangement, the design and construction functions are performed sequentially, with the project design being finalized before the construction contract is awarded or the construction work is started. The completed plans and specifications prepared by the architect are used by the developer to define the scope of work specified in the contract awarded by the developer to the contractor.

The tripartite, contractual arrangement evidenced by the design-bid-build system is described graphically in the following diagram.[34]

---

31. A report jointly published by the American Institute of Architects and the Associated General Contractors of America defines "project delivery" as "the method for assigning responsibility to an organization or an individual for providing design and construction services." *See* JOINT COMMITTEE OF THE AMERICAN INSTITUTE OF ARCHITECTS AND THE ASSOCIATED GENERAL CONTRACTORS OF AMERICA, PRIMER ON PROJECT DELIVERY (2004) (the "JOINT AIA/AGC REPORT").

32. These are the three categories identified in the JOINT AIA/AGC REPORT. The JOINT AIA/AGC REPORT acknowledges that there a multitude of hybrid, project delivery systems (*see infra* Pages 415–417, for a discussion of two such hybrid delivery system) and further notes that one of the goals of that report is "to create definitions broad enough that all hybrids fall within the three primary delivery methods." *See* JOINT AIA/AGC REPORT, *supra* note 31, at 1.

33. For a detailed discussion of the advantages and disadvantages of the different project delivery methods, *see generally* CAMERON, A PRACTITIONER'S GUIDE, *supra* note 10, at 8–15 through 8–17 of 2009 Supplement; Stanley P. Sklar, *An Overview of Architect and Construction Contracts*, in ALI–ABA COURSE OF STUDY MATERIALS, MODERN REAL ESTATE TRANSACTIONS, Course #SM–002, 2–5 (July 2006); Beck, *supra* note 6, at 4–9 through 4–22; and Robert A. Rubin and Linda M. Thomas–Mobley, *Delivery Systems*, in FUNDAMENTALS OF CONSTRUCTION LAW, Chapter 6 (Carina Y. Enhada, Cheri Turnage Gatlin and Fred D. Wilshusen eds., 2001). The discussion in the remainder of this section of the advantages and disadvantages of the three principal project delivery systems is based on my own practical experience in the field and on the excellent discussions of that topic in the authorities cited in this footnote.

34. Throughout this discussion of project delivery systems, it will be assumed that the architect performs in-house all architectural, engineering and other design services required for the developer's project. Were that not to be the case, the architect would typically subcontract that work to other design and engineering firms.

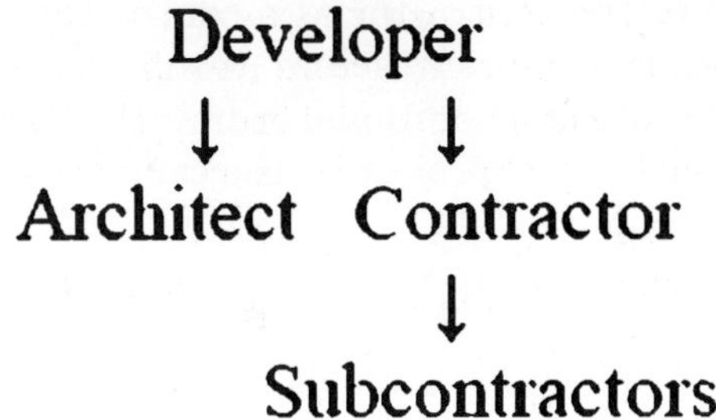

In the design-bid-build system, the developer enters into two separate contracts—one with the architect for the performance of the project design and one with the contractor for the performance of the project construction. There is no direct contractual relationship between the architect and the contractor, nor is there any privity of contract between the developer and the subcontractors (all of whom report directly to the contractor).

The following are the principal advantages and disadvantages of the design-bid-build system.

Advantages—

- The existence of two separate contracts creates a natural check and balance between the authority of the architect and that of the contractor.

- The design-bid-build method can produce certainty and lower construction costs (assuming that the contractor's contract is awarded on the basis of final plans prepared by the architect).

- The segregation of the design and construction functions and the performance of those functions in a neat, sequential order lend predictability and certainty to the construction process, which, in turn, reduces the developer's risk.

- The contractor has full responsibility and liability for the performance (or non-performance) of all the subcontractors and suppliers.

Disadvantages—

- The segregation of the design and construction functions into two contractual "silos" creates a natural tension between the architect and the contractor. This tension inhibits productive communications between the design and construction professionals and creates an environment in which there is an increased potential for disputes.

- The design-bid-build method does not lend itself to fast-track construction, where the design and construction phases of the project overlap to a significant extent.

- The sequencing of the design and construction phases can cause a protracted construction schedule.

- The insertion of the contractor as a contractual buffer between the developer and the subcontractors results in higher construction costs, because of the additional administrative costs and profit mark-up charged to the project by the contractor.

B. CONSTRUCTION MANAGEMENT

A second project delivery system is construction management. In a "pure" construction management system (frequently referred to as the ***construction management—agency system*** or ***CMa***),[35] the developer adds a fourth player to the design and construction process by hiring an independent construction manager to provide the developer with advice concerning the design and construction of the project. The construction manager (usually a construction professional, but occasionally an architect or engineer) is typically hired by the developer prior to the completion of the project design. The construction manager serves as an agent of the owner in reviewing the architect's proposed design, developing an overall budget for the project, obtaining and negotiating project bids and supervising the contractor's performance of its construction work.

The following diagram illustrates the interrelationship of the four parties under the CMa system.

Developer → Construction Manager

↓   ↓

Architect Contractor

↓

Subcontractors

The construction manager in a CMa arrangement has no contractual relationship with either the architect or the contractor, but simply serves as an advisor to the developer in the developer's oversight of the functions performed by the architect and the contractor.

A variation of the pure construction management system described above is the ***construction management at risk system*** or ***CM@R***.[36] In the construction management at risk system, the construction manager serves in two capacities—as (1) the owner's advisor during the planning and design phases of the construction process and (2) the contractor during the construction phase. The arrangement of the players in a CM@R system is diagrammed in the following manner.

---

35. *See* Rubin *supra* note 33, at 182; and John G. Cameron, *The Wonderful World of Construction*, in ALI–ABA COURSE OF STUDY MATERIALS, MODERN REAL ESTATE TRANSACTIONS, Course #SR–001, 3 (August 2009).

36. *See* JOINT AIA/AGC REPORT, *supra* note 31, at 3. The construction management at risk system is also sometimes referred to as the "construction management-constructor" system or "CMc." *Id. See also* Cameron, *Wonderful World*, *supra* note 35, at 3.

Developer

↓   ↓

Architect   Construction Manager

↓

Subcontractors

The CM@R arrangement is similar in all respects but one to the design-bid-build method described in the prior section of this Chapter. The one difference between the design-bid-build system and CM@R is that in the CM@R method, the construction manager provides advisory services to the developer during the planning and design phases of the construction process (***pre-construction services***). Once those phases of the process are completed, the construction manager sheds its advisory role and assumes direct contractual responsibility for the prosecution of the construction work. The continuity of the construction manager's efforts throughout the entirety of the construction process (including the planning and design phases) has made the CM@R method a more popular delivery system choice for developers than the pure, construction management-agency method.[37]

Advantages—

- The primary advantage of the CMa arrangement is that it provides a developer that does not have in-house capabilities with an effective means of managing the activities of the architect and the contractor throughout the construction process.

- In addition to the advantages summarized previously with respect to the design-bid-build method, the CM@R method provides the developer with the added benefit of its receipt of advice from an independent professional during the planning and design phases of the construction process.

Disadvantages—

- The disadvantage of the CMa method is that the additional fee payable to the construction manager increases the developer's total project costs.

- Unlike the design-bid-build method, there is a notable lack of case law interpreting the role that a construction manager serves during the construction process.[38]

- Because the CM@R method is largely indistinguishable from the design-bid-build method, the disadvantages of that construction

---

37. *See* Cameron, A Practitioner's Guide, *supra* note 10, at 8–55 of the 2009 Supplement.

38. *See id.* at 8–57 of the 2009 Supplement.

management system are similar to those applicable to the design-bid-build methodology.

C. DESIGN–BUILD

Over the last 20 years, the design-build delivery system has become a very popular choice of developers. It is now estimated that approximately 40% of all non-residential projects are constructed using the design-build method, with that figure being projected to grow to more than 50% by 2015.[39]

Under the design-build system, the design and construction functions are combined and delegated to a single entity known as the ***design-builder***. The developer enters into a single contract with the design-builder, who contractually agrees to be responsible for both the design of the project and its ultimate construction. The design-builder is typically a contractor, who hires the necessary design professionals either as part of its in-house staff or as subcontractors.[40]

The following is a diagrammatic depiction of the relationship of the parties in a typical design-build arrangement.

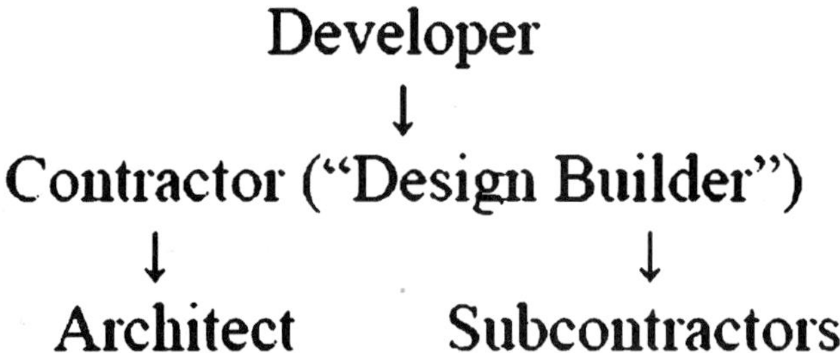

The use of a design-build delivery system is restricted in some states where licensing laws require the design function to be performed directly by a licensed architectural firm.[41] The real estate development lawyer should investigate the laws of the state where the developer's project is located to make sure that the design-build delivery system can be utilized in that state.

Advantages—

- The developer has a single point of contact and responsibility for all aspects of the design and construction of its project. As such, the developer doesn't have to waste time trying to figure out whether a particular construction defect or delay was caused by the architect or the contractor (both of whom are quite expert at pointing the finger at the other when a problem arises).

---

39. *See id.* at 8–95 of the 2009 Supplement; and Beck, *supra* note 6, at 4–16.

40. The design-builder can also be an architect or a joint venture entity created for the project by a contractor and an architect. *See* Harvey W. Berman, *Understanding Project Delivery Methods,* 15 No. 2 PRACTICAL REAL ESTATE LAWYER 4 (March 1999).

41. *See* CAMERON, PRACTITIONER'S GUIDE, *supra* note 10, at 8–99 of 2009 Supplement.

- Because the construction and design professionals are working together as a team (and not as separate, functional silos), there is a greater potential to reduce project costs (through value engineering) and expedite project completion (by overlapping the design and construction phases in a fast-track approach to the construction process).[42]

- The design-build method has been shown to significantly reduce the number of disputes between and claims filed by members of the construction and design teams.[43]

Disadvantages—

- The principal disadvantage of the design-build system is that it eliminates the checks and balances provided by the separation of the design and construction functions into separate contracts. In non-design-build structures, the architect's primary allegiance is to the developer. Reversing that arrangement by having the architect be responsible to the contractor creates a developer fear that "the fox would be guarding the hen house" and that construction and design problems might be "swept under the rug."[44]

- The developer's contact with the architect (and hence its control over the design process) is limited in a design-build structure.

- There is a potential for a cheapening of the overall quality of the project because all design and construction decisions are being made jointly by the design-builder. This potential for a reduction in the project's overall quality standards is heightened in those instances where the developer fails to provide the design-builder with detailed program requirements for its project.[45]

D. HYBRID DELIVERY SYSTEMS

There are countless hybrid delivery systems that mix and match various elements of the three principal categories of delivery systems discussed above. Two hybrid systems that have gained some traction in the construction industry in the last several years are (1) the ***multiple prime contractor method***[46] and (2) the ***integrated project delivery***

---

42. *See* Beck, *supra* note 6, at 4–17, for the assertion that "studies have suggested that design/build projects are approximately one-third faster than traditional 'design—then bid—then build' projects and approximately one-fourth faster than projects utilizing a 'construction manager at-risk'."

43. *See id.* at 4–18.

44. *See id.*

45. It is, therefore, essential that a developer choosing to use the design-build system put together detailed programmatic requirements for both the aesthetics and functionality of the proposed project. If the developer does not have an in-house staff capable of compiling such a fulsome set of program requirements, it should consider hiring its own, independent design professional to aid it in that effort. *See* CAMERON, A PRACTITIONER'S GUIDE, *supra* note 10, at 8–98 and 8–99.

46. *See generally*, Berman, *supra* note 40, at 8; and Beck, *supra* note 6, at 4–12.

method.[47]

Under the multiple prime contractor method, the owner enters into contracts with the architect and each of the prime trade contractors involved in the construction of the project. In this arrangement, there is no general contractor assigned with the task of coordinating the activities of the various trade contractors and suppliers. The owner effectively plays the role of the general contractor and, as such, is directly responsible for the scheduling, oversight and payment of all the players in the construction process. The multiple prime contractor method provides the owner with the maximum control over the construction process and further permits it to fast-track the construction process by entering into contracts for components of the project (e.g., excavation and site work) before the project design is completed. The multiple prime system also reduces the developer's overall project costs by eliminating the developer's obligation to pay a general contractor's fee and overhead. The obvious disadvantage of the multiple prime structure is that it places an incredible burden on the developer to assume responsibility for managing all aspects of the construction process. A developer can lessen the impact of that burden by hiring a construction manager-agent to help it coordinate the construction efforts of the trade contractors and suppliers.

The integrated project delivery method is a relatively new and quite revolutionary theory of project delivery that stresses the collaboration of the developer, contractor and architect throughout all phases of the construction process. Characteristics of the integrated project delivery system include the following:[48]

- The involvement of all three of the key players (that is, the developer, contractor and architect) at all time during the planning, design and construction phases of the construction process;

- The collaborative design of the project to meet agreed-upon performance requirements and budgetary constraints;

- The joint management of the project by consensus of the developer, contractor and architect;

- The establishment of a targeted project cost determined through the collaborative efforts of all three players;[49]

- The establishment of compensation incentives for each of the three players that are designed to reward (and, where appropriate, punish) the players based upon the financial outcome of the project; and

---

47. *See generally* Howard W. Ashcraft, Jr., *Negotiating an Integrated Project Delivery Agreement*, in DRAFTING AND NEGOTIATING TOMORROW'S CONSTRUCTION CONTRACTS TODAY 353 (Stanley P. Sklar chair 2009); and O'Connor, *supra* note 6.

48. *See* Ashcraft, *supra* note 48, at 372–390.

49. The targeted project cost is an estimate derived through the consensus of the three participants and is not guaranteed in any sense by any one of the participants.

• A waiver or limitation of the liability of the three participants to each other with respect to their respective project performances.

The integrated project delivery system is a largely untested theory that is intended to use emerging technologies and collaborative delivery models in an effort to reduce project costs, eliminate construction delays and minimize construction disputes. While the integrated project delivery system may have a positive application for certain types of projects (primarily public projects such as schools, hospitals and the like), the ceding of developer control that is a key component of the system makes its utility for private development projects highly suspect.

E. FACTORS DRIVING THE SELECTION OF A DELIVERY SYSTEM

So how does a developer decide which project delivery system it should use for its project? The developer must first understand that just as there is no one set of clothes that fits every person, there is no one delivery system that is the best choice for all commercial real estate projects. The selection of the right delivery system for a particular project will depend on the nature of the project and the business objectives and capabilities of the developer.

The following chart lists a number of common project/developer attributes and then indicates which of the three, primary, project delivery system is best suited to deal with that attribute (with the following short-hand references being used to describe the project delivery system alternatives: DBB = design-bid-build; CM = construction management; and DB = design-build).

The aesthetics of the project are important and novel → DBB or CM.
The project design has been used on prior projects in other locales → DB.
The developer has an experienced, in-house design and construction staff → DBB or DB.
The developer does not have any in-house design or construction capabilities → CM.
The project needs to be fast-tracked → DB.
The developer has plenty of time to complete design and bid out the work → DBB.
The project's program requirements are well-defined by the developer → DB.
The project's program requirements are not well-defined → DBB or CM.
The developer is a "control freak" → DBB.
The developer wants to secure pricing at the lowest possible number → DBB.

When selecting a project delivery system, the developer must identify and prioritize all of its design and construction goals for the subject project and then determine which project delivery system will best enable it to meet those goals in a timely and cost-effective manner.

VII. DESIGN AND CONSTRUCTION CONTRACTS

Once the developer[50] (with the advice and counsel of its lawyer) has selected the appropriate delivery system, the lawyer must set about the task of drafting and negotiating design and construction contracts for the project. The remainder of this Chapter will focus on the key legal issues that the real estate development lawyer must take into consideration when preparing those contracts.

A. CONTRACT FORMS

Stage 6 is unique in that most of the design and construction contracts drafted by the real estate development lawyer make use of pre-printed, standard forms published by trade associations representing either the architect or the contractor. The American Institute of Architects (**AIA**), the Associated General Contractors of America (**AGC**) and the Engineers Joint Contract Documents Committee (**EJCDC**) have all produced a series of contract forms designed for each of the basic project delivery systems described in the preceding section of this Chapter. The Design Build Institute of America has published a series of standard form contracts for use on design-build projects. Finally, in 2007, a group of 24 construction industry associations representing designers, owners, contractors, subcontractors and sureties joined together to create a new alternative set of standard contract forms called the ***ConsensusDOCS***.[51]

The standard forms attempt both to set forth the specific business deal struck by the parties and to establish a general set of rules governing the assignment and allocation of rights, responsibilities and liabilities among the owner, the architect, the contractor and its subcontractors.[52] The standard forms prepared by the noted industry groups are extremely thorough in describing the relationship between the players in the construction process and, hence, serve as an excellent starting point for the real estate development lawyer's preparation of design and construction contracts for its client's project.[53]

The real estate development lawyer must, however, keep in mind that the standard contract forms published by the AIA, AGC, EJCDC and other industry groups all have a decided bias in favor of the player represented

---

50. The terms "developer" and "owner" are used interchangeably throughout the remainder of this Chapter.

51. ConsensusDOCS Construction Contracts (2007), available at http://www.consensusdocs. org/catalog.

52. The AIA set of forms consist of two separate documents—(1) the specific agreement between the owner and the contractor or architect and (2) the general rules governing the construction process, referred to in the AIA documents as "general conditions."

53. The contract documents promulgated by the AIA remain the contract forms most commonly used during Stage 6 of a development project (although the ConsensusDOCS referred to in note 51, *supra*, have gained a strong following since their introduction in 2007).

by the author of those documents—which, in all instances, is someone other than the developer. As one practicing lawyer accurately noted, "from the developer's perspective, there are three things which must be understood about printed forms of design and construction contracts: (a) they are not fair; (b) they are not adequate; and (c) they generally do not reflect the agreement between the parties."[54] It is, therefore, imperative that the real estate development lawyer read every single word of the proffered standard forms and then revise them to better protect the developer and reflect the deal struck with the other players in the construction process.[55]

The discussion in the remainder of this Chapter will not deal with any specific set of industry-sponsored contract forms.[56] The limited purpose of this Chapter is to highlight those key legal issues that a real estate development lawyer needs to think about during the course of his negotiation of design and construction contracts—all of which are equally applicable to each of the project delivery systems discussed in the preceding section of this Chapter. Those of you interested in learning the specific ins and outs of revising the AIA, EJCDC or ConsensusDOCS forms should consult the excellent articles on that topic noted in the accompanying footnote.[57]

Practice Tip #10–2: Drafting Design and Construction Contracts

The first tip I will offer up about the drafting of design and construction contracts is that the lawyer's first job is to try to convince his developer clients that it really is a good idea for the lawyer to review the contracts BEFORE *the clients execute them. Developers for some unfathomable reason*

---

54. *See* Hastie, *supra* note 24, at 2.

55. Alternatively, the real estate development lawyer could prepare original construction and design documents, tailored to meet the needs of his developer client and the subject project. For a host of reasons (primarily a lack of opportunity, time and expertise), the real estate development lawyer rarely wins the "battle of the forms" with a contractor or an architect and, therefore, is forced to navigate his way through the maze of the standard pre-printed forms created by the construction and design industry.

56. The industry-sponsored forms are so complex as to render any examination of their specific provisions well beyond the scope of this Chapter. Moreover, those standard forms are in a constant state of revision and, therefore, any analysis of their specific provisions would be outdated almost as soon as it was written.

57. *See e.g.,* CAMERON, A PRACTITIONER'S GUIDE, *supra* note 10, at Chapters 6, 8 and 10; Mark C. Friedlander, *Drafting an Effective Design Agreement Using the 2007 AIA Documents: A Practical Guide to New and Controversial Issues in AIA B101—2007,* in DRAFTING AND NEGOTIATING TOMORROW'S CONSTRUCTION CONTRACTS TODAY 107 (Stanley P. Sklar chair, 2009); Steve G.M. Stein and Ronald O. Wietecha, *A Comparison of ConsensusDOCS and AIA Form Construction Contract Agreements,* in DRAFTING AND NEGOTIATING TOMORROW'S CONSTRUCTION CONTRACTS TODAY 207 (Stanley P. Sklar chair, 2009); DANIEL S. BRENNAN, MICHAEL J. HANAHAN, JENNIFER A. NIELSEN AND I. SPANGLER III, THE CONSTRUCTION CONTRACTS BOOK: HOW TO FIND COMMON GROUND IN NEGOTIATING DESIGN AND CONSTRUCTION CLAUSES (2d ed. 2008); and Lynn R. Axelroth, *There Must Be Some Way Out of Here: The Ten Top Issues in Negotiating AIA Form Contracts,* in ACREL PAPERS 21 (ALI–ABA, Spring 2005).

often fail to involve their lawyers in the negotiation of the design and construction contracts, preferring instead to delegate that task to those internal, non-lawyer, staff members, who are assigned responsibility for overseeing the construction process. Design and construction contracts are highly complex, legal documents that directly impact the success or failure of the developer's project. The real estate development lawyer's participation in the preparation, review and negotiation of those documents is every bit as warranted as is the lawyer's involvement in preparing the land purchase contract, the LLC operating agreement or the project lease.

The following are three additional tips related to the drafting of design and construction contracts.

- ***Make sure all of the contracts are internally consistent.*** *It is common for there to be a number of contract documents executed in connection with the design and construction of the developer's project (including loan documents evidencing the developer's construction loan). It is important that all these documents treat the same topic in the same way. By way of example, if the developer's loan agreement with its construction lender requires the sign-off of the architect on any draw request submitted to the lender for payment, the developer's contracts with the architect and contractor should contain a similar requirement.*

- ***Don't overreach in an effort to protect the developer.*** *The Stage 6 contracts establish the relationships among the various members of the design and construction team, all of whom must work together to produce a successful development project. Each such contract "resembles a marriage contract more than a sales transaction or real estate deal."*[58] *One practitioner provided the following sage advice on how to approach a negotiation of those "marriage contracts"—"[i]f the process of negotiating the design and construction documents is undertaken with a patently adversarial attitude, the confrontations which exist during the negotiation phase might well infect the project throughout its duration and provide impetus for the architect or contractor to 'get even' during the course of producing the project."*[59] *The real estate development lawyer must resist the natural urge to protect his client at all costs and, instead, remember that his client will be best served by the production of legal documents that foster cooperation (and not conflict) among the players in the construction process.*

- ***Follow the guiding principle that "risk and responsibility should follow control."***[60] *The focus of design and construction contracts is the assignment of responsibility for the performance of a particular task and the allocation of liability should that responsibility not be performed in the contemplated manner. While the*

---

58. *See* Beck, *supra* note 6, at 4–9.

59. *See* Hastie, *supra* note 24, at 2.

60. *See* Beck, *supra* note 6, at 4–63.

> *contracting parties are generally free to assign responsibility and allocate risk in whatever fashion they deem appropriate, the inclusion of contract provisions which assign risk or responsibility for the performance of a particular task to a party who is not in control of such performance can be counter-productive and lead to the generation of unnecessary disputes among the players in the construction process.*[61]

B. KEY LEGAL ISSUES IN DESIGN CONTRACT

This section will address some of the key legal issues that arise during the course of the real estate development lawyer's negotiation of the design contract with the project architect.[62] The noted issues exist regardless which project delivery system is selected by the developer for its project.[63]

1. Scope of Services

The first issue that the real estate developer must resolve is exactly what services the architect will be required to perform for the project. There are two prongs to the scope of services issue—(1) what is the project that the architect is supposed to design and (2) what specific services and documents is the architect required to furnish in connection with the project design?

With respect to the first prong, it is incumbent upon the developer to provide the architect with program requirements for the project, which set out in as much detail as reasonably practicable the developer's vision for the project. That vision will include the location, type and size of the proposed project (e.g., a 100,000 square foot office building on a specific ten acre site in Orlando, Florida), as well as any aesthetic considerations, performance requirements or budgetary constraints identified by the developer as part of its design definition for the project. The provision of a detailed set of program requirements will better enable the architect to

---

61. Provisions which seek to assign risk and responsibility to a party who has little, if any, power to control or influence an outcome are commonly referred to as "killer clauses." *See* Beck, *supra* note 6, at 4–56 through 4–58, for an analysis of killer clauses. As Mr. Beck notes in the cited article, "*generally speaking*, a court will give effect to a contract provision placing an inordinate amount of risk on one party even though the result may appear to be 'unfair' or 'unreasonable.' As with most rules, however, there are exceptions; and in this area of the law, the exceptions sometimes seem to swallow the rule." *Id.* at 4–58.

62. For a more thorough discussion of the issues that flow out of the negotiation of the design contract, *see generally* CAMERON, A PRACTITIONER'S GUIDE, *supra* note 10, at *Chapter 5, Preparing a Design Services Agreement*; and Keranen, *supra* note 9.

63. To the extent the design-build method is selected, the issues noted in this section will need to be resolved in the agreement entered into between the owner and the design-builder. Under the remaining project delivery systems, those issues will arise as part of the negotiation of the contract between the owner and the architect. For the purposes of this section, the reference to the "architect's contract" or "design contract" will include both a design-build agreement and any contract to which the architect and the owner are parties.

get the project design right on its first try, thereby avoiding the delays and added costs triggered by the architect having to redesign the project.

The architect's contract should also detail the specific services that the architect is required to perform in connection with its work on the developer's project. The following are samples of questions that should be raised and resolved by the real estate development lawyer with respect to this second prong of the scope of services issue.[64]

- Will the architect be required to prepare schematic design, design development and construction drawings for the project (or just a limited subset of those categories of drawings)?[65]

- Will the architect be required to provide the developer with ***as-built drawings*** at the completion of the project that reflect any modifications made to the agreed-upon construction drawings prior to completion of the project's construction?

- Will the architect serve in the role of an ***inspecting architect*** during the project's construction phase?[66]

- What role, if any, will the architect have in communicating with the contractor and resolving any disputes between the owner and the contractor concerning the compliance of the contractor's work with the final plans?[67]

- Will the architect be required to attend periodic job meetings with representatives of the developer and contractor throughout the construction process?

- Will the architect be required to appear at public meetings (e.g., hearings before a planning and zoning board or a neighborhood commission) to help the developer secure any required approvals for the project?

- Will any specific individuals be required to work on the project on the architect's behalf?

The lawyer's objective should be to prepare a scope of work for the architect, which describes in sufficient detail all those services which the architect will be required to perform during the design and construction

---

64. *See generally* Carl J. Circo, *Building a Better Construction and Design Contract*, 46 No. 2 PRACTICAL LAWYER 2 (July 2000).

65. *See supra* notes 11 and 12 and accompanying text.

66. An inspecting architect is the person assigned responsibility for making regular jobsite visits to confirm that the progress of construction conforms to the final plans and that the contractor's draw requests relate to work actually completed on the project. *See* Cameron, *The Wonderful World of Construction, supra note 35, at 2. See also supra* Chapter 9, Page 393, for a discussion of the construction lender's requirement that an inspecting architect participate in some fashion in the loan disbursement process.

67. The 2007 version of the AIA's standard form documents generally provide that (a) the owner should endeavor to run all of its communications with the contractor through the architect and (b) the architect will be the initial arbiter of all owner-contractor disputes, unless the parties agree to designate some other person to serve as the "Initial Decision Maker." *See* Friedlander, *supra* note 57, at 131 and 125, respectively. Both of these provisions are unacceptable to most developers.

phases. A skimpy or overly general scope of services provision will provide the architect with grounds to argue that a particular service requested by the developer is an "additional service" for which the architect is entitled additional compensation—a result that is extremely distasteful to the developer.[68]

2. Time for Performance

The design contract should include a timeline which lists the outside date by which the architect is required to perform each component of its design services (e.g., the delivery of schematic design drawings within 30 days after contract execution and the delivery of design development drawings within 45 days after the developer's approval of the schematic design). The failure to provide time requirements for the architect's performance of its design services can result in a delayed construction start, which, in turn, can jeopardize the success of the developer's project.

3. Compensation

There are a variety of ways in which the architect can be compensated for its provision of design services. The most common compensation methods are: (1) a fixed fee;[69] (2) a flexible fee based on the number of hours billed to the project and the hourly rates of the design professionals working on the project design;[70] and (3) a fee equal to a stated percentage of the overall project costs.[71] The architect's contract should clearly state which compensation method will be used to determine the architect's fee and when that fee will be paid (e.g., monthly progress payments on an "as incurred" basis, incremental fees payable at the conclusion of each phase of the design process or a lump sum fee payable on the completion of the architect's services).

There are two other issues related to the architect's compensation scheme which merit further discussion. The first issue is what happens to the architect's fee arrangement if the developer rejects the architect's project design and instructs the architect to "go back to the drawing table"? Is the architect entitled to an additional fee to compensate it for the time and effort spent on the redesign of the project or does the architect have to eat all of its additional redesign costs? The answer to that question is customarily tied to the nature of the reason underlying

---

68. *See* Circo, *supra* note 64, at 2.

69. While this compensation vehicle is attractive to the developer because of its certainty, most architects will resist the imposition of a fixed fee arrangement, unless the owner's program requirements and the architect's scope of services are both tightly defined.

70. If the hourly rates method is used to compensate the architect, the developer would be well-advised to include a "not to exceed" compensation figure in the architect's contract to put a cap on architect's total compensation. *See* Hastie, *supra* note 24, at 9. The developer might also want to consider requesting the use of declining hourly rates once the time spent on the project exceeds an agreed-upon limit. *See* Cameron, *The Wonderful World of Construction, supra* note 35, at 5.

71. Basing the architect's fee on a percentage of the overall project costs is often unacceptable to the developer, because it can provide the architect with an incentive to design a more costly than necessary project. *See* Cameron, A Practitioner's Guide, *supra* note 10, at 5–5.

the developer's rejection of the architect's initial design proposals—that is, was the design rejected because of the developer's imposition of a new program requirement (in which event the architect has a strong argument for its receipt of an additional redesign fee) or was the design rejected because it failed to satisfy the specified program requirements or the developer's aesthetic sensibilities (in which event the developer has a sound argument that the architect should do the redesign work for no additional fee).[72]

A second issue is whether the architect is entitled to be reimbursed for the business expenses it incurs during the course of its design work and, if so, which business expenses are reimbursable and at what rate? It is fairly typical for the design contract to permit the architect to recover certain of its out-of-pocket expenses, such as copying charges, delivery fees, postage, airfare, hotel charges and the cost of materials used in producing architectural renderings and models of the project. The careful real estate development lawyer should, however, insist that those reimbursable expenses be limited to the actual amount of the incurred expense—thereby preventing the architect from marking up the amount of its business expenses to provide itself with an additional profit center for its work on the project.[73]

4. Ownership of Plans

At common law, the construction drawings, plans and specifications prepared by the architect for a particular project remain the property of the architect.[74] The principle that the architect owns the plans is also reflected in the AIA's form documents and most of the other standard pre-printed forms used in the construction industry.[75]

The issue of who owns the design plans involves the clash of two very legitimate, but conflicting views held by the developer and the architect. The developer will argue that it has paid for the plans and, therefore, it should have the right to own the plans and use them in any way that it deems appropriate. The architect, on the other hand, will assert that the

---

72. One practitioner nicely sums up the developer's position on the architect's obligation to redesign the project (an obligation which is negated in the standard architect's contract published by the AIA) by noting that "aesthetics are at the heart of the owner-architect relationship, and the owner's taste should prevail.... Thus, the owner may wish to ... require the architect to redesign the project if the owner is not satisfied with the architect's work." *See* CAMERON, A PRACTITIONER'S GUIDE, *supra* note 10, at 6–17. I agree with Mr. Cameron's sentiment and also believe that it is well within the developer's rights to further require that the architect undertake the project redesign at its cost (and not at the developer's cost).

73. *See* Hastie *supra* note 24, at 9; and CAMERON, A PRACTITIONER'S GUIDE, *supra* note 10, at 5–6 and 5–7.

74. *See* Hastie *supra* note 24, at 8.

75. *See e.g.*, AIA DOCUMENT B101—STANDARD FORM OF AGREEMENT BETWEEN OWNER AND ARCHITECT (2007), §§ 7.1–7.3. *But see* CONSENSUSDOCS 410—OWNER/DESIGN-BUILDER GMP AGREEMENT (2007), which contains provisions transferring ownership of design plans created in the context of a design-build arrangement to the developer upon the developer's making of its final payment to the architect. Note, however, that CONSENSUSDOCS 410 still does not permit the developer's unfettered re-use of the plans for another project without the architect's authorization. *See* Beck, *supra* note 6, at 4–45.

plans represent its unique work product and that the developer's re-use of those plans would unfairly deprive the architect of its pecuniary interest in the project design and could potentially subject the architect to increased liability. The developer does not want to see the unique design features of its project replicated in competing buildings and the architect is loath to accept the possibility that its created design might appear on a building developed by the developer in another location, without the architect being compensated for the developer's re-use of that design.

The resolution of the issue of who owns the plans will turn on the uniqueness of the project design and the relative negotiating leverage of the developer and the architect. At the bare minimum, the developer should require the inclusion in the design contract of the confirmation of three points[76]—(1) the right of the developer to use the plans to complete construction of the project in the event the architect's role in the project is voluntarily or involuntarily terminated, (2) the right of the developer's lender to use the plans if it takes over ownership of the project due to the developer's default under its construction loan[77] and (3) the right of the developer to use the plans in connection with any future alteration or expansion of the project.[78]

5. Allocation of Risk

There are two primary design risks that should be addressed during the negotiation of the design contract—(1) the risk that the condition of the site (e.g., the existence of bad soils) will render the project design infeasible or make the construction of the designed project more costly than anticipated and (2) the risk that the project design does not comply with all applicable governmental requirements (e.g., local building and zoning codes or the Americans with Disabilities Act). Architects will typically seek to allocate those risks to the owner, while the owner will return the favor and argue that the architect should indemnify the owner against such risks. A common resolution of this issue is for the architect to assume responsibility for the governmental compliance risk and for the owner to assume (and then try to pass on to the contractor) the site condition risk.[79]

6. Insurance

An architect is generally liable at common law for all damages incurred by the owner as a result of the architect's negligent performance

---

76. *See* Hastie, *supra* note 24, at 8; and Circo, *supra* note 67, at 2.

77. As noted *supra* Chapter 9, Pages 353–354, the developer should also receive the architect's express consent to the developer's collateral assignment of the architect's contract to its construction lender.

78. Counsel for the architect may counter this point by insisting that the developer indemnify the architect from any liability associated with the developer's re-use of the plans without the architect's express written authorization. *See* Circo, *supra* note 64, at 3.

79. *See infra* Pages 435–436, for a discussion of the contractor's assumption of the risk of unforeseen site conditions.

of its design services.[80] The owner's protection against the architect's negligence is, however, only as good as the architect's credit standing. It is, therefore, crucial that the real estate development lawyer incorporate into the design contract a requirement that the architect maintain professional errors and omissions insurance coverage throughout the duration of the construction process and for a fixed period after the final completion of the project.[81] The real estate development lawyer should consult with the developer's insurance carrier to get a sense of the precise scope and amount of the architect's required insurance coverage. The real estate development lawyer should also make sure to exclude the architect's errors and omissions insurance premiums from the list of "reimbursable expenses" that the architect is contractually permitted to charge back to the owner.[82]

7. Termination

Virtually every design contract contains a provision expressly permitting the developer to terminate the contract if the architect defaults in the performance of its contractual obligations (a "for cause" termination). The owner may, however, also want to terminate its contract with the architect for reasons other than the architect's obvious non-performance. By way of example, the owner may simply decide that the architect, while technically in compliance with its contractual obligations, does not possess the level of creativity, core competency or communication skills that the developer wants for its project. In such a situation, it may be in the long-term best interests of the project for the developer to terminate the design contract and hire a new architect to provide the project design.

Contract terminations which fall outside of the "for cause" category are commonly known as *for convenience terminations*.[83] If possible, the developer should always seek to reserve the right to terminate the architect's contract for convenience. Doing so will give the developer the flexibility to respond to a situation where the developer no longer has confidence in the design capabilities of the original, selected architect. The price the developer has to pay for preserving the right to effect such a for convenience termination may be its payment to the architect of a negotiated break-up fee (much like a property settlement called for in a pre-nuptial agreement).[84]

---

80. *See generally* CAMERON, A PRACTITIONER'S GUIDE, *supra* note 10, at Chapter 7.

81. E&O policies are generally issued on a "claims made" basis—meaning that the E&O policy will only cover the architect's liability if a claim is made by the owner during the term of the E&O policy. It is, therefore, customary for the developer to require the architect to maintain E&O coverage for some extended period after the completion of construction (referred to in the insurance industry as a "tail" period) to give the developer sufficient time to discover any design defects and file a claim against the architect's E&O policy. *See* Axelroth, *The Owner's Perspective, supra* note 25, at 15.

82. *See* supra Page 424, for a discussion of the architect's "reimbursable expenses."

83. *See* discussion of "for convenience" terminations of the architect's contract in Lynn R. Axelroth, *The Owner's Perspective,* in FUNDAMENTALS OF CONSTRUCTION LAW 1, 18 (Carina Y. Enhada, Cheri Turnage Gatlin and Fred D. Wilshusen, eds., 2001).

84. *See id.* at 18; and CAMERON, A PRACTITIONER'S GUIDE, *supra* note 10, at 5–17.

C. KEY LEGAL ISSUES IN CONSTRUCTION CONTRACT

The dynamic nature of the construction process creates a number of issues that the real estate development lawyer must take into consideration when crafting the contract that will govern the contractor's construction of the developer's project.[85] The discussion which follows touches on those issues which are most frequently the topic of vigorous negotiations between counsel for the developer and the contractor.[86]

1. Construction Pricing

The most important issue that needs to be addressed in the construction contract is the setting of the price that the developer will have to pay the contractor to complete construction of the project. There are three basic components of the construction price—(1) the actual cost of completing the project (i.e., the cost of all labor and materials paid to trade contractors and suppliers), (2) the contractor's costs of administering the project, including temporary utilities, trash removal and job supervision costs (contractor's *general conditions*) and (3) the contractor's fee (which is intended to cover both the contractor's unreimbursed overhead expenses and its profit on the project). The sum of those three components is often referred to as the "cost of the work."

The central question that must be resolved when describing the price in the construction contract is who will be bear the risk and who will receive the reward if the actual cost of the work differs from the developer's budgeted cost of the work. A difference between the actual and budgeted cost of work numbers can be produced by a variety of circumstances—e.g., an increase in the cost of construction materials or labor after the date of the execution of the construction contract or an error made by the parties when establishing the initial budget for the cost of the work.[87]

---

85. For the purposes of the ensuing discussion, the term "contractor" will be used to refer to the firm that is principally responsible for the prosecution of the work and will expressly include the general contractor in a design-bid-build or CMa structure, the construction manager in a CM@R structure, the design-builder in a design-build structure and each contractor under a multiple prime contractors arrangement. It should also be noted that the contractor-owner issues discussed in this section are also applicable to the contractor's negotiation of contracts with its subcontractors. It is common for the owner's contract with the contractor to contain a "flow-through" clause, which "requires the . . . contractor to tie the subcontractors to provisions of the prime contract that affect their work." *See* SWEET, *supra* note 12, at § 28.04; and CAMERON, A PRACTITIONER'S GUIDE, *supra* note 10, at 11–13. The substantive points negotiated by the real estate development lawyer in the developer's contract with its contractor will, therefore, typically define the entirety of the construction work, including the performance of components of the work by the contractor's subcontractors and suppliers.

86. Other issues which arise during the course of the negotiation of the construction contract are noted in the construction contract checklists appearing in Beck, *supra* note 6, at 4–54 through 4–56; and Miles, *supra* note 1, at 422–424.

87. An actual vs. budget difference in the cost of work can also result from (1) a change in the project scope (*see infra* Pages 436–438), (2) a delay in completing construction (*see infra* Page 432) and (3) the presence of unforeseen site conditions (*see infra* Page 435). The impact of those cost

The three pricing mechanisms used in construction contracts are (1) a ***stipulated sum***, (2) the ***cost of the work, plus a fee***; and (3) a ***guaranteed maximum price***.[88] The developer's selection of the pricing method it wishes to use for a particular project is largely dependent on the status of the plans and specifications when the construction contract is executed; the project delivery system being utilized for the project; the projected construction schedule; and the developer's tolerance for risk. The pros and cons of each of the three construction pricing mechanisms are discussed below.

Stipulated Sum: The stipulated sum method is the simplest way of establishing the construction price to be paid by the developer. In a stipulated sum arrangement, the parties agree to a fixed construction price (e.g., $20 million), which will be paid by the developer to the contractor, regardless of the actual cost of the work. The contractor's fees, overhead and anticipated profit are all subsumed under the stipulated price.[89] In a stipulated sum contract, the contractor assumes the risk that the actual cost of the work will be greater than the stipulated contract price (thereby putting in jeopardy the contractor's anticipated profit from the job). However, the contractor also gets to retain the additional profit that is produced if the actual cost of the work is less than the stipulated price.

Stipulated sum pricing is attractive to a developer because it fixes the construction cost component of the overall project costs. However, the stipulated sum pricing model only works when the scope of the contractor's work is tightly defined and the project plans and specifications are complete. If that is not the case, the parties will likely not be able to reach agreement on a stipulated price because the contractor will, quite rightly, inflate its offered price by adding in a large fudge factor to compensate for the uncertainty surrounding the scope and design of the project.[90] The contractor's risk-adjusted price will almost always be unacceptable to the developer. For this reason, the stipulated sum pricing model works best in a design-bid-build arrangement and doesn't work well at all for projects

---

adjustments will be discussed under the indicated section headings. This discussion of construction pricing will focus on how to deal with those actual vs. budget cost differentials produced from a change in market conditions or an error in the initial budgeting process.

88. *See generally* Axelroth, *The Owner's Perspective, supra* note 83, at 20–24; Stanley P. Sklar, *What You Should Know Before You Start the Construction Project—Tips for Dirt Lawyers,* in ACREL PAPERS 1, 5–7 (ALI–ABA, Spring 2005); and CAMERON, A PRACTITIONER'S GUIDE, *supra* note 10, at 8–120 through 8–124 of the 2009 Supplement.

89. The contractor may seek to have the owner pay its general condition costs as an add-on to the stipulated price. To the extent the developer agrees with that approach (and it typically does not), its lawyer would be well-advised to read the discussion on general condition costs that is included under the "cost of work, plus a fee" subheading which immediately follows this section.

90. Another way that the contractor can protect itself against the risks associated with stipulated sum pricing is through the use of allowances. An allowance represents the contractor's estimate of the costs that will be incurred for a particular component of the construction work (e.g., $50,000 for carpeting). If the actual cost of the construction component is more than the stated allowance, the stipulated price will be increased by an amount equal to such excess costs. For this reason, most developers are extremely hesitant to permit the contractor's use of an allowance for any component of the work, other than items such as tenant improvements, which cannot be determined until very late in the construction process. *See* Hastie, *supra* note 24, at 5.

that are being fast-tracked in a design-build or construction management structure.

Cost of Work, Plus a Fee: Cost plus pricing is often utilized when the precise scope and design of the project has not yet been defined. In a cost of work, plus a fee arrangement, the developer is responsible for reimbursing the contractor for its actual construction costs (labor and materials provided by trade contractors and suppliers and the contractor's general condition costs), plus a fee that is typically calculated as a percentage of the project's construction costs (e.g., 3% of the total costs). A cost plus pricing structure places the risk that the actual cost of the work will be greater than the budgeted costs entirely on the developer, who is required to pay the contractor its full fee, plus reimburse the contractor for whatever its actual construction costs turn out to be.

If the construction price is going to be set using the cost plus approach, the developer must retain a right to review and verify all of the contractor's construction cost records. One issue that demands the real estate development lawyer's special attention is the identification of those general conditions costs that fall within the definition of the ***reimbursable costs*** that the developer is required to pay to the contractor. The contractor will want to recover as reimbursable costs as much of its home office and overhead expenses as possible (e.g., a portion of the salaries and benefits payable to its accounting staff and other personnel having some role, no matter how limited, in administering the contractor's construction of the project). The developer, on the other hand, will strive to limit the contractor's reimbursable costs to those contractor-incurred expenses which are specifically attributable to the developer's project (e.g., the direct cost of furnishing temporary utilities and trash removal services to the jobsite).[91] A compromise that is commonly reached on this issue is either for the cost of the contractor's general conditions to be expressed as a fixed number (e.g., $100,000) or for the entire concept to be jettisoned with a concomitant increase in the amount of the contractor's fee.[92]

While the cost plus pricing mechanism has the advantage of permitting the developer to kick off its construction project before the design and scope of the project are fully-developed, the disadvantages of the cost plus method far outweigh that single advantage. From the developer's perspective, a pure cost of work, plus a fee pricing model has two principal disadvantages—(1) it doesn't provide the developer with any certainty whatsoever as to the level of the project's construction costs and (2) it doesn't create any incentive for the contractor to try to lower its costs through competitive bidding or the efficient prosecution of the work.[93] For

---

91.   *See* Axelroth, *The Owner's Perspective, supra* note 83, at 21; and CAMERON, A PRACTITIONER'S GUIDE, *supra* note 10, at 8–122 of the 2009 Supplement.

92.   *See* Sklar, *What You Should Know Before You Start the Construction Project, supra* note 88, at 6.

93.   The developer can partially mitigate this state of affairs by including a requirement in the construction contract that all subcontract work must be competitively bid out and awarded to the low bidder. This arrangement is not, however, particularly useful in the typical, fast-track

these reasons, a pure cost plus pricing structure is seldom used for private commercial real estate projects.[94]

Guaranteed Maximum Price: The guaranteed maximum price model is a hybrid of the cost of work, plus a fee arrangement discussed under the preceding heading. In a guaranteed maximum price contract, the parties acknowledge that the construction price will be equal to the lesser of (1) the actual cost of the work, plus the contractor's fee and (2) a fixed sum agreed to by the contractor (the ***guaranteed maximum price*** or ***GMP***). The GMP can be set either at the time of the execution of the construction contract (the developer's preference) or at a later date in the construction process when the project scope and design is sufficiently well-defined for the contractor to make a reasonable estimate of its construction costs.[95] In either circumstance, the GMP is usually pegged at a cost level which the contractor is relatively confident can be achieved for the project—in other words, it includes an added cushion over the contractor's best estimate of the project's cost of work.[96]

The guaranteed maximum price model provides for a sharing between the owner and the contractor of the risk that the actual cost of work will exceed budget. The contractor assumes the risk that the actual cost of work will exceed the agreed-upon GMP and the developer takes the risk that the contractor, lacking any financial incentive to keep project costs below the GMP, will eschew cost savings that would otherwise be achievable for the project. Developers often try to create an incentive for the contractor to keep construction costs as low as possible by agreeing to increase the contractor's fee by an agreed-upon percentage (typically in the 25 to 50% range) of the difference between the GMP and the actual cost of work. Construction incentives of this type are known as ***shared savings*** clauses.[97]

---

construction project where the contractor does not have the luxury of taking the time to formally bid out all components of the work.

94. *See* Sklar, *What You Should Know Before You Start the Construction Project, supra* note 88, at 2.

95. If the GMP is not set at the time of contract execution, the contract should include a default method for dealing with a situation where the owner and the contractor cannot reach mutual agreement on the GMP. In such a circumstance, the developer should reserve the right to either terminate the construction contract or proceed with the contract with the added requirement that all subcontract work must be awarded to the low bidder as part of a competitive bidding process. *See* Hackenbrach, *supra* note 15, at 5.

96. The GMP can be phrased as either an overall cap on the total cost of the work or as a series of caps on individual components of the work (e.g., $4 million for steelwork, $2 million for site work, etc.). Most contractors resist the developer's request for line item GMPs, because they want to be able to use cost savings on one line item to cover costs overruns on another line item. The developer should, in all events, try to fix or otherwise put a cap on the contractor's general condition costs, so that the contractor is not tempted to augment its profit on the project by charging additional general condition costs to the project until the GMP threshold is met. *See* Axelroth, *The Owner's Perspective; supra* note 83, at 23.

97. If the developer agrees to share cost savings with the contractor, the contractor will have a strong incentive to set the GMP at an artificially high number, thereby creating a very real prospect that it can add its share of the savings to its profit on the project. It is, therefore, incumbent on the developer to closely scrutinize the contractor's offered GMP to try to make sure that the GMP is set at a realistic number and is not inflated simply to augment the contractor's fee on the project. *See* Hastie, *supra* note 24, at 12, for a discussion of shared savings clauses,

The guaranteed maximum price model is the pricing mechanism most commonly used on projects where the plans and specifications are not fully complete on the date the construction contract is signed by the contractor and the owner. While it can be used in connection with any of the three basic project delivery systems discussed earlier in this Chapter,[98] it frequently linked with fast track construction projects utilizing a construction management or design-build delivery system.[99]

2. Method of Payment

Once the construction price is determined, the next question that needs to be addressed in the construction contract is how and when that price will be paid to the contractor. In most construction projects, the construction price is paid monthly based upon the portion of the work completed (in a stipulated sum contract) or the construction costs incurred (in a cost plus or GMP arrangement) during the prior month.[100]

The developer's counsel should include in the construction contract a statement of those procedures that must be followed to permit the developer to verify that the work has progressed sufficiently to merit the making of each such monthly payment.[101] The construction contract should recite that the contractor must use the monthly progress payments it receives from the developer to make timely payment of all amounts then owed to its subcontractors and suppliers. Otherwise, the developer will run the risk of having a subcontractor or supplier file a mechanics' lien against its project. The payment procedures typically followed by the developer to protect its interests and those of its construction lender are discussed at length in *Chapter 9, Obtaining Construction Financing.*[102] The real estate development lawyer will want to make sure that the construction contract and all related subcontracts contain payment provisions that are fully consistent with the requirements set forth in the construction loan agreement.

---

which concludes with the insightful recommendation that "if the developer finds that the general contractor is heatedly negotiating for a savings clause, it is time for the developer to put an estimator on the developer's payroll."

98. *See supra* Pages 409–417. By way of example, the Pizzuti Companies used a GMP pricing mechanism and a design-bid-build model for all of the office buildings constructed in its HIBC project. *See infra HIBC Case Study—Design and Construction Issues.*

99. *See* Axelroth, *The Owner's Perspective, supra* note 83, at 23–24.

100. The monthly progress payments made to a contractor under a cost plus or GMP contract will normally also include the portion of the contractor's fee that is proportionate to the portion of the overall construction costs incurred during the month covered by the subject progress payment. *See* Cameron, *The Wonderful World of Construction, supra* note 35 at 11.

101. The developer should include a provision in the construction contract requiring the contractor to provide it with a schedule describing its best estimate of the timing and amount of the monthly progress payments that the contractor will be requesting during the construction phase. The developer should closely review that schedule to try to prevent the contractor from "front loading" its receipt of the construction price. "Front loading" is an attempt by the contractor to better its cash flow position (and worsen the developer's) by receiving a greater portion of the construction price than is warranted in the early months of the construction process. *See* Hastie, *supra* note 24, at 5.

102. *See supra* Chapter 9, Pages 392–394. *See also* Hackenbrach, *supra* note 15, at 8–9; and Axelroth, *The Owner's Perspective, supra* note 83, at 30–32.

Construction contracts typically contain provisions permitting the owner to withhold a stated percentage (normally 5–10%) from each monthly progress payment made to the contractor. Similar provisions are also included in the contractor's agreements with its subcontractors and suppliers. The withheld amounts (known as ***retainage***) are typically not disbursed to the contractor and its subcontractors and suppliers until the project is completed, thereby providing all those firms working on the construction project with an added incentive to complete construction on a timely basis. Contractors frequently request (and developers often agree) to eliminate retainage once the construction of the project is 50% complete, based on the theory that the developer's risk that the project will not be completed is significantly lessened once the project reaches that stage of completion.[103]

3. Construction Schedule

A principal business objective of the developer during Stage 6 is the on time completion of its development project. In an attempt to create expectations and avoid unintended construction delays, the real estate development lawyer should include in the construction contract a clear statement as to when construction must begin and when it must be completed. The concept of completion has two distinct components—(1) ***substantial completion***, which is generally defined as the stage in the progress of the work when the project is sufficiently complete so that the owner can occupy or utilize the project for its intended use,[104] and (2) ***final completion***, which is the date on which all aspects of the contractor's performance are fully completed.

A delay in the contractor's completion of construction can produce serious and sometimes devastating financial consequences for the developer.[105] A delay will result in the developer having to pay additional interest on its construction loan and could endanger the financial health of the entire project if, for example, the project leases contain provisions permitting the tenants to terminate their leases if the project is not contemplated by a certain date.[106]

---

103. See Axelroth, *The Owner's Perspective, supra* note 83, at 32. It is also quite common for the developer and its lender to agree to disburse a subcontractor's share of the retainage upon the full completion of that subcontractor's portion of the work (even though substantial completion of the entire project has not yet been achieved). *See supra* Chapter 9, Page 355.

104. *See e.g.*, AIA DOCUMENT A201—GENERAL CONDITIONS FOR THE CONTRACT FOR CONSTRUCTION § 9.8 (2007).

105. Although the focus of this text and this Chapter is on the developer's plight, I would be remiss if I failed to mention that a construction delay can also prove costly to the contractor. One practitioner correctly writes that "[o]n the contractor's side, delays translate into additional home office overhead, as well as increased jobsite overhead and supervision ('general conditions'), additional labor costs, and delays in transferring resources to another project or endeavor." *See* Beck, *supra* note 6, at 4–63.

106. The contractor's failure to complete the project on time could also trigger a default under the developer's construction loan (*see supra* Chapter 9, Page 346) or jeopardize the developer's ability to obtain permanent financing under the terms of a take-out commitment that is conditioned upon construction of the project being completed by a date certain. *See* Beck, *supra* note 6, at 4–63.

The developer has a number of options at its disposal to try to prevent a construction delay. First and foremost, the developer should select a contractor that has both a solid reputation for completing projects on time and the financial wherewithal to take whatever remedial measures may be necessary to avoid a delay (e.g., the scheduling of a second construction shift or the payment of overtime to its trade contractors). The developer should also closely monitor the progress of construction, so that it can detect any early warning signs that the contractor may have trouble meeting its completion deadline.[107] Finally, the developer should, if possible, establish a completion deadline which is realistic and which has at least some flexibility (called *float* in the construction industry) built into it to compensate for unavoidable delays.[108]

The real estate development lawyer can provide additional comfort to the developer by inserting language in the construction contract that is designed to incentivize the contractor to complete the project on time and to mitigate the financial impact to the developer of a construction delay. The following are examples of contractual techniques that the real estate development lawyer can employ to try to combat the prospect of a construction delay.

- *Written Notice of Delay*—The developer is often not in a position to independently discover the existence of a potential construction delay. The real estate development lawyer should consider adding a provision to the construction contract that requires the contractor to provide the developer with written notice of a potential construction delay promptly following the occurrence of the event that gave rise to the delay. The inclusion of such a notice requirement permits the developer to learn of the potential delay when there is still time to take remedial measures to overcome the delay. The contractor's right to receive an extension of the completion deadline or an increase in the construction price should be conditioned upon its delivery of the required written notice to the developer.[109]

- *Milestone Dates*—It is in the best interests of the developer to learn of the potential for a construction delay as early as possible in the construction process. One way that the developer can accomplish that goal is to set forth in the construction contract interim *milestone dates* for the completion of certain portions of the work (e.g., site excavation, foundation work or steel erection).

---

107. For a description of some early indicia that a contractor may be have trouble meeting the completion deadline, *see* Sklar, *What You Should Know Before You Start Construction, supra* note 88, at 12–13.

108. *See id.* at 13.

109. *See* Dugan & Meyers Construction Co. v. Ohio Department of Administrative Services, 113 Ohio St.3d 226 (2007), for a case holding that a contractor's right to receive a construction extension is conditioned upon its full compliance with the notice of delay provisions of the construction contract (even if the owner has actual knowledge of the potential delay and orally informs the contractor that no extension will be forthcoming). *See also* Thomas L. Rosenberg, *Essential Construction Contract Terms: Avoiding Future Problems by Addressing Key Issues*, REAL ESTATE FINANCE JOURNAL 50, 54 (Spring 2007).

If the contractor fails to meet one of the milestone dates, the owner might want to reserve a contractual right to require the contractor, at its expense, to take whatever actions are required to get the project back on schedule, including, furnishing additional labor and working overtime or multiple shifts.[110]

- *Liquidated Damages*—Finally, the real estate development lawyer should consider including a requirement for the contractor's payment of liquidated damages to the developer if construction of the project is not completed by the deadline date specified in the construction contract.[111] Liquidated damage clauses in construction contracts typically provide for the payment of a per diem charge for each day after the targeted completion deadline that the contractor fails to achieve substantial completion of the construction project. The lawyer's objective when drafting a liquidated damages clause is to include a per diem damages amount that is high enough to catch the contractor's attention and incentivize it to complete the project on schedule, but not so high as to render it an unenforceable penalty.[112]

All of the above provisions serve the developer's overriding goal of allocating the responsibility and risk of a construction delay to the contractor. The contractor will, however, generally resist an attempt by the developer to make the contractor responsible for a delay that is caused by events or circumstances beyond the contractor's control (an *excusable delay*). While the developer is often willing to accept that distinction, its view of what constitutes an excusable delay is usually light years away from the contractor's view.

The two generally accepted categories of excusable delays are (1) delays caused by the owner and (2) *force majeure* delays (meaning delays caused by unforeseen events beyond the contractor's control, including severe weather and other so-called acts of God). The negotiations over owner-caused delays will generally involve a heated discussion concerning the precise obligations to be placed on the owner during the construction phase, with the owner typically taking the position that its only obligation is to pay the construction price and the contractor vigorously arguing that the developer is responsible for everything from the accuracy and com-

---

110. *See* Cameron, A PRACTITIONER'S GUIDE, *supra* note 10, at 8–33 of the 2009 Supplement.

111. When faced with a request for liquidated damages, a contractor often tries to turn the table on the developer and ask for a bonus if it completes construction prior to the targeted completion date. Developers will typically agree to such a bonus provision only if an early completion of construction will provide it with a readily discernible financial benefit—such as the early commencement of a tenant's rent obligation. In many situations, the early completion of the project will not have any direct benefit to the developer and, hence, will not merit its payment of a bonus of any type to the contractor. *See* Hastie, *supra* note 24, at 12.

112. See Cameron, A PRACTITIONER'S GUIDE, supra note 10, at 8–34 and 8–35 of the 2009 Supplement. Generally speaking, a liquidated damages clause will be held enforceable if "at the time of contracting, the provisions were intended not to establish a penalty but rather to reasonably estimate the amount of actual damages that would result from a delay but would otherwise be difficult to ascertain and prove." *See* Beck, *supra* note 6, at 4–66. *See also* Rosenberg, *supra* note 109, at 53.

pleteness of the plans and specifications[113] to its warranty that the site conditions are appropriate for the construction of the project.

The parties will also take markedly different positions as to what constitutes an excusable, force majeure delay. The contractor will want the list of force majeure events to be "broad and long," while the developer will want that list to be "specific and short." By way of example, the contractor will often seek to have "inclement weather" treated as an excusable delay, while the developer will insist that only "abnormal and unusually severe weather conditions for the season and location" be included within the definition of an excusable delay.[114] Heated negotiations will frequently also take place over the issue of whether the contractor should be held responsible for delays caused by labor disputes or subcontractor bankruptcies (on the theory that those events could reasonably have been anticipated by the contractor and, hence, should have been taken into consideration by the contractor when it agreed to the project completion deadline).

The resolution of what events and circumstances will be treated as excusable delays for which the contractor is entitled to an extension of time or additional compensation (or both)[115] will ultimately come down to which side has the most "juice" in the negotiations. The tighter the construction schedule, the more heated those negotiations will be.

4. Unforeseen Site Conditions

A particularly sensitive topic in the owner-contractor negotiations is the treatment of the risk that ***unforeseen site conditions*** delay completion of construction or increase the cost of the work. In this context, unforeseen site conditions generally mean those site conditions that are not readily detectable by a visual inspection of the site. Examples of site conditions that can dramatically affect the project's schedule and costs are the presence on the site of bad soils, environmental contamination or protected wetlands. The unexpected presence of any of these site conditions will dramatically affect the project's costs and schedule.

The general rule is that the contractor is responsible for the risk of bad site conditions. As noted by the Supreme Court in the landmark case of *United States v. Spearin,* "one who undertakes to erect a structure upon a particular site assumes ordinarily the risk of subsidence of

---

113. Absent a provision in the construction contract to the contrary, the owner (and not the contractor) will be responsible for any defects in the plans and specifications. *See* United States v. Spearin, 248 U.S. 132, 136 (1918), where the Supreme Court stated that "if the contractor is bound to build according to plans and specifications prepared by the owner, the contractor will not be responsible for the consequences of defects in the plans and specifications." The *Spearin* doctrine is not, however, applicable to a design-build contractual arrangement, where the plans are provided by the design-builder and, hence, responsibility for design defects is placed on the design-builder and not the owner *See* discussion of the *Spearin* doctrine in Beck, *supra* note 6, at 4–49 through 4–51.

114. One practitioner has framed this issue from the developer's perspective by noting that "a contractor working on the Florida coast during hurricane season may not be able to claim that a hurricane was unanticipated and therefore an excusable delay." *See* Beck, *supra* note 6, at 4–64.

115. *See infra* Pages 437–438, for a discussion of constructive changes for excusable delays.

soils."[116] The parties to a construction contract are, however, free to allocate the risk of unforeseen site conditions in any specific manner they see fit.[117]

The construction contract should clearly state whether responsibility for the condition of the site falls on the contractor or the owner. Whichever party is assigned that responsibility should conduct thorough due diligence of the project's site conditions (by obtaining an environmental assessment, wetlands report, soils test and other site reviews certified by qualified, licensed professionals) to provide it with comfort that the site conditions are, in fact, suitable for the proposed project.

In most situations, the developer will seek to place the risk of unforeseen site conditions on the party that it considers to be an expert on all construction matters—the contractor. If the developer is successful in that effort and adverse site conditions are subsequently unearthed, the contractor will be the party responsible for paying the excess construction costs needed to solve the problem and get the project back on schedule. If the developer expressly assumes the site condition risk in the construction contract (and it is not all that unusual for it to do so), then the contractor will be entitled to an extension and additional compensation if adverse site conditions are discovered during the construction phase.[118]

5. Changes in the Work

Change is the norm in the construction of commercial real estate projects. In a typical project, there will be tens and maybe hundreds of changes made to the original plans and specifications. The owner may simply change its mind about the desired look or composition of the project. The contractor may determine that there is a better way to go about completing the project. Finally, circumstances beyond the control of both the owner and the contractor may dictate the need for a change in the scope of work, the project schedule or the construction price.

It is the real estate development lawyer's job to include provisions in the construction contract that are designed to give the parties clarity and guidance about the manner in which changes to the work may be made and the impact that such changes will have upon the construction schedule and pricing. In drafting the changes to work provisions of the construction contract, the lawyer needs to deal with three categories of potential changes—(1) ***change orders***, (2) ***change directives*** and (3) ***constructive changes***. The developer's goals and objectives with respect to each of those change categories are discussed below.

- ***Change Orders***—A change order is a modification to the contractor's scope of work that is voluntarily agreed to by the contractor

---

116. *See* United States v. Spearin, 248 U.S. 132, 136 (1918).

117. *See* CAMERON, A PRACTITIONER'S GUIDE, *supra* note 10, at 9–25.

118. *See* Edward Neal Pollard, *Changes in the Work*, in FUNDAMENTALS OF CONSTRUCTION LAW, 227, 230–232 (Carina Y. Enhada, Cheri Turnage Gatlin and Fred D. Wilshusen eds., 2001); and Beck, *supra* note 6, at 4–80 through 4–84.

and the owner.[119] A request for a change order can be issued by either the contractor or the owner. The contract should specifically provide that all change orders must be in writing and that they will not be effective until signed by both the contractor and the owner. The written change order should specify the nature of the agreed-upon change and the schedule and cost implications of those changes.[120]

- ***Change Directives***—In certain situations, the owner may want to reserve the unilateral right to compel the contractor to make changes to its scope of work, even if all of the terms associated with that change have not yet been agreed to by the contractor. This is especially true in fast-track projects where the owner cannot tolerate a work stoppage while the parties haggle over the precise terms of a formal change order. To deal with this type of scenario, the real estate development lawyer often includes a provision in the construction contract, which empowers the owner to issue a construction change directive compelling the contractor to proceed with the changed work in advance of the parties' mutual execution of a formal change order.[121] If the contract authorizes the owner to issue a construction change directive, the contract should also establish general parameters for determining the modifications to be made to the contract price and schedule if the owner and the contractor are not able to agree to the terms of a written change order. For example, the contract might recite that the contract price will be increased by an amount equal to the actual cost of the changed work, plus a fee equal to a fixed percentage of such cost.[122]

- ***Constructive Changes***—A constructive change is a change in the scope of the contractor's work that is caused by the occurrence of unforeseen events or circumstances after the date of the parties' execution of the construction contract. The two most obvious examples of constructive changes are those changes caused by the

---

119. Some industry published standard forms (e.g., those published by the AIA) also require the architect's approval of any change order. *See e.g.*, AIA DOCUMENT A201—GENERAL CONDITIONS FOR THE CONTRACT FOR CONSTRUCTION § 7.1.2 (2007). For the purposes of the discussion in this section, it will be assumed that the architect either is not required to approve change orders or that its approval will always be forthcoming if requested by the owner.

120. Contractors frequently seek to profit from work changes by asking at the time of the submission of a change order for a percentage mark-up on change order costs that is higher than the fee it charges on the base cost of the work. Owners prefer to fix the mark-up on change orders at the same percentage fee that is applicable to the remainder of the contractor's work. The owner's lawyer should, if possible, include a provision in the construction contract that specifies the percentage fee that the contractor will be entitled to for all changes in the work. *See* Sklar, *Drafting and Negotiating Construction Contracts, supra* note 5, at 37.

121. The construction contract typically places some limitation n the type of changes that can be subject to an owner's construction change directive. By way of example, AIA DOCUMENT A201, GENERAL CONDITIONS OF THE CONTRACT FOR CONSTRUCTION § 7.3.1 (2007) states that a construction change directive must be "within the general scope of the Contract." Some courts have also held that a change may be so "cardinal" as to render it unenforceable, absent the full agreement of the contractor. *See* CAMERON, A PRACTITIONER'S GUIDE, *supra* note 10, at 9–11 and 9–12; and Rosenberg, *supra* note 109, at 51.

122. *See* Pollard, *supra* note 118, at 228.

existence of excusable delays or unforeseen site conditions. If the nature of the contractor's work performance is delayed or made more costly as a result of the occurrence of either of those two circumstances, the contractor will want to receive the owner's acknowledgement that the completion deadline will be extended or the construction price increased (or both).[123] The best way for the lawyer to protect his client from constructive change requests is to include very tight, restrictive language in the construction contract, which (1) limits the scope and number of the contractor's excusable delays and (2) transfers the risk of unforeseen conditions to the contractor. The developer's lawyer should also place provisions in the construction contract that waive the contractor's claims for any constructive change if the contractor fails to submit a written change order to the developer within a relatively short period of time after the occurrence of the event that supports the contractor's claim for a constructive change.[124] Such a provision will preclude the contractor from routinely making a request for more time and more money at the end of every construction project.

HIBC Case Study—Design and Construction Issues

One of the primary factors contributing to the overall success of the HIBC project was The Pizzuti Companies' ability to put together a quality team of design and construction professionals and to then keep that team intact throughout the ten year duration of the HIBC project. Pizzuti's objective when assembling its design and construction team was to select seasoned and highly talented professionals and to assign them responsibility and authority commensurate with their respective core competencies. While Pizzuti encouraged collaboration among all the team members, it was extremely careful not to permit blurred lines of authority or tolerate overlapping or redundant responsibilities.

Pizzuti believed that aesthetics would be an important driver for the project's profitability, so it selected an architect (Hunton Brady Architects) that was well-known in the Orlando market for its crisp and inventive architectural designs. Pizzuti was also well aware that the sheer size and

---

123. The contractor is customarily entitled to an increase in the construction price only if the excusable delay is an owner-caused delay (and not a delay caused by an event beyond the control of both parties to the construction contract). *See* CAMERON, A PRACTITIONER'S GUIDE, *supra* note 10, at 17–8 through 17–10. Developers often attempt to alter this conclusion by inserting into the construction contract a so-called "no damage for delay" provision, which expressly states that the contractor's sole and exclusive remedy for the occurrence of an excusable delay is an extension of the completion deadline (and specifically not an increase in the construction price). Courts are sometimes hesitant to enforce a no damages for delay provision against a contractor with clean hands, based on the theory that such a provision is unconscionable and works an extreme hardship on the contractor. *See* Rosenberg, *supra* note 109, at 53; and Beck, *supra* note 6, at 4–9 through 4–73.

124. *See supra* note 109 and accompanying text. *See also* Beck, supra note 6, at 4–65.

complexity of the project would place incredible financial, manpower and logistical demands on whichever construction firm was selected as the contractor of record for the project. After interviewing a number of qualified general contractors, Pizzuti hired Brasfield & Gorrie, a construction firm headquartered in Birmingham, Alabama, that had very deep financial pockets and a reputation for consistently bringing its projects in on time and on budget. Finally, Pizzuti was adamant that it wanted to be an active participant in and retain control over every aspect of the design and construction of the HIBC project. Given this desire, Pizzuti hired three seasoned professionals to head up its in-house, development team—a senior executive to be responsible for all aspects of the HIBC project, a construction manager to supervise all vertical improvement projects and a project manager to oversee Pizzuti's land development activities at HIBC.

Once its team members were selected, Pizzuti's senior executives conveyed three principal messages to the selected design and construction professionals—Hunton Brady is responsible for design; Brasfield & Gorrie is responsible for construction; and Pizzuti is in charge of everything. Because it realized the importance of maintaining continuity throughout the project's history, Pizzuti promised (in the moral, not the legal sense) Hunton Brady and Brasfield & Gorrie that they would serve in their respective roles on the HIBC project for as long as their performance merited their retention—which, as it turned out, would be for the entire ten year history of the project.

That is more than enough discussion of what the business people did to dictate the success of the HIBC project during Stage 6. What you all want to know is what the real estate development lawyer did to contribute to the project's good fortune. The short answer to that question is fairly obvious—not too much. Having said that, Pizzuti's legal team (yours truly and two much more qualified legal professionals—one in-house and one out-house),[125] were responsible for selecting a project delivery system and negotiating design and construction contracts that, at the very least, facilitated Pizzuti's implementation of the sage business decisions made by the company during Stage 6 of the development process.[126]

The following are the mundane (but, hopefully, somewhat instructive) details regarding the actions taken by Pizzuti and its lawyers during Stage 6 of the HIBC project.[127]

- *All design and construction professionals who worked on the HIBC project were selected through negotiation (and not by a competitive*

---

125. This is an excellent opportunity for me to extend my appreciation and gratitude to Scott West (the in-house guy) and Jim Seay (the out-house guy) for doing most of the work and always being there to bail me out when I ventured outside of my competency level (which, admittedly, was most of the time).

126. That is, after all, the essence of the real estate development lawyer's job—paving the way for the developer to achieve its business objectives.

127. Pizzuti's approach to the design and construction phases remained constant throughout the ten year history of the HIBC project. It used the same architect and contractor, project delivery system and contractual arrangement for each of the buildings it developed in the HIBC park.

bidding process). Pizzuti believed that this approach fostered a greater sense of teamwork among the selected professionals and produced a higher quality product.

- *Pizzuti adopted a traditional, design-bid-build, delivery system for every project it developed in HIBC. The design and construction phases were implemented in a neat, sequential order,[128] thereby insuring that (1) the architectural design of each building would be given paramount importance and (2) the contractor could establish its construction price based on its review of a full set of completed plans and specifications. The depth and sophistication of Pizzuti's in-house, development staff permitted it to appropriately coordinate the design and construction silos that characterize the design-bid-build structure.*

- *The lawyers representing Pizzuti, Hunton Brady and Brasfield & Gorrie agreed that they would use standard AIA forms to document their contractual relationships. The AIA contract format was selected because all of the parties were familiar with the substantive provisions of the AIA documents. The contract negotiations on the first office building developed by the Pizzuti–Hunton Brady–Brasfield & Gorrie team were quite spirited and took a fair amount of time to complete. The end result, however, was a set of contract documents that clearly articulated the authority, responsibility and risk of each of the players and served as a template for the contracts used on all of the HIBC construction projects.*

- *The following are some of the negotiated features of the owner-architect contract used for all HIBC projects:*

  - *The architect's compensation was stated as a fixed fee (thereby giving Pizzuti the certainty that it desired concerning its project design costs);*

  - *The architect's reimbursable costs were tightly defined and the architect's ability to mark up any of those costs was eliminated;*

  - *The contract deleted all of the standard AIA references to the architect providing construction cost estimates for the project (because Pizzuti knew that asking an architect to estimate project costs is like asking an artist to fix your car);*

  - *All provisions seeking to give the architect a primary role in arbitrating owner-contractor disputes, setting the terms of change orders and communicating the owner's thoughts to the contractor were excised from the contract;*

---

128. Although Pizzuti developed a number of office projects under very tight construction schedules (principally single-tenant buildings), those projects did not fit the classic definition of fast track projects, because their design was always substantially complete before the kick-off of construction.

- *The contract included a "termination for convenience" feature, with no requirement that the owner pay the architect a break-up fee prior to exercising such feature; and*

- *Pizzuti was given the unfettered right to use the design plans on any other project of its choosing, as long as it paid Hunton Brady a relatively small fee each time it re-used such plans.[129]*

- *The owner-contractor agreement used for all HIBC projects contained the following features:*

  - *A guaranteed maximum price (without any contingency factor) was established on the date of contract execution, with Brasfield & Gorrie being entitled to 25% of any actual cost savings;*

  - *A liquidated damages clause was inserted into all of the contracts requiring Brasfield & Gorrie to pay a per diem amount to Pizzuti for every day that it was late in achieving substantial completion;[130]*

  - *The definition of "excusable delays" was phrased in a very restrictive fashion to eliminate adverse weather and labor conditions that were reasonably foreseeable by the contractor;*

  - *The risk of unforeseen site conditions was placed on the owner (and not the contractor)—an allocation of responsibility that was acceptable to Pizzuti because of the rigorous soils tests it performed on all of its Florida projects;*

  - *Pizzuti retained the right to issue unilateral change directives and agreed to pay the contractor a fee of 5% of the cost of all such directives (1% higher than the percentage fee paid to Brasfield & Gorrie on the base work); and*

  - *Retainage was set at 10%, until the project was 50% complete, at which time retainage on all subsequent construction disbursements was eliminated.*

The end result of the lawyers' work during Stage 6 of the HIBC project was the creation of design and construction contracts, which specifically delineated the respective rights, responsibilities and liabilities of the owner, architect and contractor. The fact that those contracts were used for the development of more than 1 million square feet of commercial space, without a single lawsuit or lien ever being filed against Pizzuti or the

---

129. The negotiated, re-use fee was less than one-third of the fee paid for the initial set of design plans.

130. The amount of the per diem charge varied from project to project based on the tightness of the construction schedule and the contractual demands of the project tenants. In those situations where a tenant lease included a liquidated damages clause, Pizzuti always endeavored to include a mirror image of that liquidated damages clause in its construction contract with Brasfield & Gorrie.

HIBC project, stands as a testament to the ultimate fairness of the contracts and the professionalism of the players that were parties to such contracts.

VIII. SUMMARY

The real estate lawyer's primary assignment during Stage 6 is to craft contracts that advance the developer's goals of completing its project on time, on budget and in accordance with sound design and construction practices. In order to properly do his job, the lawyer must gain a sound working knowledge of the dynamics of the construction process and the roles served by all the players in that process. The lawyer must then use that base of knowledge to put together a set of contract documents, which require and empower the architect, contractor and developer to effectively work together as a team to turn the developer's 20–page business plan into a fully operational building. In doing so, the lawyer would be well-advised to keep in mind the following advice offered up by a practicing construction lawyer:

> [B]uilding financial incentives and disincentives into a contract often tends to be more practical and effective than simply drafting stringent "commandments" to act in a particular way.[131]

Stated in a more colloquial fashion, you can catch more flies with honey than you can with a fly swatter.

---

131. *See* Hackenbrach, *supra* note 15, at 3.

CHAPTER 11

STAGE 7: NEGOTIATING THE
PROJECT LEASE

■ ■ ■

I. INTRODUCTION

The first six stages of the real estate development process are all focused on the cost side of the developer's business—how much the project will cost and how the developer will fund its project costs. Stage 7 is where the developer makes its money by leasing its project to rent-paying tenants.

The lawyer's role in the leasing stage also undergoes a significant change of focus. The previous chapters of this book have focused on the lawyer's role in helping the developer preserve the integrity of the project's cost structure by managing the various risks inherent in the real estate development process. During the leasing stage, the real estate development lawyer's attention turns to the income side of the developer's business. The lawyer's job is to carefully negotiate and draft the terms of the project lease, so as to enhance the predictability and stability of the income stream generated from the developer's leasing of space in its project.

The manner in which the lawyer approaches the representation of his developer client also shifts in a somewhat subtle, but extremely important way during the leasing stage. It is at this stage of the development process that the lawyer needs to realize that he is a member of the developer's marketing team. While the lawyer may not be on the front lines in seeking to identify and entice prospective tenants to lease space in the developer's project, the manner in which the lawyer approaches the preparation and negotiation of the lease will have a significant impact (hopefully a positive one) on the developer's ability to lease its project in a timely fashion.

Consistent with the approach taken in previous chapters of this book, this Chapter will begin by examining the competing business objectives of the parties involved in the leasing stage of the development process— primarily those of the landlord and tenant, but also the interests of the mortgage lender and the equity investor. It will then touch on the legal nature of a lease, as well as the various types of leases involved in the

443

commercial real estate world. The remainder of the Chapter will be devoted to an analysis of the key provisions of a multi-tenant, office lease, with particular emphasis being placed on the varying perspectives of the landlord and tenant on each of those provisions.[1] The Form Office Lease used by the author for the Heathrow International Business Center project in Orlando, Florida, will serve as the primary frame of reference for the discussion of those lease provisions.[2]

II. BUSINESS OBJECTIVES OF THE PARTIES TO A LEASE

Let's start by setting some ground rules for the terminology to be used to identify the parties to a lease. The person who owns the real estate project and is trying to lease it to third parties is generally referred to in the commercial world as either the *landlord* or the *lessor*. The person who wants to lease space in the project is generally referred to as either the *tenant* or the *lessee*. Because the similarity of the "lessor" and "lessee" references creates the potential for confusion and error, the terms "landlord" and "tenant" will be used throughout this Chapter.

A. BUSINESS OBJECTIVES OF THE LANDLORD

The developer/landlord has three business objectives during the leasing stage of the development process.

- The project should be leased at rents that are consistent with or better than those set forth in its financial projections for the project.

- The project should be leased as soon as possible and, in all events, within the time frames set forth in the project's initial business plan.

- The project should be leased on business and legal terms that are consistent with the expectations and requirements of the institutional investor community.

The profitability of the developer's project will be determined by how well it fares in its attempt to achieve these three objectives.

B. BUSINESS OBJECTIVES OF THE TENANT

Unlike the landlord, the prospective tenant has no specific, real estate, business objectives. Its goal is to conduct its business as efficiently and productively as possible, so as to foster the growth, profitability and

---

1. While the focus of this Chapter is on the provisions typically found in a multi-tenant office lease, I will, where appropriate, comment on those lease clauses which are uniquely found in other types of leases—especially retail leases.

2. *See* Document #6 in the Document Appendix (hereinafter referred to as the "Form Office Lease").

stability of its business operations. The prospective tenant simply wants to make sure that its leasing decision does not detract from its ability to meet its overall business goals.

In this regard, it is important to keep in mind why Corporate America typically opts to satisfy its space needs by leasing and not owning real estate.[3] First, it generally costs less to lease real estate than it does to own real estate (at least in the short-term). Most companies prefer to preserve their financial resources to fund the operation and growth of their core businesses, rather than to use those resources to pay for the development or acquisition of real estate. Similarly, members of Corporate America are also reluctant to deploy their human resources to deal with the operational and financial risks associated with the ownership of real estate. Shareholders and directors want their employees to spend their working hours formulating strategies to satisfy the demands of the company's customers and not responding to complaints about leaky toilets and faulty HVAC systems.

In the context of the negotiation of the project lease, the tenant has the following goals.

- It wants to lease space that will permit it to further its enterprise mission. The space should be conveniently located to its targeted customer base and targeted labor pool and should be configured and sized to fit its business model. Finally, the look and feel of the building in which its leased space is located should be consistent with the corporate image that the tenant desires to project to its customers and employees.

- It wants to negotiate ***occupancy costs*** that are consistent with the operating budget for its business. The tenant's occupancy costs refer not just to the fixed rental payment that the tenant is required to make each month to the landlord, but also to all other costs that are directly associated with its occupancy of the leased space. Those other occupancy costs include: its reimbursement of the landlord's building expenses; utility charges; parking fees; the cost of making improvements to its leased space; and the benefit of any tax or economic incentives tied to its occupancy of the project in question. The fact that the tenant's fixed rent payment at Location A might be lower than that at Location B is of little importance to the tenant if its all-in occupancy costs at Location B are higher than those for Location B (because, for example, the cost of making tenant improvements to its space in Location B is significantly higher than the cost of making comparable improvements to its space in Location A).

---

3. *See supra* Chapter 1, Pages 4–5, for a further discussion of Corporate America's inclination to lease rather than own real estate. The term "Corporate America" will used in this Chapter in its broadest sense to refer to all operating entities, both foreign and domestic, that have a business need to house their employees and products in buildings constructed by developers.

- It wants to avoid economic surprises with respect to its occupancy of its leased space. Once the tenant determines that its occupancy costs at a particular location are within its budget, the last thing that the tenant wants to have happen is for an unanticipated event to occur which permits the landlord to exact additional charges that increase the tenant's actual costs of occupying the leased space above the budgeted amount.

- Finally, it wants the lease document to maximize its flexibility to make space decisions that are responsive to its business needs. By way of example, if a tenant needs to hire new employees to respond to a spurt in its business growth, it will want to be able to expand the size of the space it leases in its current location so as to maximize the control and business synergy generated from having all of its employees located under the same roof.

All of the above goals have a central theme—the tenant does not want its leasing decision to hinder its ability to independently conduct its business operations. The tenant's quest to reach its leasing goals is made more challenging by the fact that an office lease customarily is for a term of anywhere from three to 20 years—a period of time in which any number of changes can occur with respect to the tenant's underlying business operations.

C. BUSINESS OBJECTIVES OF THE LENDER AND EQUITY INVESTOR

When negotiating the project lease, the landlord needs to be mindful of the interests of its lender and equity investor. The lender and equity investor share the following business objectives with respect to the leasing of the project by the landlord.

- They want to enhance to the maximum extent practicable the income stream generated from leases of space in project. Their focus is not only on making sure that the project leases provide for rentals that are consistent with the project's financial projections, but also that such leases are with creditworthy tenants and do not allow the tenants to unilaterally trigger a reduction in their rent obligations or an increase in the landlord's operating costs.

- Under certain circumstances, a lender or equity investor might succeed to the leasehold interest of the landlord—for example, if the project mortgage is foreclosed on by the lender or if the equity investor buys out the landlord's ownership interest in the project. The lender and the equity investor will, therefore, each be very focused during the leasing stage on making sure that the lease documents permit it, if necessary, to step into the landlord's shoes, without any diminution in the obligations that the tenant owes to the titular landlord.

In order to protect their business interests, lenders and equity investors usually insist that any lease executed by the project owner must either (a) be pre-approved by the lender/equity investor or (b) conform to leasing guidelines agreed to in advance by the project owner and the lender/equity investor.

III. WHAT IS A LEASE?

A *lease* is a "contract transferring the right to the possession and enjoyment of property for a definite period of time."[4] This definition contains two separate and distinct legal concepts—(1) a contract and (2) a conveyance or transfer of a real property interest. Anyone reading this book has already taken the basic law school courses in Contracts and Property and, hence, is familiar with the differing legal treatments afforded bilateral contracts and real property conveyances. The basic nature of that difference and why the real estate practitioner should care about it are discussed in the next section of this Chapter.

A. IS IT A CONTRACT OR A REAL ESTATE CONVEYANCE?

This book is clearly written from the perspective of the practicing lawyer. So why should a lawyer practicing real estate development law in the urbanized, global economy of the 21st century care whether a lease is interpreted in accordance with modern contract principles or the ancient tenets of English common law governing real property conveyances? Isn't that subject better suited to a law review paean to the virtues of common law than it is to a textbook that purports to be driven by the practical demands of the "real world"?

The answer to these questions lies in something called the doctrine of independent covenants. Based on the traditional common law rule that a lease is a conveyance of a real property interest, it has long been held that the covenants contained in a lease are independent of each other.[5] If the doctrine of independent covenants were to be deemed wholly applicable to the field of commercial leasing, the import for the landlord and the tenant would be as follows:

- A tenant's failure to pay rent or otherwise perform its obligations under the lease would not give the landlord grounds to evict the tenant from the leased space;[6] and

---

4. *See* ICSC's DICTIONARY OF SHOPPING CENTER TERMS 63 (3rd ed. 2009).

5. *See generally* MARK A. SENN, COMMERCIAL REAL ESTATE LEASES 1–5 through 1–10 (4th ed. 2008).

6. Most states now have statutes in place which permit the landlord to evict a tenant that has not paid its rent (usually only after the giving of notice and the failure of the tenant to cure its non-payment within some stated period of time). *See* Patrick G. Moran and Martin H. Orlick, *Litigating Commercial Leases, Default and Remedies; Those Pesky and Expensive Frequently Litigated Lease Issues*, in ACREL PAPERS 65, 72 (Spring 2007).

- A landlord's failure to perform its obligations under the lease would not give the tenant the right to terminate the lease and cease paying rent.

Both of these results assault our basic senses of logic and fairness. Why should a landlord not be able to kick out a tenant who is not paying its rent? Why shouldn't a tenant be able to walk away from its lease obligations if the landlord isn't providing basic HVAC services to the tenant's space? Incredible as it may seem, the vestiges of the English common law rules on the independence of lease covenants still remain alive in the courts of many states in this country. The following case illustrates a developing judicial trend to replace the traditional common law rules with modern contract principles.

<hr>

WESSON v. LEONE ENTERPRISES[7]

Supreme Judicial Court of Massachusetts
437 Mass. 708
Decided September 9, 2002

In this case, we abandon the common-law rule of independent covenants in commercial leases in favor of the modern rule of mutually dependent covenants.... In applying the rule of mutually dependent covenants to the facts present in this case, we conclude that a landlord's failure to keep the roof of his building in good repair deprived the tenant of a substantial benefit significant to the purpose for which the lease was entered. Consequently, the tenant had the right to terminate the lease and recover reasonable relocation costs....

The plaintiff landlord ... owned a multi-tenanted commercial building.... The lease ran for five years, commencing on March 31, 1988.

The tenant first complained to the landlord about "significant leaks in the roof" in April, 1991. The parties met soon afterward and the tenant pointed out "more than one," but less than five, leaks in the premises. The landlord agreed to fix the roof and called on his son, Wayne Wesson, who periodically managed the building, to oversee the repairs. Wayne patched the roof himself. The leaks reappeared later that spring, and the landlord hired a professional roofing contractor to make further repairs.

In early August, 1991, the roof began leaking in some of the same places previously repaired. The tenant complained several times to the landlord and Wayne about the leaks, and claimed that he and his subtenant were "forced to take necessary precautions to protect [their] businesses from more water damage." ... On November 4, 1991, the tenant notified the landlord that he would be "vacating the premises on or before December 31, 1991," for reasons "well known to you. The constant lack of minimal heat as well as the serious leakage problem."

<hr>

7. All footnotes and citations have omitted from this opinion.

The landlord filed a complaint in the District Court alleging breach of contract and damage to the demised premises.... [T]he judge concluded that ... the tenant could have lawfully withheld the rent under the dependent covenants rule, where the landlord had failed to provide a "dry space," a service "essential" to the lease.... The landlord appealed, claiming the trial judge erred in ... applying the "dependent covenants" rule to the parties' commercial lease. We affirm the judgment....

At common law, covenants in leases were considered "independent, in the absence of clear indications to the contrary, and the lessee [was] relieved from performance of his covenants only by actual or constructive eviction." ... The independent covenants rule applied to both residential and commercial leases and was based on the assumption that "a lease is primarily a conveyance of an interest in real estate," and "reflected the parties' expectations in a rural agrarian society where the right to possession of the land constituted the chief element of the exchange." "The theory of a lease as a conveyance ... fitted in well with the ancient farm lease. The lease was essentially of land; the house was incidental. Tenant got no services from landlord and expected none. Tenant was there, landlord absent. Tenant had tools that he was well versed in using. He could make such repairs as might be necessary." As a result, "[e]ven if the landlord made express maintenance promises in the lease, courts often held that the landlord's breach of these 'secondary' obligations did not affect the tenant's obligation to pay rent." This apparent unfairness was balanced under the same doctrine by the inability of the landlord to recover possession of his property from a tenant even if the tenant breached its covenant to pay rent. Both lessor and lessee were limited in their remedies to seeking damages for breach of the lease covenants. Any equilibrium that may have existed in this application of the rule was lost with the enactment of statutory dispossession actions, permitting landlords to regain possession of the premises if the tenant failed to pay rent even though the landlord may have breached express covenants within the lease.

Exceptions to the independent covenants rule first emerged in the context of residential leases.... As it applied to residential leases, the independent covenants rule was completely supplanted in 1973, when we recognized that a residential "lease is essentially a contract between the landlord and the tenant wherein the landlord promises to deliver and maintain the demised premises in habitable condition and the tenant promises to pay rent for such habitable premises." "These promises constitute interdependent and mutual considerations."

That decision was consistent with the national trend in residential leases away from interpretations based on classic property law doctrine that treated leases as "conveyances," and toward modern notions of leases as contracts for the possession of property, and modern notions of consumer protection.... This trend culminated in the almost universally recognized warranty of habitability implied in residential leases.

The development of the law of commercial leases has followed divergent paths. Some courts interpret commercial leases as they would any other commercial contract; while others have taken a step in that direction by abolishing the independent covenants rule in favor of a rule of mutually dependent covenants. Still other courts have acted at the extremes, either by continuing strictly to apply the independent covenants rule, or by moving to the other end of the spectrum and recognizing an implied warranty of suitability in commercial leases. While we conclude that there is a need to move away from the rule of independent covenants, we continue to recognize that there are significant differences between commercial and residential tenancies and the policy considerations appropriate to each.

The landlord claims that the judge erred by applying the dependent covenants rule to the parties' lease and concluding that the landlord's failure "to provide an essential service, a dry space" would have permitted the tenant "lawfully [to withhold] rent had he not vacated the Wesson building." He contends that this court has not supplanted the independent covenants rule in Massachusetts, and therefore a commercial landlord's breach of the covenant to repair does not relieve the tenant of his covenant to pay rent. As noted previously, the premise underlying the continued viability of the independent covenants rule is that a commercial lease is a conveyance of property where the right to possession of the land constitutes the chief element of the exchange. This premise no longer comports with the reality of the typical modern commercial lease, which is intended to secure the right to occupy improvements to the land rather than the land itself, and which usually contemplates a continuing flow of necessary services from landlord to tenant, services that are normally under the landlord's control.

We conclude that the better rule is the rule of mutually dependent covenants set forth in the Restatement (Second) of Property (Landlord and Tenant) § 7.1(1977), the principles of which we adopt to the extent necessary to resolve the issues in this case. Specifically, we adopt so much of the Restatement that provides as follows:

> "Except to the extent the parties to a lease validly agree otherwise, if the landlord fails to perform a valid promise contained in the lease to do, or to refrain from doing, something . . . and as a consequence thereof, the tenant is deprived of a significant inducement to the making of the lease, and if the landlord does not perform his promise within a reasonable period of time after being requested to do so, the tenant may . . . terminate the lease."

It also reflects our view of the better reasoned path to follow in modernizing the law of commercial leases.

The requirements of the rule we have adopted today . . . [do] not require that the premises be "untenantable for the purposes for which they were used," in order for the tenant to terminate the lease and vacate the premises. It is sufficient for the tenant to demonstrate the landlord's failure, after notice, to perform a promise that was a significant induce-ment to the tenant's entering the lease in the first instance. We interpret this language to include promises that constitute a substantial benefit understood at the time the lease was entered to be significant to the purpose thereof. Here that substantial benefit was a dry space necessary to safely conduct the high technology printing business for which the landlord knew the premises were to be used. . . .

Based on the judge's findings of fact, all of the requirements of the rule have been met in this case: the landlord breached his covenant to maintain the roof by failing to adequately repair its chronic leaking; the breach directly interfered with the tenant's business by depriving it of a substantial benefit significant to the purpose of the lease; and, after adequate notice, the landlord's efforts to correct the problem were both "shoddy and unsuccessful." The tenant was entitled to terminate the lease and recover relocation costs in the amount determined by the judge.

———————

NOTES AND QUESTIONS ABOUT THE WESSON CASE

The first thing which must be noted about the *Wesson* case is that its ruling that lease covenants are mutually dependent is still the minority rule in the United States. Indeed, only a handful of courts have overturned the common law doctrine of independent covenants.[8] Therefore, the law in most states remains firmly rooted in common law rules that emphasize the convey-ance aspect of a real estate lease.

One argument that is made against the notion of rejecting the common law rule of independent covenants is that "trade practices have grown up around the existing lease rules, and parties' expectations are founded on those rules. Except where the market is unable to address distortions and 'bargain around' rules that are difficult or unfair, it may be best to leave things alone."[9] The Pennsylvania Supreme Court made this same point when concluding that "[l]eases have been drafted and bargained for in reliance on this rule. Business decisions and structured financial arrangements have been made with the expectation that this rule, which has been the law, will continue to be the law."[10] Do you agree with this "if it's not broke, don't fix it" approach?

There are two very important lessons to be learned from the *Wesson* case. First, a lease is very clearly both a contract and a conveyance. The *Wesson* court opted to tilt the legal landscape dramatically in favor of the application of modern contract principles to determine the rights and remedies available

---

8. *See* MILTON R. FRIEDMAN AND PATRICK A. RANDOLPH, JR., FRIEDMAN ON LEASES 1–21 (5th ed. 2010). The Friedman treatise also notes that "[a]lthough a remarkable challenge to precedent, the [*Wesson*] case apparently has been overlooked since being decided and no other case has cited it." *See id.* at note 126.

9. *See id.* at 1–26.

10. *See* Stonehedge Square Limited Partnership v. Movie Merchants Inc., 552 Pa. 412, 415 (1998).

to landlords and tenants. However, even the *Wesson* court continued to recognize the common law principle of constructive eviction and declined to make a finding that the implied warranty of habitability is applicable to commercial leases.[11] The lesson to be learned from this case (and even more so from the more conservative majority rule followed in states other than Massachusetts) is that a practitioner must learn the common law and statutory rules that govern the rights and remedies available to the landlord and tenant in a commercial lease setting. A lawyer who thinks he can draft and negotiate a lease based solely on his understanding of general contract principles will quickly be proven wrong.

Second, all courts make it clear that the landlord and tenant can modify a jurisdiction's rules on the independence of lease covenants by expressly stating in the body of the lease document exactly which covenants are dependent and which covenants are independent. At the one extreme, tenant's counsel should seek to have the lease specifically state that the tenant will have the right to withhold rent and terminate the lease if the landlord fails to provide the bargained for services to the leased premises. Aggressive landlord's counsel will, on the other hand, want the lease to include language which negates the tenant's right to take either of those actions (leaving the tenant with the sole remedy of filing a damages action against landlord for its breach of its performance obligations).[12] The key point to keep in mind is that the lawyer should not leave these very important issues to the vagaries of the developing common law, but rather should adopt the power of the pen to solve its problems. Keep in mind that, even if the current state of the law in a particular jurisdiction is acceptable to landlord's counsel (for example, a jurisdiction which still follows the rule that the covenant to pay rent is independent of the landlord's covenant to provide services to the leased premises), the playing field can instantly be changed if a court takes the approach followed in the *Wesson* case and decides (1) to overrule existing common law principles and (2) to apply the new rules retroactively to all leases signed prior to the rendering of the court's decision.

Practice Tip #11–1: Drafting Around the Law

The prior section's admonition that a lawyer should rely on "the power of the pen" when representing his client in the negotiation of a lease reminds me of a lunch meeting I had with a senior professor shortly after I agreed to join the law school faculty at The Ohio State University. The professor, an expert in contract and commercial law, asked me, "Are there a lot of cases that you can use in teaching your course on Real Estate Development Law"? My reply (which was received in a less than accepting manner by the commercial law professor) was "not really." I went on to try

---

11. *See* Wesson v. Leone Enterprises, Inc., 437 Mass. 708, 713, 721 (2002). *See infra* Pages 508–509, for a discussion of the doctrine of constructive eviction.

12. *See e.g.,* the last sentence of §4 of the Form Office Lease. *See infra* Pages 508–510, for a discussion of a tenant's remedies upon an interruption of service.

to explain to the professor that a business lawyer's job is not merely to research and understand the applicable case law, but, much more importantly, to "draft around it."

One of the hardest things for law students (and apparently most law professors) to understand is that it is a business lawyer's job is to create the law for his client by spelling out in a contract exactly what obligations, rights and remedies are available to his client. There are no immutable legal principles on which the lawyer can rely for his client's protection. In the very first law school class I taught at Ohio State, I held up a 30 page lease document and told my students "this is my law." I recognized the looks on their faces as being the same stunned, uncomprehending visage that I saw when I talked to the senior professor about the need to draft around case law. It took my students the entire semester (and some probably even longer) to gain an understanding of what I was talking about in that first class.

B. MUST A LEASE BE IN WRITING?

Most states have statutes which, at a minimum, require that commercial leases having a term beyond a stated number of years (one or three years being the most commonly used term) must be in writing and signed by the party against whom enforcement of the lease is being sought.[13] Some states require that, in order to be held enforceable, a lease must be signed by both the landlord and tenant, while other states require that the signature of one or both of the parties to the lease must be acknowledged before witnesses or a notary public.[14]

It is absolutely essential that the practitioner make sure that the execution of the lease complies with all of the requirements and formalities specified by the applicable state statutes. Otherwise, a carefully crafted and cagily negotiated lease might end up being unenforceable against the other party to the lease negotiations.

IV. TYPES OF COMMERCIAL LEASES

The term "lease" encompasses a wide variety of commercial transactions. In its broadest sense, a lease can cover either real or personal property, including intangible personal property. As befits the nature of this book, the focus of this Chapter is on the leasing of space in a commercial building.[15]

---

13. *See, e.g.*, Ohio Revised Code Annotated §§ 5301.01 and 5301.08 (West 2010) (requiring that a lease having a term of more than three years must be in writing and signed by the landlord).

14. *See* Kirsten J. Day and Cristina C. Perez, *Don't Lose the Deal: Make Sure Your Lease Is Properly Executed*, 12 No. 3 Commercial Leasing Law and Strategy 2–3 (August 1999).

15. The law governing residential leases has developed in a fashion quite dissimilar from that applicable to commercial leases. *See e.g., Wesson*, 437 Mass. at 718. Most states have enacted

There are three principal types of commercial leases. While all commercial leases present the same core business and legal issues, each particular type of lease involves certain issues which are unique to the type of building in which the leased space is located.

- ***Office Lease***—Because its provisions are generally applicable to all types of space leases, the office lease will be the platform used throughout the remainder of this Chapter to discuss the key provisions of a commercial lease. The substantive provisions of an office lease will vary based on the type and location of the landlord's building (e.g., a one-story, suburban office building vs. a downtown skyscraper).

- ***Industrial Lease***—The most common form of industrial lease is the lease of space in a warehouse building. Industrial leases can, however, also involve the leasing of space for the conduct of more intense uses, such as manufacturing, light assembly, and research and development. The heightened nature of the use of industrial space gives rise to unique environmental, safety and noise issues that must be addressed by the lawyers representing the landlord and the tenant.[16]

- ***Retail Lease***—A retail lease is a broad category, which includes the lease of space in regional shopping malls, lifestyle centers, neighborhood strip centers and entertainment districts.[17] Retail leases often include provisions that are not found in other types of space leases—e.g., percentage rent, exclusive use, co-tenancy and continuous operation clauses. Those retail-specific clauses will be discussed in some detail later in this Chapter.[18]

A commercial space lease (be it an office, industrial or retail lease) is further subject to classification based on whether the tenant is leasing the entirety of the building or only a portion of the building. A ***multi-tenant lease*** is a lease where a building is leased to two or more separate and distinct tenants, while a ***single tenant lease*** (also known as a ***build-to-suit lease***) is a lease where one tenant leases the entirety of the available space in a building. This Chapter will, for the most part, center on a multi-tenant office lease. Occasional note will, however, be taken of the unique construction and operational issues presented by a single tenant lease.

---

legislation which specifically defines the rights, duties and liabilities of the residential landlord and tenant. A discussion of residential landlord-tenant statutes is outside of the commercial scope of this text and, hence, will not be addressed in this Chapter.

16. *See generally* Peter Aitelli, *Industrial Leases*, in COMMERCIAL REAL ESTATE TRANSACTIONS HANDBOOK, Chapter 13 (Mark A. Senn ed. 2009).

17. *Se generally* Richard R. Goldberg, *Retail Leases*, in COMMERCIAL REAL ESTATE TRANSACTIONS HANDBOOK, Chapter 14 (Mark A. Senn ed. 2009).

18. *See infra* Pages 494–496, 510–515.

V. INTRODUCTION TO KEY LEASE PROVISIONS

The focus of the remainder of this Chapter will be on an analysis of the key provisions found in a typical, multi-tenant office lease. For this purpose, the provisions of an office lease have been slotted into the following broad categories.

- ***Parties***—This subsection will focus on the description of the parties involved in the leasing transaction, including the landlord, the tenant and any guarantor of the tenant's lease obligations.

- ***Space***—This subsection will explore the identification, measurement and improvement of the space that is being leased to the tenant.

- ***Term***—This subsection will address the time period during which the tenant will have the right to possess and occupy the leased space.

- ***Rent***—This subsection will address the various rental payments to be made to the landlord by the tenant and how those rental payments are calculated.

- ***Use***— This subsection will deal with the contractual parameters established for the tenant's use of its leased space, including provisions that govern what the tenant can and cannot do in the leased space and provisions that address the nature and scope of the services that the landlord is obligated to furnish to its tenants.

- ***Tenant Flexibility Provisions***—This subsection will focus on those provisions that a tenant can insert into the lease to provide it with the needed flexibility to respond to a change in the size or nature of its business operations.

- ***Risk Allocation and Other Leasing Issues***—Finally, this subsection will address those provisions of the typical office lease that seek to allocate certain risks between the landlord and tenant, including the risks associated with the occurrence of a default, casualty or condemnation. The discussion of the key provisions of a lease will conclude with an examination of other contractual clauses that are unique to a commercial leasing transaction.

The discussion of each of these lease provisions will begin with an analysis of the competing perspectives of the landlord and the tenant with respect to the subject matter of each such provision. The focus of that discussion will be on why the landlord and the tenant adopt their respective positions—in other words, what business purpose is being served by the stance taken by the landlord or tenant. Suggestions will then be offered concerning possible compromises available to the parties to resolve their differences.[19]

---

19. Where the parties land on each of the key lease provisions will, of course, be dependent both on the skill of their respective negotiators and the relative leverage that they bring to the lease negotiations. There is no one right or wrong answer as to what should be contained in a particular lease clause. In this regard, I am reminded of the following quote from a book authored by a seasoned practitioner—"There are form books aplenty. How to draft clauses, with examples.

The Form Office Lease included in the Document Appendix will serve as the platform for the examination of the import of the various provisions of an office lease. Parenthetical reference is made in the caption describing each of the key provisions to the section of the form Office Lease where the subject provision is addressed.

The Form Office Lease is a relatively short and succinct form that I designed to lease space in the Heathrow International Business Center in Orlando, Florida. A description of the thought process which went into my development of the HIBC lease form follows.

HIBC Case Study—The Development of a User-friendly Lease Form

As mentioned earlier in this book, The Pizzuti Companies (where I served as general counsel) purchased the Heathrow International Business Center in 1994. The first lease deal done at HIBC was a single-tenant lease with Cincinnati Bell Information Services ("CBIS"). Because I had precious little experience in doing lease deals in the State of Florida and because I was at the time bogged down in closing the acquisition and equity financing for the HIBC land, I asked a senior lawyer from my former law firm to take the lead on preparing the first draft of the CBIS lease. The lawyer was a partner at a national law firm and was a card-carrying member of the prestigious American College of Real Estate Lawyers. As I expected, the lawyer produced a first-rate lease draft that was approximately 50 pages long. Over the next several months, I spent countless hours haggling with counsel for CBIS over every single line of that 50 page document. The negotiations were long, painful and frequently confrontational. Somehow, with the help of the lawyer I had retained for the CBIS job, we finally got the CBIS lease signed in February of 1995 (almost ten months to the day after the letter of intent with CBIS was first signed).

With the CBIS deal behind it, Pizzuti decided that it was time to build its first speculative, multi-tenant office building in HIBC. It was my job to put together the standard form lease that Pizzuti was going to use to market space in its HIBC office buildings. I had the CBIS lease in hand and also asked a number of prominent Florida lawyers to send me their standard office leases, so that I could synthesize the various forms and come up with a workable standard lease form for the HIBC project. The first thing I noticed about all the lease forms that I received from my Florida lawyer buddies is that they were all long—really long (the shortest being 25 pages). My life flashed before my eyes as I envisioned the hours of pain and misery I would be forced to endure while negotiating a 30 page

---

They all assume there is nobody to negotiate against. I have always found it to be great fun to negotiate with oneself. . . . One is never troubled with arguments this way. And one makes the most brilliant deals, as long as there is no one on the other side." *See* MARTIN A. ZANKEL, NEGOTIATING COMMERCIAL REAL ESTATE LEASES ix–x (2001).

lease on each leased space in the 15 or so office buildings which were planned for the HIBC project. My gut reaction was that life was too short and office leases were too long.

I decided to test the validity of my gut by talking to the folks who really mattered in the leasing process—leasing brokers, office developers, property managers, the heads of corporate real estate departments and institutional investors (you will note that I decided not to talk to any more lawyers). What I heard from my eclectic discussion group was really quite interesting. The consistent theme voiced by the group was that they were all sick and tired of having to deal with 30–40 page lease forms. The brokers and developers bemoaned the fact that the length and complexity of the lease forms slowed down the deal, ticked off the tenants and inevitably caused bad feelings and project delays for all involved. The property managers and institutional investors said that the sheer length of the leases made it incredibly difficult for them to review and administer the leases once the tenants were in the building. Finally, the heads of the corporate real estate departments (who are basically the developer's customers) expressed unending frustration with having to deal over and over again with lawyers for the landlord demanding that they sign 30 page lease documents, every line of which tried to hammer home the point that the interests of the landlord were supreme in every respect to those of the tenant.

With all these thoughts in mind, I decided to see if I could dramatically shorten the office lease forms, without adversely affecting the developer's legitimate business interests. What I found when I looked through the various office lease forms was that they all suffered, in varying degrees, from three basic drafting maladies:

- *They said the same thing over and over again, using different words each time;*

- *They contained overreaching provisions that the landlord's lawyer would almost always agree to delete from the lease if ever asked to do so by tenant's counsel; and*

- *They spent page after page dealing with lawyer-invented complexities and so-called "legal issues" that had only marginal importance to the business deal.*

I was surprised by how easy it was to reduce the length and complexity of an office lease by simply remaining faithful to the proposition that I would not fall prey to the above-noted drafting errors. The end result of my efforts was the Form Office Lease that is included in the Document Appendix. I will let you judge for yourself whether I successfully achieved my drafting objectives—with the most important of those objectives being the preparation of a short, user-friendly lease form that fully serves and protects the legitimate business interests of the landlord.[20]

---

20. The facts that Pizzuti used the shorter lease form to lease over 20 million square feet of office and industrial space over a period of eight years and then sold the entirety of its real estate

VI. PARTIES TO THE LEASE.
(¶¶B–E of Lease Summary)

The lease must set forth the full name and mailing address of the landlord and the tenant. If a party to the lease is an entity, the lease should also recite the jurisdiction in which the entity was formed (e.g., a Delaware corporation). If the tenant is an entity, the landlord should search the public records to make sure that the lease accurately recites the tenant's legal name and that the tenant is in good standing and authorized to do business in both the jurisdiction of its formation and, if different, the jurisdiction in which the landlord's building is located. A landlord who makes a sloppy mistake and fails to verify this most basic information will be hard-pressed to enforce the provisions of the lease in the courts of the state where its property is situated.

As noted at the outset of this Chapter, one of the landlord's primary objectives is to lease space in its building to creditworthy tenants—i.e., to tenants who can afford to pay the rent recited in the lease. In order to verify a prospective tenant's creditworthiness, the landlord should closely scrutinize the tenant's financial statements prior to its execution of the lease. The landlord's review of the tenant's financials should not only confirm the acceptability of the net worth and income numbers disclosed in the financial statements, but should also verify that the entity that will be signing the lease is the same entity identified in the financial statements.

If the landlord determines that the credit standing of the prospective tenant is not to its liking, the landlord should require the involvement in the lease transaction of a third person—a ***guarantor*** who will personally guaranty of the tenant's obligations under the lease. The guarantor is usually a high net worth entity or individual, who is affiliated in some fashion with the tenant named in the lease, and who executes a separate written, lease guaranty, pursuant to which the guarantor agrees to guarantee the performance of all or a designated portion of the tenant's lease obligations.[21] If a third party guaranties the tenant's obligations, the lease should recite the guarantor's legal name and mailing address and the landlord should take the same precautions concerning the accuracy of the proposed guarantor's name and financial statements that were described earlier in this section with respect to the identity and financial wherewithal of the tenant. The landlord will want the guaranty to include the following provisions—(1) a clear statement that the landlord may pursue an action against the guarantor prior to and independent of any action it

---

portfolio to of institutional investors serves as anecdotal support for my view that "shorter is better."

21. The landlord will want the guarantor to personally guarantee both the payment and performance of all of the tenant's obligations under the lease. The guarantor, on the other hand, will routinely seek to limit its obligations by placing a cap on the amount of the guaranteed obligations or limiting the duration of the guaranty. *See* Andrew R. Lubin, *Lease Guaranties—A Practical Approach*, 17 No. 3 PRACTICAL REAL ESTATE LAWYER 27, 28 (May 2001).

elects to take against the tenant and (2) a confirmation that the guarantor's liability will not be affected by any lease amendment, release of security or dissolution or reorganization of the named tenant.[22]

VII.   THE LEASED SPACE. *(¶¶G and Q of Lease Summary, §§6 and 9, Exhibit D)*

Once the parties to the lease are properly named, the next issue that needs to be addressed is the identification of the space that the tenant is leasing from the landlord. In the context of a multi-tenant, office building, the lease provides the tenant with the right to use two separate spaces—(1) its **leased premises** (sometimes referred to as the "demised premises") and (2) the building's **common areas** (referred to by more professorial types as "appurtenances"). The location, dimensions and character of each of these space elements need to be precisely described in the lease.

The leased premises is the space over which the tenant has the exclusive right of possession. In an office lease, it is the space located within the four corners of the tenant's office suite. The leased premises can either be described by reference to a specific suite number (e.g., Suite 101) or by the attachment to the lease of a floor plan establishing the exact dimensions and configuration of the space. The goal in either such event is to specifically identify the space that is reserved exclusively for the tenant's conduct of its business.

The common areas are those spaces within the landlord's project that the tenant may use in common with other tenants in the building. Common areas include both **building common areas** and **site common areas**. Building common areas are further broken down into two categories—(1) building-wide common areas, such as the first floor lobby, freight elevators, mechanical equipment rooms and other spaces that are used by all building tenants, and (2) single floor common areas, such as the restrooms and corridors located on a particular floor of the building that are available for use only by the tenants whose leased premises are located on that floor. Site common areas refer to those areas located outside of the landlord's building that a tenant can use in common with other tenants, such as a parking lot, driveways, sidewalks and patios.

The lease should describe, at least in general terms, the tenant's right to use the building and site common areas. The Form Office Lease achieves that objective by reciting that "Tenant will also have the non-exclusive right to use the common areas which serve the Building, including, without limitation, the Building's common lobbies, hallways, elevators, risers, restrooms, parking areas and sidewalks."[23]

The common area issue that is most frequently debated by counsel for the landlord and tenant is the standard provision contained in most

---

22.   *See* Susan Fowler McNally, *Get Guaranty When Renting Space to Limited Liability Entity,* in Commercial Lease Law Insider 5–6 (July 2008).

23.   *See* the penultimate sentence of §6 of the Form Office Lease.

landlord leases that reserves a right for the landlord to reconfigure the common areas after the tenant's execution of the lease.[24] The landlord wants to reserve a right to reconfigure the common areas to respond to changes in the real estate market and to attract new tenants to its project.[25] By way of example, a landlord might decide that it needs to dramatically increase the size of its surface parking lot to lure a new tenant to the project and that its only option for doing so is to eliminate the building's green space and picnic area—a feature which may have attracted certain of its existing tenants to the building in the first instance. Similarly, a landlord might want to take advantage of a hot real estate market by constructing a new building in the area immediately adjacent to its existing building, with the end result that the number of parking spaces serving the existing building will be permanently reduced by 20% and the views from the existing building will be totally obstructed by the newly-constructed edifice. To the extent the landlord has reserved in its lease a broad right to change the building's common areas, the existing tenants in the above scenarios will probably be out of luck, even if they could, with a straight face, make the argument that they never would have moved into the landlord's building if the common area changes had been in place prior to lease execution.[26]

The tenant often seeks to limit the landlord's open-ended right to reconfigure the common areas, because it fears that such a reconfiguration could have an adverse effect on its conduct of business in its leased premises.[27] The best way for the tenant to accomplish that goal is to attach a site plan to the lease, which specifically identifies the location, size and configuration of all existing common areas, and to then expressly prohibit the landlord from changing the designated common areas without the tenant's consent. A one-sided clause of that type is, however, seldom acceptable to a well-represented landlord.[28] The best that the tenant can usually hope to achieve is to render off-limits changes to the specific common area characteristics that are most important to it (e.g., a parking lot containing not less than 200 parking spaces) and to include soft language in the lease that further precludes the landlord from making other common area changes to the extent "such changes would materially interfere with the Tenant's ability to conduct its business operations in the Leased Premises"—a standard that the landlord's lawyer will promptly try to modify to address only those "changes which would permanently deprive the Tenant of the substantial benefit and enjoyment of the Leased Premises."[29]

---

24. *See e.g.*, the last sentence of §6 of the form Office Lease.

25. *See* ZANKEL, *supra* note 19, at 98–99; and SENN, *supra* note 5, at 18–3.

26. *See* SENN, *supra* note 5, at 18–4 and 18–5.

27. A reconfiguration of common areas is of particular concern to the retail tenant, because the level of customer traffic to its store is directly tied to the quality of the retail center's common areas.

28. *See* ZANKEL, *supra* note 19, at 99; and David L. Grobart, *Common Areas*, in LEASE NEGOTIATION HANDBOOK 325 (Edward Chupack ed., 2003)

29. *See e.g.*, the last sentence of §6 of the Form Office lease.

A. MEASUREMENT OF LEASED PREMISES.
(¶G of Lease Summary)

Most commercial leases contain prominent statements of the number of square feet contained within the leased premises. The landlord insists on this because it quotes and calculates its rent on a per square foot basis—e.g., rent of $20 per square foot. The tenant wants the lease to recite the number of square feet contained within its leased premises, so that it can make a rational determination as to whether the size of the leased premises will appropriately support the conduct of the its business operations. The tenant, of course, is also interested in determining the number of square feet in its leased premises, because it has been told by the landlord (and every other landlord it has ever talked to) that its rent will be calculated based on the number of square feet contained within the leased premises.

Having agreed that the lease should recite the number of square feet contained within the leased premises, the next challenge facing the landlord and tenant is to figure out how to measure the leased premises. That task is not nearly as clear-cut as it might seem. The square footage of an office building can be expressed in terms of its ***gross*** area, its ***usable*** area or its ***rentable*** area.

- ***Gross Area***—The gross area of a building includes all the constructed space within a building's footprint. To measure a building's gross area, one practitioner suggests that one should "wrap a tape measure around the building's exterior."[30] A popular measurement standard adopted in 1996 by the Building Owners and Managers Association (the ***BOMA Standard***) states that "gross building area is computed by measuring the outside finished surface of permanent outer building walls."[31] Gross area includes both building common areas and the leased premises of all building tenants and is calculated without any deduction for elevator shafts, building atrium or other so-called "vertical penetrations."[32]

- ***Usable Area***—Usable area is the space within the four walls of each tenant's leased premises, or, as one author has put it, "the space for which a tenant might buy carpet."[33] The usable area of a building is the sum of the usable areas of the leased premises of all building tenants and expressly excludes any space devoted to building common areas.

---

30. *See* Theodore I. Yi and Dov Pinchot, *Space and Term Issues in Commercial Leases*, in The Practical Real Estate Lawyer's Manual on Commercial Leasing in Troubled Times—Forms, Checklists, and Advice 3, 5 (2009).

31. *See* Building Owners and Management Association International, Standard Method for Measuring Floor Area in Office Buildings, ANSI/BOMA Z65.1, 10 (1996).

32. The BOMA Standard defines "vertical penetrations" as "stairs, elevator shafts, flues, pipe shafts, vertical ducts, and the like and their enclosing walls. Atria, lightwells and similar penetrations above the finished floor are included in this definition." *See id.* at 2.

33. *See* Senn, *supra* note 5, at 4–18.

- ***Rentable Area***—The rentable area of a building is equal to the sum of the building's usable area, PLUS an allocation for the building's common areas.[34] Rentable area is a fictional number used by the landlord to calculate the amount of a tenant's rent. The rentable area of a building is always greater than the building's usable area, but is not necessarily equal to the building's gross area. The difference between the square footage of a building's rentable and usable space is known as the ***common area load factor***. The common area load factor is typically expressed as a percentage that is calculated in accordance with the following formula: [rentable square feet − usable square feet] ÷ rentable square feet. A building with a high common area load factor is labeled an "inefficient" building, because a higher percentage of the building's constructed space is devoted to common areas than is the case in a building with a lower common area load factor.

The interplay of the three space measurement modes is illustrated in the following example.

Example 11–1: Building A is a three story office building. The gross area contained on each floor is 10,000 square feet. The usable area of the tenant space located on each of the three floors measures 8,000 square feet, leaving 2,000 square feet on each floor to lobby corridors, restrooms and other common areas.[35]

The above assumptions produce the following space calculations for Building A:

- Gross area = 30,000 square feet;

- Usable area = 24,000 square feet;

- Common area = 6,000 square feet;

- Rentable area = 30,000 square feet; and

- Common area load factor = 20%.

So why do lawyers have to know all this stuff (it seems like it should be discussed in an engineering school text and not in a law school book)? As noted earlier, most landlords compute their tenants' rent based on the number of rentable square feet contained within the tenant's leased premises. Charging rents based on a building's rentable square footage theoretically permits the landlord to receive a rental return on ALL space located in the building and not just the space located within the four walls of the tenants' suites (or at least that is the common justification proffered by landlords for why they charge rents on a per rentable square foot basis). From a more practical perspective, it allows the landlord to quote

---

34. Building-wide common areas and single floor common areas are often allocated to the tenants in accordance with different allocation ratios—e.g., the building-wide common areas may be allocated to all building tenants, while the single floor common areas may be allocated only to the tenants occupying leased premises on the subject floor.

35. In order to simplify the calculations, no deduction is made in any of the numbers for vertical penetrations. *See supra* note 32.

lower per square foot rents than it would if it were quoting rents on a usable square foot basis—because there are always more rentable square feet in a building than there are usable square feet. Thus, if the landlord in Example 11–1 needs to collect $600,000 per year in rent from its tenants in order to meet its targeted financial goals, it could meet those goals by charging rent of either $20 per rentable square foot or $25 per usable square foot. Logic tells the landlord that using rentable square feet as a basis for its rent quotes produces a better marketing optic for its building. In addition, because the concept of rentable space is a fiction, the landlord is afforded greater flexibility in calculating its tenants' rent obligations on the basis of rentable area than it would if it were forced to calculate rents on the basis of the more exacting, usable area method of space measurement.

It should be clear by now that the use of rentable square feet to measure a tenant's leased premises does not serve the tenant's goal of making sure that the leased premises is properly sized for the conduct of its business operations. Moreover, having its rent computed based on the fictional number of rentable square feet contained with its leased premises provides the tenant with little solace that it is paying a competitive rent for its leased space.

So what should a tenant do when it receives a proposal from a landlord to lease 10,000 square feet of rentable space at a rent of $20 per rentable square foot (other than to call someone who has read this Chapter and actually understands all this space measurement mumbo jumbo)? The first thing that the tenant should do is ask the landlord to tell it how many usable square feet are contained within its leased premises. Getting the answer to that question (which, ideally, should be provided in the form of a landlord representation in the lease) will permit the tenant to consult its operations people to determine if the leased premises are right-sized for its business.

The tenant should next try to unearth the precise method used by the landlord to calculate the rentable square footage of the tenant's leased premises—i.e., exactly how much space in the building is devoted to common areas and what percentage of that space is being allocated to the tenant. Discovering the method behind the madness of the landlord's rentable space calculations will permit the tenant to compare the landlord's lease proposal on an "apples to apples" basis with proposals made to the tenant by other property owners. The best way to achieve that objective is to require the landlord to make a certification in the lease that it calculated the usable and rentable square feet contained within both the building and the leased premises in accordance with a well-recognized measurement benchmark, such as the BOMA standard referred to earlier in this Chapter.[36] The tenant should then reserve the right to re-measure

---

36. The Building Owners and Managers Association International issued a new measurement standard in 2010. *See* BUILDING OWNERS AND MANAGERS ASSOCIATION INTERNATIONAL, OFFICE BUILDINGS: STANDARD METHODS OF MEASUREMENT, ANSI/BOMA Z65.1 (2010). The 2010 standard may one day supplant the 1996 BOMA standard as the measurement standard most widely referred to in

its leased premises in accordance with the selected standard and to adjust its rent downward if its re-measurement of the leased premises shows that the leased premises contain less rentable square feet than initially certified by the landlord.[37]

The following example illustrates the benefits that redound to the favor of a tenant who successfully adopts the suggested negotiating tactic.

> **Example 11–2**: Tenant receives lease proposals from two local landlords (Landlord A and Landlord B). Each proposal calls for the tenant to lease 10,000 square feet of rentable space for an annual rental of $20 per rentable square foot (producing a total rent payment under each of the proposals of $200,000 per year). Tenant asks for and receives the following certifications from Landlord A and B concerning their respective calculations of the rentable square footage of tenant's leased premises.

Calculation Components	Landlord A	Landlord B
Rentable square feet contained within leased premises	10,000	10,000
Usable square feet contained within leased premises	8,000	9,000
Square feet contained within building common areas	6,000	3,000
Percentage of building common areas allocated to the tenant (computed in accordance with the BOMA Standard)	33%	33%
Common area load factor	20%	10%

Based on this information, the tenant knows that, while its rent is the same for both buildings ($200,000 per year), the usable square footage of its leased premises in Landlord B's building is significantly greater than in Landlord A's building (9,000 vs. 8,000 square feet). The usable square footage variance between the two buildings is attributable to the higher level of common area space found in Landlord A's building. With this information in hand, the tenant can make an "apples to apples" comparison of the two buildings to determine if the additional common area amenities provided in Landlord A's building outweigh the relative inefficiency of that building.

The above example nicely portrays a theme that will run throughout the rest of this Chapter—that is, the tenant's desire for transactional transparency and the landlord's preference for obfuscation.

---

commercial leases. However, as of the date of the writing of this Chapter (the third quarter of 2010), the 1996 BOMA standard remains the favored space measurement standard for tenants (presumably because of its familiarity to tenants and their legal counsel).

37. *See e.g.,* RODNEY J. DILLMAN, THE LEASE MANUAL—A PRACTICAL GUIDE TO NEGOTIATING OFFICE, RETAIL AND INDUSTRIAL LEASES 6–9 (2007); and SENN, *supra* note 6, at 4–17 (Form 4–5).

HIBC Case Study—The Use of a
"Modified BOMA Method"

The Form Office Lease makes no reference whatsoever to any standard of measurement (be it the BOMA standard or any other benchmark). Rather, all that the Standard Office Lease says is that the "Leased Premises is deemed to contain ___ square feet of rentable space."[38] I did not want to invite an argument with the tenant about the manner in which rentable space was calculated—hence, the reference to the "deemed" rentable square footage of the leased premises.

My desire to wholly avoid the rentable space controversy was regularly met with derision from tenant's counsel, who would insist that the lease include provisions confirming that the rentable area of the leased premises had been calculated in accordance with the BOMA standard and requiring a rent adjustment if the tenant's measurement of the leased premises produced a rentable square footage number that was different from that recited in the lease. My first reaction when braced with such a tenant-sponsored request was to point out to the tenant's lawyer that the landlord used a "modified BOMA standard" in its calculation of the rentable area of the building and the leased premises. This usually satisfied the tenant's lawyer, even though there is no specific benchmark defining what is meant by a modified BOMA standard. I used that term simply to buy my client some flexibility in the way it performed its rentable space calculations. In those rare instances where the modified BOMA standard ploy didn't work, I would agree that the space would be measured in strict accordance with the BOMA standard, but would then argue till my last dying breath that the tenant's monthly rent payment would remain as recited in the lease and would not be adjusted in any fashion. In other words, the monthly base rent would be $20,000, regardless whether the tenant's leased premises contained 10,000 rentable square feet or 9,500 rentable square feet. My reluctance to give the tenant a rent adjustment had less to do with my natural stubbornness than it did with my desire to protect the landlord's projected rental stream from its building (which was based on the project's costs and not any space calculation).

B. TENANT IMPROVEMENTS. *(¶Q of*
Lease Summary, §9 and Exhibit D)

When the landlord and tenant sit down to begin their lease negotiations, the leased premises are seldom in move-in condition. Significant improvements and modifications invariably have to be made to the physical condition of the leased premises to render them suitable for the tenant's conduct of its business. This is true for both **virgin space** (i.e, space that has not previously been occupied by a tenant) and **second**

---

38. *See* ¶G of the Lease Summary to the Form Office Lease.

generation space (i.e., space that has previously been occupied by a tenant or tenants).[39] The improvements and modifications which must be made to fit the tenant's planned use of the space are known as ***tenant improvements*** or ***TI***.

Tenant improvements are in addition to those core and structural improvements that the landlord makes to the leased premises as part of its construction of the overall building—i.e., those improvements that the landlord must make to facilitate any occupancy of the leased premises and not just the specific nature of the tenant's planned occupancy. Those core and structural improvements are commonly referred to as ***base building improvements*** and typically include, at the minimum, load-bearing walls, carpet-ready floors, life safety systems, windows and stubbed-in utilities. Because the landlord bears the sole economic responsibility for constructing the base building improvements, it is in the tenant's best interests to define base building improvements in as expansive a manner as possible.[40]

A commercial lease usually includes lengthy provisions addressing the tenant improvements for the leased premises.[41] Those provisions can either be included within the text of the base lease or in a separate agreement often referred to as a ***work letter***. Regardless which drafting technique is utilized, the tenant improvement clause must address and answer all of the following questions.

- What specific improvements will be made to the leased premises?
- Who will be responsible for designing and constructing the tenant improvements?
- Who will be responsible for paying the costs of designing and constructing the improvements?
- When must the improvements be completed?[42]

In the typical office lease, the landlord is designated as the person responsible for designing and constructing the leased premises.[43] It is in

---

39. The improvements made to suit one tenant are seldom universally acceptable to a successor tenant (although, hopefully, some elements of the initial improvements can be re-used by the successor).

40. *See* SENN, *supra* note 5, at 5–17 and 5–18.

41. *See, e.g.* §9 and Exhibit D of the Form Office Lease, which contemplate a fairly simple, straightforward build-out plan. By contrast, the tenant improvement provisions for a single tenant building are highly complex and often consist of several pages. *See e.g.*, Richard R. Goldberg, *Complex Work Letter*, in ALI–ABA COURSE OF STUDY MATERIALS, COMMERCIAL REAL ESTATE LEASES: SELECTED ISSUES IN DRAFTING AND NEGOTIATING IN CURRENT MARKETS Course No. SN–013, 155 (May 2008).

42. The issue of the timing of the completion of the tenant improvements is addressed as part of the lease term discussion in Pages 472–475, *infra*.

43. National retail tenants normally take responsibility for designing and constructing their own tenant improvements (which are substantially similar for all their stores throughout the country). When dealing with a national tenant, the landlord's responsibility is limited to (1) its delivery of a "vanilla shell" to the tenant, which basically means that the tenant's space is unimproved, except for the construction of four walls, a roof and stubbed-in utilities, and (2) its payment of a cash allowance to the tenant to defray some or all of the costs incurred by the tenant in connection with its build-out of its leased premises. *See* SENN, *supra* note 5, at 5–48 and 5–49; and ZANKEL, *supra* note 19, at 14.

the best interests of the landlord to control that process, because it wants to make sure that the improvements enhance the long-term value of its office building. In addition, the landlord has a vested interest in seeing to it that the tenant improvements are completed ASAP because the completion of the tenant improvements is the usual trigger for the commencement of the tenant's rent obligation. Finally, the tenant seldom has either the expertise or the inclination to immerse itself in the intricacies of designing and constructing the tenant improvements.

Answering the remaining three tenant improvement questions is relatively straightforward if detailed plans and specifications showing the desired tenant improvements are in place in advance of the lease negotiations. If that is the case, the landlord can secure pricing and scheduling commitments from its selected design and construction professionals and then instruct its counsel to complete the tenant improvement clause by stating that (1) the improvements will be constructed in accordance with a specified set of plans and specifications, (2) the landlord will assume the cost of constructing the tenant improvements (in exchange for the tenant's agreement to pay rent at a stipulated level) and (3) the landlord will use its reasonable efforts to complete construction of the tenant improvements by a mutually agreeable target date. An arrangement of this type is commonly referred to as a *turnkey* build-out—meaning that the landlord will do all of the work and all the tenant has to do is "turn the key, open the door and commence business."[44] A turnkey arrangement is most often used for large, single tenant, build-to-suit projects, where the tenant has expended the time and effort needed to determine in advance precisely what type of build-out it needs to serve its operational needs.

Unfortunately, in the customary office lease transaction, the tenant does not enter the lease negotiations with a fixed sense of the precise nature and scope of its tenant improvement package. As such, the lawyers representing the landlord and the tenant must draft a tenant improvement clause which describes the process that will be followed to determine the specifics of the tenant improvements that will be made to the leased premises. That process typically involves the tenant's delivery to the landlord of its general program requirements for the space (e.g., ten exterior offices, two conference rooms and a reception lobby); the landlord's preparation of preliminary design plans implementing the tenant's program requirements; and, once the preliminary plans are approved by the tenant, the landlord's preparation of final plans and specifications, which will also be subject to the tenant's approval.[45] The tenant improvement clause drafted by landlord's counsel will usually impose a timeline for all of the above actions—e.g., tenant's delivery of its program requirements to landlord within ten days after lease execution and tenant's approval of the preliminary plans within five days after the landlord's

---

44. *See* Zankel, *supra* note 19, at 13.

45. The tenant's right to disapprove the final plans and specifications is often limited to matters which are inconsistent with the previously-approved preliminary plans. *See e.g.*, the second paragraph of §9 of the Form Office Lease.

submission of such plans to the tenant. Once the final plans and specifications are approved by the tenant, the landlord will then assume responsibility for constructing the tenant improvements in accordance with the approved plans and specifications.

While it is fairly easy to describe the process that will be followed to design and construct the tenant improvements, it is a much tougher task to determine the economic consequences of a tenant improvement build-out when the specific nature of that build-out is not known when the parties sign the lease. When the landlord quotes a rent figure to a tenant, it will have accounted for its budgeted costs for constructing tenant improvements to the tenant's leased premises. Similarly, when the tenant determines what rent it is willing to pay for particular space, it does so in anticipation that the landlord will improve the space in a manner that is designed to fit the operational needs of the tenant's business. All is well, as long as the cost of the build-out needed by the tenant is less than or equal to the landlord's budgeted tenant improvement costs for the space. The issue that comes to the fore in every negotiation is what happens if the actual cost of the build-out exceeds the landlord's tenant improvement budget for the leased space. Who will be responsible for the payment of the excess costs?

1. Tenant Improvement Allowance

Landlords attempt to respond to the economic issue presented by an uncertain scope of the tenant improvement work by agreeing to pay tenant improvement costs up to a stipulated level (the ***tenant improvement*** or ***TI allowance***), with the tenant then being responsible for the payment of any costs in excess of the allowance amount (***excess TI costs***). This contractual arrangement permits the landlord to fix its maximum lease costs and preserve the integrity of its financial returns, even though it does not have a handle on the precise amount of the tenant improvement costs on the date of its execution of the lease.

The TI allowance arrangement does not protect the tenant against the risk that the actual cost of the build-out will exceed the amount of the TI allowance. There are a number of tactics that the tenant can employ to attempt to mitigate its risks under a typical, pro-landlord, TI allowance provision. The most obvious thing that the tenant can do when presented with a lease draft that includes a TI allowance clause is to delay execution of the lease until the scope of the tenant improvement work has been finalized and, hence, the actual cost of the tenant improvement work has been determined.

If the circumstances surrounding the lease transaction make that option impractical,[46] the tenant would be well-advised to retain the

---

46. This option is usually rendered impractical due to (a) the time pressure felt by both the landlord and the tenant to lock in their lease deal ASAP and (b) their shared reluctance to spend the time and money needed to prepare, review and approve the tenant improvement plans and specifications, without first having reached a definitive, enforceable agreement on the tenant's leasing of the designated space from the landlord.

services of a space planner or other design professional to try to get a preliminary sense as to whether what the tenant has in mind for the build-out of its leased premises can be designed and constructed at a cost which is consistent with the TI allowance. If it cannot, then the tenant should consider either downsizing its build-out expectations (e.g., using carpet squares instead of granite tile in the receptionist area) or asking the landlord to increase the amount of its allowance (which, as one might expect, is usually a futile inquiry).[47]

2.   Rent Amortization of Excess TI Costs

Once it has done everything it can to try to properly align the scope of the anticipated build-out with the amount of the landlord's TI allowance, the tenant should next consider asking the landlord to absorb any excess TI costs in exchange for an increase in the tenant's future rental obligations. The standard, landlord-oriented, TI allowance provision states that all excess TI costs will be paid in cash by the tenant.[48] Such an upfront cash payment can be overly burdensome to a tenant, particularly one whose liquidity is not boundless. Asking the landlord to amortize the excess TI costs as a rent increase can significantly ease the tenant's cash flow burden in the event the actual cost of the build-out substantially exceeds the amount of the established TI allowance. The landlord's willingness to agree to a rent amortization option will depend largely on the landlord's own liquidity position and on the amount of the rent increase that the tenant is willing to accept for the landlord's agreement to front the payment of the excess TI costs. If a landlord has the funds available to pay the excess costs and the tenant agrees to a rent amortization equation that actually increases the landlord's financial returns for its project, then the landlord may well look kindly upon the tenant's request for a rent amortization option.

The setting of a ***rent amortization factor*** (i.e., the percentage number by which the excess TI costs are multiplied to determine the tenant's annual rent increase) is a fairly complicated task, which involves an analysis of the genesis of the excess TI costs against the backdrop of the landlord's financial return expectations. Too many lawyers fail to appreciate the nuanced nature of the negotiations over the setting of the rent amortization factor and, instead, spend their time simply trying to negotiate a high amortization factor for the landlord or a low amortization

---

47. There are, however, a variety of tactics that the tenant's counsel can employ to try to chip away at the issue of the sufficiency of the stated TI allowance. By way of example, the tenant's counsel can try to negotiate provisions which (1) limit the landlord's ability to charge its supervisory fees and overhead costs against the TI allowance (2) require the landlord to competitively bid out the tenant improvement work and (3) force feed as many construction costs as possible into the category of base building improvements that will not be charged against the TI allowance. The nuances of these provisions are beyond the scope of this Chapter, but are discussed in detail at SENN, *supra* note 5, at 5–10 through 5–46; and Ray Kwasnick, *Construction Issues in Leases: The Tenant's Perspective*, 20 No. 2 PRACTICAL REAL ESTATE LAWYER 51 (March 2004).

48. *See e.g.*, the first sentence of §9 of the Form Office Lease.

factor for the tenant (without having any real clue as to the logical underpinning of the amortization factor).

The tenant's starting point in the negotiation is to assert that the landlord should receive the same return on the excess TI costs that it does on any other project cost. Based on that assertion, the tenant might expect its annual rent to increase by somewhere around 8–12% of the excess TI costs.[49] The landlord's counterpoint will be that it is simply extending a loan to the tenant to pay the excess TI costs and all principal and interest on that loan must be repaid over the initial term of the lease. That argument would produce a rent amortization factor far in excess of that produced on the basis of the tenant's "just another project cost" argument (somewhere in the 25% range assuming an initial lease term of five years and an interest rate of 8%).

The ultimate resolution of this issue will be dependent upon the amount of the excess TI costs and the nature of the tenant improvements which gave rise to the existence of such excess costs.[50] If the excess TI costs are relatively small in amount and are attributable to the construction of improvements that will likely be re-used by a future tenant (e.g., a high-efficiency HVAC system), then the tenant should be in a relatively strong position to argue for the setting of the rent amortization factor in the 8–12% range (on the theory that the excess costs are just like any other project cost). If, however, the excess TI costs are significant in amount and are triggered by exotic improvements that will in all likelihood need to be demolished before the next tenant assumes occupancy of the space, then the landlord should prevail in it argument that it is simply acting as a lender and the rent amortization factor should be set at a percentage that will result in the excess costs, plus interest, being repaid over the initial term of the tenant's lease.[51] There is, obviously, plenty of room for negotiation between the two noted extremes and it is not uncommon for the landlord and the tenant to strike a compromise whereby the landlord will agree to amortize a portion of the excess TI costs at one percentage and another portion of such costs at a much higher percentage (with an overall cap then being placed on the amount of the excess TI costs that will be funded by the landlord).

---

49. This percentage will fluctuate with changes in the prevailing market conditions.

50. *See* ZANKEL, *supra* note 19, at 15–17 for an interesting and entertaining take on this point.

51. The math works as follows. Assume that the excess tenant improvement costs are $100,000 and that the tenant is paying annual rent of $200,000 during each year of its five year lease. If the "just another project cost" approach is adopted, the landlord will agree to pay the $100,000 of excess TI costs in consideration for the tenant's agreement to increase its annual rent by $10,000 (computed using a rent amortization factor of 10%). If the landlord treats its payment of the $100,000 of excess TI costs as a "loan" to the tenant, then the tenant's annual rent will increase by $25,000 (assuming the use of a rent amortization factor of 25%, which is designed to pay off the excess TI cost "loan" in five years at an interest rate of 8%). The upshot of the varying treatments is that under the "just another project cost" approach, the tenant will pay $50,000 of additional rent over the five year term of its lease, while it will pay additional rent of $125,000 over the five year term under the "loan" perspective—a sizable difference which certainly merits the attention of the lawyers for both the landlord and the tenant.

VIII. THE LEASE TERM. *(¶¶I, J and K of Lease Summary and §§9, 18 and 21)*

The ***lease term*** is the period during which the tenant has the right to exclusive possession of the leased premises. A typical lease term for a commercial lease is five to ten years. The length of a commercial lease term stands in sharp contrast to the usual six to 12 month term of a residential lease. The longer term of the commercial lease is driven by two factors—(1) the tenant's need for continuity in its business location and (2) the landlord's desire to lock in a financial return on its capital investment for as long a period as possible.

The ***commencement date*** of the lease term is the date on which the tenant first gains the right to exclusively possess the leased premises and the ***termination date*** is the date specified in the lease when the tenant's right to possess the leased premises ends. The commencement date can be expressed either as a date certain (e.g., January 1, 2012) or as the date on which certain conditions are satisfied (e.g., the date on which construction of the tenant improvements is completed). It is important to keep in mind that the commencement date is almost never the same date as the date of the parties' execution of the lease (due primarily to the landlord's need to make tenant improvements to the space before delivering possession of the space to the tenant) and only sometimes the same as the date on which the tenant's rent obligation commences or the date on which the tenant first opens for business in the leased premises. The termination date is usually described as being a number of years/months after the commencement date (e.g., five years after the commencement date).

The lease should specifically recite both the commencement and termination dates of the lease term. The term of the lease recited in the lease is typically referred to as the ***initial lease term*** and may be extended or renewed for an additional term or terms by the agreement of the parties.[52] The lease should also specify what the tenant's obligations are on the termination of the lease term—specifically, in what condition it is required to re-deliver the leased premises to the landlord and whether it is obligated to remove any improvements made by it in the leased premises.[53]

A. INABILITY TO DELIVER POSSESSION— AMERICAN vs. ENGLISH RULES

The biggest issue that arises concerning the lease term is what happens if the landlord is not able to deliver possession of the leased premises to the tenant on the commencement date specified in the lease, either because another tenant is holding over in the leased premises or

---

52. *See infra* Pages 522–526, for a discussion of extension and renewal terms.

53. *See e.g.,* §18 of the Form Office Lease. *See also* the discussion of the tenant's termination obligations in Ruth A. Schoenmeyer and Michelle M. McAtee, *Surrender Dorothy: Restoration Obligations in Office Leases*, 23 No. 3 Practical Real Estate Lawyer 17 (May 2007).

because the landlord has not yet completed construction of the leased premises. This topic necessarily begins with the discussion of two contrasting common law rules—the "American rule" (the minority position) and the "English rule" (the majority position).[54] Under the American rule (which is mentioned first solely for patriotic reasons), the landlord is only obligated to deliver "legal possession" of the leased premises to the tenant on the commencement date. The landlord is not required to put the tenant in "actual possession" of the leased space. As such, the tenant has no legal recourse against the landlord[55] and must begin paying rent on its leased space, even though a holdover tenant or trespasser is in possession of the leased premises—a crazy result, but one that is still followed in a number of states.[56]

The English rule more appropriately requires the landlord to deliver both legal and actual possession of the leased premises to the tenant on the commencement date. If someone other than the tenant is in actual possession of the leased premises, the tenant can withhold its rent, terminate its lease or sue the landlord for damages.[57]

The most important thing to remember about the American and English rules is that both rules can be abrogated by contract.[58] Most landlord leases make it clear that the tenant cannot sue the landlord for damages if the landlord is unable to deliver actual possession of the leased premises to the tenant on the scheduled date. It is, however, also the norm (to the extent there is ever a norm in commercial leasing) for the tenant's rent obligation to be abated if it is prevented from taking possession of the leased premises by the acts of a third party.

B. TENANT IMPROVEMENT CONSTRUCTION DELAYS

The source of most commencement date problems is the landlord's failure to complete construction of the tenant improvements by the commencement date contemplated by the lease. While both parties are naturally motivated to cause the tenant improvements to be completed by the commencement date, any number of things can go wrong to thwart the timely completion of the landlord's construction efforts. The following are some of the more common reasons for the occurrence of a construction delay:

- The tenant improvement plans and specifications are not finalized in a timely fashion;

---

54. *See* Yi, *supra* note 30, at 6; and SENN, *supra* note 5, at 5–6 and 5–7.

55. Under the American rule, the tenant has the right to sue the holdover tenant/trespasser for damages. *See* Yi, *supra* note 30, at 6; and SENN, *supra* note 5, at 5–6.

56. *See* FRIEDMAN, *supra* note 8, at 4–17.

57. *See* SENN, *supra* note 5, at 5–6.

58. *See id.* at 5–7; and Yi, *supra* note 30, at 6. Most leases also contain holdover penalties which discourage the existing tenant from staying in possession of its leased space beyond the termination date set forth in the lease. *See e.g.*, §21 of the Form Office Lease.

- The landlord fails to secure a building permit on the date contemplated in its construction schedule;

- The landlord sets an overly optimistic construction schedule that its contractor cannot meet;

- The contractor simply fouls up and misses its completion deadline;

- The tenant requests changes to the work that delay construction;

- The materials called for in the specifications are on back order;

- A trade contractor files for bankruptcy or goes on strike; or

- Bad weather or other acts of God slow down the progress of construction.

The consequences of a construction delay can be severe for both the tenant and the landlord. If a tenant cannot open for business on the targeted date, it may suffer a loss of profits and will almost certainly incur additional costs triggered by it having to stop and later re-start the process of moving into its new space. In addition, the tenant may have to pay a penalty rent to hold over in its existing leased space or, worse yet, have no place whatsoever to conduct its business.

The impact on the landlord of a construction delay can be equally disastrous. At best, the landlord's rental stream will be deferred until construction of the tenant improvements is completed. At worst, the landlord's lease with the tenant will be terminated, thereby forcing the landlord to go back in the market to try to find a replacement tenant. Even if it fortunate enough to secure a replacement tenant, the landlord will lose rent for a period of time and will likely have to pay additional leasing commission and tenant improvement costs to secure the new tenant.

The construction delay issue should be tackled head on in the text of the lease and not left to the vagaries of the American, English or other common law rules dealing with delays in the delivery of possession of the leased premises. The landlord and the tenant normally stake out polar opposite positions when the issue of possible construction delays is first raised during the lease negotiations. The landlord will graciously (and somewhat disingenuously) acknowledge that the American rule probably doesn't make a lot of sense in the context of a tenant improvement construction delay (unless, of course, the delay was the tenant's fault, in which event the landlord will do a lot of flag-waving). The landlord's proffered solution will be to stipulate that the only consequence of a construction delay should be the deferral of the commencement and termination dates by the number of days of the construction delay. The tenant, on the other hand, will insist that (1) it be given the right to terminate the lease if the tenant improvements are not completed by the deadline specified in the lease and (2) the landlord be held responsible for the payment of liquidated damages for each day of the construction delay.

The lawyers for the landlord and tenant will then embark on a negotiation which is very similar to the owner-contractor negotiation concerning construction delays discussed in an earlier chapter of this text.[59] Some of the issues that will be discussed during the course of that negotiation and the lawyers' respective takes on those issues are summarized below.[60]

- *Definition of Substantial Completion.*[61]

  - *Landlord's Take*—The tenant improvements should be deemed substantially complete on the earlier of (1) the date on which the landlord's architect certifies that the improvements are sufficiently complete to permit the tenant to occupy the leased premises or (2) the date on which the local building department issues a temporary certificate of occupancy[62] for the leased premises.

  - *Tenant's Take*— The tenant improvements should be deemed substantially complete only upon the occurrence of both of the following events (1) the issuance by the local building department of a permanent certificate of occupancy and (2) the tenant's inspection and acceptance of the leased premises (subject to a small construction punchlist authored and agreed to by the tenant).

- *Liquidated Damages.*

  - *Landlord's Take*—Liquidated damages should not apply to any excusable delay; should be in a fairly nominal amount; and should be imposed only after the expiration of a lengthy grace period (e.g., 60 days after the completion deadline specified in the lease).

  - *Tenant's Take*—Liquidated damages should be charged without regard to excusable delays; should be in an amount sufficient to incentivize the landlord to complete the project on time; and should be imposed immediately upon the passage of the completion deadline.

---

59. *See supra* Chapter 10, Pages 432–435.

60. *See generally* Lisa Rosen, *Construction Issues in Leases: The Landlord's Perspective*, in LEASE NEGOTIATION HANDBOOK 93 (Edward Chupack ed., 2003); and Kwasnick, *supra* note 47.

61. Most commercial leases use the concept of "substantial completion" (rather than "final completion") to define the point in time when the tenant improvements are sufficiently complete to trigger the commencement of the tenant's lease term. *See supra* Chapter 10, Page 432, for a discussion of the difference between substantial and final completion.

62. A temporary certificate of occupancy permits the tenant to occupy the leased premises on the condition that the landlord completes certain additional improvements within a fixed period of time established by the local governmental authorities. It is, therefore, a revocable occupancy permit. A permanent certificate of occupancy is, on the other hand, a final, irrevocable authorization for the tenant to assume occupancy of its leased premises for the conduct of its business.

- ***Excusable Delays.***
    - ***Landlord's Take***—Excusable delays should be a long, broad and non-exclusive list of events beyond the landlord's control.
    - ***Tenant's Take***—Excusable delays should be a short, specific and all-inclusive list of unforeseeable events beyond the landlord's reasonable control (to the extent the tenant even recognizes the concept of an excusable delay).
- ***Standard of Performance.***
    - ***Landlord's Take***—The landlord should be required to pursue the completion of the tenant improvements "in the due course," with no requirement that it take any extraordinary measures to meet the completion deadline.
    - ***Tenant's Take***—The landlord should be required to use "all commercially reasonable efforts" to meet the completion deadline (specifically including the payment of overtime).
- ***Consequences of Tenant-caused Delays.***[63]
    - ***Landlord's Take***—A tenant-caused delay should result in the tenant being required to pay its rent effective as of the regularly-scheduled commencement date, regardless when construction of the improvements is actually completed.
    - ***Tenant's Take***—A tenant-caused delay should result in a deferral of the commencement and termination dates (and nothing more).
- ***Termination remedy.***
    - ***Landlord's Take***—No way, no how (except after the passage of an extremely lengthy grace period and any extension granted for excusable delays).
    - ***Tenant's Take***—The tenant must have the right to terminate the lease if the work is not done within a reasonable period of time after the targeted commencement date.

The ultimate resolution of the above issues will depend on how important the schedule is to the tenant, how achievable the schedule is by the landlord and what, if any, other leasing options are available to the landlord and the tenant. The negotiation of the construction delay provisions are particularly important in the context of the landlord's development of a build-to-suit project which will be 100% occupied by a single tenant.

---

63. The definition of a "tenant-caused delay" is usually not a topic of great controversy in the lease negotiations. A representative example of such a definition is included in the last paragraph of §9 of the Form Office Lease, which specifically cites the two most common types of tenant-caused delays—i.e., the tenant's failure to review design submissions within the time period stated in the lease and the tenant's requests for changes in the final, tenant improvement plans and specifications.

IX. RENT. *(¶¶M–P of Lease Summary, §§1–3 and Exhibit B)*

The developer's primary objective during stage 7 is to lease the project to creditworthy tenants, who agree to pay rents at or above the rent levels projected in the developer's operating budget for the project. While the real estate development lawyer needs to understand the economic drivers behind his client's establishment of its quoted rent levels, the lawyer is rarely assigned the task of negotiating the per square foot rental rates that will be included in the lease. The lawyer is, however, responsible for structuring a rent clause that is designed to protect the landlord against a potential reduction of its rental income from either (1) an unbudgeted increase in its building expenses, (2) the existence of inflation in the general economy or (3) the tenants' failure to pay their agreed-upon rents.

Conversely, it is the job of the tenant's lawyer to craft a rent clause that protects the tenant against economic surprises and keeps its rent at or below the level contemplated in the operating budget for the business that it will be conducting in the leased premises. Once again, it is not the job of the tenant lawyer to negotiate the per square foot rental rates recited in the lease, but rather to make sure that the tenant does not have to make additional payments under its lease that are in any way inconsistent with the financial parameters set forth in its operating budget.

The next portion of the discussion will focus on the tactics and techniques at the lawyers' disposals to help their respective clients achieve their rent objectives. The following simple example will be used as a touchstone for that discussion.

Example 11–3: Landlord owns an office building containing 100,000 square feet of rentable space. Landlord's total development costs for the building were $20 million (or $200 per rentable square foot).[64] In order to achieve its desired total return on costs of 10%, Landlord needs to produce an annual net operating income[65] for the building of at least $2 million (or $20 prsf). Landlord's projections call for its building expenses[66] during the building's first full year of operation to be $1million ($10 prsf). Landlord's projection is for the economy to experience inflation at the rate of 3% per year.

---

64. The remainder of this section will utilize the acronym "prsf" as a short-hand reference to "per rentable square foot."

65. The landlord's "net operating income" is generally equal to the landlord's rental revenues less its building expenses. *See supra* Chapter 3, Page 39.

66. For reasons that will become obvious as the remainder of this section unfolds, I have opted to use the term "building expenses" in lieu of the more commonly used term "operating expenses." The building expenses for a multi-tenant, office project typically include the following categories of expenses: real estate taxes; insurance premiums; utility charges; maintenance and repair costs; janitorial fees; property management fees; landscaping, snow removal and trash disposal costs; legal, accounting and other professional service fees; and other miscellaneous expenses and project reserves.

A. RENT STRUCTURES

The primary economic issue presented during stage 7 is, can the landlord structure a rent clause that will preserve the stability of its net operating income if its operating expenses are greater than projected? Providing a satisfactory resolution of this issue is paramount to the landlord's achievement of its desired financial returns because (1) the tenant's annual rent obligation is set at a fixed amount during each year of the lease term and (2) the landlord's building expenses will fluctuate from year-to-year based on market conditions, project needs, inflation and a variety of other circumstances. In the context of Example 11–3, the issue that the real estate development lawyer needs to answer is, what can be done to maintain the project's net operating income at or above $2 million if the building's expenses in any year exceed the $1 million projected threshold.

Answering this question requires an understanding of the three fundamental types of rent structures—(1) *gross*, (2) *net* and (3) *expense stop rents*.[67] The three rent structures provide different answers to the basic question of who bears the risk that landlord's building expenses will be greater than projected by the landlord.

Each of the three rent structures involves the tenant's payment of a fixed amount of rent (commonly known as *base rent*) that will be payable by the tenant regardless of the level of the landlord's building expenses. Two of the structures contemplate the tenant's payment of an additional sum tied in some measure to the level of the landlord's building expenses. The variable component of the tenant's rent obligation is referred to as *additional rent*. The levels of base and additional rent paid by the tenant under the gross, net and expense stop rent structures are discussed below.

Gross Lease: In a gross lease, the tenant pays a fixed amount of base rent that is not tied in any way to the level of the landlord's building expenses. The tenant is not required to pay any additional rent whatsoever. If the landlord in Example 11–3 were to lease space in its building under a gross lease, it would need to charge each of its tenants annual base rent of $30 prsf in order to generate net operating income of $20 prsf (assuming that the landlord's actual building expenses are equal to the landlord's projected expense load of $10 prsf). In a gross lease, all of the risk that the landlord's actual building expenses will be greater than the budgeted expenses is placed on the landlord, because the tenant's rent

---

67. Different people use different labels to describe these three rent structures. Additional terms used to describe the rent structures include "full service gross" (comparable to "gross" in the above discussion), "triple net ("net" in the above discussion) and "modified gross" (the "expense stop" arrangement in the above discussion). *See e.g.*, Terry L. Barger and Marc A. Maiona, *Operating Cost Escalation Theory and Practice under Commercial Leases*, in ACREL Papers 159, 161 (ALI–ABA, Spring 2007). As is the case with most things in life, it is the substance of the arrangements (and not the labels used to describe those arrangements) that is important.

payment will remain fixed at the $30 prsf level, regardless whether the actual building expenses are $10, $15 or $20 prsf.

Net Lease: In a net lease structure, the tenant makes two rental payments—(1) a fixed base rent payment, PLUS (2) an additional rent payment equal to the tenant's proportionate share[68] of the landlord's actual building expenses—whatever those expenses may be. If the landlord in Example 11–3 were to lease space in its building under a net lease, it could satisfy its financial goals by charging each of its tenants fixed base rent equal to $20 prsf and then further requiring each such tenant to pay additional rent equal to its share of the landlord's actual building expenses. In a net lease, all of the risk that the landlord's actual building expenses will exceed the landlord's budgeted expenses is placed on the tenants, because the tenants will be required to reimburse the landlord for 100% of the actual building expenses, regardless whether they come in at $10, $15 or $20 prsf.

Expense Stop Lease: An expense stop lease is a hybrid of a gross lease and a net lease. As is the case in a net lease, the tenant in an expense stop lease makes two rental payments—(1) a fixed base rent payment, *PLUS* (2) an additional rent payment that fluctuates based on the level of the landlord's actual building expenses. The difference between an expense stop lease and a net lease is that, in an expense stop lease, the tenant is required to pay additional rent only if and to the extent that the actual building expenses exceed a pre-determined base amount (the ***expense stop***). As such, the tenant's additional rent payment is defined as its proportionate share of any INCREASE in the building expenses over the applicable expense stop. The expense stop can be defined either as a ***stipulated sum*** (e.g., $10 prsf) or, more commonly, as the "actual building expenses incurred by the landlord in a specified base year" (a ***base year expense stop***), with the selected ***base year*** typically being the first calendar year during which the tenant occupies its leased premises.[69]

If the landlord in Example 11–3 were to adopt an expense stop rent structure (with a base year expense stop equal to the landlord's actual building expenses during its first year of operations), the tenant's annual rent obligation would be equal to the sum of (1) fixed base rent of $30 prsf, plus (2) for all years subsequent to the base year, the tenant's share of any increase in the actual building expenses over the amount of the base year expense stop. For example, if the actual building expenses in the base year were $12 prsf and the building expenses increased in the next year to $14 prsf, then the tenant would be required to make an additional rent payment in that next year equal to $2 prsf. In an expense stop lease,

---

68. The manner in which the tenant's "proportionate share" of building expenses is calculated is discussed later in this Chapter. *See infra* Pages 486–487. For the purposes of the discussion of the three basic rent structures, it will be assumed that the tenant's proportionate share has been determined in a fair and objective manner that is acceptable to both the landlord and the tenant.

69. The selection of the proper base year under an expense stop lease is often the subject of heated negotiations between the landlord and the tenant. The reasons why are discussed *infra* Pages 488–490.

the risk that the landlord's actual building expenses will exceed its budgeted building expenses is shared by the landlord and the tenant. The landlord assumes the risk that its actual building expenses in the base year will be greater than the budgeted $10 prsf figure and the tenant bears the risk that the building's expenses will increase after the base year.

The operation of the gross, net and expense stop structures can best be shown through the use of an example.

Example 11–4: Assume the same facts used in Example 11–3 (that is, Landlord has a projected NOI goal of $20 prsf and projected building expenses for the first year of $10 prsf), plus the following additional facts:

- Actual Year 1 building expenses—$10 prsf (the same as budgeted);

- Tenant's annual base rent—

    - Gross lease—$30 prsf,

    - Net lease—$20 prsf, and

    - Expense Stop—$30 prsf (with an expense stop = actual Year 1 building expenses).

The financial results produced for the landlord and the tenant under each of the three rent structures are shown in the following table (with all numbers being shown on a per rentable square foot basis).

Year 1 Results	Gross	Net	Expense Stop
Base Rent	$30	$20	$30
Additional Rent	–0–	$10	–0–
Less: Actual Expenses	($10)	($10)	($10)
Net Operating Income	$20	$20	$20

The above table illustrates that the three rent structures produce identical results for both the landlord (an NOI of $20 prsf) and the tenant (a total rent payment of $30 prsf), when the landlord's actual building expenses equal its budgeted building expenses. But, as the next example shows, the three alternative rent structures produce markedly different results when the actual building expenses exceed budget.

Example 11–5: Assume all of the same facts as used in Example 11–4, except that the actual building expenses in Year 1 are $12 prsf, and the actual building expenses in Year 2 are $15 prsf.

The financial impact of the changed assumptions under each of the three rent structures is indicated in the following table.

Year 1 and 2 Results	Gross	Net	Expense Stop
Year 1			
Base Rent	$30	$20	$30
Additional Rent	–0–	$12	–0–
Less: Actual Expenses	($12)	($12)	($12)
Year 1 Net Operating Income	$18	$20	$18
Year 2			
Base Rent	$30	$20	$30
Additional Rent	–0–	$15	$3
Less: Actual Expenses	($15)	($15)	($15)
Year 2 Net Operating Income	$15	$20	$18
Total Net Operating Income	$33	$40	$36

This table shows that the three rent structures produce different financial results for the landlord and the tenant, when the landlord underestimates the amount of its building expenses. Based on the facts assumed in Example 11–5, the landlord's total net operating income for Years 1 and 2 is $40 prsf under a net lease; $36 prsf under an expense stop lease; and $33 prsf under a gross lease. Conversely, the tenant's total rent payments in Years 1 and 2 are $60 prsf under a gross lease; $63 prsf under an expense stop lease; and $67 prsf under a net lease. The clear narrative produced by those numbers is that the risk that the actual building expenses will exceed the budgeted expenses is placed on the tenant under a net lease, placed on the landlord under a gross lease and shared by the landlord and the tenant under an expense stop lease.

B. SELECTING THE RIGHT RENT STRUCTURE

A gross lease is seldom used in a commercial transaction (despite the obvious attraction it holds for the tenant). There are a couple reasons why commercial leases so infrequently adopt a gross rent structure. The first reason is fairly obvious—the commercial leasing process remains largely landlord-controlled and landlords don't like gross leases because they place all of the risk of an unbudgeted expense increase squarely on the landlord's shoulders.

The second, less obvious reason that gross leases are viewed with general disfavor has more to do with human nature than it does with economic theory. When asked to provide a rent quote under a gross lease arrangement, a landlord's natural, human inclination is to include a cushion in its quote to insulate it against the risk that the actual amount of its building expenses will outstrip the level of those expenses included in its project budget. A landlord who has budgeted an NOI of $20 prsf and building expenses of $10 prsf might well quote gross rents of $32 prsf in the first lease year and seek to bump the gross rent by $2–3 prsf for each subsequent year during the remainder of the tenant's lease term. The tendency of landlords to include such cushions in gross rent quotes runs directly counter to the tenant's primary objective of keeping its occupancy costs as low as possible. A tenant may, therefore, be better served by using a net or expense stop lease and instructing its lawyers to vigorously negotiate lease changes designed to protect the tenant from an unwarranted increase in its additional rent obligation.

The selection of a net or expense stop lease is, to a large extent, predicated on the nature of the landlord's project. By way of example, net leases tend to be the favored choice for retail, industrial and single-tenant office projects, while expense stop arrangements are more the norm for multi-tenant, office buildings. The custom of the real estate market where the landlord's project is located also is a major factor affecting the selection of a rent structure. Some office markets, like Orlando, Florida, have a strong preference for expense stop leases, while others, like Columbus, Ohio, tend to favor the use of net leases for multi-tenant office projects.[70]

To the extent market forces do not dictate the selection of a particular rent structure, the landlord tends to prefer the use of a true net lease structure because of the more ironclad protection it affords the landlord against unbudgeted expense increases. Similarly, the expense stop arrangement is preferred by most office tenants because it gives the tenant a bit more predictability concerning the amount of its annual rent obligation (and, if a base year expense stop is used, forces the landlord to stand behind its projection of base year building expenses).

It should be noted that most commercial leases are hybrids of the three basic rent structures. A lease may place an obligation on the tenant to reimburse the landlord for certain types of expenses (a net lease arrangement), but preclude the landlord from seeking reimbursement of other expenses (a gross lease approach). Similarly, a lease that generally adopts an expense stop structure might nonetheless require the tenant to pay 100% of certain specific expenses (e.g., real estate taxes and insurance premiums). The lawyer's job, therefore, is only partly done when a general form of rent structure is selected. The lawyer must next determine whether each particular building expense merits a treatment that is disparate from the treatment otherwise contemplated by the selected rent structure.

C. TENANT'S SCRUTINY OF EXPENSE PASS-THROUGH PROVISIONS

As noted in the preceding section, most commercial leases contain a feature placing the financial responsibility on the tenant for the payment of at least some portion of the landlord's building expenses. Multi-tenant office and retail leases tend to contemplate that the landlord will pay those

---

70. The Form Office Lease (which was prepared for use in connection with the leasing of multi-tenant office buildings in the Orlando, Florida market) adopts an expense stop rent structure.

expenses in the first instance and then seek reimbursement from the tenants in the form of the payment of additional rent. Warehouse and single-tenant leases usually require the tenant to pay the expenses directly to the person providing the subject service or materials to the building. In either event, the placement on the tenant of the ultimate financial burden for the payment of a certain building expense is colloquially referred to by leasing professionals as an ***expense pass-through***.

Expense pass-throughs are an added component of the tenant's overall occupancy costs. Unlike base rent, the amount of the tenant's expense pass-through obligation is neither fixed, nor easily determinable and can vary widely from period-to-period based on unforeseeable fluctuations in the nature and amount of the building expenses being passed through to the tenant. The expense pass-through concept threatens the tenant's ability to meet two of its principal financial objectives in any lease transaction—(1) the avoidance of economic surprises and (2) the maintenance of all-in occupancy costs at levels which are consistent with its overall operating budget. For this reason, the lease's purported treatment of expense pass-throughs draws closer scrutiny from tenant's counsel than any other provision of the lease.[71]

The primary goal of tenant's counsel when negotiating the expense pass-through clause is to try to limit the amount and categories of those building expenses that the tenant is obligated to pay. The tenant is legitimately fearful that the landlord will treat the expense pass-through provision as an open checkbook that permits the landlord to incur any costs of its choosing and then pass the financial obligation for the payment of those costs onto the tenant. As long as the ultimate financial responsibility for the expenses rests with the tenant, the landlord arguably has no incentive to keep its building expenses under control.[72] Its net operating income from the project will remain stable even if the amount of its building expenses increase dramatically. With a full-bodied, expense pass-through clause in hand, the landlord is free to increase the level and quality of its building services to attract new tenants to the project, because the associated cost increases will be subsidized by the expense pass-throughs paid by its existing tenants.

The tenant's lawyer has a variety of weapons in its arsenal to try to limit the adverse impact of expense pass-throughs on its client's finances. Some of those weapons are discussed below.[73]

---

71. For detailed examinations of the tenant's perspective on expense pass-through clauses, *see* Thomas C. Barbuti and Alan A. Lascher, *CAM/Operating Expenses: Devil or Angel . . . So Whose Clause Is It Anyway?,* in ACREL PAPERS 518 (ALI–ABA, Spring 2004); Marc E. Betesh, *Rent Escalation Clauses in Office Leases,* in ACREL PAPERS 148 (ALI–ABA, Spring 2007); Barger, *supra* note 69; and Gary Goldman, *Tenant Triage: Operating on a Landlord's Operating Expense Clause,* 16 No. 2 PRACTICAL REAL ESTATE LAWYER 19 (March 2000).

72. The landlord's counter to the tenant's "open checkbook" argument is that the landlord always has the incentive to keep its building expenses as low as possible, because doing so has a direct impact on its ability to retain its existing tenants.

73. For a discussion of those expense pass-through issues which are unique to an expense stop lease, *see infra* Pages 488–490.

__Exclusions:__ The prototypical landlord lease describes the pass-through expenses in an extremely expansive fashion (e.g., "all expenses of any kind or nature related to the ownership, operation, management, maintenance and repair of the building"), followed by a purely illustrative, non-exclusive listing of every conceivable category of expense conjured up by the landlord's lawyer. Tenant's counsel will try to slash the landlord's expense list to include only those specific expenses that must be incurred to provide the tenant with the level of service that it needs to efficiently conduct its business in the leased premises. The tenant's lawyer will also usually try to limit the permitted pass-throughs to those expenses that are classified as "operating expenses" under generally accepted accounting principles.

Landlord's counsel will customarily agree to exclusions for the landlord's debt service costs, income tax payments, leasing commissions and tenant improvement costs. The battle will then focus on whether expenses such as the following will be passed through to the tenant—e.g., capital expenditures; payments to affiliates of the landlord; corporate overhead; art purchases; real estate tax increases triggered by a building sale; property management fees; terrorism insurance; professional fees; and building promotion costs.[74] The landlord's lawyer will counter his opponent's thrust that "we can't give you an open checkbook," with his own parry that "if you don't agree to pay for it, we won't do it." The end result is often a complex and very specific listing of expense inclusions and exclusions, which, if the lawyers are not extremely careful, will be internally inconsistent and, on occasion, flat out contradictory.

__Caps:__ A less artful, but often more effective way of limiting the tenant's additional rent exposure is to include a cap on the amount of the tenant's annual, additional rent payments. The cap can be expressed either as an absolute number (e.g., no more than $5 prsf in any one calendar year) or as a limited increase over the amount of the prior year's expenses (e.g., an increase of not more than 3% over the prior calendar year's expenses). In either such event, the use of a cap is the tenant's attempt to use a machete rather than a stiletto to reduce the potential for a dramatic increase in its additional rent obligation. If the landlord is willing to agree to a cap (and it typically is only if it has limited leverage in the lease negotiations or if the negotiated cap provides it with a substantial cushion over its projected future expenses), its counsel should resist the imposition of a cap on any expense that is not within the landlord's control (so-called *__uncontrollable expenses__*), such as real estate taxes, insurance premiums and utility charges.[75]

__Audit Rights.__ Tenant's counsel frequently seeks to guard against landlord errors[76] in the calculation of its pass-through expenses by insert-

---

74. *See* sources cited *supra* note 71. For a representative sample of a tenant's wish list of expense exclusions, *see* Mark S. Henigh, *Office Lease Operating Expense Exclusions*, in ALI–ABA COURSE OF STUDY MATERIALS, COMMERCIAL REAL ESTATE LEASES: SELECTED ISSUES IN DRAFTING AND NEGOTIATING IN CURRENT MARKETS Course No. SN–013, 129 (May 2008).

75. *See* SENN, *supra* note 5, at 7–20 and 7–21; and Barbuti, *supra* note 71, at 8.

ing a clause into the lease that gives the tenant the right to audit the landlord's expense records.[77] The following are issues that are often the subject of negotiation when a tenant asks for an audit right:

- What level of information must the landlord provide to the tenant's auditors?

- Who can perform the audit on the tenant's behalf (e.g., a contingent fee auditor or only a certified public accountant)?[78]

- Who pays for the costs of the audit?[79]

- Can the audit be performed at any time (the tenant's preference) or only within a limited period of time after the tenant's receipt of landlord's notice quantifying the amount of the tenant's expense payments (the landlord's preference)?

- Where will the audit be conducted?[80]

An interesting aspect of the tenant's audit right is that neither the landlord, nor the tenant wants the right to actually be exercised. The landlord is leery of an audit, because it will burden its property management staff and potentially result in a refund of an overpayment. The tenant does not want to take the time to conduct a thorough audit of the landlord's books and records, because doing so will distract the tenant from its real focus—successfully conducting its business operations in the leased premises. The real purpose of the insertion of an audit right in a commercial lease is the creation of an *in terrorem* effect that is intended to incentivize the landlord to calculate the tenant's pass-through obligations in a careful manner and in full compliance with the negotiated provisions of the tenant's lease.

---

76. The practical reality is that landlords often err in the calculation of pass-through expenses. This is especially true in a multi-tenant project, where the landlord is faced with the prospect of trying to keep track of the intricate details of the many separate pass-through clauses negotiated by the landlord with its roster of tenants.

77. The tenant may also have certain rights at common law to review the landlord's expense records. *See e.g.,* P.V. Properties, Inc. v. Rock Creek Village Associates Limited Partnership, 549 A.2d 403 (Md. App. 1988), where a Maryland appeals court effectively held that a tenant has an implied right to audit the landlord's books. The well-represented tenant will not rely on common law rights, but will instead seek to include an express audit right in its lease. *See* Barbuti, *supra* note 71, at 7; and SENN, *supra* note 5, at 7–43.

78. Most landlords try to preclude the tenant from hiring a contingent fee auditor due to their fears that (1) the tenant will be incentivized to routinely audit the landlord's books, because it will not have to pay the contingent auditor unless the auditor actually unearths a landlord error and (2) if the auditor discovers a landlord error, it will then solicit business from all of the other tenants in the landlord's building. *See* SENN, *supra* note 5, at 7–46.

79. This issue is frequently resolved by the landlord agreeing that it will reimburse the tenant for its audit costs, only if the audit discloses an expense overpayment by the tenant of a specified magnitude (e.g., an overpayment of more than 3% of the amount that should have been charged). *See, e.g.,* Barger, *supra* note 67, at 186.

80. The landlord will usually take the position that the audit must be performed in its offices, so that it can monitor the tenant's review of its records and prevent those records from being copied and distributed to third parties. Landlords often gild the lily on this point by requiring the tenant to execute a confidentiality agreement as a condition to its review of any of the landlord's financial records.

Purpose Clause: One of the more useful tools available to tenant's counsel when negotiating the expense pass-through clause is a "purpose clause." The purpose of a purpose clause is to impose general guidelines and limitations on the landlord's calculation of its pass-through expenses. The following is a representative example of a pro-tenant purpose clause:

The following general principles will apply with respect to the calculation of Landlord's Building Expenses:

A. *Landlord will not recover the cost of any item more than once, nor will Landlord seek reimbursement from Tenant for an amount greater than the actual cost incurred by Tenant with respect to any item; it being expressly acknowledged by Landlord that it is not the intention or purpose of this section of the Lease to produce or generate an economic profit or windfall to Landlord;*

B. *Landlord will operate and maintain the Building in a fair, commercially reasonable and cost-effective manner;*

C. *Any additional costs incurred by Landlord due to its adoption after the Commencement Date of any change of policy or practice related to its operation of the Building (including, without limitation, increased premiums for new or different insurance coverages or additional costs related to any change in the frequency or level of any service provided by Landlord) will be excluded from the definition of those Building Expenses for which Tenant is financially responsible under this section;*

D. *All services rendered and all materials supplied to the Building will be of a nature and scope that are consistent with those rendered or supplied to comparable buildings and the cost of such services and materials will be of a cost no greater than those charged in arm's length transactions for comparable services or materials rendered or supplied for comparable purposes to comparable buildings; and*

E. *In determining the nature, amount and allocation of any cost to be included as a Building Expense, Landlord will comply with and respect generally accepted accounting principles, consistently applied.*

Landlords object to purpose clauses for several reasons: (1) they limit the landlord's discretion in determining how best to operate its building; (2) they foster a "lowest common denominator" approach to building operations by creating unfair and limiting comparisons with other buildings; (3) they restrict the landlord's prerogative to respond to changed market conditions by constraining its right to upgrade the building's physical plant and services; and (4) the use of soft and ambiguous terms like "fair," "commercially reasonable," and "cost-effective" creates inappropriate opportunities for the tenant to second guess the landlord's operational decisions. These are, of course, precisely the reasons why tenants want to include purpose clauses in their leases.[81] While a landlord will be hard-pressed to resist the tenant's entreaties to include clauses A (no mark-up of expenses) and E (the use of generally accepted accounting principles), it will almost certainly instruct its counsel to try to excise the remaining elements of the purpose clause.

All of the above-described tactics (i.e., exclusions, caps, audit rights and purpose clauses) have the same basic objective—limiting the amount of the tenant's additional rent obligation. Of course, any provision which limits the tenant's additional rent obligation has the automatic effect of decreasing the landlord's net operating income. When the lawyers sit down to negotiate the terms of the expense pass-through clause, they are doing battle over the one thing that is the most near and dear to their clients' hearts—real money.

D. TENANT'S PROPORTIONATE SHARE OF BUILDING EXPENSES

In a multi-tenant building, the amount of the tenant's additional rent obligation is determined by multiplying the total amount of the landlord's pass-through expenses by a percentage which represents the ***tenant's proportionate share*** of those expenses. The tenant's proportionate share is generally calculated in one of two ways—either by comparing the square footage of the tenant's leased premises to the square footage of all "rentable" space in the building or by comparing the square footage of the tenant's leased premises only to that portion of the building which is actually "leased"[82] to tenants.

The following example illustrates the consequences of determining the tenant's proportionate share under the two methods described in the preceding paragraph.

> **Example 11–6:** Landlord owns an office building that contains 100,-000 square feet of rentable space. There are only two tenants in the building—Tenant A, who leases 10,000 rentable square feet, and Tenant B, who leases 30,000 rentable square feet of rentable space. The remaining 60,000 rentable square feet of space is vacant and unleased. Landlord's total pass-through expenses in Year 1 are $500,000. Each tenant is obligated to pay its proportionate share of all pass-through expenses under a net lease arrangement.

The following table shows how financial responsibility for the payment of the pass-through expenses is allocated among Tenant A, Tenant B and Landlord.

---

81. *See* Goldman, *supra* note 73, at 25–26.

82. A similar comparative that is even less advantageous to the tenant is all "occupied space."

Responsible Party	"Rentable" Allocation	"Leased" Allocation
Tenant A	$50,000 (10%)	$125,000 (25%)
Tenant B	$150,000 (30%)	$375,000 (75%)
Landlord	$300,000 (60%)	$0 (0%)

Under the "rentable" allocation method, Landlord bears the burden of paying the expenses allocable to the building's vacant space. Under the "leased" allocation method, Tenants A and B are allocated responsibility for paying all of the building's expenses, including the expenses attributable to the vacant space. Because it is difficult for the landlord to logically maintain that the tenants should bear the economic risk of a vacancy in the building (when they have no ability to control the vacancy factor), most commercial leases calculate the tenant's proportionate share based on the "rentable" method—i.e., the tenant's proportionate share is deemed to equal the number of rentable square feet contained in the tenant's leased premises, divided by the rentable square feet contained in the entire building.[83]

There is, however, one circumstance where allocating building expenses in accordance with the "rentable" method produces an illogical result.

Example 11–7: Assume all of the same facts of Example 11–6, except that included in Landlord's pass-through expenses are $100,000 of janitorial fees, all of which are attributable to the cleaning of the space leased by Tenant A ($25,000) and Tenant B ($75,000).

If the tenants' proportionate shares were to be calculated in accordance with the preferred "rentable" method, Tenant A would pay $10,000 for janitorial fees; Tenant B would pay $30,000; and Landlord would bear the ultimate financial responsibility for the remaining $60,000 of janitorial fees—even though janitorial fees were not tied in any way to any of the building's vacant space. In that situation, a more logical result would be for each of Tenant A and Tenant B to pay the janitorial fees incurred to clean its leased space—i.e., $25,000 for Tenant A and $75,000 for Tenant B.

The desired result can be achieved by the insertion in the lease of a *gross-up clause*. A gross-up clause authorizes the landlord to increase the amount of its pass-through expenses to include those hypothetical expenses that the landlord would have incurred if the building had been fully occupied.[84] The breadth of the gross-up clause should be limited to those building expenses that fluctuate with occupancy (e.g., janitorial fees and utility charges).[85] The importance to the tenant of having a gross-up clause included in an expense stop lease is discussed in more detail in the next section of this Chapter.

---

83. *See* Zankel, *supra* note 19, at 68–70; Barger, *supra* note 67, at 167–168; Barbuti, supra note 71, at 521; and Mark S. Hennigh, *Office Leases*, in COMMERCIAL REAL ESTATE TRANSACTIONS HANDBOOK 15–39 through 15–42 (Mark A. Senn ed., 2009).

84. Gross-up clauses in office leases require the hypothetical expenses to be calculated based on a specific assumed level of occupancy—typically either 90, 95 or 100%.

85. *See* Hennigh, *Office Leases*, *supra* note 83, at 15–40.

E. ISSUES UNIQUE TO BASE YEAR EXPENSE STOP LEASE

There are certain issues that are unique to base year expense stop leases.[86] Those issues are triggered by the natural incentives and singular opportunities created under the expense stop structure for the landlord to manipulate its base year expenses to enhance its net operating income. A landlord can significantly boost the value of an expense stop lease by (1) keeping its base year expenses artificially low and (2) selecting a base year which the landlord knows will produce an expense stop that is less than the expense load included in its base rent quote.

The following example illustrates how a landlord can use a base year expense stop to its advantage.

> **Example 11–8**: It is July 2011 and Landlord and Tenant are diligently trying to finalize the terms of a base year expense stop lease for Tenant's leasing of space in Landlord's new office building (which was completed in December 2010). When its lease term begins on December 1, 2011, Tenant will be the first tenant to assume occupancy of space in Landlord's new office building. Landlord's lawyer designates the "2011 calendar year" as the lease's "base year" after speaking to Landlord's property management staff and learning that (1) Landlord's building should be fully occupied by no later than February of 2012, (2) Landlord's budgeted building expenses for a fully-occupied building are $10 prsf and (3) Landlord's actual building expenses for the calendar year 2011 should be no more than $4 prsf (because (a) the building will be vacant for most of the 2011 calendar year, (b) the real estate taxes for 2011 will not reflect the existence of an office building on Landlord's property[87] and (c) Landlord plans to defer payment of most of its expenses until January, 2012).

The end result of the lawyer's insertion in the lease of the simple statement that "the expense stop will be equal to the actual expenses incurred by Landlord during the 2011 calendar year" is that Tenant will likely begin making additional rent payments earlier than expected (potentially as early as January, 2012)[88] and at a much higher level than expected (at least $6 prsf).

---

86. A stipulated sum expense stop lease is essentially nothing more than a net lease. If the landlord sets its stipulated sum expense stop at $5 prsf and its base rent at $15 prsf, the landlord will achieve the same financial results that it would have achieved if it used a net lease arrangement with a base rent equal to $10 prsf. The only exception to that rule is where the stipulated expense stop turns out to be higher than the landlord's actual building expenses. In that rare circumstance, the landlord's net operating income will be increased to the extent of the excess of the stop over the landlord's actual expenses.

87. It is quite common in certain jurisdictions for the assessment of real estate taxes on a new building to lag at least a year behind the date on which the building is completed and placed in service.

88. Additional rent is ordinarily paid in advance based on the landlord's estimate of what its actual building expenses will be for the upcoming calendar year. *See e.g.*, §2 of the Form Office Lease ("Tenant's Proportionate Share of such Excess Expenses will be paid by Tenant in advance

Tenant's counsel could have protected its client from the indignities it suffered in Example 11–8 by adding the following provisions to the lease:

- The designation of the base year as "calendar year 2012";[89]

- A requirement that the landlord calculate its building expenses in accordance with generally accepted accounting principles; and

- A gross-up clause.

A tenant should always seek to select a base year that is as far in the future as possible.[90] Doing so will force the landlord to assume the risk that its actual building expenses will be greater than its budgeted expenses (something that Landlord in Example 11–8 did not have to do). The selection of a base year that concludes well after the commencement date of the tenant's lease term will also serve to defer the tenant's obligation to begin paying additional rent. The usual formulation of a tenant-friendly, base year definition is "the first full calendar year following the commencement date of the lease term."[91]

The insertion of a "generally accepted accounting principles" provision in the lease will prevent the landlord from inappropriately accelerating or deferring the payment of an expense from one calendar year to another. Under generally accepted accounting principles, the landlord must use the accrual method of accounting to allocate each expense (regardless when actually paid) to the period in which the services or materials giving rise to such expense were actually provided.[92]

In the context of an expense stop lease, a gross-up clause is a lease provision that requires the landlord to increase its base year expenses to include those hypothetical expenses that the landlord would have incurred in the base year if the building had been fully occupied and fully assessed for tax purposes.[93] The inclusion of a gross-up requirement in an expense stop lease serves two purposes—(1) it places the economic risk of a building vacancy on the landlord and (2) it creates a more apt "apples to apples" comparison of the expense loads incurred during the base year and later years of the lease term (often referred to in commercial leases as "comparison years"). Tenants try to buttress the "apples to apples"

---

based upon Landlord's estimate of the Excess Expenses which will be incurred during each Comparison Year during the Lease Term"). In the context of Example 11–8, this would mean that, beginning in January 2012, Landlord could charge Tenant additional rent in a monthly amount equal to \$.50 prsf (Landlord's estimate of the amount by which the 2012 expenses will exceed the 2011 base year expenses—that is, \$6 prsf—divided by 12).

89. In multi-tenant leases, the landlord has a strong motivation to select a calendar year as the base year (rather than, for example, the first 12 months of the tenant's lease term), because otherwise it might have a different base year formulation for each tenant in the building—a circumstance that would create an operational nightmare for the landlord's property manager. *See* Phil Skinner, *The Use of "Base Year" Provisions in Leases*, in Lease Negotiation Handbook 201, 204 (Edward Chupack ed., 2003).

90. *See id. at* 208–209.

91. *See* Dillman, *supra* note 37, at 43.

92. *See* Barger, *supra* note 67, at 170.

93. As is the case with respect to the net lease gross-up discussed *supra* Page 487, the gross-up clause in an expense stop lease should only cover those variable expenses that fluctuate with occupancy (e.g., janitorial fees, utility costs and the like).

comparative between the base and comparison years by requiring the landlord to retroactively gross up its base year expenses to account for any added expenses incurred in a comparison year that are attributable to a landlord decision to either upgrade the nature, scope or frequency of its building services (e.g., the addition of a concierge desk or an increase in the frequency of window washing from once a month to once a week) or otherwise change its methods of operating the building (e.g., the lowering of its property insurance deductibles, which, in turn, results in an increase in its insurance premiums).[94]

At the risk of stating the obvious, the landlord's lawyer will seldom voluntarily include the above-described, tenant-protective measures in the landlord's standard lease form. However, when braced with a need to include something in the lease to prevent the landlord from artificially keeping its base year expenses low and its comparison year expenses high (which, after all, is precisely what the landlord wants to do),[95] the landlord's lawyer will often make a few concession to partially respond to the tenant's concerns. By way of example, the lawyer representing Landlord in Example 11–8 might agree to a "GAAP accounting" clause, a gross-up of base year expenses and, if he is in a good mood, a re-set of the base year to calendar year 2012 (although a sound argument could be made that a re-set of the base year is not needed if a gross-up clause is included in the lease). Landlord's lawyer would likely strongly oppose the tenant's request that the base year gross-up be retroactively adjusted to reflect the added expenses incurred in any comparison year due to an upgrade in building services or some other change in the landlord's mode of operation (on the theory that doing so unduly limits the landlord's ability to respond to changes in the marketplace).[96] Finally, Landlord's lawyer would make the point that "what's good for the goose is good for the gander" and insist that its expenses in each comparison year also be grossed up to account for any unanticipated decline in the building's occupancy rate.[97]

HIBC Case Study—An Aggressive Use of Base Year Economics

In the early years of the HIBC project, Pizzuti was extremely concerned about its ability to control the expenses of owning and operating office

---

94. *See* Michael Pollack, *Base Year Issues: "More Is Less,"* in LEASE NEGOTIATION HANDBOOK 217 (Edward Chupack ed., 2003); and Barger, *supra* note 67, at 181–183.

95. In the simplest of terms, the landlord is advantaged if its base year expenses are low and its comparison year expenses are high. The tenant's additional rent obligation will be minimized if the reverse is true—that is the base year expenses are high and the comparison year expenses are low.

96. The landlord's view of retroactive gross-up adjustments is substantively similar to its view of the provision contained in clause C. of the purpose clause discussed *supra* Pages 485–486.

97. *See* Dillman *supra* note 37, at 59–61 (especially the last sentence of clause #8 on p. 61).

buildings in the HIBC park. Expense control is a challenge on any new development project because the landlord is forced to predict the unknown—that is, both the speed with which its project will lease up and the expense load that will be required to efficiently operate the building. Pizzuti's dilemma at the outset of the HIBC project was compounded by the fact that it had limited experience in operating suburban office buildings in Florida and, hence, did not have a raft of historical cost data that it could rely on when trying to project its HIBC building expenses.

The author's recommendation to solve Pizzuti's expense problem was simple—Pizzuti should use a net lease that passed all building expenses through to the tenant, regardless of what those expenses actually turned out to be. That solution, while theoretically sublime, was practically useless, because Orlando was an expense stop market. Pizzuti was already pushing the development envelope by introducing a product with an innovative design in a pioneering market. Trying to further change the market dynamic by introducing a new lease structure was quickly determined not to be a viable option.

Left with the singular choice of using an expense stop rent structure, I crafted a lease that sought to protect the landlord as best it could from the economic risk of an underestimation of its building expenses. The standard lease form that Pizzuti used in the marketing of its first HIBC office building contained the following provisions—(1) a gross-up of expenses only for the comparison years (and not the base year), (2) the designation of the base year as the first calendar year following completion of construction (annualized to the extent the first calendar year consisted of less than a full 12 calendar months), (3) an express reservation of the landlord's right to change its operating policies and practices at any time after the commencement date of the initial lease term and (4) the establishment of separate caps on the base year expenses for real estate taxes (e.g., $3 prsf) and electricity (e.g., $2 prsf).[98] These provisions were designed to permit Pizzuti to keep its base year expenses as low as possible and to shift the risk of the volatility of the real estate tax and electricity expenses to the tenant.

The inclusion of the above provisions in Pizzuti's standard lease form was met with less scorn than I anticipated. A few tenants insisted that wholesale changes be made to the expense stop provisions (e.g., the inclusion of a full gross-up for base year expenses and the deferral of the base year until the first full calendar year after the commencement date). However, many other tenants either accepted the provisions as is or required only minor tweaks in the lease language. As a result, Pizzuti was able to maintain a fairly stable stream of income, despite the fact that its expense projections were often significantly understated (particularly in the early years of its development efforts at HIBC).[99]

---

98. Pizzuti was extremely wary of the accuracy of its projections for real estate taxes and electricity. By including an expense stop cap for each of those expense categories, Pizzuti effectively made its lease "net" for the purpose of determining the tenant's share of real estate taxes and electricity. *See supra* note 86 for a narrative on the practical effect of a stipulated sum expense stop.

I decided to discuss Pizzuti's treatment of base year expenses in this case study to underscore two important lessons that the real estate development lawyer must learn. First, the lawyer's drafting approach needs to be adapted to fit the norms and customs followed in the market in which his client is engaged (hence, Pizzuti's use of an expense stop lease when it would have preferred to use a net lease). Second, there is nothing intrinsically wrong with a lawyer's inclusion in the lease of unusually aggressive provisions, if those provisions are designed to protect his client against real world risks. In drafting and negotiating a lease, the lawyer should not worry about whether a particularly provision is "fair," but rather whether its inclusion (or exclusion) will help the landlord achieve its stated business objective of leasing its building as soon as possible and on rental and other terms that are consistent with its business plan.

F. PROTECTING THE LANDLORD FROM THE RISK OF INFLATION

The last several sections of this Chapter concentrated on how a landlord can structure an additional rent provision to protect itself from the risk that the actual expenses of operating its building prove to be greater than its advance estimate of such expenses. Inflation is a second economic risk that the real estate development lawyer must take into consideration when drafting the rent provisions of a commercial lease.

The inflation risk is not directly linked to the operation of the landlord's specific building, but rather is a function of the overall condition of the economy. Inflation is generally defined as a loss of purchasing power due to a general increase in the cost of goods and services.[100] In the context of a commercial real estate project, inflation can impact the landlord either as a result of an increase in interest rates on real estate mortgage loans or a general increase in the cost of living in the locale where the landlord resides. The end result is that the net operating income generated from the landlord's project may remain stable (due to the appropriate use of a net lease or expense stop rent structure), but that the landlord's net operating income doesn't buy what it used to buy.

So how can a landlord protect the value of its base rent against the potential ravages of inflation? The simplest way that the landlord can try to mitigate the risk of inflation is to include a cushion in the amount of the base rent it charges its tenants (e.g., by charging base rent of $21 prsf

---

99. Pizzuti's concern over the management of its expense load lessened as it gained experience in operating office buildings in the HIBC environment. As a result, the lease provisions noted in this case study became less important over time and I was able to revise the standard HIBC lease to be a bit more user-friendly on the topic of the computation of the tenant's base year expenses. The Form Office Lease incorporates the "kinder, gentler," expense stop provisions.

100. *See supra* Chapter 3, Page 55 for a discussion of the inflation risk.

instead of $20 prsf). Market forces, however, seldom let the landlord hedge its inflation risk by overstating its base rent (and if they do, landlords view that cushion as a profit to which they are entitled and not a protection from the risk of inflation).

There are three ways that the landlord's lawyer can structure the base rent provisions to provide the landlord with a modicum of comfort that inflation will not adversely affect its net operating income.[101] All three techniques involve an increase (or **bump**) in the initial base rent payable by the tenant.

- ● *Fixed Bumps*—The most direct way that a landlord can try to deal with inflation is to establish fixed base rent increases at scheduled times during the tenant's lease term (e.g., base rent of $20 prsf in Year 1, $20.60 prsf in Year 2, $21.22 in Year 3, etc.). This approach requires the parties to guess what the rate of inflation will be during the lease term. The fixed bump strategy will work from the landlord's perspective only if the actual rate of inflation is less than the amount of the negotiated rent bump (i.e., 3% per year in the above example).

- ● *Indexed Bumps*—A technique commonly used to try to combat the risk of inflation is to periodically adjust the tenant's base rent to reflect increases in a cost of living index, such as the Consumer Price Index. The use of indexed bumps is favored by many practitioners because the bumps are not merely the parties' guess of future inflation (as is the case with fixed bumps), but rather are tied to an objective measure of inflation. The only negative associated with the use of such cost of living adjustments is that there is no published index that accurately measures inflation in the commercial real estate industry.[102]

- ● *Market Rent Bumps*—Adjusting base rent periodically to reflect the change in market rents is viewed by some practitioners as theoretically the best way to deal with the prospect of inflation. Under the market rate method, the parties agree that the base rent will be reset at a specific point during the lease term to reflect the then fair rental value of comparable properties in the market in which the building is located. The fair rental value is customarily determined by an appraiser or real estate broker designated in the lease. The problems associated with market rent bumps are three-fold—(1) the fair rental value of a property may increase for reasons other than inflation (e.g., for external reasons of supply and demand), (2) the process of appraising the fair rental value of a leased space is time-consuming and costly and (3) the appraisal of a leasehold interest is more art than science and can produce an

---

101. *See* Edward Chupack, *Rent*, in Lease Negotiation Handbook 189, 195 (Edward Chupack ed., 2003); and David Geltner, Norman G. Miller, Jim Clayton and Piet Eichholtz, Commercial Real Estate Analysis and Investment 809–811 (2nd ed. 2006).

102. *See* Senn, *supra* note 5, at 6–11; and Dillman, *supra* note 37, at 63.

unexpected result that may be extremely prejudicial to either the tenant or the landlord. For these reasons, market rent bumps are seldom used to adjust base rent during the initial term of a commercial space lease.[103]

Landlords generally take the position that base rent will never decrease during the lease term, but may increase based on fixed, indexed or market rent adjustments. In order to counter the economic uncertainty associated with indexed or market rent bumps, counsel for the tenant will frequently request (and often receive) the establishment of a ceiling on the amount of any base rent adjustment (e.g., an increase of not more than 3% in any one year).

G. PERCENTAGE RENT

The discussion thus far in this Chapter has centered on the office tenant's obligation to pay base and additional rent. A third type of rent that is peculiar to retail leases is ***percentage rent***. While the topic of percentage rent is far too complex to be fully covered in this Chapter, a discussion of rent would not be complete without at least a passing nod being given to the nature and scope of a retail tenant's percentage rent obligation.

Percentage rent is the portion of a retail tenant's rent obligation that is equal to a percentage of the ***gross sales*** produced from the tenant's conduct of retail operations in its leased store. The concept of percentage rent was created to ease the fixed rental burden of a retail tenant when it first opens its store.[104] A retail lease involves a higher degree of site-specific risk than does an office or warehouse lease, because the success of the retail tenant's business operations is as dependent on the location and quality of the landlord's retail center as it is on the sustainability of the tenant's business model.

For this reason, the retail landlord is often willing to reduce the tenant's fixed rent obligation[105] in exchange for the tenant's commitment to pay the landlord a percentage of its store revenues. The landlord does so not because it is a kind and caring soul, but because it hopes that, if the tenant's store is profitable, it will be able to recoup the entirety of the fixed rent discount AND MORE from the tenant's payment of percentage rent. Percentage rent is, therefore, basically a risk-reward allocation model, where the landlord takes a little more risk on the front-end of the deal in exchange for its potential receipt of an above market rate of return on the backside of the lease transaction.

---

103. Bumping the rent to a market rate comparable is, however, a technique that is commonly used to set the base rent payable by a tenant following the exercise of its option to extend its lease term. *See infra* Pages 525–526.

104. *See* SENN, *supra* note 5, at 6–29.

105. A retail tenant's additional rent obligation (commonly referred to in the retail leasing industry as "common area maintenance" or "CAM" charges) is generally unaffected by its agreement to pay percentage rent.

The following is a fairly typical phrasing of the retail tenant's percentage rent requirement:

In addition to its payment of Base Rent and Additional Rent, Tenant will pay Percentage Rent in an amount equal to the product of (a) the amount by which the Tenant's Gross Sales exceeds its Breakpoint, multiplied by (b) ____%.

The calculation of the tenant's percentage rent obligation requires the landlord and the tenant to agree on the answers to three key questions.

- What revenues are included in the tenant's **gross sales**?[106]

- What is the tenant's **breakpoint**?

- What is the **percentage** used to compute the tenant's percentage rent?

The tenor of the negotiations over the revenues that are included in and excluded from the tenant's **gross sales** is similar to that of the negotiations concerning the categories of expenses that can be passed through to the office tenant as additional rent—in other words, they are very detailed, nuanced and frequently strident. The landlord's objective is to define gross sales as broadly as possible to include every single penny of revenue that ever touches the tenant's store in any way. The tenant, on the other hand, will strive to limit the revenues included under the gross sales umbrella by specifically excluding any receipts that do not produce a direct profit to the tenant (e.g., sales taxes, vending machine receipts, lottery ticket sales, employee discount sales, returned merchandise and the like).[107] An issue that is the subject of much current debate is whether internet sales should be included in gross sales.[108]

A tenant's **breakpoint** is the maximum level of gross sales that the tenant can attain without having to pay percentage rent. In this respect the breakpoint is akin to the expense stop, in that the tenant will only be required to pay percentage rent if the gross sales produced from its store operations exceed the breakpoint. The tenant's breakpoint can be any number selected by the parties, but is most commonly set at what is called a **natural breakpoint**.[109] A natural breakpoint is equal to the volume of gross sales determined by dividing the tenant's base rent by the percentage used to calculate its percentage rent. Therefore, the natural break-

---

106. Net income is seldom used as the basis for a percentage rent clause for a couple of reasons—(1) the calculation of net income can be manipulated by the tenant to produce little or no income even though the tenant's store is very successful and (2) the use of a net income standard to compute the tenant's rent obligation serves as a disincentive for it to efficiently operate its business in the leased premises. *See* SENN, *supra* note 5, at 6–30.

107. *See* ZANKEL, *supra* note 19, at 52–53.

108. *See generally* Julian Rackow, *Implications of E–Commerce for Commercial and Retail Leasing Transactions*, in ALI–ABA COURSE OF STUDY MATERIALS, COMMERCIAL REAL ESTATE LEASES: SELECTED ISSUES IN DRAFTING AND NEGOTIATING IN CURRENT MARKETS, Course No. SL–017, 1169 (June 2006); and John C. Murray, *Percentage Rent Provisions in Shopping Center Leases: A Changing World?*, 35 REAL PROPERTY, PROBATE AND TRUST JOURNAL 731, 747–752 (Winter 2001).

109. An "unnatural breakpoint" is any threshold sales amount other than the natural breakpoint.

point of a tenant that pays base rent of $200,000 per year and percentage rent at a 4% rate will be $5 million.[110]

The final component of the percentage rent calculation is the percentage that will be used as a multiplier against the tenant's excess gross sales. The landlord obviously wants to select a high percentage number, while the tenant prefers a low percentage. A useful rule of thumb to keep in mind when negotiating the economic terms of a retail lease is that high volume/low profit margin stores (e.g., a grocery store) usually merit a low percentage, while low volume/high profit margin stores (e.g., a jewelry shop) typically draw a high percentage.[111]

In an effort to bolster the prospects for its receipt of substantial percentage rent payments, the retail landlord will usually include in its lease a series of provisions that are designed to maximize the level of gross sales produced in its center by dictating the manner in which the center's tenants will conduct their retail businesses. Restrictive use clauses, continuous operation covenants and radius restrictions are examples of provisions that are intended to augment the landlord's receipt of percentage rent. Those provisions and other clauses that are unique to a retail lease are discussed in greater detail later in this Chapter.[112]

H. PAYMENT OF RENT. *(§§2 and 3)*

The lease must also cover the following practical considerations associated with the tenant's rent obligations.

- When will the tenant's base rent be paid? (Answer—usually monthly on or before the first day of each calendar month during the lease term).[113]

- How should tenant's rent be paid? (Answer—either in cash or by an electronic wire transfer).

- Where should the tenant's rent payments be sent? (Answer—usually to the landlord's primary mailing address or, if the payment is to be made electronically, to a bank account designated in the lease).

---

110. The concept of a natural breakpoint was originally linked to the level of sales at which the tenant would be able to "break even" in its store operations. It is now just a mathematical calculation—although one that is used in most retail leases. *See* ZANKEL, *supra* note 19, at 53.

111. *See* SENN, *supra* note 5, at 6–46 and 6–47, for a table showing the range of percentage rental rates commonly paid by various types of retail stores.

112. *See infra* Pages 510–515.

113. The landlord typically requires the tenant to pay additional rent monthly in advance based on the landlord's estimate of its building expenses for the then current year. This payment method allows the landlord to make an approximate match between the date on which a particular expense is incurred and the date on which the landlord receives tenant's reimbursement—thus bowing to the time value of money concepts discussed in more detail *supra* Chapter 3, Pages 54–55. If additional rent is paid in advance, the lease should include a clause providing for an annual reconciliation of the tenant's estimated payments and the actual amount of the pass-through expenses that the tenant is responsible for under the terms of the lease. *See e.g.*, the second paragraph of §2 of the Form Office Lease. The tenant's lawyer should also consider limiting in some manner the amount of the tenant's advance expense payments—e.g., no more than 103% of its actual expense payments in the prior calendar year.

- What happens if the tenant does not pay its rent by the due date specified in the lease? (Answer—typically the tenant will be charged a late fee and interest will accrue on the delinquent rent).

- Will the tenant be entitled to withhold any portion of its rent if it is dissatisfied with the landlord's performance of its lease obligations? (Answer—"no way" for the landlord and "yes way" for the tenant).[114]

Section 3 of the Form Office Lease is a representative sample of a pro-landlord, rent payment clause.

X. USE. (*¶H of Lease Summary, §§4–7 and 10, Exhibits C and E*)

The prior sections of this Chapter centered on three fundamental themes that drive the drafting and negotiation of a commercial lease—(1) the *SPACE* that is leased by the tenant, (2) the *TERM* of tenant's leasing of the designated space and (3) the *RENT* that the tenant must pay to the landlord. The fourth leg of the leasing table relates to the following provisions of the lease that seek to regulate the tenant's *USE* of its leased space.

- The general use clause;
- The compliance with laws clause;
- The alterations clause;
- The maintenance clause; and
- The building services clause.

The shared objective of the landlord and tenant when negotiating all of the above clauses is to clearly delineate what the tenant can and cannot do in its leased premises and what, if anything, the landlord must do to enable the tenant's use of its leased premises. The landlord wants the use provisions to be structured in a fashion that will permit it to control its building expenses and preserve and enhance the value of its project. The tenant's objective is to negotiate a set of use provisions that will allow it to operate its business in a manner which is fully consistent with its business plan—both as that plan exists at the outset of the lease term and as it evolves over the course of the lease term in response to market conditions and changes in the tenant's business model.

A. GENERAL USE CLAUSE. (*¶H of Lease Summary and §6*)

It is essential that the lease articulate the parties' understanding of the purpose(s) for which the tenant may use the leased premises.[115] The

---

114. *See infra* Pages 509–510 for a discussion of rent offsets.

115. Absent a more limiting clause in the lease, a tenant may use the leased premises for any purpose that is not illegal. *See* SENN, *supra* note 5, at 11–5; and FRIEDMAN, *supra* note 8, at 27–6.

tenant's use may be prescribed in one of two ways—in a (1) *permissive use clause* or (2) a *restrictive use clause*

A permissive use clause empowers the tenant to use the leased premises for a specified purpose, but does not expressly limit the tenant's use to the specified purpose. An example of a permissive use clause is "tenant *MAY* use the leased premises for the operation of an accounting firm." The use of a permissive lease clause is favored by the tenant because it accomplishes the tenant's two-pronged goal of blessing its present, intended use and preserving its option to change its use in the future.

A restrictive use clause limits the tenant's use to the purpose specified in the lease. The following is an example of a restrictive use clause— "tenant *WILL* use the leased premises for the operation of an accounting firm and *FOR NO OTHER PURPOSE.*" Landlords prefer a restrictive use clause because it permits them to retain control over the manner in which their projects will be used by their tenants.

Given the opportunity, the courts will interpret a use clause as being permissive and not restrictive.[116] Therefore, to the extent the landlord prevails in its argument that the lease should contain a restrictive clause, it is imperative that its lawyer draft the tenant's use clause in a crisp and unambiguous fashion to make it clear that the leased premises will be used "solely" in the specified manner "and for no other purpose, without the express written consent of the landlord." Clauses incorporating that level of clarity will be enforced by the courts as restricting (and not just permitting) the nature of the tenant's use of the leased premises.[117]

The level of control afforded the landlord by its adoption of a restrictive use clause is dependent on the way in which the tenant's specific use of the leased premises is described. Landlord's counsel should endeavor to define the tenant's permitted use in as narrow a fashion as is reasonably practicable given the nature of the landlord's project. Tenant's counsel, conversely, will lobby in favor of a general description of the tenant's use of the leased premises in order to maximize the tenant's operational flexibility and provide it with a readily executable exit strategy.[118]

The following is a continuum of the ways in which an office tenant's use of its leased premises can be described in the lease (listed in the order of the tenant's preference):

---

116. *See* SENN *supra* note 5, at 11–5 through 11–7; and FRIEDMAN, *supra* note 8, at 27–9 through 27–14. By way of example of the courts' general inclination to interpret use clauses in favor of the tenant, an Ohio court ruled that a provision that said that "the leased premises may be used for the purposes of . . . a supermarket" permitted a successor tenant to use the leased premises as a karate school. *See* Juhasz v. Quik Shops, Inc., 55 Ohio App.2d 51 (1977). A lease stating that the leased premises were "to be used primarily as an auto dealership" was construed by a South Carolina court as authorizing the use of the leased premises as a saloon. *See* Chassereau v. Stuckey, 288 S.C. 368 (Ct. App. 1986).

117. *See* SENN *supra* note 5, at 11–7; and FRIEDMAN, *supra* note 8, at 27–8.

118. *See infra* Pages 530–532, for a description of the negative impact that a narrowly-defined, restrictive use clause can have on the tenant's ability to transfer its leasehold interest to a third party.

- Any lawful use;

- General office use;

- Use as a law firm;

- Use as a patent law firm; and

- Use as a patent law firm with no more than seven practicing attorneys and five support staff.

The first choice provides the landlord virtually no control over the tenant's ultimate use of the leased premises, while the last choice probably provides the office landlord more control than it realistically needs.[119] The landlord should determine, in consultation with its lawyer, just how much control it needs over the activities of its tenants. For example, does the landlord of a suburban office building really care if a tenant uses its space for the purpose of operating a law firm rather than an advertising agency? Once the landlord determines precisely how restrictive it needs to be in describing the tenant's use, it can then turn its lawyer loose in an effort to try to get even more control than it actually needs (on the theory that control is always a good thing, even if it is not actually exercised to its fullest extent).

Although a landlord may not really care if a particular office suite is used as a law firm or an advertising agency, it may not want to see the space used as a call center, governmental office, ticket brokerage or other use that might unduly tax the building's systems or potentially detract from the quality of the building's tenant roster—all of which would presumably be permitted under a clause restricting the tenant's use to "general office use." A landlord whose lease broadly describes the tenant's permitted use (e.g., "general office use") can exert additional control over the tenant's use of the leased premises by including in the lease a listing of those uses that are expressly prohibited in the leased premises. The "prohibited uses" can be specifically listed (e.g., "the operation of call center") or described in a more generic fashion (e.g., "any use which could unreasonably interfere with the business operations of other tenants in the building or which could adversely affect the character or reputation of the building as a Class A office building").[120]

---

119. The retail landlord has a much greater interest than does the office landlord in restricting each of its tenants to a tightly defined use. *See infra* Pages 511–512, for a discussion of the unique use provisions found in a retail lease.

120. Landlords often try to impose additional use restrictions by incorporating into the lease a set of building rules and regulations that delineate specific "dos and don'ts" associated with their tenants' business operations—e.g., prohibitions on smoking or the installation of vending machines in the leased premises. *See e.g.,* §6 and Exhibit C of the Form Office Lease. The tenant and its lawyers should carefully review the rules and regulations to determine whether they present any obstacle to the tenant's operation of its business in the contemplated fashion. The tenant's lawyer should also ask for written confirmation that the rules and regulations will not be modified without the tenant's consent and that the landlord will enforce the rules and regulations in a consistent manner as to all of the building's tenants—two propositions that will run directly counter to the provisions contained in most landlord-authored rules and regulations (including the Form Office Lease).

A tenant faced with what it believes is an unduly restrictive description of its permitted use can attempt to ease the restriction by introducing into the lease the concept of "incidental uses." By way of example, if the landlord's initial draft of the lease provides that the "tenant will use the leased premises solely for the operation of a law firm," tenant's counsel might suggest that the phrase "and all other incidental or related uses" be added at the end of the landlord's restrictive use clause. The incorporation of such "incidental use" language can provide the tenant with additional flexibility should it decide at a later time to add to or change the nature of its business operations (e.g., the law firm's decision to open a title insurance agency in the leased premises). To the extent the tenant is aware of a potential change in its business model, it should pass that information onto its counsel, so that the lawyer can try to enhance the tenant's position under the lease by adding the following language at the end of the incidental use clause mentioned above—"including, without limitation, the following uses . . ."[121]

B. COMPLIANCE WITH LAWS CLAUSE. *(§7)*

The compliance with laws clause deals with the issue of who is responsible for making sure that the condition of the leased premises complies with all applicable legal requirements. The legal requirements that are the proper subject of this clause are not those rules that govern the licenses and governmental approvals that a tenant is required to secure as a precursor to its conduct of its business in the leased premises (clearly a tenant responsibility), nor are they the building codes applicable to the landlord's initial construction of its building (clearly a landlord responsibility). Rather the crux of the issue at this stage of the lease negotiations is who is responsible to make those repairs and improvements to the leased premises that are required to be made as a result of a specific governmental requirement—e.g., the Americans with Disabilities Act,[122] the Comprehensive Environmental Response, Compensation, and Liability Act[123] or a state statute imposing indoor air quality standards. Because the dollars at stake can be substantial (easily running into six or seven figures), the compliance with laws clause is one of the most heavily negotiated provisions of a commercial lease.[124]

The starting point in the negotiation is usually a clause in landlord's standard lease form that purports to place the obligation on the tenant to comply with all laws and other governmental requirements affecting the leased premises in any way (specifically including the obligation to make

---

121. *See e.g.,* SENN, *supra* note 5, at 11–14.

122. *See* 42 U.S.C. §§ 12101–12213 (2010).

123. *See* 42 U.S.C. §§ 9601–9675 (2010). For a provision attempting to allocate the responsibility for compliance with environmental laws, *see e.g.,* §17 of the Form Office Lease. *See also* the extensive discussions of the environmental compliance risk in SENN, *supra* note 5, at 12–15 through 12–39; and Dillman, *supra* note 37, at 125–129.

124. *See generally* Hennigh, *Office Leases, supra* note 83, at 15–47 through 15–50; ZANKEL, *supra* note 19, at 84–85; and SENN, *supra* note 5, at Chapter 12.

any repairs or improvements mandated by such governmental require-ments). The tenant's knee-jerk response when it reads that clause is to point out to the landlord that "you own the building, so it's your problem not mine." The landlord's equally pithy response is "if it has to do with the leased premises, it is your problem."

The resolution of the landlord-tenant conflict over the proper alloca-tion of the legal compliance risk requires the negotiators to address the following three questions:

- Was the law enacted before or after the lease was executed?

- Is the application of the legal requirement triggered by the tenant's unique use of the leased premises (or is the legal requirement generally applicable to all owners of real property)?

- Does the required legal compliance require the construction of permanent improvements that can be re-used by the landlord after the expiration of the tenant's lease term?

A well-represented tenant with bargaining power relatively equal to that of the landlord should be able to get the landlord to agree to assume responsibility for making those improvements to the leased premises that satisfy all of the following requirements: (1) the repairs or improvements are attributable to the imposition of a legal requirement that was in place prior to the tenant's execution of the lease; (2) the legal requirement is generally applicable to all owners of real property; and (3) the improve-ments are permanent, will increase the value of the landlord's property, and will be re-usable by the landlord after the expiration of the tenant's lease. Similarly, the landlord is almost always successful in its efforts to place the obligation on the tenant to make those repairs and improve-ments to the leased premises, which are directly tied to the tenant's unique use of the leased premises, and which are required as a result of the enactment of a governmental requirement after the parties' execution of the lease.

The normative allocation of risks described in the preceding para-graph leaves an ample stable of legal compliance risks which remain to be negotiated by the landlord and the tenant—principally who is responsible for making those repairs and improvements to the leased premises that (1) are required as a result of the enactment of a law after the date on which the lease was executed and (2) are not directly linked to the tenant's unique use of the leased premises? The following are tactics that can be employed by the tenant's lawyer (sometimes successfully) in an effort to allocate some of the unresolved risks back to the landlord:[125]

- Requiring the landlord to provide the tenant with a representation confirming that the building was in full compliance with all laws in place as of the date of the execution of the lease;

- Limiting the tenant's obligation to the making of non-structural improvements that exclusively serve the leased premises;

---

125. *See* Hennigh, *Office Leases, supra* note 83, at 15–48 through 15–50

- Placing a cap on the amount of any costs that the tenant has to incur in making improvements to the leased premises;

- Granting the tenant a right to terminate its lease if the costs of the required legal compliance exceed a specific number or if the required compliance takes place in the last year of the tenant's lease term; or

- Requiring the landlord to amortize the cost of any required improvement over the useful life of such improvement (determined in accordance with generally accepted accounting principles),with the tenant then assuming responsibility for the payment of only that portion of the amortized cost that is allocable to its lease term.

As always, the outcome of this negotiation will be dependent on the knowledge and guile of the competing lawyers and the relative bargaining strength of their respective clients. The landlord's lawyer will, however, have the upper hand in the negotiations if the tenant occupies the entirety or a substantial part of the landlord's building and if the initial term of the tenant's lease is ten years or more.

C. ALTERATIONS CLAUSE. *(§10)*

At some point during the lease term, the tenant may have a desire to alter the physical condition of the leased premises to better suit the needs of its business operations. For example, a tenant might want to replace the carpeting in its reception area with granite tiles, build a new conference room or install a new technological advance throughout the leased premises. The issue addressed in the alterations clause is whether and under what circumstances the tenant may make such alterations.

The landlord would prefer to retain the right to approve each and every alteration that the tenant proposes to make to the leased premises. The landlord does not want the tenant to have the right to make any alteration that could adversely impact the value of the landlord's reversionary interest in the building—by either affecting the structural integrity of the building or hindering the landlord's ability to attract and retain other building tenants.

For this reason, most landlord lease forms contain an absolute prohibition against the tenant making any alterations to the leased premises. A standard tenant-sponsored incursion on that prohibition permits the tenant to make non-structural alterations up to a fixed dollar limit (e.g., $10,000).[126]

The tenant will next ask the landlord to agree that it will not unreasonably withhold its consent to any tenant-requested alteration. While most landlords (at least the reasonable ones) will accede to that request, they often do so only with the following attached conditions:[127]

---

126. *See e.g.*, the definition of "minor alterations" in §6 of the Form Office Lease.

127. *See generally* SENN, *supra* note 5, at 20–11 through 20–13; and David L. Grobart, *Alterations*, in LEASE NEGOTIATION HANDBOOK 349 (Edward Chupack ed., 2003)

- The tenant will be required to provide the landlord with complete plans and specifications depicting the proposed alteration;

- The landlord will retain the right to either construct the alteration itself or approve the contractor selected by the tenant to perform the alteration work;

- The tenant will be obligated to promptly pay all costs of constructing the alteration and to immediately discharge any mechanics' lien filed against landlord's reversionary interest in the building;[128] and

- If requested by landlord, the tenant will remove the alteration at the end of the lease term and repair any damage to the leased premises caused by such removal.

D. MAINTENANCE CLAUSE. *(§5)*

The landlord and the tenant share a goal of wanting the leased premises to be maintained throughout the lease term in the same physical and operating conditions that existed as of the commencement date of the lease term. The landlord wants the leased premises to be properly maintained to preserve the value of its reversionary interest in the leased premises, while the tenant is focused on making sure that the leased premises are maintained in a manner that is conducive to the effective conduct of its business. Given the fact that the landlord and the tenant share the same overall objective, the principal issue to be addressed in the maintenance clause is not what has to be done, but who has to do it.

Unfortunately, the maintenance clause is one of the least understood provisions of a commercial lease. The mistake that most practitioners make when drafting the clause is that they try to allocate responsibility for maintaining the leased premises, without first accurately identifying the various components of the maintenance obligation. There are two separate aspects of the maintenance obligation that a lawyer needs to take into consideration when negotiating the maintenance clause—specifically (1) what functions have to be performed to properly maintain the leased premises, and (2) what elements of the leased premises have to be so maintained?

The maintenance obligation actually consists of three distinct functions:[129]

- *Maintenance*—keeping the leased premises in the same approximate condition that existed as of the commencement date, subject to ordinary wear and tear;

- *Repair*—fixing what is broken in the leased premises; and

- *Replacement*—improving the condition of the leased premises by removing something that is irretrievably broken and substituting in its place something that is new or better.

---

128. *See e.g.*, §11 of the Form Office Lease.

129. *See* Hennigh, *Office Leases*, *supra* note 83, at 15–52 and 15–53.

The maintenance function is the least costly to perform, while the replacement function is the most costly.

Once the component functions of the maintenance obligation are identified, the next thing that the practitioner must do is to prepare a listing of what needs to be maintained and, potentially, repaired and replaced. The following are the subjects of the maintenance obligation:

- **Common areas**—including both building common areas (e.g., lobbies, hallways, elevators and other building-wide mechanical systems) and site common areas (e.g., landscaping, parking lots and sidewalks); and

- **Leased premises**—including both base building improvements (e.g., floors, windows, load-bearing walls and mechanical systems located in the leased premises) and tenant improvements (e.g., carpeting, painted surfaces, light fixtures and demising walls); and

- **Tenant's furniture, fixtures and equipment** (e.g., computers, copiers and conference room furniture).

Once all of the functions and subjects of the maintenance obligation are properly identified, the lawyers representing the landlord and tenant should then allocate responsibility for the performance of each of the functions (maintenance, repair and replacement) as to each component of the tenant's leased space (the common areas, the base building and tenant improvements, and FF&E). The key to the preparation and negotiation of a workable maintenance clause is for the lawyers to "close all the gaps"[130] and clearly and thoughtfully assign responsibility for the performance of each component of the maintenance obligation to either the landlord or the tenant.

In the context of a multi-tenant office lease, the landlord is usually allocated the responsibility for maintaining, repairing and replacing all of the building's common areas, as well as the base building improvements located within the leased premises.[131] The tenant customarily assumes responsibility for maintaining, repairing and replacing its furniture, fixtures and equipment. The allocation of responsibility for the maintenance, repair and replacement of the tenant improvements located within the leased premises is where the action is really at during the negotiation of the maintenance clause. Factors that will influence the outcome of that negotiation are the type of the project (with the tenant being more likely to assume all or a portion of the maintenance obligation in a warehouse or single tenant lease) and the length of the tenant's lease term (with the tenant being more likely to assume responsibility for the maintenance obligation in a long-term lease).

Finally, the practitioner needs to keep in mind that the allocation to the landlord of responsibility for performing a particular maintenance obligation does not necessarily mean that the landlord will bear the

---

130. *See* SENN, *supra* note 5, at 19–11.

131. *See* Hennigh, *Office Leases, supra* note 84, at 15–53.

financial responsibility for paying the costs associated with such perform-ance. As noted earlier in this Chapter, it is quite common for the landlord to try to pass through to its tenants some or all of the costs it incurs in connection with the performance of its maintenance obligation. If the landlord opts to pass through some of those expenses to its tenants, landlord's counsel should be careful to eliminate any unintended inference that the performance provisions of the maintenance clause somehow override any inconsistent financial provision of the expense pass-through clause.

E. BUILDING SERVICES CLAUSE. *(§4)*

In a multi-tenant office building,[132] the landlord customarily provides most, if not all, of the building services that the tenant requires to conduct its business in the leased premises. The basic services typically required by the tenant include: utilities (water, electricity and heating, ventilating and air conditioning services);[133] elevator service; window washing; parking; landscaping and snow removal; trash pick-up; and janitorial services. Landlords of high-end office buildings are increasingly providing the following additional services and facilities to entice new tenants to choose their buildings—24/7 security;[134] concierge services; valet parking; state of the art video conferencing and telecommunication services; and on-site fitness centers.

The following are three issues that the lawyers must resolve when drafting and negotiating the building services clause.

- What services is the landlord required to furnish to the tenant?
- How will the tenant pay for the cost of such services?
- What are the consequences of an interruption in the provision of any such service?

The answers provided by counsel for the landlord and the tenant are, understandably, quite different. The divergent positions of the landlord and tenant, as well as some commonly adopted compromises, are discussed below.

1. List of Building Services

The required provision of any service has two consequences to the landlord—(1) it increases the landlord's building expenses and (2) it

---

132. In warehouse and single tenant, office leases, the tenant often self-performs or directly contracts with third party vendors for the provision of many of the required building services. In retail leases, the tenant generally "requires less from the landlord with regard to the premises but more with regard to the maintenance and control of the common areas." *See* SENN, *supra* note 5, at 17–3.

133. Office tenants are generally responsible for handling their own telephone and other telecommunication services. *See e.g.*, §4 of the Form Office Lease.

134. Some office landlords try to avoid acknowledging in the lease that they have any obligation to provide security to the tenants out of a concern that doing so will subject them to liability if a tenant is attacked or its property is stolen. *See* Hennigh, *Office Leases, supra* note 83, at 15–11.

subjects the landlord to potential liability for failing to provide the service to its tenants. As a result, the landlord's lawyer will try to minimize the number of the services its client is required to provide to its tenants and to negate any exacting standard related to the nature, scope or frequency of the listed services. The landlord's lawyer will seek to accomplish this goal by putting together a fairly skimpy, but exclusive listing of the general building services that the landlord is required to furnish to its tenants (e.g., electricity, water, HVAC, elevator and janitorial services) and then stating that all of the listed services "will be furnished as required for the use of the leased premises for general office purposes during normal business hours."[135]

The lawyer representing the tenant will have a decidedly different agenda concerning the description of the building services that the landlord is required to provide to the tenant. First, the tenant's lawyer will seek to incorporate into the lease a very long and non-exclusive list of the specific services that the landlord must provide to the leased premises. Tenant's lawyer will try to conclude that list with a catch-all concerning the landlord's provision of "all such other services that are reasonably required to permit the tenant's efficient operation of its business in the leased premises." Tenant's counsel will then do its best to introduce the landlord to the reality of a 24/7 economy by asking the landlord's lawyer to strike the "normal business hours" limitation from the building services clause. Finally, tenant's counsel will attempt to insert into the building services clause specific performance standards for each of the listed building services—e.g., the provision of HVAC service to continuously maintain a specific range of temperatures inside the leased premises regardless of the outside temperature.[136]

Well-represented landlords and tenants usually end up with a lease that describes with reasonable specificity the nature, scope and frequency of those services that the landlord intends to furnish to all of its tenants during the building's normal business hours.[137] It is then left to the best graces of the lawyers for the landlord and the tenant to determine whether the landlord's standard list of building services is acceptable to the tenant and, if not, what, if anything will be done to rectify that situation. If the landlord is capable of ramping up or otherwise changing its building operations to satisfy the tenant's needs, the next question that

---

135. *See e.g.*, the first sentence of §4 of the Form Office Lease. The specific designation of what constitutes "normal business hours" will vary by building.

136. *See e.g.*, LAWRENCE EISENBERG, JONATHON MECHANIC AND DAVID ALAN RICHARDS, THE OFFICIAL COMMERCIAL OFFICE LEASE HANDBOOK 263 (2003). Commercial office leases often include specific performance standards for the provision of electrical and janitorial services. *See* John S. Hollyfield, *Landlord's Services*, in ALI–ABA COURSE OF STUDY MATERIALS, COMMERCIAL REAL ESTATE LEASES: SELECTED ISSUES IN DRAFTING AND NEGOTIATING IN CURRENT MARKETS, Course No. SL–017, 189, 191 (June 2006).

137. The landlord should make sure that the delineated levels of building services are consistent with (1) the building's capabilities (e.g., the building is designed to provide electrical service to meet the watts per square foot standard specified in the lease) and (2) the levels of building services contemplated in the landlord's lease quotes and operating budget for the building. *See* EISENBERG, *supra* note 136, at 269.

arises is who will bear the economic burden of paying the increased costs associated with such change—a topic that is addressed under the next subheading.

2. Allocation of Cost of Providing Building Services

The tenant can pay its share of the landlord's cost of furnishing the required building services in one of three ways—either as (1) part of its base rent obligation, (2) an expense pass-through or (3) a direct payment to the vendor that provides the service. The determination of which of these methods will be employed as to a particular cost is generally resolved as part of the rent structure negotiation discussed earlier in this Chapter.[138]

The key economic issue that must be resolved as part of the independent negotiations over the content of the building services clause is who will pay the increased costs triggered by the tenant's excessive use of a particular building service. For this purpose, a tenant's use of a building service will be viewed by the landlord as being "excessive" if such use is greater than the baseline use projected by the landlord for its general tenant population. The two most common examples of a tenant's excessive use of a building service are (1) the tenant's consumption during normal business hours of a higher level of service than that consumed by the landlord's remaining roster of tenants (e.g., the tenant's excessive use of electricity due to its operation of a computer help desk in its leased premises) and (2) the tenant's required use of a service outside of the normal business hours for the building (e.g., the tenant's operation of a call center on a 24/7 cycle).[139]

Conceptually, most landlords and tenants will agree that the increased costs associated with a tenant's excessive use of a building service should be paid by the tenant. It is, however, much tougher for them to reach a consensus on either the definition of an excessive use or the calculation of the increased costs attributable to the excessive use. The landlord wants to retain wide latitude to identify the existence of an excessive use and then measure the amount of the surcharge that it will impose on the tenant to reimburse the landlord for the increased costs produced by the tenant's excessive use.[140] The tenant, on the other hand, wants the excessive use concept to be very narrowly defined and for the related costs to be objectively measured to prevent the landlord from profiting from the service surcharge imposed on the tenant. Counsel for

---

138. *See supra* Pages 476–481.

139. *See* SENN, *supra* note 5, at 9–8 through 9–10, for an excellent discussion of the options available to measure the tenant's use of electricity in its leased premises. The best way to deal with the tenant's excessive use of electricity is to install a separate meter in the tenant's leased premises that will measure the exact amount of the tenant's actual electrical consumption. The tenant can then pay its electricity costs directly to the electricity provider. If the installation of a separate electrical meter is not an option (and, for a variety of technical reasons, it often is not), then the landlord and the tenant will be left with the challenge of negotiating an excessive use provision that balances the competing interests discussed in the next paragraph of this section.

140. *See e.g.*, the first sentence of the second paragraph of §4 of the Form Office Lease.

the landlord and the tenant will seek to bridge the gap between their clients' diametrically opposite positions by (1) agreeing on a compromised definition of "normal business hours" (something greater than "9 to 5" and less than "24/7"), (2) specifying performance standards for each building service that the landlord is required to provide to the tenant (thereby providing an objective benchmark to identify the tenant's excessive use) and (3) stipulating a fixed amount of the surcharge that the landlord can impose for the tenant's excessive use of certain building services (e.g., $__ per hour for after-hours HVAC service provided to the tenant's leased premises).[141]

3. Interruption of Service

The final question that counsel for the landlord and the tenant must answer as part of their negotiation of the building services clause is what happens if the provision of a required building service is interrupted for some reason. What, if anything, can the tenant do to protect itself from the burden placed on its business operations due to the elevators being out of service for an hour on a Tuesday morning, the parking garage being closed for two weeks while the landlord renovates the parking decks, or electric service being cut off to the building for a week due to a windstorm? The remainder of this section will discuss the common law and contractual remedies available to the tenant to deal with such interruptions of service.

Based on the common law doctrine of independent covenants that is followed in the majority of states, a tenant's sole remedy for the interruption of a required service is the filing of a damages action against the landlord. Absent a specific provision in the lease to the contrary, the tenant does not have the right to suspend its rent obligation or terminate its lease, unless the interruption of service is so severe that it amounts to a constructive eviction of the tenant's right to occupy and use the leased premises.

The common law doctrine of constructive eviction affords only limited protection to a tenant faced with the interruption of a required building service. In order to establish that an interruption of service has resulted in the tenant's constructive eviction from its leased premises (thereby permitting the tenant to terminate its lease and its ongoing obligation to pay rent), the tenant must establish that (1) the landlord caused the interruption of service, (2) the interruption permanently deprived the tenant of its use and enjoyment of the leased premises, and (3) the tenant vacated the leased premises within a reasonable period of time following the occurrence of the landlord-caused interruption of service.[142] Few tenants can satisfy this burden of proof and even fewer are willing to move out of the leased premises and take the risk that the landlord will later sue it for a

---

141. *See generally* Hennigh, *Office Lease, supra* note 83, at 15–14; and DILLMAN, *supra* note 37, at 219–223.

142. *See* David H. Fishman, *Get Me Out of This Lease*, 24 No. 2 PRACTICAL REAL ESTATE LAWYER 13, 14 (March 2008).

breach of its lease obligations. The doctrine of constructive eviction is, therefore, useful to a tenant only in the most egregious of settings.

As noted earlier in this Chapter, the courts in a minority of states have declined to follow the doctrine of independent covenants.[143] In those states, a tenant may have the right to terminate its lease or suspend its payment of rent if the landlord breaches a "promise that was a significant inducement to the tenant's entering the lease in the first instance"[144]—a lower burden of proof than that customarily placed upon the tenant in a constructive eviction action. A few states have also hinted at the possibility that the tenant might have the right to withhold its rent based on the landlord's breach of an implied warranty of suitability of the leased premises for its intended use.[145] The dependent covenant rule and the implied warranty of suitability are, however, clearly minority positions and, hence, do not provide any comfort to the majority of commercial tenants. In addition, because they apparently have application only to those significant interruptions of service that are caused by a material breach of the landlord's performance obligations, the doctrine of dependent covenants and the implied warranty of suitability fail to provide the tenant with any useful means to deal with an interruption of service that is caused by a third party or one that does not rise to the level of significance contemplated by those minority rules.

The tenant can, however, override all the common law strictures by including a provision in the lease that provides it with specific remedies to deal with an interruption in service. The following constitutes the tenant's wish list of remedies that it would like to reserve to address the impact of an interruption of service:[146]

- The right to abate its rent during the continuance of the interruption of service;
- The self-help right to do whatever is necessary to cure the interruption and then offset the costs of the cure against its rent obligation; and
- The right to terminate the lease if the service is not reinstated within a stated period of time.

As noted above, the tenant will not have any of these remedies, unless its lawyer is successful in expressly including such remedies in the lease document.

The landlord will, of course, strenuously object to the inclusion in the lease of any rent abatement, self-help or termination remedy. The landlord wants to continue to receive the full benefit of its negotiated rental stream, notwithstanding the occurrence of an interruption of service. In

---

143. *See supra* Page 451.

144. *See* Wesson v. Leone Enterprises, Inc., 437 Mass. 708, 722. *See also* Richard Barton Enterprises, Inc. v. Tsern, 928 P.2d 368 (Utah 1996).

145. *See* Fishman, *supra* note 142, at 17–18; and Senn, *supra* note 5, at 5–57 through 5–62.

146. *See* Hennigh, *Office Leases, supra* note 83, at 15–14 through 15–16; Dillman, *supra* note 37, at 139–140; and Hollyfield, *supra* note 136, at 192.

the landlord's view, the only remedy that the tenant needs to protect itself against a service interruption is the right to file a damages action against the landlord. The grant to tenant of any additional remedies significantly shifts in tenant's favor the negotiating leverage over a service dispute. Suddenly, a tenant who feels that it is "just way too hot" in its leased premises might avail itself of its rent abatement or self-help remedy to reduce the rent it pays to the landlord and then force the landlord to file a legal action against the tenant to try to recover the full amount of the rent that the landlord believes was due in the first instance. Worse yet, the tenant might actually try to get out of its lease by exercising its termination remedy.[147]

The following are factors that color the parties' determination of the remedies available to the tenant to deal with an interruption of service.

- Does the service interruption prevent the tenant from conducting its business in the leased premises (or is the interruption simply an inconvenience for the tenant)?

- How long does the interruption last (e.g., one hour versus one month)?

- Was the landlord at fault in causing the interruption (or was the interruption caused by an event or circumstance beyond the landlord's control)?

- Is the event or circumstance giving rise to the interruption covered by the tenant's business interruption insurance or the landlord's rent loss insurance?[148]

In most situations, the landlord will be extremely reluctant to give the tenant any specific right to terminate the lease as a result of the occurrence of an interruption of service (no matter how long or how severe that interruption may be). Most landlords are also hesitant to give their tenants a self-help remedy, because of the perceived negative impact that a tenant-sponsored corrective action can have on the building's residual value. Landlords tend to be more willing to entertain the grant of a limited rent abatement right to the tenant, so long as that right is exercisable only if the interruption was caused by the landlord and then only after the expiration of a substantial grace period (e.g., an interruption lasting more than ten consecutive days).

F. UNIQUE USE ISSUES IN A RETAIL LEASE

Before leaving the "use" topic, some mention should be made of the unique provisions found in the use clauses of retail leases. The following are retail-specific provisions that will be discussed in this subsection:

---

147. *See* the last sentence of §4 of the Form Office Lease for an example of a provision that attempts to eliminate any landlord liability for an interruption of service that is caused by a reason beyond Landlord's reasonable control. For a more aggressive, pro-landlord provision that wholly eliminates any tenant remedy for a service interruption (including one caused by the landlord), *see Form 1–1, Office Lease with Modifications,* in THE COMMERCIAL LEASE FORMBOOK: EXPERT TOOLS FOR DRAFTING AND NEGOTIATION 8, 32 (Dennis M. Horn ed., 2004).

148. *See infra* Page 542 and note 239, for a discussion of rent loss and business interruption insurance.

- A *restrictive use* clause;

- An *exclusive use* clause;

- A *radius restriction*;

- A *continuous operation covenant*;

- A *go dark right*; and

- A *co-tenancy requirement.*

The genesis of all of the above clauses is the reality that a retail lease is significantly different from other commercial leases in two principal respects—(1) the profitability of the tenant's store is inextricably linked to the vibrancy and success of the landlord's center as a whole and (2) a significant portion of the landlord's financial returns (specifically the income stream represented by the tenants' percentage rent obligation) is tied to the sales revenues generated in the tenants' stores. As a result, the retail landlord and tenant have a shared goal of maximizing the customer traffic to and the sales generated from the tenant's store and the landlord's retail center. The restrictive use clause, the continuous operation covenant and the radius restriction are tools used by the landlord to enhance the sales revenues produced from the operation of the center as a whole, while the exclusive use clause, the go-dark right and the co-tenancy requirement are the means used by the tenant to aid the profitability of its particular store.

1. Restrictive Use Clause

The retail landlord knows that having the right mix and balance of tenants is the key driver for increasing customer traffic to its center. The best way for the landlord to achieve the optimal tenant mix is for it to employ a *restrictive use clause*[149] to clearly articulate in the lease of each of its tenants exactly what the tenant can and cannot sell in its store. The landlord's consistent use of tightly worded, restrictive use clauses will help it create and maintain a synergistic mix of tenants and will also help it avoid the unfortunate circumstance of having multiple tenants selling the same product line (e.g., five candle stores in the same center) or mismatched tenants being located in close proximity to each other (a discount liquidation store situated next to a high-end, fashion retailer).

The tenant has an entirely different perspective on the use clause of a retail lease. The retail tenant desires to maintain maximum flexibility to change its retail operations and introduce new product lines if it determines that doing so will increase the profitability of the retail business.[150]

---

149. *See supra* Pages 497–500, for a general discussion of restrictive and permissive use clauses in the context of a multi-tenant office lease. For detailed discussion of the use clause of a retail lease, *see* Joel R. Hall, *Use Clauses*, in ALI–ABA Course of Study Materials, Commercial Real Estate Leases: Selected Issues in Drafting and Negotiating in Current Markets, Course No. SN–013, 499 (May 2008).

150. *See* Zankel, *supra* note 19, at 28. As will be discussed *infra* Page 532, the breadth of the use clause of the retail lease also is an important factor in determining whether the retail tenant can transfer its leasehold interest to another retailer.

Its clear preference is a use clause that says that "the leased premises can be used for any lawful retail purpose."[151] This stands in stark contrast to the landlord's desire to have the tenant's use clause restrict it to the use of the leased premises for the sale of a specific type of product—e.g., the "sale of women's shoes." The tug of war that ensues between the lawyers for the landlord and the tenant is frequently resolved by the inclusion in the lease of concepts designed to permit the tenant to introduce new product lines in its store, so long as the "primary use" of its store is for a specific retail use (which will likely be defined more broadly than the landlord would prefer and more narrowly than the tenant would prefer).[152]

2. Exclusive Use Clause

Major retailers are occasionally successful in negotiating the right to be the only tenant in the landlord's center that can engage in a particular retail business (e.g., the operation of a bookstore). In those situations, the landlord will expressly grant to the tenant the exclusive right to sell a particular product line in the center and will agree to prohibit all of its other tenants from selling products covered by the granted exclusive. The receipt of an ***exclusive use clause*** gives the retail tenant a mini-monopoly and permits it to grow its revenue base without fear of competition from any other tenant in the center.

The landlord views the grant of an exclusive use as marketing handcuffs that unduly limit its ability to attain the desired mix of tenants in the center.[153] As such, the landlord will resist the grant of an exclusive to anyone other than the most powerful of destination tenants, whose presence is considered to be a crucial factor in driving the level of the customer traffic in the landlord's center. If the landlord feels that it has no choice but to grant an exclusive to a particular tenant, its next battle will be to try to define the scope of the exclusive in a fashion that does not totally tie its hands in its efforts to lease space in the center. The landlord would, therefore, like to phrase the exclusive use by stating that it will not lease any other space in its center to a tenant whose "primary business is the operation of a bookstore." This description of the tenant's exclusive use would permit the landlord to lease space in its center to other tenants who sell books, so long as their sale of books is incidental to the conduct of their primary business.[154]

---

151. *See* Goldberg, *Retail Leases, supra* note 17, at 14–25; and Hall, *Use Clauses, supra* note 149, at 502.

152. *See* Goldberg, *Retail Leases, supra* note 17, at 14–25.

153. *See generally,* Kathleen A. Crocco and Jeffrey H. Kaplan, *"Good for the Goose, Good for the Gander": The Interplay between Radius Restrictions and Exclusive Use Clauses in Shopping Center Leases,* in materials for INTERNATIONAL SHOPPING CENTERS LAW CONFERENCE (2005), available online at http://library.icsc.org/dbtw-wpd/textbase/docs/L2005–S49.pdf.

154. *See* Joel R. Hall, *Exclusive Clauses,* in ALI–ABA COURSE OF STUDY MATERIALS, COMMERCIAL REAL ESTATE LEASES: SELECTED ISSUES IN DRAFTING AND NEGOTIATING IN CURRENT MARKETS, Course No. SN–013, 509, 515–516 (May 2008).

3. Radius Restriction

A ***radius restriction*** is the landlord's version of an exclusive use clause. A radius restriction limits the tenant's ability to operate a competing store within a specified proximity to the landlord's retail center. The radius restriction is designed to protect the landlord's percentage rent receipts from a reduction occasioned by the tenant's diversion of some of its potential sales to a nearby store located in a center owned by a competitor of the landlord.[155]

There are two types of radius restrictions—(1) an absolute prohibition against the tenant's opening of another store within the designated radius and (2) a requirement that any gross sales derived from the tenant's new store must be included in the base for the computation of the tenant's percentage rent in the landlord's center.[156] The enforceability of a radius restriction and its acceptability to a prospective tenant are dependent on the geographic scope of the restriction (typically no more than five miles from the boundaries of the landlord's center) and the duration of the restriction (usually no longer than the length of the tenant's existing lease term).[157]

4. Continuous Operation Covenant

In an effort to maximize the gross sales generated from its center (and, hence, the amount of its percentage rent receipts), a retail landlord will routinely insist that the tenant expressly agree to continuously operate its retail business in the leased premises during the center's normal business hours and to staff, fixture and stock its store in a manner designed to maximize its gross sales.[158] The landlord's inclusion in the lease of a ***continuous operation covenant*** is especially important if the landlord is willing to give the tenant a significant base rent discount based on the landlord's expected receipt of a sizable amount of percentage rent.[159]

5. Go Dark Right

The tenant's counterpoint to the continuous operation covenant is a ***go dark right***. Under a go dark right, the tenant expressly reserves the right to close or curtail its store operations at any time and for any reason. The tenant's exercise of its go dark right does not effect a termination of

---

155. *See generally*, Crocco, *supra* note 153, at 9–20.

156. *See* Goldberg, *Retail Leases, supra* note 17, at 14–26.

157. *See id.* at 14–27; and Crocco, *supra* note 153, at 13–18.

158. *See generally*, Marie Moore, *Shedding Light on Going Dark: Continuous Operation Clauses*, in materials for INTERNATIONAL SHOPPING CENTERS LAW CONFERENCE (2005), available online at http://library.icsc.org/dbtw-wpd/textbase/docs/L2005–S11A.pdf.

159. Courts in some jurisdictions have held that there is an implied covenant of continuous operation if (1) the lease provides for the payment of insubstantial minimum rent (when compared to the tenant's percentage rent obligation) or (2) the provisions of the lease make it clear that the tenant is economically interdependent with other tenants in the center. *See* SENN, *supra* note 5, at 11–56 through 11–63. Best practices call for the landlord and the tenant to expressly address the continuous operation issue in the lease and not leave the resolution of that important issue to the whim of the judicial branch. *See* Moore, *supra* note 158, at 5–11

its lease, but simply eliminates its need to continue conducting business in its leased space. By closing a bad store, the tenant will save money by eliminating both its percentage rent obligation and the costs of staffing and stocking the store.

The resolution of the continuous operations vs. go dark riddle boils down to a simple matter of which party to the lease is the most motivated to have the tenant lease space in the landlord's retail center. The landlord and tenant often compromise their competing positions by agreeing to limit the time period in which the tenant has the right to go dark (e.g., only during the last year of the lease term) or conditioning the tenant's exercise of its go dark right upon the occurrence of an objectively verifiable event or circumstance (e.g., the tenant's gross sales dropping below a threshold amount).

6. Co-tenancy Requirement

A ***co-tenancy requirement*** is a pro-tenant provision that conditions the tenant's obligation to perform its lease obligations upon the status of other tenants in the retail center.[160] Co-tenancy requirements come in two distinctly different forms—(1) an ***opening co-tenancy requirement*** that conditions the obligation of the tenant to open for business and begin paying rent on the occupancy status of the center as a whole and (2) a ***continuing co-tenancy requirement*** that permits the tenant to terminate its lease or reduce its rent if the occupancy of the center falls below an agreed-upon standard.[161] The co-tenancy requirement can be expressed in a variety of ways, including a requirement that "at least 80% of the retail center must be subject to binding written leases" or a requirement that "Barnes and Noble and Cheesecake Factory must be open and actively conducting business in the retail center." Regardless of how the co-tenancy requirement is phrased, its purpose from the tenant's perspective is always the same—that is, the tenant does not want to be obligated to fully perform its obligations in a "dead" or "dying" retail center.

If the landlord is willing to entertain the inclusion of a co-tenancy requirement in its lease (and with some national retail chains, it has no other choice), the landlord's lawyer will try to limit the co-tenancy to an opening only requirement. If the tenant insists on a continuing co-tenancy requirement, the landlord's lawyer can soften the impact of that requirement by inserting a provision in the lease that gives the landlord a right for a specified period of time (ideally six months or more) to cure the co-tenancy violation by replacing the closed or departed tenants with suitable new tenants.[162]

---

160. *See generally*, Eric D. Rapkin, *Co-tenancy Provisions in Retail Lease Agreements*, in materials for INTERNATIONAL SHOPPING CENTERS LAW CONFERENCE (2005), available online at http://library.icsc.org/dbtw-wpd/textbase/docs/L2005–S11B.pdf.

161. *See* Goldberg, *Retail Leases*, *supra* note 17, at 14–31 and 14–32.

162. *See* Rapkin, *supra* note 160 at 6. If the co-tenancy provision requires the co-tenant to be open and operating for business, the landlord should reserve the right in the co-tenant's lease to terminate its lease if the co-tenant closes its store. This right (commonly referred to as a "recapture right") affords the landlord the opportunity to cure the breach of the co-tenancy

7. Interplay of Retail Use Provisions

A landlord of a regional mall or lifestyle center might have upwards of a hundred tenants. It is, therefore, crucial that the landlord use its best efforts to limit both the number and scope of the special use provisions it includes in its tenants' leases. If a landlord is not careful, the interplay of the special use provisions can cause irreparable financial harm to the landlord's center.

The following are a few illustrative examples of the traps that await the unwary retail landlord:

- The grant of an exclusive to one tenant, coupled with the inclusion in another tenant's lease of a permissive use clause permitting the tenant to use its leased premises for "any lawful retail use";

- The grant of opening co-tenancy requirements to two tenants, with each such requirement stating that the tenant's obligation to open its store is expressly conditioned upon the other tenant being open and operating for business (a classic "chicken or the egg" scenario); and

- The grant of a go dark right to a tenant named in another tenant's co-tenancy requirement.

A leading expert on retail leasing notes that because the special use provisions of a retail lease "can give rise to a house of cards that can come crashing down if one of the linchpins closes, it is vital that the landlord carefully control . . . remedies in order to avoid a catastrophic collapse of the rent structure."[163]

XI. TENANT FLEXIBILITY PROVISIONS

This section will explore lease provisions that give the tenant flexibility to alter its lease arrangement to respond to changes in its business operations. The tenant flexibility clauses generally fall into one of three categories—(1) clauses that provide the tenant with a right to expand or contract the size of its leased premises, (2) clauses that give the tenant the right to shorten or extend the term of its occupancy of the leased premises, and (3) clauses that authorize the tenant to transfer its lease-hold interests to a third party.

Before moving on to an examination of the specific tenant-sponsored clauses, it should first be noted that any provision that is structured to provide the tenant with flexibility will generally work to the landlord's disadvantage. The tenant flexibility provisions all share one common characteristic—they provide the tenant with the *OPTION* (and not the *OBLI-GATION*) to take an action in the future that will change the nature of the landlord-tenant relationship. The tenant will exercise its flexibility only if

---

requirement by finding a new tenant to take over the co-tenant's space. *See* Goldberg, *Retail Leases, supra* note 17, at 14–32.

163. *See* Goldberg, *Retail Leases, supra* note 17, at 14–33.

that option produces a result for the tenant that is more favorable than that which characterizes its then existing lease arrangement. A result that is more favorable to the tenant is almost always unfavorable to the landlord.[164]

Why then does the landlord permit the tenant to include flexibility options in the lease? The answer to that question is relatively simple—in some situations, the landlord has no other choice. Many tenants place paramount importance during the lease negotiations on their retention of flexibility to properly deal with changes in their business models and will simply not sign any lease that locks them into a rigidly defined, business dynamic for the duration of the lease term. Because the tenants adopting that stance are typically the tenants that are most attractive to the landlord (for example, large national tenants, who have deep pockets and are willing to sign leases for large spaces and long terms), the real estate development lawyer often has no realistic alternative other than to try to craft lease clauses that grant the tenant a measure of flexibility, while still protecting the landlord's overarching business interests.

Landlords seldom provide the requested flexibility to tenants whose importance to the project's financial success is marginal, either because of the size of their leased premises or the depth of their pocket books. Throughout the remainder of this section, it will be assumed that the tenant asking for a flexibility option is a person that the landlord very much wants to have in its building (although, to keep the playing field level, it will also be assumed that the landlord does not feel compelled to accede to each and every request made by the tenant).

A. SPACE FLEXIBILITY OPTIONS

Any number of changes can occur during the course of a tenant's lease term that might cause the tenant to want to change the size and configuration of its leased premises. If the tenant's business has grown, it may want to increase the size of its leased premises so that it can secure the efficiencies associated with having its employees working under the same roof. If its business has declined, the tenant may need less space than it originally contracted for when it signed its lease. Finally, if the tenant's business has been sold or closed, the tenant may have no need whatsoever for any leased space.

The following are alternative clauses that the tenant's lawyer can try to include in the lease to provide the tenant with a right to expand the size of its leased premises at some point following the date of its execution of the original lease. The alternatives are presented in order from the most to the least desirable from the tenant's perspective.

---

164. Lenders and institutional investors will closely scrutinize tenant flexibility options to determine whether the existence of any such options materially undermines the value of the landlord's project. Termination and contraction options are viewed with particular disfavor by debt and equity providers. *See supra* Chapter 1, Pages 6–7.

1. Expansion Option

The optimal way to preserve the tenant's right to increase the size of its leased premises is to give it an ***expansion option*** to lease additional space in the building at any time during the lease term. If the tenant has an option to lease all or a designated portion of the vacant space in a building, the landlord will have no choice but to keep that space vacant and off the market throughout the pendency of the tenant's option— which means that the landlord will not receive any rental income from that space, unless and until the tenant exercises its expansion option. For that reason, landlords will strenuously resist the grant of an expansion option to a tenant or, at the very least, endeavor to limit both the duration of the tenant's option (e.g., only for the first 12 months of the lease term) and the identity of the space that is the subject of the option (e.g., only the 10,000 square feet of contiguous space located on the same floor as the tenant's original leased premises). The landlord might also try to receive partial compensation for keeping the option space off the market by insisting that the tenant pay the landlord an annual fee to keep the option alive.[165]

2. Right of First Refusal

A ***right of first refusal*** permits the landlord to continue to market the vacant space in its building, but gives the tenant a priority right to match any third party offer to lease that space (referred to in this section as the "RFR Space"). If a third party offers to lease the RFR space, the landlord is first required to tender that offer to the tenant, who will then have a fixed period of time to decide whether it wants to lease the RFR Space. If the tenant exercises its right of first refusal, the third party offeror is out of luck and the size of the tenant's leased premises will be expanded to include the RFR Space.

Although a right of first refusal does not prevent the landlord from marketing its vacant space, it does have a decided chilling effect on its ability to do so.[166] Few companies are willing to take the time and spend the money required to negotiate a lease if there is a realistic prospect that an existing tenant might swoop in at the end of the negotiations and pull the rug out from underneath it by exercising a right of first refusal on the targeted space. A landlord can try to limit the chilling effect of a right of first refusal[167] by (1) limiting the duration and space covered by the right, (2) requiring a very short turnaround time for the tenant's exercise of its right (e.g., two business days after its receipt of the third party offer), (3) triggering the time period for the tenant's exercise of its refusal right by the landlord's delivery to the tenant of a letter of intent or term sheet signed by a third party (rather than a fully-negotiated lease document), (4) requiring the tenant to match every part of the third party offer, even if

---

165. *See generally* ZANKEL, *supra* note 19, at 22–23; and Yi, *supra* note 30, at 4.

166. *See* Hennigh, *Office Leases,* supra note 83, at 15–18.

167. *See generally* ZANKEL, *supra* note 19, at 24; and Yi, *supra* note 30, at 4.

that offer applies to space in more than one building or imposes a condition that is impossible for the tenant to satisfy (e.g., a minimum net worth covenant or a use prohibition) and (5) providing that the right of first refusal will automatically terminate if the tenant ever opts not to exercise such right.[168]

3. Right of First Offer

A *right of first offer* is one step removed from a right of first refusal. In a right of first offer, the landlord is required to extend an offer to the tenant to lease certain space in the building before the landlord begins marketing that space to other prospective tenants. The existing tenant will have a fixed period of time (e.g., ten to 30 days) in which to decide whether it will exercise the right of first offer and lease the subject space on the terms and conditions specified in the landlord's offer. If the tenant declines to exercise the right of first offer within the designated time frame, the landlord will then be fully empowered to begin actively marketing the space for lease to third parties.

A landlord will be more inclined to grant a right of first offer than it would an expansion option or a right of first refusal, because the right of first offer simply requires the landlord to do something that it would likely do in any event—try to "pick the low hanging fruit" by contacting all of its existing tenants before marketing the space to third parties.[169] This is especially true if the right of first offer does not impose any limitation on the terms on which the landlord can lease the space to a third party following the tenant's waiver of its right of first offer. Given the lack of any such limitations, the landlord would be free to present a high-ball offer to the holder of the right of first offer and then later lease the space to a third party at a much lower rent. For this reason, most tenants will insist that the right of first offer contain a "re-offer" requirement that precludes the landlord from leasing the space to a third party on terms less favorable to the landlord than those specified in the landlord's initial offer to the existing tenant, unless the landlord first re-offers the space to the tenant on the less favorable terms.[170]

4. "Must Take" Agreement

This last alternative is the only flexibility provision that actually places an obligation on the tenant to expand the size of its leased premise (and, hence, is the alternative that is the most palatable to the landlord). Under a *"must take" agreement*, the tenant is obligated to lease additional space in the building effective as of a specified date following

---

168. A right of first refusal which automatically expires whenever the tenant declines to exercise that right is commonly referred to as a "one bite out of the apple" right. That type of right of first refusal stands in sharp contrast to the type favored by the tenant (a so-called "evergreen right"), which would keep the tenant's right of first refusal intact as to all other RFR space in the building, even after the tenant declines to exercise its right of first refusal as to a specific portion of the RFR space.

169. *See* ZANKEL, supra note 19, at 24–25; and Yi, *supra* note 30, at 3–4.

170. *See* Hennigh, *Office Leases, supra* note 84, at 15–17

the date of the parties' execution of the lease term (e.g., the first anniversary of the commencement date of the lease term). Tenants are typically reluctant to agree to a must take provision, unless they are reasonably confident that an external force will trigger its need for additional space in the future (e.g., a pre-existing arrangement for the transfer of a portion of the tenant's workforce to the landlord's building at a predictable future date).[171]

5. Additional Factors in the Negotiation of Space Flexibility Provisions

Regardless which of the above space flexibility alternatives finds its way into the lease, the landlord and the tenant will both want to make sure that the lease provision clearly describes all of the terms that will govern the tenant's leasing of the expansion space. One common way to deal with that issue is to say that the lease of the expansion space will be upon all of the same terms and conditions that are set forth in the tenant's original lease, with the exception of certain specific terms such as the rent, lease term and tenant improvement allowance that will be newly applicable to the tenant's leasing of the expansion space. The tenant will customarily want to preserve the economic benefit of the bargain it struck in its initial lease by having the rent it pays for the expansion space set at the per square foot rental rates specified in the initial lease. The landlord, on the other hand, will typically insist that the tenant's rental rate for the expansion space be tied to changes in market conditions, either by using the rental rate specified in the lease offer under the right of first refusal or right of first offer or by requiring that the rental be equal to the greater of (1) the then prevailing market rental rate for the expansion space and (2) the rental rate specified in the original lease.[172]

There are a number of limitations that the landlord will seek to impose on any space flexibility provision included in the lease.[173] By way of example, the landlord might want to insert provisions in the lease which:

- Condition the tenant's exercise of any of its expansion rights upon the tenant being in full compliance with all of its lease obligations;

- Make the expansion rights personal to the tenant—i.e., such rights will not be exercisable by any assignee or subtenant; and

- Subordinate the tenant's expansion rights to all rights previously granted on the expansion space to other tenants and third parties.

6. Contraction Option

The conservative tenant also wants to preserve flexibility to downsize its leased premises should the vitality of its business decline due to an

---

171. *See generally* SENN, *supra* note 5, at 4–41.

172. *See infra* Pages 525–526, for a discussion of "market rent."

173. For a discussion of the tenant's perspective on such limitations, *see* Linda D. White, *Issues to Consider for The Growing Tenant (with Sample Clauses)*, in THE PRACTICAL REAL ESTATE LAWYER'S MANUAL ON COMMERCIAL LEASING IN TROUBLED TIMES—FORMS, CHECKLISTS, AND ADVICE 123, 126 (2009).

internal or external force. The tenant's ability to downsize its leased premises is commonly referred to as a ***contraction option***. Under a contraction option, the tenant will be given the option to terminate its obligations with respect to all or a portion of its leased premises. Landlords despise contraction options and will grant them only when their backs are fully pressed to the wall by a tenant who wields incredible negotiating clout. The landlord's distaste for such options is driven by its fear that the project's net operating income will be adversely affected, either because the contracted space will remain vacant for an extended period of time or because the rent produced on the re-leasing of the contracted space will be less than the rent specified in the tenant's original lease.

If a landlord is forced into granting the tenant a contraction option, it will seek to ameliorate the negative impact of the tenant's exercise of such option by including modifications to the contraction option which:

- Limit the amount and location of the space that is the subject of the option;

- Make the contraction option a one-time right that can only be exercised during a short window of time (e.g., only during the 36th month of the initial lease term);

- Condition the option's exercise upon the occurrence of some objectively quantifiable event (e.g., the tenant's loss of a major customer contract);

- Preclude the tenant from leasing any other space in the market for a specified period of time after its exercise of its contraction option (so that the tenant cannot use the contraction option as a convenient means to get out of an unfavorable lease);

- Insist that the contracted space be of a location and configuration that can be readily marketed by the landlord;

- Require the tenant to provide the landlord with a long lead time between the date of the tenant's exercise of its contraction option and the date on which the contraction becomes effective (e.g., 12 months after landlord's receipt of the tenant's written exercise of its contraction option, so that the landlord will have sufficient time to locate a substitute tenant for the contracted space); and

- Mandate the tenant's payment to the landlord of a significant economic penalty immediately upon its exercise of its contraction option (e.g., a payment equal to the sum of (a) the landlord's unamortized tenant improvement costs and leasing commissions and (b) 12 months of base rent, so as to give the landlord some economic cushion to absorb the rental loss resulting from the tenant's exercise of its contraction option).[174]

---

174. *See generally* Hennigh, *Office Leases, supra* note 83, at 15–20 and 15–21; and Yi, *supra* note 30, at 7–8.

7. Relocation Clause

Before leaving the topic of a change in the tenant's leased space, note should be made of a pro-landlord provision—specifically the ***relocation clause***.[175] The relocation clause presents the landlord with the opportunity to utter hackneyed phrases such as "what's good for the goose is good for the gander" and "turnabout is fair play." At its essence, a relocation clause gives the landlord the contractual right to move the tenant's leased premises to another location in the landlord's building (or, for that matter, in some other building owned by the landlord or one of its affiliates). The inclusion of a relocation clause in a tenant's lease provides the landlord with the flexibility it needs to reposition that tenant to make room for a bigger and better tenant.[176] By way of example, assume that IBM Corporation is interested in leasing 20,000 square feet of space in the landlord's building and that the landlord has exactly 20,000 square feet of vacant space. Unfortunately for the landlord, its vacant space consists of 18,000 square feet on the top floor of its building and 2,000 square feet located on the second floor. The landlord's inability to provide IBM with 20,000 square feet of contiguous space could result in the landlord's loss of the IBM deal, unless it can somehow figure out a way to move the tenant who occupies 2,000 square feet of space on the top floor to the vacant space located on the second floor—enter the relocation clause which would permit the landlord to do just that.

The tenant views a relocation clause with as much disfavor as the landlord does an expansion option. The tenant's concerns are threefold—(1) the move will disrupt its business operations and potentially reduce its profitability, (2) the space to which it is relocated may be inferior to the tenant's existing leased premises (due to the comparative size, configuration or location of the two spaces), and (3) significant costs will have to be incurred to make the move, order new stationery, send out notices to customers, etc. Large tenants will usually be successful in having the relocation clause deleted in its entirety from the lease. Smaller tenants are frequently left to try to negotiate modifications to the relocation clause that condition the landlord's exercise of its relocation right upon (a) the tenant being moved into space that is comparable in all respects to its original leased premises and (b) the landlord's prompt reimbursement of all costs reasonably incurred by the tenant in connection with the move. Tenants also regularly ask for assurances that the landlord will move the tenant over a weekend and will otherwise use its best efforts to minimize any disruption of the tenant's business operations.[177]

---

175. *See e.g.*, §28 of the Form Office Lease.

176. *See* SENN, *supra* note 5, at 4–68.

177. *See generally*, Yi, *supra* note 30, at 8–9; and SENN, *supra* note 5, at 4–72 through 4–75.

HIBC Case Study—A Matter of Too Much Flexibility

The rent rolls of Pizzuti's HIBC office buildings were dotted with dynamic, high technology companies, all of which shared the same messianic conviction concerning the growth trajectories of their respective business units. In an effort to land these high-growth companies as tenants in its business park, Pizzuti routinely gave in to their demands for the inclusion in their leases of expansion rights (primarily rights of first offer and first refusal, with an occasional, limited expansion option thrown in for good measure). From Pizzuti's vantage point, the grant of the expansion rights seemed like a small price to pay for the privilege of securing high net worth, growth-oriented firms as tenants for its HIBC buildings.

The inherent danger in handing out expansion rights in a liberal fashion was brought home to me when I received a phone call from Pizzuti's in-house leasing broker giving me the "good news" that five of our existing tenants had expressed an interest in leasing the last 20,000 square feet of vacant space located in our newest HIBC office building. The "bad news" was that each of the tenants felt that it had a right to lease the vacant space under a specific provision contained in its lease—two rights of first refusal and three rights of first offer (which our leasing broker failed to trigger because she never sent the requisite written lease offers to the holders of the rights of first offer). My failure to track and properly prioritize the expansion rights of the HIBC tenants had resulted in the outbreak of a donnybrook among five of the park's most important tenants, with each of them pointing a finger at Pizzuti and accusing it of double-dealing and other nefarious acts. While I was ultimately able to calm everyone down and lease the last of our vacant space to two of the five tenants, that success came at a significant cost—both in terms of the general loss of goodwill and the specific lease concessions that I had to make to allay the concerns of the five affected tenants. From that point forward, I adopted a much more restrictive policy on the grant of tenant expansion rights and insisted that Pizzuti's leasing brokers at all times carry a cheat sheet in their back pockets describing the scope and relative priorities of all expansion rights granted to HIBC tenants.

B.   TERM FLEXIBILITY OPTIONS

The tenant's right to an early exit from its lease obligations with respect to some or all of its space was examined as part of the earlier discussion of a tenant's contraction option. But what if the tenant wants to stay in its leased premises after the scheduled termination date of the initial lease term? The tenant seeks to gain the flexibility to remain in its leased space after the expiration of the initial term by including an **extension option** in its lease. An extension option is simply a provision included in the original lease that gives the tenant the option (but not the obligation) to extend the term of its lease beyond the termination date specified for the initial term.[178]

A tenant will exercise its extension option only if all of the following conditions exist as of the end of the initial lease term—(1) the leased premises remain well-suited for the conduct of the tenant's business, (2) the tenant does not want to pay the added cost or put up with the hassle of moving to new space and (3) the rent applicable to the extension term is satisfactory to the tenant. If all these conditions are not met, the tenant will opt to move out of the landlord's building and into new space owned by a competitor of the landlord.[179]

Because there is no way for a tenant to know when it signs its lease whether it will want to extend the lease beyond the initial term, it is customary for a tenant to request the inclusion in the lease of an extension option. The extension option, if exercised, will permit the tenant to continue to possess and occupy the leased premises for an additional period of time (typically somewhere between three to ten years, depending on the length of the initial lease term).[180]

From the tenant's perspective, the ideal extension option will identify all of the salient terms that will govern the tenant's leasing of its space during the extension term and will give it the unfettered right to exercise its option at any time prior to the expiration of the initial lease term. If the tenant wants to stay in the leased premises and likes the terms of the extension, it will exercise its extension option. If the tenant wants to stay in the leased premises, but doesn't like the terms of the extension, it will try to renegotiate the extension terms prior to the outside date for its exercise of the extension option. If it fails in its attempt to renegotiate the extension terms or is otherwise unhappy with the leased premises, it will not exercise its extension option and will find another spot to conduct its business.[181]

The above description of the process that the tenant undertakes when making a decision whether it will exercise its extension option speaks volumes as to why the landlord generally does not like extension options. While the landlord recognizes that the grant of an extension option is often a marketing necessity,[182] it is also very much aware that the essence of an extension option works to the tenant's advantage and the landlord's disadvantage. Landlords know that if the tenant exercises its extension option as written, it is likely because the tenant has determined that the

---

178. Practitioners tend to use the terms "extension option" and "renewal option" interchangeably. However, a renewal option is technically a new lease entered into by the landlord and the tenant to govern the tenant's leasing of the leased premises after the termination of the stated term of its lease. An extension option, on the other hand, is a continuation of the stated term of the tenant's lease pursuant to an express option set forth in the tenant's lease. *See* Hennigh, *Office Leases, supra* note 83, at 15–64 and 15–65.

179. *See generally* ZANKEL, *supra* note 19, at 42; and Yi, *supra* note 30, at 11.

180. *See e.g.,* ¶1 of Exhibit E of the Form Office Lease for a representative example of a simple, pro-landlord, extension option.

181. *See* Ronald R. Pollina, *Maximizing Tenant Flexibility Through Creative Lease Negotiations,* in LEASE NEGOTIATION HANDBOOK 37, 38–39 (Edward Chupack ed., 2003).

182. *See* ZANKEL, *supra* note 19, at 41.

terms of the extension option are below market—otherwise the tenant would be knocking on the landlord's door seeking to renegotiate the rent and other business terms applicable to its leasing of the leased premises during the extension term.

1. Extension Option—Key Issues

There are three issues that the lawyers must resolve when negotiating the terms of an extension option. Those issues and the resolutions favored by the landlord and the tenant are discussed below.

- *Issue #1—How and when must the tenant exercise its extension option?* The landlord and the tenant can usually agree on the proposition that the tenant's exercise of its extension option must be in the form of a written statement delivered to the landlord sometime prior to the expiration of the then existing term of the lease. However, agreement is not as easily reached on the issue of the specifics of the required timing of the tenant's exercise of its extension option. The tenant would prefer to have the right to exercise its extension option at any time prior to the expiration of the initial lease term, so that it can make a real time determination as to whether the prevailing market conditions and the unique needs of its business merit its exercise of the extension option. The landlord, on the other hand, would like the tenant to be required to notify it as far in advance as possible as to whether it will be exercising its extension option, so that the landlord will, if necessary, have adequate time to try to re-lease the space to another party. The outside date for the tenant's exercise of its extension option usually falls somewhere between 30 days to a year prior to the scheduled expiration of the then existing term of the tenant's lease.

- *Issue #2—What conditions, if any, will be placed on the tenant's right to exercise its extension option?* The tenant will not want any conditions to be placed on its right to exercise its extension option (although it will often begrudgingly accept a limitation that it may not exercise its extension option if it is currently in default in the performance of its lease obligations). In addition to the "no current default" condition, the landlord will customarily try to preclude the tenant from exercising its extension option if it has been late on the payment of its rent more than a proscribed number of times during the initial lease term or if its net worth is appreciably below what it was as of the commencement date of the initial lease term. Landlords will also try to prevent the tenant from shopping a favorable extension option by asserting that the extension option is personal to the named tenant and cannot be sold or otherwise transferred by the tenant to a third party.[183]

---

183. *See* Yi, *supra* note 30, at 11.

- *Issue #3—What terms will govern the tenant's leasing of its leased premises during the extension term?* The extension option should specify the exact terms that will apply during the tenant's extension term. This goal is usually accomplished by the insertion into the lease of a clause that states that "the extension term will be upon all of the same terms and conditions set forth in this lease with respect to the initial lease term, except ....,"[184] followed by a specific listing of those provisions of the base lease that will not carry over to the extension term (typically, the TI allowance, number of further extension options and the base rent).

2.   Extension Term Rent

The key business point that needs to be addressed within the text of the extension option is the level of base rent that the tenant will be required to pay during the extension term. The extension term rent can be expressed in one of three ways—as (1) fixed rent (e.g., $20 prsf), (2) indexed rent (e.g., the base rent payable during the initial term adjusted to reflect increases in the Consumer Price Index) or (3) market rent. The advantages and disadvantages of the fixed and indexed rent alternatives were addressed earlier in this Chapter as part of a discussion of the ways in which a landlord can protect its rental income from being eroded by the onset of inflationary conditions in the general economy.[185] The rest of this subsection will focus on the merits and demerits associated with the use of a market rent standard to determine the tenant's base rent obligation during the extension term.

The market rent standard is frequently used to set the base rent that the tenant will pay if it exercises its extension option. The primary advantage of a market rent standard is that it is difficult for either the landlord or the tenant to logically resist the contention that the tenant's rent should be tied to prevailing market rental rates for comparable properties. The disadvantage of using a market rent benchmark is that no one really knows what the term means and, hence, its use introduces a level of uncertainty into the computation of the tenant's base rent obligation.

There are three fundamental issues that need to be taken into consideration with respect to the determination of the market rent for a particular leased premises—specifically (1) what market will be used as a comparative for the leased premises, (2) what is the prevailing rent in the designated market, and (3) who gets to make the market rent determination?

The identification of the comparable market for a tenant's office suite should take into account all of the following considerations—the specific location of the office building (e.g., the Orlando central business district or the Lake Mary suburban market); the type of office building (e.g., low-rise

---

184.   *See* ¶ 1 of Exhibit E of the Form Office Lease.

185.   *See supra* Pages 492–494.

or high-rise, Class A or Class B, multi-tenant or single tenant, new or old, brick or glass curtain wall); and the nature of the leased premises (e.g., its square footage, floor location and the quality of its tenant improvements). In theory, the lawyers should strive to put together a market narrative that permits the value arbiter to zero in on the specifics of "comparable space, in comparable buildings, in a comparable location."

The determination of the prevailing market rents in the designated comparable market is equally troublesome and complex. The estimation of market rent requires an analysis of each of the following factors as they relate both to the tenant's existing lease and all the leases that are being used as benchmarks to establish the market rent in the designated market—the rent structure (i.e., gross, net, expense stop or a hybrid of those three structures); any rent concessions; the quality and level of building services provided to the tenant by the landlord; the common area load factor; the tenant's creditworthiness; the amount of the landlord's contribution to the cost of the tenant improvements; the leasing commissions and other transactional costs paid by the landlord; and all other lease provisions that impact the lease's overall economic position (e.g., expense pass-through caps or the existence of expansion and contraction rights).[186]

The final piece of the market rent puzzle involves the selection of the person or persons who will be responsible for setting the market rent for the tenant's leased premises. The choices are: (1) the landlord (seldom a palatable alternative for the tenant); (2) the landlord and the tenant (by mutual agreement); (3) a published source (e.g., CB Richard Ellis' annual report for the designated market); (4) a single expert (usually a licensed commercial real estate broker or appraiser identified in the lease or chosen by the mutual agreement of the landlord and the tenant); or (5) a panel of experts selected in accordance with a procedure established in the lease.[187] One of the most common methods employed to determine market rent is something called a ***baseball appraisal***, where each of the landlord and tenant submits its determination of market rent and an expert or panel of experts is then required to select one of the submitted determinations as the true market rent for the tenant's leased premises.[188]

---

186. *See generally* Yi, *supra* note 30, at 12–13.

187. If the decision is going to be made by a panel of experts (a fairly common circumstance), the drafters of the extension option will need to address the following issues within the skin of the extension option clause: how will the experts be selected; what will be their minimum, required qualifications; and how will variances in their respective rent determinations be reconciled? *See* ZANKEL, *supra* note 19, at 45–46.

188. This appraisal method gets its name from the fact that it is closely patterned after the arbitration method used to establish the salaries of major league baseball players. In a baseball appraisal, the expert is compelled to choose either the landlord's or the tenant's market rent determination and is not permitted to average or otherwise compromise the differing rent determinations in any way. *See* Hennigh, *Office Leases*, *supra* note 83, at 15–68.

C. ASSIGNMENT AND SUBLEASING. *(§12)*

The assignment and subleasing clause is the tenant's final avenue for the creation of flexibility to deal with its leased space. That clause provides the tenant with an opportunity to transfer its lease rights to a third party if the tenant believes that it makes sound business sense to do so—either as an exit strategy (if the tenant wants to downsize, sell or close its business) or as a potential profit center (if the tenant's rent is below market and it wants to monetize the intrinsic value of its lease by selling it to a third party). The tenant will want as much freedom as possible to transfer its leasehold interest to any person of its choosing and on whatever terms and conditions it deems appropriate.[189]

The landlord's position on the assignment and sublease clause is antithetical to that of the tenant. The landlord wants to restrict, to the maximum extent possible, the tenant's ability to transfer its leasehold interest to a third party. In that respect, the landlord has two separate objectives—(1) it wants to retain the right to approve the identity of the person who will be paying rent and using the leased premises and (2) it wants to capture for its own account any profit attributable to a future increase in rental rates above those specified in the tenant's lease.[190]

An assignment and a sublease are distinct legal transactions. An *assignment* is a transfer by the tenant to a third party of all of its rights and interests in the lease and leased premises. In an assignment, the tenant has no reversionary interest in the lease or the leased premises and the recipient of the assignment (the *assignee*) has privity with the landlord.[191] A *sublease* is a transfer by the tenant to a third party of part of its rights and interests in the leased premises (but not the underlying lease). In a sublease, the tenant retains a reversionary interest in the lease and the leased premises and the recipient of the sublease (the *subtenant*) has no privity with the landlord.[192]

To illustrate the legal difference between an assignment and a sublease, assume that Tenant A leases 10,000 square feet of space from Landlord and that Tenant A has four years remaining on its initial lease term. If Tenant A opts to transfer its interest in all of the space for the remainder of the term to Tenant B, its transfer would be an assignment. If, however, Tenant B decides to transfer only its interest to use and occupy the space for two of the four remaining years of the lease term, then the transfer would be a sublease.

---

189. *See* DILLMAN, *supra* note 37, at 71; and ZANKEL, *supra* note 19, at 117–118.

190. *See* Elizabeth H. Belkin, *Assignment and Subleasing: What a Landlord Wants and Why*, in LEASE NEGOTIATION HANDBOOK 407, 407–408 (Edward Chupack ed., 2003); and ZANKEL, *supra* note 23, at 116.

191. Unless the landlord and the assignee enter into a separate agreement agreeing to be contractually bound to each other, an assignment creates only privity of estate (and not privity of contract) between the landlord and the tenant. Privity of estate allows the enforcement of only those covenants that are deemed to "run with the land" (such as those covenants related to the payment of rent, the use of the leased premises and the restriction on the tenant's ability to transfer its leasehold interests), while privity of contract permits the enforcement of the entirety of the lease as written. *See* SENN, *supra* note 5, at 13–9 through 13–13.

192. *See generally id.* at 13–5 through 13–9.

While there is a clear legal distinction between an assignment and a sublease, both transactions accomplish the same basic purpose of facilitating a transfer by the tenant of all or a portion of its leasehold interest to a third party. The legal and contractual considerations impacting assignments and subleases are similar in most respects.[193] For the purposes of this Chapter, an assignment and a sublease will be jointly referred to as a "transfer," the recipient of the transfer will be referred to as the "transferee" and the portion of the tenant's interest in the lease and the leased premises that is being transferred to the transferee will be referred to as the "leasehold interest."

1. Case Law on Assignment and Subleasing

The lease transfer topic is somewhat unique in the commercial leasing universe because there is a well-developed body of case law addressing the scope of the tenant's right to transfer all or some part of its leasehold interest to a third party. That case law generally establishes the following three general rules: (1) the tenant has the right to freely transfer its lease interest in any manner and to any person of its choosing;[194] (2) the transferring tenant will remain liable under the lease following the transfer;[195] and (3) both of the above rules can be abrogated and limited by the specific contractual agreement of the landlord and the tenant.[196] Landlords and tenants have fully embraced rule (3) and almost always include a specific clause in the lease that addresses the right of the tenant to transfer its leasehold interest to another person. The focus of the remainder of this section will be on the issues faced by the practitioner when crafting the assignment and sublease clause.

The case law in most states validates the ability of the landlord to include in the lease an absolute prohibition on the tenant's right to make any lease transfers whatsoever.[197] The parties could, therefore, theoretically include in the lease a simple statement to the effect that "the tenant will not assign all or any part of its interest in the lease or sublease all or any part of its interest in the leased premises." Similarly, the courts in most states support the enforceability of a lease clause that requires the landlord's consent to any transfer, but then permits the landlord to withhold its consent "arbitrarily," "capriciously" or "in its sole discretion."[198] A landlord who holds the clear upper hand in a lease negotiation would be well-advised to include one of the above types of clauses in its lease, so as to preserve its unfettered ability to deny the tenant's right to

---

193. *See* Brent C. Shaffer, *Counseling the Client on the Reasonable Consent Standard to Assignments*, 19 No. 4 PRACTICAL REAL ESTATE LAWYER 7 (July 2003); and SENN, *supra* note 5, at 13–13.

194. *See* FRIEDMAN, *supra* note 8, at 7–10.

195. *See id.* at 7–101.

196. *See id.* at 7–42

197. *See id.* at 7–39 through 7–41.

198. *See* SENN, *supra* note 5, at 13–17 through 13–24.

transfer its leasehold interest to someone who does not meet with the landlord's approval.

In most instances, the landlord does not have sufficient bargaining strength to carry the day on its assertion that it should have the sole discretion to determine when, whether and to whom the tenant may transfer its leasehold interest.[199] The default position in most landlord-tenant negotiations is an assignment and sublease clause that provides that the tenant may not transfer its leasehold interest "without the prior written consent of the landlord, which consent may not be unreasonably withheld or delayed."[200]

2. The Reasonable Consent Standard

There is an abundance of case law analyzing what it means for a landlord to act reasonably when responding to a lease transfer request from its tenant.[201] There are three guiding principles adopted by the courts to measure the reasonableness of a landlord's action:

- The landlord cannot use its consent right to get a better deal than it had with its original tenant (i.e., the landlord can deny consent only for reasons related specifically to the lease that is the subject of the proposed transfer and not to the landlord's broader economic or business concerns);[202]

- The landlord cannot deny its consent for reasons of "personal taste, sensibility or convenience"[203] (i.e., only objective and not subjective factors may be taken into consideration by the landlord); and

- The reasonableness of the landlord's actions will be determined by looking beyond the pretextual reasons for landlord's actions to the real reasons underlying its denial of a tenant's transfer proposal (i.e., the landlord must act in good faith in determining the reasons

---

199. The use of a "sole discretion" standard is more common in retail leases than it is in office leases. *See* Mark S. Hennigh, *Negotiating Assignment and Subletting Provisions*, in ALI–ABA Course of Study Materials, Commercial Real Estate Leases: Selected Issues in Drafting and Negotiating in Current markets, Course No. SN–013, 1131, 1136 (May 2008). *See also supra* text accompanying notes 209–211 for a discussion of the assignment and sublease clause in the context of a retail lease

200. The majority rule is that the landlord may withhold its consent in its sole discretion if the lease fails to set forth any standard for its consent—that is, the lease simply says that the "tenant may not assign this lease or sublease all or any part of the leased premises, without the prior written consent of the landlord." *See* Friedman, *supra note* 8, at 7–42; and Senn, *supra* note 5, at 13–17. There is, however, an "emerging trend [that] requires the landlord to be reasonable if no standard is stated." Senn, *supra* note 5, at 13–17 and 13–18. The discussion in the remainder of this section will assume that the landlord may not unreasonably withhold its consent, either because that is what the lease says or because the lease is silent on the standard and the landlord's building is located in a jurisdiction that implies a standard of reasonable consent.

201. *See generally*, Friedman, *supra* note 8, at 7–54 through 7–71; Senn, *supra* note 5, at 13–24 through 13–39; Shaffer, *supra* note 193; and Hennigh, *Negotiating Assignment and Subletting Provisions, supra* note 199, at Appendix 1.

202. *See* Shaffer, *supra* note 193, at 13.

203. *See* Broad & Branford Place Corp. v. J. J. Hockenjos Co., 39 A.2d 80, 82 (N.J. Sup. Ct. 1944); and Senn, *supra* note 5, at 13–25.

for its denial of the tenant's transfer request and the landlord's conduct may belie its stated intentions to the contrary).[204]

On the all-important topic of who has the burden of proof on the subject of the reasonableness of the landlord's behavior, the rule followed in the majority of the states is that the burden is on the tenant to prove that the landlord acted unreasonably.[205]

The following is a quick summary of some of the most prominent "reasonable" and "unreasonable" reasons cited by the courts for a landlord's denial of a tenant's request to transfer its leasehold interest to a third party.[206]

- *"Reasonable" Reasons*:

    - The creditworthiness of the proposed transferee calls into question the proposed transferee's ability to pay its rent;

    - The lack of business experience of the proposed transferee raises legitimate questions about the transferee's ability to perform its obligations under the transferred lease; and

    - The nature of the transferee's proposed use is markedly different from and more intense than that of the original tenant.

- *"Unreasonable" Reasons*:

    - The landlord just doesn't like the proposed transferee;

    - The tenant fails to meet a landlord demand that the proposed transferee agree to pay the landlord increased rent or a consent fee of some kind—i.e., good old, all-American greed;

    - The tenant's rent is below market and the landlord wants to share in any profit that might be realized by the tenant on the transfer of the favorable lease to the proposed transferee;

    - The proposed transferee is an existing occupant of the landlord's building; and

    - The landlord wants the proposed transferee to lease vacant space in the landlord's building (and not take over the space of an existing tenant).

The cases divining the landlord's relative reasonableness are so fact-sensitive as to raise interpretive questions even on the "reasonable"

---

204. *See* Toys R Us, Inc. v. NBD Trust Co, 1995 WL 591459 (N.D. Ill. 1995); and Economy Rentals, Inc. v. Garcia, 819 P.2d 1306 (N.M. 1991).

205. Most states also hold that the burden is on the tenant to provide the landlord with sufficient information to permit it to make a reasoned decision on the tenant's transfer request. *See* Shaffer, *supra* note 193, at 9–10.

206. For a more detailed discussion of representative cases weighing in on the topic of the reasonable consent standard, *see generally* Shaffer, *supra* note 193; and SENN, *supra* note 5, at 13–24 through 13–39.

reasons mentioned above. By way of example, is the mere fact that the transferee's net worth is less than the tenant's sufficient grounds to support the reasonableness of the landlord's denial of its consent to the proposed lease transfer (even if the tenant is Bill Gates and the proposed transferee is Warren Buffet)? Is the fact that the proposed transferee has an unsavory business reputation (e.g., Jeff Skilling) adequate reason for the landlord to disapprove the transfer request, even though the transferee has an established record of success in the business world? In determining the unacceptability of the proposed transferee's use, can the landlord take into consideration the actual use of the leased premises by its existing tenant (the operation of a law firm) or only the permitted use specified in the lease (any lawful use)?

There is a growing trend among lawyers representing commercial landlords to include expansive language in the assignment and sublease clause that specifically sanctions the reasonableness of certain grounds for the landlord's disapproval of its tenant's transfer request.[207] By way of example, the landlord's lawyer might try to resolve one of the uncertainties noted at the end of the prior paragraph by clearly stating that the landlord will be deemed to be acting reasonably if it denies the tenant's transfer request because the proposed transferee's net worth (even though substantial) is less than that of the existing tenant. Similarly, the lawyer might attempt to move a couple of reasons from the "unreasonable" list noted above into the "deemed reasonable category"—most notably the landlord's right to say "no" to the transfer request if the proposed transferee is an existing occupant of the landlord's building or if the landlord is negotiating with the proposed transferee to lease vacant space in the landlord's building. Most practitioners believe that provisions of this type should be upheld by the courts.[208]

3. Assignment and Subleasing in Retail Leases

There is much more at stake in the battle over the landlord's reasonableness standard in the context of a retail lease than there is in the context of an office lease.[209] The landlord of an office building usually does not get too worked up over a potential lease transfer, so long as the proposed transferee is a creditworthy entity and its proposed use of the leased premises is not something totally out of character for an office building. As noted earlier in this Chapter, the success of a retail center is directly linked to the mix of the retail tenants doing business in that center and their respective abilities to generate customer traffic. The

---

207. *See, e.g.*, Henigh, *Negotiating Assignment and Subletting Provisions, supra* note 199, at 1137–1138; SENN, *supra* note 5, at 13–38 and 13–39 (Form 13–5); and Richard R. Goldberg, *Retail Lease Agreement*, in ALI–ABA COURSE OF STUDY MATERIALS, COMMERCIAL REAL ESTATE LEASES: SELECTED ISSUES IN DRAFTING AND NEGOTIATING IN CURRENT MARKETS, Course No. SN–013, 223, 259–260, (May 2008).

208. *See* Shaffer, *supra* note 193, at 6.

209. For a detailed discussion of the assignment and sublease clause of a retail lease, *see* Joel R. Hall, *Assignment*, in ALI–ABA COURSE OF STUDY MATERIALS, COMMERCIAL REAL ESTATE LEASES: SELECTED ISSUES IN DRAFTING AND NEGOTIATING IN CURRENT MARKETS, Course No. SN–013, 579, (May 2008).

financial viability of the entire center can be jeopardized if an existing tenant transfers its lease to a transferee whose operations do not fit with the rest of the center (e.g., Saks Fifth Avenue transferring its lease to Dollar General or a jewelry store assigning its lease to a candle store when there are already three stores in the center selling candles). An inappropriate lease transfer can also significantly reduce the landlord's percentage rent revenues (under both the transferred lease and the leases of other tenants in the center) and potentially result in a violation of a co-tenancy or exclusive use provision found in the lease of one of the landlord's other tenants.

For these reasons, the negotiations over the assignment and sublease clause in a retail lease are often long and frenzied, with the landlord adopting the expansive drafting approach noted above to try to make it clear that the landlord will, in all events, have the right to deny a proposed lease transfer on the grounds that the proposed transfer could (1) reduce the amount of the landlord's percentage rent receipts, (2) trigger a violation of the provision of another tenant lease or (3) result in a reduction of customer traffic to the center (either due to a duplication of another tenant's use or the reduced drawing power of the proposed transferee's store).[210] The retail landlord can obtain added protection against an unwanted lease transfer by including a tightly worded, restrictive use clause in its lease—e.g., "the leased premises may be used for the operation of the retail sale of candles and for no other purpose."[211]

4. Additional Assignment and Subleasing Issues

There are three collateral issues that should also be considered by the lawyers during their negotiations over the content of the assignment and sublease clause. The first is whether the landlord's consent will be needed for the tenant's transfer of a leasehold interest to one of its affiliates or for its transfer of a leasehold interest to an entity that is acquiring substantially all of the tenant's business operations by way of a merger, stock sale, consolidation, asset sale, etc. A tenant generally does not want a landlord to be able to stand in the way of the reorganization or sale of its business and, therefore, typically will ask for a specific statement that the tenant may effect such a transfer without the landlord's consent. Most commercial landlords will grant such a request, as long as the landlord receives prompt written notice of the transfer and the tenant (or a related entity having a comparable net worth) remains fully liable following the transfer.[212]

The second collateral issue is who is entitled to receive the profit realized from the tenant's transfer of its leasehold interest to a third party. If its rent is below market, a tenant may be able to generate a profit by either assigning its lease in exchange for a cash payment from the

---

210. *See id.* at 586–600.

211. *See supra* Pages 511–512, for a discussion of restrictive use clauses in retail leases.

212. *See* Hall, *Assignment, supra* note 209, at 613–618; and Hennigh, *Office Leases, supra* note 83, at 15–59 and 15–60.

transferee (paid either upfront or over a period of time) or subleasing the leased premises to the transferee for a sublease rental that is greater than the rent provided in the tenant's lease with the landlord. The landlord can attempt to recover some or all of the generated profit by including either a recapture or a profit-sharing clause in its original lease with the tenant. Under a **recapture clause**, the landlord reserves the right to terminate its lease with the original tenant and then capture any potential profit by entering into a new lease with the proposed transferee. A **profit-sharing clause** requires the tenant to share with the landlord a portion (e.g., 50%) of any profit it derives from a lease transfer. If a tenant is willing to agree to the inclusion of a recapture or profit-sharing clause in its lease (and only those with inferior bargaining positions are), the tenant's lawyer will need to carefully address a wide variety of issues, including (1) the identification of the trigger for the landlord's exercise of its recapture right (e.g., just the tenant' statement that it is contemplating a transfer of its leasehold interest or the tenant's actual receipt of an offer to acquire the leasehold interest from an interested third party), and (2) the manner in which the tenant's profit on the transaction will be computed (this computation is particularly difficult when the tenant is also transferring other property to the transferee in addition to its leasehold interest).[213]

Finally, the parties should carefully think through the remedies that will be available to the tenant if the landlord breaches its covenant to act reasonably. The financial loss experienced by a tenant due to a landlord's breach of the reasonable consent standard can be quite severe—particularly if the landlord's denial of its consent results in the demise of a much larger deal (e.g., the sale of an entire business division). Landlords will frequently seek to insulate themselves from liability for the tenant's financial loss by including a statement in the lease that equitable relief (e.g., an injunction or declaratory judgment action) will be the tenant's sole and exclusive remedy for the landlord's breach of its covenant to not unreasonably withhold or delay its consent to a proposed lease transfer. The well-advised tenant will resist such a landlord ploy or, at the very least, reserve a right to sue the landlord for damages if the landlord is found to have acted in bad faith in denying its consent to a proposed tenant transfer.[214]

XII. ALLOCATION OF RISK AND OTHER LEGAL ISSUES

The concluding section of this Chapter will examine the provisions of a commercial lease that address the following topics:

- The consequences of a default by the tenant or the landlord;
- The impact of a casualty on the landlord-tenant relationship;

---

213. *See generally* Hennigh, *Office Leases, supra* note 83, at 15–60 through 15–64; and ZANKEL, *supra* note 19, at 123–125.

214. *See* SENN, *supra* note 5, at 13–39 through 13–42; and Hall, *Assignment, supra* note 209, at 84–86.

- The impact of a condemnation on the landlord-tenant relationship;

- The subordination of the tenant's leasehold interest to the mortgage lien of the landlord's lender;

- The allocation of responsibility for the payment of leasing commissions;

- The tenant's responsibility to provide the landlord with estoppel certificates confirming the status of the tenant's leasehold interest;

- The tenant's posting of a security deposit and its provision of periodic financial statements for the landlord's review; and

- Other so-called "boilerplate" matters.

A. DEFAULT CLAUSE. *(§22)*

The discussion of the tenant default clause starts with the definition of an ***event of default***. An event of default exists if an event has occurred or a circumstance has arisen that permits the landlord to exercise its remedies. In most situations, an event of default requires both the tenant's non-performance of a lease obligation AND the passage of a specified period of time without the tenant's cure of such non-performance.

The landlord's lawyer's job in structuring the default clause is threefold. First, he must identify all those events or circumstances (the ***default***) that can give rise to an event of default. Examples of such events or circumstances are: a tenant's failure to pay its rent by the due date; the tenant's use of the leased premises in a manner not permitted by the lease; and the death or bankruptcy of a lease guarantor. The lawyer's next task is to determine whether the tenant will be given a period of time (called a ***grace period***) in which to perform the subject lease obligation. Finally, the lawyer must make a reasoned determination whether the tenant will be entitled to receive written notice of the existence of the alleged default and an additional period of time (the ***cure period***) to cure such default before the landlord can declare an event of default and exercise its remedies under the lease.

The landlord's preference would be for the definition of "default" and "event of default" to be identical—that is, for the occurrence of each listed event or circumstance to immediately authorize the landlord to pursue its remedies against the tenant. Time is the enemy of the landlord when the tenant defaults. If the landlord senses that the tenant is having financial trouble, it will want to move immediately to oust the tenant from possession of its leased premises and pave the way for a new tenant to take over occupancy of the space. If the tenant is financially stable, the landlord will want to get its hands on the money to which it is due as quickly as possible. In either event, the passage of time works to the landlord's detriment.

The tenant, on the other hand, wants to make sure that it is not in jeopardy of either losing its right to conduct its business in the leased premises or being penalized economically for the occurrence of an inadvertent or immaterial event of non-performance. As such, the tenant will always seek to require the landlord to provide it with written notice of the alleged existence of any default and an ample period of time in which the tenant can cure the alleged default.

The lawyers for the landlord and the tenant begin their efforts to bridge their client's differences by focusing on two different types of default—a *monetary default* versus a *non-monetary default*. A monetary default is defined as any failure of the tenant to pay its rent on or before the due date specified in the lease. A non-monetary default is any default other than a monetary default.

The landlord is most concerned with the treatment afforded monetary defaults. Stated succinctly, the landlord wants its money and it wants it now. The landlord's lawyer will typically adopt a firm stance that the tenant knows when its rent is due and that there is no need for any grace period, written notice or cure period for a monetary default. The tenant's lawyer will, in turn, point out that it would be grossly unfair to penalize the tenant for a bookkeeping error or other inadvertent failure to pay its rent. When all the shouting is done, the lawyers usually craft a middle ground position that takes into account the landlord's need to get paid on time and the tenant's desire to not be penalized for an unintentional error. The following is a representative example of a compromise that might be reached on the topic of monetary defaults:

- A grace period of three days before the landlord can impose a late fee on the delinquent payment;

- The imposition of a late fee of 3–5% of the amount of the delinquent payment immediately upon the expiration of the grace period (without the need for any notice);

- A requirement that the landlord provide the tenant with written notice of the monetary default not more than once during any 12 month period; and

- The grant of a ten day cure period in which the tenant can cure its non-payment (again subject to the not more than once during any 12 month period limitation noted above).[215]

The landlord is generally receptive to providing the tenant with written notice of a non-monetary default and the right to cure that default for a cure period of somewhere between 20–30 days after the notice date. The tenant frequently asks for (and usually gets) a reasonable extension of the cure period for those defaults that are not readily susceptible of being cured within the normal 20–30 day cure period—e.g., a repair

---

215. *See generally* Russell B. Bershad, *Default*, in Lease Negotiation Handbook 531, 532–533 (Edward Chupack ed., 2003); Moran, *supra* note 6, at 70; Zankel, *supra* note 19, at 153–157; and Dillman, *supra* note 37, at 107–109.

requiring a new part that is on back order and won't be available for two months. Landlord's counsel will often counter by seeking to eliminate the notice requirement and cure period for certain defaults that cannot be cured—e.g., the death or insolvency of a guarantor. Tenants are usually amenable to exempting a limited number of such uncurable defaults from the general notice and cure period requirements of the default clause.[216]

1. Remedies for a Tenant Default

Once agreement is reached on what constitutes an event of default under the lease, the parties next turn to a discussion of the remedies that will be available to the landlord to respond to the event of default. Once an event of default has occurred, the landlord wants to have the rights (1) to regain possession of the leased premises, so that it can try to re-lease the premises to a new tenant and (2) to collect rent or damages from the defaulted tenant, so that it can maintain its targeted financial returns for the project while it searches for a substitute tenant.[217]

There are three ways that the landlord can go about regaining possession of the leased premises. First, it can try to convince the tenant to voluntarily surrender possession of the leased premises by returning its keys and removing its property from the leased premises. This is by far the most cost-effective method for the landlord to recover possession of the leased premises. The landlord must, however, be careful to avoid releasing the tenant from its continuing rent obligations by accepting the tenant's voluntary surrender of the leased premises.[218] A letter to the tenant from landlord's counsel confirming that the landlord will continue to hold the tenant liable for the payment of its rent and other financial obligations, notwithstanding the tenant's voluntary vacation of the leased premises, should be a part of the landlord's standard operating procedures following the occurrence of an event of default.

If the tenant refuses to gracefully surrender possession of the leased premises, the landlord has two remaining options. It can either institute an eviction proceeding against the tenant under the applicable state statute[219] or exercise its self-help remedy by changing the locks on the building or taking some other affirmative action designed to prevent the tenant from continuing to possess the leased premises. Going the self-help

---

216. *See* Moran, *supra* note 6, at 71; and Bershad, *supra* note 215, at 533–534.

217. The mere existence of an event of default does not, of course, mean that the landlord will automatically exercise all of its legal remedies against the tenant. Depending on the nature of the event of the default, the creditworthiness of the tenant and the overall health of the real estate economy, the landlord may choose to defer the exercise of its remedies and, instead, work with the tenant to resolve the dispute. Having said that, the landlord clearly wants to have the RIGHT to take immediate action against the tenant, even if it opts not to exercise that right for a period of time. The remainder of the discussion on the topic of tenant defaults will assume that the landlord wants the tenant out of the leased premises right away.

218. *See* SENN, *supra* note 5, at 31–27.

219. Most states have enacted statutes (commonly referred to as forcible, entry and detainer or FE & D statutes), which are designed to facilitate the landlord's expeditious recovery of possession of the leased premises upon the occurrence of a tenant event of default. *See, e.g.,* the discussion of Illinois' and California's FE & D statutes in Moran, *supra* note 6, at 72–74, 77–78.

route can, however, subject the landlord to an open-ended liability to the tenant for a wrongful eviction.[220] A landlord should, therefore, avoid exercising its self-help remedies, except in those extreme situations where it is concerned that the tenant will deliberately damage the leased premises or otherwise engage in prohibited conduct that will have a deleterious impact on the value of the landlord's project.

In most situations, the occurrence of an event of default means that the tenant is out of money and does not have the financial wherewithal to continue to pay its rent. In those situations, the landlord's sole goal is to recover possession of the leased premises, so that it can find a new tenant and once again begin receiving rental income from the leased premises. That is not, however, always the case. On occasion, the event of default will consist of a non-monetary default and the tenant will still be fully capable of paying its rent. More commonly, the tenant may be in financial trouble, but the lease guarantor will remain a creditworthy person. In those situations, the landlord has the added goal of collecting money from the tenant/guarantor to preserve the benefit of the economic bargain it originally struck with the tenant.[221]

At common law, the tenant's obligation to pay rent terminates coincident with the termination of its right of possession.[222] This rule can, however, be overridden by the inclusion in the lease of a ***survival clause***. A survival clause is an affirmative statement that the tenant's obligation to pay rent will survive the termination of its right of possession of the leased premises.[223] It is essential that the lease contain a survival clause to preserve the landlord's right to collect rent or damages from the tenant after possession of the leased space reverts back to the landlord.

The landlord has two possible contractual remedies that it can include in the lease to try to collect additional sums of money from the tenant after the landlord's recovery of possession of the leased premises. The landlord can either terminate the lease and sue for damages or it can elect to maintain the lease in place and continue to hold the tenant liable for the payment of rent when and as it comes due.

When the landlord elects to terminate the lease, the tenant's obligation to continue to make rent payments automatically ceases.[224] The landlord can, however, sue for damages based on the tenant's breach of the lease contract. The measure of damages is generally the difference

---

220. *See id.* at 72; and Bershad, *supra* note 215, at 538.

221. Guarantors often seek to eliminate their obligation to guaranty the payment of rent after the tenant's voluntary surrender of possession of the leased premises by posting what is commonly referred to as a "good guy guaranty." A good guy guaranty limits the guaranteed rent obligations to those that accrued prior to the date on which the tenant voluntarily vacates the leased premises. *See* Lubin, *supra* note 21, at 2.

222. *See* SENN, *supra* note 5, at 31–23; and Robert Harms Bliss, *Mitigation of Damages and Calculation of "Future Rentals": The Difference between Rent and Damages* in ACREL PAPERS 1, 1–2 (ALI–ABA, Spring 2007)

223. *See e.g.,* clause (b) of §22 of the Form Office Lease.

224. The tenant will, however, continue to be liable for the payment of all accrued and unpaid rent through the date of the termination of lease. *See* Moran, *supra* note 6, at 72.

between the present value of the rent reserved under the lease and the present value of the current fair market rental value of the leased premises.[225] In determining the fair market rental value of the leased premises, the courts will typically adjust such value downward to reflect both the rent hiatus that the landlord will experience during the time it takes to re-lease the leased premises and the reasonable costs that the landlord will have to incur as part of its efforts to re-lease the leased premises (including additional tenant improvement costs and leasing commissions).

If the landlord elects to maintain the lease in place (notwithstanding its termination of the tenant's ongoing right of possession), the tenant will remain liable for the payment of the rent specified in the lease, when and as such payments become due and payable under the lease. The landlord can either file legal actions to collect the rent periodically throughout the lease term (e.g., every six months) or it can wait until the end of the lease term and file a single legal action covering all of the unpaid rent for the entirety of the lease term. If the landlord re-leases the leased premises at any time during the defaulted tenant's original lease term, then the rental payments received by the landlord from such re-leasing (net of any tenant improvement costs, leasing commissions and other reasonable re-leasing costs incurred by the landlord) will be offset against the rent owed to the landlord by the tenant.[226]

Once the landlord decides to exercise its lease remedies, it next needs to choose whether it will terminate the lease and sue for damages or maintain the lease and sue for accrued and unpaid rent at a later date. That decision will be dictated by a number of considerations including the length of the tenant's remaining lease term, the prevailing conditions in the local real estate market and the soundness of the tenant's credit (which, for this purpose, also includes the credit of any lease guarantor).

If the tenant is in clear, financial trouble, the landlord should always elect to terminate its lease as quickly as possible. Based on the old adage that "you can't squeeze blood out of a turnip," it is unlikely that the landlord is going to collect any money from the tenant, regardless which remedy it selects. More importantly, if the tenant files for bankruptcy while its lease is still in force, the pro-tenant provisions of the federal bankruptcy laws will become fully applicable and the landlord's efforts to re-lease the leased premises may be frustrated for an extended period of time.[227]

---

225. *See e.g.,* clause (a) of §22 of the Form Office Lease. There are a few cases that seem to allow the landlord to collect the full, accelerated amount of the rent provided in the lease, without giving the tenant any credit for the fair market rental value of the lease during the remainder of the lease term. *See* SENN, *supra* note 5, at 31–31. Those cases are, however, in the clear minority and, in any event, would require the landlord to pay back to the tenant any rent the landlord subsequently collects from a new tenant. Because a full rent acceleration clause (without any credit being given to the tenant for the fair market rental value of the leased premises) works an extreme hardship upon the tenant, most lawyers representing the tenant will insist that the lease contain a damages remedy that is styled in the manner consistent with that described in the text.

226. *See* Bliss, *supra* note 222, at 3.

227. *See Bershad, supra* note 215, at 538. The impact of federal bankruptcy laws on the landlord-tenant relationship is an important topic, but one which, unfortunately is well beyond

2. Landlord's Duty to Mitigate

The final topic that needs to be covered as part of the discussion of the tenant default clause is the landlord's duty to mitigate its damages. Most states, either by statute or common law, now impose a duty on the commercial landlord to mitigate its damages.[228] Moreover, the well-represented tenant is often successful in including an express covenant in the lease requiring the landlord to mitigate its damages, even if the jurisdiction in which the landlord's building is located does not require the imposition of such a duty.

If the landlord has a duty to mitigate its damages, it will generally be required to use reasonable efforts to find a new tenant to take over the defaulted tenant's leased premises.[229] There are some relatively obvious measures that a landlord should adopt if it wants to satisfy its mitigation duty—for example, advertising the space as being available "for lease"; hiring a leasing broker to market the space; responding in a timely fashion to inquiries from prospective tenants; and putting the leased premises into a rentable condition. There are, however, a number of gray areas concerning the scope of the landlord's duty to mitigate damages. Specifically, the courts have not provided consistent, clear-cut answers to the following questions.[230]

- Is the landlord required to accept a below market rent from a new tenant?

- Is the landlord required to re-lease the space to a person whose credit standing is somewhat questionable (and worse than that of the defaulted tenant)?

- Is the landlord required to accept a new lease that has a term that is significantly shorter or longer than the defaulted tenant's term?

- Is the landlord required to spend significant dollars on additional tenant improvements and leasing commissions?

- Is the landlord required to re-lease the leased premises if it has other vacant space in its building (or in a nearby building)?

To the extent the tenant is successful in its efforts to impose a duty to mitigate on the landlord, the landlord may want to adopt a similar

---

the scope of this Chapter. Helpful and thorough discussions of the treatment of commercial leases under the bankruptcy laws can be found in Steven E. Ostrow, *What You Need to Know about the Treatment of Commercial Leases under the Bankruptcy Reform Act*, 22 No. 1 Practical Real Estate Lawyer 27 (January 2006); Trev E. Peterson, *The ABC's of Landlord Claims in Bankruptcy*, in ACREL Papers 47 (ALI–ABA, Spring 2009); and David L. Pollack, *Defaults, Landlord and Tenant Litigation and Bankruptcies*, in ALI–ABA Course of Study Materials, Commercial Real Estate Leases: Selected Issues in Drafting and Negotiating in Current Markets, Course No. SN–013, 1255 (May 2008).

228. *See* Friedman, *supra* note 8, at Appendix 16A, where the authors report that 28 states now require commercial landlords to mitigate their damages, while only 15 states impose no duty to mitigate.

229. *See generally* Senn, *supra* note 5, at 31–37.

230. *See* Friedman, *supra* note 8, at 16–78 through 16–90; and Senn, *supra* note 5, at 31–37 through 31–46.

approach to that suggested in the earlier discussion of the assignment and sublease clause and specify certain actions that the landlord need not take to satisfy the duty (such as the gray areas noted above).[231]

3. Landlord Default Clause

The discussion of the default clause has now covered several pages without a single mention of the prospect or consequences of a default by the landlord. That topic is also notably absent from most landlord-authored lease forms. If the tenant does not request the inclusion in the lease of a specific landlord default clause (and they often fail to do so), then the tenant will be left with the very limited remedies that are available to it under common law—quite possibly nothing other than the right to sue the landlord for damages.[232]

To the extent the tenant is able to convince the landlord that it makes sense to include a landlord default clause in the lease, the parties will need to address many of the same issues discussed previously with respect to the tenant default clause—most notably the existence of notice and cure rights. The most contentious part of the discussion will undoubtedly focus on the tenant's demands that it be given the rights to withhold its rent and terminate its lease if a landlord event of default occurs. The landlord's lawyer will, of course, resist those demands and try its best to effectively limit the tenant's recourse to the "go ahead and sue me" alternative provided at common law.[233]

B. CASUALTY CLAUSE. *(§19)*

Virtually every commercial lease has a clause devoted to sorting out the impact on the landlord-tenant relationship of the occurrence of a building fire or other casualty. Because the subject of that clause is the occurrence of an unusual event, many practitioners go through their entire careers without ever having the efficacy of their casualty clauses tested in a real world application. For that reason, casualty clauses are often given short shrift during the lease negotiations. However, those landlords and tenants who have been unfortunate enough to experience the aftermath of the occurrence of a fire will be quick to remind their respective counsel of the importance of drafting a thoughtful and thorough casualty clause.

The term *casualty* is often used in a commercial lease as a shorthand reference to the occurrence of a fire, explosion, storm, flood, earthquake or other calamitous event that damages the landlord's building or interferes with the tenant's use of its leased premises. The occurrence of a casualty triggers two questions that the lawyers must consider when

---

231. *See* Bershad, *supra* note 215, at 539; and SENN, *supra* note 5, at 31–45 (From 31–5).

232. *See generally* Ronald R. Pollina, *"So, Sue Me"—What is the Tenant's Recourse*, in LEASE NEGOTIATION HANDBOOK 583 (Edward Chupack ed., 2003).

233. *See supra* Pages 509–510, for a discussion of the competing perspectives of the landlord and the tenant on the rent abatement, self-help and termination remedies.

negotiating the casualty clause—(1) will the tenant's rent obligation abate as a result of the casualty and (2) will either the landlord or the tenant have the right to terminate the lease following the casualty?[234]

The answers to those two questions are largely dependent on the severity of the damage caused to the landlord's building by the occurrence of the casualty. In the context of the total destruction of a multi-tenant office building, counsel for the landlord and the tenant are typically willing to stipulate that both the landlord and the tenant will have the right to terminate the lease. If neither party exercises its termination right, the landlord will then be obligated to reconstruct its building and the tenant's rent will be abated during the reconstruction period.

The questions become much tougher to answer when the casualty does not result in the total destruction of landlord's project. Should a tenant have the right to terminate its lease or reduce its rent if a fire damages a portion (but not all) of the tenant's leased premises? What if a flash flood results in the building lobby and parking lot being rendered unusable for a period of time? Should either the tenant or the landlord have the right to walk away from the lease if it will take the landlord 90 days and a projected expenditure of $200,000 to repair the damaged areas?

A significant portion of the casualty clause negotiations is devoted to an attempt to delineate when the damage is so severe that the tenant should have the right to abate its rent or terminate its lease. The severity of the damage caused by the casualty can be measured in a number of ways—by the nature and amount of the space damaged by the casualty (e.g., more than 50% of the square footage contained in the leased premises is rendered untenantable); by the cost of repairing the damage (e.g., the estimated cost of repairing the damage exceeds 20% of the building's replacement cost); or by the time it will take to repair the damage (e.g., more than 120 days).[235]

It is usually in the landlord's best interests to keep in full force the tenant's lease and its obligation to pay rent. The landlord will, therefore, seek to establish a high threshold quantifying the severity of the damage that will permit the tenant to terminate its lease. By way of example, a landlord-oriented lease might provide that the tenant will have the right to terminate its lease only if "the tenant is wholly deprived of the beneficial use and occupancy of the leased premises, and the landlord's

---

234. Common law, as one might expect, is singularly unhelpful in answering these questions—at least from the tenant's perspective. Common law principles place no obligation on the landlord to repair its damaged building, nor do they afford the tenant the right to abate its rent or terminate its lease. While a few modern courts have softened the application of these common law rules in the context of a total destruction of the leased premises, lawyers are well-advised, as always, to put their stock in the written word contained in their clients' leases and not in the wisdom of the judiciary. Several states have enacted legislation designed to explicate the consequences of a casualty. Practitioners practicing in those states should closely review the legislation to determine whether the provisions of the statute can be modified by contract and, if so, whether they believe it is appropriate to do so. *See* Richard E. Strauss, *Damage and Destruction*, in LEASE NEGOTIATION HANDBOOK 481, 481–482 (Edward Chupack ed., 2003).

235. *See generally* SENN, *supra* note 5, at 23–5 through 23–10.

contractor determines that the damage to the leased premises cannot be repaired within 365 days after the occurrence of the casualty."

The tenant, of course, will want the flexibility to exit from its lease if the damage produced from the casualty adversely affects its ability to operate its business in the leased premises for any significant period of time.[236] The tenant will negotiate for its receipt of a right to terminate the lease if the damage is not repaired within a relatively short time frame (e.g., 60 days after the date of the casualty). The tenant will also want to make sure that the scope of the damage covered in the casualty clause extends not just to the leased premises, but also to all of the common areas that serve the leased premises.[237]

Once the parties have agreed upon the damage standard that will trigger their respective rights to terminate the lease (usually somewhere between the two extreme standards noted in the preceding two paragraphs), they next turn to the issue of the abatement of the tenant's rent during the repair period. The landlord will sometimes agree to the insertion of a clause that provides that the tenant's rent "will be equitably and proportionately abated to reflect the untenantable portion of the leased premises."[238] The landlord's willingness to grant this concession is linked to its expectation that it will recover the full amount of any granted abatement under the rent loss insurance policy it maintains for the project.[239]

Two additional points should be made concerning the parties' respective rights to terminate the lease following the occurrence of a casualty. The tenant will usually seek to negotiate for a heightened right to terminate the lease if the casualty occurs during the latter part of the lease term (e.g., the last 12 months of the term).[240] Absent such a right, the tenant could be forced to move back into the leased premises for a brief tail period after the completion of the repairs, even if its business interests would be better served by a permanent relocation to other space.

The landlord, on the other hand, will want to condition its obligation to repair the leased premises on the availability of insurance proceeds to fund its repair efforts.[241] If the casualty is not insured under the insur-

---

236. *See* DILLMAN, *supra* note 37, at 82.

237. This is especially true for retail tenants, where damage to the parking lot or other common areas can produce a significant economic hardship for the tenant. *See* SENN, *supra* note 5, at 23–21.

238. *See e.g.,* §19 of the Form Office Lease.

239. *See* Richard R. Goldberg, *Insurance*, in ALI–ABA COURSE OF STUDY MATERIALS, COMMERCIAL REAL ESTATE LEASES: SELECTED ISSUES IN DRAFTING AND NEGOTIATING IN CURRENT MARKETS, Course No. SN–013, 1313, 1321–1322 (May 2008);

240. *See* DILLMAN, *supra* note 37, at 82.

241. A commercial lease typically includes a clause that identifies the various insurance coverages that the landlord and the tenant must maintain throughout the lease term. *See e.g.,* §15 of the Form Office Lease. The insurance topic is quite technical and, as such, is beyond the scope of this Chapter. For a thorough-going discussion of the insurance clause, *see generally* Goldberg, *Insurance*, *supra* note 239; and Raymond S. Iwamoto, *Insurance and the Commercial Lease*, in THE PRACTICAL REAL ESTATE LAWYER'S MANUAL ON COMMERCIAL LEASING IN TROUBLED TIMES— FORMS, CHECKLISTS, AND ADVICE 225 (2009).

ance policy that it is required to maintain under the insurance clause of the lease, the landlord should reserve the right to terminate the lease. Similarly, if the insurance proceeds are insufficient to fund the full cost of the repair, the landlord should reserve the right to either terminate the lease or alter the scope of its repairs to fit within its insurance budget.[242]

C. CONDEMNATION CLAUSE. *(§20)*

The negotiation of the condemnation clause involves many of the same issues discussed above with respect to the casualty clause—specifically, the nature and scope of the tenant's right to receive a rent abatement and the respective rights of the landlord and the tenant to terminate the lease as a result of a taking by the government of all or part of the landlord's project through the exercise (or threatened exercise) of its eminent domain powers. There are, however, a few lease issues that are unique to the condemnation context.[243]

A governmental taking permanently changes the nature of the landlord's project. This result is unlike the situation following the occurrence of a casualty, where the parties are focused on the landlord restoring the leased premises and its building to the same condition that existed prior to the occurrence of the casualty. That is not possible in the context of a condemnation, because a part of the landlord's project is permanently taken away. As a result, the lawyers assigned with the task of negotiating the condemnation clause must tackle two issues that are not present in their negotiation of the casualty clause—(1) is the portion of the leased premises and the common areas remaining after the condemnation sufficient to permit the tenant to conduct its business in the leased premises in a substantially similar manner to that which characterized its use of the leased premises prior to the condemnation, and (2) is the tenant entitled to a permanent reduction in its rent to reflect the fact that the post-condemnation property is inherently different from the property the tenant was leasing before the condemnation? Because both of these questions rely on the evaluation of subjective considerations, the condemnation clause will usually include equally subjective standards to determine the impact of a condemnation on the landlord-tenant relationship—e.g., does the condemnation "materially interfere with the tenant's use of the leased premises" and is the tenant entitled to an "equitable adjustment" of rent to reflect the changed condition of the leased premises after the condemnation?[244]

The other issue that the condemnation clause needs to address is how the landlord and tenant will split the monetary award paid by the condemning authority—particularly an award related to the taking of the entirety of the project? Most tenants will ask for the right to share in the award to reflect the value of the tenant's leasehold interest that was taken

---

242. *See* DILLMAN, *supra* note 37, at 81.

243. *See generally* ZANKEL, *supra* note 19, at 150–151.

244. *See id.* at 150.

by the condemning authority. The landlord will respond that the tenant is free to make a separate application to the condemning authority for an award compensating the tenant for its moving expenses, but that the tenant will not be entitled to any portion of the authority's award for the value of the taken property. This is one battle that is fairly typically by the landlord.[245]

Practice Tip #11–2—Focus on What Matters

Every year I invite Brian Ellis, a prominent Columbus, Ohio developer, to speak to my law school class and share his thoughts on what it takes to be a successful real estate development lawyer. The first words out of his mouth every year are "YOU NEED TO FOCUS ON WHAT MATTERS." Brian drives homes this point by telling a story about a young lawyer who camped out in his office one day to complain about the difficulty he was having in trying to get the tenant's lawyer to agree to the substance of a condemnation clause. After listening for a few moments to the young lawyer's saga, Brian lost his patience and blurted out "IT DOESN'T MATTER!" Once he regained his composure, Brian calmly explained to his legal counsel that this particular tenant was negotiating to take space in a brand new, downtown office building and that its lease term was only five years. The likelihood that the building would be condemned in the ensuing five years was so slim that the intricacies of the condemnation clause "JUST DIDN'T MATTER."

I relish hearing Brian's story every year because it provides me with the perfect opening to make the point to my class that the successful transactional lawyer first needs to understand what matters most to his client. Only once the lawyer has figured out what matters to the client can the lawyer then follow Brian's sage advice to "FOCUS ON WHAT MATTERS."

D. SUBORDINATION CLAUSE. *(§13)*

The subordination clause attempts to deal with the status of the tenant's lease following the foreclosure of a lender's mortgage on the landlord's building. Specifically, the question is will the tenant have the right after a foreclosure to continue to occupy the leased premises pursuant to the terms of the lease it negotiated with the landlord?

The tenant does not want its lease to be terminated or otherwise affected in any way by the landlord's failure to comply with the terms of its mortgage loan. The lender, on the other hand, wants the right to pick and choose those leases that it will recognize following the foreclosure of its mortgage—keeping the good leases in place and rejecting the bad

---

245. *See* ESIENBERG, *supra* note 136, at 138.

leases. The lender also wants to make sure that its interest in any insurance or condemnation proceeds are superior to the interests of the project's tenants. Finally, in a rare show of apathy, the landlord really doesn't care one way or the other what happens to the tenant after the lender forecloses on the landlord's building. As a result, the landlord's sole motivation when negotiating the subordination clause is to arrive at language that is mutually acceptable to the tenant and the lender.

The rule established at common law is that the tenant will have an unrestricted right to remain in possession of the leased premises following a foreclosure, only if its lease is deemed to have priority over the lender's mortgage. If the lease is found to be subordinate to the lender's mortgage, then the lender will have the right to terminate the tenant's lease and evict the tenant from possession of the leased premises.[246]

A lease will be deemed subordinate to the lien of the lender's mortgage if either (1) the mortgage was recorded prior to the tenant's execution of its lease or (2) the lease expressly provides that the tenant's interest is subordinate to the mortgage.[247] To provide its lender with the maximum available protection, the landlord will often include in its standard lease a provision stating that, unless otherwise specifically elected by the lender, the lease will automatically be deemed to be subordinate to the lien of any mortgage, regardless of the comparative dates on which the lease and the mortgage were made. The effect of such a provision is quite clear—if the landlord's lender ever forecloses on its mortgage, it (and not the tenant) will have the right to determine whether the tenant's lease remains intact or is terminated.

If the tenant has any negotiating clout whatsoever, it will insist that its agreement to voluntarily subordinate its leasehold interest to the lien of the lender's mortgage be expressly conditioned upon its receipt of a written agreement from the lender acknowledging that the tenant will have the continuing right to occupy the leased premises so long as it remains in compliance with the terms of the lease. Assuming that the tenant making the above request is of a sufficient size and stature to merit the lender's respect, the tenant and the lender will then set about trying to negotiate the terms of a comprehensive document (known in the parlance of the lending industry as a ***subordination, non-disturbance and attornment agreement*** or ***SNDA***) that contains the following general features:[248]

---

246. There is a split in jurisdictions as to whether a foreclosure automatically terminates all subordinate leases (the "automatic termination" rule) or only terminates those leases designated by the foreclosing lender (the "pick and choose" rule). *See* Thomas Arendt, *Subordination, Attornment and Nondisturbance*, in Lease Negotiation Handbook 469, 471–472 (Edward Chupack ed., 2003); and Senn, *supra* note 5, at 25–7 and 25–8. Under either rule, the tenant's leasehold interest is in danger of being eliminated if that leasehold interest is found to be subordinate to the lien of the lender's mortgage.

247. *See* Senn, *supra* note 5, at 25–4 through 25–7.

248. *See* Arendt, *supra* note 251, at 472–477; and Senn, *supra* note 5, at 25–18 through 25–38 (including Form 25–3).

- The tenant's agreement to subordinate its leasehold interest to the lien of the lender's mortgage, unless the lender expressly elects to grant priority to the tenant's lease (the **subordination** feature);[249]

- The lender's agreement not to disturb the tenant's right to possess the leased premises, so long as the tenant complies with all of its lease obligations (the **nondisturbance** feature); and

- The tenant's agreement to attorn to and recognize the lender as the "landlord" under its lease following the lender's foreclosure of its mortgage (the **attornment** feature).

The lender will customarily also request that the subordination clause contain provisions relieving the lender from liability for and requiring the tenant to provide the lender with an opportunity to cure any pre-foreclosure landlord defaults.

A tenant who does not have the negotiating power to demand the execution of an SNDA will remain at risk that the lender will decide to terminate its lease if and when the lender forecloses its mortgage. The lender's ultimate decision to keep or terminate a subordinate lease will be driven by its perception of the vibrancy of the leasing market and the fair rental value of the leased premises. A foreclosing lender will seldom elect to terminate a tenant's lease, unless doing so is a necessary adjunct to the lender signing a lease with a known user whose credit and rent is superior to that of the tenant. The lender will, however, frequently use its termination right as a bargaining chip in its effort to renegotiate the terms of an existing tenant's lease.

E. BROKERAGE COMMISSION CLAUSE.
(¶U of Lease Summary and §27)

A commercial lease should contain a clause that (1) identifies the brokers who are entitled to receive a commission from the subject lease transaction and (2) assigns responsibility for the payment of the commission to either the landlord or the tenant.[250] The brokerage commission clause typically also includes a mutual representation and indemnity comparable to the following provision:

> *Each of Landlord and Tenant hereby represents that it has not dealt or consulted with any real estate broker or agent in connection with this Lease, other than those real estate brokers specifically identified in the Lease Summary. Each of Landlord and Tenant agrees to indemnify and hold the other harmless from and against any liability or expense occasioned by a breach of the foregoing representation.*

---

249. A clause that gives the lender the unilateral right to grant the tenant's lease priority over the mortgage is routinely used in those states that follow the automatic termination rule mentioned *supra* note 246. The use of such a clause effectively permits the lender to "pick and choose" those leases that it wants to survive the foreclosure by opting to subordinate the lien of its mortgage to the chosen, favorable leases. *See* Arendt, *supra* note 246, at 476.

250. *See* DILLMAN, *supra* note 37, at 179–180.

The inclusion of such a clause significantly lessens the landlord's concern that an unknown broker will suddenly show up with his hand extended looking for a commission after the lease is fully executed—a frightening prospect considering that leasing commissions on major lease transactions can easily run into seven figures.

F. ESTOPPEL CERTIFICATE CLAUSE. *(§13)*

As noted on numerous occasions throughout this text, the value of the landlord's real estate project is a direct product of the terms of its tenant leases. As such, any lender, buyer or equity provider seeking to make an investment in a real estate project will universally ask for written confirmations from the tenants that the terms of their leases are as represented by the project owner. An ***estoppel certificate*** is a written statement made by a tenant confirming the terms of its lease and representing that its lease is in full force and effect, without any default on the part of either the landlord or the tenant.

A tenant who balks at furnishing an estoppel certificate (or who seeks to get a "little something extra" in exchange for its provision of the required certificate) can jeopardize the viability of an entire loan, sale or equity transaction. In an attempt to protect the landlord against that scenario, the landlord's counsel will normally include a provision in the lease that requires the tenant to execute an estoppel certificate within a stated number of days after its receipt of the proffered certificate. Some landlords attempt to include language in the estoppel certificate clause that (1) affirms that the tenant will be liable for consequential damages should it breach its obligation to provide an executed estoppel certificate within the time period specified in the lease,[251] and (2) appoints the landlord as the tenant's attorney-in-fact to execute the certificate on the tenant's behalf if the tenant fails to provide the required certificate on a timely basis.[252]

Tenants will, of course, resist both of those provisions as unnecessary and overly draconian remedies for a simple failure by the tenant to turn around the landlord's request for an estoppel certificate within the short time frame specified in the lease. Tenants should also be mindful of the frequent attempt by the landlord and its buyer/lender/investor to include substantive provisions in the estoppel certificate that are intended to effect a modification of the lease terms or a waiver of all claims that the tenant may have against the landlord.[253] For this reason, tenants are well-advised to expressly limit the content of any required estoppel certificate to a confirmation that the lease attached to the estoppel certificate is in full force and effect, without any known default by the landlord.

---

251. *See* ZANKEL, *supra* note 19, at 162.

252. Although this provision is frequently found in commercial leases, my experience has been that it has no real practical significance because a lender/buyer/equity provider will rarely, if ever, accept an estoppel certificate signed by the landlord pursuant to an attorney-in-fact clause.

253. *See* ZANKEL, *supra* note 19, at 162.

G. SECURITY DEPOSIT/FINANCIAL STATEMENTS CLAUSE. *(¶R of Lease Summary and §§33 and 34)*

The landlord will usually require all but the most creditworthy of tenants to post collateral to partially secure the tenant's performance of its obligations under the lease. A ***security deposit*** can take any number of forms, with the most common being a cash deposit or a letter of credit. The amount of the security deposit is typically tied in some fashion to the level of the tenant's base rent obligation—e.g., a deposit equal to one or two months base rent for a tenant with a decent credit standing and six months to a year or more for a tenant with questionable credit. Regardless of the type or amount of the security deposit, the landlord will want the lease to make clear that (1) the landlord can take the deposit down immediately upon the occurrence of an event of default, and (2) the tenant will be obligated to promptly replenish the security deposit to its full original amount.[254]

In an effort to monitor the evolving financial position of each of its tenants, the landlord should include a provision in its standard lease form that requires the tenant and any guarantor to provide the landlord with at least annual financial statements documenting their then current financial condition. The landlord will often couple such a provision with a covenant that requires the tenant and the guarantor to maintain a minimum net worth at all times throughout the lease term.

H. BOILERPLATE CLAUSES

The commercial lease often contains a number of other clauses that landlords and tenants (but hopefully not their counsel) lump into the category of ***boilerplate clauses***—meaning clauses that one does not need to read or worry about. Example of lease clauses commonly referred to as boilerplate are the successors and assigns; no waiver; amendment; governing law; notices; and memorandum of lease clauses contained in the Form Office Lease (§§25, 26, 30, 31, 32, and 35, respectively). As noted in an earlier discussion of the boilerplate provisions of the land purchase contract,[255] it is essential that the lawyer heed the admonition that he should never include a clause in the lease without having a legitimate reason for doing so—even if it is commonly relegated to the scrap heap of so-called boilerplate clauses.

XIII. SUMMARY

Leasing is all about the creation of value. The value of a commercial real estate project is not a function of the project's location, design, construction or financing structure, but rather of the income stream

---

254. *See* Ira Fierstein, *Security Deposits*, in LEASE NEGOTIATION HANDBOOK 545, 545–546 (Edward Chupack ed., 2003).

255. *See supra* Chapter 5, Pages 145–148.

generated from the project. As such, the leases signed by the developer during Stage 7 will dictate whether its development project is a financial success or a bust.

The real estate development lawyer plays an important role in helping his client create value for its project. While the lawyer certainly does not (and should not) become directly involved in setting the annual rental rates for the project, it is his job to include provisions in the lease that are designed to enhance the predictability that the net rental income will actually be received by the developer at the projected times and in the projected amounts. Similarly, while the lawyer is not out front marketing the project to prospective tenants, the manner in which he conducts himself during the course of the lease negotiations will significantly affect how the prospective tenant views the landlord. Finally, the real estate development lawyer, as the preparer and primary negotiator of the lease document, serves as the gatekeeper to insure that the executed lease appropriately serves the landlord's business goals and insulates it to the fullest extent reasonably practicable from the risks inherent in the land-lord-tenant relationship.

I want to leave you with one concluding thought about the negotiation of a commercial lease. A successful negotiation has nothing to do with body language or polemics, but it has everything to do with knowledge and preparation. As noted by a well-known author on the topic of commercial leasing—"If you know the impacts on finances, risk, operations and services of all the sections of a typical sophisticated commercial lease and if you understand the needs of your client, negotiation is simply a default condition."[256]

---

256. *See* JOHN BUSEY WOOD, OUTLINE FOR COMMERCIAL LEASES, SEMINAR FOR NEW YORK UNIVERSITY/REAL ESTATE INSTITUTE SCHOOL OF CONTINUING AND PROFESSIONAL STUDIES 1 (2010), available online at http://www.officeleasingusa.com/downloads/nyucourseoutline.pdf.

CHAPTER 12

STAGES 8–10: SELECTING
AN EXIT STRATEGY

■ ■ ■

I. INTRODUCTION

The final chapter of this book will take a consolidated look at the final three stages of a development project—that is, Stage 8 (executing an interim exit strategy), Stage 9 (operating the project) and Stage 10 (selling the project). All three of these stages address the central question of what the developer should do once its development project is fully leased and cash flowing.

The real estate development lawyer's job during the final project stages is twofold—(1) he first needs to counsel his client on which of the potential exit strategies will best serve the developer's overall business objectives and (2) he must then execute the exit strategy selected by the developer. Developers often opt to skip Stages 8 and 9 entirely and instead sell the project as soon as it is leased and cash flowing. For the purposes of this Chapter, it will be assumed that the developer has decided to adopt an interim exit strategy and operate the project for an extended period of time before selling it outright to a third party.

The specific tasks performed by the development lawyer during Stages 8 through 10 are similar in many respects to those tasks discussed in earlier chapters of this book (specifically, *Chapter 5: Gaining Control of the Site* and *Chapter 9: Securing Construction Financing*). This Chapter will not repeat the material covered in those earlier chapters, but will instead focus on the special factors that the lawyer must take into consideration when advising the developer during the final three stages of a real estate development project.

II. ALTERNATIVE EXIT STRATEGIES

The developer's goal is always to stabilize its project as soon as possible. A ***stabilized project*** is one that is leased and producing positive

550

cash flow.[1] Once that goal is achieved, the developer is faced with the question of what to do next—either sell the project outright or retain full or partial ownership of the project for a period of time. The answer to that question involves a balancing of the developer's desire to maximize its after-tax economic returns from the project against the developer's equally strong objective of limiting its exposure to ongoing real estate risk.

There are a host of considerations that the developer must weigh when making its "hold or sell" decision. The most salient of these considerations are summarized below.

- *Financial Performance*—The threshold question that the developer must answer is whether the project's stabilized financial performance is sufficiently robust to merit the developer retention of a long-term ownership interest in the project. If the project's cash flow is marginal or the creditworthiness of its tenant roster is questionable, the developer may want to offload all of its real estate risk by immediately selling the project to a third party.

- *Market Conditions*—The conditions prevailing in the real estate and capital markets will also impact the developer's exit strategy choice. During the period from 2002 through 2007, institutional investors were so anxious to invest in real estate that they were willing to buy stabilized commercial projects at price levels that conjured up images of Don Corleone uttering his infamous statement in the Godfather that "I will make him an offer he can't refuse."[2] Since the financial crash of 2008, capitalization rates have soared, making the sale of a real estate project much less profitable than in years past. The availability and pricing of permanent debt are additional factors that the developer must take into account when deciding whether to hold or sell its project.

- *Personal Risk Profile*—Some developers are simply more risk averse than others. Those developers (often referred to as *merchant builders*) seek to limit their exposure to real estate risk by selling their projects as soon as they reach stabilization. Other developers (so-called *portfolio builders*), due to their financial position and innate disposition, are more inclined to try to maximize their after-tax financial returns by holding on to their projects for a longer term.

- *Tax Considerations*. An outright sale of the project will subject the developer to the payment of federal income tax on the difference between the sales price and the project's cost basis.[3] If the

---

1. Most developers use a 95% lease-up convention when preparing their financial projections for a stabilized project. The reference to a project producing "positive cash flow" means that the collected rents are sufficient to cover all project expenses (including both operating expenses and debt service costs), plus provide a current financial return to the developer and its equity investors. *See supra* Chapter 3, Page 48.

2. THE GODFATHER, screenplay by Mario Puzo, directed by Francis Ford Coppola (Paramount Pictures 1972).

3. *See* INTERNAL REVENUE CODE § 1001.

developer has an established track record of selling its projects once they achieve stabilization, the developer may be treated as a ***dealer*** and compelled to pay tax on the sales profit at ordinary income rates (currently 35% versus the 15% rate imposed on capital gains).[4] The developer can defer the recognition of income on the project's profit component by choosing to hold the project for an extended period of time.[5]

- ***Contractual Restrictions***—A developer's hold vs. sell decision may, on occasion, be dictated by the content of the debt and equity documents that it signed during the course of its raising of the funds needed to pay the project's development costs. By way of example, an LLC operating agreement may require the equity investor's consent to a sale of the project or the refinancing of its mortgage debt. The real estate development lawyer's job is, of course, to try to limit both the number and scope of any contractual restrictions placed on the developer's decision-making authority.[6]

There is no single right or wrong answer to the question of whether a developer should hold or sell its project. The advantage of skipping Stages 8 and 9 and moving directly to a sale of the project is that it provides a quick cash return to the developer of both its invested capital and the profit inherent in the stabilized project. The quick sale approach also fixes the developer's project profit by eliminating the risk that a future event will unexpectedly diminish the project's value (e.g., a tenant bankruptcy or a general market decline). On the other hand, the developer's decision to hold the project may permit it to enhance its financial returns by benefitting from (1) the ongoing positive cash flow generated from the project (which, presumably, is higher than the return produced from more conservative cash investments),[7] (2) an appreciation in the value of the project, and (3) the deferral of the imposition of any income tax on the project's incremental value. The long-term hold strategy does, however, subject the developer to the added risk that an event will occur in the future that will negatively impact the profitability of the project.

A developer's hold vs. sell decision will vary by project and time. An ardent portfolio builder may adopt the stance of a merchant builder because of its need to raise cash to deal with other financial challenges. Similarly, a developer who, by natural inclination, is a merchant builder, may decide to hold on to ownership of a particular project because its long-

---

4. *See generally*, Stefan F. Tucker, Brian S. Masterson and Tammara F. Langlieb, *Real Estate—Preserving Capital Gains, Dealer Issues*, in ALI–ABA COURSE OF STUDY MATERIALS, MODERN REAL ESTATE TRANSACTIONS: PRACTICAL STRATEGIES FOR REAL ESTATE ACQUISITION, DISPOSITION AND OWNERSHIP, Course No. SS–012, 1227 (July 2010).

5. A developer can also defer the current recognition of federal income tax by entering into a like-kind exchange of its project for another real property interest. *See* INTERNAL REVENUE CODE § 1031. *See also* Stefan F. Tucker and Tammara F. Langlieb, *The Like Kind Exchange: A Current Review*, in ALI–ABA COURSE OF STUDY MATERIALS, MODERN REAL ESTATE TRANSACTIONS: PRACTICAL STRATEGIES FOR REAL ESTATE ACQUISITION, DISPOSITION AND OWNERSHIP, Course No. SS–012, 1003 (July 2010).

6. *See infra Practice Tip #12–2: Don't Mess with the Developer's Timing*, Page 576.

7. *See supra* Chapter 3, Pages 47–49.

term financial prospects are solid and the then prevailing capitalization rates are inordinately high.[8]

The remainder of this Chapter will assume that the developer has opted to hold its project for an extended period of time (five to ten years) and to then sell it outright to an institutional investor. As such, the discussion that follows will examine the business objectives of the developer and the roles played by the developer's lawyer during each of Stages 8, 9 and 10.

III. STAGE 8: EXECUTING AN INTERIM EXIT STRATEGY

At the advent of Stage 8, the developer is faced with a good news/bad news conundrum. The good news is that its project is fully leased and generating positive cash flow. The bad news is that the developer's project is probably encumbered by a construction loan that includes the following unwanted features:

- A rapidly approaching due date for the repayment of the loan (typically only two to three years after the initial loan closing);

- An interest rate that fluctuates with changes in a financial index (e.g., the prime rate or LIBOR); and

- The developer's personal guaranty that the construction loan will be paid in full at maturity.

The developer's primary business objective during Stage 8 is to devise an interim exit strategy that permits it to refinance the construction loan with a loan that is not characterized by any of these negative features—in other words, a loan that has an extended term and fixed interest rate and is nonrecourse to the developer.

A. PERMANENT MORTGAGE LOAN

A loan that is used to retire the construction loan is known as a **permanent mortgage loan**. Permanent loans generally fall into one of two categories—(1) a **portfolio loan** that is originated and held by a single mortgage lender (e.g., a life insurance company, pension fund, bank or other financial institution), or (2) a **securitized loan** that is originated by a mortgage lender and then pooled with other mortgage loans and sold off in varying pieces and parts to investors.[9]

A permanent loan (be it a portfolio loan or a securitized loan) differs in many respects from a construction loan.[10] The following are some of the

---

8. *See infra* Pages 575–576, for a discussion of the impact that variances in capitalization rates can have on the profit produced from a project sale.

9. *See* Eric M. Schiller, Know *Your Financing Sources: Differences in Loan Documentation and Closing Requirements*, in ALI–ABA COURSE OF STUDY MATERIALS, COMMERCIAL REAL ESTATE FINANCING: STRATEGIES FOR CHANGING MARKETS AND UNCERTAIN TIMES, Course No. SP–008, 111, 113 (January 2009). While portfolio and securitized loans share many common provisions, there are a number of features that are unique to securitized loans. Those features are addressed *infra* Pages 561–563.

principal ways in which a permanent mortgage loan is different from a construction loan.

- *Term*—The term of a permanent loan is generally five to ten years (as contrasted to the typical two or three year term of a construction loan).

- *Payment Schedule*—A permanent loan will call for the borrower to make a fixed monthly payment of principal and interest based on a fixed interest rate and an amortization schedule of anywhere from 15 to 30 years. Because the term of a permanent loan is almost always less than the assumed amortization period, a permanent loan will require the borrower to make a sizable principal payment at the maturity of the loan (commonly referred to as a *balloon payment*).[11]

- *Nonrecourse Clause*—A permanent loan is typically nonrecourse to the borrower and its affiliates. The nonrecourse nature of the permanent loan is, however, frequently subject to a laundry list of exceptions.

- *Prepayment Restrictions*—A permanent loan usually contains a restriction on the ability of the borrower to pay off the loan prior to the loan's stated maturity date.

- *Due on Sale or Encumbrance Clauses*—A permanent loan also customarily limits the borrower's ability to sell or further mortgage the project that serves as collateral for the repayment of the loan.

The remainder of this section will focus on a discussion of the nonrecourse, prepayment and due on sale or encumbrance clauses of a permanent mortgage loan.

1. The Nonrecourse Clause

The inclusion in the permanent loan documents of a nonrecourse clause will generally insulate the borrower from any personal liability for the repayment of the permanent loan. The permanent lender's sole recourse in the event of a borrower default will be to foreclose on the mortgage and any other collateral that secures the permanent loan. The following is a representative sample of a nonrecourse clause.

Neither Borrower, nor any shareholder, member or partner of Borrower, shall be personally liable for the payment of any principal, interest or other sum evidenced by the Loan or for any deficiency judgment that Lender may obtain following the foreclosure of the Mortgage. Lender's

---

10. *See supra* Chapter 9, Pages 315–323, for a general discussion of the differences between a construction and a permanent loan. The one overriding similarity between a construction loan and a permanent loan is that the primary security for both loans is a mortgage on the land and improvements that comprise the developer's real estate project.

11. By way of example, a $10 million permanent loan that has a stated term of seven years, an assumed amortization period of 20 years and a fixed interest rate of 8% will have a balloon principal payment due on the maturity date of the loan of approximately $8.1 million.

sole recourse for any default under the Loan shall be limited to the property encumbered by the Mortgage and any other collateral given to secure the Loan.[12]

A permanent lender will consider extending a nonrecourse loan to any stabilized project that has (1) sufficient cash flow to cover its debt service and (2) a residual value in excess of the principal amount of the loan.[13] In the last several years, permanent lenders have, however, begun to impose a number of exceptions to the nonrecourse clause. Those exceptions (commonly referred to as ***nonrecourse carveouts***) have become so numerous and invasive as to cause one author to wonder whether "the exceptions have now come to swallow the rule."[14]

A nonrecourse carveout seeks to place personal liability on a creditworthy entity[15] for the reimbursement of losses incurred by the lender as a result of the occurrence of certain proscribed events or circumstances. Most permanent loans now contain exclusions from the nonrecourse clause for so-called "bad boy" acts, where the borrower engages in some type of particularly blameworthy conduct. The following are examples of some typical, "bad boy" carveouts—(1) fraud or misrepresentation in securing the loan, (2) intentional waste of the lender's collateral, (3) the misapplication of project receipts to pay expenses not related to the project and (4) the violation of environmental laws. Permanent lenders are increasingly attempting to further broaden their nonrecourse carveouts to include events or circumstances that might hinder the lender's ability to secure a quick and full repayment of its loan, even though such events or circumstances are not the product of any borrower wrongdoing. By way of example, permanent lenders sometimes seek to impose personal liability on the borrower or one of its affiliates for losses suffered by the lender due to the borrower's bankruptcy, the borrower's assertion of defenses to the foreclosure of the lender's mortgage and the borrower's breach of a covenant contained in the loan documents (other than the covenant to pay principal and interest).[16]

---

12. This nonrecourse clause was closely patterned after a sample clause set forth in Alan Wayte, *Selected Issues in the Negotiation of Real Estate Financing Documents*, in ALI–ABA COURSE OF STUDY MATERIALS, COMMERCIAL REAL ESTATE FINANCING: STRATEGIES FOR CHANGING MARKETS AND UNCERTAIN TIMES, Course No. SP–008, 1, 19 (January 2009).

13. Historically, nonrecourse permanent loans have been made at a debt service coverage ratio of somewhere between 1.1 and 1.2 to 1 and a loan-to-value ratio in the 75–90% range. However, a report published jointly in 2010 by the Urban Land Institute and Pricewaterhouse-Coopers noted that permanent loans are now being made only "at 'expensive,' back-to-the-future pricing—60 to 65 percent loan-to-value ratios . . . and 1.4 debt-service coverage." *See* URBAN LAND INSTITUTE AND PRICEWATERHOUSECOOPERS, EMERGING TRENDS IN REAL ESTATE 19 (October 2009).

14. *See* Marc S. Intrilligator and R. David Walker, *Nonrecourse Carveout Provisions in Mortgage Loan Documents—A Trap for the Unwary*, THE REAL ESTATE FINANCE JOURNAL 5, 6 (Summer 2010).

15. Most developers now place ownership of their projects in single purpose limited liability companies that have no assets other than the project. *See supra* Chapter 7, Page 217. As a result, lenders are now insisting that the developer (or its principals) execute personal guaranties supporting the nonrecourse carveouts.

16. *See generally* John C. Murray, *Carveouts to Nonrecourse Loans: They Mean What They Say*, 19 No. 3 PRACTICAL REAL ESTATE LAWYER 19; and Portia Owen Morrison and Mark A. Senn, *Carving Up the "Carve-outs" in Nonrecourse Loans*, 9 PROBATE AND PROPERTY 8, 12 (June 1995).

The contest between the lender and the borrower over the scope and breadth of the nonrecourse carveouts is grounded in the parties' disparate views of the purpose that should be served by such carveouts. The borrower ideally wants to be in a position to give the lender the keys to the project if the project proves not to be financially viable for any reason. While the borrower is normally willing to accept carveouts for its "bad boy" acts, it wants to make sure that the carveouts only cover those intentional, overt actions that are deliberately taken by the borrower to decrease the value of the lender's collateral. The borrower believes that the lender should bear the risk of a decline in the financial performance of the borrower's project, unless the borrower has deliberately done something designed to hurt that performance. The borrower will also try to limit its personal liability to the actual damages suffered by the lender as a direct result of the borrower's prohibited conduct (e.g., the cost of remedying an environmental spill or the amount of any misapplied project revenues).[17]

The permanent lender, on the other hand, "is less focused on culpability than it is on risk allocation."[18] The carveouts represent the lender's attempt to place as much liability as possible on the borrower for a decline in the value of the collateral that secures its loan—regardless whether that decline is directly attributable to a wrongful act by the borrower or the occurrence of an event or circumstance with respect to which the borrower has no culpability whatsoever. The permanent lender will also initially take the stance that a violation of any nonrecourse carveout makes the person standing behind the carveouts personally liable for the repayment of the entirety of the permanent loan (and not just for any damages actually sustained by the lender due to the carveout violation).[19]

The outcome of the negotiations over the nonrecourse provisions will largely depend on the economic risk assumed by the lender in making the permanent loan. If the permanent loan is made at a 50% loan-to-value ratio, the lender is more likely to limit the nonrecourse carveouts to true "bad boy" acts than it is if the loan carries a loan-to-value ratio of 85%.

2. Prepayment Restrictions

The permanent lender's motivation in making its loan is notably different than that of the construction lender. The construction lender primary goal is to mitigate its risk by getting the construction loan repaid as soon as possible.[20] The permanent lender, on the other hand, faces

---

17. *See* Joshua Stein, *Lender's Model State-of-the-Art Nonrecourse Clause (with Carveouts)*, 43 No. 7 PRACTICAL LAWYER 31, 34–36 (October 1997); and Gregory M. Stein, *When Can a Nonrecourse Lender Reach the Personal Assets of Its Borrower*, 17 No. 2 PRACTICAL REAL ESTATE LAWYER 33, 51–55 (March 2001).

18. *See* Morrison and Senn, *supra* note 16, at 12

19. *See* generally John C. Murray, *Exploding and Springing Guaranties*, in ALI–ABA COURSE OF STUDY MATERIALS, MODERN REAL ESTATE TRANSACTIONS: PRACTICAL STRATEGIES FOR REAL ESTATE ACQUISITION, DISPOSITION AND OWNERSHIP, Course No. SS–012, 1457 (July 2010); Intrilligator, *supra* note 14, at 6; and Morrison and Senn, *supra* note 16, at 9.

20. *See* Robert A. Thompson and Brian D. Smith, *Negotiating Loan Transactions*, in COMMERCIAL REAL ESTATE TRANSACTIONS HANDBOOK 9–39 (Mark A. Senn ed., 4th ed. 2009). As noted by

much less risk than does the construction lender and, as a result, is primarily focused on maintaining a consistent return on its debt throughout the stated term of the loan. The lender's prospects of achieving that consistent financial return is threatened if the borrower is able to pay its loan at par[21] prior to the loan's stated maturity date, because the lender may not be able to invest the repaid funds in a fashion that produces a return equivalent to the percentage interest rate applicable to the permanent loan.

The permanent lender tries to preserve the consistency of its loan return by either (1) prohibiting the repayment of the permanent loan for a stated period of time (a ***lock-out period***)[22] or (2) requiring the borrower to pay a negotiated premium for the privilege of prepaying the loan prior to maturity (a ***prepayment penalty***). A permanent lender will often combine these two protective measures by prohibiting any prepayments for a lock-out period of two or three years and then requiring the payment of a penalty for any prepayment occurring after the expiration of the lock-out period.

A prepayment penalty can be expressed in a variety of ways, including as a fixed percentage of the prepaid amount (e.g., 1% of the principal prepayment). The most common formulation of a prepayment penalty is the ***yield maintenance penalty***.[23] A yield maintenance penalty attempts to protect the lender from a loss of its investment yield by requiring the prepaying borrower to pay the lender an additional sum that is equal to the difference between (i) the present value of the yield that would have been produced had the loan been held to maturity (roughly equivalent to the loan's fixed interest rate) and (ii) the present value of the yield that the lender could achieve by investing the prepaid amount in some other investment vehicle.[24] The yield differential is typically calculated by comparing the permanent loan's fixed interest rate to the rate of return payable on U.S. Treasury instruments having a term comparable to the remaining term of the permanent loan. This formulation is often referred to as a ***Treasury-flat penalty***.[25] Best practice (at least from the borrower's perspective) would be to adjust the comparable yield calculation by adding to the Treasury-flat figure the ***spread*** that existed on the date the permanent loan was first made between the return on comparable term

---

Messrs. Thompson and Smith, "loan fees and other payments, rather than interest, are the primary remuneration" for the construction lender. *See id.* at 9–39.

21.   Repayment of a loan "at par" means that the borrower is not required to pay any amount other than the outstanding principal balance and accrued and unpaid interest.

22.   A lock-out clause is a common feature of securitized loans "where long-term investment is the premise, rather than simply a benefit, of the transaction." *See* Thompson, *supra* note 20, at 9–40.

23.   *See id.* at 9–40 and 9–41.

24.   *See* WILLIAM B. BRUEGGEMAN AND JEFFREY D. FISHER, REAL ESTATE FINANCE AND INVESTMENTS 361–362 (13th ed. 2008).

25.   *See e.g.*, River East Plaza, LLC v. Variable Annuity Life Insurance Company, 498 F.3d 718, 719 (7th Cir. 2007).

U.S. Treasuries and the fixed interest rate payable under the permanent loan.[26]

The enforceability of a prepayment penalty has been the subject of a great deal of litigation in the past several years.[27] The general rule produced from those cases is that a prepayment penalty is enforceable in the context of a voluntary prepayment made by a borrower as part of its sale of the underlying collateral or the refinancing of the permanent loan.[28] The courts are split on whether a prepayment penalty is enforceable in the context of an involuntary prepayment engendered due to a condemnation, casualty or borrower default.[29] A borrower under a nonrecourse loan is, of course, not particularly concerned about the enforceability of a prepayment penalty following a borrower default, because it views the prepayment penalty as just "one more obligation of the borrower that cannot be collected."[30] The borrower should, however, seek to clarify in the loan documents that a prepayment penalty cannot be imposed on a prepayment triggered by the occurrence of a casualty or condemnation.[31]

3. Due on Sale and Encumbrance Clauses

Permanent loan documents typically contain prohibitions against the borrower's sale of an interest in the mortgaged property (a ***due on sale clause***) and the borrower's placement of secondary mortgage financing on the mortgaged property (a ***due on encumbrance clause***). The following are typical examples of those two clauses.

> *Due on Sale. Borrower shall not, directly or indirectly, sell, convey, assign, transfer, alienate, or otherwise dispose of, or grant a security interest in, its interest in the property, or any part thereof, either*

---

26. If the yield maintenance differential is not adjusted to reflect a "spread" over the yield paid on the comparable term U.S. Treasury instrument, the lender will receive a windfall from the prepayment if the lender is able to re-invest the prepaid amount in an instrument (e.g., another permanent loan) that pays a return in excess of that payable on the Treasury instrument. *See* BRUEGGEMAN, *supra* note 24, at 361–362 and note 5.

27. *See generally* Rod Clement, *Turmoil in Prepayment Land: An Update of Recent Prepayment Cases*, in ACREL PAPERS 355 (ALI–ABA Fall 2007). *See also* River East, 498 F.3d 718 (7th Cir. 2007), where the Seventh Circuit Court of Appeals sustained the enforceability of a Treasury-flat yield maintenance penalty (overturning a district court opinion cited in the previously-cited article by Rod Clement).

28. *See e.g.,* River East, 498 F.3d at 723–724; Chillicothe Telephone Co. v. Variable Annuity Life Insurance Company, 2007 WL 397058 (S.D. Ohio, January 31, 2007); In re CP Holdings, 332 B.R. 380 (W.D. Mo. 2005), *aff'd per curiam* 2006 WL 3203751 (8th Cir. 2006); and United States v. Harris, 246 F.3d 566 (6th Cir. 2001). In all of the above cases, the courts rejected the notion that a prepayment penalty should be viewed as an unenforceable penalty under a liquidated damages analysis and, instead, embraced the concept that a prepayment penalty negotiated by sophisticated parties is enforceable as "bargained-for form of alternative performance." *See* River East, 498 F.3d at 721. *See also* Dale A. Whitman, *Mortgage Prepayment: A Legal and Economic Analysis*, 40 UCLA LAW REVIEW 851, 890 (1993), where Professor Whitman notes that "a freely-bargained prepayment fee clause ought to be enforced against the borrower who makes a voluntary prepayment, irrespective of the amount of money that the lender's clause demands."

29. *See* Clement, *supra* note 27, at 359–364; and Thompson, *supra* note 20, at 9–40.

30. *See* Thompson, *supra* note 20, at 9–40.

31. *See id.* at 9–41; and Morton P. Fisher, Jr. and Faith Pettis, *Loan Commitments*, in ALI–ABA COURSE OF STUDY MATERIALS, MODERN REAL ESTATE TRANSACTIONS, Course No. SL–004, 837, 849 (July 2005).

voluntarily or by operation of law, or agree to do so, without the prior written consent of Lender.[32]

Due on Encumbrance. Borrower shall not create or permit to continue in existence, any mortgage, pledge, security interest, lien, or charge of any kind (including purchase money and conditional sale liens), or other encumbrances upon any of the property, except for the lien of taxes and assessments not yet delinquent.[33]

Both of these clauses are intended to preclude the borrower from taking an action that could adversely affect the security of the lender's collateral position under the permanent loan.[34] While the lender's primary concern when making a permanent loan is the value of the mortgaged property, the lender is also focused on the business acumen and financial capacity of the borrower. A due on sale clause is designed to insulate the lender from the risk of a change in the identity of the borrower, without the lender's prior approval.[35]

The lender includes a due on encumbrance clause in the permanent loan documents to combat its fear that the placement of additional debt on the property will render the project financially unsustainable and, hence, increase the likelihood of a payment default by the borrower. A due on encumbrance clause also works to allay the permanent lender's concern that the introduction of another lender to the project's capital stack might impede the permanent lender's exercise of its legal rights and remedies in the event of a borrower default.[36]

Due on sale and encumbrance clauses are anathema to the borrower, because they limit the borrower's flexibility to preserve and enhance the value of its project by responding to changes in market conditions.[37] While borrowers are seldom successful in having due on sale and due on encumbrance clauses deleted in their entirety from the permanent loan documents, they often are able to negotiate limited exceptions to the blanket prohibitions contained in such clauses. The following is a brief summary of some of the exceptions that a borrower might want to consider incorporating into the due on sale and due on encumbrance clauses.

---

32. *See* Thompson, *supra* note 20, at 9–68.

33. *See id.* at 9–75 and 9–76.

34. Prior to the passage of the Garn–St. Germain Depository Institutions Act of 1982, 12 U.S.C. § 1701j–3, a number of legal challenges were filed in state courts contesting the enforceability of due on sale and due on encumbrance clauses. *See* John C. Murray, *Due-on-Sale Clauses: Can They Still Be Challenged,* 17 No. 4 PRACTICAL REAL ESTATE LAWYER 7 (July 2001). The Garn–St. Germain Act sanctioned Federal preemption of state law limitations on the enforceability of such clauses. *See* Thompson, *supra* note 20, at 9–69 and 9–76.

35. *See* Thompson, *supra* note 20, at 9–69, where the authors point out that a collateral effect of a due on sale clause is that it "presents the lender with an opportunity to protect its economic position in the loan. If interest rates have increased, a sale of a property subject to a transfer restriction gives the lender the opportunity to increase the yield on its investment to current market rates by placing the funds in a new or revised loan."

36. *See* Wayte, *supra* note 12, at 7; and Thompson, *supra* note 20, at 9–76.

37. *See generally* Patricia Frobes and Frank Crance, *Anticipating the Future in Loan Documentation,* 18 No. 2 PRACTICAL REAL ESTATE LAWYER 41, 48–49 and 54 (March 2002).

- ***Due on Sale Exceptions:***[38]

  - The sale of the mortgaged property to a "qualified buyer" (meaning a buyer who meets certain negotiated parameters concerning the buyer's financial condition and business experience);

  - The transfer of the mortgaged property to an affiliate of the borrower;

  - The right to substitute collateral for the mortgaged property, so long as the substituted collateral has an appraised value equal to or greater than the mortgaged property and the substituted collateral satisfies certain other performance tests;

  - The transfer of equity interests in the borrower (so long as control of the borrower is not changed as a result of such transfers);

  - The lease of space in the mortgaged property in accordance with pre-determined standards as to the form and content of the leases and the creditworthiness of the tenants;[39]

  - The grant of easements required to operate the mortgaged property; and

  - The sale of vacant land that is not needed to operate the mortgaged property, so long as the borrower pays the lender a negotiated release price (e.g., $100,000 per acre).

- ***Due on Encumbrance Exceptions:***[40]

  - Secondary mortgage financing designed to refurbish, expand or reposition the mortgaged property, so long as stipulated loan-to-value and debt service coverage ratios are met for the combined loans;

  - Mezzanine financing in which equity interests in the borrower (but not a direct interest in the mortgaged property) are pledged as security to the mezzanine lender;[41] and

  - Equipment leasing and financing that is required to permit the operation of the mortgaged property in the ordinary course of the borrower's business.

If the permanent lender agrees to any of the above exceptions, it will likely insist that the borrower may rely on such exception only if (1) the

---

38. *See generally* Charles L. Edwards, *Commercial Mortgage Loan Commitments: A Borrower's Perspective*, 8 Probate and Property 28, 29–30 (August 1994); Thompson, *supra* note 20, at 9–70 through 9–72; and Frobes, supra note 37, at 48–51.

39. *See supra* Chapter 9, Pages 384–387, for a discussion of the construction lender's right to approve project leases.

40. *See generally* Frobes, *supra* note 37, at 52–55; Wayte, *supra* note 12, at 7–10; Thompson, *supra* note 20, at 9–70 through 9–72; and Edwards, *supra* note 38, at 29–30.

41. *See* Steven Horowitz and Lise Morrow, *What You Need to Know about Mezzanine Financing*, 16 No. 3 Practical Real Estate Lawyer 9, 10–12 (May 2000).

borrower is not in default in the performance of any of its loan obligations and (2) the junior lender enters into an inter-creditor agreement with the permanent lender, expressly subordinating the interests of the junior lender to those of the permanent lender.[42]

4. Unique Provisions of Securitized Loans

A securitized loan is a permanent loan that is pooled with other similar mortgage loans, with interests in the combined mortgage pool then being sold to third party investors. The theory behind securitized loans (also referred to as ***commercial mortgage backed securities*** or ***CMBS***) is summarized in the following excerpt from a brochure jointly published by the Commercial Mortgage Securities Association and the Mortgage Bankers Association.

> CMBS has become an attractive capital source for commercial mortgage lending because the bonds backed by a pool of loans are generally worth more than the sum of the value of the whole loans. The enhanced liquidity and structure of CMBS attracts a broader range of investors to the commercial mortgage market. This value creation effect allows loans intended for securitization to be aggressively priced, benefitting Borrowers.[43]

The use of securitized loans for commercial real estate experienced dramatic growth in the early and mid–2000s. At its peak in 2007, the CMBS industry packaged over $230 billion of securitized commercial real estate loans in the U.S.[44] The CMBS market collapsed in 2008 (along with the rest of the United States economy).[45] It is, however, the considered opinion of most industry insiders and experts that the CMBS market, in some revamped form, will at some point in the future once again become a staple of the commercial real estate marketplace.[46]

While a full discussion of securitized loans is beyond the scope of this Chapter, it is important to take note of several ways in which securitized loans differ from the more traditional, portfolio loans that have thus far been the focus of the discussion of Stage 8 of a real estate development project.

---

42. *See* Frobes, *supra* note 37, at 55; and Edwards, *supra* note 38, at 30.

43. *See* COMMERCIAL MORTGAGE SECURITIES ASSOCIATION AND MORTGAGE BANKERS ASSOCIATION, BORROWER GUIDE TO CMBS 2 (2004)

44. *See* CRE FINANCE COUNCIL, COMPENDIUM OF STATISTICS Exhibit 1 (2010), available online at http://www.crefc.org/uploadedFiles/CMSA _ Site _ Home/Industry _ Resources/Research/Industry _ Statistics/CMSA _ Compendium.pdf.

45. *See generally* Joseph P. Forte, *Disruption in the Capital Markets: What Happened*, in ACREL PAPERS 1 (ALI–ABA, March 2008). The total CMBS issuance in 2008 was slightly over $12 billion (almost all of which was placed during the first half of 2008). CMBS issuances in 2009 declined to $2.9 billion. The CMBS market experienced a gentle increase in 2010 when CMBS issuances were projected to top out at approximately $3.8 billion. *See* CRE FINANCE COUNCIL, *supra* note 44, at Appendix A–2.

46. *See* URBAN LAND INSTITUTE, *supra* note 13, at 16 ; and Richard R. Goldberg, *The Future of Real Estate Financing: What to Expect after the Crash*, in ALI–ABA COURSE OF STUDY MATERIALS, MODERN REAL ESTATE TRANSACTIONS: PRACTICAL STRATEGIES FOR REAL ESTATE ACQUISITION, DISPOSITION, AND OWNERSHIP, Course No. SS–012, 1505, 1508–1509.

- ***Standardized Documentation***—CMBS issuers (as well as rating agencies like Moody's that rate the credit of the CMBS issuances) insist on the use of consistent, standard documents to evidence each mortgage loan included in their mortgage pools. As a result, the originators of securitized loans are much less likely to respond favorably to borrower requests for changes to the permanent loan documents.[47]

- ***Bankruptcy Remote Borrowing Entity***—In order to lessen the risk that a borrower will file for bankruptcy for reasons unrelated to the operation of the mortgaged property, a securitized loan will customarily require the borrower to be a bankruptcy remote entity.[48] A bankruptcy remote entity is a single purpose entity (usually an LLC) that is prohibited from having any assets or liabilities other than those directly related to the ownership and operation of the mortgaged property. The borrowing entity will also be required to make a series of so-called ***separateness covenants*** that are designed to insure that the borrower will be operated independently of any of its affiliated entities. Finally, most CMBS issuers and rating agencies will require that the borrower appoint an independent director approved by the lender, whose consent will be required prior to the borrower's institution of a bankruptcy proceeding.[49]

- ***Defeasance***—In order to preserve the consistency and predictability of the yield to CMBS investors, each securitized loan will typically require a lock-out period of at least two years. After the expiration of the lock-out period, the borrower will not have any right to prepay the loan (either at par or accompanied by a prepayment penalty). The borrower will, however, have the right to obtain a release of the mortgage on its project through a ***defeasance*** of its loan.[50] Defeasance entails the borrower's posting of Treasury instruments in an amount sufficient to fund all principal and interest payments when and as they become due under the securitized loan. From the borrower's perspective, defeasance is a more costly and complex alternative to the borrower's right to prepay the loan with a yield maintenance penalty—but an alternative that the borrower must nonetheless accept if it opts to obtain financing through a securitized loan[51]

---

47. *See* Mark A. Hill and Richard D. Jones, *A Miranda Warning for Potential Conduit Borrowers*, 17 No. 1 PRACTICAL REAL ESTATE LAWYER 7 (January 2002).

48. *See generally* Schiller, *supra* note 9, at 119–120; Portia Owen Morrison and Peter B. Ross, *Financial Covenants and Bankruptcy Remote Structures in Real Estate Loan Transactions with Forms*, 17 No. 1 PRACTICAL REAL ESTATE LAWYER 7 (January 2001); and Hill, *supra* note 47, at 8–9.

49. *See* Thompson, *supra* note 20, at 9–134. *See also supra* Chapter 9, note 81 and the accompanying text, for a discussion of bankruptcy remote entities in the context of construction loans.

50. *See generally* John C. Murray, *Defeasance Provisions in Securitized–Loan Documents*, in ACREL PAPERS 401 (ALI–ABA, March 2004); Hill, *supra* note 47, at 12; and Thompson, *supra* note 20, at 9–136.

51. *See* Hill, *supra* note 47, at 12; and Thompson, *supra* note 20, at 9–136.

- *Lack of Lender Relationship*—Unlike a portfolio loan that is originated and held by a single lender, a securitized loan quickly becomes co-mingled with a pool of other mortgages, all of which are administered by a loan servicing agent who has no affiliation with the originator of the borrower's loan. The borrower's lack of a direct relationship with the loan servicer makes it much more difficult for the borrower to negotiate loan modifications or waivers after the loan is first funded—a definite disadvantage for most commercial borrowers.[52]

For the above reasons, the securitized loan model may not be a fit for every real estate borrower. A borrower who values flexibility and creativity in the structuring and administration of its permanent loan might want to stay away from a securitized loan and instead stick with a traditional, portfolio loan made by a single financial institution.

B. THE EQUITY PLAY

The prior section centered on the developer's use of debt (in the form of a permanent loan) to facilitate its decision to retain ownership of its project after stabilization. A developer can also make an equity play during Stage 8 by contributing the stabilized project to a joint venture formed with one or more institutional investors. The institutional investors will then make a cash contribution to the venture in an amount sufficient to retire the construction loan (if no permanent loan is secured) or in a lesser amount (if a permanent loan is part of the developer's interim exit strategy).

The developer's primary objective when implementing an equity play is to extract cash to return its equity in the stabilized project. For this purpose, the developer's "equity" consists of two separate components— (1) its actual cash contribution to the project (the 10–30% of the project development costs that were not funded under the construction loan) and (2) its interest in the incremental value of the project over and above its development costs. The following example illustrates how a developer might extract its equity in the project by entering into a joint venture with an institutional investor.

Example 12–1: Developer constructs an office building at a total cost of $8 million, $6 million of which is funded with the proceeds of a construction loan and $2 million of which is funded by equity contributions made by Developer. The office building is fully leased and has a fair market value of $10 million. Developer contributes the office building to LLC, a limited liability company in which Developer and Equity Investor are the sole members. Equity Investor makes a cash contribution to LLC of $9 million, $6 million of which is used to repay the construction loan and $3 million of which is distributed to Developer as a partial return of its equity in the project. Developer

---

52. *See* Hill, *supra* note 47, at 9; and Schiller, *supra* note 9, at 121–122.

and Equity Investor agree to split all LLC cash flow 90% to Equity Investor and 10% to Developer.

Under the above example, Developer accomplishes its goal of retaining partial ownership of its project (its 10% membership interest in LLC), while at the same time putting $3 million in its pocket.

The next example shows how a developer can optimize its position by combining an equity play with the placement of a permanent loan on the stabilized project.

> **Example 12–2:** Assume the same facts as Example 12–1, except that (1) LLC secures a nonrecourse permanent loan of $8 million to repay the construction debt and (2) Equity Investor makes a cash contribution to LLC of $3 million, all of which is distributed to Developer as a partial return of its project equity. Developer and Equity Investor agree to split all LLC cash flow 75% to Equity Investor and 25% to Developer.

By introducing leverage as a component of its interim exit strategy, Developer increases its ongoing interest in the project's future cash flow from 10 to 25%, while still receiving a current payday of $3 million.[53]

Developer's ultimate financial return on the above-described equity play is, of course, further dependent on the tax treatment afforded its $3 million cash distribution. The substance of the transaction described in Example 12–2 is that Developer has sold 75% of its interest in the project to Equity Investor for $3 million. If the equity play were to be treated as a sale for federal income tax purposes, Developer would have a taxable gain of $1.5 million (the $3 million cash distribution, less Developer's $1.5 million cost basis in the 75% project interest it sold to Equity Investor). If taxed at the current capital gains rate of 15%, Developer's after-tax return would be reduced by $225,000 (the $1.5 million gain, multiplied by 15%). While a detailed discussion of the rules of Subchapter K of the Internal Revenue Code is well beyond the scope of this Chapter, it is certainly worth mentioning that, under the right circumstances, a creative and diligent lawyer might be able to defer Developer's taxable gain on all or a substantial portion of the $3 million cash distribution.[54]

An equity play of the type described above involves most of the same legal and business issues discussed previously in Chapter 7, *Stage 3: Forming and Capitalizing the Project Entity.* The following are some of

---

53. As noted in an earlier chapter of this book (*see supra* Chapter 3, Pages 50–52) the use of debt to fund project costs will increase the equity participants' return on equity if the cost of the debt is less than the project's total return on cost—so-called "positive leverage." As such, Developer's 25% equity interest in Example 12–2 will prove to be more valuable to Developer than its 10% equity interest in Example 12–1, if the cost of obtaining the permanent loan (i.e., the interest rate and other loan fees paid by LLC) is less than the office building's return on costs.

54. *See* Blake D. Rubin, Andrea Macintosh Whiteway and Shane C. Orr, *Take the Money and Run: Extracting Equity on a Tax-free Basis*, in ALI–ABA COURSE OF STUDY MATERIALS, CREATIVE TAX PLANNING FOR REAL ESTATE TRANSACTIONS, Course No. SR–057, 1375 (October 2009); and WILLIAM S. McKEE, WILLIAM F. NELSON AND ROBERT L. WHITMIRE, FEDERAL TAXATION OF PARTNERSHIPS AND PARTNERS ¶ 14.03[3][b] (4th ed. 2007).

the key issues involved in the formation of an equity joint venture to house the ownership of a stabilized commercial real estate project:

- The preferred return payable on the investors' capital contributions;[55]

- The promote or carried interest given to the developer;[56]

- The allocation of decision-making control over the entity's operations;[57]

- The fees, if any, payable to the developer;[58] and

- The buy-sell and other negotiated exits available to the parties to end their relationship.[59]

The seizing up of the real estate debt markets following the market crash of 2008 has underscored the developer's need to obtain equity funding as part of its execution of an interim exit strategy for a stabilized project. Loan-to-value ratios have dropped from a norm of 80–90% just a few short years ago to 50–70% in today's market. The funding gap left by the deleveraging of the real estate markets must be covered by additional equity contributed to the project either by the developer or, hopefully, a willing and interested institutional investor. Unfortunately (at least for the developer), the heightened need for the infusion of additional equity to fill that funding gap has significantly shifted the relative bargaining power in equity negotiations away from the developer and in favor of the equity investor.[60]

HIBC Case Study—An Interim Exit Strategy

By 1999, the Pizzuti organization had developed nine office projects in the Heathrow International Business Center. All nine of the projects were producing above-market financial returns and were supported by a creditworthy roster of tenants. As such, the HIBC office projects were prime candidates for the execution of a limited, interim exit strategy involving the placement of nonrecourse permanent debt to retire the construction debt that was then encumbering those projects.[61]

---

55. *See supra* Chapter 7, Pages 243–245.

56. *See id.* at Pages 242–243.

57. *See id.* at Pages 263–266.

58. *See id.* at Pages 267–268.

59. *See id.* at Pages 278–282.

60. *See* Scott A. Lundquist and Eric M. Schiller, *A Real Estate Lawyer's Guide to Equity Investment (With Forms)*, 25 No. 2 Practical Real Estate Lawyer 41 (March 2009); and Dean C. Pappas, Steven A. Waters, Vicki R. Harding, Gary E. Fluhrer and Robert G. Gottlieb, *The Changing World of Real Estate Equity Investment*, in ACREL Papers 45 (ALI–ABA, March 2008).

61. Pizzuti had placed nonrecourse permanent debt on five of the HIBC properties as part of a portfolio loan that it obtained from a life insurance company in November 1997. The remaining four HIBC office projects were subject to short-term construction loans.

However, Pizzuti had broader business concerns that weighed against the execution of a simple, permanent debt strategy. The company had embarked on a development binge during the prior five years that had wholly exhausted its independent financial resources.[62] Moreover, Pizzuti believed (quite correctly) that its land holdings in Ohio, Florida, Indiana and Illinois provided it with a golden opportunity to ramp up its development efforts even further in the upcoming years. The end result was that Pizzuti felt that it needed money—and a lot of it—in order to restore its liquidity and position the company to take advantage of future development opportunities.

Prior to 1999, Pizzuti had funded the equity required for its development projects through a combination of its own cash resources and those provided by the principals of Newport Partners.[63] Pizzuti's liquidity was largely depleted by 1999 and Newport's capital was both limited in amount and more expensive than the equity typically provided by institutional investors.[64]

Pizzuti's challenge, therefore, was to devise an interim exit strategy that would facilitate its achievement of both of the following objectives:

- *The repatriation to the organization of a significant portion of the equity it had previously committed to its development projects; and*

- *The securing of a readily available capital source for its future development efforts that was both "cheaper" and "deeper" than that available from Newport Partners.*

The interim exit strategy identified and then executed by Pizzuti's senior financial and legal team centered on the equity participation of Nationwide Realty Investors, Ltd. ("NRI")[65] in both Pizzuti's existing real estate assets and its future development projects.[66] NRI and Pizzuti agreed to form a new joint venture entity ("Pizzuti Properties LLC") to own Pizzuti's existing real estate portfolio and all of its future development projects. NRI agreed in principal that it would (1) acquire an approximate-

---

62. In addition to the nine HIBC office buildings, Pizzuti had also developed and still owned 21 warehouses located in various cities throughout the Midwest, several suburban office buildings in Central Ohio, and a luxury condominium project in downtown Columbus.

63. *See supra* Chapter 4, Pages 66–68, and Chapter 7, Pages 219–220, 233–234, for a discussion of the equity arrangement struck by Pizzuti with the two principals of Newport Partners.

64. The equity deal initially struck by Pizzuti and Newport contemplated that all cash flow produced from the HIBC projects would be split in the same 50–50 ratio that characterized their respective obligations to contribute capital to and guaranty the construction loan for each office project. Because the Newport principals were willing to commit their capital and debt support at the outset of each development project (and not just once the projects reached stabilization), it was agreed that Pizzuti would not receive any promoted interest from the HIBC ventures. The absence of a promote in Pizzuti's favor made Newport's capital more expensive than the capital then being provided by institutional investors to similar commercial real estate projects (albeit at a later stage in the development of those projects).

65. NRI is the real estate arm of Nationwide Mutual Insurance Company, a large insurance and financial services company headquartered in Columbus, Ohio.

66. Pizzuti was able to use its grant to NRI of an equity interest in a sizable portfolio of stabilized real estate projects as a carrot to entice NRI to agree to contribute capital on the front-side of future development projects—a proposition that most risk-averse, institutional investors are reluctant to embrace.

ly 60% equity interest in Pizzuti's portfolio of Florida office and Ohio warehouse projects (an equity investment that would fund a return of equity to Pizzuti well into eight figures) and (2) provide 90% of the capital required for Pizzuti's future development projects in Columbus, Orlando, Indianapolis and Chicago. The final piece of the financial puzzle was provided by NRI's agreement to give Pizzuti and its senior executives a 5% promoted profits interest in the existing portfolio and a 35% promote on all new development projects.

One obstacle remained to Pizzuti's grand plan to solve all of its problems by entering into a new joint venture with NRI. Newport Partners owned a 25% equity interest in all of Pizzuti's warehouse projects and a 50% equity interest in the nine HIBC office buildings and the approximately 140 acres of undeveloped HIBC land—and Newport had no intention of consenting to the roll-up of its equity interests into the new Pizzuti–NRI entity. Newport's intransigence left Pizzuti with no choice but to negotiate what proved to be a very expensive exit from its relationship with Newport. After lengthy and occasionally hostile negotiations,[67] Pizzuti and Newport agreed to structure a termination of their partnership relationship along the following lines—(1) the newly-formed Pizzuti–NRI would purchase Newport's 25% interest in Pizzuti's warehouse properties, (2) Pizzuti (acting alone and not in concert with NRI) would purchase Newport's 50% interest in the undeveloped HIBC land, (3) Pizzuti (but not Newport) would contribute its 50% interest in the HIBC office buildings to the new Pizzuti–NRI entity, and (4) Pizzuti would immediately retain a broker to try to sell the nine HIBC office buildings that would then be owned jointly by Pizzuti Properties LLC and Newport Partners.[68]

While the negotiated exit deal struck with Newport was far from ideal, Pizzuti believed that the consummation of that deal was a sacrifice worth making to serve its broader business goals of establishing a long-term relationship with a deep-pocketed and reputable investor like NRI. The exit agreements between Pizzuti and Newport were executed on January 28, 2000, paving the way for Pizzuti and NRI to close their equity deal three days later on February 1, 2000.

IV. STAGE 9: OPERATING THE PROJECT

Once the developer makes the decision to execute an interim strategy to further its long-term ownership of an interest in a development project,

---

67. *See supra* Chapter 7, Pages 282–284, for a discussion of the tactics employed by Pizzuti during the course of its exit negotiations with Newport, including its decision to exercise the buy-sell provisions contained in the various Pizzuti–Newport partnership agreements.

68. The marketing for sale of the nine HIBC buildings was especially galling to Pizzuti, because it viewed the HIBC office buildings as perfect candidates for a long-term hold by the Pizzuti–NRI venture. As noted later in this Chapter (*see infra HIBC Case Study—The Sale of the Project*), Pizzuti and NRI agreed in September 2000 to buy out most of Newport's interests in the HIBC buildings.

its attention necessarily turns to Stage 9—the operation of the project. The developer's business objectives during Stage 9 are to:

- Keep the project full with tenants paying rents at or above the pro forma rents for the project;

- Hold the project expenses at or below budget;

- Keep its two customers happy—that is, its tenants and equity investors; and

- Maintain the project in good condition and order of repair.

The developer typically delegates the achievement of these objectives to two real estate professionals—specifically, a licensed real estate broker as to the first of the listed objectives and a property manager as to the remaining three objectives. These professional positions can be staffed either with in-house personnel (as Pizzuti opted to do with respect to the HIBC project) or by the hiring of independent real estate firms. The issues that must be addressed by the real estate development lawyer when papering the owning entity's relationship with the broker and the property manager are the same regardless whether those roles are filled by affiliates of the developer or independent third parties—the only difference is the identity of the person who gets to keep the fees paid for the provision of those services.

A. THE BROKERAGE AGREEMENT

A commercial leasing broker is an important player in any development project. The broker is typically tasked with primary responsibility for finding tenants to fill the developer's building and later securing replacements for those tenants who opt to relocate to another building. Good leasing brokers are indispensable to the leasing process due to their superior knowledge of both the space that is available for lease in a particular market and the potential users that might be interested in leasing that space.

The developer's relationship with a leasing broker can be structured in one of three ways—as (1) an ***open listing***, (2) an ***exclusive agency*** or (3) an ***exclusive listing***.[69] In an open listing, the developer agrees to pay a commission to any broker in the community, who actually procures a tenant for its building. In an exclusive agency, the developer selects a particular broker to lease space in its building and agrees to pay the selected broker a commission on any lease that is signed for the building, unless the developer, without the assistance of any other broker, is the procuring cause of the signed lease. Finally, an exclusive listing obligates the developer to pay the broker a commission on any lease, even if that lease is procured directly by the developer or another broker.

---

69. *See generally* John S. Hollyfield, *Property Management and Listing Brokerage Agreements: Part Two*, 1 PROBATE AND PROPERTY 55 (October 1987); GEORGE LEFCOE, REAL ESTATE TRANSACTIONS, FINANCE AND DEVELOPMENT 40–42 (6th ed. 2009); and Bruce B. May, *Real Estate Brokers: Agreements and Conduct*, in COMMERCIAL REAL ESTATE TRANSACTIONS HANDBOOK 3–18 through 3–44 and 3–79 through 3–87.

Most good brokers will refuse to undertake the leasing of space in a developer's building, unless they receive the full protection afforded by an exclusive listing. The following are the key provisions that should be addressed in the written, exclusive listing agreement entered into by a developer and a commercial leasing broker.

- **Term of Engagement**—The term of an exclusive listing agreement typically runs between three to 24 months. The broker wants a sufficiently long term to permit it to work its contacts in the community and maximize its ability to earn commissions. The developer, on the other hand, wishes to keep the term as short as possible, so that it can, if necessary, replace an ineffective broker.[70]

- **Definition of Commissionable Event**—Under common law, the general rule is that a broker is entitled to a commission if it procures a tenant who is "ready, willing and able" to lease space in the developer's building, even if a lease is never signed or the tenant never takes occupancy of the space.[71] Most developers will seek to circumvent the operation of this common law rule by specifically stating in the exclusive leasing agreement that the broker will not be entitled to any commission, unless the developer and the tenant sign a fully binding lease. A collateral issue is whether the broker is entitled to a commission for the tenant's renewal or extension of its lease, with the broker, quite predictably, taking the position that a renewal or extension is a commissionable event, and the developer adopting a totally contrary stance.

- **Exclusions**—If the developer has identified and/or contacted a prospective tenant prior to the execution of its listing agreement with the broker, the developer should specifically exclude a lease with that prospective tenant from the list of transactions on which the broker will be entitled to a commission.

- **Commission for Post-termination Leases**—The broker will want to make sure that its entitlement to a commission is protected if the landlord signs a lease after the expiration of the term of the listing agreement with a tenant introduced to the landlord by the broker during the term of the listing.[72] If a clause affording the broker that protection is not inserted into the listing agreement, the developer might be able to wholly avoid its commission obligation by simply deferring the date of its execution of the lease to a date which is beyond the last day of the listing term.[73] The

---

70. *See* Pearl A. Zager, *Brokerage Issues*, in PLI COURSE HANDBOOK, NEGOTIATING COMMERCIAL LEASES: HOW OWNERS AND CORPORATE OCCUPANTS CAN AVOID COSTLY ERRORS, Order No. 8608, 461, 470 (May 2006).

71. *See generally* May, *supra* note 69, *at* 3–60 through 3–64; and Zager, *supra* note 70, at 472–474. *But see* Ellsworth Dobbs, Inc. v. Johnson, 236 A.2d 843 (N.J. 1967), where the New Jersey Supreme Court rejected the majority rule and held that a broker is not entitled to a sales commission, unless the sale is actually consummated.

72. *See* Zager, *supra* note 70, at 471–472; and May, *supra* note 69, at 3–80.

73. *See e.g.,* Parker v. Compton, 511 S.W.2d 708 (Tenn. App. 1973). *See also Recent Development*, 42 TENNESSEE LAW REVIEW 405 (Winter 1975).

developer will want to limit the scope of its obligation to pay a post-termination commission to leases signed within a relatively short period of time following the expiration of the listing agreement (e.g., 60 days) and then only to leases signed with tenant prospects "registered" by the broker before the expiration of the term of the listing agreement. The "registered" tenants should include only those tenants specifically noted on a written list of prospective users to whom the broker showed the property and made a marketing presentation during the term of the listing agreement.[74]

- *Amount of Commission*—The commission payable to a commercial leasing broker is usually stated as a fixed percentage of the rent payable by the tenant during the lease term. The commission percentage will vary by market and product type.[75] In some communities, the percentage will be stated at a higher number for the earlier years of the lease term.[76] Leasing commissions are typically (although not always) calculated against the base rent payable by the tenant, expressly excluding any indexed base rent bumps, expense pass-through payments or amortization of excess tenant improvement costs.

- *Timing of Payment of Commission*—The broker believes that its job is done and that it should be paid the entirety of its commission upon the tenant's execution of its lease. A provision to that effect in the exclusive listing agreement places the entire risk of a tenant default on the landlord. The landlord will often try to mitigate its exposure to the risk of a tenant default by providing that a portion of the leasing commission (typically 50%) will be deferred until at least the date on which the tenant assumes occupancy of the leased space.[77]

- *Duties of the Broker*—Best practice calls for the listing agreement to specifically recite what the broker must do as part of its efforts to market the developer's property. By way of example, the property owner might want to include in the listing agreement specific requirements that the broker advertise the property as being "for lease" in a specific business journal of wide circulation in the community in which the developer's building is located; list the developer's building in a multiple listing service; attend periodic marketing meetings with the developer's principals; provide regu-

---

74. If the listing agreement fails to so limit the identity of the "registered" tenants, the broker will be sorely tempted to "register the phone book" by listing every conceivable user for the space, even though the broker may not have had any contact whatsoever with the user during the term of the listing agreement. *See* Zager, *supra* note 70, at 472.

75. In some markets, leasing commissions are calculated based on a specific dollar amount per square foot of space leased—e.g., $2 prsf. *See e.g.,* May, *supra* note 69, at Form 3–7, ¶ 6.2 (Alternative B), 3–83 and 3–84

76. *See* Zager, *supra* note 70, at 471. The percentage used to calculate the amount of the commission, if any, payable for a renewal or extension term is almost always less than the percentage used to calculate the commission for the initial lease term.

77. *See* May, *supra* note 69, at 3–80.

lar, written reports to the developer identifying the prospective tenants to whom it has shown the property or made a marketing presentation; and assign specific individual leasing agents to market the developer's building. The listing agreement should also specifically require the broker to cooperate with all other brokers in the market and to pay any and all commissions that are payable to any cooperating broker involved in the transaction.[78]

● *Duties of the Owner*—Finally, the exclusive listing agreement should recite exactly what the property owner is required to do to assist the broker in its efforts to procure tenants for the owner's building.[79] The broker will generally want to require the owner to refer to the broker all prospective tenants that contact the owner about the available space. The owner should also be required to provide the broker with all written materials needed by the broker to market the space, (including, floor plans, building photographs and a standard lease form) and to provide the broker with rent quotes and other approved parameters for the leasing of the space.

A copy of a pro-landlord Exclusive Listing Agreement is included in the Document Appendix as Document #7.

Practice Tip #12–1: The Lawyer's Relationship With the Broker[80]

The relationship between the landlord's lawyer and its leasing broker is frequently characterized by terms such as "antagonistic" and "distrustful." The lawyer views the broker as nothing more than a matchmaker, who cares only about making the deal happen so that it can get paid, and who cares nothing at all about whether the terms of the deal actually serve the developer's business interests. The lawyer often bemoans the fact that the broker is going to receive a crazy, high commission for doing nothing other than making a phone call to a prospective tenant and then turning all the dirty work over to the developer's lawyer. The broker, on the other hand, frequently views the lawyer as a deal killer, whose sole motivation is to raise a bunch of legal issues that have nothing to do with the economics of the deal and everything to do with costing the broker a hard-earned commission.

Unfortunately, the genesis of the above stereotypes of both the real estate development lawyer and the leasing broker is based on reality.

---

78. See May, *supra* note 69, at 3–88 through 3–93; and Hollyfield, *Part Two, supra* note 69, at 57. If the listing agreement fails to place an obligation on the listing broker to pay all commissions owed to cooperating brokers, the developer might find itself in the extremely unenviable position of owing two commissions on the same lease transaction—i.e., a full commission to its listing broker and an additional commission to the cooperating broker who served as the procuring cause for the tenant's lease.

79. *See* Hollyfield, *Part Two supra* note 69, at 56.

80. *See* May, *supra* note 69, at 3–4 through 3–6, for an interesting narrative on the lawyer-broker relationship.

During my years of practice, I noted that lawyers (regrettably, including me) and brokers often butt heads for no apparent reason. Instead of acting as an efficient team to consummate a quick and favorable lease transaction, the lawyer and the broker often spend an inordinate amount of time covering the same ground in different and frequently contradictory ways and then blaming the other if the deal falters or eventually blows up.

I tried to overcome the natural bias against brokers that is inbred in real estate lawyers by following three simple rules.

- *Rule #1—Recognize the value that the broker brings to the deal. The truth is that the value added to the deal by the broker's procurement of a tenant is much greater than the value added by the lawyer's negotiation of a pluperfect lease document. That is undoubtedly why the developer is happy to pay the broker a six figure commission, but consistently grouses about paying the lawyer his four figure fee.*

- *Rule #2—Establish sensible ground rules for the roles to be played by the lawyer and the broker. The broker and the lawyer should allocate responsibility for the lease transaction by acknowledging what they do best and what they don't do well at all. As such, the broker should be the person who keeps things together by taking primary responsibility for schmoozing the tenant and helping the developer maintain a cooperative (and not contentious) relationship with the tenant. The lawyer should be the person who gets the deal done by serving in the role of the primary negotiator of the lease document. If the lawyer and the broker embrace their separate roles, the lease transaction will proceed much more smoothly than if each of them tries to be all things to all people.*

- *Build a reputation as a deal maker and not a deal killer. If the broker knows that the lawyer is a deal maker, he will be much more likely to adopt the limited negotiating role noted in Rule #2 and stay out of the lawyer's way (which I have found is the best way to get the deal done).*

B.   THE PROPERTY MANAGEMENT AGREEMENT

The property manager is the person charged with operating the developer's project once it achieves stabilization. It is the property manager's job to make sure that the project is properly maintained, the rent is collected and the bills are paid. While the property manager was once viewed as little more than a custodian and toilet cleaner, that is no longer the case. Developers and institutional investors are now acutely aware of the impact that a professional property manager can have on the financial viability of a stabilized, commercial real estate project.

The need for quality property management has been heightened by the trend toward the ownership of stabilized real estate projects by financial institutions that have no operating presence whatsoever in the community where the project is located.[81] The absentee institutional owner has no choice but to delegate responsibility for the operation of its project to a reputable, independent property manager. National firms such as CB Richard Ellis, Cushman & Wakefield and Jones Lang LaSalle all now have strong property management divisions that are responsible for managing millions of square feet of commercial space throughout the United States.

Regardless whether a project is being managed by an affiliate of the developer or by a national property management company, the property management agreement entered into by the property owner should address all of the following considerations.

- ***Status and Authority of Property Manager***—Most property management agreements contain a clear statement that the property manager is an independent contractor and not an agent of the property owner. As such, the property manager may act on the owner's behalf only to the extent it is expressly authorized to do so under the specific terms of the management agreement.[82]

- ***Duties of Property Manager***—The property manager is charged with responsibility for managing, maintaining, repairing and operating the owner's project. The specific duties delegated by the owner to the property manager will vary widely based on project location and type and the business philosophy of the person that owns the project. Among other tasks, the property manager may be assigned responsibility for entering into all service contracts related to the day-to-day operation of the project (e.g., snow removal and window washing agreements); supervising the making of all required repairs and capital improvements (including tenant improvements); securing all requisite insurance policies; complying with all applicable laws affecting the project's operation; and collecting all rents and otherwise administering and enforcing the provisions of the project leases. It is essential that the property management agreement specifically describe the nature, scope and performance standards for all the services to be provided by the property manager.

- ***Compensation***—The property manager's fee is typically expressed as a percentage of the rents collected under the project leases (e.g., 3% of collected rents). The property management agreement should specifically define all payments that are intended to be included within the definition of "rents"—e.g., just base rent or all tenant receipts, including indexed rent bumps, expense pass-throughs, amortization of excess tenant improvement costs, parking charges

---

81. *See* Earl L. Segal and Michael A. Segal, *Dissecting the Commercial Property Management Agreement (with Checklist)*, 20 No. 1 Practical Real Estate Lawyer 31 (January 2004).

82. *See* John S. Hollyfield, *Property Management and Listing Brokerage Agreements: Part One*, 1 Probate and Property 24, 25 (August 1987).

and late fees. The property manager is also frequently reimbursed for expenses it incurs in connection with its performance of the required services under the property management agreement. The categories of the manager's reimbursable expenses is often the subject of heated negotiations, with the owner taking the position that all such expenses should be subsumed within the percentage fee paid to the property manager and the property manager seeking to preserve its fee as a pure profit by passing through to the project owner all conceivable expenses, including the salaries paid to the property manager's on-site personnel and a portion of the manager's general administrative and overhead costs.[83]

- *Budgets and Operating Statements*—The property manager is usually charged with responsibility for preparing an annual operating budget for the owner's approval. Once the operating budget is approved by the owner, the property manager is then authorized to incur and pay expenses in accordance with the approved budget. Any unbudgeted or excess expenses should, however, require fresh approval by the project owner. The property manager is also customarily required to furnish the project owner with periodic operating statements comparing the actual and budgeted financial results for the property.

- *Collection and Disbursement of Rents*—In most situations, the property manager is delegated responsibility for collecting all rents and other receipts from the project's tenants and depositing those receipts in an operating account maintained specifically for the owner's project. The property manager is usually empowered and directed to disburse funds from the operating account to pay those expenses that fall within the parameters established in the approved project budget (with the owner being required to fund any shortfalls between the project's collected receipts and the approved project expenses).[84]

- *Key Employees*—The owner may want the agreement to require the property management company to assign a specific person as its on-site property manager. If the named employee is no longer assigned to the project, the owner should reserve the right to terminate the property management agreement.[85]

- *Term of Agreement*—From the owner's perspective, the ideal property management agreement is one that provides that it may be terminated by the owner on 30 days (or less) notice. The

---

83. See *id.* at 33, 43–45.

84. Some project owners prohibit the property manager from paying its property management fee out of the operating account (based on a fear that the property manager may pay its fee before paying other more pressing project expenses). *See* Hollyfield, *Part One, supra* note 82, at 26.

85. *See* Hollyfield, *Part One, supra* note 82, at 25.

property manager wants the guaranteed term of its engagement to be as long as possible (at least a year or two), so that it has sufficient time to recover its start-up costs and maximize the profitability of its contract. The initial stated term of the agreement usually falls somewhere between those two extremes, with the agreement being automatically renewed for a like term, unless either party to the agreement specifically opts to cancel the term by delivering a written cancellation notice to the other party prior to the expiration of the then existing term of the property management agreement.[86]

A copy of a fairly balanced property management agreement is included in the Document Appendix as Document #8.

V. STAGE 10: SELLING THE PROJECT

Stage 10 is, alas, the end of the road for the developer's involvement in the development of a real estate project. The developer has decided, based upon the status of its project, its personal financial condition, and the state of the overall economy, that it is time to sell the project. The developer's business objective at this stage is quite simple—it wants to maximize its profit by choosing the optimal time to sell the project.

The developer's selection of the right time to sell the project is a major contributing factor to the determination of the project's ultimate profitability. The following example illustrates how accelerating or deferring the sale of a project can affect the developer's bottom line.

Example 12–3: It is the spring of 2007 and the Developer has just leased the last available space in its office building. Developer knows that the sales market is hot (with capitalization rates hovering in the 5–6% range for Class A office projects), but is confident that things will only get better in the coming years (and certainly will not get worse). As a result, Developer makes a decision to defer the sale of its project for at least a couple of years and exercises its right to extend the maturity date of its mortgage loan until the spring of 2010. Now fast forward to the spring of 2010 when Developer's loan is due. Unfortunately for Developer, the unimaginable has come true in the wake of the financial crisis of 2008—that is, thing really have gotten worse, with the prevailing capitalization rates for the sale of office buildings topping out at 8–9%.[87] The following chart illustrates the financial impact to the developer of its decision to postpone selling its project until 2010.

---

86. *See* Segal, *supra* note 81, at 34–35.

87. *See* URBAN LAND INSTITUTE, *supra* note 13, at 9. Many prospective sellers faced an even worse dilemma in the years following the financial crash of 2008—that is, they could not find a buyer for their projects, even at the elevated capitalization rates noted in Example 12–3.

Assumptions	Sale in 2007	Sale in 2010
Project Cost	$15 million	$15 million
Annual NOI	$1.5 million	$1.5 million
Capitalization Rate	6%	9%
Sales Price	$25 million	$16.67 million
Profit on Sale	$10 million	$1.67 million

The end result of Developer's decision to delay the sale of its project was a reduction of its profit on sale by $8.33 million—even though the project was producing the same NOI in 2010 as it was in 2007. Unfortunately, this scenario was played out all too frequently for developers in the years following the 2008 real estate crash—and, as of the date of this writing in 2010, is still being played out.

Practice Tip #12–2: Don't Mess With the Developer's Timing

Example 12–3 clearly points out the danger of the developer mistiming the market. But what does that mean for the developer's lawyer? The answer is that a real estate development lawyer should strive to craft legal documents that create sufficient flexibility for the developer to choose the optimal time to sell its project. A lawyer who acquiesces to an absolute lock-out period on the prepayment of a permanent loan, without advising the developer of the danger of doing so, might find that the last work he does for that developer is the closing of the permanent loan. The lawyer should always take into account the possibility of a future change in the real estate markets or in the financial condition or perspective of his developer client and seek to infuse the developer's transactional documents with as many contractual exits as reasonably practicable. A permanent loan that includes a yield maintenance prepayment penalty throughout the loan term might, therefore, better serve the developer's interests than would a permanent loan with a three year lock-out period and an unrestricted right to prepay the loan after the expiration of the lock-out period.

The sale of a stabilized development project involves many of the same legal issues that were addressed earlier in this text as part of the discussion of the developer's attempt to gain control of the project site.[88] The developer's view of those issues, however, takes on a decidedly different tack when the developer is the seller and not the buyer. A developer who is selling a completed project will, for example, want to limit the scope and duration of the buyer's contingency and sell the project in an "as is" condition, without any significant representations and warranties being made by the developer (just the opposite of the positions it took during Stage 1 of the development process).

---

88. *See supra* Chapter 5, Pages 94–148.

In addition to switching sides of the negotiating table on those legal issues that are common to both the developer's initial purchase of the project site and its ultimate sale of the stabilized project, the real estate development lawyer must also address in the sales contract certain issues that are unique to the sale of improved real property. Those additional issues are triggered by the fact that the sale of a stabilized real estate project involves not just the sale of land and a building, but also the transfer of a living and breathing operating business.

The following are some of the unique issues that a real estate lawyer must consider when preparing and negotiating a contract for the sale of a stabilized commercial real estate project.

- **Sale of Personal Property**—The sale of a stabilized project typically involves the sale of two property components that are not part of the developer's initial land acquisition—specifically, the sale of (1) tangible personal property (e.g., cleaning supplies, lobby furnishings and window coverings), and (2) intangible personal property (e.g., trade names, development rights, construction warranties and occupancy permits). The buyer will want to use expansive language to describe the personal property it is buying (i.e., all tangible and intangible, personal property used in connection with the operation of the project), coupled with a specific listing of each known item of personal property that the buyer wants to acquire in connection with its purchase of the subject project (e.g., the "Heathrow International Business Center" trade name or the Alexander Calder mobile hanging in the building lobby).

- **Assignment of Leases**—The sales contract should specifically list the tenant leases that are being assigned by the developer to the project buyer. Each lease should be identified by the name of the tenant, the date on which the lease was executed and the location and size of the tenant's leased premises. The project leases are typically described in a rent roll prepared by the developer and attached to the sales contract as an exhibit. The sales contract should (1) require the developer to furnish the buyer with accurate and complete copies of all project leases[89] and (2) provide the buyer with a right to terminate the contract if its review of the leases disclose provisions that are inconsistent with the rent roll or are otherwise unacceptable to the buyer. The buyer is usually given a relatively short period of time to review and approve the project leases (e.g., 30–90 days after the execution of the sales contract).

- **Loan Assumption**—It is fairly common for the project buyer to assume the permanent loan that encumbers the project. If the permanent loan is going to be assumed, the sales contract should (1) specify the terms of the proposed assumption (including who will be charged with the obligation to pay any assumption fees charged by the permanent lender) and (2) condition the buyer's

---

89. It is common in today's digital age for the developer to place electronic copies of the leases and other documents pertaining to its project in an e-data room that can be securely accessed online by a prospective buyer of the project. *See* Dorothea W. Dickerman, *Navigating Commercial Real Estate Closings—Part 1*, 26 No. 2 PRACTICAL REAL ESTATE LAWYER 45, 57 (March 2010).

obligation to purchase the project upon the permanent lender's approval of the buyer's assumption of the loan.[90]

- *Rent Prorations*—The sales contract typically contains detailed provisions concerning the manner in which rents will be prorated between the seller and the buyer. The principal questions that must be answered as part of the rent proration provisions are (1) who will bear the risk that the tenants do not pay their rent for the month of closing (i.e., will the rents be prorated based on "collected" or "accrued" rents), (2) how will any year-end, expense-pass-through reconciliations be handled (i.e., who will be obligated to refund any tenant overpayment of expense payments and who will be entitled to collect any tenant underpayments) and (3) who will be obligated to collect any delinquent rent receivables that are outstanding as of the date of closing.[91]

- *Representations and Warranties on Physical Plant and Leases*—The developer will resist making any representations and warranties concerning the status or condition of the project, preferring, instead, to sell the project in an "as is, where is" condition. The buyer will be equally forceful in seeking to include in the sales contract specific seller representations and warranties concerning (1) the conformity of the tenant leases with the rent roll attached to the sales contract and (2) the soundness of the physical condition of the building and its operating systems and equipment. The gulf that exists between the positions adopted by the seller and the buyer on these issues is often bridged by the introduction of "materiality" and "knowledge" qualifiers to the seller's representation about tenant leases and the limitation of the seller's representation on the physical condition of the property to "latent, structural defects" that are not readily discoverable as part of a thorough engineering inspection of the project.[92]

- *Tenant Estoppel Certificates*—The buyer will demand that it receive written confirmation from the tenants that (1) the project leases are in full force and effect, without any default by the landlord, and (2) the form and content of those leases are fully consistent with the rent roll attached to the sales contract and the lease documents previously furnished to the buyer by the developer. A point of contention that frequently arises during the negotiation of this provision is whether the seller is obligated to deliver accept-

---

90. Permanent loan documents frequently permit the permanent loan to be assumed by a "qualified buyer"—meaning a buyer who has comparable experience and financial standing to the original borrower under the permanent loan. *See supra* Pages 559–561.

91. For a representative sample of a rent proration provision, *see* Peter Aitelli, *Purchase and Sale Agreement for Real Property*, in ALI–ABA COURSE OF STUDY MATERIALS, MODERN REAL ESTATE TRANSACTIONS: PRACTICAL STRATEGIES FOR REAL ESTATE ACQUISITION, DISPOSITION, AND OWNERSHIP, Course No. SS–012, 167, §§ 10.1 and 10.2 (July 2010).

92. *See* Billie J. Ellis and Douglas A. Yeager, *Practical Implications of a Seller's Representations and Warranties in a Highly Competitive Commercial Real Estate Transaction*, in ACREL Papers 57,74–75, 81–82, 86 (ALI–ABA, October 2006).

able, signed estoppel certificates for every tenant in the building (the buyer's preference) or just a limited subset of the building's tenants—e.g., those tenants occupying 80% of the rentable square feet contained within the building (the seller's preference).

- ***Interim Operating Covenant***—Finally, a provision should be included in the sales contract that requires the seller to continue to operate the project prior to closing in accordance with its past practices and to refrain from entering into any new leases or contracts or amending any existing leases or contracts, without first obtaining the buyer's written consent.[93]

HIBC Case Study—The Sale of the Project

The Heathrow International Business Center has been the case study used throughout this text to examine the roles played by the real estate development lawyer during each of the ten stages of a development project. The time has now come to tie a bow around both this text and the HIBC case study by briefly mentioning the circumstances surrounding the Pizzuti organization's sale of the HIBC project to Colonial Properties Trust on August 1, 2002.

As noted earlier in this Chapter, Pizzuti contributed its 50% interest in nine HIBC office buildings to a joint venture formed by it and Nationwide Realty Investors, Ltd. on February 1, 2000. At the time of the formation of the Pizzuti Properties LLC joint venture, it was the understanding of Pizzuti, NRI and Newport Partners (as the owner of the remaining 50% equity interest in the nine HIBC buildings) that Pizzuti would engage a real estate broker to pursue the sale of all of the HIBC buildings.[94] Part of that strategy was implemented in September 2000, when Pizzuti sold the two office buildings that were 100% leased by First USA to Lexington Properties Trust for $41.7 million.

Because Pizzuti and NRI were both extremely bullish on the HIBC project, an agreement was struck with Newport Partners in late 2000 for the joint venture's purchase of Newport Partners' remaining 50% interest in five of the remaining seven HIBC office buildings. It was further agreed that Pizzuti would indefinitely suspend its efforts to sell the two office buildings in which Newport Partners continued to own an interest.

The 2001 redemption/reorganization of Newport Partners' interest in the HIBC project was undertaken to facilitate a long-term hold of the HIBC office buildings by the Pizzuti–NRI joint venture. That venture was also committed to an aggressive schedule for the development of the undevel-

---

93. *See* GREGORY M. STEIN, MORTON P. FISHER, JR. AND GAIL M. STERN, A PRACTICAL GUIDE TO COMMERCIAL REAL ESTATE TRANSACTIONS—FROM CONTRACT TO CLOSING 35 (2001).

94. Pizzuti grudgingly agreed to the required marketing of the HIBC buildings in order to secure Newport Partners' consent to the closing of the Pizzuti–NRI equity deal. *See supra HIBC Case Study—An Interim Exit Strategy.*

oped HIBC land, which, at the end of 2000, consisted of approximately 140 acres of office and commercial ground. In 2001, Pizzuti Properties LLC kicked off its first new office development project by starting construction of a 192,000 square foot office building on an approximately 20 acre tract in HIBC. It was then the anticipation of Pizzuti and NRI that the venture would complete development of ten additional office buildings within the HIBC park within a horizon of five to seven years. The expectation was that the HIBC buildings would be a long-term hold for the NRI–Pizzuti joint venture.

Pizzuti Properties' long-term investment strategy for the HIBC project came crashing to a halt in late 2001 when Pizzuti experienced a severe liquidity crisis.[95] Pizzuti's immediate need for cash precipitated its request that NRI consent to an immediate sale of the entirety of the HIBC office building portfolio. NRI eventually consented to the sale of the HIBC portfolio and Pizzuti promptly retained a real estate broker to find a buyer for both the eight office buildings still owned by the Pizzuti–NRI joint venture entity and the approximately 120 acres of undeveloped land owned outright by Pizzuti. On August 1, 2002, Pizzuti sold the HIBC property to Colonial Properties Trust, a real estate investment trust headquartered in Birmingham, Alabama, for a combined purchase price of $143 million.

The sale of the HIBC project was a particularly bittersweet moment for me. I had been intimately involved in every aspect of Pizzuti's development of the HIBC project, dating from Pizzuti's acquisition of its first HIBC building in 1992 through its sale of the project to Colonial Properties Trust in August of 2002. The HIBC project afforded me the opportunity to work with some extraordinary people and to put my knowledge and skills to the test in the context of an incredibly challenging real estate project.

The sale of the HIBC project on August 1, 2002, brought an end to a wonderfully successful development project. It also served as the effective end to my career as a practicing lawyer. In March, 2003, I retired from The Pizzuti Companies and, in the words of my then 11 year old son, became a "housewife." I joined the faculty of the Moritz College of Law at The Ohio State University in the spring of 2006 and set about writing a book on real estate development law—a venture which, among other things, has permitted me to re-live the challenges and excitement presented by my participation in the development of the HIBC project.

VI. SUMMARY

The final three stages of a development project are an interesting time for a real estate development lawyer. During each of these stages, other real estate professionals pour over the documents created by the real

---

95. Pizzuti's financial crisis was precipitated by causes wholly unrelated to the HIBC project, which was continuing to produce stable, above-market rates of return for all of its equity owners.

estate development lawyer during the seven formative stages of a development project to determine whether the developer can refinance, operate, and ultimately sell its project on terms favorable to the developer. Stages 8, 9 and 10 are, therefore, the true test as to whether the lawyer did what he was hired to do—that is, add value to the developer's project.

Document Appendix

The following are the core legal documents that are included in this Document Appendix and referred to in the text of REAL ESTATE DEVELOPMENT LAW.

Document #1: *Letter of Intent*

Document #2: *Real Estate Purchase Agreement*

Document #3: *Operating Agreement*

Document #4: *Closing Statement*

Document #5: *Construction Loan Agreement*

Document #6: *Office Lease*

Document #7: *Exclusive Listing Agreement*

Document #8: *Property Management Agreement*

These documents are standard form agreements that I used during my years in the active practice of real estate development law. I believe that they are representative samples of the types of documents that real estate development lawyers regularly encounter in their daily practices. However, three important caveats need to be made concerning these documents—(1) they are standard forms that must be tailored to reflect the specifics of the business deal struck by the parties to the agreements, (2) they have been modified to create some "teaching moments" for the Real Estate Development Law course that I teach at the Moritz College of Law at The Ohio State University, and (3) they all have a slight (but hopefully not unconscionable) developer bias. For these reasons, I strongly advise you not to use any of the forms in your practice, until such time as you have thoroughly read and vetted each and every provision of the subject document.

DOCUMENT #1

LETTER OF INTENT FOR LAND ACQUISITION

■ ■ ■

__________, 20__

[Insert Name and Address of Seller]

    Subject: Letter of Intent to Purchase **[insert general description of the property]**

Dear **[insert seller's name]**:

We are interested in purchasing **[insert general description of the property]** ("Property"). The general terms upon which we would consider purchasing your Property are outlined below.

1. **Description of Property**. The Property contains approximately ___ acres and is located in ________, ________. A legal description of the Property is attached to this letter of intent as Exhibit A.

2. **Purchase Price**. The purchase price for the Property will be **[insert price or method for calculating the price]** and will be paid in cash at closing.

3. **Buyer's Contingency**. We will need a period of ________ days after the date of our mutual execution of a definitive purchase agreement in which to conduct our due diligence of the Property. We will have no obligation to purchase the Property, unless **[include specific statement of contingency]**.

4. **Closing**. We will close on the purchase of the Property within ________ days after the satisfactory completion of our due diligence efforts under ¶ 3, above. You will be responsible for paying the following closing costs: **[insert list of closing costs to be paid by seller and those closing costs, if any, to be paid by buyer]**. Real estate taxes for the taxable year of closing will be prorated through the date of closing.

584

5. **<u>Non-binding Nature of Letter of Intent</u>**. This letter of intent is merely an expression of our general interest in pursuing a purchase of your Property and is not intended to create any obligation for either of us concerning the purchase and sale of the Property. Neither of us will be bound to the other in any way, unless and until we both execute a definitive purchase agreement that sets forth the detailed terms and conditions that will govern our purchase of the Property.

If you are interested in selling us the Property in general accordance with the terms outlined above, please so indicate by signing and returning a copy of this letter to us at your earliest convenience (but, in any event, by no later than the close of business on _______, 20__). Once we receive an executed copy of this letter of intent, we will see to it that a draft purchase contract is immediately prepared and submitted to you for your review and comment.

We look forward to working with you on this matter.

Sincerely,

____

                 Accepted as of _______, 20__.

                 By: ___________________________

DOCUMENT #2

REAL ESTATE PURCHASE AGREEMENT
FOR LAND ACQUISITION

■ ■ ■

REAL ESTATE PURCHASE AGREEMENT

This Real Estate Purchase Agreement (“**Agreement**”) is entered into by _______ (“**Seller**”) and _______ (“**Buyer**”). The “**Effective Date**” of this Agreement will be the date on which both Seller and Buyer have executed this Agreement. For the parties’ convenience in reviewing this Agreement, all defined terms will be highlighted by **boldface print** when first defined in this Agreement.

Seller and Buyer hereby agree as follows:

§ 1. **Sale of the Property**. Upon the terms and subject to the conditions set forth in this Agreement, Seller will sell to Buyer the approximately ___ acre tract of land which is located off of _______ in _______, _______, and which is further described in the legal description attached hereto as Exhibit A (**“Property”**). For the purposes of this Agreement, the term “Property” will be deemed to refer not only to the above-described land, but also to all rights and interests appurtenant to such land, including, without limitation, all water and mineral rights, development rights, easements, licenses, permits, rights-of-way, utility agreements and improvements located on or related in any way to such land.

§ 2. **Deposit**. Within two business days after the Effective Date, Buyer will deposit with _______ (“**Escrow Agent**”) cash in the sum of $_______ as an earnest money deposit. Such earnest money deposit will be held in an interest-bearing account, with all references herein to the “**Deposit**” specifically including not only the initial principal sum of $_______ deposited hereunder, but also the interest earned on such initial principal sum. The Deposit will be disbursed in the following manner:

    (a) If the closing occurs in the manner contemplated in this Agreement, then the Deposit will be paid to Seller and applied as a credit against the Purchase Price payable at closing;

    (b) If this Agreement is terminated by Buyer pursuant to any right granted to it in this Agreement (including, without limitation, the

586

termination rights set forth in §§ 4, 7, 8, 11 and 12), then the Deposit will be returned to Buyer, without prejudice, however, to Buyer's right to pursue any remedies it may have against Seller, at law or in equity, to redress any default by Seller hereunder; and

(c) If the closing fails to occur as a result of Buyer's default hereunder, then the Deposit will be paid to Seller as liquidated damages, in full and complete settlement of all claims it might otherwise have against Buyer as a result of such default.

If required by Escrow Agent, Seller and Buyer will enter into a separate agreement with Escrow Agent in order to evidence Escrow Agent's rights, duties, liabilities and obligations with respect to its holding and disbursement of the Deposit under this § 2.

§ 3. **Purchase Price**. The purchase price for the Property will be $______ ("**Purchase Price**"). The Purchase Price will be paid in cash at closing by means of a federal funds wire transfer of immediately available funds. The Purchase Price will be subject to such prorations, credits, allowances and other adjustments as are provided for in this Agreement, including, without limitation, those set forth in § 10.

§ 4. **Buyer's Contingency**. Buyer's obligations under this Agreement are expressly contingent upon Buyer determining, within ___ days after the Effective Date ("**Contingency Period**"), that the condition of the Property is suitable for Buyer's intended use and that Buyer's proposed development of the Property is economically feasible. If Buyer gives Seller written notice within the Contingency Period that the foregoing contingency has been satisfied ("**Approval Notice**"), then the parties will thereafter proceed to close on Buyer's purchase of the Property in the manner contemplated in this Agreement. If Buyer fails to give Seller an Approval Notice within the Contingency Period, then the Deposit will be returned to Buyer, this Agreement will automatically terminate and, except as otherwise expressly provided in this Agreement, Buyer and Seller will be relieved of all further rights, liabilities and obligations hereunder.

§ 5. **Buyer's Due Diligence**. Seller will permit Buyer and Buyer's agents access to the Property at all reasonable times prior to closing, so that Buyer can conduct such tests, studies, inspections and other due diligence of the Property as Buyer deems appropriate. Buyer agrees to indemnify and hold Seller harmless from any liability or loss incurred by Seller as a direct result of Buyer's conduct of its due diligence activities on the Property and to promptly repair any damage caused to the Property thereby.

In order to further facilitate Buyer's due diligence efforts, Seller will, within ten days after the Effective Date, provide Buyer with copies of all written reports in Seller's possession or control related to the condition of the Property, including, without limitation, all environmental reports, utility studies, surveys, topographical studies, wetland delineations and any other site-specific written materials related to the Property. If for any reason Buyer fails to close on its purchase of the Property, Buyer will return all such written reports to Seller within ten days after Buyer's receipt of a written request from Seller for the return of the same.

§ 6. **Representations and Warranties**. For the purpose of inducing Buyer to enter into this Agreement and consummate its purchase of the Property, Seller hereby makes the following representations and warranties to Buyer as of the date of Seller's execution of this Agreement.

(a) **Seller's Authority**. Seller has the full right, power and authority to execute this Agreement and consummate the transactions contemplated hereunder, without first having to obtain the consent or approval of any other person or governmental authority.

(b) **Off-record Title Matters**. Seller owns fee simple title to the Property, free and clear of all liens and encumbrances whatsoever (including without limitation, any easement, mortgage, restrictive covenant, lease, option, right of first refusal, right of first offer or purchase contract), except for those matters and exceptions appearing of public record in the real estate records of the county in which the Property is located.

(c) **Rights of Possession and Use**. There are no adverse parties in possession of the Property and no party has been granted any license, lease or other right relating to its use or possession of the Property.

(d) **No Proceedings**. There is no action, suit, proceeding or investigation pending, threatened or contemplated before any agency, court or governmental authority, which relates to the Seller or the Property.

(e) **Public Improvements and Taxes**. Seller has not received notice of, nor does it have any other knowledge or information concerning, (i) any proposed or contemplated improvements to the Property by any public authority, the cost of which could be assessed as a special tax against the Property in the future or (ii) any proposed or contemplated increase in the valuation of the Property for real estate tax purposes.

(f) **Creditor Problems**. There are no attachments, executions, receiverships, assignments for the benefit of creditors or voluntary or involuntary proceedings in bankruptcy or under any other debtor relief law, pending, threatened or contemplated against Seller or the Property.

(g) **Termination of Access/Utilities**. No fact, condition or proceeding exists which could result in the termination or impairment of any current access from the Property to any presently existing highway or road adjoining or situated on the Property or to any existing sewer, water or other utility lines or facilities serving, adjoining or situated on the Property.

(h) **Mechanics Liens**. All bills and claims for labor performed or materials furnished to or for the benefit of the Property for all periods of time prior to the Effective Date have been paid in full and there are no mechanics liens (whether or not perfected) pending against or otherwise affecting the Property.

(i) **Hazardous Materials**. There are no Hazardous Materials located on the Property and neither Seller, nor any previous owner of the Property, has ever violated or received any notice of the claimed violation of any federal, state or local law or regulation relating to the health, safety or environment, including, without limitation, the Clean Air Act, the Clean Water Act, the Federal Water Pollution Control Act, the Resource Conservation and Recovery Act, the Hazardous Materials Transportation Act, the Comprehensive Environmental Response Compensation and Liability Act, the Toxic Substances Control Act or any amendments or extensions of any of the foregoing. No underground storage tanks exist at the Property. For the purposes of this Agreement, the term "**Hazardous Material**" means any chemical, pollutant, contaminant, waste, toxic substance or petroleum product defined in, governed by, or regulated pursuant to any of the laws or regulations referred to in the first sentence of this subparagraph (i).

(j) **Compliance with Laws and Private Restrictions**. The Property is not in violation of: (i) any statute, law, regulation, rule, ordinance, permit, requirement or other government order or degree of any kind whatsoever (including, without limitation, any zoning ordinance); or (ii) any condition, easement, right-of-way, parking agreement, covenant, restriction or other private agreement affecting the Property.

(k) **Zoning**. The Property is zoned _______. Seller has not received any written notice of, nor has it initiated or participated in, any proposed action for a change or modification of the Property's current zoning classification or the enactment, change or modification of any other governmental requirement which could have the effect of limiting the future use of the Property.

(*l*) **Separate Tax Parcel**. The Property constitutes a separate, free-standing tax parcel for real estate tax purposes.

(m) **Condemnation**. There is no condemnation or eminent domain proceeding pending, threatened or contemplated against the Property.

(n) **Wetland and Flood Hazard Areas**. No portion of the Property is located in (a) a wetland area (as that term is defined or used in any applicable federal or state law or regulation, including, without limitation, the Clean Water Act) or (b) a designated flood plain or flood hazard area.

(*o*) **Seller's Deliveries**. All of the information and other materials delivered by Seller with respect to the Property pursuant to this Agreement, including, without limitation, those items delivered pursuant to § 5, above, are, to the best of Seller's knowledge and belief, true, accurate, correct and complete in all material respects.

Each of the representations and warranties set forth in this § 6 will be deemed to have been remade by Seller as of the closing date, with the same force and effect as if first made on and as of such date. Each of such representations and warranties will survive the closing. The Buyer's remedies for Seller's breach (both before and after the closing) of any of the above representations and warranties are set forth in § 11.

§ 7. **Title Commitment and Survey**. Within 30 days after the Effective Date, Seller will cause ________ or some other nationally-recognized title insurance company acceptable to Buyer ("**Title Company**") to furnish to Buyer a commitment for an ALTA Owner's Title Insurance Policy (2006) in the face amount of the Purchase Price, together with legible copies of all title exceptions noted in such title commitment ("**Title Commitment**").

Also within 30 days after the Effective Date, Seller will cause ________ or some other land surveyor duly licensed in the state where the Property is located ("**Surveyor**") to furnish to Buyer a survey of the Property certified to Buyer and the Title Company and dated after the Effective Date ("**Survey**"). The Survey will be prepared in conformity with the Minimum Standard Detail Requirements for ALTA/ACSM Land Title Surveys and will show the location of all improvements, easements, roads, rights-of-way, encroachments and other title matters affecting the Property.

If the Title Commitment or Survey discloses any exception to title, which Buyer, in the exercise of its reasonable judgment, finds unacceptable, then Buyer will have 20 days after its receipt of the last of the Title Commitment and Survey in which to deliver in writing to Seller any objection which Buyer may have to such exception ("**Title Notice**"). Buyer will be deemed to have approved any title exceptions appearing in the Title Commitment or Survey, which are not objected to in a timely delivered Title Notice and, thereafter, such title exceptions will be treated as "**Permitted Exceptions**" for the purposes of this Agreement.

If Buyer objects to any title exception by delivering a Title Notice to Seller within the aforementioned 20–day period, then Seller, at its expense, will use its reasonable efforts to satisfy Buyer's title objections within ten days after Seller's receipt of the Title Notice. If Seller is successful in satisfying any of Buyer's objections, then Seller will deliver to Buyer proof of such satisfaction and will also cause the Title Company to take all requisite actions to remove the subject title exception from Schedule B to the Title Commitment. If Seller fails to satisfy all of Buyer's objections within the aforementioned ten-day period, then Buyer will have the option, as its sole and exclusive remedy, of either: (a) terminating all of its rights and obligations under this Agreement by delivering written notice of termination to Seller within five days after the expiration of the aforementioned ten-day period, in which event, the Deposit will be returned to Buyer and, excerpt as otherwise expressly provided in this Agreement, Buyer and Seller will be relieved from all further rights, liabilities or obligations hereunder; or (b) waiving its objections under the Title Notice and proceeding to close on the purchase of the Property.

§ 8. **Conditions to Closing**. Seller's obligation to sell the Property to Buyer is subject to Buyer's performance of all of its obligations under this Agreement (or Seller's waiver of such performance), including, without limitation, Buyer's payment of the Purchase Price to Seller in the manner set forth in §§ 3 and 10 hereof, and its execution and delivery to Seller of all of those documents required to be executed and delivered by it pursuant to § 10.

Buyer's obligation to purchase the Property from Seller is subject to the satisfaction (or Buyer's waiver) on or before the date of closing, of all of the following conditions precedent:

(a) Buyer's delivery of an Approval Notice to Seller within the Contingency Period specified in § 4;

(b) Seller's performance of all of its obligations under this Agreement, including, without limitation, Seller's timely delivery of a Title Commitment and Survey to Buyer in the manner set forth in § 7, and its execution and delivery of all of those documents required to be executed and delivered by it pursuant to § 10; and

(c) All of Seller's representations and warranties under § 6 being true and correct as of the date of closing.

If any of the above conditions has not been satisfied as of the outside date for closing specified in § 9, then the party in whose favor such condition runs will have the right to terminate this Agreement and all of its obligations hereunder by delivering a written notice of termination to the other party to this Agreement. The legal effect of any such termination (that is, the prescribed disposition of the Deposit and the existence of any remedies for the failure of such condition) will be determined under either § 4 (with respect to the failure of the condition specified in subparagraph (a), above) or § 11 of this Agreement (with respect to the failure of all other conditions).

§ 9. **Date and Place of Closing**. The closing will occur within ___ days after Buyer's delivery of an Approval Notice to Seller under § 4, at such specific date, time and place as are mutually agreed to by the Seller and Buyer. At the option of either Seller or Buyer, the closing of the transaction contemplated hereunder may be effected by the delivery by Seller and Buyer of all closing documents and other required deliveries into escrow with the Escrow Agent and the Escrow Agent's holding, recordation and disbursement of all such closing documents and deliveries in accordance with escrow instructions delivered to the Escrow Agent by Seller and Buyer.

Possession of the Property (subject only to the Permitted Exceptions) will be delivered to Buyer at closing. All references in this Agreement to the "**closing**", the "**closing date**" or the "**date of closing**" will mean the closing of the transaction contemplated in this Agreement at the time and place and in the manner contemplated by this Agreement.

§ 10.   **Closing Obligations/Procedures**. Seller's sale of the Property to Buyer will be effected by Seller and Buyer taking the following described obligatory actions at closing.

    (a) **Purchase Price Payment**. Buyer will pay the Purchase Price to Seller by means of a federal funds wire transfer of immediately available funds. The amount of such payment will be adjusted in the manner contemplated in subparagraphs (h) and (i), below, with respect to closing credits, charges and other adjustments.

    (b) **Transfer of Property**. Seller will execute and deliver to Buyer a general warranty deed, in recordable form, pursuant to which Seller will transfer to Buyer fee simple title to the Property, free and clear of all liens and encumbrances, except for the Permitted Exceptions.

    (c) **Closing Affidavits**. Seller will execute and deliver to Buyer (i) an affidavit stating that Seller is not a "foreign person" within the meaning of § 1445 of the Internal Revenue Code, (ii) an affidavit with respect to off-record title matters, which is sufficient to permit the Title Company to issue a title policy for the Property in the form contemplated in subparagraph (g), below and (iii) an affidavit affirming the continuing truth and accuracy as of the date of closing of all of Seller's representations and warranties set forth in § 6.

    (d) **Entity Resolutions**. Seller and Buyer will execute and deliver to the other (i) a certificate of good standing affirming such party's authority to do business in the state of its organization and in the state in which the Property is located, and (ii) an entity resolution affirming the authority of such party to enter into the transaction contemplated in this Agreement and further authorizing an individual officer or representative of such party to execute this Agreement and all closing documents in the name and on behalf of such party.

    (e) **Closing Statement**. Seller and Buyer will execute and deliver to the other a closing statement which sets forth the economics of Buyer's purchase of the Property from Seller, including the amount of the purchase price and all those closing credits, charges and other adjustments specified in subparagraphs (h) and (i), below.

(f) **Miscellaneous Closing Documents**. Seller and Buyer will execute and deliver to each other such other documents as are reasonably requested by Seller or Buyer to further evidence or effect the sale of the Property to Buyer in the manner contemplated in this Agreement.

(g) **Title Policy**. Seller will cause the Title Company to issue to Buyer an ALTA Owner's Title Insurance Policy (2006) in the face amount of the Purchase Price, insuring in Buyer fee simple title to the Property, free and clear of all liens and encumbrances, excepting only the Permitted Exceptions. The title insurance policy will expressly reflect the Title Company's deletion of the standard, preprinted exceptions set forth in Schedule B–1 to such policy.

(h) **Closing Costs**. Seller will pay the following costs at closing: (i) all premiums and other charges required to permit the Title Company to issue the title insurance policy referred to in subparagraph (g) above; (ii) all costs required to permit the Surveyor to issue and certify the Survey in the manner required under § 7; (iii) all state, municipal and county transfer taxes, documentary stamps and other fees payable as a condition to Seller's transfer of the Property to Buyer; and (iv) the real estate commission owed to the broker identified in § 13. Buyer will pay the following costs at closing: (v) all recording fees associated with the recordation of the general warranty deed referred to in subparagraph (b) above; and (vi) all costs associated with Buyer's conduct of its due diligence under § 5. Any escrow fees payable to the Escrow Agent will be split equally by Seller and Buyer. Seller and Buyer will each separately pay any attorney's fees incurred by such party in connection with the preparation and negotiation of this Agreement and the consummation of the transactions contemplated in this Agreement. Any costs associated with the closing of this transaction, which are not otherwise specifically addressed in this Agreement, will be paid by the party who, in accordance with the custom and practice in the area in which the Property is located, is normally required to pay such closing costs.

(i) **Closing Credits**. Seller will pay or credit on the Purchase Price the amount of all special assessments and delinquent real estate taxes (including penalties and interest thereon), which are a lien on the Property as of the date of closing. Seller will also credit on the Purchase Price an amount equal to that portion of all non-delinquent real estate taxes which are attributable to the period of time prior to the closing. If a final real estate tax bill for the taxable year of closing has not been issued by the taxing authority as of the date of closing, then the calculation of the Purchase Price credit to be given to Buyer pursuant to the immediately preceding sentence will be determined based upon the most recently available tax use, tax rate and tax valuation for the Property. Buyer will have the right to have the amount of such Purchase Price credit recalculated once the final real estate tax bill for the taxable year of closing is issued by the taxing authority. Buyer may exercise such right by delivering a written recalculation notice to Seller at any time within two years after the date on which the final real estate tax bill for the taxable year of closing is issued by the taxing authority. Any additional amount owed to Buyer as a result of the recalculation of such Purchase Price credit will be paid to Buyer by Seller within 30 days after Seller's receipt of Buyer's recalculation notice.

All other items of income and expense related to the Property will be prorated through the date of closing, with Seller being entitled to receive or obligated to pay (with any required payment being made by Seller at or prior to closing), as the case may be, all such items of income or expense attributable to the period prior to the date of closing, and Buyer being entitled to receive or obligated to pay, as the case may be, all such items of income and expenses attributable to the period from and after the date of closing.

For the purposes of this subparagraph (i), the determination of whether an item is "**attributable to**" a particular period will, except as otherwise expressly provided herein, be made in accordance with generally accepted accounting principles, consistently applied.

§ 11. **Defaults/Remedies**. If Seller defaults in the performance of any of its obligations hereunder and if such default continues for a period of ten days after written notice of the alleged existence of such default is given to Seller by Buyer, then Buyer may pursue any remedy available to it at law or in equity to redress such default, including, without limitation, the right to specific performance. Except as otherwise provided in this § 11, Seller will be deemed to have defaulted in the performance of its obligations if it breaches any representation and warranty made by it under § 6 (regardless whether such representation and warranty was made as of the Effective Date or remade as of the date of closing). Notwithstanding anything to the contrary contained herein, Seller will not be deemed to be in default under this Agreement if any fact or circumstance occurs after the Effective Date, which renders any of Seller's representations and warranties false, so long as any such fact or circumstance is not within the reasonable control of Seller; provided, however, that, the occurrence of any such fact or circumstance will nonetheless permit Buyer to terminate its obligations under this Agreement and receive a refund of the Deposit.

If Buyer defaults in the performance of any of its obligations hereunder and such default continues for a period of ten days after written notice of the alleged existence of such default is given to Buyer, then Seller will be entitled to receive payment of the Deposit as liquidated damages, in full and complete settlement of all claims it might otherwise have against

Buyer as a result of such default; it being expressly acknowledged by the parties hereto that Seller's actual damages in the event of a default by Buyer hereunder would be difficult to ascertain and that the receipt of the Deposit represents the parties' reasonable estimate of the damages that would be caused by such default. Seller's right to receive the Deposit as liquidated damages will be Seller's sole and exclusive remedy to redress a default by Buyer and Seller hereby waives all other available remedies, including the remedy of specific performance.

§ 12. **Risk of Loss**. The risk of loss to the Property from the occurrence of a casualty or a taking by any public authority under the power or right of eminent domain (or by the threat thereof) will be borne by Seller until the closing of Buyer's purchase of the Property. If any such casualty or taking occurs prior to closing, then Seller will promptly notify Buyer of the occurrence of such event and Buyer will have the sole option of either: (a) proceeding with the closing and receiving all insurance proceeds or condemnation awards payable as a result of such casualty or taking; or (b) terminating its obligations under this Agreement by delivering written notice of termination to Seller within ten days after Buyer's receipt of notice from Seller of the occurrence of such event, in which event, the Deposit will be returned to Buyer and, except as otherwise expressly provided in this Agreement, the parties will be relieved of all further rights, liabilities and obligations hereunder. If Buyer fails to make the required election pursuant to this § 12 within ten days after its receipt of Seller's written notice of the occurrence of any such casualty or taking, then Buyer will be deemed to have elected to close the transaction pursuant to clause (a) of this § 12.

§ 13. **Brokerage Commissions**. Seller will be responsible for paying all commissions and other amounts owed to _______ in connection with the transaction contemplated in this Agreement. Except as otherwise expressly provided above, each of the parties hereto represents and warrants to the other that it has not contacted or entered into any agreement with any real estate broker, agent, finder or any other party in connection with this transaction or taken any other action which could result in any fee being due and payable to any real estate broker, finder, or other party with respect to the transaction contemplated hereunder. Each party indemnifies and agrees to hold the other party harmless from any loss, liability, damage, cost or expense (including, without limitation, reasonable attorneys' fees) incurred by or claimed against the other party by reason of a breach of this representation and warranty. The provisions of this § 13 will survive the closing.

§ 14. **Interim Operations**. At all times during the pendency of this Agreement, Seller will refrain from taking any of the following actions, without first obtaining the written consent of the Buyer:

> (a) Selling, transferring, encumbering or otherwise conveying any legal, beneficial or equitable interest in the Property (including,

without limitation, any easement, lease, option, purchase right or license affecting any part of the Property);

(b) Undertaking any excavation or construction activities or taking any other action with respect to the Property which has the effect of disturbing the natural condition of the same; or

(c) Seeking, accepting or acquiescing in any rezoning or other governmental approval or change related to the Property.

Also at all times during the pendency of this Agreement, Seller will cooperate with Buyer in Buyer's efforts to plan for its ultimate development of the Property. Seller's obligations to so cooperate with Buyer will extend to and include, without limitation, Seller's execution and delivery of zoning, utility, governmental incentive and other land use applications. Notwithstanding anything to the contrary contained herein, Seller will not be required to take any action which would result in Seller incurring any out-of-pocket expense or which would be legally binding on Seller or the Property prior to the closing of Buyer's purchase of the Property.

§ 15. <u>Assignment of Agreement</u>. Neither Buyer, nor Seller may assign all or any part of this Agreement, without first obtaining the written consent of the other party to this Agreement; provided, however, that Buyer may assign this Agreement to any affiliate of Buyer, without first having to obtain Seller's consent.

§ 16. <u>Governing Law</u>. This Agreement will be construed in accordance with the laws of the State of ________.

§ 17. <u>Counterparts</u>. This Agreement may be executed in counterparts, each of which will be deemed an original, and all such counterparts will collectively constitute a single agreement. This Agreement will not be binding on the parties hereto, until such time as a counterpart of this Agreement has been executed by each such party and a copy thereof delivered to the other party to this Agreement.

§ 18. <u>Attorneys' Fees</u>. If any legal action is commenced by either Seller or Buyer to enforce its rights hereunder, then all reasonable attorneys' fees and other expenses incurred by the prevailing party in such action will be immediately due and payable to the prevailing party by the non-prevailing party.

§ 19. <u>Entire Agreement</u>. This Agreement contains the entire agreement of the parties with respect to the subject matter hereof and may not be modified or amended in any manner, except by a written instrument executed by all parties to this Agreement.

§ 20. <u>Reasonableness of Consent</u>. Except as otherwise expressly provided herein, any consent or approval, which is required or permitted to be given hereunder by either Seller or Buyer, will not be unreasonably withheld or delayed by such party.

§ 21. <u>Notices</u>. All notices required or permitted to be given under this Agreement must be in writing and must be delivered to Seller or Buyer at its address set forth below (or such other address as may hereafter be designated by such party). Any such notice must be personally delivered or sent by certified mail, overnight courier or facsimile transmission. For the purposes of this Agreement, any such notice will be deemed "delivered," "given" or "effective" only when received (if sent by personal delivery, overnight courier or facsimile transmission) or on the date which is three days after the date on which such notice is deposited in the United States mail (if sent by certified mail). The parties' addresses for the delivery of all such notices are as follows:

Seller's Address: _______________________
With a Copy to: _______________________

Buyer's Address: _______________________
With a Copy to: _______________________

§ 22. **Time is of the Essence**. Time is of the essence for all purposes of this Agreement. Any time period specified herein which would otherwise end on a weekend day or a legal holiday will, for all purposes of this Agreement, be deemed to instead end on the next business day following such weekend day or legal holiday.

§ 23. **Confidentiality**. Buyer and Seller will each keep the terms and conditions of this Agreement confidential and neither of them will release such terms and conditions to the media or the general public, without first obtaining the written consent of the other party. This § 23 will survive the termination of this Agreement.

§ 24. **Defined Terms**. For the purpose of this Agreement, the following terms will have the meanings attributed to such terms in the noted sections of this Agreement:

"Agreement" is defined in the preamble.

"Approval Notice" is defined in § 4.

"Attributable to" is defined in § 10.

"Buyer" is defined in the preamble.

"Closing", **"Closing Date"** and **"Date of Closing"** are defined in § 9.

"Contingency Period" is defined in § 4.

"Deposit" is defined in § 3.

"Effective Date" is defined in the preamble.

"Escrow Agent" is defined in § 3.

"Hazardous Material" is defined in § 6.

"Permitted Exceptions" is defined in § 7.

"Purchase Price" is defined in § 3.

"Property" is defined in § 1.

"Seller" is defined in the preamble.

"Survey" is defined in § 7.

"Surveyor" is defined in § 7.

"Title Company" is defined in § 7.

"Title Commitment" is defined in § 7.

"Title Notice" is defined in § 7.

All the meanings attributed to the above terms will be equally applicable to both the singular and plural forms of such terms.

Seller and Buyer have executed this Agreement as of the date set forth opposite their respective names below.

SELLER:

Date of Execution: _____ By: _________________
              (Name) (Title)

BUYER:

Date of Execution: _____ By: _________________
              (Name) (Title)

EXHIBIT A
LEGAL DESCRIPTION OF LAND

DOCUMENT #3

OPERATING AGREEMENT FOR DELAWARE LLC

■ ■ ■

_______________________ LLC

(A Delaware Limited Liability Company)

OPERATING AGREEMENT

_______________, 20___

This is a sample form of Operating Agreement for a limited liability company being formed under the Delaware Limited Liability Company Act. The form assumes that there are only two members—a developer and an institutional investor—and that all capital contributions made to the LLC will be made in cash. The form assumes that capital contributions will be made 75% by the investor and 25% by the developer, with the developer receiving an additional 25% "promote" in the LLC's profits. The form further assumes that the LLC will be "manager-managed," with management authority being vested in the developer (acting in the dual capacity of both a member and a manager), subject, however, to the requirement that the investor's prior approval must be obtained for certain "major decisions." Finally, the Operating Agreement is premised on the assumption that the developer and the investor have relatively equal bargaining power (although the form does have a slight, pro-developer bias).

TABLE OF CONTENTS

<u>**Page #**</u>

_________________________ **LLC**

(A Delaware Limited Liability Company)

OPERATING AGREEMENT

________, 20__

This Agreement is entered into as the date first set forth above by ________ (“**Developer**”) and ________ (“**Investor**”).

STATEMENT OF AGREEMENT

The parties to this Agreement, each in consideration of the acts, capital contributions and promises of the other, agree as follows:

ARTICLE 1: ORGANIZATION

§ 1.1 Formation of Company. The Members hereby agree to form the Company as a limited liability company pursuant to the Act and upon the terms and conditions set forth in this Agreement.

§ 1.2 Name of Company. The name of the Company will be “________ LLC.”

§ 1.3 Names and Addresses of Members. The full names and addresses of the Members are as follows:

[Name of Developer]	[Name of Investor]
[Address of Developer]	[Address of Investor]

§ 1.4 Business Purpose. The business purpose of the Company is: (a) to own, develop, finance, lease, operate and manage the Project as an investment for the production of income; and (b) to engage in all other activities incidental or related to the foregoing, including, without limitation the ultimate sale, exchange or other transfer of the Project, when and to the extent permitted in this Agreement. Except as restricted by this Agreement, the Company will have all such powers and rights which a limited liability company may lawfully possess and exercise under the Act.

§ 1.5 Principal Office. The address of the Company’s principal office is ________. Such address may be changed from time to time by the Developer.

§ 1.6 Registered Agent for Service of Process. The name and address of the Company’s registered agent for service of process are ________, ________, Delaware. Such name and address may be changed from time to time by Developer.

§ 1.7 Governmental Filings. Coincident with the full execution of this Agreement, Developer will file with the Delaware Secretary of State a certificate of formation, which certificate of formation will include the information required by the Act and such other information as Developer deems appropriate. Developer is empowered to make all such other governmental filings as it may deem necessary or appropriate to qualify the

Company to do business in any jurisdiction or to otherwise carry out the purposes and intent of this Agreement.

§ 1.8   Term. The term of the Company's existence will begin on the date on which the Company's certificate of formation is filed with the Delaware Secretary of State. The Company will exist in perpetuity, unless it is earlier terminated pursuant to the provisions of this Agreement.

§ 1.9.   Limited Liability. Except as otherwise expressly set forth in this Agreement or required by law, no Member will be personally liable for any debt, obligation or liability of the Company, regardless whether that debt, obligation or liability arises in contract, tort or otherwise.

§ 1.10   Definitions. All capitalized words and phrases used in this Agreement (other than the full names and addresses of the Company, the Members and governmental subdivisions and agencies) will have the meanings set forth in Exhibit A.

ARTICLE 2: COMPANY CAPITALIZATION

§ 2.1   Initial Capital Contributions. Coincident with the full execution of this Agreement, the Members will make those cash Capital Contributions to the Company in the amount set forth after their respective names below:

> Developer—$____________ [75% of total Capital Contributions]
> Investor— $____________ [25% of total Capital Contributions]

§ 2.2   Additional Capital Contributions. The Members acknowledge that the Company may from time to time need additional funds for the funding of cost overruns, operating deficits and other costs related to the Project and for a variety of other purposes related to the Company's business (collectively, "**Additional Funds**"). If Developer determines that any such Additional Funds are needed by the Company and that such Additional Funds cannot be borrowed on commercially reasonable terms or otherwise drawn from cash reserves previously established by Developer in the manner contemplated in this Agreement, then Developer will deliver written notice to Investor of the need for such Additional Funds ("**Additional Funds Notice**"). The Additional Funds Notice will specify the amount of the needed Additional Funds and the specific purpose for which such Additional Funds are needed. To the extent the Additional Funds are needed for an Approved Purpose (as that term is defined in this § 2.2), then, within ten business days after Investor's receipt of the Additional Funds Notice, Investor will make a cash Capital Contribution in an amount equal to 75% of the Additional Funds and Developer will make a cash Capital Contribution in an amount equal to 25% of such Additional Funds.

For the purposes of this § 2.2, the term "**Approved Purpose**" will mean the funding of any cost which Developer is authorized to incur pursuant to the authority granted to it in Article 5 of this Agreement and which is consistent with an Approved Budget or which is otherwise approved in advance by Investor.

Except for those Additional Capital Contributions required to provide Additional Funds for an Approved Purpose, no Member will have any obligation to make any Additional Capital Contributions to the Company, without its prior written consent.

§ 2.3 Defaulted Capital Contributions. If any Member defaults in its obligation to make any Capital Contribution to the Company, then the Company and the other Members will have all such rights and remedies against the defaulting Member as are provided at law or in equity, including, without limitation, any rights or remedies specifically provided for in this Agreement.

§ 2.4 Loans. Developer may loan to the Company any funds needed by the Company for use in the operation of its business. Any loans made to the Company by Developer will be payable upon demand and at an interest rate equal to the prime published lending rate of Bank of America (or any successor to Bank of America). Any loans made to the Company by Developer, together with any accrued and unpaid interest thereon, will be paid in full prior to the distribution of any Operating Cash Flow, Capital Proceeds or Liquidation Proceeds to any Member. Notwithstanding anything to the contrary contained herein, Developer may not make any loans to the Company which, in the aggregate, exceed $100,000, without first obtaining the prior written consent of Investor. Developer will promptly notify Investor of any loans which it makes to the Company and any repayments of or against such loans.

§ 2.5 Withdrawal and Return of Capital Contributions. Except as otherwise expressly provided herein, no Member will have the right: (a) to withdraw any part of its Capital Contributions; (b) to demand a return of any part of its Capital Contributions; or (c) to receive property other than cash in return for its Capital Contributions.

§ 2.6 Capital Accounts. The Company will maintain for each Member a separate Capital Account in accordance with § 1.704–1(b) of the Regulations. Except as otherwise required under the aforementioned Regulations, the Capital Account of each Member will initially be credited with the amount of its initial Capital Contributions under § 2.1, and will be increased by (a) the amount of any cash paid by it to the Company as an additional Capital Contribution under § 2.2, (b) the agreed-upon fair market value of any property contributed by it to the Company as an additional Capital Contribution under § 2.2, (c) the amount of any Company liability assumed by such Member and (d) its allocable share of Profits, and will be decreased by (a) the amount of any cash distributed to it, (b) the fair market value of any property distributed to it, (c) the amount of any liability of such Member assumed by the Company, and (d) its allocable share of Losses. If any Membership Interest is transferred in accordance with the terms of this Agreement, then the transferee will succeed to the Capital Account of the transferor to the extent it relates to the transferred Membership Interest.

The foregoing provisions and all other provisions of this Agreement relating to the maintenance of Capital Accounts are intended to comply with § 1.704–1(b) of the Regulations and will be interpreted and applied in a manner consistent with such Regulations. If Developer determines that it is prudent to modify the manner in which the Capital Accounts are computed in order to comply with such Regulations, then Developer may make such modification; provided that any such modification is designed to be consistent with and effect the Members' intentions concerning the manner in which Operating Cash Flow, Capital Proceeds and Liquidation Proceeds are to be distributed pursuant to this Agreement.

ARTICLE 3: DISTRIBUTIONS

§ 3.1 Distribution of Operating Cash Flow. Operating Cash Flow for each Fiscal Quarter will be distributed to the Members in the following manner and order of priority:

(a) First, pro rata to Developer and Investor in proportion to their relative unpaid Preferred Returns, until such time as each of them has received the full amount of its unpaid Preferred Return; and

(b) The remainder, if any, 50% to Developer and 50% to Investor.

§ 3.2 Distribution of Capital Proceeds. Capital Proceeds will be distributed as follows:

(a) First, pro rata to Developer and Investor in proportion to their relative Unreturned Capital Contributions, until such time as each of them has received the full amount of its Unreturned Capital Contribution;

(b) Second, pro rata to Developer and Investor in proportion to their relative unpaid Preferred Returns, until such time as each of them has received the full amount of its unpaid Preferred Return; and

(c) The remainder, if any, 50% to Developer and 50% to Investor.

§ 3.3 Timing of Distributions. The distribution of Operating Cash Flow will be made quarterly, within 45 days after the end of each Fiscal Quarter. The distribution of Capital Proceeds will be made within 45 days after the Company's receipt of such Capital Proceeds.

ARTICLE 4: ALLOCATION OF PROFITS AND LOSSES

§ 4.1 General Allocation Scheme. Profits and Losses for each Fiscal Year will be allocated among the Members in the following manner and order of priority:

(a) First, Profits and Losses will be allocated in a manner consistent with those "Allocations Required by the Treasury Regulations," which are itemized in subparagraph (a) of the Tax Provisions included in Exhibit B; and

(b) The remainder of the Profits and Losses will be allocated among the Members so that the Capital Account of each Member is, as nearly as possible, equal to the aggregate amount that would be distributed to such Member pursuant to § 3.2 if all of the Company's assets were to be sold for cash in an amount equal to their Carrying Values and all of the Company's liabilities were to be satisfied at par.

§ 4.2 Tax Allocations. All allocations of items of taxable income, gain, loss, deduction and credit will otherwise be made in a manner consistent with the tax rules which are set forth in Exhibit B.

ARTICLE 5: MANAGEMENT

§ 5.1 Management of Company. The Company will be a "manager managed" limited liability company, with the Developer being designated as its sole "manager" (as those terms are used in the context of the Act). In its capacity as the "manager" of the Company, Developer will have full and exclusive authority over the management of the Company's business, subject, however, to those limitations and restrictions on its authority set forth in § 5.2 and elsewhere in this Agreement. Developer will manage the business of the Company in good faith, in a manner it reasonably believes to be in the best interests of the Company and with the care that an experienced, knowledgeable professional in a similar position would use under similar circumstances. Subject to the limitations and restrictions on its authority set forth in § 5.2 and elsewhere in this Agreement, Developer will have, on behalf of and in the name of the Company, the full right, power and authority to take all actions which a limited liability company may lawfully take under the Act.

§ 5.2 Limitations on Developer's Authority. Notwithstanding anything to the contrary contained in this Agreement, Developer will not be permitted to take any of the following actions, unless such actions are: (i) expressly authorized in an Approved Budget; (ii) otherwise approved in advance by Investor; or (iii) required by law or by the terms of any agreement previously approved by Investor pursuant to the terms of this Agreement (including, without limitation, any lease or financing agreement):

(a) Sell or otherwise dispose of all or substantially all of the Project;

(b) Merge or consolidate with another Person;

(c) Acquire, commence development or otherwise invest in any new real estate project or other asset, other than any acquisition, development or investment effected in the ordinary course of the Company's business for a total consideration of less than $100,000;

(d) File a voluntary petition in or otherwise initiate or consent to the institution of any proceeding against the Company under any law relating to the bankruptcy, insolvency, reorganization or relief of debtors;

(e) Institute, voluntarily dismiss, terminate or settle any litigation or arbitration against any Person involving claims for damages and penalties in excess of $500,000 other than any litigation instituted against any tenant which is in default under any lease of any part of the Project;

(f) Distribute any cash, property or other assets to the Members, except pursuant to the provisions of this Agreement;

(g) Incur any new Debt, other than any draws or borrowings under any line of credit, construction financing or other financing arrangement which has previously been approved by Investor, which draws or borrowings may be effected by Developer without first obtaining any further advance approval from Investor;

(h) Issue any Membership Interests or any other equity interests (including any interest convertible into any equity interest) in the Company;

(i) Enter into any Major Lease;

(j) Effect a dissolution, liquidation or termination of the Company;

(k) Take any action or engage in any activity which is not consistent with the purposes of the Company set forth in § 1.4;

(l) Take any action which would cause the aggregate, actual, development costs (exclusive of Uncontrollable Expenses) for the Project to exceed the aggregate, budgeted, development costs (exclusive of Uncontrollable Expenses) specified in the Approved Development Budget by more than 5%;

(m) Take any action which would cause the aggregate operating expenses or capital expenditures (exclusive of Uncontrollable Expenses) for the Project to exceed the aggregate budgeted operating expenses or capital expenditures (exclusive of Uncontrollable Expenses) specified in a current Approved Operating Budget by more than 5%;

(n) Mortgage or otherwise encumber the Project, other than any mortgage or encumbrance required under any line of credit, construction financing or other financing arrangement which has previously been approved by Investor, which mortgage or encumbrance may be effected by Developer in a manner consistent with the specific provisions approved by Investor (including, without limitation, all economic, recourse and identity of collateral provisions), without first obtaining any further advance approval from Investor;

(o) Enter into any transaction with any Affiliate of any Member, other than those transactions effected in accordance with the Affiliate Agreements or any other agreement which has previously been approved by Investor;

(p) Materially change the nature of the Company's business;

(q) Do any other act which contravenes the terms of this Agreement or which would make it impossible to carry on the ordinary business of the Company; or

(r) Make any tax election inconsistent with the intentions of the Members expressed in this Agreement.

§ 5.3   Specific Duties of Developer. Developer will, on behalf of and in the name of the Company and in addition to the general management duties and obligations placed upon it elsewhere in this Agreement, have the following specific duties:

(a) File such documents and do such other acts as may be required to form and maintain the Company as a limited liability company under the Act and to qualify the Company to transact business in all such jurisdictions as may be required under applicable provisions of law;

(b) Serve as the "Tax Matters Partner" of the Company and, as such, exercise all of the rights and obligations given to a Tax Matters Partner under Subchapter C of Chapter 63 of the Code;

(c) Maintain at the principal office of the Company all books, records and information required to be maintained by the Company pursuant to the Act, and make all such books, records and information available for inspection and copying at the reasonable request and expense of any Member during ordinary business hours;

(d) Cause the Company to diligently prosecute the completion of the construction of the Project in a good and workmanlike fashion and in a manner consistent with the Approved Development Budget;

(e) Use all reasonable efforts to carry out those activities contemplated under and otherwise comply with the terms and conditions of each Approved Budget;

(f) Use all reasonable efforts to cause the Company to secure on commercially reasonable terms (i) financing for the acquisition and development of the Project and (ii) a refinancing of any maturing Debt, subject, however, in each and every instance to Investor's approval concerning any such financing or refinancing pursuant to § 5.2; and

(g) Maintain in full force and effect such insurance coverage with respect to the Company's ownership of the Project and the conduct of its business as is consistent with sound commercial practices for companies similar to the Company.

§ 5.4 Developer's Compensation. In consideration of its performance of services for the Company, Developer will be entitled to receive the following fees and expense reimbursements from the Company:

(a) A development fee equal to 5% of the total budgeted development costs set forth in the Approved Development Budget;

(b) A property management fee equal to 3% of all rents payable under all leases of the Project;

(c) Fees for Developer's provision of services not otherwise covered by the fees payable under (a) and (b), above, but only to the extent that such fees are comparable in amount to fees which would be paid to an independent third party in an arm's length transaction for the provision of comparable services in the locale where the Project is located; and

(d) A reimbursement of all reasonable out-of-pocket expenses incurred by Developer in connection with the formation of the Company or the management and conduct of the Company's business.

Such fees and reimbursements will be paid to Developer prior to the distribution of any Operating Cash Flow, Capital Proceeds or Liquidation Proceeds to the Members and otherwise at such commercially reasonable times as Developer determines in the exercise of its reasonable discretion. Developer is hereby authorized to delegate to any of its Affiliates the responsibility for the performance of any of the services contemplated hereunder and, accordingly, to pay to any such Affiliate any of the above-described fees and reimbursements.

§ 5.5 Dealing with Affiliates. Developer may engage any of its Affiliates to provide services or materials to the Company, so long as (a) such services or materials are otherwise required to be provided hereunder by Developer, in which case Developer will have the authority to delegate its obligations hereunder to such Affiliate or (b) the terms and conditions governing the provision of such services and materials (including, without limitation, the fees and reimbursements payable with respect thereto) are comparable to those which would govern the provision by an independent third party in an arm's length transaction of comparable services and materials in the locale in which the Project is located. Notwithstanding anything to the contrary contained herein, Investor will have the right (but not the obligation) to monitor performance, declare defaults, grant approvals and exercise options and other rights and remedies on behalf of the Company with respect to any agreement entered into by Developer with any of its Affiliates and will, for such purposes, have all rights and powers which Developer enjoys and be subject to all limitations thereon, which are set forth in §§ 5.1 and 5.2 hereof.

§ 5.6 Other Business Ventures. Any Member may engage in or possess an interest in any other business venture of any type or description, independently or with others (including, without limitation, any venture which may be competitive with the business being conducted by the Company), and neither the Company, nor any Member will, by virtue of this Agreement or otherwise, have any right, title or interest in or to such outside venture or the income or other benefits derived therefrom.

§ 5.7　Development Budget. The "**Approved Development Budget**" for the acquisition and development of the Project is attached hereto as Exhibit C. Subject to the express limitations set forth in § 5.2, Developer will at all times hereafter be fully authorized to take any and all actions which are consistent with the Approved Development Budget, without the need to obtain any further approval from Investor. Developer will not, however, have the authority to amend the Approved Development Budget in any material respect, without first obtaining the Investor's written approval of any such amendment.

§ 5.8　Operating Budgets. For each Fiscal Year, Developer and Investor will work together in good faith to finalize and agree upon an operating budget for the Project. Once any such operating budget is approved by Developer and Investor ("**Approved Operating Budget**"), Developer will at all times thereafter be fully authorized to take any and all actions which are consistent with such Approved Operating Budget, without the need to obtain any further approval from Investor (subject, however, to the express limitations set forth in § 5.2). Developer will not, however, have the authority to amend any Approved Operating Budget, without first obtaining the Investor's written approval of any such amendment.

The Approved Operating Budget for the 20＿ Fiscal Year is attached hereto as Exhibit D. On or before November 1, 20＿ and November 1 of each year thereafter during the term of the Company's existence, Developer will prepare and deliver to Investor a proposed Operating Budget for the Project for the next ensuing Fiscal Year. Each such proposed Operating Budget will be consistent with the budget format set forth in the Approved Operating Budget for the 20＿ Fiscal Year which is attached hereto as Exhibit D. Each Operating Budget will include Leasing Guidelines for the Project.

Investor will have 30 days after its receipt of any proposed Operating Budget (together with all supporting information required herein or otherwise reasonably requested by Investor) to approve or disapprove the same. If Investor disapproves any proposed Operating Budget, then it will give written notice of such disapproval to Developer, specifying the particular elements of the proposed Operating Budget of which it disapproves. Developer and Investor will thereafter endeavor in good faith to resolve any disagreement over the specified, objectionable elements of the proposed Operating Budget. All elements of the proposed Operating Budget which are not specifically disapproved by Investor in the manner and within the time period described above will be deemed to be part of an Approved Operating Budget for all purposes of this Agreement, including, without limitation, the purposes of § 5.2. If Developer and Investor are unable to agree on any component of an Operating Budget by December 1 of the year prior to the beginning of the Fiscal Year to which any such Operating Budget relates, then, until such time as such agreement is reached, the like component of the prior Fiscal Year's Operating Budget will be deemed replicated as part of an approved Operating Budget for the next ensuing Fiscal Year, with the like line item of such Operating Budget increased or decreased, as applicable, based upon the percentage increase or decrease, as applicable, in the Consumer Price Index, as published by the Bureau of Labor Statistics of the United States Department of Labor for all Urban Consumers, U.S. City Average and to reflect actual increases or decreases in all Uncontrollable Expenses.

§ 5.9 Indemnification. The Company will indemnify and hold each Indemnified Person harmless from and against any losses, claims, damages, liabilities or expenses (including, without limitation, all legal fees and expenses), judgments, fines, settlements and other amounts arising from any and all claims, demands, actions, suits or proceedings (civil, criminal, administrative or investigative), related to the Company's business brought by any person other than the Company or any Member (or any Affiliate of a Member) in which any such Indemnified Person may be involved or is threatened to be involved, as a party or otherwise, to the fullest extent permitted under the Act, as the same exists or may hereafter be amended (but, in the case of any such amendment to the Act, such amendment will apply in determining the indemnification of the Indemnified Persons hereunder only if such amendment permits the Company to provide broader indemnification rights than such law permitted the Company to provide prior to such amendment). The rights granted pursuant to this § 5.9 are deemed contract rights and no amendment, modification or repeal of this § 5.9 will have the effect of limiting or denying any such rights with respect to actions taken or proceedings arising prior to any such amendment, modification or repeal. It is expressly acknowledged that the indemnification provided in this § 5.9 could involve indemnification against claims by third parties (i.e. not by the Company or any Member or any Affiliate of any Member alleging any breach of this Agreement) for negligence or under theories of strict liability. The right to indemnification conferred in this § 5.9 will not be exclusive of any other right which any Indemnified Person may have or hereafter acquire under any law, any provision of this Agreement or any other agreement or the vote of the Members or otherwise.

If agreed to by Developer and Investor, reasonable expenses incurred by an Indemnified Person who is a party to a proceeding may be paid or reimbursed by the Company in advance of the final disposition of the proceeding. The Company may purchase and maintain insurance, on behalf of the Indemnified Persons, against any liability that may be asserted against or expenses that may be incurred by any such Indemnified Person in connection with the Company's business.

§ 5.10 Limitations on Member's Authority. Except as otherwise provided herein or in the Act, no Member other than Developer will have the right to consent to any action, to take part in the control or management of the Company's business or to sign for or otherwise bind the Company in any manner whatsoever.

§ 5.11　Buy–Sell. If, at any time after the third anniversary of the date of this Agreement, a Deadlock occurs, then either Member ("**Electing Member**") may provide a written notice of its desire to sell its Membership Interest ("**Liquidity Notice**") to the other Member ("**Recipient Member**"). Promptly after the delivery of such Liquidity Notice, the Electing and Recipient Members will meet to discuss and negotiate, in good faith, a resolution of dispute that gave rise to the Deadlock.

If the Electing and Recipient Members fail to resolve the dispute that gave rise to the Deadlock within 30 days after the Recipient Member's receipt of the Liquidity Notice, then the Electing Member will thereafter have the right to give a written buy-sell notice ("**Buy–Sell Notice**") to the Recipient Member. Such Buy–Sell Notice must set forth the gross value that the Electing Member places on all of the Company's assets, including the Project ("**Entity Value**"). The Entity Value specified by the Electing Member in its Buy–Sell Notice may be any value selected by the Electing Member, without regard to the actual value of the Company's assets or the Electing Member's estimation of such actual value.

Within 180 days after the its receipt of the Electing Member's Buy–Sell Notice, the Recipient Member will elect either to sell its entire Membership Interest to the Electing Member or to purchase the Electing Member's entire Membership Interest. If the Electing Member is not notified in writing of the Recipient Member's election to buy or sell within such 180 day period, then the Recipient Member will be deemed to have elected to purchase all of the Electing Member's Membership Interest.

The purchase price ("**Buy–Sell Price**") for any Membership Interest sold pursuant to this § 5.11 will be equal to the amount the selling Member would receive if all of the Company's assets were to be sold for the Entity Value specified in the Buy–Sell Notice and all of the partnership liabilities were to be satisfied at par, with the remaining net cash proceeds then be in distributed in accordance with § 3.2. The Buy–Sell Price will be paid in cash at the closing of the purchase and sale of the Membership Interest hereunder. Such closing will occur within 30 days after the expiration of the aforementioned 180 day period. In addition to the payment of the purchase price to the selling Member), the purchasing Member will also execute and deliver to the selling Member a written instrument indemnifying the selling Member (and any Affiliate of the selling Member who may have guaranteed any Company liability) from any Company liability. The purchasing Member will also make a good faith effort to cause the selling Member (and any Affiliate of the selling Member who may have guaranteed any Company liability) to be fully relieved from all personal liability for any Company liability. The purchasing Member will also pay and satisfy any loan made to the Company by the selling Member pursuant to § 2.4. To the extent either the selling or purchasing Member defaults in the performance of its obligations hereunder, then the other Member will have all such remedies and rights which are available at law or in equity to redress such default, including, without limitation, the right to reverse its role hereunder and become a selling Member (if the defaulting Member was initially a selling Member) or a purchasing Member (if the defaulting Member was originally a purchasing Member). If any Member elects to reverse its role in the manner contemplated in the immediately preceding sentence, it will provide written notice of such election to the defaulting Member at any time after the occurrence of the defaulting member's default hereunder and the Membership Interest sale resulting from such election will then be closed in accordance with the provisions of this § 5.11 at a time designated by the non-defaulting Member within 60 days after the defaulting Member's receipt of such election.

For the purposes of this § 5.11, a "**Deadlock**" will be deemed to have occurred if Investor fails to approve Developer's taking of any action which requires the approval of Investor under § 5.2 and such failure to approve continues for a period of ten days after Investor's receipt of a written notice from Developer specifying the nature of the action which Developer proposes to take on behalf of the Company. Notwithstanding anything to the contrary contained herein, Developer will have the right to negate the existence of a Deadlock by providing written notice to Investor that Developer is withdrawing its proposal to take the subject action on behalf of the Company, which notice must be delivered, if at all, prior to the date on which a Recipient Member receives a Buy–Sell Notice under this § 5.11.

ARTICLE 6: ACCOUNTING AND FISCAL AFFAIRS

§ 6.1 Fiscal Year and Accounting Method. The Company's Fiscal Year will end on December 31. All books of account and financial reports and information prepared by or on behalf of the Company will be prepared in accordance with generally accepted accounting principles, consistently applied.

§ 6.2 Financial Statements and Reports. Developer will cause to be delivered to each Member the financial statements listed in paragraphs (a) and (b), below. All such financial statements will be prepared in accordance with generally accepted accounting principles, consistently applied.

    (a) Within 90 days after the end of each Fiscal Year, the Company's balance sheet, income statement, cash flow statement, budget variance report and statement of changes in the Members' capital balances for the most recently concluded Fiscal Year; and

    (b) Within 30 days after the end of each Fiscal Quarter, the Company's balance sheet, income statement, cash flow statement and budget variance report for the most recently-concluded Fiscal Quarter and for the Fiscal Year to date.

The annual and quarterly financial statements described above will be accompanied by the written certification of the chief financial officer of Developer that such statements have been prepared in accordance with generally accepted accounting principles, consistently applied. At the request of Investor, Developer will cause the Company's annual financial statements to be annually reviewed or audited by a nationally-recognized firm of independent public accountants selected by Developer, with Investor's advance approval.

§ 6.3 Tax Information. As soon as reasonably practicable after the end of each Fiscal Year, Developer will cause to be delivered to each Member a statement showing all items of the Company's taxable income, gain, loss, deduction and credit for the most recently-concluded Fiscal Year and each Member's allocable share thereof. Developer will cause all tax returns and reports required to be filed by the Company to be prepared and timely filed with the appropriate authorities. Developer will retain such tax returns and reports for as long as is required by applicable law.

Developer is expressly authorized and directed to file all documents and take all other actions required to elect the "Safe Harbor" described in IRS Revenue Procedure _______ *[the successor to IRS Notice 2005–43]*. Such election will be binding on the Company and all of its Members and the Company and each of its Members (including any person to whom a Membership Interest is transferred in connection with the performance of services) agrees to comply with all requirements of the Safe Harbor described in the aforementioned revenue procedure with respect to all Membership Interests transferred in connection with the performance of services while the election remains effective.

ARTICLE 7: TRANSFER OF MEMBERSHIP INTERESTS

§ 7.1 No Transfer of Membership Interests. Except as expressly provided in this Agreement, no Member may sell, assign, pledge, encumber or in any manner transfer all or any part of its Membership Interest.

§ 7.2 Compliance with Securities Act of 1933. The Membership Interests have not been registered under the Securities Act of 1933 in reliance upon the exemption provided in § 4(2) of such Act. Notwithstanding any other provision in this Agreement, no Membership Interest may be offered for sale, sold, transferred or otherwise disposed of, unless, at the expense of the transferring Member, Developer has received an acceptable opinion of counsel to the effect that such transfer is exempt from registration under the Securities Act of 1933 and is in compliance with all applicable Federal and state securities laws and regulations. Developer may, in its sole discretion, waive the requirements of this section with respect to the transfer of any Membership Interest, but any such waiver will not constitute a waiver of any subsequent transfer of such Membership Interest or any other Membership Interest.

§ 7.3 Transfer of Membership Interests to Other Members and Affiliates. Notwithstanding anything to the contrary contained herein, any Member may sell, assign or otherwise transfer all or any part of its Membership Interest to another Member or to an Affiliate of any Member (so long as any such Affiliate controls, is controlled by or is under common control with any original Member of the Company, using 51% of the ownership of outstanding voting or equity interests as the standard to determine such commonality), at such price and on such other terms as the parties may determine provided, however, that any such sale, assignment or transfer to an Affiliate of any Member will not effect: (a) a release of the selling, assigning or transferring Member's financial and other obligations under this Agreement; or (b) a termination of the Company for federal income tax purposes under § 708 of the Code.

§ 7.4 Other Transfers Permitted if Other Member Approves. A Member may also sell, assign or transfer all or any part of its Membership Interest to any Person who is not a Member or an Affiliate thereof, so long as such transfer is approved by the other Member, which approval may be arbitrarily withheld. The Members' approval of the transfer of any Membership Interest will not constitute approval of any subsequent transfer of such Membership Interest or the transfer of any other Membership Interest or the approval of the admission of the transferee as a substituted Member in the Company.

§ 7.5 Admission of Transferee as Substituted Member. An assignee of a Membership Interest will not become a substituted Member, unless and until the other Member consents in writing to such substitution, which consent may be arbitrarily withheld. Neither the assignor of a Membership Interest, nor an assignee who is not admitted as a substituted Member, will be entitled to: (a) require any accounting of the Company's transactions; (b) inspect the Company's books and records; (c) require any information from the Company; or (d) exercise any privilege or right of a Member which is not specifically granted to a non-substituted assignee of a limited liability company interest under the Act.

ARTICLE 8: WITHDRAWAL OF MEMBERS

§ 8.1 No Withdrawal. No Member may withdraw from the Company.

§ 8.2 Death, Bankruptcy, Liquidation, etc. of a Member. A Member will not cease to be a "member" within the meaning of the Act upon the occurrence of any of the items listed in § 18–801(b)of the Act. The occurrence of any such event will not cause the dissolution of the Company.

ARTICLE 9: DISSOLUTION, WINDING UP AND TERMINATION

§ 9.1 Dissolution. The Company will dissolve upon the occurrence of any of the following events:

(a) The agreement in writing of all the Members to dissolve the Company;

(b) The sale of all or substantially all of the Project;

(c) The entry of a decree of judicial dissolution of the Company under § 18–802 of the Act; or

(d) At any time when there are no Members of the Company, unless the Company is continued in accordance with the Act.

§ 9.2 **Winding Up and Termination**. Upon the dissolution of the Company, the affairs and business of the Company will be wound up and terminated, the Company's liabilities will be discharged and the Company's assets will be liquidated and distributed in the manner hereinafter described. A reasonable time will be allowed for the orderly winding up of the affairs and business of the Company, so as to enable the Company to minimize the normal losses attendant to the winding up and termination period. The winding up and termination of the affairs and business of the Company will be supervised and conducted by Developer. Developer will have the exclusive power and authority to act on behalf of the Company to wind up and terminate the affairs and business of the Company, to sell and convey the Company's assets to such Persons (including, without limitation, Developer, any Member or any of their respective Affiliates) for such consideration and upon such terms and conditions as it deems necessary or appropriate, to discharge the Company's liabilities, to establish any reserves that it deems necessary or appropriate for any contingent or unforeseen liabilities or obligations of the Company, and to distribute the Liquidation Proceeds in the manner hereinafter described.

Upon completion of the winding up of the affairs and business of the Company, the Liquidation Proceeds will be distributed by Developer in the following manner and order of priority:

(a) First, such Liquidation Proceeds will be applied to the payment of debts and liabilities of the Company (including, without limitation, any debts or liabilities owed to Developer, any Member or any of their respective Affiliates) and the payment of expenses of the winding up of the affairs and business of the Company;

(b) Second, such Liquidation Proceeds will be applied to the setting up of any reserves (to be held by Developer in an interest-bearing account) which Developer may deem necessary or appropriate for any contingent or unforeseen liabilities or obligations of the Company; provided, however, that at the expiration of such time as Developer deems necessary or appropriate, the balance of such reserves remaining after payment of such liabilities or obligations will be distributed by Developer the manner hereinafter set forth in this § 9.2; and

(c) Third, the remainder of such Liquidation Proceeds will be distributed to the Members in accordance with the provisions of § 3.2.

§ 9.3 **Final Accounting**. Developer will furnish all Members with a statement setting forth the assets and liabilities of the Company as of the date of the completion of the winding up and termination of the affairs and business of the Company. Upon completion of the distribution plan set forth in this Article 9, Developer will cause to be executed by the appropriate parties and filed in such public offices as will be required under the Act a cancellation of the Company's certificate of formation and any and all other documents which Developer deems necessary or appropriate to effect the dissolution and termination of the Company.

§ 9.4 <u>Return of Contribution Nonrecourse to Other Members</u>. Except as otherwise required under the Act or as expressly provided in this § 9.4, each Member will look solely to the assets of the Company for the return of its Capital Contributions and if the Company's assets remaining after the payment or discharge of the debts and liabilities of the Company is insufficient to return the Capital Contributions of one or more Members, such Member or Members will have no recourse against the Company, Developer or any other Member. Notwithstanding anything to the contrary contained herein, no Member shall be required to restore a deficit in its Capital Account.

ARTICLE 10: MISCELLANEOUS

§ 10.1 <u>Notices and Addresses</u>. All notices, authorizations, consents, elections, approvals, waivers, requirements, directions or other communications which may or are required to be given hereunder will be in writing and will be sent by facsimile, overnight courier or United States mail, registered or certified, return receipt requested, postage prepaid to the Company at the address of the Company's principal office and to the Members at the addresses set forth after their respective names in § 1.3. The Company and any Member may change its address for the giving of notices, consents, demands, requests, or other communications by delivering written notice to the Company and to the other Member of its new address for such purpose.

§ 10.2 <u>Pronouns and Plurals</u>. All pronouns and any variations thereof will be deemed to refer to the masculine, feminine, neuter, singular or plural, as the identity of the Person or Persons may require.

§ 10.3 <u>Counterparts</u>. This Agreement may be executed in several counterparts all of which will constitute one agreement, binding on all parties hereto, notwithstanding that all the parties are not signatories to the same counterpart.

§ 10.4 <u>Applicable Law</u>. This Agreement and the rights of the Members hereunder will be interpreted in accordance with the laws of the State of Delaware.

§ 10.5 <u>Successors</u>. This Agreement will inure to the benefit of and will be binding upon and enforceable by and against the parties hereto and their respective successors and permitted assigns.

§ 10.6 <u>Severability</u>. The invalidity or unenforceability of any provision of this Agreement in a particular respect will not affect the validity and enforceability of any other provisions of this Agreement or of the same provision in any other respect.

§ 10.7 Exhibits. All exhibits attached hereto or referred to herein are incorporated herein by this reference.

§ 10.8 Amendment of Agreement. This Agreement may not be amended, except by a written instrument signed by all of the Members.

§ 10.9 Further Action. Each Member, upon the request of the other Member, agrees to perform all further acts and execute, acknowledge and deliver any documents which may be reasonably necessary, appropriate or desirable to carry out the purposes and intent of this Agreement.

§ 10.10 Entire Agreement. This Agreement constitutes the complete understanding and agreement of the parties hereto and supersedes all previous understandings and agreements, written or oral, relating to the subject matter hereof.

§ 10.11 No Waiver. No failure by either Member to exercise and no delay by it in exercising any right, power or privilege under this Agreement will operate as a waiver thereof; nor will any single or partial exercise of any right, power or privilege hereunder preclude the future exercise thereof or the exercise of any other right, power or privilege.

§ 10.12 Cumulative Remedies. The rights and remedies under this Agreement are cumulative and not exclusive of any rights or remedies provided by law or in equity.

§ 10.13 Waiver of Partition. Each Member hereby waives any right to partition or cause a partition of the Company's assets or to compel any sale or appraisement of any Company Property.

§ 10.14 Aids in Construction. All section and other headings contained in this Agreement are for reference purposes only and are not intended to describe, interpret, define or limit the scope, extent or intent of this Agreement or any provision thereof. Every covenant, term and provision of this Agreement will be construed simply according to its fair meaning and not strictly for or against any Member. If any time period referred to in this Agreement expires by its terms on a weekend day or a legal holiday, then such time period will automatically be deemed extended until the close of business on the next succeeding business day.

§ 10.15 Standard for Consents. Except as otherwise expressly stated in this Agreement, all consents or approvals from any Member may be withheld in the sole and unfettered discretion of the affected Member.

§ 10.16 Default. For the purposes of this Agreement (including, without limitation, the purposes of §§ 2.3 and 5.11), no party will be considered to be in "default" in the performance of any of its obligations hereunder, unless such Member fails to cure any alleged default within the time period set forth below:

> (a) As to any failure to make any Capital Contribution pursuant to § 2.2, within ten days after the subject Member's receipt of an Additional Funds Notice issued pursuant to § 2.2; and

(b) With respect to all other matters, within 30 days after the subject Member's receipt of written notice from the other Member alleging the existence of such default (or, if the alleged default is not readily susceptible of being cured within a 30 day period, then, such longer period of time, not to exceed 90 days, as is reasonably required to effect such cure, so long as the subject Member commences the cure of such alleged default within the aforementioned 30 day period and at all times thereafter diligently pursues such cure to completion).

Once a default has occurred (within the meaning of this § 10.16), then the non-defaulting party (be it the Company or any other Member) will have all such rights and remedies as are provided in this Agreement and at law or in equity.

§ **10.17** **No Prior Activity**. Developer hereby represents and warrants to Investor that, prior to the date of the parties' execution of this Agreement and the taking of those actions expressly contemplated herein, the Company has not conducted any business, owned any assets or incurred any liabilities.

Each of the Members have executed this Agreement as of the date first set forth at the beginning hereof.

DEVELOPER: **INVESTOR:**

_______________________   _______________________

By: _____________________   By: _____________________
     (Name)   (Title)   (Name)   (Title)

EXHIBIT A

DEFINITIONS

The capitalized words and phrases used in the Operating Agreement for
_______ LLC will have the following meanings (such meanings to be equally
applicable to both the singular and plural forms of such words and phrases):

1. **"Act"** means the Delaware Limited Liability Company Act, as set forth in
   6 Delaware Code Sections 18–8–1 et seq., as the same may be amended
   from time to time (or any corresponding provisions of any successor law).

2. **"Additional Capital Contributions"** means all cash or property contributed to the Company by its Members pursuant to § 2.2.

3. **"Additional Funds"** has the meaning set forth in § 2.2.

4. **"Additional Funds Notice"** has the meaning set forth in § 2.2.

5. **"Affiliate"** means, with respect to any Person: (i) any Person directly or
   indirectly controlling, controlled by or under common control with such
   Person; (ii) any Person owning or controlling 10% or more of the outstanding voting or equity interests of such Person; (iii) any officer,
   director or general partner of such Person; (iv) any Person who is an
   officer, director, general partner, trustee or holder of 10% or more of the
   voting or equity interests of any Person described in clauses (i) through
   (iii) of this subparagraph; or (v) the spouse or lineal descendant of any
   such Person or any trust established for the benefit of any of the
   foregoing.

6. **"Agreement"** means the Company's Operating Agreement, as the same
   may be amended from time to time. Words such as "herein," "hereinafter," "hereof," "hereto" and "hereunder" refer to this Agreement as a
   whole, unless the context otherwise requires.

7. **"Approved Development Budget"** means the development budget
   referred to in § 5.7 and attached hereto as Exhibit C.

8. **"Approved Operating Budget"** means any Operating Budget approved
   (or deemed to have been approved) by Investor pursuant to the provisions
   of § 5.8.

9. **"Approved Purpose"** has the meaning set forth in § 2.2.

10. **"Buy–Sell Notice"** has the meaning set forth in § 5.11.

11. **"Buy–Sell Price"** has the meaning set forth in § 5.11.

12. **"Capital Account"** means, with respect to any Member, the capital
    account maintained for such Member in accordance with § 2.6 and
    adjusted in the manner required under Exhibit B.

13. **"Capital Contribution"** means, with respect to any Member, the
    amount of cash or the agreed-upon fair market value of any property

contributed to the capital of the Company by such Member pursuant to § 2.1 and § 2.2.

14. **"Capital Event"** means of the following (a) the sale of all or substantially all of the Project; (b) the placement and funding of any Debt secured by a mortgage or other encumbrance on the Project (including, without limitation, the refinancing of any such secured Debt) (c)the condemnation of all or any material part of the Project; or (d) any loss of any part of the Project due to the occurrence of a casualty, failure of title or otherwise that results in excess proceeds after the restoration or repair of the Project.

15. **"Capital Proceeds"** means the gross cash receipts of the Company produced from the occurrence of a Capital Event, reduced by the sum of the following: (a) all cash expenditures made by the Company in connection with the Capital Event, including, without limitation, any brokerage fees or commissions paid to any party; (b) repayment of the principal and any accrued and unpaid interest on any debt being refinanced or retired as part of the Capital Event and (c) such cash reserves as Developer may decide to establish, with the consent of the Investor, to cover future occurrences and contingencies.

16. **"Carrying Value"** has the meaning set forth in Exhibit B.

17. **"Code"** means the Internal Revenue Code of 1986, as the same may be amended from time to time (or any corresponding provisions of any successor law).

18. **"Company"** means _______ LLC.

19. **"Deadlock"** has the meaning set forth in § 5.11.

20. **"Debt"** means any indebtedness of the Company for borrowed money or for the deferred purchase price of property, including, without limitation, amounts owed by any of the foregoing Persons in respect of any reimbursement obligations under letters of credit, surety bonds and other similar instruments guarantying payment or other performance of obligations by such Person, but expressly excluding any trade payables incurred in the ordinary course of business and any lease obligations pertaining solely to personal property which is not affixed to real property, regardless whether such lease obligations are treated as financing or operating leases under generally accepted accounting principles.

21. **"Default"** has the meaning set forth in § 10.16.

22. **"Developer"** means _______ and any Person who becomes a successor to _______ pursuant to the terms of this Agreement.

23. **"Electing Member"** has the meaning set forth in § 5.11.

24. **"Entity Value"** has the meaning set forth in § 5.11.

25. **"Fiscal Year"** means: (a) the period beginning on the commencement date of the Company's existence and ending on the next succeeding

December 31; and (b) each successive 12 month period thereafter through-out the term of the Company's existence, each of which such period will begin on January 1 and end on December 31.

26. **"Fiscal Quarter"** means each successive three month period throughout the Company's existence, which ends on March 31, June 30, September 30 or December 31, respectively.

27. **"Indemnified Person"** means any Person made a party reason of his or her status as: (a) a Member; (b) a manager, director, officer, committee member to any action, suit or proceeding or claiming any loss, damage, liability, expense or other amount by, employee or agent of the Company or any Member; (c) an Affiliate of any Member; and (d) such other Persons as the Members, by their mutual agreement, may designate from time to time.

28. **"Investor"** means ________ and any Person who becomes a successor to ________ pursuant to the terms of this Agreement.

29. **"Leasing Guidelines"** means the pro forma net rental income applicable to the Project, as the same is set forth in any Approved Operating Budget, and such other terms and conditions related to the projected leasing of the Project as are reasonably required by Investor.

30. **"Liquidation Proceeds"** means the cash or other property distributable to the Members pursuant to § 9.2 upon the dissolution and termination of the Company.

31. **"Liquidity Notice"** has the meaning set forth in § 5.11.

32. **"Major Lease"** means: (a) any new lease of more than 25,000 square feet of rentable space in the Project; and (b) any new lease of space in the Project which produces an annual net effective rental which is less than the annual net effective rental specified in the current Leasing Guidelines for the Project.

33. **"Member"** means ________, ________, any Person hereafter admitted to the Company as a "Member" and any Person who becomes a successor to any of the foregoing Persons pursuant to the terms of this Agreement.

34. **"Membership Interest"** means the ownership interest of a Member in the Company, including, without limitation, the rights and obligations of such Member under this Agreement and the Act.

35. **"Operating Budget"** has the meaning set forth in § 5.8.

36. **"Operating Cash Flow"** means, with respect to each Fiscal Quarter of the Company, the sum of the gross cash receipts of the Company from any source other than Capital Proceeds, plus the amount of any previously-established, but unused cash reserves, reduced by the sum of the following items paid by the Company: (a) all principal and interest payments and all other sums paid on or with respect to any indebtedness; (b) all operating expenses incurred incident to the operation of the Project; (c) all capital expenditures incurred incident to the construction, repair or replacement

of the Project; (c) such cash reserves as Developer may from time to time decide to establish, with the consent of the Investor, to cover future occurrences and contingencies; and (d) all other cash expenditures made by the Company related to the ownership, operation or management of the Project and the Company's business (other than any expenditure made in connection with the occurrence of any Capital Event).

37. **"Person"** means any individual, general or limited partnership, corporation, trust, limited liability company or other entity.

38. **"Preferred Return"** means, with respect to each Member, an amount equal to a return of __% per annum, compounded daily, on the balance of such Member's Unreturned Capital Contribution. Any Preferred Return that has accrued, but remains unpaid under §§ 3.1(a) and 3.2(b), will bear interest at __%, compounded daily, and will be considered part of the "Preferred Return" for all purposes of this Agreement.

39. **"Profits" and "Losses"** has the meaning set forth in Exhibit B.

40. **"Project"** means the approximately _______ square foot _______ building to be developed by the Company on the approximately ___ acre tract of land located in _______, _______.

41. **"Recipient Member"** has the meaning set forth in § 5.11.

42. **"Regulations"** means the Federal Income Tax Regulations (including Temporary Regulations) promulgated under the Code, as the same may be amended from time to time (including corresponding provisions of successor regulations).

43. **"Uncontrollable Expenses"** means all costs and expenses of the Company which are not reasonably capable of being controlled by Developer either as to the amount or the timing of the incurring of such costs or expenses, and expressly includes, without limitation, utility charges, insurance premiums, real estate taxes and assessments, debt service increases resulting from an increase in interest rates, costs associated with unforeseeable repairs or replacements required to be made to the Project and the incurring of any other cost or expense which is required by law or pursuant to any agreement to which the Company is legally bound.

44. **"Unreturned Capital Contribution"** means, with respect to each Member, the amount of all Capital Contributions made by such Member to the Company, reduced by the amount of any distributions made to such Member under § 3.2(a).

EXHIBIT B

SPECIAL TAX PROVISIONS

The following provisions apply for all purposes of the Agreement.

(a) **Allocations Required by Treasury Regulations**.

(i)   Subject to the exceptions set forth in Treas. Reg. §§ 1.704–2(f)(2)—(5), if there is a net decrease in Minimum Gain during any fiscal year, each Member shall be specially allocated items of Company income and gain for such year (and, if necessary, subsequent years) in an amount equal to such Member's share of the net decrease in Minimum Gain, determined in accordance with Treas. Reg. § 1.704–2(g)(2). "**Minimum Gain**" shall have the meaning set forth in Treas. Reg. §§ 1.704–2(b)(2) and 1.704–2(d). This paragraph is intended to comply with the minimum gain chargeback requirement in Treas. Reg. §§ 1.704–2(b)(2) and (f) and shall be interpreted consistently therewith.

(ii)   Subject to the exceptions set forth in Treas. Reg. § 1.704–2(i)(4), if there is a net decrease in Member Nonrecourse Debt Minimum Gain during any fiscal year of the Company, each Member who has a share of the Member Nonrecourse Debt Minimum Gain, determined in accordance with Treas. Reg. § 1.704–2(i)(3), shall be specially allocated items of Company income and gain for such year (and, if necessary, subsequent years) in an amount equal to such Member's share of the net decrease in Member Nonrecourse Debt Minimum Gain, determined in accordance with Treas. Reg. § 1.704–2(i)(5). This paragraph is intended to comply with the minimum gain chargeback requirement in Treas. Reg. § 1.704–2(i)(4) and shall be interpreted consistently therewith. "**Member Nonrecourse Debt Minimum Gain**" means an amount, with respect to each Member Nonrecourse Debt, determined in accordance with Treas. Reg. § 1.704–2(i) with respect to "partner nonrecourse debt minimum gain." "**Member Nonrecourse Debt**" shall have the meaning set forth in Treas. Reg. § 1.704–2(b)(4) for "partner nonrecourse debt."

(iii)   In the event any Member unexpectedly receives any adjustments, allocations or distributions described in Treas. Reg. § 1.704–1(b)(2)(ii)(d)(4), (5) or (6), items of Company income and gain shall be specially allocated to such Member in an amount and manner sufficient to eliminate the deficits in its Adjusted Capital Account Balance created by such adjustments, allocations or distributions as quickly as possible. This paragraph is intended to constitute a "qualified income offset" within the meaning of Treas. Reg. § 1.704–1(b)(2)(ii)(d), and shall be interpreted consistently therewith. "**Adjusted Capital Account Balance**" means the balance in the Capital Account of a Member as of the end of the relevant fiscal year of the Company, after giving effect to the following: (a) credit to such Capital Account any amounts the Member is obligated to restore, pursuant to the terms of this Agreement or otherwise, or is deemed obligated to restore pursuant to the penultimate sentences of Treas. Reg. §§ 1.704–2(g)(1) and 1.704–2(i)(5) or any other statutory, administrative or judicial authority, and (b) debit to such capital account the items described in Treas. Reg. §§ 1.704–1(b)(2)(ii)(d)(4), (5) and (6).

(iv)   Nonrecourse Deductions for any fiscal year or other period shall be specially allocated to the Members in accordance with their Percentage Interests. "**Nonrecourse Deductions**" shall have the meaning set forth in Treas. Reg. § 1.704–2(b) (1). The amount of Nonrecourse Deductions for a fiscal year of the Company equals the excess, if any, of the net increase, if any, in the amount of Minimum Gain during that fiscal year over the aggregate amount of any distributions during that fiscal year of proceeds of a Nonrecourse Liability that are allocable to an increase in Minimum Gain, determined according to the provisions of Treas. Reg. § 1.704–2(c). "**Nonrecourse Liability**" shall have the meaning set forth in Treas. Reg. § 1.704–2(b) (3).

(v)   Member Nonrecourse Deductions for any fiscal year or other period shall be specially allocated to the Member who bears the economic risk of loss with respect to the Member Nonrecourse Debt to which such Member Nonrecourse Deductions are attributable in accordance with Treas. Reg. § 1.704–2(i). "**Member Nonrecourse Deductions**" shall have the meaning set forth in Treas. Reg. § 1.704–2(i) (2) for "partner nonrecourse deductions." For any Company taxable year, the amount of Member Nonrecourse Deductions with respect to a Member Nonrecourse Debt equals the net increase during the year, if any, in the amount of Member Nonrecourse Debt Minimum Gain reduced (but not below zero) by proceeds of the liability that are both attributable to the liability and allocable to an increase in the Member Nonrecourse Debt Minimum Gain.

(vi)   The allocations set forth in paragraph (a) are intended to comply with certain requirements of Treasury Regulations promulgated under Code Section 704. Such allocations shall be taken into account in allocating other Profits, Losses, and items of income, gain, loss, and deduction to each Member so that, to the extent possible, and to the extent permitted by Treasury Regulations, the net amount of such allocations of other Profits, Losses, and other items and such allocations to each Member shall be equal to the net amount that would have been allocated to each Member if such allocations had not been made.

(b) <u>Rules of Application</u>.

(i)   Profits and Losses and other items of income, gain, loss and deduction shall be allocated to the Members in accordance with the portion of the year during which the Members have held their respective interests. All items of income, loss and deduction shall be considered to have been earned ratably over the period of the fiscal year of the Company, except that (A) gains and losses arising from the disposition of assets shall be taken into account as of the date thereof, and (B) with the consent of the Manager and all affected parties, the preceding items may be allocated by using an "interim closing of the books" method.

(ii) In the event the Company is entitled to a deduction for interest imputed under any provision of the Code on any loan or advance from a Member or its Affiliate (whether such interest is currently deducted, capitalized or amortized), such deduction shall be allocated solely to such Member.

(iii) To the extent any payments in the nature of fees to a Member or its Affiliate are recharacterized by the Internal Revenue Service as distributions to a Member for federal income tax purposes, and such recharacterization is sustained in a non-appealable administrative or judicial forum, there will be a gross income allocation to such Member in the amount of such distribution in the year in which such recharacterization is sustained.

(iv) Losses (or any item thereof) that would otherwise be allocated to a Member under this Agreement shall not be allocated to any Member to the extent that such allocation would result in a deficit in its Adjusted Capital Account Balance (determined, for this purpose, after tentatively making all allocations under this Agreement for the applicable period) while any other Member continues to have a positive Adjusted Capital Account Balance; in such event Losses shall first be allocated to Members with positive Adjusted Capital Account Balances in proportion to such balances, until their positive Adjusted Capital Account Balances have been reduced to zero. To the extent that any Losses are allocated pursuant to this paragraph, Profits shall thereafter be allocated in reverse order of such allocations of Losses to the extent of such Losses.

(v) The allocation of Profits and Losses to any Member shall be deemed to be an allocation to that Member of the same proportionate part of each separate item of taxable income, gain, loss, deduction or credit that comprises such Profits and Losses.

(vi) For purposes of allocating nonrecourse liabilities of the Company pursuant to Treas. Reg. § 1.752–3(a)(3), each Member's share of Profits shall be (A) with respect to excess nonrecourse liabilities up to the amount of gain calculated pursuant to this clause, that percentage of the gain calculated pursuant to this clause that would be allocated to such Member pursuant to Code Section 704(c) if (1) all of the Company Properties were sold at their Carrying Value in excess of (2) the liabilities allocated to each such Member under Treas. Reg. § 1.752–3(a)(2), and (B) with respect to the remaining excess nonrecourse liabilities, each Member's interest in distributions from Existing Properties or New Properties, whichever secures the excess nonrecourse liabilities.

(vii) The allocations in paragraphs (a) and (b) shall be made in the order listed therein.

(viii) Each Member having a deficit Capital Account at the end of any Fiscal Year that is in excess of the amount the Member is obligated to restore under this Agreement, including, any amount which each Member is deemed to be obligated to restore under Regulation

§ 1.704–2(g)(1) and Regulation § 1.704–2(i)(5), will be specially allocated items of Company income and gain in the amount of the excess as quickly as possible.

(ix) Investor and its tax advisors will have the opportunity to review and comment on any federal, state or local tax returns prepared by the Company or its accountants prior to the filing of such returns by the Company. The Members agree to cooperate in good faith in resolving any differences that they might have concerning reporting positions which the Company's accountants and other Members propose to take in any such returns, so that all such reporting positions fairly and properly reflect the parties' intentions with respect to their respective economic interests in the Company and the various tax and economic allocations set forth in the Agreement and this Exhibit B.

(x) Investor will have the option, but not the obligation, to indemnify Developer and its Affiliates against all or any portion of any liability associated with any debt which is non-recourse to the borrower, but which is personally guaranteed by Developer or any of its Affiliates.

(c) **Rules Concerning Calculations of Profits and Losses and Code Section 704(c) Tax Allocations**.

(i) For purposes of computing Profits and Losses "**Carrying Value**" shall mean (a) with respect to contributed property, the agreed value of such property, (b) with respect to property the book value of which is adjusted pursuant to Treas. Reg. §§ 1.704–1(b)(2)(iv)(d), (e) or (f), the amount determined pursuant to paragraphs (c)(iii) or (iv), and (c) with respect to any other property, the adjusted basis of such property for federal income tax purposes as of the time of determination, in all cases reduced by Depreciation.

(ii) Upon the occurrence of any of the following events, the Carrying Value of the Company's assets shall be adjusted to their fair market value, as such fair market value is agreed to by both Members:

(A) The acquisition of an interest in the Company by a new or existing Member in exchange for more than a *de minimis* contribution of money or property;

(B) The distribution by the Company to a continuing or retiring Member of more than a *de minimis* amount of property or money in consideration for an interest in the Company; or

(C) The "liquidation" of the Company within the meaning of Treas. Reg. § 1.704–1(b)(2)(ii)(g).

The revaluation of the Properties referred to in the immediately preceding sentence shall be made in accordance with Treas. Reg. § 1.704–1(b)(2)(iv)(f).

(iii) Upon an issuance of additional interests in the Company for cash or contributed property, the Carrying Value of the Company's assets shall, immediately prior to issuance, be adjusted (consistent with the provisions hereof) upward or downward to reflect any unrealized gain or unrealized loss attributable to each such asset (as if such unrealized gain or unrealized loss had been recognized upon an actual sale of such property at the fair market value thereof immediately prior to such issuance, and had been allocated to the Members, at such time, pursuant to the Agreement). In determining such unrealized gain or unrealized loss attributable to the Company's assets, they shall be deemed to be sold at their Fair Market Value.

(iv) Immediately prior to the distribution of any Company asset in liquidation of the Company or in redemption of all or part of any Member's interest in the Company, the Carrying Values of all the Company's assets shall be adjusted (consistent with the provisions hereof) upward or downward to reflect any unrealized gain or unrealized loss attributable to each such asset (as if such unrealized gain or unrealized loss had been recognized upon an actual sale of each such asset, immediately prior to such distribution, and had been allocated to the Members, at such time, pursuant to the Agreement). In determining such unrealized gain or unrealized loss attributable to such assets, they shall be deemed sold at their Fair Market Value.

(v) In accordance with Code Section 704(c) and the Regulations thereunder, income, gain, loss and deduction with respect to any contributed property shall, solely for tax purposes, be allocated among the Members so as to take account of any variation between the adjusted basis of such property to the Company for income tax purposes and its agreed value. To the extent any contributed property consists of an interest in any partnership or limited liability company which, in turn, owns any interest in real estate, it is the Members' intentions that income, gain, loss and deduction with respect to such contributed property (expressly including any so-called "built-in gain" attributable to such contributed property) will, solely for tax purposes, be allocated among the Members in the manner which would be mandated under Code § 704(c) and the Regulations promulgated thereunder if the contributed property were to have consisted of the real estate and other assets owned by the partnership or limited liability company whose equity interests are being contributed to the Company.

(vi) In the event the Carrying Value of any Company asset is adjusted as described in paragraph (iii) or (iv) above, subsequent allocations of income, gain, loss and deduction with respect to such asset shall take account of any variation between the adjusted basis of such asset for federal income tax purposes and its Carrying Value in the same manner as under Code Section 704(c) and the regulations thereunder.

(vii) The Company shall use the "traditional method with curative allocations" under Regulations § 1.704–3(c) (1). In the event that there is not sufficient depreciation to allocate to the non-contributing Member under the "traditional method with curative allocations", then Manager will allocate any other items of income, gain, loss or deduction to correct distortions created by the so-called "ceiling rule" under the applicable Regulations to Code § 704(c). It is the intent of the Members that the non-contributing Member will be allocated, in all instances, tax items that are equal to their Code § 704(b) book items.

(viii) Upon the contribution of any asset by any Member (either directly as fee simple interest or indirectly as an interest in any entity owning such asset), the Carrying Value of each such asset will be restated at the current § 704(b) value that has been agreed to by the Members pursuant to the terms of this Agreement.

(ix) To the extent any property contributed by any Member consists of partnership interests, membership interests or other equity interests in any entity which will continue in existence for tax purposes following the date of such contribution, it is the Members' intentions that the contributing Member will receive all of the benefits and bear all of the burdens of all taxes levied, imposed or otherwise attributable to the activities of the underlying entities to which such interests relate for all periods prior to the date of the contribution of such interests to the Company, including, without limitation, all benefits and burdens associated with any audits or other adjustments of the returns filed by such entities for any period prior to the date of the contribution of such equity interests to the Company.

(d) **Definitions**.

"Profits" and "Losses" means, for each Fiscal Year of the Company, an amount equal to the Company's taxable income or loss, respectively, for any period from all sources, determined in accordance with Code Section 703(a), adjusted in the following manner: (i) the income of the Company that is exempt from federal income tax or not otherwise taken into account in computing Profits and Losses pursuant to this definition shall be added to such taxable income or loss; (ii) any expenditures of the Company described in Code Section 705(a)(2)(B) or treated as described in such Section pursuant to Treas. Reg. § 1.704–1(b)(2)(iv)(i) or not otherwise taken into account in computing Profits or Losses pursuant to this definition shall be subtracted from such taxable income or loss; (iii) in the event the Carrying Value of any Company asset is adjusted pursuant to paragraphs (c)(ii), (iii) or (iv) of Exhibit B, the amount of such adjustment shall be taken into account as gain or loss from the disposition of such asset for purposes of computing Profits and Losses; (iv) gain or loss resulting from the disposition of an asset shall be computed by reference to the Carrying Value of such asset; (v) a deduction for Depreciation shall be taken in lieu of a deduction for depreciation, amortization or cost recovery allowable for federal income tax purposes for such fiscal year; (vi) to the extent an adjustment under Code Section 734(b) is required by Treas. Reg. § 1.704–1(b)(2)(iv)(m)(4) to be taken into account in determining Capital Accounts as a result of a distribution other than in liquidation of a Member's interest, the amount of such item shall be treated as an item of gain or loss from the disposition of the asset and shall be taken into account for purposes of computing Profits or Losses; and (vii) any items that are specially allocated pursuant to Exhibit B shall not be taken into account in computing Profits and Losses.

"Depreciation" means, for each fiscal period, an amount equal to the depreciation, amortization or cost recovery deduction allowable for federal income tax purposes for such fiscal period, unless the Carrying Value for an asset differs from the adjusted basis of such asset for federal income tax purposes, in which case "Depreciation" means an amount that bears the same ratio to the beginning Carrying Value as the depreciation, amortization or cost recovery deduction bears to the beginning adjusted tax basis; provided, however, that if the adjusted basis of an asset is zero at the beginning of a fiscal period, "Depreciation" will be determined by the Manager by using any reasonable method.

<u>**EXHIBIT C**</u>

<u>**APPROVED DEVELOPMENT BUDGET**</u>

See attached Schedule C–1.

<u>EXHIBIT D</u>

<u>APPROVED OPERATING BUDGET–FISCAL YEAR 20__</u>

See attached Schedule D–1.

DOCUMENT #4

CLOSING STATEMENT FOR LAND SALE

■ ■ ■

CLOSING STATEMENT

PROPERTY:	Approximately 120 acres of undeveloped land located in the Heathrow International Business Center in Seminole County, Florida
SELLER:	HIBC Development Company
BUYER:	Colonial Realty Limited Partnership
TITLE COMPANY:	First American Title Insurance Company
SURVEYOR:	Tinkelpaugh Surveying
ESCROW AGENT:	First American Title Insurance Company
REAL ESTATE BROKER:	Greenwich Group International LLC
SELLER'S COUNSEL:	Holland & Knight
BUYER'S COUNSEL:	Leitman, Seigal & Payne, P.C.
DATE OF CLOSING:	August 1, 2002
PLACE OF CLOSING:	Offices of Holland & Knight 200 South Orange Avenue, Suite 2600 Orlando, Florida 32801

This Closing Statement was prepared based on the sale of the HIBC land by The Pizzuti Companies to Colonial Real Properties Trust in August, 2002. The numbers used in the Closing Statement (other than the purchase price, which is a matter of public record) are, however, simply approximations of the actual costs incurred in connection with the land sale closing.

Seller's Statement

	Credits	(Charges)
Purchase Price	$13,000,000.00	
Deposit		($300,000.00)
Loan Pay-offs		
First Union National Bank		($4,000,000.00)
Newport Partners XIV		
Ltd.		($6,000,000.00)
Title Insurance Costs		($25,000.00)
Documentary Stamps		($91,000.00)
Real Estate Commission		($84,500.00)
Real Estate Tax Proration		($130,000.00)
Owners Association Dues		
Proration	$12,000.00	
Legal Fees of Seller's Counsel		($20,000.00)
Total Credits (Charges)	$13,012,000.00	($10,650,500.00)
Net Cash Payable to Seller	**$2,361,500.00**	

Buyer's Statement

	(Credits)	Charges
Purchase Price		$13,000,000.00
Deposit	($300,000.00)	
Survey Costs		$10,000.00
Recording Costs		$200.00
Real Estate Tax Proration	($130,000.00)	
Owners Association Dues		
Proration		$12,000.00
Legal Fees of Buyer's Counsel		Paid outside of closing
Total Credits (Charges)	($430,000.00)	$13,022,200.00
Net Cash Payable by Buyer	**$12,592,200.00**	

Disbursements/Reconciliations

Funds Available for Disbursement:
Net Cash Payable by Buyer   **$12,592,200.00**

Actual Disbursements:

First Union National Bank	$4,000,000.00
(Loan Pay-off)	
Newport Partners XIV, Ltd.	$6,000,000.00
(Loan Pay-off)	
First American Title Insurance Company	
(Title Insurance Costs)	$25,000.00
Greenwich Group International LLC	
(Real Estate Commission)	$84,500.00
Seminole County Clerk of Circuit Court	
(Documentary Stamps)	$91,000.00
Holland & Knight	
(Legal Fees of Seller's Counsel)	$20,000.00
Tinkelpaugh Surveying	
(Survey Costs)	$10,000.00
Seminole County Recorder	
(Recording Costs)	$200.00
HIBC Development Company	
(Net Cash Payable to Seller)	$2,361,500.00

Total Disbursements: **$12,592,200.00**

Notes to Closing Statement

1. All closing credits, charges and prorations have been calculated in accordance with the provisions of the Real Estate Purchase Agreement entered into by Seller and Buyer as of May 26, 2002 ("Purchase Contract"). All capitalized terms which are used, but not defined in this Closing Statement, will have the meanings attributed to such terms in the Purchase Contract.

2. All prorations set forth in this Closing Statement have been calculated, apportioned and prorated between Seller and Buyer as of 11:59 p.m. on the day prior to the Date of Closing.

3. At closing, the Escrow Agent will pay the principal amount of the Deposit ($300,000) to Seller and will refund all interest earned on the Deposit to Buyer.

4. Attached to this Closing Statement as Schedule 1 are loan pay-off letters from First Union National Bank and Newport Partners XIV, Ltd.

5. Attached to this Closing Statement as Schedule 2 is the proposed real estate tax bill issued by Seminole County for the Property for the 2002 taxable year. Because the real estate taxes are not yet due and payable, Buyer has been given a closing credit for 212/365ths of the proposed real estate tax bill (the number of days included in taxable year 2002 prior to the date of closing). The real estate tax credit is subject to being reprorated at the time and in the manner specified in § 7(a) of the Purchase Contract.

6. Attached to this Closing Statement as Schedule 3 is the invoice paid by Seller for the 2002 annual dues payable to the Heathrow International Center Owner's Association. Seller has been given a closing credit for 153/365ths of the paid dues (the number of days included in calendar year 2002 from and after the date of closing).

7. Attached to this Closing Statement as Schedules 4, 5, 6 and 7, respectively, are the invoices submitted for payment at closing by First American Title Insurance Company (title insurance costs), Tinkelpaugh Surveying (survey costs), Holland & Knight (legal fees for Seller's counsel) and Greenwich Group International LLC (real estate commission).

8. The net cash payable by Buyer at closing (as set forth in this Closing Statement under the caption "Disbursements/Reconciliations") will be wire transferred by Buyer in advance to the account of Escrow Agent for disbursement at closing in accordance with the "Disbursements/Reconciliations" section of this Closing Statement. Upon its receipt of a fully-executed copy of this Closing Statement and its receipt of further specific telephonic, electronic or written confirmation from each of Seller and Buyer, Escrow Agent will then disburse all available funds to the parties in the manner contemplated in this Closing Statement and otherwise in accordance with wiring or

other funding instructions provided to Escrow Agent by the intended recipients of such disbursements. The Escrow Agent's wiring instructions are attached to this Closing Statement as Schedule 8.

Seller, Buyer and Escrow Agent have each executed this Closing Statement as of Date of Closing.

Seller: **Buyer:**   **Escrow Agent:**

By: __________   **By:** __________   **By:** __________

Document #5

Construction Loan Agreement for Ohio Development Project

■ ■ ■

CONSTRUCTION LOAN AGREEMENT

Dated as of _______, 20__

Between

____

("Lender")

And

____

("Borrower")

This document was provided for use in this text through the good graces of David Conrad, a partner of the Bricker & Eckler law firm headquartered in Columbus, Ohio. David has extensive experience representing construction lenders throughout the United States. This form of Construction Loan Agreement was prepared by David for use on Ohio mortgage loans.

ARTICLE I

Particular Terms and Definitions/Terms of Loan

1.1   The following terms, as used herein, shall have the following meanings:

"Aggregate Change Order Amount"—_________ Dollars ($________).

"Borrower's Architects"—The architects and/or engineers approved by Lender who are responsible for preparing the Plans and supervising construction of the Improvements, and any successor engaged with Lender's consent.

"Change Orders"—Any amendments or modifications to the Plans, General Contract or Subcontracts.

"Commitment Fee"—_________ Dollars ($________).

"Completion Date"—_________.

"Construction Loan Checking Account"—A separate non-interest bearing checking account with Lender which shall not be drawn upon except to pay Hard Costs and Soft Costs approved by Lender.

"Draw Request"—A statement by Borrower on AIA Form G702/703 or other form acceptable to Lender and executed by Borrower's Requisition Agent setting forth the amount of the Loan advance requested in each instance and including:

(a) Lien waivers from the General Contractor for all work performed through the date of the Draw Request ("Lien Waivers");

(b) Lien Waivers from all Subcontractors for all work performed through the date of the immediately preceding Draw Request;

(c) Proof of payment of all Soft Costs covered by the immediately preceding Draw Request; and

(d) Bills or invoices for all Soft Costs covered by the Draw Request.

"Event of Default"—Any of the following shall constitute an "Event of Default":

(a) Borrower shall fail to pay any installment of principal or interest under the Note when and as the same shall become due and payable, whether monthly, at maturity, at a date fixed for prepayment or by acceleration or otherwise; or

(b) Borrower shall fail to make any other payment when due, and such failure shall continue for a period of ten (10) calendar days after written notice thereof from Lender; or

(c) any representation or warranty made in writing by or on behalf of Borrower in any Loan Document or in any writing furnished by Borrower to Lender in connection with the transactions contemplated hereby, proves to have been false or incorrect in any respect on the date as of which made; provided that if such false or incorrect statement is capable of being cured, an Event of Default shall not occur unless and until

Borrower fails to cause such misrepresentation or breach of warranty to be cured within thirty (30) days after receipt of written notice thereof from Lender; or

(d) Borrower (i) is generally not paying, or admits in writing its inability to pay, its debts as they become due, (ii) files, or consents by answer or otherwise to the filing against it of, or fails to secure the dismissal within ninety (90) days after filing of, a petition for relief or reorganization or arrangement or any other petition in bankruptcy, for liquidation or to take advantage of any bankruptcy, insolvency, reorganization, moratorium or other similar law of any jurisdiction, (iii) makes an assignment for the benefit of its creditors, (iv) consents to the appointment of a custodian, receiver, trustee or other officer with similar powers with respect to it or with respect to any substantial part of its Project, (v) is adjudicated as insolvent or to be liquidated, or (vi) takes corporate action for the purpose of any of the foregoing;

(e) A court or Governmental Authority of competent jurisdiction enters an order appointing, without consent by Borrower, a custodian, receiver, trustee or other officer with similar powers with respect to it or with respect to any substantial part of its property, or constituting an order for relief or approving a petition for relief or reorganization or any other petition in bankruptcy or for liquidation or to take advantage of any bankruptcy or insolvency law of any jurisdiction, or ordering the dissolution, winding-up or liquidation of Borrower, or any such petition shall be filed against Borrower and such petition shall not be dismissed within ninety (90) days;

(f) Borrower shall fail to perform any obligation or comply with any term applicable to it contained herein or in any other Loan Document and such failure is not remedied within thirty (30) days after Borrower' receipt of written notice thereof from Lender; or

(g) Any Guarantor fails to perform any obligation or comply with any term applicable to it under the Guaranty and such failure is not remedied within thirty (30) days after such Guarantor's receipt of written notice thereof from Lender.

"Extended Maturity Date"—________, 20__.

"Financial Statements"—Statements of the assets, liabilities (direct or contingent), income, expenses and cash flow of Borrower and each Guarantor, as required by the Mortgage.

"General Contractor"; "General Contract"—Any general contractor engaged by Borrower and approved by Lender under any General Contract; any contract (together with all riders, addenda and other instruments referred to therein as "Contract Documents") between Borrower and the General Contractor which requires the General Contractor to provide, or supervise or manage the procurement of, substantially all labor and materials needed for completion of the Improvements.

"Governmental Authorities"—The United States, the state in which the Premises are located and any political subdivision, agency, department, commission, board, bureau or instrumentality of either of them, including any local authorities, which exercises jurisdiction over the Premises or the Improvements.

"Guarantor"—________, ________ and ________, or any one of them, each of whom has jointly and severally guaranteed payment and performance by Borrower of Borrower's obligations to Lender.

"Guaranty"—The guaranty of the performance of all or part of Borrower's obligations which shall be executed by each Guarantor.

"Hard Costs"—The aggregate costs of all labor, materials, equipment, fixtures and furnishings necessary for completion of the Improvements.

"Improvements"; "Project"—The ________.

"Initial Advance"—The first advance of Loan proceeds to be made hereunder.

"Leases"—Any leases for space of the rentable area of the Improvements.

"Loan"—The loan to be advanced by Lender to Borrower pursuant to the terms and conditions of this Agreement, as the same is further defined in Section 1.2.

"Loan Amount"—________ Dollars ($________).

"Loan Budget Amounts"—The portion of the Loan Amount set forth in the Project Budget to be advanced for each line item and category of Hard Costs and Soft Costs.

"Loan Documents"—This Agreement, the Note, Mortgage, Guaranty, the Assignment of Construction Documents, the Assignment of Design Documents, UCC Financing Statements and any other instrument, document, certificate or affidavit heretofore, now or hereafter given by Borrower evidencing or securing or by any Guarantor guaranteeing all or any part of the foregoing.

"Maturity Date"—________, 200__.

"Mortgage"—That certain Open–End Mortgage, Assignment of Rents and Security Agreement to be made by Borrower to Lender to secure the Note and any sums in addition to the Loan Amount advanced by Lender for completion of the Improvements.

"Mortgaged Property"—The Premises and other property constituting the "Mortgaged Property," as said quoted term is defined in the Mortgage.

"Note"—That certain Mortgage Note for a principal sum equal to the Loan Amount to be made by Borrower to Lender to evidence the Loan.

"Option to Extend"—Borrower's option, subject to the terms and conditions of Section 1.2, to extend the term of the Loan from the Maturity Date to the Extended Maturity Date.

"Plans"—All final drawings, plans and specifications prepared by Borrower, Borrower's Architects, the General Contractor or Subcontractors, and approved by Lender, which describe and show the labor, materials, equipment, fixtures and furnishings necessary for the construction of the Improvements, including all amendments and modifications thereof made by approved Change Orders (and also showing minimum grade of finishes and furnishings for all areas of the Improvements to be leased or sold in ready-for-occupancy conditions).

"Premises"—The real property described on Exhibit "A" to the Mortgage, upon all or part of which the Improvements are to be constructed.

"Project Budget"—The statement attached hereto as Exhibit "A", setting forth, by line item and category, the Hard Costs and Soft Costs of completion of the Improvements.

"Requisition Agent"—________ who is hereby authorized by Borrower to execute and deliver each Draw Request.

"Retainage Percentage"—________.

"Retained Amounts"—The greater of the Retainage Percentage of the Hard Costs or the actual retained amounts specified on the Draw Request.

"Single Change Order Amount"—________ Dollars ($________).

"Soft Costs"—All costs of acquisition of the Premises and completion of the Improvements other than Hard Costs, including, without limitation, architects' and attorneys' fees, ground rents, interest, real estate taxes, survey costs and insurance premiums.

"Subcontractor"; "Subcontract"—Any subcontractor or supplier engaged by the General Contractor and any contractor other than the General Contractor or supplier engaged by Borrower, under one or more contracts or work orders; any such contract or work order.

"Title Insurer"—The issuer(s), approved by Lender, of the title insurance policy or policies insuring the Mortgage.

"Variable Rate"—The rate of interest equal to (a) .5% plus (b) Lender's "Prime Rate" in effect from time to time that serves as the basis upon which effective rates of interest are calculated for those loans making reference thereto (any change in the rate of interest on the Loan due to a change in the Prime Rate shall become effective on the date each change in the Prime Rate is announced by Lender).

1.2   Certain salient terms of the Loan are summarized below.

(a) The Loan. In connection with the construction of the Improvements on the Premises, Borrower desires to borrow from Lender a loan (the "Loan") in an amount equal to the Loan Amount, the proceeds of which are to be used for the payment of certain costs and expenses related to the Project, all as set forth in the Project Budget. Any amounts of the Loan disbursed by Lender shall not, in total, exceed the Loan Amount and shall be deemed evidenced by the Note and shall be payable to Lender on or before the Maturity Date or, if applicable, the Extended Maturity Date and shall bear interest at the Variable Rate.

(b) <u>Commitment Fee</u>. Borrower shall pay Lender the Commitment Fee in the amount set forth in Article 1. The Commitment Fee shall be deemed fully earned, payable and non-refundable upon the Borrower's execution of this Agreement.

(c) <u>Loan Documents</u>. Borrower shall deliver to Lender concurrently with this Agreement each of the Loan Documents, properly executed and, where applicable, in recordable form.

(d) <u>Maturity Date</u>. Except as otherwise provided in Subparagraph e., below, all sums due and owing under this Agreement, the Note and the other Loan Documents shall be repaid in full on or before the Maturity Date.

(e) <u>Option to Extend</u>. Borrower shall have the option to extend the term of the Loan from the Maturity Date to the Extended Maturity Date, upon satisfaction of each of the following conditions precedent:

(i) Borrower shall provide Lender with written notice of Borrower's request to exercise the Option to Extend not more than 90 days but not less than 30 days prior to the Maturity Date;

(ii) As of the date of Borrower's delivery of notice of request to exercise the Option to Extend and as of the Maturity Date, no Event of Default shall have occurred and be continuing, and no event or condition which, with the giving of notice or the passage of time or both, would constitute an Event of Default shall have occurred and be continuing, and Borrower shall so certify in writing;

(iii) On or before the Maturity Date, Borrower shall pay to Lender an extension fee in an amount equal to .5% of the Loan Amount; and

(iv) Borrower shall execute all documents reasonably required by Lender to exercise the Option to Extend and shall deliver to Lender, at Borrower's sole cost and expense, such title insurance endorsements as may be reasonably required by Lender.

ARTICLE II

Loan Advances

2.1 Subject to the provisions of this Agreement, Lender will advance and Borrower will accept the Loan Amount in installments as follows:

The Initial Advance will be made upon the satisfaction of the applicable conditions set forth in Article III hereof, and all subsequent advances shall be made monthly thereafter, upon satisfaction of the applicable conditions set forth in Article IV hereof, in amounts which shall be equal to the aggregate of the Hard Costs and Soft Costs incurred by Borrower through the end of the period covered by the Draw Request <u>less</u>:

(a) the Retained Amounts; <u>and</u>

(b) the total of the Loan advances theretofore made;

<u>and</u>, at the election of Lender, <u>less</u> any combination of the following further amounts:

(c) all or a portion of the amount by which any Hard Costs or Soft Costs are or are reasonably estimated by Lender to be greater than the respective Loan Budget Amounts for such costs; and

(d) any costs covered by the Draw Request not approved, certified or verified as provided in Section 2.2 hereof, any Soft Costs covered by a previous Draw Request for which proof of payment has not been received by Lender, and any Hard Costs covered by a previous Draw Request for which Lien Waivers have not been received by Lender.

2.2 Hard Costs are to be certified by the General Contractor. Verification of the monthly progress and Hard Costs and Soft Costs which have been incurred by Borrower shall be subject to the reasonable approval and verification by Lender. Lender reserves the right to utilize its own in-house engineers, architects and inspectors for purposes of such inspections, verifications and approvals, and to engage the services of independent contractors, engineers, architects or inspectors where Lender so desires, and Borrower agrees to assume and pay all costs, including, without limitation, fees and travel expenses, associated with each engineer, architect, contractor and inspector, in-house and independent.

2.3 All advances to Borrower are to be made at Lender's principal office or at such other place as Lender may designate and shall be deposited in the Construction Loan Checking Account. Draw Requests shall be received by Lender at least five (5) business days prior to the date of the requested advance. Lender may, at Lender's sole discretion and at Borrower's expense, make any or all advances through the Title Insurer, in which case interest shall accrue to Lender from the time such funds are deposited with the Title Insurer.

2.4 Retained Amounts not advanced pursuant to Section 2.1 hereof during the course of construction of the Improvements shall be advanced upon the satisfaction of the conditions set forth in Section 4.2 hereof. Loan Budget Amounts for Soft Costs not advanced prior to completion of construction of the Improvements shall be advanced until exhausted, not more frequently than once a month, for Soft Costs as incurred after such completion.

2.5 Lender shall not make Loan advances for building materials or furnishings which are stored but not yet affixed to or incorporated into the Improvements.

2.6 Lender may, in its sole discretion, accelerate all or any portion of the amounts to be advanced hereunder without regard to Borrower's satisfaction of the conditions to its entitlement to Loan proceeds and no person dealing with Borrower or the General Contractor or any other person shall have standing to demand any different performance from Lender.

2.7 If at any time the undisbursed balance of the Loan Budget Amount for any line item or category of cost shown on the Project Budget is, in Lender's reasonable judgment, excessive, the excess may be reallocated to any other Loan Budget Amount balance which Lender reasonably deems to be insufficient.

2.8 A drawing under any letter of credit which Lender has issued or hereafter issues in connection with the Premises or Improvements, irrespective of the account party thereunder, shall constitute an advance of Loan proceeds under this Agreement and the amount thereof shall be evidenced and secured, respectively, by the Note and Mortgage. The issuance of any such letter of credit shall effect a reduction, by the amount and during the existence thereof, of available Loan proceeds and Lender, in its reasonable discretion, shall allocate such reduction to the Loan Budget Amounts which it deems most appropriate.

ARTICLE III

Conditions Precedent to Lender's Obligation to Make the Initial Advance

3.1 Lender shall not be obligated to make the Initial Advance until the following conditions shall have been satisfied:

(a) Lender shall have received and approved the items specified in Section 3.2 below;

(b) The representations and warranties made in Article V hereof shall be true and correct on and as of the date of the Initial Advance with the same effect as if made on such date;

(c) Existing improvements on the Premises, if any, shall not have been materially injured or damaged by fire or other casualty unless Lender shall have received insurance proceeds sufficient in the reasonable judgment of Lender to effect the satisfactory restoration of the said improvements and to permit completion of said improvements prior to the Completion Date pursuant to terms of disbursement satisfactory to Lender; and

(d) There shall exist no Event of Default, as therein defined, under the Note or Mortgage, or any event or state of facts which after notice or the passage of time, or both, could give rise to such an Event of Default.

3.2 The items to be received and approved by Lender prior to the Initial Advance shall be:

(a) The Commitment Fee, to be retained by Lender whether or not any advances are made under this Agreement;

(b) The executed Note, Mortgage, Guaranty, Borrower's Closing Certificate, this Agreement and UCC–1 Financing Statements relating to the Mortgaged Property and any other documents to be executed in connection with, or property given as security for the Loan;

(c) A paid title insurance policy, in the amount of the Note, in form approved by Lender, issued by the Title Insurer which shall insure the Mortgage to be a valid lien on Borrower's interest in the Premises free and clear of all defects and encumbrances except those previously approved by Lender, and shall contain:

(i) full coverage against mechanics' liens (filed and inchoate);

(ii) a reference to the survey but no survey exceptions except those theretofore approved by Lender; and

(iii) a pending disbursements clause in the form of Exhibit "B" hereto;

(d) A survey (current to within thirty (30) days of the Initial Advance) of the Premises certified to Lender and the Title Insurer;

(e) The policies of hazard insurance required by the Mortgage (together with evidence of the payment of the premiums therefor) which policies will contain an endorsement specifically providing that, in the case of any damage, all insurance proceeds will be paid to Lender in accordance with the terms and conditions of the Mortgage;

(f) If Borrower, any Guarantor or any general partner of Borrower or any Guarantor is a corporation, copies of the following documents with respect to each:

(i) a good-standing certificate from the state of its incorporation and, as to Borrower only, from the state in which the Premises are located;

(ii) certified copies of the articles of incorporation and by-laws or code of regulations;

(iii) resolutions, certified by the corporate secretary, of the shareholders or directors of the corporation authorizing the consummation of the transactions contemplated hereby or by the Guaranty; and

(iv) a certificate of the corporate secretary as to the incumbency of the officers executing this Agreement, the Guaranty or any of the other documents required hereby;

and, if Borrower, any Guarantor or any general partner of Borrower or any Guarantor is a partnership or venture:

(v) the partnership agreement and all amendments and attachments thereto, certified by the general partners to be true and complete;

(vi) any certificates filed or required to be filed by the partnership in the state of its formation and the state where the

Premises are located in order for it to do business in those states; and

(vii) any consents by other partners required for the borrowing contemplated hereby, the consummation of this Agreement or the execution of the Guaranty, and an acknowledgment by each general partner of his continued membership in the partnership;

(g) An opinion of Borrower's counsel, which counsel shall have been approved by Lender, which opinion shall be in form and content satisfactory to Lender;

(h) Current Financial Statements and such other financial data as Lender shall require;

(i) Certified and correct copies of all Leases, Subordination and Attornment Agreements and Estoppel Certificates, in form satisfactory to Lender, from tenants under all Leases, and all contracts of sale for all or any portion of the Premises, together with the standard form of lease or contract of sale, as the case may be, Borrower intends to use in connection with the leasing of space in the Improvements or the sale of all or any portion of the Premises;

(j) A copy of the purchase agreement, closing statement and deed pursuant to which the Premises have been or will be acquired by Borrower;

(k) A copy of the following documents, each of which shall be in form and content acceptable to Lender: (i) General Contract; (ii) all Subcontracts requested by Lender; (iii) Borrower's agreement with Borrower's Architect; and (iv) any management agreement or franchise agreement relating to the Premises and Improvements; and (v) ________;

(*l*) Assignments of all contracts from Borrower to Lender and acknowledgments of and consents to such assignments of all contracts required to be provided to Lender as set forth in subsection ((k)) of this Section;

(m) An appraisal of the Premises and Improvements and, if required by Lender, a market feasibility study;

(n) A progress schedule or chart showing the interval of time over which each item of Hard Costs is projected to be incurred or paid;

(*o*) The Project Budget;

(p) A Draw Request for the Initial Advance;

(q) The Plans;

(r) Evidence satisfactory to Lender, to the effect that: (i) the Plans have been approved by Governmental Authorities and all tenants under Leases and purchasers under sales contracts which contain any requirements or specifications in respect of construction of the Improvements; (ii) the Improvements as shown by the Plans will comply with applicable zoning ordinances and regulations; (iii) a General Contract and/or Subcontracts are in effect which satisfactorily provide for the construction of the

Improvements; (iv) all roads and utilities necessary for the full utilization of the Improvements for their intended purposes have been completed or the presently installed and proposed roads and utilities will be sufficient for the full utilization of the Improvements for their intended purposes; and (v) the construction of the Improvements theretofore performed, if any, was performed in accordance with the Plans;

(s) Copies of all inspection and test records and reports made by or for Borrower's Architects;

(t) Copies of the applicable zoning resolutions, ordinances and map (marked to show the location of the Premises), certified by an appropriate official to be complete and accurate;

(u) Copies of any and all authorizations including plot plan and subdivision approvals, zoning variances, sewer, building and other permits required by Governmental Authorities for the construction, use, occupancy and operation of the Mortgaged Property or the Improvements for the purposes contemplated by the Plans in accordance with all applicable building, environmental, ecological, landmark, subdivision and zoning codes, laws and regulations;

(v) Letters from local utility companies or Governmental Authorities stating that gas, electric power, sanitary and storm sewer and water facilities and any other necessary utilities will be available to service the Premises in adequate capacities upon completion of construction of the Improvements, and that the same shall enter the Premises through public rights-of-way or through recorded private easements reviewed and approved by Lender;

(w) A site plan (showing all necessary approvals, utility connections and site improvements);

(x) A soil-engineer's report;

(y) An environmental site assessment;

(z) A copy of the Notice of Commencement prepared in accordance with Ohio Revised Code Section 1311.04 and to be recorded with the _______ County Recorder's Office immediately following the recording of the Mortgage; and

(aa) UCC searches against Borrower or other owner of the Mortgaged Property or any portion thereof and advice from the Title Insurer to the effect that searches of proper public records disclose no leases of personalty or financing statements filed or recorded against the Premises, Borrower or other owner of any portion of the Mortgaged Property.

ARTICLE IV

Conditions Precedent to Lender's Obligation to Make Advances After the Initial Advance

4.1 Lender's obligation to make Loan advances after the Initial Advance shall be subject to the satisfaction of the following conditions:

(a) Any requirement of Article III that has not been satisfied or waived in writing by Lender must be satisfied;

(b) Lender shall have received a Draw Request for the advance;

(c) Lender shall have received a continuation report or endorsement to the title policy insuring the Mortgage to the date of such advance, in the form approved by Lender and setting forth no additional exceptions except those approved by Lender;

(d) For any advance immediately subsequent to the completion of the foundation of any building, Lender shall have received a survey certified to Lender and the Title Insurer, indicating the location of each such foundation, and updated, with respect to all relevant requirements and information, to within ten (10) days of the advance;

(e) The representations and warranties made in Article V hereof shall be true and correct on and as of the date of the advance with the same effect as if made on such date;

(f) There shall exist no Event of Default, as therein defined under the Note or Mortgage, or any event or state of facts which after notice or the passage of time, or both, could give rise to such an Event of Default;

(g) Existing improvements on the Premises, if any, shall not have been materially injured or damaged by fire or other casualty unless Lender shall have received insurance proceeds sufficient in the reasonable judgment of Lender to effect the satisfactory restoration of the said improvements and to permit completion of said improvements prior to the Completion Date pursuant to terms of disbursement satisfactory to Lender; and

(h) Copies of any amended Notice of Commencement filed in accordance with Ohio Revised Code Section 1311.04.

4.2 In the case of the final Hard Costs advance as provided in Section 2.4 hereof, Lender shall also have received and approved:

(a) Evidence satisfactory to Lender to the effect that construction of the Improvements has been completed and any necessary utilities and roads have been finished and made available for use, in accordance with the Plans, and that all approvals have been received from all Governmental Authorities of the Improvements in their entirety for permanent occupancy, and of the contemplated uses thereof, to the extent any such approval is a condition of the lawful use and occupancy thereof;

(b) A current, final, "as built" survey of the Premises, certified to Lender and the Title Insurer, showing the completed Improvements;

(c) Certificate of substantial completion from Borrower's Architects; and

(d) Certificates by all tenants under Leases to the effect that the Improvements have been satisfactorily completed.

ARTICLE V

Borrower's Representations, Warranties and Covenants

5.1   Borrower represents and warrants that:

(a) If Borrower, any Guarantor or any general partner of Borrower or any Guarantor is a corporation, each such entity is duly organized, validly existing and in good standing under the laws of the state of its incorporation, has stock outstanding which has been duly and validly issued, is qualified to do business and is in good standing in the state in which the Premises are located with full power and authority to consummate the transactions contemplated hereby;

(b) If Borrower, Guarantor or any general partner of Borrower or any Guarantor is a partnership or venture, each such entity is duly formed and validly existing, is fully qualified under the laws of the state in which the Premises are located to do business therein, and has full power and authority to consummate the transactions contemplated hereby;

(c) The Plans are satisfactory to Borrower, have been reviewed and approved by each Guarantor, the General Contractor, the tenants under any Leases which require approval of the Plans, the purchasers under any sales contracts which require approval of the Plans, Borrower's Architects and, to the extent required by applicable law or any effective restrictive covenant, by all Governmental Authorities and the beneficiary of any such covenant; all construction, if any, already performed on the Improvements has been performed on the Premises in accordance with the Plans approved by the persons named above and with any restrictive covenants applicable thereto; there are no structural defects in the Improvements or violations of any requirement of any Governmental Authorities with respect thereto; the planned use of the Improvements complies with applicable zoning ordinances, regulations and restrictive covenants affecting the Premises as well as all environmental, ecological, landmark and other applicable laws and regulations; and all requirements for such use have been satisfied;

(d) Financial Statements have been heretofore delivered to Lender which are true, correct and current in all respects and which fairly present the respective financial conditions of the subjects thereof as of the respective dates thereof; no material adverse change has occurred in the financial conditions reflected therein since the respective dates thereof and no borrowings (other than the Loan) which might give rise to a lien or claim against the Mortgaged Property or Loan proceeds have been made by Borrower, any Guarantor or others since the date thereof;

(e) There are no actions, suits or proceedings pending, or to the knowledge of Borrower, threatened against or affecting Borrower, any Guarantor, the Premises, the validity or enforceability of the Mortgage or the priority of the lien thereof at law, in equity or before or by any Governmental Authorities; neither Borrower nor any Guarantor is in default with respect to any order, writ, injunction, decree or demand of any court or Governmental Authorities;

(f) The consummation of the transactions contemplated hereby and performance of this Agreement, the Note, Mortgage and Guaranty have not and will not result in any breach of, or constitute a default under, any mortgage, deed of trust, lease, bank loan or credit agreement, corporate charter, by-laws, partnership agreement or other instrument to which Borrower or any Guarantor is a party or by which any of them may be bound or affected;

(g) All utility services necessary for the construction of the Improvements and the operation thereof for their intended purposes are available in adequate capacities at the boundaries of the Premises, including water supply, storm and sanitary sewer, gas, electric power and telephone facilities, and all of such utility services enter the Premises through public rights-of-way or through recorded private easements reviewed and approved by Lender;

(h) Each Draw Request presented to Lender, and the receipt of the funds requested thereby, shall constitute an affirmation that the representations and warranties contained in Sections 5.1 and 5.2 remain true and correct as of the respective dates thereof;

(i) Borrower has entered into no contract or arrangement of any kind the performance of which by the other party thereto would give rise to a lien on the Mortgaged Property except for its arrangements with Borrower's Architects, the General Contractor, and Subcontractors who have been paid in full and have provided Lien Waivers for all payment due under said arrangements as of the end of the period covered by the last Draw Request;

(j) All roads necessary for the full utilization of the Improvements for their intended purposes have either been completed or the necessary rights-of-way therefor have been acquired by appropriate Governmental Authorities or dedicated to public use and accepted by said Governmental Authorities, and all necessary steps have been taken by Borrower and said Governmental Authorities to assure the complete construction and installation thereof no later than the Completion Date or any earlier date required by any law, order or regulation, or any Lease;

(k) Each of the Leases is unmodified and in full force and effect, there are no defaults under any provision thereof and all conditions to the effectiveness and continuing effectiveness thereof required to be satisfied as of the date hereof have been satisfied;

(*l*) There exists no Event of Default, as therein defined, under the Note or Mortgage, and no event or state of facts exists which after notice or the passage of time, or both, could give rise to an Event of Default thereunder;

(m) The approved Plans referred to in subsection ((c)) of this Section are the same as the filed plans referred to in the building permits for the Improvements;

(n) Borrower advised the Title Insurer in writing prior to the issuance of the title policy insuring the Mortgage whether any survey, soils-testing, site development, excavation or other work related to construction of the Improvements was begun or done before the Mortgage was recorded;

(o) No assessments (except installments not yet due and payable) of any nature will remain unpaid after the last Hard Costs advance, including, without limitation, assessments relating to streets, roads, entrances, waterlines, sanitary and storm sewers, gas lines and all other utilities including, without limitation, acreage fees and trunk sewers;

(p) Borrower shall indemnify and hold Lender harmless from all claims of every kind, of every person, including, without limitation, employees of Borrower, contractors and employees of contractors, tenants of Borrower, subtenants or concessionaires of any tenants, and employees and business invitees of any tenants, which claims arise from or out of the construction, use, occupancy or possession of the Improvements or the Mortgaged Property;

(q) The Mortgaged Property has not been damaged or injured as a result of any fire, explosion, accident, flood, gasoline or chemical leakage or other casualty;

(r) Borrower shall prepare and file a Notice of Commencement and amendments thereto as required under Ohio Revised Code Section 1311.04. Borrower represents and warrants that a Notice of Commencement has not been and will not be recorded prior to the recording of the Mortgage. Borrower shall post and keep posted the Notice of Commencement and all amendments thereto in a conspicuous place on the Premises during the course of construction of the Project. Borrower shall serve a copy of the Notice of Commencement and all amendments thereto on the original contractor in accordance with Ohio Revised Code Section 1311.04. Borrower further represents and warrants to timely comply with all provisions of Ohio Revised Code Section 1311.04 and failure to do so shall be deemed an Event of Default as defined under the Note and Mortgage;

(s) General Contractor and all Subcontractors have performed all work in connection with the Project for which they have been paid and General Contractor and all Subcontractors have been paid for all work in connection with the Project performed through the cutoff date of the immediately preceding Draw Request; and

(t) Borrower shall provide Lender with a copy of each Notice of Furnishing (as defined in Ohio Revised Code Section 1311.05) received by Borrower during the course of construction of any Improvements on the Premises.

5.2 Borrower covenants and agrees with Lender that Borrower will:

(a) Promptly comply with all laws, ordinances, orders, rules, statutes and regulations of Governmental Authorities and promptly furnish Lender with reports of any official searches made by Governmental Authorities and any claims of violations thereof;

(b) Permit Lender and its representatives to enter upon the Premises, inspect the Improvements and all materials to be used in the construction thereof and examine all detailed plans and shop drawings which are or may be kept at the construction site; Borrower will cooperate and cause the General Contractor and Subcontractors to cooperate with Lender to enable Lender to perform its inspections hereunder;

(c) Pay all Hard Costs and Soft Costs and expenses required for completion of the Improvements and the satisfaction of the conditions of this Agreement, including, without limitation:

> (i) all document and stamp taxes, recording and filing expenses and fees and commissions lawfully due to brokers in connection with the transactions contemplated hereby;

> (ii) the fees and expenses of Lender's counsel, in connection with the preparation for and consummation of the transactions contemplated hereby, and for any services of such parties which may be required in addition to those normally and reasonably contemplated hereby; and

> (iii) any taxes, insurance premiums, liens, security interests or other claims or charges against the Mortgaged Property;

(d) Commence construction of the Improvements no later than thirty (30) days from the date hereof; submit a Draw Request for the Initial Advance within thirty (30) days after such commencement and subsequent advances on a monthly basis thereafter; cause the construction thus begun to be prosecuted with diligence and continuity in a good and workmanlike manner in accordance with the Plans; use only materials, fixtures, furnishings and equipment in connection with construction of the Improvements that are not used or obsolete; and complete construction of the Improvements, and the installation of all necessary roads and utilities, in accordance with the Plans, on or before the Completion Date, free and clear of defects and liens or claims for liens for material supplied or labor or services performed in connection with the construction of the Improvements;

(e) Promptly following the execution of this Agreement, place a sign, at Borrower's own expense, on the Premises at a location satisfactory to Lender indicating, inter alia, that Lender is providing the "Construction Financing" and containing Lender's address and otherwise conforming to Lender's reasonable sign specifications;

(f) Receive and deposit in the Construction Loan Checking Account all advances made hereunder; hold the same and the right to receive the same as a trust fund for the purpose of paying only Hard Costs and Soft Costs;

(g) Indemnify Lender against claims of brokers arising by reason of the execution hereof or the consummation of the transactions contemplated hereby;

(h) Deliver to Lender copies of all contracts, bills of sale, statements, receipted vouchers and agreements under which Borrower claims title to any materials, fixtures or articles incorporated into the Improvements or subject to the lien of the Mortgage, or under which Borrower has incurred costs for which Borrower is entitled to a Loan advance, and deliver to Lender such other data or documents in connection with the Improvements as Lender may from time to time request;

(i) Upon demand of Lender, correct any defects (structural or otherwise) in the Improvements or any departures from the Plans not approved by Lender;

(j) Deliver to Lender a certified and correct copy of all Leases of the Premises whether executed before or after the date hereof and keep all of same in full force and effect in accordance with the covenants of Borrower contained in the Mortgage;

(k) Not permit the performance of any work pursuant to any Change Order until Lender: (i) shall have received a copy thereof; and (ii) in the case of Change Orders which will result in (A) a change in the aggregate of the contract prices for the construction of the Improvements in excess of the Single Change Order Amount or which, together with the aggregate of Change Orders theretofore executed by Borrower (excluding those approved by Lender pursuant to this subsection) will result in a change in such prices in excess of the Aggregate Change Order Amount or (B) a change in the character of the Improvements, shall have given specific written approval thereof; it being understood that approval of any Change Order will not obligate Lender to increase or advance any Loan Budget Amount on account of any such Change Order;

(*l*) Require covenants from the General Contractor to the same effect as the covenant made by Borrower in the immediately preceding subsection; and Borrower will provide in every General Contract that the General Contractor will deliver to Lender upon request of Lender, copies of all Subcontracts, Change Orders and any other contract, purchase order or subcontract covering labor, materials, equipment or furnishings to or for the Improvements, and the names of all persons with whom the General Contractor has contracted or intends to contract for the construction of the Improvements or for the furnishing of labor or materials therefor;

(m) Employ suitable means to protect from theft and vandalism all portions of the Improvements and all tools and building materials stored on the Premises; and

(n) Comply with all restrictions, covenants and easements affecting the Premises or the Improvements and cause the satisfaction of all conditions of this Agreement.

5.3 Borrower covenants that the representations and warranties made by it in Sections 5.1 and 5.2 hereof, and by each Guarantor in the Guaranty, will be continuously true and correct.

ARTICLE VI

General Conditions

6.1 The following conditions shall be applicable at all times during the term of the Loan:

(a) Any advance by Lender of Loan proceeds hereunder made prior to or without the fulfillment by Borrower of all of the conditions precedent thereto, whether or not known to Lender, shall not constitute a waiver by Lender of the requirement that all conditions, including the non-performed conditions, shall be required with respect to all future advances;

(b) All documentation and proceedings deemed by Lender to be necessary or required in connection with this Agreement and the documents relating hereto shall be subject to the prior approval of, and satisfactory to, Lender as to form and substance. In addition, the persons or parties responsible for the execution and delivery of, and signatories to, all of such documentation, shall be acceptable to, and subject to the approval of, Lender;

(c) If at any time Lender notifies Borrower that, in Lender's reasonable judgment, the undisbursed balance of the Loan is insufficient to pay the remaining Hard Costs and Soft Costs, Borrower shall either: (i) deposit with Lender an amount equal to such deficiency which Lender may from time to time apply, or allow Borrower to apply, to such Hard Costs and Soft Costs; or (ii) pay for such Hard Costs and Soft Costs in the amount of such deficiency so that the amount of the Loan which remains to be disbursed shall be sufficient to complete the Improvements, and Borrower shall furnish Lender with such evidence thereof as Lender shall require. Borrower hereby agrees that Lender shall have a lien on and security interest in any sums deposited pursuant to clause (i) above and that Borrower shall have no right to withdraw any such sums except for the payment of the aforesaid Hard Costs and Soft Costs as approved by Lender. Any such sums not used as provided in said clause (i) shall be released to Borrower when and to the extent that Lender determines that the amount thereof is more than the excess, if any, of the total remaining Hard Costs and Soft Costs of completion of the Improvements over the undisbursed balance of the Loan; provided, however, that should an Event of Default occur under the Note or Mortgage, Lender may, at its option, apply such amounts either to the costs of completion of the Improvements or to the immediate reduction of outstanding principal and/or interest under the Note;

(d) Upon the occurrence of any Event of Default under the Note or Mortgage, Borrower does hereby irrevocably authorize Lender to advance any undisbursed Loan proceeds directly to the General Contractor, Subcontractors and other persons to pay for completion of the Improvements but Lender is under no obligation to do so. No further direction or authorization from Borrower shall be necessary to warrant such direct advances and all such advances shall satisfy pro tanto the obligations of Lender hereunder and shall be secured by the Mortgage as fully as if made to Borrower regardless of the disposition thereof by the General Contractor, any Subcontractor or other person;

(e) All conditions of the obligation of Lender to make advances hereunder are imposed solely and exclusively for the benefit of Lender and may be freely waived or modified in whole or in part by Lender at any time if in its sole discretion it deems it advisable to do so, and no person other than Borrower (provided, however, that all conditions have been satisfied) shall have standing to require Lender to make any Loan advances or to be a beneficiary of this Agreement or any advances to be made hereunder. Any waiver or modification asserted by Borrower to have been agreed to by Lender must be in writing and comply with the provisions of subsection (h) of this Section;

(f) Borrower hereby irrevocably authorizes Lender to disburse proceeds of the Loan to pay: (i) interest accrued on the Note as it comes due; (ii) any and all commitment or loan fees; (iii) travel and inspection fees of Lender; (iv) fees and expenses of Lender's counsel; and (v) to satisfy any of the conditions of this Agreement; notwithstanding that Borrower may not have requested disbursement of such amounts and whether or not Borrower may be in default under the Note or Mortgage. Any such disbursements shall be added to the outstanding principal balance of the Note and shall be secured by the Mortgage. The authorization granted hereby shall not prevent Borrower from paying interest, or satisfying said conditions, from its own funds and shall in no event be construed so as to relieve Borrower from its obligation to pay interest as and when due under the Note, or to satisfy said conditions, or to obligate Lender to disburse Loan proceeds for the payment of interest or the satisfaction of said conditions;

(g) All notices to be given hereunder shall be sufficient if given in accordance with the provisions contained in Section 23 of the Mortgage;

(h) No provisions of the Note, Mortgage, UCC–1 Financing Statements, Guaranty or this Agreement may be changed, waived, discharged or terminated orally, by telephone or by any other means except an instrument in writing signed by the party against whom enforcement of the change, waiver, discharge or termination is sought;

(i) Except as herein provided, this Agreement shall be binding upon and inure to the benefit of Borrower and Lender and their respective heirs, personal representatives, successors and assigns. Notwithstanding the foregoing, Borrower, without the prior written consent of Lender, which consent may be withheld in Lender's sole discretion, may not assign, transfer or set over to another, in whole or in part, all or any part of its benefits, rights, duties and obligations hereunder, including, without limitation, performance of and compliance with conditions hereof and the right to receive the proceeds of current or future advances; and

(j) Borrower acknowledges that Borrower has selected or will select all architects, engineers, contractors, subcontractors, materialmen, and others furnishing services or materials for the Improvements and that Lender shall have no responsibility whatsoever for them or for any inspection reports or for the quality of their materials or workmanship. It is understood that Lender's sole function is that of lender and that the only consideration passing from Lender to Borrower are the Loan proceeds in accordance with and subject to the terms of this Agreement. Borrower shall have no right to rely on any procedures required by Lender herein, such procedures being solely for the benefit and protection of Lender.

6.2   The cover page and the Exhibits annexed hereto are incorporated as a part of this Agreement with the same effect as if set forth in the body hereof.

IN WITNESS WHEREOF, the parties have executed this Agreement as of the day and year first above written, the execution hereof by Borrower constituting: (a) a certification by the party or parties executing on its behalf that the representations and warranties made in Article V are true and correct as of the date hereof and that each of them duly holds and is incumbent in the position indicated under his name; and (b) the undertaking of said party or parties that each Draw Request, whether or not personally made by any or all of them, shall constitute the personal affirmation on the part of each of them that at the time thereof said representations and warranties are true and correct.

LENDER: BORROWER:

_______________________________   _______________________________

A National Banking Association

By: _________________________   By: _________________________

Its: _________________________   Its: _________________________

EXHIBIT "A"

PROJECT BUDGET

EXHIBIT "B"

Pending disbursement of the full proceeds of the loan secured by the mortgage set forth under Schedule A hereof, this policy insures only to the extent of the amount actually disbursed, but increases as each disbursement is made up to the face amount of the policy. However, if disbursements are made which the holder of such mortgage was not obligated to make after holder's receipt of a written notice of a lien or encumbrance or of work or labor performed or to be performed or of machinery, material or fuel furnished or to be furnished as provided in Section 5301.232 of the Ohio Revised Code, said mortgage, to the extent of said disbursements, shall be subordinate to the lien or encumbrance specified in such notice or to a valid mechanic's lien for the work or labor actually performed or machinery, material or fuel actually furnished as specified in such notice.

DOCUMENT #6

OFFICE LEASE—EXPENSE STOP

■ ■ ■

OFFICE LEASE

Between

____

("Landlord")

And

____

("Tenant")

Project: _______________

This form is based on an office lease that I used during my stint as General Counsel for the Pizzuti Companies. I intentionally used a small font (10 pt.) in an effort to keep the main text of the lease document under ten pages—a perceived marketing advantage in the markets in which Pizzuti was then doing business.

LEASE SUMMARY

A. **Date of Execution:** ______, 20___.

B. **Landlord:** ___________.

C. **Address of Landlord:** ___________.

D. **Tenant:** ___________.

E. **Address of Tenant:** ___________.

F. **Building:** The office building located at ______ in ______, ______, together with the approximately ______ acre tract of land on which the building is located. The Building contains approximately ______ square feet of rentable space.

G. **Leased Premises:** That portion of the Building outlined on Exhibit A and known as Suite #___. The Leased Premises is deemed to contain ______ square feet of rentable space.

H. **Permitted Use:** ___________.

I. **Initial Lease Term:** ______ years, commencing on the Commencement Date and terminating on the Termination Date. The "Lease Term" will include the Initial Lease Term, plus the term(s) applicable to any extension options which are expressly granted to Tenant in this Lease and which are exercised by Tenant in strict accordance with the provisions of this Lease.

J. **Commencement Date:** ______ (subject to deferral per § 9 of the Lease).

K. **Termination Date:** ______ (subject to deferral per § 9 of the Lease).

L. **Extension Option:** ______ —See Exhibit E.

M. **Base Rent:**

Lease Period	**Annual Base Rent**	**Monthly Base Rent**

N. **Base Year:** The 20__ calendar year.

O. **Base Expenses:** The Building Expenses incurred by Landlord in the Base Year.

P. **Tenant's Proportionate Share:** ___________%.

Q. **Tenant Improvement Allowance:** $___________.

R. **Security Deposit:** $___________.

S. **Guarantor:** ___________.

T. **Guarantor's Address:** ___________.

U. **Real Estate Brokers:** ______ (commission to be paid by ______).

The following exhibits are attached to and made a part of the Lease:

    Exhibit A   Description of Leased Premises
    Exhibit B   List of Operating Expenses
    Exhibit C   Building Rules and Regulations
    Exhibit D   Landlord's Work
    Exhibit E   Special Terms

THE PROVISIONS OF THIS LEASE SUMMARY ARE INCORPORATED BY THIS REFERENCE INTO THE LEASE.

OFFICE LEASE

Landlord hereby leases the Leased Premises to Tenant for the duration of the Lease Term. The leasing of the Leased Premises to Tenant will be upon the terms and conditions set forth in this Lease and the attached Lease Summary.

§ 1. Base Rent. Tenant will pay Base Rent in the amount set forth in the Lease Summary.

§ 2. Excess Expense Payments. For each full or partial calendar year included within the Lease Term after the Base Year identified in the Lease Summary ("Comparison Year"), Tenant will pay as additional rent its Proportionate Share of the excess, if any, of the Building Expenses incurred by Landlord during such Comparison Year over the Base Expenses identified in the Lease Summary ("Excess Expenses"). Those expenses which are included within the definition of "Building Expenses" are set forth in Exhibit B. Tenant's Proportionate Share of such Excess Expenses will be paid by Tenant in advance based upon Landlord's estimate of the Excess Expenses which will be incurred during each Comparison Year during the Lease Term. Landlord will use its best efforts to notify Tenant by December 1 of each calendar year during the Lease Term of the amount of the estimated Excess Expense payment which Tenant will be required to make for each month of the upcoming Comparison Year.

As soon as reasonably practicable after the end of each Comparison Year, Landlord will deliver to Tenant a written statement showing its actual Building Expenses for such Comparison Year and Tenant's actual Proportionate Share of the Excess Expenses. If the sum of the estimated Excess Expense payments paid by Tenant during such Calendar Year exceeds Tenant's Proportionate Share of the actual Excess Expenses incurred during such Comparison Year, then Landlord will refund such excess amount to Tenant within ten days after the date on which the amount of such Excess Expenses are actually determined. If the sum of the estimated Excess Expense payments paid by Tenant during such Comparison Year is less than Tenant's Proportionate Share of the actual Excess Expenses incurred during such Comparison Year, then Tenant will pay the deficiency to Landlord within ten days after Tenant's receipt of Landlord's written demand for the payment thereof. If the Lease Term begins on a day other than January 1 or expires on a date other than December 31, then Tenant's Proportionate Share of the Excess Expenses for the first and last Comparison Year during which the Lease Term is in effect will be prorated to take into consideration the number of days during such Comparison Year in which the Lease Term is in effect.

§ 3. Manner and Timing of Rent Payments. Monthly installments of Base Rent and Excess Expenses will be due and payable in advance on or before the first day of each calendar month during the Lease Term. Each such installment will be paid to Landlord by electronic funds transfer to an account designated by Landlord (or by such other means as Landlord may designate from time to time). If the Lease Term commences on a day other than the first day of a calendar month or terminates on a day other than the last day of a calendar month, then the amount of the installments of Base Rent and Excess Expenses payable by Tenant for any such partial calendar month will be prorated to take into consideration the number of days during such calendar month in which the Lease Term is in effect. If any installment of Base Rent or Excess Expenses or any other sum payable under this Lease is not received by Landlord on or before its due date, then a late payment charge of 5% of such past due amount will be assessed and will be immediately due and payable from Tenant. In addition, if any such installment, payment or sum is not received by Landlord within ten days after its due date, then the unpaid amount will thereafter accrue interest until paid at a rate equal to four percent in excess of the rate from time to time announced as its prime lending rate by Bank of America (or its successor). Landlord's acceptance of any payment which constitutes less than all of the balance then owed to it by Tenant will be treated as its receipt of a payment "on account" and not as an accord and satisfaction and landlord may accept any such payment (regardless of the existence of any endorsement or statement to the contrary contained on any check or letter accompanying such payment) without prejudice to Landlord's rights to recover the balance of the amount owed to it by Tenant or to pursue any other remedy provided to it under this Lease. All installments of Base Rent and Excess Expenses and every other sum payable under this Lease will be paid by Tenant without notice or demand and without reduction, abatement, counterclaim or offset in any amount or for any reason whatsoever, including, without limitation, any alleged default by Landlord in the performance of its obligations under this Lease.

§ 4. Services. Landlord will provide all utility, HVAC, janitorial and elevator services that are required for the use of the Leased Premises for general office purposes during normal business hours (7:00 a.m. to 6:00 p.m. Monday through Friday, and 8:00 a.m. to noon on Saturday, national holidays excepted). Notwithstanding the foregoing, Tenant will contract directly for and pay all costs related to the provision of telephone and other telecommunication services to the Leased Premises.

If Tenant's usage of any such service is excessive when compared to the normal, anticipated usage of other tenants in the Building or if the nature of Tenant's business requires the provision of any such service outside of normal business hours or at a level in excess of that normally provided for the Building, then, in either such event, Tenant agrees to pay a service surcharge to Landlord in an amount which Landlord determines fairly reflects Tenant's excessive or after-hours usage of such service. Landlord will not be liable to Tenant, nor will Tenant be relieved of any obligation hereunder by reason of constructive eviction or any other legal theory or claim if any service to the Leased Premises is interrupted for any reason beyond Landlord's reasonable control.

§ 5. **Maintenance and Repair**. Landlord will maintain, repair and replace the common areas and all Base Building Improvements located within the Leased Premises in good condition and order; provided, however, that Tenant (and not Landlord) will be required to pay all costs of maintaining, repairing and replacing the same if the need therefore arises due to the fault or negligence of Tenant or its agents, employees or guests. Landlord's cost s of maintaining, repairing and replacing the common areas and Base Building Improvements will be reimbursable by Tenant in accordance with the provisions of § 2 and Exhibit B. Except as otherwise expressly set forth in this § 5, Tenant will be responsible and pay for all costs associated with maintaining, repairing and replacing the interior of the Leased Premises in good condition and order, including, without limitation, all costs associated with the painting of interior walls, the cleaning or replacing of wall coverings and floor coverings and the replacing of light bulbs and light fixtures. Landlord will not be liable to Tenant, nor will Tenant be relieved of any obligation hereunder if Tenant's use of the Leased Premises is interrupted as a result of Landlord's required entry into the Leased Premises for the purpose of making any repairs, alterations or improvements to any element or system located within the Leased Premises (including, without limitation, the HVAC system).

§ 6. **Use of Leased Premises**. Tenant will use the Leased Premises solely for the Permitted Use and for no other purpose. Tenant will not cause or permit any waste or damage to the Leased Premises or the Building and will not occupy or use the Leased Premises for any business or purpose which is unlawful, hazardous, unsanitary, noxious or offensive or which unreasonably interferes with the business operations of other tenants in the Building. Tenant will comply with the Rules and Regulations for the Building which are set forth in Exhibit C (and any modifications or additions thereto which are not inconsistent with the provisions of this Lease). Tenant will also have the non-exclusive right to use the common areas which serve the Building, including, without limitation, the Building's common lobbies, hallways, elevators, risers, restrooms, parking areas and sidewalks. Landlord reserves the right to change the size, use, shape or nature of the Building and its common areas and to expand or add on to the Building and to construct additional improvements in the common areas, so long as any such action by Landlord does not permanently deprive Tenant of the substantial benefit and enjoyment of the Leased Premises.

§ 7. **Compliance with Law**. Tenant will, at its sole expense, comply with all laws, governmental requirements and recorded covenants or conditions which are now or hereafter in force pertaining to Tenant's occupancy and use of the Leased Premises, including, without limitation, the Americans with Disabilities Act.

§ 8. **Signs**. Tenant will not place any sign or other advertising material on the exterior of the Leased Premises or the Building, without the prior written consent of Landlord. Landlord will, at its expense, provide Tenant with the Building's standard graphics and signage for identification of Tenant on the first floor business directory and the entranceway to the Leased Premises.

§ 9. **Leasehold Improvements**. Attached to this Lease as Exhibit D are the preliminary plans and specifications for the improvements to be made to the Leased Premises ("Improvements"). Exhibit D also lists those "Base Building Improvements" which have been or will be made to the Leased Premises by Landlord, but which will not be charged against the Tenant Improvement Allowance provided to Tenant hereunder (as the amount of such Tenant Improvement Allowance is set forth in the Lease Summary).

Promptly following the parties' execution of this Lease, Landlord will proceed with the preparation of the final architectural and engineering drawings, plans and specifications for the Improvements. Once those drawings, plans and specifications are completed, Landlord will deliver a full set thereof to Tenant for its review and approval, with any objections to be made by Tenant to anything contained therein being limited to any objections it may have which are premised solely upon the fact that such drawings, plans and specifications are inconsistent with the preliminary specifications which are delineated in Exhibit D. The approved final drawings, plans and specifications ("Final Plans") will be deemed incorporated herein by this reference.

If the cost of constructing the Improvements in accordance with the approved Final Plans (as such cost is determined by Landlord's general contractor) exceeds the amount of the Tenant Improvement Allowance, then, in such event, Tenant will pay any such excess costs within ten days after Landlord's written demand for the payment thereof. If, following the approval of the Final Plans, Tenant expresses a desire to make any revisions thereto, Tenant will so notify Landlord and Landlord will then ask its general contractor to prepare a cost estimate for the making of such changes. Landlord will promptly notify Tenant of any increased costs resulting from such changes and Tenant will have the right to require Landlord to cause such a change to be made to the Final Plans; provided, however, that such changes will not unreasonably affect the exterior aesthetics, structural integrity or value of the Building. If the aggregate of all such changes results in a net increase in the cost of the construction of the Improvements, (net of any savings), then Tenant will pay such net increase to Landlord within ten days after Landlord's written demand for the payment thereof.

Landlord will cause the Improvements to be constructed in accordance with the Final Plans. Landlord will use its best efforts to substantially complete construction of the Improvements on or before the targeted Commencement Date set forth in the Lease Summary, subject to delays caused by the occurrence of any event which is beyond Landlord's reasonable control, including, without limitation, labor disputes, civil commotion, war or war-like operations, sabotage, governmental regulations or controls, unseasonable weather, fire or other casualty, inability to obtain any material or service or any act of God ("Delay Events"). The establishment of the substantial completion date referred in the immediately preceding sentence is further predicated upon Tenant's timely review and approval of all plans, specifications and other matters submitted to it for its review and approval pursuant to the provisions of this § 9. Tenant agrees that it will review and either approve or specify its objections to any documents or drawings submitted to it for its review and approval hereunder within five days after its receipt of the same. If Tenant fails to respond to any submission to it within five days after its receipt of same, then it will be deemed to have approved the same for all the purposes of this Lease.

If the Improvements are not substantially completed on or before the target Commencement Date set forth in the Lease Summary, then the Commencement Date will be deferred until the date on which the Improvements are substantially completed and the Termination Date will be deferred by the number of days equal to the deferral in the Commencement Date. Notwithstanding anything to the contrary contained herein, if Landlord's inability to substantially complete the improvements on or before the targeted Commencement Date set forth in the Lease Summary is attributable to Tenant-caused delays (including, without limitation, Tenant's failure to timely respond to any manner submitted for its review or delays caused by Tenant's requested change orders), then the Commencement Date will remain as set forth in the Lease Summary, notwithstanding the fact that the Improvements are not yet substantially completed, and Tenant will, from and after the stated Commencement Date, have an obligation to pay Base Rent, Excess Expenses and all other sums payable by it under this Lease and perform all of its other obligations and duties set forth in this Lease. For the purposes of this Lease, the Improvements will be deemed substantially completed on the date on which a temporary or permanent certificate of occupancy for the Improvements is issued by the appropriate governmental authority.

§ 10. Alterations. Except for "Minor Alterations" (as that term is hereinafter defined), Tenant will not at any time prior to or during the Lease Term make any alterations, additions or improvements to the Leased Premises, without the prior written consent of Landlord. For the purposes of this section, "Minor Alterations" will mean any alteration, addition or improvements to the Leased Premises, which costs less than $5,000 and which does not alter the exterior aesthetics or structural integrity of the Building. All improvements, alterations and additions made at one time in connection with any one job will be aggregated for the purposes of determining whether the $5,000 limit has been exceeded. All alterations, additions or improvements made to the Leased Premises (expressly including those made pursuant to this section, as well as the Improvements and Base Building Improvements made by Landlord pursuant to § 9 and Exhibit D) will at all times remain the property of Landlord and will remain as part of the Leased Premises upon the expiration of the Lease Term.

§ 11. Mechanics Liens. Tenant will indemnify and hold Landlord harmless from any liability or expense associated with Tenant's construction of any alteration, addition or improvement to the Leased Premises. Tenant will immediately discharge or bond off any mechanics lien filed against the Leased Premises or the Building in connection with any work performed by Tenant.

§ 12. **Assignment and Subleasing**. Tenant may not assign this Lease or sublet all or any part of the Leased Premises without the prior written consent of Landlord. Unless otherwise expressly agreed to by Landlord, Landlord's consent to any such assignment or sublease will not relieve the "Tenant" named in the Lease Summary from its obligations under this Lease.

§ 13. **Subordination/Estoppel Certificate**. Tenant's rights and interest under this Lease are subordinate to all mortgages and other encumbrances now or hereafter affecting any portion of the Building; provided, however, that the holder of any such mortgage or encumbrance will have the unilateral right to elect to grant priority to Tenant's rights and interests under this Lease over the rights and interests of such holder. In the event of the foreclosure of any mortgage or other encumbrance, Tenant will, upon request of any person succeeding to the interest of Landlord, attorn to and automatically become the tenant of such successor without change in the terms or conditions of this Lease; provided, however, that such successor shall not be liable for any act or omission of any prior landlord or subject to any offsets or defenses which Tenant may have against any such prior landlord. This paragraph will be self-operative and no further instrument will be required to effect the subordination provided for herein. Tenant may not terminate this Lease because of any default by Landlord, unless Tenant first gives written notice of the alleged default to any mortgagee of Landlord whose name and address have been provided to Tenant, and such mortgagee fails to cure such default within 30 days after its receipt of such written notice.

Within ten days after its receipt of a written request for the same from Landlord, Tenant will execute and deliver to Landlord a written estoppel certificate certifying to Landlord and any other person designated by Landlord that (a) the Lease is unmodified and in full force and effect, without any default on the part of Landlord thereunder and (b) such other matters concerning the status of the Lease and Tenant's occupancy of the Leased Premises as are reasonably requested by Landlord. If Tenant fails to deliver an estoppel certificate to Landlord within the aforementioned ten day period, then Tenant will be liable to Landlord for all damages incurred by Landlord as a result of such failure by Tenant, including, without limitation, loss of profits and consequential damages.

§ 14. **Limitation of Landlord's Personal Liability**. Tenant will look solely to Landlord's interest in the Building (including, without limitation, all insurance proceeds or condemnation awards paid with respect to the Building) for the recovery of any judgment against Landlord; it being the express intent of the parties hereto that neither Landlord, nor any of its partners, members, affiliates, shareholders, officers or employees will ever be personally liable for any such judgment. Landlord's obligations hereunder will be binding upon Landlord only for the period of time that Landlord is the fee simple owner of the Building. Upon termination of that ownership, Tenant will look solely to Landlord's successor-in-interest in the Building for the satisfaction of each and every obligation of the "Landlord" hereunder.

§ 15. **Indemnification and Insurance**. Landlord will not be liable for and Tenant hereby releases Landlord from any liability or expense associated with any damage or injury to any person or property (including any person or property of Tenant or anyone claiming by, through or under Tenant) which arises directly or indirectly in connection with the Leased Premises or Tenant's use or occupancy of the Leased Premises or any common areas serving the Building. Tenant will indemnify and hold Landlord harmless from any of the above-described liabilities and expenses. Landlord will not be responsible or liable to Tenant or to anyone claiming by, through or under Tenant for any injury, loss or damage that may be occasioned by or through the acts or omissions of persons occupying other leased space in the Building.

Tenant will, at its sole expense, maintain in full force and effect at all times during the Lease Term: (a) commercial general liability insurance for personal injury and property damage with liability limits of not less than $2,000,000 for injury to one person, $5,000,000 for injury from one occurrence and $1,000,000 for property damage; and (b) commercial property insurance (a Causes of Loss—Special Form policy, with coverage extended to cover floods and earthquakes) on all property stored or placed by Tenant in or about the Leased Premises in an amount equal to the full replacement value thereof. All insurance required to be maintained by Tenant under this section will be issued by insurance companies having a policyholder rating of at least "A" and a financial size category of at least "Class X" under the A.M/ Best's Key Rating Guide for insurance companies (or any comparable rating under any successor publication or index). The commercial general liability insurance policy required to be maintained by Tenant hereunder will name Landlord as an additional insured and will specifically provide that such insurance policy cannot be terminated without giving at least 30 days prior written notice to Landlord. Prior to the Commencement Date, Tenant will furnish Landlord with a certificate of insurance showing compliance with the insurance requirements set forth in this section.

Landlord will, at its initial expense, but as a Building Expense subject to being passed through to Tenant under § 2 hereof, maintain in full force and effect at all times during the Lease Term: (a) commercial property insurance (a Cause of Loss—Special Form policy, with coverage extended to cover floods and earthquakes) on the Building in an amount equal to the full replacement value thereof; (b) commercial general liability insurance for personal injury and property damage with limits of not less than $2,000,000 for injury to one person, $5,000,000 for injury from one occurrence and $1,000,000 for property damage; and (c) rental loss insurance. Any insurance required to be carried by Landlord may be provided under a blanket policy (or policies covering other properties of Landlord or its related or affiliated entities).

§ 16. **Waiver of Subrogation**. Landlord and Tenant each hereby waives its right to receive damages against the other party with respect to any loss or claim occasioned by the occurrence of any hazard or peril covered by any insurance policy required to be carried under the provisions of this Lease to the extent of the amount of insurance proceeds that the damaged party is entitled to receive under any such insurance policy; provided, however, that the foregoing waiver will not be applicable to the portion of any loss or claim which is not reimbursable by the damaged party's insurer because of any "deductible" permitted under such insurance policy. Any insurance policy procured by either Tenant or Landlord hereunder will contain an express waiver of any right of subrogation by the insurance company against Landlord or Tenant, as the case may be.

§ 17. **Hazardous Substances**. Tenant will not use, store or dispose of any "Hazardous Substance", (as that term is hereinafter defined) on or about the Leased Premises, except for immaterial amounts that are exempt from or do not give rise to any violation of applicable law. Tenant will indemnify and hold Landlord harmless from any liability or expense (including, without limitation, reasonable attorney's fees and expenses, court costs, expenses and costs incurred in the investigation, settlement and defense of claims and any cost or expense incurred in connection with any environmental clean-up) incurred by or claimed against Landlord as a result of Tenant's breach of the covenant contained in this section. For the purposes of this section, the term "Hazardous Substance" will mean any "hazardous" or "toxic" substance (as those terms are defined in the Comprehensive Environmental Response Compensation Liability Act) "hazardous waste" (as that term is defined in the Resource Conservation Recovery Act), polychlorinated biphenyls, asbestos, radioactive material or any other pollutant, contaminant or hazardous, dangerous or toxic chemical, material or substance, which is regulated by any federal, state or local law, regulation, ordinance or requirement. All of the indemnifications contained in this section will survive the expiration or sooner termination of the Lease Term.

§ 18. **Surrender of Premises**. Upon the expiration or sooner termination of the Lease Term, Tenant will immediately surrender possession of the Leased Premises to Landlord in good repair and "broom clean" condition, reasonable wear and tear and damage by fire or other casualty excepted. Tenant will at the same time remove all of its movable trade fixtures from the Leased Premises. Tenant will promptly repair any damage caused to the Leased Premises by the removal of any of such property.

§ 19. **Casualty**. Except as otherwise provided in this section, if the Building or the Leased Premises is damaged by fire or other casualty, then Landlord will proceed to repair the damaged area at its sole expense; provided, however, that Landlord will in no event be required to repair or replace any property owned by Tenant or any alterations, additions or improvements made to the Leased Premises by or at the request of Tenant pursuant to § 10. If the Leased Premises are rendered untenantable in whole or in part as a result of a fire or other casualty, then all rent and other payments accruing after the occurrence of any such fire or other casualty and prior to the completion of the repair of the Leased Premises will be equitably and proportionately abated to reflect the untenantable portion of the Leased Premises. Landlord will not be liable to Tenant for any inconvenience or interruption to Tenant's business occasioned by such fire or other casualty or the concomitant repair of the damaged area.

Notwithstanding anything to the contrary contained herein, if the occurrence of any fire or other casualty renders more than 50% of the rentable square footage of the Leased Premises untenantable and if Landlord reasonably determines that the damaged portion of the Leased Premises cannot be reasonably repaired within 180 days after the date on which all requisite permits and licenses for the repair thereof are obtained from the appropriate governmental authorities, then Tenant will have the right to terminate this Lease by delivering written notice of termination to Landlord within 30 days after Tenant's receipt of written determination from Landlord that the damaged portion of the Leased Premises cannot be so repaired within such 180 day period; provided, however, that Tenant will not have any such right to terminate this Lease if the fire or other casualty was caused by the negligence or willful misconduct of Tenant or any of its employees, agents, guests or invitees. In addition, if the Building is "substantially damaged" (as that term is hereinafter defined) by fire or other casualty, then Landlord may terminate this Lease by giving written notice to Tenant within 90 days after the occurrence of such fire or other casualty. For the purposes of this § 19, the Building will be deemed "substantially damaged" if Landlord reasonably determines that the cost of repairing the damaged area is greater than 50% of the replacement value of the Building immediately prior to the occurrence of such casualty.

§ 20. **Condemnation**. If all or any substantial portion of the Building or the means or access to the Building is taken by or under threat of condemnation so as to render the Leased Premises wholly untenantable, then this Lease will automatically terminate as of the date of the vesting of title to such property in the condemning authority. If such taking does not render the Leased Premises wholly untenantable, then this Lease will not terminate but will continue in full force and effect in accordance with its terms and Landlord will promptly take all reasonably practicable steps to constitute the Building as a complete architectural unit. Landlord will not be liable to Tenant for any inconvenience or interruption to Tenant's business occasioned by any such taking. Landlord will be entitled to receive the entire award made by the condemning authority for any such taking; provided, however, that Tenant will have the right to seek and receive a separate award (so long as it does not diminish the amount of the award otherwise payable to Landlord) for any damage to Tenant's personal property and for Tenant's moving expenses.

§ 21. **Holding Over**. Tenant will not hold over in its occupancy of the Leased Premises after the expiration of the Lease Term, without the prior written consent of Landlord. If Tenant holds over in its occupancy of the Leased Premises after the expiration of the Lease Term, Tenant will pay 200% of the Base Rent and Estimated Operating Expense Payment in effect for the last month of the Lease Term. Tenant will also be required to pay Landlord all damages sustained by reason of Tenant's holding over after the expiration of the Lease Term (including, without limitation, all damages caused by Landlord's loss of any prospective tenancy resulting from Tenant's holdover hereunder).

§ 22. **Default**. If Tenant fails to pay any installment of Base Rent or Excess Expenses or any other sum payable by it hereunder within ten days after Tenant's receipt of written notice from Landlord that any such sum is due and unpaid, or if Tenant defaults in the performance of any of its other obligations under this Lease and such default continues for 30 days after written notice thereof is received by Tenant, then, in addition to any other legal rights and remedies available to Landlord at law or in equity, Landlord may: (a) terminate this Lease and all rights and interests of Tenant hereunder (including Tenant's right of possession under this Lease) and declare immediately due and payable as liquidated damages the amount by which Landlord's commercially reasonable estimate of the aggregate amount of Base Rent, Excess Expenses and other sums payable by Tenant under this Lease for the remainder of the Lease Term, exceeds Landlord's commercially reasonable estimate of the fair rental value of the Leased Premises for the same period (after giving effect to the time needed to relct the Leased Premises and the costs which Landlord might have to incur in connection with any such reletting, including, without limitation, brokerage commissions, tenant improvement costs and other tenant allowances and concessions), with both amounts being discounted to present value using a discount rate of 4%; or (b) terminate Tenant's right of possession of the Leased Premises without terminating this Lease and re-enter and attempt to relet the Leased Premises, in which event Tenant will remain obligated to pay to Landlord any deficiency between all sums payable by Tenant pursuant to this Lease and any sums collected by Landlord from any reletting of the Leased Premises (net of any sums paid by Landlord in connection with such reletting, including, without limitation, brokerage commissions, tenant improvement costs and other tenant allowances and concessions).

§ 23. **Quiet Enjoyment**. Landlord covenants and agrees with Tenant that, upon Tenant paying all sums required to be paid by it hereunder and performing all of the other terms and conditions required to be performed by it hereunder, Tenant may peacefully and quietly enjoy the Leased Premises during the Lease Term, free from any interference by Landlord, subject, nonetheless, to the terms of this Lease and to any mortgage, ground lease or other agreement to which this Lease is subordinated.

§ 24. **Prevailing Party's Fees**. If any legal action is commenced by either Landlord or Tenant, to enforce its rights hereunder, then all attorneys' fees, paralegal fees and other costs and expenses incurred by the prevailing party in such action will be promptly paid by the non-prevailing party.

§ 25. <u>Successors and Assigns</u>. This Lease will be binding upon and inure to the benefit of the successors and assigns of Landlord and the permitted successors and permitted assigns of Tenant.

§ 26. <u>No Waiver</u>. No waiver of any covenant or condition of this Lease by either party will be deemed to constitute a future waiver of the same or any other covenant or condition of this Lease. In order to be effective, any such waiver must be in writing and must be delivered to the other party to this Lease.

§ 27. <u>Brokerage Commissions</u>. Each of Landlord and Tenant hereby represents and warrants that it has not dealt or consulted with any real estate broker or agent in connection with this Lease, other than those real estate brokers specifically identified in the Lease Summary. The commissions payable to any real estate broker identified in the Lease Summary will be paid by the party (that is, Landlord or Tenant) identified in Lease Summary. Each of Landlord and Tenant agrees to indemnify and hold the other harmless from and against any liability or expense occasioned by a breach of the foregoing representation and warranty.

§ 28. <u>Relocation</u>. Landlord will have the right to relocate Tenant to other space in the Building, so long as the size, configuration, improvements and amenities of the new space are substantially similar to those of the Leased Premises. Landlord will pay all reasonable expenses incurred by Tenant in connection with the relocation of its space. Landlord will effect such relocation in a manner intended to minimize any interference with Tenant's business operations. If such a relocation occurs, this Lease will continue in full force and effect without any change in the terms and conditions thereof, except that the new space will thereafter be substituted as the Leased Premises for the purposes of this Lease and, if the new space is smaller or larger than the initial Leased Premises, then the Base Rent and Tenant's Proportionate Share of Operating Expense will be proportionately decreased or increased, as the case may be.

§ 29. <u>Reasonableness of Consent</u>. Neither Landlord nor Tenant will unreasonably withhold, delay or condition any consent or approval which is required to be given by it pursuant to the terms of this Lease.

§ 30. <u>Amendment</u>. This Lease may not be amended except by a written instrument signed by both Landlord and Tenant.

§ 31. <u>Governing Law</u>. This Lease will be governed by and construed in accordance with the laws of the State of ________.

§ 32. <u>Notices</u>. All notices required or permitted under this Lease must be in writing and must be delivered to Landlord and Tenant at their addresses set forth in the Lease Summary (or such other address as may hereafter be designated by such party). Any such notice must be personally delivered or sent by either registered or certified mail, fax or overnight courier.

§ 33. <u>Security Deposit</u>. Concurrently with its execution of this Lease, Tenant has deposited with Landlord a Security Deposit in the amount identified in the Lease Summary. The Security Deposit will be retained by Landlord as partial security for Tenant's performance of all its obligations under this Lease. If Tenant defaults in the performance of any of its obligations under this Lease, then Landlord will have the right to use all or a portion of the Security Deposit to cure such default and Tenant will immediately deposit additional sums with Landlord in an amount sufficient to restore the Security Deposit to its original amount. Any portion of the Security Deposit remaining unutilized following the expiration of the Lease Term and Tenant's full performance of all its obligations under this Lease will be returned to Tenant without interest.

§ 34. <u>Financial Statements</u>. On or before April 1 of each year during the Lease Term, Tenant will provide Landlord with its then most current financial statements (a balance sheet, statement of cash flows and income and loss statement). Each such financial statement will be certified as being true and correct by an authorized officer of Tenant. The provisions of this section will not apply during any period that Tenant is subject to the reporting requirements of § 13 or § 15(d) of the Securities Exchange Act of 1934, as amended, and in accordance therewith files periodic reports with the Securities and Exchange Commission.

§ 35. <u>Memorandum of Lease</u>. If requested by either Landlord or Tenant, the other party to this Lease will execute a memorandum of lease which complies with the statutory requirements of § ___ of ________ and which otherwise sets forth only the following information—(a) the names and addresses of Landlord and Tenant, (b) the address of the Leased Premises, (c) the commencement and termination dates of the initial lease term and any extension term(s) specifically set forth in the Lease and (d) such other information as is mutually acceptable to Landlord and Tenant. The requesting party may, at its expense, record the executed memorandum of lease in the public real estate records of the jurisdiction in which the Building is located

§ **36.** **Special Terms**. Exhibit E sets forth those special provisions, if any, which supplement and modify the provisions of this Lease Agreement.

[Signatures and Acknowledgements Appear on Next Page]

SIGNATURES AND ACKNOWLEDGEMENTS

Landlord and Tenant have executed this Lease as of the date specified in the Lease Summary.

LANDLORD:

____

By _______________________________________
        (Name)   (Title)

TENANT:

____

By _______________________________________
        (Name)   (Title)

STATE OF _________
COUNTY OF _______ : SS

Before me, a notary public in and for said state and county, personally appeared _______, the _______ of the Landlord in the foregoing Lease, who acknowledged the signing of the Lease to be his or her free act and deed on behalf of the Landlord.

Date: ______________   ______________
                                Notary Public

STATE OF _________
COUNTY OF _______ : SS

Before me, a notary public in and for said state and county, personally appeared _______, the _______ of the Tenant in the foregoing Lease, who acknowledged the signing of the Lease to be his or her free act and deed on behalf of Tenant.

Date: ______________   ______________
                                Notary Public

<u>**EXHIBIT A**</u>

<u>DESCRIPTION OF LEASED PREMISES</u>

See floor plan(s) attached hereto as Schedule A–1.

       Initialed and Approved by   Initialed and Approved by
       Landlord: Tenant:

       _______________________________   _______________________________

EXHIBIT B

LIST OF BUILDING EXPENSES

The following are those expenses which are included within the definition of "Building Expenses":

1. Costs of maintaining, repairing and replacing the Building, all common areas and all Base Building Improvements located within the Leased Premises;

2. The cost of providing janitorial, landscaping, window cleaning and snow and ice removal services for the Building and all common areas serving the Building;

3. The cost of providing any security for the Building;

4. Real estate taxes and assessments on the Building, including, without limitation, any assessments imposed by any property owner's association;

5. Insurance premiums for all insurance policies maintained by Landlord on or with respect to the Building, including, without limitation, insurance against liability for personal injury, death and property damage, fire and extended coverage insurance on the Building and rent loss insurance);

6. Costs related to the provision of utilities and all other services to the Building (including, without limitation, electricity, water, HVAC, sewer, elevator and trash removal services);

7. Salaries and related costs (including, without limitation, fringe benefits and payroll taxes) of personnel spending time directly associated with the operation, management and maintenance of the Building, including, without limitation, those paid to any on-site property management or maintenance personnel;

8. A reasonable property management fee;

9. The cost of any Building improvement that Landlord is required to make to operate the Building at levels of efficiency and quality that are comparable to those maintained by comparable buildings in the submarket in which the Building is located;

10. The cost of any cost-saving utility device installed in the Building, but only to the extent of the actual cost-savings obtained therefrom;

11. The cost of any Building improvement that Landlord is required to make as a result of the enactment or promulgation of any governmental law or regulation after the date of the execution of this Lease;

12. The cost of cleaning goods and supplies;

13. Accounting, legal and other professional services rendered in connection with the ownership, operation, management and maintenance of the Building;

14. Fees and charges payable under service agreements and other payments made to Landlord's agents or independent contractors for the performance of any services for the Building;

15. The cost of securing and maintaining all licenses, permits and inspections required in connection with the operation, management and maintenance of the Building;

16. The cost of successfully contesting any real estate tax assessment or the validity or applicability of any law or governmental requirement to the Building; provided, however, that the cost of any such contest which may be included in Operating Expenses for any calendar year will not exceed the amount by which Operating Expenses for such calendar year were actually reduced as a result of such contest; and

17. All other costs related to the ownership, operation, management, maintenance and repair of the Building. and the common areas that serve the Building

The following are those expenses that are excluded from the definition of "Operating Expenses":

1. Expenses related to leasing space in the Building or preparing space for lease or for occupancy (including, without limitation, tenant improvements, leasing commissions and advertising expenses);

2. Any inheritance, estate, gift, net profits or similar tax which may be assessed against or imposed upon Landlord;

3. Debt service payments made on any financing in place with respect to the Building; and

4. Salaries and related costs of Landlord's off-site administrative personnel above the level of Building manager.

Building Expenses will be computed for the Base Year and each Comparison Year during the Lease Term based upon the accrual method of accounting. If, during the Base Year or any Comparison Year, the Building is ever less than 100% occupied, then the Building Expenses for each such period will be grossed up an calculated as if the Building had been 100% occupied and the results will constitute Landlord's Building Expenses for such period for all purposes of this Lease.

Initialed and Approved by
Landlord:

Initialed and Approved by
Tenant:

<u>**EXHIBIT C**</u>

<u>**RULES AND REGULATIONS**</u>

1. No sign, placard, picture, advertisement, name or notice visible from outside the Premises shall be installed or displayed on any part of the outside or inside of the Building without the prior written consent of Landlord. Landlord shall have the right to remove, at Tenant's expense and without notice, any sign installed or displayed in violation of this rule. All approved signs or lettering on doors and walls shall be printed, painted, affixed or inscribed at the expense of Tenant by a person chosen by Landlord, using materials of Landlord's choice and in a style and format approved by Landlord.

2. Tenant must use Landlord's blinds in all exterior and atrium window offices. No awning shall be permitted on any part of the Premises. Tenant shall not place anything against or near glass partitions or doors or windows which may appear unsightly from outside the Premises.

3. Tenant shall not obstruct any sidewalks, halls, passages, exits, entrances, elevators, escalators or stairways of the Building. The halls, passages, exits, entrances, shopping malls, elevators, escalators and stairways are not for the general public, and Landlord shall in all cases retain the right to control and prevent access thereto of all persons whose presence in the judgment of Landlord would be prejudicial to the safety, character, reputation and interests of the Building and its tenants; provided that nothing herein contained shall be construed to prevent such access to persons with whom any tenant normally deals in the ordinary course of its business, unless such persons are engaged in illegal activities. No tenant and no employee or invitee of any tenant shall go upon the roof of the Building.

4. The directory of the Building will be provided by Landlord and shall consist exclusively of the display of the name and location of tenants only.

5. All cleaning and janitorial services for the Building and the Premises shall be provided exclusively through Landlord, and except with the written consent of Landlord, no person or persons other than those approved by Landlord shall be employed by Tenant or permitted to enter the Building for the purpose of cleaning the same. Landlord shall not in any way be responsible to any Tenant for any loss of property on the Premises, however occurring, or for any damage to any Tenant's property by the Janitor or any other employee or any other person.

6. Landlord will furnish Tenant, free of charge, with two keys to each door lock in the Premises and one key card per employee. Landlord may make a reasonable charge for any additional keys. Tenant shall not make or have made additional keys, and Tenant shall not alter any lock or install a new additional lock or bolt on any door of its Premises. Tenant, upon the termination of its tenancy, shall deliver to Landlord the keys of all doors which have been furnished to Tenant, and in the event of loss of any keys so furnished, shall pay Landlord the reasonable cost of replacing such keys. Landlord will be allowed to maintain a master pass key permitting it to enter the Leased Premises at any and all times during the lease term.

7. Any freight elevator shall be available for use by all tenants in the Building, subject to such reasonable scheduling as Landlord in its discretion shall deem appropriate. No equipment, materials, furniture, packages, supplies, merchandise or other property will be received in the Building or carried in the elevators except between such hours and in such elevators as may be designated by Landlord.

8. Tenant shall not place a load upon any floor of the Premises which exceeds the load per square foot which such floor was designed to carry and which is allowed by law. Landlord shall have the right to prescribe the weight, size and position of all equipment, materials, furniture or other property brought into the Building. Heavy objects, if such objects are considered necessary by Tenant, as determined by Landlord, shall stand on such platforms as determined by Landlord to be necessary to properly distribute the weight. Business machines and mechanical that may be transmitted to the structure of the Building or to any space therein to such degree as to be objectionable to Landlord or to any tenants in the Building, shall be placed and maintained by Tenant, at Tenant's expense, on vibration eliminators or other devices sufficient to eliminate noise or vibration. The persons employed to move such equipment in or out of the Building must be acceptable to Landlord. Landlord will not be responsible for loss of, or damage to, any such equipment or other property from any cause, and all damage done to the Building by maintaining or moving such equipment or other property shall be repaired at the expense of Tenant.

9. Tenant shall not use or keep in the Premises any kerosene, gasoline or inflammable or combustible fluid or material other than those limited quantities necessary for the operation or maintenance of office equipment. Tenant shall not use or permit to be used in the Premises any foul or noxious gas or substance, or permit or allow the Premises to be occupied or used in a manner offensive or objectionable to Landlord or other occupants of the Building by reason of noise, odors or vibrations, nor shall Tenant bring into or keep in or about the Premises any birds or animals, except those permitted by ADA regulations.

10. Tenant shall not waste electricity, water or air conditioning and agrees to cooperate fully with Landlord to assure the most effective operation of the Building's heating, air conditioning and lighting to comply with any governmental energy saving rules, laws or regulations of which Tenant has actual notice, and shall refrain from attempting to adjust control. Tenant shall keep corridor doors closed, and shall close window coverings at the end of each business day.

11. Landlord reserves the right, exercisable without notice and without liability to Tenant, to change the name and street address of the Building.

12. Landlord reserves the right to exclude from the Building between the hours of 8 p.m. and 7 a.m. the following day, or such other hours as may be established from time to time by Landlord, and on Sundays and legal holidays, any person unless that person is known to the person or employee in charge of the Building and has a pass or is properly identified. Tenant shall be responsible for all persons for whom it requests passes and shall be liable to Landlord for all acts of such persons. Tenant shall pay the cost of replacing any security cards provided by Landlord. Landlord shall not be liable for damages for any error with regard to the admission to or exclusion from the Building of any person, Landlord reserves the right to prevent access to the Building in case of invasion, mob, riot, public excitement or other commotion by closing the doors or by other appropriate action.

13. Tenant shall close and lock the doors of its Premises and entirely shut off all water faucets or other water apparatus, and electricity, gas or air outlets before Tenant and its employees leave the Premises. Tenant shall be responsible for any damage or injuries sustained by other tenants or occupants of the Building or by Landlord for noncompliance with this rule.

14. Tenant shall not obtain for use on the Premises ice, drinking water, food, beverage, towel or other similar services or accept barbering or boot blacking services upon the Premises, except at such hours and under such regulations as may be fixed by Landlord.

15. The toilet rooms, toilets, urinals, wash bowls, kitchen sinks and garbage disposals and other apparatus shall not be used for any purpose other than that for which they were constructed and no foreign substance of any kind whatsoever shall be thrown therein. The expense of any breakage, stoppage or damage resulting from the violation of this rule shall be borne by the tenant who, or whose employees or invitees, shall have caused it.

16. Tenant shall not sell, or permit the sale at retail, of newspapers, magazines, periodicals, theater tickets or any other goods or merchandise to the general public in or on the Premises. Tenant shall not make any room-to-room solicitation of business from other tenants in the Building. Tenant shall not use the Premises for any business or activity other than that specifically provided for in Tenant's Lease.

17. Tenant shall not install any radio or television antenna, loudspeaker or other device on the roof or exterior walls of the Building. Tenant shall not interfere with radio or television broadcasting or reception from or in the Building or elsewhere.

18. Tenant shall not mark, drive nails, screw or drill into the partitions, woodwork or plaster or in any way deface the Premises or any part thereof, except to install normal wall hangings. Landlord reserves the right to direct electricians as to where and how telephone and telegraph wires are to be introduced to the Premises. Tenant shall not cut or bore holes for wires. Tenant shall not affix any floor covering to the floor of the Premises in any manner except as approved by Landlord. Tenant shall repair any damage resulting from noncompliance with this rule.

19. Tenant shall not install, maintain or operate upon the Premises any vending machine without the written consent of Landlord.

20. Canvassing, soliciting and distribution of handbills or any other written material, and peddling in the Building are prohibited, and each tenant shall cooperate to prevent same.

21. Landlord reserves the right to exclude or expel from the Building any person who, in Landlord's judgment, is intoxicated or under the influence of liquor or drugs or who is in violation of any of the Rules and Regulations of the Building.

22. Tenant shall store all its trash and garbage within its Premises. Tenant shall not place in any trash box or receptacle any material which cannot be disposed of in the ordinary and customary manner of trash and garbage disposal. All garbage and refuse disposal shall be made in accordance with directions issued from time to time by Landlord.

23. The Premises shall not be used for the storage of merchandise held for sale to the general public, or for lodging or for manufacturing of any kind, nor shall the Premises be used for any improper, immoral or objectionable purpose. No cooking shall be done or permitted by any tenant on the Premises, except that use by Tenant of Underwriters' Laboratory approved equipment for brewing coffee, tea, hot chocolate and similar beverages shall be permitted, and the use of microwave shall be permitted, provided that such equipment and its use is in accordance with all applicable federal, state, county and city laws, codes, ordinances, rules and regulations.

24. Tenant shall not use in any space or in the public halls of the Building any hand trucks except those equipped with rubber tires and side guards or such other material handling equipment as Landlord may approve. Tenant shall not bring any other vehicles, including bicycles, of any kind into the Building.

25. Without the written consent of Landlord, Tenant shall not use the name of the Building in connection with or in promoting or advertising the business of Tenant except as Tenant's address.

26. Tenant shall comply with all safety, fire protection and evacuation procedures and regulations established by Landlord or any governmental agency.

27. Tenant assumes any and all responsibility for protecting its Premises from theft, robbery and pilferage, which includes keeping doors locked and other means of entry to the Premises closed.

28. The requirements of Tenant will be attended to only upon appropriate application to the office of the Building by an authorized individual. Employees of Landlord shall not perform any work or do anything outside of their regular duties unless under special instructions from landlord, and no employee of Landlord will admit any person (Tenant or otherwise) to any office without specific instructions from Landlord.

29. In the event Tenant fails to deliver to Landlord its keys to the Premises upon termination of Tenant's right to possession under the Lease, or Tenant's vacating of the Premises, the cost of replacing the locks and keys shall be borne by Tenant.

30. Bicycles, motorbikes and motorcycles are prohibited within the Building and must be kept in designated parking areas.

31. No pets or other animals of any type whatsoever are permitted in the Building at any time, except those permitted by ADA regulations.

32. Landlord may waive any one or more of these Rules and Regulations for the benefit of Tenant or any other tenant, but no such waiver by Landlord shall be construed as a waiver of such Rules and Regulations in favor of Tenant or any other tenant, nor prevent Landlord from thereafter enforcing any such Rules and Regulations against any or all of the tenants of the Building.

33. These Rules and Regulations are in addition to, and shall not be construed to in any way modify or amend, in whole or in part, the terms, covenants, agreements and conditions of any lease of premises in the Building.

34. Landlord reserves the right to make such other and reasonable Rules and Regulations as, in its judgment, may from time to time be needed for safety and security, for care and cleanliness of the Building and for the preservation of good order therein. Tenant agrees to

abide by all such Rules and Regulations hereinabove stated and any additional rules and regulations which are adopted.

35. Tenant shall be responsible for the observance of all of the foregoing rules by Tenant's employees, agents, clients, customers, invitees and guests.

36. Tenant understands that the building is a no-smoking facility. Tenant is permitted to smoke only in the areas outside which have been designated by the Landlord as the "smoking area". Tenant will properly dispose of cigarette butts and matches in the containers provided. Failure to comply will result in the revocation of Tenant's smoking privileges.

37. Areas under construction are not common areas. They are restricted to construction personnel only and Tenant shall not enter these or any other vacant space in the building.

Initialed and Approved by
Landlord:

Initialed and Approved by
Tenant:

____

____

LANDLORD'S WORK

Landlord will provide a Tenant Improvement Allowance for the construction of the Improvements to the Leased Premises in the amount set forth in the Lease Summary. The preliminary plans and specifications for such Improvements are attached hereto as Schedule D–1. If the cost of the construction of the Improvements (as the same is determined by Landlord's contractor) exceeds the amount of the aforementioned Tenant Improvement Allowance, then such excess costs will be paid by Tenant in accordance with the provisions of § 9 of the Lease.

The Base Building Improvements which have been or will be constructed by Landlord and which are not to be charged against the Tenant Improvement Allowance improvement allowance are set forth in ScheduleD–2.

<table>
<tr><td>Initialed and Approved by
Landlord:</td><td>Initialed and Approved by
Tenant:</td></tr>
<tr><td>___________________________</td><td>___________________________</td></tr>
</table>

SPECIAL TERMS

The following special terms modify and supplement the provisions of the Lease between Landlord and Tenant. All capitalized terms used but not defined in this Exhibit E will have the meanings attributed thereto in the Lease Agreement.

Extension Option: Tenant will have the option to extend this Lease for one extension term of five years. Such extension option must be exercised, if at all, by Tenant's delivery of written notice of exercise to Landlord at least 12 months prior to the scheduled expiration of the initial lease term. Tenant's right to extend this Lease will be conditioned upon this Lease being in full force and effect, without any default on the part of Tenant, both at the time of Tenant's exercise of such extension option and at the time of the scheduled commencement of the extension term. The extension term will be upon all of the same terms and conditions set forth in this Lease with respect to the initial Lease Term, except that (a) Tenant will not have any further extension options, (b) Landlord will not be obligated to pay any tenant improvement or other allowances in connection with any such extension term and (c) the Base Rent for such extension term will be equal to the then fair market rent for comparable space in comparable buildings in the _______ submarket, but, in no event, will the Base Rent payable during such extension term be less than 115% of the Base Rent payable during the last month of the initial lease term. Landlord will provide Tenant with Landlord's determination of such fair market rent within 30 days after Tenant's written exercise of its extension option. If Tenant disagrees with Landlord's determination of such fair market rent, then, as its sole option, Tenant will have the right to rescind its exercise of such extension option at any time with ten days after its receipt of Landlord's rent determination.

        Initialed and Approved by   Initialed and Approved by
        Landlord: Tenant:

        ________________________   ________________________

Pro–Tenant Lease Modifications

The following are examples of provisions that a tenant might want to include in Exhibit E of the Office Lease (i.e., those "Special Terms" that are intended to modify and supplement the provisions of the form Office Lease). Please keep in mind that, while these provisions are representative of lease modifications that might be requested by a tenant, they are not intended to be an exhaustive listing of a tenant's desired modifications. There is literally no limit to the imagination of a tenant's lawyer when he or she takes on the task of negotiating changes to the landlord's standard form of lease. Moreover, each of the provisions listed below can be further modified to reflect the needs and desires of a particular tenant.

Finally, it should be noted that most landlords will resist (at least initially) the inclusion of any of the following provisions in the lease. To the extent landlord's lawyer is persuaded to include any of the suggested provisions in the lease, one can rest assured that those provisions will be massaged and manipulated in any number of ways so as to more appropriately address the landlord's business concerns and objectives.

---

1. **BOMA Method of Space Measurement**. Landlord represents that the rentable areas of the Building and the Leased Premises (as set forth in the Lease Summary) have been determined using the method of measurement mandated in the Building Owners and Managers Association International's Publication ANSI Z65.1, copyright 1996 ("BOMA Method"). Tenant reserves the right to have such rentable areas remeasured and recalculated by a licensed engineer selected by Tenant. If Tenant's engineer determines that the rentable area of the Building or the Leased Premises (calculated in accordance with the BOMA Method) is different from that specified in the Lease Summary, then Tenant's annual Base Rent and its Proportionate Share of Excess Expenses will be adjusted to take into consideration the new rentable area calculations.

2. **Usable Area of Leased Premises**. Landlord represents and warrants that:

    (a) The Leased Premises contain ___ square feet of usable area;
    (b) The R/U ratio used by Landlord to calculate the rentable area of the Leased Premises is ___%; and
    (c) The calculations made in (a) and (b), above, were made in strict accordance with the BOMA method.

    Landlord will indemnify and hold Tenant harmless from any damage or injury caused to Tenant as a result of Landlord's breach of any of the foregoing representations and warranties.

3. **GMP for Tenant Improvements**. Before commencing construction of the Improvements to the Leased Premises, Landlord will be required to provide Tenant with a written notice setting forth Landlord's guaranteed maximum price for the construction of all such Improvements ("GMP"). If the GMP exceeds the amount of the Tenant Improvement Allowance being provided to Tenant under this Lease, then Tenant will have the right to either:

    (a) Cause Landlord to competitively bid the construction of the Improvements to at least three additional general contractors approved by Tenant, with Landlord then being required to award the contract for the construction of the Improvements to the low bidder; or

    (b) Take over direct responsibility for the construction of the Improvements with a contractor of Tenant's choosing.

    Tenant may exercise either of the above rights by delivering a written election notice to Landlord within ten days after Tenant's receipt of Landlord's written GMP notice. If Tenant elects to proceed under alternative (b), above, then, within ten days after Landlord's receipt of Tenant's written exercise notice, Landlord will assign to Tenant all of Landlord's rights and interest in the Final Plans and will pay Tenant the full amount of the Tenant Improvement Allowance.

4. **Modification to Leasehold Improvements Section of Lease**. Notwithstanding anything to the contrary contained in § 9 or Exhibit D to this Lease, the following rules will apply in connection with Landlord's construction of the Improvements to the Leased Premises:

    (a) Landlord will construct all such Improvements (i) in a good and workmanlike manner, (ii) free of any defects in design, materials or workmanship and (ii) in compliance with all applicable laws, governmental requirements and recorded covenants or conditions; and

    (b) Landlord will not charge against the Tenant Improvement Allowance any construction, design or other fee or payment made to Landlord or any affiliate of Landlord.

5. **Amortization of Excess Tenant Improvement Costs**. Notwithstanding anything to the contrary contained in § 9 or Exhibit D of this Lease, if the cost of the construction of the Improvements to the Leased Premises exceeds the amount of the Tenant Improvement Allowance being provided to Tenant under this Lease ("Excess Costs"), Tenant will have the option to require Landlord to provide the funding for the payment of all such Excess Costs. The Base Rent payable by Tenant during each year of the Lease Term will then be increased by an amount equal to 10% of the amount of such Excess Costs.

6. **Reconfiguration of Common Areas**. A site plan depicting the present location of the Building and all of the common areas serving the Building is attached to this Rider as Schedule ____. The attached site plan is a material inducement for Tenant to enter into this Lease and Landlord may not make any significant change, alteration, improvement or addition to the site plan or any of the common areas shown on such site plan, without first obtaining Tenant's written consent.

7. **Parking**. Tenant will have the right to use parking spaces in the parking lot located adjacent to the Building on a first come, first served basis in common with other occupants of the building and their respective employees, agents, guests and invitees. Landlord hereby represents that the parking lot located adjacent to the Building currently contains ____ regular parking spaces and ____ handicapped spaces and that all such spaces are reserved for the exclusive use of occupants of the Building and their respective agents, employees, guests and invitees. Landlord hereby acknowledges and agrees that, without Tenant's prior written consent, Landlord will not be permitted (a) to reduce the total number of parking spaces located in the Building's parking lot, (b) to change the location or configuration of the parking lot or (c) to grant any right to use the parking lot to any persons other than occupants of the Building and their respective agents, employees, guests and invitees. Finally, Landlord agrees that, at all times during the Lease Term, it will reserve and designate ______ parking spaces for the exclusive use of Tenant's senior management and ______ parking spaces for the exclusive use of visitors to occupants of the Building, with all such reserved parking spaces being located where indicated on the parking plan attached hereto as Schedule 1 or in such other areas of the parking lot as are specifically approved in writing by Tenant.

8. **Expansion Option**. Tenant will have the option to expand its Leased Premises to include the ______ rentable square feet of space which is located on the ______ floor of the Building and which is more particularly shown on the floor plan attached to this Rider as Schedule ____ ("Expansion Space"). Tenant will exercise its expansion option, if at all, by delivering written notice of the exercise of such option to Landlord at any time prior to the ____ anniversary of the Commencement Date. If Tenant so exercises its expansion option, then its leasing of the Expansion Space will be upon all of the same terms and conditions set forth in this Lease with respect to the original Leased Premises (including, without limitation, the Termination Date of the Lease Term and the per rentable square foot amount of Tenant's Base Rent), except that (a) the Commencement Date applicable to Tenant's leasing of the Expansion Space will be the date on which all "Improvements" to the Expansion Space are "substantially completed" (as those terms are defined in § 9 of this Lease), (b) the Tenant Improvement Allowance for the Expansion Space will be equal to ______ per rentable square foot contained within the Expansion Space and (c) Tenant's Proportionate Share for the Expansion Space will be deemed to be ___%. If Tenant exercises its expansion option at the time and in the manner required in this paragraph, then Landlord and Tenant will execute an amendment to this Lease, which reflects the terms and conditions applicable to Tenant's leasing of the Expansion Space (as such terms and conditions are described in the immediately preceding sentence of this paragraph).

9. **Right of First Refusal**. Tenant will have a right of first refusal on all vacant space located on the ______ floor(s) of the Building ("RFR Space"). If at any time during the Lease Term,

Landlord receives a bona fide written offer from any third party ("Third Party Offer") to lease any space ("Offer Space") which includes all or any part of the RFR Space and if Landlord, in good faith, is willing to accept such offer, then Landlord will promptly provide Tenant with written notice of the terms and conditions of such Third Party Offer. Tenant will then have ten business days after its receipt of Landlord's notice to provide Landlord with written notice that Tenant elects to lease such Offer Space upon the identical terms and conditions set forth in the Third Party Offer. If Tenant fails to provide Landlord with such written notice within the aforementioned ten business day period or if Tenant expressly declines to exercise its right of first refusal hereunder, then, in either such event, Landlord will thereafter have the unrestricted right for a period of 60 days to lease the Offer Space to the third party who submitted the Third Party Offer upon the identical terms and conditions set forth in such Third Party Offer. If Landlord does not so lease the Offer Space within such 60 day period, then Tenant's right of first refusal hereunder will be fully reinstated.

10. **Right of First Offer**. Tenant will have a right of first offer on all space which "becomes available" (as that term is hereinafter defined) on the ________ floor of the Building. For the purposes of this paragraph, the space on the ________ floor of the Building will be deemed to have "become available" only after it has been leased to a third party and such third party's right to occupy the subject space terminates (other than as a result of any assignment or subleasing by any such tenant) and will expressly exclude any space which has never been leased to a third party or any space which is subject to an expiring lease if the tenant then occupying that space extends or renews its lease pursuant to a right granted to it under its lease or pursuant to a separate agreement entered into by such tenant and Landlord.

If at any time during the Lease Term, any space on the ________ floor of the Building so becomes available ("Available Space"), then Landlord will promptly provide Tenant with written notice of such availability ("RFO Notice"), specifying (a) the size, location and configuration of the Available Space, (b) the projected commencement and termination dates for Tenant's leasing of the Available Space, (c) the improvements which Landlord proposes to make to the Available Space (or the tenant improvement allowance which Landlord proposes to make available to Tenant for the construction of such improvements), (d) the Base Rent which Landlord proposes that Tenant pay for its leasing of the Available Space and (e) any other provisions of which Landlord proposes to include in Tenant's lease of the Available Space, which would be inconsistent with the provisions specified in this Lease with respect to Tenant's leasing of the Leased Premises (all of the terms specified in clauses (a) through (e) being hereinafter referred to as the "RFO Terms"). Tenant will have 20 business days after its receipt of Landlord's RFO Notice in which to provide Landlord with written notice of Tenant's exercise of its right of first offer. If Tenant so exercises its right of first offer, then Landlord and Tenant will execute a lease for the Available Space, which incorporates the RFO Terms and all those provisions of this Lease which are not inconsistent with the RFO Terms. If Tenant fails to provide Landlord with notice of its exercise of its right of first offer within the aforementioned 20 business day period or if Tenant expressly declines to exercise its right of first offer hereunder, then, in either such event Landlord will thereafter have the unrestricted right for a period of 60 days to lease the Available Space to any third party upon terms and conditions which are at least as favorable to Landlord as are the RFO Terms. If Landlord does not so lease the Available Space within such 60 day period, then Tenant's right of first offer will be fully reinstated.

11. **Right of First Negotiation**. Tenant will have a right of first negotiation on all space which "becomes available" (as that term is hereinafter defined) on the ________ floor of the Building. For the purposes of this paragraph, the space on the ________ floor of the Building will be deemed to have "become available" only after it has been leased to a third party and such third party's right to occupy the subject space terminates (other than as a result of any assignment or subleasing by any such tenant) and will expressly exclude any space which has never been leased to a third party or any space which is subject to an expiring lease if the tenant then occupying that space extends or renews its lease pursuant to a right granted to it under its lease or pursuant to a separate agreement entered into by such tenant and Landlord.

If at any time during the Lease Term, any space on the ________ floor of the Building so becomes available ("Available Space"), then Landlord will promptly provide Tenant with written notice of such availability ("RFN Notice"), specifying the size, location and configuration of the Available Space. Tenant will thereafter have a period of 30 days in which to negotiate with Landlord to reach final agreement on the terms and conditions which will govern Tenant's leasing of the Available Space. If Landlord and Tenant do not execute a lease or lease amendment for the Available Space within such 30 day period, then Tenant's right of first negotiation will terminate as to the then Available Space (but not as to the remainder on the space located on the _____ floor of the Building) and Landlord will thereafter have the unrestricted right to lease all or any part of such Available Space to any third party upon such terms and conditions as Landlord deems appropriate.

12. **Contraction Option**. Tenant will have the option to contract the size of the Leased Premises by canceling this Lease as to the _______ rentable square feet of space which is identified in the floor plan attached to this Rider as Schedule ____ ("Contraction Space"). Tenant will exercise its contraction option, if at all, by delivering written notice of the exercise of such option to Landlord at any time prior to the _______ anniversary of the Commencement Date. The cancellation of this Lease as to the Contraction Space will be deemed to be effective ____ days after the date on which Tenant delivers its written notice of the exercise of its contraction option to Landlord ("Contraction Date"). It will be a condition to Tenant's exercise of such contraction option that Tenant pay to Landlord, at the same time as it delivers written notice to Landlord of the exercise of such contraction option, cash in a sum equal to (a) the unamortized balance of all leasing commissions and tenant improvement costs paid by Landlord with respect to the Leased Premises (with such unamortized balance being computed as of the Contraction Date, based upon an initial amortization schedule equal to the length of the initial Lease Term and an annual interest rate of ____% per year), multiplied by the percentage determined by dividing the rentable square feet contained within the Contraction Space by the rentable square feet contained within the entirety of the original Leased Premises, plus (b) a contraction fee of $_______. If Tenant exercises its contraction option at the time and in the manner required in this paragraph, then, prior to the Contraction Date, Landlord and Tenant will execute an amendment to this Lease, which reflects the cancellation of this Lease as to the Contraction Space. Such amendment will be prepared by Landlord and will confirm (i) the size, location and dimensions of the remaining Leased Premises, (ii) the Contraction Date, (iii) the reduction, from and after the Contraction Date, of Tenant's Proportionate Share to ____% and its monthly Base Rent to $_______, (iv) Landlord's right to enter the Leased Premises, at all reasonable times prior to the Contraction Date, to do all work necessary to separate the Contraction Space from the remaining Leased Premises, including, without limitation, the construction of demising walls and the reconfiguration of any of the mechanical and electrical systems serving the respective spaces, (v) Tenant's ongoing obligation, from and after the Contraction Date, to abide by all of the terms and conditions of this Lease as they relate to the remaining Leased Premises, (vi) the survival of all of Tenant's obligations with respect to the Contraction Space, which accrued prior to the Contraction Date and (vi) such other matters as are required to properly reflect the effect of Tenant's exercise of its contraction option.

13. **Deletion of Relocation Section**. Section 28 of the Lease is deleted in its entirety.

14. **Cancellation Option**. Tenant will have the option to cancel this Lease effective as of _______, 20__ ("Cancellation Date"). Tenant will exercise its cancellation option, if at all, by delivering written notice of the exercise of such option to Landlord at any time which is at least _______ days prior to the Cancellation Date. It will be a condition to Tenant's exercise of such cancellation option that Tenant pay to Landlord, at the same time as it delivers written notice to Landlord of the exercise of such cancellation option, cash in a sum equal to (a) the unamortized balance of all leasing commissions and tenant improvement costs paid by Landlord with respect to the Leased Premises, with such unamortized balance being computed as of the Cancellation Date, based upon an initial amortization schedule equal to the length of the initial Lease Term and an annual interest rate of ____% per year, plus (b) a cancellation fee of $_______.

15. **Tenant's Remedies for Construction Delays**. Notwithstanding anything to the contrary contained in § 9 and Exhibit C to this Lease, if the Improvements required to be constructed by Landlord are not substantially completed by the targeted Commencement Date specified in the Lease Summary for any reason other than a "Tenant-caused delay" (as that term is used in § 9 of the Lease), then Landlord will pay to Tenant liquidated damages in an amount equal to $_______ per day for each day of delay beginning on the targeted Commencement Date specified in the Lease Summary and ending on the date on which the Improvements are substantially completed. Such liquidated damages will be paid by Landlord within ten days after the date on which the Improvements are substantially completed. If Landlord fails to pay such liquidated damages to Tenant within the aforementioned ten day period, then Tenant will have the right to offset the amount of any unpaid liquidated damages against its next succeeding installment(s) of Base Rent and Excess Expenses. Landlord and Tenant hereby acknowledge and agree that the Tenant's damages in the event the Improvements

are not substantially completed on time will be difficult to ascertain and the receipt of the amount set forth above constitutes a reasonable liquidation of such damages and is not intended as a penalty.

Tenant will have the further right to cancel this Lease if the Improvements are not substantially completed on or before the date which is 60 days after the targeted Commencement Date set forth in the Lease Summary; provided, however, that Tenant will not have any such cancellation right if the cause for the delay in the substantial completion of the Improvements is solely attributable to a Tenant–Caused Delay. Tenant may exercise such cancellation right by delivering a written notice of cancellation to Landlord at any time before the actual substantial completion of the Improvements.

16. **Early Occupancy**. Tenant will be permitted access to the Leased Premises 30 days prior to the Commencement Date for the purpose of installing its furniture, fixtures and equipment in the Leased Premises. During such early occupancy period, Tenant will have in place the insurance required to be maintained by Tenant pursuant to § 15 of the Lease and will otherwise abide by all other provisions of the Lease, with the express exception of its covenant to pay Base Rent and Excess Expenses pursuant to §§ 1–3 of the Lease. Tenant will, at all times during such early occupancy period, use its best efforts to minimize any interference with Landlord's construction of the Improvements to the Leased Premises.

17. **Extension Option**. Tenant will have the option to extend this Lease for _____ renewal terms of _______ years each. Each such extension option will be exercised, if at all, by Tenant's delivery of written notice of exercise to Landlord at least 45 days prior to the scheduled expiration of the then existing term of the Lease (be it the initial term or any subsequently exercised extension term). Each such extension term will be upon all of the same terms and conditions set forth in this Lease with respect to the initial lease term, except that (a) in lieu of the Tenant Improvement Allowance referenced in the Lease Summary, Landlord will provide Tenant with a refurbishment allowance of $_______ for each exercised extension term, which amount may be used by Tenant to defray the costs of repainting, recarpeting and otherwise redecorating its Leased Premises; and (b) the annual Base Rent payable during each year of each such extension term will be equal to 90% of the "Fair Market Rent" for the Leased Premises. For the purposes of this section, "Fair Market Rent" means the average annual rental rate (expressed in an amount per square foot of net rentable area) then being charged in the _______ submarket for space comparable to the Leased Premises, taking into consideration (1) the specific provisions of the Lease which will remain constant during the extension term, (2) the relative condition, quality, design, age and location of the Leased Premises and all comparable space, (3) the building amenities and services available to the tenants of all the subject buildings, (4) the creditworthiness of Tenant and (5) the provisions of all leases of comparable spaces, including without limitation, the tenant improvement allowances, rent structures and concessions provided under such leases.

Landlord and Tenant will have 30 days after Tenant's exercise of its extension option in which to reach mutual agreement on the Fair Market Rent for the Leased Premises (and, hence, the amount of the Base Rent which will be payable by Tenant during the exercises extension term). If Landlord and Tenant are not able to reach agreement on such Fair Market Rent within such 30 day period, then the Fair Market Rent for the Leased Premises will be determined in accordance with the appraisal procedures specified in the next succeeding paragraph of this section.

Within five days after the expiration of the 30 day period referenced in the immediately preceding paragraph, Landlord and Tenant will each separately appoint a licensed real estate broker with at least five years' full-time commercial brokerage experience in the _______ submarket to appraise the Fair Market Rent for the Leased Premises. Within 30 days after the appointment of the last broker, Landlord and Tenant will each submit to the appointed brokers its written statement ("Rent Statement") of the Fair Market Rent for the Leased Premises (including whatever support for such contention the party wishes to have considered by the brokers). The appointed brokers will then have ten days to reach agreement on the selection of the Rent Statement which is nearest to their belief of the Fair Market Rent for the Leased Premises. The brokers must select either Landlord's Rent Statement or Tenant's Rent Statement and cannot compromise the two Rent Statements or otherwise determine a Fair Market Rent for the Leased Premises which is different from that set forth in one of the two Rent Statements. If the brokers cannot agree upon the selection of one of the two Rent Statements, then the brokers will have an additional period of seven days in which to appoint a third real estate broker with at least five years' full-time commercial brokerage experience in the _______ submarket. The third broker will then have fifteen days to select which of the two Rent Statements he or she believes is closest to the actual Fair Market Rent for the Leased Premises. The selection of such Fair Market Rent by the third broker will then be binding on Landlord and Tenant for all the purposes specified in this Lease.

18. **Modification to Holdover Section of Lease**. Section 21 of the Lease is modified by deleting the number "200%" in the second sentence of such section and inserting the number "110%."

19. **Gross-up Adjustments**. The Building Expense gross-up adjustments required to be made under the last sentence of Exhibit B to this Lease will be made in accordance with the following rules:

    (a)   Such adjustments will be made in accordance with industry standards and generally accepted accounting principles, consistently applied;

    (b)   Only those Building Expense components which fluctuate based upon occupancy levels in the Building will be grossed up;

    (c)   Landlord will include a reasonably detailed description of how the gross-up adjustments were calculated in the written Building Expense statement for each Calendar Year that Landlord is required to provide to Tenant pursuant to § 2 of this Lease;

    (d)   If, during any Calendar Year, Landlord incurs additional costs because of a change of policy or practice related to its operation, management, maintenance or ownership of the Building (including, without limitation, increased premiums for new or different insurance coverages or additional costs related to any change in the frequency or levels of Building services provided by Landlord), then the Base Expenses will be deemed increased to include those additional costs which Landlord would have incurred if such change in policy or practice had been in effect at all times during the Base Year;

    (e)   If any portion of the Building was covered by a warranty during the Base Year, then the Base Expenses will be deemed increased to include those additional costs which Landlord would have incurred if such warranty had not been in effect during the Base Year; and

    (f)   If the Building is not fully assessed for real estate tax purposes during the Base Year or, then the Base Expenses will be deemed increased to include the additional real estate taxes that would have been incurred by Landlord if the Building had been fully assessed during the Base Year.

20. **Replacement of Building Expense Exclusions**. The exclusions from the definition of Building Expenses set forth as items 1 through 5 of the penultimate paragraph of Exhibit B to this Lease are hereby deleted and replaced with the list of Building Expense exclusions set forth in Schedule ___ to this Exhibit. Notwithstanding anything to the contrary contained in the Lease, Building Expenses will expressly not include any cost or expense that is not considered to be an "operating expense" under generally accepted accounting principles.

21. **Rules Governing Calculation of Building Expenses**. Notwithstanding anything to the contrary contained in § 2 or Exhibit B to this Lease, the following general principles shall apply with respect to the calculation of Landlord's Building Expenses and Tenant's Excess Expense payments:

    (a)   Landlord will not recover the cost of any item more than once, nor will Landlord seek reimbursement from Tenant for an amount greater than the actual cost incurred by Tenant with respect to any item; it being expressly acknowledged by Landlord that it is not the intention or purpose of this Lease to produce or generate an economic profit or windfall to Landlord;

    (b)   Landlord will operate and maintain the Building in a cost-effective and economically responsible manner;

    (c)   Landlord will calculate its Building Expenses in a fair, accurate and commercially reasonable manner;

    (d)   All services rendered to and all materials supplied to the Building will be of a nature and scope which are consistent with those rendered or supplied to comparable buildings and the cost of such services and materials will be of a cost no greater than those charged in arm's length transactions for similar services or materials rendered or supplied for similar purposes to comparable buildings; and

(e) In determining the nature and amount of any costs to be included as Building Expenses hereunder, Landlord will comply with and respect generally accepted accounting principles, consistently applied.

22. **Cap on Controllable Expenses**. Notwithstanding anything to the contrary contained in § 2 or Exhibit B of this Lease, the amount of "Controllable Expenses" (as that term is hereinafter defined) to be taken in consideration when computing Tenant's Proportionate Share of Excess Expenses in the 20__ calendar year will be capped $_______ per rentable square foot contained within the Leased Premises. The amount of Controllable Expenses to be taken into consideration when computing Tenant's Proportionate Share of Excess Expenses for each calendar year subsequent to the 20__ calendar year will be capped at 105% of the Controllable Expenses taken into consideration for such purposes during the immediately preceding calendar year. For the purposes of this Lease, the term "Controllable Expenses" will mean those expenses referred to in paragraphs ____, ____, ___ and ___ of Exhibit B.

23. **Audit of Operating Expenses**. Tenant will have the right, upon reasonable prior written notice to Landlord, to audit Landlord's books and records with respect to Landlord's computation of its Building Expenses for any calendar year during the Lease Term (including, without limitation, all invoices, executed contracts, canceled checks and general legers related to such Operating Expenses). Any such right of audit as to a particular calendar year must be exercised, if at all, within three years after Tenant's receipt from Landlord of a written statement showing Landlord's actual Building Expenses for such calendar year. If any audit conducted by Tenant discloses an overage in the amount billed to Tenant over the amounts actually due from Tenant hereunder, then Landlord will reimburse Tenant for the amount of such overage, plus interest thereon at ___% from the date paid through the date reimbursed. To the extent such overage exceeds 2% of the amount actually due from Tenant, Landlord will also reimburse Tenant for all reasonable out-of-pocket costs and professional fees incurred by Tenant in connection with its auditing of Landlord's books and records. The payments referred to in the immediately preceding sentences will be made by Landlord to Tenant within ten days after Landlord's receipt of a detailed invoice identifying the amount of such payments. Except as otherwise expressly provided herein, Tenant will bear all costs associated with the auditing of Landlord's books and records.

24. **Grace Period for Rent Payments**. Notwithstanding anything to the contrary contained in § 3 of the Lease, Tenant will not be liable for the payment of any late fee, unless Tenant has been delinquent in the making of any required payment on more than two occasions in the last 12 months.

25. **Modification to Security Deposit Section of Lease**. Notwithstanding anything to the contrary contained in § 33 of the Lease, the following provisions will apply with respect to the posting, holding and disbursement of the Security Deposit identified in the Lease Summary.
    (a) Landlord will hold any cash Security Deposit in a separate, interest-bearing account and will not co-mingle the Security Deposit with any of Landlord's other funds.
    (b) In lieu of a cash Security Deposit, Tenant may deliver to Landlord an irrevocable letter of, issued by a FDIC-insured bank, in the amount of the Security Deposit identified in the Lease Summary. Upon its receipt of any such letter of credit, Landlord will promptly refund to Tenant any cash Security Deposit previously paid to it by Tenant.
    (c) If, as of the _______ anniversary of the Commencement Date, Landlord has not yet drawn down on any portion of the Security Deposit to cure any default by Tenant under the Lease, then Tenant's obligation to post a Security Deposit will automatically terminate and Landlord will promptly return the Security Deposit to Tenant.

26. **Modification to Financial Statements Section of Lease**. Landlord acknowledges that it has received a copy of Tenant's most current financial statement as of the date of the parties' execution of this Lease. Landlord covenants that it will hold Tenant's financial statement in the strictest of confidences and that it will not disclose the same to any person, firm or entity, other than to any lender who has executed a subordination, nondisturbance and attornment agreement with Tenant. Tenant will not have any obligation whatsoever to provide any further financial statements or other financial information to Landlord. As such, § 34 of the Lease is hereby deleted in its entirety.

27. **Administration of Rules and Regulations**. Notwithstanding anything to the contrary in § 6 or Exhibit C to the Lease, Landlord will not issue any new rules or regulations which would unreasonably interfere with Tenant's conduct of its business in the Leased Premises. Landlord will enforce the Building's rules and regulations in a fair, consistent and even-handed manner, In the case of any conflict between any rule or regulation established by Landlord and any provision of this Lease, the provision of this Lease will control.

28. **Modification to Alterations Section of Lease.** Section 10 of the Lease is modified by deleting the number "$5,000" found in the second and third sentences of such section and inserting the number "$20,000."

29. **Limitations on Tenant's Compliance with Law Obligation**. Notwithstanding anything to the contrary contained in § 7 of this Lease, Landlord (and not Tenant) will, at its sole expense, comply with all laws, governmental requirements and recorded covenants or conditions which are now or hereafter in force pertaining to the ownership or use of office buildings generally (and not solely to Tenant's specific use of the Leased Premises). Tenant's compliance obligation under § 7 of this Lease is further made subject to the following limitations:

   (a) Tenant will not be required to spend more than $_______ in making any alteration, addition or improvement to the Leased Premises;

   (b) Tenant will not be required to make any alteration, addition or improvement to the Leased Premises during the last 12 months of the Lease Term (unless Tenant has previously exercised any option set forth in the Lease to extend the Lease Term); and

   (c) Tenant will not be required to make any alteration, addition or improvement to the Building's common areas or to any structural element or mechanical or electrical system which does not exclusively serve the Leased Premises.

Landlord will be required to pay all compliance costs in excess of the $_______ limit set forth in subparagraph (a) and will be further required, at its sole expense, to make all those alterations, additions and improvements described in subparagraphs (b) and (c).

30. **Landlord's Representations and Warranties**. Landlord hereby makes the following representations and warranties to Tenant for the express purpose of inducing Tenant to execute this Lease and occupy the Leased Premises. All such representations and warranties will be deemed made by Landlord both as of the date of the parties' execution of this Lease and as of the Commencement Date.

   (a) The Building does not contain any Hazardous Substance (as that term is defined in § 17 of the Lease), except for immaterial amounts that are exempt from or do not give rise to a violation of applicable law.

   (b) The Building complies with all laws, governmental requirements and recorded covenants and conditions which are applicable to the ownership, use and operation of the Building, including, without limitation, the Americans with Disabilities Act of 1990, as amended.

   (c) The Permitted Use identified in the Lease Summary is permitted under applicable zoning and other laws and regulations, including, without limitation, those applicable to the zoning classification under which the Building is classified.

   (d) There are no restrictive covenants, exclusive use provisions or any other agreements, any of which would prevent Tenant from occupying the Leased Premises for the Permitted Use.

   (e) The Building has no latent, structural defects and all mechanical and electrical systems serving the Building (including, without limitation, the HVAC system) are in good operating condition.

   (f) The Building's HVAC system complies with the minimum operating standards set forth in the Ventilation for Acceptable Air Quality Standard 82–1989 promulgated by The American Society of Heating, Refrigerating and Air Conditioning Engineers.

Landlord will indemnify and hold Tenant harmless from any liability or expense incurred by or claimed against Tenant as a result of Landlord's breach of any of the foregoing representations and warranties.

31. **Landlord's Environmental Covenant**. Landlord agrees that if any cleanup, repair, detoxification or other similar action is required by any governmental or quasi-governmental agency as a result of the use, storage or disposal in or about the Building of any "Hazardous

Substance" (as that term is defined in § 17 of the Lease) by Landlord, any other Building tenant or any of their respective agents, contractors, employees, guest or invitees, and if such action requires that Tenant be closed for business for greater than a 24–hour period, then Tenant's obligation to pay Base Rent and Excess Expenses will abate throughout the period of Tenant's closure. If any such required closure continues for more than 14 consecutive days, then Tenant will at all times thereafter have the right to cancel this Lease effective as of the date of Tenant's delivery of a written cancellation notice to Landlord.

32. **Limitations on Tenant's Maintenance and Repair Obligation.** Notwithstanding anything to the contrary contained in § 5 of the Lease, Tenant will not be obligated to (a) replace any item, component, equipment or system located within the Leased Premises if the useful life of any such item, component, equipment or system (determined in accordance with generally accepted accounting principles) extends beyond the Lease Term or (b) to repair any damage to the interior of the Leased Premises caused by the fault or negligence of Landlord or its other tenants, agents, employees or guests.

33. **Level of Building Services.** The level of services currently applicable to the Building (including, without limitation, HVAC, electrical, elevator, janitorial and security services) are described in Schedule ___ to this Rider ("Current Services"). Landlord agrees that, without first obtaining Tenant's written consent, Landlord will not take any action which could result in the level of the Current Services being reduced or otherwise changed in any manner which could adversely affect Tenant's use of the Leased Premises.

34. **After Hours HVAC Service/Separate Meter.** Notwithstanding anything to the contrary contained in § 4 of the Lease, the agreed-upon surcharge for the provision of HVAC services to the Leased Premises outside of normal business hours will be the lesser of (a) $___ per hour or (b) the actual cost incurred by Landlord in providing such after-hour HVAC service to the Leased Premises. Tenant will have the right throughout the Lease Term to elect to have electricity supplied to the Leased Premises directly from the public utility company that furnishes electricity to the Building and to have the level of Tenant's consumption of electrical service measured by an electrical meter installed in the Leased Premises. If Tenant notifies Landlord that it elects to have electricity supplied and measured in the manner set forth in the immediately preceding sentence, then Landlord will promptly install all meters and additional wiring and equipment that are required to permit electricity to be supplied directly from such public utility company to the Leased Premises. From and after the completion of all the required installations, Tenant will pay all costs of providing electricity to the Leased Premises directly to the public utility company and Landlord will thereafter exclude all such costs from the calculation of its Operating Expenses. Tenant will reimburse Landlord for all reasonable, out-of-pocket costs incurred by Landlord in connection with its installation of the aforementioned meters, wiring and equipment. Such reimbursement will be paid to Landlord within 30 days after Tenant's receipt from Landlord of a detailed invoice itemizing Landlord's installation costs.

35. **Interruption of Building Services.** Notwithstanding anything to the contrary contained in § 4 of the Lease, if the provision of any service required to be provided to the Leased Premises by Landlord (including, without limitation, HVAC, electrical, elevator and security services) is interrupted for any reason other than the negligence or willful misconduct of Tenant and if such interruption substantially impairs Tenant's ability to conduct its business in the Leased Premises, then Tenant's obligation to pay Base Rent and Excess Expenses will abate throughout the period of such interruption. If any such interruption continues for more than 14 consecutive days, then Tenant will at all times thereafter have the right to cancel this Lease effective as of the date of Tenant's delivery of a written cancellation notice to Landlord.

36. **Identification on Exterior Building Signage.** Notwithstanding anything to the contrary contained in § 8 of the Lease, Tenant will have the right to be identified (using its standard corporate logo and trade name) on any Building monument sign or other sign erected or installed by Landlord on the exterior of the Building. Tenant agrees to pay all costs of including Tenant's name and logo on any such sign.

37. **Permitted Transfers.** Notwithstanding anything to the contrary contained in § 12 of the Lease, Tenant may, without having to obtain Landlord's prior written consent, sublet the Leased Premises or assign its interest in the Lease to (a) any successor-in-interest to Tenant resulting from a merger, consolidation or sale of Tenant's entire business, or (b) any subsidiary or affiliate of Tenant; provided, however, that Tenant will be required to provide Landlord with written notice at least ten business days prior to the scheduled occurrence of

any such sublease or assignment and provided further that no such sublease or assignment will release Tenant from the performance of its obligations under this Lease.

38. **Self-help Remedy**. If Landlord fails to fully perform any of its obligations under this Lease within 30 days after its receipt of written notice from Tenant of the non-performance of such obligation, then, in addition to any other right or remedy that Tenant may have at law or in equity to redress such non-performance, Tenant will have the right to perform such obligation and to offset its performance costs against its next succeeding installment(s) of Base Rent and Excess Expenses.

39. **Landlord's Duty to Mitigate Losses**. Notwithstanding anything to the contrary contained in § 22 of the Lease, Landlord must at all times following any default by Tenant use commercially reasonable efforts to mitigate its damages.

40. **Mediation**. Notwithstanding anything to the contrary contained in § 22 of the Lease, no judicial or administrative proceeding may be commenced to enforce the provisions of this Lease or make any determination thereunder, until after the parties shall have attempted, without success, for a minimum of 60 days, to resolve the dispute consensually by means of an informal process involving the services of a neutral mediator experienced in mediation, early neutral evaluation, mini-trial or some other comparable, alternative dispute resolution procedure.

41. **Modification to Insurance Section of Lease**. Section 15 of the Lease is modified by adding the following sentence at the end of such section:

> "All insurance required to be maintained by Landlord under this section will be issued by insurance companies having a policyholder rating of at least "A" and a financial size category of at least "Class X" under the A.M/ Best's Key Rating Guide for insurance companies (or any comparable rating under any successor publication or index)."

42. **Modification to Casualty Section of Lease**. Notwithstanding anything to the contrary contained in § 19 of the Lease, if the Leased Premises or any common area serving the Leased Premises is damaged by fire or other casualty during the last 12 months of the Lease Term and such damage cannot be repaired in 30 days or less, then Tenant will have the further right to cancel this Lease effective as of the date of Tenant's delivery of a written cancellation notice to Landlord.

43. **Modification to Condemnation Section of Lease**. Notwithstanding anything to the contrary contained in § 20 of the Lease, Tenant will have the further right to cancel the Lease if a taking of any of the common areas serving the Leased Premises (including, without limitation, any parking area or means of access) materially interferes with Tenant's ability to conduct its business in the same manner and space as it conducted such business immediately prior the occurrence of such taking. Tenant will exercise such cancellation right, if at all, by delivering written notice of cancellation to Landlord. The effective date of such cancellation will be the later of (a) the date of Tenant's delivery to Landlord of such written notice of cancellation and (b) the date on which title to the taken area vests in the condemning authority.

44. **SNDA**. Notwithstanding anything to the contrary contained in § 13 of the Lease, Tenant's subordination and attornment obligations set forth therein will be expressly conditioned upon Tenant's execution with Landlord's lender of a subordination, non-disturbance and attornment agreement, which provides that Tenant's leasing and possession of the Leased Premises will, in no event, be disturbed by Landlord's lender, so long as Tenant is in full compliance with all of the provisions of this Lease. The subordination, non-disturbance and attornment agreement will otherwise be in such form and content as are reasonably acceptable to Landlord, Tenant and Landlord's lender.

45. **Modification to Subordination/Estoppel Certificate Section of Lease**. The last sentence of § 13 is deleted.

DOCUMENT #7

EXCLUSIVE LISTING AGREEMENT FOR NEW OFFICE BUILDING

■ ■ ■

EXCLUSIVE LISTING AGREEMENT

______, 20__

This Exclusive Leasing Agreement ("Agreement") is entered into as of the date first set forth above by ______ ("Owner") and ______ ("Broker"). Owner and Broker agree as follows:

§ 1. **Identification of Property**. The real property which is the subject of this Agreement ("Property") is located in ______, ______, and is further described as ____________. For the purposes of this Agreement, the term "Property" will be deemed to refer to all or any part of the above-described real estate.

§ 2. **Appointment of Broker**. Owner hereby appoints Broker as its exclusive agent to procure tenants to lease improved office space in the Property. Broker agrees that it will use its best efforts throughout the term of this Agreement to procure tenants for the Property upon the terms and conditions specified in § 4. Broker further agrees that ______ and ______ will be assigned primary responsibility for performing Broker's services throughout the term of this Agreement. Notwithstanding anything to the contrary contained herein, Owner will have the right to terminate this Agreement effective immediately if either of the above-named salespersons is no longer assigned to Owner's account.

§ 3. **Term of Agreement**. The term of this Agreement will begin on the date first set forth above, and will end on the earlier of: (a) the first anniversary of the date first set forth above; or (b) the date on which all improved office space in the Property is leased to tenants.

§ 4. **Acceptable Lease Terms**. Owner will from time to time during the term of this Agreement specify those terms and conditions that are generally acceptable to Owner with respect to the leasing of space in the Property. Notwithstanding Owner's delivery of such generally acceptable terms to Broker, Owner and Broker hereby acknowledge and agree that no terms with respect to the leasing of any space in the Property will be deemed acceptable to Owner, unless Owner has executed a fully-binding written lease ("Lease") incorporating the terms and conditions upon which it will lease space in the Property to any tenant.

§ 5. **Broker's Compensation**. Broker's right to receive any leasing commissions will be governed by the provisions of this § 5. The amount of any leasing commissions payable to Broker will be calculated in the manner set forth in § 6 of this Agreement.

> (a) **Occurrences During Term of Agreement**. Broker will be entitled to receive a leasing commission only upon the execution of a Lease by Owner and any tenant at any time during the term of this Agreement.

> (b) **Occurrences after Expiration of Term**. Broker will also be entitled to receive a leasing commission upon the Owner's execution of a Lease within 60 days after the expiration of the term of this Agreement with any tenant who was identified as a "Prospect" in the list furnished to Owner by Broker pursuant to § 13 of this Agreement.

For all purposes of this Agreement, a "Lease" will include a modification to any existing Lease, pursuant to which an existing tenant agrees to lease additional space in the Property. The term "Lease" will not, however, include any renewal, extension, assignment, sublease or transfer of an existing lease.

§ 6. **Commission Schedule**. With respect to any Lease in which a "Cooperating Broker" is involved (as that term is defined in § 8, below), the commission payable to Broker hereunder will be equal to 6% of the rent payable during the initial lease term of such Lease. With respect to any Lease in which a "Cooperating Broker" is not involved, the commission payable to Broker hereunder will be equal to 4% of the rent payable during the initial lease term of such Lease. For the purposes of this Agreement, the term "rent" includes all payments which are to be made by Tenant under the lease and which are the fixed, minimum rents payable during the initial lease term of the Lease (generally designated as "Base Rent" under Owner's standard form of lease) and will not include any expense payments or escalators or of any nature whatsoever.

§ 7. **Payment of Commissions**. Any commissions payable to Broker hereunder will be paid one-half upon the execution of the Lease by Owner and the tenant and one-half upon the occupancy of the leased premises by such tenant. All commissions payable to Broker hereunder will be fully paid in cash at the times specified above. If Owner fails to make any payment to Broker within 30 days after the date when due hereunder, then, from and after the expiration of such 30–day period, the delinquent amount will bear interest at a rate equal to the prime lending rate published during the pendency of such delinquency by the Wall Street Journal.

§ 8. **Cooperating Brokers**. Broker is hereby authorized and directed to cooperate with and share its commission with other licensed real estate brokers ("Cooperating Broker(s)"), regardless whether said brokers act as Broker's subagents or in some other capacity. If a Cooperating Broker is involved in connection with any Lease, then Broker will pay a commission to such Cooperating Broker (in such amount as is negotiated by Broker) out of the commission payable to Broker pursuant to this Agreement. Broker will indemnify and hold Owner harmless from and against any claims from commissions made by any Cooperating Broker; it being expressly understood and agreed by the parties hereto that Owner will not, under any circumstances, be obligated to pay any commission or other sums directly to any Cooperating Broker.

§ 9. **Specific Duties of Broker**. In addition to any other duties assigned to Broker under this Agreement, Broker agrees that it will, at Owner's request, do all of the following at its sole cost and expense: advertise the Property as being "for lease" in a commercial multiple listing service and a business journal of wide circulation in the community in which the Property is located; attend weekly marketing meetings with representatives of Owner; and provide Owner with a monthly written report identifying the prospective tenants to whom Broker has shown the Property, made a marketing presentation or delivered written materials concerning the availability of the Property.

§ 10. **Duties of Owner**. Owner will cooperate with and assist Broker in effecting Leases of the Property. Owner will refer to Broker all inquiries of any party interested in leasing any space in the Property.

§ 11. **Owner's Disclosure Obligations**. Owner hereby agrees that, upon Broker's request, it will disclose to Broker all pertinent information that Owner has in its possession regarding the environmental condition of the Property, including, without limitation, the presence of asbestos, PCB transformers, underground storage tanks, or other toxic, hazardous or contaminated substances on the Property. Broker is hereby specifically authorized to disclose all information furnished by it to Owner hereunder to prospective tenants of the Property. Owner hereby further represents that: (a) it is the sole owner of the Property and has the legal right and authority to enter into this Agreement and lease the Property; and (b) unless otherwise disclosed to Broker, no person or entity who has an ownership interest in the Property is a "foreign person" within the meaning of the Foreign Investment in Real Property Tax Act.

§ 12. **Advertising and Signage**. Owner will erect a project sign on the Property, which specifically includes the Broker's name and telephone number and the name of the listing agent assigned to the Property. The location, size and format of such project sign will be determined by Owner. Unless otherwise agreed to by Owner, Broker will not erect any other sign on the Property.

§ 13. **Prospects List**. Within 30 days after the expiration of the term of this Agreement, Broker will deliver to Owner a list of all those persons to whom Broker has made a marketing presentation and physically shown the Property during the term of this Agreement ("Prospects"). Such list will set forth the name, address, phone number, contact person and status of each such Prospect.

§ 14. **Non–Discrimination**. It is acknowledged by both parties hereto that it is illegal for either Owner or Broker to refuse to lease the Property to any person because of race, color, religion, national origin, sex, marital status, sexual orientation or physical disability.

§ 15. **Amendment**. This Agreement may not be amended except by a written instrument executed and delivered by both Broker and Owner.

§ 16. **Applicable Law**. This Agreement will be governed and construed in accordance with the laws of the State of _______.

§ 17. **Successors and Assigns**. Neither party hereto may assign its interest in this Agreement to any third party, without first receiving the written consent of the other party hereto.

§ 18. **Default**. Notwithstanding anything to the contrary contained herein, Owner will have the right to terminate this Agreement if Broker is in material breach of any provision of this Agreement and Broker fails to cure such material breach within 30 days after its receipt of written notice from Owner of the alleged existence of such material breach.

§ 19. **Legal Documents**. Owner and its counsel will be solely responsible for determining the legal sufficiency of any Lease or other document related to any transaction contemplated by this Agreement. Owner hereby agrees to include in any such Lease, a recital concerning Broker's representation of Owner and a provision committing Owner to pay all commissions owed to Broker hereunder.

§ 20. **Arbitration**. If any dispute arises hereunder between Owner and Broker, then such dispute will be resolved by means of binding arbitration conducted in accordance with the commercial arbitration rules of the American Arbitration Association. A judgment based upon any award rendered by the arbitrator(s) may be entered in any court of competent jurisdiction. The arbitrator(s) will be limited to awarding compensatory damages and will have no authority to award punitive, exemplary or similar type damages. The prevailing party in the arbitration proceeding will be entitled to recover its expenses from the non-prevailing party, including, without limitation, all the costs of the arbitration proceeding and its reasonable attorneys fees. Depositions may be taken and other discovery obtained during such arbitration proceeding to the same extent as authorized in civil judicial proceedings in the state in which the Property is located.

§ 21. **Tenant Exclusions**. Notwithstanding anything to the contrary contained in this Agreement, Broker will not under any circumstance be entitle to receive a leasing commission if Owner executes a Lease at any time with any of the prospective tenants named below (or any of affiliate of any such prospective tenant).

Excluded Prospective Tenants: _________________.

Owner and Broker have executed this Agreement as of the date first set forth above.

OWNER: **BROKER:**

_________________________   _________________________

By: _______________________   By: _______________________
    (Name)   (Title)   (Name)   (Title)

DOCUMENT #8

PROPERTY MANAGEMENT AGREEMENT
FOR OFFICE BUILDING

■ ■ ■

PROPERTY MANAGEMENT AGREEMENT

This Property Management Agreement ("Agreement") is entered into as of the date first set forth above by _______ ("Owner") and _______ ("Manager").

Owner and Manager agree as follows:

§ 1. **Appointment of Manager**. Owner hereby appoints Manager as its sole and exclusive agent to manage and operate the buildings located at _______, _______, _______ ("Property"). Manager agrees that _______ will be assigned primary responsibility for performing Manager's services throughout the term of this Agreement. Notwithstanding anything to the contrary contained herein, Owner will have the right to terminate this Agreement effective immediately if the above-named person is no longer assigned to Owner's account.

§ 2. **Term of Agreement**. The initial term of this Agreement will begin on the date first set forth above and will end on the first anniversary of such date. The term of this Agreement will automatically renew for consecutive renewal terms of one year each, unless either Owner or Manger elects to terminate this Agreement by giving written notice of termination to the other party at least 60 days prior to the scheduled commencement date of such renewal term.

§ 3. **Manager's Duties**. Manager will perform all of the duties set forth in this § 3 in a diligent and competent manner so as to protect and promote Owner's interest in the Property. Notwithstanding anything to the contrary contained herein, Manager may not incur any cost without first obtaining Owner's prior consent thereto, unless (i) the incurring of such cost is consistent with an Approved Budget (as that term is defined in subparagraph (a) below) or (ii) the incurring of such cost is immediately required for the preservation and safety of the Property or to avoid the suspension of any essential service to the Property.

696

(a) **Operating Budgets**. Manager will prepare an operating budget for the Property for each calendar year during the term of this Agreement. The operating budget for the first such calendar year will be prepared and submitted to Owner for its review and approval within 30 days after the execution of this Agreement. The operating budget for each subsequent calendar year will be prepared and submitted to Owner for its review and approval at least 30 days prior to the beginning of such calendar year. Each operating budget approved by Owner is hereinafter referred to as an "Approved Budget".

(b) **Maintenance of Property**. Manager will maintain the Property in good order and condition of repair. Manager will not, however, have any authority to make any structural changes to the Property, without first obtaining the consent of Owner.

(c) **Rent Collection**. Manager will invoice tenants for and use its best efforts to collect all rent and other charges payable by tenants under leases of space in the Property. Manager may, with the prior consent of Owner, pursue all available legal remedies to collect delinquent rents from any tenants of the Property and retain legal counsel to aid it in such efforts. Manager will also collect all applicable sales tax and remit the same to the appropriate public authorities.

(d) **Services and Utilities**. Manager will negotiate contracts on behalf of Owner for the provision to the Property of water, electricity, telecommunications, security, trash collection, janitorial, elevator, landscaping, snow removal and other similar services and utilities. The costs payable by Owner under each such contract shall be reflected in an Approved Budget. Unless otherwise approved in writing by Owner, each contract negotiated under this subparagraph shall provide for its cancellation by Owner without penalty on 30 days' prior written notice.

(e) **Leasing Files**. Manager will establish and maintain complete records and files of all leases of space within the Property and all correspondence with existing and prospective tenants. All such records and files will be available for inspection by Owner throughout the term of this Agreement and will be delivered to Owner within ten days after the termination of this Agreement.

(f) **Operating Statements**. Manager will prepare and submit to Owner a monthly operating statement for the Property for each calendar month during the term of this Agreement. Each such operating statement will delineate in reasonable detail all items of income and expense flowing from the Property for such month and for the year to date and will also compare actual results with the estimates set forth in the Approved Budget. A monthly operating statement will be submitted to Owner no more than ten days after the end of each calendar month during the term of this Agreement. Manager will also prepare and submit to Owner an annual operating statement that summarizes the income and expense flowing from the Property for the entire calendar year. The annual operating statement will be submitted to Owner no later than 30 days after the end of each calendar year during the term of this Agreement.

(g) **Personnel**. Manager will hire, supervise, pay and discharge such employees, contractors and other personnel as Manger deems necessary or appropriate to properly manager and operate the Property. All persons so hired by Manager will be deemed to be the employees or contractors of Manager. Manager may also contract with third parties to perform any or all of the duties otherwise required to be performed by Manager pursuant to this Agreement. All personnel and contract costs incurred under this subparagraph shall be paid by Manager.

(h) **Tenant Improvements**. Manager will administer and supervise the making of all tenant improvements to the Property, including, without limitation, the preliminary design and preparation of working drawings and specifications for the tenant improvements and the supervision, scheduling and accounting for the construction of such tenant improvements.

(i) **Insurance Review**. At Owner's request, Manager will review Owner's insurance policies for the Property, including without limitation, policies for fire, theft, public liability, plate glass, rent loss, elevator, boiler and workers compensation. It is, however, acknowledged and agreed by both Owner and Manager that the services to be provided by Manager pursuant to this subparagraph are advisory only and that the sole responsibility for placing, maintaining and otherwise administering such insurance policies rests with Owner.

(j) **Additional Services**. Manager will perform such additional management, advisory, consulting, supervisory, design, construction or other services as are requested by Owner. Manager's compensation for the provision of any such additional services will be determined based upon the hourly rate then in effect for the person who ultimately renders the services on Manager's behalf.

§ 4. **Management Account**. All monies collected by Manager under this Agreement (including, without limitation, all rents collected from tenants) will be promptly deposited by Manager in a separate bank account ("Management Account") opened and maintained by Manager for the sole benefit of the Property. If directed by Owner, Manager will open and maintain a separate bank account for the purpose of holding tenant security deposits. All bank accounts opened and maintained by Manager under this § 4 will be with financial institutions approved by Owner and will be held in Manager's name as Owner's agent. Owner and Manager will both be named as authorized signatories on such bank accounts.

Owner reserves the unilateral right to suspend Manager's status as a signatory on any such account or to limit Manager's authority to withdraw funds from such account without Owner's co-signature to a specified maximum dollar amount. The amounts deposited in the Management Account or any other bank account opened and maintained under this § 4 will not be commingled with any other funds of Manager.

Manager may withdraw from the Management Account such amounts as are required to pay those costs that Manager is authorized to incur under the first paragraph of § 3 of this Agreement. Manager may also withdraw from the Management Account all fees, reimbursements and other compensation payable to Manager pursuant to this Agreement; provided, however, that Manager will first pay all other current costs owed with respect to the Property prior to its withdrawal of any funds from the Management Account to pay its fees, reimbursements or other compensation.

Any funds in the Management Account that are not required for the payment of current Property expenses will be paid to Owner in accordance with Owner's instructions to Manager. If at any time the funds in the Management Account are insufficient to permit Manager to pay all expenses required to be paid by it hereunder, then Manager will so notify Owner in writing and Owner will promptly deposit in the Management Account any additional funds required for such purposes.

Manager will not under any circumstances be obligated to make any advance for the account of Owner or to pay any expense associated with the Property with funds other than those deposited in the Management Account, nor will Manager be obligated to incur any liability unless Owner furnishes Manager with the necessary funds for the discharge of such liability. Manager will deliver an accounting of the balance in the Management Account to the Owner on or before the tenth day of each calendar month during the term of this Agreement.

§ 5. **Manager's Compensation**. Manager will be paid a monthly management fee in an amount equal to ___% of the Gross Rent actually collected from tenants of the Property during the preceding calendar month. For this purpose, "Gross Rent" will mean all fixed base rent, any rent increases tied to an index and any expense payments payable by tenants of the Property. Manager will be reimbursed on a monthly basis for: (a) all wages, salaries, benefits, payroll taxes and other compensation paid by manager to its maintenance personnel for time spent directly in connection with maintenance work performed at the Property; (b) all wages, salaries, benefits, payroll taxes and other compensation paid by Manager to any on-site assistant property manager retained by Manager at the express instruction of Owner; and (c) all compensation payable to Manager for its provision of additional services under § 3(j) of this Agreement. Manager will maintain and submit to Owner on a monthly basis adequate records substantiating all expenses for which Manager is entitled to reimbursement hereunder.

All fees, reimbursements and other compensation payable to Manager for each calendar month during the term of this Agreement will be paid to Manager within ten days after the end of each such month. If sufficient funds are in the Management Account to permit the payment of such fees, reimbursements and other compensation to Manager after the payment of all other current costs owed with respect to the Property, then Manager may pay the same out of the Management Account without obtaining any further consent or direction of Owner.

§ 6. **Indemnification of Manager**. Owner will indemnify, defend and hold Manager harmless from and against any and all claims, losses, costs, expenses and liabilities incurred by or asserted against Manager in connection with the Property or Manager's performance of services pursuant to this Agreement, including, without limitation, any such claims, losses, costs, expenses or liabilities arising under the Comprehensive Environmental Response, Compensation and Liability Act or any other federal, state or local law or regulation pertaining to the environment. Notwithstanding the foregoing, Owner will be under no obligation to indemnify Manager with respect to any claims, losses, costs, expenses or liabilities occasioned by Manager's gross negligence, willful misconduct or material breach of any obligation or covenant contained in this Agreement. Manager will indemnify, defend and hold Owner harmless from and against any and all claims, losses, costs, expenses and liabilities incurred by or asserted against Owner arising out of Manager's gross negligence, willful misconduct or material breach of any obligation or covenant contained in this Agreement. The provisions of this § 6 will survive the termination of this Agreement.

§ 7. **Independent Contractor Status**. Manager is an independent contractor and no provision of this Agreement shall be construed to treat Manager as a partner, co-venturer or employee of Owner. Manager's authority to act on behalf of Owner will be strictly limited to that expressly delegated to it in this Agreement.

§ 8. **Amendment**. This Agreement may not be amended except by a written instrument executed and delivered by both Manager and Owner.

§ 9. **Applicable Law**. This Agreement will be governed and construed in accordance with the laws of the State of ________.

§ 10. **Successors and Assigns**. Neither party hereto may assign its interest in this Agreement to any third party, without first receiving the written consent of the other party hereto.

§ 11. **Default**. Notwithstanding anything to the contrary contained herein, Owner will have the right to terminate this Agreement if Manager is in material breach of any provision of this Agreement and Manager fails to cure such material breach within 30 days after its receipt of written notice from Owner of the alleged existence of such material breach.

§ 12. **Prevailing Party's Fees**. If any legal action is commenced by either party against the other to enforce its rights hereunder, then the prevailing party shall be entitled to recover all attorney's fees and other expenses incurred by the prevailing party in any such action (including any such fees or expenses incurred in connection with or otherwise recoverable in any bankruptcy or other administrative proceeding).

Owner and Manager have executed this Agreement as of the date first set forth above.

OWNER: **MANAGER:**

___________________________   ___________________________

By: _______________________   By: _______________________
    (Name)   (Title)   (Name)   (Title)

Glossary of Terms

All of the following terms are highlighted in ***boldface italic*** print in the text of REAL ESTATE DEVELOPMENT LAW. The chapter and page where each such term is defined are noted parenthetically.

Access and utility study: A report that confirms that the land has direct access to public roads and that utilities of sufficient size and capacity to service the developer's proposed project are available to the boundaries of the land.

Additional rent: The variable component of the tenant's rent payment that is tied to the level of the landlord's building expenses.

AIA, AGC, EJCDC and ConsensusDOCS contract forms: Pre-printed, standard forms developed by trade associations for use in the construction process.

ALTA survey: A survey prepared in accordance with the surveying standards jointly promulgated by the American Land Title Association and the American Congress on Surveying and Mapping.

Amortization period: The benchmark period of time selected by the lender for the repayment of a real estate loan. Most commercial real estate loans assume an amortization period that is significantly longer than the actual term of the loan.

Application for payment: A form prescribed by a lender (often AIA Document G–702) for the borrower's submission of its draw requests.

As-built drawings: Drawings prepared by the architect at the completion of construction that reflect any modifications made to the original construction drawings during the construction period.

"As is" clause: A clause inserted into a purchase contract that states that the buyer is purchasing the real property in its "as is, where is" condition, without any representations or warranties from the seller concerning the condition or character of the real property.

Assignment of intangible property: A document that assigns to the buyer all of the seller's rights and interests in trade names, contractual rights and other intangible property.

Assignment of lease: A transfer by a tenant to a third party (the ***assignee***) of all of its rights and interests in the lease and the leased premises.

Back-end equity: Capital contributions that are funded after the disbursement of all of the construction loan proceeds.

Balloon payment: The sizable principal payment that is payable on the maturity of a permanent loan (due to the use of an amortization period that is longer than the term of the permanent loan).

Bankruptcy remote entity: An entity that is not permitted to own any assets other than a single real estate project. The entity is structured to protect a lender from the possibility that the entity owning the real estate project might be forced into bankruptcy for a reason unrelated to the financial performance of the subject project.

Baseball appraisal: A method used to determine the fair market rental value of leased space, where each of the landlord and the tenant submits its determination of the fair market rental value and an expert or panel of experts is then required to select one of the submitted determinations as the market rent applicable to the tenant's leased premises.

Base building improvements: Those core and structural improvements that the landlord must make to facilitate any occupancy of the leased premises. They typically include, at a minimum, load-bearing walls, carpet-ready floors, life safety systems, windows and stubbed-in utilities.

Base rent: The fixed amount of rent payable by a tenant during each year of the lease term.

Before tax cash flow: The cash distributed to an equity investor by the entity that owns a real estate project. It is, by definition, calculated before the investor's payment of any income tax on its receipt of the distributed cash.

Bill of sale: A document that transfers title to personal property to the buyer.

Boilerplate: A misnomer used to describe provisions that are customarily included in all real estate documents.

BOMA standard: A standard for the measurement of space in a commercial building adopted by the Building Owners and Management Association.

Book/tax disparity: The difference between the agreed value and the tax basis of property contributed to a pass-through entity.

Breakpoint: The maximum level of gross sales that a retail tenant can attain without having to pay percentage rent. A breakpoint can be either a ***natural breakpoint*** (i.e., the result produced by dividing the tenant's base rent by the percentage used to calculate its percentage rent) or an ***unnatural breakpoint*** (any breakpoint other than a natural breakpoint).

Bring-down certificate: A document signed by the seller that confirms that all of its representations and warranties remain true and accurate as of the closing date.

Brownfield: A parcel of real property whose expansion, redevelopment or reuse is complicated by reason of the presence of hazardous substances, pollutants or contaminants—contrasted with **greenfield** properties that have no environmental problems whatsoever.

Builders risk insurance: An insurance policy that insures the owner against damage caused to a development project during the construction period by fire, wind, explosion, lightning, hail and other causes beyond the owner's control.

Bump: An increase in the tenant' base rent intended to provide the landlord with a modicum of comfort that inflation will not adversely affect its net operating income. A rent bump can be expressed either as a fixed rent increase (a **fixed bump**) or tied to an increase in a financial index (an **indexed bump**) or a change in the fair market rental value of the leased premises (a **market bump**).

"But for" test: A test used by governments to determine whether the provision of a governmental incentive to a private real estate project serves a public purpose—i.e., the subject project would not have been developed "but for" the receipt of the incentive.

C corporation: A corporation taxed as a separate entity under Subchapter C of the Internal Revenue Code.

Capitalization rate: The percentage return that a buyer will demand as a condition to its purchase of a particular property. A project's value is often estimated by dividing a project's stabilized net operating income by the capitalization rate then prevailing in the market for comparable properties.

Capital interest: An equity interest received by a developer in exchange for its contribution of services to a pass-through entity that gives the developer an immediate share of the value of all of the entity's existing assets.

Capital proceeds: The portion of an entity's cash flow that is attributable to the occurrence of certain capital transactions, such as the sale of all or a part of a project or the refinancing of the project debt.

Capital split: An equity owner's percentage share of all capital contributed to an entity. The Delaware Limited Liability Company Act (as well as many other state LLC statutes) states that an LLC's cash flow will be distributed to the LLC's members in accordance with their respective capital splits, unless the operating agreement provides otherwise.

Carried interest: Another name for the profits interest granted to an equity participant in exchange for its contribution of services to the entity. The "carried interest" nomenclature is commonly used in the context of venture capital deals.

Cash flow: All cash that is available for distribution to the equity owners of a project. It is equivalent to before tax cash flow and includes both operating cash flow and capital proceeds.

Cash on cash return: A financial return standard used to measure the return achieved by an investor on its equity investment in a project. It is equal to the investor's before tax cash flow, divided by the total equity contributed to the project by the investor.

Cash reserve: The portion of an entity's cash flow that is held back from distributions to the equity participants and deposited into a "rainy day" account to protect the entity against foreseeable and unforeseeable future contingencies.

Casualty: A short-hand reference used in a commercial lease to refer to the occurrence of a fire, explosion, storm, flood, earthquake or other calamitous event that damages the landlord's building or interferes with the tenant's use of its leased premises.

Caveat emptor: The "let the buyer beware" doctrine that is generally applicable to commercial real estate transactions and that supports the dual proposition that (1) the seller has no obligation to disclose to the buyer any defects or other problems related to the condition of the real property being sold to the buyer, and (2) the buyer has no inherent legal right to sue the seller if the condition of the real property purchased by the buyer ultimately proves to be at odds with the buyer's expectations.

Certificate of good standing: A document issued by the state in which an entity is formed affirming that the entity exists and is in good standing under the laws of such state.

Certification: A statement made by a third party expert concerning the condition or character of real property—e.g., statements received by a title insurance company, environmental engineer or wetlands consultant.

Change directive: A contractual right reserved by the developer to compel the contractor to proceed with a change in the nature or scope of a construction project, before the parties reach final agreement on the substance of a change order.

Change order: A change in the nature or scope of a construction project. It typically requires the agreement of both the contractor and the owner and may result in an adjustment to the construction price or schedule.

Closing: The consummation of all of the transactions contemplated in a purchase contract.

Closing bible: The compilation of all those documents that are pertinent to the closing of a real estate transaction.

Closing deliverables: All documents and other materials that the buyer and seller are responsible for executing and delivering at the closing.

Closing statement: The document that shows how much money the buyer needs to pay to close a real estate acquisition and to whom that money is to be disbursed.

Commencement Date: The date specified in the lease on which the tenant first has the right to exclusively possess the leased premises.

Commercial mortgage backed securities (CMBS): A securitized loan made with respect to a commercial real estate project.

Commitment letter: A letter issued by a lender to indicate its intention to make a loan to a borrower upon the specific terms and conditions set forth in the letter.

Common areas: Those spaces within the landlord's project that the tenant may use in common with other tenants in the building. Common areas include both ***building common areas*** (those contained within the four corners of the building) and ***site common areas*** (those located on the land parcel on which the building is situated).

Common area load factor: The difference between the square footage of a building's rentable and usable space. It is typically expressed as a percentage equal to [the building's rentable square feet − the building's usable square feet] ÷ the building's rentable square feet.

Completion guaranty: A promise made to a lender by a guarantor (typically a creditworthy affiliate of the borrower) that the guarantor will do whatever is necessary to completion construction of a project in accordance with the approved plans and specifications and by the outside completion date specified in the construction loan documents.

Construction loan agreement: The document that establishes the rules that will govern the construction lender's disbursement of loan proceeds under a construction loan.

Construction, future advance or open-end mortgage: A mortgage that contemplates that advances of loan proceeds will be made periodically throughout the loan term and that affords such periodic advances priority over liens filed subsequent to the initial loan closing.

Construction management-agency system: A project delivery system in which the developer adds a fourth person to the design and construction process (in addition to the developer, contractor and architect) by hiring an independent construction manager to provide the developer with advice concerning the design and construction of the a project.

Construction management at risk system: A variation of the pure construction management-agency system in which the construction manager serves in two capacities—as (1) the owner's advisor during the planning and design phases, and (2) the contractor during the construction phase.

Constructive change: A change in the scope of the contractor's work that is caused by the occurrence of unforeseen events or circumstances.

Contingency: A clause that conditions a party's contractual obligation to the occurrence of a stated circumstance or event.

Contingency reserve: A line item in a development cost budget that allows for unforeseen costs that may have to be incurred to deal with the specter that "something bad may happen" during the construction period or the term of any applicable loan.

Continuous operation covenant: A lease clause that obligates a retail tenant to continuously operate its retail business in the leased premises during the retail center's normal business hours and to staff, fixture and stock its store in a manner designed to maximize its gross sales (Chapter 11, page ___).

Contraction option: A lease clause that gives the tenant an option to terminate its obligations with respect to all or a portion of its leased premises.

Cooperating broker: A broker who is retained to represent the interests of the buyer or the tenant and who shares in the commission paid to the listing broker.

Cost of funds: A convention used to determine the cost to a lender of securing the funds needed to make a real estate loan. A bank's cost of funds is a factor of (1) the interest rate it pays on money deposited with it by its depositors, and (2) the interest rate that it pays on any money borrowed by it from the Federal Reserve Bank or any other source.

Cost of the work, plus a fee contract: A construction contract in which the developer agrees to reimburse the contractor for its actual construction costs, plus a fee equal to a stated percentage of the project's construction costs.

Co-tenancy requirement: A lease clause that conditions a retail tenant's obligation to perform its lease obligations upon the status of other tenants in the retail center. The requirement can either relate to the tenant's obligation to open for business (an ***opening co-tenancy requirement***) or to the tenant's ongoing obligation to perform its lease obligations after it opens for business (a ***continuing co-tenancy requirement***).

Date-down endorsement: A title policy endorsement issued by a title insurance company confirming that no mechanics' lien has been filed against a project since the date of the construction loan closing.

Deadlock: The circumstance that exists when the members of an entity agree to disagree on a major decision that the manager or managing member proposes to make on behalf of the entity.

Dealer: A status assigned for federal income tax purposes to a developer who has an established track record of selling its projects once they reach stabilization. The sale profit realized by a dealer upon the sale of a real estate project is taxed as ordinary income (and not as a capital gain).

Deal maker: A lawyer who has a reputation for doing that which is required to consummate a transaction in a manner that serves his client's stated business objectives—contrasted with a lawyer who becomes a ***deal killer*** by placing "the law" and his or her personal, competitive interests above the interests of the client.

Deal momentum: A circumstance where the parties to a transaction feel committed mentally and emotionally to doing a deal, even though they are not legally committed to do so—often produced by the execution of a non-binding letter of intent.

Debt service coverage ratio: A test used by a real estate lender to limit the principal amount of a loan by requiring that the projected income stream produced from the project must be a fixed multiple of the debt service payable on the loan. The maximum loan amount sanctioned by the application of a debt service coverage test is determined by dividing the project's maximum debt service by the mortgage constant applicable to the loan.

Debt yield test: A test used by a real estate lender to limit the principal amount of a loan by dividing the project's annual projected net operating income by a fixed percentage yield.

Defeasance: An alternative to a borrower's prepayment of a securitized loan involving the borrower's posting of Treasury instruments in an amount sufficient to fund all principal and interest payments when and as they become due under the loan.

Design-bid-build system: A traditional project delivery system in which the developer assigns responsibility for the design function to the architect under one contract and the responsibility for the construction function to the contractor under a separate contract.

Design-build system: A project delivery system in which the design and construction functions are combined and delegated to a single entity known as the ***design-builder***.

Design development drawings: Detailed architectural drawings that incorporate the general features of the approved schematic drawings, plus add new detail concerning the building's architectural design and the specifics of the building's structural, mechanical and electrical systems.

Discounted cash flow model: A real estate valuation methodology that takes into consideration both the volume and timing of future cash flows generated from a real estate project.

Drag along: The right of an equity owner to sell its equity interest to a third party and to compel its fellow equity owners to similarly sell their equity interests to the designated third party.

Draw request: A written request periodically delivered to a construction lender by a borrower asking the lender to disburse loan proceeds to pay those development costs incurred by the borrower during the preceding period.

Due diligence: An investigatory process conducted by a buyer to determine whether a particular parcel of real property is suitable for its intended use.

Due on sale and due on encumbrance clauses: Prohibitions contained in permanent loan documents against the borrower's sale of an interest in the mortgaged property (a ***due on sale clause***) and the borrower's placement of secondary mortgage financing on the mortgaged property (a ***due on encumbrance clause***).

Earnest money deposit: Cash paid or property delivered by a buyer to partially secure its commitment to purchase real property.

Economic development: A principle that supports the government's provision of assistance to a real estate project if the development of the project will create new jobs and spur further development in the vicinity of the assisted project.

Entitlement: A governmental approval that is required to be issued to the developer if its proposed development plan complies with governmental rules applicable to all similarly situated projects.

Environmental assessment: A report prepared by an environmental engineer that identifies any environmental problems associated with a particular parcel of land. A ***Phase One environmental assessment*** is one that is prepared based on a routine walk-through of the land and an examination of the public records of the state and federal environmental protection agencies, while a ***Phase Two environmental assessment*** involves an additional round of testing of the soils and ground water located on the land.

Equity: The cash or other property contributed by the owners of an entity to pay the portion of a project's development costs that are not funded with debt—also commonly referred to as ***capital***.

Escrow agent: A neutral third party designated to hold and disburse the earnest money deposit and transactional documents placed in escrow by the parties to a contract.

Escrow closing: A closing effected by the parties' delivery of all requisite documents and funds to an escrow agent, with written ***escrow instructions*** specifying the circumstances under which the escrow agent is authorized to disburse such documents and funds.

Estoppel certificate: A written statement made by a tenant confirming the terms of its lease and representing that its lease is in full force and effect, without any default on the part of either the landlord or the tenant.

Event of default: The occurrence of an event or circumstance that permits the landlord to exercise its remedies for a tenant's nonperformance of its lease obligations.

Exclusive agency: A brokerage arrangement where a developer selects a particular broker to lease space in its building and agrees to pay the selected broker a commission on any lease that is signed for the building, unless the developer, without the assistance of any other broker, is the procuring cause of the signed lease.

Exclusive listing: A brokerage arrangement where the developer is obligated to pay its selected broker a commission on any lease signed for the building, even if that lease is procured directly by the developer or another broker.

Exclusive use clause: A lease clause that gives a retail tenant the exclusive right to sell a particular product line in a retail center.

Excusable delay: Those construction delays for which the contractor is entitled to an extension of the construction schedule or an adjustment of the construction price.

Exit strategy: The developer's plan to realize its profit and eliminate its ongoing risk by selling all or a part of a project to an institutional investor or placing permanent financing on the project. An exit strategy can be either ***interim*** or ***permanent***.

Expansion option: An option granted to an existing tenant to lease additional space in the landlord's building.

Expense pass-through: A lease provision that places the ultimate financial burden for the payment of a building expense on the tenant.

Expense stop lease: A hybrid of a gross lease and a net lease where the tenant makes two rental payments—(1) a fixed base rent payment, plus (2) an additional rent payment equal to the tenant's share of the excess, if any, of the landlord's actual building expenses over a pre-determined base amount (i.e., the ***expense stop***). The expense stop can be expressed either as a fixed number (a ***stipulated sum expense stop***) or as the landlord's building expenses is a specified ***base year*** (a ***base year expense stop***).

Extension option: A lease clause that gives a tenant the option (but not the obligation) to extend the term of its lease beyond the termination date specified for the initial lease term.

Fast-track construction: A compressed construction process that is characterized by the commencement of construction of a portion of a project before the planning and design of the entirety of the project is completed.

Final completion: The date on which all aspects of the contractor's performance of its work is fully completed.

FIRPTA affidavit: An affidavit confirming that the seller is not a "foreign person" subject to the withholding of taxes under the Foreign Investment in Real Property Tax Act.

Float: A term used in the construction industry to describe the added time built into a construction schedule to compensate for force majeure and other potential construction delays.

Floating interest rate: A variable interest rate used on construction loans that is adjusted throughout the loan term to reflect changes in a specified financial index.

Forced sale: An entity dispute resolution method where one member reserves the right to compel the entity to market its assets for sale to a third party.

Force majeure: The risk of an occurrence of an event which is beyond a party's anticipation or control, but which nonetheless delays or prevents the construction of a real estate project.

For convenience termination: A clause that permits the developer to terminate the architect's contract for any reason and without cause.

Front-end equity: A construction lender's requirement that all capital contributions of the equity investors must be funded before the construction lender will disburse any construction loan proceeds.

Full warranty sale: A purchase contract that contains an extensive litany of representations and warranties concerning the condition and character of the real property and the seller's authority and capacity to sell the real property, including a statement that the seller has completely and accurately disclosed to the buyer all material facts concerning the real property and the contemplated transaction.

General conditions: A contractor's costs of administering a construction project, including temporary utility, trash removal and job supervision costs.

General partnership: An unincorporated organization in which two or more persons agree to share profits and losses associated with the conduct of a business or investment activity.

General warranty deed: A document that conveys title to real property and includes a warranty from the seller that it is conveying good title to the land and that the buyer may bring a cause of action against the seller if the title is defective, regardless whether the title defect arose during or prior to the seller's ownership of the land.

Go dark right: A lease clause that expressly grants a retail tenant the right to close or curtail its store operations during the lease term.

Gross area: All constructed space within a building's footprint.

Gross lease A lease where the tenant pays a fixed amount of rent that is not tied in any way to the level of the landlord's building expenses.

Gross revenues: The sum of all rents and other income received by the owner of a real estate project.

Gross sales: The benchmark used to determine a retail tenant's percentage rent obligation. Gross sales are generally considered to be all those revenues generated from the tenant's conduct of retail operations in its leased store.

Gross-up clause: A clause that authorizes the landlord to increase the amount of its expense pass-throughs to include those hypothetical expenses that the landlord would have incurred if its building had been fully occupied.

Guaranteed maximum price: A ceiling placed on the construction price payable under a cost of the work, plus a fee construction contract.

Hard costs: Those expenses that are directly incurred in connection with the construction of a building, the build-out of tenant space and the making of other site improvements.

Hurdle rate: An investor's minimum acceptable rate of return for its investment in a particular real estate project.

Incentive: Governmental assistance provided to encourage a developer to move forward with its development of a particular project.

Incentive zoning: A phenomenon of recent vintage where a local government provides a developer with a zoning bonus (usually in the form of increased density for its project) in exchange for the developer agreeing to develop its project in a manner that advances a governmentally embraced agenda—e.g., the adoption of green building practices.

Inspecting architect: The design professional assigned responsibility for making regular jobsite visits to confirm that the progress of construction conforms to the approved construction drawings and that the contractor's draw requests relate to work actually completed on the project.

Institutional controls: Limited clean-up standards sanctioned by state and local governments to encourage the development of brownfield sites. The most common example of a permitted institutional control is the elimination of a developer's obligation to remove mildly contaminated soils if those soils are capped with a concrete pad for a building or parking lot.

Institutional-grade property: A real estate project that is deemed worthy of investment by institutional investors because (1) the creditworthiness of the project's tenant roster is sufficiently solid as to give the investor comfort that the expected income stream will be realized, and (2) the project location, design and quality of construction are such that it is reasonable to assume that replacement tenants will be found if and when the existing tenants vacate the project.

Institutional investors: Life insurance companies, pension plans, equity funds and other financial institutions, both domestic and foreign, who have huge sums of money to invest in real estate each year.

Integrated project delivery method: A hybrid project delivery system in which the developer, contractor and architect collaborate at all times during the planning, design and construction phases of the construction process.

Interest rate hedges: Techniques used to mitigate the risk to the borrower and the lender of a fluctuation in a loan's floating interest rate. ***Caps***, ***collars*** and ***swaps*** are types of interest rate hedges commonly used in the commercial real estate industry.

Internal rate of return: The percentage rate at which the present value of a series of future cash flows equals an investor's required equity investment.

Irrevocable, standby letter of credit: A form of collateral often posted to secure a party's performance under a contract (e.g., a construction loan agreement or lease), whereby a financial institution provides its unconditional commitment that it will pay the letter of credit beneficiary a specified sum upon its receipt of a demand for payment specifying that a default has occurred under the contract.

Killer forms: A legal form that is unduly long, complex and overreaching in its efforts to eliminate every conceivable risk faced by a party to a real estate document.

Landlord or lessor: The person who owns a real estate project and is trying to lease it to third parties.

Land risk: Any circumstance or event that could lead a buyer of land to conclude that it no longer wants to buy the land. ***Site-specific land risks*** are those risks that are specific to the to-be acquired land, while ***non-site-specific land risks*** are those risks that relate to broader concerns about the viability of the project that the buyer intends to develop on the land.

Lease: A contract transferring the right to the possession and enjoyment of property for a definite period of time.

Leased premises: The space over which the tenant has the exclusive right of possession.

Lease term: The period during which the tenant has the right to exclusive possession of the leased premises. The lease term includes the ***initial lease term*** specified in the lease and may be extended or renewed for an additional term or terms by the agreement of the parties.

Letter of intent: A short-form document (typically two to three pages in length) that is a preliminary expression of certain key deal points on which both parties to a transaction have reached consensus.

Leverage: The use of debt to pay the costs of developing or acquiring a real estate project. Leverage is ***positive*** to the extent that a project's total return on costs is greater than the mortgage constant of the project's mortgage loan and is ***negative*** to the extent the project's total return on costs is less than the mortgage constant.

LIBOR: The London Inter-bank Offered Rate is an index commonly used by construction lenders to measure the fluctuating rate of interest payable on a construction loan.

Lien waiver: A written waiver executed by a contractor, subcontractor, laborer, supplier or material provider confirming that it has been paid for all work performed by it on a construction project and expressly waiving its right to file a mechanics' lien against the project to the extent of such prior or contemporaneous payments.

Limited liability company: An entity that blends the best of both the corporate and partnership worlds, by combining the limited liability status of corporations, with the pass-through tax status and operational and investment flexibility of partnerships. It is the entity of choice for most private real estate projects.

Limited partnership: An entity that possesses all of the attributes of a general partnership, except that certain partners are afforded limited liability status as limited partners.

Limited warranty deed: A document that conveys title to real property and includes a title warranty from the seller covering only those title defects that arose during the seller's ownership of the land.

Listing broker: The broker hired by a seller or landlord to find a buyer or tenants for its project.

Loan balancing provision: A loan provision that requires the borrower to contribute additional capital or post additional collateral if the lender determines that the construction loan is ***out of balance***—i.e., that the costs of completing construction of a project are greater than the amount of the funds then reserved for the funding of such costs.

Loan remargining provision: A loan provision that obligates the borrower/guarantor to make additional capital contributions or post additional collateral if the lender determines that the value of a development project is less that that projected at the inception of the lender's underwriting of the loan.

Loan-to-cost ratio: A test used by a real estate lender to limit the principal amount of a loan to a fixed percentage of a project's total development costs.

Loan-to-value ratio: A test used by a real estate lender to limit the principal amount of a loan to a fixed percentage of the appraised value of the project that serves as collateral for the lender's mortgage loan.

Lock-out period: A period of time during which the members are prohibited from exercising a buy-sell right or the borrower is prohibited from prepaying a permanent loan.

Major decisions: Those fundamental actions and decisions that require the approval of all or a super-majority of an entity's equity participants.

Manager: The person assigned responsibility for the management and control of the business and affairs of a manager-managed LLC.

Manager-managed LLC: A limited liability company in which the management and control of the business and affairs of the limited liability company is centralized in one or more managers (who may or may not be members of the limited liability company).

Marketable title: A state of title that is legally presumed to be acceptable to all owners of real estate—i.e., title that permits the owner to possess, use and dispose of the subject property, without any unreasonable legal impediment.

Mechanics' lien: Right created by statute whereby a person who works on or provides labor or materials to a construction project can file a lien against that project if such person is not paid in full for its efforts.

Member-managed LLC: A limited liability company in which the management and control of the business and affairs of the limited liability company is vested in its members (who may, in turn, delegate such management and control to a specific ***managing member***).

Merchant builder: A developer who customarily seeks to limit its exposure to real estate risk by selling its projects as soon as they reach stabilization.

Milestone dates: Interim dates established for the completion of certain portions of the construction work—e.g., site excavation, foundation work or steel erection.

Mini-perm loan: A construction loan that affords the borrower a right to extend the loan's maturity date for an additional term of years if certain conditions are satisfied by the borrower.

Monetary default: A failure of a tenant to pay its rent on or before the due date specified in the lease.

Monetary liens: Those real property liens that can be discharged by the payment of an ascertainable sum of money—e.g., mortgages and judgment liens.

Mortgage constant: The percentage of a real estate loan that must be paid every year to repay all principal and interest over the loan's assumed amortization period.

Multiple prime contractor method: A hybrid project delivery system in which the developer enters into contracts with the architect and each of the prime trade contractors involved in the construction of the project.

Multi-tenant lease: A lease where a building is leased to two or more tenants.

"Must take" agreement: A lease clause that obligates an existing tenant to lease additional space in the building effective as of a specified future date.

Net lease: A lease where the tenant pays a fixed base rent payment, plus an additional rent payment equal to the tenant's share of the landlord's actual building expenses.

Net operating income: The current operating profit produced from a real estate project, represented by the project's gross revenues minus its operating expenses.

New York style closing: A closing where all the parties and their lawyers gather in one physical location to hammer out the final details of a transaction and execute and deliver all required legal documents.

Non-monetary default: Any tenant default other than a monetary default.

Nonrecourse: A feature common to permanent loans where the borrower has no personal liability for the repayment of the loan and the lender's sole recourse for a borrower default is a foreclosure on its mortgage.

Nonrecourse carveouts: Exceptions to the operation of a nonrecourse clause that seek to place personal liability on a creditworthy entity for the reimbursement of losses incurred by a lender as a result of the occurrence of certain proscribed events or circumstances.

No shopping clause: A clause inserted into a letter of intent that seeks to place a legally binding limitation on a property owner's right to solicit or receive offers for the sale or leasing of its property from any party other than its counterpart under the letter of intent.

No work affidavit: An affidavit signed by a developer attesting to the fact that neither it, nor any contractor, subcontractor, supplier or material provider has performed any work or provided any materials to the project site prior to the closing of the construction loan.

Obligatory advance: A loan advance that a construction lender is required to make to a borrower under the terms of the applicable loan documents. Such an advance is customarily afforded priority over mechanics' liens filed after the construction loan closing.

Occupancy costs: All costs associated with a tenant's occupancy of leased space, including not only its fixed rental payment, but also: its reimbursement of the landlord's building expenses; utility charges; parking fees; the cost of making improvements to the leased premises; and the benefit of any tax or economic incentives tied to its occupancy of the subject project.

Open listing: A brokerage arrangement where a developer agrees to pay a commission to any broker who procures a tenant for the developer's building.

Operating agreement: The document that governs the relationship of the members of a limited liability company and the operation of the limited liability company's business.

Operating cash flow: The portion of an entity's cash flow that is attributable to the entity's day-to-day conduct of its rental and development operations.

Operating expenses: Those expenses that are paid to operate and maintain a real estate project, including real estate taxes, janitorial fees, maintenance and repair costs, insurance premiums, utility costs and property management fees. Principal and interest paid on project debt and capital expenditures (e.g., leasing commissions and the cost of adding to or replacing the structural components of a project) are usually excluded from the definition of "operating expenses".

Optional advance: A loan advance that a construction lender is not required to make to a borrower under the terms of the applicable loan documents. Such an advance is often held to be subordinate to a mechanics' liens filed after the construction loan closing, but prior to the date on which the optional advance is made by the lender.

Origination, commitment or loan processing fee: An upfront fee charged by a lender to either reimburse it for its costs of making a loan or augment the lender's profit on the loan transaction.

Owner's title insurance policy: A contract in which a title insurance company indemnifies an owner of real property against any loss that the owner suffers due to the quality of the owner's title being other than that specified in the title insurance policy.

Pass-through tax entity: An entity formed to own a real estate project that does not pay any taxes on the income stream generated by the project, but rather passes all tax attributes and consequences on to the entity's equity owners.

Payment and performance bonds: Separate bonds pursuant to which a surety guaranties (1) the payment of all construction costs owed to subcontractors, laborers, suppliers and material providers under a construction contract (the ***payment bond***) and (2) the completion of construction of a project at the time and otherwise in accordance with the terms of the construction contract.

Payment guaranty: A promise made to a lender by a guarantor (typically a creditworthy affiliate of the borrower) that the guarantor will repay all or a designated portion of a real estate loan.

Pay rate: The return payable on an equity contribution or debt disbursement.

Percentage rent: The portion of a retail tenant's rent obligation that is equal to a percentage of the gross sales produced from the tenant's conduct of retail operations in its leased store.

Permanent loan: A mortgage loan placed on a real estate project to refinance a construction loan. A permanent loan typically has a term of five to ten years and is nonrecourse to the borrower.

Permanent take-out commitment: An agreement by a permanent lender that it will close a permanent loan to the borrower and pay off the construction loan upon the occurrence of certain conditions.

Permissive use clause: A lease clause that empowers the tenant to use the leased premises for a specified purpose, but does not expressly limit the tenant's use to the specified purpose.

Permitted exceptions: Those liens, easements, restrictions and other exceptions to a perfectly clean title that are contractually deemed to be acceptable to the buyer.

Portfolio builder: A developer who, due to its financial position and innate disposition, is inclined to try to maximize its after-tax financial returns by holding on to its projects for a long term.

Portfolio loan: A permanent loan that is originated and held by a single mortgage lender.

Pre-construction services: Advisory services provided to the developer (typically by a construction manager) during the planning and design phases of the construction process.

Preferred return: The required priority return payable to an equity investor on the amount of its contributed capital.

Prepayment penalty: A negotiated premium payable by a borrower for the privilege of prepaying a permanent loan prior to maturity. The most common formulation of a prepayment penalty is a ***yield maintenance penalty,*** where the borrower is required to pay the lender an additional sum that is equal to the difference between (1) the present value of the yield that would have been produced had the loan been held to maturity, and (2) the present value of the yield that the lender could achieve by investing the prepaid amount in some other investment vehicle.

Present value: The current value of a future payment, discounted to reflect time value of money concepts.

Prime rate: A benchmark frequently used to set the floating interest rate payable by a borrower under a construction loan. It is generally viewed as the interest rate charged on loans made by a financial institution to its most creditworthy customers.

Profit-sharing clause: A lease clause that requires a tenant to share with the landlord a portion of any profit it derives from an assignment of its lease or a sublease of its leased premises.

Profits interest: An equity interest received by a developer in exchange for its contribution of services to a pass-through entity that gives the developer an interest only in the profits that are attributable to the entity's future operations or a future appreciation in the value of the entity's assets.

Program: The developer's requirements concerning the design and function of a development project that the developer furnishes to its architect at the inception of the project.

Project delivery system: A method for assigning construction and design responsibility and authority to the developer, architect and contractor.

Promoted interest or promote: The portion of a developer's profits interest that is disproportionate to its share of an entity's contributed capital.

Public-private partnership: A collaborative effort between a private developer and the public sector involving the government's provision of affirmative support for a particular project.

Push-pull, buy-sell: A provision that provides deadlocked members with a mechanism they can use to go their separate ways, with one member acquiring the equity interest of the other member. Under this mechanism (also often referred to as a ***Russian roulette*** buy-sell), one member establishes the price to be paid for the equity interest, while the other member makes the decision whether to sell its interest at the established price or buy the other member's interest at that price.

Quitclaim deed: A document that conveys title to real property, but does not contain any title warranty whatsoever from the seller.

Radius restriction: A lease clause that limits a retail tenant's ability to operate a competing store within a specified proximity to the landlord's retail center.

Real estate investment trust: A creature of the federal tax laws that may be organized as either a corporation or an unincorporated trust or association for state law purposes. It is not subject to any entity-level tax, as long as it satisfies a series of complex tests specified in the Internal Revenue Code, including the requirement that it distribute at least 90% of its qualifying income each year to its equity owners.

Recapture clause: A lease clause that permits a landlord to terminate its lease with a tenant for the purpose of entering into a new lease with a proposed assignee or subtenant of the original tenant.

Reimbursable costs: Those general condition costs that the developer is required to pay to the contractor in additional to its payment of the construction price.

Relocation clause: A lease clause that gives the landlord a contractual right to move the tenant's leased premises to another location controlled by the landlord.

Rentable area: A fictional number used by a landlord to calculate a tenant's rent that equals the usable area of a designated space, plus an allocation of the building's common areas.

Rent amortization factor: The percentage number by which excess tenant improvement costs (i.e., those in excess of the agreed-upon tenant improvement allowance) are multiplied to determine the tenant's annual rent increase (assuming that the landlord is willing to front such excess costs in exchange for the tenant's agreement to increase its annual rent).

Representation: An affirmative statement made by a party to a contract concerning a current fact.

Residual value: The net cash produced on the sale of the project, represented by the gross sales proceeds minus any selling expenses.

Resolution: A document certified by an authorized officer of an entity confirming that all requisite action has been taken by the entity to authorize its participation in the subject transaction and that the person who is signing the closing documents on behalf of the entity is duly authorized to do so.

Restrictive use clause: A lease clause that limits the tenant's use of the leased premises to the purpose specified in the lease.

Retainage: Amounts withheld from advances made under a construction loan until a contractor completes its work on a project.

Return on debt: A financial return standard used to measure the lender's return on its advancement of the principal amount of a construction loan. It is roughly equal to the interest rate payable on the loan, plus the amount of any fees received by the lender that are not in the nature of a reimbursement of a lender's transactional costs.

Return on equity: A financial return standard used to measure an investor's return on the equity it contributes to a real estate project (also referred to as an investor's ***cash on cash return***). It is equal to the investor's before tax cash flow, divided by the total equity contributed to the project by the investor

Return on total costs: A financial return standard used to measure the overall productivity of a real estate project. It is equal to the project's net operating income, divided by the project's total development costs.

Right of first offer: A lease clause that requires the landlord to extend an offer to an existing tenant to lease space in the building before the landlord begins marketing that space to other prospective tenants.

Right of first refusal: A lease clause that permits an existing tenant to lease additional space in the building by matching any lease offer received by the landlord from a third party.

Schedule B–1 and B–2 exceptions: The exceptions to coverage set forth in a title commitment or title insurance policy, with the schedule B–1 exceptions being those applicable to all properties and the B–2 exceptions being those applicable only to the specific insured parcel.

Schematic drawings: General design drawings and guidelines prepared by the architect for the developer's review at the earliest stage of the design phase.

S corporation: A corporation that is exempt from most (but not all) entity level income taxes under Subchapter S of the Internal Revenue Code.

Second generation space: Space in a building that has previously been occupied by a tenant.

Securitized loan: A permanent loan that is originated by a mortgage lender and then pooled with other mortgage loans and sold off in varying pieces and parts to investors.

Security deposit: Collateral posted by a tenant to partially secure the performance of its obligations under a lease.

Selling expenses: Those transactional costs that reduce the amount of cash available for distribution to the project participants following a sale of the project—e.g., real estate brokerage commissions, legal fees and title insurance premiums.

Separateness covenants: A series of covenants made by a borrower that are designed to insure the bankruptcy remote status of the borrowing entity by requiring that the entity must be operated independently of any affiliate.

Shared savings clause: A clause pursuant to which the developer agrees to increase the contractor's fee by an agreed-upon percentage of the excess of the guaranteed maximum price over the actual cost of the work.

Single member LLC: A limited liability company that has only one member (Chapter 7, page ___). It is often referred to as a ***tax nothing***

entity, because it is wholly disregarded for federal income tax purposes and is not required to file an informational tax return.

Single tenant or build-to-suit lease: A lease where one tenant leases the entirety of a building.

Soft costs: All those costs, other than hard costs, that would not have been incurred but for the development of the project.

Soils report: A report that is intended to confirm that the soils located on the land will support the construction of the proposed project.

Spread: The difference between the lender's cost of funds and the interest rate charged by it on a mortgage loan.

Squeeze-down: A right granted to a non-defaulting member of a pass-through entity to cause the entity to recalculate the ratios in which the members will share in the entity's profits and losses to take into consideration a member's default in its obligation to make additional capital contributions to the entity. The exercise of this right will typically seek to punish the defaulting member by reducing the member's share of future profits and losses below its share of the total contributed capital.

Stabilized project—A real estate project that is leased and producing positive cash flow.

Stipulated sum contract: A construction contract in which the developer and the contractor agree to a fixed construction price.

Sublease: A transfer by the tenant to a third party (the ***subtenant***) of part of its rights and interests in the lease premises (but not the underlying lease).

Subordination, nondisturbance and attornment agreement: A document entered into by a tenant and the landlord's mortgagee that delineates the relationship of the tenant and the mortgagee following the mortgagee's foreclosure of its mortgage on the landlord's building.

Substantial completion: The stage in the progress of the construction of a project when the project is sufficiently complete to permit the owner to occupy and utilize the project for its intended use.

Suitability or free look contingency: A clause inserted into a purchase contract that conditions the buyer's purchase obligation on its determination that the real property is suitable for its intended use.

Survey: A document prepared by a licensed land surveyor that depicts the dimensions and boundaries of a land parcel and the location of any improvements, easements, roads and encroachments affecting the parcel.

Survival clause: A clause inserted into a purchase contract that states that certain seller representations, warranties and covenants will survive the closing of the sale of the real property for a stated period of time (Chapter 5, page ___). Also used to refer to an affirmative statement in a lease that the tenant's obligation to pay rent will survive the termination of its right of possession of the leased premises.

Tax abatement: A governmental incentive pursuant to which a taxpayer's tax liability is reduced or eliminated for a fixed period of time.

Tax credit: A governmental incentive pursuant to which the taxpayer is provided with a credit to offset its existing tax liability.

Tax increment financing: A financing device used by state and local governments to provide a source for the developer's funding of a portion of its development costs. The ***incremental taxes*** created by a project (i.e., the taxes that would not exist but for the development of the subject project) are used to pay certain statutorily approved development costs. A tax increment financing arrangement can be either a ***pay as you go TIF*** (where the developer is responsible for fronting the development costs) or a ***bonded TIF*** (where the government is responsible for fronting those costs).

Tax rebate: A governmental incentive pursuant to which the government refunds taxes previously paid by a taxpayer.

Tenancy in common: An ownership structure whereby two or more persons hold undivided interests in the same real estate.

Tenant or lessee: The person who wants to lease space in a project.

Tenant improvement allowance: A maximum dollar amount that the landlord will pay for the construction of tenant improvements to a tenant's leased premises.

Tenant improvements: The improvements and modifications that must be made to the leased premises to fit a particular tenant's planned use of the space.

Tenant's proportionate share: The tenant's percentage share of an expense pass-through.

Termination date: The date specified in the lease when the tenant's right to possess the leased premises ends.

Time value of money: The economic concept that states that a dollar received today is more valuable than a dollar received in the future.

Title affidavit: A document that sets forth the seller's certification that there are no off-record title matters affecting the subject real property.

Title commitment: A title insurance company's written promise to issue a title insurance policy on the terms and conditions stated in the commitment.

Turnkey build-out: A method used for the design and construction of tenant improvements where the landlord does all of the work and all the tenant has to do is "turn the key, open the door and commence business".

Uncontrollable expenses: Those expenses that are not susceptible to control by a manager/managing member or a landlord.

Underwriting: The process undertaken by a lender to determine whether it should make a loan to a particular developer on a particular project.

Unforeseen site conditions: Those site conditions which are not readily detectable by a visual inspection of the site, but which nonetheless cause a delay in the performance of the work or an increase in the cost of the work.

Usable area: The space within the four walls of each tenant's leased premises.

Vertical improvements: The buildings and other structures constructed on the project land.

Virgin space: Space in a building that has never been occupied by a tenant.

Voluntary action program: State programs designed to encourage the development of brownfield sites through the provision of grants and other financial incentives and the issuance of covenants not to sue.

Warranty: A promise made by a party to a contract concerning a future fact.

Wetlands report: A report prepared by a wetlands consultant that identifies the location, size and nature of any protected wetlands located on the land.

Work letter: A supplement to a lease that addresses all aspects of the making of tenant improvements to the leased premises, including the scope and timing of the improvements and the party who will be responsible for designing, constructing and paying for such improvements.

Zero sum game: A public policy argument that says that governmental incentives should not be provided to a private development project if the benefits garnered from a developer's decision to locate its development project in jurisdiction A (and not jurisdiction B) are directly and fully offset by losses suffered by jurisdiction B.

Zoning report: A report that recites the current zoning classification of the land and states whether the development plans for the proposed project conform to the requirements imposed by the applicable zoning classification.

INDEX

References are to Pages

References are to Pages

†